P9-AQU-189

Why Do You Need This New Edition?

If you're wondering why you should buy this new edition of *Understanding American Politics and Government*, here are six good reasons!

1. Learning Objectives help you efficiently preview, study, and review key chapter concepts.

2. Critical thinking questions within the How Do We Know? sections will help you apply a deeper level of analysis to the techniques political scientists use to answer key questions within the discipline.

3. Seven new case studies on topics ranging from the Tea Party to "Race to the Top" to gays in the military show the immediate relevance of constitutional concerns to contemporary culture.

4. An annotated version of the Constitution now appears between Chapters 3 and 4 of the text, providing you with straight-forward language to understand constitutional provisions.

5. To help you understand, analyze, and apply founding principles, annotated versions of the Declaration of Independence, *Federalist 10*, and *Federalist 51* appear in the Appendix.

6. Critical thinking questions now accompany many of the photos and figures, encouraging you to reflect and analyze.

PEARSON

ELECTORAL COLLEGE VOTES IN THE 2008 ELECTION

THE UNITED STATES
A political map showing the number of electoral votes per state

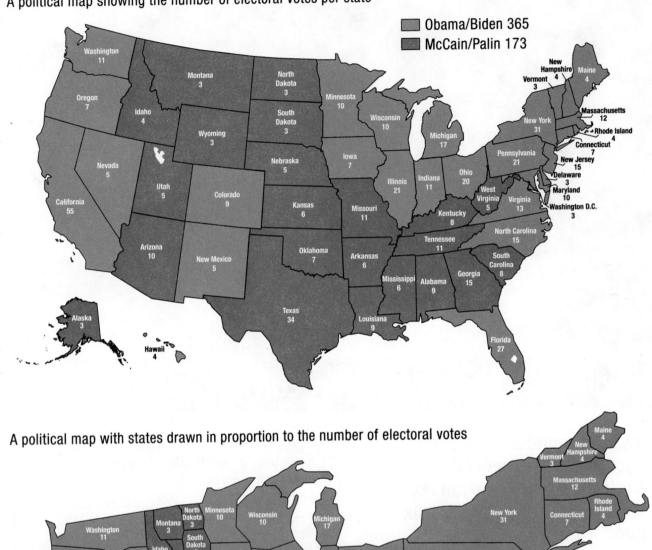

Obama/Biden 365
McCain/Palin 173

A political map with states drawn in proportion to the number of electoral votes

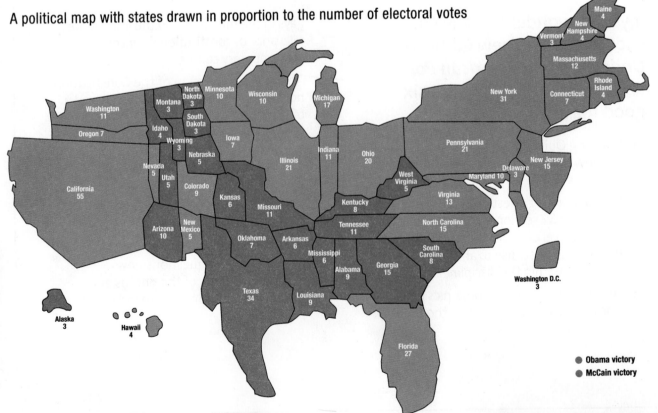

Obama victory
McCain victory

Understanding American Politics and Government

Understanding American Politics and Government

Second Edition

JOHN J. COLEMAN
University of Wisconsin-Madison

KENNETH M. GOLDSTEIN
University of Wisconsin-Madison

WILLIAM G. HOWELL
University of Chicago

Longman
New York   San Francisco   Boston   Columbus   Indianapolis   Upper Saddle River
Amsterdam   Cape Town   Dubai   London   Madrid   Milan   Munich   Paris   Montreal
Toronto   Delhi   Mexico City   Sao Paulo   Sydney   Hong Kong   Seoul   Singapore   Taipei Tokyo

Executive Editor: Reid Hester
Director of Development: Meg Botteon
Development Editor: Barbara Conover
Editorial Assistant: Elizabeth Alimena
Senior Marketing Manager: Lindsey Prudhomme
Supplements Editor: Donna Garnier
Senior Media Producer: Regina Vertiz
Production Manager: Stacey Kulig
Project Coordination, Text Design, and Electronic Page Makeup: Electronic Publishing
Services Inc., NYC
Cover Designer/Manager: John Callahan
Cover Image: © Volker Moehrke/Corbis
Photo Researcher: Teri Stratford
Manufacturing Manager: Mary Fischer
Printer and Binder: Von Hoffman
Cover Printer: Coral Graphics

For permission to use copyrighted material, grateful acknowledgment is made to the
copyright holders on pp. 773–776, which are hereby made part of this copyright page.

Library of Congress Cataloging-in-Publication Data

Coleman, John J., 1959–
  Understanding American politics and government / John Coleman, Ken Goldstein,
William Howell. — 2nd ed.
      p. cm.
  Includes bibliographical references and index.
  ISBN-13: 978-0-205-80659-1
  ISBN-10: 0-205-80659-7
  ISBN-13: 978-0-205-82933-0
  ISBN-10: 0-205-82933-3
  1. United States—Politics and government.   I. Goldstein, Kenneth M., 1965–
II. Howell, William G. III. Title.
  JK275.C65 2011b
  320.473—dc22

                                                                    2010044215

Copyright © 2011, 2010, 2009 by Pearson Education, Inc.

All rights reserved. Printed in the United States of America. This publication is protected by
Copyright and permission should be obtained from the publisher prior to any prohibited
reproduction, storage in a retrieval system, or transmission in any form or by any means,
electronic, mechanical, photocopying, recording, or likewise. To obtain permission(s) to
use material from this work, please submit a written request to Pearson Education, Inc.,
Permissions Department, One Lake Street, Upper Saddle River, New Jersey 07458 or you
may fax your request to 201-236-3290.

2 3 4 5 6 7 8 9 10—DJM—13 12 11

Longman
is an imprint of

(Hardcover) ISBN-13: 978-0-205-80659-1
            ISBN-10:   0-205-80659-7
(Paperback) ISBN-13: 978-0-205-82933-0
            ISBN-10:   0-205-82933-3

Brief Contents

Detailed Contents

CHAPTER 3

The Constitution 67

No Permission Required? Searching Without a Warrant 68

Annotated Constitution of the United States 107

CHAPTER 4

Federalism 121

The State of Their Unions: Marriage as a Federalism Issue 122

CHAPTER 5

Civil Liberties   165

The Battle over Corporate Political Speech   166

CHAPTER 6

Civil Rights   213

Apologizing for the Past   214

CHAPTER 7

Public Opinion   253

Guessing Weights   254

CHAPTER 8

Political Participation 279

Literacy Tests 280

CHAPTER 9

Voting, Elections, and Campaigns   315

The Puzzle of the 2000 Election   316

The Basic Rules Governing American Elections   317

The first objective of a candidate that is running for president is to receive his or her party's nomination.   317

The presidential nomination process has changed significantly in American history.   319

Presidential election rules are complicated.   322

Figuring out the winner in general elections for Congress is easy.   324

Understanding Individual Vote Choice   325

Primary voting is less studied and understood than general election voting.   325

Partisanship can both influence and be influenced by the general election vote.   325

Issue and policy preferences have a complex and uncertain impact on voter choice.   329

Voters appraise candidates in three big ways.   333

Party ID, issues, and candidate appraisals come together to produce a vote choice.   333

Understanding Election Outcomes   334

Frontrunners have a great advantage in presidential nomination contests.   334

Key factors allow political scientists to accurately forecast presidential election results.   336

CaseStudy ELECTION 2000: FAILED FORECAST   338

Congressional Elections 339

The Campaign   340

Turnout, loyalty, defection, and persuasion are the ingredients of a successful campaign.   341

Campaign messages are meticulously researched and targeted.   342

Field operations encourage voting and make it more convenient to vote.   343

Campaign finance laws govern the way campaigns raise and spend money.   345

HOW DO WE KNOW? CAN CONGRESSIONAL CANDIDATES BUY VICTORY WITH CAMPAIGN SPENDING?   348

Chapter Summary   351

Key Terms   352

Suggested Readings   352

Suggested Websites   352

CHAPTER 10

Media and Politics   353

Obama Versus Fox News   354

The Unique Role of the American Mass Media   355

American mass media are largely privately owned.   355

American mass media stress objective political coverage.   356

American mass media play a watchdog role in government and politics.   358

American mass media operate largely unfettered by government restriction.   359

Constraints on American Media Freedom   360

The freedom the American press enjoys was not won quickly.   361

The media can be both forbidden and compelled to provide certain information.   361

Reporters may be compelled by the federal government to reveal their sources.   362

Types of Media and Patterns of Media Use   363

The World Wide Web is becoming an increasingly important source of information.   366

CaseStudy THE ALWAYS PUBLIC POLITICAL LIFE   368

The Nature of Media Coverage of Politics and Government   369

The media devote most of their attention to explaining and interpreting the president's actions.   369

Reporters receive much more airtime than candidates do.   369

Since Vietnam and Watergate, TV coverage of politics has become conspicuously cynical.   370

TV coverage generally focuses on strategy over substance.   371

CHAPTER 11

Political Parties   387

On the Wrong Side of the Party Line   388

CHAPTER 12

Interest Groups   429

Human Nature   430

CHAPTER 13

Congress   459

Distributing Homeland Security Funds   460

CHAPTER 14

The Presidency   495

Surrounded by Challenges   496

CHAPTER 15
The Federal Court System 533

The Courts Rule on Campaign Finance 534

CHAPTER 16
The Bureaucracy 563

Building a Bureaucracy to Combat Terrorism 564

CHAPTER 17

Economic and Social Policy 597

CHAPTER 18

Foreign Policy 629

CHAPTER 19

State and Local Governments 665

Appendices

Preface

- Did Barack Obama's race help or hurt his chances of winning the presidency?

- Have the federal government's economic policies helped, hindered, or had no effect on the country's economic situation as the United States slowly emerges from the Great Recession of 2008 and 2009?

- Did the activities of the Tea Party movement in 2009 and 2010 shift public opinion on health care reform?

These **causal questions** are among the dozens asked during the historic 2008 election and during Barack Obama's first two years as president. Despite the certainty of the answers offered by journalists, pundits, and other "talking heads," we saw that throughout the twists and turns of the long presidential contest and through the eventful first years of Obama's presidency, the answers and predictions of the "chattering class" often were very, very wrong.

Why? Because many of us—not just talking heads—often attempt to explain events in our political world by oversimplifying and making causal connections where there are none. Our explanations flow from our own political viewpoints or the need to explain something quickly. Although such answers make for good television debates and effective headlines,they fail to give us the understanding of the political world that we need to make informed decisions and demand real accountability from our political leaders.

Political scientists, on the other hand, see the world differently. We believe that there are rarely simple answers and that sorting out fact from fiction can be a challenge. We gather and analyze evidence. We evaluate research and interpret arguments. We use the tools of political science to go beyond simplistic answers in a quest to explain and provide real understanding of politics and government. Here are some examples of questions for which political scientists suggest different answers from those you might hear in the media or around the dinner table:

- Do the media influence the way people think about politics and government?

- Does money influence election outcomes?

- Does the president get his way in foreign policy?

The tools of political science are not just for political scientists, however. Our goal in writing *Understanding*

American Politics and Government, as in our own teaching, is to give students these same critical thinking tools so they are empowered to make sense of the political world themselves.

In this book, we lay out the fundamentals of American politics—the political, cultural, and historical background of American government, the mechanisms and groups that link citizens to their leaders, the political institutions and the policies they generate—in clear, straightforward terms. We pull our examples right from the real world of politics and attempt to convey our own excitement about the political world that we hope students will share. What we attempt to do in the following pages is shake away any notions that the "book is closed" on American politics. Rather, we present the study of American politics and government as a dynamic field full of interesting questions, controversies, and puzzles, for which we give students the analytical tools and perspectives needed to explore, evaluate, and solve.

To that end, throughout the text, we emphasize the importance of understanding the actual causal factors behind political developments, and we help students distinguish between correlation and causation, starting in Chapter 1. In every chapter, we cover the strategies that political scientists use—and the challenges they face—in answering political questions. We also take a comparative perspective on many aspects of American government, enabling students to understand how our unique political system and history—in and of themselves—help create particular outcomes.

New to This Edition
General Themes

In this second edition of *Understanding American Politics and Government*, we have extended the rationale for the correlation versus causation theme to one that more explicitly and expressly prepares students to be informed and engaged citizens, able to analyze events in the world around them and make informed political decisions. Going beyond simple answers and sound bites in the media and viewing various contemporary issues as a social scientist helps give students the tools they need to be critical thinkers and consumers of information.

Among the more specific changes and additions in the second edition are:

- Expansion of the use of the U.S. Constitution, building on the book's inherent historical perspective. An annotated version of the Constitution now appears between Chapters 3 and 4 of the text, providing a touchstone throughout the book, providing students with straightforward language to understand constitutional provisions. Within chapters, topics have been situated within a constitutional framework, specific articles and amendments have been referenced, and the language of the Constitution has been included. To further assist students in their understanding, analysis, and application of founding principles, annotated versions of the Declaration of Independence, *Federalist 10*, and *Federalist 51* appear in the Appendix.

- Chapter 1 has been revised to include more coverage of the social contract, Hobbes, Locke, Rousseau, the types of government, and why government is necessary. We emphasize the idea that students need to be informed citizens (i.e., critical thinkers who can discern cause and effect) in order to keep American democracy functioning.

- "After reading this chapter, you will be able to" provides a set of learning objectives that are referenced at the beginning of major chapter sections and linked explicitly with the summary at the end of the chapter. These features "bookend" the chapter and give students a clear idea of what information they should take away from it.

- Throughout the text, we have updated examples and brought the latest political developments, events, court decisions, and legislation to students, and referenced the latest scholarship.

- Throughout the text, we reinforce and expand the focus on causal thinking:

- Chapter opening stories have been updated throughout and linked explicitly to questions of causality. New chapter opening stories appear in Chapter 2 (Church and State on the Campaign Trail), Chapter 4 (The State of Their Unions: A Federal Issue), Chapter 5 (The Battle over Corporate Political Speech), Chapter 10 (Obama Versus Fox News), Chapter 14 (Surrounded by Challenges), Chapter 15 (Courts Rule on Campaign Finance), Chapter 17 (An Economy in Collapse), and Chapter 18 (Afghanistan). All other chapter-opening stories have been updated and revised.

- ThinkingCausally and ThinkingComparatively flags have been updated, and new flags have been added throughout to reflect text additions that emphasize this focus.

- Among the new and heavily revised How Do We Know? features are Why Was the Path to Universal Health Insurance Coverage So Difficult? (Chapter 2), Can Congressional Candidates Buy Victory with Campaign Spending? (Chapter 9), Is American Polarized? (Chapter 11), Has Congress Abdicated Its War-Making Authority? (Chapter 13).

  - We have added critical thinking questions to encourage students to form their own reactions.

- Case Studies have been updated throughout. New case studies appear in Chapter 6 (Gays in the Military), Chapter 8 (The Tea Party Movement and Conservative Mobilization), Chapter 10 (The Always Political Public Life), Chapter 12 (Health Care Lobbying), Chapter 13 (Immigration Reform in 2010), Chapter 14 (Health Care Reform), Chapter 17 (Obama's "Race to the Top" Initiative).

- We have added critical thinking questions to many of the photos and figures, to encourage students to reflect and analyze.

In many chapters, following the Chapter Summary, students will find a set of 10 questions, spanning Bloom's Taxonomy, to enable them to test their knowledge, understanding, and application of analytical and critical thinking.

Given that the introductory American government course is often the first and only social science course many students will take, we think it is important that they come away from it being able to think and view their world critically, as social scientists do and as truly educated citizens must.

An Emphasis on Causal Questions

From the very first chapter, the book trains students to distinguish between the concepts of *correlation* and *causation* as they examine political phenomena, helping them become better critical thinkers and more thoughtful citizens.

Answering causal questions in the realm of politics and government is what political science and this book are all about. The question of Sarah Palin and her impact on the outcome of the 2008 election is a particular causal question. However, before you address this sort of question and identify what factors determine different sorts of political behaviors or outcomes, you should first be able to describe and understand the basic characteristics and organization of American government and society. Furthermore, questions regarding a specific politician's impact on the outcome of a presidential election lead to larger questions about who and what forces influence election outcomes, policy decisions, and governing more generally. What factors combine for a successful campaign? How can politicians and groups influence voters? Who decides what goes on the policy agenda? How do politicians of different parties and ideologies govern together?

Public officials, political activists, journalists, and pundits often have simple answers to such questions. Sorting out fact from fiction in the hurly-burly of political debate can be difficult, however, and can make citizens wary about getting involved in political arguments or political activity. Although you do not need to run for office or get involved in every political campaign, knowing the fundamentals of your political system and the fundamentals of good thinking allows you to keep your leaders—not to mention your friends and family—accountable. How health care will be funded, what sorts of taxes you will pay, and the shape of your retirement are all major issues that will surely be debated in the coming years. The wars in Iraq and Afghanistan will certainly not be the last wars debated by public officials and political activists.

This book provides you with the tools to see through simplistic answers that often get put forward in political debates, cable talk shows, and dinner-table conversations and to help you become a more informed and active citizen. The text will talk a lot about power and how it is wielded. The authors want to give you the confidence to take part in politics and influence how power is wielded in America's democracy. Throughout this text, you will encounter political scientists' answers to important questions in American politics in each of these areas. As you study each topic, pay close attention to the different ways researchers gather and analyze evidence as they try to understand politics and political decisions. Whatever the topic, we encourage you to take a critical view of how these arguments are framed and made. This will not only enable you to make sense of class material but will also give you the confidence to evaluate research and make arguments in other settings—academic, political, professional, or even social.

We will certainly discuss topics such as which factors influence presidential election outcomes—the questions that concluded the vignette about Sarah Palin and the 2008 election. Other examples of causal questions include

change in the specific outcome they are studying. If the president's approval rating is the outcome to be studied, one of the explanatory causes would be the state of the national economy. This is just another way of saying that the performance of the U.S. economy is one factor that affects presidential job approval.

There are rarely simple solutions to political questions.

Most good studies associate more than one causal or explanatory factor with each outcome. Political scientists tend to believe, for example, that while the state of the economy has an important influence on presidential approval, it is not the only relevant factor. The percentage of the electorate that has an attachment to the political party of the president (Republican or Democrat) is another factor that influences presidential approval. Another would be whether the nation is at war or at peace or whether the president is perceived as responding well to a natural disaster like Hurricane Katrina.

Whereas political scientists see a world in which more than one factor contributes to an outcome, journalists and politicians often focus on one major cause, even claiming it is the sole cause of something. If the economy is bad, it is because taxes are too high. If a candidate loses an election, it is because he or she ran a poor campaign. If the president suffers a legislative defeat, it is because the media covered his proposal in negative ways. If a political protest evolves into a riot, it is because the police failed to keep order. Simple answers make the journalist's job and the politician's job much easier.

Often these single-cause explanations flow from a particular viewpoint or partisan posture, or—in today's world—the need to explain something in a quick sound bite. Generally, they do not represent good theory or good social science research, or even the whole story. Political scientists see the world as complex, with most conditions having not just one but a variety of causes. One of our goals in this book is to help you get beyond the shouting matches on television news shows and give you the tools to make, interpret, and evaluate arguments on your own—and thus to be an informed and critical citizen who can question the black-and-white world of sound bites and television talk shows and see the issues in more realistic, more complex terms.

Correlation does not equal causation.

Challenges arise when analysts conduct research on politics. One challenge occurs with such frequency that it needs special attention as you learn about others' research and come up with your own answers: correlation is not the same as causation. Consider a fairly simple example from outside the world of politics. Imagine that when ice cream sales went up, so did residential burglaries. Likewise, when ice cream sales went down, residential burglaries went down as well. What would you conclude from this? One conclusion would be that the increase in ice cream sales was somehow causing the rise in burglaries. Perhaps when criminals eat ice cream, they get a sudden rush of carbohydrate energy and break into the nearest house they can find. Or maybe it works the other way. Criminals who have just broken into a home have more money to spend. With more money to spend, they buy more of all the things they normally buy—including ice cream. Most likely, however, neither of these scenarios is correct. Instead, it is probably the case that during the summer, people buy more ice cream in order to cool down. Also during the summer, people tend to go on vacation, leaving their homes empty. These homes then become attractive targets for burglars.

Obama versus Fox News

As long as there has been a United States president, there has been friction between that office and the press. But there have been times when that long-standing rivalry has taken on unusually mean turns. Newspaper editorials savaged Abraham Lincoln during the Civil War, calling him a "blockhead," a "moron," and a "widow maker." The majority of daily newspapers, led by the powerful *Chicago Tribune*, opposed Franklin Roosevelt politically. And Richard Nixon took the *New York Times* and *Washington Post* all the way to the Supreme Court over the Pentagon Papers, when he tried and failed to stop those newspapers from publishing the government's secret reports on Vietnam. Later, it was the *Post* that kept up the investigation of the Watergate scandal, which eventually brought down the Nixon presidency (with a special assist from CBS White House correspondent Dan Rather).

In the fall of 2009, Barack Obama began his own conflict with Fox News, a cable network that was harshly critical of his young presidency. After a hugely successful campaign a year earlier, tremendous popularity in the polls, and with a large democratic majority in both houses of Congress, the administration thought it was in a position to force its opponents in the media to cave in. But the new president would quickly learn what previous administrations had learned before: taking on a free press in the United States in head-to-head combat is rarely a winning proposition. This skirmish also came at a time when the entire landscape of the news media in America was in the midst of a seismic makeover. Newspapers were losing their influence, and alternative media, like the Internet and cable news channels, were changing the basic assumptions about how Americans get their information.

Since the beginning of network television in 1948, three companies held sole ownership of that domain: NBC (National Broadcasting Company), CBS (Columbia Broadcasting System), and ABC (American Broadcasting Company). Their news divisions created several evening news broadcasts in the 1950s. At first, solemn men simply read the news with very little video. But as technology expanded, television reporters like Walter Cronkite, Chet

Huntley, and David Brinkley became known as anchormen and began to exercise tremendous influence on national political debates. One event catapulted television news beyond every other form as the chief purveyor of information—the assassination of President John F. Kennedy. From the first bulletins at 12:40 P.M. on Friday, November 22, 1963, until the end of the funeral the following Monday, practically the entire country shared the grieving experience through these three channels. Americans began to shift from newspapers and radio to television, and from that point on, the vast majority got their news from the "big three."

In 1980, that dominance began to erode when CNN, the first 24-hour, all-news cable channel, premiered. The big three paid little attention to CNN at first. Many Americans still did not have access to cable. Again, it was a major news event that changed the equation. On January 15, 1991, a U.S.-led coalition attacked Iraq after that country had invaded Kuwait. Unlike the big three, CNN had placed reporters in downtown Baghdad and had the ability to broadcast live from a city that was being bombarded by American war planes. It was the first war that viewers could watch live. As cable's influence grew over the next decade, new channels were created. Microsoft teamed up with NBC to create MSNBC. In 1996, media king Rupert Murdoch hired longtime Republican strategist Roger Ailes to start another channel, Fox News. But, unlike the others, Ailes concentrated Fox News on opinion journalism, and that opinion often leaned to the conservative side of American politics.

Ailes was prescient. After the terrorist attacks on September 11, 2001, and the subsequent invasions of Afghanistan and Iraq, Americans were drawn to this form of opinion news. Soon, Fox sailed past CNN in number of viewers with its "fair and balanced" trademark. Fox also

▼ **OBAMA VERSUS FOX**
Frustrated with the tone of the network's coverage, the Obama administration picked a fight with Fox News.

Each chapter opens with a **vignette** designed to grab students' attention and draw them into the chapter's subject matter. These stories will pique students' interest and begin to suggest some of the causal questions one might ask regarding the chapter's topic.

benchmark that assumed that government restrictions on speech were likely to be inherently unreasonable. Government now had the burden to show, through a stringent two-part test, that limiting speech was necessary and desirable.

The Supreme Court determines which categories of speech merit constitutional protection and which do not.

The Supreme Court has determined that some categories of speech do not merit constitutional protection. These include fighting words, defamation, commercial speech, student speech by minors, and obscenity. Fighting words or inflammatory words that create an immediate threat to public safety are not constitutionally protected.[37] The person who uses such words could, for example, be validly charged with disturbing the peace. Defamation means speaking (slander) or writing (libel) a false statement that is heard or read by a third party and harms the target's reputation.[38] For public figures—public officials and others, such as celebrities who are frequently in the public's attention—defamation also requires that the person who spoke or wrote the offensive words did so knowing they were false.[39] Commercial speech has gained growing protection from the courts, as it, like political speech, transmits information. Unlike political speech, however, the government can regulate commercial speech to be sure it is accurate and not misleading.[40] Minors have generally not been accorded the same speech rights as adults, but that is not the same as being without rights, as the Court noted when it declared that "students do not shed their constitutional rights . . . at the schoolhouse gate."[41] Striking down a federal law in 2010, the Supreme Court declined to add depictions of animal cruelty as another area of speech that did not merit First Amendment protection. Doing so would have been the first category of speech the Court added to the list of categories unprotected by the First Amendment since child pornography was added in 1982.[42]

Governments have passed numerous laws attempting to thwart the distribution of obscene materials, and challenges to these laws have generated a lengthy trail of court decisions. In 1973, a 5–4 Court ruling revised the definition of obscenity and, in the process, increased the range of speech protected by the Constitution. The ruling retained the "community standards" provision from an earlier decision, which stated that material was obscene if, by average community standards, the material mainly appealed to prurient interest.[43] The Court now added that to be obscene and thus subject to government restrictions, a work also must depict or describe sexual conduct "in a patently offensive way" and have no serious literary, artistic, political, or scientific value. Federal law and court rulings have established that any sexually explicit depictions of children or depictions of children in sexual acts inherently violate these guidelines and are not constitutionally protected.[44] In 2008, the Court upheld the Protect Act of 2003. The law prohibited the offering or soliciting of any form of child pornography, including computer-generated pornography. By a 7–2 vote, the Court concluded in *U.S. v. Williams* that offers to provide or obtain child pornography were excluded from First Amendment protection. The difficulty of defining obscenity in other instances was most famously reflected in the comment of Justice Potter Stewart when he wrote that although he could not easily define hard-core pornography, "I know it when I see it."[45]

Controlling the spread of obscene materials in the Internet era provides a test of the Supreme Court's impact on political outcomes and on society—known to political scientists as judicial impact studies. The

Freedom of Speech

187

ThinkingCausally
Do Supreme Court actions change political outcomes?

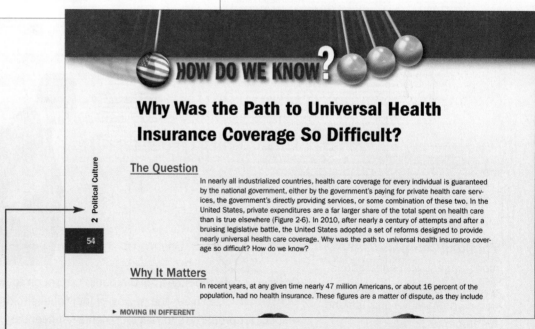

2 Political Culture

54

HOW DO WE KNOW?

Why Was the Path to Universal Health Insurance Coverage So Difficult?

The Question

In nearly all industrialized countries, health care coverage for every individual is guaranteed by the national government, either by the government's paying for private health care services, the government's directly providing services, or some combination of these two. In the United States, private expenditures are a far larger share of the total spent on health care than is true elsewhere (Figure 2-6). In 2010, after nearly a century of attempts and after a bruising legislative battle, the United States adopted a set of reforms designed to provide nearly universal health care coverage. Why was the path to universal health insurance coverage so difficult? How do we know?

Why It Matters

In recent years, at any given time nearly 47 million Americans, or about 16 percent of the population, had no health insurance. These figures are a matter of dispute, as they include

▶ MOVING IN DIFFERENT

Marginal **ThinkingCausally** icons are used throughout to highlight discussions in the chapters where particular causal questions are explored. The icons are accompanied by questions that prompt students to actively consider causal relationships.

The **How Do We Know?** feature in every chapter poses a provocative political question and then demonstrates the techniques political scientists use to answer it. Each box provides context for—and underscores the importance of—the question, highlights the means and challenges of answering it, includes Critical Thinking questions, and ends with a Bottom Line summary on what conclusions social scientists have reached.

Comparative and Cultural Perspectives

Understanding how politics and political institutions in the United States differ from those of other countries can shed light on causal relationships. Substantive comparative examples provide answers to students who wonder "Why don't we do this?" or "What are the alternatives?"

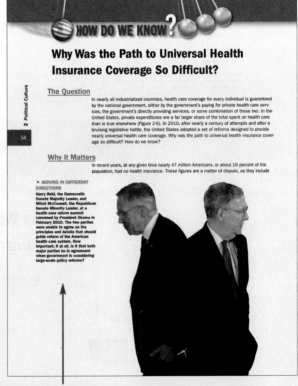

ThinkingComparatively
icons appear with annotations in the margins to highlight these comparative discussions for students.

Chapter 2 sets the stage for the book's attention to how American political culture—the prizing of individualism, democracy, liberty, respect for property, and religious rights—influences our politics and government. Students will learn how these beliefs are balanced against each other, how they are defined and change, and how they compete and coexist with other beliefs such as communitarianism and multiculturalism. Values and beliefs motivate participants in the political process, and they also make some policy paths more likely than others in American politics. When students become involved in politics and passionate about it, it is due in large part to their excitement and interest in competing ideas, values, and beliefs.

Critical Thinking

The **CaseStudy** in each chapter tells an engaging story about recent major political events. These high-interest, in-depth examples apply the ideas developed in the text to the real world, bringing our political system to life and making abstract concepts concrete.

Each CaseStudy concludes with **Thinking Critically** questions that help students understand, apply, and synthesize key points.

campaigns actually get interesting—will be unable to cast a ballot. States that allow early voting or make it easier to vote absentee by mail when a voter cannot make it to the polls also tend to see higher turnout.

In general, over time, the movement has been toward a reduction in the legal barriers to registration and voting. For example, thanks to the efforts of political parties, civic groups, and the courts, registration offices are now required to stay open during standard business hours. Also, since the passage of Motor Voter legislation in 1993, citizens are allowed to register by mail and at many different government offices (including motor vehicle agencies, which gave the law its nickname). Furthermore, the maximum number of days before an election that one must register is now 30 days, rather than 60 or 90 days, which had been the deadlines in some states.

CaseStudy: The Tea Party Movement and Conservative Mobilization

In 1773, a group of 200 colonists boarded three ships docked in the Boston harbor and dumped 342 chests of tea overboard. It was a passionate act of defiance against taxation without representation, and it would become the rallying cry of a similar movement 236 years later after CNBC's Rick Santelli voiced outrage at the mortgage relief plan being proposed by the Obama administration. This much-viewed clip, in which Santelli and a group of bond traders talked about a Chicago tea party to protest federal spending, spurred a conservative movement urging fiscal responsibility, a constitutionally limited government, and free markets. It demonstrates the power of political participation and the clear factions that exist among the populace.

The twenty-first-century Tea Party rallies are nationally organized events that specifically and publicly oppose government spending. President Barack Obama, the federal deficit, the stimulus package, and increased taxes. And, despite their conservative base, leaders of the movement are not afraid to lash out against Republicans, as they do when speaking against former President George W. Bush's heavy spending and what they consider his disregard for free markets late in his second term.

Whether their arguments are correct or not is not as important to us as is the movement's ability to garner a wide range of support and media coverage for their cause. Organizers held rallies and protests all around the country, from Atlanta to Santa Monica to Washington, D.C., bringing thousands into the movement, many of whom had never before participated in politics. They were shown on CNN, Fox News, and MSNBC, and were mocked on shows like *The Daily Show* and *The Colbert Report*. People became interested, and the movement grew. Many were angry, and

▶ THE BIRTH OF TEA PARTY POLITICS
CNBC bond analyst Rick Santelli shown during his now famous tirade against the Obama administration's economic and financial policies.

followers were encouraged to speak out, leading to contentious town hall meetings held by congressional representatives to discuss health care reform. Spurred on by social media networks like Facebook and Twitter, written about in countless blogs, and discussed on talk radio, the movement reached millions. Skeptics emerged, claiming that many of the protests and rallies were a form of "astro-turfing," a carefully planned and meticulously funded PR campaign to disrupt the Democratic Party and the initiatives of President Obama. The Tea Party organizers countered, claiming that many of the participants were first-time protesters and all were part of purely grassroots activities.

The Tea Party movement has garnered so much attention, and in some cases support, that many mainstream politicians (primarily Republicans) are attempting to latch onto the group's ideals and popularity. In fact, the results of an NBC/Wall Street Journal poll released in December 2009 show greater support for the "Tea Party" than either the Democratic or Republican Party. According to the poll, 41 percent of respondents said they have a favorable opinion of the Tea Party, compared with 35 percent for Democrats and 28 percent for Republicans.[15] Whether this movement will play a significant impact in the 2010 elections and beyond is yet to be seen, but it is clear that it has mobilized the conservative base around a clear cause and attracted many people to the political process that would have otherwise remained inactive. Organizers of the Tea Party hope that the same type of community activism that helped elect Obama will work for them, too. We shall see how big an impact, if any, the Tea Party movement will have in the years to come, and whether they can mobilize enough supporters to bring the changes they seek. Are they a viable movement? Or will they wither and fade like many movements before them? As we wait for the answers to these questions, it is apparent that the movement has mobilized a base and given people an avenue to participate in politics.

Thinking Critically

1. Do you expect the Tea Party movement to be a big factor in the 2012 elections? How about elections 10 years from now?

2. Do you think the Tea Party movement is good for America? Do you think this type of political participation is healthy?

3. Looking into the future, how do you expect the costs of political participation to change in the next 10, 20, or 30 years? What impact will this have on political participation? What role did media, both old and new, have in creating the Tea Party movement?

The political environment also influences voter turnout decisions.

In addition to personal and legal factors, the nature of the candidates, campaigns, and issues in an election year can also influence who turns out to vote. As noted above, people who have stronger attachments to one of the parties are more likely to participate in politics. Again, the 2008 election stands as a watershed event in American political history. The first African American nominee of a major party, Barack Obama, created tremendous pride in African American voters who cast ballots in record numbers and increased their share of the electorate from 11 percent in 2004 to 13 percent in 2008. Hispanics and young voters also voted overwhelmingly for Obama, greatly increasing their turnout by 2.7 percent and 2.1 percent, respectively, in the 2008 election.[16] A powerful image or message of a minority president was the benefit that gave both groups the added incentive to cast their ballots.

A similar phenomenon takes place every election year, primarily at the state level. About half of the states have a process for putting issues directly on the ballot for consideration and approval or rejection by voters. In November 1996, for example, California voters approved Proposition 209, which prohibited government agencies, colleges, and public schools from using affirmative action procedures when making purchasing, hiring, or admissions decisions. In 2004, 11 states had measures on their ballots that sought to ban same-sex marriage. Research has shown that states with this kind of referendum tend to have higher turnout than those without such a process.[17] The presence of specific issues on the ballot apparently can induce some citizens to perceive benefits in participation that they might not otherwise see.

Similarly, the presence on the ballot of more interesting or important races and candidates can boost turnout. A race for president, governor, or U.S. Senate would

Resources in Print and Online

Name of Supplement	Print	Online	Available to	Description
MyClassPrep		✓	Instructor	This new resource provides a rich database of figures, photos, videos, simulations, activities, and much more that instructors can use to create their own lecture presentation. For more information visit www.mypoliscilab.com.
Instructor's Manual 0205066763		✓	Instructor	Offers chapter overviews, lecture outlines, teaching ideas, discussion topics, and research activities. All resources hyperlinked for ease of navigation.
Test Bank 0205066755		✓	Instructor	Contains over 100 questions per chapter in multiple-choice, true-false, short answer, and essay format. Questions are tied to text Learning Objectives and have been reviewed for accuracy and effectiveness.
MyTest 0205043372		✓	Instructor	All questions from the Test Bank can be accessed in this flexible, online test generating software.
PowerPoint Presentation 0205060374		✓	Instructor	Slides include a lecture outline of the text, graphics from the book, and quick-check questions for immediate feedback on student comprehension.
Transparencies 020506681X		✓	Instructor	These slides contain all maps, figures, and tables found in the text.
Pearson Political Science Video Program	✓		Instructor	Qualified adopters can peruse our list of videos for the American government classroom. Contact your local Pearson representative for more details.
Classroom Response System (CRS) 0205082289	✓		Instructor	A set of lecture questions, organized by American government topics, for use with "clickers" to garner student opinion and assess comprehension.
American Government Study Site	✓		Instructor/ Student	Online package of practice tests, flashcards, and more, organized by major course topics. Visit **www.pearsonamericangovernment.com.**
You Decide! Current Debates in American Politics, 2011 Edition 020511489X	✓		Student	This debate-style reader by John Rourke of the University of Connecticut examines provocative issues in American politics today by presenting contrasting views of key political topics.
Voices of Dissent: Critical Readings in American Politics, Eighth Edition 0205697976	✓		Student	This collection of critical essays assembled by William Grover of St.Michaels College and Joseph Peschek of Hamline University goes beyond the debate between mainstream liberalism and conservatism to fundamentally challenge the status quo.
Diversity in Contemporary American Politics and Government 0205550363	✓		Student	Edited by David Dulio of Oakland University, Erin E. O'Brien of Kent State University, and John Klemanski of Oakland University, this reader examines the significant role that demographic diversity plays in our political outcomes and policy processes, using both academic and popular sources.
Writing in Political Science, Fourth Edition 0205617360	✓		Student	This guide, written by Diane Schmidt of California State University, Chico, takes students step by step through all aspects of writing in political science.
Choices: An American Government Database Reader	✓		Student	This customizable reader allows instructors to choose from a database of over 300 readings to create a reader that exactly matches their course needs. For more information, go to www.pearsoncustom.com/database/choices.html.
Ten Things That Every American Government Student Should Read 020528969X	✓		Student	Edited by Karen O'Connor of American University. We asked American government instructors across the country to vote for the 10 things beyond the text that they believe every student should read, which are now included in this brief and useful reader. Available at no additional charge when packaged with the text.
American Government: Readings and Cases, Eighteenth Edition 0205697984	✓		Student	Edited by Peter Woll of Brandeis University, this longtime best-selling reader provides a strong, balanced blend of classic readings and cases that illustrate and amplify important concepts in American government, alongside extremely current selections drawn from today's issues and literature. Available at a discount when ordered packaged with this text.
Penguin-Longman Value Bundles	✓		Student	Longman offers 25 Penguin Putnam titles at more than a 60 percent discount when packaged with any Longman text. Go to www.pearsonhighered.com/penguin for more information.
Longman State Politics Series	✓		Student	These primers on state and local government and political issues are available at no extra cost when shrink-wrapped with the text. Available for Texas, California, and Georgia.

* Instructor Resource Center available at **www.pearsonhighered.com/educator**

Save Time and Improve Results with

PEARSON

mypoliscilab™

The most popular online teaching/learning solution for American government, MyPoliSciLab moves students from studying and applying concepts to participating in politics. Completely redesigned and now organized by the book's chapters and learning objectives, the new MyPoliSciLab is easier to integrate into any course.

✔ STUDY A flexible learning path in every chapter.

Pre-Tests. See the relevance of politics with these diagnostic assessments and get personalized study plans driven by learning objectives.

Pearson eText. Navigate by learning objective, take notes, print key passages, and more. From page numbers to photos, the eText is identical to the print book.

Flashcards. Learn key terms by word, definition, or learning objective.

Post-Tests. Featuring over 50% new questions, the pre-tests produce updated study plans with follow-up reading, video, and multimedia

Chapter Exams. Also featuring over 50% new questions, test mastery of each chapter using the chapter exams.

✔ APPLY Over 150 videos and multimedia activities.

Video. Analyze current events by watching streaming video from the AP and ABC News.

Simulations. Engage the political process by experiencing how political actors make decisions.

Comparative Exercises. Think critically about how American politics compares with the politics of other countries.

Timelines. Get historical context by following issues that have influenced the evolution of American democracy.

Visual Literacy Exercises. Learn how to interpret political data in figures and tables.

MyPoliSciLibrary. Read full-text primary source documents from the nation's founding to the present.

✔ PARTICIPATE Join the political conversation.

PoliSci News Review. Read analysis of—and comment on—major new stories.

AP Newsfeeds. Follow political news in the United States and around the world.

Weekly Quiz. Master the headlines in this review of current events.

Weekly Poll. Take the poll and see how your politics compare.

Voter Registration. Voting is a right—and a responsibility.

Citizenship Test. See what it takes to become an American citizen.

✔ MANAGE Designed for online or traditional courses.

Grade Tracker. Assign and assess nearly everything in MyPoliSciLab.

Instructor Resources. Download supplements at the Instructor Resource Center.

Sample Syllabus. Get ideas for assigning the book and MyPoliSciLab.

MyClassPrep. Download many of the resources in MyPoliSciLab for lectures.

 The icons in the book and eText point to resources in MyPoliSciLab.

With proven book-specific and course-specific content, MyPoliSciLab is part of a better teaching/learning system only available from Pearson Longman.

✔ To see demos, read case studies, and learn about training, visit www.mypoliscilab.com.

✔ To order this book with MyPoliSciLab at no extra charge, ask your local Pearson representative for a unique ISBN.

✔ Questions? Contact us: www.pearsonhighered.com/replocator.

 Follow MyPoliSciLab on Twitter.

Acknowledgments

Understanding American Politics and Government is the result of an extensive development process that included the input of instructors and students through reviews, focus groups, and class tests. We are grateful to all of them and here name the instructors who participated in the development of the first and second editions.

Jean Abshire, Indiana University, Southeast Campus
Martin Adamian, California State University, Los Angeles
Randall Adkins, University of Nebraska at Omaha
Dave Adler, Idaho State University
Scott Adler, University of Colorado
Beth Admiral, Kings College
Ruth Ann Alsobrook, Paris Junior College
Lydia Andrade, University of the Incarnate Word
Phillip Ardoin, Appalachian State University
Chad Atkinson, Wright State University
Wayne Ault, Southwestern Illinois College
Augustine Ayuk, Clayton State University
Nivedita Bagchi, Millersville University
John Baker, Wittenberg University
Perry Ballard, Daytona Beach Community College
Robert Ballinger, South Texas College
Jack Barbour, Angelo State University
Michelle Barnello, Christopher Newport University
John H. Barnett, Emporia State University
Andrew Battista, East Tennessee State University
Chris Baxter, University of Tennessee, Martin
Brian Bearry, University of Texas at Dallas
Lawrence Becker, California State University, Northridge
Cynthia Benson, University of Central Florida
Prosper Bernard, Baruch College of CUNY
Matt Beverlin, Rockhurst University
Phillip Beverly, Chicago State University
Alicia Biagioni, Cisco Junior College
Amanda Bigelow, Illinois Valley Community College
Jeff Birdsong, Northeastern Oklahoma A&M
Amy Black, Wheaton College
Jeff Blankenship, University of South Alabama
Louis Bolce, Baruch College of CUNY
Julio Borquez, University of Michigan, Dearborn
Stephen Borrelli, University of Alabama
Catherine Bottrell, Tarrant County Community College, Southeast
James Bourbeau, University of Hartford
Janet Box-Steffensmeier, The Ohio State University
Tim Boylan, Winthrop University
Todd Bradley, Indiana University, Kokomo
James Brazier, St. Cloud State University
Robert Brem, College of Alameda
Beau Breslin, Skidmore College
Mark Brewer, University of Maine, Orono
Danette Brickman, St. Bonaventure University
John David Briley, East Tennessee State University
Wendall Broadwell, Georgia Perimeter College, Dunwoody
Joseph Brown, Baylor University
Lee Brown, Blinn Community College
Michael Brown, Emerson College
Theodore Brown, Virginia State University
Scott Buchanan, Columbus State University
Kelly Bucy, Sonoma State University
Randolph Burnside, Southern Illinois University, Carbondale
William Byrne, St. John's University
Charles Cameron, Princeton University
Juliet Carlisle, Idaho State University
Pamela Carriveau, Black Hills State University
William Carroll, Sam Houston State University
Jamie Carson, University of Georgia

Colette Carter, Colorado State University
Cynthia Carter, Florida Community College at Jacksonville, North
Larry Carter, University of Texas, Tyler
Jason Casellas, University of Texas, Austin
Heather Casey, Brenau University
Douglas Casson, Wake Forest University
David Chadwick-Brown, Palomar College
Elsa Chen, Santa Clara University
Jeff Christansen, Northeastern Oklahoma A&M
Brad Clark, Colorado State University
Ann Clemmer, University of Arkansas, Little Rock
Michael Cobb, North Carolina State University
Daniel Coffey, University of Akron
Scott Cole, Longwood University
Michael Collins, University of Memphis
Kim Conger, Iowa State University
Richard Conley, University of Florida
Paul Cooke, Cy Fair College and American Military University
Matthew Costello, Saint Xavier University
Michael Crespin, University of Georgia
David Crockett, Trinity University
Matthew Cross, Macomb Community College, South Campus
Gregory Culver, University of Southern Indiana
William Cunion, Mount Union College
Nicholas Damask, Scottsdale Community College
Debbie Daniels, University of Minnesota
David Darmofal, University of South Carolina
Roger Davidson, University of California, Santa Barbara
Darren Davis, University of Notre Dame
Kevin Davis, North Central Texas College
Paul Davis, Truckee Meadows Community College
Christine Day, University of New Orleans
Frank DeCaria, West Virginia Northern Community College, Weirto
Denise Degarmo, Southern Illinois University, Edwardsville
Joseph Denman, Blinn College
Sarah Dennis, Grambling State University
Matthew DeSantis, Highpoint University
Jay DeSart, Utah Valley State University
Iva Ellen Deutchman, Hobart and William Smith Colleges
Jeff Dewitt, Kennesaw State University
David Dillman, Abilene Christian University
Johnny Dollar, Pulaski Technical College
John Domino, Sam Houston State University
Keith Dougherty, University of Georgia
Jay Dow, University of Missouri, Columbia
Amy Shriver Dreussi, University of Akron
Bryan Dubin, Oakland Community College, Highland Lakes
Tony Dudik, Tarleton State University
Gavan Duffy, Syracuse University
Patricia Dunham, Duquesne University
Pamela Dunning, Christopher Newport University
Francisco Durand, University of Texas at San Antonio
Manar Elkhaldi, University of Central Florida
Elisabeth Ellis, Texas A&M University
Tom Esch, Seattle Central Community College
Rodolfo Espino, Arizona State University
Marcy Everest, South Florida Community College

Teri Fair, Suffolk University
Tim Faltyn, Oklahoma State University
Bruce Farcau, University of Central Florida
Femi Ferreira, Hutchinson Community College
Charles Finocchiaro, University of South Carolina
Rich Flanagan, College of Staten Island
Julianne Flowers, Loyola University Chicago
Joseph Fonseca, St. Mary's University
Linda Fowler, Dartmouth College
Heidi Franco, University Utah
Kenneth Frank, Brenau University
Erich Frankland, Casper College
Michael Franz, Bowdoin College
Samuel Freeman, University of Texas, Pan American
Kim Fridkin, Arizona State University
William Galston, Brookings Institute
Alejandro Gancedo, Miami Dade College, Hialeah Campus
John Garcia, University of Arizona
Dale Garrett, Evangel University
G. David Garson, North Carolina State University
Michele Gay, El Centro Community College
Sarah Gershon, Georgia State University
Frank Gilbert, Southeastern Oklahoma State University
William Gillespie, Kennesaw State University
Lawrence Giventer, California State University, Stanislaus
Michael Good, California State University, Hayward
Jay Goodman, Wheaton College
Sanford Gordon, New York University
Charles Gossett, Cal Poly State Pomona
Steven Greene, North Carolina State University
Caren Griffen, Jones County Junior College
Mark Griffith, University of West Alabama
Nathan Griffith, Belmont University
Jeannie Grussendorf, Georgia State University
Dan Guerrant, Middle Georgia College
Baogang Guo, Dalton State College
William Hall, Bradley University
Stephanie Hallock, Harford Community College
Lori Han, Chapman University
Sally Hansen, Daytona Beach Community College
Robert Harding, Spring Hill College
Rose Harris, Grambling State University
Kenneth Hartman, Longview Community College
Brian Harward, Southern Illinois University Edwardsville
Ed Hasecke, Wittenberg University
William Hatcher, Eastern Kentucky University
Griffin Hathaway, Illinois Central College
Kenji Hayao, Boston College
Ahad Hayaud-Din, Brookhaven College
Daniel Hayes, Syracuse University
Audrey Haynes, University of Georgia
Alexander C. Heckman, Capital University
Steven Hellerman, Crafton Hills College
David Henry, Alma College
Jeffrey Herndon, Texas A&M University, Commerce
Chrissie Herrera, University of New Orleans
Richard Herrera, Arizona State University
John Hibbing, University of Nebraska, Lincoln
Kim Hill, Texas A&M University
Marshall Hobbs, Brookhaven College
M.V. Hood, University of Georgia
Randolph Horn, Samford University

John Howell, Southern Utah University
Lisa Huffstetler, University of Memphis
Steve Hughes, California State University, Stanislaus
Elizabeth Hull, Rutgers University
Carl Iannacone, University of Arkansas, Little Rock
Robert Jackson, Florida State University
W. Martin James, Henderson State University
Kevin Jefferies, Alvin Community College
Mark Jendrysik, University of North Dakota
Jeffrey Jenkins, University of Virginia
Shannon Jenkins, University of Massachusetts, Dartmouth
Timothy Johnson, University of Minnesota
Jean-Gabriel Jolivet, Southwestern College
Brenda Jones, Houston Community College, Central
Sharon Jones, Columbia College
Terry Jones, University of Missouri, St. Louis
Carlos Juarez, Hawaii Pacific University
Jane Junn, Rutgers University
Jeffrey Karp, University of Exeter
Nina Therese Kasniunas, Allegheny College
Christine Kelly, William Paterson University
Sean Kelly, California State University, Channel Islands
William Kelly, Auburn University
Kenneth Kersch, Boston College
Richard Kiefer, Waubonsee Community College
Bob King, Georgia Perimeter College
Chad King, Texas A & M University, Commerce
Elizabeth Kloss, Ohio State University
Patricia Knol, Triton College
Perry Knop, John A Logan College
Keith Knutson, Viterbo University
Stuart Koch, College of New Jersey
Chris Koski, James Madison University
Timothy Krebs, University Of New Mexico
Jon Kreger, Schoolcraft College
Dina Krois, Lansing Community College
Melvin Kulbicki, York College of Pennsylvania
Todd Kunioka, California State University, Los Angeles
Paul Labedz, Valencia Community College, East
Jonathon Lair, South Plains College, Reese
June Lang, Suffolk County Community College
Lisa Langenbach, MIddle Tennessee State University
Drew Lanier, University of Central Florida
Melvin Laracey, University of Texas, San Antonio
David Larkin, Paris Junior College
Michael Latner, Cal Poly State University
Christopher Lawrence, Tulane University
Jeffrey Lazarus, Georgia State University
Dedric Lee, Jefferson College
Sooho Lee, University of West Georgia
William Lester, Jacksonville State University
David Levenbach, Arkansas State University
Karen Levin, Lake Sumter Community College
Tal Levy, Marygrove College
Angela Lewis, University of Alabama, Birmingham
Joel Lieske, Cleveland State University
Nancy Lind, Illinois State University
Kara Lindaman, Winona State University
Lisa Langenbach, Middle Tennessee State University
John Liscano, Napa Valley College
Robert Little, Brookhaven College
Bob Lively, Southern Nazarene University
Ian Loadman, Arkansas State University
Bob Locander, North Harris Montgomery County Community College, Kingwood
Brad Lockerbie, University of Georgia
Burdett Loomis, University of Kansas
Claude Louishomme, University of Nebraska, Kearney
Mario Love, St. Louis Community College, Meramec

Arthur Lupia, University of Michigan
James Lutz, Indiana-Purdue Fort Wayne
Henry Lyon, University of Kentucky
Bill Lyons, University of Akron
Eric Mackey, University of Arkansas, Little Rock
James Magee, University of Delaware
Eloise Malone, U.S. Naval Academy
Maurice Mangum, Texas Southern University
David Mann, College of Charleston
Paul Manna, College of William and Mary
Roger Marietta, Darton College
Khalil Marrar, DePaul University
Bryan Marshall, Miami University
Christopher Martin, Ohio University, Main Campus
Wendy Martinek, Binghamton University, SUNY
Seth Masket, University of Denver
Aaron Mason, Northwestern Oklahoma State University
Charles Mastrangelo, Massasoit Community College
Adrienne Mathews, Valencia Community College, West
Elizabeth Matthews, California State University, San Marcos
Ronald Matthews, Mount Union College
Sean Mattie, Clayton State University
John Maynor, Middle Tennessee State University
Mike Mayo, St. Petersburg Junior College
Steve Mazurana, University of Northern Colorado
Mark McBeth, Idaho State University
John McCormack, Pittsburg State University
Ian McDonald, Portland University
Stephen McDougal, University of Wisconsin, La-Crosse
Nancy McFadden, Fox Valley Technical College
Patrick McGovern, University of Arizona
Mary McHugh, Merrimack College
Aman McLeod, Rutgers University, Camden
Lauri McNown, University of Colorado
Bryan McQuide, University of Idaho
Linda Medcalf, South Puget Sound Community College
Edward Mihalkanin, Southwest Texas State University
Mark Milewicz, Gordon College
Fiona Miller, Arkansas State University
Steve Millies, University of South Carolina, Aiken
Chris Mobley, Chattanooga State Tech Community College
Ken Moffett, Southern Illinois University Edwardsville
Randy Moffett, Savannah College of Art and Design
Fred Monardi, Community College of Southern Nevada
Charles Moore, Georgia State University
Michael Moore, University of Texas–Arlington
William Moore, College of Charleston, University of Charleston
Jonathan Morris, East Carolina University
Laura Moyer, Louisiana State University
Katrina Moyon, Winthrop University
Sophia Mrouri, Cy-Fair College
Kenneth Mulligan, Southern Illinois University
William Murin, University of Wisconsin-Parkside
Kay Murnan, Ozarks Technical Community College
Gregg Murray, Texas Tech University
Leah Murray, Weber State University
Martha Musgrove, Tarrant County Community College–South
Carolyn Myers, Southwestern Illinois College–Belleville
Mike Nagle, West Shore Community College
Richard Niemi, University of Rochester
Garrison Nelson, University of Vermont
Bruce Newman, Western Oklahoma State University

James Newman, Idaho State University
Adam Newmark, Appalachian State University
David Nice, Washington State University
Stephen Nicholson, University of California–Merced
Jim Norris, Texas A & M International University
Anthony Nownes, University of Tennessee
Bruce Odom, Trinity Valley Community College
Kwasi Ofori-Yeboah, Southwest Baptist University
Elizabeth Oldmixon, University Of North Texas–Denton
L. Marvin Overby, University of Missouri
Patricia Owens, Wabash Valley College
Lynn Paredes-Manfredi, Valencia Community College–Osceola
David Parker, Montana State University
Mike Parkin, Oberlin College
Kevin Parsneau, Minnesota State University
Kant Patel, Missouri State University
David Paul, Ohio State University–Newark
Michelle Pautz, University of Dayton
Richard Pearlstein, Southeastern Oklahoma State University
Stacey Pelika, College of William & Mary
Luke Perry, Southern Utah University
Geoff Peterson, University of Wisconsin–Eau Claire
Steven Peterson, Pennsylvania State University
Greg Petrow, University of Nebraska–Omaha
Justin Phillips, Columbia University
Jason Pigg, Louisiana Tech University
Fernando Pinon, San Antonio College
Dennis Pohlman, East Central College
Dennis Pope, Farleigh Dickinson University
Robert Porter, Ventura College
Richard Powell, University of Maine–Orono
Lou Prozesky, Southern Illinois University–Edwardsville
A.J. Quackenbush, Valencia Community College–East
Chapman Rackaway, Fort Hays State University
Eric Rader, Henry Ford Community College
LeeAnn Rasmussen, Mississippi Gulf Coast Community College
Tom Raven, Syracuse University
Sherri Replogle, Illinois State University
Philip Resnick, Northern Kentucky University
Tim Reynolds, Alvin Community College
James Rhodes, Luther College
Sondra Ricar, West Valley College
Jesse Richman, Old Dominion University
Travis Ridout, Washington State University
Jack Riley, Coastal Carolina University
Joseph Rish, King's College
Jason Roberts, University of North Carolina
Naomi Robertson, Macon State College
Donald Robinson, Casper College
Mark Rom, Georgetown University
Bernard Rowan, Chicago State University
Jennifer Sacco, Quinnipiac University
Jeffrey Sadow, Louisiana State University Shreveport
Gabriel Sanchez, University of New Mexico
Arlene Sanders, Delta State University
Denise Scheberle, University of Wisconsin–Green Bay
Al Schendan, San Jose State University
Katherine Scheurer, University of North Dakota
Sara Schiavoni, John Carroll University
Eric Schickler, University of California–Berkeley
Deborah Schildkraut, Tufts University
Gilbert Schorlemmer, Blinn College
Ronnee Schreiber, San Diego State University
Joanna Scott, Eastern Michigan University
Margaret Scranton, University of Arkansas—Little Rock
Mary Kay Scullion, Lansing Community College
Allen Settle, California State University–San Luis Obispo

Mark Setzler, High Point University
Jocelyn Shadforth, North Central College
Brett Sharp, University of Central Oklahoma
Sam Shelton, Troy University
Maurice Sheppard, Madison Area Technical College
Clifton Sherrill, Mississippi College
Andrew Sidman, John Jay College of Criminal Justice
Linda Simmons, Northern Virginia Community
    College
Kevin Sims, Cedarville University
Barbara Sinclair, University of California–Los Angeles
Brian Smith, St. Edward's University
Candy Smith, Texarkana College
Joseph Smith, University of Alabama
Mark Smith, University of Washington
Mark Smith, Cedarville University
Michael Smith, South Plains College
Kathy Smith, Wake Forest University
Paul Sondrol, University of Colorado–Colorado
    Springs
Chris Soper, Pepperdine University
David Sosar, King's College
Robert Speel, Penn State Erie
Rorie Spill Solberg, Oregon State University
Sheldon Stanton, University of New Mexico
Katherine Stenger, Gustavus Adolphus College
Robert Sterken, The University of Texas at Tyler
Charles Stewart, MIT
Atiya Stokes-Brown, Bucknell University

Patricia Strach, University at Albany
Pamela Stricker, California State University–San Marcos
John Sutherlin, University of Louisiana–Monroe
Martin Sweet, Florida Atlantic University
Dari Sylvester, University of the Pacific
Bea Talpos, Wayne County Community
    College–Downtown
Andrew Theising, Southern Illinois
    University–Edwardsville
Baldino Thomas, Wilkes University
Leslie Tischauser, Prairie State Community College
Maj. Kevin Toner, United States Military
    Academy–West Point
Bob Trotter, El Centro College
Jovan Trpovski, Valencia Community College
Kelly Tzoumis, DePaul University
Matt Udie, Eastern Kentucky University
Jamie Underwood, Montana State
    University–Northern
James Van Arsdall, Metropolitan
    Community College
John Van Doorn, Columbus State University
Robert Van Sickel, Indiana State University
John Victor, California State University–Sacramento
Darren Walhof, Grand Valley State University
Sherrie Wallace, University of Louisville
William Wallis, California State University–Northridge
Adam Warber, Clemson University
Cynthia Warner, Coastal Carolina University

Alissa Warters, Francis Marion University
Andrew Waskey, Dalton State College
Donna Wasserman, Washtenaw Community College
Wendy Watson, Southern Methodist University
David Weiden, Illinois State University
Darrell West, Brown University
Jonathan Wharton, Stevens Institute of Technology
Robert Whitaker, Hudson Valley Community College
James Whitt, Ozarks Technical Community College
David Wigg, St. Louis Community College–Florissant
    Valley
Christine Williams, Bentley College
Kenneth Williams, Michigan State University
Ted Williams, Kennedy-King College
Dwight Wilson, University of Georgia
Matthew Wilson, Southern Methodist University
Patrick Wilson, University of Idaho
Paul Wilson, San Antonio College
John Winkle, University of Mississippi
Christy Woodward-Kaupert, San Antonio College
Jaclyn Woolf, McNeese State University
Mark Wrighton, University of New Hampshire
Mikel Wyckoff, Northern Illinois University
Chunmei Young, Southeastern Oklahoma State
    University
Katherin Young, Colorado State University
Melanie Young, University of Nevada Las Vegas
Maryann Zihala, Ozarks Technical Community
    College

We would also like to thank Donald Haider-Markel of the University of Wisconsin for his work on the state and local government chapter, Jon Pevehouse of the University of Wisconsin for his assistance with the foreign policy chapter, and Randall Adkins for developing the marginal annotations for the "Thinking About Causality/Comparison" flags.

William Howell recognizes Sarah Anzia, Tana Johnson, and Anton Zietsman, who made significant contributions to the research and writing of the chapters on political institutions and public policy.

Kenneth Goldstein recognizes David Dodenhoff, an extraordinarily talented writer and careful social scientist, for his extensive help drafting Chapters 1, 7–10, and 12. Thanks are also due to Ben Tabileson for his research help in the early stages of this project.

We are also grateful to the first-rate team at Pearson Longman that it was our distinct pleasure to work with. Authors could not ask for a more talented or more supportive group. This book is better because of them. Roth Wilkofsky, Longman's president, provided great support and patience as we embarked on this project. Development Manager Meg Botteon expertly guided us through the development and production process. We also benefited from the excellent work of Laura Coaty, Barbara Conover, Brandy Dawson, Michael Dew, Daryl Fox, Donna Garnier, Lindsey Prudhomme, Paula Soloway, Lori Sullivan, Linda Sykes, John Tweeddale, and Nancy Wolitzer. We also thank the terrific team of Pearson Longman sales representatives for their commitment to this book.

Eric Stano, editor-in-chief of political science for the first edition, deserves special thanks. This book simply would not have happened without Eric's knowledge, enthusiasm, and persistence. He took a deep interest in this project from its earliest stages and never wavered in his support or enthusiasm for the book's pedagogical vision as we moved from a general vision to an actual text. He is a phenomenally talented and dedicated editor and we thank him. Reid Hester, our new executive editor, provided great assistance on this second edition.

About the Authors

JOHN J. COLEMAN

John Coleman is a professor and chair of the Political Science Department at the University of Wisconsin, Madison. Professor Coleman is the author or co-editor of five books, including *Party Decline in America: Policy, Politics, and the Fiscal State* (Princeton University Press, 1996). His articles on political parties, elections, public knowledge, Congress and the presidency, divided government, campaign finance, and American political development have appeared in the *American Political Science Review, American Journal of Political Science, Journal of Politics,* and *Studies in American Political Development,* among other journals. His current research includes projects on campaign finance and party accountability in elections.

KENNETH M. GOLDSTEIN

Ken Goldstein is a professor of political science at the University of Wisconsin, Madison. He is the author of *Interest Groups, Lobbying, and Participation in America* (Cambridge University Press, 1999) and *Campaign Advertising and American Democracy* (Temple University Press, 2007) as well as over 30 refereed journal articles and book chapters on political communication, voter turnout, campaign finance, survey methodology, Israeli politics, presidential elections, and news coverage of health issues. Professor Goldstein is a consultant for the ABC News Elections Unit and a member of their election-night decision team. He has worked on network election-night coverage in every U.S. federal election since 1988.

WILLIAM G. HOWELL

William Howell is the Sydney Stein Professor in American Politics at the University of Chicago. He holds appointments in the Harris School of Public Policy, the Department of Political Science, and the College. He has written widely on separation of powers issues and American political institutions, especially the presidency. His recent research examines the relationships between war and presidential power. He is the co-author (with Jon Pevehouse) of *While Dangers Gather: Congressional Checks on Presidential War Powers* (Princeton University Press, 2007), author of *Power Without Persuasion: The Politics of Direct Presidential Action* (Princeton University Press, 2003), co-author (with Paul Peterson) of *The Education Gap: Vouchers and Urban Schools* (Brookings Institution Press, 2002), co-editor (with George Edwards) of *The Oxford Handbook on the American Presidency* (Oxford University Press, 2009), and editor of *Besieged: School Boards and the Future of Education Politics* (Brookings Institution Press, 2005). His research has appeared in such journals as *International Organization, American Political Science Review, American Journal of Political Science,* and *Journal of Politics,* as well as in numerous edited volumes.

1

Thinking About American Politics

Sarah Palin and the 2008 Election

On the night of September 3, 2008, the relatively unknown governor of Alaska saved the Republican national convention for presidential candidate John McCain. With her charm, folksiness, and brisk frankness, vice presidential nominee Sarah Palin electrified the large gathering in St. Paul, Minnesota, along with millions of people watching across the country. Just 48 hours earlier, the convention had seemed dead on arrival— the first night had been cancelled due to a hurricane in the Gulf of Mexico, and the incumbent president and vice president had not set foot in the hall because they were so unpopular. Palin was a breath of fresh air.

McCain, an Arizona senator who as a Navy pilot had made split-second, life-and-death decisions, appeared to have come up with a last-minute call that saved the ticket. With Palin as his

▼ PALIN FACES COURIC

Katie Couric's interview of vice presidential candidate Sarah Palin aired on *CBS Evening News* over the course of a week in late September. Palin's performance was not strong, and the nightly airing of different clips was a prolonged, painful experience for the McCain campaign.

running mate, he brought back the base of the party, which had doubted his conservative credentials. Perhaps even more important, Palin seemed to intrigue undecided voters as well as women who had supported former Democratic presidential candidate Hillary Clinton. These voters would ultimately decide the winner of the 2008 presidential election. Now, at a time when Americans were calling for change, these two mavericks promised to change the status quo in Washington, D.C. McCain already had a long history of crossing the aisle and working with Democrats when he thought it was in the interest of his country. And Palin had taken on entrenched Alaskan Republican Party officials, whom she accused of corruption. In the end, this woman from a very ordinary background prevailed, defeating a powerful incumbent governor and enjoying an approval rating of 90 percent in her home state. The McCain-Palin ticket drew enormous and enthusiastic crowds as they traveled together after the Republican convention. The polls tightened and the Republican ticket even pulled ahead by some accounts. Democrats were nervous.

However, just two months later, the McCain-Palin ticket lay in ruins, swamped by an Obama-Biden tsunami that swept across the nation on election night. In the aftermath of such a defeat, when finger-pointing is often part of the political terrain, many of the fingers pointed to Sarah Palin and to John McCain for choosing her as his running mate. Anonymous McCain aides sniped at her, accusing her of "going rogue," being a "diva," and not knowing that Africa was a continent. Late-night comedian Conan O'Brien summed up the conventional wisdom: "President-elect Barack Obama spent the day thanking the people who helped him win the election. . . . Yeah, and actually, Obama's first phone call was to Sarah Palin. He sent her flowers."

What happened in just two months—from September 3 to November 4—that would have caused this dramatic reversal from Republican savior to national joke? Too inexperienced, was one popular criticism. Not ready for the Oval Office. No foreign policy expertise. Palin's handlers didn't

CBS EVENING NEWS EXCLUSIVE

help. They sequestered her from most of the press at the start, and when they finally allowed interviews, it was with two of the biggest and most seasoned journalists, Charlie Gibson of ABC and Katie Couric of CBS. For these prime-time broadcasts, the McCain team had not set ground rules, and they gave the networks discretionary power to air clips of the interviews. When the Alaska governor slipped up on foreign policy, those clips played over and over on network television and went viral on the Internet. Even more damage was done by comedian Tina Fey's satiric portrayal of Palin in skits on *Saturday Night Live,* earning that television show its highest ratings in decades. Added to the mix was "clothing-gate," where it was discovered that the Republican National Committee had spent over $150,000 on clothes for Palin and her family. Palin had been reduced to a joke and became a drag on the ticket. But did

Sarah Palin actually *cause* the defeat of the Republican ticket just 62 days after her electrifying convention speech?

As we will see in politics, rarely does one single factor decide a presidential election, especially in a year when so many other factors are at play. The McCain-Palin ticket pulled even with Obama-Biden and was ahead in important battleground states up to September 15. But on that critical date, Lehman Brothers, one of the oldest and most venerable financial institutions on Wall Street, failed. For the first time since the Great Depression, Americans worried about the solvency of their bank accounts. For one week, it was unclear whether the entire financial system would topple—not just in the United States but throughout the world.

Sarah Palin did not cause this unprecedented financial crisis. Nor did she cause the approval rating of the sitting Republican president, George

W. Bush, to fall lower than Richard Nixon's numbers just before the tarnished Nixon resigned. Palin did not cause Republican Party identification to fall 8 points in just four years. She did not send troops into Iraq looking for weapons of mass destruction that never materialized, and she was not the sole reason that Barack Obama put together the most astounding fund-raising machine in modern times, allowing him to outspend McCain in some states by 5 to 1. Finally, Sarah Palin did not tell John McCain to announce the suspension of his campaign to go to Washington to deal with the financial crisis, thus drawing more attention to the charge that the problem was caused by the Republicans. Could she have had an impact on the race in other ways? Did she make it difficult for McCain to talk about experience? Did she cause Democrats to come home to their nominee?

CHAPTER LEARNING OBJECTIVES

After reading this chapter you will be able to:

1-1 Assess the challenges that researchers face when studying causal relationships within politics.

1-2 Analyze the purposes of government and explain why government is necessary.

1-3 Compare and contrast the U.S. government to other democratic systems and identify core values and beliefs within American political culture.

Thinking About Politics

1-1 Assess the challenges that researchers face when studying causal relationships within politics.

Causal questions are concerned with "what causes what." Such questions address the roots or origins of particular events or behaviors. They attempt to explain which factor or factors made a particular outcome occur. You deal with causal questions every day: Did I get a "C" on that exam because I didn't study hard enough, or because I didn't study the right material? Which major gives me the best chance of getting into law school—political science or economics? Which will improve my job prospects more—taking extra classes during the summer, or working in an unpaid internship? In all of these cases, you are trying to understand an actual or potential outcome— getting a "C," getting into law school, getting a good job—in terms of factors that may bring it about. In this sense, you are always asking causal questions, and coming up with answers, as you seek to understand your world.

causal question a question regarding the factors responsible for a particular outcome.

"You are always asking causal questions, and coming up with answers, as you seek to understand your world."

Answering causal questions in the realm of politics and government is what political science and this book are all about. The question of Sarah Palin and her impact on the outcome of the 2008 election is a particular causal question. However, before you address this sort of question and identify what factors determine different sorts of political behaviors or outcomes, you should first be able to describe and understand the basic characteristics and organization of American government and society. Furthermore, questions regarding a specific politician's impact on the outcome of a presidential election lead to larger questions about who and what forces influence election outcomes, policy decisions, and governing more generally. What factors combine for a successful campaign? How can politicians and groups influence voters? Who decides what goes on the policy agenda? How do politicians of different parties and ideologies govern together?

Public officials, political activists, journalists, and pundits often have simple answers to such questions. Sorting out fact from fiction in the hurly-burly of political debate can be difficult, however, and can make citizens wary about getting involved in political arguments or political activity. Although you do not need to run for office or get involved in every political campaign, knowing the fundamentals of your political system and the fundamentals of good thinking allows you to keep your leaders—not to mention your friends and family—accountable. How health care will be funded, what sorts of taxes you will pay, and the shape of your retirement are all major issues that will surely be debated in the coming years. The wars in Iraq and Afghanistan will certainly not be the last wars debated by public officials and political activists.

This book provides you with the tools to see through simplistic answers that often get put forward in political debates, cable talk shows, and dinner-table conversations and to help you become a more informed and active citizen. The text will talk a lot about power and how it is wielded. The authors want to give you the confidence to take part in politics and influence how power is wielded in America's democracy. Throughout this text, you will encounter political scientists' answers to important questions in American politics in each of these areas. As you study each topic, pay close attention to the different ways researchers gather and analyze evidence as they try to understand politics and political decisions. Whatever the topic, we encourage you to take a critical view of how these arguments are framed and made. This will not only enable you to make sense of class material but will also give you the confidence to evaluate research and make arguments in other settings—academic, political, professional, or even social.

We will certainly discuss topics such as which factors influence presidential election outcomes—the questions that concluded the vignette about Sarah Palin and the 2008 election. Other examples of causal questions include

- Why do some people become Democrats, others Republicans, and others independents?
- Why does the United States have low rates of voter turnout compared with other countries?
- Do the major media in this country give preferential treatment to one political party over the other?
- Why are members of Congress reelected at such high rates?
- Why do views of the president fluctuate so much over the course of a term in office?

All of these questions have outcomes that political scientists try to explain: party attachments, voter turnout, media bias, congressional election outcomes, and presidential approval. In addressing these questions and explaining these outcomes, the first step for researchers is identifying which factors could influence or cause change in the specific outcome they are studying. If the president's approval rating is the outcome to be studied, one of the explanatory causes would be the state of the national economy. This is just another way of saying that the performance of the U.S. economy is one factor that affects presidential job approval.

There are rarely simple solutions to political questions.

Most good studies associate more than one causal or explanatory factor with each outcome. Political scientists tend to believe, for example, that while the state of the economy has an important influence on presidential approval, it is not the only relevant factor. The percentage of the electorate that has an attachment to the political party of the president (Republican or Democrat) is another factor that influences presidential approval. Another would be whether the nation is at war or at peace or whether the president is perceived as responding well to a natural disaster like Hurricane Katrina.

Whereas political scientists see a world in which more than one factor contributes to an outcome, journalists and politicians often focus on one major cause, even claiming it is the sole cause of something. If the economy is bad, it is because taxes are too high. If a candidate loses an election, it is because he or she ran a poor campaign. If the president suffers a legislative defeat, it is because the media covered his proposal in negative ways. If a political protest evolves into a riot, it is because the police failed to keep order. Simple answers make the journalist's job and the politician's job much easier.

Often these single-cause explanations flow from a particular viewpoint or partisan posture, or—in today's world—the need to explain something in a quick sound bite. Generally, they do not represent good theory or good social science research, or even the whole story. Political scientists see the world as complex, with most conditions having not just one but a variety of causes. One of our goals in this book is to help you get beyond the shouting matches on television news shows and give you the tools to make, interpret, and evaluate arguments on your own—and thus to be an informed and critical citizen who can question the black-and-white world of sound bites and television talk shows and see the issues in more realistic, more complex terms.

Correlation does not equal causation.

Challenges arise when analysts conduct research on politics. One challenge occurs with such frequency that it needs special attention as you learn about others' research and come up with your own answers: correlation is not the same as causation. Consider a fairly silly example from outside the world of politics. Imagine that when ice cream sales went up, so did residential burglaries. Likewise, when ice cream sales went down, residential burglaries went down as well. What would you conclude from this? One conclusion would be that the increase in ice cream sales was somehow causing the rise in burglaries. Perhaps when criminals eat ice cream, they get a sudden rush of carbohydrate energy and break into the nearest house they can find. Or maybe it works the other way. Criminals who have just broken into a home have more money to spend. With more money to spend, they buy more of all the things they normally buy—including ice cream. Most likely, however, neither of these scenarios is correct. Instead, it is probably the case that during the summer, people buy more ice cream in order to cool down. Also during the summer, people tend to go on vacation, leaving their homes empty. These homes then become attractive targets for burglars.

correlation a relationship between factors such that change in one is accompanied by change in the other.

causation a relationship between variables such that change in the value of one is directly responsible for change in the value of the other.

spurious relationship a relationship between variables that reflects correlation but not causation.

Thus, ice cream sales and residential burglaries move up and down together; they are **correlated** and therefore are associated with one another. But, in this case, correlation does not necessarily mean **causation**; that is, increased ice cream sales do not cause increased burglary; they are not responsible for increased burglary.

Consider another example. It is a fact that the more firefighters who respond to a fire, the worse the damage and the injuries. What possibly could be happening here? More firefighters get in the way of each other and cause injuries? Not likely. A more likely explanation is that this is another case of two factors that occur together—they are related but their relationship is not causal. Political scientists call this a **spurious relationship**. The more serious the fire, the more firefighters that respond. Of course, the more serious the fire, the more likely it is that damage and injuries will occur. The same factor that is influencing the number of firefighters that are sent is also influencing the amount of damages and injuries that result.

The concept of a relationship that is correlated but not causal is illustrated in the simple "inverted V" diagram in Figure 1-1. It illustrates how a third factor is influencing both of the other two outcomes. In this case, the seriousness of the fire influences both the number of firefighters who are called to the fire and the amount of damage from the fire.

Now, consider an example from the world of politics. Congressional studies show that politicians tend to vote in ways consistent with the preferences of the interest groups that contribute to their campaigns. Politicians who receive funds from the National Rifle Association (NRA), for example, reliably vote against gun control legislation and in support of an expansive interpretation of the Second Amendment to the Constitution, which guarantees citizens the right to bear arms.

You could conclude from this example that the NRA is buying votes—that the correlation between their campaign contributions and the votes of members of Congress is actually evidence of causation. This is precisely the sort of case, however, in which one must exercise caution. Perhaps causation is working in reverse here. Maybe the NRA supports those candidates who vote in favor of its issue positions. Rather than the NRA buying votes with its contributions, maybe members of Congress are attracting NRA contributions with their votes. Again, what at first appears

to be a case of correlation and causation is not so straightforward. Something else may be happening. There may be another more complex, more realistic explanation.

How do you sort through such issues? First, for a change in a particular factor or situation to cause a change in an outcome, the situation must precede the outcome. World War II could not have caused World War I. If you want to assert a causal relationship between two factors, make sure that any change in the value of the one precedes a change in the value of the other. Second, try to rule out the possibility of outside factors that may be responsible for the movement or change. For example, a researcher in France found a strong, positive correlation between young men who play sports and those who took part in riots in the suburbs of France's biggest cities. The argument was that playing sports made young men more aggressive and prone to violence. Still, this finding seems surprising since conventional wisdom and the rationale behind the funding of many sports programs is that they instill discipline and keep kids off the streets—helping to decrease crime. The positive correlation between playing sports and violent behavior could be driven by a third factor. We know that those without jobs are more likely to engage in crime. Perhaps those without jobs also have more time to play sports (Figure 1-2)?

This example reinforces an earlier point: the world is complex, and there is rarely a single cause for any observed effect. We should always be careful, therefore, to consider all variables that might be driving a relationship we have observed. Throughout this text, we will be examining causal relationships. Such discussions will be highlighted by a marginal causation flag like the one in the margin here.

ThinkingCausally

Causality flags in subsequent chapters provide a question that highlights the causal question being explored.

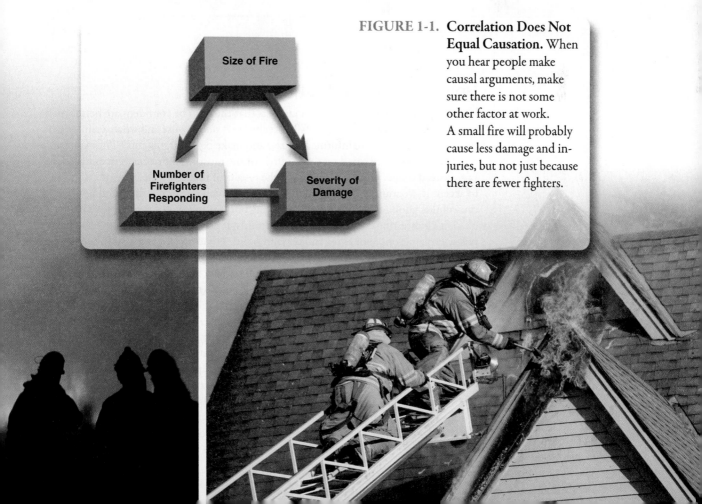

FIGURE 1-1. Correlation Does Not Equal Causation. When you hear people make causal arguments, make sure there is not some other factor at work. A small fire will probably cause less damage and injuries, but not just because there are fewer fighters.

Size of Fire

Number of Firefighters Responding

Severity of Damage

Riots among the youth in France began in the suburbs of Paris in October 2005. Although many of the rioters played sports, their criminal behavior was not caused by playing sports. Other factors may have caused both of these behaviors, such as not having jobs and thus having more time for both sports and criminal activity.

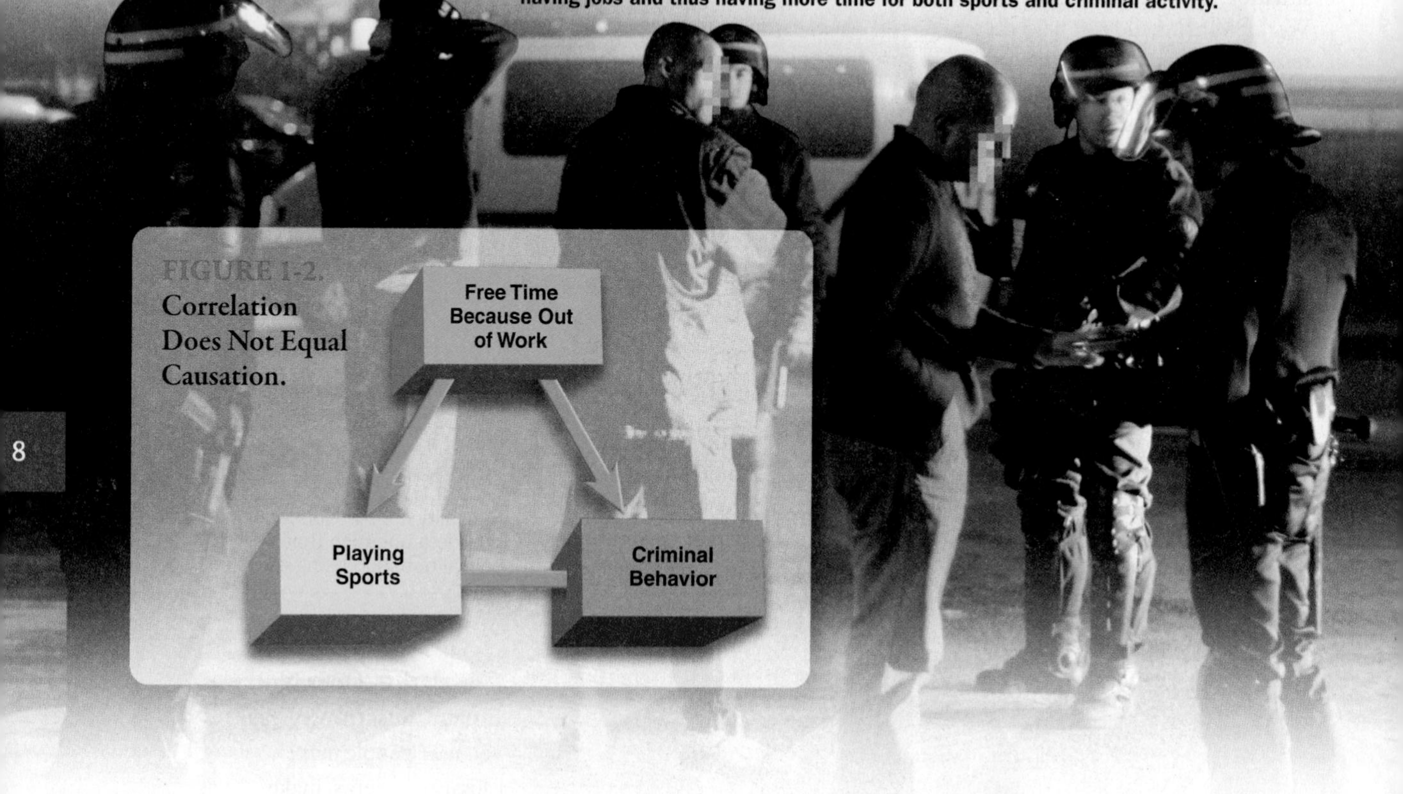

FIGURE 1-2.
Correlation
Does Not Equal
Causation.

Free Time
Because Out
of Work

Playing
Sports

Criminal
Behavior

8

How do we know that we are right?

How do political scientists arrive at answers that they can be confident are better than the simple, single-cause answers? What techniques do they use and what techniques can you use to be a more informed citizen and make better arguments? The explanations in this book are based on the findings of the most recent research in our field. But, instead of just presenting you with the results of that research and expecting you to accept it, we want to help you understand how such research is done and how you can employ good research and good thinking both in and out of the classroom. First of all, it's interesting stuff, but more importantly, it will help you see beyond the simplistic explanations about government and politics that you see and hear in the media. Hence, each chapter contains a feature called "How Do We Know?"

The "How Do We Know?" features begin with an important research question, puzzle, or serious methodological challenge relevant to the material in the chapter and to being a good citizen. For example, when we study political participation, we will examine how we know how to calculate voter turnout. And when we study elections, we will examine the challenges involved in determining the effect of campaign spending on election outcomes. We describe each question, puzzle, or challenge in some detail and tell you why political scientists consider it important. We then explain how scholars have tried to answer the question, solve the puzzle, or meet the challenge—often using the methods and principles discussed in this chapter. Through the "How Do We Know?" features, we hope you will see how political scientists approach their work, and will begin to use some of those methods as you observe the activities of American government and the coverage of those events in the media.

We also want you to see how many of the concepts we discuss in the book have tangible, real-world consequences. We study politics and tackle causal questions because we find issues revolving around elections, presidential power, congressional decisions, and public policy debates to be interesting and important. Put another way, we enjoy following current politics and political battles. Accordingly, throughout this book, we will illustrate important concepts and arguments with up-to-date and exciting examples of politics and political decision making. Every chapter will begin with a short story that illustrates a key puzzle for the subject at hand. In addition, each chapter contains a Case Study section that examines in more depth how citizens or our leaders went about making political decisions or how a particular political event played itself out.

Government and Why It Is Necessary

1-2 Analyze the purposes of government and explain why government is necessary.

When this book refers to **government**, it means the institutions that create and enforce rules for a specific territory and people. As we noted previously, there are many governments in the United States. Although this book focuses almost

government the institutions that have the authority and capacity to create and enforce public policies (rules) for a specific territory and people.

◄ **EQUAL AT THE STARTING LINE, BUT A WINNER EMERGES**
Most Americans hold that citizens should have equal opportunities, but—like runners in a race—they understand that our society, economy, and politics will generate both winners and losers. Are there any areas in which you think there should be an equal outcome?

exclusively on the central or national government based in Washington, D.C., a citizen of the United States is also subject to the authority of many other governments. These include state government, county government, city and town councils, local school boards, and special entities that cross the boundaries of local governments such as water, tourism, and transportation authorities. Although each of these governments is distinctive, all are related in that, as the definition states, they consist of institutions that create and administer public policies for a particular territory and the people within it. All may have direct relevance to you and your family as they determine the amount of local taxes you pay, the quality of your schools, and the size of your community's police force.

Citizens in a democracy make a fundamental bargain with their government.

Government is different from other institutions in society in that it has a broad right to use force. To put the matter bluntly, government can make citizens do things they otherwise might not do (such as pay taxes, educate their children, carry car insurance, and pay for lost library books). If citizens refuse to do these things, or insist on doing things that are prohibited by law, government can take

▼ WHOSE JOB IS IT?
One of the core definitions of government is that it has the sole authority to enforce laws. On the U.S.-Mexican border, some citizens and groups like the Minutemen are taking the law into their own hands to discourage illegal immigration. What should citizens do if they believe the government is not providing essential services?

Government:
U. S. Border Patrol

Authority

Civilian:
Minutemen

Senor Fox, The King of England
Didn't like the Minuteman either

action against them—imposing financial or other penalties, including extreme penalties, such as life imprisonment or, in some states, death.

No other segment of society has such wide-ranging authority or ability to enforce its rules. Even corporations and wealthy individuals, which many Americans think of as very powerful, ultimately must use the court system—that is, the government—to get others to do what they want.

Why do people willingly grant government this monopoly on force and compulsion? Because, as people often say about getting older, it beats the alternative. The alternative to a government monopoly on force is a collection of individuals trying to impose their will on each other. Imagine, for example, that you and your neighbor enter into a dispute over where your property ends and his or hers begins. Without a government available to mediate the dispute, you would be left to resolve it on your own. If you could not resolve it on peaceful, mutually agreeable terms, one or both of you might seek to enforce your will through force or even violence.

Or imagine that your neighbor was hungry, while you had abundant food. If you did not wish to share, your neighbor might attempt to steal some of your food in order to feed his family. Without government, the only way to stop this would be to take matters into your own hands. You would have to forcibly prevent your neighbor from stealing, and maybe leave him with a lump on his head as a token of your displeasure. He, of course, would try to resist all of this, perhaps leaving you with a lump on your head. Now imagine these scenarios multiplied tens of thousands of times per day, as men and women pursue their own self-interest without any restrictions, regulations, or protection provided by a governing authority. This sort of arrangement would obviously be unacceptable. In the words of Thomas Hobbes, a famous political thinker writing during the English Civil War in the 1600s in his treatise *Leviathan*, it would soon lead to "a war of all against all," and a world in which life was "solitary, poor, nasty, brutish, and short."[1] We will have more to say about the influence of Hobbes and his co-thinkers below.

Governments arise or must arise because individuals do not wish to live in such a world. Accordingly, they enter into a **social contract** with one another to create, and give authority to, a governing body with a legal monopoly on power or force. Under this arrangement, individuals give up any claim to use force to get what they want. They give the instruments of compulsion—laws, courts, police, prosecutors, and prisons, for example—to the arms of government. In exchange for these, individuals get to enjoy life, liberty, and property without constant fear of outside interference. In the United States, the social contract is the Constitution. In Chapter 3, we will discuss in great depth the nature and logic behind this document that has defined the relationship between the people and their leaders in the United States for over two hundred years. And, throughout the text, we will discuss how the Constitution structures the institutions and the political decisions and debates that happen today.

This is the essence of the idea that government is a social contract, an idea popularized by its main proponents—the political thinkers Thomas Hobbes, John Locke, and Jean-Jacques Rousseau.[2] Among those Enlightenment philosophers who influenced the framers of the U.S. Constitution, few loomed larger than Locke. Writing in seventeenth-Century Britain, Locke laid a logical foundation for the creation of government and civil society. Locke was primarily concerned with the protection of individual property, by which he meant each individual's "life, liberty, and estate." Locke shared Hobbes' concern that in the state of nature individual property was

social contract an agreement among members of a society to form and recognize the authority of a centralized government that is empowered to make and enforce laws governing the members of that society.

◄ A WAR OF ALL AGAINST ALL

Thomas Hobbes, shown here with the cover of his famous treatise *Leviathan*, popularized the idea of a social contract that people enter into with one another to create and give authority to government.

continually threatened. Individuals, then, logically surrendered some rights to a government so that their property might be protected. Note, though, that for Locke the existence of government presupposed the existence of basic rights to property that every individual naturally enjoyed. The justification for government lay in the protections it afforded to individual property and not to its ability to foster any larger social good (e.g., virtue).

Notice that in Locke's thinking, government receives its authority from the people. It is decidedly not the case that government grants rights. Rather, the reverse is true—the people decide, through their contract with one another, which rights and authorities they will give over to government and which they will retain for themselves. Moreover, if the government breaks its side of the contract and engages in tyranny, the people retain the right to revolt. Indeed, for philosophers like Locke, revolution constituted the ultimate check on government tyranny.

Because in a democracy governmental authority rests on an agreement among the governed, that authority can be modified. In the United States, for example, the people can change government's authority by changing or amending the Constitution. Or if they wish, the people can revoke the authority of government altogether. This is one check against the possibility of government overstepping its bounds in the social-contract agreement. In **authoritarian systems**, where one person or group enjoys total power, there are no such checks.

authoritarian (or totalitarian) system a political system in which one person or group has absolute control over the apparatus of government, and in which popular input in government is minimal or nonexistent.

▲ WHO'S GOING TO CLEAR
THE ROAD?
Although it is certainly in every
motorist's best interest to have
the road cleared of snow, there is
no incentive for any car owner to
clear the road on his or her own.
This is one public good that
government can provide to all
residents.

Government provides public goods and services.

Government is not only about protecting us from each other. Government also
provides its citizens with **public goods**. Public goods are products or services that
are enjoyed by all citizens and unlikely to be provided by anyone other than government. Nongovernmental institutions generally cannot, or will not, provide public
goods because

public goods goods (and
services) that are enjoyed by all
citizens and unlikely to be
provided by any organization other
than government.

- it would be too difficult for them to marshal sufficient resources to provide the
  good; and
- it is difficult, if not impossible, to exclude nonpayers from receiving the good.

The best example of a public good is national defense. The United States
currently spends more than $400 billion per year on various elements of its national
defense. This kind of investment, year in and year out, is simply beyond the reach of
any private-sector institution.

National defense is also difficult to exclude from those unwilling to pay for it.
Imagine that U.S. national defense was provided by a private company, and that
individual consumers could choose whether they wished to pay to be defended.
Now imagine that only half of the homeowners in a particular state decided to pay
for this service. If a missile were headed toward this state, there would be no way
for the defense company to protect only those homeowners who had paid its services. Instead, the company would have to defend all of the state's residents.

Such a scenario is problematic in two respects. First, the company is providing a
service and not being compensated by everyone benefiting from it. Why would the
company want to stay in this business? Second, homeowners who did pay for the
service would quickly begin to think they were being taken advantage of. Why should
they continue to pay for the service if others will receive the service for free?
Obviously, either the company will get out of the business, or individuals who are
currently paying for defense will stop doing so. Either way, national defense will not
be provided.

Government overcomes such problems by providing the service itself and then compelling everyone to contribute by paying taxes. Any situation that has the characteristics of a public good will be a prime area for government involvement.

Although government's primary responsibilities are to keep order, protect individual rights, and provide public goods, in practice, government's activities extend well beyond these areas. One of the federal government's largest areas of responsibility, for example, is providing retirement security for workers and their families through the Social Security system. The government does this even though provision of Social Security is unrelated to ensuring public order or preserving individual rights. Furthermore, government provides Social Security even though it is not a public good—private companies do sell retirement securities, and it is a simple matter to provide them only to those willing to pay.

▼ BILLIONS OF DOLLARS IN MILITARY HARDWARE

The funding of the military is a classic example of a public good. Everyone shares in the benefits of advanced national defense. No single citizen could fund it, and those who might choose to not contribute to it cannot be excluded from its benefits.

Politics is about influencing decisions.

Of course, exactly which goods and services are public and how they are provided can vary significantly depending on who gets to decide how and which public goods and services are provided. In the context of this book, **politics** refers to individual and collective efforts to influence the workings of government. Engaging in politics, therefore, means trying to influence

politics individual and collective efforts to influence the workings of government.

- who will lead government,
- how government will operate and make decisions,
- what the nature and substance of government decisions will be, and
- how government enforces its decisions.

As for specific examples, politics means working to elect a particular person as mayor, or state senator, or judge, or president. Politics means collecting signatures to put on the ballot a requirement that raising taxes would need more than a majority vote in the state legislature. Politics means attending a town hall meeting to voice concerns about proposed health care reforms. Politics means forming a group to demonstrate outside a prison as a way to protest the death penalty. And politics means participating in an organized effort for a higher minimum wage, increased student loan programs, bringing American troops home from a war, job training, small business assistance, and agricultural subsidies.

Often, politics is referred to in a negative manner: "it was all about politics," or so and so "was just playing politics." But there is nothing inherently negative in the definition of politics. Certainly, politics can in some ways be distasteful to people. But efforts to influence the workings of government can also be noble and high minded.

Furthermore, although we might cringe at times at the way politics is conducted—petty partisanship, shrill language, naked appeals to selfish interests, broken promises, and so on—again, it is surely better than the alternative. Without politics, many differences would be settled violently, outside the accepted processes of government. Americans experienced that most clearly in the Civil War, when differences over slavery were settled on the battlefield and at the cost of hundreds of thousands of lives.

One of the differences Americans have with each other is over which issues are appropriate for government consideration. For example, is the content of movies, music, and video games a purely private matter, or is it a public concern? Some would say that this matter can be dealt with appropriately by individual businesses and consumers. Others say that government should have the right to require that movies, music, and video games come with a rating label.

One policy debate that resulted in legislation during the Obama administration was whether the federal government should provide every citizen with health insurance. The debate was really about whether health care was mostly a private concern or a public concern. Should health insurance coverage be a public matter decided by the government? Should it be a private matter, decided by individual citizens and their employers? Or does it fall somewhere in the middle?

Clearly, then, politics "starts" even before an issue makes it to the governmental agenda. As this book will frequently note, much of the substance of politics is devoted to the complex questions about which issues belong on that agenda in the first place.

▲ **MAKING YOUR VOICE HEARD**

Attending town hall meetings is one of the many ways you have of influencing policy and politics.

Contexts for Studying American Government and Politics

1-3 Compare and contrast the U.S. government to other democratic systems and identify core values and beliefs within American political culture.

Understanding the answers to—and how to answer—fundamental questions in American politics and government is a main goal of this book. You will learn about American politics in light of two important contexts: the comparative context and the cultural context. We also want to help you begin to think logically and carefully in investigating important causal questions related to American government. We think that understanding how your government works and how politics in America works is important and even exciting. Today, however, lots of partisan bickering and hyperbolic media coverage of politics can turn people off and make them cynical about their government. Pundits and politicians make causal claims at every turn, and it can be difficult—even intimidating—to think about wading into these arguments and participating in politics. That said, for American democracy to survive and thrive, students must engage in politics and in political arguments. We believe that providing you with the tools to explore answers to political questions and make political arguments can make you more confident and give you the skills to be more thoughtful, critical, and empowered citizens.

The presidential system and rights are central to American government.

democracy a form of government in which the people rule. This can take place directly, through participation by the people in actual lawmaking, or indirectly, through free elections in which the people choose representatives to make laws on their behalf.

autocracy a form of government in which a single person rules with effectively unlimited power.

direct democracy a form of democracy in which the people themselves make the laws and set the policies adopted by the government.

representative democracy a form of democracy in which the people, through free elections, select representatives to make laws on their behalf and set policies adopted by the government.

Democracy, a word derived from ancient Greek, means "rule by the many" (in contrast to its opposite, **autocracy**, which means "rule by a single person," such as a king or emperor). The defining principle in a democracy is that government is based on the consent of the governed. In other words, democratic government operates at the pleasure or will of the people.

Democracy in its purest form is known as **direct democracy**. In a direct democracy, the people vote directly on laws. Many U.S. states, such as California, have a form of direct democracy in which citizens can both initiate and vote on ballot measures to change state law. (Examples are the initiatives in a number of states to amend the state constitution to ban same-sex marriage.)

The U.S. federal government, however, has no such mechanism. It is organized entirely as a **representative democracy**. In a representative democracy, people vote for their leaders through elections. But those leaders, not the people themselves, make the laws. Whether direct or representative, democracy implies more than just providing avenues for individuals to influence government. American democracy, for example, is also characterized by the following principles:

- **Political equality.** All adult Americans (with some narrow exceptions) have the right to vote, and each American's vote counts equally. Furthermore, all adult Americans have an equal right to participate in politics at every level.

- **Plurality rule and minority rights.** Plurality rule means that whoever or whatever gets the most votes wins, and in American politics the will of the plurality of people usually prevails. Whoever gets the most votes wins elective office; bills pass with a plurality vote in the legislature; Supreme Court decisions must command a plurality in order to have the force of law. In any of these settings, however, pluralities may not use their dominant status to trample the rights of those in the minority. Specific minority rights are guaranteed in state and federal law, in state and federal constitutions, in state and federal court decisions, and in the operating rules at various levels of government. Thus, even if one group could muster a winning margin for the proposition that a smaller group be denied the right to vote, state and federal constitutions would prevent this from happening.

- **Equality before the law.** With only a few exceptions, every American has the same legal rights and obligations as do all other Americans. Every American is subject to the same laws as every other. And every American must be treated the same by government. In other words, American government is not permitted to discriminate arbitrarily among groups or individuals. Of course, in reality, this is a principle or goal that has not been fully accomplished in American democracy. Certain individuals or groups can have advantages over their fellow citizens (such instances of unequal power will be identified throughout this text).

America is a **constitutional democracy**. Thus, the U.S. Constitution is a document with the force of law that defines and constrains government's exercise of power. It expressly identifies, for example, the responsibilities of each branch of government, ensuring that the president, Congress, or the courts will not overreach. The Constitution also makes clear, through the Bill of Rights, that the government must do certain things and may not do certain things. For example, it must ensure that criminal defendants receive a speedy and fair trial. And it must not limit freedom of speech, religion, or assembly.

As we will discuss in Chapter 2 on political culture, people's attitudes toward their government, their role as citizens in a democracy, and their support for the freedoms that government is supposed to protect are highly important to the healthy functioning of a democratic government. As the legendary U.S. Circuit Court Judge Learned Hand (1872–1971) reminded us,

constitutional democracy a form of democracy in which there is a foundational document (such as the U.S. Constitution) that describes the structure, powers, and limits of government.

◄ ONE PERSON, ONE VOTE
Representative democracy is the fundamental element of the American political system. Although people may have more or less of a resource, all votes, cast in secret, are equal.

> Liberty lies in the hearts of men and women; when it dies there, no constitution, no law, no court can save it; no constitution, no law, no court can even do much to help it. While it lies there it needs no constitution, no law, no court to save it.[3]

In more colloquial terms, Hand means that the American public is the ultimate guardian of its own rights and freedoms. As long as Americans believe in their democratic system and are willing to engage in it, there can be no serious threat to liberty or democratic stability. If Americans, however, lose faith in the system, fail to hold it accountable, or abandon the democratic values that support it, the very concepts of self-rule and liberty may be at risk.

Politics in America is not the only model for politics or democracy.

ThinkingComparatively
Some countries rely on an evolving set of laws or customs to preserve democratic features of government, while others, like the United States, do this through a constitution.

America is one among a number of the world's democracies. It shares some common features with all of them, such as a commitment to majority rule through elections. It also differs from them in many respects. The U.S. Constitution, for example, is rightly seen as a limiting document, one intended by the founders as a bulwark against the possibility of governmental tyranny. Not all democracies set such limits on themselves at their founding. When Israel became a state, major political interests there were unable to agree on a constitution. In place of a single constitutional document, therefore, Israel has a series of "basic laws" and court decisions that have accumulated over the years. These define the contours of government responsibility. Similarly, the United Kingdom has no single, limiting document like the U.S. Constitution. Instead, it has an evolving set of laws, judicial decisions, customs, and practices that are the rough equivalent of American constitutional law.

American democracy also differs from others in that it is a federal system in which there is a national government with responsibility for the affairs of the nation as a whole, and 50 separate state governments, each with responsibility for affairs within state borders. Thus, as we will discuss in Chapter 4, much of the federal governing apparatus—a president, a Congress, and federal courts—is duplicated at the state level, with governors, state legislatures, and state courts.

Federalism is not the only structure by which a democracy can be organized. France, Japan, and Uruguay, on the one hand, have only one layer of decision-making authority—at the national level. In these countries, there are no equivalents to American governors or state legislatures. Canada, Germany, and India, on the other hand, are organized as federal systems—with a national government and regional governments, just as in the United States.

presidential system a political system in which the head of the executive branch is selected by some form of popular vote and serves a fixed term of office. The United States has a presidential system.

parliamentary system a political system in which the head of the executive branch is selected by members of the legislature rather than by popular vote.

Finally, the United States differs from most other democracies in being a presidential system rather than a parliamentary one. In a **presidential system**, the voters select separately their chief executive and their legislators. (In 2008, for example, a voter living in North Carolina could have "split the ticket," casting one vote for Republican presidential candidate John McCain and a separate vote for Democratic senatorial candidate Kay Hagan.)

In a **parliamentary system**, this kind of split-ticket voting in which one votes for one party for president and another for Congress would be impossible. In fact, in the United Kingdom, voters do not cast a ballot for the chief executive at all. Instead, they vote for representatives to the national legislative assembly, the House of Commons. From among their ranks, the members of that body then choose the chief executive, the prime minister.

On occasion, this book will make these sorts of comparisons, contrasting American politics and government with the corresponding processes and institutions in other countries. These sorts of comparisons will clarify the unique features of American government. These cross-national comparisons can also shed light on underlying causal processes here in the United States and help us make causal arguments about the roles of parties, elections, culture, and other aspects of American politics. As with discussions of causation, discussions of comparisons will be indicated by a marginal flag, as this one was on the previous page.

Unique values and attitudes define politics in America.

American politics and government are continually shaped by the uniquely American **political culture**. Political culture refers to the orientation of citizens toward the political system and toward themselves as actors in it—the basic values, beliefs, attitudes, predispositions, and expectations that citizens bring to political life.

The United States has a dominant political culture, sometimes referred to as the American creed. Chapter 2 will explain the American political culture in detail. The main ideas and values that make up the creed are individualism, democracy, equality, and liberty, as well as respect for private property and religion. Most Americans strongly embrace these concepts in the abstract, and often in specific cases as well. Often these values, however, can clash with one another. For example, does equality dictate that everyone in America should have equal incomes? Not necessarily. When Americans express their belief in the value of equality, they generally mean equality of opportunity—everyone having an equal chance to rise as high as their talents will carry them. This is not the same, however, as everyone enjoying equal outcomes. That is an idea that most Americans do not embrace.

American political culture gives a sense of what is politically possible in the United States: what the American people demand, expect, and will tolerate from government; which public policy undertakings are likely to be viewed favorably and which negatively; which political messages are consistent winners and losers with American voters; and which social, political, and demographic trends are likely to put pressure on government.

The American political culture is not a perfectly harmonious set of beliefs. When it comes to specific cases, some values and ideas in the culture clash, and others give way to more practical considerations. Although it establishes some clear boundaries for American political discourse and governmental action, those boundaries are fairly expansive. Chapter 2 will explain the American political culture in comparative and historical contexts, and this text throughout will periodically invoke American political culture as a useful lens through which you can view U.S. politics and government.

political culture the values and beliefs of citizens toward the political system and toward themselves as actors in it.

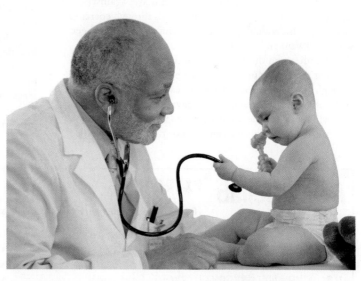

▲ **THE ROLE OF GOVERNMENT**

Debates about the role of government in issues like health care continue to rage in American politics. Although many other industrialized democracies provide health care for their citizens, health care and health insurance are generally in private hands in America. How might this preference result from the political culture of the United States?

CHAPTER SUMMARY

In this chapter you have learned to:

1-1   Assess the challenges that researchers face when studying causal relationships within politics. Political science focuses on politics and government and how government leaders and citizens behave. Political scientists typically try to determine what factor, or combination of factors, produced a particular outcome. Political scientists strive to be rigorous, thorough, and scientific researchers. To be good citizens and understand how your government and society work, students of American politics should also understand some basic rules of rigorous thinking. One important rule, often violated by politicians and pundits alike, is the fact that correlation does not equal causation. Just because two factors may move together—ice cream sales and burglaries, number of firefighters and fire damage—does not mean that one is causing the other.

1-2   Analyze the purposes of government and explain why government is necessary. Government is necessary because only government has the broad right to force citizens to do things they otherwise might not do. Citizens grant government this monopoly on force and coercion in order to gain public goods such as roads, military defense, clean water, and education, and to protect themselves against fellow citizens trying to enforce their wills through coercion or violence. Individuals give up any claim to use force to get what they want and, in return, get security for themselves, their families, and their property. Still, in a democracy, government receives its power from the people—citizens decide, through a social contract with their leaders, which rights and authorities they will relinquish to government and which they will retain for themselves. Politics in America is a competition about which rights and authorities are best handled

by government and what government will do with its authority. America is a constitutional democracy in which the U.S. Constitution identifies the responsibilities of each branch of government: executive, legislative, and judicial. The Constitution also makes clear, through the Bill of Rights, that the government may not do certain things—abridge freedom of speech, religion, or assembly, for example—and that it must do certain things, such as ensure that criminal defendants receive a speedy and fair trial.

1-3   Compare and contrast the U.S. government to other democratic systems and identify core values and beliefs within American political culture. The American model of government is one sort among many. By studying models and practices in other countries, we can learn a great deal about our own. America is a democracy and like all democracies is committed to majority rule through elections. Differences in governmental structure and the core values of citizens influence the path of politics in different democracies. Understanding the major features of American politics, and the major factors that drive political decisions and outcomes, can be made easier by comparing our system to government systems in other countries. Decisions made throughout our history also influence the path of politics today. We can learn much about how American leaders and citizens behave today by looking at how previous situations were dealt with and how that affects decisions and outcomes in today's politics. American politics and government are influenced by the uniquely American, dominant political culture, sometimes referred to as the American creed. The main ideas and values that make up the creed are individualism, democracy, equality, and liberty, as well as respect for private property and religion.

EXERCISES

Apply what you learned in this chapter by starting with these resources on MyPoliSciLab.

📖 **Read** on **mypoliscilab.com**

    eText: Chapter 1

✔ **Study** and **Review** on **mypoliscilab.com**

    Pre-Test
    Post-Test
    Chapter Exam
    Flashcards

👁 **Watch** on **mypoliscilab.com**

    Video: Mexico Border Security
    Video: The Bailout Hearings
    Video: Vaccines: Mandatory Protection

✳ **Explore** on **mypoliscilab.com**

    Comparative: Comparing Political Landscapes

KEY TERMS

authoritarian (or totalitarian)
    system, p. 12
autocracy, p. 16

causal question, p. 3
causation, p. 6
constitutional democracy, p. 17

correlation, p. 6
democracy, p. 16
direct democracy, p. 16

SUGGESTED READINGS

David Friedman. 1996. *Hidden Order: The Economics of Everyday Life.* New York: Harper Business. Argues that economics can explain everything from general wants, choices, and values to consumer preferences, street crimes, financial speculations, and political campaign spending.

John Gerring. 2001. *Social Science Methodology: A Critical Framework.* New York: Cambridge University Press. An introduction to social science methodology suggesting that task and criteria, not fixed rules of procedure, lead to methodological adequacy.

Gary King, Robert O. Keohane, and Sidney Verba. 1994. *Designing Social Inquiry: Scientific Inference in Qualitative Research.* Princeton: Princeton University Press. A unified approach to developing valid descriptive and causal inference, arguing that qualitative and quantitative researchers face similar difficulties that can be overcome in similar ways.

Steven Levitt and Stephen Dubner. 2006. *Freakonomics: A Rogue Economist Explores the Hidden Side of Everything.* New York: William Morrow. Looks at different puzzles in American society, providing a good illustration of how one social science method can help us understand vexing social issues.

Michael M. Lewis. 2003. *Moneyball: The Art of Winning an Unfair Game.* New York: Norton. How Billy Bean, manager of the Oakland Athletics baseball team, took a modernized, statistics-heavy approach to running an organization and recruiting valuable players overlooked by better-resourced teams.

SUGGESTED WEBSITES

Freakonomics Blog: www.freakonomics.blogs.nytimes.com
The authors of Freakonomics continue their search for new and interesting social science puzzles.

United Kingdom Parliament: www.parliament.uk
Information on the workings of the British government as well as links to the House of Lords and House of Commons.

Constitution for Israel: www.cfisrael.org//home.html
Explains the continuous work of the Constitution, Law, and Justice Committee of the Knesset toward drafting a constitution for the State of Israel.

Robert Wood Johnson Foundation: Coverage for the Uninsured: www.rwjf.org/coverage/index.jsp
Information about various health care issues and health reform plans by a major foundation in the medical policy field.

Initiative and Referendum Institute at the University of Southern California: www.iandrinstitute.org/ statewide_i&r.htm
Describes the government processes for placing issues on the ballot in each of the 50 states.

2 Political Culture

Church and State on the Campaign Trail

The words were stunning and, to many Americans, shocking.

"The government . . . wants us to sing 'God Bless America.' No, no, no, not God Bless America. God damn America—that's in the Bible—for killing innocent people. God damn America, for treating our citizens as less than human."

These comments by Reverend Jeremiah Wright, senior pastor of Chicago's Trinity United Church of

▼ FAITH BECOMES
A POLITICAL ISSUE
Provocative statements by Reverend Jeremiah Wright created shockwaves in the 2008 presidential nomination contest. Wright was the pastor at the church long attended by Barack Obama, and the Democratic candidate considered him a spiritual mentor. In his response, Obama explained the historical context for his pastor's remarks while at the same time rejecting them.

Christ through early 2008, exploded into the 2008 presidential nomination battle. Excerpts from Wright's sermons broadly condemned actions of the U.S. government, saw the terrorist attacks of September 11, 2001, as America's "chickens coming home to roost" because of American misdeeds abroad, and addressed in stark terms the country's racial divisions.

America's sense of self, as enshrined in a set of values and beliefs, is always something candidates must attend to. Most often, this is uneventful and candidates steer clear of any comments that seem to question the American way of life. A controversy over values and beliefs can detour or even derail a candidacy.

Wright's remarks posed a difficult challenge for Barack Obama. The Democratic contender had a close relationship with Wright, considering him a spiritual mentor who had aided him

in his Christian walk. Wright had officiated at Obama's wedding, baptized his two children, and one of his sermons served as the inspiration for the title of Obama's memoir, *The Audacity of Hope*. Obama had been a member of Wright's church for over 20 years.

At first, Obama tried a middle-ground approach. He repudiated Wright's most inflammatory comments, endorsed the positive role and message of the pastor in other aspects, and said the excerpts were not reflective of Wright's typical message. When the controversy did not die down, the candidate gave a major speech on race in which he placed Wright's comments, particularly those touching on race, in historical context. Soon after the speech, Wright made several media appearances in which he amplified the most controversial of his rhetoric. Obama responded with his strongest distancing yet, saying that Wright's

latest comments "do not portray accurately the perspective of the black church. They certainly don't portray accurately my values and beliefs." The candidate added, "whatever relationship I had with Reverend Wright has changed, as a consequence of this." Obama later resigned his membership in Trinity United.

2008 was not the first time religion emerged as a presidential campaign issue. In 1960, critics charged that Democratic nominee John F. Kennedy, a Roman Catholic, would be guided in his decision-making by the pope in Rome. In a speech before Protestant ministers in September 1960, Kennedy rejected the accusation and emphasized his belief in the separation of church and state. "I do not speak for my church on public matters—and the church does not speak for me," he stated. His faith, though, did matter to him: "I do not intend to apologize for these views . . . nor do I intend to disavow either my views or my church in order to win this election."

These episodes reveal that American political culture and the national identity entwined within it can have significant effects in politics. Candidates work hard to demonstrate that they are in the mainstream and embrace a shared set of values with voters. Reverend Wright's comments had a particularly strong impact on the presidential campaign precisely because he was a man of religion. Had the comments been made by Obama's longtime electrician or accountant, they would not likely have had the same effect.

The symbolic importance of religion in American political life reappeared at President Obama's inauguration in January 2009. Whereas conservatives were critical of candidate Obama for his affiliation with Reverend Wright, now it was liberals who were critical of President Obama for having Rick Warren, one of the country's most prominent evangelical pastors and an opponent of abortion and same-sex marriage, deliver the inauguration's opening prayer.

More so than in most other economically advanced countries, religious belief is an important part of America's self-perception.[1] But religion is only one aspect of American political culture. Beliefs in individualism, democracy, liberty, and property rights also guide people in how they vote, how they want the government to spend their tax dollars, and who should benefit from such spending. Americans have certain expectations about how religion or liberty, for example, fit into American political life, and these expectations are so deep that they become assumptions or habits. Most Americans do not, for example, spend much time on a daily basis thinking through the costs and benefits of freedom of speech to decide whether it is a good thing. "Of course" freedom of speech is good, they would think. "Of course" religious belief has a place in American political life.

But sometimes, the assumptions and habits of "of course" are challenged. Of course free speech is deeply cherished, but what about speech that is vile and hateful toward particular groups? Of course religion has an appropriate place, but to what degree should a public official bring his or her religious values into decisions about public policy or be held accountable for the beliefs of a particular religion? Of course individuals should be able to achieve all they can achieve, but is it appropriate through taxation to take hard-earned resources from one group in order to improve the opportunities for another? As in 2008, religious and other beliefs often present candidates and the larger political community with difficult choices and questions. At their deepest, the choices and questions affect Americans' self-identity, their understanding of what America is and what it means to be American.

CHAPTER LEARNING OBJECTIVES

After reading this chapter you will be able to:

2-1 Define political culture and explain how certain values and beliefs achieve dominance within a society.

2-2 Illustrate how the key values and beliefs of the American creed shape politics and government today.

2-3 Evaluate the consequences of American political culture such as limited government and a weak sense of sovereign power.

2-4 Identify the major challenges and alternatives to the dominant political culture.

What Does It Mean to Be an American?

2-1 Define political culture and explain how certain values and beliefs achieve dominance within a society.

What makes Americans *American*? Given the country's remarkable diversity, it cannot be a shared ethnic heritage. Nor can it be a long, shared history—Americans arrived here in waves of immigration, so the starting point of their sense of being

American varies tremendously. For most Americans, what defines being an American is a set of beliefs or ideals. The idea that individuals pursuing opportunity can make a better life for themselves, often referred to as the American Dream, is widely shared. This is part of American political culture.

Culture refers to a way of thinking or mode of behavior. **Political culture** refers to the basic values, beliefs, attitudes, predispositions, and expectations of citizens toward the political system and toward themselves as participants in it. Take, for example, the value of freedom of speech. Survey results over a long period of time suggest that freedom of speech is a bedrock value in the United States, enshrined in the Constitution, with 90 percent or more of the public agreeing with statements such as "I believe in free speech for all no matter what their views might be." When evaluating an issue concerning speech, most Americans start from the premise that free speech is important and should be encouraged and that they have a right to speak their minds. Freedom of speech is part of American political culture.

Political culture is not the same as public opinion. Public opinion focuses more on the issues of the day and is more susceptible to change, even over relatively short periods. It reveals, for example, how the public feels about a particular candidate or issue. Political culture is a broader, more permanent set of beliefs. Which candidate the public will vote for in the next presidential election is the realm of public opinion; the centrality of competitive elections to Americans' sense of democracy is the realm of political culture. Culture is pervasive and present in ways that you may not even be aware of, in the symbols used by candidates and organizations, in the language used to appeal to people, in the kinds of themes in popular culture that Americans seem to "naturally" gravitate toward, in what Americans assume to be important. Off-the-cuff comments like "it's a free country" convey how deeply political culture influences our thinking and carry many layers of meaning for most Americans.

political culture the values and beliefs of citizens toward the political system and toward themselves as actors in it.

Political culture provides a framework for political evaluation.

Political culture does not necessarily explain how Americans will respond to every situation. For instance, we noted that consistently over 90 percent of Americans say they believe in free speech for all, regardless of the views of the speakers. But when pushed, Americans will sometimes back away from this commitment. In one survey taken about a decade after World War II, for example, less than 15 percent of Americans were willing to allow fascists and communists to hold meetings and express their political views. Table 2-1 gives other examples of Americans' support for free speech in specific circumstances, including racist and anti-religious speech. Even though support for free speech has been increasing in recent decades, many Americans find their principles wavering in certain scenarios.

Often there are significant inconsistencies when moving from abstract beliefs to concrete decisions and issues. But abstract principles still matter. Most of you would agree with the old saying that "honesty is the best policy." You likely also believe that people should obey the law, that laws should be enforced, and that enforcement of the law should be done fairly. Yet few people think being brutally honest is right if it would needlessly hurt someone. And most of us who drive have probably found ourselves, on occasion, driving over the posted speed limit when there were no police watching (we plead guilty).

Does that inconsistency mean your general belief that honesty is the best policy is a farce? No. You start with that policy when you evaluate what to do. The belief provides a framework for decision-making. The confirmation that beliefs and values matter is that, even when we violate them, we feel compelled to understand and justify why we do so.

TABLE 2-1. Support for Free Speech in Specific Circumstances (percentages)

	YEAR OF SURVEY			
Allow book in library that	**1977**	**1988**	**1998**	**2008**
States blacks are genetically inferior	61%	62%	63%	64%
Is against churches and religion	60	64	69	71
Advocates homosexuality	55	60	70	76
Argues against elections and for military rule	55	57	67	69
Allow someone to teach in college who				
Believes blacks are genetically inferior	41	41	47	45
Is against churches and religion	39	45	57	60
Is a homosexual man	49	57	74	79
Argues against elections and for military rule	34	37	51	51
Allow someone to make a speech in your community who				
Believes blacks are genetically inferior	59	61	63	58
Is against churches and religion	64	70	74	76
Is a homosexual man	62	70	81	82
Argues against elections and for military rule	50	56	66	65

Source: General Social Survey.

Political culture works the same way. It provides a general framework and a starting point to evaluate issues, candidates, and the actions of public officials. It can also be exploited by politicians or political activists looking to score a victory. They know that these themes and beliefs resonate with the public, so they adjust their language accordingly.

The American creed is the dominant political culture in the United States.

The dominant political culture in the United States consists of beliefs in individualism, democracy, liberty, property rights, and religion, all tied together by the value of equality. This set of beliefs has been labeled with many terms; we will call it the **American creed**.[2] It provides the frame of reference most Americans use to evaluate candidates and specific issues. For that reason, politicians make heavy use of this frame of reference to reach Americans, which then reinforces its importance. President Barack Obama provided an example in his victory speech on election night in 2008, noting that America's strength comes "from the enduring power of our ideals: democracy, liberty, opportunity, and unyielding hope."

These beliefs are ideals, and as such they are general rather than specific. To say there is a widely shared political culture is *not* to say that Americans agree on all the specifics about politics and that there is no conflict in the United States. It is also not to say that these beliefs always describe the political reality for all groups. Even a passing glance at American political history reveals that not all groups have had full property rights or access to democratic politics. Instead, to say that there is a strong, widely held political culture is to say that most Americans start with a general set of beliefs and predispositions when they think about issues. It is to say that most Americans share a set of general presumptions about politics and that most political debate operates within those general boundaries. The debate within those boundaries, however, can be intense. Rivals to the American creed have also had a significant place in American politics, and they will be discussed later in this chapter.

American creed the dominant political culture in the United States, marked by a set of beliefs in individualism, democracy, liberty, property, and religion, tied together by the value of equality.

► **DEFINING VISIONS**

Great Britain has had a long history of highly-charged ideological conflict between its parties. Here, Liberal Democrats party head Nick Clegg (left), Conservative party leader David Cameron (center), and Labour party chief Gordon Brown (right) face off in the first-ever live televised debate between potential prime ministers, April 2010.

ThinkingComparatively

Rather than a widely shared political culture, competing political cultures oriented around factors such as social class, religion, language, and ethnicity are common outside the United States.

In many countries, including those with far less diverse populations than the United States, competing political cultures are at the core of politics. There might be competition between a capitalist orientation and a socialist orientation, between a secular and a religious outlook, between one language and another, or even between one region of the country and others. European countries such as Spain and France regularly pit evenly matched socialist parties against capitalist parties. Canada has weathered deep regional splits based on language and cultural differences between French-speaking Quebec and the remaining provinces. These different perspectives offer fundamentally different beliefs to guide citizens and politicians.

The population of the United States is among the most diverse of any country in history. Although less so around the time of the Revolution, the population of the United States gradually became more varied as waves of immigration reshaped the demographic landscape. Americans named over one hundred ethnicities when identifying their ancestry in the 2009 American Community Survey conducted by the U.S. Census. In some parts of the country, notably California and Texas, the terms "minority" and "majority" are becoming outmoded as the non-Hispanic white majority becomes a minority of the population and current minority groups such as blacks, Hispanic whites, and Asians together become the majority, a development that is likely to be mirrored elsewhere.[3] This extraordinary diversity makes American political culture all the more interesting. We might expect that such demographic diversity would lead to sharply competing sets of basic political values and beliefs—competing political cultures—but that has not been the case.

Considering the varied backgrounds of the American population, the agreement in the United States around a set of general political beliefs is remarkable. Other beliefs, discussed at the end of this chapter, have played an important role in American politics, but there is nonetheless a widespread adherence in spirit, if not always in day-to-day politics, to the general ideals embodied in the American creed. However, that agreement has not been without significant racial, ethnic, and religious strife. Through all the waves of immigration, there have been charges that new immigrants were too "different" to fit into American life. As the children and grandchildren of immigrants grow up within American culture, they often find themselves culturally at odds with their ancestors. Efforts to "Americanize" immigrants through instruction in values, culture, language, childrearing, household management, and dress were explicit in past immigration waves and implicit in more recent attempts to make English the official language of the United States. One argument has been that without knowledge of the dominant language, immigrants cannot fully partake of political and economic liberty, democracy, or equality, which will set them apart from the American creed and corrode American social cohesion. Those who offer this argument believe that a highly diverse country requires a shared identity of some sort, and that in the United States this identity has been based on fundamental beliefs of political culture.[4]

American creed beliefs became dominant for several reasons.

Why one particular set of values and beliefs would become dominant in the face of such diversity is a puzzle. One explanation is that Americans hear numerous messages from politicians, economic leaders, and educators that reinforce and tout the superiority of those beliefs. Other messages that reinforce political culture come from outside politics, for example, the entertainment media. Popular culture, whether fictional or based on actual events, tends to embrace the individualistic ideals and wants of Americans, celebrating the self-reliant individual who overcomes the odds.

This explanation is helpful, but it does not tell us why Americans believe and "buy into" these repeated messages. Scholars have proposed other explanations for the dominance of the American creed. Addressing the question "Why is there no

▼ **DOES IMMIGRATION THREATEN NATIONAL COHESION?**

While acknowledging the contributions of immigrants to society, and often being children or grandchildren of immigrants themselves, many Americans worry that immigration threatens the sense of national identity conveyed by shared values. Advocates for expanded immigration stress that the historical record shows that immigrants are united around core American creed beliefs.

ThinkingCausally

Given the tremendous diversity of groups in the American population, how would one particular set of values and beliefs become dominant?

socialism in the United States?" one scholar offered three reasons.[5] First, because voting rights spread early to white men, the political system in the United States was relatively more open to working-class influence than in other countries. It did not take a socialist movement or party for workers to gain these rights. Second, prosperity in the United States made it difficult for competing political cultures to take firm root; the creed seemed to work. And last, the United States did not experience the same history of class relations as did European countries, and that history, with its very strict and hierarchical relationships between classes, may have been necessary for an alternative to the creed to take root.[6]

Other scholars have been less optimistic, arguing that government use of repressive tactics and judicial rulings played a stronger role in thwarting opposition to the creed than these interpretations suggest. They point to examples ranging from nineteenth-century labor activists being beaten and jailed, to investigations like those launched by Senator Joseph McCarthy in the 1950s to root out suspected communists in government, entertainment, and other industries, to dissident groups being infiltrated and monitored by government agents, as evidence that the government has often taken action to squelch dissent against the American creed.[7] Although these efforts to thwart alternative views are important, in comparative context they fall short of the widespread repression seen in some other regimes or the complete denial of rights, such as freedom of the press, found in others.

These competing explanations are insufficient on their own, but together they show there are many factors at play that sustain the preeminence of the American creed. A widespread popular mindset, based on life experience, that the creed works and produces individual opportunity is the broad foundation for the creed's success. Upon that foundation, government tactics have likely had chilling effects on targeted groups. And because the public is already receptive to the message, the reiteration of the culture's beliefs by politicians, media figures, and entertainers reinforces the place of these beliefs in American life and carries them to new generations. These repeated messages discourage cracks from forming in the foundation.

In sum, it is reasonable to describe American political culture as one based in the American creed, but—as this chapter will show—consensus does not eliminate conflict. There is substantial conflict in American politics within the confines of the creed. How much weight to place on each belief and what the beliefs themselves mean are often up for debate. In addition, other competing beliefs have had important impacts on American political life. These alternative approaches have mixed and mingled with the beliefs of the creed, proving that American political culture is dynamic and changing.

The Beliefs of the American Creed

2-2 Illustrate how the key values and beliefs of the American creed shape politics and government today.

equality the value that all Americans should be treated the same under the law, be able to influence government, and have equal opportunity to succeed in life.

The central value of the American creed is **equality**. A sense of equality underlies each of the specific beliefs of the creed—individualism, democracy, liberty, property, and religion.[8] Americans value every person's being treated the same under law, being able to influence government, and having equal opportunity to succeed in life. These expectations do not mean that everyone will or should have equal results, but that all people should "play by the same rules." The perception that some individuals have advantages not based on merit severely violates this norm of equality. The American experience has fallen short of these ideals many times in many places, however. These shortfalls will be discussed in this and other chapters. For now, as you read the descriptions below, remember that the emphasis in this part of the chapter is on the general ideals to which Americans say they aspire and how they affect the ways Americans think about politics and government.

Americans generally prefer that individuals have an equal chance for success rather than a guarantee that all people will have equal results. A 2009 survey found that about two-thirds of Americans disagree that success in life is mostly beyond an individual's control. The same proportion agreed with the idea that hard work leads to success. Ninety percent said they admired people who got rich by working hard. About 90 percent of adult Americans agreed that "our society should do what is necessary to make sure that everyone has an equal opportunity to succeed." Only about 30 percent, however, agreed that "we should make every possible effort to improve the position of blacks and other minorities, even if it means giving them preferential treatment." To most Americans, treating a group "preferentially," even to rectify past injustices, is inconsistent with equal opportunity. And most Americans in an earlier survey—by a margin of 3 to 1—placed the responsibility for failure to succeed on the individual rather than on society. This disparity held by nearly the same margin even when considering only the opinions of former or current welfare recipients.[9] These views do not mean that Americans oppose government helping those in need, especially in targeted fashion such as financial aid for college, food aid programs, and medical assistance, or that they do not believe in private charity for the poor, but they show that Americans place a strong emphasis on individual responsibility.

▲ **PERSONAL VERSUS PUBLIC RESPONSIBILITY**

A wave of mortgage foreclosures across the country led President Obama and Congress to enact mortgage restructuring programs in 2009 and 2010. Critics of the programs argued that if homeowners had gotten in over their heads financially, that was a matter of personal irresponsibility. Supporters said the mortgages were sometimes sold in misleading ways and that ultimately it was in a community's interest to keep people in their homes.

Individualism: People should choose their own path through life.

For Americans, individuals—not groups or classes—are the fundamental political unit. Americans believe in **individualism**, meaning that all individuals should be able to succeed to the maximum extent possible given their talents and abilities. The leading example of what Americans mean by freedom is the ability of individuals to choose their own path in life (see Table 2-2). The notion that the individual is entitled to a sphere of unfettered freedom is much less established in other countries than

individualism a belief that all individuals should be able to succeed to the maximum extent possible given their talents and abilities, regardless of race, religion, or other group characteristics.

TABLE 2-2. What Freedom Means to Americans (in percentages)

CHARACTERISTICS OF FREEDOM	ONE OF THE MOST IMPORTANT THINGS ABOUT FREEDOM	EXTREMELY IMPORTANT	VERY IMPORTANT	MODERATELY, SOMEWHAT, OR NOT TOO IMPORTANT
Having the power to choose and do what I want in life	45%	27%	22%	6%
Being able to express unpopular ideas without fearing for my safety	40	29	24	7
The right to participate in politics and elections	36	27	26	11
Having a government that doesn't spy on me or interfere in my life	30	26	32	12
Being left alone to do what I want	27	23	28	22

Source: General Social Survey 2000.

Note: Percentages add across each row. Survey respondents were asked for each characteristic of freedom whether it was one of the most important things about freedom, extremely important, very important, or moderately, somewhat, or not too important an aspect of freedom.

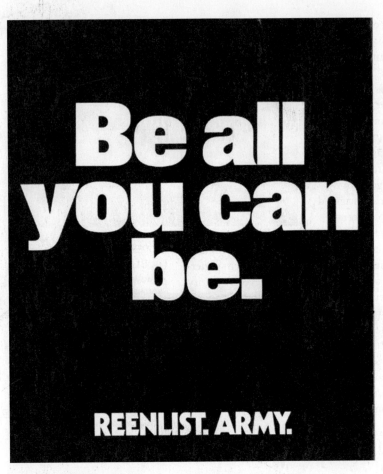

in the United States.[10] To Americans, individuals should be treated equally, regardless of group membership or other characteristics, and be free to pursue their dreams and aspirations. Organizations, even those that epitomize teamwork, recognize the power of these cultural beliefs. From 1980 through 2006, the U.S. Army used "Be All You Can Be" as its main recruiting slogan. This is precisely what Americans think of when they think about individualism—which is, of course, why savvy marketers would tap into this message. The Army briefly replaced this slogan with another that tapped into individualism: Army of One. For even this organization—in which cohesion, unity, and selflessness are prized and literally a matter of life and death—to use this language indicates the importance of individualism in American thinking. (Today's slogan is Army Strong.) Presidential candidates are similarly not shy about casting their biographies as triumphs of American individualism. From Ronald Reagan's rising from his modest, Midwestern roots, through Barack Obama as a mixed-race child raised largely by a single parent and grandparents, candidates hope their stories relate with voters as examples of American opportunity and success.

▲ THE MARKETING APPEAL OF INDIVIDUALISM

The Army's "Be All You Can Be" recruitment campaign effectively tapped into American political culture's emphasis on individuals reaching their maximum potential and seeking to achieve their personal dreams.

ThinkingComparatively

Citizens of other countries place great weight on government's role in reducing income differences, while Americans have tended to focus more on government's role in fostering equal opportunity.

In preferring equality of opportunity over equality of outcome, the United States is unique. In a 2006 survey of 33 countries, the United States ranked 32nd in the percentage of respondents saying that it "definitely should be" or "probably should be" a responsibility of government to "reduce income differences between the rich and the poor." New Zealand scored lower, by less than one percentage point. Only about a quarter of Americans saw reducing income differences as a responsibility government should "definitely" be concerned about, and a larger proportion of Americans than citizens of other countries saw this objective as one government definitely should not consider a responsibility. Almost 95 percent of citizens in Portugal saw reducing income differences as something government definitely or probably should be involved in; about 85 percent in Spain and Israel; and 75 to 80 percent in France, Finland, Venezuela, and Ireland. About half of Americans considered this as definitely or probably a government responsibility.[11] Asking about "people with high incomes and people with low incomes" rather than "the rich and the poor" reduces the support in the United States to 35 percent.[12] Examining surveys across a broader time period produces the same result: Americans are just as likely as citizens in other countries to think that income inequality is a problem, but they are less likely than citizens of other countries to believe that government has an obligation to reduce income differences.[13] And Americans are more likely to see economic inequality as something created by personal opportunities rather than by fate or the actions of others (see Table 2-3).

TABLE 2-3. Public Perceptions of the Causes of Income Inequality

Survey Question: Next, we'd like to know why you think it is, that in America today, some people have better jobs and higher incomes than others do. I'm going to read you some possible explanations, and I want you to tell me how important you think each is. Because . . .	VERY IMPORTANT	SOMEWHAT IMPORTANT	NOT IMPORTANT
Some people don't get a chance to get a good education	55%	35%	9%
Some people just don't work as hard	45	42	13
Some people have more in-born ability to learn	33	43	23
Discrimination holds some people back	26	50	23
Government policies have helped high-income workers more	25	39	35
Some people just choose low-paying jobs	19	38	41
God made people different from one another	22	26	49

Source: Data presented in Larry Bartels, *Unequal Democracy: The Political Economy of the New Gilded Age* (Princeton, NJ: Princeton University Press, 2008).

Note: Percentages add across rows.

Democracy: Government actions should reflect the will of the people.

The second belief of the American creed is that government should adhere to democratic principles. Democracy, as described in Chapter 1, is a form of government in which the people rule. This rule can take place directly, through participation by the people in actual lawmaking, or indirectly, through free elections in which the people choose representatives to make laws. Between elections, people have indirect input in democracy through a variety of means—hearings, writing to public officials, signing petitions, and lobbying, for example, and they partake of these more than citizens in other countries. Because voting and these other activities are not participated in equally by all segments of American society, many political observers are highly critical of the performance of American democracy compared to the ideal. To Americans, the ideal suggests four criteria in particular.

The will of the people   First, government actions should reflect the will of the people. The people's wishes are not always easy to identify, but the general principle is that government should be guided by them as much as possible.[14] Frequent elections allow the people to remove officials who have not lived up to this standard. In many other countries, legislative elections at the national level can be as many as five years apart and have to be "called" by government officials rather than being held on a predictable, regular schedule as in the United States.

The consent of the governed   Second, and closely related, power is granted to public officials by the consent of the governed. In this view, power that is exercised by a public official is always an extension of the public will and can potentially be reclaimed by the people. At its most extreme, the notion of consent means that citizens have a right to abolish the government altogether if they conclude that it is using power inappropriately.[15]

Equal opportunity to influence government   Third, to Americans, democracy also means an equal opportunity to influence government. This includes not only the opportunity to vote, but also access to government by citizens from all

▲ **HOW CLOSE IS
TOO CLOSE?**

**The linkage of business and
government troubles many
Americans. Here, Barack Obama
shakes hands with Verizon CEO
Ivan Seidenberg at a 2010
meeting of the Business
Roundtable, a group of the
country's largest corporations. Is
this unfair access, or is a
president right to lend an ear and
share his thoughts with the
heads of companies employing
thousands of Americans and
generating billions of dollars in
revenue?**

walks of life. Americans are uneasy with the idea—while recognizing it is the
reality—that some individuals or groups may appear to have "inside connections"
with government officials, so that their views are more influential than that of the
"average" person.[16] In April 2009, over 75 percent of Americans agreed "there is
too much power concentrated in the hands of a few big companies," about the
same percentage as over the previous 20 years.[17] Candidates and public officials go
to great lengths to clobber their opponents for being cronies of "special interests."
President Obama began his term with restrictions on lobbyists serving in his
administration, but soon he was critiqued for a number of exceptions he made to
that policy.

Equal treatment by the law Fourth, to Americans, democracy means equal
treatment by the law. Laws, regulations, and penalties should be enforced regardless of the social stature of the individual. This does not mean that judges, juries,
or public officials should ignore circumstances when determining penalties or
benefits. Rather, it means that the same actions taken under the same set of circumstances should result in equal penalties or benefits, regardless of the social
status, religion, ethnicity, race, income, or other characteristics of the individuals
involved. Of course, Americans recognize and lament that these ideals are violated
in everyday life. For example, wealthier individuals can hire more talented lawyers
and thus increase the odds that a case works out to their advantage. The fact that
Americans are troubled by such inequities is a sign of the potency of the idea of
equal treatment.

Liberty: Government restraint on individual behavior should be minimal.

The third belief in the American creed is liberty, which was the dominant demand of the American Revolution. Americans often define **liberty** as freedom from government restriction on the exercise of one's rights; that is, whenever possible, government should let people do as they please. Government's obligation, in this view, is not to make decisions for you about what would make your life better, but to protect your right to decide what a "better life" is and to protect your freedom to go for it.

Natural rights   Associated with this belief is the conviction that government does not grant rights. Rather, rights are inherent, part of what makes people human: these are **natural rights**. Americans consider the rights to free speech, to associate in groups, and to hold and practice religious faith to be effectively sewn into human beings upon birth, not rights that government gives us. The Declaration of Independence provides a clear statement of this idea: "we hold these truths to be self-evident, that all men are created equal, that they are endowed by their Creator with certain unalienable rights, that among these are life, liberty, and the pursuit of happiness." Government's job is to protect these rights from other citizens and from government at other levels. That people had natural rights, and the idea that government exists to protect these rights, not grant them, was central to the thinking of philosopher John Locke, who had a strong influence on the Founders. And for political theorist Thomas Hobbes, the idea that government had a role in protecting individuals from the threatening actions of other individuals was central.

Government's role in securing liberty   To Americans, government secures liberty either by not restricting rights or by restricting them only when their expression imposes excessively on the rights of other individuals. The freedoms of speech and assembly are considered fundamental rights, but even these are commonly restricted by government. Slanderous and libelous speech can lead to punishment. Marching and demonstrating without a permit can result in fines or other sanctions. And, when they believe national security is threatened, Americans often tolerate what would be considered unacceptable infringements on liberty at other times. All these limitations can be a matter of great political controversy.

Individuals in other countries view liberty in somewhat different ways from those in America. In Scandinavian countries, liberty requires being given something by government in order to thrive fully as a human being. This may mean health care, education, housing, or any number of other services. In this view, the freedom to speak or to earn a living is weak unless citizens are given the tools to use these freedoms effectively. For example, without a health care system to provide for all citizens, the promise of "life" or the "pursuit of happiness" is empty. Or, without high-quality education for all, "free speech" quickly becomes the province of a relatively small elite. Without both of these, one's opportunities to pursue success, whether in one's career or elsewhere, are sharply limited.

In the United States, the perspective is a different one. Many or even most Americans may agree that universal health care and quality education are important goals for government. However, relatively few

▲ **LIBERTIES IN WAR AND PEACE**

Americans generally tolerate greater inconveniences and limits to their liberties in times of war. Security checks at airports, railway stations, and subways became more extensive following the terrorist attacks on September 11, 2001. Is this flexible response of Americans desirable?

liberty   the belief that government should leave people free to do as they please and exercise their natural rights to the maximum extent possible.

natural rights   rights inherent in the essence of people as human beings; government does not provide these rights but can restrict the exercise of them.

ThinkingComparatively

The concept of liberty in the United States traditionally emphasizes being left alone by government, but government provision of services like health care and education is seen in some other countries as an essential part of liberty and freedom.

would say that liberty is absent if these government services are not provided. Even in the major debate over health care reform in 2009 and 2010, the argument that reform was necessary to promote liberty was rarely heard. Arguments for reform were made on other grounds. Liberty was more often entered into the debate by those opposed to expanding the government's role in this policy area.

Property: Individuals should be free to acquire, own, and use goods and assets.

property rights the belief that people should be able to acquire, own, and use goods and assets free from government constraints, as long as their acquisition and use does not interfere with the rights of other individuals.

Americans believe in extensive **property rights**—that people should be able to acquire, own, and use goods and assets free from government constraints, so long as their acquisition and use does not interfere with the rights of other individuals. Property rights are therefore twofold: freedom to acquire property and freedom to use property.

▼ BUILDING IN A DANGER ZONE

Property rights generally confer on individuals the right to use their property as they see fit. However, around the country individuals build houses in zones where tornadoes, fires, landslides, floods, and hurricanes are common. How far should government go to restrict or regulate such building?

Freedom to acquire property   First, people should have the right to acquire private property without limitations. This means that individuals should be paid whatever they can command in the economic marketplace for their goods or their work. With their talents or resources, individuals should be able to obtain property—money, goods, services, real estate, stocks—with minimal meddling by society or government. You may think it excessive that a professional athlete or movie star makes $20 million a year, or that a corporate executive receives $100 million when leaving a company, but few Americans believe that this should be prohibited. As Americans considered the idea of restricting executive compensation following the banking and financial problems of 2008 and 2009, they voiced strong majority support for limiting the pay of executives whose firms had received government bailout funds. However, despite their anger toward banks and financial institutions, Americans were split on whether government should restrict executive pay in this industry in general or for executives at firms that had paid back their bailout funds.[18]

Freedom to use property   Second, individuals should be free to use property with few restrictions. Some acceptable restrictions protect the property of others or protect some societal interest. Many communities prohibit the use of jet skis on lakes, or at certain hours, and most have noise ordinances of some type. You cannot build your house on sensitive wetlands.

Exactly how property rights coexist with democracy in the confines of a single political culture is an enduring puzzle. Historically, one prominent school of thought feared that the growth of democracy would lead to property rights being tossed aside: voters with little property would use government to take wealth from others. The Framers of the U.S. Constitution shared this fear. Because democracy might pose a risk to property rights, they believed a careful structure of institutions, rules, and procedures was needed to protect property from the people's "passions." Another approach saw property rights and political freedoms as mutually reinforcing.[19] The individual freedoms prized in a market economy—the ability to make choices, having minimal restrictions on one's action—will be attractive as political liberties as well.

Political scientists have noted a third, ironic, way in which the two can fit together: Property rights as expressed in activities such as shopping could lead to skepticism about government, as individuals might see the free market as ultimately more democratic and equal than the political system. Not everyone can afford every product, but if you can gain sufficient resources through hard work or luck, you have the same opportunity to obtain that item as anyone else. By contrast, the political system might not seem nearly so open, accessible, and understandable. In the market, you can buy the product—like anyone else—if you can afford it. With government, on the other hand, the process for

ThinkingCausally

How do democratic rights and property rights, which are potentially at odds, coexist?

you to get an economic benefit can appear to be much more time consuming, complicated, and conflictual. This perceived difficulty of getting economic gains through government may reduce the number of demands placed on government to take property from one group and give it to another.[20]

Religion: Individuals should be free to practice their religious faith.

religious freedom   a belief that individuals should be free to choose and practice their religious faith and that government should not establish any particular religion as the official or preferred religion.

Americans believe in **religious freedom**, the idea that individuals should be free to choose and practice their religious faith and that government should not establish any particular religion as the official or preferred religion.[21]

Freedom of religious expression   Americans view the freedom to practice one's religion as akin to the right to free speech. Early in the nation's history, so-called dissenting Protestants emigrated to the colonies in part as a way to practice their faith. They fled societies, England in particular, where official government religions made it difficult for individuals with other religious beliefs to practice their faith. The idea that government should remain neutral among religions was therefore closely linked to the idea of freedom of religious practice. In this perspective, freedom of religious expression was likely only if government did not take sides. Such freedom was more easily stated than accomplished, however, and religious intolerance in the colonies was common. Favoring a particular religion—and effectively discriminating against others—was also a practice of many local and state governments into the twentieth century. Anti-Catholicism, in particular, was a strong force in many areas. The twin beliefs in freedom of expression and noninterference by government, although not common at the time of the American Revolution, were enshrined in the Constitution and have grown gradually over time.

▼ **FAITH AS AN AMERICAN TOUCHSTONE**
References to faith appear frequently in American political culture. Presidents routinely end their speeches by saying "God bless the United States of America," and other references abound in places such as the Pledge of Allegiance, the Declaration of Independence, and U.S. currency.

Importance of religion in American political life   Religious belief has been central to American political discourse. Major efforts such as the anti-slavery, civil rights, and anti-abortion movements relied on religious language and principles. Presidents of both parties, including Presidents George W. Bush and Barack Obama, have sprinkled religious language in their speeches and ended major addresses with the exhortation "God Bless America." Faced with the issue of whether to allow stem-cell research on frozen embryos—a process that destroys the embryos—Bush leaned heavily on his faith in disallowing the development of any new stem-cell lines and later vetoed an attempt to change his policy.[22] American beliefs lean against the idea of an official religion or church, but *religiosity*, the tendency of people to have some sort of religion, pervades political culture.

Survey results provide a sense of just how important religion is to Americans today. Over 80 percent of Americans in 2009 said they completely or mostly agree that they never doubt the existence of God, while nearly that many said that prayer is an important part of their daily life, and that everyone will have to answer to God for their sins.[23] Nearly three-quarters of Americans in 2008 said it was important for a president to have strong religious beliefs, and only about 30 percent thought politicians expressed their religious faith too much.[24]

This degree of religiosity is unusually high (see Figure 2-1). The general pattern around the globe is that countries that are wealthier, more developed, and industrialized tend to place less emphasis on religious belief. Perhaps scientific and rationalistic reasoning have moved people away from faith-based beliefs or the vast

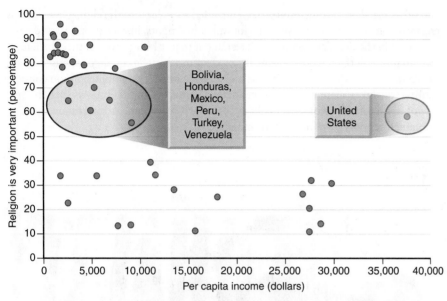

FIGURE 2-1. **Relationship Between Religion's Importance in People's Lives and Economic Development.** High percentages of Americans state that religion is a very important part of their daily lives. Countries with similar levels of belief tend to be much poorer than the United States.

Note: Survey question asked in 44 countries, 2002. "How important is religion in your life— very important, somewhat important, not too important, or not at all important?"

entertainment and leisure options of the modern world draw attention away from spiritual matters. The United States, however, bucks the trend. The exceptionally diverse scope of religious denominational choices in the United States may be one reason. This competitive marketplace draws attention to religion while also providing many niches that can satisfy Americans' differing spiritual needs.

ThinkingComparatively

The level of religious belief in the United States is more typical of that found in lesser developed countries than in wealthy countries.

The American creed provides a starting point for most Americans to evaluate issues, candidates, and government actions.

The five beliefs of the American creed have endured even though these ideals have not always been honored in practice. For much of the nation's history, not all groups have shared equally in the promises and benefits of creedal beliefs or the overarching value of equality. During the Revolutionary era, only about 15 to 30 percent of the adult population could take full advantage of the promises of life, liberty, and the pursuit of happiness. Laws and customs made sure that women, blacks, white indentured servants, and nonpropertied adult white males could not.[25]

Despite this widespread exclusion, the remarkable fact is that these groups still believed in the promise of the American creed. They did not argue that this set of beliefs should be discarded. Instead, women, white men without property, blacks, and other racial and ethnic minorities demanded to be let into the club. These groups engaged in massive social movements for individual rights, liberty, property, and participation in the democratic process, a testament to just how powerful these beliefs were to those on the outside looking in. By championing the equality promised by the American creed, these movements had a strong impact on public opinion concerning equal treatment across race, gender, and group. Figure 2-2 shows that, in the case of equal roles for women, equality as defined by the women's rights movement has gained support from the American public.

▼ EQUAL RIGHTS
Marchers in New York supporting the addition of the Equal Rights Amendment to the U.S. Constitution. Although the attempt to ratify the amendment fell short by three states, the women's rights movement had a profound effect on American laws, business practices, and society.

Consequences and Implications of the American Creed

2-3 Evaluate the consequences of American political culture such as limited government and a weak sense of sovereign power.

Political scientists ask the "so what?" question: why should we care about political culture? The American creed matters because its consequences and implications are far-reaching. A brief survey of some of these consequences and implications will demonstrate the important influence of political culture on American life.

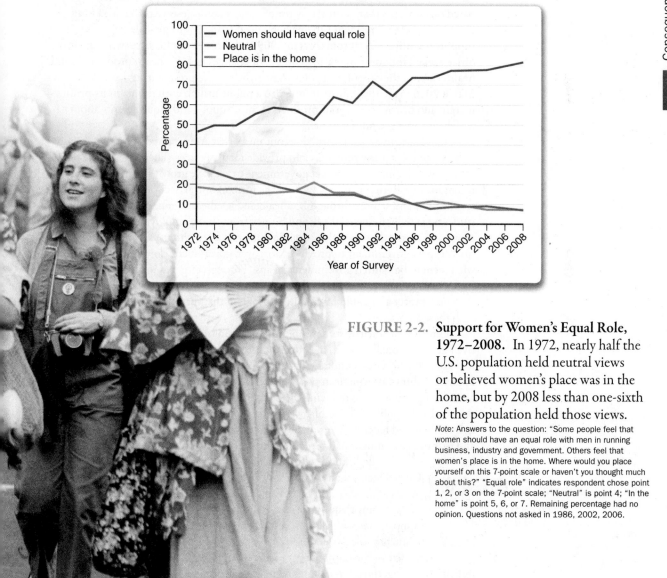

FIGURE 2-2. Support for Women's Equal Role, 1972–2008. In 1972, nearly half the U.S. population held neutral views or believed women's place was in the home, but by 2008 less than one-sixth of the population held those views.

Note: Answers to the question: "Some people feel that women should have an equal role with men in running business, industry and government. Others feel that women's place is in the home. Where would you place yourself on this 7-point scale or haven't you thought much about this?" "Equal role" indicates respondent chose point 1, 2, or 3 on the 7-point scale; "Neutral" is point 4; "In the home" is point 5, 6, or 7. Remaining percentage had no opinion. Questions not asked in 1986, 2002, 2006.

limited government the idea
that the scope of government
activities should be narrow and
that government should act only
when the need is great and other
sectors of society are unable to
meet the need.

Americans prefer government to be limited in the scope of its activities.

One consequence of the American creed is a preference for the idea of **limited government** rather than a large, active government. This means government is seen as a last resort to solving problems. People do not need to be convinced that it is appropriate for real estate developers to build houses, for instance, but they may need to be convinced that it is appropriate for government to build housing, to subsidize mortgages for home buyers, or to pay part of the costs for certain people to rent housing. Americans tend to rely first on other arenas—family, church, the marketplace, nonprofit institutions, self-improvement—and they turn to government only when these alternatives fail or they are overwhelmed by the scope of a problem. Lawmakers in 2008 enacted a $700 billion rescue of financial institutions, largely based on concerns that no other sector of society could resolve the crisis. Using similar reasoning, President Obama convinced Congress to provide government support for ailing U.S. automakers in 2009 and throughout his first two years in office argued for government to prod major changes in U.S. energy production and health care. In the case of health insurance, the bill the president signed into law in March 2010 made the industry similar to a public utility, with limits on its profit margin and prices, rules about products it must supply, and requirements about which customers it must accept.

"Government as last resort" does not mean that Americans do not look to government to solve many problems and provide many services. They do, and the policy areas in which Americans expect government to act have grown significantly during recent history. Retirement payments in the form of Social Security, health insurance for the poor and seniors through Medicaid and Medicare, grants and loans for college students via federal financial aid, and money from the unemployment insurance program to assist those who lose their jobs are just a few things Americans today routinely expect government to provide. Moreover, government can be active while using what seem to be limited government means. Through targeted incentives—tax credits for buying energy efficient appliances, for example—government can create much the same impact as it could by creating a program that directly provides individuals with these appliances.[26]

Some political scientists describe American opinion as philosophically conservative but operationally liberal, meaning that Americans may genuinely believe in limited government while simultaneously supporting specific government programs.[27] Figure 2-3 shows an American public reluctant to cut federal government spending, even during a time when reducing the federal budget deficit was considered a high priority by the public. The public was reluctant to cut even though about 60 percent in 2009 believed federal government programs were usually inefficient and wasteful and that the government had too much influence in their daily lives.[28]

The dedication to the idea of limited government is stronger in the United States than in other industrialized democracies. In general, governments in these countries are larger and have more control over society and the economy than is true in the United States. We need to interpret these comparisons with caution, as there are many different ways to measure government's role. Nonetheless, when we compare the size of government to the size of the economy, especially when focusing on domestic rather than military spending, the United States regularly falls at the low end of the list. Government in the United States often hires private sector firms to do a wide range of work, including counseling, job skills training, rubbish collection, and more, that in other countries might be done by government employees. Faith-based organizations, for

ThinkingComparatively

The concept of limited government has been more popular in the United States than elsewhere.

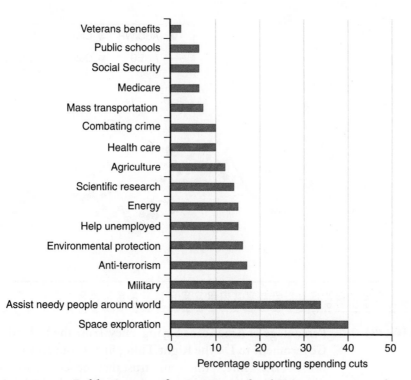

FIGURE 2-3. **Public Support for Cutting Federal Government Spending, 2009.** Americans generally support the idea of a small, efficient government, but they find it difficult to identify areas they would like to see cut. Although 60 percent of Republicans, Democrats, and independents cited the federal budget deficit as a top national priority, there was no majority support for cutting any of the programs listed above.

Note: Data from Pew Center on the People and the Press, 2009. Questions on Social Security, mass transportation, and space exploration from General Social Survey, 2008.

example, have been involved in providing services and training to welfare recipients to ready them for the labor force. In the United States, expanding government's reach through the use of private sector firms and organizations can be less politically controversial than hiring scores of new public employees.[29]

Americans often do not trust that government will do the right thing.

A second consequence of the American creed has been a pervasive skepticism about the effectiveness of American government. At some times in American history, this skepticism has been deeper than at others. In 1958, according to the American National Election Studies, a major academic public opinion survey, about three-fourths of Americans believed they could trust the federal government to do what is right most or all of the time. In 2008, fewer than one-third believed so.[30] Surveys in 2010 (see Figure 2-4) showed overall trust in government to do what is right at about 20 to 25 percent.[31]

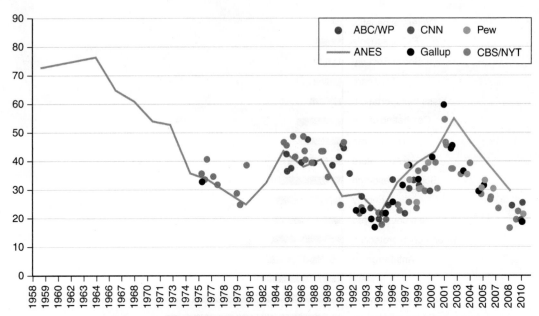

FIGURE 2-4. **Percentage of Americans Saying They Trust the Federal Government to Do the Right Thing Just About Always or Most of the Time.** Americans' trust that the federal government will do the right thing has dropped from the high levels recorded 50 years ago by the American National Election Studies. Despite fluctuations and differences between partisan groups— Democrats will be more trusting when Democrats control the presidency and Congress than when Republicans do, and vice versa—the general trend is a decline in trust since the mid-1960s.

ThinkingCausally

Why has trust in government declined?

What might explain this decline in trust? A succession of difficult events in American politics plays some role—Vietnam, Watergate, the protracted period of high inflation and high unemployment in the 1970s, escalating economic competition from other countries, scandals, the Iraq War beginning in 2003, and the economic troubles more recently would be on this list.

But other factors play a role also. As we cautioned in Chapter 1, political life tends to be complicated. Thus, political scientists have proposed and established some validity for a variety of additional factors:

■ Trust was artificially inflated in the years after the Great Depression and World War II. After those calamities were overcome and the United States stood atop the world in economics, science, and many other categories, trust was high. This high trust, rather than the more recent period of low trust, may be the anomaly, and trust has simply declined to more "normal" levels.

■ American politics at the elite level has become more divisive, and news coverage in turn has focused disproportionately on conflict and stalemate rather than cooperation and accomplishment.

- American economic life has become less secure, traditional moral values have been challenged, and government has been unwilling or unable to do much to reverse these trends, to the dismay of the various groups concerned about them.

- There has been declining respect for all large institutions, not simply government.

- There has been a decline in trust across advanced industrial democracies, suggesting some non-America-specific causes may play a role also.[32]

Governing within the American constitutional system of separation of powers and checks and balances has never been easy. Low levels of trust may complicate the job of political leaders.[33] On one hand, that might be a reasonable price to pay to keep government in check, consistent with American political culture. On the other hand, high levels of distrust can increase the difficulty of making necessary and tough policy decisions, thus reinforcing the skepticism about government's ability to perform effectively.

There is a weak sense of sovereign power in the United States.

A third consequence of the American creed, related closely to the idea of limited government, is that there is a weak sense of sovereign power in the United States. **Sovereign power** suggests a final authority, a final decision maker. In the United States, it is difficult to think of any truly "final" authority. American government is structured so that one part of government can challenge and check other parts of government. For example, Congress can pass legislation, but the president can veto it. With enough votes, Congress can then override that veto. The Supreme Court can declare unconstitutional the actions of both Congress and the president. Congress and the states can pass constitutional amendments that will guide future Court decisions, or the president can nominate and the Senate can approve new Supreme Court justices who might render different decisions. There is no ultimate seat of power in the system at the national level.

But what about the claim that the American people are sovereign? In the abstract, this is true. Their opinion influences policy makers. And the people reserve the ultimate right to push for a rewriting of the Constitution or to enter into a revolution. But on a practical, day-to-day level, it is a limited sovereignty. This is not an accident but an intended result of the Constitution. American government is designed to hear the voice of the people, but not to translate that voice into immediate action. When the American people are dissatisfied, the strongest practical recourse they have is to replace members of government. But there is never a time when Americans can vote out all members of government in a single election. And members of the federal judiciary and bureaucracy, who are unelected, are never up for direct public removal. Thus, the sovereign power of the people is limited and some parts of government are only indirectly controlled.

Competing ideas are viewed with suspicion.

A fourth consequence of the American creed is that competing ideas are often viewed with suspicion. In general, the American people and their leaders tend to assume the superiority of the creed's values. For a long time in the United States, one way to discredit an idea has been to label it socialistic. And only rarely do U.S. policy makers, at least publicly, seriously talk about the policies and programs of other countries as examples to be followed, the assumption being that the underlying values and beliefs

sovereign power the individual or institution in a political system whose decisions are binding and unable to be overturned by other individuals or institutions.

guiding these programs would not be relevant in the American context. Conservative critics of President Obama repeatedly have aimed to tie him to both of these sensitive cultural critiques, depicting him as a "socialist" whose policies are geared toward making the United States look more like Europe.

"Un-American" beliefs Competing ideas not only challenge the American creed but also are sometimes deemed "un-American." Throughout U.S. history, ideas that have challenged the creed were often seen as infections on the body politic caused by outsiders. In few countries is a set of political beliefs so intertwined with national identity that to oppose or challenge these beliefs can sometimes be perceived as a challenge to the nation itself.

In the 1950s, the House Un-American Activities Committee investigated a large number of individuals suspected of holding or being sympathetic to "un-American" ideas, chiefly socialism and communism. At other points in American history, efforts to remove immigrants and to restrict the future flow of immigration were based on the idea that these individuals brought disruptive beliefs and values to the United States. At one time or another in American history, Catholics, Irish, Chinese, Japanese, Eastern and Southern Europeans, Jews, and others have been deemed dangerous because of the cultural practices and beliefs they might import into the United States.

Appeals to social class Attempts to appeal to Americans as members of social classes are often considered a danger to national harmony. With the exception of references to the middle class—which is widely used and tends to be defined in very broad terms—directly appealing to class interest is often denounced. When President Obama promised that he would raise taxes "on the wealthiest Americans" while leaving other "hardworking Americans" untouched, critics denounced him for advocating "class warfare" and demonizing financially successful Americans. President Obama and other Democrats have asserted that, on the contrary, it was President Bush and Republicans who were engaged in class politics by skewing their policies toward the interests of higher-income individuals and families. The concerns on

► **AMERICAN IDEAS**

American national identity is closely linked to the widely shared beliefs of the American creed. Political activists use this linkage to suggest that some ideas are not simply wrong, but directly violate the country's Founding principles and basic beliefs. Supporters of the Tea Party movement, as seen here in April 2010, argue that the actions and policies of the federal government have become inconsistent with the Constitution, the intentions of the Framers, and the American way of life.

both sides that policy is being devised to promote one class at the expense of another are often sincerely held, as are the fears that class-based politics invites disharmony and division. But the provocative charge that the rich are warring on the poor or the poor are warring on the rich can also be a strategy for halting serious discussion about a particular policy.

Other countries have been more comfortable talking about class and challenging individualistic political culture. Socialism, which views society through the lens of social class and envisions an expansive role for government, has had a more sympathetic reception elsewhere, particularly in the form of strong labor unions and a Labour Party (Australia, Ireland, New Zealand, United Kingdom), Social Democratic Party or New Democrat Party (Canada, Germany, Sweden), or Socialist Party (France). Although socialist parties in the early twentieth century had some success in industrial cities in the United States, they have made little impact on the national scene. The causality can be reciprocal: class-oriented political parties may have thrived in countries with political cultures and electoral rules that encouraged multiparty elections, and the success of class-based parties might have in turn made the publics in these countries more comfortable with class as being at the center of political discussion.

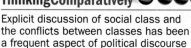

ThinkingComparatively

Explicit discussion of social class and the conflicts between classes has been a frequent aspect of political discourse outside the United States.

Appeals to the public interest are difficult in an individualistic political culture.

A fifth consequence of the American creed is that it can be difficult for politicians and the public to act in the public interest or even to define it. In a nation where individualism and skepticism of government are strong, references to "the public interest" might be interpreted by the public as a rhetorical gloss employed to make someone's individual interest sound more noble. Because American political culture has such a strong emphasis on individual freedom, opportunity, and rights, can you convince people to sacrifice their self-interest for the public interest? When advocating policies, politicians and political activists continually wrestle with the tension between appealing to the interests of the community and the interests of the individual. Barack Obama in the 2008 election asked Americans to "look after not only ourselves, but each other," while his opponent John McCain implored Americans to "put country first."

> "When advocating policies, politicians and political activists continually wrestle with the tension between appealing to the interests of the community and the interests of the individual."

Alexis de Tocqueville, a French historian and political theorist, visited the United States in the 1830s and wrote a sweeping analysis of the nature of American politics and society that is still considered one of the most perceptive studies ever written about the United States. He was particularly interested in the interplay of liberty, individualism, democracy, and equality in the young American republic. In his famous *Democracy in America*, published in 1835 when he was 30 years old, Tocqueville suggested that Americans engage in "self interest rightly understood." In Tocqueville's view, one way Americans reconciled the conflict between pursuing their self-interest and sacrificing for the public interest was by seeing how engaging in kind acts toward others and being concerned about the public interest could also serve their self-interest. In other words, the "sacrifice" could reap personal dividends. Vote for a school referendum that will "help the children" and the community, and your property value will increase because communities with good schools are attractive to home buyers. Help others, and you will feel good about yourself. Volunteer for community service and do good things, and you will have another impressive line on your résumé.

Political conflict emerges from tension among the creed's beliefs and from debate over the meaning of the beliefs.

An important and ironic final consequence of the widely shared American creed is that it also produces much of the political conflict in the United States. The creed creates political tension because, first, its beliefs are often in conflict with one another, and second, the meaning of the individual beliefs is open to debate.[34] Both of these sources of tension have led to significant amounts of political debate and struggle in the United States. Much of the conflict between the two major political parties may be attributed to the differential emphasis they place on American creed beliefs when these beliefs—for example, property versus democracy—are in conflict, or to the different meaning parties may attach to a belief such as liberty.

Tension among the creed's beliefs Consider a low-income high school student. She is an excellent student, qualified for admission at a prestigious university. Her ability to maximize her potential depends on her going to college, the most prestigious one for which she is qualified. Being poor, however, she cannot afford such a university. Her situation poses a conflict between two beliefs. According to the belief in individualism, this young woman should be able to achieve all she can achieve without any artificial barriers, certainly not the barrier of her parents' income. On the other hand, according to the belief in property, your property is your property; when you work hard to earn income, that money is yours. If you want to donate voluntarily to a scholarship fund, you can do that, but you should not be forced by government to give your money to someone else.

As a society, Americans have resolved this particular conflict between American creed beliefs by deemphasizing property rights to elevate individual opportunity. That is, we have created federal financial aid programs that take tax dollars and redistribute them to individuals like this student. The government takes property from one group and gives it to another. This example reinforces the point made earlier that beliefs can prevail at the abstract level but weaken in specific circumstances. Americans do believe that, on the whole, people should be able to do with their property as they wish. When this belief collides with the belief in individual opportunity, Americans, through government, have to decide how heavily to weigh each belief to reach a decision in a specific case.

Cultural differences across regions When the beliefs of the American creed are in conflict, there is no balance that is inherently right or wrong. Instead, there is a balance that can gain the strongest political support nationally at a particular moment in time. But what does this national balance mean at the state or regional level?

Even a quick glance at the United States shows significant variation across the states in partisan strength, public opinion, and the content of laws and policies. In addition to federal student financial aid programs, for example, most states have their own programs, ranging from modest to generous. If national political culture is important, it is puzzling that there is such diversity across states. Why do states vary? Is the variation simply random, or do particular factors contribute to it? More specifically, does political culture play a systematic role in this cross-state variation?

The regional variety in laws and political behavior has led some political scientists to suggest that, although there is a balance of creedal beliefs at the national level that shapes policy, the balance among creedal beliefs also varies systematically from region to region, state to state, and even within states. Migration and immigration have contributed to this variation. Ethnic groups and nationalities have

---

ThinkingCausally

If national political culture is so important, why do we see variations across the states in party strength, public opinion, and laws?

been distributed unevenly across the country, and their heavy presence in a particular state or city would encourage further immigration to that area. This was as true of European immigrants in the 1890s as it is of Asian and Latino immigrants today. Their beliefs have influenced the practice of politics where they lived. In one part of the country, property rights might get more emphasis. In another, it might be religious freedom. These areas would then be appealing relocation destinations for other Americans who shared those preferences. This geographical variation in political culture is one factor that helps explain differences in state laws and politics.

One famous classification speaks of moralistic, traditionalistic, and individualistic subcultures that dominate or mix in different parts of the United States.[35] The moralistic subculture has been most present in the northern states and the Pacific Northwest, the traditionalistic in the southern states, and the individualistic through the middle tier of states and in California. The moralistic subculture views government as a positive force and tends to place heavy emphasis on the needs of the community and government's ability to satisfy those needs. A more active government is welcomed and popular participation is encouraged. A traditionalist subculture favors limited government that works to sustain the social relations and values already dominant in society and the economy. Popular participation is not strongly encouraged and historically was actively discouraged for some groups. The individualistic subculture sees politics neither as a means to transform society (like moralism) nor to preserve society (like traditionalism), but a mechanism through which private interests are advanced and in which government is expected to encourage, enable, and support private initiative. Political scientists have used these regional cultural differences as one factor among many to try to explain differences in voting turnout, election outcomes, and social policy across states.

CaseStudy: Defining Democracy When Drawing District Lines

Political tension results not only from the conflict between beliefs, but also from different interpretations of beliefs in the American creed.[36] For example, consider the process of redistricting, which will be in the news throughout 2011 and 2012, following the 2010 U.S. Census. Redistricting refers to the drawing of boundaries around legislative districts. Each district elects one legislator.[37] Prior to 1964, congressional and state legislative district boundaries often followed county lines. They were redrawn for U.S. House districts only when the U.S. Census, taken every 10 years, indicated that a change in a state's share of the national population meant it should have more or fewer House members than it currently had. If the census showed no need to change the state's number of seats in Congress, the state could go a very long time without changing the congressional district boundaries. For state legislatures, whose size would not change because of the census—a state can have as many members in its own legislature as it wishes—there was even less reason to redraw the lines. Under this system, districts could vary enormously in population from one House district to another or one state legislative district to another, yet each would have the same number of legislators: one.

What does a seemingly technical matter like redistricting have to do with the American creed or beliefs in democracy? A lot, as it turns out. In 1964, the Supreme Court, in two famous decisions, concluded that democracy hinges on the principle of "one person, one vote," the idea that every citizen has one vote, each voter is equally powerful in selecting legislators, and each voter is equally represented in the legislature.[38] If one district had 1,000 potential voters and another had 600,000, the power of each voter in selecting a representative in the first district would be 600 times greater than in the second. The 1,000 voters of the first district would have one vote in the legislature, as would the 600,000 voters in the second district. Such unequally sized districts, which were common around the country, violated constitutional norms of equality that were fundamental to the American democratic process. Moreover, given residential patterns in which populations of minority racial and ethnic groups tend to be clustered together, district lines can either deliberately attempt to keep these groups in a single district, disperse them across districts, or not take account of race or ethnicity at all when drawing the lines. Are either of these three approaches inherently more "democratic"?

(continued)

The Court's one person, one vote principle provides no explicit guidance about how to draw the lines that separate districts. Every 10 years, states need to redraw their district lines to be sure that population is approximately equal in the House districts (if the state has more than one representative in the U.S. House) and in state legislative districts. Which way of drawing the lines would most enhance democracy? Is democracy better served if lines are drawn in a way that some districts are likely to be heavily Republican and others heavily Democratic? The individuals elected to the legislature in these districts are apt to represent their citizens very well because they tend to share common viewpoints. However, competitive elections will be rare in these districts—the weaker party is unlikely to have any chance to win, so voters might not have much real choice. If the lines are drawn with an intent to spread Democratic and Republican voters about equally across the two districts, elections may be more competitive—considered by many people to be a fundamental sign of a healthy democracy—but large numbers of people in the districts may feel they share few beliefs and values with the elected officials who represent them in the legislature. They might feel unrepresented, and that hardly seems democratic.[39]

Every decade, after the census is finished, there are bitter battles to draw up district lines. These will occur again in 2011 and 2012. In most states, the job falls to the legislature. And most often, the pattern is predictable. First, lines are drawn in a way to protect incumbents of both major parties. Then, the majority party seeks to draw lines around remaining districts in such a way as to maximize the number of seats the party will win. This process, known as gerrymandering, often produces districts with contorted, convoluted boundaries. And last, the minority party might file suit against the new district lines, usually to no avail. In a split decision in 2004, the U.S. Supreme Court declined to intervene in a case involving partisan bias in congressional redistricting in Pennsylvania (Figure 2-5 shows one of the disputed districts). The Court concluded it had no clear standard to apply to determine how much partisan bias is "too much" and is contrary to democratic principles and equality. But it did not rule out the possibility that it might determine such a standard in the future.[40]

The most widely publicized dispute in recent years over district lines occurred in Texas. Following the 2000 census, the Texas legislature, with one house controlled by each party, was unable to agree on a new districting plan and, under state law, the districting process went before a panel of federal judges. The judges drew new lines that kept in place a Democratic majority in the Texas delegation

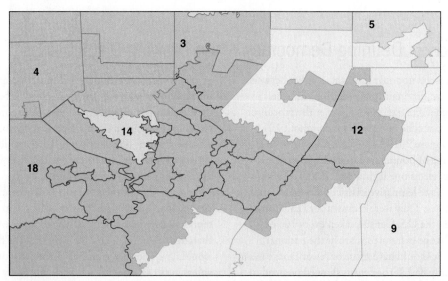

FIGURE 2-5. Contested Congressional District 12 in Pennsylvania Partisan Redistricting Case, 2004. The boundaries of Pennsylvania's 12th congressional district, located in the state's southwest corner, were carefully crafted to advantage the candidates of one political party. In an effort to build a safe Democratic seat, the district's boundary twists and turns, picking up disparate pockets of neighborhoods along the way and almost completely surrounding portions of the adjacent district 18. The Supreme Court concluded that it did not have any clear standard to determine whether partisan bias in drawing the boundary of this district, shaded here in purple, violated norms of democracy and equality.

to the U.S. House. In the 2002 Texas state legislative elections, however, Republicans gained control of the legislature and in 2003 passed a new district map much more favorable to Republican candidates. Predictably, in the 2004 U.S. House election, the Republicans won 21 seats, compared to 15 in 2002.

Challenges to the new Texas district lines landed in the U.S. Supreme Court in 2006, arguing two points.[41] First, Democrats charged there was no lawful reason to change the lines that had just been established in 2001. The mid-decade redrawing, the suit argued, was done solely for partisan advantage. Rather than treating individuals equally under the law, the suit alleged, the redistricting targeted and discriminated against Democratic voters for their political viewpoints. Second, minority groups claimed that the Texas legislature illegally sought to distribute Hispanic and black voters across districts in order to decrease the likelihood of electing Democrats to the House. Since the late 1980s, the Supreme Court has frowned on using race as a primary factor in drawing district lines, including deliberate attempts to weaken the voting clout of minority groups. In 2006, the Court concluded that the critics of the plan had not established that the partisan rearrangement was inherently unequal or undemocratic, but it did strike down one district for unconstitutionally weakening minority voting power.

These conflicts show again that Americans believe in democracy in general but can disagree on precisely what that belief requires them to do in the specific case of drawing district lines. In the real world of politics, ideals about democratic principles and values often jostle with hardheaded aspirations for political power. Americans may generally believe in democracy, or liberty, or the other beliefs of the American creed, but their understanding of what those terms mean will always be a battleground for public officials, political activists, and other citizens. Most Americans share the general ideals of the American creed, but the tension inherent in the creed leaves plenty of room for political debate, conflict, and struggle.

ThinkingCritically

1. In your view, what are the considerations line drawers should have in mind if they want to draw the most democratic, equal district lines?

2. In a democracy, should district lines be drawn to maximize the competitiveness of elections, even if that means about one-half of the residents will not believe their elected officials represent their policy viewpoints?

Challenges to the American Creed

2-4 Identify the major challenges and alternatives to the dominant political culture.

Although the American creed has had strong allegiance, alternative beliefs have also influenced American politics. At times, people might profess the creed's beliefs while also agreeing with some of the alternatives. This combination may seem logically impossible, but individuals often put ideas together in surprising ways. Even within a society like the United States where one set of general beliefs generally predominates, the mosaic of cultural beliefs and values can be incredibly rich and complex because of the way that American creed ideals are mixed and mingled with other beliefs. American political culture is dynamic, not fixed and unchanging.

Communitarianism emphasizes the contributions and interests of the community.

Whereas the American creed gives primacy to the individual in society, **communitarianism** focuses on society and the community.[42] In the communitarian view, individuals are not self-made: society makes us and we owe something to society in return. In the words of Revolutionary leader Samuel Adams, "A citizen owes everything to the Commonwealth."[43] The communitarian approach does not dispute that individuals are personally responsible and need to work hard. But it would point out that we all depend on the resources provided by others and by the community, whether education, transportation, an array of commercial and cultural choices, or the bounty of the earth and water. These resources do not determine whether we will reach our goals, but they influence our ability to reach them, and we rely on others to provide them.

communitarianism the view that the needs of the community are of higher priority in government than the needs of the individual, even if the result is a restriction of individual liberties.

Communitarianism also says that the goal of self-improvement should not focus only on the self, but on how self-improvement serves the community and society more broadly. This way of thinking suggests that it is not an inherently bad thing for an individual to make a lot of money, but it asks whether society is served in the process.

Communitarian beliefs in American history   Communitarianism has been influential throughout American history. In the colonial and Revolutionary eras, this was the dominant mode of thought, often referred to by historians and political scientists as classical republicanism.[44] Political rhetoric of those eras placed great emphasis on having self-sacrificing virtuous people—those who would pursue the common good—as political leaders. Communitarian themes were emphasized along with individualistic ones. It was common practice for government to regulate wages, prices, and the entry of new businesses into the marketplace, all to maintain social stability and, it was believed, to produce a just society. Gradually, individualistic beliefs gained ascendancy. Communitarian ideals survived, but in a less prominent position than previously.

Periodically, these ideals flourished in the advocacy of social, political, or economic reform. Populists from 1875 through 1900 expressed deep concern about the disruption of communities by industrial capitalism and proposed many reforms to rectify the perceived exploitation of government by private interests. Communitarian ideas alone were not enough to lead to reform—political activists and politicians needed to organize people who held these views. Major reform movements like Progressivism (1904–1918), the New Deal (1930s), and the Great Society (1960s) were successfully infused with the idea that politics or economics needed to be reformed for the greater interest of the community. Proposed reforms such as income taxes, retirement and social welfare programs, and extensive regulation of business practices were criticized as contrary to the American creed. But right up to today, language condemning a politics of "the powerful versus the people," such as President Obama's critique of insurance companies and Wall Street investment firms, can resonate with many Americans.

▼ SUPPLY, DEMAND, AND QUESTIONS

When gas prices escalated in recent years, many Americans were suspicious that big oil companies were "gouging" consumers with high prices. Despite the reassurances of most economists that the oil and gasoline markets were not being manipulated by large corporations, Americans remained skeptical as oil company profits hit all-time highs. Defenders of the industry noted that it still had a profit rate much lower than that of many other industries.

Private interest and the public good   To communitarians, the rights of individuals and the interests of the community are not necessarily in conflict. But when they are, the public good should trump private interest.[45] For example, in some states and municipalities, police set up sobriety checkpoints and stop drivers at random to screen them for drunk driving. These checkpoints bypass the normal requirement that police can stop drivers only if they believe they have probable cause to investigate them. Sobriety checkpoints are clearly an infringement on the privacy rights of individuals, but they have been defended as serving the community's interests. If drivers realize they might get pulled over even when they are not driving erratically, they will be more cautious about drinking and driving, thereby enhancing everyone's safety and reducing the social costs involved with car crashes, injuries, and loss of life.[46]

Refining the American creed   One way to look at communitarianism is that it refines the American creed without necessarily rejecting it.[47] On their own, creedal beliefs about individualism can appear harsh, advocating a "sink or swim" society in which individuals either succeed or fail, with little compassion for those who fall behind. Communitarian ideas remove this harsh edge by supporting government programs to provide social resources and services for individuals who are struggling, if that is in the community's interest. Consider unemployment compensation. Whereas a strict application of the creed's emphasis on individual responsibility would see unemployment compensation as unnecessary—people could land new jobs by moving, accepting lower wages, or being flexible about the jobs they would take—communitarianism would view such compensation as necessary, at least for a time, to prevent the social disruption of unpaid rent and mortgages, delinquent bills, and families in disarray. Similar beliefs motivated some of the advocates for national health insurance (see *How Do We Know? Why Was the Path to Universal Health Insurance Coverage So Difficult?*).

Public Support for Communitarianism   Public opinion reveals the persistence of communitarian ideals today. Americans are not anti-business. In 2009, over 75 percent believed that "the strength of this country today is mostly based on the success of American business." Over half believed government regulation of business usually does more harm than good. However, about three-fifths of Americans charged that business fails to strike "a fair balance between making profits and serving the public interest." And the same proportion concluded that "business corporations make too much profit."[48] The very notion of "too much profit" is telling. In the creedal beliefs of property, liberty, and individualism, the idea of "too much" profit makes no sense. If an individual or business is clever enough to make a product for which there is high demand, how can we say "too much" profit is being made? Assuming you have choices, you are not forced to buy the product. If you believe the price is too high, you should not purchase it. Whereas the creedal view holds that substantial profit indicates a good business plan, communitarianism worries that businesses may be taking advantage of customers individually and society more generally.

Many Americans, such as those upset at oil companies when gasoline prices spike up sharply, share the communitarian belief that it is wrong for businesses to "exploit" certain situations—such as a shortage of a key resource—and increase their profit. When investment bankers in 2008 and 2009 received large bonuses even while their banks received taxpayer assistance to stay afloat as the economy soured and foreclosures soared, many Americans who were upset similarly saw this as disregarding the interest of the community.

2 Political Culture

54

Why Was the Path to Universal Health Insurance Coverage So Difficult?

The Question

In nearly all industrialized countries, health care coverage for every individual is guaranteed by the national government, either by the government's paying for private health care services, the government's directly providing services, or some combination of these two. In the United States, private expenditures are a far larger share of the total spent on health care than is true elsewhere (Figure 2-6). In 2010, after nearly a century of attempts and after a bruising legislative battle, the United States adopted a set of reforms designed to provide nearly universal health care coverage. Why was the path to universal health insurance coverage so difficult? How do we know?

Why It Matters

In recent years, at any given time nearly 47 million Americans, or about 16 percent of the population, had no health insurance. These figures are a matter of dispute, as they include

▶ **MOVING IN DIFFERENT DIRECTIONS**
Harry Reid, the Democratic Senate Majority Leader, and Mitch McConnell, the Republican Senate Minority Leader, at a health care reform summit convened by President Obama in February 2010. The two parties were unable to agree on the principles and details that should guide reform of the American health care system. How important, if at all, is it that both major parties be in agreement when government is considering large-scale policy reforms?

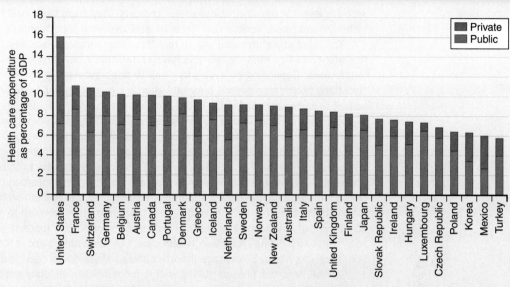

FIGURE 2-6. **Public and Private Health Care Expenditures as Percentage of Gross Domestic Product, 2007.** The United States devotes a much larger share of its economy to health care expenditures than other countries and has a much larger role for the private sector. American national and state governments also spend substantial sums on health care.

not only those who are unable to find insurance they can afford, but individuals who have chosen not to purchase insurance (for example, the young and healthy), those who qualify for health insurance from their employer or government but do not sign up, and individuals in the United States illegally. Nonetheless, they are the most widely cited figures. Among the unemployed, the poor, and racial and ethnic minorities, the rate is even higher, and many Americans drop into and out of heath care coverage for short periods of time over a two- or three-year period. In public opinion surveys, Americans frequently express fears that they will lose their insurance and will not be able to afford their medical expenses.[49] Whether you believe that universal health insurance is crucially important to individuals' health and life opportunities, or you believe that it will harm medical care overall more than help it, the answer to the question matters. By understanding what made the adoption of national health insurance so difficult, you learn the ingredients that contributed to its success in 2010.

Investigating the Answer

For political scientists, explaining why something did not happen is similar to explaining why something did happen: a researcher needs to come up with an idea that connects the outcome to factors that might explain the outcome. The outcome we are interested in is the absence or presence of national health insurance that covers all individuals. The possible cause we are especially interested in is political culture. The hunch is that the American creed's emphasis on individualism, liberty, and property is incompatible with the idea that health care should be considered a federal government responsibility. Individualism demands personal responsibility. Liberty means allowing choices, and if some people choose not to have insurance, why force it on them? Moreover, in the American free enterprise economy, health insurance has been a benefit offered by employers to entice prospective employees and retain their current workers. This competition might give employers the incentive to offer more generous insurance packages as they compete for employees. If different jobs provide different levels of benefits, workers have choices. They might trade health insurance for higher income, more flexible work schedules, or overtime opportunities.

The most straightforward way to test this idea is through examining public opinion. Regarding health insurance, surveys have shown that Americans express some communitarian views. Depending on the survey, half to three-quarters of Americans say they favor "providing health care coverage for all," even if it means raising taxes. American political culture is rooted predominantly in the American creed, however, and we see its influence in public opinion also. In one survey, a majority said they favored national health insurance provided by government, but support dropped off if the program would limit one's choice of doctors or if there were waiting lists for nonemergency treatments or if the respondent personally had to pay higher taxes. Adding these new opponents to those who initially opposed a universal health insurance program would make opposition the majority view.[50] During the 2009–2010 debate, the measurement of public opinion on health reform was highly susceptible to question wording and the information provided to respondents. About 90 percent of Americans in mid-2009 expressed support for "fundamental changes" in or "completely rebuilding" American health care, but when asked about their personal situation, nearly as high a percentage reported being satisfied with their health care.[51]

Overall, American political culture seems a deterrent to adopting national health insurance. The idea that there was no support for universal health insurance certainly is not correct, but support for a national plan was vulnerable to political arguments—and survey question wording—about service quality, availability, and choice. So it is fair to say that American political culture did not rule out national health insurance, but it also did not lend clear support for it if advantages of the current system might be lost. Certainly there was both vociferous opposition to President Obama's plans and massive mobilization against its passage, with references to the beliefs of the American creed highly prominent in these critiques. Is it that simple? Was the difficult path to universal coverage all due to culture? Case closed?

The answer, in fact, is not so simple. The United States has not had universal national health insurance, and the new plan will not be fully in place until 2014. But America does have the Medicare and Medicaid programs, which provide insurance for the elderly and the poor, respectively. U.S. national and state governments spend huge sums on health care, even more than in many other countries (Figure 2-6). If American political culture prior to 2010 simply would not allow any form of national health insurance, the existence of these two programs and all that spending would be a real puzzle. What if the explanation was modified to say that Americans opposed government-funded health insurance except for those individuals who are unable to provide for themselves? That seems to fit Medicare. But what about Medicaid? American creedal beliefs in individualism might argue that low-income persons, unlike the elderly, are in a position to better their financial standing and acquire health care, so government should not provide it. But government has, for decades.[52]

Given the mixed public opinion results and the presence of these two partial forms of national health insurance in the United States, how might we further try to explain the long, difficult path toward universal health insurance? Remember from Chapter 1 that there are rarely simple solutions. So one possibility is to add another factor: American political institutions.[53] For something as massive as national health insurance—which entails changes throughout the health care industry—the president, Congress, different parts of the federal bureaucracy, state governments, and possibly even the Supreme Court would be involved in the policy-making process. The health care industry is huge and well established, so efforts to change it are necessarily long and complicated, requiring a great deal of political dedication throughout multiple levels of political power. With influence dispersed across institutions and across majority and minority parties, there are many locations in the American political process where legislation can be defeated. Add a political culture that is only partly supportive of national health insurance, and the intersection of culture and institutions posed significant hurdles for national health insurance.

The political activity of "special interests" is another factor to consider.[54] Adding this factor further helps explain the complexity in this area of public policy. Traditionally, one part of the health care industry or another was likely to oppose movements toward national health insurance because they feared bureaucratic oversight of their business practices, interference with patient care, and depression of prices and salaries that would make the industry less efficient economically and less desirable as a career.[55] The interests opposed to national health insurance were likely to be already very well organized and very persistent on the issue because they had a lot at stake financially. Those individuals or groups in favor of national health insurance, on the other hand, needed to get organized to fight this battle, frequently had many different points of view, and often did not have as intense an interest in creating national health insurance as opponents had in stopping it.[56] A battle between a movement divided across several different reform plans and groups relatively unified to protect their turf will usually be won by the latter, even if there are more people in the former.

Thinking Critically

- Based on what you heard and read about the push for health care reform during 2009–2010, which of these factors do you believe might have changed enough to make reform possible?
- If you were a political strategist, how would you convince Americans that universal health care coverage guaranteed by the federal government is consistent with American political culture?
- Do any of these causal factors—culture, institutions, or interests—seem more important than the others, or does each seem about equally important in explaining the long path toward universal coverage?

The Bottom Line

Political culture, institutional features of American government, and the politics of special interests historically formed a thicket of obstacles to the adoption of national health insurance. So what made 2010 different from past years? Considering political culture, the argument that the president's health care agenda went against the grain of American political culture was one of the strongest rallying cries of the president's opponents. The president replied that "we are proud of our individualism, we are proud of our liberty, but we also have a sense of neighborliness and a sense of community," suggesting American political culture's communitarian aspects supported government's ensuring that all citizens had health care coverage.[57]

The role of culture in 2010 ultimately is best thought of neither as advancing nor defeating universal health insurance, but as shaping the construction of the program. Coverage for illegal immigrants, for example, was not included, and efforts to create a new government-run insurance company were defeated. Where the health care reform effort in 2009–2010 differed most from previous experiences is in the institutions involved with it. Lowering some of the institutional barriers to reform were a president who made health insurance a major priority, the substantial majority of seats held by his party in the House and Senate, adroit use of legislative procedures by Democratic leaders, and a fear that failure would lead to deep discontent among their staunchest party activists and supporters. As for interests, the growing worry, even among former opponents of reform, that health care costs had become economically unsustainable for businesses, governments, and individuals, prodded a recalculation about the desirability of some kind of universal coverage. Organizations representing senior citizens, physicians, pharmaceutical companies, hospitals, businesses, labor, and many others, including even the insurance companies themselves, committed early in the process to work with, or at least not actively oppose, the reform efforts. The change of heart among former opponents was due in part to the odds looking better than on previous occasions that reform might pass—better to be on the reform bus and try to steer its path rather than be run over by it. Despite this historically friendly institutional and interest environment in 2009-2010, the path to reform was still extraordinarily difficult, in part because of the mobilization of those Americans who saw government-guaranteed health insurance coverage as inconsistent with basic American political beliefs.

Discrimination stresses that not all groups deserve equal treatment.

discrimination the view that not all groups in society are deserving of equal rights and opportunities.

Another challenge to the American creed, particularly the value of equality, is **discrimination**. According to this view, society is a hierarchy where not all groups deserve all the rights and benefits the American creed can offer—some groups are favored and others are disfavored. The most glaring example of discrimination in American history was the treatment of racial minorities, especially blacks. Those holding hierarchical ideas considered blacks inherently inferior to whites. Some of the language used to describe blacks in comparison to whites was degrading and offensive, depicting blacks as anything from children to savages. Racism was so pervasive in American history that even many of those who opposed slavery did not consider blacks fully equal and fully deserving of the same rights as whites.

Discrimination cannot be dismissed as an inconvenient blip on history, or an unpleasant set of ideas held by relatively few people on the bottom rungs of society, or the distorted worldview of a few white supremacist organizations such as the Ku Klux Klan. Political, educational, and business leaders believed in these ideas. Well into the twentieth century, American public policy at the national and state levels was greatly influenced by the racist, anti-equality premises of discrimination, denying minorities equal access to the opportunities in America's society, economy, and polity. University researchers of the late nineteenth and early twentieth centuries measured the brain size of blacks and whites to demonstrate "objectively" the innate superiority of whites. The research lent an air of scientific justification to the denial of economic, social, and political rights to blacks. Across the country businesses refused to hire minorities, paid them less when they did, and often refused to serve them as customers. And many public officials pandered to racist views held by the public.

The same group inferiority and social hierarchy arguments used to limit the individual rights of blacks were also historically used against other ethnic groups, Native Americans, and women. The derogatory labels questioning the maturity, character, intelligence, and emotional stability of blacks were applied to these groups as well. Some people today argue that homosexuals face some of the same kinds of unequal treatment. Visions of the United States as a social hierarchy are still part of the mixture of American political culture, but not in the same bold, public, and widespread manner as in previous eras.[58]

Multiculturalism questions the desirability of a common American political culture.

Multicultural thought began sweeping through the United States in the 1980s, particularly on college campuses and in popular culture. The defining characteristics

◀ **BIG INTERESTS, BIG CHALLENGES**

In the late nineteenth century, the trusts—combinations of corporations that wielded significant market power—were seen by many Americans as being harmful to the interests of the community. President Theodore Roosevelt, when he took office in 1901, declared that one of his goals was to "bust" the trusts. The political movement known as Progressivism flourished at this time, emphasizing the need to regulate some trusts and remove others because of their perceived adverse impact on the public good.

multiculturalism   the view that group identity influences political beliefs and that, because groups are naturally diverse in their beliefs, the idea of a shared or dominant political culture merely reflects the imposition of a dominant group's beliefs on subordinate groups.

of **multiculturalism** are a belief that American society consists of multiple cultures and a focus on group identity rather than on the individualism strongly emphasized in the American creed. Advocates of multiculturalism are skeptical about the notion of any common American political culture. If there is such a culture, it is seen as reflecting the domination of one group in society—white men of European descent in particular—over other groups. Rather than bringing people together in social cohesion, the notion that there is one American political culture to which most individuals subscribe is seen as an exercise of power by dominant groups in society over weaker groups. In this view, as groups become more aware of how the dominant culture has cemented their subordinate position in society, they become more determined to protect and advocate their separate group identity and culture. They may interact with "mainstream" American society, but they also wish to preserve their distinctive language, customs, and beliefs.[59] Identity politics is a recent term used to describe such political activity.

Recognition and tolerance of diversity   In its least controversial version, multiculturalism simply calls for a recognition that the United States is composed of many different ethnic, racial, religious, gender, sexual preference, class, and nationality groups with distinctive contributions to bring to American society. If we view it in this way, it is possible to conceive of the American creed as a national political

▼ **NO WELCOME MAT**
Efforts to integrate the nation's schools during the civil rights movement faced strong opposition in some areas of the country.

culture, even while acknowledging that many other aspects of culture and behavior might differ from one group to another. It is from this version of multiculturalism that frequent calls for toleration, diversity, and "embracing our differences" are heard in public discourse.

Rejection of a common culture   In a more controversial version, multiculturalism means that any concept of a unified national political culture is false and is inherently an attempt by dominant groups to exert their power. Some multiculturalists contend not only that national political culture is highly diverse rather than unified, but also that individuals themselves reflect multiple cultural beliefs. Because of unique histories and life experiences, people look at the world differently. People "carry" a culture with them based on their group identity, but usually people have a collection of identities based on race, gender, ethnicity, and other characteristics, so the mix of beliefs may differ markedly from person to person.

Conflict with the American creed   This approach can lead to direct conflicts with beliefs in the American creed. One area that has been especially controversial and delicate is how multiculturalism intersects with the focus on equality and individualism in the American creed. For example, the nature of gender relations in some cultures has led to the rise of "cultural defenses" in court cases.[60] The cases are inherently inflammatory and controversial. Some have involved men charged with kidnap and rape who defended their actions as part of a particular marriage custom in their culture, and men who explained their murder of their wives as a culturally sanctioned response to their wives' adultery or mistreatment. In other cases, mothers who killed their children have explained their actions as instigated by the shame of a husband's infidelity and as part of a cultural practice of mother–child suicide. Expert testimony about a defendant's cultural background has sometimes led to dropped or reduced charges or reduced sentences.[61]

Cases like these raise challenging questions. Advocates of the American creed would ask whether equality is better served by emphasizing the equal and free status of each individual or by emphasizing the equal status of different cultural beliefs, which might differentiate between the rights accorded to men and women. Advocates of multiculturalism would ask whether these

▼ **DOMINANT CULTURE OR DOMINATING CULTURE?**
Some proponents of multiculturalism argue that, given people's diverse experiences and worldviews, there can be no true consensus around a single set of political beliefs and values. Instead, any claim that there is a unified political culture is better seen as an attempt by a majority group to impose its set of beliefs on minority groups. Does the presence of a widely shared political culture in fact mean that the majority is dominating minority groups?

► **CULTURAL DEFENSES**

In a society that wishes to embrace diverse groups and backgrounds, what happens when that diversity clashes with established legal standards? Khalid Adem, an Ethiopian immigrant to the United States, was convicted for cruelty to children for the circumcision of his two-year-old daughter, though he denied being responsible for the act. Defenders of Adem argued that his behavior needed to be understood within the context of his cultural heritage, which was more accepting of female circumcision than was the case in the United States.

defenses are any different from those offered earlier in American history by individuals whose cultural heritage was European. For a long time in the United States, they note, legal rights were sharply different for men and women, largely because of Western cultural understandings about gender relations.

Libertarianism argues for a very limited government role.

libertarianism a view that emphasizes the importance of individual choice and responsibility, the private sector, and the free market, in which government's primary obligations are to defend the country militarily, protect individuals from crime, and ensure that people fulfill contracts entered into freely.

Libertarianism argues that individuals are responsible for their own lives, and society is best off with individuals maximally free from government restraints. Government's responsibilities should be very limited, libertarians argue, and should not intrude on individual property rights or liberties. Its fundamental duties are to defend the country militarily, to protect individuals from crime, and to ensure that people fulfill contracts entered into freely. Beyond those duties, individual choice, the market, and voluntary action are what drive society, and government should not interfere. Outside these core responsibilities, each and every act of government compromises individual freedom.

In the United States, many citizens and politicians of both major political parties profess to hold some libertarian beliefs. This pick-and-choose method is usually unsatisfactory to libertarians: limited government activity and the primacy of the individual and a free market are core principles that should apply across all policy areas, not just be applied when politically convenient. The American creed prizes individualism and limited government, but to libertarians the creed tolerates too big a role for government.

American political culture is a mosaic of beliefs.

The beliefs of the American creed have been powerful guides for public thinking about politics. As noted above, these beliefs are ideals that mark out the starting point for most Americans when they think about political issues. Americans may be convinced to change their understanding of the meaning of these beliefs, or they may find the beliefs in severe tension and have to determine the acceptable balance between them. They may in some cases simply choose to ignore, or be persuaded to ignore, one of the beliefs that they profess to support.

For some Americans, American creed beliefs may be displaced by alternative sets of beliefs. More common, however, is that Americans hold many of these beliefs simultaneously and in some tension—supporting the American creed's beliefs, for example, but also holding strong communitarian beliefs or even views supportive of discrimination. Perhaps some hold beliefs from all three of these streams—American creed, communitarianism, discrimination—simultaneously. Or they could embrace the joining of other beliefs like multiculturalism or libertarianism with the American creed beliefs.

The beliefs of the American creed—democracy, individualism, liberty, property rights, religion—and the fundamental value of equality are powerful touchstones in American politics that guide the way most individuals think about politics and government, but they do not preclude other beliefs and ideals holding important places in the mosaic of American political culture. Each generation works with the political culture template left by previous generations and makes its own adjustments, either minor or major, of what is permissible and impermissible, proper and improper, in American politics and government. The remarkable and dynamic mosaic of American political culture endures but also is periodically redefined and reshaped.

CHAPTER SUMMARY

In this chapter you have learned to:

2-1 Define political culture and explain how certain values and beliefs achieve dominance within a society. Political culture consists of the basic values, beliefs, attitudes, predispositions, and expectations within which politics operates. It is where citizens start as they process and assess issues, causes, groups, parties, candidates, and public officials. Political culture provides a language used by politicians in speaking to the public.

2-2 Illustrate how the key values and beliefs of the American creed shape politics and government today. The American creed is built around beliefs in individualism, democracy, liberty, property rights, and religion, all tied together by the value of equality. These beliefs are frequently discussed during the formation of public policy. One of the key storylines of American history is that over time additional groups, such as racial minorities and women, demanded that they, too, be able to receive the benefits of the creed.

2-3 Evaluate the consequences of American political culture such as limited government and a weak sense of sovereign power. Several consequences emerge from the creed's dominance in American political culture, including a preference for limited government, a weak sense of sovereign power, tension between private and public interests, and concern about the impact of competing beliefs. The beliefs of the

creed can sometimes conflict. The belief in liberty might lead toward one policy solution, but the belief in democracy might lead toward another. Tension also arises because the beliefs themselves may be defined differently or might change over time. A term like "democracy" or "liberty" might mean different things to different people. Tension between beliefs and over the definition of each belief creates much of the debate in American politics.

2-4 Identify the major challenges and alternatives to the dominant political culture. Throughout American history other views have challenged the creed. Alternative modes of thinking about political life have had important effects in the United States. Communitarianism emphasized the role of society or community rather than the centrality of the individual. Communitarianism was prominent during the colonial and Revolutionary periods and continues to influence politics. Discrimination also has had a profound influence on American politics. Justification and defense of social hierarchy and inequality, particularly those based on race and gender, have had a long place in American history. Multiculturalism questions the desirability of a consensus in political culture, arguing that any such consensus is more likely the imposition of the values and beliefs of dominant groups upon groups that are weaker politically. Libertarianism tolerates only the most minimal role for government.

PEARSON
mypoliscilab

EXERCISES

Apply what you learned in this chapter on MyPoliSciLab.

📖—Read on **mypoliscilab.com**

eText: Chapter 2

✓—Study and Review on **mypoliscilab.com**

Pre-Test
Post-Test
Chapter Exam
Flashcards

👁—Watch on **mypoliscilab.com**

Video: The President Addresses School Children
Video: Facebook Privacy Concerns
Video: Who is in the Middle Class?

☀—Explore on **mypoliscilab.com**

Simulation: What Are American Civic Values?
Timeline: Major Technological Innovations that Have Changed the Political Landscape
Visual Literacy: Using the Census to Understand Who Americans Are
Visual Literacy: Who Are Liberals and Conservatives? What's the Difference?

CHAPTER TEST

1. What is the difference between political culture and public opinion?
2. Why has the United States had a shared political culture despite the country's extensive diversity?
3. How does the value of equality tie together the five beliefs of the American creed?
4. What expectations about politics and government are contained in the American creed belief in democracy?
5. How can the preference for limited government in the American creed coincide with the existence of an array of government programs?
6. In what ways is the sense of sovereign power in the United States weak?

7. How do tension among American creed beliefs and different interpretations of the meaning of the beliefs create conflict in the United States, despite a shared political culture?
8. How do the major communitarian beliefs compare to the American creed, and how prominent has this alternative outlook on politics been in the United States?
9. What are the chief conflicts between multiculturalism and the American creed?
10. In what ways might American political culture be thought of as a mosaic of beliefs?

KEY TERMS

American creed, p. 27
communitarianism, p. 51
discrimination, p. 58
equality, p. 30
individualism, p. 31

libertarianism, p. 62
liberty, p. 35
limited government, p. 42
multiculturalism, p. 60
natural rights, p. 35

political culture, p. 26
property rights, p. 36
religious freedom, p. 38
sovereign power, p. 45

SUGGESTED READINGS

Jim Cullen. 2003. *The American Dream: A Short History of an Idea That Shaped a Nation*. New York: Oxford University Press. The history of the "American dream" and its continuing power in American thought today.

Alexis de Tocqueville. 1835. *Democracy in America*. Still a remarkably perceptive and insightful analysis of the nature of American society, politics, and identity and how they differ from other countries.

Jennifer L. Hochschild. 1981. *What's Fair: American Beliefs About Distributive Justice*. Cambridge, MA: Harvard University Press. Argues that support for equality thrives in political and private life, but that there is less support for equality in economic matters.

Samuel P. Huntington. 1981. *American Politics: The Promise of Disharmony*. Cambridge, MA: Harvard University Press. Suggests that American politics has been cyclically driven by gaps that emerge between the ideals of the American creed and the reality of American institutions, and that the timing of the cycle is related to the rise and fall of religious "great awakenings."

Calvin C. Jillson. 2004. *Pursuing the American Dream: Opportunity and Exclusion over Four Centuries*. Lawrence: University Press of Kansas. A sweeping overview of the idea of opportunity in American thought and its institutionalization in social, economic, and political life.

Seymour Martin Lipset. 1996. *American Exceptionalism: A Double-Edged Sword*. New York: W. W. Norton. Examines whether America is distinctive from other societies in culture, economics, and politics, and concludes that overall it is.

Richard M. Merelman. 1991. *Partial Visions: Culture and Politics in Britain, Canada, and the United States*. Madison: University of Wisconsin Press. How embedded political messages and values in popular culture weaken and distort democratic participation.

Benjamin I. Page and Lawrence R. Jacobs. 2009. *Class War? What Americans Really Think About Economic Inequality*. Chicago: University of Chicago Press. Argues that Americans are more supportive of measures to address income inequality than is typically assumed.

Michael Sandel. 1996. *Democracy's Discontent: America in Search of a Public Philosophy*. Cambridge, MA: Harvard University Press. An accessible discussion of American political culture, noting particularly the strain between individualism and communitarianism.

Patricia Strach. 2007. *All in the Family: The Private Roots of American Public Policy*. Stanford, CA: Stanford University Press. Argues that to understand the full scope of American government, one must examine how government uses the family to implement many policies.

SUGGESTED WEBSITES

American Ethnic Geography: A Cultural Geography of the United States and Canada: www.valpo.edu/geomet/geo/courses/geo200/HomePage.html

A course website at Valparaiso University with a wealth of interesting maps demonstrating various kinds of diversity across the United States. A simplified map of the division of the United States into regions of political culture can be found under the Politics link.

E Pluribus Unum: The Bradley Project on America's National Identity: www.bradleyproject.org/bradleyprojectreport.html

Data and analysis exploring the idea of a shared national identity, perceived threats to that identity, and differences between demographic groups.

U.S. Religious Landscape Survey: religions.pewforum.org

A survey of over 35,000 adult Americans on their religious practices, beliefs, and opinions on issues.

Trends in Political Values and Core Attitudes: 1987–2009: people-press.org/report/517/political-values-and-core-attitudes

A survey of American attitudes across an array of fundamental beliefs as well as some specific policy areas.

Public Agenda: www.publicagenda.org/citizen

Of particular interest are the issue guides, which examine major issues and present the basic policy choices. The choices provide a good sense of different tradeoffs in American creed beliefs, as well as competing beliefs such as communitarianism and libertarianism. See also the surveys of immigrants in 2002 and 2009 ("A Place to Call Home").

World's Smallest Political Quiz: www.theadvocates.org/quizp/index.html

A quiz published by the Advocates for Self-Government, a libertarian group. The quiz analyzes your answers and labels your political ideology.

CHAPTER

3   The Constitution

No Permission Required? Searching Without a Warrant

By shaping and constraining the actions of the three branches of government, the U.S. Constitution has direct causal effects on American politics. Ironically, because the Constitution constrains, it also leads these branches
to take actions to expand their authority and influence.

Consider the issue of searches conducted without a warrant. For the most part, such searches are prohibited by the Constitution. But, presidents argue, not always.

"We will direct every resource at our command—every means of diplomacy, every tool of intelligence, every instrument of law enforcement, every financial influence, and every necessary weapon of war—to the disruption and to the defeat of the global terror network." President

▼ **TRACKING COMMUNICATIONS**

Federal government arguments that it has the right to access e-mail messages and records of the location of cell phone calls as part of the executive branch's national security duties have been highly controversial. In 2010, the Justice Department dropped its demand that Yahoo provide e-mail messages to investigators, but maintained that it had a right to the messages.

George W. Bush spoke these words before Congress in a nationally televised address on September 20, 2001. In his speech, the president promised bold, aggressive action against those responsible for terrorist activity.

In the heat of the immediate aftermath of the September 11 terrorist attacks on the United States, the president's words garnered wide support and approval. Four years later, however, the president's vision had become more controversial. What does "every resource at our command" mean? What are the limits to the resources and to the president's command? The Constitution provides for a government of carefully balanced legislative, executive, and judicial powers, centered chiefly in Congress, the president, and the courts, respectively. How far could the president go and remain faithful to this constitutional principle?

In December 2005, the *New York Times* revealed the existence of a program in which the National Security Agency, without authorization from the courts, monitored communications that the administration said involved individuals and members of terrorist organizations in the United

States. Under the 1978 Foreign Intelligence Surveillance Act (FISA), the government is normally expected to obtain a warrant from the Foreign Intelligence Surveillance Court to eavesdrop on the international communication of individuals in the United States when at least one party to the communication is suspected of having ties to terrorism.

The revelation that the government had been conducting surveillance without requesting warrants prior to intercepting messages provoked a firestorm of protest. In emergencies, FISA allowed surveillance to be done, with three days granted to obtain a warrant after the surveillance, but the administration had not obtained these warrants. Moreover, although a few members of Congress had been informed about the program, they were not permitted to divulge any information to their colleagues, so Congress as an institution had no knowledge of the surveillance.

The president's position was that as commander in chief, his obligation was to win a war, and warrantless searches were one of the tools at his disposal. Congress's authorization of military action to root out terrorism after September 11, 2001, implicitly gave the president wartime authority to order the National Security Agency to monitor e-mail and telephone calls in which one of the persons in the communication—either in the United States or abroad—might have terrorist links, the administration argued in defense of its Terrorist Surveillance Program. National security, in this view, is Job One of a president.

To critics, the president was taking unilateral, unchecked action in a manner inconsistent with the Constitution. The failure to obtain warrants or advise Congress about the surveillance program indicated that the president had taken a far too expansive view of the executive

branch's power, threatening the constitutional balance between the branches. The president's theory of his commander in chief powers, they charged, had no logical stopping point, and yet the U.S. Constitution is all about providing stopping points to power.[1]

Many of these critics thought that a new president would mean a change in these policies. But, as noted earlier, the causal effects of the Constitution are twofold: it may constrain presidential behavior, but for that very reason it may also encourage presidents to take actions that establish their independent authority and influence.

President Barack Obama's Department of Justice has repeatedly defended the surveillance program from legal challenges and argued that being required to reveal any information gathered by the program would cause substantial harm to national security. As one writer noted, the legal arguments about "state secrets" made by the Obama administration defending the surveillance program and the information it obtained were nearly identical in wording to those offered by the Bush administration.[2] Although the administration has not been explicit about its thoughts on the program itself, it asserts it has shielded the program from lawsuits to protect national security and, by extension, the president's role as commander in chief in taking what

he sees as necessary measures to enhance that security.

The administration has defended warrantless searches in other cases. In spring 2010, the Department of Justice filed suit against Yahoo to obtain messages in its Yahoo Mail service, stating it did not need a warrant to obtain the mail. The dispute turned in part on whether e-mails that had been opened and read were in "electronic storage" and therefore required a warrant to search. The Justice Department argued they were not, and thus no warrant was needed. A large coalition of groups opposed the demand, including Yahoo, Google, the Electronic Frontier Foundation, and the Computer and Communications Industry Association. The Department ultimately dropped its demand, but not its position that it had a right to the mail.

Other cases have involved the authority of government investigators to demand, without a search warrant, records from cell phone companies recording the location of cell phone calls as determined by cell tower tracking information. The administration has argued that individuals' constitutional rights are not violated when a phone company, responding to a government demand made without a search warrant, provides records showing where a cell phone made or received a call. Like the surveillance program and the e-mail case, the

administration's position on cell phone tracking alarmed civil liberties groups, who argued the administration was unconstitutionally prioritizing executive branch authority over individual citizen privacy.[3]

Although the Framers of the U.S. Constitution could not have foreseen the precise issues leading to the recent battles over warrantless searches, or imagined the new technologies available to store and transmit information, the questions raised by the controversies are the same kinds the Framers wrestled with nearly 225 years earlier. What are the responsibilities of the different branches of government? How can the Constitution ensure that no one part of American government becomes too powerful or too unchecked in its exercise of power? How can it protect the liberties and rights of the people, and what are the limits to those liberties and rights? In this chapter, we explore how the Framers answered these questions as they wrote the Constitution. Based on their experience with Great Britain, as well as their experience in governing the new country after the Revolution in 1776, the Framers were deeply concerned with power—its use, abuse, extent, and proper exercise—as they designed a new system of government. Over the centuries since, public officials would work within the Constitution's constraints, but also, in turn, seek to reshape and redefine those constraints.

CHAPTER LEARNING OBJECTIVES

After reading this chapter you will be able to:

3-1 Trace developments from events leading to the American Revolution through problems with the country's first constitution.

3-2 Outline the problems the Framers of the Constitution attempted to resolve and the solutions they devised.

3-3 Compare and contrast the arguments of Anti-Federalists and Federalists.

3-4 Explain the processes of constitutional change.

From Revolution to Constitution

3-1 Trace developments from events leading to the American Revolution through problems with the country's first constitution.

Momentous in its impact, the American Revolution has been difficult for historians to classify. Unlike other revolutions, it was not a revolt of one social class against another or a replacement of one economic system by another. If it was not a revolution in these ways, then what was it?

The American Revolution changed ideas about governance.

▼ TAXATION WITHOUT REPRESENTATION

Taxes are rarely popular. They are even more unpopular when people believe they have been imposed without fair representation of their point of view. One of the chief debates between the colonists and the British government was over the nature of representation. Actions like the Stamp Act convinced Americans that they had no genuine representation in the British political system.

One answer provided by political scientists and historians is that the American Revolution was an "ideological" revolution, which is to say a revolution most notably in ideas and philosophy of government. With this answer, scholars agree with former president John Adams, who wrote in 1818 that the "radical change in the principles, opinions, sentiments, and affections of the people was the real American Revolution."[4]

It was a revolution about ideas, particularly ideas about governing.[5] To colonial leaders, power, because of human corruption, tended to be too aggressive and to extend beyond its legitimate boundaries. The victim of power was liberty. To defend liberty and thwart excessive power required vigilance and virtue from ordinary people.

The colonists drew insights from their own experience and borrowed liberally from various political theorists and writers. As we discussed in Chapter 1, British political theorist John Locke's ideas on limited government and social contracts were especially influential. The idea of the social contract was that the relationship between the governed and those in power was equivalent to a business contract in which each side had obligations to fulfill or the contract would become void.[6] The governed were not bound indefinitely to corrupt or dysfunctional political institutions.

From this basis, the colonists built a new understanding of politics based on the concepts of representation, constitutional rights, and sovereignty. During the decade prior to the colonists' formal declaration of independence, the language of democratic representation was a key rallying cry to build enthusiasm for the prospect of a separation from Great Britain. The expression "no taxation without representation" highlights one of the most famous demands from the American Revolution and has been learned by every school child since then as a key to what the revolution was about. British government officials attempted to convince the colonists they were "virtually represented"—even though the colonists did not elect members of Parliament, members of Parliament in effect represented their interests because they tended to the interests of the British Empire in general, and these two sets of interests were the same. The colonists, instead, touted the concept of direct representation: the job of the representative was to reflect faithfully the opinions of the constituents who elected him or her. Citizens should send representatives to the legislature with specific instructions about how to vote.

In addition, constitutions should mark the boundaries of legitimate government power. People had natural, inherent rights that preceded any government action, and written constitutions were needed to protect these rights.

Lastly, the colonists challenged the dominant view of sovereignty. In Britain, the idea that there could only be one final, ultimate authority—sovereignty—was undisputed. The colonists, however, argued that sovereignty could be divided. Authority could be located in different geographical locations, for example at the local and national levels, as well as in different institutions, such as the executive and legislative branches.

The combination of these beliefs generated a radical view of the people as self-governing. The concept of "the people" as a positive, active force, rather than just passive subjects of government, became a touchstone for much of the oratory of the period.[7] The people's role had been transformed from occasional watchdog to partici-pant: the people were not only a check on government, they in effect were the government. In this new conceptual understanding of how politics should work, the active and continuous consent of the governed was necessary.[8]

The colonists rebelled against taxes imposed unilaterally by the British government.

The immediate impetus for the revolution was a series of economic and po-litical events, many of which received prominent billing in the Declaration of Independence. The causal forces are difficult to disentangle. Would the events have had such resonance in the absence of new ideas about the right of the people to self-government? For decades, the colonists had been out of practical reach of British rulers and had been allowed to operate with exten-sive freedom. This experience built their confidence in their ability to self-govern. So we can flip the question and ask: would those ideas about self-government have flourished as thoroughly in the absence of a set of provocative events? After all, the revolutionary leaders were not simply dreamily concocting new political ideas from the sidelines—they were very practical and strategic politicians whose ideas about government were forged in the political battles within the colonies and with Britain.

ThinkingCausally

Did powerful ideas or dramatic events push the colonies toward revolution?

The best resolution to these questions is to see the events and ideas as mutually reinforcing. When Britain began to clamp down on the colonies, the colonists believed the freedom they had already achieved was being threatened, and this threat reinforced the appeal of self-governance. To colonists, the revolution was needed to maintain their freedom, not to create it. As they saw it, an orchestrated campaign was afoot to demolish American liberty. These causal factors—ideas and events—cannot be completely separated, as each furthered the other and both in turn fostered senti-ment for revolution.

The two most influential economic groups of the day were New England merchants and southern planters. These two groups had long been fiercely loyal to the British government, and by controlling key positions of power in the colonies they prevented more radical elements in the colonies from pushing toward conflict with the mother country. Now, however, they were agitated by recent changes in

British policies, particularly tax policies. For seven years, Britain had been engaged in the French and Indian War, an engagement that depleted the British treasury. Believing that many of its costs were related to maintaining the safety of the American colonists, that the colonists had had a free ride for some time, and that British citizens had subsidized the colonies extensively, the British government instituted new policies designed to extract some revenue from this growing part of its empire.

Stamp Act   One new law was the Stamp Act, passed by Parliament in 1765. This law required all legal documents, licenses, commercial contracts, newspapers, and pamphlets to obtain a tax stamp. The colonists rebelled. Stamp agents were attacked by mobs, and many had their property destroyed. Several colonial assemblies passed resolutions of protest against the act. The Stamp Act Congress sent a protest to the king and Parliament. A boycott of British goods finally led Parliament to repeal the tax. But Parliament then passed the Declaratory Act, stating the right of the British government to pass laws that would be binding on the colonists. The British government wanted to send a clear message that the colonies were indeed part of the British Empire and subject to its edicts.

Townshend Acts   That message would soon be reinforced with the Townshend Acts. Passed in 1767, one of these acts suspended the New York legislature because that colony had not complied with a law requiring that British soldiers be quartered in (that is, reside in) housing owned by the colonists. The Revenue Act, the second of the Townshend Acts, imposed customs duties on colonial imports of glass, lead, paint, paper, and tea. Generally, the cost of these fees was passed along to the colonists by raising the price tag on these products.

Resistance to the Revenue Act was considerable. The Massachusetts Assembly, indicating its unwillingness to enforce the law, was disbanded by the British in 1768. Tensions rose over the next 18 months, culminating with the Boston Massacre in March 1770. British soldiers, enduring another day of taunting from a crowd gathered at the Customs House, killed five colonists. The event and the subsequent acquittals further agitated the colonists. Ultimately, boycotts and merchants' refusal to import goods led to the repeal of all the Townshend duties except that on tea.

Tea Act   Following a three-year lull, the British government enacted a particularly controversial new economic policy in 1773, the Tea Act. Tea was an extremely important industry in that era. Leaders of the economically advanced countries of the day believed that tea, much like high technology today or automobiles 40 years ago, stimulated the national economy. Nearly every country wanted a piece of this industry. Competition was brisk, but the profit potential was enormous. The Tea Act allowed the British-controlled East India Company to export its tea to America without paying the tea duty that had been imposed by the Townshend Acts. This made the British tea cheaper than Dutch tea, which dominated the American market and was sold by colonial merchants. The colonial merchants were squeezed out by the new law, because the East India Company would use its own British agents, not colonial merchants, to sell the tea.

The colonists' response was the incident known as the Boston Tea Party. Inflammatory language unmistakably threatened death to anyone who assisted the East India Company in unloading its tea. In December 1773, protesters prevented the unloading of the East India Company tea and threw the tea in the harbor. The British government viewed the Tea Party as an act of terrorism—random violence and property damage coupled with random threats designed to intimidate colonists and British officials alike, all to prevent a company from carrying out its legal activities.

To Americans, however, the Tea Party became a symbol of reaction against powerful government, a symbol that every schoolchild for generations has learned. The Tea Party movement that emerged in 2009 is the latest in a long line of protests that use Boston Tea Party imagery to link back to this iconic event.

When the Boston Town Meeting refused Parliament's demand for compensation for the tea, the British government retaliated with what colonists referred to as the Intolerable Acts. These acts closed the port of Boston, restricted the power of the Massachusetts Assembly and local town meetings, quartered troops in private houses, and exempted British officials from trial in Massachusetts. In response, 12 of the 13 colonies banded together to establish the First Continental Congress in September and October 1774.[9] The Congress issued demands to the king in the form of a Declaration of Rights and Grievances and developed plans for colonial resistance to what they deemed as an overbearing imperial government.

The Declaration of Independence aimed to build a nation.

The Continental Congress met again from May 1775 through December 1776 in a charged atmosphere. In April 1775, skirmishes had broken out in Lexington and Concord, Massachusetts. Parliament had rejected the First Continental Congress's Declaration of Rights and Grievances, which set out complaints about economic policies, lack of representation, British domination of the colonial judicial system, and disbanding of colonial legislatures. Communications within and between the colonies about the trouble with the British government were frequent and impassioned, with writers like Thomas Paine using pamphlets and his book *Common Sense* to arouse opposition to the royal government.

Recognizing the drift of events and opinion, the Second Continental Congress began the process of building a new government by creating an army, approving the issuance of currency, and establishing diplomatic and trade relations with other

▼ ATTENTION-GETTING VIOLENCE

The environmental group Earth Liberation Front was believed responsible for this fire and two other house fires on a single night in Seattle in 2008. When groups use violent methods like this, referred to as eco-terrorism, they often gain attention for their cause but also invite a crackdown from government. This was the pattern seen with the Boston Tea Party. These methods are often controversial, even among those who agree with the cause.

Declaration of Independence the document announcing the intention of the colonies to separate from Great Britain based on shared grievances about the treatment of the colonists by the British government.

nation A shared sense of understanding and belonging among a people, that they are different and separate from other peoples with particular characteristics and that they have a right to self-government over a defined territory.

▼ **THE DECLARATION OF INDEPENDENCE**
The Declaration was adopted by the Second Continental Congress on July 4, 1776. It sought to build a sense of national unity. Creating a nation, and the shared goals and sacrifices that go with it, was one contributing factor in the success of the revolutionary effort.

countries. Influenced by experience, their reading of history, the lessons of the republics of antiquity in Greece and Rome, and the ideas of a range of writers, political leaders were building the intellectual framework necessary to justify revolution. On July 4, 1776, their efforts bore fruit, as the Second Congress approved the **Declaration of Independence** drafted by Thomas Jefferson. (An annotated Declaration of Independence can be found at the end of this book, in the Appendix.)

The Declaration asserted that rights of life, liberty, property, and the pursuit of happiness were "unalienable," meaning they cannot be given away. Similarly, as expressed earlier by John Locke, these rights were natural, born in people as an essential part of their being. Government did not provide these rights—the most it could do was restrict them. When it restricted them arbitrarily and unjustly, then revolution was an appropriate response. The Declaration was also an attempt to find common ground that would join the colonists as "Americans." Although "nation" is often used as synonymous with "country," from a political science perspective a **nation** is a distinctive concept. It refers to a shared sense of understanding among a people that they are different and separate from other peoples, that basic principles, values, and outlooks unite them, and that they have a right to self-government. The Declaration attempted to inspire that sense of nationhood.

The Articles of Confederation aimed to build a government.

The next step was to build a set of government institutions infused by fundamental principles, rules of operation, values, and beliefs.[10] A government enhances a population's sense of nationhood. Constructing a government that can rule effectively and is

consistent with a population's sense of nationhood was a significant challenge in 1776, just as it is in emerging democracies today. Rules and procedures guide how governments operate. And rules laid down early can be very difficult to change later. The stakes, therefore, are high.

The first attempt to devise governing principles and draft a national constitution was the **Articles of Confederation.** The Articles were approved in November 1777 by the Third Continental Congress, which had begun meeting in December 1776. Each of the former colonies, now called states, had to ratify the document. The ratification process was completed in March 1781, and the Articles remained in effect until 1789. The Revolutionary War, which had begun in April 1775, ended in April 1783.[11]

The challenge facing the authors of the Articles of Confederation was to create a government that embraced the sense of nationhood expressed in the Declaration of Independence, while also recognizing that Americans primarily identified themselves by the individual states in which they lived. The Articles of Confederation reflected a deep fear of centralized political power, born out of the Americans' experience with Parliament and British monarchs and expressed in the Declaration of Independence. It also provided a leading role for the states. For both these reasons, it seemed a reasonable fit for the new country.

Articles of Confederation the first constitution of the United States, which based most power in the states.

Under the Articles, the national government was based in Congress. Members of Congress were selected by state legislatures, paid by the states, and able to be recalled and removed from office by the states. Laws were to be implemented by the individual states. There was neither an executive branch nor a judiciary. It was difficult for Congress to pass legislation. Although state legislatures typically sent three representatives to Congress, each state cast only one vote. For a bill to pass, a simple majority of seven of the 13 states was not enough. Instead, a supermajority—a set amount that is more than a simple majority—of nine states had to agree. Changing the Articles required the approval of all 13 states.

Problems with the Articles as a governing framework   Difficulties set in almost immediately. Congress's powers were limited. Although this was consistent with American ideas about limited government, the government also needed to perform basic functions. Congress could declare war—but there was no standing national army. It could regulate trade with Native Americans—but it could not regulate trade between the states. It could borrow money or coin money—but it could not institute taxes. Effectively, the system of government built under the Articles made the national government almost entirely dependent on the voluntary cooperation of the states. There was little this government controlled and little it could do to force action.

Action was sometimes needed internationally, but the United States had no coherent way to deal with other countries. Economic treaties were a free-for-all, with states making their own arrangements with foreign countries. Under the Articles, Congress would have had no way to enforce international treaties even if it had been able to negotiate them. Although Congress could declare war and could name senior army officers, any military action required pulling together the disparate state militias. Given the control of portions of North America by European countries, and the ongoing interactions with Indian tribes, a more coordinated effort with national leadership was an appealing idea to many public officials.

Action was sometimes needed internally. Politicians, merchants, and creditors were shaken by domestic upheaval during the 1780s. Many events worried them. For example, Rhode Island printed paper money for use in repaying debts, but creditors considered it worthless. Some states instituted one-year terms for legislators, to limit their power and make them more responsive to public opinion. However, to leaders

Shays's Rebellion a protest by farmers in western Massachusetts in 1786–1787 to stop foreclosures on property by state courts; it convinced many political leaders that the Articles of Confederation were insufficient to govern the United States.

▼ **COURTING TROUBLE**
The ability of rebels in western Massachusetts to take control of courthouses, as shown here, was a wake-up call to political and business leaders around the country.

in government and business, democracy had degenerated into rule by the mob, or "mobocracy."

In their view, all that was wrong under the Articles was on view in the incident known as **Shays's Rebellion** in 1786–1787. Daniel Shays was a former army officer angered by the growing number of people being thrown off their land in western Massachusetts, mostly for inability to pay land taxes. To prevent further foreclosures, Shays joined and then, perhaps reluctantly, led like-minded men from August 1786 through February 1787. Bearing firearms, they assembled outside courthouses to prevent the courts from opening. Punctuating the incident, his supporters attempted to raid the federal arsenal in Springfield, where weapons were stockpiled. Massachusetts officials asked the Continental Congress for assistance, but the national government was ill equipped to pull together either financial resources or military personnel. The state itself had no permanent militia. To displace Shays and his supporters, Boston businessmen raised private money to fund the state militia. Although Massachusetts then successfully put down the rebellion within a few days, the incident sent shockwaves around the country.

The political system created by the Articles of Confederation seemed unable to manage either international or domestic affairs. As a result, the political and economic leaders concluded that the new nation's first constitution had already failed.

Frustration with the Articles led to the writing of a new Constitution.

The 1780s were unsettling. Schooled in the communitarian belief that concern for the public good should outweigh personal interests, many political leaders worried that the people's capacity for restrained self-government had failed. Self-government required that the people use their power cautiously and not to advantage one group at the expense of another. In the view of these leaders, a critical juncture had been reached. Not everyone agreed that the experience of the 1780s was so dire—the real concern of political leaders, they suggested, was the erosion of the leaders' political power. But those who did share a sense of worry over the country's direction concluded that change was necessary.[12]

The first attempt to repair the Articles had occurred before Shays's Rebellion. In the fall of 1786, accepting an invitation from the Virginia legislature, delegates from five states met in Annapolis, Maryland, to discuss the problems facing the young national government. With only five states present, the Annapolis Convention was not in a position to make specific proposals for changes in the Articles. Instead, the delegates approved a resolution drafted by Alexander Hamilton that called for possible revision of the Articles. Hamilton had been an assistant to George Washington in the

Revolutionary War and would later play a large role in the ratification of the Constitution and as secretary of the Treasury in Washington's administration.[13] His resolution called for Congress to send delegates to Philadelphia at some future date to make the Articles more effective in managing domestic and international affairs.

Soon, Congress did just that. Shocked by Shays's Rebellion, Congress called on each state to send delegates to Philadelphia in May 1787 to discuss revision of the Articles. Every state except Rhode Island participated. They met with a sense of crisis in the air: the national government appeared to be unable to handle international disputes, establish civility and cooperation between the states, or react to domestic insurrection. The delegates quickly concluded that revision of the Articles was pointless. They decided to start over and establish a new set of ground rules for an effective American government.[14]

Those efforts would culminate in the Constitution, the young country's second attempt to build a government that would rule effectively and unify the new American nation. (An annotated Constitution is at the end of this chapter.) The delegates were still concerned about threats to personal liberty posed by the concentration of too much power in a national government, but they now believed that too weak a national government was just as severe a threat. As they struggled to devise a new set of rules for the national government, the Framers would need to find a way to blend power with liberty, freedom with order, and national authority with state sovereignty.

Crafting the Constitution

3-2 Outline the problems the Framers of the Constitution attempted to resolve and the solutions they devised.

America's constitutional structure has held remarkable legitimacy. Although Americans may often be skeptical about the individuals in power, they tend to be proud of their Constitution and the system of government, liberties, and responsibilities it created. Indeed, for many Americans, government in the American form essentially defines democracy. People may be critical of politicians, but they believe that the constitutional system works fairly and effectively. If a system of rules is legitimate, people will agree to challenge policies and actions through constitutionally established procedures. In its protection for liberty, property rights, religion, democracy, and equality, the Constitution adheres to beliefs deeply held by most Americans across many diverse groupings, which enhances the esteem in which it is held.

> "They met with a sense of crisis in the air: the national government appeared to be unable to handle international disputes, establish civility and cooperation between the states, or react to domestic insurrection."

For the most part, this satisfaction is reasonable. The U.S. Constitution is now the oldest national written constitution in the world, and the vast majority of countries have followed the American model of a written constitution. Great Britain is the primary example of an unwritten constitution. The British constitution might be thought of as "an understanding" that has emerged from statutes and traditions. In the United States and other countries with written constitutions, such as Canada, Mexico, France, and Germany, the interpretation of the text might change, but "the constitution" is a well-defined, explicit document. Similarly, the means to amend it are precisely stated, normally requiring a procedure that differs from the one used to pass legislation.

Fashioning a constitution is an exercise in problem-solving that reflects the particular circumstances present at the document's creation. This was no less true for Americans in 1787 than it was for constitution writers in West Germany after World War II or those attempting to construct a constitution in Iraq in 2005. In their problem-solving, the Germans prohibited political parties based on Nazism. The drafters of

ThinkingComparatively

Constitutions around the world attempt to resolve or minimize the political stresses and conflicts that existed prior to their writing.

Iraq's constitution sought ways to give different ethnic and religious groups a stake in the broader sense of nationhood, and to determine the balance between central and regional authority that would be best for governing and most practical for the political task of ratifying the constitution.

Constitutions are complex. The resolution of one problem might well create new problems and unintended consequences. The more detailed and complicated the document, the higher the risk that it may institutionalize ideas that have only passing or temporary allegiance. This criticism has been lodged against state constitutions in the United States. Too thin a framework, however, runs the risk that the document will not be taken seriously as a guide to behavior or a limit on the abuse of power. As they worked on the draft, the Framers of the new American constitution were well aware of these considerations.[15]

There are many ways to think about and categorize the results of the deliberations of the convention. Table 3-1 lists the seven articles of the Constitution. Rather than review the Constitution article by article, however, we will discuss the crafting of the new constitution as an exercise in problem-solving. In particular, the Framers had five major objectives:

- Overcoming fundamental disputes over representation in the new government.
- Encouraging public input while limiting both "excessive" democracy and concentrated power.

TABLE 3-1. The Constitution

ARTICLE I: THE LEGISLATIVE BRANCH
Bicameral legislature
Nature of election
Powers and duties
ARTICLE II: THE EXECUTIVE BRANCH
Nature of election
Qualifications
Powers and duties
ARTICLE III: THE JUDICIAL BRANCH
Nature of appointment and tenure
Creation of Supreme Court
Types of cases
ARTICLE IV: NATIONAL UNITY
"Full faith and credit" to acts of other states
All "privileges and immunities" to be same whether or not a state's citizen
Guarantee of republican government
Admitting new states
ARTICLE V: THE AMENDING PROCESS
Procedures to amend Constitution
ARTICLE VI: NATIONAL SUPREMACY
Constitution to be "supreme law" of the land
No religious test for public office
ARTICLE VII: RATIFICATION PROCESS
Procedure to ratify Constitution

- Protecting commerce and property.
- Creating legitimacy for the new system.
- Providing a coordinated approach to international relations and national defense.

The Great Compromise and Three-fifths Compromise resolved fundamental splits over representation.

Two issues facing the delegates absolutely had to be resolved if the convention were to succeed. Both involved the distribution of political power. The delegates' solutions did not guarantee success, but without them failure was assured.

More so than many of us can understand or appreciate today, the delegates were oriented toward their individual states. Political history, tradition, and loyalty, as they knew it, had much more to do with their colonies, now states, than with the American nation at large. In their view, the creation of the Union was less a union of disparate individuals and more a union of sovereign states.

The name of the new country—the United States—is significant in that regard. Indeed, it was not until 80 years later, when Abraham Lincoln would aim to rebuild the Union in the Civil War, that Americans would routinely refer to the "United States" in the singular rather than the plural—"the United States is" rather than "the United States are." We see this conception directly reflected in Article III of the Constitution: "Treason against the United States, shall consist only in levying War against them, or in adhering to their Enemies."

"The delegates' solutions did not guarantee success, but without them failure was assured."

The large state–small state split   Given this strong allegiance to the states, the relative influence of the various states in the new system rose immediately as a contentious issue. The first split was the division between large and small states. If the new system were to be based at least in part on a representative legislature, how would states be represented in that body? Should representation be based on a state's population or should each state have equal representation?

The battle lines were predictable. Large states gravitated around the **Virginia Plan** offered by Virginia governor Edmund Randolph.[16] This plan called for state representation in the national legislature to be based on state population: the larger a state's population, the more representatives it would send to the legislature. The so-called lower house would be elected by the people; in turn it would select the members of the upper house, based on lists of candidates provided by state legislatures.

Delegates from small states saw this plan as an unacceptable push toward large-state domination of the new political system. Their response was the **New Jersey Plan,** introduced by William Paterson (the former attorney general of New Jersey, who would go on to become a U.S. senator, governor of New Jersey, and justice on the U.S. Supreme Court). Like the Virginia Plan, the New Jersey Plan concerned more than just the issue of representation, but it was on this issue that the two competing visions of the new government were especially divided.[17] The New Jersey Plan called for equal state representation in a single-house legislature. Regardless of a state's population, it would send the same number of representatives to the legislature as any other state.

With the two plans on the table, each side staked out strong stances. If the small states wanted to destroy the Union, the large-state delegates opined, then so be it. If the large states wanted to throw their power around, declared the small states, any number of foreign countries would be more than happy to create a new government

Virginia Plan   one of the rival plans at the Constitutional Convention, it argued for a two-house legislature, with representation based on a state's population; the lower house would be elected directly by the people, and that house would then select the members of the upper house.

New Jersey Plan   one of the rival plans at the Constitutional Convention, it called for, among other things, equal representation of the states in a single-house legislature.

with the small states. The convention and the task of writing a new constitution faced a deep fracture, but returning to what nearly all the delegates concluded was a defunct and ineffective status quo was not a reassuring prospect for either side, so they were open to compromise.

Although sometimes in politics there is an obvious compromise or consensus position when developing rules, policies, or institutions, often this position is not reached until rounds of bargaining and negotiation have been conducted. There may even be a solution no one offered at the outset. With regard to the big state–small state split, the solution came in the form of the Connecticut Plan, also known as the **Great Compromise.** Under this plan, representation in the House of Representatives would be based on population, as the large states preferred, and legislators would be elected by the people. A second legislative body, the Senate, would have equal representation of all the states, as the small states preferred, and be elected by the state legislatures. The idea of a bicameral, or two-house, legislature itself was not new: Great Britain had a House of Commons and House of Lords, and the existence of two legislative houses was the norm in the colonies and in the states.

Great Compromise the agreement between small states and large states that representation in the Senate would be equal for each state, as small states preferred, and representation in the House would be based on population, as large states preferred.

The vote for the Great Compromise was close: five states voted in favor, four were opposed, two others did not vote, and two more were not in attendance. Although the plan was not entirely satisfactory to either side, it did prevent either group of states from dominating the new system of government. Bicameral arrangements are a common feature of political systems in which power is shared by governments at the national and subnational levels. As in the Great Compromise model, typically the upper house represents geographical units and the lower house represents "the people" (see Figure 3-1).

The slave state–free state split   Similar calculations drove the other critical division between political leaders. This split was between states where slavery was forbidden and states where slavery was allowed, which geographically meant a split between northern and southern states, respectively. If representation in the House of Representatives were to be determined by a state's population, how would population

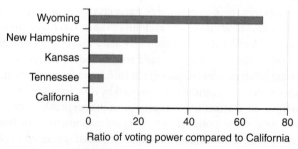

Ratio of voting power compared to California

FIGURE 3-1. **Ratio of Residents' Voting Power in U.S. Senate.** As a result of the Great Compromise, each state has equal voting power in the Senate. However, because populations differ among states, people who live in states with smaller populations, like Wyoming, effectively have greater voting power per person than people who live in states with large populations, like California. This chart shows the ratio of state residents' voting power in the Senate, compared to California residents. Equal state representation in the Senate was seen by the Framers as a way to protect the interests of the various states.

be determined? In particular, do slaves count as part of the population? Southern states argued that slaves should count. Delegates from northern states saw this as hypocrisy. Slave states certainly did not consider slaves to be citizens and it was doubtful whether they even considered them persons, northerners charged.

Once again, both sides were concerned with the balance of power in the new legislature. There were more free states than slave states, so the South was disadvantaged in the Senate. And the population of the North exceeded that of the South, so the South faced the prospect of being outvoted in the House as well. Southern delegates made it clear that this was a make-or-break issue: either include slaves in the population count or the convention ends.

A resolution was reached through the **Three-fifths Compromise.** Under this plan, each slave would count as three-fifths of a person in the population count for each state. Sixty percent was chosen not as a philosophical statement, but because this number would balance representation between the North and South in the House. Neither side could dominate the other.[18]

It is a popular misconception, hundreds of years after the convention, to say that the delegates ignored the issue of slavery and were uniformly uninterested in the plight of slaves. The evidence usually offered for this assertion is the lack of direct discussion of slavery in the Constitution. If the issue does not appear prominently in the Constitution, the logic goes, the cause must be lack of interest or concern about the issue.

But the critics' contention makes the analytical mistake of assuming that what we can see is a reliable indicator of what matters most to politicians. In politics, however, sometimes what is not visible is equally as important as that which is visible. Rather than ignore slavery, the delegates were consumed by the issue. Some were ardent defenders of slavery. Others opposed the practice on economic or moral grounds. Individual states had wrestled with the issue in years prior to the convention. Everyone recognized the explosive nature of the issue. It was ironically the importance of the issue, not the lack of interest in it, that led to its being given less visibility in the Constitution than critics today might wish.

Believing that politicians usually act strategically in important situations, political scientists would reject the analytical leap made by critics and reframe the question: if it was not due to lack of interest or concern, what would cause the Framers to avoid placing heavy emphasis on slavery in the Constitution? The answer is the immediate strategic imperative of crafting a constitution—this is the causal force contributing most heavily to slavery's lack of prominence in the Constitution. The Framers had to find a way to address the issue of slavery in a way that did not undermine their interest in producing a new document. It was clear to the delegates that the issue of slavery could destroy the convention. On the surface, it might appear that the delegates avoided the issue, but in reality they were strategically accommodating competing points of view on slavery in order to produce a constitution. Would a constitution have been possible if opponents of slavery were determined to use the document to eliminate it? Most of the Framers thought not, and ultimately they were more determined to write a constitution. In the twenty-first century, our moral revulsion against slavery makes it deeply disturbing to even think about this kind of tradeoff, but that was the real-world situation as the Framers perceived it.[19]

Three-fifths Compromise an agreement between slave states and free states that a state's slave population would be counted at 60 percent for purposes of determining a state's representation in the House of Representatives.

ThinkingCausally

Does the lack of emphasis on slavery in the Constitution demonstrate the Framers' lack of interest in the plight of slaves?

▼ **PEOPLE AS PROPERTY**

Delegates from slaveholding states wanted to count slaves toward their state population, to boost their representation in the House of Representatives. Delegates from other states saw this as inconsistent with the usual treatment in slave states of slaves as property, not people. Why, they asked, should these states now benefit from treating slaves as people for the purpose of gaining more representation in the House? The dispute was resolved by the Three-fifths Compromise.

Although the terms *slave* and *slavery* do not appear in the Constitution, three provisions directly concerned slavery. The first is the Three-fifths Compromise, which boosted southern representation in the House of Representatives. Second, the Constitution forbade Congress from prohibiting the importation of slaves prior to 1808. And third, any slave escaping to a free state would have to be returned to his or her master. Those who opposed slavery and saw it as a violation of the tenets of the Declaration of Independence were frustrated by these provisions, but they also realized that no new government would be formed if they pressed the issue. Their hope was that the new government would, over time, devise a way to deal with this problem. Bargains in the first half of the nineteenth century gradually confined slavery to the southern states, but they were unable to resolve the issue, which exploded in the calamity of the Civil War.

The Framers wanted public officials to hear the voice of the people but also wanted to prevent "excessive" democracy.

The Framers believed that the people should have a voice in government. How should that be accomplished? One option would be to allow direct rule by the people—the classic definition of democracy. The Framers had experience with that kind of government, because many municipalities in America did much of their important business in town meetings where citizens directly voted on matters of public policy. Despite that experience, or perhaps because of it, they did not believe that the people's voice should dictate the behavior of public officials. The people's input should influence the decisions of government, they concluded, but there must be a buffer between the people's demands and the government's actions. They feared that a government that was too close to the people would get swept up in the people's passions and impulsive decisions. Such a government would weaken the rights of the minority, particularly the minority that owned significant amounts of property.[20]

To the Framers, those were the risks of democracy. The political system needed to be structured in a way that took account of the people's views but also allowed for a "cooling off" of those views. At the same time, the people's voice would be

▶ **PROTECTING CITIZENS FROM EACH OTHER**
In one highly publicized Supreme Court decision in the 1990s, the Court concluded that a Florida community's law against animal sacrifice was explicitly targeted toward restricting the ceremonial religious practice of the Santeria religion. Other forms of animal slaughter for commercial use, private hunting, and other nonreligious uses were exempted in the law. Groups upset with this particular religion used the power of government to restrict the freedom of Santeria's adherents to practice their religion. The Court struck down the law as oppressive to the rights of the followers of this religion.

impotent if government were weak. Power and authority needed to be both encouraged and restrained.

For these reasons, the Framers did not create a democracy in the technical sense, in which the people themselves directly rule. Rather, they created a **republic,** in which the people select representatives who are entrusted to make the laws.[21] Preventing excessive democracy meant not only protecting government from the people's passions, but also protecting citizens from each other—preventing groups from using government to oppress other groups. The Framers accomplished these goals in several ways.

Selection of public officials   The Constitution provided for staggered terms of office for elected officials (Articles I, II). House members would serve two-year terms; senators would serve six-year terms, with one-third of the senators up for election in any given election year; and the president would serve a four-year term. This arrangement means that Americans can never dismiss all government officials at once because all officials are never up for election in the same year. Americans can "clean house" in government, but it is always only a partial cleaning: in any given election year, two-thirds of the senators will not be up for election, while the president will be up for election only every other election year. Regardless of the passions that may be stirring the public, it would take six years before they could completely replace all the elected officials in the national government. And the public has no direct way to choose federal judges. Once nominated by the president and confirmed by the Senate, federal judges—unlike judges in many states—have lifetime tenure and do not face elections. This provision again provides a buffer between the people's voice and the government's actions.

Should the people try to change the system to make it more immediately responsive to the people's demands, they would have to work through the difficult process of amending the Constitution (Article V). The Framers did not want the people to be able to easily rewrite the rules. Such a process was not just for the Framers' benefit, however—it reduced the likelihood that one group would amend the Constitution in a manner to reject or restrict the rights of another group.

In the Constitution as ratified, the people directly elected only the members of the House of Representatives. Senators were selected by state legislatures. The people voted for state legislators, who then selected the state's U.S. senators, a process known as **indirect election.** Not until the passage of the Seventeenth Amendment in 1913 would the people directly elect their U.S. senators. Presidents were also elected indirectly. The public in a state voted for electors (in some states, the state legislature selected the electors), and these electors then met in their states in the Electoral College to cast ballots for president and vice president. The candidate who received a majority of the electoral vote would be the president. Even today, although ballots list the presidential candidates, voters are technically voting for a group of electors who have pledged to cast their electoral vote for the particular candidate. The logic was that the people could select the electors, but the electors, presumably individuals who were wise, knowledgeable, and distinguished, would evaluate the presidential candidates more carefully.

Separation of powers   The Framers most famously attempted to protect against the effects of excessive democracy with separation of powers and checks and balances. The idea of balancing power was not new. In the colonists' eyes prior to 1763, this had been the defining achievement of British politics and a source of great pride. The colonies, too, relied on the idea of balancing power against power, with legislators checking the power of the governor, who served on the behalf of Britain.

republic   a system in which people elect representatives to make policy and write laws; also known as a representative democracy

indirect election   an election in which voters select other individuals who directly vote for candidates for a particular office; U.S. Senate and presidential elections were of this type in the Constitution, but Senate elections are now direct elections.

separation of powers the principle that the executive, legislative, and judicial functions of government should be primarily performed by different institutions in government.

Recall that in the Articles of Confederation the legislature was the national government, albeit a weak one. By contrast, in the Constitution the Framers provided for three independent centers of authority in a legislature, executive, and judiciary (in Articles I, II, and III, respectively). **Separation of powers** means that the major branches of government would have different primary functions and responsibilities—the legislature would make law; the executive would implement law; and the judiciary would interpret law (see Figure 3-2). The separation would be reinforced by alternative methods of selecting the leadership of each branch— legislators were directly and indirectly elected (House and Senate, respectively), the president was indirectly elected, and judges were appointed. In practice, the division in functions has not been quite this neat and tidy, so some observers suggest that a better description of separation of powers is "separated institutions

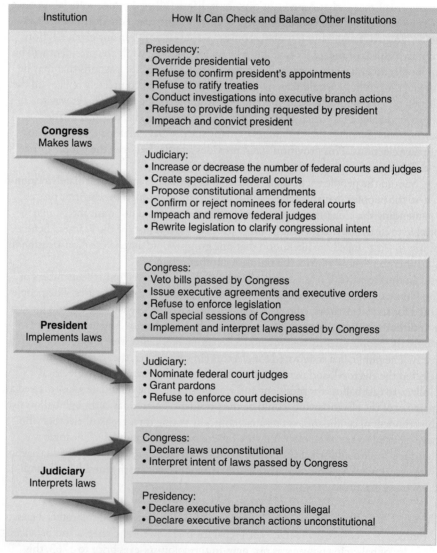

Institution	How It Can Check and Balance Other Institutions
Congress Makes laws	Presidency: • Override presidential veto • Refuse to confirm president's appointments • Refuse to ratify treaties • Conduct investigations into executive branch actions • Refuse to provide funding requested by president • Impeach and convict president
	Judiciary: • Increase or decrease the number of federal courts and judges • Create specialized federal courts • Propose constitutional amendments • Confirm or reject nominees for federal courts • Impeach and remove federal judges • Rewrite legislation to clarify congressional intent
President Implements laws	Congress: • Veto bills passed by Congress • Issue executive agreements and executive orders • Refuse to enforce legislation • Call special sessions of Congress • Implement and interpret laws passed by Congress
	Judiciary: • Nominate federal court judges • Grant pardons • Refuse to enforce court decisions
Judiciary Interprets laws	Congress: • Declare laws unconstitutional • Interpret intent of laws passed by Congress
	Presidency: • Declare executive branch actions illegal • Declare executive branch actions unconstitutional

FIGURE 3-2. **Separation of Powers and Checks and Balances.** With separation of powers and checks and balances, each branch of government has distinct but overlapping responsibilities.

sharing powers." Rather than rigid demarcation between branches, this formulation suggests that each institution trespasses somewhat on the jurisdiction of the others.

Checks and balances   The system of **checks and balances** provides the main set of mechanisms through which the branches monitor each other. Checks and balances means that each branch of government has a way to affect and, in some instances, to stop, the actions of the others. Many of the checks and balances techniques are likely familiar; they are listed in Figure 3-2. They reinforce the idea of separated institutions sharing power. Lawmaking, for example, is not the province of Congress alone. The president has to approve any bills before they can become law.[22] And, because of legislative bicameralism—Congress is divided into two houses, each of which must approve the same version of a bill before it can be sent to the president for approval—Congress has internal checks and balances. In some areas, notably approval of treaties and confirmation of judges, the Framers wanted the people involved, but only through their indirectly elected representatives in the Senate. Lastly, although the judiciary's power was only thinly described in the Constitution, this branch soon asserted the power of **judicial review,** meaning it would decide whether the laws and other actions of government officials were or were not constitutional. This meant the judiciary could strike down a federal or state law altogether, and overturn nonlegislative actions such as a policy or procedure implemented by an executive-branch agency. Thus, the judiciary has the power to determine what the text of the Constitution means. As for checks on this branch, Congress and the president can counteract the judiciary's power through constitutional amendments, new appointments to the courts, and restructuring of the courts.[23]

There were competing views early in the convention on how to check and balance power. In the Virginia Plan, the president and judiciary, who had been selected by the legislature, would form a Council of Revision that could veto legislative acts. However, the legislature could override those vetoes, and would also have the authority to veto state laws. The New Jersey Plan called for a single-chamber Congress in which

checks and balances the principle that each branch of the federal government has the means to thwart or influence actions by other branches of government.

judicial review the power of the judiciary to interpret and overturn actions taken by the legislative and executive branches of government.

▶ FIRST AMONG EQUALS

General Washington's reputation towered above all others of his generation. As commander in chief of the Revolutionary forces, his remarkable organizational, military, and political skills held the war effort together and led the American troops to victory. He came out of retirement to preside over the Constitutional Convention. There was no doubt among the delegates that he would be selected as the country's first president.

▲ CONFIRMING A JUSTICE

Supreme Court justices are unelected and have lifetime terms, raising issues of democratic accountability. For this reason, both elected branches of government are involved in selecting Supreme Court justices. President Obama's nominee, Elena Kagan, appears here before the Senate Judiciary Committee for her confirmation hearing in 2010. What difference, if any, would it make if federal judges served fixed terms rather than lifetime tenure?

each state had one vote. Congress would appoint a multiperson Executive, which would in turn appoint the judiciary. The New Jersey Plan declared that the Constitution and federal laws would supersede state constitutions and laws, but given that state governors were given the power to remove the Executive, this "supremacy" was effectively conditional on the states' acceptance.

Both these plans gave the legislature the strongest position in American government, as Congress selected the members of the other branches. The Framers ultimately did choose to prioritize Congress—it is Article I in the Constitution and the institution with the most detailed list of responsibilities and duties—but they dispersed power and increased the independence of the other branches more than either the Virginia or New Jersey plans.[24] The Framers wanted to make sure that any pressure from the people was heard by government, but that it was diffused across the three branches. If one branch reached too far in pushing a new policy demanded by the people, the other branches could slow it down or stop it altogether. Moreover, the Framers wanted a strong national government, but they also wanted to be sure that it would not become so powerful as to threaten liberty and property. The proposed government was designed to thwart the power-grabbing tendencies of human nature, according to James Madison. "If men were angels, no government would be necessary," he wrote. "If angels were to govern men, neither external nor internal controls on government would be necessary."[25]

The checks and balances system was one aspect of the careful balancing act between government power and personal freedom. Each seemed necessary, yet each could dominate the other. The task of the Framers was to keep the two in balance. As they saw it, disaggregating power this way both protected against abuse of the people by government and made it more difficult for any one part of the public to capture all of the power centers in government. Madison referred to this system, in combination with federalism (described in the following section), as a "double security" against tyrannical government.[26]

Federalism   Despite differences concerning the relative power and authority of the national and state governments, delegates agreed that federalism would be an underlying principle of the new system. **Federalism** is a governing arrangement that provides multiple levels of government with independent ruling authority over certain policy areas, and guarantees the survival of these different levels of government. As noted, resolving the distribution of power between the states and the national government was a key practical concern. At the level of principle, however, federalism was a bulwark against the risk of concentrated power and excessive democracy. The states check the power of the national government, but the national government checks the power of the states. We will have much more to say about federalism in Chapter 4.

The parliamentary system as an alternative distribution of power   The choices made by the Constitutional Convention delegates differ significantly from the choices made in later years in other parts of the world. In Europe, especially, the **parliamentary system** was the structure of choice for those constructing governments. In a parliamentary system, the prime minister, who serves as the chief executive, is selected from the parliament (the legislature) by other members. Although voters are usually well aware of the candidates for prime minister, they do not vote on the position nationally or directly. The prime minister then selects department heads from among his fellow partisans in the legislature. Typically in a parliamentary system, the legislature ultimately interprets what the constitution means (even if the constitution is unwritten, as in Great Britain). In this system, the legislature is supreme, and the notions of checks and balances and separation of powers are not particularly relevant.

Opponents of the parliamentary system charge that it puts too much power in the hands of the majority party. Unlike in the American system, control of the executive branch and the legislature cannot be split between two parties, even if that would be the voters' preference. In the view of these critics, parliamentary systems leave voters who do not support the majority party powerless. Advocates of the parliamentary system respond that it is a government that is not at cross-purposes with itself. Rather than checking and balancing power, parceling power out to different parts of government, and having branches of government intentionally frustrate each other and the majority's will, the ideal behind the parliamentary system is to gather power in the leading party in the legislature to enable swift action. The Framers of the American Constitution were wary of giving any entity, including the majority of the population, so much power.

Numerous constitutional provisions were designed to protect commerce and property.

Events in the states in the 1780s, such as Shays's Rebellion and the printing of currency of questionable worth, panicked New England merchants, southern planters, and the entire spectrum of businesspeople in between. Therefore, one chief concern of the Framers was to protect commerce and property from the designs of the national government, the state governments, and states pitted against states.

Delegates included many provisions in the Constitution to do this. First, they established that the national government would have primary regulatory control over commerce and finance. The national government would regulate commerce between the states and with other countries and be responsible for producing coinage and currency, establishing bankruptcy laws, and creating protections for copyrights and patents (Article I in the Constitution). This arrangement still allowed differences between the states—for example, states could have different insurance or banking regulations—but it prevented states from creating alliances with each other or with

federalism   a form of government that distributes power across a national government and subnational governments and ensures the existence of the subnational governments.

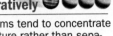

ThinkingComparatively

Parliamentary systems tend to concentrate power in the legislature rather than separating it across branches of government.

parliamentary system   a political system in which the head of the executive branch is selected by members of the legislature rather than by popular vote.

▲ FAST FORWARD

Toyota began a recall of nearly 4 million cars in late 2009 to address problems with stuck accelerator pedals. Although technically the recall was voluntary, federal officials at the National Highway Traffic Safety Administration (NHTSA) and legislators in Congress had begun pressuring Toyota to fix the problem. NHTSA had been investigating reports of accidents caused by the defect, and Congress was gearing up for hearings on Toyota's safety procedures. The federal government's constitutional power to regulate interstate commerce provided the legal authority for the agency and Congress to act.

supremacy clause a clause in the Constitution that declares that national laws and treaties have supremacy over state laws and treaties.

full faith and credit clause a clause in the Constitution stating that states are to honor the official acts of other states.

equal privileges and immunities clause a clause in the Constitution stating that states are to treat equally their citizens and the citizens of other states.

another country that harmed the commercial or property interests of citizens in other states. It also prevented states from inflating currency or devising other schemes to make it easy for their citizens to escape from debt obligations.

Second, the Constitution's **supremacy clause** declared that national laws and treaties would have supremacy over state laws and treaties (Article VI). State laws could differ from the national law, but they had to be consistent with it. For example, states can enact anti-pollution laws more stringent than those the federal government requires, but not more relaxed. Federal law can, however, preempt the states from deviating from federal standards. For example, the Federal Cigarette Labeling and Advertising Act imposes national rules on cigarette advertising and prohibits state governments from imposing additional advertising regulations.[27]

States were also to be nondiscriminatory toward each other (Article IV). Through the **full faith and credit clause,** states are to honor the official acts of other states, such as public records and the results of judicial proceedings. Under the **equal privileges and immunities clause,** states are to treat their citizens and citizens of other states similarly. Congress and the president can override these provisions if they choose to do so. Such an override happened in 1996 with the passage of the Defense of Marriage Act, which stipulated that states need not honor same-sex marriages performed in other states. Normally, the free faith and credit clause would dictate that a marriage that is legal in one state will be recognized as legal in the others, but states were given an exemption in this instance.

The Constitution included additional protections for commerce and property. Article VI stipulated that any contracts entered into before the Constitution must still be honored after the Constitution was ratified: the adoption of a new political system did not negate ongoing economic commitments. This provision was motivated chiefly by concern that debts incurred during the Revolutionary War be paid, but it applied to debts incurred after the war also. The national government also guaranteed each state a republican—that is, representative—form of government and pledged to protect the states against domestic violence, a reaction to Shays's Rebellion.

Lastly, the Framers provided for a president who would be a counterweight to Congress. As the Framers saw it, representatives would often allow the narrow interests of their districts to guide their decisions, whereas senators would have the somewhat broader but still biased self-interests of their states in mind. Only the president would represent the country as a whole and have an ongoing commitment to the national interest rather than to any special interest of a state or district.

Certain measures and principles were emphasized to enhance the proposed system's legitimacy.

Legitimacy is about trust. When you believe that an arrangement is legitimate, you believe it is fair and reasonable. You may not trust individual officials, but you trust the system. Americans had come to see the British government, or at least its control over the colonies, as illegitimate. The idea that the colonies were "virtually represented" though not actually directly represented in Parliament struck many Americans as folly. Americans then placed their trust in the new governmental system of the Articles of Confederation, but many saw that, too, as a failure. To the Framers, establishing legitimacy for the new government was critical, and they addressed the challenge in three ways.

First, they emphasized the representativeness of the new government. In the House, Senate, and presidency, they noted, distinct parts of society were represented—parts of states, states, and the country, respectively. Direct popular election of the House of Representatives was another legitimacy-building feature. The House would be the "people's house." Its members would have shorter terms than any other part of government, giving the people frequent input into its composition. And, because of the system of checks and balances, relatively little could be done that did not have to pass through the people's house.

Second, the Framers built the case for legitimacy around the notion that the new government would not be dominating. It would have more power than it did under the Articles, but constrained power. The checks-and-balances system would prevent government from acting recklessly. With its concept of federalism, the Constitution delegated specific powers to the federal government and left others to the states. Public officials would take the Constitution seriously—Article VI required public officials to swear to uphold the Constitution, not the wishes of a monarch, church, or select group. The Constitution, the Framers noted, was a social contract between rulers and ruled (see Chapter 1 for more on the social contract). If the rulers violated this contract, the people had a right to remove them, and if the violations were extensive, the people had a right to scrap the contract and construct a new system of government. Further, the Framers promised that a bill of rights guaranteeing personal liberties would be added to the Constitution as the first order of business after ratification.

Third, they created an enduring but flexible framework for government. They wanted the people to believe that the Constitution had roots—that its meaning and content would have some stability—but they also wanted the people to believe that the system could be changed if necessary. By providing for amendments, the Framers created a document that would be flexible. By making the amending process difficult, they created a document that would be enduring. We discuss the amendment process in detail later.

Balancing stability and flexibility was also achieved by writing a Constitution that provided a basic framework for government and politics. The Constitution lays down the essential rules of how government will work and how officials will be selected. It also indicates the responsibilities of government officials. It presents a general outline for how public policy will be made, but it contains very little actual policy.

For example, it gives Congress the power to regulate interstate commerce, declare war, and establish currency, but it does not set in stone any particular policy about how interstate commerce should take place or when declarations of war should and should not occur. Nothing in the Constitution says how much should be spent on national defense, how many roads should be built, and so on. The Framers left that kind of detail to the branches of government to work out in the form of laws. They realized that preferences about particular issues would change over time, so enshrining them in the Constitution would be problematic in two respects. If the Constitution were difficult to change, citizens would be stuck with policies they no longer agreed with. If the Constitution were made easy to change, it would lose the sense that it had permanency and was above competitive politics.

The Civil War provides the most glaring exception to the rule that Americans believe their political differences can be worked out through constitutional provisions. The Constitution could not contain the depth of division between North and South. And for much of American history, the Constitution was seen as compatible with discrimination of the rankest sort against racial, ethnic, and religious minorities and women. Americans today, however, are more likely to fault the people and the politicians in power during those times rather than the Constitution itself, because the Constitution also provided the means to change these patterns.[28]

The new system provided the means for a coordinated approach to international relations and national defense.

The foreign threats facing Americans in the 1780s were significant. Britain controlled the territory around the Great Lakes. Aside from Britain's own disagreements with the United States, the tension between Britain and France meant that being caught in their crossfire was a distinct possibility. Spain controlled Florida and areas to the west. Skirmishes with Native American tribes were frequent. The Constitution provided the promise of executive and legislative leadership and coordination to respond to these challenges. The president would be the operational head of military actions and the representative of the United States to other countries. He would appoint ambassadors and negotiate treaties, but both of these would require the Senate's approval. Congress's control over military budgets and taxes and the declaration of war was intended to make foreign policy a cooperative venture. States would have to follow the national lead on military matters, including those with Native American tribes. They could not enter into treaties or alliances with other countries or tribes, arrange discriminatory tariffs, or enter into military conflict unless invaded or facing a similar immediate emergency.[29]

The Battle for Ratification

3-3 Compare and contrast the arguments of Anti-Federalists and Federalists.

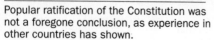
ThinkingComparatively
Popular ratification of the Constitution was not a foregone conclusion, as experience in other countries has shown.

Sending the Constitution to the states for ratification was a risky gambit. The Framers could not look to other countries to see how a national ratification effort would fare, or what the risks and rewards were of giving the people this much influence. The experience of other countries in later years shows just how risky it was. In France, popular ratification failed in 1789, 1791, 1793, and 1830. Canadian leaders chose not to risk a popular ratification process for its constitution. Britain's unwritten constitution was similarly not subject to a ratification process. Among English-speaking countries, only Australia followed the U.S. ratification model, more than a century later.[30] In the American context, however, supporters of the Constitution believed that ratification in the states was a political necessity. It was also, they realized, an opportunity for opponents to derail the document.

Battle lines over ratification of the Constitution were drawn between the **Federalists,** who supported ratification, and the **Anti-Federalists,** who opposed it.[31] The central debate concerned not democracy, which might be the center-stage issue today, but liberty: what kind of governmental arrangement would best preserve liberty? See *How Do We Know? What Motivated the Framers of the Constitution?* for an analysis of how political scientists have examined the Framers' motivations.

Anti-Federalists argued that the Constitution threatened liberty.

Anti-Federalists argued that the proposed Constitution threatened the people's liberty. Distant from the people, this kind of government might begin to tax heavily, override state court decisions, have a permanent army at its disposal, or absorb functions performed by the states—fears that later history showed were not far-fetched. Legendary patriots such as Patrick Henry, a stalwart supporter of the Revolution, saw the proposed Constitution as a counterrevolution, pushing back toward more central authority, reducing democratic influence on government, and protecting the interests of political and economic leaders.

To the Anti-Federalists, a different kind of government was needed. Their ideal was, like in the New Jersey Plan, a government more along the lines of the one established by the Articles of Confederation. The loose union of states that characterized the Articles was the ideal arrangement to protect liberty—the central government's powers were so limited, it lacked the means to restrict liberty, even if public officials were so inclined.[32]

Given the public's apparent preference for a stronger national government, the Anti-Federalists offered some principles to guide its development. They argued that such a government should have many restrictions on its power. For example, they suggested reducing the range of cases the Supreme Court could hear; creating a council to review all presidential decisions; leaving military affairs to state militias; enlarging the House

Federalists individuals who supported the proposed Constitution and favored its ratification.

Anti-Federalists individuals opposed to the proposed Constitution, fearing it concentrated too much power in the national government.

▼ **PATRICK HENRY AND JAMES MADISON**
Patrick Henry (left) was one of the leading voices in opposition to the Constitution. To him, the document granted too much power to the national government. James Madison, a delegate at the Constitutional Convention, was one of the Constitution's most ardent proponents.

of Representatives, which would mean creating smaller districts so that representatives would feel more closely bound to their constituents; and adding a "bill of rights" to protect individual freedoms.

Only on this last item were the Anti-Federalists successful. Supporters of the Constitution initially argued that a bill of rights was unnecessary—unless the Constitution gave Congress the right, for example, to establish an official religion, then government should not be presumed to have that right. And a listing of rights or liberties could become effectively a limitation on rights and liberties if misinterpreted as a comprehensive list. In the climate of the ratification debate, however, a strong symbolic statement was needed, so the proponents of ratification agreed to a bill of rights. They did not want to send the document to states and have states begin revising it. They knew their best chance of success would be if states were forced to make an up-or-down vote—this document or nothing. As ultimately ratified by the states, the **Bill of Rights** refers to the first 10 amendments to the Constitution, which focus on preserving individual freedoms.

Bill of Rights the first 10 amendments to the U.S. Constitution, intended to protect individual liberties from federal government intrusion.

Madison responded in the *Federalist Papers* that a large republic is the best defense for liberty.

The argument between Federalists and Anti-Federalists was fought out in speeches, handbills, and newspaper columns. The most famous of all these was a set of newspaper opinion columns penned under a pseudonym by James Madison, Alexander Hamilton, and John Jay. Collectively, these columns would come to be called the *Federalist Papers*. These columns discussed the many nuances of the proposed government. They presented the theoretical basis of American government, discussing such concepts as federalism, the separation of powers, and checks and balances. Although it is unlikely that the columns were widely read, those who did read them were likely to be opinion leaders—individuals who, because of their status, could shape the opinions of others.

The Anti-Federalist argument about the desirability of democracies and small republics was rejected in the most famous of the *Federalist Papers*, number 10. (An annotated *Federalist 10* appears in the Appendix.) In *Federalist 10*, James Madison argued that liberty is actually most at risk in direct democracies and small republics. It is safest in precisely the kind of large republic being proposed in the Constitution.

Like politicians today, Madison was making causal claims. The outcome to be explained is the preservation of liberty. Madison begins by stating that the most severe threat to liberty is the presence of factions. To Madison, factions are defined by having some self-interest or common passion that threatens the rights of other citizens, and they can be either a majority or minority of the population. Factions are natural, Madison argues, as people naturally cluster with like-minded individuals. Trying to prevent the emergence of factions would require authoritarian and conformist measures that would be a "cure worse than the disease." The real question, therefore, is how to control factions and their effects, especially, for Madison, their effects on property rights.

ThinkingCausally
What best preserves liberty?

Could democracy cure the effects of factions? Madison says no. In a democracy, a majority faction has no check on its behavior—it would be quite easy for a majority of the population to deny rights or otherwise oppress a minority.

The proposed republic, on the other hand, could control excessive factional influence. This is Madison's key causal link between the proposed Constitution and the protection of liberty. First, in Madison's view, having a relatively small number of representatives increases the likelihood that voters are selecting individuals of honor, merit, and virtue for public office. Second, larger, more diverse districts will send mixed policy messages to representatives, encouraging them to sift out the bad ideas and keep the good. Representatives with large districts are less likely to be "captured" by any one interest, because they will try to represent a broader cross-section of their constituency. Third, in a geographically large political system, more opposing interests will be vying for attention; as interest battles interest, a majority faction is less likely to form. Madison thought it unlikely that the same dangerous idea would arise in far-flung parts of the country, and if it did, it would be difficult logistically to organize a majority faction over a large area, which again protects liberty.

The bottom line of Madison's argument was a remarkable rejection of the conventional causal wisdom of his day. Rather than holding onto communitarian hopes about civic virtue—selfless political participants concerned only for the common welfare—Madison suggested the country allow self-interest to serve public ends. Each individual's self-interest, he reasoned, gives that person an incentive to ensure that other individuals do not abuse power, thus producing precisely the best outcome for society. Madison took this argument one step further in *Federalist 51* (an annotated version appears in the Appendix), where he noted that governmental power would be distributed across the national and state governments and across the three major branches of government, whose officials would challenge each other and thus prevent the monopolization of power. Their self-interest would protect liberty.[33]

Are today's high-tech communications a threat to the Madisonian model? Individuals anywhere in the United States can communicate with others rapidly and frequently. Pressure can be placed on members of Congress very quickly. Political figures—as Barack Obama showed in 2008—can build followings and organizations that are truly national in scope and that can be reached, mobilized, and spurred to action with great speed. On the other hand, as Madison noted, power remains dispersed across branches and levels of government, which may not be equally responsive to public desires. And, as Madison also noted, the more interests that are brought into politics, the more likely it is that other interests will seek to participate, reducing the likelihood of any interest having a monopoly on what legislators hear. The relationship between the people and government is much tighter and potentially more immediate today than Madison would likely recommend, but on the whole, his analysis remains relevant for understanding American politics.

▲ **THE REACH OF MEDIA**

National television figures like Glenn Beck express strong opinions and reach viewers coast to coast instantly. Does contemporary communication technology negate James Madison's arguments about the advantages of a large republic?

Belief that change was necessary assisted the Federalists' ratification campaign.

Citizens in the states voted for delegates to attend state ratifying conventions. Nine states needed to approve the Constitution for it to be in effect. The first state to ratify was Delaware, in December 1787. Seven months later, when New Hampshire became the ninth state to approve, the Constitution was ratified. In eight states, the Constitution received the support of at least 65 percent of the delegates. In the

continued on page 96 ▶

HOW DO WE KNOW?

What Motivated the Framers of the Constitution?

The Question

The men sent to the Constitutional Convention in Philadelphia in 1787 had risen to prominence in their respective states. Overall, however, the U.S. Constitution reduced the autonomy of the states. For political scientists, this outcome raises a research puzzle: why would ambitious, intelligent political leaders agree to a system that might reduce the power of the states in which they had been politically influential? What motivated the Framers of the Constitution? How do we know?

Why It Matters

Why should any of us care what motivated the Framers of the Constitution so long ago? The reason is simple: if Americans wish to know whether contemporary American politics and government live up to founding values, they must know why the system was designed the way it is.

▼ THE CONSTITUTIONAL CONVENTION, 1787

Delegates gathered in Philadelphia to revise the Articles of Confederation, but quickly concluded that a new constitution was necessary. The crafting of the Constitution involved a sequence of decisions, and scholars have examined the evidence to disentangle causality from correlation in explaining the outcome of the convention.

Investigating the Answer

One answer, offered by economist Charles Beard early in the twentieth century, is that the Constitution reflected the economic self-interest of those drafting and voting for it.[34] Beard complained that previous accounts of the Constitution had been based on ideals and wishful thinking. He called for social scientists to conduct hardheaded, systematic analyses of the world as it was. Politics, including the writing of the Constitution, was about the political will, conflict, and interests of people or groups of people in power.

Beard wanted to explain the votes of delegates at the Constitutional Convention. Assuming that political action is guided by self-interest, Beard hypothesized that delegates' financial self-interest determined how they voted on the Constitution. By analyzing the financial holdings and economic interests of the delegates, he concluded that the Framers protected their commercial interests, including currency, public securities, manufacturing, and trade and shipping. Opponents in the convention, he argued, were also influenced by their self-interest and were mostly farmers who had land holdings, those without property, and those in debt. Knowing the economic interests of those who supported or opposed the document, he argued, reveals the motivations of the document's writers. He did not suggest the Framers should be indicted on this account, however. If it had not been one group's interests that were primarily served by the crafting of the document, it would have been another's.[35]

Beard's critics offer a different answer to the question about the Framers' motivations, and a different approach to political investigation. They took more interest in the convention delegates' ideas and rhetoric. They saw the Framers' actions as grounded more in their practical political assessment of what was necessary to keep the country united and afloat, or in their sincere interest in the political ideals they were espousing.[36] To the critics, Beard mistakenly assumed that correlation equals causation: the fact that delegates' financial self-interest and their votes in the convention were correlated did not prove that the interests caused the votes.

Having also analyzed the delegates' financial interests, the critics pointed out that Beard did a poor job of identifying them. Reanalysis of Beard's data showed that the delegates in favor of the Constitution also had substantial land ownership, which was a prime characteristic Beard identified among the opponents. In fact, those favoring the Constitution had more land ownership than ownership of commercial interests.[37] If landholders had a self-interest in opposing the Constitution, then even the supporters of the Constitution should have opposed it because they had a larger financial stake in land than in commerce.

Beard may have been too quick to leap from correlation to causation. But by assuming that the ideals of those who supported the Constitution were unified and that therefore their motives were the same, Beard's critics may also have erred. For example, James Madison and Alexander Hamilton wrote the bulk of the *Federalist Papers*, but within a few years it was clear that their political ideologies were radically different from one another.[38] They may have both supported the Constitution, but their motivations were likely not identical.

Rather than looking at a political outcome and then assuming that the result reflects some group's motives, political scientists can look to the historical record—memoirs, journals, interviews, and other sources—to determine what drove individuals to take particular actions. Individuals may not be completely aware of or candid about their motivations, but this approach can reveal important insights. In a study of the crafting of the Constitution, for example, one political scientist concluded that the final document was a defeat for some of its most ardent proponents, such as Madison.[39] The most successful bloc in the convention sought to preserve the states' autonomy within an environment of international and domestic uncertainty that was leading many to call for a strong national government. Throughout the convention, Madison unsuccessfully pushed for a more powerful national government than created in the final document. Careful analysis of the day-by-day proceedings shows Madison to be frequently on the defensive. Rather than Madison's rhetoric in the *Federalist Papers* being a completely clear signal of his true preferences, he shaped his argument around the Constitution that was approved by the convention.

Such analysis highlights the importance of sequence and timing in explaining political outcomes. Early decisions, even small decisions, can have tremendous impact because they begin a process that influences future decisions. Once the delegates decided on an elected presidency, for example, that decision affected their votes on other aspects of the Constitution, and rethinking that decision would have been very difficult, because everything else afterward depended on it. Some decisions become "locked in" and shape future decisions. The document was created by a series of decisions. This sequence produced a document much more deferential toward the states than Madison and many others wanted. Scholars have also shown that the voting rules at the convention—each state's delegation would cast a single vote—gave disproportionate influence to certain delegates. A different set of rules where, for example, each delegate voted individually, would have likely produced a different Constitution.[40] And yet, after the Constitutional Convention sent the document to the states for ratification, Madison strongly supported the document, and scholars ever since, influenced by that strong support, have seen the Constitution as a victory for him.

Thinking Critically

■ In what ways might you imagine the American political system would be different if the delegates had decided early in their deliberations to have a president elected for a single six-year term?

■ Offer your strongest argument for having delegates at the convention vote by state rather than each delegate casting an individual vote. How about the other way around?

■ When is it acceptable or unacceptable for a representative—for example, a delegate to a convention or a legislature in a legislative body—to vote in a manner consistent with his or her economic interests?

The Bottom Line

The Framers of the Constitution were motivated by a number of factors, including political ideals and principles, a belief that the status quo was unacceptable, concerns about what would be politically palatable to the states, and likely some political and economic self-interest as well. But to correlate the convention votes with economic self-interest and then assume that self-interest was the primary causal motivation behind the Constitution is faulty social science. In political analysis, it is important to consider multiple causal factors and to realize that the sequence and timing of decisions, as well as the rules for making decisions, affect the outcome. These factors can even lead an individual to support something he or she believes falls short. Just as Madison vigorously supported a document that did not entirely reflect his preferences, a president must sometimes sign legislation that does not precisely reflect his or her leanings.

remaining five states, support ran from about 51 to 55 percent. One state, North Carolina, had originally voted against the Constitution but voted to support it after the Constitution had been ratified.

In the end, the Federalists won the debate. The main causes are straightforward. In part, this victory appears due to the more convincing arguments of the Federalists. In part, it owes to the absence of a comprehensive Anti-Federalist alternative. Many who voted for the Constitution might well have shared some of the Anti-Federalists' fears about a strong central government, but they also feared domestic disturbances and foreign threats. At bottom, the decision became whether to adopt the Constitution, stick with the Articles, or start over again. Given the sense that the young country faced both foreign and domestic challenges, the appeal of continuing with the Articles or renewing the debate was limited. Change was needed, most people believed, and the Constitution provided that change. The Constitution was also politically attractive because it incorporated the beliefs of the American creed. Liberty, religious freedom, property, and democracy were the focus of many constitutional rules and principles. And underlying many of these constitutional principles was the belief in the notion of individual opportunity and the value of equality.

Amending the Constitution

3-4 Explain the processes of constitutional change.

The structure of the constitutional system sometimes frustrates Americans. Features usually thought of as strengths can sometimes be seen as negatives. The separation of powers and checks and balances can be seen as protectors of liberty, but they can also slow government responses to important national problems. The American system is designed for the cautious use of power, consistent with the American creed, but Americans often get upset when government does not act. Federalism allows for diversity and innovation, but it can frustrate those who believe that national standards in some areas are necessary. Thus, the structure of the Constitution can lead to some frustration, but on the whole this frustration is outweighed by a belief among Americans that the system works.

Part of the process of establishing legitimacy for the Constitution, however, was providing a procedure by which it could be revised. With the Constitution established as a broad framework for government, the Framers were free to create amending procedures that were difficult but not impossible. The underlying premise of the Constitution's amendment process is that any change in the Constitution has to have broad consensus throughout society. The consensus required is not as extensive as that in the Articles of Confederation, however, which required the congressional representatives of every state to agree to any proposed change.[41]

Amendments should have broad societal acceptance.

The introduction of amendments is essentially a national-level process, while the ratification of amendments is a state-level process (see Figure 3-3). Moreover, supermajorities are a requirement of all four paths to amendment. Amendments will not be added to the Constitution unless they receive supermajority support at two stages—three stages, if we consider that a proposed amendment must have supermajority support separately in the House and in the Senate. (The president has no formal role in the amending process.) The premise that amendments should have broad social acceptance is therefore built into the process, and the presence or absence of such acceptance is often a chief point of debate, as in the discussion of a proposed amendment banning same-sex marriage.[42]

In the two paths used for the introduction of all amendments to date (paths A and C in Figure 3-3), it is not enough to get the support of just over half the members of Congress, a simple majority. Rather, two-thirds of the members of the House and two-thirds of the members of the Senate who are present and voting are needed to approve a proposed constitutional amendment. Echoing the Great Compromise, the process in paths A and C ensures that two-thirds of the representatives of the entire population—House members—must agree to the amendment, as well as two-thirds of the representatives of the states—U.S. senators.

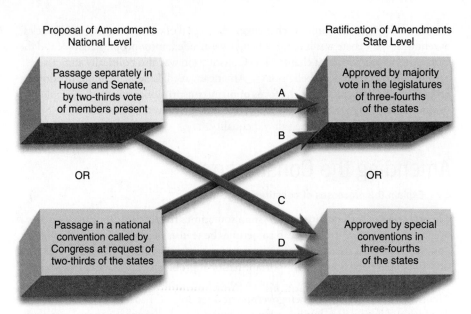

Proposal of Amendments
National Level

Ratification of Amendments
State Level

Passage separately in House and Senate, by two-thirds vote of members present

Approved by majority vote in the legislatures of three-fourths of the states

A

B

OR

OR

C

Passage in a national convention called by Congress at request of two-thirds of the states

Approved by special conventions in three-fourths of the states

D

FIGURE 3-3. Paths to Amending the Constitution. The amending process is based on supermajorities at both the proposal and ratification stages.

Note: Congress chooses which path is used. Path A: Used for 26 Amendments. Path B: Never used. Path C: Used for one amendment (21st). Path D: Never used.

The constitutional rules for introduction of an amendment using paths B and D are less clear, as this method has never been used. The Constitution does not indicate whether votes at a national convention would need to be supermajorities. Most likely, given that the Constitution gives Congress the power to call the convention if two-thirds of the states request it, Congress would set the rules for how the convention would be run. Some observers worry that a convention could become a "runaway convention," proposing amendments on any number of issues. The Constitution seems to imply that Congress could prevent this possibility by establishing ground rules for the convention.

At the ratification level, we again see the Framers' desire that constitutional changes have broad societal acceptance. Three-quarters of the states, or 38 today, either in the state legislature or specially convened state conventions, are needed to ratify an approved amendment. Table 3-2 lists potential amendments since 1980 that had supermajority support in at least one house of Congress but failed in the other house or in the states. Table 3-3 lists all the proposed constitutional amendments in U.S. history that were passed by both houses of Congress but did not receive the necessary support in the states. The shortness of the list in Table 3-3 may seem surprising, but it makes sense. Members of Congress have little incentive to approve a proposed amendment that seems to lack sufficient support in the states to be ratified. On some occasions, however, initial supportive conditions can deteriorate as opponents mobilize against the proposal. When members of Congress sent the Equal Rights Amendment (ERA) to the states in the 1970s, they had good reason to believe it would be ratified. After a rapid string of state ratifications, however, the ERA proved susceptible to the arguments of opponents in some states that its implications were vague and its interpretation so uncertain that extensive litigation would be a likely result.[43] Supporters were unable to build sufficient societal consensus in the wake of these critiques. What looked like a relatively easy victory at the outset turned into defeat.

TABLE 3-2. **Failed Attempts to Amend the Constitution Since 1980**

AMENDMENT	YEAR DEFEATED
Equal Rights Amendment*	1982
No right to abortion	1983
School prayer allowable	1984
Grant District of Columbia residents full voting rights*	1985
Term limits for Congress	1995
Prohibit flag "desecration"	1995, 2006
Require supermajority to increase taxes	1996
Require balanced budget (multiple attempts)	1982–97

*Amendment was rejected by the states. In all other cases, amendment passed one house of Congress only.

TABLE 3-3. **Proposed Amendments Rejected by the States**

AMENDMENT	YEAR APPROVED BY CONGRESS
Regulate size of House	1789
U.S. citizens cannot accept titles of nobility	1810
Prohibit any amendments that would interfere with slavery	1861
Give Congress power to limit child labor	1926
Equal Rights Amendment	1972
Grant District of Columbia residents full voting rights	1978

Note: Years indicate when these proposed amendments passed the second house of Congress.

Congress has the responsibility to decide which ratification path a proposed amendment will take. Congress also determines whether proposed amendments have any time limits attached to their ratification. The most recent amendment, the Twenty-seventh, was actually introduced at the same time as the Bill of Rights but did not gather enough state support to be ratified—mostly because it had been forgotten—until 1992. This amendment states that a congressional pay raise cannot take effect until after the next election. On the other hand, the ERA fell just short of receiving the support of three-fourths of the states and died with the expiration of its 10-year time limit, which Congress had already extended from the original seven years.

CaseStudy: Lowering the Voting Age to 18

The uniform adoption of an 18-year-old voting age across the United States was accomplished through the ratification of the Twenty-sixth Amendment in 1971. A handful of states had lowered their voting age before this, at least for some elections. Most states, however, still had 21 as the legal age for voting entering the 1970s. This was consistent with the societal consensus that 21 was the age of maturity. This consensus would need to shift to lower the voting age.[44]

War provided one key catalyst to changing thoughts about the age of maturity. Eighteen- to twenty-year-olds were dying in the Vietnam War in large numbers, but did not have the right to vote. Similar pressure had arisen following previous wars. During World War II, Republican Senator Arthur Vandenberg joined Democratic Representative Randolph Jennings to introduce a constitutional amendment in 1942 to lower the voting age. Large numbers of the military forces were not of voting age—one-half of the Marines, one-third of the Navy, and one-quarter of the Army. The proposal, however, did not make it out of committee. Only one state, Georgia, lowered its voting age during World War II.

Some organizations continued the pressure after World War II. The National Education Association argued that the national increase in high school graduates suggested that 18-year-olds were more ready to assume the duties of citizenship than ever before. Veterans' organizations like the American Legion and youth organizations also argued for the change. Primarily, these groups focused their energy on changing state laws rather than a national constitutional amendment. Only Alaska, Hawaii, and Kentucky agreed to lower the age to vote.

At the national level, Republican President Dwight Eisenhower, who had a long military history, publicly supported the idea of a constitutional amendment in 1954, right on the heels of the Korean War. Some prominent legislators, including future Democratic Vice President Hubert Humphrey, agreed with Eisenhower. Although by this time a majority of Americans favored a lower voting age, the voting age amendment went nowhere. In part, this failure was because the support was not overwhelming, and many Americans saw the ages of 18–20 as those of rebellion, uncertainty, and susceptibility to emotional appeals and rabble rousing rather than sober and thoughtful citizenship. In addition, it was not a strongly felt issue for most Americans who believed the voting age should be lowered, and most

legislators who supported the idea also had higher-priority concerns.

Vietnam changed everything. Unlike the previous conflicts, this one became tremendously controversial and highly unpopular among large, though not always majority, parts of the population. It was especially unpopular among younger Americans, at least in part because of the military draft. Youth protested in unconventional ways rather than through the ballot box, because they could not vote. The contradiction between eligibility for military service and ineligibility to vote was more pronounced, at least symbolically, under these circumstances. States began to reconsider their laws, and support grew again at the national level for an amendment. In addition to the organizations that had supported the idea for decades, a number of the youth organizations that emerged during the war pressed for the 18-year-old vote, as did labor unions, some church groups, and organizations linked to the civil rights movement. The societal consensus for an 18-year-old voting age had grown.

The path to an amendment was accelerated in 1970, with the addition of a provision in the Senate's renewal of the Voting Rights Act (originally passed in 1965) that lowered the age for all elections to 18. Although many members of the House suspected the provision was unconstitutional, they agreed to it so that the renewal of the Voting Rights Act would not be derailed. President Nixon, similarly skeptical about the provision's constitutionality, nonetheless signed the bill.

◄ FIT TO SERVE BUT NOT TO VOTE

Young American soldiers of the 9th Infantry fire at enemy troops along the South Vietnamese–Cambodian border in May 1970. The contrast between young adults aged 18–20 serving in combat but being unable to vote led to demands, as during previous wars, that the voting age be lowered. One reason the demand succeeded at this time and not the others was the controversy over the war itself. Not only were the troops unable to vote, but the young adults who marched in large numbers against and for the war were also shut out of the ballot box.

A challenge to the provision quickly reached the Supreme Court. In *Oregon v. Mitchell* (1970), four members of the Court believed the provision was constitutional, and that Congress could legislate the voting age for all elections. Four others argued that it was up to the states to decide the voting age for all elections. The final justice, Hugo Black, concluded that Congress could set the age for federal elections but not state elections. Therefore, the country was now faced with an 18-year-old voting age for federal elections (president, U.S. House, U.S. Senate) and whatever age each state set for its own elections.

This scenario promised a very difficult election in 1972. Many states would have to monitor different voting ages for different parts of the ballot. Even if they wanted to change their voting age to 18, in many states that change required voter approval of a proposed state constitutional amendment at two subsequent elections. The national consensus was now nearly complete that lowering the voting age uniformly was right, whether on policy grounds or because of the horrors facing election administration without a uniform age.

Spurred by the Court's action, Congress moved quickly. A decision of the Supreme Court has been a causal factor leading Congress to push for constitutional change in other instances as well. In *Chisholm v. Georgia* (1793), the Court denied states' immunity from citizen lawsuits in federal courts; this "sovereign immunity" was embedded in the Constitution with the Eleventh Amendment (1795). *Pollock v. Farmers' Loan & Trust* (1895) declared particular forms of income tax unconstitutional, and this was superseded by the Sixteenth Amendment (1913). Within a month of the

Oregon v. Mitchell decision, Randolph Jennings, who had proposed the first constitutional amendment on the issue in 1942, introduced another constitutional amendment to lower the voting age. The amendment was approved unanimously in the Senate, with fewer than 20 dissenting votes in the House, and sent to the states for ratification. The amendment needed quick passage to be in effect for 1972. In the states, ratification was accomplished in record time. A little over three months after being sent to the states, the Twenty-sixth Amendment had been ratified and added to the Constitution.

The quick response across the states marks this amendment as unusual—ratification looked much the same in every state. In the importance of causal factors such as societal consensus, interest-group pressure, and politicians who believed in the proposal for reasons of good policy or electoral advantage, or both, however, the story of the Twenty-sixth Amendment looks like those of other successful amendments.[45]

ThinkingCritically

1. Some reformers have proposed that the voting age today be lowered to 16. What criteria would you use to decide if this is a good idea?

2. In your view, what are the valid reasons, if any, to deny someone the ability to vote? Should that denial be permanent or temporary?

3. War was a key causal factor in lowering the voting age to 18. Should we generally expect war to lead to social change or instead to preserve the status quo?

Twenty-seven amendments have been added to the Constitution.

The proof that the federal amending process is difficult is in the numbers. Since 1789, over 10,000 proposals for constitutional amendments have been introduced in Congress. Of these, only 27 have been ratified. Ten were ratified almost immediately, as part of the Bill of Rights. Since 1791, only 17 amendments have been added to the Constitution, less than one per decade on average. The country can go long periods without any amendments—over 60 years elapsed between the Twelfth and Thirteenth Amendments, and over 40 between the Fifteenth and Sixteenth Amendments—and then have a number of amendments over a short period. Between 1961 and 1971, four amendments were added to the Constitution.[46]

As Table 3-4 shows, amendments have followed the logic of the articles of the Constitution, emphasizing the basic framework of government, the powers of government, the size of the electorate, and the relationship between people and government. The amendments have generally not dealt with matters of social or economic policy, with three exceptions: the elimination of slavery, the approval of a federal income tax, and the prohibition—and then repeal of the prohibition—of alcohol production and sales. Slavery and taxation were issues addressed in the Constitution, implicitly and explicitly, respectively, so these amendments did not address new areas. The failure of Prohibition

TABLE 3-4. Amendments to the Constitution

AMENDMENT	PURPOSE	YEAR ADOPTED
	Relationship of People and Government	
1st	Freedom of religion, speech, press, assembly, petition	1791
2nd	Right of people to keep arms	1791
3rd	No housing of militia without due process	1791
4th	Restrictions on search and seizure	1791
5th–8th	Rights in judicial proceedings	1791
9th–10th	Non-enumerated rights reserved to the states or people	1791
13th	Slavery prohibited	1865
14th	Civil liberties and civil rights protections extended to states	1865
	Government Structure	
12th	Changes in Electoral College process	1804
17th	Direct election of U.S. senators	1913
20th	Starting dates for terms; procedure when president-elect dies	1933
22nd	Presidents limited to two terms	1951
25th	Succession in cases of president's death or disability	1967
27th	Congressional pay raises require intervening election	1992
	Size of the Electorate	
15th	Extend voting rights to all races	1870
19th	Extend voting rights to women	1920
23rd	Extend voting rights to residents of District of Columbia	1961
24th	Eliminate payment of "poll tax" as requirement to vote	1964
26th	Extend voting rights to citizens 18 years of age and over	1971
	Powers of Government	
11th	Restricts federal courts' role in cases involving states	1795
16th	National income tax	1913
18th	Prohibition of sale, manufacture, and transportation of alcohol	1919
21st	Repeal of 18th Amendment	1933

is often considered a prime example of why specific social policy should not be included in the Constitution.[47]

The Constitution can be "amended" through judicial interpretation.

Although the amending process does provide some flexibility to the Constitution that enhances system legitimacy, it is, as we have seen, infrequently successful, and the country can go long periods without any formal change to the Constitution. Whether the Framers expected this degree of structural stability in the Constitution is difficult to say. After all, they saw the Constitution amended 10 times—the Bill of Rights—within two years. By 1804, another two amendments had been ratified, so that 12 of the 27 amendments, or nearly 45 percent, had been added to the Constitution within 15 years of its adoption.

The infrequent amendment of the Constitution since then therefore presents a puzzle. The easy answer, often given, is that the Framers disdained the idea of frequent revision of the document and provided a role model of

ThinkingCausally

Why has the Constitution been amended so infrequently?

appropriate behavior for later generations. From the view of political science, however, the empirical record is difficult to match up with this answer. Yes, the Framers were concerned conceptually about overly frequent revision to the document, but they also had to deal with practical political reality. Americans are sometimes so swept up with notions of wise, philosophical Framers, that they neglect how astute and capable the Framers were as politicians. In the world of practical politics, they were not adamantly opposed to the idea of amending the document to achieve their goals. In addition to the 12 successful amendments noted above, they proposed two more as part of the set of Bill of Rights amendments—one, on the size of House districts, was unsuccessful, and the other, on congressional pay raises, was finally ratified as the Twenty-seventh Amendment in 1992. The bottom line is that if the Framers were setting an example for future generations to follow, it was not one of restraint in the amendment process.

If infrequent amendments cannot be attributed to the Framers as role models, what other factors might be important? One key factor noted by political scientists is that the supermajority processes involved in the proposal and ratification stages create a high barrier to adding new amendments. Another key factor is that the formal amending process is not the only means of constitutional change: when the Supreme Court interprets the Constitution, it can change the meaning of the Constitution. Most likely, the causality runs both ways: the difficulty of the formal amending process leads individuals to look to the Supreme Court for new interpretations of the Constitution, and because the Court engages in constitutional interpretation, individuals may see less need to engage in the lengthy formal amendment process.

Consider the Court's *Plessy v. Ferguson* decision of 1896. The Supreme Court declared that racial segregation was legally permissible under the Constitution. Nearly 60 years later, however, in the *Brown v. Board of Education* decision, the Court concluded precisely the opposite. The language of the Constitution had not changed in the meantime with regard to this issue, yet the Court, with different members, in a different time, read the meaning of the Constitution differently.

Think of the amending process detailed in the Constitution as producing formal amendments: they actually change the text of the document. Constitutional interpretation as performed by the courts produces what might be considered informal amendments: the constitutional text remains the same, but the meaning of that text is read differently. To some observers of American politics, this practice creates the risk of allowing judges to insert their policy preferences into the Constitution, by decreeing the Constitution requires or prohibits something that had previously been left to elected officials to decide. In this view, too much power is placed in the hands of unelected federal judges, rather than the elected officials who would have to pass constitutional amendments. On the other hand, informal amendments undeniably provide additional adaptability to the system, which was a goal of the Framers. Most likely, it would have proved impossible to pass a formal constitutional amendment between 1896 and 1954 stating that segregation was unconstitutional, but through a change in interpretation, the Constitution was, in effect, amended.

Both formal and informal amendments have been involved in what some scholars refer to as "constitutional moments"—times of great debate on the fundamental principles of American government, politics, and the Constitution.[48] The 1780s, with the creation of the Articles and Constitution, are often seen as one such period. The 1860s, with a new relationship between the national and state governments, as well as the social revolution brought by the end of slavery, are another. The 1930s and 1940s, with the rise of a federal government of larger and more extensive scope and power than that seen previously, is a third. Formal amendments and constitution writing dominated the first two moments, while informal amendments dominated the latter.

CHAPTER SUMMARY

In this chapter you have learned to:

3-1 Trace developments from events leading to the American Revolution through problems with the country's first constitution. Although scholars still debate the causes and effects of the American Revolution, we can safely say that ideas about liberty and democracy were prominent rallying cries of the colonists. After a series of acts by the British government led to support for independence, the Americans turned their attention to building a structure of governance. The first attempt at a constitution, the Articles of Confederation, proved to be insufficient in building a national government with sufficient power and authority over the states.

3-2 Outline the problems the Framers of the Constitution attempted to resolve and the solutions they devised. The Framers focused on resolving five problems: overcoming fundamental disputes on representation in the new government; allowing for public input while limiting "excessive" democracy and concentrated power through election procedures, separation of powers, checks and balances, and federalism; protecting commerce and property; creating legitimacy by constructing an adaptable but stable governing framework; and providing for national defense. As they wrote a new constitution, the Framers sought to meld power and liberty, freedom and order, and national authority and state sovereignty.

3-3 Compare and contrast the arguments of Anti-Federalists and Federalists. Federalists and Anti-Federalists debated the system of government set out in the Constitution. The Federalists argued that the best protection for liberty would be a stronger national government, a large republic rather than a small democracy, and a system with some distance between the people and government power, so that any "passions" that swept through the population would not immediately find their way into law. The Anti-Federalists favored a system closer to that provided by the Articles of Confederation—a loose union of the states in which the national government was clearly subordinate. At the very least, they wanted a national government that was very close to the people and had many checks on its power.

3-4 Explain the processes of constitutional change. The amending process includes introduction or proposal of an amendment, which happens at the national level, and the ratification of a proposed amendment, which happens at the state level. Through this two-level process, and through the use of supermajorities in Congress and the states, the Framers hoped to ensure that only those amendments with broad societal approval would be added to the Constitution. To date, only 27 out of more than 10,000 amendments proposed have made it through both levels of the amending process. The Constitution does not change only when the text is changed, however. When judges interpret the Constitution, they give it specific meaning. When those interpretations change, the meaning of the Constitution changes also, even though the text remains unchanged.

PEARSON mypoliscilab EXERCISES

Apply what you learned in this chapter on MyPoliSciLab.

📖 **Read** on **mypoliscilab.com**

> **eText:** Chapter 3

✓ **Study** and **Review** on **mypoliscilab.com**

> **Pre-Test**
> **Post-Test**
> **Chapter Exam**
> **Flashcards**

👁 **Watch** on **mypoliscilab.com**

> **Video:** Animal Sacrifice and Free Exercise
> **Video:** Polygamy and the U.S. Constitution

✳ **Explore** on **mypoliscilab.com**

> **Simulation:** You Are James Madison
> **Simulation:** You Are Proposing a Constitutional Amendment
> **Comparative:** Comparing Constitutions
> **Timeline:** The History of Constitutional Amendments
> **Visual Literacy:** The American System of Checks and Balances

KEY TERMS

CHAPTER TEST

1. In what ways did the Articles of Confederation make it difficult for national government to act?
2. How did the Declaration of Independence, the Articles of Confederation, and the Constitution differ in purpose?
3. What were three key problems the Framers sought to address in the Constitution, and what were some of the ways they did so?
4. How would the Framers respond to someone who argued "American government is supposed to be about 'the will of the people'"?
5. With what provisions does the Constitution attempt to improve relations among the states?
6. What were the major steps the Framers took to protect commerce and property?
7. Would Federalists or Anti-Federalists be more likely to support the idea of having all senators, representatives, and the president serve the same length term and be up for election at the same time, and why?
8. How, in the Federalists' view, would the Constitution defend liberty?
9. How do the paths to amend the Constitution provide for a high degree of consensus before the document is changed?
10. What are the differences between formal and informal amendments?

SUGGESTED READINGS

George A. Billias. 2009. *American Constitutionalism Heard Round the World, 1776–1989: A Global Perspective*. New York: New York University Press. A sweeping study that explores the effect of the U.S. Constitution on the spread of democracy around the globe up through the end of the Cold War in 1989.

Catherine Drinker Bowen. 1966. *Miracle at Philadelphia: The Story of the Constitutional Convention*. Boston: Little, Brown. A popular and easy-to-read account of the events prior to the Constitutional Convention and the competing ideas and individuals at the convention.

Robert A. Dahl. 2002. *How Democratic Is the American Constitution?* New Haven: Yale University Press. A comparison of the U.S. Constitution to others around the world.

James A. Gardner. 2005. *Interpreting State Constitutions: A Jurisprudence of Function in a Federal System*. Chicago: University of Chicago Press. A sophisticated analysis of the place of state constitutions within the national constitutional framework.

Alexander Hamilton, John Jay, and James Madison. *The Federalist Papers*. 1787–1788, any edition. Considered by many political scientists the single best distillation of American political philosophy, *The Federalist Papers* presented arguments in favor of the proposed Constitution.

Merrill Jensen. 1959. *The Articles of Confederation: An Interpretation of the Social-Constitutional History of the American Revolution, 1774–1781*. Madison: University of Wisconsin Press. A lively review of the political and economic factions among the colonists as they debated independence from Great Britain and the form of the new American government.

Edmund S. Morgan. 1992. *The Birth of the Republic: 1763–89*. Chicago: University of Chicago Press. A classic overview of the separation from Great Britain and the struggles to build a national government following independence.

David Brian Robertson. 2005. *The Constitution and America's Destiny*. New York: Cambridge University Press. An account of the Constitutional Convention that emphasizes the practical politics as well as principles involved in shaping the Constitution, profiling the defeats suffered by James Madison to delegates wary of national government power.

Herbert J. Storing. 1981. *What the Anti-Federalists Were For: The Political Thought of the Opponents of the Constitution*. Chicago: University of Chicago Press. A brief overview of the philosophy and principles that drove the Anti-Federalists and gave them lasting relevance in American politics.

Gordon S. Wood. 1969. *The Creation of the American Republic, 1776–1787*. New York: W.W. Norton. A beautifully written account of the events between independence and the Constitution, focusing especially on the significance of the classical republican, communitarian vision in America.

SUGGESTED WEBSITES

Library of Congress, Primary Documents in American History: www.memory.loc.gov/ammem/help/constRedir.html

Site with links and discussion of the key documents in American political history, including draft versions. Includes key documents that preceded and contributed to the Declaration of Independence, Articles of Confederation, and U.S. Constitution.

Congressional Research Service Annotated Constitution: www.law.cornell.edu/constitution

A helpful guide that includes commentary, background, historical developments, and relevant court cases for each article, section, and amendment of the Constitution.

Avalon Project: The U.S. Constitution: www.yale.edu/lawweb/avalon/constpap.htm

An outstanding collection of documents related to the development of the Constitution. From the Avalon Project home page, you can access document collections on many other topics in American politics and law.

Constitution Finder: http://confinder.richmond.edu/confinder.html

Constitutions from around the world.

Constitution of the Confederate States of America: www.civilwarhome.com/csconstitution.htm

The Confederate Constitution used the U.S. Constitution as a framework. This site shows where the two constitutions matched and where they diverged.

American Law Sources Online: www.lawsource.com/also

Provides a gateway to state constitutions and other state legal documents and information.

The Constitution of the United States of America*

The Preamble

We the People of the United States, in Order to form a more perfect Union, establish Justice, insure domestic Tranquility, provide for the common defense, promote the general Welfare, and secure the Blessings of Liberty to ourselves and our Posterity, do ordain and establish this Constitution for the United States of America.

"We, the people." Three simple words, yet of profound importance and contentious origin. Every national government in the world at the time of the Constitutional Convention was some type of monarchy in which sovereign power flowed from the top. The Framers of the Constitution rejected monarchy as a form of government and proposed instead a republic, which would draw its sovereignty from the people.

The remainder of the preamble describes the generic functions of government.

Article I—The Legislative Article

Legislative Power

The very first article in the Constitution established the legislative branch of the new national government. Why did the Framers start with the legislative branch instead of the executive branch? Under the Articles of Confederation, the legislature was the only functional instrument of government. The Framers believed it was the most important component of a government, where sovereignty rested directly or indirectly with the people.

Section 1 All legislative Powers herein granted shall be vested in a Congress of the United States, which shall consist of a Senate and House of Representatives.

Section 1 established a bicameral (two-chamber) legislature including an upper (Senate) and lower (House of Representatives) chamber.

House of Representatives: Composition; Qualifications; Apportionment; Impeachment Power

Section 2 *Clause 1.* The House of Representatives shall be composed of Members chosen every second Year by the People of the several States, and the Electors in each State shall have the Qualifications requisite for Electors of the most numerous Branch of the State Legislature.

This section sets the term of office for House members (2 years) and indicates that those voting for Congress will have the same qualifications as those voting for the state legislatures. Originally, states limited voters to white property owners. Some states had religious disqualifications, such as prohibition of voting by Catholics or Jews. Most property and religious qualifications for voting were removed by the 1840s, but race and gender restrictions remained until the 15th and 19th Amendments were passed.

Clause 2. No Person shall be a Representative who shall not have attained to the Age of twenty five Years, and been seven Years a Citizen of the United States, and who shall not, when elected, be an inhabitant of that State in which he shall be chosen.

This section sets forth the basic qualifications of a representative: at least 25 years of age, a U.S. citizen for at least 7 years, and a resident of a state. Note that the Constitution does not require a person to be a resident of the district he or she represents, nor does it require that each district be represented by only one representative. Despite some earlier legislative actions, it was not until 1967 that states with more than one representative were prohibited from electing the representatives at large (representing the entire state) or electing multiple representatives in a district.

Clause 2 does not specify how many terms a representative can serve in Congress. Some states passed legislation to limit the terms of their U.S. representatives. Because of the specificity of the qualifications for office, however, the Supreme Court ruled in *U.S. Term Limits, Inc. v. Thornton* (1995) that term limits for U.S. legislators could not be imposed by any state but would instead require a constitutional amendment.

Clause 3. Representatives and direct Taxes[1] shall be apportioned among the several States which may be included within this Union, according to their respective Numbers, which shall be determined by adding to the whole Number of free Persons, including those bound to Service for a Term of Years, and excluding Indians not taxed, three fifths of all other Persons.[2] The actual Enumeration shall be made within three Years after the first Meeting of the Congress of the United States, and within every subsequent Term of ten Years in such Manner as they shall by Law direct. The Number of Representatives shall not exceed one for every thirty Thousand, but each State shall have at Least one Representative, and until such enumeration shall be made, the State of New Hampshire shall be entitled to chuse three, Massachusetts eight, Rhode Island and Providence Plantations one, Connecticut five, New York six, New Jersey four, Pennsylvania eight, Delaware one, Maryland six, Virginia ten, North Carolina five, South Carolina five, and Georgia three.

This clause contains the Three-fifths Compromise in which, to compute a state's population for congressional representation purposes, slaves were counted as three-fifths of a person. This clause also addresses the question of congressional reapportionment every 10 years, which requires a census. Since the 1911 Reapportionment Act, the size of the House of Representatives has been set at 435. This is the designated size that is reapportioned every 10 years. Based on changes of population, some states gain and some states lose representatives. This clause also provides that every state, regardless of population, will have at least one representative. Currently, seven states have only one representative.

Clause 4. When vacancies happen in the Representation from any State, the Executive Authority thereof shall issue Writs of Election to fill such Vacancies.

This clause provides a procedure for replacing a U.S. representative in the case of death, resignation, or expulsion from the House. Generally, if less than half a term is left, the governor will appoint a successor. If more than half a term is remaining, most states require a special election to fill the vacancy.

---

*Annotations by the authors, based on annotations originally written by James Corey, previously of High Point University.
[1]Modified by the Sixteenth Amendment.
[2]Replaced by Section 2, Fourteenth Amendment.

Clause 5. The House of Representatives shall chuse their Speaker and other Officers, and shall have the sole Power of Impeachment.

> Only one officer of the House is specified—the Speaker. All other officers are decided by the House. This clause also gives the House authority for impeachments (accusations) against officials of the executive and judicial branches. Thus, it is the House that determines whether there are charges against the official that are worthy of trial in the Senate.

Senate Composition: Qualifications, Impeachment Trials

Section 3   *Clause 1.* The Senate of the United States shall be composed of two Senators from each State, chosen by the Legislature thereof,[3] for six Years and each Senator shall have one Vote.

> This clause treats each state equally—all have two senators each. Originally, senators were chosen by state legislatures, but since the ratification of the Seventeenth Amendment, they are now elected by popular vote. This clause also establishes the term of a senator—6 years—three times longer than that of a House member.

Clause 2. Immediately after they shall be assembled in Consequence of the first Election, they shall be divided as equally as may be into three Classes. The Seats of the Senators of the first Class shall be vacated at the Expiration of the second Year, of the second Class at the Expiration of the fourth Year, and of the third Class at the Expiration of the sixth Year, so that one third may be chosen every second Year and if Vacancies happen by Resignation, or otherwise, during the Recess of the Legislature of any State, the Executive thereof may make temporary Appointments until the next Meeting of the Legislature which shall then fill such Vacancies.[4]

> This clause provides that one-third of the Senate will be elected every two years. Senate vacancies are filled similar to those in the House—either by appointment by the governor or by a special election.

Clause 3. No person shall be a Senator who shall not have attained to the Age of thirty Years, and been nine Years a Citizen of the United States, and who shall not, when elected, be an Inhabitant of that State for which he shall be chosen.

> This clause sets forth the qualifications for U.S. senator: at least 30 years old, a U.S. citizen for at least nine years, and a resident of the state he or she represents.

Clause 4. The Vice President of the United States shall be President of the Senate but shall have no Vote, unless they be equally divided.

> The only constitutional duty of the vice president is specified in this clause—president of the Senate. The Senate president has a vote only when there is a tie vote in the Senate; then the vice president's vote breaks the tie.

Clause 5. The Senate shall chuse their other Officers, and also a President pro tempore, in the Absence of the Vice President, or when he shall exercise the Office of President of the United States.

> One official office in the U.S. Senate is specified—temporary president, who fills in during the vice president's absence (which is normally the case). All other Senate officers are designated and selected by the Senate.

Clause 6. The Senate shall have the sole Power to try all Impeachments. When sitting for that Purpose, they shall be on Oath or Affirmation. When the President of the United States is tried, the Chief Justice shall preside. And no Person shall be convicted without the Concurrence of two thirds of the Members present.

Judgment in Cases of impeachment shall not extend further than to removal from Office, and disqualification to hold and enjoy any Office of honor, Trust or Profit under the United States, but the Party convicted shall nevertheless be liable and subject to Indictment, Trial, Judgment and Punishment according to Law.

> The Senate acts as a trial court for impeached federal officials. If the accused is the president, the chief justice of the U.S. Supreme Court presides. Otherwise, the vice president normally presides. Conviction of the charges requires a two-thirds majority vote of those senators present at the time of the vote. Conviction results in the federal official's removal from office and, at the Senate's discretion, disqualification to hold any other appointed federal office. Removal from office does not bar further prosecution under applicable criminal or civil laws.

Congressional Elections: Times, Places, Manner

Section 4   The Times, Places and Manner of holding Elections for Senators and Representatives, shall be prescribed in each State by the Legislature thereof, but the Congress may at any time by Law make or alter such Regulations, except as to the Places of chusing Senators.

The Congress shall assemble at least once in every Year, and such Meeting shall be on the first Monday in December, unless they shall by Law appoint a different Day.[5]

> The states determine the place and manner of electing representatives and senators, but Congress has the right to make or change these laws or regulations, except for the election sites. Congress is required to meet annually, and now, by law, annual meetings begin in January.

Powers and Duties of the Houses

Section 5   *Clause 1.* Each House shall be the Judge of the Elections, Returns and Qualifications of its own Members, and a Majority of each shall constitute a Quorum to do Business, but a smaller Number may adjourn from day to day, and may be authorized to compel the Attendance of absent Members, in such Manner, and under the Penalties as each House may provide.

> This clause enables each legislative branch to make its own rules. Normally, to take a vote, a quorum is necessary. But if no votes are scheduled, fewer than a quorum can convene a session.

Clause 2. Each House may determine the Rules of its Proceedings, punish its Members for disorderly Behaviour, and with the Concurrence of two thirds, expel a Member.

> Each branch promulgates its own rules and punishes its own members. The ultimate punishment is expulsion of the member, which requires a two-thirds vote. Expulsion does not prevent the member from running again.

Clause 3. Each House shall keep a Journal of its Proceedings, and from time to time publish the same, excepting such Parts as may in their Judgment require Secrecy, and the Yeas and Nays of the Members of either House on any question shall, at the Desire of one fifth of those Present, be entered on the Journal.

---

[3]Repealed by the Seventeenth Amendment.
[4]Modified by the Seventeenth Amendment.

[5]Changed by the Twentieth Amendment.

An official record called the *Congressional Record* or *House Journal* is kept for all sessions. It is a daily account of Senate and House floor debates, votes, and members' remarks. However, a record is not printed if a proceeding is closed to the public for security reasons. Many votes are by voice vote, but if at least one-fifth of the members request a recorded vote of Yeas and Nays, the members will vote individually and their votes will be recorded. This procedure permits analysis of congressional roll-call votes.

Clause 4. Neither House, during the Session of Congress shall, without the Consent of the other, adjourn for more than three days, nor to any other Place than that in which the two Houses shall be sitting.

This clause prevents one branch from adjourning for a long period or to some other location without the consent of the other branch.

Rights of Members

Section 6   Clause 1. The Senators and Representatives shall receive a Compensation for their Services, to be ascertained by Law, and paid out of the Treasury of the United States. They shall in all Cases, except Treason, Felony and Breach of the Peace, be privileged from Arrest during their Attendance at the Session of their respective Houses, and in going to and returning from the same, and for any Speech or Debate in either House, they shall not be questioned in any other Place.

This section ensures that senators and congressional representatives will be paid a salary from the U.S. Treasury. This salary is determined by the legislature. The salary for members of Congress in 2010 was $174,000. The Speaker of the House and the Majority Leader and Minority Leader in both the House and Senate receive higher salaries. Under current law, legislators receive a cost-of-living-adjustment to their salary annually. Members of Congress receive many other benefits as part of their compensation, including health care, a pension, access to athletic facilities, and travel to their home state or district. This section also provides immunity from arrest or prosecution for congressional actions on the floor or in travel to and from the Congress.

Clause 2. No Senator or Representative, shall, during the Time for which he was elected, be appointed to any civil Office under the Authority of the United States, which shall have been created, or the Emoluments whereof shall have been encreased during such time; and no Person holding any Office under the United States, shall be a Member of either House during his Continuance in Office.

This section prevents the United States from adopting a parliamentary democracy, since congressional members cannot hold executive offices and members of the executive branch cannot be members of Congress.

Legislative Powers: Bills and Resolutions

Section 7   Clause 1. All Bills for raising Revenue shall originate in the House of Representatives; but the Senate may propose or concur with Amendments as on other Bills.

This clause specifies one of the few powers specific to the U.S. House—revenue bills.

Clause 2. Every Bill which shall have passed the House of Representatives and the Senate, shall, before it becomes a Law, be presented to the President of the United States; If he approve he shall sign it, but if not he shall return it, with his Objections to that House in which it shall have originated, who shall enter the Objections at large on their Journal, and proceed to reconsider it. If after such Reconsideration two thirds of that House shall agree to pass the Bill, it shall be sent, together with the Objections, to the other House, by which it shall likewise be reconsidered, and if approved by two thirds of that House, it shall become a Law. But in all such Cases the Votes of both Houses shall be determined by yeas and Nays, and the Names of the Persons voting for and against the Bill shall be entered on the Journal of each House respectively. If any Bill shall not be returned by the President within ten Days (Sundays excepted) after it shall have been presented to him, the Same shall be a Law, in like Manner as if he had signed it, unless the Congress by their Adjournment prevent its Return, in which Case it shall not be a Law.

The heart of the checks and balances system is contained in this clause. Both the House and Senate must pass a bill and present it to the president. If the president fails to act on the bill within 10 days (not including Sundays), the bill will automatically become law. If the president signs the bill, it becomes law. If the president vetoes the bill and sends it back to Congress, this body may override the veto by a two-thirds vote in each house. This vote must be a recorded vote.

Clause 3. Every Order, Resolution, or Vote to which the Concurrence of the Senate and House of Representatives may be necessary (except on a question of Adjournment) shall be presented to the President of the United States; and before the Same shall take Effect, shall be approved by him, or being disapproved by him, shall be repassed by two thirds of the Senate and House of Representatives, according to the Rules and Limitations prescribed in the Case of a Bill.

This clause covers every other type of legislative action other than a bill. The same procedures apply in most cases.

Powers of Congress

Section 8   Clause 1. The Congress shall have Power to lay and collect Taxes, Duties, Imposts and Excises, to pay the Debts and provide for the common Defence and general Welfare of the United States, but all Duties, Imposts and Excises shall be uniform throughout the United States.

To borrow Money on the credit of the United States;

To regulate Commerce with foreign Nations, and among the several States, and with the Indian Tribes;

To establish an uniform Rule of Naturalization, and uniform Laws on the subject of Bankruptcies throughout the United States;

To coin Money, regulate the Value thereof, and of foreign Coin, and fix the Standard of Weights and Measures;

To provide for the Punishment of counterfeiting the Securities and current Coin of the United States;

To establish Post Offices and post Roads;

To promote the Progress of Science and useful Arts, by securing for limited Times to Authors and Inventors the exclusive Right to their respective Writings and Discoveries;

To constitute Tribunals inferior to the supreme Court;

To define and punish Piracies and Felonies committed on the high Seas, and Offences against the Law of Nations;

To declare War, grant Letters of Marque and Reprisal, and make Rules concerning Captures on Land and Water;

To raise and support Armies, but no Appropriation of Money to that Use shall be for a longer Term than two Years;

To provide and maintain a Navy;

To make Rules for the Government and Regulation of the land and naval Forces;

To provide for calling for the Militia to execute the Laws of the Union, suppress Insurrections and repel Invasions;

To provide for organizing, arming, and disciplining, the Militia, and for governing such Part of them as may be employed in the Service of the United States, reserving to the States respectively, the Appointment of the Officers, and the Authority of training the Militia according to the discipline prescribed by Congress;

This extensive clause establishes what are known as the "expressed" or "enumerated" powers of Congress. In theory, this clause serves as a limit or brake on congressional power. Among the many important powers listed in this clause, that of regulating commerce between the states has been highly consequential. As the Supreme Court revised its interpretation of interstate commerce, it expanded the policy areas where the federal government could act. The most recent major debate concerned whether, as a part of Congress's regulation of interstate commerce, the federal government could require individuals to purchase health insurance.

Clause 2. To exercise exclusive Legislation in all Cases whatsoever, over such District (not exceeding ten Miles square) as may, by Cession of particular States, and the Acceptance of Congress, become the Seat of the Government of the United States, and to exercise like Authority over all Places purchased by the Consent of the Legislature of the State in which the Same shall be, for the Erection of Forts, Magazines, Arsenals, dock Yards, and other needful Buildings—And

This clause establishes the seat of the federal government, which was first located in New York but eventually was moved to Washington, D.C., when both Maryland and Virginia ceded land to the new national government, which then established the District of Columbia.

Clause 3. To make all Laws which shall be necessary and proper for carrying into Execution the foregoing Powers, and all other Powers vested by this Constitution in the Government of the United States, or in any Department or Officer thereof.

This clause, known as the "elastic clause" or the "necessary and proper clause," provides the basis for the concept of "implied" congressional powers, which was first introduced in the U.S. Supreme Court decision in *McCulloch v. Maryland* (1819). This concept greatly expanded the range of legislative and regulatory actions Congress could take. Even if an action was not explicitly enumerated above, Congress could now assert that it had the authority to take the action in order to implement one of the enumerated powers.

Powers Denied to Congress

Section 9   Clause 1. The Migration or Importation of such Persons as any of the States now existing shall think proper to admit, shall not be prohibited by the Congress prior to the Year one thousand eight hundred and eight, but a Tax or duty may be imposed on such Importation, not exceeding ten dollars for each Person.

The new Congress was prohibited from stopping the importation of slaves until 1808, but it could impose a head tax, not to exceed ten dollars for each slave.

Clause 2. The Privilege of the Writ of Habeas Corpus shall not be suspended, unless when in Cases of Rebellion or Invasion the public Safety may require it.

Congress cannot suspend the writ of habeas corpus except in cases of rebellion or invasion. The writ of habeas corpus permits a judge to inquire about the legality of detention or deprivation of liberty of any citizen.

Clause 3. No Bill of Attainder or ex post facto Law shall be passed.

This provision prohibits Congress from passing either a bill of attainder (forfeiture of property in capital cases) or ex post facto laws (making an earlier action criminal retroactively). Similar restrictions were enshrined in many state constitutions.

Clause 4. No Capitation, or other direct Tax shall be laid, unless in Proportion to the Census or Enumeration herein before directed to be taken.[6]

This clause prevented Congress from passing an income tax. Only with passage of the Sixteenth Amendment in 1913 did Congress gain this power.

Clause 5. No Tax or Duty shall be laid on Articles exported from any State.

This section establishes free trade within the United States. The federal government cannot tax state exports.

Clause 6. No Preference shall be given by any Regulation of Commerce or Revenue to the Ports of one State over those of another; nor shall Vessels bound to, or from one State, be obliged to enter, clear, or pay Duties in another.

This clause also applies to free trade within the United States. The national government cannot show any preference to any state or maritime movements among the states.

Clause 7. No Money shall be drawn from the Treasury, but in Consequence of Appropriations made by Law, and a regular Statement and Account of the Receipts and Expenditures of all public Money shall be published from time to time.

This provision prevents any expenditure unless it has been specifically provided for in an appropriations bill. If Congress has not completed work on the budget at the beginning of the fiscal year, it will pass a "continuing resolution" providing temporary authority to continue to spend money until the new appropriations bill is approved and signed into law.

Clause 8. No Title of Nobility shall be granted by the United States. And no Person holding any Office of Profit or Trust under them, shall, without the Consent of Congress, accept of any present, Emolument, Office, or Title, of any kind whatever, from any King, Prince, or foreign State.

Feudalism would not be established in the new country. There would be no nobles. No federal official can even accept a title of nobility (even honorary) without permission of Congress.

[6]Modified by the Sixteenth Amendment.

Powers Denied to the States

This section sets out the prohibitions on state actions.

Section 10 *Clause 1.* No State shall enter into any Treaty, Alliance, or Confederation, grant Letters of Marque and Reprisal, coin Money, emit Bills of Credit, make any Thing but gold and silver Coin a Tender in Payment of Debts, pass any Bill of Attainder, ex post facto Law, or Law impairing the Obligation of Contracts or grant any Title of Nobility.

This particular clause provides a list of denied powers. Note that these restrictions cannot even be waived by Congress. States are not to engage in foreign relations nor acts of war. A "letter of marque and reprisal" was used during these times to provide legal cover for privateers. The federal government's currency monopoly is established. The sanctity of contracts is specified. State prohibitions are specified for bills of attainder and ex post facto laws.

Clause 2. No State shall, without the Consent of the Congress, lay any Imposts or Duties on Imports or Exports, except what may be absolutely necessary for executing its inspection Laws: and the net Produce of all Duties and Imposts, laid by any State on Imports or Exports, shall be for the Use of the Treasury of the United States, and all such Laws shall be subject to the Revision and Control of the Congress.

This section establishes the monopoly control of the national government in matters of both national and international trade. The only concession to states is health and safety inspections.

Clause 3. No State shall, without the Consent of Congress, lay any Duty of Tonnage, keep Troops, or Ships of War in time of Peace, enter into any Agreement or Compact with another State, or with a foreign Power, or engage in War, unless actually invaded, or in such imminent Danger as will not admit of delay.

This final section of the legislative article establishes the war power to be held exclusively by the national government. The only exception to state action is actual invasion or threat of imminent danger.

Article II—The Executive Article

This article establishes an entirely new concept in government—an elected executive power.

Nature and Scope of Presidential Power

Section 1 *Clause 1.* The executive Power shall be vested in a President of the United States of America. He shall hold his Office during the Term of four Years and, together with the Vice President, chosen for the same Term, be elected, as follows.

This clause establishes the executive power in the office of the president of the United States of America. It also establishes a second office—vice president. A four-year term was established, but no limit on the number of terms. A limit was later established by the Twenty-second Amendment.

Clause 2. Each State shall appoint, in such Manner as the Legislature thereof may direct, a Number of Electors, equal to the whole Number of Senators and Representatives to which the State may be entitled in the Congress: but no Senator or Representative, or Person holding an Office of Trust or Profit under the United States, shall be appointed an Elector.

This paragraph establishes the Electoral College to choose the president and vice president.

Clause 3. The Electors shall meet in their respective States, and vote by Ballot for two Persons, of whom one at least shall not be an Inhabitant of the same State with themselves. And they shall make a List of all the Persons voted for, and of the Number of Votes for each; which List they shall sign and certify, and transmit sealed to the Seat of the Government of the United States, directed to the President of the Senate. The President of the Senate shall, in the Presence of the Senate and House of Representatives, open all the Certificates, and the Votes shall then be counted. The Person having the greatest Number of Votes shall be the President, if such Number be a Majority of the whole Number of Electors appointed; and if there be more than one who have such Majority and have an equal Number of Votes, then the House of Representatives shall immediately chuse by Ballot one of them for President; and if no Person have a Majority, then from the five highest on the List the said House shall in like Manner chuse the President. But in chusing the President, the Votes shall be taken by States, the Representation from each State having one Vote; a quorum for this Purpose shall consist of a Member or Members from two thirds of the States, and a Majority of all the States shall be necessary to a Choice. In every Case, after the Choice of the President, the Person having the greatest Number of Votes of the Electors shall be the Vice President. But if there should remain two or more who have equal Votes, the Senate shall chuse from them by Ballot the Vice President.[7]

This paragraph has been superseded by the Twelfth Amendment. The original language did not require a separate vote for president and vice president. Instead, each elector cast two votes. Only one of the two can be from the state of the elector. When one candidate received a majority of the electoral votes cast and there was no tie, the second-place finisher became the vice president. Thus, two candidates who had just opposed each other could now find themselves as president and vice president. The Twelfth Amendment requires a separate vote for each office.

The original language provided for the House to elect the president in the case where two candidates both received an equal number of electoral votes and had a majority—it was possible for two candidates to receive a majority because each elector cast two votes and the "majority" being referred to here was a majority of the number of electors casting votes, not the number of votes. There would also be a House election among the top five candidates if no candidate received a majority. The Twelfth Amendment lowered the number of candidates to the top three.

In both these instances, each state delegation in the House casts a single vote. The Senate is to select the vice president if a candidate does not have an electoral majority or in the case of a tie vote. The Senate considers only the top two candidates. The Twelfth Amendment later clarified that the age, citizenship, and residency requirements of the vice president are the same as those for president.

Clause 4. The Congress may determine the Time of chusing the Electors, and the Day on which they shall give their Votes; which Day shall be the same throughout the United States.

Congress is given the power to establish a uniform day and time for the state selection of electors.

[7]Changed by the Twelfth and Twentieth Amendments.

Clause 5. No Person except a natural born Citizen, or a Citizen of the United States, at the time of the Adoption of this Constitution, shall be eligible to the Office of President, neither shall any Person be eligible to that Office who shall not have attained to the Age of thirty five Years, and been fourteen Years a Resident within the United States.

The qualifications for the office of president (and, as the Twelfth Amendment made clear, by implication the vice president) are specified here—at least 35 years old, 14 years' resident in the United States, and born in the United States (or a citizen of the United States when the Constitution was adopted). Congress has addressed by statute—as early as 1790—that someone born to American parents while in a foreign country is a citizen and effectively considered to have been born in the United States. The rules concerning children born to one American citizen in a foreign country have varied over time.

Clause 6. In Case of the Removal of the President from Office, or of his Death, Resignation, or Inability to discharge the Powers and Duties of the said Office, the Same shall devolve on the Vice President, and the Congress may by Law provide for the Case of Removal, Death, Resignation, or Inability, both of the President and Vice President, declaring what Officer shall then act as president, and such Officer shall act accordingly, until the Disability be removed, or a President shall be elected.[8]

This clause has been modified by the Twenty-fifth Amendment. Upon the death, resignation, or impeachment and conviction of the president, the vice president becomes president. The new president nominates a new vice president, who assumes the office, if approved by a majority vote in both congressional branches. The president is also now able to notify the Congress of his inability to perform his office.

Clause 7. The President shall, at stated Times, receive for his Services, a Compensation which shall neither be encreased nor diminished during the Period of which he shall have been elected, and he shall not receive within that Period any other Emolument from the United States, or any of them.

This section covers the compensation of the president, which cannot be increased or decreased during the term in office. The current salary is $400,000 per year. Unlike legislators, judges, and the heads of federal agencies, the president's salary does not receive an annual cost-of-living adjustment.

Clause 8. Before he enter on the Execution of his Office, he shall take the following Oath or Affirmation—"I do solemnly swear (or affirm) that I will faithfully execute the Office of President of the United States, and will to the best of my Ability, preserve, protect and defend the Constitution of the United States."

This final clause in Section 1 is the oath of office administered to the new president.

Powers and Duties of the President

Section 2   Clause 1. The President shall be the Commander in Chief of the Army and Navy of the United States, and of the Militia of the several States; when called into the actual Service of the United States, he may require the Opinion, in writing, of the principal Officer in each of the executive Departments, upon any Subject relating to the Duties of their respective Offices, and he shall have the Power to grant Reprieves and Pardons for Offences against the United States, except in Cases of Impeachment.

[8]Modified by the Twenty-fifth Amendment.

This clause establishes the president as commander in chief of the U.S. armed forces. The second provision provides the basis for Cabinet meetings that are used to acquire the opinions of executive department heads. The last provision provides an absolute pardon or reprieve power from the president.

Clause 2. He shall have Power, by and with the Advice and Consent of the Senate to make Treaties, provided two thirds of the Senators present concur, and he shall nominate, and by and with the Advice and Consent of the Senate, shall appoint Ambassadors, other public Ministers and Consuls, Judges of the supreme Court, and all other Officers of the United States, whose Appointments are not herein otherwise provided for, and which shall be established by Law but the Congress may by Law vest the Appointment of such inferior Officers, as they think proper in the President alone, in the Courts of Law, or in the Heads of Departments.

This clause covers two important presidential powers, treaty making and appointments. The president (via the State Department) can negotiate treaties with other nations, but these do not become official until ratified by a two-thirds vote of the U.S. Senate. The president is empowered to appoint judges, ambassadors, and other U.S. officials (such as Cabinet officers, military officers, and agency heads), subject to Senate approval. The Congress can and does delegate this approval to the president in the case of inferior officers. For example, junior military officer promotions are not submitted to the Senate, but senior officer promotions are.

Clause 3. The President shall have Power to fill up all Vacancies that may happen during the Recess of the Senate, by granting Commissions which shall expire at the End of their next Session.

This provision allows recess appointments of the officials listed in clause 2 above. These commissions automatically expire unless approved by the Senate by the end of the next session. Presidents have used this provision, sometimes controversially, to fill jobs when the nomination process is stalled.

Section 3 He shall from time to time give to the Congress Information of the State of the Union, and recommend to their Consideration such Measures as he shall judge necessary and expedient, he may, on extraordinary Occasions convene both Houses, or either of them and in Case of Disagreement between them, with Respect to the Time of Adjournment, he may adjourn them to such Time as he shall think proper, he shall receive Ambassadors and other public Ministers, he shall take Care that the Laws be faithfully executed, and shall Commission all the Officers of the United States.

This section provides for a report on the state of the union during the president's term. Although today this report is delivered in person in the form of the televised State of the Union Address, presidents can also simply submit a report to Congress. "From time to time" has come to mean annual, but in some years, usually a transition year to a new president, there has been no report. The "necessary and expedient" clause indicates that the Framers expected that presidents would have some role in prodding the legislature to act. The president is also authorized to call special meetings of either the House or Senate. If there is disagreement between the House and Senate regarding adjournment, the president is empowered to adjourn them. This would be extremely rare. The president formally receives other nations' ambassadors. The next to last provision, to faithfully execute laws, provides the constitutional basis for the whole administrative apparatus of the presidency. All officers of the United States receive a formal commission from the president.

Section 4 The President, Vice President and all civil Officers of the United States, shall be removed from Office on Impeachment for, and Conviction of, Treason, Bribery, or other high Crimes and Misdemeanors.

This section provides the constitutional authority for the impeachment and trial of the president, vice president, and all civil officers of the United States for treason, bribery, or other high crimes and misdemeanors. In practice, precisely what constitutes a high crime or misdemeanor has been a matter of great debate.

Article III—The Judicial Article
Judicial Power, Courts, Judges

Section 1 The judicial Power of the United States, shall be vested in one supreme Court, and in such inferior Courts as the Congress may from time to time ordain and establish. The Judges, both of the supreme and inferior Courts, shall hold their Offices during good Behaviour, and shall, at stated Times, receive for their Services, a Compensation, which shall not be diminished during their Continuance in Office.

This section establishes the judicial branch in very general terms. It specifically provides only for the Supreme Court. Congress is given the responsibility to develop the remainder of the court system. It initially did so in the Judiciary Act of 1789, when it established 13 district courts (one for each state), and 3 appellate courts. All federal judges hold their offices for life and can be removed only for breaches of good behavior; judges have been removed for drunkenness, accepting bribes, and other offenses. To date, no justice of the U.S. Supreme Court has ever been removed. The number of Supreme Court justices is not set by the Constitution but is instead determined by statute.

The salary of federal judges is set by Congress and can not be cut while the judge serves. Federal district judges earned $174,000 in 2010, appellate judges $184,500, and Supreme Court justices $213,900. The chief justice was paid $223,500.

Jurisdiction

Section 2 The judicial Power shall extend to all Cases, in Law and Equity, arising under this Constitution, the Laws of the United States, and Treaties made, or which shall be made, under their Authority,—to all Cases affecting Ambassadors, other public Ministers and Consuls;—to all Cases of admiralty and maritime Jurisdiction;—to Controversies to which the United States shall be a Party;—to Controversies between two or more States; between a State and Citizens of another State[9];—between Citizens of different States;—between Citizens of the same State claiming Lands under Grants of different States, and between a State, or the Citizens thereof, and foreign States, Citizens, or Subjects.

In all Cases affecting Ambassadors, other public Ministers and Consuls, and those in which a State shall be Party, the supreme Court shall have original Jurisdiction. In all the other Cases before mentioned, the supreme Court shall have appellate Jurisdiction, both as to Law and Fact, with such Exceptions, and under such Regulations as Congress shall make.

The Trial of all Crimes, except in Cases of Impeachment, shall be by Jury; and such Trial shall be held in the State where the said Crimes shall have been committed; but when not committed within any State, the Trial shall be at such Place or Places as the Congress may by Law have directed.

[9]Modified by the Twelfth Amendment.

This section establishes the Supreme Court's original jurisdiction (the Supreme Court alone hears the case) and appellate jurisdiction (the Court hears the case on appeal from another court). With the Congress of Vienna's 1815 establishment of "diplomatic immunity," the U.S. Supreme Court no longer hears cases involving ambassadors. Since 1925, the Supreme Court no longer hears every case on appeal but can select which cases it will accept, which is now about 100 cases per year. This section also establishes the right of trial by jury for federal crimes.

Treason

Section 3 Treason against the United States, shall consist only in levying War against them, or in adhering to their Enemies, giving them Aid and Comfort. No Person shall be convicted of Treason unless on the Testimony of two Witnesses to the same overt Act, or on Confession in open Court.

The Congress shall have Power to declare the Punishment of Treason, but no Attainder of Treason shall work Corruption of Blood, or Forfeiture except during the Life of the Person attainted.

Treason is the only crime defined in the U.S. Constitution. Congress established the penalty of death for treason convictions. Note that two witnesses are required to convict anyone of treason. Even in cases of treasonable conduct, seizure of estates is prohibited.

Article IV—Interstate Relations
Full Faith and Credit Clause

Section 1 Full Faith and Credit shall be given in each State to the public Acts, Records, and judicial Proceedings of every other State. And the Congress may by general Laws prescribe the Manner in which such Acts, Records and Proceedings shall be proved, and the Effect thereof.

This section provides that the official acts and records of one state will be recognized and given credence by other states—for example, marriages and divorces.

Privileges and Immunities, Interstate Extradition

Section 2 *Clause 1.* The Citizens of each State shall be entitled to all Privileges and Immunities of Citizens in the several States.

This clause requires states to treat citizens of other states equally. For example, when driving in another state, one's driver's license is recognized and the traffic laws apply equally to state citizens and visitors from other states.

Clause 2. A person charged in any State with Treason, Felony or other Crime, who shall flee from Justice, and be found in another State, shall on Demand of the executive Authority of the State from which he fled, be delivered up, to be removed to the State having Jurisdiction of the Crime.

This clause refers to the concept of extradition—a criminal fleeing to another state, if captured, can be returned to the state where the crime was committed. But this is not an absolute. A state's governor can refuse to extradite someone to another state.

Clause 3. No person held to Service or Labour in one State, under the Laws thereof, escaping into another, shall, in Consequence of any Law or Regulation therein, be discharged from such Service or Labour, but shall be delivered up on Claim of the Party to whom such Service or Labour may be due.[10]

[10]Repealed by the Thirteenth Amendment.

This clause was included to cover runaway slaves and provide for their return. It was overruled by the Thirteenth Amendment, which abolished slavery.

Admission of States

Section 3 New States may be admitted by the Congress into this Union but no new State shall be formed or erected within the Jurisdiction of any other State, nor any State to be formed by the Junction of two or more States, or Parts of States, without the Consent of the Legislatures of the States concerned as well as of the Congress.

The Congress shall have Power to dispose of and make all needful Rules and Regulations respecting the Territory or other Property belonging to the United States, and nothing in this Constitution shall be so construed as to Prejudice any Claims of the United States, or of any particular State.

This section concerns the admission of new states to the Union. Although no new state can be created from part of another state without permission of the state legislature, there is one historical exception: West Virginia was formed from Virginia during the Civil War without the permission of Virginia, which was part of the Confederacy.

Republican Form of Government

Section 4 The United States shall guarantee to every State in this Union a Republican Form of Government, and shall protect each of them against Invasion, and on Application of the Legislature, or of the Executive (when the Legislature cannot be convened) against domestic Violence.

This section commits the federal government to guarantee a republican form of government to each state and protect the state against foreign invasion or domestic insurrection.

Article V—The Amending Power

The Congress, whenever two thirds of both Houses shall deem it necessary, shall propose Amendments to this Constitution, or, on the Application of the Legislatures of two thirds of the several States, shall call a Convention for proposing Amendments, which, in either Case, shall be valid to all Intents and Purposes, as Part of this Constitution, when ratified by the Legislatures of three fourths of the several States, or by Conventions in three fourths thereof, as the one or the other Mode of Ratification may be proposed by the Congress; Provided that no Amendment which may be made prior to the Year One thousand eight hundred and eight shall in any Manner affect the first and fourth Clauses in the Ninth Section of the first Article; and that no State, without its Consent, shall be deprived of its equal Suffrage in the Senate.

Amendments to the U.S. Constitution can be originated by a two-thirds vote in both the U.S. House and the Senate or by two-thirds of the state legislatures asking for a convention to propose amendments. Proposed amendments, by either route, must be approved by three-fourths of state legislatures or by three-fourths of conventions convened in the states for purposes of ratification. Only one amendment has been ratified by the convention method: the Twenty-first Amendment, to repeal the Eighteenth Amendment establishing prohibition of alcohol. There have only been 27 successful amendments to the U.S. Constitution.

Article VI—The Supremacy Clause

Clause 1. All Debts contracted and Engagements entered into, before the Adoption of this Constitution, shall be as valid against the United States under the Constitution, as under the Confederation.

This clause made the new national government responsible for all debts incurred during the Revolutionary War. This provision was very important to those interests concerned that debts and contracts might be discarded in the transition from the Articles of Confederation to the Constitution.

Clause 2. This Constitution, and the Laws of the United States which shall be made in Pursuance thereof, and all Treaties made, or which shall be made, under the Authority of the United States, shall be the supreme Law of the Land, and the Judges in every State shall be bound thereby any Thing in the Constitution or Laws of any State to the Contrary notwithstanding.

The national supremacy clause provides the basis for the supremacy of the national government over the states in policy areas where the national government has constitutional authority to act.

Clause 3. The Senators and Representatives before mentioned, and the Members of the several State Legislatures, and all executive and judicial Officers, both of the United States and of the several States, shall be bound by Oath or Affirmation, to support this Constitution, but no religious Test shall ever be required as a Qualification to any Office or public Trust under the United States.

This clause requires all federal and state officials to swear or affirm their allegiance to and support of the U.S. Constitution. A religious test was prohibited for federal office. However, some states used religious affiliation as a criterion for state office until the 1830s.

Article VII—Ratification

The Ratification of the Conventions of nine States, shall be sufficient for the Establishment of this Constitution between the States so ratifying the Same.

Done in Convention by the Unanimous Consent of the States present the Seventeenth Day of September in the Year of our Lord one thousand seven hundred and Eighty seven and of the Independence of the United States of America the Twelfth. In Witness whereof We have hereunto subscribed our Names.

Realizing the unanimous ratification of the 13 states of the new Constitution might never have occurred, the Framers specified that only 9 states would be needed for ratification. The ratification campaign posed the Federalists, who supported the Constitution, against the Anti-Federalists, who opposed it.

AMENDMENTS
The Bill of Rights

The first 10 amendments were ratified on December 15, 1791, and form what is known as the Bill of Rights. The Bill of Rights applied initially only to the federal government and not to state or local governments. Beginning in 1897 in the case of *Chicago, Burlington and Quincy Railroad v. City of Chicago*, the Supreme Court began to selectively and gradually make the provisions of the Bill of Rights applicable to state and local governments. There are only a few exceptions, which will be discussed at the appropriate amendment.

Amendment 1—Religion, Speech, Assembly, and Politics

Congress shall make no law respecting an establishment of religion, or prohibiting the free exercise thereof; or abridging the freedom of speech, or of the press; or the right of the people peaceably to assemble, and to petition the Government for a redress of grievances.

This amendment has vast range, in that it protects five fundamental freedoms: religion, speech, press, assembly, and petition.

Amendment 2—Militia and the Right to Bear Arms

A well-regulated Militia, being necessary to the security of a free State, the right of the people to keep and bear Arms, shall not be infringed.

In 2010, the Supreme Court determined that this amendment applied to the actions of state and local governments in addition to the federal government. The Court had, one year earlier, established that the amendment protected an individual's right to possess firearms. Previously, the Court had seen this amendment as protecting a collective right of the people as organized in official militias, not an individual right.

Amendment 3—Quartering of Soldiers

No Soldier shall, in time of peace be quartered in any house, without the consent of the Owner, nor in time of war, but in manner to be prescribed by law.

It was the practice of the British government to insist that colonists provide room and board to British troops. This amendment was designed to prohibit this practice. Today, military and naval bases provide the necessary quarters. The Supreme Court has not said that this amendment applies to state and local governments.

Amendment 4—Searches and Seizures

The right of the people to be secure in their persons, houses, papers, and effects, against unreasonable searches and seizures, shall not be violated, and no Warrants shall issue, but upon probable cause, supported by Oath or affirmation, and particularly describing the place to be searched, and the persons or things to be seized.

This amendment provides protection for individuals subject to investigation. Searches or seizures of homes, persons, or property cannot be undertaken without probable cause or a warrant that specifically describes the place to be searched, the person involved, and suspicious things to be seized.

Amendment 5—Grand Juries, Self-Incrimination, Double Jeopardy, Due Process, and Eminent Domain

No person shall be held to answer for a capital, or otherwise infamous crime, unless on a presentment or indictment of a Grand jury, except in cases arising in the land or naval forces, or in the Militia, when in actual service in time of War or public danger; nor shall any person be subject for the same offence to be twice put in jeopardy of life or limb, nor shall be compelled in any criminal case to be a witness against himself, nor be deprived of life, liberty, or property, without due process of law, nor shall private property be taken for public use, without just compensation.

Only a grand jury can indict a person for a federal crime. This provision does not apply to state or local governments. This amendment also covers double jeopardy: being tried twice for the same crime in the same jurisdiction. However, because the federal government and state governments are different jurisdictions, an individual could be tried in each jurisdiction for the same act. For example, it is a federal crime to kill a congressperson. It is also a state crime to murder anyone. Further, this amendment also covers the prohibition of self-incrimination. "Pleading the Fifth Amendment" is common among defendants. The deprivation of life, liberty, or property is prohibited unless due process of law is applied. Finally, private property may not be taken under the doctrine of "eminent domain" unless the government provides just compensation and the taking is for public purposes.

Amendment 6—Criminal Court Procedures

In all criminal prosecutions, the accused shall enjoy the right to a speedy and public trial, by an impartial jury of the State and district wherein the crime shall have been committed, which district shall have been previously ascertained by law, and to be informed of the nature and cause of the accusation, to be confronted with the witnesses against him, to have compulsory process for obtaining witnesses in his favor, and to have the Assistance of Counsel for his defence.

This amendment requires public trials by jury for criminal prosecutions. Anyone accused of a crime is guaranteed the right to be informed of the charges, to confront witnesses, to subpoena witnesses for his or her defense, and to have a lawyer for his or her defense. The government must provide a lawyer for a defendant unable to afford one.

Amendment 7—Trial by Jury in Common Law Cases

In Suits at common law, where the value in controversy shall exceed twenty dollars, the right of trial by jury shall be preserved, and no fact tried by a jury shall be otherwise re-examined in any Court of the United States, than according to the rules of the common law.

Federal civil lawsuits with a guaranteed jury are now restricted to cases that exceed $50,000. The Supreme Court has not required that trial by jury be applied to the states: some state and local governments have trials by judges, not by juries.

Amendment 8—Bail, Cruel and Unusual Punishment

Excessive bail shall not be required, nor excessive fines imposed, nor cruel and unusual punishments inflicted.

Capital punishment is covered by this amendment, which also prohibits excessive bail. The Supreme Court has outlawed capital punishment for minors and those with severe mental development disabilities as being inherently cruel and unusual.

Amendment 9—Rights Retained by the People

The enumeration in the Constitution of certain rights, shall not be construed to deny or disparage others retained by the people.

This amendment implies that there may be other rights of the people not specified by the previous amendments. For the most part, the Supreme Court has established that the people have additional rights through other provisions of the Constitution, especially the Fourteenth Amendment. The Ninth Amendment is often mentioned in these decisions but is usually not at the root of the Court's decision.

Amendment 10—Reserved Powers of the States

The powers not delegated to the United States by the Constitution, nor prohibited by it to the States, are reserved to the States respectively, or to the people.

The Tenth Amendment was seen as the reservoir of reserved powers for state governments and is frequently cited today by individuals concerned that federal government is involved in too many areas that should be the responsibility of the states. The doctrine of implied national government powers, established by the Supreme Court in *McCulloch v. Maryland* (1819), complicates to some degree the application of this amendment. The amendment refers to "powers not delegated," yet the Court validated as constitutional the federal government taking actions that were not specifically delegated to it. The meaning and application of the Tenth Amendment are a battleground for those involved in politics who are wrestling over the appropriate reach of and limits on federal government power.

Amendment 11—Suits Against the States
[Ratified February 7, 1795]

The Judicial power of the United States shall not be construed to extend to any suit in law or equity, commenced or prosecuted against one of the United States by Citizens of another State, or by Citizens or Subjects of any Foreign State.

Article 3 of the U.S. Constitution originally allowed federal jurisdiction in cases of one state citizen against another state citizen or state. This amendment removes federal jurisdiction in this area. States may not be sued in federal court by citizens of another state or country.

Amendment 12—Election of the President
[Ratified June 15, 1804]

The Electors shall meet in their respective states, and vote by ballot for President and Vice-President, one of whom, at least, shall not be an inhabitant of the same state with themselves; they shall name in their ballots the person voted for as President, and in distinct ballots the person voted for as Vice-President, and they shall make distinct lists of all persons voted for as President, and of all persons voted for as Vice-President, and of the number of votes for each, which lists they shall sign and certify, and transmit sealed to the seat of the government of the United States, directed to the President of the Senate;—The President of the Senate shall, in presence of the Senate and House of Representatives, open all the certificates and the votes shall then be counted;—The person having the greatest number of votes for President, shall be the President, if such number be a majority of the whole number of Electors appointed; and if no person have such majority, then from the persons having the highest numbers not exceeding three on the list of those voted for as President, the House of Representatives shall choose immediately, by ballot, the President. But in choosing the President, the votes shall be taken by states, the representation from each state having one vote; a quorum for this purpose shall consist of a member or members from two-thirds of the states, and a majority of all states shall be necessary to a choice. And if the House of Representatives shall not choose a President whenever the right of choice shall devolve upon them, before the fourth day of March next following, then the Vice-President shall act as President, as in the case of the death or other constitutional disability of the President.[11] The person having the greatest number of votes as Vice-President, shall be the Vice-President, if such a number be a majority of the whole numbers of Electors appointed, and if no person have a

majority, then from the two highest numbers on the list, the Senate shall choose the Vice-President, a quorum for the purpose shall consist of two-thirds of the whole number of Senators, and a majority of the whole number shall be necessary to a choice. But no person constitutionally ineligible to the office of President shall be eligible to that of Vice-President of the United States.

Article II of the original Constitution specified that each elector would cast two ballots. It did not specify for whom. This amendment clarifies that the electoral vote must be specific for president and vice president. The original Constitution provided that if no candidate received a majority of electoral votes, the House would decide from the candidates with the top five vote totals. This amendment reduces the candidate field to the top three vote totals. If the House delays in this selection past the fourth day of March, the elected vice president will act as president until the House selects the president. The original Constitution provided that the candidate with the second highest number of electoral votes would become vice president; this provision is superseded by this amendment's requirement that there be a separate vote tally for the position of vice president. The amendment provides for selection by the U.S. Senate if no vice presidential candidate receives an electoral vote majority.

Amendment 13—Prohibition of Slavery
[Ratified December 6, 1865]

Section 1   Neither slavery nor involuntary servitude, except as a punishment for crime whereof the party shall have been duly convicted, shall exist within the United States, or any place subject to their jurisdiction.

Section 2   Congress shall have power to enforce this article by appropriate legislation.

This is the first of the three Civil War amendments. Slavery is prohibited under all circumstances. Involuntary servitude is also prohibited unless it is a punishment for a convicted crime.

Amendment 14—Citizenship, Due Process, and Equal Protection of the Laws
[Ratified July 9, 1868]

Section 1   All persons born or naturalized in the United States, and subject to the jurisdiction thereof, are citizens of the United States and of the State wherein they reside. No State shall make or enforce any law which shall abridge the privileges or immunities of citizens of the United States; nor shall any State deprive any person of life, liberty, or property, without due process of law; nor deny to any person within its jurisdiction the equal protection of the laws.

This section defines the meaning of U.S. citizenship and protection of these citizenship rights. It also establishes that each state must guarantee the equal protection of the laws. It extended the provisions of the Fifth Amendment of due process and protection of life, liberty, and property and made these applicable to the states.

Section 2   Representatives shall be apportioned among the several States according to their respective numbers, counting the whole number of persons in each State, excluding Indians not taxed. But when the right to vote at any election for the choice of electors for President and Vice President of the United States, Representatives in Congress, the Executive and Judicial officers

[11]Changed by the Twentieth Amendment.

of a State, or the members of the Legislature thereof, is denied to any of the male inhabitants of such State, being twenty-one[12] years of age, and citizens of the United States, or in any way abridged, except for participation in rebellion, or other crime, the basis of representation therein shall be reduced in the proportion which the number of such male citizens shall bear to the whole number of male citizens twenty-one years of age in such State.

This section changes the three-fifths clause of the original Constitution. Now all persons in the state, excluding certain Indians, will be included in the population count used to calculate representation in the House of Representatives. If a state denies the right to vote to any male 21 or older, the number of denied citizens will be deducted from the overall state total to determine representation.

Section 3 No person shall be a Senator or Representative in Congress, or elector of President and Vice President, or hold any office, civil or military under the United States, or under any State, who, having previously taken an oath, as a member of Congress, or as an officer of the United States, or as a member of any State legislature, or as an executive or judicial officer of any State, to support the Constitution of the United States, shall have engaged in insurrection or rebellion against the same, or given aid or comfort to the enemies thereof. But Congress may by a vote of two-thirds of each House, remove such disability.

This section disqualifies from federal office or elector for president or vice president anyone who rebelled or participated in an insurrection against the Constitution. This was specifically directed against citizens of southern states. Congress by a two-thirds vote could override this provision.

Section 4 The validity of the public debt of the United States, authorized by law, including debts incurred for payment of pensions and bounties for services in suppressing insurrection or rebellion, shall not be questioned. But neither the United States nor any State shall assume or pay any debt or obligation incurred in aid of insurrection or rebellion against the United States or any claim for the loss or emancipation of any slave, but all such debts, obligations and claims shall be held illegal and void.

This section guarantees payment of Civil War debts incurred by the U.S. government but declares void any debts incurred by the Confederacy.

Section 5 The Congress shall have power to enforce, by appropriate legislation, the provisions of this article.

Amendment 15—The Right to Vote
[Ratified February 3, 1870]

Section 1 The right of citizens of the United States to vote shall not be denied or abridged by the United States or by any State on account of race, color, or previous condition of servitude.

Section 2 The Congress shall have power to enforce this article by appropriate legislation.

This final Civil War amendment guarantees that voting rights cannot be denied by any states on account of race, color, or previous servitude. Gender and age would be addressed in future amendments.

Amendment 16—Income Taxes
[Ratified February 3, 1913]

The Congress shall have power to lay and collect taxes on incomes, from whatever source derived, without apportionment among the several States, and without regard to any census or enumeration.

Article I, section 9, of the original Constitution prohibited Congress from enacting a direct tax (head tax) unless in proportion to population as indicated by a census. Congress in 1894 passed an income tax law, levying a 2 percent tax on incomes over $4,000. In 1895, the Supreme Court found that this income tax was a direct tax not apportioned among the states and was thus unconstitutional. This amendment gave Congress the power to enact an income tax without the revenues needing to be proportional among the states.

Amendment 17—Direct Election of Senators
[Ratified April 8, 1913]

The Senate of the United States shall be composed of two Senators from each State, elected by the people thereof, for six years and each Senator shall have one vote. The electors in each State shall have the qualifications requisite for electors of the most numerous branch of the State legislatures.

When vacancies happen in the representation of any State in the Senate, the executive authority of such State shall issue writs of election to fill such vacancies: Provided, That the legislature of any State may empower the executive thereof to make temporary appointment until the people fill the vacancies by election as the legislature may direct.

This amendment shall not be so construed as to affect the election or term of any Senator chosen before it becomes valid as part of the Constitution.

Prior to this amendment, U.S. senators were selected by state legislatures. Now U.S. senators would be selected by popular vote in each state. Further, the governor of each state may fill vacancies, subject to state laws.

Amendment 18—Prohibition
[Ratified January 16, 1919, Repealed December 5, 1933, by Amendment 21]

Section 1 After one year from the ratification of this article the manufacture, sale, or transportation of intoxicating liquors within, the importation thereof into, or the exportation thereof from the United States and all territory subject to the jurisdiction thereof for beverage purposes is hereby prohibited.

Section 2 The Congress and the several States shall have concurrent power to enforce this article by appropriate legislation.

Section 3 This article shall be inoperative unless it shall have been ratified as an amendment to the Constitution by the legislatures of the several States, as provided in the Constitution, within seven years from the date of the submission hereof to the States by the Congress.[13]

This amendment banned the manufacture, sale, or transportation of alcoholic beverages. The amendment was repealed 14 years later by the Twenty-first Amendment. The Eighteenth Amendment is the first for which Congress set a time limit for ratification.

---

[12]Changed by the Twenty-sixth Amendment.

[13]Repealed by the Twenty-first Amendment.

Amendment 19—Women's Suffrage
[Ratified August 18, 1920]

The right of the citizens of the United States to vote shall not be denied or abridged by the United States or by any State on account of sex.

Congress shall have power to enforce this article by appropriate legislation.

This amendment provides that the right for a citizen to vote cannot be denied on account of sex. Women in some states had the right to vote prior to 1920. This amendment applied that right nationwide.

Amendment 20—Ending Lame Duck Sessions
[Ratified January 23, 1933]

Section 1   The terms of the President and Vice President shall end at noon on the 20th day of January, and the terms of the Senators and Representatives at noon on the 3d day of January, of the years in which such terms would have ended if this article had not been ratified, and the terms of their successors shall then begin.

Section 2   The Congress shall assemble at least once in every year, and such meeting shall begin at noon on the 3d day of January, unless they shall by law appoint a different day.

Section 3   If, at the time fixed for the beginning of the term of the President, the President elect shall have died, the Vice President elect shall become President. If a President shall not have been chosen before the time fixed for the beginning of his term, or if the President elect shall have failed to qualify, then the Vice President elect shall act as President until a President shall have qualified, and the Congress may by law provide for the case wherein neither a President elect nor a Vice President elect shall have qualified, declaring who shall then act as President, or the manner in which one who is to act shall be selected, and such person shall act accordingly until a President or Vice President shall have qualified.

Section 4   The Congress may by law provide for the case of the death of any of the persons from whom the House of Representatives may choose a President whenever the right of choice shall have devolved upon them, and for the case of the death of any of the persons from whom the Senate may choose a Vice President whenever the right of choice shall have devolved upon them.

Section 5   Sections 1 and 2 shall take effect on the 15th day of October following the ratification of this article.

Section 6   This article shall be inoperative unless it shall have been ratified as an amendment to the Constitution by the legislatures of three-fourths of the several States within seven years from the date of its submission.

Prior to this amendment, the term of the new Congress and president did not begin until March of an odd-numbered year, which was four months following the November elections. And the actual congressional session often did not start until December of the odd-numbered year, another eight months after March. Thus, elected officials might not begin a legislative session until 13 months after their election, and "lame-duck" sessions of Congress ran from December of the even-numbered year through

March when the new term started. This amendment sets the dates for the end and beginning of presidential and legislative terms to end these lame-duck sessions, and requires the new Congress to assemble on January 3, just two months after the elections. The president's term begins a little over two weeks later, on January 20. The amendment also makes provisions for situations where the president-elect dies prior to taking office.

Amendment 21—Repeal of Prohibition
[Ratified December 5, 1933]

Section 1   The eighteenth article of amendment to the Constitution of the United States is hereby repealed.

Section 2   The transportation or importation into any State, Territory, or possession of the United States for delivery or use therein of intoxicating liquors, in violation of the laws thereof, is hereby prohibited.

Section 3   This article shall be inoperative unless it shall have been ratified as an amendment to the Constitution by conventions in the several States, as provided in the Constitution, within seven years from the date of the submission hereof to the States by the Congress.

This amendment nullified the Eighteenth Amendment. It ended federal Prohibition and placed regulation of liquor at the state level.

Amendment 22—Number of Presidential Terms
[Ratified February 27, 1951]

Section 1   No person shall be elected to the office of the President more than twice, and no person who has held the office of President, or acted as President, for more than two years of a term to which some other person was elected President shall be elected to the office of the President more than once. But this article shall not apply to any person holding the office of President when this article was proposed by the Congress, and shall not prevent any person who may be holding the office of President, or acting as President, during the term within which this article becomes operative from holding the office of President or acting as President during the remainder of such term.

Section 2   This article shall be inoperative unless it shall have been ratified as an amendment to the Constitution by the legislatures of three-fourths of the several states within seven years from the date of its submission to the states by the Congress.

Franklin D. Roosevelt won an unprecedented four terms as president. All previous presidents had adhered to a maximum of two terms in office, though the Constitution had no such requirement. This amendment limits presidents to two terms.

Amendment 23—Presidential Electors for the District of Columbia
[Ratified March 29, 1961]

Section 1   The District constituting the seat of government of the United States shall appoint in such manner as the Congress may direct:

A number of electors of President and Vice President equal to the whole number of Senators and Representatives in Congress to which the District would be entitled if it were a state, but in no event more than the least populous state, they shall be in addition to those appointed by the states, but they shall be considered for the purposes of the election of President and Vice President, to be electors appointed by a state, and they shall meet in the District and perform such duties as provided by the twelfth article of amendment.

Section 2 The Congress shall have power to enforce this article by appropriate legislation.

This amendment gave electoral votes in presidential elections to the citizens of Washington, D.C., which is not a state and thus not included in the original arrangement of state electoral votes. Currently, Washington, D.C., has three electoral votes, bringing the total of presidential electoral votes to 538. Each state has electoral votes equal in number to the sum of the state's members of Congress in the House and Senate.

Amendment 24—Elimination of the Poll Tax
[Ratified January 23, 1964]

Section 1 The right of citizens of the United States to vote in any primary or other election for President or Vice President, for electors for President or Vice President or for Senator or Representative in Congress, shall not be denied or abridged by the United States or any state by reason of failure to pay any poll tax or other tax.

Section 2 The Congress shall have power to enforce this article by appropriate legislation.

The poll tax was a procedure used mostly in southern states to discourage poor white and black voters from registering to vote. An individual would have to pay a tax to register to vote, and in some places one would have to pay the cumulative back taxes for elections in which the individual did not register. The tax was usually not much but might still be enough to deter a potential voter, especially if back taxes were involved. Literacy tests, another device to disqualify voters, were abolished by the Voting Rights Act of 1965.

Amendment 25—Presidential Disability, Vice Presidential Vacancies
[Ratified February 10, 1967]

Section 1 In case of the removal of the President from office or his death or resignation, the Vice President shall become President.

Section 2 Whenever there is a vacancy in the office of the Vice President, the President shall nominate a Vice President who shall take the office upon confirmation by a majority vote of both Houses of Congress.

Section 3 Whenever the President transmits to the President pro tempore of the Senate and the Speaker of the House of Representatives his written declaration that he is unable to discharge the powers and duties of his office, and until he transmits to them a written declaration to the contrary, such powers and duties shall be discharged by the Vice President as Acting President.

Section 4 Whenever the Vice President and a majority of either the principal officers of the executive departments or of such

other body as Congress may by law provide, transmit to the President pro tempore of the Senate and the Speaker of the House of Representatives their written declaration that the President is unable to discharge the powers and duties of his office, the Vice President shall immediately assume the powers and duties of the office as Acting President.

Thereafter, when the President transmits to the President pro tempore of the Senate and the Speaker of the House of Representatives his written declaration that no inability exists, he shall resume the powers and duties of his office unless the Vice President and a majority of either the principal officers of the executive departments, or of such other body as Congress may by law provide, transmit within four days to the President pro tempore of the Senate and the Speaker of the House of Representatives their written declaration that the President is unable to discharge the powers and duties of his office. Thereupon Congress shall decide the issue, assembling within forty-eight hours for that purpose if not in session. If the Congress, within twenty-one days after receipt of the latter written declaration, or, if Congress is not in session, within twenty-one days after Congress is required to assemble, determines by two-thirds vote of both Houses that the President is unable to discharge the powers and duties of his office, the Vice President shall continue to discharge the same as Acting President; otherwise the President shall resume the powers and duties of his office.

This amendment provides procedures for handling an incapacitating illness of a president. One path is that the president informs congressional leaders of incapacitation and the vice president takes over. On recovery, the president can so inform congressional leaders and resume office. A second path recognizes that the president may not be able or wish to indicate this debilitation, so the vice president and a majority of Cabinet members can inform congressional leaders. Again, the vice president would assume the presidency temporarily. On recovery, the president so informs congressional leadership and resumes the presidency, unless the vice president and a majority of the cabinet disagree. Then Congress must decide.

The most immediate importance of this amendment concerned the office of vice president. The original Constitution did not address the issue of a vacancy in this office. Six years after ratification, in 1973, the sitting vice president, Spiro Agnew, resigned his office. Under the provisions of this amendment, President Nixon nominated Gerald Ford as vice president. When Nixon resigned in 1974, Ford became president and he in turn nominated a new vice president, Nelson Rockefeller.

Amendment 26—Eighteen-Year-Old Vote
[Ratified July 1, 1971]

Section 1 The right of citizens of the United States, who are 18 years of age or older, to vote, shall not be denied or abridged by the United States or by any state on account of age.

Section 2 The Congress shall have power to enforce this article by appropriate legislation.

The Twenty-sixth Amendment prohibited denying citizens 18 years or older the right to vote because of their age.

Amendment 27—Congressional Salaries
[Ratified May 7, 1992]

No law varying the compensation for the services of the Senators and Representatives shall take effect until an election of Representatives shall be intervened.

This amendment was part of 12 amendments originally submitted by the first Congress to the states for ratification. The states in short order ratified 10 of the 12, which collectively became known as the Bill of Rights. Because Congress did not set a time limit for ratification, the other two amendments remained alive, though largely forgotten until the 1980s. By 1992, three-fourths of the states had ratified this amendment, thus adding it to the Constitution. The amendment delays any increase of compensation for at least one election cycle.

The State of Their Unions: Marriage as a Federalism Issue

Among the issues that gay and lesbian advocacy groups currently see as fundamental to equality, the most publicly prominent has been same-sex marriage. The issue is characteristic of many civil rights battles: the struggle between tradition and change; the appeals to American political culture and its embrace of equality; and strategic calculations about whether to seek change via legislatures or courts. Also characteristic is the way the issue raises debates about federalism and features political activity at the state and national levels. Same-sex marriage illustrates several causal questions at the heart of federalism. How is federal policy influenced by state policy, and how is state policy influenced by federal policy? Under what conditions are federal policy makers likely to intervene to impose uniform rules and regulations across the states, and when do they prefer to

▼ MARRIAGE AND FEDERALISM

The debate over same-sex marriage has occurred at the national and state levels. Protesters outside a federal courthouse in California in 2010 support overturning California's ban on same-sex marriage. The first federal challenge to state laws prohibiting gay marriage, the case could ultimately end up before the U.S. Supreme Court.

have states make their own choices? How do outcomes at the federal level or in one state affect political strategy and outcomes in others?

Marriage confers favorable treatment in a range of areas—inheritance, taxation, health care, child custody, immigration, property rights, hospital visitation, and Social Security survivor benefits. Over 1,000 federal laws include reference to marital status.

Typically, marriage has been a legal status determined by state law. The issue of same-sex marriage first entered national political conversation in the mid-1990s when it appeared the state of Hawaii might—though ultimately it did not—legalize this type of marriage. The 1996 Defense of Marriage Act (DOMA) signed by President Clinton was the federal response. This act stipulates that, for the purpose of federal programs and benefits, marriage consists of "the legal union between one man and one woman as husband and wife." As the Constitution allows, the law also creates an exemption to the usual requirement that states honor the official acts of other states, by specifying that they need not honor same-sex marriages that are legal in

another state. It is left up to the individual states to decide. Because of the heterosexual definition of marriage in DOMA, same-sex marriage is not recognized by federal programs like Social Security.

Because marriage has traditionally been a state-level issue, and because the chances for success have been greater in the states than at the federal level, gay and lesbian civil rights organizations have focused most of their attention on this issue in the states. In 2004, the Massachusetts Supreme Judicial Court was the first to decide that banning same-sex marriage violated the state constitution's guarantee of equal protection under the law. Supreme courts in Connecticut and Iowa reached the same decision in 2008 and 2009, respectively. Legislatively, in 2009 the District of Columbia city council and legislatures in Maine, New Hampshire, and Vermont approved same-sex marriage, but voters in Maine overturned the law later that year. California voters in November 2008 amended the state constitution to ban same-sex marriage, reversing a state Supreme Court ruling. Supporters of same-sex marriage filed a federal lawsuit arguing that California's ban on same-sex marriage violated the U.S. Constitution's guarantee of equal protection of the law.[1] A federal district court agreed and overturned the California ban. The decision was appealed and same-sex marriages were put on hold pending the outcome of that decision. The case may well end up in the U.S. Supreme Court. In sum, same-sex marriage is legal in six states, pending the result of the California case.

There have been other victories for the pro-same-sex-marriage forces. Colorado, Hawaii, Maine, Maryland, New Jersey, Oregon, Washington, and Wisconsin all have a form of "civil union" or "domestic partnership," either as a result of legislation or court decisions. The Washington law was upheld by voters in a 2009 referendum.

Unions or partnerships are a legal status that can provide some or nearly all of the benefits of marriage. Unlike marriage, however, civil unions and domestic partnerships have no meaning outside the state in which they were created; other states do not acknowledge them. Prior to their 2008 court rulings, California and Connecticut allowed these alternatives to marriage.

Although marriage is usually a state issue, the U.S. Supreme Court has upheld the federal government's authority to pass laws banning certain state-approved marriage arrangements, such as polygamy. It has also struck down some state marriage restrictions. In *Loving v. Virginia* (1967), the Court declared Virginia's ban on interracial marriage to be a violation of the U.S. Constitution's promise of equal protection of the laws. In the Court's view, the law had no purpose outside of "invidious racial discrimination." Gay and lesbian civil rights activists point to the ban on same-sex marriage as presenting precisely the same discriminatory issues as *Loving*. Opponents of same-sex marriage reject this parallel, saying the two situations are worlds apart—banning interracial marriage was purely discrimination, while banning same-sex marriage is about the basic definition of a social institution.[2]

Accordingly, these critics led a countermovement designed to stop the legal recognition of same-sex marriages. Part of the strategy has been passage of laws and constitutional amendments in the states to prohibit same-sex marriage. These efforts have been highly successful. Another part of the strategy was the proposal of an amendment to the U.S. Constitution to prohibit same-sex marriage. This effort has not been successful. The proposed Marriage Protection Amendment states that "Marriage in the United States shall consist only of the union of a man and a woman. Neither this Constitution, nor the constitution of any State, shall be construed to require that marriage or the legal incidents thereof be conferred upon any union other than the union of a man and a woman."

Gay and lesbian rights advocates argue against the idea of a constitutional amendment on substantive grounds and on federalism grounds. Substantively, they see same-sex marriage as a matter of civil rights and equality. Regarding federalism, they note that 41 states have laws and 30 have constitutional language prohibiting same-sex marriage. Therefore, they suggest, there is little need for a federal constitutional amendment. The main task for the gay and lesbian rights movement at the national level is avoiding an amendment to the U.S. Constitution. Like the supporters of such an amendment, they realize that once added, an amendment would be very difficult to dislodge.

Politically, the issue is delicate for both sides. Those opposed to same-sex marriage seem to have public opinion on their side, but public opinion is not necessarily supportive of a U.S. constitutional amendment or of prohibiting civil unions and domestic partnerships. The majority of the public also recoils from appeals that appear to be hostile to homosexuals.[3] Meanwhile, those who support same-sex marriage recognize they are working in an environment in which the public overall does not currently support same-sex marriage and votes against it when given the chance. This public mindset makes it hard to achieve gains on this issue through legislative means. A majority of Americans under age 30, however, support same-sex marriage, so legislative strategies may be more successful over time.[4] At the national level, although the Obama administration defended DOMA as constitutional in a 2009 suit in federal court, the president has indicated he believes it is bad policy and supports its repeal.

Same-sex marriage illuminates the principles and practices of federalism and the fault lines in American politics between different levels of government and among different institutions. It raises questions about where the responsibilities of the state governments end and the federal government begins. And it shows us how federalism has strong causal effects in American politics, with state actions leading to federal responses, federal actions leading to interest group recalculations of their best strategy to achieve their ends, and actions by governments and activists in one state prompted by developments in other states.[5]

This chapter explores these principles and practices of federalism and the politics surrounding them.

CHAPTER LEARNING OBJECTIVES

After reading this chapter you will be able to:

4-1 Show how the Constitution serves as a framework for federalism and why debates remain.

4-2 Outline the principles of dual federalism and their basis in the Supreme Court's traditional understanding of interstate commerce.

4-3 Trace the evolution from dual to cooperative federalism and identify methods of cooperative federalism.

4-4 Assess the extent and nature of changes in federalism over the past two decades.

The Nature of the Union

4-1 Show how the Constitution serves as a framework for federalism and why debates remain.

When the Constitution was written and sent to the states for ratification, the debate between Federalists and Anti-Federalists was not only about liberty. As the names of the two sides suggest, it was also about federalism. And it was about the interaction of liberty and federalism.

This clash between Federalists and Anti-Federalists was about ideas, but it was also an intensely political battle. Both groups had views about public policy, and they realized some arrangements of national and state power would be more likely to advance these policies than would others. This clash started a long trend of federalism being a political battleground where politicians, judges, and activist groups jostle to advance their positions. Politicians frequently evoke federalism to justify particular policies or to argue against their opponents. Those arguments can be inconsistent, arguing for more national control in one area and more state control in another. Philosophy about federalism and the Constitution can drive the actions of politicians, but politicians can also be federalism opportunists, willing to support strengthening Washington or strengthening the states depending on how the issue suits their own policy preferences, ideology, or reelection prospects. Federal judges also can be influenced by ideology or by particular outcomes they wish to see. Federalism is not a settled topic of constitutional doctrine—it is a matter of intense debate that brings together philosophy, power, politics, and policy.

Confederal and unitary arrangements are two ways to organize power between national and subnational governments.

What was the appropriate relationship between the state governments and the national government? The question was important not in the dry sense of deciding who should do what. Individuals on the two sides of the debate believed it was

▼ **PRESIDENT OBAMA ADDRESSING THE NATIONAL GOVERNORS ASSOCIATION, FEBRUARY 2009**

The nation's governors meet annually to share ideas on education, transportation, budgets, and other issues they share in common. They also discuss the appropriate relationship between the national and state levels of government. Governors welcome federal assistance but worry about too much federal control of their activities.

important mainly because it had significant implications for liberty, a key element of American political culture embodied in the proposed new government. To the Anti-Federalists, a system with a powerful, remote national government was likely to lead to the erosion of individual liberty. State governments could be better monitored and controlled by the people and, thus, were less a danger to liberty. Anti-Federalists therefore preferred a **confederation**. In this type of government, independent entities—states, in the American case—join together to pursue some common purposes. The joint government in a confederation tends to have very limited authority over the individual member governments, and that authority must usually be explicitly granted by the members—the joint government does not itself have ongoing powers independent of the members. As in the case of the Articles of Confederation, citizens in a confederation often do not directly elect representatives to the confederation. Rather, representatives or delegates are selected by the individual member governments. Under the Articles, for example, state governments selected their representatives in the national Congress.

Governing a confederation can be a challenge. Under the Articles of Confederation, American government was similar to the structure we see today in the United Nations (UN). UN decisions can be difficult to enforce because they depend on countries to comply voluntarily. Resources can be hard to come by because members can choose to withhold their contribution to the organization. Member countries are frequently in competition, trying to best or disadvantage each other, especially economically. Most countries have strong norms of independence, and ambitious politicians might rail against outsiders dictating their country's policies. As detailed in Chapter 3, these governing difficulties were paralleled in the United States under the Articles of Confederation. Nonetheless, the Anti-Federalists were so concerned with the risks of a powerful central government that they considered a confederal arrangement to be a better choice.

Many Federalists agreed with the Anti-Federalists that the states should have an important role, but they argued that a strong national government could help protect liberty by preventing control by factions, as James Madison explained in *Federalist 10* (see Chapter 3). Other Federalists, such as Alexander Hamilton, took a much more aggressive view and desired the formation of a strong central government that would be very active in the economy and build a powerful military to rival those in Europe.

The Framers did not share the Anti-Federalists' enthusiasm for a confederal arrangement that made the national government dependent on the states, but neither did they construct a **unitary system** that would make the states dependent on the national government. In a unitary system, lower levels of government are subordinate to the national government and have little, if any, independent governing authority. The upper level government is free to create, combine, or disband lower level governments. Lower levels of government typically have limited ability to raise funds on their own. In the United States, the District of Columbia is an example of this type of arrangement. Washington, D.C. has its own city government, but that government's independent authority is limited by Congress, which controls the city budget and can revoke laws passed by the city government. Although there have been movements and proposed constitutional amendments to give the District a representative in the U.S. House and two senators, as the states have, these attempts have so far been unsuccessful.

State governments are essentially unitary systems with respect to local municipalities. Typically they allow substantial independence to the localities within their borders, but this arrangement is at the convenience of the state government. The Constitution makes no mention of cities and counties or other substate governments, nor does it guarantee their existence: their creation is up to the states.

Around the world, the unitary system of government is the norm. France, Great Britain, The Netherlands, Japan, and Italy are unitary systems, and South America

confederation a loose grouping of independent political units, such as states or countries, whose main purpose is to govern the relationship between those units.

ThinkingComparatively

Governing a confederation, as the United Nations shows, presents multiple challenges.

unitary system a form of government in which government at the highest level has the power to create, combine, or disband lower-level governments and determine what powers will be allowed at the lower levels.

ThinkingComparatively 🌐 ●●●

Unitary systems, the norm around the world, are harder to establish in places where a functioning set of lower-level governments already exists, as in the United States.

and Africa are dominated by unitary systems as well. The amount of independence granted to lower-level governments is determined by the national government. In some cases, national governments have granted increasing authority to their sub-national governments. Regions in Italy, for example, have governing units that have been given increasing freedoms since the establishment of the 1948 constitution. And over the past decade, the United Kingdom has allowed more autonomy for Scotland and Wales, including the establishment of their own parliaments. In the United States, by contrast, a functioning set of state governments already existed when the Constitution was being debated. Their existence made a move to a unitary form of government difficult.

The Constitution provides the framework for intergovernmental relations through federalism.

The Framers steered a middle course between a confederation and a unitary government. They were not unanimous in their vision. Some would have favored a unitary system, with power centralized at the national level. Some preferred a confederal arrangement, in which the states were supreme. Some preferred federalism, in which the national and state governments shared power. Federalism was a middle-ground position between the unitary and confederal extremes (Figure 4-1).

Confederal

Subnational governments create the national government and grant it some limited areas of responsibility. The national government relies on the subnational governments for funding and to implement decisions made by the national government. The national government typically lacks enforcement mechanisms and relies on the voluntary compliance of the subnational governments. Sovereign power (the ultimate decision maker) is at the subnational level.

Federal

Both the national government and the subnational governments have areas in which they hold primary sovereign power and have their own sources of funds and ability to implement policies. They have some areas of shared authority and may compete for control. The existence of the subnational governments is guaranteed. Sovereign power exists at both levels.

Unitary

The national government creates the subnational governments. It may grant governing authority to the subnational governments in certain policy areas, but this authority is not independent or guaranteed—it can be eliminated by the national government, as can the subnational governments themselves. Sovereign power is at the national level.

FIGURE 4-1. **Flow of Power in Three Systems of Government.** The confederal, federal, and unitary systems of government provide alternative distributions of political power. The confederal system places sovereignty in the subnational governments while the unitary system places it in the national government. The federal system is blended, with sovereignty at both the national and subnational levels.

Federalism is a system that distributes political power across a national government and subnational governments. In the United States, these subnational governments are the states. Federalism ensures that the subnational units can make some final decisions and have their existence protected. In addition to the United States, other federal systems include Austria, Australia, Brazil, Canada, Germany, India, Mexico, and Tanzania.

The Constitution distributed power and decision-making between the national government and the states. According to the *supremacy clause*, when the two are in conflict, national laws overrule state laws. And powers delegated to the national government are not available to the states. On the other hand, the Tenth Amendment provides that powers not delegated to the national government by the Constitution, and not prohibited for state governments, are reserved for the states or for the people—the **reserved powers**. States also are guaranteed equal voting rights in the U.S. Senate, protection against domestic insurrection and foreign invasion, and the preservation of a representative form of government. Existing states, via their representation in the U.S. Congress, have a role in the admission of new states, and existing states cannot have any of their territory shifted to a new state without their consent.

The Constitution also mandates fair play between the states with three crucial provisions that are intended to prevent states from discriminating against one another or cutting special deals that would aggravate relations with other states or potentially other countries. The *full faith and credit clause* requires states to honor the official acts of other states, such as public records and the results of judicial proceedings. The *equal privileges and immunities clause* requires states to treat similarly their citizens and citizens of other states. And the *commerce clause* places the regulation of interstate commerce and foreign economic trade in the federal government, not the individual states. The evolution of interstate commerce has played a key role in the evolution of federalism and so is discussed at length later in this chapter.

Federalism and the "federal system" refer to the arrangement of power distributed across the national and state levels. As a practical matter, however, in the United States the term "federal government" refers to the government created by the U.S. Constitution and ratified by the states. This term is used interchangeably with "national government." In common usage, references to the federal government or to the national government both mean the government created by the Constitution and based in Washington, D.C.

The appropriate balance of national and state power creates significant debate.

Ratification of the Constitution did not end disputes over the nature of the new system. From the start, the question of precisely how much control the national government had over the states was a matter of contention. Sovereignty was a key point of difference. **Sovereignty** refers to a government's having the ultimate authority to make decisions about what happens within its borders, free from interference by other governments. Advocates of a limited national role preferred a **compact theory** of federalism, which suggested the states were sovereign entities that joined together. As discussed in Chapter 3, "the United States are" would be an appealing phrase for this group. The Constitution was an instrument for these sovereign states to coordinate and pursue their interests. The states gave up some limited and specific powers, but they retained their sovereignty. The national government could make no other demands on state governments beyond those in the Constitution, nor could it intrude into relations between these sovereign states and their citizens. Except in ways that they explicitly consented to, the states were to be left alone. Although individuals supporting the compact

federalism a form of government that distributes power across a national government and subnational governments and ensures the existence of the subnational governments.

reserved powers Tenth Amendment guarantee to state governments of any powers other than those granted to the national government or those specifically prohibited for the states.

sovereignty having the ultimate authority to make decisions within one's borders, without interference by other governments.

compact theory a theory of the founding of the American government that argues states were sovereign units that joined together in the new national government but did not give up their status as sovereign, independent governments.

theory did not agree on all the details, the idea that the states were sovereign was a powerful idea held by important figures such as Thomas Jefferson.

This approach to understanding federalism was particularly prominent in the South, where it led to the doctrine of **nullification**—the idea that states could nullify national government laws with which they disagreed and which they believed violated the letter or spirit of the U.S. Constitution. Identified most strongly with Vice President John Calhoun of South Carolina (1825–1832), nullification was frequently and controversially employed in the decades prior to the Civil War, especially with regard to the slavery issue, but it had been present in political circles long before that.[6]

In later years, the compact theory would sometimes be referred to as the "states' rights" position. This became a controversial term in the 1950s and 1960s when it was most commonly invoked to thwart the push of the national government to end racial segregation, particularly in southern states. The compact view of federalism, however, should not be seen as limited to issues concerning civil rights, nor does it inherently advocate a limited, minimalist government. State governments could be quite active within the compact framework. The key concern for the politicians advocating it was less about the reach of government authority in the abstract than it was that decisions made by government be made by that government closest to home, over which they had more influence.

The **nationalist theory**, more prominent in northern states, provided an alternative to the compact theory. Nationalists would be more comfortable with "the United States is" rather than "are." This approach stressed that the Constitution was intended to be a departure from the limited government of the Articles of Confederation. The Constitution represented "the people," not the states, coming together. The preamble to the Constitution could have begun "We the people of the states," an option the delegates considered, but it did not. The very language "We the people," according to the nationalist view, indicates that the Constitution's purpose is to provide the institutions and rules by which a nation of people, rather than a collection of states, can be governed. This does not mean abusing the states or ignoring their independence, but it does mean that national

nullification the theory that states have the right to nullify national laws to which they object and believe violate the U.S. Constitution.

nationalist theory a theory of the founding of the American government that sees the Constitution more as the joining together of the people than the joining together of the states.

▶ **POLICE OFFICER CHECKS DRIVER'S LICENSE**
Should states and cities be responsible for enforcing federal immigration laws? Some states and cities have bristled at the idea. It is illegal under federal law for states and cities to adopt formal sanctuary policies, but many nonetheless prohibit their employees from asking about immigration status or contacting federal officials if they discover someone is not in the United States legally. In 2010, however, Arizona passed a controversial law that supporters said enhanced the enforcement of existing federal immigration law, while opponents said the law made arbitrary harassment of Hispanics more likely.

needs override states' wishes. At times, states will have to accept national direction and demands, regardless of their approval or disapproval of those demands, especially if the national action can be portrayed as promoting the general well-being of the country. Like advocates for the compact view, politicians stating a nationalist vision also had an assessment of where they were likely to be most successful in pushing their policy agenda. In the case of nationalists, they saw their influence likely to be stronger at the national level than in the many state capitals.

Strongly identified with this view is Alexander Hamilton, secretary of the Treasury under President Washington. Among executive branch officials in the early years of the republic, Hamilton had the most expansive vision for national government power, especially with regard to establishing the national government as the clear leader in economic matters. He proposed that the national government establish a bank and that it invest heavily in building the roads, canals, and other infrastructure that would help unite the new country and advance economic development.

Given the unhappy experience of centralized British power during the colonial era, how could Hamilton go about creating the political coalition to support such a plan? His answer was to mastermind a deal in which the federal government assumed all the debt that state governments had incurred in fighting the Revolutionary War. To Hamilton, this plan would link wealthy individuals and institutions in financial arrangements with the national government rather than with the states, and the stability, power, and authority of the national government would become critical in their eyes. To many who subscribed to the compact theory, however, Hamilton's nationalist vision veered toward monarchy.

Across the course of American politics, debate has flourished concerning the appropriate balance of power between the national and state governments. And the debate matters in very concrete ways. Issues as diverse as slavery, punishment for violence against women, regulation of business, environmental protection, minimum wages, end-of-life decisions, and enforcement of anti-discrimination statutes, among many others, are influenced heavily by interpretations of federalism. People who care about these issues need to care about federalism, because in the American political system prevailing interpretations of federalism will strongly shape what, if anything, government can or should do about these matters, and which level of government should do it. In the case of national health care reform, a major debating point was whether the national government had the constitutional authority to do what the president and his allies in Congress were proposing. This was a battle over the meaning of the Constitution, but it was also a practical political battle. To achieve his policy goals and satisfy his supporters who wanted to see some version of health care reform pass, President Obama argued for pulling major aspects of health policy away from the states and setting national rules and requirements. He ultimately settled for less of a national role than he or many of his supporters originally desired.[7] To achieve their policy objectives and satisfy their supporters, opponents of his plan argued for maintaining state control and enhancing consumer choice. Some of their favored proposals, like allowing consumers to purchase insurance across state lines, would have required a convergence of insurance regulations across the states to work effectively.[8]

Federalism has evolved over time and is still in flux. Dual federalism would give way to cooperative federalism. Over time, cooperative federalism would develop different variants. Today's federalism features a mix of cooperative federalism and renewed elements of dual federalism.

Dual Federalism

4-2 Outline the principles of dual federalism and their basis in the Supreme Court's traditional understanding of interstate commerce.

dual federalism a form of federalism in which the national and state governments have distinct areas of authority and power, and individuals have rights as both citizens of states and citizens of the United States.

Distinct lines separating the national and state governments are the hallmark of the system of **dual federalism**, which dominated American politics through the mid-1930s. This model of federalism embraces the ideas of dual sovereignty and dual citizenship. Sovereignty refers to a final say—the sovereign power is the one who speaks last and most authoritatively. In dual federalism, the national government is sovereign in some areas and the state governments are sovereign in others. Described sometimes as "layer-cake federalism," with one layer representing national government responsibilities and the other representing state government responsibilities, the essence of dual federalism is the idea of a constitutional division of labor between the national and state governments.

Dual sovereignty provides separate areas of authority for the national and state governments.

dual sovereignty the idea that both the national and state governments have sovereignty, but over different policy areas and functions.

In dual federalism, the two levels of government have separate functions and areas of authority. They are both dominant over their respective areas of concern in this system of **dual sovereignty**. Each has policy responsibilities in which it has the final say, the defining aspect of sovereignty. In the nineteenth century, the federal government had control over setting tariffs on foreign goods, granting patents and copyright protection, managing the country's currency, establishing agreements with other countries, and providing defense and postal services. Some concurrent powers were shared by the two levels of government: both could collect taxes; establish courts; create roads and other internal improvements, such as canals and opening public lands to development; and borrow and spend money. States in the nineteenth century were concerned with pretty much everything else: banking and insurance law; family and morals regulation; public health; education; criminal law; construction codes; water use; health, safety, and environmental regulations, and so on. For ambitious politicians, a career in state politics might well have been more satisfying than a career in national politics, simply because of the broader range of activity afforded to state governments. Collectively, this list of duties is often referred to as the **police power**

police power the protection of public safety, health, welfare, and morality by a government.

reserved to state governments by the Tenth Amendment—protection of public safety, health, welfare, and morality. This power was thought to be closer to the people if centered at the state level.

Observers have often noted that state constitutions are longer than the U.S Constitution. On average, they have more than three times as many words. The federal Constitution falls short of 9,000 words; several state constitutions exceed 90,000. Why are state constitutions longer? It is not due to the age of the constitutions: only Massachusetts and New Hampshire have constitutions older than the U.S. Constitution.[9] And 37 of the 50 states did not even exist when the U.S. Constitution was ratified. Instead, the reserved powers, plus the idea that the states are closer to the people than is the national government, help explain why state constitutions are longer. First, the list of state areas of responsibility, which includes any duties not granted to the national government or specifically prohibited for states, is extensive. Second, there are about four dozen references to the states in the U.S. Constitution, and many of these are shorthand for areas that state constitutions would need to fill out in detail. For example, the U.S. Constitution as originally passed provided little guidance on who was qualified to vote—the state constitutions had to fill in this

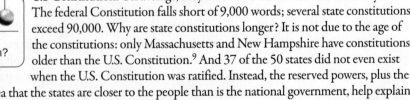

ThinkingCausally

Why are state constitutions typically much longer than the U.S. Constitution?

gap. The U.S. Constitution could be shorter because the state constitutions would contain the longer detail. And, third, because state governments were seen as closer to the people, their constitutions are easier to amend than is the federal constitution. Much of the length of state constitutions is due to the amendments, which often number in the hundreds. These amendments, unlike the "rules of the game" amendments that are typical at the national level, often contain a significant amount of policy detail and prescriptions. If the amending process is not inordinately difficult, then legislators have an incentive to put policy provisions into constitutions, as they will still be harder for future legislators to change than a law would be.[10]

Citizens of the United States are also citizens of a state.

If you are a U.S. citizen, you are also a citizen of a state.[11] Under dual federalism, this is known as **dual citizenship**. As a citizen of the United States, you have the same rights as other citizens of the United States. As a citizen of your state, you will have rights and responsibilities that may be different from citizens of another state. For example, in many states, citizens have a constitutional guarantee of what may be referred to alternatively as a "uniform" or "equal" or "suitable" education system. This language has led to lawsuits charging that students have a right to equal education funding across districts. In seven states, your right to hunt or fish is constitutionally protected; more than a dozen others are considering similar amendments. The ability to purchase alcohol legally, to be married, to drive a car, and so on, varies from state to state. Responsibilities regarding jury duty, an obligation to help strangers, the process by which life support can be terminated, or who is legally allowed to marry also vary across the states.

dual citizenship the idea that an individual is a citizen of both his or her state and the United States. Rights and responsibilities can vary from state to state and can be different on the state and national levels.

▼ **MIXING OIL AND WATER**
Due to the 2010 oil spill in the Gulf of Mexico, authorities in Escambia County, Florida, issued a health advisory for beach visitors, This action is an example of the "police power" reserved for states under the Constitution. Construction standards and zoning laws are other examples of areas left to the states under their police power.

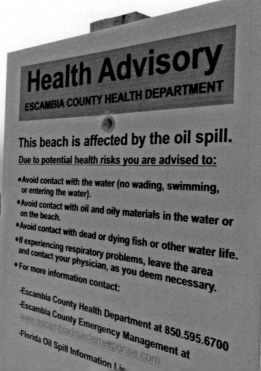

The case of *Barron v. Baltimore* (1833) illustrates the principle of dual citizenship under dual federalism. John Barron operated a commercial wharf in Baltimore. During construction projects, the city began dumping dirt and fill in the harbor. With ships facing great difficulty navigating in or out of the area near Barron's wharf, his business collapsed. Barron sued the city, arguing that the Fifth Amendment to the U.S. Constitution guarantees that citizens will be compensated when government takes their property for public purposes (known as the *takings clause*). Barron won his case, but the city appealed and won in the Maryland appeals court. Barron appealed that decision to the U.S. Supreme Court. The Court agreed that Barron was injured by Baltimore but said he was not entitled to any compensation. In the Court's view, the Fifth Amendment—indeed, the Bill of Rights as a whole—applied only to Barron as a citizen of the United States, not as a citizen of Maryland. In this case, Barron was not injured by the U.S. government—he was injured by a state government. If Maryland's constitution had a "takings" clause, then Barron would have recourse through the state's courts.

What would cause the Court to reach this conclusion? The distinction between Barron's rights as a state citizen and as a national citizen may seem odd, but it is consistent with the forces that led to the Bill of Rights. Recall that the Federalists agreed to add a Bill of Rights to respond to the charge that the Constitution did not sufficiently protect the people from the national government. Anti-Federalist agitation for the Bill of Rights was based not on the premise that the people needed to be protected from state governments—the Anti-Federalists surely would have said that citizens worried about state government power should work through the state legislature to rectify their concern—but on the premise that the national government needed to be constrained. Had it been the U.S. government rather than a state government that had taken Barron's property, he would have had a valid claim as a citizen of the United States.

For reasons discussed in Chapter 5 (Civil Liberties), the Supreme Court would decide Barron's case differently today. Nonetheless, the concept of dual citizenship remains an important part of American federalism.

▼ YOUR HOUSE OR OUR HOUSE?

A divided U.S. Supreme Court in 2005 ruled that the city of New London, Connecticut, could constitutionally justify as a "public use" the taking and transfer of property from one private party to another for the purpose of economic development. Susette Kelo's refusal to sell her house in the city's Fort Trumbull area led to the lawsuit. In response to the decision, many states passed laws revising the eminent domain laws within their borders to prohibit such transfers of property. Should government be able to take property, with compensation, in order to make the land available to another private entity who promises substantial economic benefits for the community?

Interpretation of the commerce clause affects national government power.

Interstate commerce has been a central political and legal battleground on which the meaning of federalism has been fought. Consistent with dual federalism, the Constitution marks out the regulation of interstate commerce as within the realm of federal government authority. The Constitution's **commerce clause**, in Article 1, section 8, gave Congress the power to "regulate commerce with foreign nations, and among the several states, and with the Indian tribes." Intrastate commerce was, implicitly, under the jurisdiction of the states.

Regarding interstate commerce, the Supreme Court confirmed the national government's primacy in this policy area in its decision in *Gibbons v. Ogden* (1824). The state of New York granted exclusive rights to two individuals to operate steamboats on the state's waters. This policy created problems because the water flowed into and from other states—New York required boats entering from another state to obtain a permit to navigate on New York waters. A steamboat owner whose business required him to travel between New Jersey and New York challenged this law. In its decision, the Court concluded that, because of the Constitution's supremacy clause, New York's licensing requirement was overridden by a federal law that regulated coastal trade. Chief Justice John Marshall's opinion made it clear that, in addition to the buying and selling of goods and services, commerce included navigation on interstate waterways, and thus was an arena solely for federal government regulation.

Gibbons v. Ogden was a judicial victory for national commercial authority over the states. The Sherman Anti-Trust Act of 1890 was a legislative victory. The law was a response to the growth of huge corporations that monopolized sales in their particular industries. For many Americans, the sheer size of these corporations brought into question the promises of equality and democracy in the American creed, particularly because corporations were treated as "persons" as far as law was concerned. For others, these corporations were seen as a threat to property rights as embodied in the creed. As monopolies or nearly so, they could price their products excessively high to gain extra profit, or they could price excessively low to drive out any remaining competitors. In response, the antitrust act prohibited contracts, mergers, or conspiracy that restrained trade or commerce between states or with other countries.

Subsequent Court decisions refined and limited the federal government's control over interstate commerce. By 1892, the E. C. Knight Company, through stock purchases of other sugar refining companies, controlled about 98 percent of the sugar-refining business in the United States. In a blow to the federal government's regulation over interstate commerce, however, the Supreme Court ruled in 1895 that "commerce" did not include manufacturing and that the Sherman Act only applied to commerce, the actual sale and moving of goods across state lines, not to monopolies in manufacturing.[12] To the Court, manufacturing was a local activity that preceded commerce, regardless of the fact that E. C. Knight controlled firms in more than one state. Although the Court recognized that monopoly over manufacturing might be linked to restraint of commerce, it sought to keep the two separate in the interests of dual federalist principles. States, but not the federal government, could regulate manufacturing; the federal government, but not the states, could regulate commerce.[13]

The Court's interpretation of interstate commerce was reiterated in other controversial cases. For example, the Keating-Owen Child Labor Act prohibited the interstate shipment of goods produced by child labor.[14] A father challenged the law on

commerce clause a provision in the U.S. Constitution that gives Congress the power to regulate commerce with other countries, among the states, and with Indian tribes.

▲ **YOU ARE WHAT YOU EAT**

As part of its authority to regulate commerce, the national government has the authority to require health and safety labeling on food and other products. The information on the label and its formatting are determined by the Food and Drug Administration.

cooperative federalism a form of federalism in which the national and state governments share many functions and areas of authority.

behalf of his two sons, one younger than 14 and one younger than 16. Both children worked in a cotton mill in Charlotte, North Carolina. The Court ruled that the law was unconstitutional because the regulation of manufacturing, which was not part of commerce, was reserved to the states by the Tenth Amendment.[15] If states wanted to limit child labor, they could, but the federal government could not use its commerce powers to do so.

Although this judicial definition of interstate commerce placed limits on what the federal government could do, it did not leave that government powerless. In the early twentieth century the government expanded its reach into economic matters. The Pure Food and Drug Act of 1906 gave the federal government the regulatory authority to monitor food and drug safety and, in particular, to ensure that labeling of these products was accurate. Regulating misleading information was acceptable because such information could affect commercial transactions. The agency responsible for these tasks was later named the Food and Drug Administration. Prior to the 1906 law, most regulation of this type had been at the state level. The Federal Trade Commission (FTC) is another example of increased federal power under the traditional definition of commerce. Created in 1914 in the Federal Trade Commission Act, the FTC monitors false and deceptive advertising as well as corporate mergers with implications for commerce.

Cooperative Federalism

4-3 Trace the evolution from dual to cooperative federalism and identify methods of cooperative federalism.

Dual federalism's sharp line of separation between national and state responsibilities was blurred by **cooperative federalism**, which rose to prominence beginning in the 1930s. In this form of federalism, still prominent today, the national and state governments share many functions and areas of authority. For political activists frustrated by their inability to pursue their policy goals due to the Court's dual federalist orientation, this new form of federalism provided some hope. Cooperative federalism diminished the notion of separate spheres of state and national authority that was embodied in dual federalism. Accordingly, rather than a layer cake, cooperative federalism has been described as "marble-cake federalism," with the swirls of vanilla and chocolate in a marble cake representing the intersecting areas of state and federal involvement, rather than strict demarcation between the two levels of government. For the liberal reformers of the 1910s and especially the 1930s, this new way of thinking about federalism opened the doors to policy successes that were impossible as long as dual federalism held sway.

Many of the new social programs adopted by the national government during the 1930s, including welfare, unemployment insurance, and jobs programs, were jointly financed and administered by the national and state governments. This is a puzzle. Why would power-seeking national politicians, particularly Democrats who had just swept into office with huge majorities, place partial control of these programs at the state level? Why not centralize all the control in Washington, D.C.? Political scientists have suggested that the national-state blend was often done for practical political reasons rather than for reasons of grand philosophy. The national government in the early 1930s

ThinkingCausally

Why would power-seeking national politicians share control of important government programs with politicians at the state level, rather than centralizing all control in Washington?

was small. The New Deal, as the collection of new programs in the 1930s was known, called for a significant expansion of the role of the national government in American life. Instantly expanding federal agencies would be difficult—state agencies could be helpful in launching programs. And although the misery of the Great Depression pushed even state politicians toward supporting this new federal role, state officials were sure to be reluctant to give up power. So a joint program might have been necessary in some instances to ensure passage through Congress.

Often, the support of state officials hinged on whether they would have a piece of the action in administering the new program. If benefits were to be distributed to their constituents, they wanted some say in the matter and some of the political credit. In other cases, if a program seemed likely to have significant and possibly disruptive social and economic effects, state officials would want to have some flexibility in managing the program. For example, the new national minimum wage law was crafted in a way to omit agricultural workers, meaning that a large proportion of blacks in southern states fell outside the protection of the national minimum wage law.[16] This design was motivated by southern political leaders' dual goals of holding down costs in agriculture and maintaining racial order. For northern politicians, this was the price they had to pay to pass a national minimum wage law. They also recognized that southern support for a range of other New Deal policies might hinge on the negotiations over the minimum wage.

Since the 1930s, minimum wage policy has been consistently cooperative. The national government sets minimum wage standards that states have to meet. States, however, are free to exceed those wages if they so choose and may establish minimum wages for workers not covered under federal law. Figure 4-2 shows how states vary on the minimum wage. Where the map indicates the state level is lower, the federal rate prevails except for workers who are not covered by the federal minimum wage law—the state minimum wage for those workers is less than the standard federal minimum wage.[17]

The practice in minimum wage is similar to that in other contentious policy areas, such as welfare. Prior to 1996, the national government had specific programs designed to address the needs of poor families with children. The states, however, had substantial leeway in administering these programs, most notably in the benefit levels. After the passage of welfare reform legislation in 1996, state-by-state variation became even more pronounced. National law set a few guidelines for states to work within—most importantly, there were national limits on the number of years an individual could receive welfare benefits, and state programs needed to focus on moving recipients from welfare to work—but the programs themselves were entirely the creation of the states. Before 1996, states administered one national program but in 50 different ways; now states are administering 50 different state programs within broad national guidelines. Each of these two approaches is an example of cooperative federalism.

In practice, cooperative federalism has sometimes been referred to as "picket-fence federalism," but this imagery seems outdated today as a depiction of policies and problems in the American federal system. The idea is that each horizontal band of the fence represents a level of government: federal, state, and local. Each vertical picket represents a separate policy area, such as transportation, health care, or education. The main implication of the picket-fence metaphor is that within each level of government, officials may be relatively unaware of the practices and needs of officials in the other areas. For example, transportation officials in the federal government might have much closer connections with state and local transportation officials (the other officials up and down the vertical picket) than they do with federal officials in energy or housing or environmental affairs, even though the issues concerning these areas overlap in important ways. However accurate this description might once have been, policy makers at all levels today are aware of the cross-cutting nature of issues. The food stamp program and free school lunch programs, for example, link

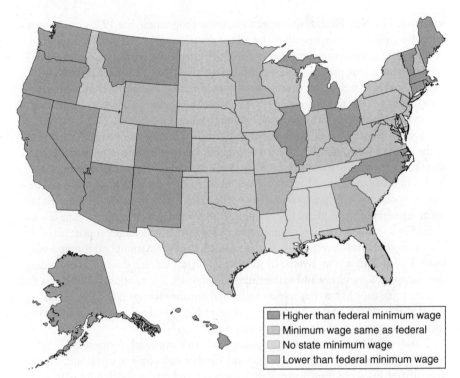

Higher than federal minimum wage
Minimum wage same as federal
No state minimum wage
Lower than federal minimum wage

FIGURE 4.2. **Differences in State Minimum Wages, 2011.** State minimum wages can match or exceed the federal wage. For work categories not covered by the federal law, states may set a minimum wage below the wage assigned for categories that are federally covered, or can go without a minimum wage. Until the federal minimum wage was increased to $7.25 in 2009, many more states exceeded the federal wage than is true today.

officials concerned with agriculture, K–12 education, and welfare. Energy policies connect the environment, foreign policy, and economic development. Instead of a picket fence, today's image might be a chain-link fence, where connections between officials and issues are multiple.

Implied powers increased the scope of permissible federal government activity.

Changes in constitutional interpretation were necessary to facilitate the evolution from dual federalism to cooperative federalism. One important step happened early in American history, in the case of *McCulloch v. Maryland* (1819). The Supreme Court's decision in this case expanded Congress's ability to interlope on policy areas previously considered to be the responsibility of the states. The case involved the Second Bank of the United States. The bank, chartered by Congress, had a branch in Baltimore, Maryland. Traditionally, states had chartered banks, so this new national role was eyed warily by the states. In response, Maryland taxed the bank. The U.S. government challenged this tax and filed suit against Maryland in the Supreme Court.

The Court had to resolve two questions. Could Congress charter a national bank? The Court's answer was yes. Its justification was twofold. First, Chief Justice John Marshall, the author of the Court's decision, argued against the compact theory of the

Constitution in favor of the nationalist theory. Maryland presented the argument that the states had created the federal government and owed no deference to it in banking. Marshall responded that it was not the states, but the people, who had formed the national government, and the national government therefore did not require the consent of the states to carry out its powers, nor was it subordinate to the states.

Second, the Court pointed to the **necessary and proper clause**, sometimes referred to as the *elastic clause*. Article 1, section 8, of the Constitution gives Congress the authority "to make all laws which shall be necessary and proper for carrying into execution the foregoing powers, and all other powers vested by this Constitution in the Government of the United States, or in any Department or Officer thereof." The "foregoing powers" refers to a list of duties prescribed in Article 1 as the responsibilities of Congress. These listed duties, specifically mentioned in the Constitution, are known as Congress's **enumerated powers**.

What the Court said in *McCulloch* is that the necessary and proper clause gave Congress **implied powers**, meaning it could make laws needed to carry out its enumerated powers. It was reasonable, in the Court's view, for a Congress given the power to pay debts, borrow money, regulate commerce, and coin money, to create a bank to facilitate the performance of these duties. The creation of the bank was an implied power that resulted from Congress's need to carry out its enumerated powers.

Having answered the first question by ruling that the bank was constitutional, the Court now had to answer the second question—whether Maryland could tax the bank. The Court's answer was no. The power to tax, the Court famously stated, is the power to destroy. Under a federal system, a single state government has no right to destroy an entity of the national government. Maryland could not force the national government out of banking by onerous taxation.

▲ **HARD TIMES IN MICHIGAN**

Hoping for better times, unemployed workers line up in the early morning cold. Financing and administering unemployment compensation has been a joint federal and state effort since 1935. States are allowed flexibility in eligibility requirements and benefits.

necessary and proper clause a provision in the U.S. Constitution that gives Congress the authority to make the laws needed to carry out the specific duties assigned to Congress by the Constitution.

enumerated powers the specifically listed duties that the U.S. Constitution assigns to Congress.

implied powers functions and actions that Congress could perform in order to implement and exercise its enumerated powers.

► **WORKPLACE SAFETY**
The Supreme Court's 1937 *Jones & Laughlin* decision opened the door to federal regulation of workplace safety. The Mine Safety Health Administration conducts inspections to make sure mines are in compliance with health and safety standards. Here, Massey Energy and MSHA officials confer in West Virginia following a mine explosion that killed over two dozen miners in 2010.

The *McCulloch* decision opened the door for Congress to expand the reach of the national government and chip away some of the wall separating state and national government functions and responsibilities. The decision certainly broadened the scope of what could be considered legitimate federal government activity. Congress did not rush to move the national government onto the policy turf of the state governments, but the precedent was established that Congress potentially could do so.[18]

Redefining interstate commerce expands federal government power.

If the door to cooperative federalism cracked open in 1819, it swung fully open in 1937, much to the relief of public officials looking for a more active role for the federal government in American life. In *National Labor Relations Board v. Jones & Laughlin Steel Corporation* (1937), the Supreme Court expanded the scope of what was meant by interstate commerce.

Jones & Laughlin had fired workers for labor union activity. The recently enacted National Labor Relations Act (1935) prohibited employers engaged in interstate commerce from taking such actions. The act declared that labor-management relations were an aspect of commerce and thus subject to federal government regulation. When challenged by the National Labor Relations Board, which was created by the 1935 law, the steel company argued that labor-management relations were not part of commerce and therefore were not subject to federal regulation. Traditionally, the Supreme Court interpreted interstate commerce to mean not what happened inside a factory—that was manufacturing, not commerce—but what was involved in the transfer of products from one state to another. The national government could regulate shipping rates, for example, and it could regulate the entry of firms into the business of shipping steel, but what happened inside a steel plant was not in and of itself interstate commerce. Using this definition of commerce, Jones & Laughlin argued that the National Labor Relations Act was an invalid federal intrusion into its business practices.

In its decision in *Jones & Laughlin*, the Supreme Court concluded that this conception was too narrow. Instead, a company that uses any interstate products in its business or sells any product interstate is part of the stream of interstate commerce, and the stream involves the company's entire operations. Poor labor-management relations can lead to industrial strife, and this strife can affect the stream of commerce. In the Court's view, the fundamental principle was that some activities may appear to be intrastate when considered alone, but if they had a close relationship to interstate commerce, then Congress must be given the authority to regulate those activities to prevent obstructions to commerce.

The *Jones & Laughlin* decision meant, in effect, that national government action on issues such as worker safety, environmental controls, health codes, work hours and conditions, and overtime pay were justified by the government's responsibility to regulate interstate commerce. The Court's decision in *Wickard v. Filburn* (1942) underlined this point. Under authority granted by the Agricultural Adjustment Act of 1938, the U.S. Department of Agriculture, in an attempt to avoid overproduction and plummeting prices, allocated about 11 acres for Roscoe Filburn to grow wheat. Filburn grew wheat on another dozen acres, and although he said this was for his local use on his farm, the Court ruled Filburn could be ordered to stop. By growing wheat beyond his quota, Filburn was having an effect on interstate commerce by not purchasing the needed wheat from another farm. Any activity that has a "a substantial economic effect on interstate commerce," the Court ruled, is within Congress's regulatory reach.

Everything in the stream of commerce was now ripe for federal involvement. Once solely under the purview of the states, these responsibilities would now be shared. And in accordance with the Constitution's premise of the supremacy of national laws, it would be the states that would have to conform with federal standards in these areas, not the other way around.

Although the Court cautioned that its new definition of interstate commerce must be "a matter of degree," the principle of the stream of interstate commerce provided a nearly limitless range to congressional action. Anything in the stream or any action or practice that might affect the stream was now open to national government involvement. The Court declared that it was up to Congress to decide the appropriate use of its newly expanded interstate commerce powers.[19] The constitutional basis of cooperative federalism was now firmly established, the role of Congress and the president in deciding what activities came under the interstate umbrella was in place, and the scope of federal government activity in society and in the economy was poised to grow accordingly.

The scope of activity and the debate over it have continued right up to today. The interpretation of the federal government's role in regulating interstate commerce has, for example, been a central point of debate since the passage of health care reform legislation in early 2010. The federal requirement that individuals purchase insurance is a particular flashpoint. If insurers must provide coverage to individuals with preexisting health conditions, everyone, healthy or not, needs to be in the insurance market. Obviously, insurers cannot afford a situation where individuals do not have insurance, then have a disease or accident that requires it, and they can simply then decide to buy it. This would be akin to having a car accident, then buying auto insurance, and the insurance company is required to pay the cost of the damage in the accident. Until health care reform, the federal government had not used an interstate commerce justification to compel someone to purchase a product under threat of penalty. To opponents of the health care reform law, forcing an individual to enter interstate commerce by buying insurance when she does not choose to do so is not consistent with the Framers' vision of regulating commerce between the states. To supporters, this mandate is needed to make universal health coverage work, and it is not qualitatively different from other federal requirements imposed on individuals. Governors or attorneys general in over twenty states cited this mandate as one way the law violates the commerce clause, and filed lawsuits to block it. More states will join the suits as a result of the Republican victories in the 2010 elections. Ultimately, the Supreme Court will decide the matter.

CaseStudy: Federalism and the Regulation of Native American Casinos

Long before the Founding Fathers led a revolution and crafted a constitution, Native Americans governed territory in what would come to be the United States. This history created a particularly difficult problem for governance in the United States: how would these Native American, or Indian, nations be incorporated into the American political system?

The answer was to grant tribes some degree of sovereignty within the United States and within the states. The tribes, in other words, are part of the American system of federalism. The Supreme Court has upheld this principle, noting that the tribes hold "attributes of sovereignty over both their members and their territory."[20] In the Constitution's commerce clause (Article 1, section 8), Indian tribes are made the equivalent of other sovereign entities: Congress is responsible "To regulate Commerce with foreign Nations, and among the several States, and with the Indian Tribes." In an executive memorandum in April 1994, President Clinton reaffirmed that federal government agencies are to operate on a "government to government" basis with Indian tribes.[21]

American Indians are citizens of their tribe, the state they live in, and the United States. They pay individual federal income tax and pay state income tax unless they work for the tribe and live on tribal lands. As governmental entities, the 564 federally recognized tribes do not pay taxes to other governments, just as the federal and state governments do not pay taxes to each other.[22]

The questions raised by tribal sovereignty are similar to those raised by the relationship between states and the national government in American federalism. In what areas does the national government prevail? What areas are the province of tribal law and regulation rather than the U.S. government? How do the states fit in?

In recent years, the status of Indians in the federal system has been particularly salient because of gambling and the revenues it generates. Prior to 1988, casinos on Indian reservations were rare, but by 2008, about 230 tribes ran over 400 casinos in 30 states. Casino gambling has generated huge revenues for tribes. From 1987 to 2008, revenues from tribal-owned casinos increased from barely $100 million to more than $20 billion.[23] The world's largest casino is the tribal-owned Foxwoods Resort in Connecticut.

One of the controversies in federalism raised by Indian gaming is the ability of state governments to regulate tribal-run casinos. In 1987, the Supreme Court ruled that a state could not enforce its gaming laws within tribal reservations, unless Congress had specifically given the states that authority.[24] Overall, federal, not state, authority prevails when it comes to the tribes. In this case, the Court said that state restrictions on Indian casinos conflicted with the federal

government's attempt to further tribal self-sufficiency and economic development through tribal gaming. Other Court decisions confirmed that American federalism made Indian tribal sovereignty subordinate to the federal, not state, government.[25]

Recognizing the difficult political issues that might arise with the expansion of tribal gaming in the states, the federal government provided a role for the states in regulating this gambling. The Indian Gaming Regulatory Act (IGRA), signed into law in 1988, established three classes of Indian gambling activity: (1) social and traditional games with stakes or prizes of minimal value, commonly associated

▲ INDIAN GAMING AND FEDERALISM

Indian tribes, as a part of American federalism, often need to negotiate with the federal and state governments. Gaming is no exception. Under a federal law, the tribes enter into agreements with state governments concerning the nature of the gaming and the share of the proceeds that will go to the state. This profit sharing encourages states to sign the agreements.

with tribal customs or celebrations; (2) bingo and other games played against other players, not against "the house"; and (3) any games not in the first two groups, such as slot machines, blackjack, and roulette. Tribes are essentially free to offer the first two classes of games; the third requires the tribes to negotiate a "compact" with a state that would determine casino size, games, hours, and the share of the profits that would go to the state.

Intended to regulate gambling on Indian reservations, the IGRA also gave the states some incentive to encourage, or at least not discourage, Indian gaming, because now states would receive a portion of the profits. Because they are sovereign entities, Indian tribes could not be taxed directly by the federal or state governments.[26] Thus the tribes were not sources of tax revenue in the states. However, under IGRA, states were assured part of the financial windfall from casino gambling. The law also provided for a mediator to choose between the final offers of tribes and states if a tribe could convince a federal court that a state was not negotiating in good faith. Knowing the mediator might agree with the tribe and leave the states with a smaller share of the profit, states had a strong financial incentive to reach agreements with the tribes.[27]

To its critics, IGRA was a disaster. They describe it as reckless—in effect establishing a national policy that encourages loose affiliations of Native Americans to petition the Bureau of Indian Affairs to be declared tribes in order to enter into casino gambling operations. Once acknowledged as tribes, sovereignty leaves them free to develop their lands without being subject to state environmental, safety, zoning, or other ordinances. As the critics see it, the control of states over their own future development is imperiled.

States seemed to regain some leverage in 1996. The Seminole tribe in Florida filed suit in federal court, complaining that the state had violated IGRA by not bargaining in good faith to establish a gaming compact. In *Seminole Tribe v. Florida*, the Supreme Court rejected the tribe's case. The Court concluded in a 5–4 decision that the Eleventh Amendment gave states, as sovereign bodies, immunity from lawsuits in federal courts without their consent. Just as a sovereign body can be undermined if another entity taxes it, it can be undermined if another entity encourages lawsuits against it. In the Court's view, Congress did not have the constitutional authority to remove state immunity simply because of its interstate commerce powers to regulate the tribes and states.[28]

As it turns out, with significant financial resources likely to flow from gambling, states did not use the *Seminole* decision to prevent Indian casinos. Instead, they used the decision as leverage to negotiate more lucrative agreements with the tribes. Suffering from revenue shortfalls, states saw casino gambling on reservations as a potential windfall, now that they could force better deals. By 2008, states were collecting $2.5 billion in revenues from the casinos.[29] At the same time, they could continue to prohibit commercial casino gambling outside the reservations.[30]

With state budgets depleted during the weakened economy of the past few years, extracting more revenue from Indian casinos has been a tempting strategy for state governments. In April 2010, a federal appeals court struck down California governor Arnold Schwarzenegger's attempt to extract more revenue from the Rincon tribe's casino operations. The tribe and the state had been deadlocked for over five years on the tribe's desire to add more slot machines to its casino operations, and the state's insistence that the tribe pay a fee into the state's general fund in exchange. The court ruled that the state was bargaining in bad faith and was in effect illegally imposing a tax on the tribe—IGRA prohibits states from taxing tribes. The decision may encourage tribes in other states to challenge what they consider bad faith demands by states desperate for more revenue.[31]

The sovereign status of Indian tribes intersects American federalism at both the national and state levels. Although states sometimes complain that Indian sovereignty compromises their own sovereignty, they have been able to use the *Seminole* decision—itself based on state sovereignty—to wrest more profitable deals with the casinos in difficult budgetary times. At the same time, states without casinos or with less attractive gaming options see their citizens and other tourists pouring into neighboring states to gamble at Indian casinos, which gives some negotiating power back to the tribes. And, as California learned, there are limits to what states can demand. Within states, Indian casino gambling has emerged as a political football, as governors and legislatures battle to determine who has the authority to negotiate and sign the gaming compacts.

ThinkingCritically

1. Should states or the federal government have the primary regulatory role regarding Native American tribes?

2. Should tribes have to negotiate with states or should they, as sovereign entities, be free to determine how they will run their gaming enterprises?

3. Consider the case of tribes that have members scattered geographically and do not control any land as a group. Are these the equivalent of tribes on reservations? Should these individuals, because of tribal sovereignty, have a right to receive land from the federal and state governments for the purpose of establishing casino operations?

The federal and state governments collaborate to implement policy in some issue areas.

The regulation of Indian gaming indicates the complexity that arises when multiple levels of government are involved in the same policy area. The national–state relationship in cooperative federalism can likewise take on different forms: collaboration, mandates, and persuasion.

To understand collaboration, consider environmental policy. State governments and the national government collect and share significant amounts of data and information on the environment. They work together to identify and create rules to protect endangered species. They will respond jointly to disasters such as the massive oil spill in the Gulf of Mexico in 2010. State offices often provide personnel who implement, at the state level, programs that are created at the national level, such as water and air pollution control. Sometimes these agreements and sharing of information and personnel involve multiple states in a region, such as the states bordering the Great Lakes, in addition to the federal government.

As a form of collaboration, the national government may set standards and then allow states to exceed those standards, as is the case in air pollution control. A provision added to the Clean Air Act in 1967 allowed California to seek exemptions from federal air pollution rules. If these exemptions were granted, other states then had the option of following the federal or California standards, whichever were more stringent. Thirteen states opted to use the stronger California standards. In 2007, the Environmental Protection Agency (EPA) for the first time denied a California exemption request. A year later, another three states had decided they would adopt the proposed California automobile emissions standards if the state ultimately received its exemption. The EPA under the Obama administration in 2009 reversed the prior ruling and granted California the exemption. In 2010, the EPA folded the stronger California standards into new national emissions and fuel mileage standards that apply across the country.[32]

Ideally, officials at all levels of government have common environmental goals, so these collaborations are considered mutually beneficial. Freedom for states to tailor policy to fit their needs, while still falling within federal guidelines, increases the likelihood of mutually beneficial collaboration.[33]

Even while collaborating, the state and national governments will often still have separate areas of responsibility, the hallmark of dual federalism. For example, states are responsible for noise pollution and nonendangered wildlife management policy within their borders. The national government, on the other hand, controls the management and disposal of nuclear waste generated by national defense needs. Both of these are environmental concerns, but the two levels of government work on them independently. Similarly, the federal government sets policy on which pesticides can be made, but a state, or a city if allowed by the state, can decide which of these allowable pesticides can be used within its borders and in what ways.

Immigration has been another area of federal and state collaboration. In 2009, states passed over 200 laws concerning immigrants and immigration. Federal law is supreme, but states have enforcement roles and can make decisions about which benefits and services immigrants may receive. Although laws requiring strict enforcement and verification of legal immigrant status receive the most publicity, many of the laws enacted offer benefits to immigrants. Similarly, laws are not always about illegal immigration, but about the obligations and privileges of legal immigrants as well. Issues addressed include health care benefits, driver's licenses, eligibility for in-state college tuition rates, allowed and disallowed techniques to verify legal immigration status, and sanctions on employers who hire illegal immigrants. States often pass laws that address issues related to immigration or that arise because of immigration, but not strictly about immigration itself, which is the job of the federal government. Although states sometimes act because they have concluded the federal government will not—most prominently when Arizona enacted a controversial immigration enforcement law in 2010—collaboration has been more common than conflict, despite the headlines.[34]

The federal government may enact policy mandates to direct the states to take certain actions.

Another possibility is for the national government to issue a **mandate** that orders state governments to take certain actions. Beginning in the 1960s, the volume of federal government mandates upon the states increased sharply. For example, in the area of education, states must follow the rules established by the national government in the Individuals with Disabilities Education Act. This law sets out the kinds of services that states and localities must provide to students with learning or other disabilities and provides some federal funding. Here "cooperative" federalism need not mean that there is harmony and agreement between the two levels of government. Instead, the national government may set the rules that states are required to follow, regardless of the view of the states toward these rules. Some analysts refer to this practice as "coercive federalism."

Federal mandates have rankled state officials for two reasons. First, the mandates may force states to do things they would prefer not to do or for which there is only modest support from state residents. Second, mandates impose demands on the states but often do not provide federal financial assistance to carry out the demands. States long complained that they were spending far too much to meet the policy demands and policy preferences of federal government officials and politicians, draining money from policies of more interest to state politicians and residents. Columbus,

mandate an order from the federal government that requires state governments to take a certain action.

▼ WHOSE WATER IS IT, ANYWAY?

A collaborative program involving 25 agencies of the federal government and California state government, CalFed is an example of cooperative federalism. The effort manages water use and ecosystem protection in the San Francisco Bay/Sacramento-San Joaquin River Delta, the state's most important source of water for homes, businesses, and farms. Farmers and environmentalists have battled for years over limits on the water that can be pumped from the delta for farm use.

unfunded mandate a law requiring certain actions without appropriating the necessary funds to carry them out.

Ohio, reported it would need to raise $1 billion from 1991 through 2000 to meet federal environmental mandates. Danville, Virginia, complained in 1993 that federal mandates absorbed 16 percent of its local revenue. The state of Texas estimated it would need to spend $11.4 billion in 1994–1995 to accommodate mandates. Examples like these made the elimination of **unfunded mandates** a major priority of the Republican Party when it gained control of the U.S. House and Senate following the 1994 election. Unfunded mandates are federal requirements that states take some action, but without provision of sufficient resources to do so.

The result, after lengthy controversy and extensive lobbying by groups such as the National Association of Counties, the National Conference of State Legislatures, and the U.S. Conference of Mayors, was the 1995 Unfunded Mandates Reform Act. The bill required congressional committees to get estimates of the cost of proposed legislation that would mandate new expenses on states, localities, or businesses. If the cost exceeded $50 million on states and localities or $100 million on the private sector, legislators could then be required to vote that the benefits of the bill exceeded the costs. These figures were adjusted for inflation, reaching $69 million and $139 million, respectively, in 2009.[35] The act did not apply to existing unfunded mandates and did not apply to mandates that protected the constitutional rights of individuals, prohibited discrimination, or were labeled emergency legislation.

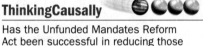

ThinkingCausally

Has the Unfunded Mandates Reform Act been successful in reducing those mandates?

Unfunded mandates seemingly declined after the act was passed. By one accounting, only five new mandates had been passed during the decade after the law's enactment, and the law had changed the way Congress interacted with the states. However, this correlation between the law and the drop in unfunded mandates may be misleading. Evidence on the effectiveness of the act has been mixed. Another accounting argues the law looked effective only because its exemptions allowed major new unfunded mandates that simply were not labeled as such, including education reforms in the No Child Left Behind Act, education services for disabled children, Medicaid, and a requirement after 2000 that states meet standards for voting technology.[36] The U.S. Government Accountability Office noted, in its examination of unfunded mandates, that the most common complaint it heard from academic and think tank experts, public interest advocacy organizations, businesspeople, federal agencies, and state and local government officials was that the law defined unfunded mandates too narrowly.[37] The National Conference of State Legislatures (NCSL) discontinued its Mandate Monitor in 1995 but restarted it in 2004 because of state complaints about a renewed escalation of unfunded mandates. The NCSL estimated that unfunded mandates, interpreted more broadly than the federal law, totaled approximately $131 billion from 2004 through 2009.[38] These data suggest that some of the "success" of the federal law resulted from narrowly labeling what counts as an unfunded mandate, rather than from actually reducing the fiscal burdens imposed on the states.

preemption legislation legislation that declares, or mandates, certain actions off-limits for state governments.

Similarly to mandating that states take some action, the federal government can pass **preemption legislation** that declares, or mandates, certain actions off-limits for state governments. For example, federal law passed in 2005 prohibits certain kinds of liability suits from being filed against firearms manufacturers in state courts.[39] The Family Smoking Prevention and Tobacco Control Act of 2009 preempts state laws in areas such as tobacco product standards—flavored cigarettes except for menthol, for example, are prohibited—and warning labels. The health care reform legislation enacted in 2010 (the Affordable Care Act) contained an extensive array of preemptive measures. These measures will require many complicated adjustments of state law and regulations to conform to new federal standards. Insurance has traditionally been an area primarily regulated by state law, but the reform bill created an array of new requirements on health insurance companies that preempt state law, such as who is eligible for benefits, the particular benefits that insurance policies must offer, and the

TABLE 4-1. Tools of Federal Influence over State Governments

TOOLS	DESCRIPTION
Mandates	**States are required to follow federal policy orders**
Direct orders	An order is imposed by the federal government on state governments requiring that it carry out a federal policy or program
Total preemption	A state is prohibited from implementing its own program or law in a policy area
Partial preemption	A state is partially prohibited from implementing its own standards and regulations in a policy area—typically it may implement a standard higher than the federal standard but not below the federal standard
Persuasion	**States are prodded to follow federal policy preferences through financial inducements**
Conditions on grants	A state must meet conditions and requirements established by the federal government in order to receive a federal grant
Crosscutting requirements	The federal government places the same set of requirements across a large number of grant and funding programs, making it more difficult for a state to choose not to meet the requirement
Crossover sanctions	The federal government requires compliance with requirements on small grant programs in order for a state to continue to receive federal funds in larger, often unrelated, federal funding programs

Source: Paul L. Posner, *The Politics of Unfunded Mandates: Whither Federalism?* Washington, DC: Georgetown University Press, 1998.

Note: The federal government imposes these tools directly on local governments as well. Within states, state governments use similar tools in relation to local governments.

allowable rate differentials in individual insurance policies for different groups of individuals (such as younger and older policy holders).

The federal government may use fiscal persuasion to influence states' behavior.

In addition to collaboration and mandates, cooperative federalism can work through persuasion (see Table 4-1). The national government might try to influence or persuade a state government to take some action in the area of education, the environment, or some other policy area, but not require it. Typically, this will involve providing some incentive for states to agree to take the desired action.

One of the best incentives is money. **Fiscal federalism** refers to the national government's use of its financial resources to persuade the states to take particular actions. The restrictions on the use of the money might be specific or general. With a **categorical grant**, the federal government provides money that is to be used for very specific purposes. Funds might be provided for a particular form of science instruction for children in grades 1–3 who attend schools with a large proportion of low-income students. To receive the categorical grant funds, the state or locality would have to agree to these and any other restrictions on their use. As Table 4-1 shows, the tools the federal government can employ can make it difficult for a state not to comply with federal demands. Various rules about discrimination, environmental protection, and employment and contract requirements, for example, are built into a large group of federal grants (see crosscutting requirements in Table 4-1). A state not willing to accept any one of these rules is shutting itself out of dozens or hundreds of programs.

Categorical grants can be either formula based or competitive. Formula-based grants are, as the name suggests, based on a formula that determines the amount of funds a state will receive. Precisely what should be in the formula is the focus of intense political maneuvering. Usually, several factors are included, and each will

fiscal federalism a technique of persuasion in which the federal government offers resources to states that agree to take certain actions.

categorical grant funds provided by the federal government to a state or local government for a specific, defined purpose.

reward some states more than others.[40] A formula based on state unemployment rates may funnel more funds to state A than state B, while a formula based on the increase in the state unemployment rate over the prior 12 months might provide more funds to state B instead. The Individuals with Disabilities Education Act, mentioned above, has three formula-based programs that provide funds for the education of students who qualify for special services. Competitive grants require an application or proposal and are rated based on criteria specified by the granting agency. The highest-rated applications would then be funded. Applicants typically have to meet eligibility criteria. For example, states were unable to apply for "Race to the Top" funds from the U.S. Department of Education in 2010 unless they agreed to allow evaluation of teachers and principals to be linked to students' academic achievement.

block grant funds provided by the federal government to a state or local government in general support of a broad government function such as education or transportation.

Block grants, which began during the presidency of Richard Nixon (1969–1974), are more general and provide greater flexibility to the states. These grants are for broad categories of spending: transportation funds, welfare program funds, homeland security, and so on. States are free to spend those funds more or less as they please, within those particular policy areas, and the amounts states receive are based on formulas determined by the federal government. Block grants can come with conditions, however. For example, in 1984, a new federal law required a portion of transportation block grants to be withheld from any state that did not raise its legal drinking age to 21. Similarly, states that do not comply with portions of the federal Clean Air Act will lose some of their highway funding.

Since 1987, the federal government has provided funds to state and local governments through block grants and categorical grants that comprise over 20 percent of all state and local expenditures.[41] This proportion recently spiked up because of the large infusion of federal stimulus and economic recovery funds sent to state government beginning in 2009. Federal assistance increased over 20 percent from fiscal year 2009 (October 2008–September 2009) to fiscal year 2010. The most rapidly growing area of federal aid to states and localities has been assistance for medical expenses, increasing from about $44 billion in 1990 to a projected $350 billion in 2015.[42] Although the percentage of state and local budgets financed by federal aid stayed about the same over the past two decades, much more of that aid is now dedicated to medical expenses (see Figure 4-3). As most medical care expenses are funneled through state governments, one hidden story in Figure 4-3 is that federal assistance directly to the nation's urban areas has declined over the past two decades.

▼ **PERSUASION THROUGH FISCAL FEDERALISM**
In order to receive their full share of federal substance abuse prevention and treatment block grant funds, states have to prohibit tobacco sales to minors. States that do not, or that inadequately enforce the law, can lose up to 40 percent of their block grant funds. Should the federal government put conditions on the receipt of its funds?

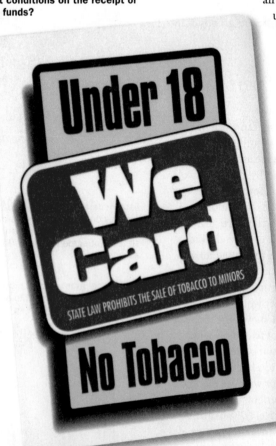

To state governments, fiscal federalism is attractive. It provides states with funding to do things they otherwise would be unable to do. If politics often concerns "who gets what" and "who will pay for it," fiscal federalism is a prime example. Whenever an elected official can provide a benefit to his or her constituents but have someone else's constituents pay the cost, it is an attractive proposition. Fiscal federalism encourages members of Congress to join together to provide more funds for the folks back home—while someone else pays the price.

But fiscal federalism creates problems as well. One problem is that these cash infusions may come with strings attached, so that the state may be creating some

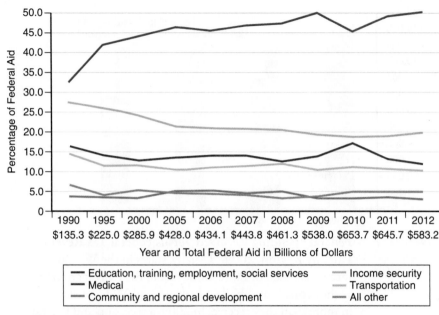

FIGURE 4-3. **Federal Aid to States and Cities by Function.** Federal grants to the states for medical expenses have been an increasing share of all federal aid provided to states and cities.

Note: Data for 2010-2012 are estimates provided in the 2011 U.S. Budget.

programs or services primarily because there is money available to do so, rather than because it is a priority of the state government or the people of the state. After September 11, 2001, the federal government sent over $25 billion in grants to the states to enhance domestic security. States complained that the grants required them to fund what they considered unnecessary counterterrorism projects. "Improvised explosive devices," or IEDs, were a problem in Baghdad, they argued, not in the streets of American cities and towns. Spending time and money to create an anti-IED plan did not, in their view, make sense. By contrast, Michael Chertoff, secretary of the Department of Homeland Security under President Bush expressed concerns in 2008 that states were trying to stretch federal antiterrorism grant funds to include programs targeting gangs, narcotics, and gun violence. Either way, federally funded programs can mean jobs and an infusion of cash to the state economy, and those can be difficult to refuse.

Republicans in Washington who opposed President Obama's economic stimulus plan found themselves at odds with Republican governors who, even if they had misgivings about the restrictions that might come with increased federal funding, found it hard to say no when their states were strapped for cash. To compete for a share of $4 billion in federal education grant funds under the president's Race to the Top program, some states began changing state law. In some states, this new federal requirement may have ironically been power enhancing: it may have allowed governors to institute changes they had long sought. In other states, changes may have been unpopular but considered necessary to compete for the federal funds.[43]

Another problem with fiscal federalism is that states may battle each other to get a larger share of federal funds. The criteria used by federal officials to distribute aid will benefit some states more than others, so they are hotly debated. In the competition for the Race to the Top grants, states had to agree to certain requirements—allowing teachers to be evaluated in part by student achievement, for example.

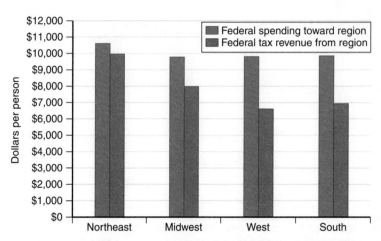

FIGURE 4-4. **Federal Spending Received Versus Federal Tax Revenue Paid, by Region, 2009.** Usually, states in the West and South receive as much or more money from the federal government as they contribute, while Northeast and Midwest states pay in more than they receive. In 2009, a recession and federal economic stimulus spending combined to make all regions net recipients of federal funds.

States that already had those provisions in place were better positioned to focus on burnishing other aspects of their proposals for funding, possibly giving them a competitive edge. In effect, states that win grant competitions like these are being subsidized by the federal tax payments made by citizens of the losing states. State officials pay acute attention to how much their citizens pay into the federal government and how much the state receives in return. Generally, over the past two decades, states that are more rural have fared better than those that are more urban, and southern and western states have fared better than eastern and northern states (see Figure 4-4).[44]

A final problem with fiscal federalism is the difficulty of a state or city in speaking with one voice. Officials at the highest levels of state and local government, such as governors or mayors, typically prefer the flexibility of block grants and lobby the federal government for more. Officials in state and city agencies, however, as well as organized interest groups, are often equally determined to obtain categorical grants that they know will be used for a defined purpose. This desire to obtain targeted funding can both arise from and perpetuate the policy silo problem. Policy silos refer to employees in government programs in similar areas—for example, unemployment offices and job training offices—working in isolation. Two seemingly related programs may have different funding sources, reporting requirements to Washington, and rules for distribution of funds in the states. The availability of specialized funds can lead employees in different parts of the same agency to remain isolated as they seek to win these narrowly targeted funds. If they are successful in winning funds, their ability to continue operating in isolation is enhanced.

In addition, states and city officials can have different political incentives. In particular, to the extent that federal grants go directly to cities, state political leaders will not receive political credit for new programs and spending. Moreover, the funds being received by the city might, in the view of state officials, be put to better use elsewhere. This view might be based on an assessment that competing needs in the state should have higher priority, or it might be based on a calculation that spreading resources to other constituents will be more politically beneficial for the state official, or both of these. One of the reasons federal officials sometimes wish to funnel funds directly to cities is precisely because they are concerned that states will shortchange the cities. City officials, of course, have the same incentive as state officials, hoping to receive federal funds directly so they can claim full credit for this success.

Members of Congress, even if they philosophically believe in the principle of block grants, gravitate toward the more defined grants because they can claim more credit for obtaining them. For members of Congress, there are few things better than a grateful constituent who can thank them for a specific program or service that came about through the initiative of the federal government. Despite the wishes of some politicians at both the federal and state levels, categorical grants have continued to grow more rapidly than block grants.

So which are better—categorical grants or block grants? The answer will vary depending on whom you ask. Categorical grants reveal the national government's priorities, or at least the priorities of those members of Congress who voted in favor of a federal agency's budget. With block grants, the national government has money spent generally where it wants, but the states decide how they want to spend it. Thus, national lawmakers can be less sure that funds are being spent in a way they would desire. For federal lawmakers, the tradeoff is between the close control of categorical grants and the potential state-level innovation and effectiveness of block grants. Within the states, political activists and government agency officials may prefer the specific funding that comes with categorical grants rather than having to compete for a share of a state's block grants. Because categorical grants do not allow state elected officials to steer funds toward favored groups and causes, governors and legislators might prefer the flexibility of block grants. Elected officials will rarely turn down what appears to be "free" federal money, however, whether block or categorical.[45]

Federalism can create both problems and solutions.

The more general question raised by the choice between categorical grants and block grants is what type of relationship one desires between the national and state governments. For those who favor more national standards and control, the concerns with allowing the states a great degree of independence in setting policy are multiple. States may simply not have access to the same expertise available to the federal government. One state's solutions may create problems for bordering states. If states are not required to meet high national standards, there may be a "race to the bottom" in which states try to provide minimal services and cut taxes and regulation in an attempt to attract business (see *How Do We Know? Are States Engaged in a Race to the Bottom?*).

Political power is a factor as well. If particular ideas and politicians dominate national politics—whether conservative or liberal—these politicians may be tempted to use that opportunity to implement uniform conservative or liberal policies, respectively, across the country. Even ardent advocates of a strong role for the states can be attracted to the idea of writing national policies and rules that the states must follow, especially if they believe their political opponents have a foothold on state governments.

For those who favor allowing states more flexibility and leeway, the advantages are also multiple. Allowed flexibility in solving problems, the states become "laboratories of democracy," a phrase coined by Supreme Court Justice Louis Brandeis early in the twentieth century to describe an environment in which numerous policy proposals can be implemented and tested. States vary tremendously in the substance of their policies in areas such as education, welfare, consumer protection, health care, and many more.

continued on page 153 ▶

HOW DO WE KNOW?

Are States Engaged in a Race to the Bottom?

The Question

Critics of welfare policy argue that states with generous welfare benefits risk becoming "magnets" that attract the poor. Furthermore, the higher taxes resulting from these policies may be a disincentive to businesses looking to locate in the state. Defenders of these policies worry that this logic leads states to compete economically by decreasing welfare benefits to the level of neighboring states, which they refer to as a "race to the bottom." Are states engaged in a race to the bottom? How do we know?

Why It Matters

The race-to-the-bottom question is one of the most contentious in the study of federalism. The policy consequences are significant for welfare recipients, taxpayers, and economic development. Philosophically, the question engages the very strong and competing points

▼ MAGNETIC BENEFITS?

Although food purchase assistance is a federal program, states are allowed some leeway on benefits and eligibility. Supporters of generous program benefits worry that states have incentives to match their neighbors by decreasing benefits, while opponents are concerned that generous states become magnets attracting more beneficiaries. This farmers market in California accepts the electronic benefit transfer cards used by Supplemental Nutrition Assistance Program recipients.

of view researchers may have about the desirability of welfare programs for individuals. And the concern about magnets and policy races in American federalism appears in other policy areas. School districts and states express concern at the financial pressures that may result if, for example, excellent special education services attract out-of-district and out-of-state parents seeking particular services for their children. Advocates for parents of these children worry that states and districts will reduce their services because of this fear of becoming a magnet.[46]

Investigating the Answer

The premise of the race-to-the-bottom debate is that states offering generous welfare policies put themselves at risk by becoming welfare magnets. With more generous policies, there will be an influx of welfare recipients because of higher benefits and an outflow of business because of higher taxes. States respond to this dilemma by reducing welfare benefits, which prompts surrounding states to do the same. The result is a downward spiral in which states follow each other toward low benefits. Federalism allows differences in state benefits: if the national government simply set a fixed benefit across all states, the race could not occur. This is the case in a program like Social Security, where states do not set benefit levels.

The basic approach in studies of the race to the bottom is twofold. One group of studies focuses on state government behavior. The outcome to be explained is whether surrounding states adjust their level of welfare benefits in reaction to changing levels of benefits by their neighbors. The causal relationship being tested by the researchers is whether lower benefits in one state lead to lower benefits in surrounding states. This requires tracking benefit levels over time.

These researchers may also seek to determine whether a state is a "welfare magnet" by looking at states that make benefits more generous and then seeing whether the poverty level in those states changes. The logic is that if increased benefits lure the poor, then at least initially a state's poverty rate would increase after benefits were raised because poor residents from other states will have migrated to the generous state.

Any investigation of state government welfare benefits needs to take account of a number of factors other than the actions of other states that might affect a state's benefit levels. Wealthier states can more easily afford higher benefits per person, because they have a smaller percentage of their population receiving benefits than do poorer states. States with more liberal public opinion might also be expected to have higher spending. On the other hand, states with declining wages might reduce welfare benefits to discourage workers from leaving jobs to enter the welfare system.

A second set of studies focuses on the behavior of individuals rather than state governments. These studies seek to determine why low-income individuals move from one state to another and, in particular, whether welfare benefits are part of that decision. Researchers tracking the movement of individuals from one state to another need to consider other factors that may lead individuals to move, particularly family concerns and greater work opportunities in another state. The latter is particularly important. A low-income individual might move to a higher-benefit state not because of the higher benefits, but because that state is more likely to be prosperous and have more available jobs. Thus, the increased economic opportunity, not the generous welfare policy, would be the magnet. Although there would be a correlation between welfare benefits and migration, the benefits would not actually be causing the migration.

Research on the race-to-the-bottom thesis faces other complications. Most studies, for example, assume that neighboring states are the relevant set of states—these are the states that a government is "competing with" in terms of welfare benefits and also the states from which migration is most likely. However, this assumption is not always accurate. California, for example, has more migrants from Texas, New York, Illinois, and Florida than from neighboring Oregon. Also, what if state officials set their benefits not in reaction to actual reductions in other states but in anticipation that other states will reduce their benefits? As a result, the cause of their behavior may well be behavior in other states that has not even happened yet and thus would be hard to demonstrate by a researcher. A similar problem is that states may reduce their welfare benefits to be more in line with nearby states even if individuals do not behave in the manner presumed by the welfare magnet thesis. State government officials might assume that individuals will migrate for benefits and therefore reduce their state welfare expenditures to preempt migration. In this scenario, state policy makers are influenced by the threat of movement, rather than by any demonstrated fact that individuals do move for welfare reasons. And while most studies focus on benefit levels, states could compete in other arenas as well. They could keep benefits per recipient largely unchanged, for example, but make access to a program more difficult. Or their focus could be on changing the overall cost to taxpayers, which could entail some combination of benefit or access revisions.

Thinking Critically

- You are a state legislator and an advocacy group wants you to support a proposal to substantially increase benefits and services for students with severe developmental disabilities, services that tend to be very expensive. Would your decision about supporting the proposal depend at all on concerns that families will move to your state to receive these benefits? Why or why not?
- What would make a policy area one where a state might choose to provide higher benefits to encourage migration to the state?
- If a state were determined to spend a fixed amount on income assistance programs, would you recommend higher benefits but less access, or lower benefits but more access? What do you think the strategy would be for legislators worried about the state becoming a welfare magnet?

The Bottom Line

Despite these research challenges, political scientists have reached some conclusions on the race-to-the-bottom theory. Overall, research has found support for the notion that states compete on benefit levels. States tend to follow each other as benefits are lowered, but they do not seem to follow each other if benefits are increased. The size and the speed of the "copying" behavior, however, are not clear. In some studies, states match nearly dollar for dollar what other states do, whereas in other studies the matching is modest, adjusting state benefits only a few cents to every dollar in a competing state.[47] Although examination of access levels and overall cost to the state are less frequently examined, some copying behavior is evident there as well.[48]

There have been fewer studies on whether individuals move to welfare magnets, but these generally conclude that factors other than welfare benefits are more important in determining the location decisions of low-income individuals. Once cost-of-living is factored in, some studies suggest, state-to-state differences in welfare benefits are not as large as they would seem initially and, thus, are less an incentive to move from one state to another. On the other hand, for policy makers, it may not matter whether welfare benefits are the only reason an individual moves or a major reason: what might matter is simply whether welfare benefits influence location decisions to any degree.[49]

The Obama administration has urged states to think more regionally about economic development, and to see these regions as being in competition with other countries rather than with each other or with other states. Achieving such a change on any large scale would require a significant shift in the thinking of both politicians and citizens. It would also require the federal government to change its practices significantly, as much of its funding flows to states and inherently pits states in competition with each other.[50]

► STATES VARY IN GRADUATION REQUIREMENTS

Setting graduation requirements is a state and local responsibility. In some states, students take high-stakes exams that they must pass in order to graduate. States can look to other states to see which requirements produce the best educational outcomes. What might be the obstacles to setting graduation requirements at the national level as is common in other countries? Would national requirements be desirable?

States also vary in their political processes. The veto power of governors, the making of state budgets, the length of legislative sessions, voter registration laws, access of minor parties to election ballots, campaign finance laws, lobbying regulations, and many other aspects of the political process are quite different from one state to another. Ultimately, the nation gains because other states can borrow those policy reforms that prove to be effective, efficient, or popular. Some examples of state innovations that were adopted by many states—known as policy diffusion— include raising standards and creating charter schools in education and "three strikes" laws and minimum sentencing standards in criminal justice. Citizens also have the advantage of choice—they can choose where to live based on a number of factors, including the different styles and roles of government across the states.[51]

States also serve as laboratories for individuals wishing to enter national-level politics. Since 1977, four presidents—Jimmy Carter, Ronald Reagan, Bill Clinton, and George W. Bush—had served as governors. Barack Obama had been a state senator before serving in the U.S. Senate. About half the members of Congress had served in state government. Indeed, political scientists find that candidates for the U.S. House and Senate who have served at other levels of government have a decided electoral advantage.

Advocates of federalism also note that societies with potentially deep divisions are best governed with federal arrangements. Federalism is not a cure-all, they concede—the tortured history of conflict between Catholics and Protestants in Northern Ireland provides one example; the mixed record of federalism in Africa provides another. In Iraq, areas like Kurdistan are relatively stable and peaceful and have control over substantial oil revenues, so their incentives for becoming more engaged with the less stable parts of Iraq are minimal. Despite these cases, supporters of federalism believe in general it provides the ingredients for sharing power and thwarting separatism.[52] Countries with distinctive clusters of ethnic groups or groups that see themselves as "nations," such as the French-speaking population in Canada, might particularly benefit from this mode of government. Critics reply that the record is not nearly so clear-cut. Federalism, for example, might help prevent conflict, but because it gives rival groups competing bases of power, it also might perpetuate conflict once it emerges. Even in Canada, federalism did not discourage separatists from seeking Quebec's independence, though they have yet to succeed.[53]

Political scientists' research into this question has produced mixed results. Overall, research suggests federalism tends to mitigate conflict, but that in certain

> **ThinkingComparatively**
>
> Federalism provides power-sharing arrangements that might be appealing for societies whose ethnic or other differences are deep.

ThinkingCausally

Does federalism reduce conflict within societies?

contexts—for example, Eastern Europe—it may have contributed to conflict. It may also be that federalism works best in societies where the economic pie provides ample slices to share. In very poor countries, federalism may spawn, or at least not deter, violent conflict.[54]

Part of the reason for mixed results in studies of federalism and domestic conflict relates to the difficulties inherent in researching these questions: the term "federalism" embraces a vast spectrum of systems, and the term "conflict" is equally difficult to pin down. Moreover, some societies prone to conflict may choose federalism precisely for that reason; if these societies continue to be fractious, is federalism really the "cause" of that conflict? Researchers also must make judgments based on time spans. Does federalism in the United States prevent conflict? One answer might be yes, with the Civil War being the exception that proves the rule. That is, however, a very large exception.[55]

Federalism in Flux

4-4   Assess the extent and nature of changes in federalism over the past two decades.

Since the early 1990s, American federalism has changed. "Revolutionary" is probably too strong a term to describe the change, but certainly there has been a significant departure from previous decades in the way elected officials and the judiciary have interpreted and implemented American federalism.

Elected officials have initiated changes in federalism.

devolution   a process in which the authority over a government program's rules and implementation is largely transferred from a higher-level government to a lower-level government.

Congress and Presidents Bill Clinton and George W. Bush instigated part of the shift. After Republicans won control of the House and Senate in the 1994 congressional elections, they pushed an agenda of devolution and block grants. **Devolution** refers to the transfer of authority over program details and implementation from a higher level of government to a lower level of government. This transfer could be from federal to state, from state to local, or from federal to local, depending on the issue. In the devolution starting in the 1990s, transfer from the federal to state level was especially prominent. The federal government remained involved, but it allowed the states to use more discretion in deciding how programs will be run. The most famous example is the reform of the national welfare system in 1996. The environment is another example. By the end of the 1990s, the federal Environmental Protection Agency had shifted the authority for nearly 760 federal environmental programs to the states. Over 80 percent of the programs related to the Clean Air Act are now run by state governments. In other policy areas as well, block grants have been used more extensively to give states more flexibility in spending federal funds.

Another way in which Congress has shifted authority to the states is through a process known as negotiated rulemaking. Here, Congress inserts into legislation a requirement that federal agencies negotiate with states over the content of the federal regulations that will implement the law. This requirement does not give states veto power over agency regulations, but it ensures them a formal, ongoing role in the process when regulations are developed that goes beyond the traditional comments that anyone in the public can offer on pending regulations.[56]

The Supreme Court has redefined contemporary federalism.

Even more dramatic than the changes initiated by elected officials were the changes produced by the Supreme Court. In a series of controversial decisions starting in the mid-1990s, the Court began to redraw the boundaries between federal and state responsibilities and authority. It did this by scaling back Congress's use of the interstate commerce clause to justify legislation and by reasserting dual sovereignty ideals. In these efforts, the Court majority believed it was breathing new life into the Tenth Amendment—powers not delegated to the United States are reserved for the states or the people—and the Eleventh Amendment—the federal judicial power does not extend to cases of private individuals against states. Many of these decisions were decided by 5–4 Court majorities and were cheered by conservatives and Republicans while being denounced by liberals and Democrats.

Reining in Congress's use of the commerce clause   Following the Supreme Court's 1937 decision in *National Labor Relations Board v. Jones & Laughlin Steel Corporation* (described earlier), Congress used the Court's new inter-pretation of the interstate commerce clause to move the federal government into areas previously relegated to the states. Until 1995, the Supreme Court acceded to this expansion of federal power. That year, however, in *United States v. Lopez*, the Supreme Court signaled a change in direction. The Gun-Free School Zones Act of 1990 prohibited the possession of firearms within 1,000 feet of a school. Congress justified its intervention in this area by arguing that guns were an item of interstate commerce, but the Court struck down the law.[57] In the Court's view, Congress was improperly involving itself in matters of local policing and using the interstate

▼ **GUNS PROHIBITED NEAR SCHOOL PROPERTY**

The Supreme Court went nearly 60 years after the *Jones & Laughlin* decision before objecting to Congress's use of the commerce clause to justify a law. In 1995, the Court did so, striking down the Gun-Free School Zone Act of 1990. The following year, a new version of the law was passed that, in the view of Congress and the president, provided a stronger justification for the law's connection to interstate commerce. The new law still stands and has not been challenged in court.

commerce clause as a thin and unconvincing rationale for its action. If states and localities wished to pass such restrictions on firearm possession, they were free to do so, but this was not a matter for federal government involvement. For the first time in nearly six decades, the Court refused to agree to Congress's use of the interstate commerce clause to expand federal power. Congress passed a revised law that took account of the Court's decision.

In 2000, the Court's decision in *United States v. Morrison* confirmed this new direction. In the Violence Against Women Act, part of President Clinton's 1994 package of anti-crime legislation, Congress allowed women to file civil suits in federal courts against their attackers. Congress supported its action on interstate commerce grounds, noting that fear of violence suppressed women's full participation in economic life. The Court struck down this provision of the law, determining once again that Congress did not have authority over local criminal activity and that Congress's interstate commerce justification for its action was not credible. Although the Court majority agreed that the violence in the case—a rape of a college student—was reprehensible, it argued that the proper remedy was to be found through the laws of Virginia, not the United States.

Reasserting dual sovereignty   Another issue in the Court's new federalism offensive was whether states could be sued by private parties, such as individuals or organizations, in federal court. In a set of controversial decisions, the Court concluded that under the Eleventh Amendment, states had **sovereign immunity** against these suits—in essence, the states could not be sued in federal court unless they chose to allow themselves to be sued or Congress made a compelling case that it should be able to override this immunity.[58] The Court majority in these decisions added that even without the Eleventh Amendment, the states were sovereign entities prior to the creation of the Constitution and had not given up that status. This view reaffirms the compact theory explained earlier in this chapter.

Under this framework, the Court restricted the use of federal courts to sue states. For example, the Court ruled that the states could not be sued in federal courts by employees complaining that they had not received overtime pay required under the federal Fair Labor Standards Act. States were not subject to age discrimination suits arising from the Age Discrimination in Employment Act or some suits arising from the Americans with Disabilities Act. As mentioned previously in the *Seminole* case, the Court also struck down the ability of Indian tribes to sue states for their failure to negotiate in good faith regarding gambling compacts.[59] Only under certain specific conditions, the Court concluded in these cases, could Congress subject the states to suit by private parties in federal courts.

Other decisions reasserted principles of dual sovereignty and were designed to limit the federal government's ability to impose its will on the states. In *Printz v. United States* (1997), the Court declared that the federal government could not require state officials to perform federal functions. The issue in this case was background checks for handgun purchasers, a function that the law known as the Brady Bill had assigned temporarily to local law enforcement officials until a federal system was in place. The Court concluded that the Constitution's necessary and proper clause did not entitle Congress to compel state or local law enforcement officials to perform federal tasks without their consent. In *City of Boerne v. Flores* (1997), the Court concluded that Congress had exceeded its power in the Religious Freedom Restoration Act by attempting to impose restrictions on local zoning, health, and other regulations in order to prevent perceived threats to religious freedom. The case concerned a complaint by the archbishop in San Antonio over the city's historic preservation zoning regulations. He charged that regulations prohibiting him from expanding his church violated his religious freedom.[60] And in *Gonzales v. Oregon*

sovereign immunity the principle that state governments cannot be sued by private parties in federal court unless they consent to the suits or Congress has constitutionally provided an exemption that allows suits to be filed.

(2006), the Court concluded that the federal government did not have the authority, under the Controlled Substances Act, to prohibit the use of regulated but legal drugs for physician-assisted suicide in Oregon. The Court majority reasoned that Congress had intended to prevent physicians from engaging in the sale and distribution of what the federal government considered legal drugs, not to define standards of medical practice, an arena traditionally left to state governments.

The cumulative effect of the Court's jurisprudence in this era was to send Congress and the president stark messages that they had to tread carefully in their attempts to intervene in states' relationships with their citizens and other areas traditionally established as matters of state concern. It was a clear attempt to restore the influence of dual federalist principles and the ideas of the compact theory, described earlier in this chapter. The narrow 5–4 majorities on many of the decisions heightened the political tension surrounding future Supreme Court nominations. Liberals did not want to lose ground, and conservatives did not want to see their 5–4 majority flip to a 4–5 minority on federalism issues.

State officials have implemented significant new policy.

As law and constitutional interpretation shifted at the federal level, policy innovation in the states expanded in the 1990s and the first decade of the twenty-first century. In areas as diverse as the minimum wage, greenhouse gas emissions, health care coverage, prescription drug imports, and embryonic stem-cell research, state governments enacted significant legislation. By 2007, California, Illinois, Connecticut, and New Jersey had dedicated funding to promote new types of stem-cell research that were generally disallowed under federal funding. Even though President Bush's policy did not allow federal funds to be used for the development of new embryonic stem-cell lines for research purposes, the research was not illegal, so there was no usurpation of national supremacy.[61]

In some of these areas, states acted because of their dissatisfaction with national government policies. In other areas, the federal government's involvement had waned as government officials' concerns were focused elsewhere. These state laws and regulations were, ironically, especially attractive to liberal political activists. With Republicans holding the majority in Congress from 1995 through 2006, and with a Republican president from 2001 through 2008, liberal activists and politicians pushed for legislation and regulation on the state level. National policies might have been preferred, but those were unlikely to happen. As we noted earlier in this chapter, politicians are often opportunistic about federalism and will favor whichever level of government gives them the best chance to win elections and to thwart their opponents.

Has there been a revolution in federalism?

Given these strong moves by Congress, the president, the Supreme Court, and the states, why consider the change in federalism to be anything short of a revolution? Many media and advocacy group critics of the moves describe the changes precisely that way, especially the Court's decisions. These conclusions, however, tend to generalize from only part of the evidence—particular laws or decisions that rankled the critic. Bringing a wider body of evidence into the analysis suggests that "revolution" is too strong a word to describe the changing balance of national and state power.

One reason is that the federal government still remains involved in those policy areas known for devolution, such as welfare. States are free to design their programs as they wish, but they are not free to eliminate those programs.

ThinkingCausally

Have elected officials and the Supreme Court produced a revolution in the balance of national and state power?

Also, federal involvement in new policy areas is possible. Complaining about "frivolous" and "junk" lawsuits, President Bush and many members of Congress argued strongly for national limits on noneconomic damages—such as pain and suffering for loss of companionship—in cases concerning matters like medical malpractice or injuries received from using a product. Traditionally, this issue has been regulated by the states, but with an increasingly globalized economy and for purposes of efficiency and competitiveness, business interests may push more strongly for nationalized standards to replace 50 separate state standards.

One example of the pull and tug of federalism links terrorism and driver's licenses—two seemingly distinct areas of federal and state responsibility, respectively. Congress, in the REAL ID Act of 2005, sought as an antiterrorism measure to require all states to demand proof of permanent residency before issuing driver's licenses; 10 states had no such requirements. In addition, licenses were to be standardized in certain ways across the states, such as the information stored on the machine-readable cards. State license databases would need to be linked to a national database. If a state's licenses were not consistent with the federal standard, individuals holding those licenses would not be able to use them for identification purposes with federal agencies, such as the Transportation Security Administration, which handles security at the nation's airports. Proponents of the law argued it would make it more difficult for terrorists to operate in the United States and more difficult for illegal immigrants to get legal employment. Some of the hijackers involved in the September 11, 2001, attacks had acquired driver's licenses and been able to board planes despite being in the United States illegally.

Opposition to the REAL ID Act spread through states in early 2007. Legislators in many states objected to this federal intervention in traditional state responsibility, its perceived threats to privacy, and the cost imposed on state governments. State governments estimated the cost to them to be $11 billion nationwide, while the federal government put the cost at $3.9 billion, but Congress has allocated only about $200 million to implement the law.[62] Quickly, a majority of states passed resolutions objecting to the law and pledging not to implement it. States with fewer people, less wealth, a more ideologically conservative population, and a tradition of privacy concerns were especially likely to voice opposition.[63] By the end of 2007, the federal government had softened its demands in an attempt to increase support from state officials, and the original May 2008 deadline to meet the act's requirements was extended. The deadline was extended again in December 2009, to May 2011. Measures to repeal REAL ID were introduced in the House and Senate in 2009. President Obama's secretary of Homeland Security, Janet Napolitano, the former governor of Arizona and an opponent of REAL ID, supported the Senate legislation known as PASS ID (Providing for Additional Security in States' Identification Act). The proposed PASS ID would still require state licenses to conform to a national standard, but numerous mandates in REAL ID would be dropped and state privacy laws would not be preempted.

The federal government's role has also become more pronounced in other areas. In the conduct of elections, which were once considered completely the province of the states, national norms have emerged over time, including who can vote. States have not been allowed to place term limits on members of Congress. The federal "Motor Voter" law of 1993 mandated that voting registration be made available at government offices such as motor vehicle bureaus. Following problems with counting votes in the 2000 presidential election, the Help America Vote Act of 2002 mandated changes in states' voting technology—eliminating punch card ballots, for example.[64] An effort in Congress to go one step further and require all states to accept "no excuse" absentee voting was unsuccessful in 2010.[65]

The most notable example in the past decade of an expanded federal role has been in education, long a bastion of state and local governments. The No Child

▼ REAL ID PROVOKES REAL OPPOSITION

The requirement that states change their driver's licenses to match a federal security standard was considered intrusive and expensive by many states. Although a number of states indicated their strong disapproval of the requirement, the state of New York issued its first enhanced driver's license in 2008. The license can be used instead of a passport for non-air travel to Canada, Mexico, and some Caribbean countries.

Left Behind Act championed by President Bush and passed by Congress in 2002 required school districts to test each child in grades 3–8 and specified penalties for schools whose students do poorly and are not improving. President Obama's Race to the Top program aims to reward states with competitive grants for innovations in curriculum standards, student assessment, teacher training, rewarding effective teachers, and improving the performance of unsuccessful schools.[66]

The increased federal role across policy areas has had multiple causes—partisan goals, interest group activism, reactions to crises, similarity of goals among federal and state officials, and disorganized state officials outmaneuvered by unified legislators at the national level.[67] And, just as we noted above that Democrats and liberals were active in innovating policy on the state level, Republican President George Bush and his Republican allies in Congress were instrumental in seeking to increase national power with No Child Left Behind and REAL ID as well as areas like providing prescription drug benefits for seniors and forcing some class-action lawsuits out of state courts and into the generally more conservative federal courts. Federalism remains a political battleground where politicians take advantage of the opportunities they have in front of them. That may mean preferring national solutions in some instances and state solutions in others.

Another reason not to overstate the extent of the new federalism "revolution" is that the Court did not completely defer to the states in its decisions about sovereign immunity from lawsuits. When cases involved Fourteenth Amendment issues of equal protection (see Chapter 6), particularly in the areas of race and gender, the Court allowed states to be subject to federal authority. For example, the Court concluded that an individual could sue a state in federal court for that state's alleged

◄ **WOULD YOU LIKE SOME HIGHS WITH THAT?**

In 2000, Colorado voters supported the use of marijuana for medicinal purposes. Medical marijuana shops soon emerged. A U.S. Supreme Court decision in 2005, however, upheld Congress's power to prohibit the growing and possession of medical marijuana, even for one's personal use, superseding the Colorado law. The U.S. Justice Department announced in 2009 that it would no longer prosecute the use of medical marijuana in states that allowed it. How aggressive should federal government enforcement be when state laws contradict federal laws?

gender-based discrimination in implementing the Family Medical Leave Act, and that these suits were consistent with Congress's intent when it passed the act.[68]

This idea, that Congress could respond to widespread and persistent discrimination, was also at the core of *Tennessee v. Lane* (2004). The case concerned a paraplegic who could not attend a court case because of a lack of elevators in the court building. To the Supreme Court, the fundamental importance of citizen access to the courts overrode the state's claim to immunity from a discrimination lawsuit. Congress was right to allow an exception to sovereign immunity, in the view of the 5–4 Court majority, because it had amassed evidence of recurrent, extensive violations of equal access by the states. If the Court believes a right is of special gravity, it will give Congress more leeway to force states to comply with federal rules that might otherwise be seen as exceeding federal constitutional authority.[69]

The Supreme Court also has been willing to trim state power. The Court rejected a California law that allowed Holocaust survivors to pursue insurance claims through lawsuits, rather than through international diplomacy as called for by federal law. The California statute, in the Court's view, interfered with the federal government's authority over foreign policy.[70] And in *Gonzales v. Raich* (2005), Congress's power to prohibit the personal growing and possession of marijuana for medical use was upheld, superseding a first-in-the-nation 1996 California law that allowed such use. The federal Controlled Substances Act did not allow exemptions for medical use of marijuana, the Court held, and the federal government could regulate those products involved in interstate commerce. Although growth for personal medicinal use might appear to be entirely local and thus not an area for federal regulation, the Court concluded that personal medicinal use nonetheless affected supply and demand and was in effect a part of the national marijuana market. Therefore, it was subject to the national government's interstate commerce power.

In October 2009, U.S. Attorney General Eric Holder announced that the Justice Department would no longer prosecute individuals who were using marijuana strictly for medical purposes in states where such use was allowed—currently over one dozen—arguing that prosecution of such cases was not an efficient use of limited federal resources.[71] California voters in 2010 rejected a measure to legalize the personal recreation use of marijuana. Touted as a source for new revenue, the defeated proposal would have allowed cities and counties to collect sales taxes on marijuana purchases. The passage of a state law would not trump the federal prohibition on marijuana growth and sales, however, and Holder indicated prior to the election that the federal ban would be enforced.

Certainly the Court has continued as well to look favorably on the demands of states for freedom from federal restrictions. In *Altria Group v. Good* (2008), a case concerning cigarettes advertised and labeled as "light" with "lowered tar and nicotine," a 5–4 Court majority ruled that federal law on cigarette labeling could not preempt a portion of a Maine unfair trade practices act. This allowed a lawsuit against a tobacco company to proceed. What made the decision especially interesting was that it was the Court's four most liberal members and the more conservative Justice Anthony Kennedy who formed the majority in favor of state government authority.

So where does federalism stand today? Early in the second decade of the twenty-first century, federalism continues to evolve. It has not returned to the dual federalism of the nineteenth century, as the federal government's intervention into areas like education, traditionally thought of as a local and state responsibility, makes clear. But it is also not simply the cooperative federalism of much of the twentieth century. It is neither strictly layer cake nor marble cake. Today's federalism remains cooperative in many respects but does so within dual federalism boundaries that have been reasserted by elected officials and by the Supreme Court.

Rather than a cake, perhaps a better metaphor today would be a pie. Dual federalism is the crust that prevents cooperative federalism from spilling too far outside the constitutional pan. Rather than the open-ended cooperative federalism in place from the mid-1930s to mid-1990s, today's is a constrained cooperative federalism, restricted and limited by the Court's enforcement of dual federalist principles via the Tenth and Eleventh Amendments. This constrained cooperative federalism, however, does not sit still. Politicians and judges push and pull it in multiple directions. Today's federalism is united with past federalism in that politicians and judges mix philosophy with desired policy outcomes as they wrestle with the balance of national and state power.

Although it is uncertain how President Obama's appointments to the Supreme Court will affect this blend of dual and cooperative federalism, they will most likely not lead to a major new direction. The president's first two appointments to the Court replaced liberal justices with new justices who are also liberal, thus suggesting the Court's overall view on issues concerning the balance of national and state power would remain about the same as previously. Among the president's legislative achievements, universal health insurance, which requires states to comply with new national standards and uses interstate commerce regulation to mandate that individuals purchase insurance, may produce the most highly charged federalism case that will reach this new Court.

CHAPTER SUMMARY

In this chapter you have learned to:

4-1 **Show how the Constitution serves as a framework for federalism and why debates remain.** The Constitution defines the framework within which American federalism operates, identifying areas where the national government is supreme to the states. But disputes about the role of the states in the federal system have never gone away. Differing interpretations of the formation of the United States contribute to the dispute. To some, the Union was a joining together of "the people," which weakens the primacy that states should have in federalism. To others, the Union was a joining together of the states in which states reserved a substantial amount of the sovereignty they held prior to creating the United States.

4-2 **Outline the principles of dual federalism and their basis in the Supreme Court's traditional understanding of interstate commerce.** The two major forms of federal–state relations in American history have been dual federalism and cooperative federalism. Dual federalism delineates separate and independent spheres of function and responsibility for the federal and state governments. All citizens have dual citizenship, being a citizen of both their state and the country. Prevailing Supreme Court interpretation of Congress's power to regulate interstate commerce reinforced dual federalism.

4-3 **Trace the evolution from dual to cooperative federalism and identify methods of cooperative federalism.** Redefining interstate commerce played a significant role in expanding the scope of federal government responsibility and moving the country from dual to cooperative federalism. Rather than relying on strict spheres of federal and state duties, cooperative federalism allows for many areas of overlapping responsibilities for these two layers of government. Collaboration, mandates, and persuasion in the form of fiscal federalism are types of federal–state interaction in cooperative federalism. Generally, the federal government was the more powerful in this "cooperative" arrangement; thus, cooperative did not always mean harmonious. Mandates are sometimes described as coercive federalism, and fiscal federalism can apply pressure on state officials to follow federal government wishes.

4-4 **Assess the extent and nature of changes in federalism over the past two decades.** Over the past two decades, the relationship between the federal and state governments has shifted. State officials became more active in policy areas where they had previously deferred to national leadership. At the national level, elected officials sought to provide states with more flexibility and responsibility over some policies. In a number of important decisions, the Supreme Court clamped down on Congress's use of the interstate commerce justification, concluded that the federal government had become improperly involved in areas of state government responsibility, and asserted the argument that the sovereignty of state governments shielded them from some federal government regulation. Not everything has moved in the direction of more state authority, however. In few policy areas has the federal government fully withdrawn, and it has inserted itself into new areas that had traditionally been the purview of the states.

mypoliscilab **EXERCISES**

Apply what you learned in this chapter on MyPoliSciLab.

Read on mypoliscilab.com

eText: Chapter 4

✓ **Study** and **Review** on mypoliscilab.com

Pre-Test
Post-Test
Chapter Exam
Flashcards

Watch on mypoliscilab.com

Video: Water Wars
Video: The Real ID
Video: Proposition 8

Explore on mypoliscilab.com

Simulation: You Are a Federal Judge
Simulation: You Are a Restaurant Owner
Comparative: Comparing Federal and Unitary Systems
Timeline: Federalism and the Supreme Court
Visual Literacy: Federalism and Regulations

KEY TERMS

block grant, p. 146
categorical grant, p. 145
commerce clause, p. 133
compact theory, p. 127
confederation, p. 125
cooperative federalism, p. 134
devolution, p. 154
dual citizenship, p. 131
dual federalism, p. 130

dual sovereignty, p. 130
enumerated powers, p. 137
federalism, p. 127
fiscal federalism, p. 145
implied powers, p. 137
mandate, p. 143
nationalist theory, p. 128
necessary and proper clause, p. 137
nullification, p. 128

police power, p. 130
preemption legislation, p. 144
reserved powers, p. 127
sovereign immunity, p. 156
sovereignty, p. 127
unfunded mandate, p. 144
unitary system, p. 125

CHAPTER TEST

1. What are the main differences between the confederal, unitary, and federal systems of organizing government?

2. How would advocates of the nationalist and compact theory views of American government evaluate the confederal, unitary, and federal systems?

3. What is the difference between dual sovereignty and dual citizenship?

4. What were the main areas of responsibility thought to be distinctively the authority of the federal government and distinctively the authority of the state governments under dual federalism?

5. How did the interpretation of interstate commerce change, and how did this matter for the evolution of federalism?

6. As a federal official, what would influence your decision whether to use a form of collaboration, mandate, or persuasion in dealing with the states?

7. As a governor of a state, how would you rank the forms of federal financial assistance from most to least attractive?

8. In what areas would you argue that states should and should not have a great degree of flexibility rather than following national standards in establishing public policy, and what are your criteria for making those distinctions?

9. What were the main themes of Supreme Court pro-state federalism decisions over the past two decades?

10. What are the strongest arguments that there has not been a revolution in federalism?

SUGGESTED READINGS

Samuel H. Beer. 1993. *To Make a Nation: The Rediscovery of American Federalism*. Cambridge, MA: Harvard University Press. A thorough analysis of the principles and philosophy of American federalism.

Martha N. Derthick. 2001. *Keeping the Compound Republic: Essays on American Federalism*. Washington, DC: Brookings Institution Press. The evolution of federalism in the United States and an analysis of a range of issues concerning federalism and intergovernmental relations.

Morton Grodzins. 1966. *The American System*. Chicago: Rand McNally. Argues that the idea of a distinct division of labor between the federal and state governments has been exaggerated.

Alison LaCroix. 2010. *The Ideological Origins of American Federalism*. Cambridge, MA: Harvard University Press. Views American federalism as not so much an adaptation to circumstances that Americans backed into, but as a major theory and ideology that held a prominent position in American political thought in the eighteenth century prior to the Constitution.

Paul Manna. 2006. *School's In: Federalism and the National Education Agenda*. Washington, DC: Georgetown University Press. How the increased role of the federal government in education was a result of building on state-level fiscal and administrative capacities created by education reformers in previous decades.

Paul E. Peterson. 1995. *The Price of Federalism*. Washington, DC: Brookings Institution Press. An exploration of the ways in which federalism works well and the political pressures that can push legislators away from it.

Paul L. Posner. 1998. *The Politics of Unfunded Mandates: Whither Federalism?* Washington, DC: Georgetown University Press. Examines the political struggle between national and state officials over paying for programs required by the national government.

Deloria Vine Jr. and Clifford M. Lytle. 1998. *The Nations Within: The Past and Future of American Indian Sovereignty*. Austin: University of Texas Press. Through a close accounting of the politics surrounding an important bill, the book explores the complexity of tribal sovereignty in the American federal system.

SUGGESTED WEBSITES

National Conference of State Legislatures: www.ncsl.org

Excellent resource with policy analysis, election results, and a range of other helpful data comparing states and examining federal–state issues.

Education Commission of the States: www.ecs.org

Useful site for comparing state education policies and implementation of the federal government's No Child Left Behind Act.

Library of Congress, American Memory Project: To Form a More Perfect Union: memory.loc.gov/ammem/collections/continental/intro01.html

Original documents related to federalism and the relationship of the states to each other and the national government. Focus on Revolutionary War era and the making of the Constitution.

Grants.gov: www.grants.gov

Easy-to-use searchable database of federal grants.

Statistical Abstract of the United States: www.census.gov/compendia/statab

Terrific collection of data published by the U.S. Census Bureau that includes hundreds of tables and downloadable spreadsheets, many at the state level, and data on intergovernmental finances.

Urban Institute: http://www.urban.org/government/federalism.cfm

Good collection of studies on a wide range of issues facing federalist systems in the United States and around the world.

The Battle over Corporate Political Speech

The scene was extraordinary. Before a national television audience and in front of the assembled members of Congress, President Barack Obama was directly criticizing the U.S. Supreme Court in his State of the Union Address, with six of the justices seated before him. One of those justices, Samuel Alito, was silently mouthing the response "Not true" to the president's criticism.

The Supreme Court had ruled in January 2010 that corporations have a right to spend their funds independently to support or oppose candidates by running television ads or other forms of communication. By extension, the ruling applied to labor unions also, and to both for-profit and nonprofit corporations. The Court was bitterly divided, 5–4. The majority argued that the First Amendment does not allow the government to choose favored and

▼ **CENTER OF ATTENTION**
Justice Samuel Alito (center) sits with five other justices during President Obama's State of the Union Address, 2010. The president had just rebuked the Supreme Court for its decision in _Citizens United v. FEC_, bringing senators and administration officials to their feet in applause. Alito silently mouthed "not true" in response to the president's critique.

disfavored speakers. The minority argued that the First Amendment was never intended to give corporate entities the same free speech protection as it provided individuals.

At issue was _Hillary Clinton: The Movie_, a critical documentary produced by Citizens United, a small nonprofit corporation funded mostly by individual contributions. Clinton was running for the Democratic Party's 2008 nomination for the presidency. The company wanted to distribute its documentary by video-on-demand services on cable television, and it also wished to air short advertisements promoting the documentary. Fearing the Federal Election Commission (FEC) would consider the documentary and ads to violate the Bipartisan Campaign Reform Act of 2002 (BCRA), Citizens United sought an injunction against any FEC action. BCRA prohibits corporations from using their general treasury funds for independent electioneering activities—that is, any broadcast, cable, or satellite communications within 30 days of a primary election or 60 days of a general election that specifically mentions a candidate for federal office. Citizens United lost and the case moved to the Supreme Court.

The response to the Supreme Court's decision was thunderous. Critics denounced the ruling in _Citizens United v. Federal Election Commission_ as a devastating blow to democracy and fair elections: "This appalling decision . . . will further weaken the quality and fairness of our politics.

much too powerful, a nuclear weapon. . . . The conservative justices savaged canons of judicial restraint they themselves have long praised." Supporters cheered the decision as a stirring victory for free speech: "Hopefully, this ruling marks an end to 20 years of jurisprudence in which the Court has provided less protection to core political speech than it has to Internet pornography . . . flag burning, commercial advertising, topless dancing, and burning a cross outside an African American church." Critics promised legislative responses that would require extensive disclosure and place limits on campaign involvement by some corporations. Supporters promised to pursue vigorous legal challenges to other campaign finance laws that in their view restricted freedom of speech or circumvented the intent of the Court's ruling. The DISCLOSE Act, the first legislative response to _Citizens United_, faltered in the summer of 2010.[1]

Praise for and condemnation of the Supreme Court's reasoning, and impassioned debate over what the First Amendment does and does not demand regarding free speech, were the basis of one major post-decision debate. The other major debate concerned causality. What would be the result of the Court's decision?

Critics charged that corporate speech would "drown out" speech from candidates and other sources. Some argued that legislators would live in fear that casting a difficult vote might unleash a large war chest of independent corporate or union spending against them—or that legislators, fearing such reaction, would avoid casting difficult votes.

Supporters claimed that the ruling would lead to more vibrant campaigns—speech begets more speech in response, and the public is ultimately the beneficiary. Many also than the other way around, so corporate campaigning would more likely be in response to government actions rather than be prompting such action.

Most political science research, when controlling for other factors that influence members of Congress, has not found a strong connection between corporate political action committee (PAC) contributions, or contributions by individuals in particular industries, and votes by legislators in Congress.[2] But PAC contributions do not come from corporate treasuries—the funds are raised separately by donations to the PAC—and there are strict dollar limits on the amount a PAC can contribute to a candidate, so the causal analogy may be weak.

Prior to *Citizens United*, about half the states already allowed unlimited campaign spending by corporations and unions. These are funds spent independently by these organizations, for example on campaign ads. The spending is not coordinated with a candidate or party and is not contributed to a candidate. One analysis soon after the Court decision found little significant difference between this set of states and the other states on party control, business climate, or policy of interest to business. Why? Perhaps business spending motivates labor and consumer groups to be more involved. Maybe different businesses are on opposite sides in a particular race. Or many businesses may fear the reputational backlash of heavy involvement in campaigns.[3] On the other hand, it could be that if many legislative seats are safe for one party or another, the relevant test of the significance of business spending would be to focus on elections where the control of the seat is up for grabs and the outcome could have major policy consequences. Helping elect the sixty-fifth Democrat or Republican in a hundred-member state legislature might not be a sound investment. Helping elect the fifty-first in a legislature that is evenly divided might.

The debates over the propriety of the Supreme Court's decision, as well as its causal impact on politics, will continue. Constitutional guarantees such as freedom of speech, freedom of religion, and the right to assemble are general principles, but politics is also about specifics, and these specifics lead to conflict. In these conflicts, choices must be made, either through law, executive action, or court decision, each of which are examined in this chapter. You will see that a number of Supreme Court decisions were decided by votes of 5–4, suggesting just how deep the conflict over defining proper protections for civil liberties can be, and how a change in the members of the Court can lead to significant changes in these definitions. You will also see how Court decisions prompt legislative action, to which the Court may have to respond in the future.

In addition to conflict, another constant of civil liberties is change. What is considered appropriate at one time might not be considered so at another. This chapter will emphasize how the scope of civil liberties protections has changed across time. Historically, three paths have led to this change in scope. First, the civil liberties restrictions placed on the federal government by the U.S. Constitution were gradually applied to state governments. Second, as membership in the Supreme Court changed, interpretation of the Constitution's meaning also changed. And third, Supreme Court decisions have established individual rights that are not specifically mentioned in the Constitution.

CHAPTER LEARNING OBJECTIVES

After reading this chapter you will be able to:

5-1 Define the civil liberties guaranteed by the Constitution and trace the process by which they became binding on state governments.

5-2 Analyze the different standards by which the Supreme Court has determined whether restrictions on freedom of speech are acceptable.

5-3 Evaluate how the Supreme Court has interpreted cases regarding religion and how Congress has reacted to the Court's actions.

5-4 Trace the expansion of the rights of the accused and their balance with the needs of police and prosecutors.

5-5 Explain how the Ninth and Fourteenth Amendments have helped to establish rights other than those specifically listed in the Constitution.

Civil Liberties in American Politics and the Constitution

5-1 Define the civil liberties guaranteed by the Constitution and trace the process by which they became binding on state governments.

Civil liberties are another name for individual rights. The Declaration of Independence makes eight references to a "right" or "rights." Equality, another important principle in the American governmental framework, is mentioned only twice. Even "the people," a staple of revolutionary thought and language, appears less frequently than rights. And this rights language is not just a thing of the past. The 2008 Democratic Party platform mentions rights over 70 times. The Republican platform does the same, mentioning rights more than 70 times. (See Table 5-1.) The parties' references range from very general mentions of rights to more specific notions such as the right not to join a union or the right to health care.

We can safely say that very few words are more important to Americans' understanding of their political system than *rights*. Political rhetoric in America is full of references to rights, whether individual rights, like the right to speak freely, or collective rights, such as the right of the people to assemble. American political culture, with its emphasis on individual independence, liberty, property ownership, religious freedom, and democratic government, is infused throughout with individual rights. Some rights might be expressed from a more communitarian perspective, such as the idea that it is in the community's interest and not only the individual's interest that everyone in the community has a right to an equal quality of education.

Civil liberties identify areas where government should not interfere.

civil liberties individual rights and freedoms that government is obliged to protect, normally by not interfering in the exercise of these rights and freedoms.

In the United States, **civil liberties** focus on individual rights that government is obliged to protect, normally by standing back and not interfering. When Americans talk about civil liberties, they are typically talking about places government should not go: speech, the press, religious expression, organizing for political purposes, and so on.[4] With civil liberties, the call is usually that government be passive and not intrude when, for example, individuals speak, worship, or engage in political action. American political culture, and its understanding of liberty, suggests that these rights are not *granted* to us or *given* to us by government—they are inherent in us as people. What government can do is protect or restrict the exercise of these individual rights.[5]

As a matter of definition, civil liberties are easy enough to understand. But politically, civil liberties can be difficult, as the campaign finance example above suggests. Civil liberties issues often create a contest between elected officials and the judiciary to define what is and what is not consistent with constitutional values and text. Causal chain reactions are common. Congress passes a law. The courts respond. Congress revisits the issue with a new law. Maybe the states pass their own versions of the federal law. The courts will often then be asked to rule again on the civil liberties issue in question.

Civil liberties differ from civil rights, the subject of Chapter 6. Civil liberties are chiefly concerned with liberty, whereas civil rights focus on equality. Civil rights are guarantees of government to provide equal opportunities, privileges, and treatment under the law for all individuals regardless of any group characteristic.

In some instances, Americans will tolerate limits on civil liberties to preserve public safety, order, or other important societal goals. For example, Americans have the right to assemble, but that does not extend into a right to assemble in the middle

TABLE 5-1. Number of References to Rights in the Republican and Democratic Party Platforms, 2008

REFERENCE	REPUBLICAN PLATFORM	DEMOCRATIC PLATFORM
Human rights	3	17
Own guns	7	4
Women's rights	3	5
Civil rights	2	5
Voting rights	2	5
Right to join/not join union, collective bargaining rights	3	4
Right of U.S. territories to self-determination	3	2
Victims' rights	4	1
Educational rights	4	1
Constitutional rights	2	2
Israel's self defense	1	2
Intellectual property rights	2	1
Uniformed service employment rights	1	2
Tibetan rights	1	1
Property rights	6	
Individual rights	4	
Religious freedom	4	
Right to liberty	4	
Right to life	3	
Right of freedom of speech and the press	3	
Rights of states in same-sex marriage and voter ID	3	
Rights of families (no international abortion funds)	1	
Cuban refugees	1	
Religious organizations freedom in hiring	1	
Rights of children	1	
Parental rights over medical decisions	1	
Iranian right to choose their own government	1	
Workers' rights		3
Rights of people with disabilities		3
Right to choose abortion		3
Health care		3
Homeowners' rights		2
Cultural rights of Native Americans and Hawaiians		2
Credit Card Bill of Rights		1
Right of individuals to challenge their detention		1
Equal rights for District of Columbia residents		1

Compiled by the authors.

Note: Each entry indicates references to a "right" or "rights" in the party platforms.

of a city street and stop traffic. Government has to be concerned with the conflicting rights of both the assemblers and those needing to go about their lives and go to work, school, or wherever they might need to travel. Part of civil liberties protection, therefore, is that when government restricts the exercise of rights, it does so with **due process**. The Fifth Amendment to the Constitution states that no person shall "be deprived of life, liberty, or property, without due process of law." This clause means

due process procedural safeguards that government officials are obligated to follow prior to restricting rights of life, liberty, and property.

► A PRAYER IN CONGRESS FOR ACTION ON POVERTY

The House of Representatives starts each day with a prayer delivered by religious figures from various faiths. Is this an unconstitutional violation of the separation between church and state or an acknowledgement of the importance of freedom of religious practice in American civil liberties? Here, former House Speaker Nancy Pelosi (center) joins with church and faith-based organization members and with other members of the House of Representatives.

that there must be procedural safeguards in place prior to the restriction of rights. Government officials exercising due process have to follow clear guidelines and established procedures. In the case of gathering in the street, for example, there are procedures by which a group can get a permit to assemble and march.

A related concept also found in the Fifth Amendment is expressed in the "takings clause," which requires that government must compensate you for taking your private property for a public use ("nor shall private property be taken for public use, without just compensation"). As with many terms in the Constitution, "public use" can be defined broadly or narrowly. In 2005, for example, a divided 5–4 Supreme Court in *Kelo v. City of New London* upheld New London, Connecticut's desire to take private property for economic development, which in practice meant building private office space and a conference hotel. In effect, property was transferred from one private party to another as a "public use." In the wake of that controversial decision, many states passed laws to prohibit this kind of government action. This response to *Kelo* demonstrates another way in which Americans' civil liberties are protected: through state-level constitutions, bills of rights, and laws. Because Americans are dual citizens, as discussed in Chapter 4, they can have additional protections for their liberty in their states. Thus, a takings like that in New London may not violate the takings clause in the U.S. Constitution, but it might be determined as violating a state's laws or the takings clause in a state's constitution.

ThinkingComparatively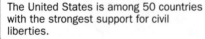

The United States is among 50 countries with the strongest support for civil liberties.

On the whole, civil liberties protections are strong in the United States. Although Americans often think of the United States as unique in this regard, the United States is 1 of 50 countries judged in 2010 to have the strongest protection for civil liberties among all 194 independent countries by Freedom House, an international political rights and civil liberties watch-dog group. Freedom House describes these countries as having freedom of expression, assembly, association, education, and religion; having an established and equitable rule of law; and enjoying free economic activity. Figure 5-1 shows the countries Freedom House considers to be free, partly free, and not free.[6]

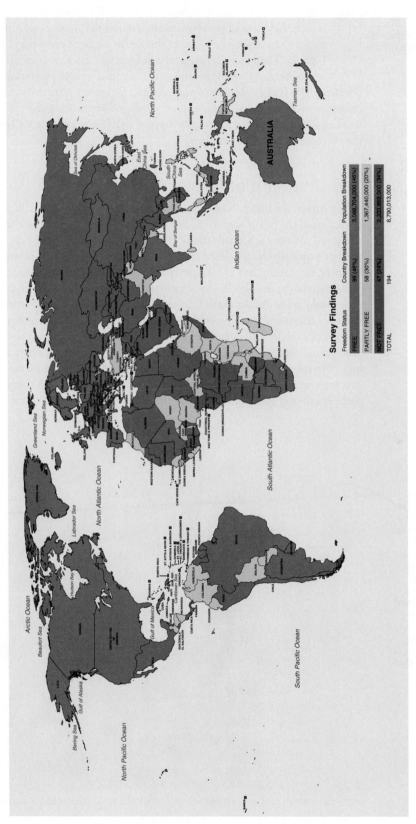

FIGURE 5-1. **Freedom Around the Globe, 2010.** The number of free or partly free countries has increased over the past decade, but there is still significant regional variation in the spread of political rights and civil liberties around the globe.

Survey Findings

Freedom Status	Country Breakdown	Population Breakdown
FREE	89 (46%)	3,088,704,000 (46%)
PARTLY FREE	58 (30%)	1,367,440,000 (20%)
NOT FREE	47 (24%)	2,333,869,000 (34%)
TOTAL	194	6,790,013,000

ThinkingCausally

Do protections for civil liberties lead to prosperity or do they result from prosperity?

In general, civil liberties protections are strongest in Europe and the Americas and weakest in Asia and Africa. These patterns correlate roughly with the distribution of prosperity around the globe, prompting social scientists to examine whether civil liberties result from prosperity or create prosperity. Their research suggests that both processes are present: civil liberties encourage economic growth, and economic growth encourages civil liberties.[7] The relationships are not automatic. Economic prosperity varies among countries with strong civil liberties protection, and countries with increasing prosperity, such as China, do not necessarily support civil liberties strongly. Overall, however, the two appear to work in tandem.

The Constitution protects civil liberties.

When Americans think about the constitutional protection of civil liberties, they think first of the Bill of Rights, the first ten amendments to the Constitution. But this is only one of the Constitution's protections of liberty. To the Framers, the structural principles in the articles of the Constitution—separation of powers, checks and balances, federalism, and limited government—all worked to enhance the general protection of the people's liberty. The Framers also included specific civil liberties protections in the articles of the Constitution. For example, the Constitution declares that only courts and juries—not the legislature—can determine whether an individual is guilty of a crime. The intent is to ensure that, before any rights are restricted, the proceedings that might lead to that outcome are fair, impartial, proper, and not subject to the political pressures that exist in a legislature. Both the federal and state governments are prohibited from passing a bill of attainder, which is legislation that declares a person guilty of a crime and establishes punishment, all without a trial.

▶ **DETAINEE AT U.S. MILITARY BASE AT GUANTANAMO BAY, CUBA**

Terrorism suspects—"enemy combatants"—were held at this military base without the usual kinds of protections afforded to prisoners in the civilian court system. In July 2008, the prisoners gained their *habeas corpus* rights, which allowed them direct access to federal courts, by a 5–4 Supreme Court decision in *Boumediene et al. v. Bush*. Early in his term, President Obama pledged to close "Gitmo" in 2010 and relocate the detainees, but that deadline was not met.

The articles of the Constitution protect civil liberties in other ways. Religious tests or oaths for federal employment are prohibited. The writ of *habeas corpus*, which gives an accused individual the right to appear in court to hear the formal charges against him or her, cannot be suspended except to enhance public safety during times of rebellion or invasion. And an individual cannot be tried based on *ex post facto* ("after the fact") laws passed by state governments or the federal government, meaning that you cannot be tried for an act that was not illegal at the time you committed it.

Freedom of expression and the rights of the accused are the two main areas of civil liberties protection in the Bill of Rights.

The Bill of Rights is at the heart of constitutional civil liberties protections. The Federalists believed that a Bill of Rights was unnecessary. In their view, the articles of the Constitution themselves contained specific guarantees of liberty, the Constitution's general structure was designed to protect liberty, and state constitutions had bills of rights. The risk of specifying rights was that government might be presumed free to ignore all rights not mentioned. But the Federalists quickly saw that the promise of additional specific protections would increase the likelihood of ratification of the Constitution.[8]

The provisions in the first eight amendments of the Bill of Rights provide protection against the actions of the legislative, executive, and judicial branches of government. Table 5-2 shows that the protections overwhelmingly regard two categories: freedom of expression and the rights of those accused of crime. A final category consists of three provisions that do not fit into the previous two categories.

TABLE 5-2. Specific Civil Liberties Protections in the Bill of Rights

CATEGORY OF SPECIFIC CIVIL LIBERTIES PROTECTED (AMENDMENT IN PARENTHESES)		
FREEDOM OF EXPRESSION	**RIGHTS OF DEFENDANTS**	**OTHER PROTECTIONS**
Freedom to exercise religion (1st)	Cannot search for or seize evidence without court warrant and probable cause (4th)	Right of people to keep and bear arms (2nd)
No establishment of religion (1st)		
Freedom of speech (1st)	Right to grand jury hearing in criminal cases (5th)	Cannot use citizen homes to house soldiers without due process (3rd)
Freedom of assembly (1st)		
Freedom to petition government (1st)	Right to jury trial in criminal and civil cases (6th and 7th)	Property cannot be taken for public use without fair compensation (5th)
Freedom of the press (1st)		
	Right to speedy trial (6th)	
	Right to hear charges against oneself (6th)	
	Right to confront witnesses and offer own witnesses (6th)	
	Cannot be forced to incriminate oneself (6th)	
	Cannot be tried for the same crime more than once (6th)	
	Right to legal counsel (6th)	
	Bail cannot be excessive and punishment cannot be cruel and unusual (8th)	

One of these, the quartering of troops in homes, has not been especially significant since its ratification into the Constitution, but the other two—the right to keep and bear arms and the compensation for public appropriation of one's property—have been the subject of extensive political and legal debate. The Ninth Amendment states that the failure to list rights in the preceding amendments should not be presumed to mean that the people do not have additional rights. The Tenth Amendment declares that powers not given to the federal government are reserved for the states or the people.[9]

Nationalization of the Bill of Rights protected individuals against the actions of state governments.

Despite its importance in the constitutional ratification debate and despite the reverence with which it is held today, the Bill of Rights had a more limited effect on American politics during the nineteenth century than it does today. During that time, government was much more active on the state level. Many states had their own bills of rights to protect their citizens from state government actions, but the U.S. Constitution's Bill of Rights was considered to apply only to the actions of the national government. After all, the words "Congress shall make no law" in the First Amendment seem pretty clearly to apply to the national level of government and not the states. Recall the case of *Barron v. Baltimore* (see Chapter 4), in which the Supreme Court declared that Barron was not entitled to compensation under the Constitution's Fifth Amendment because it was the city of Baltimore, not the federal government, that took Barron's property without compensation.

The nationalization of the Bill of Rights is the first of three paths by which the scope of civil liberties protection has been changed. Beginning in 1897, as explained below, the Supreme Court began to see the Bill of Rights as limiting the actions of state governments as well as the national government. This revolutionary shift opened the door for increased federal government authority.[10]

Incorporation and the Fourteenth Amendment   The Supreme Court used the **incorporation process** to apply the Bill of Rights to the states. The Fourteenth Amendment was key to this process. Stated technically, the Bill of Rights was incorporated into the Fourteenth Amendment and through this inclusion became binding on the states.

incorporation process   the application, through the Fourteenth Amendment, of the civil liberties protections in the Bill of Rights to state governments.

The Fourteenth Amendment has been profoundly important to American life. The amendment was ratified in July 1868 as part of the post–Civil War reconstruction of American government and society. It was the first amendment to limit state action directly, declaring that "no State shall make or enforce any law which shall abridge the privileges or immunities of citizens of the United States; nor shall any State deprive any person of life, liberty, or property, without due process of law; nor deny to any person within its jurisdiction the equal protection of the laws." If we consider the battle over state versus national power during the framing of the Constitution, and the many protections for state sovereignty in the Constitution and in law, this declaration was a remarkable turnabout. Why the change? Keep in mind that three-quarters of the states needed to ratify this amendment. In effect, they would be voting to limit their independence. Political scientists often point to the importance of ideas, interests, and institutions in explaining political change, and all three can be brought to bear on this puzzle. Some of those legislators voting to ratify the amendment may have done so based on a sincere belief in the idea that the Union needed to have some

ThinkingCausally

Why would state legislators ratify the Fourteenth Amendment, an amendment that was likely to limit their independent authority?

consistent civil liberties standards to protect all citizens, but especially the recently emancipated slaves.

Given that the collapse of a unified nation contributed to the descent into a horrific war, it is understandable that a majority of politicians and the public supported constitutional provisions that could prevent states from straying too far from fundamental protections of life, liberty, and property—it was in their self-interest. Whether ideas or interests were ultimately more important to a northern state legislator voting to ratify the amendment, an important institutional rule further helps explain the amendment's success: southern states were required to accept the amendment prior to being readmitted to the Union, and they were not allowed representation in Congress until they were readmitted. Even if they opposed the content of the amendment—and some southern states did initially vote against ratification—self-interest ultimately led them to ratify it.

The "due process clause" of the Fourteenth Amendment brings protection from state government intrusions on life, liberty, and property into the U.S. Constitution.[11] But what exactly does that mean? This is what the Supreme Court began to determine in a series of major decisions.

Selective incorporation　The Court began the process with a decision concerning property. In 1897, the Court decided that, in order for the Fourteenth Amendment's general protection of property to be a meaningful concept, it required compensation when property was taken for public use. The Fifth Amendment's "takings clause," which states that private property cannot be taken for public use

◄ **BENJAMIN GITLOW, WORKERS PARTY 1928 VICE PRESIDENTIAL CANDIDATE**

The Supreme Court in 1925 upheld the conviction of Benjamin Gitlow (right) under a New York law for promoting overthrow of the government. However, the Court established in *Gitlow v. New York* that the Bill of Rights' protection of freedom of speech also applied to the states. Over the next four decades, the remaining provisions of the First Amendment would be determined to apply to the states.

unless the property owner is compensated, was thus incorporated into the Fourteenth Amendment and, therefore, now applied to the states.

Over a quarter-century would pass before the Court took another incorporation step. In 1925, the Court decided that the Fourteenth Amendment's protection of "liberty" must include a free speech guarantee—free speech was fundamental to the concept of liberty. The First Amendment's free speech guarantee was thus incorporated into the Fourteenth Amendment's protection for "liberty" and now it, too, applied to the action of state governments.[12]

Notice that these two cases incorporated only part of the Bill of Rights guarantees into the Fourteenth Amendment. In practice, the Supreme Court has proceeded through **selective incorporation**, meaning that it incorporated civil liberties guarantees in bits and pieces. The Supreme Court has not simply declared that the entire Bill of Rights applied to the states. Rather, the Court has worked with the issues in the cases before it. As cases raised issues concerning particular parts of the amendments that comprise the Bill of Rights, the Court would decide whether that particular right was fundamental enough to the Fourteenth Amendment's protection of life, liberty, and property that it should now apply to the states.

selective incorporation the process by which protections in the Bill of Rights were gradually applied to the states, as the Supreme Court issued decisions on specific aspects of the Bill of Rights.

ThinkingCausally

What factors led the Supreme Court to engage in selective incorporation?

Over time, the Court declared that additional portions of the Bill of Rights beyond these first two would apply to state governments. Why did they take this stance? There was no guarantee that incorporation would go any further. Four factors seem chiefly important in the spread of selective incorporation. First is that dramatic events gave increased credibility and legitimacy to extending the protections of the Bill of Rights against actions by state and local governments. Abusive search and seizure cases during Prohibition, the mistreatment of blacks by southern police and court systems, and the hostility toward Jehovah's Witnesses before and during World War II because of their beliefs, including a refusal to salute the flag, were especially important. Second, the wars against fascism and communism, enemies defined in large part by their disdain for civil liberties, contributed to an environment for spreading civil liberties protections in the U.S. Constitution to the states. A third factor is the changing perspective brought by new justices on the Court. These justices received their legal training during a time that incorporation existed, so their training and the ideas and doctrines they became acquainted with were inevitably different from those of the justices before them. A final key factor is the cumulative process of incorporation itself. As one part of the Bill of Rights was incorporated, the logic of future decisions pushed toward incorporating similar constitutional provisions.[13]

Table 5-3 shows that selective incorporation has been a lengthy process. For a long time, selective incorporation was essentially limited to the First Amendment. Then, in the 1960s, the Court addressed many issues concerning the rights of defendants. Before the year of incorporation indicated in the table, it would have been possible for a state to engage in the specific behavior. For example, prior to 1961, a state or local government could allow its police to conduct searches and seize evidence without a warrant. This option does not mean that all states allowed such searches, because the state constitution or state law might have prohibited it. But there would have been no federal constitutional prohibition on states' conducting such searches as they investigated alleged violations of state or local law.

The Second Amendment right to keep and bear arms   Incorporation is an ongoing process. Only recently has the Second Amendment right to keep and bear arms been seen as an individual right, and not until 2010 did the Supreme Court incorporate this right and apply it to the states.[14]

TABLE 5-3. Selective Incorporation of the Bill of Rights into the Fourteenth Amendment

AMENDMENT	ISSUE	YEAR	KEY CASE
Amendments Fully Incorporated			
1st	Freedom of speech	1925	*Gitlow v. New York*
1st	Freedom of the press	1931	*Near v. Minnesota*
1st	Freedom of assembly	1937	*De Jonge v. Oregon*
1st	Freedom of religious exercise	1940	*Cantwell v. Connecticut*
1st	No establishment of religion	1947	*Everson v. Board of Education*
1st	Freedom of association	1958	*NAACP v. Alabama*
1st	Right to petition	1963	*NAACP v. Button*
2nd	Right to keep and bear arms	2010	*McDonald v. Chicago*
4th	No unreasonable search and seizure	1949	*Wolf v. Colorado*
4th	No search and seizure without warrant	1961	*Mapp v. Ohio*
6th	Right to counsel in capital punishment cases	1932	*Powell v. Alabama*
6th	Right to public trial	1948	*In re Oliver*
6th	Right to counsel in felony cases	1963	*Gideon v. Wainwright*
6th	Right to confront witnesses	1965	*Pointer v. Texas*
6th	Right to impartial jury	1966	*Parker v. Gladden*
6th	Right to speedy trial	1967	*Klopfer v. North Carolina*
6th	Right to compel supportive witnesses to appear in court	1967	*Washington v. Texas*
6th	Right to jury trial for serious crimes	1968	*Duncan v. Louisiana*
6th	Right to counsel for all crimes involving jail terms	1972	*Argersinger v. Hamlin*
Amendments Partially Incorporated			
5th	Compensation for public taking of private property	1897	*Chicago, Burlington, and Quincy Railroad v. Chicago*
5th	No compulsory self-incrimination	1964	*Malloy v. Hogan*
5th	No forced confession	1964	*Escobedo v. Illinois*
5th	Right to remain silent	1966	*Miranda v. Arizona*
5th	No double jeopardy	1969	*Benton v. Maryland*
5th	Right to grand jury hearing in criminal cases	Not incorp.	
8th	No cruel and unusual punishment	1962	*Robinson v. California*
8th	No excessive bail or fines	Not incorp.	
Amendments Not Incorporated			
3rd	Limits on quartering of soldiers	Not incorp.	

Prior to the Supreme Court's recent rulings, there was a long-lasting disconnect between the public debate over the right of gun ownership and the Supreme Court's interpretation of the Second Amendment. The Second Amendment states, "a well regulated Militia, being necessary to the security of a free State, the right of the people to keep and bear Arms, shall not be infringed." The Supreme Court traditionally considered this language a collective guarantee of the self-defense of the states, rather than a guarantee of individual ownership. Militias were called into action by state governments to repel threats to public order. As long as the Supreme Court considered constitutionally protected gun ownership to be connected to state militias rather than individual ownership, it was unlikely to conclude that gun control laws violate the Second Amendment. In 2008, in a case involving the prohibition of handgun ownership in the District of Columbia, the

► CONTROVERSY BREWING
Protesters in Seattle in 2010, including children, urge Starbucks to prohibit the open carry of guns in its cafes. The company had announced it was continuing its policy of allowing customers to carry guns in states and cities where it is legal.

Supreme Court declared for the first time that the Second Amendment protected an individual's right to have a gun in his or her home. The decision struck down the handgun ban in Washington, D.C., and the National Rifle Association, the country's leading advocacy group for gun owners, quickly filed challenges to gun control laws in Chicago and other cities. Because the District of Columbia is a federal entity and not a state, the Court needed to decide in a subsequent case whether its decision in *District of Columbia v. Heller* should be incorporated and thus apply to the states and their cities. It did so in *McDonald v. Chicago* (2010). That decision does not end the story, however. We can expect causal reactions between judicial and legislative action. Future cases will continue to determine the scope and limits of an individual's right to possess firearms and government's ability to regulate them. States and cities are likely to respond by passing new laws to determine exactly what the Court will and will not allow.

Denationalization allows variation in states' protection of civil liberties.

Nationalization of civil liberties means that most of the Bill of Rights guarantees now also apply to state governments. But in some areas, the Supreme Court has allowed denationalization. Federal constitutional protection has not been eliminated in these areas, but the Supreme Court allows variation in the exercise of a right from one state to another.

Consider freedom of religious practice. The freedom to practice one's religion is fundamentally the same in New Hampshire as it is in New Mexico, the same in Oregon as Ohio, the same in Tennessee as Texas. The Supreme Court considers freedom of religious practice a fundamental right, such that liberty is unthinkable as a concept without it. Religious freedom, in the Court's view, is part of the very essence of liberty.

The Court has made it clear that other rights, although undeniably of value and importance, do not rise to that level. With fundamental rights, the Supreme Court tolerates very little variation from state to state. With qualified rights, however, the Court allows states more flexibility. Abortion is the most politically charged example of denationalization. Freedom to obtain an abortion does not fall into the category of fundamental rights, so the Court has allowed significant variation in states' restriction of its exercise. The ability of a minor to obtain an abortion, for example, varies widely across the states, with some states requiring parental notification or consent. States also vary on many additional details, including whether other relatives can give consent in place of parents, whether minors get consent from a judge instead of parents, and how to proceed when both parents are no longer married or one or both parents cannot be located or are deceased. Similarly, states vary on whether they require women to receive counseling prior to an abortion, a requirement that would not be plausible in the case of a fundamental right such as free speech or freedom to practice religion.

Freedom of Speech

5-2 Analyze the different standards by which the Supreme Court has determined whether restrictions on freedom of speech are acceptable.

As noted at the beginning of this chapter, nationalization of the Bill of Rights, which gradually applied most of the protections in the Bill of Rights to the actions of state governments, is one of three paths by which the scope and reach of civil liberties protections have changed over time. A second path is when the Supreme Court or Congress expands or restricts the protections for rights and liberties listed in the Constitution as they develop new interpretations of what the Constitution requires and forbids. Political scientists have shown that a change in membership in these institutions can lead to dramatic changes in the constitutional interpretation of individual rights by introducing new ideas, judicial philosophies, and policy preferences into judicial and legislative debates. Who is elected to Congress or appointed to the Court matters.[15] The following sections will explore this path by examining the changing scope of civil liberties protection in the areas of speech, freedom of religion, and rights of the accused.

To Americans, freedom of speech is the most prized of all the rights guaranteed by the Constitution and perhaps the most definably *American* right. The freedom to speak one's mind is a hallmark of America's political and popular culture.

> **ThinkingCausally**
>
> How do new justices and new legislators affect the scope of civil liberties protection?

Government can attempt to limit speech before and after its utterance.

Government action limiting speech is of two types. Action that prevents speech from being uttered is referred to as **prior restraint**. This is censorship in its truest form: preventing certain speech from being expressed by requiring some kind of permission or pre-clearance from government that the content of the speech is acceptable, or by simply forbidding the speech. Most often this kind of restraint has concerned the news media. The Supreme Court today is reluctant to tolerate restraint of this type. The Court first established its position in *Near v. Minnesota* (1931), in which a Minnesota law that allowed government to prevent the publication of malicious material was struck down as a violation of the First Amendment. The most famous prior restraint case is *New York Times v. United States* (1971). The U.S. government attempted to prevent the newspaper from printing the "Pentagon Papers," a history of the Vietnam War based on State Department documents that had been leaked to the *Times* and the *Washington Post* by a former State Department official. Despite the government's argument that publishing the documents threatened national security, the Court agreed with the newspaper's contention that the public had a right to the information.[16]

After speech has been uttered, government may punish individuals by equating the speech with a crime. In practice, this can have the same censoring effect as prior

prior restraint government intervention to prevent the publication of material it finds objectionable.

restraint. One of the most controversial examples of this type of speech restriction concerns "hate speech."

Hate speech emerged as a major concern on college campuses and in society more broadly in the 1990s. Over 300 institutions of higher education adopted speech codes that punished the use of derogatory speech based on group characteristics such as race, gender, and ethnicity.[17] Some cities did the same. In 1992, the Court considered a case in which a cross was burned on the lawn of a black family.[18] The defendant was charged under St. Paul, Minnesota's Bias Motivated Crime Ordinance, which prohibited the display of a symbol that was known to arouse "anger, alarm or resentment in others on the basis of race, color, creed, religion or gender." The Court struck down St. Paul's law, concluding that it violated the First Amendment by criminalizing speech based on a particular viewpoint. Hate speech cannot be considered a crime simply because of its hatefulness. The speech in question in this case was symbolic speech, rather than the actual utterance or writing of words. In recent decades the Supreme Court has tended to consider symbolic speech and actual speech to be deserving of the same protection. The Court has also been generally protective of "speech plus"—the combination of speech and some activity like picketing or a demonstration.[19]

A decade later, the Court refined its stance. The case concerned a Virginia law prohibiting cross burning on someone's property, along a highway, or in any public place "with the intent of intimidating any person or group."[20] In its decision, the Court ruled that a state could constitutionally ban cross burning, because of that symbol's historical use to intimidate and terrorize targeted groups. The fact that Virginia's law automatically *assumed* that the intent of cross burning was to intimidate, however, made that aspect of the law unconstitutional. Cross burning, even though hateful, was constitutionally protected if it was not designed to be intimidating and make particular targets fear for their safety. Following these Court decisions, some colleges continued to adopt the equivalent of speech codes by including them in more general codes of conduct.[21]

The "bad tendency" standard assumed government restriction on speech was necessary.

The evolution of the Supreme Court's perspective on speech as criminal conduct shows how, over time, the scope of free speech rights has generally expanded in the United States. This might be considered the strongest test for freedom of speech: can speech that appears to be supportive of criminal actions be tolerated? The Court is often faced with balancing the need for free speech with the need for social order. How has the Court handled this difficult question?

Up until 1919, the Supreme Court was guided by the **bad tendency standard**. Using this standard, the Court sided with government, presuming that government restrictions on speech were reasonable unless proven otherwise. If certain acts were criminal, then speech that seemed to advocate such conduct was itself criminal. The burden, therefore, fell on the individual to demonstrate that the government's speech restriction was in some way unreasonable or that the speech in question was not actually supportive of illegal conduct. Convictions under this standard were frequent, particularly during World War I, when speech that might hinder the war effort was deemed a crime.[22]

bad tendency standard a free speech standard which took as its starting point a presumption that government restrictions on speech were reasonable and constitutional, thus leaving the burden of proof to those who objected to the restriction.

The "clear and present danger" standard made it more difficult for government to justify restricting speech.

The reasonableness standard was replaced in 1919 by the **clear and present danger standard**. Charles Schenck and Elizabeth Baer mailed pamphlets to men drafted to serve in World War I, arguing that the draft was motivated by the needs of Wall Street financial interests and was illegal. They encouraged draftees to "assert your rights" and "do not submit to intimidation" but did not advocate any violent or illegal activity, suggesting instead actions such as organizing petition drives to repeal the draft. The Espionage Act of 1917 prohibited actions that would cause insubordination in the military or would hinder recruiting. Schenck and Baer were found guilty of violating the Espionage Act and were sentenced to prison.

In *Schenck v. United States* (1919), the Supreme Court upheld the convictions. Although speech is technically not action, the Court concluded that it can effectively be the same thing. If speech brings about a "clear and present danger" that prohibited actions will take place, then that speech itself can be considered a criminal act. Chief Justice Oliver Wendell Holmes, writing for the Court, noted that speech that is constitutionally protected in one circumstance might not be protected in another. Holmes famously noted that "the most stringent protection of free speech would not protect a man in falsely shouting fire in a theatre and causing a panic." In *Schenck*, the distinction between wartime and peacetime was key. Words could be prohibited under this new standard if there were a clear and present danger that would encourage the kinds of actions that government is constitutionally authorized to prevent—for example, actions that hinder the war effort. Holmes's argument paralleled public thinking, which has also varied in its support for restrictions on speech and civil liberties during times of war and peace (see *How Do We Know? Did the Public's Response to 9/11 Lead to Civil Liberties Restrictions?*).

continued on page 185 ▶

clear and present danger standard used in free speech cases, this standard permitted government restrictions on speech if public officials believed that allowing the speech created a risk that some prohibited action would result from the speech.

▼ **CROSS BURNING AND FREE SPEECH**

In a 2002 decision, the Supreme Court declared that cross burning, even though hateful, was constitutionally protected free speech if it was not designed to be intimidating and make particular targets fear for their safety. In those instances, it would be protected as symbolic speech representing a point of view. If intimidating and making people fear for their safety were the intent, the cross burning would not be constitutionally protected speech. Should the same symbol be treated two different ways legally?

HOW DO WE KNOW?

Did the Public's Response to 9/11 Lead to Civil Liberties Restrictions?

The Question

As discussed in Chapter 2, American political culture includes a strong belief in liberty—at least in the abstract. Public opinion polls consistently show high levels of support among the American public for basic civil liberties principles. But support can plummet when individuals feel threatened by certain ideas or lifestyles or are worried about their physical security.[23] Following the terrorist attacks of September 11, 2001, Americans indicated greater support for measures that infringed on civil liberties. Did the public's response to 9/11 lead to civil liberties restrictions? How do we know?

Why It Matters

Extensive protection for civil liberties is a central part of the American experiment in democracy. To most Americans, freedom is synonymous with civil liberties. Therefore, it is critical to understand when civil liberties can be restricted and for what reason. Civil liberties

▼ **THE LIBERTY-SECURITY TRADEOFF**

A bomb technician examines a vehicle loaded with explosive devices in New York City's Times Square, May 2010. U.S. Attorney General Eric Holder called the failed bombing "a terrorist plot aimed at murdering Americans in one of the busiest places in our country." Americans have often tolerated restrictions on liberties during times of perceived crisis, and the Supreme Court has granted the government more leeway to act during those times.

restrictions are particularly likely during wartime, but when war ends or ebbs, those restrictions are eventually repealed, overturned by the courts, or weakened substantially.[24] For this reason, many observers are concerned about current restrictions on civil liberties as the country battles terrorism. Unlike traditional war, the conclusion of this conflict—because of the very nature of terrorism—will be difficult to define.

Investigating the Answer

Americans' commitment to civil liberties appears to weaken—alarmingly—when put to the test in specific cases. Using public opinion research, one study of public attitudes after September 11, 2001, examined individuals' depth of support for civil liberties. The analysis considered a number of possible factors that might explain an individual's level of support for civil liberties. The researchers found that the greater the perceived sense of threat to oneself or the country, the more willing individuals were to sacrifice civil liberties. Trust in government played an important role also. Regardless of whether people perceived a great or modest terrorist threat, people with less trust of government were less willing to give government additional power to reduce civil liberties. People who were more trusting toward government were more willing to make the tradeoff.[25]

To civil liberties advocates, Americans fortunately give little indication of wanting to act on their attitudes regarding a reduction in civil liberties or of demanding immediate action from public officials that would be consistent with these attitudes. But this line of argument still leaves open one possibility—Americans might not push for civil liberties restrictions, but perhaps they will accept them when politicians initiate them. Following some failed terrorist episodes in recent years—an unsuccessful attempted Christmas Day airline bombing in 2009 and a failed bombing attempt in New York City's Times Square in 2010—Americans were open to restrictions. About 70 percent approved the increased use of surveillance cameras in public places. The same percentage approved stripping U.S. citizenship from individuals "who support or affiliate with terrorist groups." Anywhere from 50 to 70 percent, depending on question wording and the date of the survey, supported extra scrutiny of airline passengers who fit terrorist profiles based on age, sex, and ethnicity. When asked in January 2010, "do you think that it is necessary to give up some civil liberties in order to make the country safe from terrorism, or [do you think] some of the government's proposals will go too far in restricting the public's civil liberties," 51 percent believed it was necessary to sacrifice some liberties, while 36 percent disagreed. On the other hand, modest to strong majorities of Americans thought terror suspects should be read their rights upon arrest.[26]

Studies of support for civil liberties show that the manner in which an issue is framed—whether it is free speech or security at stake—can influence public support for civil liberties.[27] For example, in 2005, whereas 29 percent of the public expressed a willingness to allow government to monitor telephone calls and e-mail messages of "ordinary Americans on a regular basis," 56 percent would allow such monitoring of "Americans that the government is suspicious of." Similarly, as the events of 9/11 grew more distant across time, a growing majority of Americans from 2003 through 2009 rejected the idea that it was "necessary for the average person to give up some civil liberties" to combat terrorism.[28]

What if government instituted restrictions on civil liberties with the rationale that war or other international threats demanded such action? Given the public's fears of terrorism, might people simply view these initiatives passively, as an acceptable tradeoff for security? They might. Absent an intensely hostile public attitude against civil liberties restrictions, politicians have some leeway to act. The correlation between public support for civil liberties restrictions and public policy might be just that—a correlation, not necessarily a causal link from beliefs to policy. The public may not cause politicians to restrict civil liberties but it may tolerate restrictions when they happen.[29]

The historical record indicates that the public may well be willing to sacrifice some liberty if it is given a convincing security rationale. This is not isolated to September 11 and subsequent terror threats. In fact, study of similar historical cases suggests it would have been puzzling if

Americans had not been supportive of civil liberties restrictions following the 2001 terrorist attacks.[30] Throughout American history, particularly when war or foreign disruption of American life was feared, the national government has imposed restrictions on civil liberties that usually received at least passive support from large segments of the public:

■ The Sedition Act of 1798, enacted while Americans believed their young country was vulnerable to the world's major powers and to deepening political divisions at home, made it illegal to say or write anything that might encourage hostile actions by other countries or that might bring disrepute or disfavor to the government, the president, or Congress.

■ During the Civil War, President Abraham Lincoln suspended the writ of habeas corpus, which meant prisoners could be held without charges.

■ The Espionage Act of 1917, passed during World War I, restricted speech or action that might be perceived as contributing to insubordination in the military or a hindrance to recruiting.

■ The Alien Act of 1918 promised deportation to any alien belonging to a group that advocated the overthrow of the U.S. government, while the Sedition Act of 1918 cracked down on criticism that might affect the country's military operations.

■ The Smith Act of 1940, passed while World War II was raging in Europe, prohibited any speech, action, or organization that supported the overthrow of the U.S. government.

■ During World War II, President Franklin Roosevelt ordered Japanese Americans to be relocated and held in detention camps.

■ At the outset of the Cold War, the Internal Security Act of 1950 stated that membership at any time in the Communist Party or other totalitarian party was grounds to deny an alien admission to the United States; that communist organizations needed to register with the federal government; and that individuals and groups considered threats could be ordered into detention camps.

■ As part of the "war on terror" after September 11, 2001, "enemy combatants" were indefinitely detained at Guantanamo Bay, Cuba; the National Security Agency engaged in surveillance without judicial approval; "extraordinary rendition" led to suspects being sent to other countries for potentially harsh interrogation techniques; and the USA PATRIOT Act allowed the government to engage in searches and investigations without the judicial approval typically required for other investigations.

Viewing this list as a whole, war or the fear of war was a primary motivation for the actions. The stress of these times led Americans to distinguish between their abstract preference for civil liberties and their perceived needs for the country's safety under specific circumstances.[31] In these instances, Americans seemed to be agreeing with the often-stated legal phrase that "the Constitution is not a suicide pact."[32] Certainly support was not unanimous, as these actions did arouse determined opposition. But overall the public tolerated restrictions that seemed to fit a particular context. If public opinion polling were available during World War I, for example, it might have shown strong support for government investigations of German Americans based on their ethnic background. But asking that same question today would likely provoke very little support for such an idea.

Thinking Critically

■ What level of detail about security threats should government officials provide to justify a restriction on civil liberties?

■ Should public opinion about civil liberties always be taken into account by government officials when they are crafting public policy, or are there times when the public's view should not be relevant to policy makers?

■ Should advocates for strong civil liberties protections believe there is any significant difference between the public's advocating for civil liberties restrictions and the public's accepting restrictions when they are proposed?

The Bottom Line

Did the public's response to September 11 lead to civil liberties restrictions? Research shows that the public certainly is willing to veer from its general principles in support of civil liberties, especially during times of war. But the evidence suggests it is more likely that public opinion responds to restrictive actions taken by the government or provides a supportive environment for government actions rather than directly causing those actions. The significance of difficult times or events in prompting public support for restrictions suggests that the support is likely to fade as the precipitating concerns became a more distant memory.

The clear and present danger standard was more demanding on government, in that speech that had only a "bad tendency" to produce illegal outcomes was not sufficient for a conviction. Nonetheless, convictions for speech remained common under this standard.

The "gravity of the danger" standard allowed restrictions on speech if its subject matter was sufficiently "evil."

Schenck guided Court decisions until the late 1960s, but through the 1950s and 1960s, clear and present danger proved less useful as a standard as every word—*clear, and, present, danger*—was up for debate and interpreted with great variation around the country.[33] The Court turned then to the **gravity of the danger standard**. Here, the Court asserted it would consider the potential "evil" advocated by someone's speech when deciding whether government could punish that speech.[34] The case introducing this standard concerned the Smith Act, which made it illegal to advocate overthrowing the U.S. government by force. Although such attempts were highly unlikely to be successful, and thus the "clear and present danger" was low, the Court approved convictions under the Smith Act, using the gravity of the danger standard. If the evil of the potential outcome from speech—in this case, the overthrow of the government—was great enough, the improbability of its actually happening need not deter government from restricting it. On the other hand, something that posed a danger, but of a lesser significance, would need a higher level of probability of its happening for government to restrict it.

> **gravity of the danger standard**
> a free speech standard in which the Supreme Court allowed restrictions on speech if the danger espoused by the speech was sufficiently evil, even if that evil was unlikely to occur.

Throughout the 1950s and 1960s, the Supreme Court used the gravity of the danger standard to evaluate convictions based on individuals' membership in groups deemed dangerous by a government entity. Given the Cold War era in which the standard emerged, government actions against individuals with communist affiliations were especially likely to be upheld.[35]

The "preferred position" standard presumes the unreasonableness of restrictions on speech.

Change in membership on the Court in the 1960s led to the strongest support yet for the protection of free speech rights and abandonment of the gravity of the danger standard. The Court had maintained for decades that the First Amendment and its protection for freedom of speech, the press, and religion held a "preferred position" among the amendments.[36] A **preferred position** means that First Amendment freedoms should be abridged only with great reluctance, and that if these freedoms

> **preferred position** the idea, endorsed by the Supreme Court, that protections of First Amendment rights predominates over other rights.

are in conflict with other rights, the First Amendment protections, such as free speech, should prevail. But only in the late 1960s, in *Brandenburg v. Ohio* (1969), did the Court explicitly adopt preferred position as its primary free speech standard.

Clarence Brandenburg, a speaker at a Ku Klux Klan rally in 1964, was convicted under an Ohio law—similar to laws in many states—that made it illegal to advocate or assemble with those who promote criminal behavior in the pursuit of political or economic reform. The Court concluded that Ohio's law was unconstitutional. The decision established a two-part rule to determine whether speech acts could be considered criminal: First, was the speech "directed at inciting or producing imminent lawless action"? Second, was the speech "likely to incite or produce such action"? If the answer was yes to both, then government could restrict the speech. The Court concluded that the Ohio law ignored the second part of this test. Given the preferred position of free speech, unless a speech was extremely likely to produce immediate lawless behavior, it could not be restricted or considered illegal itself. Advocating that people commit illegal acts was not in and of itself an illegal act, unless it was highly likely to result imminently in that lawbreaking.

With its strong statement in *Brandenburg*, the Court had effectively reversed the burden of proof in free speech cases. Under the bad tendency standard, prior to 1919, it was up to the individual charged with a crime related to speech to prove that a governmental restriction on speech was unreasonable. Under the clear and present danger standard and the gravity of the danger standard, up through the 1960s, the Court pushed more of the burden toward government. And with the preferred position standard, which remains in effect today, the Court moved to a

▼ **SENATOR JOSEPH McCARTHY TESTIFIES ON COMMUNIST ACTIVITY IN THE UNITED STATES, 1950**
Although his investigations raised cries of outraged opposition and complaints about their effects on individuals' livelihoods, fear of communism led many Americans to support investigations such as that by Senator McCarthy. A number of states passed restrictions or penalties on communist political activity. The federal courts frequently upheld these policies, concluding that the evil of communism was so great that it could be controlled even if its political success was highly unlikely.

benchmark that assumed that government restrictions on speech were likely to be inherently unreasonable. Government now had the burden to show, through a stringent two-part test, that limiting speech was necessary and desirable.

The Supreme Court determines which categories of speech merit constitutional protection and which do not.

The Supreme Court has determined that some categories of speech do not merit constitutional protection. These include fighting words, defamation, commercial speech, student speech by minors, and obscenity. Fighting words or inflammatory words that create an immediate threat to public safety are not constitutionally protected.[37] The person who uses such words could, for example, be validly charged with disturbing the peace. Defamation means speaking (slander) or writing (libel) a false statement that is heard or read by a third party and harms the target's reputation.[38] For public figures—public officials and others, such as celebrities who are frequently in the public's attention—defamation also requires that the person who spoke or wrote the offensive words did so knowing they were false.[39] Commercial speech has gained growing protection from the courts, as it, like political speech, transmits information. Unlike political speech, however, the government can regulate commercial speech to be sure it is accurate and not misleading.[40] Minors have generally not been accorded the same speech rights as adults, but that is not the same as being without rights, as the Court noted when it declared that "students do not shed their constitutional rights . . . at the schoolhouse gate."[41] Striking down a federal law in 2010, the Supreme Court declined to add depictions of animal cruelty as another area of speech that did not merit First Amendment protection. Doing so would have been the first category of speech the Court added to the list of categories unprotected by the First Amendment since child pornography was added in 1982.[42]

Governments have passed numerous laws attempting to thwart the distribution of obscene materials, and challenges to these laws have generated a lengthy trail of court decisions. In 1973, a 5–4 Court ruling revised the definition of obscenity and, in the process, increased the range of speech protected by the Constitution. The ruling retained the "community standards" provision from an earlier decision, which stated that material was obscene if, by average community standards, the material mainly appealed to prurient interest.[43] The Court now added that to be obscene and thus subject to government restrictions, a work also must depict or describe sexual conduct "in a patently offensive way" and have no serious literary, artistic, political, or scientific value. Federal law and court rulings have established that any sexually explicit depictions of children or depictions of children in sexual acts inherently violate these guidelines and are not constitutionally protected.[44] In 2008, the Court upheld the Protect Act of 2003. The law prohibited the offering or soliciting of any form of child pornography, including computer-generated pornography. By a 7–2 vote, the Court concluded in *U.S. v. Williams* that offers to provide or obtain child pornography were excluded from First Amendment protection. The difficulty of defining obscenity in other instances was most famously reflected in the comment of Justice Potter Stewart when he wrote that although he could not easily define hard-core pornography, "I know it when I see it."[45]

Controlling the spread of obscene materials in the Internet era provides a test of the Supreme Court's impact on political outcomes and on society—known to political scientists as judicial impact studies. The

ThinkingCausally

Do Supreme Court actions change political outcomes?

question is twofold. Did a Court ruling prompt elected officials to take new actions? And did the ruling prompt major societal changes? The impact produces four possible outcomes that political scientists can analyze: no actions, no changes; actions, no changes; no actions, changes; and actions, changes. The Communications Decency Act (CDA) of 1996 prohibited making available to minors online any obscene or indecent material that shows or describes "sexual or excretory activities or organs" in a way that would be considered offensive by community standards. The act launched the kind of causal chain reaction common in civil liberties: Congress passes a law, the Court responds, Congress often replies by revising its law, and the Supreme Court weighs in again. Responding to CDA, the Supreme Court in 1997 strongly declared the law to be an unconstitutional limit on free speech.[46] Including "indecent" materials, the Court ruled, made the law overly broad and intruded too far on the speech rights of adults—the Court distinguished between indecency, which is constitutionally protected, and obscenity, which is not. Congress responded with the Children's Online Protection Act of 1998, which required websites to provide age-verification systems (for example, providing credit card information) to keep harmful content from minors.[47] Dissatisfied, the Court suspended enforcement of the act unless Congress could demonstrate that there were no other methods available to achieve its goals that would be less intrusive on personal privacy. This time, Congress responded with a law more modest in scope than either of the previous laws. The Children's Internet Protection Act of 2000 required public libraries that received federal funds to install filtering software on their publicly accessible computers. The Supreme Court upheld the law, concluding that it did not violate patrons' First Amendment rights.[48]

So what was the judicial impact? Overall, we do see the Court prompting action by elected officials. Actions—yes. But what about societal change? Here, the outcome is murkier, and it does not appear that the Court has prompted societal change. Few would declare that the spread of obscene materials on the Web has declined or that it is significantly difficult for minors to access it. But analysts need to be careful when evaluating whether a Court decision has led to societal change, as this might not be the Court's direct intent—the justices in the majority in these decisions might argue that their job is not to stop the spread of obscenity per se, but to make sure that

▶ **HIGH SCHOOL**

In *Morse v. Frederick* (2007), the Supreme Court upheld a Seattle school principal's right to suspend an 18-year-old student for holding up this banner during a school-sponsored event, because the message contradicted the school's anti-drug policy. The students were watching an Olympic torch relay parade. Should a school principal be able to discipline students for their speech?

government attempts to do so do not violate other rights. Other decisions might arguably lead more directly to societal change, though decisions may be influenced by changes in society as well. We discuss the influences on judicial decisions more extensively in Chapter 16.

The legal treatment of pornography has varied across countries. One particularly interesting case is Canada. Rather than following the U.S. model, which places individual freedom of expression at its core, Canada has followed a communitarian approach. Although the 1982 Canadian Charter of Rights and Responsibilities guarantees protection of free speech, the protection is qualified by the need to promote gender equality and to consider what should be acceptable in a democratic society. In a key case, the Canadian Court rejected a challenge to Canada's criminalization of the possession and distribution of obscene materials. The Court concluded that degrading materials that place women in subordinate, servile, or humiliating positions violate principles of equal human dignity. This type of material, the Canadian Court ruled, would be prohibited not for moral reasons, but because public opinion considers it harmful to the community.[49]

ThinkingComparatively

Canada has approached cases involving pornography by referring chiefly to community values rather than individual freedom of expression.

Freedom of Religion

5-3 Evaluate how the Supreme Court has interpreted cases regarding religion and how Congress has reacted to the Court's actions.

As with speech, the First Amendment sets out the Constitution's basic principles regarding freedom of religion.[50] The amendment states, "Congress shall make no law respecting an establishment of religion, or prohibiting the free exercise thereof." "Respecting an establishment of religion" is referred to as the **establishment clause**. Government is not to designate any official religion, appear to embrace some religions at the expense of others, become involved in religious teaching, or, as interpreted by some scholars and justices, favor religion over nonreligion. "Prohibiting the free exercise thereof" is referred to as the **free exercise clause**. This clause declares that government should not interfere with the individual practice of religious beliefs. Because of incorporation, the establishment and free exercise clauses also apply to the states.

As with speech, the seemingly unconditional text of the First Amendment has not been interpreted by the Supreme Court to mean that there can be no restrictions on religious freedom. And regulating church–state relations also follows the speech example in that over time, the courts have altered the scope of the right to freedom of religion. What Americans would now consider violations of religious freedom were common from the colonial era, when official churches were not unusual, through the 1960s. Evangelical Christians, members of nontraditional denominations, and individuals whose worldview was guided more by science and reason were particularly active in urging church–state separation, and the Constitution represented a victory for these groups.[51] But even though the Constitution avoids religious references, and an early treaty declared that the United States was not founded specifically upon Christianity, Supreme Court decisions sometimes referred to the United States as a Christian nation as part of their reasoning.[52] Prior to the nationalization of the Bill of Rights, religious oaths for holding office were present in some states, and members of specific religions, most commonly Catholics and Jews, were prohibited from holding public office. In other states, attending Catholic parochial school was illegal. Government intrusion into religious practice and some forms of establishment did not simply disappear after the colonial era.

establishment clause a clause in the First Amendment that prevents government from establishing an official religion, treating one religion preferably to another, proselytizing, or promoting religion over nonreligion.

free exercise clause a clause in the First Amendment that prohibits government from interfering with individuals' practice of their religion.

Lemon test a three-part
establishment clause test used
by the Supreme Court that states
that, to be constitutional, a
government action must have a
plausible nonreligious purpose;
its primary or principal effect
must be to neither advance nor
inhibit religion; and it must not
foster excessive government
entanglement with religion.

Establishment clause cases have been decided using the *Lemon* test.

The Court's current standard on establishment clause issues is provided by the **Lemon test**, drawn from its decision in *Lemon v. Kurtzman* (1971). In this ruling, the Court used standards from previous cases and applied a three-part test to determine whether a government action was permissible. First, the law or action must have a plausible secular—i.e., nonreligious—purpose. Second, its primary effect must not be to either advance or inhibit religion. Third, it must not foster "excessive government entanglement with religion." A law or action violating any of these three precepts would be considered unconstitutional under this test. In the laws under review in 1971, the Court concluded that providing financial subsidies to private schools for nonreligious subject instruction excessively entangled government and religion and was therefore unconstitutional. Because the schools were religious, the Court was concerned that the need for ongoing government surveillance of church financial records involved government too intimately in church affairs.

Relaxation of the Lemon test　The *Lemon* test continues to guide establishment clause decisions, but many political scientists who study constitutional law believe the Court may be ready to formulate a new approach to these cases. For example, in 1985 the Court considered New York's deployment of public-school remedial education teachers to parochial schools to be in violation of the establishment clause because of excessive entanglement.[53] In 1997, however, the Court directly overturned this decision and concluded that New York's program was constitutional. The Court majority did not discard the *Lemon* test, but it noted that its view toward "excessive entanglement" had begun to shift over the previous decade. There was no reason to assume that public employees would advocate a religion simply because they were in religious schools, so the "pervasive monitoring" of teachers was not necessary to avoid excessive entanglement.[54]

Another sign of the Court's more lenient view toward establishment clause cases appeared in its 2002 decision regarding educational vouchers. Vouchers are public funds that provide parents or guardians with a stipend to use for a child's tuition at private schools. One such program provided need-based assistance to parents in the Cleveland school district. Ninety percent of the funds were used to send children to religious schools. The Court, by a narrow 5–4 vote, concluded that the program did not constitute establishment of religion. The program was secular on its face, and if parents used the funds to send their children to religious schools, that was their decision, not the government's.

Establishment clause cases　Many issues test the establishment clause. Three important ones are school prayer, public religious displays, and the faith-based initiative. In a long line of cases, the Court has ruled that public school prayer or similar activities constitute establishment of religion if they rely on public resources or imply the sponsorship or endorsement of the school. The Court has disallowed prayer time in classrooms, classroom Bible reading exercises, prayers delivered at graduation events, and student-initiated and student-led prayers at sporting events.[55] Individual student decisions such as wearing religious symbols to public school or praying privately while in school are not considered establishment.

Evaluating two religious displays in 2005, the Court concluded by a 5–4 vote that a Ten Commandments display in Austin, Texas, was constitutional because it had a valid secular purpose, was part of a large number of statues, and had been on display for over 40 years without complaint that it was advocating a particular religion. It determined that a courthouse display in Kentucky was unconstitutional because it had clearer religious intent, having been posted initially in courtrooms without any other historical documents and being modified later only after complaints were lodged by the American Civil Liberties Union.[56] A 2009 Court decision clarified unanimously that governments are not required to accommodate every religious group wishing to add a religious symbol to a public display. In *Pleasant Grove City v. Summum,* the Court also rejected the argument that a group's free speech rights are violated if its symbol is not added to a display. The city of Pleasant Grove, Utah, had placed a privately donated monument of the Ten Commandments in Pioneer Park, where it stood with 10 nonreligious, privately donated monuments. The Summum church argued that it, too, should be able to install a similarly sized monument, but the city denied the request, stating that its policy was to accept monuments only that concerned the city's history or that came from organizations with long-standing community ties. Justice Samuel Alito, the author of the Court's ruling, drew a distinction between monuments, which take on different meanings over time because of their permanence and history and become part of a community, and nonpermanent displays that are using a public forum (such as a park) for a short time. The government is allowed to engage in speech when it accepts a monument, Alito determined—the United States was not obliged to add a Statue of Autocracy when it received the Statue of Liberty from France. Other justices agreed with the decision, but they noted that if the case had come to the Court as an establishment clause case rather than a free speech case, they would have had more questions about the appropriateness of Pleasant Grove's denial of the Summum request.

The placement of religious symbols in public places has stirred controversy in other countries as well. In 1991, parents of elementary school children challenged a Bavarian law that required a crucifix to be placed in every public school. Based on Germany's constitution, the Basic Law, which declares freedom of faith to be "inviolable," the parents successfully argued that the Christian crucifix infringed on their religious freedom. In the justices' view, religious freedom demanded that government be neutral in matters of faith, especially because students were mandated to be

ThinkingComparatively

As in the United States, the placement of religious symbols in public places has been controversial in other countries.

◄ **A CROSS IN THE DESERT**

This cross was placed in the Mojave National Preserve in California in 1934 as a memorial to fallen soldiers. A legal challenge to its placement on public land led Congress to arrange a land swap—placing the land around the cross in private ownership while receiving an offsetting amount of property to add to the preserve. In *Salazar v. Buono* (2010), the Supreme Court did not rule directly on the constitutionality of the placement of the cross but said the lower courts had not conducted the appropriate legal analysis when they concluded that the land swap was improper. The case was sent back to federal district court.

in school.[57] In 2004, France went even further by banning students from wearing "conspicuous" religious symbols in public schools. Prohibited items include Muslim veils or headscarves, Sikh turbans, Jewish yarmulkes, and Christian crucifixes. By contrast, U.S. federal courts have made it clear that students must be allowed to wear religious symbols to school. France in mid-2010 was considering a ban on face-covering Islamic veils in all public buildings and possibly in all public places, due to concerns about security and the effect of the veils on French identity. The wearing of the veils has become a controversial issue in many European countries.[58]

Not yet fully tested is President George W. Bush's faith-based initiative, an effort to ensure that religious organizations are able to participate in providing federally funded social service programs such as drug counseling and job training. The Supreme Court made challenges of the initiative difficult in 2007. Split 5–4, the Court ruled in *Hein v. Freedom From Religion Foundation* that citizens could not challenge the initiative because taxpayers do not have the legal standing to bring the federal government to court over executive branch expenditures. The majority's opinion declared that if payment of taxes was sufficient to allow cases to be filed, the federal courts would become "general complaint bureaus." Under President Bush, religious organizations providing these services did not have to abide by federal regulations that prohibit discrimination in the hiring process based on religious beliefs. President Obama has continued the faith-based initiative with the Office of Faith-Based Initiatives and Neighborhood Partnerships. The Department of Justice is reviewing the hiring policy aspect of the program.

The balancing standard carved out a zone of protection for religious free expression.

In addition to prohibiting any establishment of religion, the First Amendment also guarantees the free exercise of religion. Are restrictions on free exercise ever permissible? If so, when and why?

As with establishment cases, the Court has answered these questions with standards that it then applied to subsequent cases. From 1963 through 1990, the Court relied on the **balancing test**, introduced in *Sherbert v. Verner* (1963). Adeil Sherbert, a Seventh-day Adventist, lost her job when she refused to work on Saturday, her Sabbath Day. After she was unable to find other work for the same reason, she applied to the state of South Carolina for temporary unemployment benefits. The state denied her any benefits, because the state believed she could have taken a job requiring Saturday work.

The Supreme Court applied a two-part test to resolve the dispute. First, did the government law or policy impose a significant burden on religious exercise? The Court concluded in this instance that South Carolina's eligibility requirements for unemployment compensation did significantly burden Sherbert's ability to practice her faith. With that established, the Court turned to the second part of the test: was a compelling government interest served by this burdensome law or policy? If it were, then the policy or law would be constitutional despite its interference with religious expression. Here, the Court determined that there was no compelling state interest that justified the burden on Sherbert's religious practice. On the basis of the two-part test, the Court ruled in favor of Sherbert.

The neutrality standard narrows the scope of religious free expression.

The two-part balancing test survived for nearly three decades before being demoted in favor of a new test.[59] The new standard made it surprisingly more difficult to carve out space for religious expression. The case establishing the new standard involved Alfred

balancing test used by the Supreme Court in free exercise of religion cases, this two-part test first determined whether a government action or law was a burden on religious practice and, if it was, whether a compelling government interest was at stake that would make the burden constitutionally acceptable.

Smith and Galen Black, who participated in Native American church ceremonies that involved the ingestion of peyote, an illegal hallucinogen. Unlike many other states, Oregon law provided no exception for use of the drug for sacramental purposes. Smith and Black were fired from their jobs at a private drug rehabilitation center because their drug use was considered work-related misconduct. They were denied state unemployment benefits on those grounds.

In *Employment Division v. Smith* (1990), the Supreme Court upheld Oregon's refusal to provide unemployment benefits. In a striking shift away from the balancing test established in *Sherbert*, the decision introduced the Court's **neutrality test** for free exercise cases: a neutral law applied in a neutral way can validly impose a burden on religious practice, even if there is no compelling government interest at stake. If a law was not neutral in intent and application, the Court would employ the balancing test. The Court would want to be convinced that such a law was justified by a compelling government interest, and that it was as narrowly constructed—meaning as minimally invasive on rights—as possible in its quest to advance that interest.

In the Court's view, the law prohibiting peyote and other drugs validly regulated something that government is allowed to regulate, and it did so in a neutral way. Its enactment was not targeted at any one group and it was applied equally across groups. Restriction of religious expression was an "incidental effect" of the law, not an intentional goal. There is no religious exemption from the law, just as there is no religious exemption if one believes one's taxes support causes that one finds spiritually repugnant.[60]

A notable example of the Court's application of the neutrality test concerned the issue of animal sacrifice. The city of Hialeah, Florida, passed several laws to forbid the practice of animal sacrifice or slaughter but exempted state-licensed activities from the new regulation, including slaughterhouses, food establishments, and some hog and cattle slaughter that did not occur in areas zoned for slaughterhouses. In its decision in *Church of the Lukumi Babalu Aye v. Hialeah* (1993), the Supreme Court struck down the city's ordinances as an undue burden on the religious practice of the Santeria religion, which used animal sacrifice. Had the laws been designed neutrally and applied neutrally, they could have been upheld even though burdening religion. They were not neutral, however. The Court concluded that the city could have found other ways to protect public health and prevent animal cruelty without targeting one group's religious practice.[61]

This test does not mean that a neutral law or policy cannot be challenged on other grounds. The Court in 1995 ruled that, even though the University of Virginia had a neutral student organization policy that allowed funding of religious groups and thus did not violate the establishment clause, it did engage in viewpoint discrimination and violate free speech protection when it refused to fund one specific religiously oriented student newspaper based on the beliefs it expressed.[62]

The Court's most significant recent ruling on free exercise came in 2010. A Christian group at the University of California's Hastings Law School was denied recognition as a registered student organization because it required adherence to a particular set of beliefs and behaviors for voting members and officers. This policy ran afoul of the university's nondiscrimination rule, which was based on state law. The rule required all groups that wished to receive registered student organization status to accept all those students interested in joining. The university argued that its rule was neutrally applied to all groups and that the Christian Legal Society, the student group, had abided by the rule until it became affiliated with a national organization. The Christian Legal Society challenged the university in federal court, arguing its constitutional free speech, freedom to associate with others of like-minded interests, and free exercise rights were violated. In a 5-4 decision, the Court upheld the constitutionality of the university's rule,

neutrality test the Supreme Court's most recent approach to deciding free exercise of religion cases, this test declares that a government law or action with a neutral intent and application is constitutional, even if it burdens religion and there is no compelling government interest at stake.

▶ THE NEUTRALITY
STANDARD IN PRACTICE
Is the requirement to remove a veil for a driver's license photo an unconstitutional burden on religious freedom? A Florida appeals court used the neutrality standard to reject Sultana Freeman's case in 2002, noting that the requirement was valid because it was created and applied in a neutral fashion.

determining that the rule was created and applied neutrally and was not targeted toward religious beliefs in general or Christian beliefs in particular.[63]

Protest over the Court's neutrality standard in free exercise cases prompted Congress to respond with legislation.

The Court's neutrality standard sparked a chain of legislative and judicial actions. Responding to a massive outcry among religious groups, Congress responded to the Court's new neutrality test by passing the Religious Freedom Restoration Act (RFRA) of 1993. Referring directly to the Court's *Smith* decision, RFRA attempted to erase the Court's use of the neutrality test by prohibiting the federal and state governments from restricting an individual's free exercise of religion unless such restriction served a compelling government interest and was narrowly tailored to meet that interest. In short, with RFRA Congress was telling the Court that balancing, not neutrality, was the standard by which to judge religious practice cases. Congress passed follow-up legislation in 1994, the American Indian Religious Freedom Act Amendments, which specifically protected Native American use of peyote.

In 1997, the Supreme Court invalidated the underlying premise of RFRA and declared its applicability to the states to be unconstitutional.[64] Regarding the underlying premise, the Court majority concluded that RFRA went too far into the judiciary's responsibilities in the American separation of powers system. Regarding the states, the Court decided the law was far too extensive and intrusive in its impact and could not be imposed on state governments. RFRA could, however, apply to the federal government because Congress has the authority to set the guidelines by which federal agencies make decisions. The Court unanimously reiterated in 2006 that federal agencies needed to abide by the balancing requirements imposed by Congress in RFRA.[65]

Rather than try to tell the Court how to interpret the Constitution and apply it to the states, supporters of RFRA passed the Religious Land Use and Institutionalized Persons Act of 2000. This time, using its power of fiscal federalism (see Chapter 4),

Congress required states that chose to receive certain federal funds to use the balancing test when deciding how to accommodate religion for institutionalized persons. In June 2005, the Supreme Court, which tends to be deferential toward Congress's spending power, ruled unanimously that Congress was free to set conditions on the receipt of federal funds.[66] Overall, through RFRA as imposed on federal agencies, state enactment of their own versions of RFRA, and Congress's use of fiscal federalism with the states, elected officials were able to ensure a prominent place for balancing, even if the Supreme Court would no longer consider it the primary constitutional standard by which it evaluated free exercise cases.

Rights of the Accused

5-4   Trace the expansion of the rights of the accused and their balance with the needs of police and prosecutors.

As with freedom of speech and freedom of religion, the scope of rights accorded to individuals accused of a crime has changed significantly over the past 50 years. Much of what Americans now take for granted as "standard operating procedure" in police procedures and criminal prosecutions in fact marked a stark change from previous practice. This procedure was mandated during the 1960s by the Supreme Court led by Chief Justice Earl Warren. Americans, although acknowledging generally the need for procedural safeguards for defendants, can nonetheless be frustrated when criminals go free because of what appear to be "technicalities."

The rights of the accused concern both the behavior of police and government prosecutors and the processes related to trials. Today Americans may wonder why the system is so concerned with the rights of those accused of crimes. But it makes perfect sense that the Framers of the Constitution, especially the Anti-Federalists who demanded a Bill of Rights, were eager to protect the rights of defendants. Remember their experience with the British government. They feared a powerful government that could fabricate charges or corrupt the legal process to get the results it desired. They chose to err on the side of caution and crafted a series of safeguards that they hoped would prevent government from imprisoning the innocent, even if sometimes letting the guilty go free. Table 5-4 lists these rights, ordered from initial investigation to subsequent trial and sentencing.

One of the chief differences between civil liberties in the United States and other countries is the nature of their legal systems. The American legal system, like that in the United Kingdom, is adversarial, unlike the inquisitorial system found in many other advanced democracies, including most in Europe. In an adversarial system, the two sides put together the arguments and evidence and present them before a judge or a jury. The assumption underlying this system is that the competition between the two sides will produce a just outcome. In this system, the rights of the accused are given great weight, and defects in procedures such as gathering evidence and informing suspects of their rights are treated very seriously. The proceedings are dominated by the attorneys presenting the cases. In an inquisitorial system, however, as seen in France, the judge is at the center. It is her or his job to direct the gathering of the evidence and conduct the inquiry that will help resolve the case. The judge can interview witnesses, communicate directly with intelligence and other investigative agencies, and detain suspects prior to the commission of a crime. The rights of the accused are important, but they are given less weight than in the adversarial system. Someone accused of a crime cannot, for example, refuse to testify in most inquisitorial systems.

ThinkingComparatively

The United States uses an adversarial legal system, but many countries around the world use an inquisitorial system.

TABLE 5-4. Constitutional Rights of the Accused from Investigation to Sentencing

Investigation and arrest

- No unreasonable or unwarranted searches and seizures (4th Amendment)
- No arrest without probable cause (4th)
- No entrapment (4th)
- Must be informed of rights (to remain silent, to counsel) (5th)
- No coerced confession and no illegal interrogation (5th)
- No self-incrimination during arrest or trial (5th)
- Be informed of charges (6th)
- Prompt arraignment (6th)
- Legal counsel (6th)
- No excessive bail (8th)
- Grand jury hearing to determine if case is viable (5th)

Trial

- Trial before a judge (Article I, Section 9)
- Speedy and public trial before an impartial jury (6th)
- Trial atmosphere free from prejudice and external interference (6th)
- Evidence obtained by illegal search not admissible during trial (4th)
- Right to confront witnesses (6th)
- No double jeopardy (5th)

Sentencing

- No cruel and unusual punishment (8th)
- Opportunity to appeal verdicts (8th)

The Supreme Court has established guidelines for the constitutional gathering of evidence.

The job of the police and prosecutors depends fundamentally on uncovering evidence that links an individual with a crime. Thus, the gathering of evidence is absolutely critical. But, as the Framers of the Constitution feared, investigators might be overzealous in their attempts to unearth damaging information. At the extreme, investigators might even manufacture evidence in order to obtain a conviction. The protections in the Bill of Rights are designed to minimize that threat.

Central to these protections is the nature of the search-and-seizure process. The Fourth Amendment of the Constitution protects citizens against "unreasonable" searches and seizures, noting that people are to be "secure in their persons, houses, papers, and effects." The amendment mandates that prior to any search, police obtain warrants specifically indicating the place to be searched and the items to be seized. To obtain a warrant, police must have probable cause—that is, they must have enough information suggesting that a crime has taken place and that an individual or location is linked to the crime. Police must also obtain a warrant before engaging in wiretaps of phone and electronic communication, but for obvious reasons, these need not be shown to the target of the investigation. Originally these provisions protected individuals from federal government action. Later, through incorporation, they became binding on the states as well.

The Fourth Amendment prohibits unreasonable searches, but it does not specify what is reasonable or what should happen if police overstep "reasonable" boundaries.

For example, can police look through your trash without a warrant? They can. According to the Supreme Court, individuals cannot assume that trash placed by public streets is covered by any expectation of privacy.[67] Can police stop you while driving even if you are not suspected of wrongdoing? They can. The Court has confirmed that police are allowed to conduct "sobriety checkpoints," in which motorists are stopped without cause in order to deter drunk driving, because the government's compelling interest in public safety outweighs the minor intrusion on personal liberty.[68] On the other hand, police cannot stop vehicles without cause or traffic violations and search them for drugs or other contraband—with no immediate safety issue, the intrusion on liberty outweighs the government's interest in regulating the contraband.[69]

Convictions may not be based on illegally obtained evidence.

In 1914, the Supreme Court prohibited federal courts from basing decisions on evidence obtained improperly—a principle known as the **exclusionary rule**. According to this rule, evidence that is gathered during an illegal search cannot be introduced in a trial, even if that evidence is absolutely necessary to obtain a conviction. In 1961, the Supreme Court applied the rule to the states also.[70] Even after a trial, a conviction can be overturned if a defendant can convince an appeals court that the evidence used for conviction was obtained improperly and should not have been introduced at trial. No other country has any provision regarding evidence that is as extensive as the exclusionary rule.[71]

exclusionary rule   principle established by the Supreme Court, according to which evidence gathered illegally cannot be introduced into trial, and convictions cannot be based on this evidence.

▼ **SEEKING EVIDENCE**

Before entering property to conduct a search, police officers need to obtain a warrant that specifies the location of the search and the items or information sought in the search. Evidence seized in the absence of a judge's warrant may be deemed inadmissible in court.

Over time, the Court has become flexible in its enforcement of the exclusionary rule. The general principle stands, but the Court has allowed for introduction of questionably obtained evidence in specific circumstances. For example, the Court has concluded that it is acceptable to introduce evidence obtained illegally if police can show that they would have eventually obtained the evidence through legal means, or needed to act because the evidence was mobile—in an automobile, for example. The Court has also allowed evidence that was technically collected improperly, but that police exercised "good faith" to collect properly or, in a 2009 decision, was collected as a result of a simple police error. In addition, if a person agrees to a search even without a warrant, these searches are legal so long as the individual did not feel intimidated into complying with the police request. Police do not need to obtain warrants to seize illegal goods that are in open view—firearms, for example.

The Constitution protects defendants during investigations and trials.

Individuals accused of crimes have a number of rights during the process of investigation and litigation. These rights leave much leeway for interpretation by the courts. What is "excessive" bail? What is a "speedy" trial? What is "cruel and unusual" punishment? Questions like these have spawned a long line of judicial clarifications of what the Constitution requires.

The Fifth Amendment and self-incrimination   As any viewer of television dramas knows, police are required to read suspects their rights when placing them under arrest. One of these rights is the right to remain silent. The basic idea is that individuals should not be coerced or intimidated into offering a confession; that individuals must be informed that they are not required to speak to the police except to respond to basic questions of identification; that anything they say can be used against them in court; that they have a right to have an attorney present during questioning; and that an attorney will be provided if they cannot afford one. Confessions made in the absence of these conditions would be inadmissible in court. This procedure is known as the **Miranda warning**, based on the Court's 1966 decision in the case of *Miranda v. Arizona*. It emerged from the Fifth Amendment's guarantee that no citizen "shall be compelled in any criminal case to be a witness against himself" and the Sixth Amendment's guarantee of the right to legal counsel. Despite occasional congressional attempts to overturn it, the *Miranda* warning remains binding on police during investigations. Over time, however, the Court has made the burden on the police less restrictive—for example, unless individuals explicitly request to speak to an attorney, police need not assume that they would like to do so.[72] Two recent 5–4 rulings continued this trend. In *Montejo v. Louisiana* (2009), the Court ruled that police may continue questioning a suspect after the suspect has requested to consult with legal counsel. And in *Berghuis v. Thompkins* (2010), the Court ruled that a suspect must state to police that he or she is invoking the right to remain silent—not talking for an extended period does not itself invoke the right. Thus, comments a suspect makes, even after a long period of silence, would be admissible as evidence if the suspect had not explicitly stated the right to remain silent.

The right not to incriminate oneself stretches back well before the U.S. Constitution. English courts honored this right by the seventeenth century, and the Supreme Court pointed to this English legal tradition in *Miranda*. English courts and Parliament, however, neither require English police to offer *Miranda*-like warnings nor require prosecutors to exclude evidence obtained from improper searches. As of 1995, an act of the British Parliament

Miranda **warning**   ruling that requires police, when arresting suspects, to inform them of their rights, including the right to remain silent and have an attorney present during questioning.

ThinkingComparatively ⚬ ⚬⚬⚬

The right not to incriminate oneself was present in English courts before the U.S. Constitution and is in place in major European countries today.

allows judges and prosecutors to assume the guilt of anyone who refuses to testify in his or her defense. Other major European countries are more consistent with the American model. Germany, France, and Italy all exclude statements from trial if the police failed to inform defendants of their right to remain silent, but the time at which suspects must be informed differs. Italy's practice is closest to that of the United States, with expectations that suspects will be informed of their right to remain silent at the time of arrest.

The Sixth Amendment and the right to counsel   One of the rights guaranteed by the Constitution and mentioned in the *Miranda* warning is the right to have the advice of legal counsel during questioning and trial. As it selectively incorporated the Sixth Amendment, the Court broadened the range of cases that fit within the right to counsel (see the entries for the Sixth Amendment in Table 5-2). Moreover, the Court made the individual's right to counsel an obligation upon governments to *provide* counsel for defendants who could not afford an attorney. The defining case was *Gideon v. Wainwright* (1963). Clarence Earl Gideon, not entitled to public counsel under Florida law unless he faced the death penalty, defended himself at trial and was convicted and sentenced. Gideon appealed to the Supreme Court, and the Court unanimously concluded that individuals in all felony cases must be provided with legal assistance if they cannot afford their own. Lawyers in criminal cases, the Court ruled, are not a luxury but, rather, a necessity for a fair trial. The broad right to counsel established in this case was extended even further in subsequent years, with defendants able to challenge convictions based on the poor quality of publicly provided legal representation they received.

The Eighth Amendment and cruel and unusual punishment   Once a defendant is found guilty, a judge or jury must declare an appropriate sentence. The Constitution forbids "cruel and unusual" punishment, and the Supreme Court has focused on the "and." A punishment can be cruel but not unusual, or unusual but not cruel. The Supreme Court is most concerned when it is both.

Capital punishment—the death penalty—is the area that most often reaches the Supreme Court for review under the Eighth Amendment's prohibition against cruel and unusual punishment. Though opponents of the practice decry it as inhumane, the Court has never declared the death penalty in general to constitute cruel and unusual punishment. It has prohibited capital punishment in cases of rape, including rape of a child.[73] In recent years, the Court has decided that the death penalty constitutes cruel and unusual punishment for individuals with severe mental developmental disabilities and for minors.[74] In 2010, the Court added in a 5–4 vote that life terms without parole also constitute cruel and unusual punishment for minors.[75]

These decisions concerning minors and the mentally disabled were notable for the references to international trends and law in the majority's rulings. Justices Stephen Breyer and Antonin Scalia have expressed publicly— and often in joint appearances—the two ends of the spectrum, with Breyer arguing that consideration of foreign trends and law is appropriate for, in this case, understanding what is currently deemed cruel and unusual punishment, whereas Scalia argues that international trends and rulings are irrelevant considerations for a court that is interpreting and applying the U.S. Constitution. It is too early to determine whether the Court is influenced by changing global opinion or whether these are merely additional facts marshaled for decisions that would have been the same even without these international references. But as more cases make these kinds of references, political scientists will be in a stronger position to sort out the influence of international court decisions, law in other countries, and legal briefs filed by international human rights organizations versus the influence of domestic opinion, legal precedent, briefs filed by domestic groups, and the changing membership of the Court, among other possible factors.

ThinkingCausally

Is the U.S. Supreme Court influenced by foreign courts and law?

▶ THE TECHNOLOGY OF CAPITAL PUNISHMENT

This chamber at San Quentin prison in California was used for execution by lethal injection through 2007, when it was replaced by a new facility. In 2008, the Supreme Court lifted the restriction it had placed on lethal injection executions. The Court determined that this method of execution did not constitute cruel and unusual punishment and was constitutional.

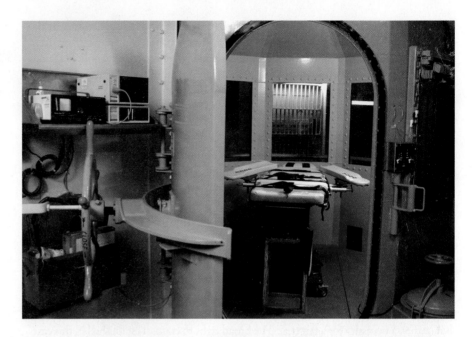

For individuals outside the categories of minors and the mentally challenged, the Court has sought to ensure that defendants' due process rights were adhered to rigorously in capital punishment cases. Although it is uncommon, the Court will, for example, overturn death sentences if it believes a defendant received a defense so inadequate that it violates the constitutional right to counsel.[76] The Court also considers whether the method of execution is cruel and unusual. In April 2008, the Supreme Court ended its eight-month moratorium on the death penalty when it decided that death by lethal injection—the primary method used in the 35 capital punishment states—did not constitute cruel and unusual punishment.

The current system of regulating capital punishment began with the Supreme Court's decision in *Furman v. Georgia* (1972). In that ruling, the justices struck down three death penalty sentences, concluding that the use of capital punishment was impermissibly arbitrary. The decision did not eliminate capital punishment, but it did lead to a five-year hiatus in its use. States needed to reexamine their procedures for imposing the penalty. This meant, first, being specific about which crimes might justify capital punishment, so that a jury could not impose the death penalty arbitrarily. Second, cases would be two-staged, with a jury first determining guilt or innocence and then, if their verdict was "guilty," determining whether the death penalty is warranted. Today, federal law and the law in 35 states allow the use of the death penalty under this procedure, with nearly all executions taking place at the state level.[77]

The death penalty is a highly charged emotional and moral issue. To opponents, it is morally wrong, applied inconsistently across racial and ethnic groups, and no more effective than other deterrents to crime. Opponents also point to the elimination of capital punishment in many countries around the world as evidence that it is widely considered inhumane. By 2010, 139 countries had either eliminated the death penalty in law or eliminated it in practice, including Mexico and Canada, while 58 countries—including India, China, Japan, and the United States—allowed it.[78] To supporters, capital punishment is justified on individualistic grounds as an appropriately harsh response to the destruction of the liberty of other individuals, and on communitarian grounds as an appropriate protection of the community's safety and sense of justice, which outweigh the life and liberty interest of the convicted criminal.

ThinkingComparatively

About two-thirds of the countries around the world, including Canada and Mexico, have eliminated the use of capital punishment.

CaseStudy: The USA PATRIOT Act

Few events truly "shock the world," but the terrorist attacks of September 11, 2001, clearly belong in that category. Americans were stunned by their country's vulnerability, saddened at the tragic loss of life, and angered by those responsible for the acts. President George W. Bush needed to respond to strengthen the country's security. And he also needed to act for political reasons: in times of crisis, a president needs to respond with strength and authority or risk a sharp drop in public support. Among President Bush's responses was organizing an international effort to attack Afghanistan, the suspected home of Osama bin Laden, mastermind of the September 11 attacks.

Inside the United States, the president's response was fourfold. First, foreigners in the United States who were suspected of possibly having knowledge about terrorist acts were indefinitely detained and questioned. Second, the government began interviewing thousands of young Middle Eastern men to get possible leads on future terrorist attacks. Third, military tribunals, which do not have many of the civil liberties safeguards of civilian courts, were formed to put some suspected terrorists on trial. Each of these tactics raised concerns about possible civil liberties violations. But it was the fourth part of the president's domestic response to the attacks that proved to be the most controversial: the Uniting and Strengthening America by Providing Appropriate Tools Required to Intercept and Obstruct Terrorism Act—the USA PATRIOT Act—typically referred to as the Patriot Act.

Defying the usually slow legislative process, the Patriot Act was passed overwhelmingly by both chambers of Congress six weeks after the September 11 attacks.[79] Some aspects of the bill raised alarms among groups, such as the American Civil Liberties Union, that see themselves as defenders of civil liberties. Many of the complaints about

these provisions centered around the federal government's ability to investigate individuals and obtain records without probable cause or a judge's approval. Supporters of the law responded that in most cases these controversial changes simply allowed law enforcement to use tactics for detecting terrorism that they had been allowed to use for other criminal activity.

Controversial provisions of the Patriot Act included the following:

- A definition of "domestic terrorism" that seemed to encompass activism designed to "influence the policy of a government by intimidation or coercion."
- Authorization of searches and wiretaps without having to show probable cause to a judge to justify a search warrant.
- Restricted entry into the United States of individuals who had engaged in speech that "undermined" American efforts to reduce terrorism.
- Expanded ability to search personal records held by a third party such as a bank or insurance company.
- Ability to obtain information on reading and viewing habits from bookstores, libraries, and video stores.
- Ability to install software to track all forms of Internet activity.
- Ability to detain immigrants without charges for up to seven days and indefinitely if any immigration violations were discovered.
- Prohibition of "material support," including training, personnel, expert advice or assistance, and service, for organizations designated as terrorist by the State Department.

The Patriot Act was under constant attack by its critics from its inception. In September 2004, a federal judge struck down a provision in the law that allowed the Federal

► **A LIBRARY PROTESTS THE PATRIOT ACT**
The American Library Association and many individual librarians were upset with a provision in the original Patriot Act that allowed FBI agents to investigate the borrowing record of individuals connected to investigations of spying or terrorism. The association argued that this practice violated the privacy assumed by patrons and that it might be abused. The FBI noted that some of the September 11 hijackers had used library computers and reading materials to hatch their plot.

Bureau of Investigation (FBI) to require Internet service providers to turn over subscriber information without informing the subscriber or being able to challenge the order in court. This was the first time that a court had limited the government's surveillance powers under the act. A handful of states and over 100 cities, towns, and counties voted not to cooperate with any provisions of the Patriot Act that officials believed violated civil liberties or civil rights.

Over time, public support for the act diminished. A Harris Poll survey compared public opinion in late September 2001 and mid-June 2005, when Congress was considering reauthorizing the Patriot Act. It found decreased support for a number of the act's more aggressive measures—stronger document and physical security checks for travelers, expanded undercover activities to investigate suspicious groups, closer monitoring of banking and credit card transactions, adoption of a national ID system for all U.S. citizens, expanded camera surveillance on streets and public places, and monitoring of Internet chat rooms and other forums.

Despite the drop in support, however, each of these investigatory activities still retained majority support, some overwhelmingly. In times of uneasiness, Americans tend to tilt the scales more toward security and somewhat away from liberty. In only one area addressed by the survey did majority support in 2001 become minority support in 2005—expanded government monitoring of e-mail and cell phones.[80]

Sixteen provisions of the Patriot Act were set to expire at the end of 2005. During the spring and summer of 2005, Congress was engaged in hearings concerning the renewal of these provisions. President Bush strongly urged Congress to continue and strengthen these parts of the act.[81] Despite the president's urging, objections from many members of Congress prevented a permanent reauthorization of the Patriot Act in 2005. The road to reauthorization looked rocky enough, given the concerns of many legislators about encroachments upon civil liberties. But the road became impassable in late 2005 when it was revealed that President Bush, separately from the Patriot Act, had authorized the National Security Agency (NSA) to intercept the communications of Americans without court approval. Democrats and some Republicans denounced the president's action as being in direct violation of a 1978 law concerning domestic wiretapping for intelligence purposes. In the ensuing uproar, a filibuster stalled reauthorization and Congress resorted to temporary extensions of the Patriot Act through March 2006.

Negotiations in early 2006 between the White House and members of Congress produced concessions from the president and swung enough votes to reauthorize 14 of the 16 main provisions permanently. The concessions allowed recipients of subpoenas to challenge, after one year, a requirement that they not discuss their case publicly. They also prevented the Federal

Bureau of Investigation from demanding the names of lawyers consulted by individuals who received secret government requests for information. And they excluded most libraries from having to turn over records on their patrons.

The revised version of the Patriot Act passed overwhelmingly in both the House and Senate. Some members of Congress who voted for the bill, such as then-Senator Barack Obama of Illinois, remained troubled by it but urged their colleagues to support the compromise and work in future legislation to provide additional civil liberties protections. Outright opponents declared the compromise to be insufficient in its defense of civil liberties. Russell Feingold, a Democratic senator from Wisconsin who was the only senator to vote against the Patriot Act in 2001 and was instrumental in leading the filibuster in late 2005, spent most of a day reading the Constitution aloud on the Senate floor to express his displeasure.[82] Despite this discontent, large majorities of legislators cast their support for the bill. In March 2006, the president had achieved his long-sought goal and signed the Patriot Act extension into law.

The next opportunity for critics to revise the legislation would come four years later. Three sections of the Patriot Act were slated to expire if not renewed by the end of February 2010, and two were especially controversial. "Roving wiretaps" allow investigators to follow suspects on multiple communication devices, rather than obtaining permission for each one. In the Patriot Act, unlike in other criminal statutes, the FBI is not required to name the person, place, or initial device it wishes to tap. The second provision concerned the government's ability to access private records when a person is not a target of an investigation or suspected of involvement in terrorism but when the FBI determines the information might be useful to an investigation. To the dismay of Patriot Act critics, Congress, now controlled by the Democrats rather than the Republicans, overwhelmingly voted to extend the provisions for one year. In late February 2010, President Obama signed the extension into law. The act's prohibition of expert assistance, including nonviolent educational aid, for organizations designated as terrorist was upheld by the Supreme Court later that year.[83]

ThinkingCritically

1. Select one of the Patriot Act provisions identified above and make the strongest argument you can for it and against it.

2. Considering both the Framers' vision and your own analysis, to what degree should public opinion about the tradeoff between civil liberties and security guide policy makers?

3. Devise and defend guidelines for the federal government's surveillance of e-mail and text messages during wartime.

Discovering New Rights That Are Protected by the Constitution

5-5 Explain how the Ninth and Fourteenth Amendments have helped to establish rights other than those specifically listed in the Constitution.

As explained above, the scope of civil liberties has changed with nationalization and denationalization. The scope has also been revised by a second path, as judicial interpretations of the Constitution with regard to freedom of speech and religion and the rights of the accused have all undergone expansion and contraction at different times in American history. The scope of civil liberties can also change by a third path, by the discovery of new rights that are protected by the Constitution.

The identification of new rights happens by two methods that we examine below. First, lawyers and Supreme Court justices may use the Ninth Amendment, which states that rights not specifically mentioned in the Constitution are reserved to the people. The second method for the identification of new rights is through the Fourteenth Amendment, and particularly through the due process clause discussed earlier in this chapter.

The right to privacy has revolutionized the law concerning birth control, abortion, and same-sex relationships.

Some of the most momentous civil liberties decisions of the past four decades have been based on a right that is not even explicitly guaranteed in the Constitution, the right to privacy. Court decisions concerning birth control, abortion, and homosexual behavior have all focused on individuals' right to privacy. This right connects deeply to beliefs in individualism and liberty in American political culture. The Court used the Ninth Amendment to discover this right.[84]

Birth control　From 1873 through 1938, the federal government criminalized the distribution of birth control material across state lines.[85] Many states, following the federal government's lead, also restricted the use of birth control within their borders. In the early 1960s, 28 states still prohibited married couples from using contraceptive devices. Challenges to such laws made only limited headway. Federal courts initially struck down state laws that were not flexible enough to allow physicians to prescribe contraceptives to protect patients' health, but the courts otherwise left the contraception bans in place.

In 1961, the Planned Parenthood League of Connecticut opened a birth control clinic in defiance of state law. The clinic provided information and instruction on contraceptive use to married couples. Ten days after opening the clinic, Estelle Griswold, the league's executive director, and Charles Lee Buxton, the medical director, were arrested and convicted for violating Connecticut's law barring the dissemination of information about birth control devices and techniques. Four years later, in *Griswold v. Connecticut* (1965), the U.S. Supreme Court overturned the convictions and declared by a 7–2 majority that there was a constitutional right to privacy for married couples, later extended to unmarried heterosexual couples.[86] The Court's majority concluded that even though the word *privacy* does not appear in the Constitution, the Ninth Amendment, combined with provisions of the First, Third, Fourth, and Fifth Amendments,

> "Some of the most momentous civil liberties decisions of the past four decades have been based on a right that is not even explicitly guaranteed in the Constitution: the right to privacy."

►**TELEMEDICINE, A NEW ABORTION DISPUTE**
In a new telemedicine abortion procedure in Iowa, a remote-control pill-dispensing and videoconference system allows doctors to deliver abortion medications to patients in clinics across the state. The doctor remotely unlocks the drawer that contains the two medicines.

implicitly suggested that the Constitution contained a right to privacy.[87] Protections in these amendments create "zones of privacy" in the Constitution. The dissenting justices in *Griswold* argued unsuccessfully that, by declaring a general right to privacy beyond the specific privacy protections mentioned in the Constitution, the unelected justices of the Supreme Court were displacing the appropriate role of elected officials in the states and of the voters who elected them.

Abortion   *Roe v. Wade* (1973) demonstrated the extensive impact of the *Griswold* decision. Abortion had been illegal by law in Texas since 1854, unless medical personnel determined it was necessary to save the life of the mother. Similar laws existed in almost every state by the 1950s; most dated back to the latter half of the nineteenth century. During the 1960s, several states liberalized their abortion statutes, but a majority still had laws similar to that in Texas. Norma McCorvey—known in the legal case as "Jane Roe"—wishing to terminate her pregnancy legally, filed a challenge to Texas's law in 1970. Building from the *Griswold* decision, the suit contended that the statute violated McCorvey's right to privacy.

The Supreme Court, by a 7–2 majority, agreed. A woman's privacy right was not absolute, however. The Court determined that the right to privacy in the abortion decision could be conditional upon important government interests in health, medical standards, and protecting potential life. The privacy interest dominates at first, but as pregnancy advances, these government interests begin to balance the woman's privacy interest. Based on this framework and on what it took to be generally consensual understandings of fetal development, the Court established a trimester arrangement. During the first three months of pregnancy, women were free to obtain abortions. During the second trimester—after the first three months but before fetal viability (i.e., before the fetus can potentially live outside the mother's womb)—*Roe* allowed the state to regulate abortion in a manner consistent with its interest in protecting maternal health. During the final trimester, a state could regulate or prohibit abortion, consistent with its interest in protecting potential human life.[88]

In later years, the Court would allow states to adopt some first-trimester restrictions consistent with their interest in protecting potential life, but none that could put an undue burden on a woman's right to obtain an abortion.[89] The Court defined an undue burden as a "substantial obstacle in the path of a woman seeking an abortion before the fetus attains viability." By this standard, in *Planned Parenthood v. Casey* (1992) the Court accepted a mandatory 24-hour waiting period before an abortion procedure could be performed, requiring doctors to counsel women on alternatives to abortion (see Figure 5-2), and requiring minors to get parental consent or a judge's approval as reasonable and constitutional restrictions on abortion access. Requiring a woman to notify her husband before obtaining an abortion was struck

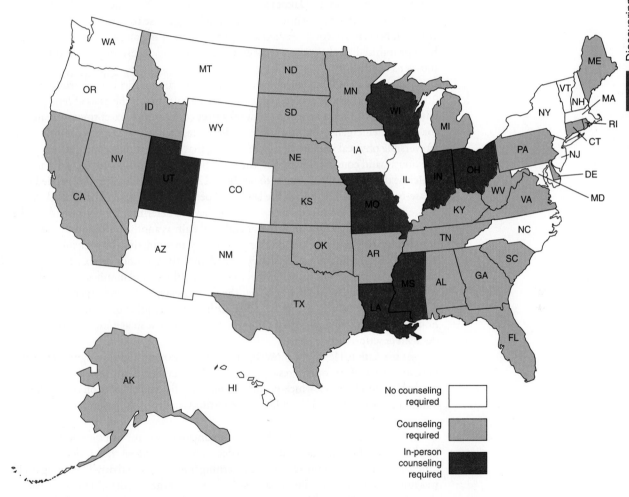

FIGURE 5-2. Counseling Requirements for Women Seeking an Abortion, 2010. The Supreme Court has declared that abortion is a protected constitutional right, meaning that states cannot prohibit it. But because access to abortion is not considered a fundamental right, significant variation in law and policy across the states is permissible, as long as states do not create an "undue burden" on access to abortion. Most states require women to obtain counseling before having an abortion, with various requirements regarding what the counseling must cover. Counseling is usually coupled with a waiting period of 24 hours prior to the abortion being performed.

down as an undue burden. No state can deny access to abortion completely, but some have made it more difficult to exercise this right than others.

In 2006, the strongest challenge yet to *Roe v. Wade* came from South Dakota, where a bill outlawing all abortions except those necessary to save the life of the mother was signed into law. The law was passed soon after Samuel Alito joined the Supreme Court, replacing former justice Sandra Day O'Connor, who had been pivotal in upholding abortion rights during her tenure. Pro-life forces believed that with the change in personnel on the Court, the time was ripe for a full-fledged challenge to *Roe* that would return decisions about abortion to the states, and they expected that pro-choice advocates would challenge the law in court. This pro-life strategy was derailed when opponents of the South Dakota law instead forced a referendum that put the law up for a statewide vote in November 2006. In that balloting, 56 percent of South Dakota voters rejected the new law, meaning that there was now no need for pro-choice advocates to bring a case to court. South Dakota voters in November 2008 rejected a revised version of the amendment that would have prohibited all abortions except in the case of rape, incest, or protection of the mother's health.

Nebraska and Oklahoma opened new fronts in the conflict over abortion in 2010. Nebraska became the first state to restrict abortions on the basis of fetal pain. The state banned most abortions 20 weeks after conception—exceptions were made for medical emergency, imminent death of the pregnant woman, and substantial and irreversible physical impairment—concluding that fetuses at that point can feel pain. Previously, and consistent with *Roe*, the state disallowed abortions after fetal viability, which at the earliest was thought to be about 22 weeks (viability was determined on a case-by-case basis). Although the law could be challenged and end up in the U.S. Supreme Court, pro-choice advocates would have to determine if they wished to take the strategic risk that the Court might add fetal pain as another criterion that states could constitutionally use, in addition to viability, in regulating the availability of abortion. In Oklahoma, the legislature passed, over the governor's veto, a law that requires providers of abortion services to set up an ultrasound monitor so that the woman can see it and to describe to her the fetus's heart, limbs, and organs. The law does not exempt victims of rape or incest. Other states require ultrasounds, but Oklahoma is the first to mandate that the woman be shown the image and be given a detailed description.

At the national level, the most significant restriction on abortion rights in the past decade came in 2003, when President George W. Bush signed into law the Partial Birth Abortion Ban Act, which prohibited one specific type of abortion procedure. The Supreme Court, by 5–4, upheld the constitutionality of the law in 2007.[90]

Sexual activity   *Griswold* and *Roe* were landmark decisions with significant social implications. The Supreme Court's 2003 decision in *Lawrence v. Texas* added a third milestone privacy decision, this time concerning homosexual activity. The ruling itself was not based on privacy considerations, but rather on the broader grounds of what the guarantee of "liberty" in the Fourteenth Amendment protects. It nonetheless had the effect of overturning an earlier ruling that had not extended privacy rights to same-sex sexual activity. Nearly 20 years earlier in *Bowers v. Hardwick* (1986), a case involving an anti-sodomy law in Georgia, the Court concluded that there was no right to privacy for homosexual conduct. But in *Lawrence* the Court sharply repudiated its previous decision, declaring that the previous court, by defining the issue narrowly as the "right to engage in sodomy," minimized the liberty at stake. Liberty, the Court concluded, demanded that homosexuals not lose "their dignity as free persons" because of their sexual behavior in the confines of their own home.

Legislative protection of the right to privacy   Privacy need not be a constitutional right for government to protect it. Government can choose legislatively or administratively to protect aspects of privacy if it wishes. For example, the Privacy Act places restrictions on how government agencies use personal information about individuals. The Family Educational Rights and Privacy Act protects the privacy of students' educational records. The Right to Financial Privacy Act governs how financial institutions collect and disclose personal financial information and how individuals can limit that disclosure. The national "do not call" registry allows phone customers to prohibit calls from telemarketers.

The privacy of consumer information online is one area in which legislation will likely be considered over the coming years.[91] What kind of privacy employees can expect may be another. In 2010, the Supreme Court ruled unanimously that police employees in Ontario, California, who were given pagers for their jobs, could not assume they have an expectation of privacy when sending text messages on the pagers.[92] Written city policy stated that e-mail messages were not private, and employees were told verbally that text messages were considered e-mails.

Debate over a general right to privacy   The constitutional right to privacy will remain contentious because it implies a much broader scope of privacy than these legislative enactments provide, and a scope that will be determined not by elected officials but by judges. Scholars, activists, and justices who see no general right to privacy argue that the Constitution prohibits some specific violations of privacy but is silent on others. Where the Constitution is silent, they argue, it should be up to legislatures, not judges, to determine whether to extend privacy protections. And just how far does a *general* right to privacy go, they ask? Does a general right to privacy require that euthanasia be legal? Suicide? Assisted suicide? What about bigamy or polygamy? Must laws prohibiting prostitution be struck down?

The Court has ruled on each of these issues. In some cases, such as upholding state or federal laws restricting bigamy, polygamy, and prostitution, the decisions came before the privacy right was fully established, but the Court today might see a compelling government interest at stake that would justify limiting privacy. In end-of-life issues, the Court's decisions have been more recent. In *Cruzan v. Director, Missouri Department of Health* (1990), the Court declared that a patient can refuse unwanted medical treatment. If the patient is incompetent and unable to articulate his or her wishes, a state is constitutionally allowed to require that there be "clear and convincing" evidence that the patient would have refused the treatment. The case of Terri Schiavo riveted national attention in 2005 as her husband and parents fought over whether to discontinue a feeding tube that had kept her alive for 15 years. Medical reviews described Schiavo as being in a "persistent vegetative state" during this time. The case drew the attention of lawmakers and courts in both Florida and Washington, D.C. Ultimately, the consensus of both the state and federal courts was that Schiavo had made her intent clear enough to her husband and that he could order her feeding tube discontinued, despite her parents' objections.

If an individual has a privacy right to reject treatment, which can passively result in death, does an individual also have a specific privacy right to end his or her life deliberately? In 1997, the Court upheld the state bans on physician-assisted suicide in Washington and New York, firmly and unanimously rejecting the idea that liberty includes a right to suicide. In 2006, however, the Court let stand Oregon's law that

207

▼ **CHARGED AFTER RAID ON A POLYGAMIST RANCH**
Raymond Jessop was found guilty in 2009 of sexually assaulting a teen with whom he had a "spiritual marriage." He was charged following the raid of a polygamist sect's ranch the previous year. In the raid, 400 children were removed but were soon placed back with the sect. Although not arguing for the validity of underage marriages, some polygamists have argued that the practice among adults should be protected by the constitutional right to privacy.

allowed physician-assisted suicide.[93] Because the Court does not see suicide as a right but has not concluded that it is constitutionally prohibited, it appears to be allowing states latitude either to prohibit or to allow physician-assisted suicide.

To defenders of the Court's discovery of a general right to privacy, these decisions show that there need be no "slippery slope" that leads to potentially problematic social outcomes in areas like prostitution, suicide, and marriage between multiple partners. They argue that—as with other liberties—privacy is outweighed when government can show that it has a compelling need to restrict it.

Substantive due process discovers new rights by applying specific guarantees to the Fourteenth Amendment's general guarantee of life, liberty, and property.

The federal courts have established that the Constitution protects many rights other than those specifically listed in the document. There is, for example, a right of association, a right against compelled association and compelled speech, a right to supervise the education of one's children, a right to an attorney's being present while one is being questioned about a crime, and a right to procreate.[94]

Where does protection for these rights come from? The answer is through the second method for the discovery of new rights, the concept of substantive due process. Due process is normally thought of as procedural—did a government official follow the specified rules and accord an individual all the rights and appeals allowed before restricting some aspect of the person's life, liberty, or property? Were the rules clear so that individuals did not inadvertently fail to defend a right because the process was unclear? Were they clear enough that the individual knew the consequence of taking certain actions? Procedural due process, then, is doing the "right thing" by way of process.

▶ **PARENTS' RIGHTS IN EDUCATION**

The Supreme Court used substantive due process to affirm key decisions in 1923 and 1925 that parents have a right to control their children's education. Home schooling is an option for parents, such as those in this Muslim family in Phoenix in 2008, who believe public schools do not meet their children's needs or that they clash with their religious or cultural values.

Substantive due process, by contrast, is doing the "right thing" by way of substance. It says that "life, liberty, and property," mentioned in the Fourteenth Amendment, have specific meanings that must be discovered by and protected by the courts because of their fundamental nature or their place in American tradition.[95] Substantive due process has had a large impact on civil liberties interpretation. The right to privacy was discussed above as an example of discovering new rights through the Ninth Amendment. It has also been considered an aspect of substantive due process by some judges, participants in legal proceedings, and political scientists.[96] Opponents of Connecticut's birth control restrictions, for example, did not claim that the state of Connecticut was violating *procedural* due process when it arrested individuals who distributed birth control materials—the state followed the law and proper procedures. The claim, instead, was that privacy to use birth control must be protected as part of the *substance* of the "liberty" protected by the Fourteenth Amendment's due process clause.

For the past two decades, the Supreme Court has been reluctant to read new rights into the Constitution via substantive due process. For example, the Court ruled unanimously against a substantive due process claim that workers have a right to be free from "unreasonable risk of harm," or that the public has a right to safety that is violated when innocent bystanders are injured during high-speed pursuit of criminal suspects by the police.[97] The general protection of "life" in the Fourteenth Amendment did not require the protection of these specific rights. However, the Court has tended to uphold and sometimes expand rights established by substantive due process in previous decisions.[98]

substantive due process
an interpretation of the due process clause in the Fourteenth Amendment that says the clause's guarantee of "life, liberty, and property" provides a means to discover new rights not mentioned elsewhere in the Constitution, and that these rights would exist at both the national and state levels of government.

CHAPTER SUMMARY

In this chapter you have learned to:

5-1   Define the civil liberties guaranteed by the Constitution and trace the process by which they became binding on state governments. Civil liberties are guaranteed in the U.S. Constitution—in the articles and in the Bill of Rights. Civil liberties address concerns such as speech, the practice of one's religion, and the use and ownership of property, with Americans usually believing that these are areas where government should not interfere unless there are fundamental and compelling reasons to do so. Through selective incorporation, the Bill of Rights gradually became binding upon the states.

5-2   Analyze the different standards by which the Supreme Court has determined whether restrictions on freedom of speech are acceptable. Over time, the Supreme Court has adopted a series of standards that have expanded the right of free speech, even in difficult cases where the speech might lead to illegal acts. The Court's interpretation of particular categories of speech, such as obscenity, has also shifted over time. First Amendment freedoms, including freedom of speech, hold a preferred position among Americans' civil liberties.

5-3   Evaluate how the Supreme Court has interpreted cases regarding religion and how Congress has reacted to the Court's actions. The Constitution's religious freedom guarantee is twofold: individuals are to be free to exercise their religion, and government is not to establish religion. Since 1990, the

Court has employed a neutrality standard, which is less likely to provide legal exemptions for religious practice as long as a law is conceived and implemented neutrally. Establishment cases since the 1970s have been decided by the three-prong *Lemon* test.

5-4   Trace the expansion of the rights of the accused and their balance with the needs of police and prosecutors. The Supreme Court in the 1960s added significant safeguards to protect the rights of the accused when evidence is gathered, during investigations and trials, and at the time of sentencing. Well-known features of the legal system such as the *Miranda* warning and the obligation of government to provide counsel were introduced during this era. Over the past two decades, the Supreme Court has given police more leeway in their investigations.

5-5   Explain how the Ninth and Fourteenth Amendments have helped to establish rights other than those specifically listed in the Constitution. The discovery of new rights that are protected by the Constitution has come about in two ways, through the Ninth Amendment and through the Fourteenth Amendment. Many significant new rights have been established by one or the other of these means. The most far reaching of these rights in terms of its social impact has been the right to privacy, which is the basis most notably for dramatic changes in government regulation of birth control, abortion, and sexual behavior.

KEY TERMS

bad tendency standard, p. 180

balancing test, p. 192

civil liberties, p. 168

clear and present danger standard, p. 181

due process, p. 169

establishment clause, p. 189

exclusionary rule, p. 197

free exercise clause, p. 189

gravity of the danger standard, p. 185

incorporation process, p. 174

Lemon test, p. 190

Miranda warning, p. 198

neutrality test, p. 193

preferred position, p. 185

prior restraint, p. 179

selective incorporation, p. 176

substantive due process, p. 209

---

mypoliscilab EXERCISES

Apply what you learned in this chapter on MyPoliSciLab.

Read on mypoliscilab.com

eText: Chapter 5

Study and Review on mypoliscilab.com

Pre-Test

Post-Test

Chapter Exam

Flashcards

Watch on mypoliscilab.com

Video: D.C.'s Right to Bear Arms

Video: Funeral Protestors Push the Limits of Free Speech

Explore on mypoliscilab.com

Simulation: You Are a Police Officer

Simulation: Balancing Liberty and Security in a Time of War

Comparative: Comparing Civil Liberties

Timeline: Civil Liberties and National Security

CHAPTER TEST

1. How did selective incorporation change the impact of the Bill of Rights on American government and society?

2. Why was the Fourteenth Amendment so significant?

3. How did the Supreme Court compare the significance and the likelihood of a particular danger when it applied the gravity of the danger standard?

4. What difference does it make for individuals challenging a government law or action that the Supreme Court now uses the preferred position standard rather than the bad tendency standard in free speech cases?

5. If you were on the Supreme Court, how would you apply the three prongs of the *Lemon* test to a challenge to the faith-based initiative begun by President Bush and continued by President Obama?

6. How do the balancing and neutrality standards in religious practice cases differ?

7. What were the responses in the legislative and judicial causal chain reaction that occurred after the Supreme Court adopted the neutrality standard?

8. With the exclusionary rule, how has the Supreme Court attempted to balance the individual rights of defendants with the community's interest, through police and prosecutors, in combating crime?

9. How has the Supreme Court's view changed on whether and when capital punishment is potentially cruel and unusual?

10. Why did the Supreme Court determine that Americans had a constitutional right to privacy despite that term not appearing explicitly in the Constitution, and what are some of the major issue areas affected by this right?

SUGGESTED READINGS

Garrett Epps. 2001. *To an Unknown God: Religious Freedom on Trial*. New York: St. Martin's Press. An examination of *Employment Division of Oregon v. Smith*, the case concerning sacramental use of peyote that ushered in the Court's neutrality standard in free exercise cases.

Amitai Etzioni. 1999. *The Limits of Privacy*. New York: Basic Books. Argues, from a communitarian perspective, that sometimes community interests need to trump the privacy concerns of individuals.

Steven M. Feldman. 2008. *Free Expression and Democracy in America*. Chicago: University of Chicago Press. Comprehensive and careful review of the changes in the law and politics of free speech doctrine in America since the colonial era.

Jon B. Gould. 2005. *Speak No Evil: The Triumph of Hate Speech Regulation*. Chicago: University of Chicago Press. Examines the rise of hate speech codes and other forms of hate speech regulation.

Anthony Lewis. 1964. *Gideon's Trumpet*. New York: Random House. A classic account of the individuals and events leading to *Gideon v. Wainwright*, in which the Court declared that government is obliged to provide an attorney for individuals charged with a felony who cannot afford legal representation.

Herbert McClosky and Alida Brill. 1983. *Dimensions of Political Tolerance: What Americans Believe About Civil Liberties*. New York: Russell Sage. A classic analysis of the civil liberties beliefs of Americans in general and in specific circumstances.

Martha Nussbaum. 2008. *Liberty of Conscience: In Defense of America's Tradition of Religious Equality*. New York: Basic Books. An accessible and wide-ranging analysis of conflicts over religious liberty and freedom across American history.

David M. Rabban. 1999. *Free Speech in its Forgotten Years, 1870–1920*. New York: Cambridge University Press. How free speech issues emerged on the judicial or political agenda during the era when government restrictions on speech were difficult to defeat.

Geoffrey R. Stone. 2004. *Perilous Times: Free Speech in Wartime from the Sedition Act of 1798 to the War on Terrorism*. New York: W. W. Norton. Focuses on six periods of war and social stress in American history and analyzes the restrictions on civil liberties in those years.

Cass R. Sunstein. 1995. *Democracy and the Problem of Free Speech*. New York: Free Press. Argues that the Supreme Court should add democratic concerns for justice and equality to its concerns for individual freedom when it decides free speech cases.

SUGGESTED WEBSITES

American Civil Liberties Union: www.aclu.org

The largest civil liberties advocacy group in the United States, active both in legislation and lawsuits. Site provides overviews of key civil liberties issues.

Institute for Justice: www.ij.org

A major civil liberties advocacy group. Their positions sometimes coincide, but the IJ is generally more aligned with conservative perspectives and the ACLU with liberal perspectives.

Electronic Frontier Foundation: www.eff.org

The leading group focused on civil liberties and free speech issues in cyberspace and digital media. Site provides issue analysis and court case updates.

First Amendment Center: www.firstamendmentcenter.org

Excellent starting point for research. "First Amendment Topics" provides gateway to description, overview, and analysis of a wide range of civil liberties issues.

Freedom House: www.freedomhouse.org

Site monitors civil liberties and democratic and economic freedom worldwide. Provides annual ranking of each country in these categories and analysis of key issues.

Oyez: www.oyez.org

Helpful and friendly site with analysis and description of U.S. Supreme Court decisions in easily understood terms. Links to audio of oral arguments and text of the Court's decision, among other features.

CHAPTER

6 Civil Rights

Civil rights tie together the guarantees of the Constitution and the hard work of politics. Groups that believe they have been unfairly discriminated against can point to the Constitution, but they often also need to engage in politics to get results. For political scientists, this basic framework raises a causal question that is both simple and important: why do political involvement and action lead to success for some groups but not for others?

Consider one of the most dramatic issues in civil rights—reparations for past injustices. On December 7, 1941, Japan's air force attacked the U.S. military base at Pearl Harbor, Hawaii, bringing World War II to American soil. Immediately, Japanese Americans

found themselves the targets of suspicion and hostility, not for anything they had done, but for who they were. Two months later, in February 1942, President Franklin D. Roosevelt directed the secretary of the Department of War to move citizens purportedly vulnerable to enemy sabotage or spying to detention centers away from military zones on the West Coast—specifically the entire western halves of California, Washington, and Oregon, and the southern third of Arizona. Everyone knew that meant Japanese Americans. A month later, Congress passed a law making it a crime to violate the president's directive.

Over 120,000 Japanese Americans were relocated, and most remained in the detention centers for more than two years. They were forced to leave behind their belongings, homes, and careers. Also devastating was that the detainees were considered un-American

and were not treated equally as citizens, simply because of their identity. In 1944, the Supreme Court ruled that excluding individuals from the military zone was constitutional as an exercise of national security, but it did not rule directly whether the subsequent relocation to detention centers was an unconstitutional violation of civil rights.[1]

The victims remained silent for decades. But in the 1970s, inspired by the successes of the black civil rights movement, the Japanese American Citizens League (JACL), an organization that lobbied on issues of interest to Japanese Americans, began to act. Under considerable pressure, President Gerald Ford issued a proclamation that rescinded President Roosevelt's order, expressing regret for this "setback to fundamental American principles." JACL passed resolutions calling for financial reimbursement for those who had been sent to the detention camps. JACL and its allies had considered several possible paths to achieve their goal. Establishing a federal commission to publicize and investigate the issue, with the hope of influencing public opinion and pressuring Congress, was one possibility. Introducing legislation immediately in Congress was another. A third strategy was bypassing the elected branches by seeking compensation through a class-action lawsuit representing all the internees. Because the 760,000 Japanese Americans in the United States were concentrated in Hawaii and California and unlikely to be much of a political force in elections elsewhere, some advocates for Japanese American compensation believed a judicial rather than legislative strategy would be more successful. Consultations with civil rights groups and members of Congress, however, suggested that this third possibility faced an uphill climb against lingering racism and a possible perception that the lawsuit was simply a financially motivated special-interest

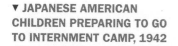

▼ **JAPANESE AMERICAN CHILDREN PREPARING TO GO TO INTERNMENT CAMP, 1942**

With the United States at war with Japan, over 120,000 Japanese Americans were relocated to internment camps under an executive order by President Franklin Roosevelt. The order was justified by the president as a military necessity, but for many Americans of Japanese descent, the order stung of racial and ethnic prejudice. Three decades later, Japanese Americans began exploring if they should seek redress for the internment and, if so, what should be sought.

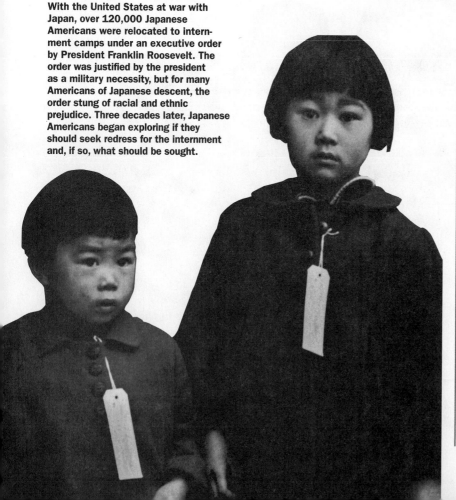

handout. JACL did not pursue this approach.

Instead, JACL pushed for Congress to create a federal investigatory commission, with the hope that compensation legislation would follow the commission's report. The Commission on Wartime Relocation and Internment of Civilians began work in 1981 and issued a report in 1983. In harsh terms, the report labeled the internment "a grave injustice" directly linked to racial prejudice. The commission called for a federal apology, $20,000 for each surviving detainee, and funds for research and education about the relocation of Japanese Americans.

After the report was issued, the four Japanese American members of Congress introduced a bill that would implement the commission's recommendations. Debate continued in Congress for over five years. To many members of Congress, the internment had been a reasonable response during a time of crisis and called for neither an apology nor financial compensation. The four members of Congress who introduced the bill played a critical role in the discussions, convincing their colleagues to support the bill and the resulting compensation. JACL also developed a sophisticated lobbying plan to influence Congress, implementing a plan for Japanese Americans and their advocates to express support for the legislation through letter writing and personal testimony. In August 1988, President Ronald Reagan signed the bill that provided funds for research and education, a $20,000 payment for each internee or a descendant, and a national apology for the relocation and detention of Japanese Americans.[2]

The success of the Japanese American effort stands in contrast to that of Mexican Americans. In the 1930s, an estimated 200,000 to 2 million individuals of Mexican

▲ **DOWN ON THE FARM**
In the 1930s, many Mexican families worked on farms in the United States. This family is returning home to Texas after working on farms in Mississippi.

descent—most of them legal residents or U.S. citizens, many of whom had lived their entire lives in the United States—were deported to Mexico as part of a "repatriation" program. The exact number is uncertain and it is not known precisely how many were involuntarily deported, how many left because other family members had been deported, or how many left because they feared forced deportation. The program was authorized by President Herbert Hoover, and though discontinued by President Franklin Roosevelt at the national level, many states and counties continued with their own efforts. The stated reason for the program was the Great Depression and the shortage of jobs. Public opinion, including from the organized labor movement, was generally supportive of the deportations.[3] As with Japanese Americans, the experience was one of financial loss and a feeling of being rejected by one's country, and in this case by the receiving country of Mexico as well, where the deportees were often considered too anglicized.

The movement for an apology and compensation for those forced to move has had some success. Although scholars began discussing the "repatriation" program in the 1970s, the full scope and extent of the deportations has become more clear, including to the victims' families themselves, only over the past 15 years. Mexican American groups have been able to study the Japanese American experience as a guide. In 2005, California Governor Arnold Schwarzenegger signed a bill authorizing an official apology, but he vetoed a bill that would establish a commission to consider financial reparations. A class-action lawsuit on behalf of the surviving deportees was not successful.[4] Congressional efforts, co-sponsored by then congresswoman Hilda Solis (who became Secretary of Labor in the Obama administration), to create a commission to study the deportations and consider a national apology and possible reparations were not successful.[5]

The experiences of the Japanese American internees and the Mexican American and Mexican deportees mirror the political courses of action often seen throughout the history of American civil rights activism. A group—based on its race, gender, or any other category—is singled out and treated differently from the rest of the population. Through shared memories, the group starts to think about its shared interests, and seeks action to correct past or present wrongs. But having shared memories and interests is not enough—the group must determine how to influence the political process. Is the group unified enough to present a clear argument for its case? Should it focus on the courts, Congress, or the president? The national government, or the state governments? Are there powerful elected officials who would lead the effort, or do they consider it too expensive, counterproductive, or divisive? What specific strategies and tactics might a group use to press its case? What is the right timing? Can the group draw on beliefs in the American creed to make its case, or does it need to change people's thinking? What kinds of redress, if any, could gain widespread support among public officials and the public? Is an apology sufficient? These are the kinds of strategic calculations and considerations that groups must consider when they consider constitutional guarantees of equal protection under the law to have been violated, and they are the kinds of strategic calculations political scientists study to understand the politics of civil rights and to unlock the puzzle of why some efforts succeed while others fall short.

CHAPTER LEARNING OBJECTIVES

After reading this chapter you will be able to:

6-1 Trace the advances and setbacks in the quest for civil rights in the nineteenth century.

6-2 Explain the demise of the separate but equal doctrine and the creation of civil rights laws and regulations.

6-3 Analyze the changes that led to the success and splintering of the civil rights movement.

6-4 Describe legal and legislative actions to extend equal protection guarantees to other groups.

Equality and Civil Rights

6-1 Trace the advances and setbacks in the quest for civil rights in the nineteenth century.

Barack Obama, an African-American of mixed racial heritage, is president of the United States. His victory does not end the American civil rights story. It does, however, shine a bright light on dramatic changes in American politics and society. A momentous election year saw African American, Hispanic, Mormon, and women candidates vie seriously for major party presidential nominations.

To understand the significance of President Obama's accomplishment requires a close look at the politics and evolution of **civil rights** in the United States. Civil rights are the guarantees of government to provide equal opportunities, privileges, and treatment under the law for all individuals. They entail sharing in the equal rights and responsibilities of citizenship and being fully part of the American nation.

When Americans claim that civil rights have been violated, they usually mean that the government needs to defend the rights of an individual or group that has been denied some form of access or opportunity based on their race, ethnicity, color, gender, religion, sexual orientation, or other group characteristic. When groups or individuals assert their civil rights, they are telling government that it needs to act on behalf of those receiving unequal treatment in society.

In American politics, discriminatory treatment toward different groups has led to angry and sometimes bloody conflict over civil rights. This experience has torn through the history of many groups. The experience of black Americans has been a

civil rights guarantees of equal opportunities, privileges, and treatment under the law that allow individuals to participate fully and equally in American society.

particular touchstone for civil rights. Most civil rights laws and court decisions arose originally in the area of black–white relations and set the framework for the legal status of other groups. Because the black civil rights movement was also the earliest to be extensively organized, it provides a historical example that has played a key role in the evolution of American civil rights for other groups.

The Constitution did not prohibit slavery.

The Framers of the Constitution faced a dilemma. Controversy over slavery was already substantial. After independence, several northern states prohibited slavery, while southern states retained it. Addressing slavery in any direct way during the Constitutional Convention might well have been a deal breaker, ending the possibility of crafting a constitution to unite the 13 colonies. But the issue could not be entirely avoided.

Although the word *slavery* did not appear in the Constitution, three provisions in the document concerned the subject. First, the Three-fifths Compromise determined that three-fifths of a state's slave population would be added to its headcount for purposes of allocating representatives in the House of Representatives. Second, the importation of slaves was to cease after 1808. Third, fugitive slaves were to be returned to their owners.[6] The net result of these provisions was that slavery, by not being prohibited, was accepted as constitutional.

For the 70 years following ratification of the Constitution, slavery repeatedly flared up as an issue. Political leaders tried to keep the nation together through legislative compromises, especially concerning the place of slavery in America's westward expansion. Throughout the period, as with the adoption of the Three-fifths Compromise during the Constitutional Convention, an important political goal was to keep the power of slave states and free states as nearly equal as possible.

Dred Scott rejects black citizenship.

One particularly dramatic development brought the issue to the Supreme Court. Dred Scott, a slave from Missouri, traveled with his owner to Illinois, a free state, and to other free territories north of the line established by the Missouri Compromise of 1820. The compromise had established in which territories and states slavery would be legal. Scott and his owner lived in these free areas for seven years, ultimately returning to Missouri, a slave state. When his owner died, Scott filed a lawsuit in Missouri, arguing that he should be considered a free man because he had been living on free soil.[7] Scott's petition was opposed by the owner's widow. After a series of court decisions in Scott's home state of Missouri, Scott brought the case to federal court. To file a federal lawsuit, however, Scott had to demonstrate that he was a citizen.

In one of the most notorious opinions in its history, the Supreme Court ruled in **Dred Scott v. Sandford** (1857) that Scott could not bring his case to federal court. To Chief Justice Roger Taney, the question was straightforward: "Can a negro, whose ancestors were imported into this country, and sold as slaves, become a member of the political community formed and brought into existence by the Constitution of the United States, and as such become entitled to all the rights, and privileges, and immunities, guaranteed by that instrument to the citizen?" Taney's answer was no: Slaves could not be citizens, and neither could the

Dred Scott v. Sandford Supreme Court decision in 1857 declaring that neither slaves nor the descendants of slaves could be U.S. citizens.

▼ DRED SCOTT, HIS WIFE, AND THEIR TWO DAUGHTERS
The Court's decision in *Dred Scott* has stood as one of the most consequential, and most criticized, in American history. Scott received support for his case in many northern newspapers similar to this one.

descendants of slaves, whether free or not. When the Constitution was written, the Court concluded, blacks were considered "subordinate and inferior" to the "dominant race." Therefore, they could not possibly be considered citizens or part of "the people" as understood by the authors of the Constitution.

The Civil War amendments bring civil rights into the Constitution.

The *Dred Scott* decision also declared the Missouri Compromise an unconstitutional use of congressional power because it deprived slaveholders of their property without due process of law. The political firestorm it triggered was one of the contributing factors to the country's move toward civil war. By mid-1865, when the Civil War drew to a close, a nation disassembled by war needed to be put back together—not on its old terms, but recast, with African Americans as citizens. From 1865 through 1877, this process, known as Reconstruction, repeated the efforts of the revolutionary and constitutional eras to build both a sense of shared nationhood and a government capable of delivering the war's hard-won gains to blacks. It was, in effect, the third time the young country would try to lay a new foundation for itself.

Following the Civil War, the Thirteenth, Fourteenth, and Fifteenth Amendments—commonly referred to as the Civil War amendments—were added to the Constitution. All concerned civil rights for blacks. Congress included a section in each amendment giving it the authority to enforce the amendment by "appropriate legislation." This was Congress's attempt to prevent the Supreme Court from saying Congress did not have constitutional authority to act, as the Court had ruled in the *Dred Scott* decision. For a country imbued with a political culture of limited government, the addition of that power-expanding language was a remarkable move by Congress. The Thirteenth Amendment, ratified in December 1865, made slavery unconstitutional anywhere within the United States. The Fifteenth Amendment, ratified in March 1870, made it unconstitutional for the national government or state governments to deny someone the right to vote based on race, color, or whether the individual had previously been a slave or was descended from a slave.

The Fourteenth Amendment, ratified in July 1868, has had an extraordinary impact on American politics and life, as discussed in Chapter 5. It establishes that anyone born or naturalized in the United States is a citizen of the United States and also the state in which he or she lives. This edict made it clear that former slaves were fully citizens. It then declares that no state shall "deny to any person within its jurisdiction the equal protection of the laws." This **equal protection clause** would be the basis of much of the subsequent legislation and many of the court decisions concerning civil rights.

equal protection clause clause in the Fourteenth Amendment stating that states are not to deny any person equal treatment under the law.

Congress passes civil rights legislation to bring blacks into American life.

In addition to the Civil War amendments, Reconstruction included other legislation that assisted the promotion of black civil rights. The Freedmen's Bureau, created in 1865, provided food, clothing, and fuel; established schools; supervised labor–management relations; and created a system by which blacks could become landowners. The Civil Rights Act of 1866 guaranteed blacks the same property and legal rights as whites.[8] It also provided for the punishment of those who violated an individual's rights because of race or color.[9] In response to violence and the rise of the Ku Klux Klan, a secretive group that terrorized blacks, four "enforcement acts" were passed

During Reconstruction, blacks advanced to new positions in southern society. In many states, blacks were elected to the legislature in significant numbers. The white backlash against this success would take firm root after Reconstruction's end in 1877. Blacks were routinely denied the right to vote and violently harassed when they sought to exercise this right, and black office-holding quickly disappeared.

in 1870–1871 to make sure these legislative promises were implemented.[10] They provided protection for black voters, ensured access to office holding and jury duty for blacks, and monitored equal treatment under the law. As a result, blacks, running as Republicans, were elected to state governments and to Congress. They began attending schools and entering professions in large numbers. The final legislative action was the Civil Rights Act of 1875, which concerned the private sector. It promised blacks the "full and equal enjoyment" of hotels, transportation, and places of entertainment such as theaters.

"Equal protection of the laws" does not prohibit private discrimination.

The Civil Rights Act of 1875 seemed to mark the end of a decade of civil rights action that promised substantial equality and integration for blacks. But reality proved otherwise. By 1877, federal troops had been removed from the South, and the former Confederate states were essentially on their own. Southern state governments came under the control of whites who had been unhappy with the changes since 1865. And the Supreme Court interpreted civil rights laws and amendments in a narrow way that significantly hampered black equality with whites.

One major stumbling block was whether the Civil War amendments covered actions in the private sector. The Court ruled they did not. *Strauder v. West Virginia* (1880) was the first case in which the Court was asked to apply the equal protection clause to black civil rights. The Court struck down a West Virginia law that limited jury duty to white males. The Court thus clearly saw the Fourteenth Amendment as applicable to the actions of state governments, known as the doctrine of **state action.** But what about private sector action? In the *Civil Rights Cases* (1883), the Court consolidated five cases from California, Kansas, Missouri, New Jersey, and Tennessee, in which blacks had been denied service in private establishments—seemingly a violation of the Civil Rights Act of 1875. The Court declared the 1875 act unconstitutional because it concerned discriminatory private, as opposed to government, action.[11] The Fourteenth Amendment, in the Court's view, applied to the actions of governments: it did not apply to discriminatory private behavior between individuals.[12] This state action view of the Fourteenth Amendment has remained a binding standard for Court decisions.

state action Supreme Court interpretation of the equal protection clause that holds the clause prohibited unfair discriminatory actions by government, not by private individuals.

The Supreme Court declares that segregating the races does not violate equal protection.

In these decisions, the Court established that government actions that discriminated against blacks violated equal protection, but that private discrimination was not unconstitutional. Working within these guidelines, some state governments proved creative in their attempts to perpetuate a society in which whites dominated. Beginning in the late 1880s, southern states enacted laws that required blacks and whites to be separated when they used public accommodations. Referred to as **Jim Crow** laws, the statutes covered a wide range of circumstances. From parks to schools, hotels, restaurants, hospitals, prisons, funeral homes, cemeteries, sporting events, restrooms, entrances, exits, transportation, and more, the laws required separate facilities for blacks and whites. Blacks were prohibited from eating at whites-only restaurants, attending whites-only state universities, or riding in the front of public buses. African Americans had separate and usually unequal hospital systems and educational systems. In 1890, Louisiana passed a law requiring all railway companies to provide "equal but separate accommodations" for blacks and whites.

Homer Plessy was arrested in June 1892 after he boarded a train in New Orleans and refused to leave the car reserved for whites.[13] In ***Plessy v. Ferguson*** (1896), the Supreme Court ruled 8–1 that Louisiana's law was constitutional. Separate accommodations were not a "badge of servitude" akin to slavery, the Court ruled, so the Thirteenth Amendment did not apply. As for the Fourteenth Amendment, there was nothing inherently discriminatory in separating the races, the Court concluded, as long as each race was accommodated. The amendment was intended to create equality before the law, not to abolish racial distinctions or enforce social integration. Indeed, the Court noted, Congress had passed acts requiring separate schools for blacks in the District of Columbia, so it would not likely disapprove of similar acts in the states. According to the **separate but equal doctrine,** it was constitutional to require separate facilities for the races, as long as the facilities were substantially equal, even though not identical. The Court interpreted Louisiana's law as a reasonable attempt to promote the public good as

Jim Crow system of laws that separated the races in schools, public accommodations, and other aspects of daily life.

Plessy v. Ferguson Supreme Court decision in 1896 upholding the constitutionality of laws and government policies that required segregated facilities for blacks and whites.

separate but equal doctrine Supreme Court doctrine that laws or policies requiring segregated facilities for the races are constitutionally acceptable as long as the facilities are of equal quality.

▶ JIM CROW IN DURHAM, NORTH CAROLINA, 1940

The separate but equal doctrine was the cornerstone of racial segregation. The Supreme Court validated the doctrine in 1896, but in *Brown v. Board of Education* in 1954, it declared that mandatory racial separation is inherently unequal and unconstitutional.

legislators saw it, not an attempt to oppress any group and not a violation of equal protection of the laws.

With these late nineteenth-century decisions, national authority over race relations was extremely limited. Neither the president nor members of Congress were likely to address racial discrimination seriously. For southern politicians, such action would be career ending. For northern politicians, there were few constituencies pushing actively for integration. And segregation itself was constitutionally protected by the Supreme Court.[14]

Equal Protection of the Laws Gains Meaning

6-2 Explain the demise of the separate but equal doctrine and the creation of civil rights laws and regulations.

Segregation proved to be separate, but certainly not equal. Facilities and services provided to blacks were notably inferior in quality, quantity, and convenience. For nearly half a century after the *Plessy* decision, federal politicians did little to improve the political, economic, social, or legal status of blacks in the United States. Jim Crow continued unabated and black voters in the South dwindled to just a very small percentage of all blacks, because of discriminatory voting restrictions. Leaders of black civil rights organizations, however, continued to press for government action. After a long period, these efforts began to succeed. In fits and starts, the legal underpinning for segregation eroded. Finally, in 1954, the separate but equal doctrine came crashing down. Soon afterward, a wave of legislative and administrative changes would follow and advance civil rights, not only for blacks but for other groups of Americans as well.

Presidents bypass Congress to chip away at racial discrimination.

Black political activists knew that elected officials needed to consider the protection of civil rights as being in their own political interests, especially given the Supreme Court's blunt acceptance of segregation. Over the first four decades of the twentieth century, activists formed organizations to represent black political interests, place pressure on politicians, and form a legal strategy for use in the courts. The most important of these organizations was the National Association for the Advancement of Colored People (NAACP), formed in 1909. The organization focused largely on legal strategies in its first two decades and began deeper consideration of legislative and administrative strategies in the 1930s. At the time of the NAACP's founding, white southern Democrats dominated Congress and thwarted any attempts to pass civil rights legislation. For this reason, the NAACP primarily concentrated its lobbying efforts on the president and the executive branch, and this strategy began to bear fruit during the presidency of Franklin Roosevelt (1933–1945).

Roosevelt used his unilateral executive powers to make some progress in civil rights. He appointed more blacks to his administration than any previous president. In June 1941, in part to forestall a massive March on Washington by blacks, but also because of the impending acceleration in military production brought on by U.S. involvement in World War II, President Roosevelt signed an executive order—a presidential proclamation with the force of law that does not require congressional approval—creating the Fair Employment Practices Committee (FEPC).[15] The order mandated an end to employment discrimination based on race, creed, color, or national origin in companies and U.S. government agencies involved in defense production, and it authorized the committee to punish offenders. The FEPC expired in 1946 when Congress refused to extend funding.

Following Roosevelt's death, President Harry Truman (1945–1952) continued the use of executive orders to advance civil rights in the face of congressional opposition. Truman took his most dramatic civil rights action by integrating the armed forces through Executive Order 9981. Issued in July 1948, the order declared that regardless of race, color, national origin, or religion, there would be "equality of treatment and opportunity" for all members of the military. A companion order, 9980, created the Fair Employment Board and forbade all racial discrimination in federal government hiring. By October 1954, the last all-black military unit had been disbanded, and the military had become the most fully integrated institution in American society.

Court decisions begin to challenge separate but equal.

Supreme Court decisions after 1937 began to challenge racial discrimination. Why this change at this time? In large part, the new perspective coincided with a major change in Court membership. Between 1937 and 1943, President Roosevelt appointed eight new justices; between 1945 and 1949, President Truman appointed three.

Civil rights for blacks began to make some progress in education. Although the Court did not challenge the separate but equal doctrine during this period, it did become more demanding in ensuring that conditions for black students and white students were somewhat comparable. In 1938, the Court struck down Missouri's practice of paying blacks' tuition at out-of-state law schools rather than enrolling them at the University of Missouri Law School.[16] This decision did not result in integration of the law school—Missouri established a separate law school for minorities—but it did indicate that the Court was looking more carefully at how "equal" the conditions facing the races really were. Forcing students of one race to leave their state to attend school elsewhere was not, in the Court's view, comparable treatment. Following this victory, blacks in other states won similar victories at professional schools.

Engaging in lawsuits that challenged the system of segregation in American education was the strategy of the newly created legal arm of the NAACP, the NAACP Legal Defense and Educational Fund, which was formed in 1940. The organization sought first to win victories at specific schools around the idea of what "equal" meant. With successes in those cases on the state level, and in federal courts if those decisions were appealed, the organization could then move to challenge separate but equal as a principle.

Victories in important cases convinced the organization that the time had come to challenge the *Plessy* decision. In 1950, the Supreme Court ruled that an alternative Texas law school for black students did not provide "substantial equality," and it ruled that a black student in the University of Oklahoma School of Education could not be separated from white students in classrooms, libraries, or cafeterias.[17] For the first time, the Court hinted that separation itself was likely to damage the quality of a student's education.[18]

Segregation is declared unconstitutional in *Brown v. Board of Education.*

With these victories, the stage had been set for an assault on the separate but equal doctrine. Four cases in 1951 and 1952, from Kansas, South Carolina, Virginia, and Delaware, challenged the doctrine in education. The Supreme Court consolidated these cases and considered them together as **Brown v. Board of Education** *of Topeka, Kansas* (1954). The lead case was prompted when Oliver Brown attempted to enroll his daughter for third grade in an all-white school and was turned away. Arguing the case on behalf of Brown was Thurgood Marshall of the NAACP, who later became the first black Supreme Court justice.

Under the leadership of Chief Justice Earl Warren, the Court unanimously struck down the separate but equal doctrine. Avoiding any definitive stand on what the Fourteenth Amendment required in public education, the Court instead emphasized the importance of education in modern society and asked whether segregating the races provided equal opportunity for black children. In the Court's view, the answer was no. Referring to psychological studies, the Court concluded that segregation could generate a permanent "feeling of inferiority as to their status in the community." In public education, the Court famously ruled, "the doctrine of 'separate but equal' has no place. Separate educational facilities are inherently unequal."

The *Brown* decision was an earthquake, bringing down the legal and constitutional edifice of enforced segregation. It struck down the laws of 21 states.[19] In practical terms, however, change was not as swift. Aware of the potential explosiveness of its decision, the Court did not set any timetable in *Brown*. In a follow-up opinion in 1955, referred

Brown v. Board of Education
Supreme Court ruling in 1954 that in public education, mandatory separation of children by race leads to inherently unequal education. The decision overturned the separate but equal doctrine.

▼ **AN INTEGRATION PIONEER IN LITTLE ROCK, ARKANSAS, 1957**
Elizabeth Eckford arrives for her first day of class at Little Rock Central High School. A federal court ordered the school to enroll her and eight other black students. The court's order was prompted by a lawsuit filed by the NAACP.

to as *Brown II*, the Court stated that school districts should move with "all deliberate speed" to desegregate their schools.[20]

Massive resistance, especially in the South, blunted the speed of change. Many school boards preferred to go to court rather than voluntarily abide by the Court's ruling. Others districts sought to disband their public schools. Incidents of violence and intimidation to keep blacks from white schools were common. A decade after *Brown*, barely 3 percent of southern black children were in schools where a majority of students were white.

In response to this foot dragging, the federal government began threatening to initiate lawsuits and withhold federal funds from states and districts that were not making progress in implementing desegregation. These tactics were effective. By 1970, about one-third of southern black children were in majority-white schools and 90 percent were in schools with at least some white students.[21]

Civil rights activists seek to extend *Brown*'s reach to cases of *de facto* segregation.

de jure segregation racial segregation that occurs because it is written into law, policy, or government procedures.

de facto segregation racial segregation that results not because of explicit law, policy, or procedures, but from patterns of behavior that have the effect of segregating the races.

Activists in the black civil rights movement pushed courts to address instances both of **de jure segregation** and **de facto segregation.** *De jure* segregation refers to segregation explicitly written into laws and regulations. It was the kind of segregation outlawed by the *Brown* decision and was common in southern states. *De facto* segregation occurs, in practice, because of patterns of behavior. If residential patterns are highly skewed racially, for example, and all children attend the school nearest to them, then schools would automatically remain highly segregated. This pattern was common in the North. The issue became whether schools were required to desegregate, which could be achieved by repealing *de jure* segregation, or whether they were required to integrate, which would also entail challenging *de facto* segregation.

The Court's early decisions leaned toward integration.[22] "Busing" was an especially controversial remedy. This called for students to be bused from one part of a school district to another in order to achieve a particular racial balance, even if there had been no history of *de jure* segregation in the district. A later Court decision scaled back this remedy. In 1974, by a 5–4 vote, the Supreme Court concluded that the Fourteenth Amendment's equal protection guarantee did not extend to *de facto* segregation if there was no evidence that a school district intended to discriminate (see Table 6-1).[23] With this ruling in place, courts could not easily order school districts to use busing to remedy *de facto* segregation in the schools.

Nonetheless, school districts could voluntarily devise busing and other integration plans in order to achieve more diversity at their schools or to thwart potential lawsuits. For three decades, many districts did precisely that. In *PICS v. Seattle* (2007), however, the Supreme Court struck down such plans in Seattle, Washington, and Louisville, Kentucky, as an unconstitutional violation of equal protection.[24] In each city, white parents whose children were denied admission to a school on racial grounds brought the lawsuit against the school districts. The decision allowed districts to continue to find ways to make their schools more diverse, through the drawing of school boundaries, magnet schools, open enrollment, and other such plans. School districts could not, however, make an individual student's enrollment in a school dependent on his or her race. Wrote Chief Justice John Roberts, "the way to stop discrimination on the basis of race is to stop discriminating on the basis of race." But as critics saw it, the decision effectively overturned *Brown* and would accelerate the resegregation of schools in the United States.[25]

TABLE 6-1. Significant Supreme Court Decisions on School Desegregation

CASE	YEAR OF DECISION	DECISION
Brown v. Board of Education of Topeka, Kansas	1954	Segregated "separate but equal" schools are inherently unequal and unconstitutional.
Green v. County School Board of New Kent County	1968	Integration and not simply repeal of discriminatory laws and practices is necessary to comply with the "unitary system" of schools implied by Brown. Examination of student assignments, faculty assignments, staff assignments, transportation, physical facilities, and extracurricular activities will determine whether a school system is unitary or dual and separate.
Swann v. Charlotte-Mecklenburg Board of Education	1971	Busing is acceptable as a remedy to desegregate schools, as are quotas. The racial balance at a school need not be identical to the overall district balance. A school district's intent to discriminate by law or practice must be proven before a court imposes a desegregation plan.
Milliken v. Bradley	1974	Court-imposed busing cannot cover multiple school districts such as a city and its suburbs, unless intentional segregation is demonstrated in each district.
Freeman v. Pitts	1992	Federal courts can gradually withdraw from oversight of school districts as they are convinced that specific aspects of a desegregation plan are being met.
PICS (Parents Involved in Community Schools) v. Seattle School District No. 1	2007	Denying students enrollment in particular schools on the basis of their race, as part of a school district's voluntary integration or diversity plan, is unconstitutional.

The debate over how best—or whether—to achieve racial integration in education will continue as districts devise plans they hope will meet the Supreme Court's approval. In its *PICS* decision, the Court did not rule out using income and other socioeconomic factors as a basis for enrollment. Because minority status is often correlated with income and wealth, this approach achieves racial integration by increasing socioeconomic diversity (see Figure 6-1). One challenge for architects of even the most creative integration and diversity plans will remain finding public support for their efforts. Public opinion data consistently show that people of all races are more concerned about the quality of education than about the racial diversity of students in schools.

New laws and executive orders expand civil rights protection.

During the 1960s, civil rights also advanced in other spheres of public and private life. As with the education system, public officials employed both legislation and executive orders in this process.

Legislation　The Civil Rights Act of 1964 is the centerpiece of American antidiscrimination law. Work on the law began under President Kennedy and, following his assassination, was completed by President Johnson. The law prohibited discrimination in public accommodations and in private employment on the basis of race, color, religion, sex, and national origin.

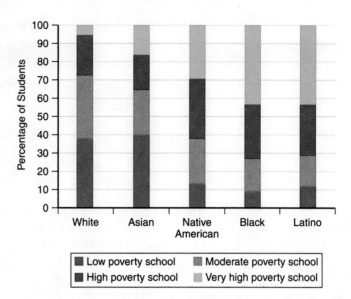

FIGURE 6-1. **Type of Elementary Public School Attended by Race and Ethnic Group, 2007–2008.** Minority students are more likely than white students to attend schools with significant percentages of students from poor families. Only a small percentage of white students attend schools with very high poverty levels, compared to over 40 percent of black and Latino students.

Note: Low poverty schools: 0–25% of students attending are poor; Moderate: 26–50%; High: 51–75%; Very high: 76–100%.

On the surface, this law sounds similar to the 1875 Civil Rights Act that was struck down in the *Civil Rights Cases*—the decision ruling that the Fourteenth Amendment gave Congress the authority to regulate only government action, not private behavior. Significantly, however, Congress justified the Civil Rights Act of 1964 not in terms of the equal protection guarantee of the Fourteenth Amendment, but by linking the law to Congress's power to regulate commerce. As noted in Chapter 4, the Supreme Court in 1937 established a generous definition of interstate commerce that vastly expanded the power of the federal government. As a result, if Congress could link discrimination to the flow of commerce, it could regulate discriminatory actions in the private sector.

Grounding Congress's action in an established constitutional power like regulation of interstate commerce was a dramatically consequential idea, opening new horizons for civil rights legislation. The Civil Rights Act of 1964 also set the mold in another way: it denied federal funds to any program or activity that discriminated. After 1964, Congress justified all civil rights legislation that affected the private sector either on interstate commerce grounds or as an extension of Congress's control over federal spending.[26] By doing so, Congress bypassed the restrictions of the state action doctrine. The Civil Rights Act of 1968, which prohibited discrimination in the sale, rental, financing, or advertising of housing on the basis of race, color, religion, or national origin, is one key example.

Another signal legislative achievement was the Voting Rights Act of 1965. Earlier laws provided modest federal oversight of southern elections. The 1965 act was much stronger than these. It prohibited the use of discriminatory methods, such as literacy tests, intended to weaken the voting power of blacks (see Chapter 8). States or parts of states with a history of such methods were required to clear any changes in their voting laws with the Department of Justice. The same pre-clearance rule applied to laws that might affect the electoral power of minorities. For example, pre-clearance would be necessary if a city with a significant minority population wished to annex neighboring suburbs that were almost completely white. The pre-clearance requirement is subject to periodic reauthorization by Congress and the president and remains in place today.[27]

Black access to voting was enhanced with the abolition of **poll taxes** in federal elections by the Twenty-fourth Amendment in 1964 and subsequently in state elections by the Supreme Court in 1966.[28] A poll tax was a fee to vote in an election. It was designed to discourage voting by blacks and recent immigrants. For example, if your father or grandfather had been able to vote in elections prior to the Thirteenth Amendment, you were "grandfathered" in and did not need to pay the tax. Some states had a cumulative tax, such that you would owe a fee for all the previous elections you had not voted in.

poll tax fee assessed on each person who wishes to vote; prohibited by the Twenty-fourth Amendment in 1964.

These changes had a significant effect. The number of black voters increased substantially. Black candidates began winning elected office. The Supreme Court's "one person, one vote" mandates of the 1960s (see *CaseStudy: Defining Democracy When Drawing District Lines*, in Chapter 2) which improved the representation of urban areas within states, further boosted black political participation and candidate success. Without these changes, Barack Obama's achievement would have been impossible. The groundwork to his victory in 2008 was laid in the victories for voting rights in the 1960s.

Executive orders   As noted earlier, Presidents Roosevelt and Truman began using executive orders to advance civil rights—a practice continued by later presidents. Presidents Eisenhower and Kennedy, for example, used executive orders to activate National Guard units in Arkansas, Mississippi, and Alabama to enforce school desegregation. President Kennedy ordered the creation of compliance mechanisms for nondiscriminatory employment policies by federal contractors. Orders by later presidents enhanced these mechanisms. Additional categories of protection were added as well, including discrimination based on sex (President Johnson), disability and age (President Carter), and sexual orientation and status as a parent (President Clinton).[29]

Affirmative action   Despite becoming one of the most controversial civil rights policies, affirmative action started out quietly in executive orders issued by Presidents Kennedy, Johnson, and Nixon in the 1960s to combat discrimination in federal hiring and contracts.[30] On its face, **affirmative action** calls for aggressive outreach efforts targeted to groups traditionally underrepresented in particular jobs and college admissions. Concerned that outreach might not be enough to satisfy the Supreme Court, many employers, colleges, and government administrators interpreted affirmative action to require setting guidelines, such as quotas, for the recruitment of minorities. Some black leaders feared that quotas would lead to a white backlash.[31] For leaders like Martin Luther King Jr., this was a dangerous risk. And to the extent that "affirmative action" was thought of strictly as "quotas," it was in fact highly unpopular among white voters (see *How Do We Know? Is White Opposition to Affirmative Action Racist?*).

affirmative action efforts to reach and attract applicants for jobs, college admissions, and business contracts from traditionally underrepresented groups, ranging from extensive publicity and outreach to quota plans.

Since 1989, the Supreme Court has been reining in the scope of these efforts. In *Richmond v. Croson* (1989), the Court struck down "set-aside" programs that required contractors on city projects to subcontract 30 percent of the business to minority businesses. The Court declared that state and local affirmative action like that in Richmond could not be initiated as a response to racism in general: there had to be a specific discriminatory practice in a specific location to justify the need for the affirmative action policy.

continued on page 231 ▶

HOW DO WE KNOW?

Is White Opposition to Affirmative Action Racist?

The Question

The opinions of whites and blacks are often far apart on policies like affirmative action, school desegregation, and spending on social programs. Such a gap could be explained by genuine principled opposition among whites to certain roles for government. It could also be explained by white racism. If whites hold inherently negative and generalized views toward racial minorities, they might be more likely to oppose policies that seem to disproportionately benefit minority groups. Is white opposition to affirmative action and similar programs racist? How do we know?

Why It Matters

Whether white opposition to policies benefiting minorities is based on bigotry or other factors matters for at least two reasons. First, as discussed in Chapter 2, political culture is negotiable. Advocates for a policy can try to convince people to balance beliefs

▼ RACIAL PROFILING—OR—APPROPRIATE POLICE RESPONSE?

To some Americans, the 2009 arrest of Harvard Professor Henry Louis Gates at his home was an illustration of subtle racial bias—a neighbor and police saw a black man attempting to enter a house and assumed the worst. To others, this interpretation racialized what was a simple matter of police responding to what looked like an attempted break-in.

in a new way, or redefine what they mean by particular beliefs. If policy opposition is based on political culture, there is some prospect that opponents and proponents can engage in dialogue. On the other hand, if policy opposition is based on racism, this more deep-seated resistance will be hard to change. Second, if bigotry, rather than different weighting of beliefs in the American creed, is the primary reason for opposition to certain policies, then the prospects for civil rights and racial and ethnic harmony would seem dim. The answer tells us something about how far the United States has evolved from the days of acute, public racism.

Investigating the Answer

Political scientists have explored this question largely through research on black and white public opinion, so that is the focus here.[32] The outcome analyzed is white opposition to affirmative action. The two competing factors that may explain the outcome are racist beliefs and general philosophical beliefs about government's appropriate role.

Public opinion data show substantial differences between whites and blacks. White and black public opinion are working at cross-purposes on matters related to race, with whites often opposing the adoption of policies favored by blacks. The differences between the races' attitudes toward race-related policies, income redistribution programs, and the fairness of American life are often larger than those of class, gender, and religion.[33]

Exploring the extent to which racial considerations drive white opinion has been a large, complex, and heated area of debate in political science research.[34] One group of scholars points to the significance of what they call racial resentment.[35] Traditional racism was cruel and blunt and built around an explicitly stated belief in white racial superiority. The success of the civil rights movement, however, blocked that kind of racism from entering public discourse. Its public legitimacy evaporated: things that were once commonly said could now no longer be said.

In its place, however, arose a more subtle racism in which blacks were not seen as inherently inferior but were critiqued for not making the best of the opportunities given to them. This racism blends traditional beliefs of American political culture, especially individualism, with disaffection for blacks or what is considered "black behavior." Discrimination, in this view, is not a significant problem and is used as an excuse by blacks. Black progress is stunted by blacks themselves—their failure to work and study hard and their expectation that government should take care of people even if they make poor choices in life. This racism is hard to detect in surface behavior, but underneath lies suppressed racist views—the old racism dressed up in the language of traditional American values. Extensive analysis of survey research has led scholars in this school to conclude that white attitudes toward affirmative action and similar programs are strongly determined by this racial resentment.

Another group of scholars believes the racial resentment argument goes too far in blaming racism for white opposition to programs like affirmative action. This view claims that the impact of any white racism on policy attitudes has been overstated and is less important than general ideological predispositions about government. Whites are not averse to assistance for blacks, but they are, on average, less likely than blacks to support the types of assistance policies and programs favored by liberals. Opposition to certain programs would exist because of ideological positions favoring limited government, regardless of whether the beneficiaries were white or black. To the extent that the racial resentment argument presumes that liberal positions favor racial equality and conservative positions do not, white public opinion will be wrongly interpreted as racist when in fact whites are simply more ideologically conservative, on average, than blacks but no less committed to equality.

One technique employed to test this possibility—the survey experiment—changes the wording of a public opinion survey question and compares responses. For example, in one study whites were split into two groups. The first group was asked if, because of past discrimination, blacks should be given preference in college admissions. Only 26 percent of whites supported this idea. The second group was asked instead whether an extra effort should be made to ensure that qualified blacks applied for college admission. About 65 percent of whites supported this form of affirmative action specifically aimed toward blacks. This softer form of affirmative action might fit more easily within the beliefs of American political culture.

Another experiment divided respondents into three groups. All three were asked about government assistance for those born into poverty. For the first group, the program was said to help blacks as a matter of racial justice for past wrongs: 31 percent of whites approved of such a program. For the second group, the program was said to help blacks, but the justification was equal opportunity rather than racial justice: 42 percent of whites supported this program. And for the third group, the program was said to help poor people, with no race indicated: 49 percent of whites supported this program. This suggests that programs that are justified by reference to American creed beliefs and that do not single out particular racial or ethnic groups as beneficiaries receive greater support from whites.

Finally, an experiment dividing respondents into two groups asked one group about blacks and the other about new immigrants from Europe. Whites were equally likely to say these two groups should "work their way up without special favors"—white views appeared more driven by ideology than by who benefited from government help.

Thinking Critically

- In a survey experiment, participants are not saturated with the media messages they might receive in a real-world setting. Does this difference make these experiments more or less useful guides of individuals' true beliefs?
- When, if ever, are generalizations about a group's behavior acceptable in either designing or evaluating public policy?
- Would you consider the results of survey experiments helpful, because they show public officials what resonates with the public, or dangerous, because they provide public officials with tools to manipulate public opinion?

The Bottom Line

The debate over the concept of racial resentment has been extensive and deeply felt among political scientists. The perceived stakes are high. Studies continue to support each side in the argument—some finding that racial resentment is a key driver of white public opinion, and others finding that belief and ideology is more important than attitudes toward blacks.[36] Many Americans are conflicted in their views, believing that individuals are responsible to improve their condition, but also believing that society may need to provide assistance under certain circumstances.[37] Virtually all scholars agree that racism at some level remains a force in American society and that bigotry continues as an everyday problem facing blacks and other minorities. Although it is complicated to measure and analyze, clear and incontrovertible evidence that racism is the predominant driver of white public opinion is lacking. Evidence in some studies shows that white public opinion is open to persuasion and appeals to principle, which seems unlikely if racism thoroughly dominated white opinion on racially oriented policies.[38] Scholars are careful to note, however, that such evidence does not mean that negative racial attitudes cannot be activated among some individuals by the way that issues are portrayed or symbolized, including in news coverage.[39] Nor does it mean that we can always be certain that the results obtained in experimental settings will apply directly to real-world situations.[40]

The Court further narrowed the scope of affirmative action programs in its 5–4 decision in *Adarand v. Pena* (1995), a case concerning extra payments supplied by the federal government to contractors who hired minority firms. The decision decreed that all racial classifications at all levels of government would be subject to strict scrutiny, meaning the Court would have to be convinced that the classification was absolutely necessary to meet a compelling government interest, and that this interest was being achieved in the least intrusive, narrowest manner possible (was "narrowly tailored"). And a 5–4 decision in 2009 concluded that New Haven, Connecticut, officials could not throw out the results of a firefighter promotion exam simply because they feared being sued when few minorities did well.

In **Regents of the University of California v. Bakke** (1978), while prohibiting racial quotas for college admissions, the Court ruled that race could be a "plus" factor considered along with other admissions criteria. More recently, the Supreme Court in *Grutter v. Bollinger* (2003) upheld in a 5–4 vote the University of Michigan Law School's "holistic" use of race to foster viewpoint diversity at the school. In *Gratz v. Bollinger* (2003), however, the Court rejected the undergraduate admissions process at the University of Michigan. The college awarded 20 points—one-fifth of the total needed to guarantee admission—to every African American, Hispanic, and Native American applicant. Although again confirming that student diversity is a compelling government interest, the Court concluded that the college's automatic point system was not, as the *Bakke* decision called for, a narrowly tailored solution.

Michigan voters in 2006 struck down the state's use of affirmative action policies—"discriminating against or granting preferential treatment"—in public hiring, contracting, and education. Voters in California and Washington had previously done the same. In 2008, Nebraska joined this list, while voters in Arizona rejected affirmative action in that state in 2010.

Regents of the University of California v. Bakke Supreme Court decision in 1978 that a rigid quota plan for admissions violates the Constitution's equal protection guarantee, but race could be considered a "plus factor" in college admissions to increase student body diversity.

Civil rights policies vary across countries.

The United States is not the only country to struggle with racial and ethnic conflict. European countries have faced tremendous internal electoral and policy tensions due to the diversity of an increasing immigrant population. The European Union in 2000 called for an end to discrimination in education, employment, housing, social welfare, and training, along the lines of American anti-discrimination law and policy. Countries remained free to add preference policies for groups long discriminated against. Progress has been uneven across Europe in implementing the decree.

Each country's particular context of political culture has shaped the extent to which it emphasizes two key tools: anti-discrimination laws and government programs. Compared to other countries, the United States has stronger anti-discrimination laws but less generous government benefits. Generous programs do not ensure nondiscrimination, but they may reduce economic inequality between groups. On the other hand, those paying for these programs may oppose the high costs.

Two of America's allies have handled the civil rights challenge differently from each other and from the United States. Britain and France have sizable minority populations, both native and immigrant. Britain has leaned toward American-style anti-discrimination laws, but enforcement has been modest. Britain also has a more generous set of government services and benefits than the United States, some tailored to particular groups. France offers generous benefits, but generally not targeted toward particular minority groups. It has not focused as strongly as the United States or Great Britain on anti-discrimination law. Affirmative action has been most deeply embedded in the United States, while Britain has allowed affirmative action but not quotas, and France

ThinkingComparatively
Governments use differing mixes of anti-discrimination laws and government programs to address problems with discrimination.

has prohibited any kind of affirmative action. Assimilation and colorblindness have been key themes in France. Racial divisiveness is highly monitored and frequently punished. For example, the wearing of religious symbols in public schools was outlawed in 2004 as divisive, Holocaust denial is illegal, convicted racists are stripped of some civil rights, and collection of racial and ethnic data is sharply limited, much more so than in the United States and Britain.[41] Variations in these countries' historical experiences, interest group pressures, and political cultures help account for these differences.

The Politics of Civil Rights

6-3 Analyze the changes that led to the success and splintering of the civil rights movement.

By the end of the 1960s, the United States had been through a civil rights revolution. The equal protection clause had been used to challenge discrimination by government. Congress advanced civil rights in the private sector through its commerce clause and spending powers. Presidents used unilateral executive power to prod civil rights in the federal government and among those doing business with it. Segregation had fallen. Voting rights were expanded. Employment discrimination was prohibited. The Supreme Court added its first black justice, Thurgood Marshall, in 1967. In later years, blacks, women, Hispanics, and other minorities would reach the highest levels of American government. Barack Obama's election in 2008 provided an exclamation point to this journey. Inequities in quality of life remained then and remain today, but the country had changed radically.

How did these seismic changes happen? To understand, we need to explore the politics of civil rights in greater detail. Some political scientists argue that the success of civil rights resulted from political opportunities that created the possibility for change. Others focus on effective appeals to American creedal beliefs. Still others emphasize overcoming the difficulties in organizing people for political action. All of these factors are important, and their reversals featured prominently in the struggles

232

▼ **FRENCH STUDENTS PROTEST RESTRICTIONS ON WEARING RELIGIOUS SYMBOLS**

To defuse ethnic and religious hostilities, students in French schools are prohibited from wearing religious symbols or clothing. These demonstrators in Paris ask "Where are liberty, equality, fraternity?"—referring to the motto of the French Republic. Would the French model of deemphasizing group difference work effectively in the United States?

civil rights advocates faced after these major successes.[42] As is common in politics, no single explanation is sufficient.

The civil rights movement led to civil rights successes for blacks.

ThinkingCausally

What were the key political factors that led to the dramatic changes in civil rights?

The pressure created by the civil rights movement contributed to the legal, legislative, and administrative successes gained by blacks. As mentioned earlier, organizations advocating for black civil rights led to significant legal victories in the first half of the twentieth century, culminating in the dramatic victory in *Brown v. Board of Education* in 1954. In December 1955, the NAACP encouraged a year-long boycott of the bus system in Montgomery, Alabama, to protest segregation of public buses. The boycott drew national attention. Rosa Parks, the NAACP member who like Homer Plessy refused to change her seat, became a household name. Martin Luther King Jr., a Baptist minister, similarly became nationally known. King and the organization he would soon head, the Southern Christian Leadership Conference (SCLC), advocated a strategy of **civil disobedience.** This practice used nonviolent tactics such as marches and demonstrations to sway public opinion and pressure public officials. Prior to the late 1950s, mass protests had been infrequent. Inequalities and injustice were severe, but organizing and encouraging mass participation in the face of entrenched and powerful opponents was not easy. Participants risked their jobs and even their lives. Each victory was important, and each victory gave future participants the sense that direct political action could succeed. Mass political activity for the right to vote and for the repeal of Jim Crow restrictions did not become widespread until the 1960s, by which time the country became filled with these forms of political action (see Figure 6-2).

civil disobedience strategy of breaking law nonviolently in order to protest a law one considers unjust and draw attention to one's cause.

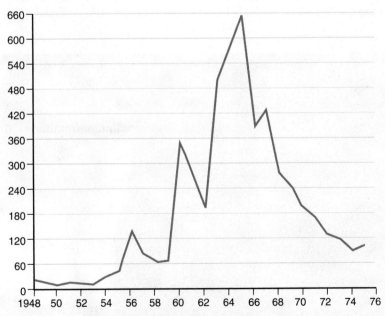

FIGURE 6-2. Number of Civil Rights Movement Marches, Speeches, Protests, Sit-ins, and Related Events Annually. The number of events initiated by civil rights movement groups and organizations peaked from 1963 to 1965 and declined swiftly after that as the movement won major legislative victories and then splintered over goals and tactics.

The Politics of Civil Rights

233

One of the most important of these protests occurred in Alabama in 1963. That spring, the SCLC decided to target Birmingham—a center of segregation—for a series of protests and boycotts. The goal was not only to force downtown stores to desegregate and end discriminatory hiring practices, but to focus national attention on similar situations throughout the South. Sheriff Bull Connors and his deputies quickly obliged civil rights leaders on the latter goal. The notorious chief of the Birmingham police unleashed fire hoses and police dogs on the peaceful protestors and jailed thousands. Many of the protesters were high school and even elementary school students. These harsh actions were widely covered by the national press and the broadcast networks.

King and his deputies skillfully capitalized on the publicity and the images that were being transmitted to the rest of the country by raising money and galvanizing support in the North.[43] Their efforts even encouraged some northern whites, mostly college students and religious leaders, to go to the South to help organize voter registration drives and other acts of protest.

In retrospect, the success of the civil rights movement and the important role that mass protest played in breaking down barriers and winning African Americans the right to vote suggest that these activities were the obvious course for African Americans in the South and their supporters in the North. But rather than being obvious, they present a puzzle. Why would people risk their livelihoods, if not their lives, to register to vote or to get others to register to vote? Why would someone face police dogs to win the right to sit at a department store lunch counter or ride a bus? Why would individuals in the North bother to write letters to legislators and send contributions in support of the protests in the South?

The answers are complex and have been studied at great length. Political scientists, when looking at movements of collective action such as the civil rights movement, approach the subject from one of two directions. Some accounts provide a top-down view of mobilization, focusing more on actions of civil rights

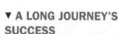

ThinkingCausally

Why, with no guarantee of success, would people engage in political action at risk to their livelihoods or their lives?

▼ **A LONG JOURNEY'S SUCCESS**

Jesse Jackson, a civil rights activist since the 1960s, sheds tears of joy as president-elect Barack Obama delivers his victory speech in Grant Park, Chicago, on November 4, 2008. Jackson himself had run for the 1984 and 1988 Democratic Party nomination. He won 11 contests in 1988 and finished second to Michael Dukakis, the eventual nominee.

group leaders and political activists to build organizations and make demands on government. In the case of the civil rights movement, some individuals sincerely believed their actions could make a difference. Among these key political entrepreneurs and patrons were the foundations that provided financial support to civil rights organizations, the interest groups that focused on civil rights, the ministers who motivated congregations to act, and the government officials who promoted policy change. Other accounts offer a bottom-up view, focusing on how grassroots action changed public opinion about black civil rights and ultimately government policy. These accounts highlight those who participated to express their support for a cause and for the benefit of feeling like a contributor to something important. These two types of explanations sometimes compete but can also be complementary, with these different modes of political action having influence at different levels of society from the individual up through government institutions.[44] And movements can have a cumulative and interactive effect. As successes mount, as more individuals have participated, and as public awareness grows, the incentives for others to participate, to be part of a winning cause, and to lead and organize that cause, can grow.[45]

Changes in the Democratic Party aided the civil rights movement.

A wave of political action by supporters of civil rights is part of the explanation of the civil rights success in the 1960s. This raises another puzzle: why did public officials respond to the movement as they did? There was no guarantee of their favorable response. Local and state officials in the South demonstrated forcefully that the demands of political movements do not always translate into victory. Yet these demands were successful with national officials. Why? The answer lies largely in the transformation of the Democratic Party. The multiple intersecting factors of a changed voter base, new party rules, and revised congressional procedures were key to public officials' political recalculations and their openness to movement demands.

In the period following the Civil War, politics in the South had been dominated by the Democratic Party. The Republican Party, considered the party of the North and of Lincoln, was almost invisible in the South, especially at the state and local levels. In many respects, the region had a one-party system. Most outcomes were essentially decided in the Democratic Party's primary election. Often, until outlawed in 1944 by the Supreme Court, this was a **white primary,** in which—as the name implies—only white voters were allowed to cast ballots.[46] So even in the rare instances when African Americans were allowed to register and vote in general elections, there were usually no contested races and no meaningful choices on the ballot.

Just as the Democratic Party dominated southern politics, so the South dominated Democratic Party politics. Democratic Party politicians had to tread carefully around issues of race or risk disrupting the party coalition. At the national level, this power of the South over the Democratic Party played out in two ways. First, the Democrats required their presidential nominee to receive two-thirds of the delegate votes at the presidential nominating convention. This rule ensured that the South could thwart an undesirable contender for the Democratic nomination. A candidate who made civil rights a major goal would have no way to win the nomination. Second, in the Senate, the ability of a minority of senators to block action on bills—known as a filibuster (discussed further in Chapter 13)—meant that civil rights legislation would face a difficult road to passage. Moreover, by the middle of the twentieth century, committee chairs were awarded almost exclusively on the basis of

ThinkingCausally

Why did national public officials respond to the demands of the civil rights movement favorably, considering that state and local officials had often shown strong hostility?

white primary   primary elections in southern states in which only white voters were allowed to participate.

seniority. With no serious two-party competition in the South, Democrats from that region tended to be the committee chairs. Because chairs had great influence over when, if, and in what form bills would leave a committee and go to the full House or Senate, it was difficult to move civil rights legislation through Congress.[47]

The grip of the South over the Democratic Party began to weaken in the 1930s. The Great Migration of blacks from the South, where they typically could not vote, to the North, where they could, gave northern Democratic politicians increased interest in cultivating the black vote. But they had to proceed cautiously, because many northern Democratic constituencies did not embrace civil rights as an issue. After the Democrats swept through the country with a massive election victory in 1932, President Franklin Roosevelt was able to have the two-thirds rule removed in 1936. As a result, the South no longer had a veto over the Democratic presidential nomination. Recognizing that the party's geographical center was increasingly moving north, every Democratic presidential nominee after 1936 expressed support for civil rights, and the party added civil rights to its 1948 platform. Democratic Presidents Roosevelt, Truman, Kennedy, and Johnson all used executive orders and other unilateral powers to advance civil rights. For each, the calculation may have involved principle, but it certainly included a substantial amount of political pragmatism as well, as the path to moving civil rights legislation through Congress was still strewn with obstacles.

Southern Democrats' grip on Congress slowly weakened as well. With the northern share of congressional Democrats growing, and with this share dominated by urban, liberal representatives, support for civil rights was increasing. Even though southern Democratic senators were still able to impede civil rights reforms by threatening or carrying out filibusters, the rule governing the termination of filibusters was modified in the mid-1960s to make filibusters easier to defeat. Subcommittees also gained additional independence to work around some of the tight control exerted by conservative southern committee leaders. All these factors combined to push the civil rights and voting rights acts through Congress in the 1960s.[48]

Obstacles in the late 1960s slowed the momentum of the civil rights movement.

ThinkingCausally

What led to the political environment for civil rights becoming unfavorable so quickly?

The civil rights achievements of the 1960s were monumental. But as the decade wore on, the politics of gaining additional civil rights advances grew daunting. Why did the political environment become so unfavorable so quickly? Political scientists focus, with varying emphasis, on three igniters of this trend. First, unity in the civil rights movement disintegrated. Second, new issues raised by the movement troubled many whites who had supported, or at least not opposed, the breakthroughs of the early 1960s. Third, blacks had the support of the Democratic Party, and the party had the support of black voters, and this mutual support created challenges as well as opportunities. The combination of these three factors created particular problems for the civil rights agenda.[49]

Collapse of unity in the black civil rights movement By the late 1960s, the black civil rights movement appeared to have peaked. Participation in civil disobedience events had dwindled, as had the number of events. The ability of leaders like Martin Luther King Jr. to maintain nonviolent civil disobedience as the movement's central strategy came under increasing pressure after 1964. In the summer of 1964, massive violence directed at blacks and white civil rights activists in Mississippi shocked the country and inflamed black public opinion—80 civil rights workers beaten, 35 shot at, 4 killed; 70 black homes, businesses, and churches burned;

1,000 activists jailed.[50] Similar scenes elsewhere shook faith in the effectiveness of nonviolent appeals. Riots sprang up in Los Angeles in 1965 and in many cities across the country following the assassination of King in April 1968. Some in the civil rights movement, such as the members of the Black Panther party, believed that the violent resistance to civil rights should be met with a violent response. Black leaders including Malcolm X argued for a black nationalism that sought to advance black equality by withdrawing from white society and developing the black community rather than by focusing on integration.

The rupture in the movement was evident in 1966 when the Student Nonviolent Coordinating Committee (founded in 1960) and the Congress of Racial Equality (founded in 1942) embraced this notion of separationist black power. Two other prominent civil rights groups, the NAACP and the Urban League (founded in 1910) rebuked this goal. In part, these debates echoed those stretching back to the early twentieth century, when black leaders such as Booker T. Washington and W.E.B. Du Bois argued over the extent to which black advancement was in the control of self-improvement by blacks and to what extent it depended on major changes in white society. In the latter half of the 1960s, the consensus over strategy that was present in the early part of the 1960s had evaporated.

Challenging issues in the late 1960s   Once the legal and political infrastructure of segregation and denial of voting rights had fallen, civil rights activists moved onto issues of social and economic equality. These issues were more difficult for many whites to support. As contentious as the issues of political equality were, they stood firmly within a political culture framework that was familiar to Americans and mostly consistent with their beliefs. Equal treatment under the law, equal opportunity, the freedom to hold a job and earn a living, the chance to go as far as one's talents allowed, to be judged not on the color of one's skin, but on the content of one's character, as King preached, echoed familiar themes.

Newer issues, however, presented a greater challenge and a range of possible solutions. Some activists advocated reparations, the idea that blacks who were descendants of slaves needed to be compensated financially for the harsh deprivations imposed by slavery. Others advocated strong outreach efforts to bring minorities into colleges and the workforce, including racial quotas if necessary. Yet others called for redistribution of wealth through government programs, benefits, and taxes to reduce economic inequality. In the eyes of many, these policies blatantly called for taking property and income from one group and giving it to another—always a controversial proposition. Many labor unions, because of the fear and opposition of their white members, struggled with civil rights issues. By the late 1960s, a white backlash to the demands of the civil rights movement had set in.

Consolidation of black political pressure in one party   Once the Democratic Party became the champion of black civil rights, black voter support for that party surged. In presidential elections, 90 percent or more

▼ MEXICO CITY, 1968
Debate over how best to advance civil rights grew more fractious in the late 1960s. Leaders of some black organizations argued that the assassination of Martin Luther King Jr. earlier in 1968 was proof that civil disobedience was too passive an approach. Americans Tommie Smith and John Carlos shocked American television viewers of the 1968 Olympics by giving a black power salute while looking downward during the playing of the national anthem.

of blacks typically voted for the Democrat. Black support for Democratic candidates at other levels was similarly high. Some scholars have suggested that this situation created a dilemma for black political power.[51] On the one hand, unified voting made blacks an important constituency for the Democratic Party and often an indispensable part of a winning coalition. On the other hand, such unified support can also be taken for granted by Democratic candidates, who might minimize blacks' concerns in order to avoid antagonizing white voters. The more that candidates highlight issues of particular interest to blacks, this argument suggests, the greater the risk of losing the votes of moderate whites and thus losing elections. And Republican candidates, given black voting patterns, might conclude they have relatively little to gain by making a strong pitch for the African American vote, which would risk alienating other factions who do not favor expanding the scope of government spending, taxation, or redistribution. Thus, according to this argument, black political interests tend to be systematically underrepresented in electoral politics.

> "Once the Democratic Party became the champion of black civil rights, black voter support for that party surged. In presidential elections, 90 percent or more of blacks typically voted for the Democrat."

As the black vote became increasingly identified as Democratic, there were feedback effects on the party. Support for Democrats in the white South, which had once been unshakable, began to wobble. Republican candidates began winning in the South, and the region became a key part of Republican Party presidential election strategy. This created a dilemma for Democrats. The more they conceded the South to Republicans, the more difficult it would be to win the presidency. Republicans sought to link Democratic candidates to plans to redistribute wealth, bus students long distances, and base hiring on racial and minority quotas. Before Barack Obama in 2008, only two Democrats won the presidency from 1968 through 2004, both from the South and both considered relatively conservative or moderate compared to the party nationwide. They did not disavow civil rights, but they did not prominently campaign on this issue.

Debate continues over how to enhance minority electoral power.

One question facing minority groups is how best to enhance their political power. Would an effective strategy be to spread minority voters out across districts so that they are a sizable and potentially influential bloc but not necessarily a majority of the district population? Or would minority interests be better served by concentrating minority voters in a small number of districts and virtually ensuring that a minority candidate will be elected who will then be able to negotiate on behalf of minority interests in the legislature? Districts where boundaries are drawn to ensure that a majority of potential voters are minority—that is, a historically disadvantaged racial or ethnic group—are known as **majority-minority districts.** Starting in the late 1980s, the U.S. Supreme Court issued decisions in a series of cases that challenged the constitutionality of creating district lines for the express purpose of creating a majority-minority district. The conclusion of these decisions was that race or ethnicity could not constitutionally be the predominant factor in drawing district lines, but they could be taken into account as one of several factors.[52]

Whether the creation of majority-minority districts assists minority political influence has become hotly debated. The answer depends in part on the changing behavior of white voters.[53] One study suggests that spreading minority voters across districts had not been an optimal strategy for minority political influence in the 1970s or 1980s, but it had become so by the 1990s. In part, reduced bloc voting by whites meant that even in districts where the minority population is 40–50 percent

majority-minority districts legislative districts in which district boundaries are drawn in a manner to ensure that a majority of the district residents are members of minority groups, intended to increase the probability of minorities being elected.

rather than a majority, a minority candidate can win about two out of three times.[54] This had not been true previously. Even if a minority does not win, this argument suggests, his or her strong share in the electorate may influence the winning candidate's voting behavior as a legislator.[55] The debate over the "best" strategy for minority influence will continue, but this research suggests the answer may change over time.

ThinkingCausally

Is minority group political power best advanced by distributing minority voters across legislative districts, or by concentrating minority voters in a smaller number of districts so that they are a majority of voters in those districts?

The way forward will also depend on the Supreme Court. The Voting Rights Act required redistricting when a majority-minority district could be formed to address minority vote dilution, which refers to minority voting power and influence being reduced by spreading minority voters in small percentages across districts. But what about a situation where a district could be created with a larger, but not majority, share of minority voters? In 2009, the Court decided 5–4 that the Voting Rights Act did not require redistricting to create a minority-influence district (sometimes called a coalition district) in which minority voting power would be enhanced but the minority presence would fall below 50 percent.[56] The dissenters in the Court's decision argued that minority-influence districts could be an effective counterweight to vote dilution.

Political strategists will be busy in coming years assessing the significance of Barack Obama's victory for these debates. Obama received 95 percent of the black vote, about 5 points higher than other Democratic presidential candidates. But he also won about 43 percent of the white vote, and whites were 60 percent of his voters overall. He lost some states with large minority populations, such as Georgia and Alabama, but he also won states with modest minority populations, such as Iowa and Maine. Whether the results of a national-level election provide direct lessons for majority-minority districting within states is another complication that will need to be factored into the meaning of Obama's win.

Extension of Equal Protection to Other Groups

6-4 Describe legal and legislative actions to extend equal protection guarantees to other groups.

Governments classify individuals into groups and use these classifications to make decisions. Federal education assistance programs classify individuals as students and nonstudents. They classify students by full-time or part-time status, by the expense of their school, by the ability of their family to provide financial support, by whether or not they have a high school diploma or equivalent, and by whether they are dependent on their parents. The government uses these classifications to make decisions about who can receive a grant or loan and for what amount. Not everyone qualifies and not everyone gets the same amount. In short, the programs discriminate among groups, and most people have no problem with that.

Other discrimination is different. Most Americans consider different treatment of individuals based on race, gender, or other factors offensive. How do the federal courts determine which kinds of group classifications resulting in differential treatment are acceptable and which are not? The courts divide these cases into three types.

The first type concerns "suspect categories," namely race and ethnicity. Because of the country's struggle with slavery and the origin and history of the Fourteenth Amendment, the courts pay particularly close attention to laws and policies involving race and ethnicity. Selecting applicants for employment or government contracts on the basis of race or ethnicity is an example. The courts employ "strict scrutiny," meaning government officials would need to prove that there was a *compelling*

▶ **STUDENTS AT A SINGLE-SEX CLASSROOM IN THE BRONX**

Classifying on the basis of gender is allowed by government policy in education. In 2002, only a dozen public schools offered single-sex classrooms within co-educational schools or were entirely single sex. By 2010, the number was over 540, with nearly 100 of those being entirely single-sex schools. Should public schools allow separate education by sex?

governmental interest at stake that *required* the distinction between racial or ethnic groups. This is normally very difficult to prove.[57]

A second type of case involves "quasi-suspect categories." Cases involving classification on the basis of sex are the prime example. Government would have to show that classifying by sex had a *substantial* relationship to an *important* government interest.[58]

The third type of case involves most other classifications, such as age, income, and disability. They are evaluated on what the courts call a rational basis standard; that is, does the classification have some *rational* connection that *contributes* to the goal of the law or policy?[59] This is an easier test for government officials to meet, and the courts will be more easily convinced that these classifications were necessary than they will for race and ethnicity. For example, the courts allow the federal government to impose higher tax rates on wealthier individuals in order to fund programs and redistribute income across income levels, but it would not allow higher tax rates to be imposed on the basis of race. Overall, in sum, the courts demand the strongest justification from government officials for classifying by race and ethnicity and next so by sex.

Many of the political and social accomplishments of the black civil rights movement had benefits for other groups. In addition to race and color, the legislative and administrative actions of the 1960s have been applied to religion, national origin, sex, disability, age, and sexual orientation. The three mechanisms to advance black civil rights—equal protection clause cases, Congress's use of its commerce clause and spending powers, and the president's authority over the executive branch—were also used to advance the civil rights of other groups that have been victims of discrimination.

Latinos, Asians, and Native Americans have experienced unique histories of discrimination.

Severe discrimination faced other racial and ethnic groups throughout U.S. history. Many states and municipalities enacted laws specifically targeting groups for differential treatment. When these laws have been challenged on constitutional grounds, the Supreme Court has generally applied reasoning similar to that in cases involving black civil rights. Segregation, until 1954, was acceptable. Laws that treated groups differently, however, were suspect. For example, in 1886 the Court struck down a San Francisco law that, despite appearing neutral on its face, the justices interpreted as intended to drive Chinese laundries out of business. The Fourteenth Amendment's guarantees of equal protection, the Court declared, "are universal in their application."[60] Similarly, legislation and presidential orders enacted as a result of the black civil rights movement in the 1960s also benefited other groups.

Each group has had its own particular history and specific issues, as well as its own interest groups to represent its concerns. Ethnic groups such as Asians and Latinos—the largest minority group in the country—are not randomly distributed throughout the country. As a consequence, laws targeting Latinos were more common in the Southwest, while laws targeting Asians were more common on the West Coast.

▲ ORGANIZING FOR HISPANIC CIVIL RIGHTS

Like blacks, other groups have had advocacy organizations play a large leadership role in advancing their civil rights. Increasing Hispanic political participation has been a recent focus, as in this voter registration drive at an immigration reform rally in Florida in 2010.

Because of the ways their histories in the United States differ from that of blacks—most notably the absence of slavery—the umbrella terms *Hispanic* and *Asian* may mean less for individuals in these categories than do national identities such as Mexican, Argentinean, Cuban, Japanese, Korean, or Chinese. "Hispanic" or "Latino" and "Asian" have not provided the same kind of common identity and widely shared political outlook that has been prevalent among African Americans. That heterogeneity has made political organization of these groups more difficult, and cross-ethnic group coordination—black, Hispanic, Asian—has been minimal. On some issues, such as immigration and language accommodation, individuals in these three groups often see more conflict than commonality among their interests.[61]

The experience of Native Americans has its own distinctive features. Prior to the passage of the Indian Citizenship Act in 1924, Native Americans were not considered U.S. citizens. As members of sovereign nations, they had to go through the same citizenship application procedures as individuals from other countries. Attempts to use the Fifteenth Amendment as a basis for the right to vote failed because of this lack of citizenship.[62] With the passage of the act, Native Americans were considered U.S. citizens without any special procedure required. This status entitled Native Americans to the rights and responsibilities of U.S. citizenship, but as with other groups, rights did not instantly materialize. They required political action.

The case of Native Americans differs from other groups in that they are considered U.S. citizens and also members of sovereign nations that exist within the United States. (See the discussion in Chapter 4, *CaseStudy: Federalism and the Regulation of Native American Casinos.*) Native Americans are protected by the anti-discrimination statutes and regulations that cover other groups. They also have tribal rights and responsibilities that differ among the various tribes and are determined by tribal authorities. Tribes have been actively involved in court cases and legislation seeking to preserve and restore their interests in land, mineral, and water resources, and defending traditional customs even if they conflict with state or national law.

Pervasive sex discrimination in law has eroded.

The movement for women's equality had two distinct phases. The early phase culminated in 1920 with the Nineteenth Amendment, which gave women the right to vote. An extensive array of legal restrictions on women remained, however, and these became the focus of women's rights organizations in the second phase, beginning in the 1960s.

Like the civil rights movement, the women's movement used legal and legislative strategies to challenge laws and policies that differentiated between men and women. The women's movement also engaged in "consciousness raising" designed to help women understand their identity and their status in law and society. Sometimes criticized as being geared toward the needs of white upper-middle-class women, this self-awareness and its call for "women's liberation" likely generated important organizational benefits by contributing to fund-raising and support for the efforts of women's rights organizations. These funds would be instrumental in filing court cases and lobbying for legislative changes. One of the key organizations involved in these efforts, the National Organization for Women (NOW), was founded in 1966.

Supreme Court rulings Prior to the 1970s, the Supreme Court had tended to uphold gender-based distinctions in law. It had sustained laws that denied women the right to vote prior to 1920, restricted their working hours to "protect the weaker sex," and prohibited admission to trades and professions. Fundamental rights and responsibilities of citizenship, such as participating on juries, were often denied to women.[63] After 1970, the Court overturned many gender-based state laws. Examples of the kinds of gender distinctions in law that the Court rejected included different treatment of men and women when calculating Social Security benefits, different ages for consuming alcohol, and permitting unwed mothers but not unwed fathers to withhold consent on the adoption of their children.

Most of the Court's discrimination-based decisions since the mid-1980s have been justified on the interpretation of civil rights statutes—what did laws mean and what did they require—rather than on Fourteenth Amendment equal protection grounds. For example, the Court ruled in 1986 that the Civil Rights Act of 1964 prohibited not only sex discrimination in hiring and firing, but also sexual harassment on the job.[64] Sexual harassment includes unwanted sexual attention, advances, or comments. The harassment can be directed toward a person or can be a part of the culture or environment of a workplace. A hostile environment on the job, whether general or targeted to a particular person, threatens the full participation in American commerce that is at the base of Congress's commerce clause justification for laws regulating discriminatory actions in the private sector.

While striking down most sex distinctions, the Court has upheld those that furthered important government interests. It has upheld limiting the military draft to men, for example. It has also supported regulations and policies that do not formally distinguish between men and women but in practice will have the effect of doing so. Giving preferences to veterans in state and federal government employment will tend to advantage men disproportionately, but the Court has upheld these as furthering an important government interest. Job screening that requires the ability to lift large weights will tend to favor men, but if this skill is related to the job being performed, the Court has accepted the practice. However, the Court may also examine whether there is any prospect for restructuring the job to eliminate the need for heavy-lifting skill, so that these skill filters are not simply indirect ways to discriminate on the basis of sex.

ThinkingComparatively

Many other economically advanced countries offer family and medical leave, usually with benefits somewhat more generous than in the United States.

Actions by Congress and presidents Congress and presidents have also addressed sex discrimination issues. The 1963 Equal Pay Act required equal pay for equal work, and the 2009 Lilly Ledbetter Fair Pay Act stated that the 180-day clock for filing a pay bias case starts again with each new paycheck, not just the first one. The Civil Rights Act of 1964 prohibited employers, employment agencies, and labor unions from discriminating on the basis of sex. Amendments to the Higher

Education Act in 1972, specifically that portion of the act known as Title IX, denied federal funds to universities that discriminated against women in any respect, including admissions, course availability, athletics, and advising.

Women's rights activists have argued that full equality sometimes needs to take account of differences. Expanded government support for child care, for example, has been advocated on gender equality grounds, so that women can more fully enter the workforce. In the United States, the need to accommodate the special demands placed on women inspired the Family and Medical Leave Act of 1993, which provides women with 12 weeks of unpaid leave following childbirth. New fathers can take this time off also, as can same-sex partners (as of 2010) and individuals needing to care for a sick family member. France, Denmark, Austria, Spain, Germany, and India provide from 12 to 26 weeks of leave with 100 percent of wages paid. The United Kingdom, Italy, Greece, and Japan offer 14–22 weeks at 60–90 percent of one's wages. And Australia offers unpaid leave, like the United States, but for a one-year period.[65]

Equal Rights Amendment   Like the black civil rights movement, the women's rights movement lost strength over time. Why? Some political scientists saw the movement as geared toward the interests of well-off white women rather than poor or minority women. Others noted that after many successes, it is difficult for any movement to maintain strong momentum. As with black civil rights, many of the issues that motivated early supporters had been addressed. A third factor is that after its early, widely appealing successes, the movement may have suffered by becoming perceived as too narrowly focused on upholding the 1973 decision in *Roe v. Wade*, which struck down anti-abortion laws around the country. The rise of a strong

▼ DIVERSITY IN UNIFORM
Women's advancement in traditionally male fields has often required overcoming *de facto* discrimination. Although a job might not be explicitly limited to men, the requirements for being hired could, in practice, advantage men. In such cases, judges will consider whether the requirement is significantly related to performing the job or seems arbitrary and unconstitutionally discriminatory against women.

243

ThinkingCausally

What factors contributed to the stalling of the women's rights movement?

conservative Christian spiritual and political movement by the late 1970s raised the question of whether the women's movement only allowed for a single, narrow identity for women—pro-choice on abortion, career oriented, in the workforce, seeking jobs traditionally held by men, believing that male–female distinctions were socially perpetuated rather than biological. Although often agreeing with the women's movement on economic and legal equality issues, women holding more conservative views did not necessarily accept the other liberal views propounded by the major women's rights organizations or share the same aspirations. This split resembles the fissures that emerged between factions in the movement for African American civil rights.

The difficulties facing the women's movement became apparent in the battle over adding an Equal Rights Amendment (ERA) to the U.S. Constitution. Introduced annually since 1923, the ERA finally passed both houses of Congress in 1972 after heavy lobbying by NOW and the National Women's Political Caucus. The proposed amendment stated, "Equality of rights under the law shall not be denied or abridged by the United States or by any State on account of sex." It was sent to the states for ratification, with 1979 set as the deadline. Twenty-two states ratified the amendment in the first year. By 1978, the amendment was three states short of the 38 needed for ratification. Congress controversially extended the ratification period through 1982. But by 1982 the amendment was still three states short, and five states that had approved the amendment rescinded their approval (see Figure 6-3). The constitutionality of the rescissions was unclear; nevertheless, the proposed amendment was never able to obtain enough state approval to add it to the Constitution. Why not?

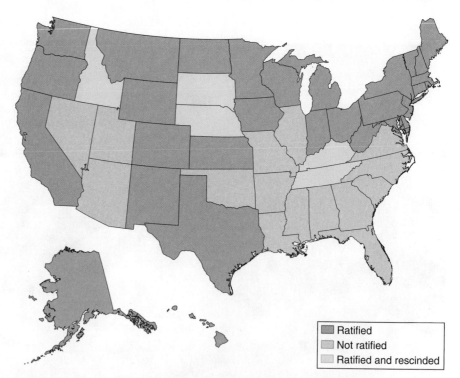

Ratified
Not ratified
Ratified and rescinded

FIGURE 6-3. **Ratification of the Equal Rights Amendment.** Ratification by 38 states was necessary for the amendment to be added to the Constitution, but only 35 ratified the proposed amendment. Five of those 35 later sought to rescind their ratification.

The three factors mentioned above—the rise of a conservative opposition, division among women, and a legacy of prior success—help explain what happened. First, the ERA faced concerted opposition by religious and conservative groups, which had used this issue to build very effective political organizations. Ironically, these groups may have actually benefited from the quick approval of the ERA in 35 states. They were able to concentrate their resources and lobbying on the remaining states, rather than fighting a national battle.[66] Second, division among women meant the pro-amendment forces were unable to marshal the same focused intensity as the opponents. Some women thought the amendment did not go far enough. Others thought women would lose some rights in the workplace—for example, accommodations for pregnancy—or would not be able to obtain support from ex-husbands. Third, the amendment may have been weakened by a perception that much of what the amendment was intended to achieve had already been accomplished by law, unilateral presidential action, and Supreme Court application of the Fourteenth Amendment's equal protection guarantee and its interpretation of civil rights laws. Together, these factors stalled the drive for the ERA.

Age and disability discrimination are subject to standards of review different from race and sex.

Not considered suspect or quasi-suspect classifications requiring the Court's strict scrutiny, the use of an age or disability classification in law must have some rational connection to the goal of the law. If it does not, the law will be struck down as inconsistent with equal protection. If it does, the law can stand. For example, the Court upheld Missouri's mandatory requirement that public officials retire at age 70.[67] Similarly, certain rights, such as voting, are limited to adults.

Laws passed by Congress and executive orders issued by presidents have also addressed discrimination based on age and disability. The Age Discrimination in Employment Act of 1967 prohibits employment discrimination against individuals between the ages of 40 and 70—the time when discrimination is considered more likely, but a split 5–4 Court decision in 2009 said that an age bias case against an employer had to show that age was the decisive factor in an adverse employment decision, not just a factor.[68] Two major laws have advanced civil rights for the disabled. The Rehabilitation Act of 1973 prohibited discrimination in federal employment on the basis of physical or mental disability, required the federal government to make reasonable accommodations for disabilities, and mandated affirmative action in hiring. The act also played a significant role in igniting the disability rights movement.[69] A key concern for the movement has been that disability law be presented as a civil rights issue and not a welfare or benefits issue.

Years of lobbying, litigation, and protest led to the Americans with Disabilities Act (ADA) of 1990. This act placed the same requirements on the private sector as the Rehabilitation Act had placed on the government. The law prohibits discrimination in employment, in all programs and services of state and local governments, and in public accommodations. Unlike in racial and gender discrimination, disability antidiscrimination remedies can be avoided if they are too costly or would impose an "undue hardship." For example, a store owner who would face prohibitive costs to redesign a store for wheelchair access might be exempted from the law's demands. Because of this possible exemption, and because "accommodation" and "disability" are subject to different interpretations, many cases have reached the courts in an attempt to sort out what is and is not reasonable with regard to accommodations and what type and severity of disability leave a person qualified or unqualified for a particular job. In response to court decisions, the ADA was amended in 2008 to

▶ **ACCESS FOR THE DISABLED**

The Americans with Disabilities Act led to improved accommodations for individuals with physical or mental disabilities. The nature of the required accommodation has been a matter of ongoing legal dispute, as has the cost. How much is too much? Should cost be irrelevant?

ThinkingComparatively

The American model for treating disability discrimination as a civil rights issue rather than a welfare and public assistance issue has become influential in other countries.

clarify that Congress intended the courts to take a broad rather than narrow view of what constituted a disability under the law.

Since the passage of the ADA, the transformation of law concerning the disabled from a welfare and assistance orientation to a civil rights orientation—integrating the disabled as full participants in the economy and society—has occurred around the world. Australia and Great Britain enacted laws prohibiting employment discrimination and calling on employers to make efforts to accommodate the disabled. Several European countries have required quotas to move disabled people into the workforce. In Germany, employers who do not meet their quotas are fined, and the funds raised from these fines go to employers who meet or exceed their quotas. Generally, quota systems have yielded disappointing results. Some were not well enforced, while in others, like Germany's, the fine proved insufficient to motivate employers. The American ADA anti-discrimination model has become attractive to many advocates for the disabled in countries with quota systems and has been endorsed by the European Union.[70]

Gay and lesbian equality has involved both civil liberties and civil rights.

Rights campaigns for gays and lesbians have concerned both civil liberties and civil rights. Regarding civil liberties, many states had prohibitions against homosexual sexual activity. The Supreme Court upheld these restrictions in 1986 but overturned them as violating basic concepts of liberty in the *Lawrence v. Texas* decision of 2003 (see Chapter 5).

Regarding civil rights, most states, many cities, and the federal government have adopted anti-discrimination hiring policies that include sexual orientation. These cover government employees and companies doing business with the government. Which aspects of federal civil rights law apply to gays and lesbians has been handled by the Supreme Court on an issue-by-issue basis. For example, the Supreme Court ruled in 1998 that same-sex sexual harassment is forbidden by the 1964 Civil Rights Act.[71] On the other hand, the Court in 2000 upheld the Boy Scouts of America's right to prohibit gays from serving as troop leaders because it conveyed a message contrary to the organization's beliefs.[72]

During his first two years in office, President Obama took unilateral steps through executive orders, proclamations, and administrative rulings to promote lesbian, gay, bisexual, and transgender rights. Sexual orientation was added as a protected class under hate crimes law. Hospital visitation must be available to gay and lesbian partners at any facility taking Medicare dollars. The Family and Medical Leave Act applies to partners in a same-sex couple to care for a sick child or newborn. The Violence Against Women Act, which in practice also covers domestic violence against men, was expanded to include victims in same-sex relationships of either gender. For federal workers, long-term health insurance, day care, and other benefits are now available to same-sex couples. The Census Bureau will be reporting the number of people in same-sex relationships.

Some advocates for LGBT rights, however, were critical of what they saw as the administration's slow movement on a range of issues. As a presidential candidate, Obama had not supported same-sex marriage, and gay and lesbian groups were disappointed that his administration defended the Defense of Marriage Act in federal court. (See the introduction to Chapter 4, *The State of Their Unions: Marriage as a Federalism Issue,* for an extensive discussion of the issue of same-sex marriage.) Activists also criticized what they considered slow movement on the issue of homosexuals serving in the military (see below, *CaseStudy: Gays in the Military*). A final set of concerns was that the president had not pushed sufficiently for employment nondiscrimination, and that where he had acted on various issues, the president relied too heavily on executive decrees that could be more easily reversed by a future administration, rather than through law, which would be more difficult to overturn.[73] The president's team may not have wanted to have these issues front and center while addressing other major items on their agenda, but LGBT activists sought to put pressure on the administration by threatening to reduce or withhold their financial support for the Democratic Party.

▲ REACHING NEW HEIGHTS
Previously a test pilot for Raytheon, Amanda Simpson was named by President Obama as senior technical adviser in the Commerce Department's Bureau of Industry and Security, monitoring U.S. weapons technology exports. She is the first openly transgender presidential appointee.

CaseStudy: Gays in the Military

At the national level, one of the most prominent civil rights issues concerns homosexuals serving in the military. Current law prohibits individuals who are openly homosexual from serving in the military, with the impact on morale, order, and unit cohesion being primary reasons stated for the ban.

Early in American history, homosexuals or bisexuals were not explicitly prohibited from military service, but engaging in same-sex sexual activity was considered grounds for dismissal. In one form or another, this policy was effectively in place for most of American history. During World War I and World War II, revisions to discharge policy added provisions for removal for homosexual status as well as conduct, and psychological prescreening aimed to bar homosexuals

from military service. A Department of Defense directive issued in 1982 reaffirmed the policy that homosexuality was incompatible with military service.

The ban on gays in the military became a major issue advanced by gay advocacy groups in the 1980s. The groups argued that the policy violated the civil rights of homosexuals, by preventing them as a class from this aspect of citizenship. They also argued the policy was inconsistent, because thousands of gays had in fact served in the military without being discharged, while others were discharged or not allowed to enlist.

During the 1980s, gay and lesbian groups were becoming important parts of the Democratic Party voter and financial base. This more prominent role led many Democratic candidates to call for a change in the military's policy. In his 1992 presidential campaign, Democratic nominee Bill Clinton advocated an end of the ban on gays serving in the military.

The issue became one of the earliest and most controversial tackled by the Clinton administration upon taking office in 1993. When it became apparent that a complete removal of the ban was politically unlikely, the administration later in the year adopted a compromise policy known as "don't ask, don't tell." Under this policy, military personnel are not to be asked about their sexual orientation nor are they to disclose it, the logic being that unit cohesion and discipline would thus be protected. Revealing that one is homosexual can lead to dismissal. According to military guidelines as of March 2010, the dismissal would be not for homosexual sexual orientation itself, but because of the risk of homosexual conduct. This conduct includes "engaging in, attempting to engage in, or soliciting another to engage in a homosexual act or acts, a statement by a Service member that he or she is a homosexual or bisexual, or words to that effect, or marriage or attempted marriage to a person known to be the same biological sex."[74] Although this policy allows gays and lesbians to serve in the military, it does not allow them to do so openly.

Public opinion on the issue has shifted over time, with most surveys now showing majority support for gays and lesbians serving openly. President Obama said during his campaign in 2008 and his State of the Union Address in 2009 that he wanted to end the policy. Congress began considering a repeal in 2010. With leading military officials suggesting openness to the idea, the Defense Department began a year-long review that same year. If both houses of Congress

approve the repeal and the military confirms it will not harm readiness or unit cohesion, don't ask, don't tell would be poised to expire sometime in 2011. A federal judge in 2010 struck down the policy, but the Obama administration, preferring a legislative solution, successfully requested the implementation of the ruling be put on hold pending an appeal.

Service in the military by gays and lesbians is widespread around the world. Most other democracies now allow homosexuals to serve openly. Of the five countries in the United Nations Security Council with veto power, the United Kingdom, France, and Russia have no ban, while the United States and China do. Argentina, Australia, Brazil, Canada, Israel, Peru, and all but one of the 27 member countries of the European Union also allow for service by gays and lesbians. Most of the changes have happened since 1993.[75]

ThinkingCritically

1. To what degree should policies in other countries affect American considerations of what is or is not appropriate civil rights policy?

2. If you were a legislator, in what order would you rank the influence of arguments made by advocacy groups supportive of or opposed to allowing gays and lesbians in the military, the opinion of military leaders, the opinion of military rank-and-file, and public opinion in determining how you would vote on repealing "don't ask, don't tell"?

3. What would you identify as the major factors explaining why the political environment today appears more favorable than it did previously toward overturning the prohibition on homosexuals serving in the military?

Noncitizens share some of the rights of citizens, but not all.

The U.S. Constitution confers rights on all persons in the United States, not just citizens. Whether citizen or not, legally in the United States or not, individuals are covered by the Constitution's due process provisions when charged with a crime, prohibition against cruel and unusual punishment, freedom to practice one's religion, equal protection of the laws, and so on.[76] The major provisions of the Bill of Rights apply to citizens and noncitizens alike.

Noncitizens are protected by First Amendment free speech rights in that they cannot be criminally prosecuted for speech, except in those same instances as for citizens where speech is not protected, such as child pornography. Speech made prior to entry in the United States, and speech deemed possible once a person arrives here can, however, be taken into account in a decision whether to grant entry. A claim that a noncitizen was selectively targeted with a technical violation of immigration law, but that his or her speech was the real motive, will generally be dismissed by the courts.[77] And although individuals who are in the United States illegally may have constitutional rights and may legally have access to certain services and benefits, they remain subject to deportation for having violated immigration law. For this reason, there has been great controversy around the country as to what extent government officials should, when they are not directly involved in immigration enforcement, inquire about citizenship status and whether someone is in the United States legally. This simmering debate boiled over in 2010 over a new Arizona law intended to increase these inquiries. The U.S. Justice Department responded by filing a successful lawsuit to block implementation of the law, arguing that portions of the legislation violated the national government's supremacy in immigration policy.

Noncitizens do not have all the same rights and privileges as citizens. They cannot, for example, run for certain public offices and they cannot vote in federal elections. Access to federal programs and funds may in some instances be limited to citizens. Because of national security concerns, there are limits placed on noncitizens, including the length of time they can be in the United States and their access to certain jobs, and immigrants in the country illegally are subject to long detentions prior to hearings or possible deportation. Because violation of immigration rules is typically treated as an administrative and not a criminal matter, noncitizens do not have a right to have counsel provided during immigration proceedings.

At the state level, issues such as whether noncitizens can obtain drivers licenses, pay in-state tuition at public universities, and qualify for public assistance programs run by a state vary across the states. However, as with other categories used by government to discriminate among groups, the Supreme Court will review whether classifying by citizenship status is constitutional. Generally, the Court has applied an intermediate to high level of scrutiny in examining cases concerning classification by citizenship status—the Court has typically approached such distinctions with skepticism and has frequently overturned distinctions based on citizenship status. The Court has ruled, for example, that public schooling cannot be denied based on whether one is a citizen.[78]

Who bears the burden of proof in discrimination cases is controversial.

Across all these various population groups, one of the issues considered by the Supreme Court and Congress is whether each individual who believes he or she has been discriminated against has to prove discrimination. In a 1989 decision, the Supreme Court declared that the burden of proof was on the person alleging discrimination to show how an employment practice was, on its own, directly discriminatory toward that particular person.[79] If each individual must prove intentional discrimination, rather than rely on statistical patterns that show disparity between groups, for example in pay, these cases would be much more difficult to win.

Congress responded to the Supreme Court in the Civil Rights Act of 1991. The act returned the burden of proof to the employer—the employer would have to defend a questionable pattern in employment and explain why it was not problematic. A Court decision in 1993 divided the burden of proof, concluding that each individual need not prove the employer set out to discriminate against him or her, but would still need to demonstrate that any discriminatory impact between groups was intentional and unreasonable.[80] In civil rights, such seemingly technical distinctions are highly consequential and are the focus of substantial political and legal conflict.

CHAPTER SUMMARY

In this chapter you have learned to:

6-1 Trace the advances and setbacks in the quest for civil rights in the nineteenth century. Amendments to the Constitution during and following the Civil War, as well as legislation enacted during the period known as Reconstruction, began the process of national recognition of civil rights for blacks. The Fourteenth Amendment's guarantee of equal protection of the laws was interpreted by the Supreme Court to limit government discrimination, not private discrimination. And the Supreme Court concluded that mandating separate facilities for blacks and whites did not violate equal protection as long as the facilities were substantially equal.

6-2 Explain the demise of the separate but equal doctrine and the creation of civil rights laws and regulations. In the twentieth century, black civil rights organizations began to challenge discriminatory laws in court, with some success, while presidents bypassed Congress to promote civil rights through executive orders and other unilateral actions. The rejection of the separate but equal doctrine by the Supreme Court in *Brown v. Board of Education* prompted a broader movement to press for civil rights. Major legislation challenging discrimination in the private sector and government, significant executive orders introducing affirmative action policies, and a constitutional amendment prohibiting use of the poll tax produced a civil rights revolution in the

United States. Congress used its interstate commerce powers and spending powers to avoid Supreme Court concerns that the Fourteenth Amendment did not apply to the private sector.

6-3 Analyze the changes that led to the success and splintering of the civil rights movement. Civil rights successes depended heavily on the rise of a strategically effective civil rights movement, appeals to key beliefs in the American creed, and changes in the Democratic Party that focused the party more on its growing northern, urban, and minority constituency. The push for civil rights encountered difficulty when the movement splintered, policies and ideas became more controversial, and white backlash worried Democratic politicians about their chances to win the presidency.

6-4 Describe legal and legislative actions to extend equal protection guarantees to other groups. Although covered by the same laws, court decisions, and presidential actions that aided black civil rights, groups based on ethnicity, gender, religion, age, and sexual orientation, among other categories, have each faced distinctive issues and formed their own organizations to challenge discriminatory laws and practices. The doctrine of equal protection extends to these groups, although the Supreme Court does not treat every classification the same. Race and ethnic classifications in laws and regulations are reviewed the most strictly, followed by gender classifications.

---

mypoliscilab EXERCISES

Apply what you learned in this chapter by starting with these resources on MyPoliSciLab.

Read on mypoliscilab.com

    eText: Chapter 6

Study and Review on mypoliscilab.com

    Pre-Test
    Post-Test
    Chapter Exam
    Flashcards

Watch on mypoliscilab.com

    Video: Supreme Court: No Race-Based Admissions
    Video: Should Don't Ask Don't Tell Go Away?

Explore on mypoliscilab.com

    Simulation: You Are Redrawing the Districts in Your State
    Simulation: You Are the Mayor and Need to Make Civil Rights Decisions
    Comparative: Comparing Civil Rights
    Timeline: The Civil Rights Movement
    Timeline: The Mexican-American Civil Rights Movement
    Timeline: The Struggle for Equal Protection
    Timeline: Women's Struggle for Equality
    Visual Literacy: Race and the Death Penalty

KEY TERMS

affirmative action, p. 227
Brown v. Board of Education, p. 223
civil disobedience, p. 233
civil rights, p. 216
de facto segregation, p. 224
de jure segregation, p. 224

Dred Scott v. Sandford, p. 217
equal protection clause, p. 218
Jim Crow, p. 220
majority-minority districts, p. 238
Plessy v. Ferguson, p. 220
poll tax, p. 227

Regents of the University of California v. Bakke, p. 231
separate but equal doctrine, p. 220
state action, p. 219
white primary, p. 235

CHAPTER TEST

1. How did the Fourteenth Amendment reverse the Dred *Scott v. Sandford* decision regarding citizenship?
2. What is the significance of the state action doctrine for civil rights?
3. What was the separate but equal doctrine, and how did the Supreme Court overturn it in *Brown v. Board of Education*?
4. What government actions were key in obtaining full voting rights for blacks in the 1960s?
5. What is the significance of the Civil Rights Act of 1964?
6. How did Congress apply civil rights statutes to the actions of private individuals and organizations rather than only to governments?
7. In what ways did presidents use their unilateral power to promote civil rights?
8. What were the strategic challenges faced by the civil rights movement and the women's movement?
9. In what major ways have the strategic challenges and issues facing civil rights movements for other racial and ethnic groups differed from the movement for African Americans?
10. What categories has the Supreme Court constructed to guide its decisions about discrimination in cases based on race, sex, age, and other categories?

SUGGESTED READINGS

Angelo N. Ancheta. 2007. *Race, Rights, and the Asian American Experience*, 2nd ed. New Brunswick, NJ: Rutgers University Press. A compelling overview of Asian American civil rights. Emphasizes the importance of considering civil rights beyond the black–white relationship.

Ward Connerly. 2002. *Creating Equal: My Fight Against Race Preferences*. New York: Encounter Books. A memoir by the chief architect of the campaign to outlaw racial preference in California state government and universities.

F. Chris Garcia and Gabriel R. Sanchez. 2008. *Hispanics and the U.S. Political System: Moving into the Mainstream*. New York: Pearson/Prentice Hall. A helpful examination of Hispanic politics and civil rights issues today.

Victoria Hattam. 2007. *In the Shadow of Race: Jews, Latinos, and Immigrant Politics in the United States*. Chicago: University of Chicago Press. Explores the distinction between race and ethnicity and how these have affected public policy and immigrant politics.

Ira Katznelson. 2005. *When Affirmative Action Was White: An Untold History of Racial Inequality in Twentieth-Century America*. New York: W. W. Norton. Argues that many of the public programs arising from the New Deal in the 1930s and 1940s were in effect affirmative action that benefited white Americans.

Jane J. Mansbridge. 1986. *Why We Lost the ERA*. Chicago: University of Chicago Press. Highlights the organizational, ideological, and strategic reasons the Equal Rights Amendment was not ratified.

Abagail M. Thernstrom. 1987. *Whose Votes Count? Affirmative Action and Minority Voting Rights*. Cambridge: Harvard University Press. Highlights the successful struggle for voting rights that culminated in the Voting Rights Act of 1965, but argues that the implementation of the law since then has undermined the law's original purpose.

Richard M. Valelly. 2004. *The Two Reconstructions: The Struggle for Black Enfranchisement*. Chicago: University of Chicago Press. Examines movements for black enfranchisement, offering an explanation of why these efforts failed in the nineteenth century but were successful in the twentieth century.

David E. Wilkins and K. Tsianina Lomawaima. 2001. *Uneven Ground: American Indian Sovereignty and Federal Law*. Norman: University of Oklahoma Press. Thoughtful examination of the nature, limits, and possibilities of sovereignty for Native American tribes.

C. Vann Woodward. 1957. *The Strange Career of Jim Crow*. New York: Oxford University Press. A classic account of the system of Jim Crow laws that prevailed throughout the southern states until the 1960s.

SUGGESTED WEBSITES

U.S. Department of Justice, Civil Rights Division: www.usdoj.gov/crt

Provides links to presidential statements on civil rights, newsletters, Department of Justice special initiatives and court cases, and guidance on compliance with civil rights policy.

American Civil Rights Institute: www.acri.org

Website of an organization dedicated to ending racial and gender preference policies around the country and challenging the philosophy of other civil rights organizations.

National Association for the Advancement of Colored People: www.naacp.org

Website of the organization that played a crucial role in the rise of black civil rights. Provides information on the organization's major policy and legal concerns and its advocacy priorities.

National Council of La Raza: www.nclr.org

One of the major Hispanic/Latino civil rights and advocacy organizations.

Human Rights Campaign: www.hrc.org

One of the leading advocacy organizations for lesbian, gay, bisexual, and transgender rights.

Human Rights Watch: www.hrw.org

Extensive investigations of human rights violations and concerns globally, organized by country and issue area.

Guessing Weights

One day in the fall of 1906, British scientist Francis Galton left his home in the town of Plymouth and headed for a country fair. As he walked through the exhibition that day, Galton came across a weight-judging competition. A fat ox was on display and members of a gathering crowd were lining up to place wagers on the weight of the ox.

Eight hundred people tried their luck. They were a diverse lot. Many of them were butchers and farmers, who were presumably expert at judging the weight of livestock, but there were also quite a few people who had no special knowledge of cattle. "Many nonexperts competed," Galton later wrote in the scientific journal *Nature*, "like those clerks and others who have no expert knowledge of horses, but who bet on races, guided by newspapers, friends, and their own fancies."

When the contest was over and the prizes had been awarded, Galton borrowed the tickets from the organizers and ran a series of statistical tests. He undoubtedly thought that the average guess would be way off the mark. After all, mix a few very informed people who may be expert at guessing weights of livestock with a slew of less well informed folks, and it seems likely the result would be a wrong answer. But Galton was wrong about getting a wrong answer. The crowd as an average had guessed that the ox, after it had been slaughtered and dressed, would weigh 1,197 pounds. After it had been slaughtered and dressed, the ox weighed 1,198 pounds. In other words, the crowd's judgment was essentially perfect.[1]

What Galton discovered that day was something of a paradox: a group of people, many of whom have little interest or expertise in a particular subject matter, can still, collectively, make appropriate judgments about it.

This chapter will consider this paradox as applied to American politics. Although the great mass of Americans have no great interest or expertise in politics or policy, somehow they tend to make appropriate, reasonable, and logical judgments about political life. These judgments fall under the heading of "public opinion," one of the most commonly used phrases in any discussion of politics and policy. During the 2008 presidential campaigns and the battle over health care reform, one could read the following sorts of comments about "public opinion."

"Does the press influence public opinion? Absolutely. Is the public often capable of ignoring the press? Absolutely, too. If you look at the way the press covered [Sarah] Palin initially, it was at a right angle to the public response to her. It was coverage that questioned her credentials and his choice."
Andrew Kohut, President, Pew Research Center[2]

"The polls carried by the media have a more significant impact on what members of Congress think [about the health care debate] because it has an impact on writers. It sets the tone for journalism coverage of an issue."
Robert Blendon, Professor of Health Policy and Political Analysis, Harvard University[3]

Political leaders focus on public opinion and strategists focus on influencing the content and direction of what people think and know. The fact that public opinion has an important role in American politics comes from our political culture and the value it places on democracy, representation, and civil liberties. Compared to other political systems (even other democratic ones), Americans seem to have a greater opportunity for their opinions to matter.

◄ **GUESSING WEIGHTS**
This team of oxen is not unlike those in the weight-guessing competition at the country fair. On average, a crowd not only may be very close to guessing an ox's correct weight but also may collectively exercise good judgment in a political context.

CHAPTER LEARNING OBJECTIVES

After reading this chapter you will be able to:

7-1 Define public opinion and identify its four basic traits.

7-2 Outline the process and agents of political socialization.

7-3 Assess the extent to which American public opinion is based on political knowledge.

7-4 Establish how American democracy functions despite the public's low levels of political knowledge.

The Nature of Public Opinion

7-1 Define public opinion and identify its four basic traits.

Public opinion is one of the most commonly used phrases in the discussion of politics and policy. **Public opinion** can be measured, obeyed, manipulated, ignored, and even misunderstood. But, what, in fact, is public opinion? A simple and useful definition is "the preferences of the adult population on matters of relevance to government."[4] Another definition provides a broader perspective: "public opinion is the collective political beliefs and attitudes of the public, or groups within the public, about issues, candidates, officials, parties, and groups." This second definition makes clear that although public opinion typically refers to the collective opinion of the public, it can also refer to opinions of groups within the public. Here, we will examine both types. Both types of public opinion are useful to examine.

Public opinion has four basic traits: salience, stability, direction, and intensity. **Salience** indicates an issue's importance to a person, or to the public in general. The public can feel strongly about an issue yet not rate that issue as particularly salient in their lives or political calculations. Similarly, the public might mildly favor or mildly oppose an issue, but that issue might be quite salient to many people.

When politicians decide whether to attempt to change public opinion or whether to follow the message the public appears to be sending, they need to consider the **stability** of public opinion. Is public opinion on an issue likely to change and, if so, is change likely to be gradual or rapid? Once changed, is opinion likely to solidify around that new position, or is this an issue on which one might expect changes to be frequent? These are crucial questions for politicians. Are attitudes, for example, about health care likely to change significantly in the short term? And, if they do, is that change likely to endure?

Along with salience and stability, direction and intensity round out the four basic traits of public opinion. The **direction** of the public's opinion about something refers to whether the public favors or opposes it. Any indication of agreement or disagreement, approval or disapproval, favor or opposition, is an example of direction.

The **intensity** of the public's opinion measures the strength of the direction. For example, some people strongly favor or oppose abortion, whereas others may not harbor such strong feelings on the issue. Some will favor abortion in most cases, but not strongly; some will oppose abortion in most cases, but not strongly.

As the above definition makes clear, public opinion can also vary significantly among different groups within the population. It is important for politicians to recognize how public opinion breaks down among these various groups so they can better understand the impact of different policies on different demographics. The same-sex marriage debate illustrates this perfectly. When Proposition 8 was put on the ballot in California in 2008 to make same-sex marriage unconstitutional, liberals assumed that

public opinion the collective political beliefs and attitudes of the public, or groups within the public, on matters of relevance to government.

salience an issue's importance to a person or to the public in general.

stability the speed with which the change will occur, and the likelihood that the new opinion will endure.

direction in public opinion, the tendency for or against some phenomenon.

intensity the strength of the direction of public opinion.

▲ **HEALTH CARE POLICY SHOWDOWN**

President Obama and Democratic Congressional leaders meet with Congressional Republicans to discuss and debate health care reform legislation. When researchers conduct a survey, they must take care to obtain unbiased results. A survey question on health care reform will yield different responses if asked at a senior citizen center than it might if asked at a skate park.

the strong turnout to elect Barack Obama would also help defeat the proposition. What they did not foresee was that African Americans would turn out in such force for the proposition. The measure passed, thus defining marriage in California as between a man and a woman only, in large part because of the black vote. It was bitter irony for the Democrats that the same people who voted so heavily to elect the more liberal presidential candidate also voted so heavily with conservatives against same-sex marriage. It was a harsh lesson for the liberals, yet it demonstrates just how important it is for policy makers to be cognizant of the varying opinions that different groups have.

As Table 7-1 shows, public opinion on specific policy issues varies greatly among different demographic groups. Race, gender, income, and political affiliation are all factors in how an individual forms an opinion on a certain issue.[5] It is important for politicians to understand how these opinions differ among these groups so they can strategically appeal to each group.

More generally it is crucial to understand the nature of public opinion. A politician has to ask, "Do I follow public opinion now, only to find that it soon will shift in another direction? Do I attempt to move public opinion in a new direction, or make it more intense or salient, when I can see that opinion on this issue tends to have great stability and is very difficult to alter?" Answering these questions about stability, and trying to gauge the direction, intensity, and salience of public opinion, can be very challenging for public officials.

Politicians do not always base their actions on public opinion, and representative democracy does not demand that office holders always follow public opinion. Still, in a well-functioning representative democracy, policy-making should generally follow the contours of public opinion on most issues. Furthermore, most politicians like to be on the "80 side of 80–20 issues." In other words, office holders who are too often on the wrong side of public opinion risk great political cost and face electoral danger. We have much more to say about this in our chapter on Congress.

TABLE 7-1. Attitudes About Major Policies by Different Demographics

VIEWS ON HEALTH CARE LEGISLATION BY DEMOGRAPHICS			
	FAVOR (%)	OPPOSE (%)	DON'T KNOW/ REFUSED (%)
Gender:			
Men	57	35	7
Women	46	42	12
Race:			
White Non-Hispanic	53	37	10
Total Non-White	46	43	11
Black Non-Hispanic	47	43	10
Income:			
$75,000 +	61	32	7
$30,000–$74,999	53	40	7
<$30,000	41	47	11
Party ID:			
Republican	65	29	6
Democrat	45	44	12
Independent	49	41	9

VIEWS ON THE AFGHANISTAN WAR BY DIFFERENT DEMOGRAPHICS			
	FAVOR (%)	OPPOSE (%)	DON'T KNOW/ REFUSED (%)
Gender:			
Male	35	50	14
Female	34	46	19
Race:			
White Non-Hispanic	30	55	16
Total Non-White	48	32	20
Black Non-Hispanic	61	18	21
Income:			
$75,000 +	37	54	8
$30,000–$74,999	36	49	15
<$30,000	36	43	20
Party ID:			
Republican	11	79	11
Democrat	59	20	21
Independent	32	52	16

Source: Pew Research Center for the People and the Press, "Unabated Economic Gloom, Divides on Afghanistan and Health Care." December 16, 2009. http://people-press.org.

Political Socialization

7-2 Outline the process and agents of political socialization.

What is the source of public opinion? How do individuals acquire their political values and attitudes in the first place? The process takes place through what political scientists call **political socialization**. Political socialization is a learning process, one in which individuals absorb information about the political world and add it, selectively, to their stock of knowledge and understanding of politics and government.

This learning tends to be governed by two important principles: primacy and persistence. **Primacy** means that what is learned first is learned best, that is, it is lodged most firmly in one's mind. **Persistence** means that political lessons, values, and attitudes learned early in life tend to structure political learning later on in life. In keeping with these two principles, what children learn about politics at a young age becomes an important determinant of the values, attitudes, and beliefs they will hold in later life.

The most common expression of values, attitudes, and beliefs is the identification of an individual's ideology. **Ideology** can be described as a consistent set of ideas about a given set of issues. The two most commonly used ideological categories are "liberal" and "conservative." Although there are no hard and fast definitions for what makes an individual "liberal" or "conservative," certain beliefs are generally associated with one ideology or the other. A liberal would generally favor a government that is active in promoting social equality and economic welfare. A conservative would generally favor a smaller government that interferes minimally in the economic sphere but actively promotes social morality.

political socialization the learning process in which individuals absorb information and selectively add it to their knowledge and understanding of politics and government.

primacy the principle that what is learned first is learned best and lodged most firmly in one's mind.

persistence the principle that political lessons, values, and attitudes learned early in life tend to structure political learning later on in life.

ideology a consistent set of ideas about a given set of issues.

continued on page 261 ▶

HOW DO WE KNOW?

Can Surveys Accurately Gauge the Opinions of Almost 300 Million Americans?

▼ THE PIECES OF PUBLIC OPINION

Hoping to influence election and legislative outcomes, politicians and political strategists—like former Democratic consultant, political strategist, and now White House staffer David Axelrod, pictured (on right) here talking with communication director Robert Gibbs (on left)—must consider the stability, direction, and intensity of public opinion.

Discussions of public opinion are a routine part of American political life. During election season, scores of polls report who is ahead and behind virtually every day. At other times, news reports frequently mention the public's perception of the president's job performance and whether the country is heading in the right direction. If the president or a member of Congress makes a significant policy proposal, major media outlets survey Americans for their reactions. Politicians seldom rely on media polls; they conduct their own surveys. Presidents have extensive polling operations. Typically they take the pulse of the nation before, during, and after a campaign, an important speech, or the introduction of a major policy initiative. Political scientists, too, use surveys to gauge the collective consciousness of the American people.

Not all surveys are created equal, however. A well-designed survey can provide accurate information on public opinion, but a poorly done one can lead to false conclusions and be

essentially useless. The question is: can surveys accurately gauge the opinions of almost 300 million Americans? How do we know?

Why It Matters

Agreement between public opinion and government action is one measure of a democratic government. However, it is not always a good one. Sometimes the opinion "snapshot" in a survey obscures important momentum—at the time of the survey, government may be in the process of moving toward the public's position, or vice versa. And sometimes what the public wants may be ill-advised or even unconstitutional. However, a critical starting point in our assessment is understanding how surveys work.

Investigating the Answer

Imagine you are making a pot of soup for some friends. You add water, chicken, vegetables, and spices, and let the soup simmer for a couple of hours. Before serving it, you want to make sure it tastes good, so you take a small spoonful. If you took the spoonful from the top, you might think the soup needed more seasoning. If you took a spoonful from the bottom, you might think the soup needed more water. A good cook mixes the soup before taking a sample spoonful to make sure all parts are represented.

sampling taking a small fraction of something that is meant to represent a larger whole: e.g., a group of people that represents a larger population.

The same logic applies to survey **sampling**, the process of choosing a small group of people to interview for a survey. A survey sample should represent all elements of the population—men, women, young, old, Democrats, Republicans, and other groups—in rough proportion to their population percentages. Such representation is accomplished by using a **random sample,** a sample of the population in which every member of the population has an equal chance of ending up in the sample.

random sample a population sample in which it is equally likely that each member of the population will be included in the sample.

Particularly with large populations, the sampling procedures for a random sample can become very complex. But consider this simple example. We begin with a population of 100 people, half men, half women. We want to take a random sample of 20. To do this, we give each man and woman a slip of paper with a number, 1 through 100. Each number is used only once. Then we have a computer generate 20 random numbers between 1 and 100. As the computer generates each number, the person holding the number is asked to step forward. Once the computer has provided 20 numbers, we have our random sample.

This sample should end up with roughly half men and half women, and in that respect be representative of the total population of 100, because every man and woman in our population had an equal probability, or chance, of being sampled. We can then have some confidence that if we pose questions to members of the sample, their answers will be very similar to the ones we would get if we posed them to the entire population.

sampling error the difference between the reported characteristics of the sample and the characteristics of the larger population that result from imperfect sampling.

Even in perfectly drawn samples, unavoidable **sampling error** occurs because no sample is an exact match for the population. Sampling error is reported in most surveys as the **margin of error**. To understand what this means, suppose that 55 percent of respondents in a survey approved of the president's job performance and the survey claims a margin of error of plus or minus 5 percentage points. Thus, if we had talked to the entire population, we would have found that somewhere between 50 percent and 60 percent approved of the president's performance—55 percent plus or minus 5 percentage points. So the result from interviewing a random sample is close to what we would get if we spoke with the entire population.

margin of error the range surrounding a sample's response within which researchers are confident the larger population's true response would fall.

One influence on sampling error is the size of the sample. The larger the sample, the smaller the sampling error. If you flipped a coin several times, you should get a roughly equal proportion of heads and tails, but you could get all heads or all tails. The more times you flip the coin, the more likely the proportion of heads to tails will be nearly equal. Try it! The same applies to survey samples. If researchers picked just 1 person at random, or 10, or even 100, to represent the entire U.S. population, the sampling error would be enormous. But if they picked 1,000 people at random, the sampling error would be 3 or 4 percentage points, a margin most researchers are comfortable with. With 1,000 people in the sample, there would likely be a fair mix of men, women, young, old, Democrats, Republicans, whites, nonwhites, and so on. In other words, 1,000 people are a large enough group to be broadly representative of the entire U.S. population.

Sampling error also can result from the diversity of the population studied. To take an extreme example, suppose you knew everyone in a state had the same opinion on every issue. If you wanted to measure public opinion on an issue in that state, you would need to ask only one person. Now suppose everyone had a slightly different opinion on every issue. If you were to interview just one person, your sampling error would be unacceptably large; one person's opinion could not possibly capture the diversity of thinking within the population. So the greater the diversity of opinion, the more people a researcher needs to survey to be confident of results.

Surveys can contain other sorts of errors. For example, questions can be poorly written or structured to encourage a particular response. Consider the following questions:

Given the recent series of murders in our state, some people say the state should reinstate the death penalty. Do you agree or disagree?

Given the recent cases of police misconduct and the freeing of inmates who had been wrongly convicted, do you agree or disagree that the state should reinstate the death penalty?

The first question is structured to elicit pro–death penalty responses, while the second question is structured to elicit anti–death penalty responses. Even if a question is asked in a straightforward manner—"Do you support or oppose the death penalty for convicted murderers?"—where that question appears in a survey also matters. If, on the one hand, it followed a long series of questions on crime, a pro–death penalty result would be more likely. If, on the other hand, it followed a series of questions on police misconduct, one might expect more anti–death penalty responses.

The demographic characteristics of interviewers can also introduce error. Evidence shows that men reply differently to male interviewers than to females on issues such as abortion and birth control, and answers to questions about race are influenced by the race of the interviewer.

Another source of error is **nonresponse bias**. Even though a researcher may have drawn a reliable sample, not everyone in that sample may agree to participate in the survey. If those who participate have attitudes different from those who decline, the results will be biased. In a survey on Social Security, for example, young workers would be expected to have opinions different from those of older workers and retired individuals. If the refusal rate for the younger group were much higher than for the older group, the survey would contain disproportionate input from older individuals and inadequate input from younger.

Certain types of surveys also suffer from their own set of problems. Despite their rising popularity, non-probability online surveys can be misleading. These online surveys, sometimes also called volunteer or opt-in surveys, have participants sign up and answer questionnaires on the Internet, usually in exchange for gifts or money. This type of survey has grown into a multibillion-dollar business in the last 10 years, mainly due to the low cost and faster survey turnaround time.[6] Yet because of the inherent nature of these surveys, they suffer from many flaws. The majority of these surveys rely solely on individuals who have Internet access, leading to significant under-coverage. As of December 2009, only 74 percent of U.S. adults use the Internet, and Internet usage tends to be positively associated with income and negatively associated with age.[7] Some demographic groups also tend to be online less frequently and are therefore underrepresented in online surveys. There can also be errors associated with the high level of nonresponse, resulting in extensive

nonresponse bias a nonrandom error that occurs when people who choose to participate in a survey have different attitudes from those of people who decline to participate.

bias. Despite these problems, non-probability online surveys continue to be used for market research in such areas as product testing and customer satisfaction. They have even become more commonly used in political polling.[8]

The increased use of online surveys in such applications has led to their heightened scrutiny, specifically from the American Association for Public Opinion Research, whose report in March of 2010 challenged the use of non-probability surveys. The AAPOR report concludes that "researchers should avoid non-probability online panels when one of the research objectives is to accurately estimate population values." The report goes on to say that "there is currently no generally accepted theoretical basis from which to claim that survey results using samples from non-probability online panels are projectable to the general population." It is the findings of the report, therefore, that claiming "representativeness" should be avoided when using online surveys.[9] Whether these warnings have a discernable influence on the use of online surveys is yet to be seen.

Thinking Critically

Suppose you were in charge of designing a survey to gauge public opinion on certain major issues. How would you word your questions, and in what order would you place your questions? How would you make sure there is little nonresponse bias?

What do you need to know about polls in order to properly understand the results? In other words, what would you need to know about a survey before you trust the results? Do you think polling via the Internet is as trustworthy as other, more established polling techniques? What are some problems Internet polls may have?

The Bottom Line

Surveys can be an incredibly useful tool for journalists, political scientists, and politicians. However, identifying good survey methods and understanding how particular surveys are conducted are highly useful skills for citizens as well. Those skills will serve you well in other courses as well as enabling you to be a good consumer of polls.

Further, liberals are often said to fall to the "left" of the political spectrum, while the "right" is occupied by political conservatives. Of course, many people do not fall squarely in either of the two camps. People who favor a smaller government that interferes minimally in the economy and does not interfere in social morality are often called "libertarians." Those who support an active government role in both the economy and social morality are sometimes dubbed "populists."

Political sophistication grows as children grow up.

Political socialization plays a crucial role in determining which ideology an individual will support. Children begin learning about politics and government surprisingly early. In their preschool years, the first representative of government that they become familiar with is often the police officer. Preschoolers generally consider the police officer a helpful, benevolent authority figure.[10] Most preschool-aged children are unfamiliar with the president, but this changes in the early grade school years.[11] As with the police officer, grade schoolers typically see the president in a positive light, believing him to be an honest, trustworthy, virtuous figure.

▲ EARLY INTERACTIONS WITH GOVERNMENT

Police and firefighters are often young children's first introduction to government. In later years, children learn about their president, mayor, and members of Congress.

These generally positive sentiments are by no means universal, however. There are certain subgroups of children who do not view political authority as favorably as the general population—for example, African Americans, Hispanics, and the low-income, white children of Appalachia.[12]

In the later grade school years, children's political thinking becomes substantially more sophisticated. In the first place, the child's awareness of political figures begins to expand. To the short list of police officer and president, many children add figures such as firefighters, soldiers, mayors, and governors.[13] At the same time, the child begins to think of government not just in terms of political figures but in terms of institutions and activities as well. These may include Congress and the political parties, for example, and activities such as voting.[14]

The child also begins to distinguish more clearly among different individuals and institutions. During the later grade school years, children come to understand the differences in the roles played by, for example, the president, the Supreme Court, and members of Congress.[15] They also begin to view some political figures more favorably than others. For example, grade schoolers tend to find the president more likeable than the police officer, and both of these more likeable than the senator.[16] Overall, however, positive feelings toward various authority figures begin to decline during the late childhood period. Though children still maintain generally favorable assessments of political figures and institutions, during the grade school years they transition toward a more realistic, less heroic view of specific political figures.[17] During these years, children also begin to gain a basic understanding of the concept of "policy," of conflict over specific issues, and of the idea of competition between the political parties.[18]

Beyond basic political knowledge, grade schoolers also develop a concept of the elements of good citizenship. Their earliest thoughts on the subject consist primarily of being a "good person." In later years, children expand the concept of good citizenship to include showing an interest in governmental affairs and participating in politics by voting.[19] As for how one should vote, children tend to think that good citizens should support those who will perform well in office, regardless of their partisanship.[20] Even so, particularly in the later grade school years, most children are able to express a preference for one political party or the other, though they often have a hard time understanding the differences between the two parties.[21]

Further political maturity comes with adolescence. High school students begin to understand major policy issues and take sides on them. They also gain an understanding of the place of interest groups in the political process, and of which groups are involved with which issues.[22] In the high school years, too, children make significant progress in understanding differences between Democrats and Republicans.[23]

The adolescent's concept of good citizenship does not change measurably during high school. It remains centered on the ideas of attention to public affairs, participation in the political process, and obedience to the laws.[24] One thing that does change, however, is the adolescent's sense of trust in the political system. Just as young children's views evolve from highly trusting to more guarded and realistic, in the high school years, idealistic views begin to give way to some distrust and cynicism. Even so, high school seniors tend to be less cynical about politics and government than their parents.[25]

What are the sources of these attitudes that children have toward the political world? Political scientists tend to think in terms of agents of socialization, that is, individuals or institutions that help confer political knowledge, and events that help socialize people to politics.

Family   The single most important socialization agent is the family, particularly parents. Even with the myriad distractions of work and modern life, children still spend a tremendous amount of time with their parents, and the bonds between parent and child are usually very close. Furthermore, parents are likely to reveal their own political beliefs in front of their children more frequently and openly than other socializing agents—teachers and peers, for example.[26]

The political attitudes of parents and their children are not always in agreement, however. A variety of factors explain the disparity. Chief among these is the communication between parents and children about politics—the quantity, clarity, and importance of that communication. If parents spend little time talking about politics in front of children, watching (and reacting to) political programming on television, or trying to teach children political values, the mechanisms of political socialization do not work as well. Therefore, if public affairs do not seem especially significant to parents, their children will also be likely to view them this way. Further, if a child does not receive a clear, consistent message about politics from his or her parents, either because the parents' views seem to be in frequent flux or because the parents in a two-parent home do not share the same beliefs, it is inevitable that the children will not fully adopt either parent's political views. Lastly, children have their own minds and can sort through information about the political world and arrive at conclusions different from those of their parents. This is particularly true when they are exposed to events or influences that are unique to their generation. For example, young people of college or draft age were more influenced by the Vietnam War than their parents and grandparents were. In addition, children—especially teenagers—sometimes take pride in small acts of rebellion against their parents. These may include adopting divergent positions on the hot political topics of the day.

The most reliable area of transmission from parent to child is identification with a political party, that is, whether one considers oneself a Democrat, Republican, independent, or something else.[27] One reason that partisanship tends to be "inherited" more easily than specific issue positions is that a parent's partisanship is much easier for a child to grasp than a parent's position on, say, Social Security reform. (Consider "My mom's a Republican" versus "My mom thinks that if the government stopped indexing retiree earnings to account for increases in average wages, the financial problems with Social Security would be much more manageable.")

▼ FAMILY MATTERS
Early time spent with family watching political programs or discussing political values helps children to develop their own political views and ideas.

▲ **VALUES AND TRADITIONS INFLUENCE IDEOLOGY**
Though churches do not often endorse a particular candidate, the religious ideals they preach can inform the values of children in the congregation.

Finally, partisanship is often deeply held and highly salient to adults. Such core beliefs tend to be transmitted most reliably.[28]

Religious institutions and traditions   Family religious traditions may also influence a child's political learning. Religious teachings are, of course, dedicated to the spiritual realm rather than the political. But different religions and denominations teach different values with respect to punishment and mercy, social justice, the importance of law and authority, equality, and so on. These values, adopted by the child in a religious context, can also play an important role in thinking about politics.

Furthermore, adherents of different religious traditions have historic affiliations with different parties and socioeconomic groups.[29] Jews, for example, tend to be Democrats, while evangelical Christians are more likely to be Republicans. In cases such as these, parents who pass their religion on to their children also may pass along part of their politics. Of course, and as we will discuss in a subsequent chapter on voting (Chapter 9), such loyalties are not set in stone. One excellent historical example of change is the movement over the last 30 years of white evangelical Christians in the South from the Democratic Party to the Republican Party.

Peer groups   The child's peer group (the friends that a child most closely associates with) will likely have a significant impact on the development of political views. This influence is particularly strong during adolescence, when children begin the transition to adulthood and spend more time with their friends, away from their parents. The salience of politics to adolescents is generally low and is largely unrelated to a child's status within peer groups.[30] Accordingly, therefore, political communication among adolescents is, in general, expected to be relatively limited, and the resulting peer-to-peer socialization is similarly limited.[31]

Educational system   Another potentially important socialization agent is the educational system. Public schools actively seek to inculcate students with a respect for the law, authority, and democratic values; an appreciation of the American political system; a sense of the meaning and importance of active democratic citizenship; and the political knowledge necessary for active, effective political participation. They also teach some of the rituals and symbolism of politics—flying the flag, reciting the Pledge of Allegiance, voting in student elections, writing to elected officials, and so on. Because schools are often homogenous, with children from similar backgrounds attending the same school, it is difficult to separate the impact of the education system from other socialization agents. Still, schools seem a very likely contributor to children's stance toward the American political system and the idea of good citizenship.[32] On the other hand, contrary to the claims of some partisans that teachers indoctrinate students with their own views, there is little evidence that school has a significant impact on partisan or issue attitudes.

The media   Political socialization depends on politically relevant information, often provided by the media. What the media choose to cover, how they choose to do so, and the accessibility of their coverage are all important political socialization questions. We will discuss the media and its effects in Chapter 10.

   Considering this brief overview of political socialization, think again about the primacy and persistence principles. Although the period from preschool through young adulthood brings dramatic change in political knowledge and sophistication, children are socialized to have generally positive predispositions toward the political system. Later in life, these positive orientations will erode somewhat, but most individuals will enter adulthood with a reservoir of support for American democratic government and, as discussed in Chapter 2, the American creed. This contributes to the relatively smooth functioning and stability of the U.S. political system.

Events that socialize can have generational, period, or life-cycle effects.

Events as well as agents contribute to political socialization. Whereas socialization by agents typically revolves around the socialization of children and young adults, events can influence the political learning of older individuals as well.

Generational effects   One kind of effect that political events can exert on public opinion is a generational effect. When a **generational effect** occurs, younger members of the body politic are influenced by events in a way that makes their attitudes and beliefs different from those of older generations. Consider the tumultuous political period of the 1960s and early 1970s, for example. For many young people coming of age in these years, the defining political events were the Vietnam War and the protest movement surrounding it. Not surprisingly, in general, those who lived through this era as young men and women, and particularly those who participated in protest politics, ended up with a distinctive—and more liberal—set of political beliefs.

   One research study found that college-educated war protesters in the 1960s did, in fact, take on a distinctive political character.[33] Because the researchers had information about the people before they went to college and knew that protesters and nonprotesters had similar backgrounds, they were able to conclude that participation in protests inspired a particular set of political attitudes, even though everyone in this generation lived through the same tumultuous time.

   For example, in 1965, the war protesters were quite similar to their college-educated, nonprotesting peers on a number of demographic and attitudinal measures. But by 1973, on the down slope of the war protest movement, the protesters differed sharply from nonprotesters in a number of ways:

- Protesters were much stronger Democratic partisans than were nonprotesters.

generational effect   the situation in which younger citizens are influenced by events in such a fashion that their attitudes and beliefs are forever rendered distinct from those of older generations.

▼ POLITICAL EXPERIENCE OFTEN SHAPES POLITICAL BELIEFS

Those involved in the Vietnam War protest movement adopted a distinctive and more liberal set of political beliefs than others in their generation.

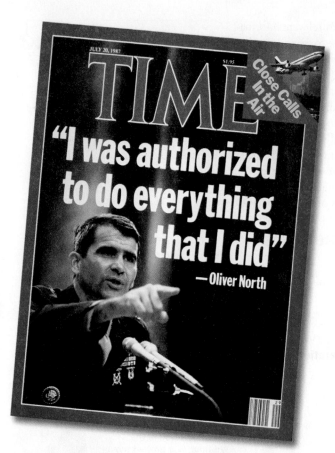

▲ **DECLINING TRUST**
Vietnam, Watergate, the protracted period of stagflation in the 1970s, the Iran-Contra affair in the late 1980s, and the Iraq War in more recent times may all have led to declining trust in government.

period effect an event that influences the attitudes and beliefs of people of all ages.

life cycle effect attitudes or physical characteristics that change as one ages, no matter the time period or generation. The graying of one's hair is a life cycle effect.

■ Protesters showed much higher support for civil liberties than did nonprotesters.

■ Protesters showed much less support for conservative groups, and much more support for women, the poor, and minorities than did nonprotesters.

■ Protesters espoused significantly more liberal issue positions than did nonprotesters.

A follow-up study in 1982 concluded that differences between the two groups were still present. Thus, those who received their "political baptism" via the Vietnam War protests maintained the distinctive set of political beliefs learned during that period. Again, because these researchers had information on the attitudes and behavior of these students before they protested, we know that "protesting" was a decisive factor and we can be confident that there was a causal relationship.

Period effects   Political events affect not only younger generations. Sometimes, events exert a noticeable impact across political generations and affect the political socialization of citizens young and old. This is known as a **period effect**. Consider, for example, responses to the following survey question:

There is much discussion as to the amount of money the government in Washington should spend for national defense and military purposes. How do you feel about this? Do you think we are spending too little, too much, or about the right amount?

Figure 7-1 presents the public's answers to this question during the period from 1969 through 2009.[34] Consider only the "too little" responses given in Figure 7-1. Note that in the early 1970s, only a small percentage of Americans thought that the country was spending too little on national defense. But by the mid-1970s, the number of Americans who held that belief doubled once, and then, surprisingly, doubled again. What caused this dramatic shift? One political scientist suggests it was a combination of two factors. First, this period saw a substantial decline in defense spending as a percentage of the federal budget and as a percentage of gross domestic product. Second, a series of disturbing foreign policy events rocked the world: the fall of South Vietnam, Cambodia, and Nicaragua to communist forces; the Soviet military build-up and takeover of Afghanistan; and the hostage crisis at the American embassy in Iran.[35] Notice also the substantial increase in those who believed we were spending too little from 1990 to 2000. In 1990, only 7 percent believed we were spending too little on national defense, yet in August 2000, that number had grown to 40 percent. To produce such substantial shifts in public opinion, these events must have pushed virtually every age group in the same direction—toward support of more defense spending. Both of these examples are clear illustrations of the period effect.

Life cycle effects   Finally, one factor that can have an impact on political opinions is less an event than a process—the process of getting older. In the **life cycle effect**,

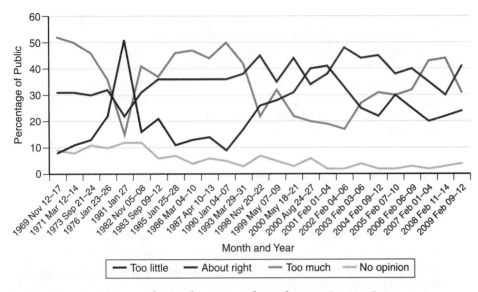

Legend: — Too little — About right — Too much — No opinion

FIGURE 7-1. Support for Defense Spending Shows a Strong Surge, 1969–2009. After reaching a low point in the early 1970s, at the end of the Vietnam War, support for defense spending surged through the late 1970s and early 1980s with the election of Ronald Reagan. Public attitudes also shifted significantly in the 1990s as conflicts in the Middle East escalated.

just as common understanding suggests, individuals tend to get more conservative as they grow older and more secure in their political beliefs. Consider again the study of Vietnam War protesters and their nonprotesting peers. As mentioned above, the impact of the war and protest politics appears to have made the protesters a substantially more left-leaning group than nonprotesters of the same age. Even so, the study found both groups moving in a more conservative direction, with the protesters doing so at a more rapid pace. In other words, although protesters remained more liberal, the groups grew more alike, and more conservative, as they aged.

The same basic phenomenon can be observed in Americans' description of themselves as "liberal" or "conservative." As they age, survey respondents are more likely to declare themselves conservative—a classic life cycle effect.[36] Americans also grow more secure in their partisan attachments as they grow older: they are increasingly likely to side with the Democratic or Republican parties and less likely to say that they are politically independent.[37]

Political Knowledge and Ideology

7-3 Assess the extent to which American public opinion is based on political knowledge.

The term "public opinion" contains the word "opinion" for a good reason: democratic governance requires the public to have opinions, or preferences, regarding candidates and policy decisions. Only by developing such opinions can the public express its will at the ballot box and through other forms of direct political action. And only by expressing these preferences can the public guide policy makers in their day-to-day decision-making, and ultimately hold political leaders accountable for the choices they make and the consequences of those choices.

Developing an informed opinion about matters of government, politics, and public policy requires some basic knowledge. For example, before deciding on a preferred presidential candidate, a citizen must at least know who is running and, in general terms, how the candidates will govern if elected. Without this basic information, a voter will be unable to make an informed choice among presidential candidates.

Americans possess less political knowledge than they should, but more than is alleged.

Unfortunately, at least from the perspective of democratic theory, American adults have generally low levels of knowledge regarding American politics, government, and current news (see Table 7-2). In a 2010 survey, only 32 percent of Americans knew the number of Republican senators who voted for the health care bill (zero), and roughly 70 percent of Americans did not know the chair of the Republican National Committee (Michael Steele). What's more, just over half of all respondents could say what the current unemployment rate is closest to (10 percent), while only 56 percent knew that there was more than one woman on the Supreme Court. Only 6 in 10 (59 percent) could correctly say which country holds the most U.S. debt (China).[38]

TABLE 7-2. Basic Political Knowledge Among Americans Adults

YEAR	QUESTION	KNOW	DON'T KNOW/ REFUSED/INCORRECT
2010	Who holds the most U.S. debt? (China)	59%	41%
2010	U.S. imports how much of the oil it consumes? (two-thirds)	57%	43%
2010	Number of women on Supreme Court of the United States? (More than one)	56%	44%
2010	What is the current unemployment rate? (10 percent)	55%	45%
2010	What country was the attempted Christmas Day bomber trained in? (Yemen)	50%	50%
2010	In 2009, were there more deaths in Iraq or Afghanistan? (Afghanistan)	43%	57%
2010	Do you know who Stephen Colbert is? (Comedian and TV host)	41%	49%
2010	Who is the majority leader of the U.S. Senate? (Harry Reid)	39%	61%
2010	What is the Dow Jones currently at or around? (Around 10,000)	36%	64%
2010	How many GOP senators voted for the health bill? (Zero)	32%	68%
2010	Who chairs the GOP National Committee? (Michael Steele)	32%	68%
2010	How many votes does it take in the Senate to break a filibuster?	26%	74%
2007	Who is the current vice president?	69%	31%
2007	Who is your current state governor?	66%	34%
2007	Who is the president of Russia?	36%	64%
2007	Who is Nancy Pelosi?	49%	51%
2007	Can you identify Dick Cheney/Robert Gates?	21%	79%

Source: "Political Knowledge Update Survey," Pew Research Center, January 14-16, 2010, and "What Americans Know: 1987–2007," Pew Research Center, April 15, 2007.

These numbers are certainly eye-opening but not sufficiently comprehensive to determine the extent of political knowledge and ignorance within the American electorate. A more thorough study conducted over 10 years ago of American knowledge of politics and government was based on more than 50 years' worth of survey questions. To excerpt the conclusions:

> Only 13 percent of the more than 2,000 political questions examined could be answered correctly by 75 percent or more of those asked, and only 41 percent could be answered correctly by more than half the public. Many of the facts known by relatively small percentages of the public seem critical to understanding—let alone effectively acting in—the political world: fundamental rules of the game; classic civil liberties; key concepts of political economy; the names of key political representatives; many important policy positions of presidential candidates or the political parties; basic social indicators; and significant public policies.[39]

Even with the advent of social media and the influx of information sharing on the Internet, low levels of political knowledge remain. A more recent study in 2007 concludes that Americans continue to possess low levels of knowledge regarding the political environment. Only 69 percent of participants could name the current vice president, while only 66 percent could name their own state's governor. Similarly, just less than half could identify Nancy Pelosi and only 21 percent could identify Dick Cheney or Robert Gates.[40] These pessimistic findings are not the whole story, however. It was also found that a significant proportion of the American public is aware of key governmental institutions and processes, civil liberties, and economic terms. The public could also identify the politicians at the very top of government along with the policies endorsed by prominent politicians—both historic and contemporary.[41] To characterize these contrasting conclusions, then, one might say that while Americans do not know as much about politics as one would wish, nor as much as they should in order to be highly effective democratic citizens, they do possess some substantial political knowledge—more, in fact, than is often alleged.

How does Americans' political knowledge stack up in comparative terms? It's a mixed picture, although one in which the United States does not fare particularly well. For example, an eight-nation survey conducted in 1994, which tested knowledge of international affairs, finds Americans finishing in the bottom three countries, ahead of only Mexico and Spain (Table 7-3). Thirty-seven percent of Americans were

TABLE 7-3. Knowledge of Foreign Affairs in Comparative Perspective (percentage correct)

	CANADA	FRANCE	GERMANY	ITALY	MEXICO	SPAIN	UNITED KINGDOM	UNITED STATES
President of Russia?	59	61	94	76	42	65	63	50
Country threatening to withdraw from nonproliferation treaty	12	7	45	26	6	5	11	22
Who is Boutros Boutros Ghali?	26	32	58	43	14	15	22	13
Ethnic group that has conquered much of Bosnia	42	55	77	51	12	24	46	28
Name of group with whom Israelis recently reached peace accord	51	60	79	56	21	29	59	40
Answered four or five correctly	19	25	58	34	8	10	18	15
Answered none correctly	27	23	3	18	41	32	22	37
Mean number correct	1.92	2.13	3.55	2.49	1.22	1.35	2.01	1.53

Source: Michael X. Delli Carpini and Scott Keeter, *What Americans Know About Politics and Why It Matters* (New Haven, CT: Yale University Press, 1996), 89–90.

unable to answer correctly any of the five survey questions—the highest percentage among the participating countries. More recent findings suggest that knowledge in foreign affairs has not gotten any better. Only 36 percent of respondents in a 2007 study could correctly name the president of Russia.[42] Barely half of respondents in another survey knew that Hugo Chavez is the president of Venezuela, while only 46 percent knew that Kosovo declared independence from Serbia.[43] More striking, however, is Americans' lack of knowledge regarding Iraq's involvement, or lack thereof, in the September 11, 2001, terrorist attacks. In a 2003 survey, only one-sixth of respondents knew that none of the hijackers were from Iraq, while almost half (44 percent) said that at least one hijacker was from Iraq.[44]

Americans fared somewhat better when the task was limited to naming world leaders. In a 1986 survey that inquired about the heads of government in the United States, United Kingdom, France, West Germany, Italy, and Japan, Americans scored at the top in terms of their ability to name their own president (compared to, say, Italians' ability to name the Italian prime minister). Americans generally lagged behind the other countries in their ability to name European heads of state, but they did as well as or better than all but one country (Italy) in naming the prime minister of Japan (Table 7-4).

ThinkingComparatively

Americans exhibit lower levels of political knowledge than citizens of most European countries.

Americans are ideologically innocent.

Having examined what Americans know about politics, the next logical question is: how well are they able to use their knowledge to form political opinions? The seminal study of this question was published in 1964 by University of Michigan scholar Philip Converse. Converse's research is still the starting point in any discussion of the sophistication of political thinking among the public at large.

The study painted a fairly gloomy picture of Americans' political sophistication. Converse concluded Americans lacked the capacity for well-developed, informed political thought. He went on to declare most of the American public "innocent" of organized, logical, structured political thinking.[45] Converse argued that Americans' political beliefs often had little internal logic, and sometimes appeared to be arrived at without any application of forethought or reasoning. Not only, said Converse, do Americans not think about politics with anywhere near the sophistication of politicians and political journalists, they probably are largely incapable of doing so.

Converse proposed a "black and white" model of public opinion. According to this model, some particularly attentive citizens have stable and coherent attitudes, but most people change attitudes on issues almost with the same frequency as if they were flipping a coin to determine what they thought.

TABLE 7-4. Knowledge of Political Leaders in Comparative Perspective (percentage correct)

	WEST GERMANS	FRENCH	BRITISH	ITALIANS	AMERICANS
President of United States	94	94	93	95	99
Prime Minister of United Kingdom	80	89	96	77	74
President of France	64	99	55	76	34
Chancellor of West Germany	95	59	17	37	16
Prime Minister of Italy	39	18	2	89	6
Prime Minister of Japan	19	17	4	23	19

Source: Michael X. Delli Carpini and Scott Keeter, *What Americans Know About Politics and Why It Matters* (New Haven, CT: Yale University Press, 1996), 91.

When asked to offer opinions on specific policy issues, large proportions of the public simply had no substantively meaningful opinions to offer. This absence of opinions did not stop the public from offering answers to survey questions. In a separate publication, Converse referred to such hollow answers as an expression of "nonattitudes."

Many scholars argue that the American public may not be politically ignorant.

One possible response to Converse is that he did his research at a particularly quiet time in American politics—the late 1950s and early 1960s. Converse had completed his analysis over 50 years ago—before the Kennedy assassination and Vietnam, before the major race riots of the 1960s, before Watergate and stagflation, before the Reagan Revolution of 1980 and the terrorist attacks of September 11, 2001. Perhaps if he had undertaken his analysis a few years later, in a more turbulent or ideologically charged period, he would have found Americans more engaged in issues of politics and government.

Another response challenging Converse's argument is that, inevitably, survey responses are flawed. The apparent flip-flopping of opinions over time, and the failure of respondents' answers to "hang together" in logical ways, may result as much from poorly worded questions as from genuine randomness of respondent opinions. The instability and lack of logical groupings one sees in survey responses are, as one commentator put it, a product of "fuzzy measures and fuzzy citizens."[46]

Another line of criticism relates to Converse's treatment of the concept of ideology. Specifically, critics have complained that a simple left/right, liberal/conservative concept of ideology is far too narrow. Americans are capable of ideological thinking, this line of argumentation goes, but only ideological thinking that can be captured in the limited terms typically used by political leaders. Furthermore, these critics argue, surveys typically are not well designed to capture the complexity of Americans' thinking about politics. How can a format that forces respondents into a limited choice among one- or two-word responses accurately capture the fullness of an opinion, or the processing of ideas and information that took place in order to arrive at that opinion?

Another interesting possibility about the nature of individual Americans' opinions on specific policy issues also has a bearing on Converse's claims. Perhaps people do not have perfectly formed attitudes that correspond to the specific answers required by survey questions. Instead, they possess a mix of considerations.[47] Think of a bunch of ping-pong balls in your head, each with a competing thought about a particular issue.

For some people, that mix of ideas might be more or less a 50–50 proposition. One person, for example, might have a head full of competing ideas on abortion, about half of which suggest that abortion should remain legal and the other half of which suggest it should be outlawed. Another person on another issue, though, might have a more lopsided mix. For example, most of what he or she knows might suggest the wisdom of tougher gun control laws, but he or she might also recognize instances in which gun laws are fine as is, or perhaps even too restrictive.

What happens when someone with a head full of different, sometimes inconsistent ideas is asked a question in a survey?

▼ MAJOR EVENTS MAY CHARGE OPINIONS

Major events like the Kennedy assassination have a tendency to engage people in politics more actively.

The survey respondent answers by making reference to whatever considerations happen to be most accessible at the moment—that is, by giving an answer based on those ideas that, at that moment, are at the forefront of his or her mind.

Think again about the person with a head full of ideas on abortion, half of which could be classified as "pro-choice" and half "pro-life." One morning, that person reads a newspaper article about pro-life activists blocking access to a family planning clinic. This action strikes her as inappropriate—as long as abortion is legal, she thinks, people should have access to clinics. That afternoon, she receives a call from a pollster who asks a question about abortion rights. Most salient in the respondent's mind is a vague feeling of unease with pro-lifers, based on her reading of the morning's newspaper article. Accordingly, she tells the pollster that she supports abortion rights and would describe herself as pro-choice, even though her enduring opinion is not so black and white.

Consider, too, the case of the person with predominantly pro–gun control ideas but also a handful of ideas sympathetic to the gun rights movement. Under normal circumstances, we would expect this person to answer a survey question about gun control in a sympathetic fashion. Most of her ideas, after all, are supportive of more gun control, so it is likely that one of those ideas will be at the top of her head when the pollster calls. But what if she has just heard a story from a neighbor who successfully defended his home against a break-in by brandishing a handgun? The burglar fled, and the neighbor and his family were safe. This kind of story does not fit with most of the ideas about gun control that our hypothetical citizen has in her head. But if a pollster should call while this story is still fresh in her mind, she might very well give an answer supportive of more gun rights. Why? Because those considerations happened to be at the top of her head when the survey interviewer telephoned.

ThinkingCausally

What factors might contribute to an individual's instability in survey response over time?

Over time, then, the same respondent might give very different answers to the same questions, depending on what considerations or ideas happen to be at the forefront of his or her mind at the time of the survey. This would produce the very thing that Converse found in his study—a high level of response instability.

This instability could suggest that many people were simply "making up" a response, on the fly, in order to accommodate the interviewer, meaning that respondents had no substantive thoughts on the issue. Although survey respondents very often do not have complete, fully formed attitudes on public policy issues, this limitation is not the same as saying that they have "nonattitudes" and simply invent answers to satisfy survey interviewers. Instead, they have a variety of ideas about a specific issue. Yet those ideas typically do not form a cohesive, stable stance that mirrors ideological categories—either with respect to one particular issue, or from one issue to the next.

▼ **RECENT EVENTS MAY DRIVE SURVEY RESPONSE**
Here students gather to mourn victims of the 2007 Virginia Tech shooting. Below, customers at a Starbucks demonstrate their right to bear arms in public. Our views in combination with the stories and ideas that we have heard most recently will influence our response to a survey question on gun control.

CaseStudy: An Experiment in Nonattitudes

The phrase "nonattitudes" refers to the hastily concocted, largely baseless opinions that some people offer when asked to comment on political topics of which they have little or no genuine knowledge. In 1978, some enterprising researchers carried the concept of the nonattitude to its logical extreme. If people are willing to essentially fabricate opinions on real political issues, they wondered, might they do the same if asked about an imaginary one?[48]

To answer this question, the researchers asked a random sample of survey respondents about a completely fictitious piece of legislation, the "1975 Public Affairs Act." Specifically, respondents were asked this question: "Some people say that the 1975 Public Affairs Act should be repealed. Do you agree or disagree with the idea that the 1975 Public Affairs Act should be repealed?"

In one version of the survey, the researchers found that one-third of respondents were willing to offer an opinion on the repeal of the imaginary legislation. Rather than volunteering the fact that they had never heard of the 1975 Public Affairs Act, respondents politely gave the pollsters an opinion. (About 16 percent supported repeal, and about 18 percent opposed it.)

The researchers then decided to make it somewhat easier for respondents to admit they had never heard of the 1975 Public Affairs Act. They asked the question somewhat differently: "Some people say that the 1975 Public Affairs Act should be repealed. Have you been interested enough in this to favor one side over the other?" Though survey respondents were given an easy out, 7 percent still insisted that they had heard of, and had an opinion on, the wholly fictitious legislation.

"IT TURNS OUT WE'RE SIXTY PERCENT INACCURATE, THIRTY PERCENT MISTAKEN, AND TEN PERCENT WRONG!"

◄ **BACK AND FORTH**
Polls may reflect fuzzy people, fuzzy questions, or a more complicated underlying process for forming and reporting opinions.

273

ThinkingCritically

1. Think of several reasons why American citizens seem to be so poorly informed politically. Should we be concerned, or is this predictable and benign?

2. What implications does this study have for researchers crafting survey questions?

Making Public Opinion Work in a Democracy

7-4 Establish how American democracy functions despite the public's low levels of political knowledge.

Although political knowledge and sophistication among Americans may be somewhat lacking, there are certain reassuring regularities in the ebb and flow of public opinion. For example, when a president performs poorly in office, the public usually recognizes this, reduces its collective approval of his job performance, and ultimately denies him reelection. Likewise, when a president performs well in office, the public recognizes this, too, and typically rewards the president with high job approval numbers and another term. Similarly, the public will often react in orderly, predictable ways to shifts in public policy.

The miracle of aggregation can compensate for low levels of information among the mass public.

miracle of aggregation the phenomenon that occurs when a group consists of individuals who are largely ignorant of a particular issue, but their collective opinion tends to make sense.

Recall the example presented at the beginning of this chapter, with common men and women accurately guessing the weight of an ox. It illustrates a paradox that has often been referred to as the **miracle of aggregation**. The "miracle" is that, even though a group of individuals can be largely ignorant of a particular phenomenon, when their opinions are aggregated, their collective opinion tends to make sense.

Here is how the miracle of aggregation works. Imagine an American public in which only 30 percent of the people paid close attention to politics and the other 70 percent were completely ignorant. Now imagine that politicians are looking for guidance from the public on whether to undertake a dramatic reform of the Social Security program. According to the terms of our example, 70 percent of the public has no real opinion on the matter. But let's assume that, of the other 30 percent, two-thirds want reform and one-third do not. Now we have 20 percent of the electorate that wants reform, 10 percent that does not, and 70 percent that have no idea.

As shown above, even completely ignorant members of the public will often give answers to survey questions just to be polite, or perhaps not to seem as ignorant of a particular issue as they really are. Let us assume, then, that the 70 percent split equally on the Social Security question—35 percent for reform and 35 percent for no reform. (There is no reason to believe that individuals essentially inventing their answers to a survey question should favor one side more than the other.)

Now the picture of public opinion on the issue looks like this: 55 percent support reform and 45 percent do not. Notice what has happened: Opinion from the public as a whole, including the great mass of ignorant individuals, conveys the same message to policy makers as opinion from only the informed 30 percent: Americans want Social Security reform. A miracle!

As long as the random opinions of uninformed members of the public cancel each other out, policy makers will get a clear, meaningful signal that accurately reflects the wishes of those who are paying attention. This result may cause some anguish for those who would like the entire public to be aware, interested, and informed. However, the miracle of aggregation at least provides a way for the truly interested and informed to see their policy preferences accurately represented to decision makers.

Opinion leaders shape what the public thinks about and what they think about it.

Studies of public opinion typically divide the American public into three segments: those who pay very close attention to politics, those who are generally indifferent to politics but pay attention sporadically, and those who pay no attention to politics at all. There are debates over the relative size of these different segments, but the most attentive group is likely to be a small one, and on particularly obscure issues, extremely small.

That this most attentive group is small, however, does not mean that it lacks significant influence. In fact, many of the members of this group can be considered "opinion

◄ A member of Congress is shown here checking his e-mail or perhaps even trying his hand at Twittering.

leaders." **Opinion leaders** are people who can legitimately claim high levels of interest and expertise in politics and seek to communicate their political beliefs to others. This group may include political writers and journalists, politicians, political professionals (lobbyists, pollsters, campaign consultants, association executives), bloggers, academic political scientists, community activists, and garden-variety "political junkies."

Opinion leaders make it their business to send strong signals to the public regarding which political issues are important and what the public ought to think about them. An opinion leader can communicate with a member of the public as impersonally as through television or as intimately as over a cup of coffee. Increasingly, leaders are attempting to communicate with people through e-mail and text messages. Many opinion leaders are also trying to take advantage of social media like Facebook and Twitter to communicate their take on issues to constituents and supporters. Either way, the mass public can become informed quickly and easily through the efforts of opinion leaders.

You can see an example of opinion leadership by looking at the results of the "most important problem" question over the years. Periodically, polling organizations have asked the American public the following question: "What do you think is the most important problem facing the country today?" In April 2009, only 9 percent of the public identified health care as America's most important problem. A mere four months later, however, in August 2009, that number had risen to 20 percent. Clearly, the health care situation in the United States had remained unchanged in those two months. What had changed, however, was that members of Congress began debating the urgent need for reform in the health care system. The media carried that message from the Congress through television and newspaper coverage of this debate, and through commentary and editorials of their own. Various opinion leaders continued this "trickle down" process, discussing the issue in town hall meetings and personal conversations. The polling data indicate that at least part of the public ultimately got the message coming out of Congress. Consider one other case: global warming. The Gallup polling organization asked the American public six times between 1992 and 2004 how well it thought it understood the issue of global warming. In 1992, when Gallup first asked the question, 22 percent responded "not at all." By 2008, however, that number was down to 2 percent.[49] Clearly, in that 16-year interim, the American public got the message from opinion leaders—most obviously the media and the president—that they ought to be paying attention to this issue.[50]

opinion leaders individuals with high levels of interest and expertise in politics who seek to communicate their political beliefs to others.

Beyond giving the public cues about what issues it should be thinking about, opinion leaders also help shape how the public thinks about certain issues. In one scholarly study, for example, researchers identified 80 different questions that were asked at least twice on a variety of surveys from 1969 to 1983. In many cases, opinion had changed noticeably between the first time the question was asked and the second. In explaining these changes, the researchers found that changes in public opinion corresponded significantly with television news commentary—in other words, messages from opinion leaders.[51]

Partisanship simplifies political judgments.

Unlike many other aspects of public opinion, most voters have a self-defined, stable affiliation with a political party. In making judgments about the political world, then, they can use partisanship as a cue.[52] The partisan affiliation of a political candidate communicates a tremendous amount of information. If you are a Democrat, for example, you know that you are much more likely to agree with the policy preferences of Democrats than those of Republicans, without having to sort through each and every position of a particular candidate. If you vote strictly along party lines, you may regret your choice occasionally, but for the most part a vote for your party versus the other party will tend to be consistent with your preferred outcome. Similarly, if you are a Republican, you know that most of the policy proposals from your party's leaders are likely to be more acceptable to you than proposals from the Democrats. Knowing that your party proposed them provides you with some assurance that the ideas make sense.[53]

The same basic logic applies to your approval or disapproval of the job performance of policy makers, from the president on down. If they share your partisan affiliation, it is likely that you will agree, on the whole, with the policy choices they are making. You may not know the details of those choices, but because you are members of the same party, you know that you probably share the same broad set of beliefs. With that knowledge, you can have some confidence that if time permits you to follow their performance closely, you will likely approve of the job they are doing.[54] We will have much more to say about partisanship and party identification in Chapter 9.

Moderately politically attentive "scorekeepers" cause most aggregate public opinion change.

One political scientist proposes that the middle stratum of Americans referred to above—the group that is only moderately attentive to politics—serves an important "scorekeeping" function.[55] This group has little passion for politics and does not think about the political world in ideological terms. It pays just enough attention to politics to pick up on signals indicating big changes—for example, a change from peace to war, from recession to recovery, from bipartisan cooperation to acrimony and scandal, or from a conservative bent in social policy to a liberal one. The scorekeepers, in other words, keep a running tally of "how things are going" in very broad, very general policy areas. When they pick up a signal that a noticeable change has occurred, they change their opinions accordingly. According to this view, those changes account for most of the movement in aggregate public opinion. Furthermore, they are connected to real-world events in a fairly logical, orderly fashion that results in government accountability.

These are just some of the shortcuts that help the public arrive at collectively rational opinions about politics and government. Certainly, these shortcuts help mitigate some of the potential consequences of low voter sophistication and keep policy makers aware of, and generally accountable to, the public. But American public opinion remains a very mixed picture, full of attitudes and nonattitudes, contradictory beliefs, loosely and fleetingly held considerations, authentic opinions, strong value commitments, vast stretches of ignorance and indifference, and isolated oases of knowledge, all mixed together.

CHAPTER SUMMARY

In this chapter you have learned to:

7-1   Define public opinion and identify its four basic traits.
Public opinion is a subject at the heart of democratic theory, and it has four basic traits: salience, stability, direction, and intensity. It is challenging but crucial for leaders to know and understand public opinion in terms of all these traits and patterns.

7-2   Outline the process and agents of political socialization. Political socialization is the process by which citizens acquire the values and attitudes that shape their thinking about politics. It tends to be governed by two important principles: primacy and persistence, both of which point to the importance of early childhood learning. There are several phases of socialization from early childhood all the way through young adulthood, and the development of ideological thinking demonstrates increased political sophistication. Socialization occurs through specific agents of socialization and socializing events. Although the family is foremost among agents of socialization, socializing events include generational effects, period effects, and life cycle effects.

7-3   Assess the extent to which American public opinion is based on political knowledge. Political knowledge among the American public is somewhat lacking. Large proportions of the public simply have no substantively meaningful opinions to offer when faced with political survey questions. Not surprisingly, Americans' capacity to translate their knowledge into opinions is also less than desirable. Political scientist Philip Converse's work was particularly important to these discoveries. Although much subsequent research has taken issue with Converse's findings and not all of the conclusions hold today, a large proportion of what we know about public opinion has come about as scholars have addressed and often challenged the findings from the original work.

7-4   Establish how American democracy functions despite the public's low levels of political knowledge.
American public opinion collectively makes sense in many cases. Despite the lack of political knowledge and sophistication at the individual level, collective opinion is often rational, ordered, and predictable. A number of shortcuts and devices enable the American public to communicate to policy makers a collectively ordered, rational set of preferences.

PEARSON mypoliscilab **EXERCISES**

Apply what you learned in this chapter by starting with these resources on MyPoliSciLab.

Read on mypoliscilab.com

eText: Chapter 7

✓• **Study and Review on mypoliscilab.com**

 Pre-Test
 Post-Test
 Chapter Exam
 Flashcards

Watch on mypoliscilab.com

 Video: Opinion Poll on the U.S. Economy
 Video: Obama Approval Rating

Explore on mypoliscilab.com

 Simulation: You Are a Polling Consultant
 Comparative: Comparing Governments and Public Opinion
 Timeline: War, Peace and Public Opinion

KEY TERMS

direction, p. 255
generational effect, p. 265
ideology, p. 257
intensity, p. 255
life cycle effect, p. 266
margin of error, p. 259
miracle of aggregation, p. 259

nonresponse bias, p. 260
opinion leaders, p. 275
period effect, p. 266
persistence, p. 257
political socialization, p. 257
primacy, p. 257
public opinion, p. 255

random sample, p. 259
salience, p. 255
sampling, p. 259
sampling error, p. 259
stability, p. 255

SUGGESTED READINGS

Robert Erickson and Kent Tedin. 2005. *American Public Opinion: Its Origins, Content, and Impact*. New York: Longman. An excellent text that covers a wide range of information about the measurement, nature, and importance of public opinion.

Morris Fiorina. 2006. *Culture War? The Myth of a Polarized America*. New York: Longman. Argues that Americans are not nearly as divided on major political issues as many commentators claim.

Paul M. Sniderman, Richard A. Brody, and Philip E. Tetlock. 1991. *Reasoning and Choice: Explorations in Political Psychology*. Cambridge: Cambridge University Press. Argues that ordinary citizens who pay little attention to politics can still make reasonable decisions based on particular shortcuts.

James Stimson. 2004. *Tides of Consent: How Public Opinion Shapes American Politics*. Cambridge: Cambridge University Press. Although the public rarely engages in politics, when public opinion is aroused, major changes in policy result.

Herbert Weisberg, Jon Krosnick, and Bruce Bowen. 1996. *An Introduction to Survey Research, Polling, and Data Analysis*. Thousand Oaks, CA: Sage. The basics of how to conduct and analyze survey research, with information on sampling, question writing, and interviewing techniques.

John Zaller. 1992. *The Nature and Origins of Mass Opinion*. New York: Cambridge University Press. Argues that people sample from a mix of political considerations in their head when confronted with the need to make political decisions or share political attitudes.

SUGGESTED WEBSITES

Gallup: www.gallup.com

Gallup conducts regular public opinion polls on timely topics. This site provides links to surveys on the 2008 elections.

The Pew Research Center for the People and the Press: people-press.org

The Pew center is an independent opinion research group that studies attitudes toward the press, politics, and public policy issues. Pew conducts regular national surveys to measure public attentiveness to major news stories. This site provides links to recent surveys.

Pollster.com: www.pollster.com

Taking advantage of the proliferation of publicly released polls, this site aggregates and tracks public opinion across a wide range of issues. It features expert commentary on the practice of polling and clear graphical presentation of data.

The Center for Information and Research on Civic Learning and Engagement (CIRCLE): www.civicyouth.org

CIRCLE conducts research on the civic and political engagement of Americans between the ages of 15 and 25.

Declare Yourself: www.declareyourself.com

This website was home to the popular "Vote or Die" campaign to raise political awareness in youth. The site provides answers to questions from inexperienced voters as well as information on voter registration.

MoveOn: www.moveon.org

MoveOn.org Civic Action is a nonprofit organization dedicated to education and advocacy on what they deem important national issues. The website links to campaigns, political advertisements, and opportunities for political participation.

Tea Party Movement: www.freedomworks.org

This website gives information on the Tea Party, its ideals, and the motives behind its members. FreedomWorks is a conservative-leaning organization that advocates less government and lower taxes.

Because this chapter mentions political socialization, here are a couple of Web sites geared to children:

White House Kids Homepage: www.whitehouse.gov/kids

The White House Kids Homepage is designed to familiarize young children with presidential history and politics. Children and their parents can read about presidential history, play games, and connect to news stories.

Congress for Kids: www.congressforkids.net

The Congress for Kids site provides an easy-to-navigate congressional tutorial and online tours of Congress.

Literacy Tests

Political participation is the effort to influence what happens in the political world—either by voting or by doing things like writing letters, signing petitions, or attending a demonstration to influence political officials or the public at large. Now, imagine that you want to participate in politics by voting in an election for president, governor, Congress, or a local office, but you are required to answer the following questions:

1. The only laws that can be passed to apply to an area in a federal arsenal are those passed by _____ provided consent for the purchase of the land is given by the _____.
2. Appropriation of money for the armed services can be only for a period limited to _____ years.
3. A United States senator elected at the general election in November takes office the following year on what date _____?

These are actual questions from a test given to African Americans attempting to vote in Alabama in the late 1950s and early 1960s.[1] The questions varied from state to state, but these are fairly typical of the obscure facts that African Americans were required to know in order to vote in many southern states. Known as literacy tests, they were a sham created primarily to bar blacks from voting. Literacy tests and other hurdles such as the poll tax (which required a person to pay a fee to register to vote) were relatively tame compared to the violence and intimidation that black Americans faced when they tried to exercise their rights to participate in American democracy.

For black Americans, freedom and the ability to participate in American politics were obtained piecemeal. The Civil War and the Emancipation Proclamation freed blacks from slavery. The Fourteenth Amendment to the U.S. Constitution, ratified in 1868, conferred citizenship upon African Americans and, through protection of civil liberties, further guaranteed political liberty to blacks, though women were still excluded from the right to vote. Although you might assume that citizenship included the right to vote, southern states nonetheless systematically turned black men away at the polls. Pressure mounted to provide a constitutional guarantee of black voting rights. Accordingly, in 1870, the Fifteenth Amendment was passed. It stated, "the right of citizens of the United States to vote shall not be denied by the United States or by any state on account of race, color, or previous condition of physical servitude."

Despite the amendment, many barriers to voting remained, including physical intimidation (even death),

▼ LITERACY TESTS

Literacy tests gained infamy as a means for denying the franchise to African Americans. In a number of states, these tests were used to disenfranchise many literate southern blacks while allowing many illiterate southern whites to vote.

literacy tests, and poll taxes. The results of these measures were striking. In 1960, nearly 100 years after the end of the Civil War, the number of African Americans registered to vote in some southern states was around one-tenth of the number of eligible voters. In Mississippi, for example, only 5.2 percent of African Americans were registered. The figure was 13.7 percent in Alabama and 12.7 percent in South Carolina. The comparable figures for white citizens in those states were 63.9 percent in Mississippi, 63.6 percent in Alabama, and 57.1 percent in South Carolina. Overall, 29.1 percent of African Americans were registered in the 11 southern states that had formerly comprised the Confederacy, compared to 61.1 percent of white citizens.[2] The differential between blacks and whites was reduced only when the 1965 Voting Rights Act gave the federal government new powers to enforce the promises made in the Fifteenth Amendment.

But it took another 45 years for African Americans to pass the next and greatest barrier. On November 4, 2008, the end of more than 200 years of disenfranchisement of an entire people could be seen in the tears streaming down the cheeks of people like Jesse Jackson and talk-show host Oprah Winfrey as they watched President-elect Barack Obama deliver his victory speech in Chicago. Up until that election, the cost/benefit perspective could explain why African Americans shied away from the voting booth. Facing severe costs—including physical violence—the benefits seemed meager. But in 2008, the prospect of the first African American president compelled many people to wait for 12 hours in line to vote and increased participation of blacks by 4.9 percent.[3] The cost was now worth the benefit. Recognizing how these costs and benefits interact is a major theme of political participation and helps political scientists understand why people choose to vote.

CHAPTER LEARNING OBJECTIVES

After reading this chapter you will be able to:

8-1 Analyze the costs and benefits of political participation for individuals and groups.

8-2 Identify the different kinds of political activities in which Americans participate.

8-3 Outline the main factors that influence political participation.

8-4 Analyze voter turnout from comparative and historical perspectives and assess explanations.

8-5 Assess whether differences in groups' political participation matters and whether participation itself matters.

The Paradox of Political Participation

8-1 Analyze the costs and benefits of political participation for individuals and groups.

If you have ever voted on Election Day, volunteered for a political campaign, or written a letter to a public official advocating a certain position, you had to make a decision beforehand about whether these actions were worth your time and effort. Many people in America engage in these sorts of activities, but just as many—and usually more—choose not to. In fact, as we will see in the next section, about half of America's citizens engage only in voting, and most do not vote in all the elections available to them.[4] Political scientists have studied why some people get involved in politics and others do not, borrowing language and ideas from another discipline—economics. These political scientists believe that decisions about whether or not to participate in politics depend in large part on individual evaluations about the costs and benefits of political activity.

Citizens weigh costs and benefits in deciding whether to vote.

Although we will illustrate the cost/benefit concept with the most common kind of political participation—voting—the basic logic we outline here holds for other sorts of political activities. Assume that your decision about whether or not to vote depends on your weighing the relative costs and benefits of voting. First, consider the costs of voting. These costs include the time and effort required for you to register to vote or to update your registration, to travel to a polling place, to wait in line, and to cast your vote. The costs also include the time you spent determining how to register or reregister, finding out where your polling place is, and perhaps the most time-consuming aspect, learning enough about the different candidates and issues to make educated choices.

Now, consider the benefits of voting. If your vote helps elect your preferred candidate, some or all of his or her policies—policies that you support—will be adopted. Depending on your political preferences, some of the benefits you would receive from voting might include lower taxes, more money for student loans, a new federal highway near your hometown, increased Social Security benefits for your grandparents, or other policy changes the candidate has promised.

The final element in your decision about whether or not to vote involves a comparison of the costs and benefits of voting. If the benefits to you outweigh the costs, you will vote. If they do not, you will stay at home.

It is unlikely that a single individual will influence an election outcome or political decision.

Initially, the potential benefits of voting would seem to outweigh the costs and you would decide to vote. For example, even if you have to spend a half-hour on the Internet figuring out how to register, or use a lunch break or hire a babysitter in order to be able to cast a ballot, those costs are minor compared to the benefits of more generous student loans, expanded health care, lower payroll taxes, and the other policy changes your candidate favors. But this calculation assumes that your candidate needs your vote in order to win.

What if your candidate could win without your vote? Then you could enjoy all of the benefits of voting—specifically, the policy changes that your candidate will bring about when he or she wins—without experiencing any of the costs of voting. And, if that were true, why would you bother voting? The only cases in which your vote would be decisive are if your vote causes or breaks a tie. In all other cases, whether you vote or not, the winner will be the same.

Looking at the history of elections, even local elections with very few voters involved, it is exceedingly rare that an election is decided by a single vote. In fact, for all intents and purposes, you can assume before any particular election that your vote will not decide the outcome. Whether you stay home or cast your ballot, the election result will be the same. From this perspective it makes no sense for you to vote ever. Yet every Election Day, Americans vote by the millions. That they do so, even though they could enjoy the benefits of voting without bearing the costs of casting a ballot, is the paradox of voting.

This paradox applies to other types of political participation, too. For this reason, the paradox of voting really can be considered a paradox of participation. In early 2010, for example, there was a major legislative and political battle over health care reform. Suppose that you are asked by a friend to make a phone call to your member of Congress requesting that she support the legislation. Faced with this situation, you might think through costs and benefits as described above. Before you even began to do so, however, you might think to yourself: "What if proponents of health care reform get 9,999 people to e-mail or call this same member of Congress? Is my one letter, making it an even 10,000, really going to matter? Probably not. There is really no difference between 9,999 letters and 10,000 letters. On the other hand, what if the supporters of the Obama health care plan are able to get only

▼ VOTE HERE

Voters line up on Election Day for many different reasons. For most, the potential benefits of showing up to the polling place, such as influencing public policy, outweigh any costs incurred.

100 letters from other people? If I write a letter, then there will be 101. But there is no real difference between 100 and 101, either. Whether or not I write a letter will not likely be critical."

Your logic here would be exactly the same as the logic about whether or not to vote. The effect of your participation is unlikely to make any meaningful difference in the outcome either way, so why bother? If the member of Congress is going to vote against the Democratic bill whether you write a letter or not, then you should not bother. But if the president is going to decide to support the bill whether you write a letter or not, not writing looks even better. You get to enjoy the benefit of the bill's passing without putting forward any effort.

There are a number of possible solutions to the paradox of participation.

As you probably realize, people do put forward the effort of political participation every day, in all walks of life, and in many different kinds of activities. In the case of the health care debate, millions of phone calls and e-mails flooded Congress and thousands traveled to Washington, D.C., to rally and lobby personally their member of Congress. This effort leaves political scientists to resolve the paradox of participation—the fact that people participate in politics, even though the impact of their individual participation would seem far too small to matter. How have they attempted to resolve this paradox?

One argument is that citizens worry that other individuals will make the same decision they make. That is, individuals might recognize that it is possible for them to collect benefits without paying the costs of participation, but they also recognize that if all citizens were to make the same calculation, then democracy would be threatened because no one would participate. Not wanting democracy to collapse, at least some citizens decide to participate.[5]

There is another possible resolution of the paradox: individuals may think about benefits of voting other than the immediate election outcome, that is, other than the victory or defeat of their preferred candidate. A candidate's victory or defeat is what political scientists call a **collective benefit**—everyone gets to enjoy it, whether they vote or not. But political scientists have also identified what can be called **selective benefits** of voting—benefits that only voters get to enjoy.[6]

What might such a selective benefit be? The one most frequently mentioned by political scientists is that only those who vote get to experience the satisfaction of having fulfilled their civic duty. You do not have to believe that you will be the deciding vote in order to receive this benefit, nor does it matter to you whether other individuals vote. For those who actually show up to vote on Election Day, this benefit is enough to outweigh the costs associated with voting. For those who do not show up, the benefit is not large enough to outweigh the costs of voting.[7]

Cost-benefit analysis can help us understand who participates.

The cost-benefit approach can be extremely useful in understanding why some people participate in politics and others do not. The argument is not that individuals are "computers" who put precise figures on costs and benefits and calculate expected outcomes. Still, there is evidence that people behave as if they are taking into account, if not making precise calculations about, costs and benefits in their heads, even if political scientists do not quite understand how or why this works. For example, in a large-scale survey of

ThinkingCausally

Why do people participate in politics even when their participation is unlikely to be the final decisive difference between success and failure?

collective benefit   a benefit everyone enjoys, regardless of whether or not they contributed to its attainment.

selective benefit   benefits that can be accessed only by those who participate in or contribute to group activity.

▲ "I VOTED!"

For some, the sense of civic duty and the personal satisfaction gained from doing that duty motivate political participation.

Americans who regularly participate in a variety of political activities, 61 percent said that one of the reasons they vote is "the chance to influence government policy."[8] To political scientists, it is absurd to think that one vote can influence government policy when more than 100 million votes may be cast in a given election. But if that idea makes sense to Americans who participate in politics, then political scientists need to take it seriously.

People are more likely to participate when expected costs are low. For example, it is easy to register to vote because registration deadlines are now closer to Election Day and opportunities to register are more plentiful. In these circumstances, potential voters need not do much advance planning. People are also more likely to vote when they can easily absorb the costs of voting and afford the cost of the time it takes to become informed: for example, when they can afford to hire a babysitter so they can get to the polls, or can afford to pay for magazines or cable television programming that will help them understand election issues.

As for expected benefits, participation in elections (typically dubbed voter turnout) is likely to be higher when the collective benefits are greater and lower when they are smaller. When, for example, the election is for the county registrar of deeds, then the expected benefit of one candidate or the other winning is unclear to many potential voters. As a result, turnout will likely be lower. If candidates seem very close on many issues, the expected benefit of voting will also be more difficult to discern, because regardless of which candidate wins, the policy outcomes would likely be quite similar. Or, if a particular candidate is running for office unopposed, the selective benefits derived from voting are negligible. Why? The sense of civic duty a voter feels and the satisfaction from doing one's duty are probably not as strong when the election has effectively been decided before Election Day.

The Nature and Extent of Political Participation in America

8-2 Discuss the different kinds of political participation in America.

How many Americans participate in politics? The answer to that question varies, depending on the type of participation. In any mention of political participation, the activity that first comes to mind is voting. Although voting is the most common type of political activity, there are many other ways that citizens can participate in politics. Whereas voting involves the direct choice of political leaders, the goal of nonvoting activities is to try to influence the decisions of leaders who have already been selected.

Much political participation goes on outside the voting booth.

Each year, Americans typically participate in a variety of political activities other than voting (see Table 8-1). These include signing petitions, attending demonstrations, organizing or attending community meetings, joining political organizations, contacting government officials, and volunteering for political campaigns. In addition, about 15 percent of Americans contribute money to political campaigns.

Another form of nonvoting political participation is the social movement. Social movements are made up of informal alliances of groups or individuals for the purpose of enacting or resisting social change. They often include several other types of the nonvoting behavior discussed previously, such as joining and attending meetings of

TABLE 8-1. Participation in Politics Outside the Voting Booth

TYPE OF ACTIVITY	PERCENTAGE OF AMERICANS PARTICIPATING IN ACTIVITY LAST YEAR
Discuss politics with family or friends	77.7
Volunteer	39.2
Work at/join organization to deal with community problem	30.6
Attend community meeting about school or community issue	22.8
Participate in protest	19.1
Contact public officials	18.5
Campaign contributions to party, candidate, or other group	14.9
Campaign-related activities (attend meeting, put up signs, etc.)	8.5
Attend campaign meetings, rallies, speeches, etc.	8

Source: Authors' analysis of 2008 National Election Study, http://www.electionstudies.org.

political organizations, contacting government officials, and participating in political protests. The civil rights movement of the 1950s and 1960s and the anti–Vietnam War movement of the 1960s and early 1970s are famously influential social movements. These examples demonstrate the potential power of this type of political participation; however, social movements no longer play as notable a role in American politics. The "sleeping giant" of nonvoting political participation came together with actual voting in January 2008, when predominantly white voters gathered in the Iowa caucuses and gave Barack Obama his first victory. This one event catapulted Obama ahead with the significant understanding that white voters would vote for a black candidate.

Still, although Americans have the reputation of being relatively inactive in politics, that reputation may be largely undeserved. Figure 8-1 compares levels of participation in various political activities across several countries.

ThinkingComparatively

While Americans may vote at lower levels than citizens of other countries, they surpass comparative participation in many other political activities.

continued on page 289 ▶

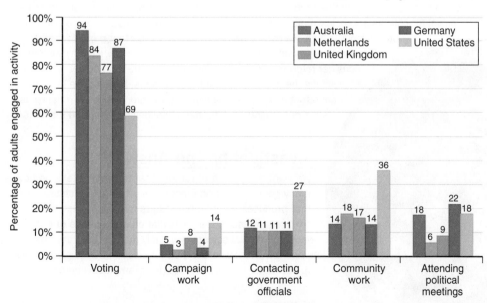

FIGURE 8-1. The United States Votes at Lower Rates than Other Countries But Has Higher Rates of Other Types of Political Participation.

HOW DO WE KNOW?

Why Is It So Difficult to Determine How Many People Vote on Election Day?

The Question

The 2008 presidential election is a great example of just how tricky it can be to get a precise figure on voter turnout. The Census Bureau's Current Population Survey, Voting and Registration Supplement, which gives information on voting behavior and trends based on surveys, indicates that the national turnout rate and registration rate decreased from 2004 to 2008, from 63.8 percent to 63.6 percent. These figures contradict aggregate findings that take into account actual voters and estimates of the voting eligible population that suggest that the turnout rate actually increased from 60.1 percent in 2004 to 61.7 percent in 2008.[9] Although both of these methods for determining turnout rates are reliable, they separately settle on different figures for the 2008 general election and come to diverse conclusions about trends in voter turnout. And although the 1.9 percent difference may seem small, it is rather a significant difference that illustrates just how difficult calculating turnout rates can be.

More generally, the success of democracy depends in part on popular participation in politics and government. Knowing how many people vote on Election Day gives an indication of whether the United States is thriving as a democracy or is struggling or even failing to live up to its democratic ideals. Because of the importance of this question, political scientists ask after every national election: How many people voted? How do we know?

Why It Matters

Voting is the most fundamental, most important act of democratic citizenship. Indeed, for government to be truly accountable to its citizens, those citizens must vote; they must express approval for policies and policy makers they like, and disapproval for those they do not. When voter turnout is high, we can be satisfied that this important part of American democracy is working as intended. When turnout is low, we may wish to consider reforms designed to stimulate registration and voting. Before weighing the merits of any of these reforms, however, we need to construct a valid, reliable measure of voter turnout in order to assess our progress—a far more challenging task than it seems.

Investigating the Answer

We want a measure of turnout that accurately tells us how many people voted on Election Day, that is consistent, and that produces comparable results from one election to the next, regardless of the particular characteristics of each election. Political scientists usually measure not the absolute number of voters who show up on Election Day (e.g., 125 million), but rather the turnout rate (for example, 50 percent).

◄ **WHO COUNTS?**
Constructing a valid, reliable measure of voter turnout is a far more challenging task than it seems. Should counts of potential voters include those who have failed to register to vote?

Calculating the turnout rate for an election entails dividing the number of people who voted in the election by the number of people who could have voted:

Turnout Rate = Actual Voters divided by Potential Voters

So, for example, if 100 people could have voted in an election, but only 50 people actually did vote, the turnout rate would be 50 percent.

Although this is a seemingly straightforward exercise, several problems arise in performing a real-world calculation of turnout based on this formula. We have to decide whether potential voters are: (a) only those people who were registered to vote and therefore could have cast a ballot on Election Day, or (b) this first group, plus those people who failed to register and so were ineligible to vote, but nonetheless met all of the other legal requirements for voting. Most political scientists prefer to use the latter definition. If we were to use the registered voter measure, a situation could arise in which, say, only 30 percent of the eligible voting population was registered to vote, but 90 percent of those who were registered actually showed up on Election Day. In this case, turnout would be 90 percent—the kind of number we would like to see in a democracy. In actuality, though, only 27 percent of individuals eligible to vote would have shown up to cast a ballot (30 percent multiplied by 90 percent)—an unhealthy number. In addition, as we have seen in this chapter, the population of registered voters has historically been subject to political manipulation. African Americans in particular were denied opportunities to register under the pre-1965 political system in the South. Thus, if we used a registered-voter measure to calculate turnout in, say, the 1960 presidential election, we would be obscuring the fact that large numbers of Americans were effectively prohibited from turning out.

Finally, using a measure based on registered voters makes it difficult to compare turnout rates in the United States with those in other countries. Why? In the United States, individuals who wish to vote are responsible for registering themselves and then keeping their registration status up-to-date. In most other democracies, however, the government assumes responsibility for registering legal voters. In those countries, therefore, all individuals who are eligible to vote are registered. If we wish to compare turnout in these countries to U.S. turnout, we must make the comparison among equivalent groups. For purposes of comparing U.S. turnout to foreign turnout, therefore, it makes sense to use the entire eligible U.S. voter population.

> If we wish to compare turnout in these countries to U.S. turnout, we must make the comparison among equivalent groups. For purposes of comparing U.S. turnout to foreign turnout, therefore, it makes sense to use the entire eligible U.S. voter population.

There are also problems, however, with using the eligible-voter population. How do we know how many members of the U.S. population are eligible to vote? In the voter turnout calculations that you are probably familiar with, statisticians estimate the number of eligible voters using census data on the "voting-age population," that is, the number of individuals 18 years of age or older living in the United States. But not everyone who lives in the U.S. is eligible to vote—citizens of other countries, for example, whether living in the United States legally or illegally, cannot vote in American elections. Furthermore, in some states convicted felons are legally prohibited from voting. But these groups, along with others who for one reason or another cannot vote, are all lumped into the pool of the voting-age population. At the same time, legally eligible American citizens living overseas are not counted as members of the voting-age population, because they do not live in the United States.

Despite these problems, many researchers—including most political scientists—typically rely on some measure of the U.S. voting-age population to determine the number of potential voters. In recent years, though, researchers have begun to refine their measures of the legally eligible voting population.[10] The Census Bureau, for example, has prepared an alternate measure that seeks to exclude noncitizens from the pool of potentially eligible voters.

Up to this point, we have addressed only half of the problem—how to measure the number of potential voters. But what about measuring the number of people who actually vote? The most common way of doing this is simply to count up all of the ballots that are cast on Election Day. With one ballot per person, the number of ballots cast would represent the number of voters. It is surprisingly difficult, however, to get an accurate count of the number of ballots cast. As we learned from the 2000 presidential election in Florida, not all of the ballots cast are counted. This omission can result from voter error, machine error, mistakes by poll workers, or some combination of those factors. Though Florida attracted most of the attention in 2000, uncounted ballots are a problem nationwide. Across the country in 2000, for example, researchers have estimated that between 4 million and 6 million ballots were uncounted.[11]

Political scientists and assorted media outlets have pursued one other avenue in estimating the number of voters: public opinion surveys. In fact, surveys can be used to determine both parts of the turnout equation. For example, survey researchers could ask a nationally representative sample of voting-age adults: (a) whether they met the legal requirements to vote, and (b) whether they did, in fact, vote. Then, they could estimate turnout on the basis of the survey as follows:

Turnout Rate = Number of Survey Respondents Who Report Having Voted divided by Number of Survey Respondents Legally Eligible to Vote

Unfortunately, as with all survey data, there are risks in using this approach. First, many surveys fail to draw a representative sample of the voting-age population. For example, if a survey is conducted by telephone, it will not include individuals without phones. Such people are likely to have lower incomes and are less likely to vote. If such individuals are omitted from telephone surveys, the resulting turnout calculations may be inflated. Similarly, surveys typically exclude residents of dormitories and those who exclusively use cell phones, thus excluding younger people, who are less likely to vote. Accordingly, excluding students from a survey sample could result in an overestimate of the turnout rate. Surveys also may overstate the number of people who actually cast a ballot. Studies comparing survey responses to actual voting records show that many survey respondents report having voted when they did not—perhaps because they were embarrassed to admit to interviewers that they had not done their "civic duty."

The combination of these two problems—excluding low-turnout voters from the denominator and overstating the number of voters in the numerator—tends to result in an inflated turnout estimate. Even so, surveys are still among the best tools for studying turnout. Although turnout rates based on survey data may be inflated, political scientists are able to use even inflated rates to compare behavior among different demographic groups and to compare rates of turnout over time. For example, assume that a standard, nationally representative survey will overstate turnout by roughly 20 percentage points every year. If a turnout calculation based on survey data shows a turnout rate of 70 percent in one year, and then 75 percent four years later, we can be confident that turnout rose by about 5 percentage points. It does not matter that the overall turnout rates are overstated, as long as they are overstated by the same amount in each survey. Similarly, an individual survey might show that self-described "strong Democrats" and "strong Republicans" turned out at a rate of 85 percent in a particular presidential election, whereas independents turned out at a rate of only 50 percent. Though these individual figures might be inflated, we can still be confident that strong partisans turned out at a rate roughly 35 percentage points higher than political independents.

Thinking Critically

- Can you think of other reasons, besides the ones stated above, that may account for the difficulty in calculating the actual number of real voters and eligible voters? How would you mitigate these factors?
- Why might it be easier to calculate turnout rates in other countries?
- As a political scientist, what steps would you take to ensure that you counted as many voters, or eligible voters, as possible? In other words, what methods best approximate the actual number of voters and eligible voters?

The Bottom Line

Even something as seemingly straightforward as measuring how many people vote in American elections presents difficult methodological issues. Nonetheless, recent work that takes into account the number of eligible voters—the voting-eligible population—makes us more confident that we are assessing the actual proportion of voters who turn out to vote in any particular election. Furthermore, although surveys almost definitely overstate turnout in any one election, they are a useful way to look at trends over time and assess how particular groups behave, such as the young, old, rich, poor, strong partisans, or weak partisans.

Only in voting do Americans lag substantially behind their peers in industrialized democracies. (We will have more to say about that later.) In the remaining four activities, American rates of participation either exceed or are roughly equivalent to those seen in other industrial democracies.

◀ **DUELING IMMIGRATION DEMONSTRATIONS**

In 2010, the politics of immigration was in the news as Americans demanded more strict enforcement of immigration laws while others protested a new law passed in Arizona.

Factors That Influence Participation

8-3 Outline the main factors that influence political participation.

ThinkingCausally

Why do lower-income Americans vote at a lower rate than those with higher income?

Political scientists have identified a number of factors that affect individuals' perceptions of the costs and benefits of participation, and therefore the likelihood that they will participate when presented with the opportunity. These include personal factors, legal factors, the political environment, and mobilization. Many of the factors we discuss below are related, and it is important for political scientists to take all into account when attempting to determine the impact of each.

Personal factors have a critical impact on participation.

By a wide margin, the most important personal factor influencing political participation is **socioeconomic status (SES).** This factor has turned up as a highly significant predictor of participation in study after study, election after election. SES influences participation directly, but also through its impact on other factors that influence participation.

socioeconomic status (SES) a combination of an individual's occupation, income, and education levels.

Socioeconomic status   SES is usually measured as a combination of an individual's occupation, income, and education levels. Someone with a high-ranking professional position, a high income, and an advanced education has a high socioeconomic status. Someone who has a low socioeconomic status has a poor education, minimal specialized skills, and a job with low earnings.

Why should occupation level have an impact on political participation? In a high-level professional position, one normally cultivates the skills of writing, speaking, analyzing, and organizing. These skills translate handily into the political arena, where political activists often have to speak, write, persuade others, think on their feet, and organize events and individuals. To someone with these **civic skills,** the costs of political participation seem lower. So the more advanced one's occupational level, the more likely one is to have the skills that make participation easier, and the more likely one is to participate in politics, other things being equal.

civic skills   the skills of writing, speaking, analyzing, and organizing that reduce the cost of political participation.

A large income clearly makes one type of political participation less costly—contributing money to political campaigns. Moreover, a substantial income also may bring one in contact with certain institutions—philanthropies, social clubs, and civic organizations—in which discussion of and participation in politics are common. Being steeped in politics in this fashion can lower the cost of participation, both by making it easier to understand the political world and by helping to develop the skills that make political participation seem less daunting.

Education is not only the most important component of SES; it is one of the most important determinants of political participation generally. For one thing, education tends to give people access to better jobs and to more income. And, as shown, those kinds of jobs, coupled with more money, can help increase participation by lowering its costs. The classroom also provides instruction and practice in the skills critical for taking part in political life—reading, writing, speaking, organizing, and critical thinking. So the better educated an individual is, the better developed these skills usually are, and the less costly participation seems. Lastly, a more advanced education level increases the likelihood that an individual has gained enough understanding of politics and government to believe that he or she can influence what happens in the political world, developing a sense of **political efficacy.**[12]

political efficacy   an individual's belief that he or she can influence what happens in the political world.

◀ **FAMILY CONNECTION**
The more families discuss politics, the more likely children are to be active politically.

◀ **CLASSROOM CONNECTION**
Even young children can learn and practice the skills critical for taking part in political life. Here children take part in a classroom election with voting booths and secret ballots.

These qualities affect one's perception of the costs and benefits of political participation. Greater interest in politics results in more satisfaction from political activity. This is just another way of saying that more education brings greater benefit from political participation than does less education. A sense of political efficacy also raises an individual's assessment of the benefits of participation. The more effective and influential you feel, the more likely you are to believe that your participation will result in some collective benefit you value. Finally, the knowledge about politics that education brings can help reduce the costs of getting involved. If your education has made you conversant in political and policy issues, you can more readily participate in politics than someone with less education.

Personal factors and voting behavior   In addition to socioeconomic status, civic skills, political efficacy, political interest, and political knowledge, a few other personal qualities can affect political participation. These include strength of political partisanship, age, and having intense feelings on particular issues, such as abortion or the death penalty.

The particular case of voting behavior demonstrates just how important some of these personal factors can be in determining who gets involved in politics and who does not. Table 8-2 indicates rates of voter turnout in 2008 among groups of individuals with varying personal characteristics. The first characteristic, education, is among the most important determinants of participation, because it has both direct and indirect effects. Notice that someone with a college diploma or an advanced degree is

TABLE 8-2.   Older, More Educated, and More Partisan Voters Were More Likely to Vote in 2008

PERSONAL QUALITIES OR CHARACTERISTICS	PERCENTAGE WHO REPORTED VOTING IN 2008
Education	
Grade school/some high school	51.3
High school diploma	70.1
Some college, no degree	80.6
College diploma or advanced degree	90.2
Income	
1st quintile	71.1
2nd quintile	68.5
3rd quintile	75.2
4th quintile	83.8
5th quintile	90.2
Age	
29 and under	65
30–45	77.5
46–61	80.2
62–77	87
78 and over	84.1
Partisanship	
Democrats (incl. leaners)	78.5
Independents and apoliticals	48.4
Republicans (incl. leaners)	84.1
Ideology	
Liberals	85.5
Moderates	75.5
Conservatives	85.9
Region	
South	76.6
Non-South	78.5

Source: Authors' analysis of 2008 American National Election Study, http://www.electionstudies.org.

nearly twice as likely to vote as someone with less than a high school education. Income also shows a strong relationship with an individual's propensity to vote. Among those in the highest income groups, nearly 90 percent turn out to vote on Election Day, or about 20 percent more than members of the lowest income groups.

Finally, note in Table 8-2 the importance of party identification, or party ID, the strength of one's attachment to one of the two major political parties. Citizens who strongly identify with either the Democratic or Republican parties are 30 and 36 percentage points, respectively, more likely to vote than citizens who consider themselves pure independents. In between these two groups are individuals who say they are independent but tend to lean toward one of the parties, and individuals who say that they identify with one of the two parties, but only weakly. Thus, according to these statistics, turnout increases across the spectrum from pure independents, to independent leaners, to weak partisans, to strong partisans. Citizens with strong partisan attachments are more likely to believe that they will enjoy meaningful benefits if their candidate wins, or that they will lose such benefits if their candidate loses. Therefore, the stronger the partisanship, the greater the perceived benefits, and the greater the likelihood of voting on Election Day.

Legal factors affect the cost of participation.

As the description of literacy tests at the outset of this chapter demonstrated, legal factors can make it more or less costly to participate in politics, particularly to vote. In the United States, **suffrage,** the right to vote, has become available to all citizens relatively recently. At various points in U.S. history, wealth, gender, race, age, and property ownership have all served as voting qualifications. Until the 1820s, most men who did not own land, regardless of their race or ethnicity, were prohibited from voting. Although allowed to vote earlier in some states, women were not allowed the right to vote by federal law until ratification of the Nineteenth Amendment in 1920. Many African Americans were effectively barred from voting in a large segment of the country until passage of the **Voting Rights Act of 1965.** Young people in the 18- through 20-year-old age range were not allowed to vote until passage of the Twenty-sixth Amendment in 1970.[13] Today, convicted felons and noncitizens are the only remaining groups of adults to whom voting rights have been denied. Thirty-two states maintain some manner of prohibition on the casting of ballots by felons, and noncitizens are universally excluded from the franchise, with the exception of a limited number of municipal and school-board elections.[14]

Even for adults who can vote, however, the United States is rare among democracies in that voting is a two-step process. All states except North Dakota require that citizens register to vote before they cast a ballot. Registration requirements vary from state to state. In some states, citizens can register at the polls on Election Day. In those states, turnout rates tend to be higher. But in those places where an individual has to register 10, 20, or 30 days before an election, a voter who becomes interested late in the campaign—the point when most

suffrage the right to vote.

Voting Rights Act of 1965 legislation that abolished literacy tests as a requirement to register to vote.

▼ **SUFFRAGISTS MAKE HISTORY**

Here women campaign and remind others to vote for their suffrage. In 1920, the Nineteenth Amendment granted all American women the right to vote.

campaigns actually get interesting—will be unable to cast a ballot. States that allow early voting or make it easier to vote absentee by mail when a voter cannot make it to the polls also tend to see higher turnout.

In general, over time, the movement has been toward a reduction in the legal barriers to registration and voting. For example, thanks to the efforts of political parties, civic groups, and the courts, registration offices are now required to stay open during standard business hours. Also, since the passage of Motor Voter legislation in 1993, citizens are allowed to register by mail and at many different government offices (including motor vehicle agencies, which gave the law its nickname). Furthermore, the maximum number of days before an election that one must register is now 30 days, rather than 60 or 90 days, which had been the deadlines in some states.

CaseStudy: The Tea Party Movement and Conservative Mobilization

In 1773, a group of 200 colonists boarded three ships docked in the Boston harbor and dumped 342 chests of tea overboard. It was a passionate act of defiance against taxation without representation, and it would become the rallying cry of a similar movement 236 years later after CNBC's Rick Santelli voiced outrage at the mortgage relief plan being proposed by the Obama administration. This much-viewed clip, in which Santelli and a group of bond traders talked about a Chicago tea party to protest federal spending, spurred a conservative movement urging fiscal responsibility, a constitutionally limited government, and free markets. It demonstrates the power of political participation and the clear factions that exist among the populace.

The twenty-first-century Tea Party rallies are nationally organized events that specifically and publicly oppose government spending, President Barack Obama, the federal

deficit, the stimulus package, and increased taxes. And, despite their conservative base, leaders of the movement are not afraid to lash out against Republicans, as they do when speaking against former President George W. Bush's heavy spending and what they consider his disregard for free markets late in his second term.

Whether their arguments are correct or not is not as important to us as is the movement's ability to garner a wide range of support and media coverage for their cause. Organizers held rallies and protests all around the country, from Atlanta to Santa Monica to Washington, D.C., bringing thousands into the movement, many of whom had never before participated in politics. They were shown on CNN, Fox News, and MSNBC, and were mocked on shows like *The Daily Show* and *The Colbert Report*. People became interested, and the movement grew. Many were angry, and

► **THE BIRTH OF TEA PARTY POLITICS**
CNBC bond analyst Rick Santelli shown during his now famous tirade against the Obama administration's economic and financial policies.

followers were encouraged to speak out, leading to contentious town hall meetings held by congressional representatives to discuss health care reform. Spurred on by social media networks like Facebook and Twitter, written about in countless blogs, and discussed on talk radio, the movement reached millions. Skeptics emerged, claiming that many of the protests and rallies were a form of "astro-turfing," a carefully planned and meticulously funded PR campaign to disrupt the Democratic Party and the initiatives of President Obama. The Tea Party organizers countered, claiming that many of the participants were first-time protesters and all were part of purely grassroots activities.

The Tea Party movement has garnered so much attention, and in some cases support, that many mainstream politicians (primarily Republicans) are attempting to latch onto the group's ideals and popularity. In fact, the results of an NBC/Wall Street Journal poll released in December 2009 show greater support for the "Tea Party" than either the Democratic or Republican Party. According to the poll, 41 percent of respondents said they have a favorable opinion of the Tea Party, compared with 35 percent for Democrats and 28 percent for Republicans.[15] Whether this movement will play a significant role in the 2010 elections and beyond is yet to be seen, but it is clear that it has mobilized the conservative base around a clear

cause and attracted many people to the political process that would have otherwise remained inactive. Organizers of the Tea Party hope that the same type of community activism that helped elect Obama will work for them, too. We shall see how big an impact, if any, the Tea Party movement will have in the years to come, and whether they can mobilize enough supporters to bring the changes they seek. Are they a viable movement? Or will they wither and fade like many movements before them? As we wait for the answers to these questions, it is apparent that the movement has mobilized a base and given people an avenue to participate in politics.

ThinkingCritically

1. Do you expect the Tea Party movement to be a big factor in the 2012 elections? How about elections 10 years from now?

2. Do you think the Tea Party movement is good for America? Do you think this type of political participation is healthy?

3. Looking into the future, how do you expect the costs of political participation to change in the next 10, 20, or 30 years? What impact will this have on political participation? What role did media, both old and new, have in creating the Tea Party movement?

The political environment also influences voter turnout decisions.

In addition to personal and legal factors, the nature of the candidates, campaigns, and issues in an election year can also influence who turns out to vote. As noted above, people who have stronger attachments to one of the parties are more likely to participate in politics. Again, the 2008 election stands as a watershed event in American political history. The first African American nominee of a major party, Barack Obama, created tremendous pride in African American voters who cast ballots in record numbers and increased their share of the electorate from 11 percent in 2004 to 13 percent in 2008. Hispanics and young voters also voted overwhelmingly for Obama, greatly increasing their turnout by 2.7 percent and 2.1 percent, respectively, in the 2008 election.[16] A powerful image or message of a minority president was the benefit that gave both groups the added incentive to cast their ballots.

A similar phenomenon takes place every election year, primarily at the state level. About half of the states have a process for putting issues directly on the ballot for consideration and approval or rejection by voters. In November 1996, for example, California voters approved Proposition 209, which prohibited government agencies, colleges, and public schools from using affirmative action procedures when making purchasing, hiring, or admissions decisions. In 2004, 11 states had measures on their ballots that sought to ban same-sex marriage. Research has shown that states with this kind of referendum tend to have higher turnout than those without such a process.[17] The presence of specific issues on the ballot apparently can induce some citizens to perceive benefits in participation that they might not otherwise see.

Similarly, the presence on the ballot of more interesting or important races and candidates can boost turnout. A race for president, governor, or U.S. Senate would likely motivate greater turnout than a race for, say, state mine inspector (an elective position in Arizona), as the potential benefits of a victory or defeat for John McCain or Barack Obama in the 2008 contest for president exemplifies.[18] Having appealing, attractive, or even "star quality" choices on the ballot also appears to elevate turnout.[19] Voters seem to find politics more interesting, and therefore more worth their time, when they can vote for a candidate with the "star power" of Arnold Schwarzenegger or John F. Kennedy.

Some research has shown, too, that elections that are perceived to be close will boost turnout.[20] Close elections stimulate more intense campaign activity and media coverage, which provide voters with more information about the campaign. Furthermore, citizens are more likely to discuss politics among themselves when an election is close. In the months preceding the 2008 presidential contest, newspapers, Internet sites, and news broadcasts were full of stories about the battle between Obama and McCain as ads saturated the airways and as the candidates barnstormed around the country. Citizens who typically do not talk about politics told various survey organizations that they were interested and engaged in the presidential election. This was especially the case in competitive or "battleground" states. These states, which drew most of the candidates' attention, produced higher turnout than states that were not as close and crucial to the respective campaigns. With all the attention and conversation about the race, especially in battleground states, citizens could more easily access the information they needed and wanted in order to vote. Close elections can also convince voters that their individual vote will "count," increasing their perception that their vote may influence the outcome and, thus, determine whether they receive benefits.

get-out-the-vote (GOTV) term used by campaign professionals to describe the various activities that candidates, political parties, activists, and interest groups use to make sure their likely supporters go to the polls on Election Day.

▼ TEA PARTY PROTESTS

Tea party protestors in what could be described as festive dismay often dressed in colonial garb during their demonstrations.

Mobilization efforts increase turnout.

Mobilization efforts, often dubbed **GOTV (get-out-the-vote)** are activities by candidates, political parties, activists, interest groups, friends, and co-workers to induce others to participate in politics. These efforts can include phone calls, personal visits, mailings, and even transportation to the polls on Election Day. If you have ever been called the night before an election and urged to vote, or had someone stop you outside the library and ask you to sign a petition, you have been the target of mobilization efforts. The Obama-Biden campaign in 2008 put together an army of volunteers through the Internet to help bring out the vote in Democratic precincts. In the 2000 election, those who reported being contacted by a party or campaign worker were 29 percentage points more likely to cast a ballot than those who were not contacted.[21]

Mobilization can increase participation in three ways. First, mobilization efforts tend to provide information about the relevant candidates and issues, making it easier for people to learn what they need to know in order to make a voting decision. And, in addition to simply asking you to help organize a community meeting on local crime, a neighbor would probably give you some background on the issue and tell you what a local meeting might accomplish. Second, mobilization efforts lower the costs of participation by providing information to individuals on exactly how to carry out the activity—where and when to vote, how to get to the rally, how to sign up to be heard at the committee hearing, and so on. In states with early and absentee voting, mobilizers can even arrange for ballots to be sent to citizens at home. Third, mobilization brings implicit social rewards for those who agree to participate, and possibly negative consequences for those who do not. Individuals who get involved in politics at the behest of others will enjoy the gratitude and esteem of those who asked them to participate.[22] This benefit can be very important, considering that these individuals are often co-workers, neighbors, or fellow parishioners.

Yet mobilization is also more than simply getting people to the voting booth. Often, politicians must first select the appropriate message. Selecting the right message actually gets voters to care, making the message the best mobilizer. Campaigns, parties, and interest groups first select the people most receptive to being contacted, then transmit this specific message to these people in the hopes that they will be motivated to participate. A significant element of mobilization, therefore, requires that the "right" message be sent to the "right" people. Basing a campaign simply on the mechanical aspects of turnout is not sufficient. Rather, it is the message that matters and the engagement of voters in what is going on in politics. Voter contact and organization do play a significant role in voter turnout, but it is often the message of campaigns or the current political situation that ultimately gets voters to the booth. In 2008, the Obama campaign spent tens of millions of dollars on GOTV activity directed at African Americans. Although this activity might have spurred turnout, the presence of Barack Obama himself on the ticket was probably a greater mobilizing factor.

One of the big stories of the 2010 election was the enthusiasm gap among Democrats and Republicans. Republicans were simply much more engaged and likely to vote than Democrats were in 2010. Samples of likely voters in pre-election polls skewed strongly Republican while surveys that included all registered voters or all adults had the Democrats doing better. Fundamentally, the 2010 electorate was a mirror image of 2008 when Democrats were more energetic, engaged, and likely to vote.

Typically, the mobilization efforts of Democrats and Republicans have taken different directions, based on their assumptions about their voters. Democrats have usually focused efforts on voters with somewhat lower SES, whereas Republicans have tended to mobilize suburbanites, church members, and hunters. In the 2004 election, both parties and their supporters were engaged in massive mobilization and GOTV efforts along these lines. Typically, Democrats have focused more of their energies than Republicans on mobilizing their voters with the assumption that their voters—who, on average, have lower SES than Republican voters—needed more of a push to get to the polls. And in 2004, groups supporting John Kerry, such as Americans Coming Together, spent tens of millions of dollars in a handful of battleground states like Ohio. But Republicans also put together an extensive field organization to identify, register, and mobilize their likely voters.

In the 2008 election, Barack Obama took advantage of relatively new media and social networking sites like Facebook, Twitter, and MySpace to mobilize millions of supporters. He effectively used online media to raise millions of dollars and generated a type of online activism never seen before. This online public engagement gave him a

TABLE 8-3. Contacting Government Officials Tops List of Nonvoting Political Behavior

ACTIVITY	PERCENTAGE ASKED[a]	PERCENTAGE OF THOSE ASKED WHO SAY YES[b]
Campaign work[c]	12	48
Campaign contribution	22	27
Contact government officials	29	57
Protest	11	28
Community activity	19	50

Source: Sidney Verba, Kay Schlozman, and Henry Brady, *Voice and Equality* (Boston: Harvard University Press, 1995), 135.

[a]Weighted cases

[b]Multiplied by percentage who were asked

[c]Or work in a campaign and contribute to it

significant advantage over John McCain, who failed to mobilize a sizeable number of people with his online outreach. Obama's use of online tools gave him an outlet for instant political mobilization and gave him a vehicle through which he could easily and directly get his message across to the millions of online followers. Many political pundits pointed, and arguably overemphasized, Obama's aggressive utilization of online media as a major reason for his victory. Still, although many who participated in Obama's online outreach were already Obama supporters, and the millions of text messages, tweets, and e-mails were "preaching to the converted," it nonetheless gave them an easy medium for communicating and a sense of community not realized in any previous presidential campaign. Social networking sites gave people a chance to engage and interact with other Obama supporters in an online environment. These important elements were crucial for generating hype and discussion, and offered a chance to participate in politics to a significant amount of people—especially younger people—who otherwise would have lost interest.

How common an occurrence is mobilization in American political life? In a typical year, between 10 and 30 percent of American adults will be asked by someone else to participate in some nonvoting form of political activity (see Table 8-3). Of those who are asked, anywhere between 27 and 57 percent actually agree to participate.

Where people are asked to participate is also interesting. You might expect requests to come primarily from those who interact regularly—co-workers, for example. Survey data indicate, however, that the workplace is actually the least common setting for mobilization. Membership organizations and churches tend to be the more common location of choice for political mobilizers.

Finally, how close a relationship usually exists between two people in order for one to ask the other to get involved in a political issue? Figure 8-2 addresses that question. For adult Americans who report having been asked to participate in various political activities, note the percentage of requests that came from: someone they knew personally; a secondary connection, that is, a "friend of a friend," or someone they did not know but whose name they recognized; or a complete stranger.

The higher effectiveness of contacts from people with a personal connection was demonstrated in the 2004 election. The Democratic Party and its allies in labor unions largely relied on paid staff to conduct GOTV efforts. The Republican Party and the Bush campaign relied on volunteers. After the election, many Democrats admitted that they were surprised by the effectiveness of the GOP efforts. One union head praised the "neighbor-to-neighbor" voter mobilization program that the GOP ran in 2004 and contrasted it with the "stranger-to-stranger" program run by Democratic allies.

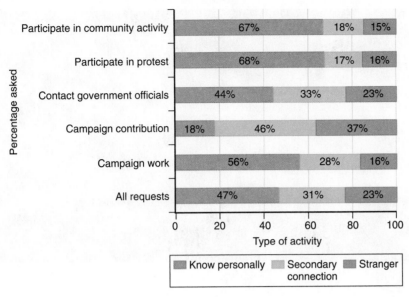

FIGURE 8-2. Personal Connections Are Most Effective in Encouraging Political Participation.

In the 2008 election, supporters of Barack Obama utilized neighbor-to-neighbor mobilization in a much more effective manner. This was demonstrated with the wildly popular viral video "The Great Schlep," in which comedian Sarah Silverman encouraged younger Jewish Americans living in nonbattleground states to visit "Nana and Papa" in Florida to convince them to vote for Obama.[23] If nothing else, the family-to-family type mobilization advocated by Silverman generated hype and discussion and made an important impact in how mobilization efforts are organized. Viral videoing also made a significant impact in the election with the release of the "Yes We Can" collage-style music video. Released in the heat of the Democratic primary, it showed popular celebrities Scarlet Johansson and John Legend, among others, supporting Barack Obama. By mid-February 2008, the video had a combined total of over 26 million viewers.[24] Americans' interest in all things celebrity gave this video traction and proved that political mobilization was entering a new frontier.

It is an empirical question whether the video worked or just made people feel good about what they were doing, but out-of-state calling and Internet calling took on an unprecedented role in the 2008 election. Barack Obama's campaign made the most effective use of phone-banking—getting people in nonbattleground states like California to call people in Ohio and other key states. The Obama campaign made it easy for people living in states like California to make a difference that they otherwise could not. These volunteers were given lists of undecided, likely, and Democratic voters in key states and then called these people persuading them to vote. Volunteers could also easily make an impact by signing up online and calling people through a virtual phone bank. Obama supporters were able to volunteer their time in the comfort of their own home, calling people on their own time. The Obama campaign also used mass texting as a way to get out the vote. People could sign up to receive alerts from the campaign, and these mass texts were used to remind people to vote and to provide information on the nearest polling station. Obama wasn't the only one to use such technology through the primaries and general election, but he was certainly the most effective at using it. In fact, one exit poll showed that Obama's team made as much as 37 percent more voter contacts than McCain's team did.[25]

► SCHLEPPING FOR VOTES
Comedian Sarah Silverman stars in an edgy video trying to convince college students to convince their grandparents to vote for Obama.

These mobilization efforts tend to add to the already substantial influence of socioeconomic status in determining participation. If you wanted to have someone help advance a political issue you cared about, you would be smart to pick someone with developed civic skills and a high-prestige job; someone with substantial amounts of money to give to the cause; someone with access to clubs and charities full of other people with money; and someone with a good education and all of the knowledge, skills, and confidence that education brings with it. In other words, you would ask a high-SES individual. In fact, high-SES individuals are the ones most likely to be asked to participate in political activities. So even though individuals who enjoy high socioeconomic status are more likely to participate in politics in the first place, they are also prime targets for mobilization campaigns.

Comparative and Historical Puzzles of Voter Turnout

8-4 Analyze voter turnout from comparative and historical perspectives and assess explanations.

American rates of voter turnout lag behind those in a handful of Western European countries (refer again to Figure 8-1). Expanding the list of countries to include Canada, Japan, New Zealand, and Iceland yields the same result. Among the 21 countries included in this larger list, American voter turnout would rank next to last in recent years. Only the Swiss vote at lower levels. Even with all the excitement of the 2008 election and pictures of long lines waiting to vote, the participation levels in America remain low when compared with other countries.

Voter registration requirements top the list of reasons for America's low voting rate.

Why does America's voter turnout lag so far behind that of other democracies? Answering this question is a challenge because comparable data on some variables are unavailable from one country to the next. Still, some important explanations are obvious.

ThinkingComparatively
Structural differences explain some of the gap in voter turnout between the United States and other countries.

Registration regulations   First, as explained earlier, voter registration requirements in the United States significantly depress turnout in comparison with other countries, where voter registration is a government responsibility and the registration process is effortless and cost free.[26] The United States has a personal registration requirement, meaning that Americans are personably responsible for registering to vote. Like buying a car, this is something most people do infrequently and so are less likely to know how to do. Some Americans, therefore, forget to register or do not realize that they need to; others attempt to do so but fail to comply with state regulations; and others try to register but give up in frustration over the process. As a result, tens of millions of Americans who are otherwise eligible to vote cannot do so, simply because they have not registered.

The personal registration requirement has significant consequences for voter turnout. Fully 30 percent of Americans who could register to vote have not done so and are thus not eligible to cast ballots. Among registered voters in the United States, turnout is about 85 percent in presidential election years, a rate that is respectable in comparison with other western democracies (though in midterm elections this percentage drops to 69 percent).[27] On the basis of this comparison, then, it appears that if the United States were to adopt a European-style voter registration system, participation in American elections would come closer to matching that in other countries.

Election scheduling   Another legal factor with implications for U.S. voter turnout has been the way elections are conducted. In America, elections are typically held on a single day—a Tuesday—during which voters are expected to find time to participate amid their other personal and professional activities. Early and absentee balloting now gives many Americans the chance to vote over the course of days or even weeks. But the evidence on whether early voting increases turnout has been mixed, with most scholarly studies showing that early voting has an insignificantly small impact on voter turnout.[28] In other democracies, elections are sometimes held on weekends or may also be declared national holidays, so that voters have the time they need to attend to their civic obligations. All of these considerations may affect participation.

Some political scientists believe that Americans suffer voting fatigue, based on the frequency with which they are asked to go to the polls. If citizens are required to vote too often, they may see less urgency in each election and be less inclined to turn out. In many democracies, voters go to the polls no more than two or three times over a four-year period. In the United States, by contrast, national elections are held every two years, and state, city, county, school-related, and special elections may be held in between. Furthermore, each election campaign may consist of both a party-level (primary) and a general election. Complicating matters, Americans also must vote on many more offices and issues than their counterparts in other countries. Some European countries, for example, do not have or do not frequently use the ballot initiative process in which citizens vote directly on legislation (instead of just leaving such votes to elected legislators). Furthermore, many democracies have far fewer elected offices and far more appointed offices than the United States has. As a result of both the frequency and the complexity of U.S. elections, then, the investment required to be an active voter in the United States is substantially more than in other countries.

Plurality decisions   The way votes are counted and apportioned in America also may depress voter turnout. Elections in the United States are predominantly plurality, or winner-take-all, affairs. Decision by plurality means that the candidate who receives the most votes wins the seat being contested; all other candidates lose. Imagine that you are a liberal Democrat living in Orange County, California, a bastion of conservative politics. In election after election, your district sends Republicans to Congress. You show up faithfully to vote in every election, but your candidate, the Democrat, always loses. Under the circumstances, it would not be surprising if you concluded, "Why bother?"

Many foreign countries—such as Israel—have a proportional representation system in which a party's share of legislative seats is proportionate to its share of votes. In such a system, even if the party you vote for finishes in second place or worse, it will likely win some seats in the legislature. As a voter, this system gives you an incentive to vote; at least some candidates of the party you favor can win seats, even if your party does not get the most votes. The net effect of this procedure is to increase the benefits of voting.

> **ThinkingComparatively** ●●●●
>
> Election rules have a significant influence on the behavior of both elites and voters and create different incentives for mobilization and participation in different countries.

The two-party system   Finally, the U.S. system has only two major political parties, and two relatively centrist parties at that, both of them battling within the confines of the American creed, which we discussed in detail in Chapter 2. This situation may also result in lower rates of voter turnout. In multiparty parliamentary systems, the parties have more narrowly focused agendas and closer links to population groups. For example, in many European countries, environmentalists can find a comfortable home in various Green parties, which are devoted almost exclusively to environmental issues. In the United States, by contrast, voters who are very environmentally conscious have to choose between Republicans and Democrats, neither of which places environmental politics at the center of their agendas. Thus, in a multiparty system, voters may feel that their vote can help deliver the specific kinds of collective benefits that interest them most. Naturally, this perception gives them a greater incentive to turn out on Election Day.

The 2004 national elections in the United States and in Spain illustrate this phenomenon. In the United States, the leadership of both the Democratic and Republican parties had agreed that the U.S. military must stay in Iraq and "finish the job," that is, ensure that stability and democracy had taken hold. In the Spanish election, however, the two major parties differed dramatically on this issue. The Partido Popular, a center-right party not unlike the Republican Party in the United States, committed to keeping Spanish troops in Iraq to help usher in a new Iraqi government. But the Partido Socialista Obrero Español (PSOE), the Spanish socialist party, vowed to quit Spain's current Iraq policy and bring Spanish troops home immediately. PSOE consistently trailed in the pre-election polling, and few political analysts thought they had any chance of winning the contest in Spain. Still, when Islamic terrorists struck a central Madrid train station just days before the election, killing 191 people and wounding about 1,800, voter turnout surged and Spanish voters handed an unexpected victory to the PSOE. Within a matter of weeks, all of Spain's troops serving in Iraq were brought home.

A variety of other factors might explain the turnout differential between the United States and other countries. Just remember two main points: First, the structure of America's government and of its election system tends to make casting a ballot more costly here than in other democracies. Second and specifically, the single largest determinant of the relatively low rate of American turnout in comparison with other countries is America's uniquely onerous voter registration system.

▲ MULTIPARTY SYSTEMS
ALLOW VOTERS MORE
SPECIFIC CHOICES

When Islamic terrorists struck a central Madrid train station just days before the election, voter turnout surged. Spanish voters put the socialist party in office, and within a matter of weeks, all of Spain's troops serving in Iraq were brought home.

Despite increases in education and the legal ease of voting, turnout has dropped since 1960.

In the close and hotly contested 1960 presidential race between Richard Nixon and John F. Kennedy, over three-fifths of eligible Americans cast their ballots. In an equally competitive presidential race in 2000 between George W. Bush and Al Gore, only about half of all eligible Americans voted. In the 40 years between those two elections, voter turnout declined (see Figure 8-3). While there were rises in the 2004 and 2008 elections, a smaller proportion of Americans vote now than did 40 years

FIGURE 8-3. **Voter Turnout in Presidential Elections, 1960–2008.**
Voter turnout in presidential elections declined after 1960 but has shown an upturn in recent years.

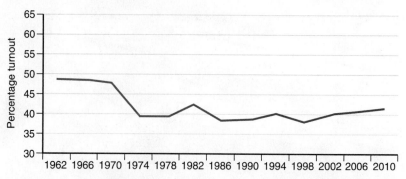

FIGURE 8-4. **Midterm Election Turnout, 1962–2006.** Midterm election turnout has also declined over the last 40 years. In the 1962 midterm elections, 47 percent of eligible Americans cast ballots. In the 2010 midterm elections, 41.5 percent of the eligible population cast a ballot.

ago. The low point in this period came in 1996, when fewer than half of those who could cast a ballot chose to do so.

A similar voter-turnout pattern emerges in midterm elections. Although there is no presidential race in midterm elections, all 435 House of Representatives seats are up for election, along with one-third of Senate seats and more than 30 state governorships. Turnout in these contests has declined by 11 percentage points in the last 40 years (see Figure 8-4).

This decline in voter turnout has been one of the most intensely studied puzzles in American politics. What makes the decrease particularly curious is that two factors that are strongly correlated with turnout—education and legal restrictions—have changed in ways that should have boosted turnout.

Americans have higher levels of education now than they did 40 years ago. In 1960, for example, only 41 percent of Americans had a high school education. In 2000, the proportion of Americans who had graduated high school had increased to 84 percent.[29] Furthermore, as noted earlier, legal restrictions on voting have become less burdensome. The poll tax was abolished by the Twenty-fourth Amendment to the Constitution in 1964, and literacy tests were eliminated via the Voting Rights Act of 1965 and its revisions in 1970. Finally, the passage of the Motor Voter Act in 1993 made voter registration forms available in scores of government offices and agencies, and in recent years, restrictions on voter registration and use of mail-in and absentee ballots were eased to make registration and voting a simpler, more inclusive process.

According to one study, given the increase in levels of education and the easing of registration and voting laws, turnout should have risen by close to 5 percentage points. Instead, turnout declined by 14 percentage points from 1960 to 1988.[30] And, even with the uptick in 2004 and 2008, it is still 6 percentage points less than 1960. How, then, can we explain the 11 percentage point drop in turnout at the same time it was expected to increase?

ThinkingCausally

Why did turnout in American elections continue to decline even as the population became more educated?

Many factors work in concert to explain the drop in turnout.

One explanation for the drop in turnout is that the electorate expanded with the ratification of the Twenty-sixth Amendment in 1970. The net impact of enfranchising millions of 18- to 20-year-olds—granting them the right to vote—was to decrease the proportion of Americans voting. Why? Because the electorate was expanded to include young people, and because young people are less likely to vote than older people, the net effect of the Twenty-sixth Amendment was to decrease voter turnout. Some scholars have calculated that the enfranchisement of 18- to 20-year-olds caused a three percentage point decline in turnout rates.[31] Others have argued that the turnout rate in the United States is measured incorrectly (an argument we discussed in "How Do We Know?"). If you correct for this, these scholars argue that the lowering of the voting age explains almost all of the drop in turnout that we have seen since the early 1970s. In spite of the excitement of younger voters for Barack Obama in 2008, the 18- to 20-year-olds, while voting in greater percentages than in the past, still had the lowest turnout of any other age group.

Other factors that relate to voting, such as the political attitudes and attachments discussed above, can also explain part of the decline in turnout. As shown in Figure 8-5, Americans have lower levels of political efficacy, lower levels of trust in government, and are less attached to political parties today than they were 40 years ago. Taken together, these factors may account for as much as three-quarters of the decline in turnout since 1960.[32]

Another study invokes the mobilization factor and argues that fewer people are voting because fewer are being urged to vote. However, National Election Studies data presented in two different studies indicate that, on the whole, mobilization by political parties increased between 1960 and 1982, and increased again after 1992.[33]

If levels of party mobilization have not declined noticeably in the past four decades, perhaps something about the nature of mobilization has changed. Scholars have speculated, for instance, that the quality of mobilization may have declined in recent decades. Whereas in the past mobilization meant friends, neighbors, and committed volunteers canvassing in person, today voter mobilization operations are often conducted by professional consultants and phone banks. It seems reasonable to believe that a contact from a friend, neighbor, or volunteer was likely to be more effective than a computerized phone call from an anonymous telemarketer at a phone bank. More research needs to be done on this theory, but the initial research shows strong potential.[34]

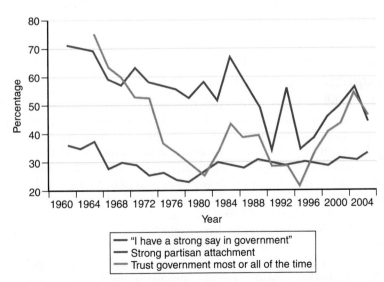

FIGURE 8-5. Political Efficacy, Attachment to Political Parties, and Trust in Government Have Declined over the Last 40 Years, 1960–2004.

One final, and intriguing, explanation for the decline in voter turnout is that, over time, Americans have been interacting with each other less and less outside of work. This steady decrease in "social connectedness" is manifested in declining church attendance, declining participation in civic and membership organizations, the sharp decrease in labor union membership, and the drop-off in social activities with families and friends.

Several arguments suggest how social connectedness plays into decisions about voting. First, the more connections an individual has with others, the more likely that he or she is in a position to mobilize and to be mobilized. Second, social connectedness may help individuals see greater meaning and consequence in the outcome of an election, which are other inducements to vote.[35] Third, social involvement can also reduce information costs by facilitating the sharing of information relevant to politics.[36] The 2008 candidacy of Barack Obama created a greater upturn in social connectedness in that the future president was the source of greater fascination and enthusiasm than, say, John Kerry, four years earlier.

Scholars disagree about the extent to which social connectedness might affect turnout. In addition, there is little consensus about how to measure social connectedness, or about the precise mechanisms whereby connectedness influences political behavior. As with the study of the quality of political mobilization, these questions remain fertile areas of inquiry.

Who Gets Heard? Does It Matter?

8-5 Assess whether differences in groups' political participation matters and whether participation itself matters.

Just below the surface of this discussion lies an important and disconcerting fact of American political life: participation in the political process is not equal among American citizens. As we well know, income, education, political attitudes, and opportunities for mobilization are not uniformly distributed across the demographic spectrum. Men and women; young and old; black, white, Hispanic, and Asian; wealthy and poor; and Republicans and Democrats all differ among the factors that help determine participation. The result is that these groups participate in American politics to very different degrees.

Political participation differs considerably across demographic categories.

Consider the different rates of participation according to race (see Figure 8-6). Whites tend to participate to a greater extent than both blacks and Latinos, except in campaign work, protests, and community activity. Latinos, on the other hand, are not the most involved group in any of the activities indicated in the figure. Though they are as likely as whites to serve as board members, in all other categories they show the lowest rates of participation among the three groups. And, as we have pointed out previously, the 2008 election proved to these communities what higher participation can accomplish with the election of Barack Obama.

Expanding this analysis to other demographic categories, it would quickly become clear that those who participate in American politics tend to be whiter, older, wealthier, better educated, more likely male, and more conservative than the populace at large. This fact has led some observers to complain that the American political system does not live up to its ideals—for example, that all have an equal say in government—and that it caters disproportionately to the needs and demands of an unrepresentative portion of the population.

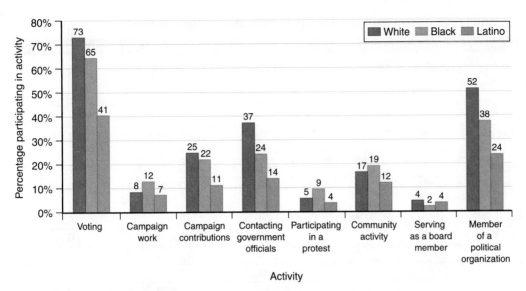

FIGURE 8-6. **Across the Board, White Americans Are More Likely to Take Part in Political Activity.** Whites participate in higher numbers in most political activities, though they are less likely to participate in campaign work, protests, and community activities.

Considering broad demographic categories, some of those needs and demands would appear to differ significantly from one group to the next. Table 8-4 compares opinions between whites and blacks on a variety of policy issues. The opinion difference between blacks and whites in each issue area is substantial—between 18 and 36 percentage points. Thus, if blacks are being underrepresented in the political process and whites are being overrepresented, that difference may have significant implications for which opinions are being aired among policy makers.

TABLE 8-4. **The Opinions of Black and White Americans Differ Significantly on Important Issues**

ISSUE	WHITES	BLACKS	DIFFERENCE
Government should make every effort to improve the economic and social condition of blacks and other minorities	17%	47%	30%
Due to past discrimination blacks should be given preferences in hiring and promotion	11%	44%	33%
Affirmative action programs needed "as long as there are no rigid quotas"	43%	79%	36%
Government should provide more services and increase spending	47%	65%	18%
Government should guarantee food and shelter	62%	80%	18%
Favor death penalty for those convicted of murder	77%	45%	32%
War in Iraq was not worth fighting	38%	74%	36%
Government collects too much information about people like me	54%	74%	20%

Source: Robert S. Erikson and Kent L. Tedin, *American Public Opinion* (New York: Pearson Education, 2005), 201–3.

TABLE 8-5. Younger and Older Americans Have Differing Attitudes on Various Issues

ISSUE	UNDER 30	55 AND OVER	DIFFERENCE
Favor the U.S government paying for all necessary medical care for all Americans	59.7%	40.4%	19.3%
Government should provide more services than it does now	43.6%	34.4%	9.2%
Favor allowing Social Security funds invested in stock market	35.6%	23.8%	11.8%
Allow same-sex marriage	59.5%	21.8%	37.7%
By law, a woman should always be able to obtain an abortion.	46.3%	29.9%	16.4%
Favor cutting the deficit by spending less on the military	47.6%	31%	16.6%
War in Iraq was not worth the cost	80.2%	74.2%	6%
Liberal	28.3%	16.7%	11.6%
Moderate	20.8%	21.8%	1%
Conservative	23.8%	37.5%	13.7%

Source: Authors' analysis of 2008 American National Election Study, http://www.electionstudies.org.

Political participation also differs considerably according to another demographic category: age (see Table 8-5). Note substantial differences in the opinions of Americans under the age of 30 and those 55 and older. In all political activities, seniors participate at significantly higher rates than younger cohorts. And in virtually every issue, older Americans support the more conservative position. In the most extreme example, older Americans oppose same-sex marriage at a rate nearly 38 percentage points higher than their younger counterparts.

We could expand this analysis to other groups—the working class and the upper class, different religious groups, and so on. It would likely become obvious that different demographic groups sometimes hold very different opinions on policy issues. This fact, combined with differential rates of political participation, raises the concern that not all voices and positions get the hearing they deserve in America.

If demographic groups participated in proportion to their percentage in the population, collective opinion would change little.

A number of researchers have attempted to determine the message that policy makers would hear from the American public if various demographic groups were to participate in proportion to their percentage of the population. They have analyzed, for example, the extent to which the message communicated to policy makers would differ if African Americans, who constitute approximately 12 percent of the population, also constituted 12 percent of the individuals engaged in various forms of political participation. Researchers have extended this analysis to all major population groups, and have compared opinions among those who actually participate in politics with those who would participate if all groups participated at rates equal to their population percentages.

When researchers construct a hypothetical public such as this, equal in its proportions to the demographic groups in the population at large, that public holds only a mildly more liberal set of beliefs than the actual participating public. But how can this be, given the very sharp differences in opinion shown above? In general, the groups that tend to be most underrepresented also tend to be small. African Americans and the poor, for example, each constitute no more than about one-seventh of the American public. Thus, even if they were to participate at full strength, it would be hard for them to change collective opinion considerably. However, they certainly could gain influence at the margin in some very competitive congressional districts and states.

Other groups, such as women, are underrepresented as well. However, their opinions tend to align more closely with the groups that are overrepresented. Again, even if women were to participate in politics at rates equivalent to their population percentages, they would not dramatically change opinion.

The most persuasive critique of this conclusion comes from those who argue that comparing responses to survey questions between political participants and nonparticipants is not the best approach. After all, one does not write a letter to a public official simply requesting "more services and increased spending," which would be a typical survey question. Usually, an individual's interests in policy are very specific. When it comes to these more specific policy preferences, the distortion created by underrepresentation of some groups may be far more significant than the survey data indicate.

Another difficulty with opinion comparisons based on surveys is that they fail to indicate the different issue agendas that different groups might bring before government. Imagine that the wealthy and the poor had precisely the same opinions on school voucher programs—programs that provide government funds for parents to send their children to private school. Such agreement might provide some comfort to those who worry that the poor are underrepresented in politics and the wealthy overrepresented. But imagine further that a federal voucher program is the number-one priority for the poor and at the bottom of the list for the wealthy. The wealthy are unlikely to bring this issue to the attention of policy makers, whereas the poor would do so if they were actively participating. In politics, as we discuss in chapters on public opinion and interest groups, who controls the agenda is a vitally important question.

Does participation matter?

This discussion about differential participation rates is entirely academic if participation does not influence the decisions that policy makers make. Does participation matter?

Considered at the level of the individual, it would be hard to argue that participation matters much. As noted above, the impact of an individual's participation in politics is minimal. Someone engaging in a one-person protest outside the offices of a business guilty of polluting the environment, or a clinic that provides free contraceptives, or a school that does a poor job educating its students would be fighting a lonely battle unlikely to succeed. Being the one-hundred-thousandth marcher in a demonstration will not materially affect its impact. We would expect these behaviors to have no effective impact. This is part of the paradox of participation.

The collective actions of individuals, though, whether coordinated or not, clearly do have an impact on political outcomes. In the 1932 presidential election, for example, a surge in voter turnout ousted the conservative Herbert Hoover and swept in the progressive New York governor, Franklin D. Roosevelt. This vote was largely a response to the dire economic conditions gripping the country in 1932, the height of the Great Depression. The coalition that came together to support Roosevelt dramatically changed the shape of American public policy in ways that continue to

ThinkingCausally

Considering what little impact individual participation is likely to have on outcomes, why do people participate in politics?

affect the country today through programs such as Social Security, welfare, unemployment compensation, housing assistance, and labor union protections.

Perhaps a less momentous, but equally dramatic, result of participation can be seen in the presidential elections of 2000 and 2004 and the midterm contest in 2006. The result in Florida, and therefore the outcome of the presidential election in 2000, came down to slightly more than 500 votes. If a relative handful of people had voted differently that day, or decided not to vote at all, the result of the election—and perhaps of American history—would have been different. Furthermore, the voting behavior of those few hundred people may have been influenced by others' participation—mobilizing them to vote, for example, or to vote one way rather than the other. Although in 2004 the margin was more decisive, the presidential election again came down to one state, and George W. Bush won Ohio and the presidency by a little more than 120,000 votes. Again, the impact of citizen participation in the election was unmistakable and decisive. In 2006, the Democrats took control of the Senate by narrow victories in two states, Virginia (where Democrat James Webb won by about 9,000 votes) and Montana (where Democrat Jon Tester won by 3,500 votes).

The impact of voter participation is also apparent from the election-year activities of political parties and organized interests. For example, the Democratic and Republican parties, as well as their interest group allies, spent tens of millions of dollars on voter mobilization efforts in the 2008 election. The parties and the groups that support them obviously believe that who shows up on Election Day, and how they vote when they show up, can determine an election outcome. Otherwise, why invest such significant resources in get-out-the-vote efforts?

Measuring the impact of nonvoting forms of participation, such as contacting elected officials or joining a protest, is more difficult. Often, evidence concerning the impact of such participation is less systematic. That does not necessarily make it less persuasive, however. For example, we know that the Clinton health care plan went down in defeat in 1994. We also know that in the battle leading up to that defeat, opponents of the Clinton plan were much more likely to contact Congress than supporters of the plan. Moreover, many of those active in the fight over Clinton's plan believed that this **grassroots lobbying** was decisive. One key architect of President Clinton's health care policy claimed, "the most effective tactic against our program was grassroots lobbying and phone banks in selected districts."[37] With this in mind, the Obama administration and the DNC orchestrated huge efforts to get constituents to contact members of Congress in the days leading up to the final health care vote in Congress in spring of 2010.

If grassroots mobilization and phone banks—selectively used—are not effective tactics, that means that the tens of millions of dollars that interest groups spent on those tactics did not work. More broadly speaking, if nonelectoral forms of political participation do not matter, we have to ask why millions of individuals and organized interests spend countless dollars and hours participating in politics, and why political insiders routinely report that these nonelectoral forms of participation do have an impact. Either participation matters, or those who act as if it matters and those who report that it matters are simply fooling themselves.

grassroots lobbying efforts to persuade citizens to contact their elected officials regarding a particular issue or piece of legislation.

▼ DOES PARTICIPATION MATTER?

Many active in the fight over universal health care in the early 1990s believe that grassroots lobbying was decisive in its defeat. How might individuals at the grassroots level make a difference in current debates?

Two key examples demonstrate how much participation matters.

We can find examples, of course, in which the impact of nonvoting forms of participation is undisputed. As we noted at the beginning of the chapter, extension of the franchise to women and minorities is a relatively new development in this country. Women were not guaranteed a constitutionally protected right to vote until 1920. It took the women's suffrage movement, which was launched with a convention at Seneca Falls, New York, in 1848, roughly 70 years to achieve this outcome.

In the second half of the nineteenth century, women volunteered in the anti-slavery movement, the temperance movement (advocating the abolition of liquor), the settlement house movement (which provided educational, health, and cultural programs for the urban poor), and assorted organizations promoting better working conditions for women and children. In the course of this work, they came to see the franchise as indispensable in promoting their concerns on a broader scale.

In 1869, therefore, two organizations promoting women's suffrage were founded: the National Woman Suffrage Association (NWSA) and the American Woman Suffrage Association (AWSA). After two decades of pursuing separate agendas, the groups merged in 1890. The new organization was named the National American Woman Suffrage Association (NAWSA). Its leader was Susan B. Anthony.

The suffrage movement was greatly aided by the skills and relationships its female members had built in their fight for prohibition, abolition of slavery, and improved living and working conditions for the poor, women, and children. Women's participation in social clubs, too, strengthened their ties to other women and helped create an organizational base for the movement. As the suffrage movement began growing in size and success through its victories in securing the franchise at the state level, it was joined by other women's groups. These included the General Federation of Women's Clubs and assorted professional organizations. Eventually, both the size of the movement and its success in securing the franchise at the state level created an irresistible momentum for a constitutional amendment guaranteeing women the right to vote. Congress proposed that amendment in 1919, and it was ratified by the required 36 states in 1920.[38]

The story of the civil rights movement is similar in many respects to the women's suffrage movement. In 1963, there were essentially no federal protections for the voting rights of African Americans (see Chapter 4). As a result, there was not a single African American member of the House of Representatives from the South, and only a handful of state and local officials such as mayor or sheriff. In Birmingham, Alabama, thousands of protesters hit the streets. By the year 2010, thanks to civil rights legislation and court decisions protecting the voting rights of African Americans, 41 members of the U.S. House of Representatives were African American, and thousands of black elected officials serve at the state and local level. In Birmingham, Alabama, site of the original clashes to attain equality, both the mayor and the sheriff are African American. Although blacks have been disproportionately underrepresented in the Senate, they have been crucial in electing Democratic governors and senators throughout the South. And in the 2008 election, Florida, North Carolina, and Virginia went to Barack Obama. The civil rights movement, a form of mass, nonelectoral participation, created irresistible pressure on policy makers to guarantee voting rights to African Americans. With those voting rights in place, African Americans have indeed changed the American political landscape.

Finally, participation also matters in a broader sense than the outcomes it produces on a particular issue. The health of representative democracy demands that citizens choose their leaders, monitor their work, and provide feedback both at the ballot box and through nonelectoral forms of participation. This is how Americans must act as responsible stewards of democratic government. Furthermore, the act of citizen participation can be beneficial to the individual citizen. It can provide skills, experience, knowledge, and a sense of efficacy that will enable individuals to play a more active, constructive role in the workplace, the church, and the community—or even in politics.

▼ THE CONGRESSIONAL BLACK CAUCUS

The Congressional Black Caucus was established by African American members of Congress in 1971 to "positively influence the course of events pertinent to African Americans and others of similar experience and situation," and "achieve greater equity for persons of African descent in the design and content of domestic and international programs and services."

CHAPTER SUMMARY

In this chapter you have learned to:

8-1 Analyze the costs and benefits of political participation for individuals and groups. People analyze the costs and benefits of voting in any particular election and decide whether or not to vote based on these perceived costs and benefits. Many Americans vote even though a rational analysis suggests they will not—this is the paradox of participation. Citizens weigh costs and benefits in deciding whether to vote. As the incremental benefit of one vote is often quite small, a confusing situation arises in which the costs seem to outweigh the benefits of voting. Although the paradox of voting remains unresolved, it seems likely that the satisfaction voters receive from performing their civic duty plays some role in encouraging voting.

8-2 Identify the different kinds of political activities in which Americans participate. There are many different ways in which citizens can participate in politics in America. Although voting is the type of participation that first comes to mind, citizens can participate in politics in many other ways. Signing petitions, attending demonstrations, organizing community meetings, joining political membership organizations, volunteering for political campaigns, and contacting elected officials are examples of other sorts of political activity. Although Americans tend to vote at lower rates than citizens in other countries, they do tend to engage in these other activities at higher rates.

8-3 Outline the main factors that influence political participation. Personal factors, legal factors, the political environment, and mobilization efforts are key elements that influence political participation. By a wide margin, the most important personal factor influencing political participation is socioeconomic status. The civic skills it implies make the costs of political participation seem lower, and levels of political efficacy are generally higher for those with higher socioeconomic status. Legal factors, like poll taxes and literacy tests, also play an important role in participation decisions. The twentieth century brought an end to a number of legal barriers that prevented women and African Americans from voting. Further, Motor Voter legislation made voter registration more convenient. The competitiveness of a race, as well as the efficacy of mobilization efforts, also affect participation. The more competitive the race and the more effective the mobilization, the higher the levels of political participation.

8-4 Analyze voter turnout from comparative and historical perspectives and assess explanations. There are many comparative and historical puzzles of political participation. One comparative puzzle is the fact that America's voter turnout lags far behind other democracies. Reasons may include America's personal registration requirement, which makes it inconvenient for citizens to register to vote. Other factors may include voter fatigue (due to the relative frequency of American elections), plurality decisions, and the two-party system. Nevertheless, the United States has high levels of nonvoting political participation relative to other advanced democracies. Historically, the United States is in a puzzling situation: both the costs and levels of participation in the United States have decreased with time. Participation should increase as costs decrease, but other reasons, including younger eligible voters, decreases in political trust and efficacy, and ineffective mobilization, may explain the puzzle.

8-5 Assess whether differences in groups' political participation matters and whether participation itself matters. Questions of whether political participation matters and whether it affects the decisions of government are particularly important because participation in the political process is not equal across demographic groups. Whites, men, and upper-class individuals tend to have higher levels of participation than their counterparts in nearly every category. Ironically, however, if demographic groups participated in proportion to their percentage in the population, there would be little change in collective opinion. This would likely occur because underrepresented groups are either relatively small or have opinions similar to the overrepresented groups. Finally, although individual participation is unlikely to cause great change, political participation collectively can change the American political landscape in vast and meaningful ways. The women's suffrage movement, the election of FDR, and the civil rights movements are just a few such examples.

PEARSON mypoliscilab **EXERCISES**

Apply what you learned in this chapter by starting with these resources on MyPoliSciLab.

Read on **mypoliscilab.com**

    eText: Chapter 8

Study and **Review** on **mypol**

    Pre-Test
    Post-Test
    Chapter Exam
    Flashcards

Watch on **mypoliscilab.com**

    Video: Teen Sues for Equal Protection
    Video: Candidates Court College Students
    Video: Chicago Worker Protest
    Video: L.A. Riots: 15 Years Later

Explore on **mypoliscilab.com**

    Simulation: You Are the Leader of Concerned Citizens for World Justice
    Simulation: You Are an Informed Voter Helping Your Classmates
    Visual Literacy: Voting Turnout: Who Votes in The United States?

KEY TERMS

civic skills, p. 290
collective benefit, p. 282
get-out-the-vote (GOTV), p. 296

grassroots lobbying, p. 310
political efficacy, p. 290
selective benefit, p. 283

socioeconomic status (SES), p. 290
suffrage, p. 293
Voting Rights Act of 1965, p. 293

SUGGESTED READINGS

Sidney Verba, Kay Schlozman, and Henry Brady. 2006. *Voice and Equality*. Boston: Harvard University Press. Argues that some have a greater voice in politics than others and that this inequality stems from both personal inclinations toward political activity and resources such as money and education.

Steve Rosenstone and Mark Hansen. 2002. *Mobilization, Participation, and Democracy in America*. New York: Longman Classics. Argues that people participate in voting based on the perceived costs and benefits of doing so and because politicians mobilize them, but that these may depend on one's income, education, age, race, efficacy, and social networks.

Robert Putnam. 1993. *Making Democracy Work*. Princeton, NJ: Princeton University Press. Argues that social capital is a necessary ingredient for government functioning and suggests that political institutions may gradually improve civic engagement.

David Campbell. 2006. *Why We Vote: How Schools and Communities Shape Our Civic Life*. Princeton, NJ: Princeton University Press. Argues that our communities shape our civic and political engagement, and that schools are especially significant communities for fostering strong civic norms.

SUGGESTED WEBSITES

Rock the Vote: www.rockthevote.org

Rock the Vote is a nonprofit organization that works to engage young people in the political process by incorporating the entertainment community and youth culture in outreach efforts. This website provides a link to voter registration.

Bus Project: busproject.org

The Oregon Bus Project was founded in 2001 to "bring voters out of the woodwork" through "zany forums" designed to teach the public about candidates and issues and encourage voters to elect progressive candidates in swing districts. This site provides links to volunteer opportunities as well as the history and goals of the organization.

MoveOn.org: moveon.org

MoveOn.org aims to help busy but concerned citizens "find their political voice." The organization's website provides links to current campaigns.

Black Congressional Caucus: www.house.gov/kilpatrick/cbc

The Black Congressional Caucus is an organization of African American members of Congress. This site provides links to caucus history, member information, news, and events.

American Association of Retired People: www.aarp.org

The AARP website provides links to information about health, travel, leisure, family, and politics.

National Voter Registration Act: www.usdoj.gov/crt/voting/nvra/activ_nvra.htm

This site provides information regarding the provisions and enforcement of the 1993 National Voter Registration Act, also known as the Motor Voter law.

United States Election Project: www.elections.gmu.edu

This website is intended to provide information on elections, election statistics, electoral laws, research reports, and other useful information that pertains specifically to American elections. By providing this information, the Election Project aims to inform United States citizens on how their electoral system works, how it can be improved, and how they can participate in it.

CHAPTER
9 Voting, Elections, and Campaigns

INSERT BALLOT

When Americans woke up on the day after the 2000 election, they did not know who their next president would be. The identity of the 43rd president would only become clear more than a month later, when Democratic Vice President Al Gore conceded victory to Republican George W. Bush. Gore's concession speech came 36 days after Election Day. It occurred only after a deeply divided Supreme Court denied Gore a statewide vote recount in Florida.

After all was said and done, a number of people had a lot of explaining to do. Television network executives had to explain why they made not one, but two mistaken calls in Florida (first calling the state for Gore, then for Bush) before finally saying it was too close to call. Voting machine manufacturers and election officials had to explain the high number of spoiled (uncountable)

▼ GORE WINS!

Television network executives had to explain to the American people why they made not one but two mistaken calls in Florida before deciding the race was too close to call.

ballots across the entire country, especially in Florida. The Democratic election supervisor in Palm Beach County, Florida, had to explain the confusing butterfly ballot design, which many voters claimed had caused them to vote unwittingly for independent candidate Pat Buchanan rather than for Democrat Al Gore. Supreme Court justices had to explain their controversial ruling, which ended the Democrats' legal challenges. And Al Gore had to explain why he had not won the election in a landslide, given his association with eight years of peace and prosperity under the Clinton administration.

Lost among the errant network calls, confusing ballots, and novel legal rulings was another embarrassing fact—embarrassing, at least, for political scientists. Using analysis that had proved highly reliable in previous presidential elections, a panel of political scientists at an American Political Science Association conference had uniformly predicted that Gore would beat Bush. Their estimates of Gore's share of the two-party vote (that is, the total number of votes cast for either the Republican or the Democrat, but

not for third-party candidates like Ralph Nader) ranged between 53 percent and 60 percent.[1]

Although political scientists had predicted a sizable Gore popular-vote victory, his actual share was 49.7 percent, only about half a percent more than George W. Bush. "It's not even going to be close," one had confidently proclaimed.[2] Furthermore, since the popular vote does not decide presidential elections, the election ended with an exceedingly narrow Gore defeat. Obviously, political scientists had some explaining to do as well. Still, to be fair, political scientists got it right in 2004, 2006, 2008, and 2010.

What went wrong in 2000 and right in all those other years? The types of analysis used to predict elections differ in some minor ways, but most share some basic characteristics. First, they assume that party identification determines individual vote choice. Citizens tend to identify with one of the two major political parties. When more voters go into an election identifying with one party more than another, that party will have an advantage. The advantage that the Democrats had heading into the 2000 election helps explain why the political scientists' models predicted a Gore victory in 2000. In that election year, more members of the electorate identified themselves as Democrats than as Republicans. In 2008, more members of the electorate identified themselves with the Democrats while the pendulum swung back the other way in 2010 with the electorate's attachments trending more toward the GOP.

Second, the models also assume that voters cast their ballots with a retrospective perspective, selecting candidates based on their or their party's past performance, rather than comparing what each candidate would do if elected. The 2000 election came after nearly a decade of robust economic growth, presided over by a Democratic administration.

Since voters' retrospective judgment of the Democrats' performance was generally positive, according to the theory, that should have been reflected more widely in the popular vote. In 2008, the economy was in trouble and voters were dissatisfied with the Bush administration. In 2010, voters were holding the Obama administration and the Democrats accountable for high unemployment and difficult economic times.

So, while the results in 2008 and 2010 seem to make sense, what happened in 2000? Did Al Gore blow the election? Or did political scientists blow their predictions? In order to answer the questions and the factors that generally explain election outcomes, in this chapter we will examine the factors that determine individual vote choice and collective election outcomes—not just party identification and incumbent performance, but also the nature of the candidates' campaigns, their issue positions, and voter assessments of them as individuals, as well as the rules that structure and finance campaigns and elections.

CHAPTER LEARNING OBJECTIVES

After reading this chapter you will be able to:

9-1 Outline election procedures, such as how candidates are nominated and how winners are determined.

9-2 Identify the key factors that determine how voters make electoral choices.

9-3 Identify the key factors that determine the outcome of presidential and general elections.

9-4 Analyze the methods candidates use to conduct and pay for election campaigns.

The Basic Rules Governing American Elections

9-1 Outline election procedures, such as how candidates are nominated and how winners are determined.

The choices available to voters in America, and the decisions voters ultimately make about who they want their leaders to be, are strongly shaped by the rules governing elections. To understand individual vote choice and collective election outcomes, then, we must understand the rules of American elections. If presidential elections were decided on the basis of the popular vote rather than an Electoral College majority, presidential candidates would probably conduct their campaigns much differently. Furthermore, the rules that govern U.S. elections are different from those in most other democracies around the world. Most parliamentary democracies, for example, employ a system known as proportional representation. In this system, seats in the legislative body are assigned according to each party's vote share. Therefore, a party whose candidates ran a consistent second in every race would still be allocated a significant number of seats in the legislature. Also, in many countries, party leaders or party committees choose the nominees to run in the general election. In Great Britain, for example, if an individual wants to run for Parliament under the Labour Party banner, his or her candidacy must be approved by a small committee of Labour Party leaders or members. This is not so in the United States, where a different set of rules decides party nominations for president and other elected offices.

ThinkingComparatively

How seats are allocated and how parties choose their nominees differ significantly from country to country and can have a large impact on the organization and actions of governments and the policies they choose to pursue.

ThinkingComparatively

Whereas a winner-takes-all system decides seats in the U.S. Congress, many countries use a system of proportional representation that awards seats based on vote share.

The first objective of a candidate that is running for president is to receive his or her party's nomination.

Only one candidate can be listed on state ballots as the Democratic candidate for president, or a House or Senate seat, and only one as the Republican candidate.[3] That is the candidate who receives the party nomination. As a result of running under the

delegates individuals who represent a state's voters in the selection of a political party's presidential candidate.

caucus a small meeting at which registered political party members select delegates to attend the national party convention and nominate a presidential candidate.

primary election in which voters choose the candidate that will represent their political party in the general election.

party label, that candidate will receive "built-in" support from the party's members in the electorate and may also get substantial financial and logistical help from the state and national party organizations.

How does a candidate receive the nomination of his or her party? In the presidential race, he or she does so by successfully accumulating a majority of **delegates**—representatives of the voters—at the party's nominating convention in the summer before the November election. Candidates earn delegates' support primarily by competing in state primaries and caucuses. All of the primaries and caucuses for presidential elections are held during a five-month period of each election year, from late January or early February through June. By tradition, Iowa always holds the country's first caucuses, and New Hampshire always holds the country's first primary.

In a **caucus** system, registered members of each political party are invited to get together in small meetings around their state. At these meetings, party members select delegates to attend regional and state-level conventions. These conventions then choose delegates to send to the national conventions. The delegates who attend the national conventions are usually pledged to specific presidential candidates.

A primary system is considerably simpler. A **primary** election is conducted just like a regular election, with voters casting ballots for the candidate of their choice. However, the voter may choose only from candidates of one party. In some primaries, delegates are assigned to candidates in proportional fashion—that is, a state's delegates are assigned to each candidate based on his or her proportion of the primary vote.

In the 2008 New Hampshire Democratic presidential primary, for example, Hillary Clinton received 39 percent of the vote; Barack Obama, 36 percent; and John Edwards, 16 percent. Bill Richardson received 5 percent of the vote and Dennis Kucinich got 1 percent. All Democratic primary delegates are allocated in proportional fashion. Under the Democratic Party's rules, a candidate must receive at least 15 percent of the primary vote in order to receive a proportional share of that primary's delegates.[4] With rounding, Clinton and Obama each ended up with nine delegates and Edwards with four. Of course, primaries in general, and New Hampshire in 2008 in particular, can be about more than just accumulating delegates. Clinton's win in New Hampshire in 2008 resurrected her campaign and gave her the momentum to continue.

▼ IOWA CAUCUS
Registered Democrats gather in this school cafeteria to voice their support for Hillary Clinton.

In Republican presidential primaries, by contrast, delegates in some states are allocated according to the **winner-take-all** rule—that is, coming in second—even if one loses by only one vote—means that the losing candidate gets no delegates. The choice between proportional and winner-take-all allocation is left up to the party in individual states. In 2008, for example, Arizona Senator John McCain received 50 percent of the Virginia Republican primary vote, while Mike Huckabee garnered a solid 40 percent. Because Virginia's Republican primary system is winner-take-all, however, McCain was awarded all of Virginia's 63 delegates to the Republican Party's national convention. Although Huckabee had received almost half of the Virginia vote, he got none of the state's delegates.[5]

Rules governing primaries may differ from state to state. In an **open primary**, a voter can participate in either party's primary (but not both), regardless of his or her party registration. In a **modified open primary**, registered voters who are not affiliated with either party can vote in either party's primary. A registered Democrat, however, cannot "cross over" and vote in a Republican primary, or vice versa. Finally, in a **closed primary**, only registered Democrats can participate in the Democratic primary, and only registered Republicans can participate in the Republican primary.

Most states have closed primaries and caucuses. The logic of this system is obvious: only registered members of the party should have a voice in selecting the party's nominee. But if party voters have more extreme views than members of the general electorate, they may end up selecting a nominee who will not have broad appeal in the general election. An open primary helps address this problem, by allowing voters outside the party to have a say in choosing the party's nominee. In the 2008 campaign, because Barack Obama did better with independents, Hillary Clinton often did better in closed primary states.

Most of our discussion here focuses on the presidential nominating process. The process for securing the nomination for a House or Senate seat is different from that for the presidential race and much more straightforward. A congressional candidate must win the party's primary election in order to run as the party's candidate in the fall election. But, unlike presidential primary contests, which occur over a series of months as candidates attempt to secure delegates, congressional primaries are conducted like a typical election in which the plurality winner receives his or her party's nomination.

As we discuss in the parties chapter, parties in the United States exert far less control over who runs under their party label than parties in other countries. In 2010, for example, the favorites of Republican party leaders lost primaries in Colorado, Delaware, Nevada, and Kentucky. And, in fact, in Alaska and Utah, incumbent Republican senators lost their contests to be re-nominated. The fact that insurgent candidates won Republican primaries in Colorado, Delaware, and Nevada most likely cost the GOP three additional Senate seats as those nominees then went down to defeat in races that most observers considered the GOP's to win.

The presidential nomination process has changed significantly in American history.

The allocation of convention delegates by presidential caucuses and primaries is a relatively new phenomenon that has come about in the last 30 years. Until 1972, state delegations were chosen not by voters but by powerful party leaders and elected officials within the states. Some states did have primaries prior to 1972, but they were usually not binding and did not actually choose delegates. Instead, they were "beauty contests," so-called because candidates ran in order to demonstrate to party leaders their appeal to voters. For example, John F. Kennedy made a strong effort in the West Virginia primary in 1960. He did not do so to win a large number of delegates

winner-take-all election in which the candidate who gets the most votes wins, while any other candidate loses and receives nothing.

open primary an election in which a voter can participate in either party's primary (but not both), regardless of party registration.

modified open primary an election in which registered voters who are not affiliated with either party can vote in either party's primary.

closed primary an election in which only registered members of a political party can participate in the party's primary election.

▶ CHAOS AT THE
CONVENTION

Police and protesters collide in
the streets of Chicago following
the Democratic convention.

to the national convention—West Virginia had few delegates, and they were not
bound to support the state's primary winner. Instead, Kennedy campaigned strongly
to prove to party leaders around the country—the ones who would actually choose
and control the delegates at the party convention—that the Catholic Kennedy could
win votes in an overwhelmingly Protestant state.

The watershed year of 1968   Party primaries began to take on much greater
importance after the tumultuous Democratic nomination campaign of 1968. In that
year, after a weaker-than-expected victory over Minnesota Senator Eugene McCarthy
in the New Hampshire primary, incumbent Democratic President Lyndon Johnson
decided not to seek reelection. With the once formidable Johnson out of the way, two
other prominent Democrats joined the race—New York Senator Robert Kennedy,
younger brother of John F. Kennedy, and Vice President Hubert Humphrey.
McCarthy and Kennedy competed in a number of primaries and mobilized many
young voters who were adamantly opposed to the ongoing war in Vietnam. After Senator Kennedy was assassinated on the night of his victory in the California primary,
the field was left to Humphrey, who supported President Johnson's Vietnam War policy, and McCarthy, who had become the standard-bearer for the anti-war movement.

Even though Humphrey did not campaign in any of the Democratic primaries,
party leaders supported his candidacy. Thus, Humphrey arrived at the 1968 Democratic convention in Chicago with a sufficient number of delegates to win the nomination. To anti-war activists and supporters of McCarthy and Kennedy, this meant a
continuation of the current Vietnam policy, which they strongly opposed. Their
anger boiled over into the streets of Chicago, where violent demonstrations and
clashes with the police ensued. All of this unrest during the convention was captured
on live television and broadcast to the entire country. Ultimately, Humphrey lost a
close election in November to Republican Richard Nixon, while independent candidate George Wallace picked up 13 percent of the popular vote and 46 electoral votes.

Democratic reforms   Aware of the damage that the convention had done to their
party's nominee, the Democratic Party appointed a commission to study ways to give

rank-and-file party members a greater voice in the choice of the party's nominee. South Dakota Senator George McGovern, who would become the Democratic Party's nominee for president in 1972, chaired the commission. The recommendations of the McGovern commission led to the system of delegate selection described above—one in which candidates accumulate delegates chiefly through primary and caucus votes, rather than through the back-room dealings of party leaders.

The Democratic reforms led to a proliferation of presidential primaries. In 2008, 38 states held Democratic primaries, and 34 states held Republican primaries. In 1968, by contrast, the numbers were 17 and 16, respectively. The remaining delegates were chosen in caucuses. All of these delegates chosen by voters in primaries and caucuses are dubbed "pledged delegates" and are committed to voting for the candidate they pledged to on the first ballot at the nominating convention.

Super-delegates and brokered conventions　One exception to the trend toward the increasing importance of primaries is the creation of Democratic "super-delegates." Since the 1980s, the Democratic Party—though not the Republican Party—has selected a bloc of about one-fifth of its convention delegates outside the primary and caucus process. These super-delegates include:

- Members of the Democratic National Committee (DNC).

- Democratic members of the U.S. House and Senate.

- Sitting Democratic governors.

- Other distinguished Democratic party leaders, such as former presidents, vice presidents, and DNC chairs.

▼ **WHOSE VOTES COUNT?**

Harold Ickes, a strategist for Hillary Clinton, argues for the full reinstatement of the delegates for Michigan and Florida. Earlier in the year, the delegates from these states had been stripped of their voting rights at the Democratic party convention for failure to abide by party rules. In the primary elections held in both states, Clinton outperformed her main opponent, Barack Obama.

STAR TRIBUNE
sack

— FASTER THAN A PRIMARY ELECTION....
— MORE POWERFUL THAN ANY CAUCUS RESULTS....
— ABLE TO DICTATE A NOMINEE NO MATTER WHO GOT THE MOST VOTES.....

SUPERDELEGATES

▲ **THE SUPERPOWERS OF SUPER-DELEGATES**

Super-delegates have the power to vote for whomever they choose at the Democratic convention. They often express their support for a particular candidate beforehand. Hillary Clinton and Barack Obama competed for the votes of these all-powerful few throughout the primary season.

Super-delegates may vote for whomever they choose at the convention, but they are typically expected to follow the preferences expressed by voters during the primary and caucus season. If a single candidate does not emerge with a majority of the delegates, however, there would be a "brokered convention," in which party leaders would have to choose a candidate to carry their party's banner in the fall election. In such a situation, the super-delegates would be expected to support the most electable candidate, and would probably induce other convention delegates to follow their lead. This brokered convention scenario, although a perennial favorite of political journalists, political scientists, and other political junkies, has not occurred since the 1968 Democratic reforms were instituted. In 2008, with Barack Obama having a lead but not a majority of pledged delegates, the battle for the Democratic nomination was actually decided by the super-delegates. Over the spring, both Hillary Clinton and Obama fought hard to convince these Democratic Party leaders that they were the most deserving and most electable.

More primaries, earlier primaries   As the number of primaries has increased over the past 30 years, primaries have also been occurring earlier in the year. In 1972, for example, the New Hampshire primary took place on March 7. In 2008, the New Hampshire primary was held on January 8. Other states, seeing the attention and money that flow to the early contests in Iowa and New Hampshire, have moved up their contests as well. In 1968, for example, fewer than 10 percent of states holding primaries had done so by the end of March. In 2008, that number was nearly 75 percent. In 2008, the states of Florida and Michigan moved up their primary days to January to get more attention. This change resulted in the Democratic Party's penalizing the two states and taking away their delegates. Ironically, primaries late in the season that few thought would matter—Ohio and Texas on March 3, Pennsylvania on April 22, and North Carolina and Indiana on May 7—became crucial and received immense attention from the campaigns and the media.

As the primary calendar has shortened, many states now hold primaries on the same day. In the 1980s, Democrats in southern states sought to turn this situation to their advantage. Concerned about what they considered the liberal tilt of the national Democratic Party, and eager to avoid a repeat of Walter Mondale's 49-state loss to Ronald Reagan in 1984, southern Democrats united to create a regional primary, dubbed Super Tuesday. The first Super Tuesday primary was held on March 9, 1988. The results of that contest were mixed, with the Reverend Jesse Jackson, Senator Al Gore, Governor Michael Dukakis, and Representative Richard Gephardt each taking at least one state.

Although the nomination went to Governor Dukakis, who represented the liberal wing of the Democratic Party, Super Tuesday also gave a boost to the candidacy of moderate Democrat Al Gore. In the next Super Tuesday contest, in 1992, the consummate Democratic centrist, Arkansas Governor Bill Clinton, swept the day's primaries and became unstoppable in his quest for the nomination.

Presidential election rules are complicated.

In a presidential election, determining winners and losers tends to be substantially more complicated than in congressional races. In the fall general election for president, the winner of the popular vote may or may not win the presidency. In

2000, for example, Al Gore won the national popular vote, but he lost the presidential election to George W. Bush. To win the presidency, a candidate must win a majority in the Electoral College—regardless of the popular vote total—and Gore did not. This scenario had also played out in the highly controversial election of 1876. Despite winning the popular vote by more than 200,000 ballots, Samuel J. Tilden lost the Electoral College and the presidency by one vote, 185 to 184, to more popular Rutherford B. Hayes.

The decision to select the president via the Electoral College rather than by popular vote resulted from a compromise during the Constitutional Convention in Philadelphia in 1787. Delegates at the convention considered two options for selection of the president—popular vote, and selection by members of the House of Representatives. The popular vote was not favored by representatives of smaller states, who imagined that their states' influence in the presidential election would be overwhelmed by the larger states.[6] At the same time, some convention members worried about whether the largely uneducated populace could be counted on to make a wise choice for president. Yet others worried about logistical issues involved in holding a single nationwide election on a specific day.[7]

The alternative to popular election—selection of the president by the House of Representatives—was more strongly favored by convention members, but it also raised concerns. The chief worry was that the president would be beholden to the legislature that had selected him, violating the principles of separation of powers and checks and balances. This scenario might lead to the very tyranny that the new system was intended to prevent.[8]

The convention reached a compromise solution, the **Electoral College**, which addressed a number of these concerns, albeit imperfectly. Small states received disproportionately high representation in the Electoral College relative to their population. Each state was granted an elector for each member it sent to the House of Representatives. But each state, regardless of size, was also granted an elector for each of its two senators. Because the Constitution needed to be ratified by 9 of the 13 states, with each state counting equally, this compromise was likely necessary to receive adequate support from small states.

For those who worried about the capacity of the people to pick an appropriate president, the Electoral College was thought of as an assembly of "wise men" who would choose a president more carefully than the masses. The electors from each state would meet in their respective states about a month after Election Day and vote for the presidential and vice presidential candidates of their choosing. If no candidate received a majority of the delegates' votes, then the House of Representatives would determine the president.[9] On Election Day, therefore, though they may not realize it, voters in presidential elections are casting their ballots for a party's slate of electors to the Electoral College, not directly for the president.

With only two exceptions, states assign their electoral votes on a winner-take-all basis. Maine and Nebraska allocate their electors somewhat differently. In these two states, the winner of a state's popular vote as a whole receives two electoral votes. Then, the remainder of the electoral votes is allocated by congressional district, with the popular vote winner in each district receiving one electoral vote. In 2008, Barack Obama was able to win one of Nebraska's Electoral College votes.

The modern Electoral College consists of 538 electors, representing the 50 states and the District of Columbia. Each state's number of electors is equivalent to its combined number of House and Senate members. (The District of Columbia does not have voting representatives in the House or Senate, but it receives three

> "For those who worried about the capacity of the people to pick an appropriate president, the Electoral College was thought of as an assembly of 'wise men' who would choose a president more carefully than the masses."

Electoral College the meeting, in each state and the District of Columbia, of electors who cast votes to elect the president.

electors in the Electoral College.) In 2000, for example, Florida had 23 members in the House of Representatives and, like every other state, two senators. Thus, Florida had 25 votes in the Electoral College. In the 2000 presidential election, with every state except Florida counted, George W. Bush had earned 246 electoral votes, and Al Gore had earned 266. (One elector abstained in protest.) Thus, the Florida race was crucial because the candidate who won would have more than the 270 electoral votes needed to win a majority of the Electoral College, and therefore the presidency. In 2004, although John Kerry lost the national popular vote by 2.5 percentage points or about 3 million votes, only 120,000 votes separated Bush and Kerry in Ohio—and if Kerry had won Ohio's 20 electoral votes, he would have won the presidency.

The evolution of the modern party system—dominated by two political parties, the Democrats and the Republicans—has changed at least one aspect of the Electoral College in a way America's founders did not envision. Local political parties and the presidential campaigns now select the electors who will participate in the Electoral College vote. Selection is based not necessarily on wisdom or experience, but on service to the party, political contributions, and other demonstrations of party loyalty. Thus, the Electoral College no longer serves as a deliberative body, consisting of wise men and women who will choose the best-qualified candidate. Instead, electors are expected to vote for their party's nominee for the presidency—whether or not they believe that nominee is the best-qualified person. In fact, in most states, they are required to do so or they face a fine.

Figuring out the winner in general elections for Congress is easy.

Determining the winner in U.S. congressional elections is easy; the person who gets the most votes wins. With one or two exceptions, Congressional elections operate by winner-take-all rules. Those who oppose the winner-take-all format and favor a proportional representation system argue that proportional representation produces a legislature that more accurately represents the various opinions of voters. In the U.S. system, they argue, the winner-take-all system leads to two major parties rather than multiple parties, creating conditions where large minorities can feel unrepresented in Congress. However, supporters of the winner-take-all format note that it avoids the factionalism caused by having too many competing parties in the legislature, as is the case in Israel or Italy. Moreover, they note, in parliamentary systems, smaller parties often have to form coalitions after the election in order to create a governing majority. In the United States, by contrast, the major parties themselves represent coalitions, so voters know the coalition they are voting for prior to the election rather than after.

plurality rule rule by which a candidate wins office by getting more votes than his or her opponent, even if that candidate does not receive an absolute majority of the votes.

Congressional and most other U.S. elections are also conducted according to the plurality rule. The **plurality rule** means that a candidate wins office by getting more votes than his or her opponent, even if that candidate does not receive an absolute majority. There are a few isolated exceptions to the plurality rule in the United States, however. Some elections have two rounds of voting. If no candidate receives a majority of the vote in the first round, the contest goes to a second round, or runoff election, in which the top two candidates face off against each other. In 2008, for example, Georgia Senator Saxby Chambliss received 49 percent of the vote on Election Day, beating his Democratic opponent and a weak third party challenger. But because he failed to get an absolute majority of the vote, he and the second place finisher—Democrat Jim Martin—had to face each other in a runoff election, which Chambliss won.

Understanding Individual Vote Choice

9-2 Identify the key factors that determine how voters make electoral choices.

In a presidential election, voters generally have two chances to cast a vote for a candidate—once in the primaries, and once in the general election. Once the campaigns are over, the advertisements have been aired, the debates have come and gone, and the media have made their endorsements, the voters must make a choice and cast a ballot. And because there are different processes for the primary election and the general election, the factors that determine those choices may be different.

Primary voting is less studied and understood than general election voting.

No single aspect of political behavior in America has been examined more often or more closely than the individual vote for president. Although political scientists know a great deal about individual vote choice during the November presidential election, they know relatively little about individual decision-making among presidential primary voters. There are two reasons for this discrepancy. First, the general election determines who will be president, and that choice, in turn, usually has major consequences in terms of domestic policy, the economy, and international affairs. But who wins a particular party's nomination may end up being little more than a historical footnote.

The second reason for political scientists' greater attention to presidential elections is that one critical factor in understanding voting behavior in the general election is not a factor in primary elections—party identification (or party ID). An individual voter's party identification is the single most important influence on vote choice in the general election. In the 2008 general election, for example, 89 percent of Democrats voted for Barack Obama, and 90 percent of Republicans voted for John McCain.[10]

In a primary, though, all of the candidates are of the same party. Political scientists, therefore, cannot explain the primary vote choice as well as they can explain the general election vote. They do, however, have some understanding of the outcome of the primary process as a whole—why a particular candidate ends up being the party's nominee. Accordingly, we will address primary election results in detail in the section on election outcomes.

Partisanship can both influence and be influenced by the general election vote.

In the 1950s, a pioneering study established enduring theories on the role of partisan identification in the behavior of individual voters. In their seminal work *The American Voter*, Angus Campbell, Philip Converse, Warren Miller, and Donald Stokes argue that in pre-adult years, most voters adopt a partisan affiliation that becomes a psychological attitude akin to the attachment a person has to a religion or racial identity. Therefore, it tends to be highly stable over time (although slow change could occur), and it is the predominant force in determining most other political attitudes and behaviors—including voting. This view has come to be known as the "traditional" view of partisan affiliation.

Direction and strength of partisan identification *The American Voter* identified two components in an individual's partisan attachment: direction and strength. Direction refers to whether a person identifies more with the Republican Party or with

Strong		Lean		Lean		Strong
Democrat	Democrat	Democrat	Independent	Republican	Republican	Republican

FIGURE 9-1. **Partisan Identification on a Seven-Point Scale.**

the Democratic Party. Strength refers to the intensity of that attachment. Accordingly, researchers typically measure partisan identification using a series of questions and a 7-point scale that captures both direction and strength, like the one in Figure 9-1.

Since the 1950s, there have been relatively few party ID panel studies that track the same group of individuals over many years. Those few suggest that partisan affiliation is a stable attachment. For example, a panel study that looked at the same group of adults at three different times—1965, 1973, and 1982—found that nearly 80 percent of these individuals maintained the same partisan status from one period to the next. A majority of the rest only moved into or out of the independent category.[11]

ThinkingCausally

Does party identification determine other beliefs and choices or are other factors causing individual party ID?

Differing views of party identification   The traditional view of partisanship sensibly emphasized party ID as a factor that determined other beliefs and behaviors—that is, a causal factor. Because the average citizen pays little attention to the fine points of politics, the voter needs some way to simplify and make sense of the political world. Partisan affiliation is a highly effective mechanism for this. Supporting one's party and opposing the other party is a relatively simple way to organize the political world. Thus, it makes sense to think of partisanship as a lens through which one sees the political world, and a handy shortcut for arriving at opinions about specific political figures and issues.

Not all political scientists are completely satisfied with this view of party ID, however. In the "revisionist" view embraced by some scholars, although party affiliation can certainly influence vote choice, issue stands, and evaluations of candidates, the reverse is also true; those same opinions about issues and candidates can influence party identification. Consistent with this view, political scientist Morris Fiorina has argued that party identification is less a "standing decision" than a mental "running tally" of party performance. Ronald Reagan, a Democrat who became a Republican in the 1950s, reflected this aspect of party identification when he stated, "I didn't leave the Democratic Party. The Democratic Party left me."

Which view of partisan attachment makes more sense: the traditional or the revisionist? Consider that each explains some of the puzzle of partisan attachment. Because of political socialization, most voters develop a partisan attachment long before they would be capable of assessing the parties' performance in office. Furthermore, there is little evidence that individuals switch from one party to another in reaction to party performance (with limited movement to the independent category).

Partisan change and instability   At the same time, partisan affiliation is not always permanent or perfectly stable, nor need it be seen only as a causal agent. Partisans, especially weaker ones, sometimes do switch sides and affiliate with the other party—particularly when extraordinary political events upset existing political arrangements. During the civil rights movement of the 1960s, for example, the national Democratic Party adopted an agenda of federal intervention to promote political, social, and economic equality for African Americans—leaving many white southern Democrats disenchanted (see Figure 9-2).

Another example of political attitudes affecting partisan affiliation instead of the reverse is the emergence in the 1980s of a group of voters known as "Reagan Democrats." These were generally white, working-class voters who had traditionally considered themselves Democrats but began to identify with the Republican Party on social issues. Accordingly, many of these individuals voted for Ronald Reagan in 1980 and 1984 and ultimately registered as Republicans. But, as the traditional theory would suggest, these conversions were not a simple calculation that it suddenly made more sense to identify with the Republican Party. These individuals had to overcome their strong, lifelong attachment to the Democrats.

Other scholars have pointed to the weakening of partisan attachments in the electorate as a whole as evidence that partisanship is not as stable as indicated by the traditional view. As Figure 9-3 shows, the direction and intensity of partisan attachments have changed noticeably since the 1960s.

In the 1960s, pure independents constituted only about 10 percent of the electorate; independents and right or left "leaners" added up to about 25 percent. The 1970s witnessed a further drop in the number of Americans identifying with one of the two major parties—particularly the Democrats.

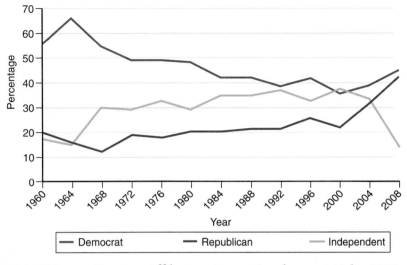

FIGURE 9-2. **Partisan Affiliation Among Southerners, 1960–2008.**

▼ **REAGAN DEMOCRATS**
Ronald Reagan shakes hands with white working-class voters. Some of these voters followed him as he moved from the Democratic to the Republican Party.

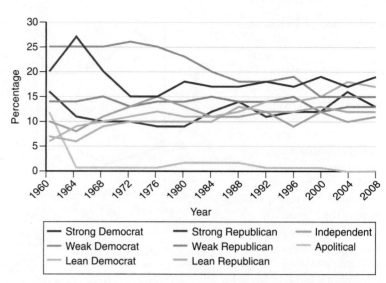

FIGURE 9-3. **Partisan Affiliation Among American Adults, 1960–2008.**

The defection of previous partisans to the independent and "leaner" categories, as shown in Figure 9-3, might raise some doubts about the traditional view of partisan stability. However, research into the dynamics of the dealignment suggests that two other factors have been more influential than partisan defections. First, individuals who came of political age in the late 1950s and early 1960s entered adulthood with weaker partisan attachments than their parents. Second, some individuals who typically would be expected to grow stronger in their partisan attachments over time—a "life cycle" effect of the sort we discussed in Chapter 7—did not do so. Therefore, only a minority of the dealignment—perhaps 30 to 40 percent—can be accounted for by defections among former Republicans and Democrats.[12]

One is generally safe in assuming the durability and stability of partisan attachments and that changes in partisan attachments occur slowly. That said, change can occur, and one of the big stories of the 2008 election was the change in party attachments. In 2004, most polls showed that there was relative parity in the number of voters identifying themselves as Democrats and Republicans. In 2008, Democrats had a double digit lead in party identification. One of the big stories of 2010 was the pendulum swinging back to a more even distribution of party identification. The swings that we have seen in recent years are some of the most dramatic that scholars have documented in the over 60 years of tracking partisan attachments.

Regardless of one's precise view of partisanship and its durability and predictive value, in the long run there is no question that, in the short term, partisan affiliation remains a singularly important predictor of vote choice, in general, and presidential voting, in particular. In recent presidential elections, typically 90 percent or more of "strong" Democratic and Republican partisans have voted for their party's candidate. Among individuals who identify themselves as Democrats and Republicans, though not strongly, the loyalty rate is somewhat lower but still impressive—generally in the range of 70 to 85 percent.[13] In 2010, according to the exit polls, 92 percent of Democrats voted for Democratic candidates for Congress and 95 percent of Republicans voted for Republicans for Congress. Thus, knowing voters' partisan affiliations will yield a tremendous insight into their probable vote choice.

Not all partisans are loyal to their party's candidate in every election, however. Furthermore, not every voter considers himself or herself a Democrat or Republican.

ThinkingCausally

Why do voters sometimes make decisions contrary to those we would expect based upon their party ID?

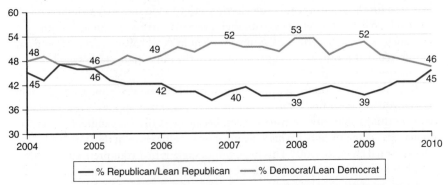

Party Identification and Leaning, Quarterly Averages, 2004 to 2010

FIGURE 9-4. Party Identification Over the Last Six Years. Party ID has been unusually volatile over the last six years moving from parity in 2004 to large Democratic advantages in 2006 and 2008 and back to parity in 2010.

Source: www.gallup.com/poll

Two other factors are thought to have an important influence on the individual vote—issue and policy preferences and candidate evaluations.

Issue and policy preferences have a complex and uncertain impact on voter choice.

Most political scientists agree that voters' opinions on specific issues and their preferences for certain policies can and do affect their presidential vote. The shorthand phrase for this phenomenon in the research literature is **issue voting**. It makes sense intuitively. For example, if you are a strong supporter of universal, government-paid health care, you will likely be inclined to vote for a candidate who also supports that concept rather than one who opposes it (other things being equal). Political scientists also agree on certain preconditions that must exist in order for a voter to engage in issue voting:

issue voting voting style in which the voter judges candidates based on the voter's and the candidates' opinions on specific issues and preferences for certain policies.

- The voter must be aware of the issue and have an opinion concerning it.
- The issue must be at least minimally important to the voter.
- The voter must be able to identify the candidates' positions on the issue accurately.
- The voter must believe that one party or candidate represents the voter's own position better than the other party or candidate.[14]

Beyond these basics, political scientists disagree about the relative importance of issues in the voting decision, the precise mechanisms by which voters compare their issue positions to those of presidential candidates, the kinds of issues that are relevant to voters, and the best ways to study issue voting.

Consistency between issue preference and voter choice Although the above list of requirements for issue voting seems daunting, V. O. Key argued that on highly salient campaign issues, voters were capable of developing meaningful issue positions and voting in part on the basis of them. Using a body of survey data, Key looked at the behaviors and attitudes of individuals in consecutive presidential elections. The most interesting data came from "party switchers"—individuals who voted for different parties in consecutive elections. In comparison with individuals who voted for the same party in both elections, Key found the party switchers much more likely to have disagreements with their previous party on major campaign issues, such as Social Security or U.S. involvement in World War II. From these data, Key inferred that those issue disagreements were the cause of the party switchers' vote changes.

Key's research methods were not without problems, however. Imagine, for example, that you as a voter find a particular candidate personally appealing for reasons having nothing to do with his issue stances. Because you like the candidate so much, you may also come to embrace his issue positions, seeing them in the "reflected glow" of his personal characteristics. This logic would suggest that your preference for the candidate led to your support of his issue positions, rather than the opposite.

Later generations of political scientists, using much more comprehensive voter databases and sophisticated analytical techniques, have addressed this and other shortcomings in Key's analysis. For example, a now classic article by Gregory Markus and Philip Converse acknowledged and adjusted for the fact that the congruence between voters' policy preferences and their vote choices, demonstrated by Key, may be a simple result of voters adopting the issue positions of candidates they prefer. Having made the appropriate statistical corrections for this possibility, Markus and Converse found that voters' ultimate evaluations of candidates were significantly affected by their policy preferences in five different issue areas: social welfare, school desegregation and busing, treatment of minority groups, women's rights, and tax reform (all salient issues in the 1970s, when the study was conducted). Voters' evaluation of candidates, in turn, also had a significant effect on their ultimate vote choice. Thus, voters' issue positions affected the vote indirectly, by contributing to voters' evaluation of candidates.

Retrospective and prospective voting   Scholars also introduced another insight on issue voting. Voters do not only try to project how candidates will perform on important issues in the future—a process known as **prospective voting**. Rather, issue voting can also be **retrospective**; voters simply assess the performance of the party that has held the presidency for the past four years. If the party has performed well on the issues the voter cares about, she will reward that party's candidate with her vote. According to this logic, presidential elections are considered more of a referendum on the incumbent party's stewardship of the country than a judgment about the relative strengths and weaknesses of two competing candidates. Key summed up the essence of this idea in fairly dramatic terms, describing the voter as "a rational god of vengeance and reward."[15]

Support for Key's argument can be seen in a number of twentieth-century presidential elections. Presidents who presided over periods of recession or slow economic growth, or who found themselves mired in serious scandal or controversy, or who were associated with conspicuous foreign policy failures, did not win reelection—Herbert Hoover, Gerald Ford, and Jimmy Carter, among others. Other presidents have served during eras of peace and general prosperity, and so have been rewarded with reelection—Dwight Eisenhower, Ronald Reagan, and Bill Clinton, for example. This same logic applies even when an incumbent president is not up for reelection. In 1988, for example, because of the peace and prosperity of the Reagan years, Reagan's vice president—George H.W. Bush—had a relatively easy path to the presidency. In 2008, although President George W. Bush was not on the ballot, the fact that the incumbent administration was Republican during an economic downturn and a time of great anxiety was clearly harmful to the McCain-Palin ticket. These patterns also hold in midterm elections, as we saw in 2010. Although he was not on the ballot,

prospective voting   voting style in which voters judge a candidate based on their assessment of what the candidate will do in office if elected.

retrospective voting   voting style in which voters judge candidates based on the performance of the candidates or their parties rather than issue stands and assessments of what each candidate would do if elected.

President Obama's plunging job approval numbers in the months leading up to the elections hurt Democratic congressional candidates.

One reason for the intuitive appeal of the retrospective voting model is that making retrospective judgments about whether a particular party deserves to be rewarded or punished is a much easier, more reasonable task than making prospective judgments based on candidate issue positions. Prospective judgments require one to learn what the two presidential candidates say they will do on various issues if elected, and then compare the candidates' positions with one's own. Retrospective voting, on the other hand, simply requires the voter to observe the results of the incumbent presidential party's policies. Furthermore, retrospective judgments require the voter to observe and pass judgment on only those things that the incumbent party has actually done, not what they say they will do.

As noted, voters tend to make retrospective judgments on the basis of "big" issues—for example, the state of the national economy, whether the country is at peace or at war, and if the latter, whether that war is being executed successfully. Furthermore, whether making retrospective or prospective judgments, one should expect issue voting to take place with respect to issues that voters, not researchers, consider important. This point may seem obvious, but in early research on issue voting, researchers often specified the issues that they considered important in national

▼ "HOOVERVILLE"
Shanty towns of the 1930s were called Hoovervilles by those frustrated and disappointed with President Hoover's involvement with the relief effort for the Great Depression.

affairs. This approach had a tendency to understate the relevance of issues in determining the vote.

Developing positions and making voting decisions   Some issues are relatively easy for voters to develop opinions on—and therefore to incorporate into their voting decisions—whereas others are much more technical and complex. For example, compare and contrast two issues: same-sex marriage, and the military action in Iraq after the 9/11 terrorist attacks. With respect to the same-sex marriage issue, there are only two options: for or against. Developing a well-informed position on this issue might require nothing more than thinking through one's own existing beliefs and values. With respect to the Iraq situation, however, a number of policy options were available:

- Maintain the status quo.
- Attempt to strengthen the existing economic sanctions against Iraq.
- Seek to overthrow Saddam Hussein's regime through covert action.
- Support Iraqi forces seeking to overthrow Hussein.
- Launch a renewed weapons inspection program.
- Seek U.N. approval to invade Iraq.
- Invade Iraq unilaterally, without U.N. approval.
- Some combination of these steps.

Although many Americans had opinions, developing a well-informed position on the appropriate Iraq policy would involve a thorough consideration of all these options and their potential costs and benefits—an expertise beyond the reach of the vast majority of Americans. In general, one should expect a greater incidence of issue voting on issues that are relatively easy for the mass electorate to consider.[16]

valence issues   issues on which virtually everyone agrees.

Perhaps the "easiest" issues of all are so-called **valence issues**—issues on which virtually everyone agrees. Almost all voters agree, for example, that less crime is better than more, that peace is better than war, and that lower unemployment is better than higher unemployment. On these issues, voters cannot be said to have conflicting positions. However, voters do have distinct beliefs about which party is better able to handle such valence issues.[17] One voter might believe, for example, that the Democratic Party is more likely to help achieve low unemployment than is the Republican Party. Another voter might believe precisely the opposite.

Some evidence suggests that voters do cast ballots in part on the basis of judgments about the parties' potential handling of valence issues.[18] When this occurs, it does not necessarily mean that voters can explain why or how one party would do a better job managing the issue than the other, or what the voters themselves would like to see done on that issue. In fact, many voters would be unable to offer any such explanation. It does mean, though, that voters are engaged in issue voting of a sort. They care about a particular set of issues, and they will vote for the party that they believe would be more capable of addressing those issues. In 2010, jobs and the economy were clearly the valence issue.

Beyond these generalities, it is difficult to draw conclusions on the circumstances under which a particular issue will affect a given election outcome. This obstacle does not stop journalists, campaign consultants, and even political scientists from claiming that a specific issue—say, abortion, gun control, or "moral values"—influenced or even determined an election. When assessing such claims, keep in mind the prerequisites for issue voting identified above. When these circumstances do not hold, or when their applicability is open to debate, then any talk about issue voting is just that—talk.

Voters appraise candidates in three big ways.

A final factor that many political scientists consider important in influencing individual vote choice is candidate evaluation. This term does not refer to which candidate has the most winning smile, the most engaging wit, or the most photogenic family. Although democratic theorists worry that such superficial characteristics may influence the vote, little political science research indicates that they do. Rather, political scientists have measured candidate evaluations in ways that are typically considered more relevant to an informed, meaningful vote choice. These include candidate ideology and certain traits that characterize their personalities or policies.

- Open-ended voter comments about aspects they like and dislike about specific candidates.[19]

- Voter assessments of whether particular presidential candidates have "the kind of personality a president ought to have."[20]

- "Feeling thermometer" ratings of presidential candidates, in which voters are asked to assign a number to a candidate on a zero to 100 scale, with zero indicating "very cold or unfavorable" and 100 indicating "very warm or favorable."[21]

Despite many studies regarding the effects of candidate evaluations on vote choice—some large, some very modest—no consensus has evolved on the best ways to measure candidate evaluations, or on the relative importance of candidate evaluations among other factors that influence the vote. Even so, it is reasonable to consider candidate evaluations, along with party ID and issue voting, as one of the "big three" determinants of vote choice.

Party ID, issues, and candidate appraisals come together to produce a vote choice.

How exactly do these three elements combine to produce an individual vote decision? This is a difficult question, for two reasons. First, individual decision-making inevitably includes elements of random, idiosyncratic behavior that are very hard to identify and describe—even for voters themselves. Second, the three elements of voter choice interact with each other in complex ways. Party identification can affect candidate evaluations, which in turn can affect a voter's thinking about the candidate's issue positions. Other things being equal, a Republican voter is more likely to evaluate a Republican candidate favorably and then to project his preferred issue positions onto that candidate. For example, "I like everything about John McCain; I'm sure I agree with him on most of the important issues." The reverse is true as well—the voter's understanding of the candidate's issue positions can affect her evaluation of the candidate.

Despite the complexity of these interactions and the degree of randomness inherent in human decision-making, a good, general rule that describes most presidential voting behavior might be:

> The voter canvasses his likes and dislikes of the two candidates involved in the election. He then votes for the candidate for whom he has the greatest net number of favorable attitudes. If no candidate has such an advantage, the voter votes consistently with his partisan affiliation, if he has one.[22]

One can test the accuracy of the rule by generating vote predictions from it using voter survey data. This basic rule, relying on candidate evaluation and party ID, can generate a correct prediction nearly 85 to 90 percent of the time (depending on the election). Thus, it would seem to be a good approximation of the way that voters actually arrive at a final decision.

You may have noticed, however, that the rule includes only two of the "big three" vote determinants: candidate evaluations and party identification. What about voter issue positions? Issue positions influence the vote by way of candidate evaluations. Specifically, the voter's assessment of candidates' issue positions affects the voter's candidate evaluation, which in turn affects the vote. Not surprisingly, party identification also affects voter evaluations of candidates. Because of these relationships, party ID influences the vote through candidate evaluation, and not just as a tie-breaker, as the rule given above would seem to indicate. Finally, party identification also affects voter issue positions, a connection that provides another avenue through which party ID can affect the vote indirectly.[23]

ThinkingCausally

How might party ID affect a voter's positions on health care or the economy?

Understanding Election Outcomes

9-3 Identify the key factors that determine the outcome of presidential and general elections.

The winners and losers of public office in the United States emerge from the interaction of three factors: the laws governing how elections are conducted, the manner in which candidates wage their campaigns, and the ways in which voters decide whom to support. How do rules and campaigns and choices and decisions all come together to determine election outcomes and the leaders who govern us?

Frontrunners have a great advantage in presidential nomination contests.

Even if political scientists do not understand all the ins and outs of vote choice, they do understand the primary election process and how it produces a particular nominee. This understanding has changed significantly over the past generation, however.

The pre-primary season   A candidate hoping to win the party's nomination needs to be prepared to make a credible run in multiple states before the primary season even begins. The candidates best equipped to do this begin the primary season having raised the most money, having already achieved frontrunner status in pre-primary polls, or both. Candidates who have reached one or both of these success milestones—who have won the **invisible primary**—almost always go on to win their party's nomination. This principle holds over most of the previous 11 contested nomination battles for the presidency, as shown in Table 9-1. (A contested nomination is one in which there is no incumbent president seeking the party's nomination.)

Note several things in particular in Table 9-1. First, in most cases the pre-primary season does produce a clear winner of the invisible primary—that is, a candidate who leads in both fund-raising and pre-primary polling. The three exceptions are 1980, 1988, and 2008. Second, when there is a clear invisible primary winner, that individual goes on to win his party's nomination, with the exceptions of 2004 and 2008. Finally, in no case has someone won the nomination unless at the end of the invisible primary period he led the field in public opinion polls, in fund-raising, or in both.

Importance of momentum in past primaries   Until the early 1980s, the key to understanding the primary process was one word: **momentum**. Thirty years ago, primary contests were few in number and spaced far enough apart that even long-shot candidates had time to build a credible campaign over the course of a primary season. An early success in Iowa or New Hampshire gave them a coveted shot of momentum, indicated by a boost in media coverage, name recognition, fund-raising, and

invisible primary   the race to raise the most money and achieve frontrunner status before the primary season begins.

momentum   the boost in media coverage, name recognition, fund-raising, and perceptions of electability that accompanies unexpected and repeated primary success.

TABLE 9-1. Pre-Primary Leaders in Fund-Raising and Opinion Poll Preference Among Party Identifiers, 1980–2008.

YEAR	PARTY	CANDIDATE WITH LEAD IN LAST POLL BEFORE IOWA CAUCUSES	CANDIDATE RAISING MOST MONEY PRIOR TO THE YEAR OF THE ELECTION	CLEAR INVISIBLE PRIMARY WINNER?	EVENTUAL NOMINEE
1980	Republican	Reagan	Connally	None	Reagan
1980	Democratic	Carter	Carter	Carter	Carter
1984	Democratic	Mondale	Mondale	Mondale	Mondale
1988	Republican	Bush	Bush	Bush	Bush
1988	Democratic	Hart	Dukakis	None	Dukakis
1992	Republican	Bush	Bush	Bush	Bush
1992	Democratic	Clinton	Clinton	Clinton	Clinton
1996	Republican	Dole	Dole	Dole	Dole
2000	Republican	Bush	Bush	Bush	Bush
2000	Democratic	Gore	Gore	Gore	Gore
2004	Democratic	Dean	Dean	Dean	Kerry
2008	Democratic	Clinton	Clinton	None	Obama
2008	Republican	Romney	Giuliani	None	McCain

perceptions of electability. They could convert these assets into a successful campaign in the next primary, and the benefits going forward would compound. In this way, by exceeding expectations in an early caucus or primary, a long-shot candidate like George McGovern in 1972, Jimmy Carter in 1976, and Barack Obama in 2008 could leverage the primary process itself to become a formidable candidate for the nomination.[24]

Still, the crowded primary calendar leaves very little time to raise money, organize local volunteers, attend campaign events, and develop and implement state-specific media strategies while the campaign is in progress. A candidate who attempts to run a credible campaign in only one or two early states, hoping to turn that into success in the next round of contests, probably will not have adequate time to make this strategy work. In 2004, for example, North Carolina Senator John Edwards devoted most of his pre-primary resources to the Iowa caucuses, and he finished a surprisingly strong second there. Pre-election polls predicted Edwards would finish further back, and the novelty of his overperforming in Iowa led to increased and favorable attention from the press. But the New Hampshire primary was just one week later, and Edwards finished fourth with 12.1 percent of the vote—receiving no delegates. In 2008, Obama not only won Iowa but had a plan, money, and staff in place for the states that followed.

Emergence of the frontrunner   As demonstrated above, the pre-primary period usually creates a clear frontrunner for the nomination. And in general, although he or she must first compete in a gamut of primaries that inevitably produce twists, surprises, tension, and drama, that individual goes on to win the party's nomination. Why should this be? As we have noted, the compressed primary calendar rewards candidates who can run a credible campaign in multiple states in a very short span of time. The candidate best equipped to do this is the one who has abundant resources and support in place before the primaries begin. He or she will be prepared to win from day one. And, when all is said and done, that candidate usually will win.

Despite the relative accuracy of this claim, there is still something unsatisfying about it. Note that it says nothing about how or why a particular individual comes to win the invisible primary in the first place. The reason we have neglected this topic is that political scientists do not fully understand invisible primary dynamics—specifically, how one builds momentum in the pre-primary period. They do know that early fund-raising success leads to favorable media coverage, which in turn leads to greater name recognition and a higher standing in the polls, which can then lead to more successful fund-raising, and so on. But these relationships simply raise the question, why are some candidates more successful than others at raising money?[25] And why do some candidates who raise large sums of money—such as businessman Steve Forbes in 1996 and 2000, or former Massachusetts Governor Mitt Romney in 2008—not succeed? Even if political scientists could answer these questions, they almost certainly would find it difficult to predict winners of the invisible primary. Those kinds of predictions, however, are the hallmark of good political science theory.

> "The compressed primary calendar rewards candidates who can run a credible campaign in multiple states in a very short span of time."

Beyond this gap in our understanding of the invisible primary, the evolution of the Internet as a political tool and communications medium may be changing some of the basic logic of the primary process. Thanks to the World Wide Web, candidates can now raise and immediately spend large sums of money as fast as interested supporters can type their credit card numbers into a digitized form. Furthermore, websites, Twitter, Facebook, and e-mail make round-the-clock mass communication and campaign coordination possible at an extremely low cost. Thus, Obama's Internet fund-raising allowed him not only to raise money quickly, but to raise it with minimal expense. The Web has also changed the news cycle significantly. Stories that used to be updated once a day, in the morning paper or on the evening news, are now updated continuously, online. Twenty-four-hour news channels and the proliferation of nationwide talk-radio programming have also contributed to this phenomenon. Thus, candidates who need to raise money, communicate with millions of supporters, recruit volunteers, raise media awareness, and get their message out in a hurry now have tools that were not available to them even 15 years ago. Eventually, these factors may change the existing primary season dynamic in which candidates who start behind almost always end behind as well.

Key factors allow political scientists to accurately forecast presidential election results.

In 2008, the American Political Science Association solicited election forecasts from nine different scholars or teams of scholars. These scholars completed their forecasts several months before the fall election. In six out of nine cases, they predicted that Barack Obama would be the new president. On average, the forecasters predicted that Obama would receive 52 percent of the two-party vote.[26] In actuality, Obama received just over 52 percent of the vote. In this instance, the forecasters were amazingly accurate, signifying the reliability and accuracy of these forecasting models.

Factors in forecasting In predicting presidential election outcomes, the political scientists' models generally take into account four different kinds of factors:

- The partisan orientations of the electorate.
- The job approval rating of the incumbent party president.
- The performance of the economy during the first half of the election year.
- Incumbency, that is, whether an incumbent president is running for reelection, and if so how long his party has held the presidency.

Inclusion of these factors should make sense in light of the earlier discussion about partisan orientations, which are obviously a critical influence on individual electoral choices. The incumbent president's job approval gives a rough sense of what kind of retrospective judgments voters will make about the performance of the party in power, about voters' comfort level with that party's issue positions, and about their personal feelings toward the party's leader (the president). Whether or not the incumbent president is running for reelection, all of these factors can influence voters' evaluation of the party's candidate in the general election. Inclusion of an economic performance variable reflects the fact that the strength of the economy has proved to be the single most important issue to voters in election after election. When the economy is performing well, the party in power tends to win. The economy was doing well in 1996 and Bill Clinton easily won reelection. The economy was slowly coming out of recession in 1992, and George H.W. Bush lost the contest to serve another term. When the economy is not doing well, the party in power tends to lose. Finally, the incumbency factor captures the generally greater name recognition and voter comfort with an incumbent president in comparison with a lesser-known challenger. However, incumbency can operate in reverse; the longer the same party holds the presidency, the more likely the voters will become disenchanted with its candidates and policies and vote for a change.

ThinkingCausally

Why would voters factor their assessment of the president and of current economic conditions into their vote choice even when he or she is not running for reelection?

From one election to the next, the factors that are most likely to change sharply, and thus exert decisive effects on election outcomes, are presidential approval ratings and economic performance. Anyone wishing to predict an election outcome, or to understand why an election turned out the way it did, would do well to study one or both of these factors. Looking at presidential elections since 1952, for example, when the incumbent party's president has an average approval rating of 49 percent or better during April, May, and June of the election year, that party's candidate wins the general election. When that number is 46.7 percent or lower, on the other hand, the incumbent party's candidate loses.[27] In between these two numbers is a sort of "no man's land," an area of uncertainty. George W. Bush was dangerously near this no man's land in 2004, barely achieving an approval rating of 49 percent during the second quarter of the election year. Thus, predictions based solely on his approval ratings would have considered him vulnerable, but with a slightly better chance of winning than losing.

Looking at economic performance as a predictor between 1952 and 2008, when gross domestic product (GDP) grows at an annualized rate of at least 2.6 percent in the second quarter of the election year, the incumbent party wins. When growth is 1.5 percent or less, the incumbent party loses. Growth rates in between are inconclusive. Looking again at 2004, GDP grew by 3 percent during the second quarter of the year. This should have put George W. Bush in a relatively good position to earn reelection, though not as strong as some of his predecessors. Richard Nixon, for example, saw 6.9 percent GDP growth in 1972 and was reelected overwhelmingly. Ronald Reagan and Bill Clinton benefited from growth rates of 5.3 percent and 4.6 percent, respectively, during their reelection years. Both were rewarded with a second term.[28] In 2008, with the country in a recession and GDP growth rates negative, even though George W. Bush was not on the ballot, fellow Republican John McCain faced an almost impossible headwind.

Party attachments in the electorate typically change at a snail's pace, and party attachments in this country were essentially even in 2000 and 2004. By 2008, however, the Democrats had a healthy advantage in party identification. Furthermore, with the economy in trouble and the war in Iraq moving into its fifth year, as well as presidential approval numbers in record low territory, all the fundamental factors seemed to be with the Democrats in 2008.

Still, these fundamental advantages that the Democrats enjoyed in 2008 did not mean that Barack Obama would definitely win. Swing voters still would have to reach a threshold level of comfort with a presidential candidate. In 1980, the fundamental factors advantaged the Republicans, but it was not until late in the campaign that Ronald Reagan achieved credibility with key blocks of voters and was able to win the election. In 2004, even with President Bush's approval level in a dangerous zone for an incumbent, John Kerry was not quite able to reach a threshold level of credibility with key swing voting blocks. In 2008, Barack Obama was able to reach that threshold level of credibility and take advantage of the fundamental factors that would have advantaged any Democrat nominee.

CaseStudy: Election 2000: Failed Forecast

We return now to the question posed at the beginning of the chapter. In light of forecasting models that predicted a big win for Al Gore in the 2000 presidential election, did Gore blow the election, or did political scientists blow their predictions? The answer is both. On the one hand, Gore did not receive the normal boost expected from having served under a president with job approval ratings as high as those of Bill Clinton. Why? One explanation is that the Gore campaign sought to distance its candidate from President Clinton, perhaps fearing that disapproval of Clinton's moral behavior might hurt Gore, or wanting Gore to emerge from Clinton's shadow and be his own man. Whatever the reason, Gore avoided running as the candidate of "four more years of good times, without the scandal"—a fact that was noted during the 2000 campaign, and that drew criticism from Democrats. As a result, Gore appears not to have received the full benefit of the Clinton administration's strong economic record.[29]

As for evaluation of the candidate as a man and a potential president, Gore did not suffer from a significant "likeability deficit" with the electorate—despite his admittedly stiff and occasionally prickly manner. He also got relatively high marks from voters for competence and experience, and for his positions on specific issues. However, he appears to have paid a price for voters' perceptions that he was too liberal—more liberal, in fact, than George W. Bush was conservative, and more liberal than the president (Clinton) with whom Gore had served.[30] The Gore campaign has to take some blame for running him as a left-leaning populist, rather than a centrist in the Clinton tradition.

And what about the political scientists? As noted above, their forecasting models do not take into account the unique aspects of a particular campaign, including candidates and their campaign strategies. To the extent that there were particular campaign effects in 2000, as suggested, they worked to Al Gore's disadvantage. This was one reason the political scientists' predictions were overly optimistic about Gore's election prospects. Also as noted, Gore did not attempt what admittedly would have been a difficult straddle—openly embracing the successful record of the Clinton administration while distancing himself from Clinton's behavior in the Lewinsky scandal. But political scientists, too, failed to make a necessary straddle—one that would have been much easier than Gore's. Although they included Clinton's job approval ratings in their models, they did not include voters' assessments of his personal behavior. Historically, these two measures have tended to track one another fairly closely. In Clinton's case, though, his personal ratings were substantially lower than his job approval. This disconnect appears to have hurt Al Gore in the election.[31] In that respect, Gore got the worst of both worlds. He failed to get full credit for his association with the economic prosperity of the Clinton years, and he was weighed down by the judgments of voters disenchanted with Clinton's behavior. It may have been no consolation to Gore, but this split embarrassed political scientists too. By failing to take into consideration Clinton's low personal ratings and include them in their models, they wrongly predicted a very sizeable Gore win.

◄ **FOUR MORE?**

Clinton and Gore campaigned together rarely in 2000. In an attempt to step out of Clinton's shadow and away from his scandals, Gore may also have distanced himself from people's memories of "the good times."

ThinkingCritically

1. If you had been an adviser to Barack Obama or John Mc-Cain in 2008, how would you have explained to them the fundamentals of American presidential elections?

2. Given what you have learned, what campaign message would you have recommended that each candidate try to convey to voters? In order to achieve the objectives of a successful campaign, how would you have communicated the message?

The reward/punishment equation   What all of these voting considerations suggest is that a basic "reward/punishment" or retrospective voting model, combined with a recognition of the importance of partisanship, is a sensible way to think about and understand election outcomes. Every election year starts with the electorate divided into three camps: Republicans, Democrats, and independents. There will be some movement among these groups during the year, but their proportions should remain fairly stable. Naturally, the vast majority of strong partisans vote loyally. Some of the weaker partisans, though, and most of the independents will likely decide on the basis of comparative candidate evaluations that are heavily influenced by the performance and leadership of the party in power. In terms of the political scientists' predictive models, if voters are generally pleased with the incumbent party and its president—as indicated in presidential approval ratings—they will be inclined to look favorably on the party's candidate for president. Likewise, if the economy has performed well with the incumbent party in charge, that party's candidate for president is likely to receive favorable voter evaluations and be rewarded with the presidency.

Those who are not political scientists tend to be uncomfortable with this logic, and with political scientists' predictive models, because they seem to omit so much. In 2004, for example, the news was full of stories on the Iraq War. Had George W. Bush misled the country about the presence of weapons of mass destruction in Iraq? Was deposing Saddam Hussein worth the cost in American lives and tax dollars? Although it might seem that the forecasting models do not take into account such important voter concerns, they do—by way of presidential approval. To the extent these concerns were important to voters, they were included in the president's job approval ratings. And, as noted above, President Bush's second quarter approval ratings were hardly in a comfortable range for him. In fact, when the president's Gallup poll rating dropped to 46 percent in early May 2004, Frank Newport of Gallup said, "Looking at [his approval rating] in context, Bush is following the trajectory of the three incumbents who ended up losing rather than the trajectory of the five incumbents who won."[32]

Congressional Elections.

In many ways the 2010 mid-term elections were the opposite of the 2006 and 2008 Congressional elections. Democrats had an advantage in party identification and the Republicans "owned" the difficult times in those years. Party identification came back to parity in 2010 and Democrats now owned the situation in which economic times were still difficult. While Democrats won independent and swing voters in 2008, independent and swing voters moved decisively to Republican candidates in 2010—by a margin of almost 20 percentage points (56 percent to 38 percent). This resulted in Republicans gaining over 60 seats in the House and six Senate seats. The most comparable postwar midterm election in scope would be 1946: the largest incumbent party loss in the House prior to 2010, and the second largest Senate loss.

The Campaign

9-4 Analyze the methods candidates use to conduct and pay for election campaigns.

The foregoing discussions of voting behavior in general, and of presidential and congressional elections in particular, have mentioned nothing about the impact of the campaign itself on the outcome of elections. What about the hundreds of millions of dollars that were spent on television advertising between Labor Day and November 4, 2008, in the most recent contest for president (see Figure 9-5)? What about the national conventions, debates, and visits to key states like Florida, Ohio, and Pennsylvania? What about all the campaign activity that went on in the run-up to the 2010 midterm elections? Did none of this matter at all?

The short answer is yes, it did matter. In fact, considered from one perspective, it mattered greatly. Imagine a hypothetical election year in which one party decided to mount an election campaign, but the other party did not. One party ran television and radio advertisements, conducted a **direct mail** campaign, organized get-out-the-vote efforts (GOTV) in important states, showed up for the debates, traveled around the country to motivate and mobilize local party activists, and held a national convention. Now, imagine that the other party did none of these things. Would it matter? Almost certainly. The party that had run a campaign could expect a higher turnout rate among partisans than the party that had done nothing. The party that had run a campaign could expect higher loyalty among its partisans—that is, fewer voter defections to the other party's candidate—than the party that had done nothing. Finally, the party that had run a campaign could expect a higher vote among weak partisans and independents than the party that had done nothing.

In the real political world, though, in competitive races both sides run very active, aggressive campaigns. In one sense, then, the parties' efforts offset one another. But the parties' and candidates' efforts are not always equally effective. In a close race, a particularly good campaign or a particularly inept one might budge the vote just enough to make a difference between winning and losing. This edge is clearly

direct mail political advertising in which messages are sent directly to potential voters in the form of mail or e-mail, rather than using a third-party medium.

Targeted states

FIGURE 9-5. Map of Advertising Buys in 2008. Advertising in the presidential race in 2008 was highly focused, with a handful of states getting the great majority of all advertising dollars.

demonstrated in debates, which have played an important role in presidential campaigns since the beginning of the modern television era. Campaigns spend countless hours preparing for debates, as they can sometimes play a pivotal role in shaping the outcome of a race. Take, for example, the events surrounding the first ever nationally televised debate in the 1960 presidential election between Vice President Richard Nixon and Senator John Kennedy. About 70 million viewers tuned in to see a pale and sickly looking Nixon side by side with the tan and telegenic Kennedy. This contrast helped Kennedy win the "image" battle, and many point to this as a significant catalyst in Kennedy's victory. This first debate serves an important lesson for those that have followed in the years since: debates can often swing a campaign just enough to make a difference.

▲ **CAMPAIGNS MATTER AT THE MARGINS**
Though it is hard to measure the impact of GOTV efforts, political scientists believe that campaigns matter for electoral outcomes.

After all, had 269 voters in Florida voted for Gore instead of Bush, Florida would have gone for Gore and he would have won the presidency. Thus, though political scientists do not think of the campaign—or debates, for that matter—as routinely decisive, they recognize that it can be—particularly when the country is closely divided politically. They also freely admit that their forecasting models, which do not explicitly account for campaign effects, often miss the mark in their predictions by a few percentage points. These misses clearly could be a result of unmeasured campaign effects—and as noted, in a close election those effects can be the difference between winning and losing. We have more to say about campaign and media effects in Chapter 10.

ThinkingCausally

What kind of "campaign effects" might influence an election outcome in a close race?

Turnout, loyalty, defection, and persuasion are the ingredients of a successful campaign.

Consistent with the arguments presented above, candidates and their campaign managers know that to win any election, they must successfully achieve as many as possible of the following objectives:

- Achieve high turnout among their own party's identifiers.
- Win a large share of the vote from their own party's identifiers.
- Encourage some of the other candidate's partisans to defect.
- Reduce turnout among the other candidate's identifiers.
- Win independents.

A winning campaign equation based on these objectives would look something like this:

Turnout + Loyalty + Defection + Persuasion = Victory

The equation begins with turnout—getting large numbers of your own partisans to show up on Election Day, and if possible, demoralizing the other candidate's partisans so that they do not vote. Loyalty is next—ensuring that the highest possible percentage of your partisans vote for your party's candidate. Defection is the reverse of loyalty—getting some of the other party's voters to cast their ballots for your party's candidate. Last comes persuasion—convincing independent voters that they should vote for your candidate rather than the other party's. Put all of these elements together, and they add up to victory.

Campaign messages are meticulously researched and targeted.

How do campaigns pursue the elements of victory? First, by developing messages or themes beneficial to their candidate. When constructed properly, these messages may induce voters to view one candidate more favorably; may generate enthusiasm among partisans, inspiring them to vote; and may demoralize the other party's voters, discouraging them to vote. Messages and themes that have these qualities are repeated endlessly in debates, campaign appearances, and television and radio advertising.

The fundamental factors mentioned above—the state of the economy and presidential approval—render some messages more plausible and effective than others. A shaky economy, for example, set the stage for Bill Clinton's successful campaign to unseat George H.W. Bush in 1992. With its mantra of "It's the economy, stupid," the Clinton team continually reminded voters of the country's sluggish employment situation, placing the blame squarely on Bush's shoulders. The substantial rise in welfare caseloads under President Bush also opened the door to the memorable Clinton pledge to "end welfare as we know it."

In other cases, the political environment significantly constrains the message options available to candidates. Consider 1980, when Jimmy Carter's reelection bid was hindered by an election-year recession and a series of foreign-policy crises, including a protracted hostage standoff at the U.S. embassy in Tehran, Iran. A "You've never had it so good" campaign did not fit the facts or the national mood. Thus, Carter unsuccessfully sought to raise serious doubts about his opponent, Ronald Reagan, and the conservative Republicans that Reagan spoke for:

> The Republican nominee advocates abandoning arms control policies which have been important and supported by every Democratic President since Harry Truman, and also by every Republican President since Dwight D. Eisenhower. This radical and irresponsible course would threaten our security and could put the whole world in peril. You and I must never let this come to pass.[33]

How do campaign managers develop such messages? Using information gathered from research on their opponents and the positions of their own candidate, they identify the most persuasive arguments for their side and against their opponent, and the most compelling language with which to couch their message. Among the methods they use toward this end are surveys and **focus groups**—in-depth interviews with a small number of people representing important voter constituencies (undecided voters, for example). Consider this excerpt from a 2004 focus group report prepared by Democracy Corps, a not-for-profit political consulting firm founded by Democratic campaign professionals:

focus group in-depth interview with a small number of people representing important voter constituencies.

> In our discussions with voters, we explored attitudes toward George W. Bush and John Kerry, [and] views on major issues impacting the vote. . . . We also compared Bush's current message with a Kerry message centered on American priorities, and looked at voters' responses to some of the candidates' television commercials.
>
> Key observations include:
>
> ■ Attitudes toward Bush remained unchanged from the many other focus groups we have conducted since 9/11. Positive feelings still revolve around his moral character, Christianity, strong family, leadership, decisiveness, and patriotism. The only policy related area where he received credit was 9/11 and his strong response during the nation's crisis. As usual, the doubts about Bush were wrapped in his close ties to big business, spending too much overseas at the expense of our problems at home, and for some, a go-it-alone foreign policy.
>
> ■ Perceptions of Kerry are forming and most participants had some opinion of him, frequently reflecting the messages delivered in the Bush and Kerry television

commercials. A dominant attitude was that Kerry changes his position on issues and tells people what they want to hear; he will also raise their taxes. And while people recognize his military service, for now, negative perceptions driven by the media dominate the positive ones.

■ Despite the even division among the number of [2000] Gore voters and Bush voters within the focus groups—which, as usual, played out with highly polarized views on Bush and the parties—the Kerry message of prioritizing and creating a strong America, and going in a new direction was far better received than Bush's message of steady leadership demanded by these times. This perception held true in all groups regardless of gender, income, or education.[34]

Once campaign messages are developed and tested, they need to be delivered. Television advertising is one major way that political campaigns deliver their messages. In the 2008 presidential campaign, over $800 million was spent on television advertising. (Tens of millions more were spent on radio and direct mail ads.) Because the Electoral College ultimately chooses the president, candidates have a strong incentive to focus their advertising on states that are expected to be especially competitive in the fall campaign because they have many Electoral College votes. With winner-take-all rules for assigning the vast majority of electoral votes, it makes little sense for candidates to invest resources in states that they can safely expect to win or lose. There is no "extra credit" for an especially large victory margin, and no credit at all for coming in second. Campaigns spend advertising dollars accordingly.

In the 2008 election, for example, the McCain and Obama campaigns bought no political advertising at all in the country's three largest states: California, New York, and Texas. Both camps were confident that Obama would win California and New York and McCain would triumph in Texas. Thus, neither had any reason to advertise there. But the McCain and Obama campaigns both invested heavily in television advertising in three states that were vote rich and thought to be competitive: Ohio, Florida, and Pennsylvania. Obama ended up winning all three.

In recent years, the list of such competitive or **battleground states**, along with those that are reliably Republican or Democrat, has been fairly stable. In 2004, the Republican states came to be known as **red states** because of media graphics that used the color red to indicate these states on election maps. For the same reason, reliably Democratic states have come to be called **blue states**. Competitive, swing, or battleground states are usually indicated with white, yellow, or gray. In 2008, the battlefield expanded with traditional red states like Indiana, Virginia, and North Carolina becoming battlegrounds. All three of these states were ultimately won by Obama. Figure 9-6 offers one picture of the states thought to be red, blue, and competitive, prior to the 2008 election. Figure 9-7 shows the actual results of the 2008 election.

In 2010, the battlefield for control of the House of Representatives expanded to almost 100 districts, and there was also a major focus on 12 states that would decide which party would control the US Senate. Senate contests in Nevada, West Virginia, and Washington drew particularly strong national attention. In many ways, 2010 was the opposite of 2008. The 2008 election was fought on the Republican side of the field while the 2010 campaign was waged on the Democratic side of the field.

Field operations encourage voting and make it more convenient to vote.

To help achieve their objectives, presidential campaigns pursue one final type of campaign tactic: **field operations**. If television advertising constitutes the air war in a political campaign, then field operations are the ground war. Field operations are intended to produce high turnout among party loyalists, particularly in battleground states. Specific tactics include phone calls, letters, e-mail, social networking, and

battleground states competitive states in which no candidate has an overwhelming advantage, and therefore Electoral College votes are in play.

red states largely uncontested states in which the Republican candidate for president is very likely to win.

blue states largely uncontested states in which the Democratic candidate for president is very likely to win.

field operations the "ground war" intended to produce high turnout among party loyalists, particularly in battleground states.

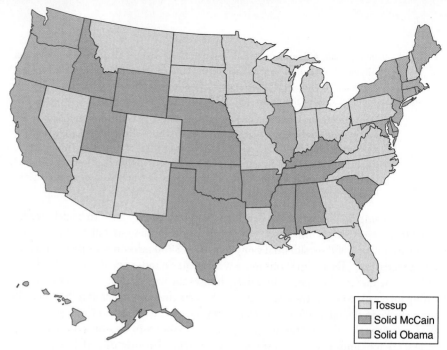

FIGURE 9-6. **Classification of States According to Competitiveness: Solid McCain, Solid Obama, Toss-up.** The 2008 election was very much played on the Republican side of the field, with Obama able to count on almost 200 Electoral College votes and most of the competitive states being places McCain needed to win.

FIGURE 9-7. **State-by-State Results from the 2008 Election.** In 2008, Barack Obama won every state won by John Kerry in 2004 while also winning Nevada, Colorado, New Mexico, Iowa, Virginia, North Carolina, Indiana, and Florida—all states won by George W. Bush in 2004.

Note: Nebraska splits its electoral votes; 4 went to McCain and 1 went to Obama.

personal visits, encouraging supporters to vote and offering resources to help them do so. For example, Democrats know that African Americans in most cases will overwhelmingly support their party's nominee. The Democratic Party has, therefore, traditionally invested significant resources in get-out-the-vote efforts targeted at African American neighborhoods in large cities within competitive states. Republicans, by contrast, invest considerable energy in turning out white, evangelical Christians, who have become core supporters of the GOP.

Campaign finance laws govern the way campaigns raise and spend money.

Running a modern campaign for the presidency or for Congress is extremely expensive. In the 2008 election, Barack Obama spent more than $650 million on his campaign. His GOP opponent, John McCain, spent more than $350 million. Candidates in competitive Senate races in 2010 typically spent over $20 million, and some House candidates spent over $5 million.

In order to spend money, campaigns first have to raise it. The rules governing campaign fund-raising are complex, and they have changed considerably in recent years. To understand campaign finance, one must begin with the three kinds of monies used to fund federal campaigns: hard money, soft money, and public money. **Hard money** refers to funds designated for the express purpose of running an election campaign, and are subject to strict limits on size and source. Federal candidates and political parties are restricted to using only hard money. **Soft money** refers to funds designated for political purposes other than running a campaign—voter registration and get-out-the-vote efforts, for example, or political advertising by interest groups unaffiliated with a campaign or political party. It can also speak to money spent trying to influence other political or legislative decisions, which is called issue advocacy. **Public money** refers to taxpayer funds designated to help finance presidential campaigns, both in the primary season and in the general election. The laws and regulations governing these three kinds of monies differ substantially. It is another sort of hard money.

hard money funds to be used by candidates or parties for the express purpose of running an election campaign, or by PACs for contributing to candidates.

soft money funds to be used for political purposes other than running a campaign, for example, get-out-the-vote efforts; or by some interest groups for political ads praising or attacking candidates.

public money taxpayer funds used to help finance presidential campaigns.

Sample Advertisement

"Pledge"

Clinton: I will not raise taxes on the middle class

Announcer: We heard this a lot.

Clinton: We gotta give middle class tax relief, no matter what else we do.

Announcer: Six months later, he gave us the largest tax increase in history. Higher income taxes, income taxes on Social Security benefits, more payroll taxes. Under Clinton, the typical American family now pays over $1,500 more in federal taxes. A big price to pay for his broken promise. Tell President Clinton you can't afford higher taxes for more wasteful spending.

FIGURE 9-8. Sample "Issue Ad" Paid for by the Republican Party. As of 2002, parties are no longer allowed to use soft money. Before this, however, they were able to raise unlimited funds to pay for ads like this one that did not use "magic" words that explicitly advocated for a vote against a candidate.

political action committee (PAC) a group that collects money from individuals and makes donations to political parties and candidates.

Hard money   For each political campaign, individuals are currently permitted to contribute up to $2,400 in hard money to candidates. The primary election and general election are considered separate elections, so an individual can contribute $4,800 per year to the same campaign. Because this amount is indexed to inflation, it will rise to keep pace with future price increases. The amount in 2008 was $2,300.

To each of the national political parties (the DNC and the RNC), an individual each year may contribute up to $30,400 in hard money—an amount that is also indexed for inflation. In addition, an individual may contribute up to $5,000 to any federal **political action committee (PAC).** A political action committee is an organization funded by 50 or more people, usually affiliated with a corporation, labor union, or some other special interest group. The PAC combines individual contributions to funnel campaign funds to federal candidates. It exists, in part, as a way to allow corporations and labor unions to make campaign contributions under tight regulations: these groups are prohibited by law from contributing directly from their corporate or union treasuries to a political campaign. Political action committees also allow individuals to pool their resources, thereby having greater influence on a campaign than they could exert on their own.

independent expenditures funds spent to elect or defeat candidates but not coordinated with any candidate's campaign.

The parties and interest groups are also able to make unlimited **independent expenditures**. These are expenditures on behalf of a candidate, but without any coordination between the party and the candidate's campaign. For example, the party might wish to pay for a campaign advertisement in a local newspaper or television station. Interest groups, as of the 2010 elections, are allowed to use hard or soft money to pay for these expenditures, but parties can only use hard money. If the party checks with the candidate's campaign on the wording of the ad, that would be a **coordinated expenditure**, and such coordination is prohibited for PACs.

coordinated expenditures legally limited purchases or payments made by a political party on behalf of, and in coordination with, a specific campaign.

Table 9-2 summarizes the amounts of hard money or express advocacy funds that can be given directly to a campaign, national party, or PAC, by an individual, PAC, or national party, respectively.

Public money and matching funds   In addition to hard money and soft money, public money has been a major source of funding in presidential campaigns. The funding structure in the primary election process is different from that in the fall general election.

matching funds public monies given to qualifying candidates to match a certain percentage of the funds they have raised from private donors.

During the primary season, candidates for their party's nomination can qualify for **matching funds**, which are public monies given to candidates to match a certain percentage of the funds they have raised from private donors. In order to receive matching funds, a candidate must raise at least $5,000 in individual contributions of $250 or less in at least 20 states. The candidate must also agree to adhere to both state-specific and total spending limits during the primary season. Finally, should the candidate fail to receive at least 10 percent of the vote in two successive primaries, he or she loses eligibility for matching funds.

TABLE 9-2. Hard Money Contribution Limits.

	TO ANY CANDIDATE CAMPAIGN	TO A NATIONAL PARTY	TO A POLITICAL ACTION COMMITTEE
An individual can give	$2,400 per election, indexed to inflation	$30,400 per year, indexed to inflation	$5,000 per year
A PAC can give	$5,000 per election	$15,000 per year	$5,000 per year
A national party can give	$5,000 per election in the House; up to $42,600 for a Senate campaign	Not applicable	$5,000 per year

Candidates who can clear the fund-raising hurdle, agree to the spending limits, and continue to get at least 10 percent of the vote in party primaries will receive matching funds. Specifically, the federal government will provide a dollar-for-dollar match for each individual contribution received by the candidate up to certain limits.

Candidates are not required to receive public money. If they accept public money, however, they must abide by the spending limits. If they do not accept public money, they are free to spend what they wish. This format is consistent with the Supreme Court's rulings on campaign finance—namely, that spending limits on campaigns are unconstitutional unless they are voluntary. Government, therefore, has to offer something to get candidates to agree to limit their spending. In determining whether or not to participate in the matching fund system, then, candidates have to assess their ability to win the nomination within the confines of the federal spending limits, and also their ability to raise the funds without the help of public financing. Furthermore, candidates often want to spend money after the primary season is over—to keep their names on voters' minds before the national conventions and fall campaigns take place. If a candidate believes that the federal spending limits will leave inadequate dollars to fund a post-primary media campaign, he or she may opt out of the public funding system.

In recent years, most major candidates have shunned public financing during the primaries. In 2000, for example, George W. Bush became the first eventual party nominee to refuse matching funds. In 2004 he refused again, as did Democratic Senator John Kerry, who went on to become his party's nominee. In 2008, none of the major candidates accepted matching funds in the primaries. On the Democratic side, Hillary Clinton and Barack Obama raised massive amounts of money—over $200 million for Clinton and over $250 million for Obama. The campaigns raised their money in significantly different ways from one another, however. The majority of Clinton's contributions came from donors giving the maximum amount. Obama relied on many more contributors—over 3 million—who gave smaller amounts, often online.

Once the parties have selected their nominees, the federal government provides financing for the fall general election campaign. In 2004, the Democratic and Republican presidential nominees each received about $75 million to spend on the presidential campaign. As a condition of receiving this money, however, the candidates had to agree that (a) their campaigns would not seek to raise or spend any additional funds from private individuals; and (b) they would not spend any more than $50,000 of their own personal funds on the campaign. If they agree to these terms, the candidates are able to spend the campaign funds largely as they see fit, with no state-specific limits on spending. In 2008, Barack Obama refused public funds for the general election campaign, while the Republican nominee, John McCain, took the $84 million. This decision allowed the Obama campaign to vastly outspend the McCain campaign and have complete control of the candidate's campaign message.

Third parties—parties other than the Democratic and Republican—can qualify for full general election campaign funding only if they receive at least 25 percent of the vote in the previous presidential election. If a party accomplished this, it would retroactively receive the same amount received by the two major parties in that year, and it would be given an equal share in the next presidential election, just like the two major parties. And just like the major parties, it would receive these funds at the outset of the general election campaign, not after the election. No third party has received full public funding, but third parties can receive some public funds by receiving at least 5 percent of the national vote in the preceding election. For example, based on the performance of presidential candidate Ross Perot in 1992 and 1996, the Reform Party qualified for partial general election funding in 1996 and 2000.

HOW DO WE KNOW?

Can Congressional Candidates Buy Victory with Campaign Spending?

The Question

Running a campaign for Congress can be very expensive. In 2010, for example, the two candidates for senator in California, Barbara Boxer and Carly Fiorina, spent a total of $41 million on their race. In the same year, in a single House district in Florida, candidates Ron Klein and Allen West spent a total of more than $9 million. Looking at all of the 2010 House and Senate races together, the Federal Election Commission reported that spending by Democratic and Republican congressional campaigns reached nearly $1.5 billion.[35] The magnitude of these dollar amounts raises serious concern about the cost of congressional campaigns. Some critics have charged that candidates are simply buying their way into the House or Senate, using vast sums of donated campaign cash. This claim is precisely the sort of issue that political scientists study. Specifically, they ask: Can congressional candidates buy victory with campaign spending? How do we know?

Why It Matters

The growing chorus of concerned observers calling for campaign finance reform stresses the need to "get money out of politics." Their argument is that as campaigns become more costly, candidates must increasingly rely on private donations to get elected. The successful candidate may then feel beholden to his or her financial supporters, making

▼ SHOW ME THE MONEY
Incumbent Barbara Boxer and challenger Carly Fiorina spent over 41 million dollars in their 2010 California battle for the U.S. Senate.

decisions that favor their narrow interests. Those interests may conflict with the broader interests of the candidate's legislative district, state, or even the nation as a whole. One way to reduce candidates' reliance on private donors is to limit the amount of money that can be spent on a campaign. But such a restriction will likely have an adverse effect on one group of candidates in particular—challengers. Challengers rely on campaign spending to level the playing field with incumbents, who enter the election season with a number of advantages. Thus, any reform designed to reduce the amount of money that candidates can spend on their election campaigns may reduce the competitiveness of congressional elections and increase the already sky-high reelection rates of incumbent members of the House and Senate.

Investigating the Answer

A basic way to investigate this question is to determine whether, in fact, candidates who spend more money than their opponents actually win their elections. Most of the time, they do. In 2010, for example, House incumbents who won with more than 60 percent of the vote spent on average nearly ten times the amount spent by challengers. In races where the incumbent won with less than 55 percent of the vote, the advantage in spending was $1.50 for every $1 spent by challengers.[36] Clearly, then, there is a correlation between the amount of campaign spending and the probability of an election victory. But a political scientist would ask whether that correlation reflects causation—that is, whether candidates who spend more win because they spend more. As we noted in Chapter 1, very few political phenomena can be explained by a single cause. Instead, most events in the political world have multiple causes. Accordingly, a political scientist seeking to determine the impact of campaign spending on election outcomes needs to build a model that takes into account not just the impact of campaign spending, but all of the other variables that affect the election result.

Political scientists have, in fact, constructed such models of the electoral process, using various statistical techniques. In these models, the outcome is typically a measure of the incumbent candidate's share of the two-party vote in the election. The two causes or variables are (a) the amount of money the incumbent candidate spent on the campaign, and (b) the amount of money the challenger spent on the campaign. Together, these two causes represent the campaign-spending variable. The purpose is to determine the extent to which campaign spending affects the election outcome, given the other variables known to influence election results, such as the party ID composition of the electorate, the challenger's political positions, the incumbent candidate's past performance, and so on. To ensure the most accurate results, all variables must be considered.

What have political scientists learned about the impact of campaign spending on election outcomes? To date, the results have been inconclusive on whether, or how much, incumbent spending affects the outcome of an election. However, challenger spending does appear to exert a large and consistent impact on election results. Specifically, the more the challenger spends on an election campaign, the higher his or her vote percentage tends to be, other things being equal. Even though the results on incumbent spending are inconclusive, let us assume for the moment that challenger spending does matter. Why would this be? An incumbent is usually well known and well liked and has the benefits of office to help preserve and promote his or her standing with the electorate. Under these circumstances, campaign spending does not help an incumbent much, precisely because the incumbent does not need much help. Because he or she starts the electoral cycle in a highly favorable position, spending money on a campaign can improve that position to a very limited extent.

Unlike incumbents, challengers often begin the election cycle with little name recognition among voters and none of the incumbent's advantages of office. At the outset of a campaign, therefore, they can be at a distinct disadvantage. Yet by spending large amounts of money during the campaign, challengers can raise their name recognition dramatically, and help create a favorable impression among voters. Put simply, money can help challengers buy some of the familiarity, respect, and good will that incumbent office holders get for free. That familiarity, respect, and good will can translate into votes for the challenger on Election Day.

These arguments make sense intuitively, and political science research supports them in most circumstances. However, imagine that an incumbent holder is facing a very strong challenger who is well known and well liked, and who has managed to raise a significant amount of money, or who has a large personal fortune available to finance a campaign. With a challenger of this quality, the campaign will be hard fought, and the election will probably be close. When an incumbent office holder expects an election to be close, he or she will usually raise and spend significant sums of money to fend off the challenge. Even so, because the challenger is strong and has also raised large sums of money, the race usually ends up being close anyway. In other words: incumbent expects close race, incumbent spends heavily, outcome is close.

If, on the other hand, the incumbent faces an unknown challenger waging a largely symbolic campaign with little or no money to spend, the incumbent has every reason to expect an easy victory. Under those circumstances, he or she usually will raise and spend relatively little money. Ultimately, because the challenger is so weak, the incumbent usually wins handily. In other words: incumbent expects easy win, incumbent spends little, incumbent wins big.

It is often the case that the more an incumbent spends, the closer the race ends up, and the less he or she spends, the greater the margin of victory. This is somewhat counter-intuitive; one might expect that when incumbents spend a lot of money, they should win big, and when they spend only a little money, the race will be close. This paradoxical result occurs, however, because the same factors—the strength, experience, and quality of the challenger—influence both how much money the incumbent spends and the closeness of the outcome on Election Day.

The Bottom Line

There is not an easy answer to the question of whether money buys elections. In fact, the topic is a classic example of a point we have made throughout this book—namely, that correlation does not equal causality. That said, a variety of studies demonstrate that challenger spending is likely to matter more than incumbent spending, and that even incumbent spending can matter at the margin—which can make all the difference in a close election. In 2010, there were an unusually large number of races decided by less than 2 percent, including the Senate races in Washington and Colorado, and as late as mid-November, about 10 House races were still too close to call.

Thinking Critically

■ What kind of impact does the rise of campaign spending have on elections overall? In particular, do you see any problems with such a dramatic rise in campaign expenditures?
■ Besides those mentioned in the previous paragraphs, what other factors may cause a rise in incumbent spending? In challenger spending?
■ Briefly explain campaign spending and victory in terms of correlation and causation.
■ Should there be limits on campaign spending? If so, how much? If not, why not?

CHAPTER SUMMARY

In this chapter you have learned to:

9-1 Outline election procedures, such as how candidates are nominated and how winners are determined.   The first objective of a candidate running for office is to receive his or her party's nomination. In the presidential race, the candidate does so by winning a majority of delegates to the party's nominating convention during the state primary elections. The Electoral College and the winner-take-all system do much to define the American political landscape.

9-2 Identify the key factors that determine how voters make electoral choices.   Certain key factors determine how voters make electoral choices. Primary among these are "the big three" determinants: party identification, issue voting (including the retrospective vote), and candidate evaluations. A voter's party ID is the single most important influence on vote choice in the general election. Other influences are voters' opinions on specific issues and retrospective voting, in which voters judge candidates based on their, or their party's, past performance. Despite idiosyncratic voter behavior and the complex interaction of "the big three," vote prediction forecasting models are highly accurate.

9-3 Identify the key factors that determine the outcome of presidential and general elections.   In order to succeed in presidential primaries, it is crucial to win the invisible primary. This includes leading the field in public opinion polls, in fund-raising, or in both at the end of the pre-primary period. Candidates who begin the heavily front-loaded primary season in the lead often go on to win. Primaries follow each other too rapidly for underdog candidates to devote resources to multiple races and build the momentum necessary to win the nomination. In general elections, presidential approval ratings and economic performance are the two variables most often included in election forecasting models—and have excellent predictive power. The partisan orientations of the electorate, whether there is an incumbent president running for reelection, and how long the party has held the presidency are also significant factors. Not to be forgotten, however, is the significance of campaign effects at the margin in close races.

9-4 Analyze the methods candidates use to conduct and pay for election campaigns.   Understanding the "victory equation" and its components—turnout, loyalty, defection, and persuasion—is crucial to understanding how presidential candidates wage a campaign. The main ways candidates attempt to secure these components are by developing messages or themes beneficial to the campaign and by effectively managing field operations. The messages and field operations are carefully planned and are targeted almost exclusively to battleground states. Forecasting models and candidates are not perfect, however, as demonstrated by the failed forecasts of the 2000 presidential election. Ultimately, the Al Gore campaign and political scientists failed to appropriately manage and account for Bill Clinton's negative association—and both suffered the consequences.

Finally, running a modern campaign for the presidency or for Congress is extremely expensive, and campaign finance laws dictate how money may be raised and spent by candidates. Campaign finance laws further distinguish between hard, soft, and public money, and are responsible for the recent proliferation of 527 organizations to circumvent restrictions on these monies.

PEARSON mypoliscilab EXERCISES

Apply what you learned in this chapter by starting with these resources on MyPoliSciLab.

Read on **mypoliscilab.com**

e-text: Chapter 9

Study and **Review** on **mypoliscilab.com**

Pre-Test
Post-Test
Chapter Exam
Flashcards

Watch on **mypoliscilab.com**

Video: Dissecting Party Primaries
Video: State Primary Race
Video: Who Are the Superdelegates?
Video: Money in the 2008 Presidential Race
Video: Oprah Fires Up Obama Campaign

Explore on **mypoliscilab.com**

Simulation: You Are a Media Consultant to a Political Candidate
Simulation: You Are a Campaign Manager: Countdown to 270!
Simulation: You Are a Campaign Manager: Lead Obama to Battleground State Victory
Simulation: You Are a Campaign Manager: McCain Navigates Campaign Financing
Comparative: Comparing Voting and Elections
Comparative: Comparing Political Campaigns
Timeline: Nominating Process
Timeline: Close Calls in Presidential Elections
Timeline: Television and Presidential Campaigns
Visual Literacy: Iowa Caucuses
Visual Literacy: The Electoral College: Campaign Consequences and Mapping the Results

KEY TERMS

battleground states, p. 343

blue states, p. 343

caucus, p. 343

closed primary, p. 319

coordinated expenditures, p. 346

delegates, p. 318

direct mail, p. 340

Electoral College, p. 323

field operations, p. 343

focus group, p. 342

hard money, p. 345

independent expenditures, p. 346

invisible primary, p. 334

issue voting, p. 329

matching funds, p. 346

modified open primary, p. 319

momentum, p. 334

open primary, p. 319

plurality rule, p. 324

political action committee (PAC), p. 346

primary, p. 318

prospective voting, p. 330

public money, p. 345

red states, p. 343

retrospective voting, p. 330

soft money, p. 345

valence issues, p. 332

winner-take-all, p. 319

SUGGESTED READINGS

Paul Abramson, John Aldrich, and David Rohde. 2007. *Change and Continuity in the 2008 Elections.* Washington, DC: CQ Press. Straightforward and accessible analysis of the 2008 election, evaluating campaign strategies and their impact on the outcome of the midterm elections.

Gary Jacobson. 2008. *Politics of Congressional Elections.* New York: Longman. A comprehensive review of the current literature on congressional elections: why people vote as they do, variance in outcomes across districts and states, changes over time in aggregate representation (who has power), and the implications for democratic governance.

Richard G. Niemi and Herbert F. Weisberg, eds. 2010. *Controversies in Voting Behavior*, 5th ed. Washington, DC: CQ Press. The key questions in political science: Why is voter turnout low and declining? Does the public lack of political information or expertise matter? What

determines vote choice? Do campaigns matter? Do voters intentionally elect a divided government? How much does politics affect party ID? Are parties changing? Also, essays on party realignment and the polarization of the American electorate.

Angus Campbell, Philip E. Converse, Warren E. Miller, and Donald E. Stokes. 1960. *The American Voter*. Chicago: University of Chicago Press. Argues that party ID is the major influence on voters' perceptions of political choice and their final vote, that party ID is stable and resistant to outside influence, and that partisanship is adopted early in life.

Jan Leighley. 2010. *The Oxford Handbook of American Elections and Political Behavior*. New York: Oxford University Press. The various approaches and issues in research design, political participation, vote choice, and the influences on individuals' political behavior.

SUGGESTED WEBSITES

Democratic National Committee: www.democrats.org

Provides links to the Democratic National Convention, action plans, and agenda as well as opportunities to register to vote and contribute to current campaigns or the party.

Republican National Committee: www.rnc.org

Offers links to blogs, calls to action, groups affiliated with the party, party issues, and state parties.

Democratic National Convention: www.demconvention. com

Links to blogs, speeches, and videos from the 2008 convention. The site is updated before each presidential election.

Republican National Convention: www. gopconvention2008.com

Videos, a schedule, and links to delegates and blogs pertaining to the 2008 election. The site is updated daily during convention years.

PoliticalMaps.org: politicalmaps.org

The best and most interesting political maps. Site managers update the site regularly during election season.

Federal Election Commission: www.fec.gov/law/feca/ feca.shtml

The FEC was created by Congress in 1975 to administer and enforce the Federal Elections Campaign Act (FECA). The FEC hosts this Campaign Finance Law site, which provides links to statutes, legislative recommendations, campaign finance reports and data, committee meetings, enforcement matters, and help with reporting and compliance.

National Institute on Money in State Politics: www.followthemoney.org/index.phtml

The institute is a nonpartisan, nonprofit organization that examines the influence of campaign money on state-level elections and public policy throughout the United States. This site provides access to the institute's data, research, and reports.

Obama versus Fox News

As long as there has been a United States president, there has been friction between that office and the press. But there have been times when that long-standing rivalry has taken some unusually mean turns. Newspaper editorials savaged Abraham Lincoln during the Civil War, calling him a "blockhead," a "moron," and a "widow maker." The majority of daily newspapers, led by the powerful *Chicago Tribune*, opposed Franklin Roosevelt politically. And Richard Nixon took the *New York Times* and *Washington Post* all the way to the Supreme Court over the Pentagon Papers, when he tried and failed to stop those newspapers from publishing the government's secret reports on Vietnam. Later, it was the *Post* that kept up the investigation of the Watergate scandal, which eventually brought down the Nixon presidency (with a special assist from CBS White House correspondent Dan Rather).

▼ OBAMA VERSUS FOX

Frustrated with the tone of the network's coverage, the Obama administration picked a fight with Fox News.

In the fall of 2009, Barack Obama began his own conflict with Fox News, a cable network that was harshly critical of his young presidency. After a hugely successful campaign a year earlier, tremendous popularity in the polls, and with a large democratic majority in both houses of Congress, the administration thought it was in a position to force its opponents in the media to cave in. But the new president would quickly learn what previous administrations had learned before: taking on a free press in the United States in head-to-head combat is rarely a winning proposition. This skirmish also came at a time when the entire landscape of the news media in America was in the midst of a seismic makeover. Newspapers were losing their influence, and alternative media, like the Internet and cable news channels, were changing the basic assumptions about how Americans get their information.

Since the beginning of network television in 1948, three companies held sole ownership of that domain: NBC (National Broadcasting Company), CBS (Columbia Broadcasting System), and ABC (American Broadcasting Company). Their news divisions created evening news broadcasts in the 1950s. At first, solemn men simply read the news with very little video. But as technology expanded, television reporters like Walter Cronkite, Chet

Huntley, and David Brinkley became known as anchormen and began to exercise tremendous influence on national political debates. One event catapulted television news beyond every other form as the chief purveyor of information—the assassination of President John F. Kennedy. From the first bulletins at 12:40 P.M. on Friday, November 22, 1963, until the end of the funeral the following Monday, practically the entire country shared the grieving experience through these three channels. Americans began to shift from newspapers and radio to television, and from that point on, the vast majority got their news from the "big three."

In 1980, that dominance began to erode when CNN, the first 24-hour, all-news cable channel, premiered. The big three paid little attention to CNN at first. Many Americans still did not have access to cable. Again, it was a major news event that changed the equation. On January 15, 1991, a U.S.-led coalition attacked Iraq after that country had invaded Kuwait. Unlike the big three, CNN had placed reporters in downtown Baghdad and had the ability to broadcast live from a city that was being bombarded by American war planes. It was the first war that viewers could watch live. As cable's influence grew over the next decade, new channels were created. Microsoft teamed up with NBC to create MSNBC. In 1996, media king Rupert Murdoch hired longtime Republican strategist Roger Ailes to start another channel, Fox News. But, unlike the others, Ailes concentrated Fox News on opinion journalism, and that opinion often leaned to the conservative side of American politics.

Ailes was prescient. After the terrorist attacks on September 11, 2001, and the subsequent invasions of Afghanistan and Iraq, Americans were drawn to this form of opinion news. Soon, Fox sailed past CNN in number of viewers with its "fair and balanced" trademark. Fox also marketed itself as an alternative to the more liberal mainstream media or "MSM." In response, MSNBC switched to a left-of-center alternative to Fox, and gained in popularity.

From the beginning of the Obama administration in January 2009, Fox News focused much of its airtime on the new president's policies in a more critical way than the other news outlets, which were accused by conservative critics of being too supportive of the White House. It was Fox News that broke the story that one of the administration's appointees, Van Jones, had a more radical past than many Americans were comfortable with. Jones quickly resigned, but the appointment was an embarrassment to the White House. Similarly, Fox broadcast a tape of White House Communications Director Anita Dunn singling

out Chinese Communist leader Mao Zedong as someone she admired. She would soon be gone as well.

In September 2009, the White House launched a counterattack against Fox. In a direct shot aimed at Fox News, President Obama appeared on every major news channel except Fox. Anita Dunn said that "Fox News often operates as either the research arm or the communications arm of the Republican Party." In an attempt to further cut off Fox, the Fox News White House correspondent was excluded from an interview with an administration economist, at which point the other networks came to Fox's defense—refusing to have one of their own singled out for retribution. And one Democratic consultant who regularly appeared on Fox was even warned by the White House to stay off the network.

In the end, what was the outcome of the White House counter offensive? By March 2010, Fox News' two major personalities, Bill O'Reilly and Glen Beck, respectively, enjoyed a 28 and 50 percent increase in ratings from a year earlier.[1] At the same time, CNN and MSNBC lost viewers. The Obama Administration gained nothing and it came at a time when the president's popularity ratings slipped as well. Clearly, the White House had miscalculated and quickly realized that although the president was seen as the most powerful man in the world, that power appeared to be inconsequential compared to the power of the American media. In the words of the old newspaper maxim, often attributed to Mark Twain: "Never get into a fight with someone who buys ink by the barrel."

355

CHAPTER LEARNING OBJECTIVES

After reading this chapter you will be able to:

10-1 Evaluate the unique role that the media play in American politics and society.

10-2 Identify the legal constraints on American media.

10-3 Differentiate the types of media that exist today.

10-4 Analyze the nature of media coverage of politics and government.

10-5 Determine whether the media are biased.

10-6 Assess the effect of the media on political attitudes and behaviors.

The Unique Role of the American Mass Media

10-1 Evaluate the unique role that the media play in American politics and society.

The **mass media, or media,** are the various modes of communication designed to reach a mass audience. These include television, radio, newspapers, news magazines, and the Internet. The term also refers to the individuals responsible for producing the content disseminated through various communications media. Thus, when this chapter refers to "the media," it may be referring to the actual communications media themselves (newspapers, for example), or to the people who are responsible for their content (such as newspaper reporters and editors). In many respects, the mass media occupy a position in American political life different from that in most other countries. We shall examine several of these differences in this section.

mass media or media various modes of communication intended to reach a mass audience—including television, radio, newspapers, newsmagazines, and the Internet.

American mass media are largely privately owned.

Unlike in other industrialized democracies, the largest media outlets in the United States are owned and operated in the private sector, rather than by the government. Prior to the 1980s, there were government restrictions on how many news and broadcast outlets one

ThinkingComparatively 🌑🌑🌑🌑

In a majority of democratic countries, the government owns at least one major news outlet.

company could own. Each of the networks could only own three local stations. But after these limitations were lifted, the United States saw a wave of takeovers and mergers. The News Corporation, a global media enterprise under the ownership of Rupert Murdoch, added Fox News and the *Wall Street Journal* to its holdings. CNN and Time Warner merged. Disney bought ABC. CBS was purchased by Westinghouse, which was then placed in the hands of Viacom. The U.S. government, however, does not own any major television networks or cable news outlets. Public broadcasting in the United States receives only a small share of its funding from the government and accounts for about 2 percent of the total television audience share.[2] By contrast, in the vast majority of European countries and the democratic countries of Asia and the Pacific, the government owns at least one major television outlet.[3] Government-owned outlets in these areas typically have at least a 30 to 40 percent audience share.[4]

Newspapers are a different story. In the industrialized democracies, including the United States, government ownership of print media is highly unusual. However, many other countries have a print tradition that is not well established in the United States—that of the national newspaper. Most American newspapers are tied to a particular city, state, or region—the *San Francisco Chronicle, New York Post, Des Moines Register*, and *Denver Post* are examples. Although *USA Today* attempted to change that, producing a national daily paper in 1982, the majority of Americans continued to rely on their local papers. The *Wall Street Journal* also turned its business format into a national daily as well, especially under the ownership of Murdoch. In other countries, though, some of the oldest, most respected, and most widely read newspapers are national in scope. These include the *Sun* in the United Kingdom, *Le Monde* in France, and *Die Zeit* in Germany.

American mass media stress objective political coverage.

A second difference lies in the American media's effort to be objective and nonpartisan in covering the news. This means that reporters and editors generally seek to present all sides completely, fairly, and accurately. It was not always this way. William Randolph Hearst created one of the most powerful and successful newspaper chains in the 1890s; by the mid 1920s, he owned 28 of the most influential papers in the country, with a brand of titillating and sometimes even false but sensational stories known as yellow journalism. (Hearst, by the way, was the inspiration behind the 1941 film *Citizen Kane.*) By the 1940s, papers and radio networks strived to play it fair. Journalists usually refrain from advocating particular views or suggesting who or what is right and wrong. They have always operated independently of government and the political parties, refusing to become spokespeople for any particular party or government administration.

But the concept that the mainstream media were unbiased was put under question in the 1990s with the advent of cable television and conservative talk radio. Personalities like Rush Limbaugh, Sean Hannity, and Bill O'Reilly argued that the "MSM," which included the *New York Times*, CBS, NBC, and ABC News, may have claimed to be unbiased but showed a penchant for reports that favored liberal viewpoints.

This accusation led to a profusion of advocacy journalism. Fox News, with its conservative focus, quickly outpaced the older and established CNN. MSNBC countered with a left of center point of view. CNN insisted on trying to run down the middle but fell far behind in ratings. In fact, CNN's decline in 2010 was so precipitous, many of its program hosts lost almost half their viewers. CNN fell behind Fox News, MSNBC,

▲ NATIONAL AND REGIONAL NEWSPAPERS

Although papers like the *New York Times*, *Wall Street Journal*, and *USA Today* have national readerships, virtually all American newspapers are based in particular cities or regions. Papers like France's *Le Monde* have a more national scope.

◄ **REMEMBER THE MAINE**

In the heyday of Yellow Journalism, newspapers—especially those owned by Hearst—actively tried to gin up public opinion in favor of war against Spain.

and even its sister network HLN in prime-time viewers.[5] Fox News and MSNBC, with their sometimes controversial and sometimes misleading television personalities who express strong opinions, usually run away with the ratings.

During this timeframe, newspapers, challenged by the growing dominance of the Internet throughout the country, began to lose readers and advertisers. Strapped for cash, many of the once mighty newspapers in major cities were on the verge of bankruptcy by the first decade of the 21st century.

Media in other countries have always had different standards than the US. In Western Europe, for example, newspapers frequently assume an advocacy role, presenting the news in ways that support a particular political party or ideology.[6] In 1997, for example, the British *Daily Mirror* newspaper openly supported the reelection of Labour Party Prime Minister Tony Blair. Topless models, so-called "Blair babes," appeared in the paper every day, giving their reasons for supporting Blair.[7] Similarly, if less provocatively, with its first edition in the 1970s, the Italian newspaper *La Republica* announced:

> "This newspaper is a bit different from others: It is a journal of information that doesn't pretend to follow an illusory political neutrality but declares explicitly that it has taken a side in the political battle. It is made by men who belong to the vast arc of the Italian left."[8]

In the United States, such open advocacy for a party, candidate, or philosophy by a mainstream newspaper might have been unthinkable. (So, too, would be the appearance of topless models.) But the editorials of papers like the *New York Times, Los Angeles Times*, and *Washington Post* have been consistently left of center, while the *Wall Street Journal* has advocated a conservative view of the world. There are almost no major newspapers in the United States that are truly centrist in their editorials.

Journalists in other countries also hold different views of the meaning of objectivity. American journalists are more likely than others to see their role as limited to reporting opposing sides' positions (see Figure 10-1). In a multinational survey, for example, only 28 percent of American journalists said that "objectivity" meant "going beyond the statements of the contending sides to the hard facts of a political dispute." In Sweden, this

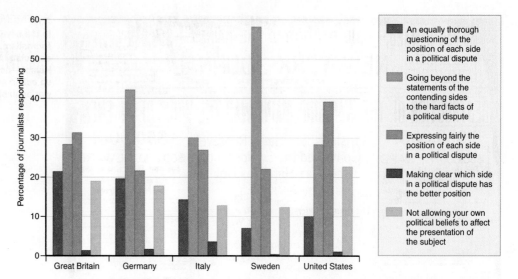

Legend:
- An equally thorough questioning of the position of each side in a political dispute
- Going beyond the statements of the contending sides to the hard facts of a political dispute
- Expressing fairly the position of each side in a political dispute
- Making clear which side in a political dispute has the better position
- Not allowing your own political beliefs to affect the presentation of the subject

FIGURE 10-1. American Journalists Are More Likely to Support Presenting Both Sides of an Issue Than Are Colleagues in Other Countries

ThinkingComparatively

Definitions of objectivity vary internationally, with American journalists less likely than journalists in many European countries to believe they should act as analysts and critics.

definition was supported by 58 percent of journalists. Moreover, 39 percent of American journalists defined objectivity as "expressing fairly the position of each side in a political dispute," whereas only 21 percent of German journalists said that this definition closely reflected their understanding of "objectivity."[9]

These differing views of objectivity have practical implications. Journalists in Sweden and Germany act not only as reporters of information but also as analysts and social critics. They attempt to reveal the "hard facts" behind and beyond what political figures say and do. Many American journalists would consider this stepping into the middle of a political debate, which would violate their objectivity standard. But foreign journalists see it as delivering a truthful version of events to audiences—a version of events not typically available from politicians.[10]

American mass media play a watchdog role in government and politics.

watchdog the media's role in keeping a close eye on politicians and presenting stories and information that politicians might not willingly reveal to the media on their own.

The job of American journalists is sometimes described as serving in a **watchdog** role. They keep a close eye on government and politics, watching for signs of dishonesty, corruption, unfair dealing, and broken promises, and investigating aggressively when they find such evidence. In other words, they often seek to "uncover" news, that is, to present stories and information that politicians might not willingly reveal to the media. The most famous example of this approach was the news coverage after the Watergate burglary in 1972 that eventually led to the resignation of President Richard Nixon on August 9, 1974. But we should remember that had it not been for two dogged reporters with the *Washington Post*, Carl Bernstein and Bob Woodward, the entire account of lies and deceit that went all the way up to the president might have been brushed aside by the media. Since then, reporters have tried and sometimes failed to find fault in government where there was none—for example, in Billie-gate, an investigation of the shenanigans of President Carter's brother; and the speculations following the suicide of President Clinton's friend Vince Foster, who was alleged to have been murdered. In other cases, the press completely missed stories like the arms-for-hostages deal in the Reagan administration until the White House announced it. And a potential Wall Street collapse in 2008 was missed by every media outlet until the problem was made public by the government.

This watchdog role, when it works, marks a third respect in which American journalists differ from some of their foreign counterparts. In Italy, Germany, and the United Kingdom, for example, print and broadcast media are more passive in their coverage of politics. Rather than actively patrolling the political arena for signs of foul play, journalists in these countries tend to take their cues from political actors on which stories deserve news coverage.[11]

American mass media operate largely unfettered by government restriction.

A fourth difference between American media and those of other countries is that the American media are largely unrestrained by government interference. Most significantly, U.S. media are allowed to publish or broadcast free from the threat of **prior restraint**—that is, government intervention to stop the publication of material it finds objectionable. This freedom has never been absolute, however. The Supreme Court has ruled that if publication of certain information "will surely result in direct, immediate, and irreparable harm to our nation or its people," then prior restraint can be exercised.[12] For instance, the government often tries and sometimes succeeds in exercising prior restraint in cases involving national security. A broadcast or print outlet could be restrained from publishing the secret locations of U.S. armed forces in enemy territory, or the names and addresses of intelligence agents overseas. Significantly, however, the Supreme Court has made it clear that the burden rests with government to demonstrate that publication would be harmful, rather than with the media to show why the information merits a public airing.

> U.S. media are allowed to publish or broadcast free from the threat of prior restraint—that is, government intervention to stop the publication of material it finds objectionable.

This principle grew out of the Pentagon Papers case in June 1971, when the *New York Times, Washington Post*, and *Boston Globe* published excerpts of a top-secret government study of U.S. involvement in Vietnam. The excerpts were provided by Daniel Ellsberg, a former government employee who had worked on the study and had become disenchanted with the Vietnam War. Initial excerpts cited repeated examples of poor presidential decision-making and failures to deal honestly with both Congress and the American public. Claiming a threat to national security, the Nixon administration sought an injunction to prevent publication of further installments. The administration won an injunction but the victory was short-lived; the U.S. Supreme Court ultimately ruled in favor of the newspapers and argued that the government did not meet the extraordinarily high burden of proof necessary to justify such a restraint.

In some instances, the media will voluntarily hold off publishing or broadcasting information. This was the case in 2005 when the *New York Times* learned of a covert program in which American scientists and special forces helped guard Pakistani nuclear material. Because of the fear of adverse reaction in Pakistan and the Muslim world if word got out about the top-secret program, the Bush administration asked the *New York Times* not to reveal its existence. The paper agreed and held the information for more than two years. In this case, the key point was that

prior restraint   government intervention to prevent the publication of material it finds objectionable.

▼ SHOWING THE COST OF WAR

The bodies of American soldiers killed in combat overseas arrive at Dover air force base in Delaware. The Obama administration overturned the Bush administration directive that forbid media coverage of these events.

the paper's restraint was voluntary. There was virtually nothing the Bush administration could have done to prevent the paper's publishing the information.

In the second year of the Iraq War, newspapers wanted to publish photographs of the returning caskets of Americans killed in action. The Bush administration did not allow this for reasons of privacy. Those opposed to the war considered publication of the photographs a way to remind Americans of the war's high cost in lives lost. When President Obama took office, the ban was reversed and the families of fallen soldiers were given the option of having the return of their sons or daughters photographed and made public.

Constraints on American Media Freedom

10-2 Identify the legal constraints on American media.

The press's ability to publish what it deems appropriate without government restriction has come a long way over the course of American history. Members of the modern media have few of the restraints faced by their earliest forebears. However, contemporary political journalists in the United States do face some significant constraints on what they can air or publish.

The freedom the American press enjoys was not won quickly.

The relative freedom that characterizes U.S. media operations today was not established by the adoption of the First Amendment in 1791. At the time of its passage, the First Amendment was thought to guarantee freedom of the press only from prior restraint by government. Expansions of freedom were won through ongoing battles between the press, the government, and public figures, many of which the press lost.

Early restrictions on the press   The most famous early restriction on the press was the Sedition Act, a federal law passed in 1798. The act effectively criminalized criticism of Congress and the president:

> if any person shall write, print, utter or publish . . . any false, scandalous and malicious writing or writings against the government of the United States, or either house of the Congress of the United States, or the President of the United States, with intent to defame the said government, or either house of the said Congress, or the said President, or to bring them, or either of them, into contempt or disrepute; or to excite against them, or either or any of them, the hatred of the good people of the United States . . . then such person, being thereof convicted before any court of the United States having jurisdiction thereof, shall be punished by a fine not exceeding two thousand dollars, and by imprisonment not exceeding two years.[13]

Ostensibly, the act was designed for national security purposes—to silence American supporters of France, a country with which President John Adams feared the United States might soon be at war.[14] Critics argued, however, that the act was intended instead to quiet the critics of President Adams and his Federalist Party allies in Congress.[15] And, in fact, all 14 individuals indicted under the act (10 of whom were convicted) were members of the Anti-federalist opposition—mostly editors of opposition newspapers.[16]

When Thomas Jefferson, leader of the Anti-Federalists, was elected president in 1800, he freed those still serving prison sentences because of Sedition Act convictions. The Sedition Act itself was allowed to expire in 1801, but the struggle for a free press was far from over. During the Civil War, the federal government limited telegraph transmissions from Washington, D.C., that it argued might compromise the successful planning and prosecution of the war. During the post–Civil War era, the federal government jailed reporters who were critical of the program of southern Reconstruction.

Reporters also were cited for contempt of court for describing pending legal cases, particularly if they criticized presiding judges.

By the turn of the twentieth century, press outlets were being sued, successfully, for printing photographs of and intimate gossip about figures of interest to the public. Legislation was enacted to restrict the ability of the press to "invad[e] the sacred precincts of private and domestic life."[17] Further restrictions on the press were enacted during World War I. The Espionage Act, passed in 1917 and expanded in 1918, made illegal any "seditious expression"—in particular, publications that might undermine military recruitment or weaken support for the military draft. Nearly one thousand individuals ultimately were convicted for engaging in such expression.[18] A similar law, the Smith Act, was passed as World War II loomed. Though it was rarely enforced during the war, it was used in the early postwar years to prosecute American communists.

Establishment of press freedoms in the twentieth century A countervailing trend began to appear during the 1930s, when the Supreme Court started to develop a more expansive interpretation of the First Amendment. The trend took decades to reach maturity, but by the end of the 1970s, the press freedoms that we recognize today had largely been established in case law and federal statute. Eventually, the press—and private individuals who wished to publish information for mass distribution—won important decisions expanding their freedom to criticize the government and public officials, guaranteeing their right to cover criminal trials and aspects of individuals' private lives, setting highly restrictive limits on prior restraint in cases related to national security, and granting access to government information that was once off-limits. Thus, in the twenty-first-century, the American press operates with substantially more latitude than it did in the first 200 years of the nation's history—and with much more freedom than the mass media in most other countries.

The media can be both forbidden and compelled to provide certain information.

There are other sorts of restrictions or standards that the media must follow. For example, defamation refers to a false or unsubstantiated attack on someone's good name or reputation. To be considered defamation, an attack must be false. If the press calls the president a liar and a thief and he can be shown to be a liar and a thief, laws against defamation do not apply. Even if he is not a liar and a thief, however, defamation can be very difficult to prove. As the case law has evolved, the courts have stated that actual malice by the media must be demonstrated in order to prove defamation of a public figure. Thus, the media outlet must have reported the defamatory information "with knowledge that it was false or with reckless disregard of whether it was false or not."[19] Given the difficulty of meeting this standard, or surviving the appeals process, public figures must rely on journalists' integrity and self-policing by media outlets, as much as on anti-defamation laws, to protect their reputations. In Great Britain, it is much easier to prove libel and, not surprisingly, there are more trials.

Authoritarian governments handle the problem of pesky journalists in a less nuanced way. In Cuba, Saudi Arabia, and other restrictive countries, dissident newspapers are not allowed, and independent journalists are jailed and sometimes executed. Even after the fall of Soviet communism, Russian journalists critical of the government have been killed and their murders never solved. The government of Iran not only disallows criticism from its own journalists but has threatened foreign journalists as well.

If the government cannot actively restrain the American media from disseminating content, can the media be compelled to publish or broadcast certain information? With respect to print media, the answer is no. The courts have ruled that no individual or institution has a right to coverage of an opinion or pet issue in the print media. The broadcast media, on the other hand, are treated differently. The broadcast spectrum is considered a public asset; unlike a newspaper or magazine, no one owns it. And whereas the broadcast spectrum can carry only a limited amount of programming, the number of potential print outlets is unlimited. The broadcast media, therefore, are considered semi-monopolies.

For both of these reasons, the federal government takes a more active role—through the Federal Communications Commission (FCC)—in regulating broadcasters. One regulation relevant to political programming is the equal time provision. Under this rule, if a television station gives time to a candidate for office, it must give all other candidates for that office equal access. Because national debates, news, and public affairs programming are exempt from this rule, its primary impact is on campaign advertising. If a local television or radio station runs a 30-second advertisement by a candidate for governor, for example, the station must offer to sell the same amount of time to the candidate's opponents at equal cost. When Arnold Schwarzenegger ran for governor of California for the first time in 2003, California TV stations did not dare to air any of his movies during his election campaign for fear that it would trigger the equal time provision.

Reporters may be compelled by the federal government to reveal their sources.

Despite their resistance to the idea, reporters can be compelled to reveal the names of confidential sources. This mandate can become an issue when the information provided by a source is germane to a legal matter. In 2003, for example, *Time* magazine published an article revealing the name of CIA officer Valerie Plame. The reporters involved in the story did nothing illegal by revealing Plame's identity, but it is illegal for a government official with authorized access to a covert agent's identity to deliberately reveal that information to a reporter. Accordingly, a federal grand jury was assembled to determine whether any criminal wrongdoing had taken place.

At the heart of the investigation was one question: who revealed Plame's identity to reporters? Two reporters involved in the story, Matthew Cooper of *Time* magazine and Judith Miller of the *New York Times*, were called to testify. Having received permission from his source to reveal the name, Cooper named presidential

◄ PROTECTING CONFIDENTIAL SOURCES
New York Times reporter Judith Miller received information on the identity of CIA official Valerie Plame from a government source but refused to identify the source to a grand jury investigating who leaked the sensitive information. Why would the federal government be resistant to shield laws?

adviser Karl Rove. But Miller either received no such permission from her source or chose not to exercise it; she would not reveal her source in testimony before the grand jury. For her refusal, she was sentenced to remain in jail until the grand jury was dismissed. She eventually revealed her source—Lewis Libby, Vice President Richard Cheney's chief of staff—when he released her from her pledge of confidentiality. But this disclosure happened only after she spent 85 days in jail.

In order to avoid the choice between spending time in jail and revealing a confidential source, reporters have advocated shield laws. These laws grant them certain exemptions from having to testify in legal matters. Just as a priest cannot be compelled to testify against a penitent, or a husband against a wife, shield laws protect journalists from having to reveal the name of a confidential source in a legal proceeding. Most states have adopted shield laws of varying leniency, but the federal government has not. However, both federal and state courts have recognized limited exemptions from the normal requirement that a reporter testify when subpoenaed—even when no explicit statutory exemption exists. In summary, then, reporters have some protections against compelled testimony, but those protections are far from absolute. Reporters argue they need this protection—without it, sources would fear to come forward and reveal crimes.

Despite these various restrictions, American mass media are still among the most free in the world. By way of comparison, consider one observer's description of working conditions for the media in Russia, at present ostensibly a democratic country:

> The Kremlin gained "nearly total control" of broadcast media in 2003 through legislation and financial pressure. While the print media provide some dissenting viewpoints, broadcast media has denied coverage to opposition parties and ideas. Although the Russian Supreme Court did curtail some government censorship legislation, many editors and journalists had already turned to self-censorship. Most unfortunately for those who have not, "independent journalists continue to be harassed, assaulted, kidnapped, and killed."[20]

ThinkingComparatively — American reporters operate with a tremendous amount of freedom compared to reporters in some other countries, like Russia, where dissent can be harshly punished.

According to Reporters without Borders, in 2008 the United States ranked 22 out of 167 countries on the index of press freedom.[21] Though American journalists sometimes complain about government restrictions on their activities, we can see that in comparative terms, they operate with tremendous latitude.

Types of Media and Patterns of Media Use

10-3 Differentiate the types of media that exist today.

A number of technological developments or inventions have had a profound impact on the way human beings learn about the world around them. The first occurred in 1440 when a German named Johannes Gutenberg invented the printing press using movable type, making it possible to distribute large quantities of printed material. It was almost 400 years until the second advance. In 1837, Samuel F.B. Morse, an American, sent the first electronic telegram using his code of dots and dashes to link up cities along the eastern U.S. coast. With the transatlantic cable of 1866, Americans could learn the news from Europe in minutes, as opposed to weeks when messages came by ship; soon both coasts of the United States were connected. Then, in the 1920s, radio offered instant and immediate news to the entire nation, followed 20 years later with pictures in a device called television.

Each of these inventions did not supersede the previous innovations. The telegraph only helped newspapers in their ability to gather information faster. And, although newspapers and magazines lost some readership to television, they still continued to flourish alongside electronic media.

But, at the dawn of the twenty-first century, a fourth wave of technology shook the foundations of the established mass media. With the Internet, cell phones, iPhones, blogs, Facebook, Twitter, and technology still to be invented, a tectonic shift has taken place in the world. Newspapers and magazines, once major forces with ad-filled pages, have gone bankrupt. Network news, which dominated information-gathering beginning in the 1950s, has lost millions of viewers to cable news and the Internet. The majority of people who still watch the network evening news are much older and not part of the prime group that advertisers seek (the 25–54 age group). When that generation passes on, the networks may have to turn off the camera.

Even though the old powers like the newspapers and networks tried to enter the new field by setting up their own sites on the Web, they failed to grasp the Internet's potential and offered their services for free. Once a practice is established, it is always difficult if not impossible to charge people for something they didn't have to pay for previously—especially when there are other free alternatives.

All of these innovations have also changed the habits of the viewer. People can self-select what they want to hear and watch. In the past, there was far less choice. By 2010, conservatives could watch, hear, and read only the news that fit their worldview. Liberals and libertarians could do the same. That people can hear just what they want to hear and not be exposed to other views is likely to have implications for how the media influence what people know.

There are definite plusses and minuses to these new technologies. Blogs have offered a true form of democracy to news gathering since everyone can offer their own opinion to any story. In the past, before the Internet, the only method of complaint was sending a letter to the editor or screaming at your television screen, which may have helped increase one's blood pressure but had no impact outside your home. Blogs have had a huge influence on the news. It was a blog that brought down the mighty CBS anchor Dan Rather for airing a false report on President George W. Bush's Air National Guard service during the 2004 campaign. And it was a blog that forced the Associated Press and Reuters to issue a retraction and institute new policies when it was shown that their photographs of supposed Israeli damage to civilians had been altered and misrepresented.

The downside of the Internet is that sometimes information presented as factual has no basis in fact at all. In the past, professional editors and fact-checkers toiled to make sure stories were accurate. Since the Internet is open to all, even racists, anti-Semites, and other hate mongers have a voice, but not necessarily any facts.

Americans do not rely equally on these media forms to get their news about the world. The dominance of television over other media is part of the long-term trend that we have discussed. Until the late 1950s, newspapers topped television as Americans' primary source of information about politics and government.[22] Since that time, however, newspaper readership has been in decline. In 1960, for example, combined circulation for morning and evening newspapers in the United States was about 59 million. By 2009, that number had fallen to 48 million—despite a nearly 60 percent increase in the U.S. population.[23] Figure 10-2 provides additional detail on this trend, illustrating the declining percentage of Americans who report reading a newspaper "regularly."

What caused the decline in newspaper readership and the ascendancy of television? Whereas reading a newspaper requires effort, attentiveness, and energy, watching television is largely passive—even relaxing. Furthermore, print media cannot compete with the sights, sounds, emotions, and attractive personalities available on television—and, increasingly, the Internet. The mass movement of women into the workforce in the second half of the twentieth century also played a role in

▼ CREDIBILITY UP IN SMOKE

In 2006, during the war in Lebanon, a Reuters photo editor altered an image—doubling an explosion—to show more damage from an Israeli airstrike.

Reuters issued a picture kill and apologized for the doctored photo by Adnan Hajj.

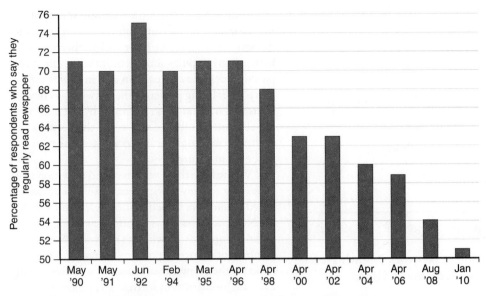

FIGURE 10-2. **There Have Been Massive Declines in Newspaper Readership.**

declining newspaper readership. Women found they had less time to read newspapers. Finally, the growth of American suburbs and exurbs increased commute times for many Americans, which also reduced the amount of leisure time available to read a daily paper.[24] The classic stereotypical 1950s father came home to a housewife who was cooking dinner; he picked up the afternoon paper, sat in his favorite chair, and read until the family sat down for dinner. By the 1990s, it was more common for both parents to work and arrive home later because of long commutes. Given this change, most of the afternoon papers ended publication by the 1990s, unable to compete with television and the increasing likelihood that the entire family no longer sat down for dinner together.

There has also been a huge decrease in coverage of news abroad.[25] Newspapers and network news organizations once had bureaus in all the major cities of the world. Beginning in the 1980s, they began to close them to save money. Those cutbacks have only increased over the past 30 years, leading news organizations to rely on stringers—freelance reporters living in various countries—who are called on only when editors deem there is news that will interest the American audience. When there is a major story, networks will send in their top personalities, most of whom have not lived in those areas and know only as much as they can cram into their heads during the flight—allowing almost no opportunity for real reporting.

Despite the continued dominance of television as a news source, even its control has begun to weaken in recent years—particularly in broadcast television and the network news programs. Note the percentage of Americans who reported getting their news from the listed sources on a daily basis in 2002 and 2008, as shown in Figure 10-3. Local

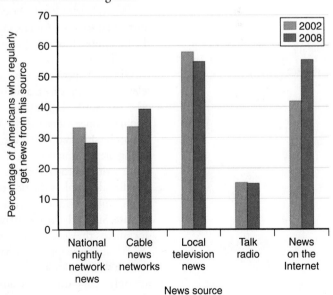

FIGURE 10-3. **Local News Continues to Dominate as an Everyday Source of News.**

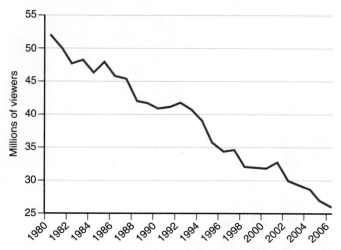

FIGURE 10-4. **Viewership of Network Nightly News Broadcasts Is on the Decline.**

television remains the most common source of news for Americans, but cable news programs, radio talk shows, and the Internet have become increasingly popular sources of information in the past decade. The comparison also indicates the sharply declining power of the networks as news sources. That reality is reinforced by the decline in the absolute number of viewers of the networks' nightly news programming over the same period, as shown in Figure 10-4.

Where have those who have fled television news gone? Not to daily newspapers, as we have already noted. Some have turned to cable television. CNN, MSNBC, and Fox News all offer news programming in direct competition with the networks. Some former network viewers appear to be tuning in to talk radio for their news. One broadcaster alone—Rush Limbaugh—attracts more than 13 million listeners per week, and the number could be much more according to some estimates.[26] Local television news has also managed to fill part of the role the networks used to fill (see Figure 10-4). Satellite technology now makes it possible for local news stations to cover national and international stories that formerly only the "big three" networks could cover.[27] As mentioned above, more Americans still get their news from local news sources than from any other source.

The World Wide Web is becoming an increasingly important source of information.

An increasingly large percentage of the population is getting its news from the Internet or, more accurately, the World Wide Web (the Internet is the infrastructure and the World Wide Web is the content). In 1995, the World Wide Web was still unfamiliar to most Americans. By September 2009, however, roughly 40 percent of the U.S. population was getting news from the Web on a daily basis.[28]

When we talk about getting news on the Web, we can mean a number of different things. Almost all of the national broadcast networks, cable networks, and local television stations have a presence on the Web. Networks and most affiliates post articles, community information, and streaming video on their sites. Often, these television news operations use the Web to post materials or provide information that cannot be shown on their broadcasts because of limited time or the difficulty of conveying the information on television. For example, ABC News might conduct a poll about attitudes toward the economy and the president. Only a few seconds of time could be devoted to the poll on one of the network's traditional broadcasts, but ABC News could post additional analysis, commentary, and a full copy of the poll on its website. Similarly, investigative reporters might post additional analysis or the source documents they used in a particular story on the Web.

Most newspapers now have online editions. However, the decision to develop one is a difficult choice for newspaper owners. Unlike television stations, newspapers not only earn money from advertising but also charge for their papers as well. People may be reluctant to buy a paper if the material is available for free on the Web. Furthermore, online editions often compete with the print editions of the same newspaper. Should an editor post a story immediately when it is completed or wait

▲ **WHERE HAVE THE VIEWERS GONE?**

More Americans are getting their news, especially their election news like the presidential debate shown here, from cable outlets like CNN, Fox News, and MSNBC. Millions of Americans also tune into talk radio for news and commentary about politics. Conservative broadcasters like Rush Limbaugh dominate the talk radio medium. What might draw viewers and listeners to these different media outlets?

until the next morning when the paper comes out? If the editor holds the story until the next day, the story may be scooped by other news outlets. At the same time, posting it on the Web decreases any incentive for buying the print edition of the paper. Nonetheless, while newspapers struggle to survive, they have little choice but to put their material on the Web. One exception to this rule is the *Wall Street Journal*, which charged an additional fee for its online version from the very beginning. Now, as papers like the *New York Times* and *Washington Post* struggle to find different ways to charge for their services, the *Wall Street Journal* has been collecting revenue for its electronic edition all along and is only getting stronger.

An increased number of news and information platforms reside solely on the World Wide Web. These can include big computer service companies such as Yahoo. Yahoo both creates news content and serves as a portal to thousands of other news sources. The Yahoo home pages attempt to organize the vast amount of data available on the Web. In addition, services like Google News track news sources around the world which are drawn mostly from independent stringers.

Finally, weblogs or "blogs" are becoming an increasingly important source of information in political life—particularly for those who are politically engaged. Blogs are online journals or diaries that invite users to comment on and add content to postings on various topics. Blogs often have links to other blogs, websites, and sources of information. They are typically specialized by subject and tend to cater to those with particular political leanings. In other words, information on blogs typically flows to those who already agree with the blogger. For example, liberals follow the Daily Kos and conservatives visit the Drudge Report. Some blogs have even become more professional with paid staff and slick graphics supported by sponsors and advertisers. Most, however, are managed by individuals who simply want to use the power of the Web to get commentary out to the world.

CaseStudy: The Always Public Political Life

In the not-too-distant past, candidates for national office controlled the amount of time they appeared on the television screens. In 1988, then presidential candidate George H.W. Bush often declined interviews with network television reporters and instead gave access to local reporters at campaign stops who were far less likely to ask tough questions. But with the advance in technology, it is increasingly difficult for political figures to control what gets recorded and how much people see or hear. Today, almost all cell phones have a camera, and instead of a dozen video cameras following an event, there can now be hundreds. With all this coverage, it is almost impossible for a candidate to escape saying the wrong thing or somehow looking foolish. When that happens, these embarrassing moments are on YouTube within minutes.

One example of a video that destroyed a political career is that of George Allen, a successful governor and senator from Virginia. During his reelection race in 2006, Allen made a comment at a campaign stop to a young staff member of his opponent, Jim Webb, that was seen as racial in its overtones. The staffer's only job was to follow Allen with a video camera and record anything embarrassing. The young staffer caught the comment on video and posted it on the Web, and this was a leading cause in the eventual defeat of Allen in his senate race and the derailing of his political career.

During the 2008 presidential campaign, video of the Reverend Jeremiah Wright showed the fiery preacher denouncing America and saying things that were considered anti-Semitic. Because presidential candidate Barack Obama had gone to Wright's church for 20 years and even called him his "spiritual father," the video was embarrassing to Obama, who was forced to break all ties with Wright. In

▲ SOMEONE'S ALWAYS WATCHING

George Allen, pictured here, campaigning in 2006, learned this lesson when an off-color remark he made to a representative of an opposing campaign was videotaped and made available widely through the internet and social media. Allen's comment can be viewed at http://www.youtube.com/watch?v=r90z0PMnKwl.

both the Wright and Allen cases, the video went up on the Internet before television picked it up, demonstrating the growing power of the new media.

ThinkingCritically

1. Explain how the behavior of political actors has changed, and will continue to change, as their lives become more and more public.

2. Do you think politicians should expect more privacy, or do you think their line of work requires them to be scrutinized whenever they are in public?

The Nature of Media Coverage of Politics and Government

10-4 Analyze the nature of media coverage of politics and government.

What kind of information do Americans get from their news sources? Because of the diversity of the media, the kinds of stories they cover, and the high variance in quality of news information, the answer is not simple. One significant problem is that most of what political scientists know about media content concerns media coverage of elections rather than day-to-day politics and governance. Not that this isn't offered in the world of cable television. C-SPAN began broadcasting the proceedings of the House and Senate in the 1980s. Watching government proceedings can be as exciting, however, as watching paint dry, so it is no surprise that the vast majority of viewers turn to more highly produced television. Nonetheless, there are a few general trends. Next we'll examine both the subjects that are covered and how the media covers them.

The media devote most of their attention to explaining and interpreting the president's actions.

When covering national politics, the media focus primarily on the president, the White House staff, and the executive branch. Collectively, they are the subject of about 70 percent of government news coverage by national and local newspapers and about 80 percent of the government news coverage on the network news. Congress receives the next highest level of coverage, with about "one-in-four discussions of government in the print press and one-in-six on television."[29] The judiciary receives so little coverage as to be almost an afterthought, except when a new Supreme Court justice is nominated. Then the confirmation hearings can hold the nation's rapt attention—as it did during the Clarence Thomas–Anita Hill battle in 1990. But, in general, Congress and the judiciary cannot compete with the amount of attention the president and the executive branch receive.

Reporters receive much more airtime than candidates do.

The second trend in media coverage is that in presidential election coverage on television, reporters tend to get substantially more camera time than the actual candidates. In the 2000 presidential election campaign, for example, reporters accounted for 74 percent of spoken airtime; Al Gore and George W. Bush accounted for 11 percent; and other sources, 15 percent.[30]

These numbers indicate that reporters assume a prominent mediating role in election coverage as they report and analyze what candidates say.[31] In the 1992 election, for example, *CBS Evening News* broadcast a brief statement by Bill Clinton regarding the proposed North American Free Trade Agreement:

> I'm reviewing it carefully, and when I have a definitive opinion, I will say so. It's a very long and complex document; it was negotiated over a long period of time. And I think we have to go through it, and check it all off.

Rather than letting the matter rest there, CBS reporter Eric Enberg added:

> Time out! Clinton has a reputation as a committed policy wonk who soaks up details like a sponge. But on an issue which will likely cost him votes no matter what side he takes, the one-time Rhodes scholar is a conveniently slow learner.[32]

370

▲ TALKING TO THEMSELVES

Evidence shows that reporters tend to receive significantly more air time than the subject they are covering, and that news shows often interview media figures and other talking heads.

Since Vietnam and Watergate, TV coverage of politics has become conspicuously cynical.

The third media trend is that media coverage of politics and government has assumed an increasingly skeptical—even cynical—tone.[33] Most media historians date this trend to the late 1960s and early 1970s, coincident with the Vietnam War and the Watergate scandal.[34] The two events convinced many reporters that government officials were capable of dishonesty and corruption on a scale previously unthinkable and the media had let them get away with such behavior for too long.

To this day, journalists frequently cast politicians in a negative light or quote sources who do. Based on ABC, CBS, and NBC network news coverage of government during 1993 and 2001, Table 10-1 shows the percentage of negative, positive, and neutral stories on the federal government. Although not overwhelmingly negative in either year, in both samples the stories reflect a tendency to portray the workings of government, and specific politicians, in a negative light. A recent contradiction to the overwhelmingly negative news coverage of government is the positive coverage that President Barack Obama enjoyed in his first 100 days in office. Almost 4 out of 10 stories, editorials, and op-ed columns about Obama were clearly positive in tone, which compares to only 2 in 10 for George W. Bush and 27 percent for Bill Clinton in their first 100 days in office.[35]

With the advent of social media, it is increasingly common for journalists to criticize politicians on websites like Twitter and Facebook. Jake Tapper, an ABC

TABLE 10-1. **Evaluative Content of Network News Stories on the U.S. Government, 1993 and 2001.** News coverage of government concentrates on the negative.

	1993	2001
Negative	59%	41%
Positive	36%	23%
Neutral	5%	36%

News senior White House correspondent, has tweeted criticizing remarks about the Obama administration, including a tweet that called out the White House for not allowing press into an awards ceremony. Social media, especially blogs, have allowed journalists to share information and commentary faster than ever before. In real time, they can write a scathing remark about a political figure, which in seconds can be read by anyone who wants to.

TV coverage generally focuses on strategy over substance.

Yet another trend is that television coverage of elections tends to neglect substantive matters, such as the content of policy proposals, candidates' positions on issues, and politicians' voting records. Instead, the focus often is on the **horse race**—who is up or down in the latest polls, what is happening behind the scenes, who has committed the latest gaffe or landed a rhetorical blow, and which candidates are winning a competitive advantage. Such reporting is also referred to as "strategy frame coverage" because it sometimes treats elections purely as a competitive game for power or a contest of political strategies rather than policy ideas.

The following are a few examples of horse race coverage from recent campaigns:

> After falling behind in the Iowa polls, Senator [Hillary] Clinton, who earlier condemned attacks by other Democrats, turned negative on Obama. Fair enough. Except her attacks were neither focused nor effective.... It's a good bet that Clinton, encouraged by her husband, is weighing a shakeup, such as bringing in former White House Chief of Staff John Podesta to direct the overall campaign. The question is whether it's too late and too awkward before those first contests, which are to be held in 3½ weeks.
>
> —Al Hunt of Bloomberg, December 10, 2007[36]

> After a series of blows, many of them self-inflicted, [Bush] aides acknowledge their message has been muffled.
>
> —Bill Whitaker of CBS, September 17, 2000[37]

horse race a focus in election coverage on who and what are up or down in the latest poll numbers.

▼ **NEW WAYS TO GET THE MESSAGE OUT**

Although campaigns continue to spend millions of dollars putting their ads on television, they can also easily post them on Internet sites like YouTube. Online video sharing sites have also become an easy way for campaigns and their supporters to post other sorts of videos that support their candidate or embarrass an opponent.

■ The first real political battle is shaping up across the country in New Hampshire where, with the primary only nine days away, Arkansas Governor Bill Clinton's lead in the Democratic race appears to be shrinking, and the other candidates have suddenly found themselves in a horse race.

—Forrest Sawyer of ABC, February 9, 1992[38]

Why do television reporters prefer this kind of coverage? It may simply be that reporters, and viewers, find such stories more entertaining than the dry stuff of policy papers and voting records.[39] Such coverage may also reflect the cynicism referred to above.[40] Reporters may believe that stories on tactics and behind-the-scenes discussions shed light on what is really driving a campaign (as opposed to what candidates and their handlers say is driving the campaign). Furthermore, candidates' issue positions and policy proposals do not change from day to day, but poll numbers, political tactics, and politicians' behavior can change on a daily basis, so they get reported as news.

Are the Media Biased?

10-5 Determine whether the media are biased.

One enduring debate among observers of American politics is whether media coverage of politics and government exhibits **bias**, that is, favorable treatment to certain politicians, policy positions, groups, and political outcomes. Certain aspects of the American media are decidedly and unapologetically partisan. Radio hosts Rush Limbaugh and Sean Hannity, for example, are openly conservative and are far more critical of Democrats than Republicans in their daily monologues. On the other hand, Keith Olbermann and Rachel Maddow of MSNBC are clearly left of center and often criticize Republican politicians and conservative viewpoints. These are not, however, instances of media bias. The media's objectivity ethic—its stated commitment to avoid partisan or political bias—applies only to hard news reporting, not to commentaries or editorials.

But what about journalists, television programs, newspapers, newsmagazines, radio programs, Internet sites, and other news outlets that are supposedly devoted primarily to reporting the basic facts of the news in an objective manner? Do the media favor some political figures and outcomes over others? Some media critics argue that the media favor Republicans and conservatives at the expense of Democrats and liberals, while others argue just the opposite.

What would a biased media mean for American politics? First, it could create a distorted democratic process—one in which the public made up its mind on certain issues on the basis of incomplete and possibly misleading information. Second, it might contribute to a climate in which the public was less informed about matters of politics and government than it could be. A public suspecting that mainstream media outlets are providing biased coverage might avoid such outlets, seeking alternative sources of information in talk radio, cable television talk shows, and weblogs. Or they might switch to more entertainment-oriented "news light" programs, such as the early morning network offerings like *Good Morning America*. Third, like the public, politicians might migrate away from media outlets they believe to be biased, and instead provide information and access only to friendlier, more specialized media. The potential significance of such developments makes it all the more important that political scientists continue to study the true extent of media bias.

bias favorable treatment to certain politicians, policy positions, groups, and political outcomes.

In the 2008 presidential election, conservatives, as well as Bill Clinton, complained that the mainstream media were far more tolerant of candidate Barack Obama and much more critical of his opponents. One example concerned the Jeremiah Wright tapes, where the mainstream reporters were thought to go easy on Senator Obama when he explained that he hadn't been in the church when Wright professed these views. The contention was that if candidate John McCain had gone to a church for 20 years where the minister used anti-black and anti-Jewish statements, reporters would have been tougher on him. In this case, the media were accused of using a double standard in the 2008 campaign.

Anecdotal evidence of bias in the media is mixed.

In the debate over media bias, much of the evidence is anecdotal—that is, it is based on a few isolated examples that may or may not represent overall media coverage. An organization called Fairness and Accuracy in Reporting (FAIR), for example, has produced studies indicating that conservative think tanks are cited more often in the media than left-leaning ones.[41] On the other hand, the Center for Media and Public Affairs found that in the 2004 election, John Kerry received the most favorable coverage of any general election candidate for the presidency since 1980.[42]

Little conclusive evidence of media bias has been found in examinations of media content.

Obviously, by choosing issues, media outlets, and time periods selectively, one can produce evidence of both liberal and conservative media bias. The question, however, is whether a comprehensive analysis across a broad range of issues, a wide variety of media outlets, and a substantial time period would indicate systematic bias. Ultimately, the proof is in the actual content of media reporting.

Self-assessment   One way to assess the content is to ask journalists themselves what they think of it. In a survey of more than 1,700 newspaper journalists, the American Society of Newspaper Editors asked the following question: "Thinking about how your newspaper tends to cover particular social or political groups, is that coverage sometimes too favorable or sometimes unfavorable?"

At first glance, the figures suggest a bias against conservatives; the reporters indicated that they report less favorably on conservatives than on liberals. This finding is not consistent throughout, however. For example, the same reporters indicated that the military and the wealthy, two groups usually associated with the American right, received overly favorable coverage. Similarly, poor people and labor union members, groups usually associated with the left, appeared to receive disproportionately unfavorable coverage. Then again, gun owners—another group associated with political conservatives—also seem to receive unfavorable coverage.

More generally, a series of surveys conducted over more than 40 years has shown journalists to be more liberal than conservative, and to be more liberal than the average American.[43] Perhaps most famously, a survey of Washington, D.C.-based reporters indicated that 89 percent had voted for Democrat Bill Clinton in the 1992 election—compared with only 42 percent of the American public. That

TABLE 10-2. Newspaper Journalists' Self-assessments. Journalists are more likely than the general public to call themselves liberal

IDEOLOGICAL SELF-RATING	GENERAL PUBLIC*	NATIONAL PRESS	LOCAL PRESS
Liberal	20%	32%	23%
Moderate	35%	53%	58%
Conservative	35%	8%	14%
Don't know	10%	7%	5%
	100%	100%	100%

*Public figures from August 2008 Pew Media Believability Study (N=1800)
Source: http://www.stateofthemedia.org.

survey has been criticized for its low response rate and allegedly unrepresentative sample.[44] The survey findings on the general ideological leanings of journalists have been replicated often enough, however, to leave little doubt that liberals outnumber conservatives substantially in American newsrooms. For example, a 2008 survey indicated that while the majority identified themselves as moderate, those journalists who identified themselves as liberal outnumbered those identifying themselves as conservative by a significant margin, and that journalists were much more liberal in their political orientations than the public as a whole (Table 10-2 shows this breakdown).

Advocates of the survey approach argue that reporters' political predispositions inevitably make their way into news stories, leading to biased reporting. Others argue that there is no correlation between journalists' personal beliefs and the content of their reporting. First, they note that journalists are trained to set aside their personal predispositions when reporting on politics and government. A Democratic journalist reporting on a Republican administration, they say, is no different from a Democratic doctor operating on a Republican patient. Second, they say that the economics of the media industry are designed to drive out biased coverage. Newspapers, television and radio programs, and newsmagazines that allowed bias to enter their coverage of politics and government would risk offending paying customers and advertisers who did not share their opinions. If for no other reason than the "bottom line" then, the media must work to keep their product bias free. Third, though many reporters may exhibit liberal tendencies, publishers and owners of radio, television, and print media outlets, being businesspeople, are presumed to exhibit more conservative ones. Somewhere, then, in the balance between reporters' and owners' politics, the media get the story right.

Content analysis   Fortunately, given the mixed nature of these findings, political scientists and other researchers have moved beyond examination of survey data into actual content analysis of media reporting. Content analysis is a technique for identifying themes, categories, and logical groupings in written material or material that can be converted into a written transcript. This could include television programming, newspaper and magazine reporting, and radio broadcasts. The methods of content analysis, therefore, can be applied to the study of media bias.

Because presidential elections are the great spectator sport of American politics, scholars have studied media bias primarily in the context of presidential election coverage. A 2000 study examined 59 studies of media bias in presidential election coverage from 1948 to 1996 that included analysis of television, newspaper, and weekly newsmagazine reporting on the presidential election. They investigated three kinds of bias:

- **Gatekeeping bias:** presenting news stories that cast a favored party or politician in a positive light while ignoring stories that would cast the party or politician in a negative light.

- **Coverage bias:** providing more news coverage to a favored party or politician and less to opponents.

- **Statement bias:** making positive statements about a favored party or politician and negative ones about opponents.

In analyzing the results of the 59 studies addressing these three kinds of bias, the authors concluded that "the results indicate an aggregate, across all media and all elections, of zero overall bias."[45]

This conclusion does not indicate that every media outlet was bias-free in every presidential election conducted between 1948 and 1996. First, the number of studies of gatekeeping bias in newspaper and television news coverage of presidential elections was too small to draw any definitive conclusions.[46] Second, bias in one medium in one election can be offset by an opposing bias in another medium. For example, the study identified small pro-Democratic coverage and statement biases in television news covering presidential elections, and even smaller pro-Republican coverage and statement biases in weekly newsmagazine reporting of the same elections. These two results effectively canceled each other, leading to a finding of zero "net" bias.

Recall, however, that Americans' consumption of the news tends to come disproportionately from television. Thus, "a little" bias in television news coverage could have a big impact on viewer beliefs. The researchers recognized that possibility but found it irrelevant. Specifically, they acknowledged that Democratic candidates received just over 10 percent more television coverage than Republican candidates, but they claimed this difference was "almost certainly undetectable by the audience." (Were they right? We discuss the impact of the mass media on public opinion in the next section.)

Presidential elections, as interesting and exciting as they can be, are not the only setting in which biased media coverage might occur. What about the day-to-day media coverage of Congress, the presidency, and current events? Is that coverage biased, and if so, in what direction? Among political scientists, there are no consensus answers to these questions. The existing studies are too few, too limited in scope, and too contradictory in their conclusions to provide any definitive conclusions. Perhaps after another generation of scholarship, it will be possible to conduct a meta-analysis of the sort described above in the context of election coverage. Until then, the jury is out.

Media Effects on Public Opinion

10-6 Assess the effect of the media on political attitudes and behaviors.

To what extent does the content of mass media coverage affect public opinion? The early research on this subject was prompted by startling demonstrations of the power of mass media in the 1920s, 1930s, and 1940s. An early instance was the panic following news of the stock market crash in 1929. Next was the rise of fascist dictators Benito Mussolini in Italy and Adolf Hitler in Germany. Both men cultivated popular support through radio addresses and newsreels that carried their fiery speeches to enraptured crowds. Then came Orson Welles's 1938 radio broadcast of H. G. Wells's science fiction book *War of the Worlds*, which set off a panic among a million Americans who mistook the dramatization for an actual news broadcast of an alien invasion.[47]

Observing these events, scholars worried that clever use of the mass media could enable leaders to inject the masses with supportive attitudes the way a hypodermic needle injects a patient with medicine. One researcher warned that "one persuasive person could, through the use of mass media, bend the world's population to his will."[48]

minimal effect the theory that change in voting intent as a result of mass media exposure was relatively rare.

▼ **THE POWER OF THE MEDIA**
When Orson Welles performed the radio play *War of the Worlds*, millions of Americans heard the broadcast and actually thought the United States was under alien invasion. This event and the massive newspaper coverage that it received suggested that people could be moved by the media to believe just about anything. How much do you think you are influenced by mass media?

Early research into the impact of media pointed to minimal effects.

Researchers in the United States first investigated the effects of the mass media on voting behavior. These seminal voting studies conducted in the 1940s and 1950s revealed an electorate surprisingly unaffected by media coverage. The studies found most voters were party loyalists whose votes could not be swayed by media messages. A number of group and personal characteristics—particularly religion, social status, and place of residence—also strongly dictated political predispositions. Partisanship and other political predispositions were so strong, in fact, that large majorities of voters in the 1950s and 1960s made their voting decision before the general election campaign and the related media coverage even began.[49] Thus, changes in voting intent as a result of mass media exposure were relatively rare.

This finding in the early literature came to be referred to as **minimal effect**. For years, media scholars accepted the minimal effect conclusion, although many found it unsatisfying. One researcher explained the scholars' dilemma as follows:

> The mass media have been a source of great frustration to social scientists. On one hand, citizens in modern democracies routinely develop opinions about political events and personalities far beyond their direct experience. It is hard to imagine where many of these opinions come from if not from the mass media. And yet it has proven maddeningly difficult to demonstrate that the mass media actually produce powerful effects on opinion.[50]

Herald Examiner
FINAL

RADIO FAKE SCARES NATION

Ultimately, scholars were able to demonstrate that the media's effect is more than minimal. But to do so, they had to overcome certain assumptions about the kinds of effects they should be looking for and how such effects might work.

The media may exert influence through agenda-setting and priming.

Early researchers into media effects focused on persuasion, or changing someone's mind about an issue, person, or group. But the media can also play a role in political socialization; in educating the public with basic information about politics, government, issues, groups, and candidates; in stimulating or discouraging political participation among the public; in helping to crystallize or reinforce existing beliefs and predispositions; and in determining which issues the public and policy makers consider important, or agenda-setting.

Of these topics, **agenda-setting**—determining which issues are considered important—has been highly influential in shaping political scientists' thinking about media effects. The issues that the media cover the most extensively are in turn the issues that the public considers most important. Conversely, the public considers the issues that the media neglect less important. In short, by covering some issues and ignoring others, the media help determine which issues the public considers important.

Researchers have also demonstrated **priming**, a media effect in which the public assesses the performance of politicians and candidates in terms of the issues that the media have emphasized. Imagine, for example, that the media devote extensive coverage to the issue of welfare fraud. If the public begins to consider welfare fraud an important problem because of this media coverage, that is evidence of agenda-setting. But if the public also begins to evaluate the performance of the president in terms of what he is doing or not doing about welfare fraud, that is evidence of priming. The experiments described in "How Do We Know?" demonstrate that people exposed to extra stories on defense preparedness tended to evaluate the president more heavily in terms of his performance in addressing defense preparedness. The same held true for the pollution and inflation issues. Thus, the media appear to have a priming effect on public opinion.

The media draw the attention of policy makers as well. For example, studies have shown that policy makers' attention to the issues of global warming, the North American Free Trade Agreement, and the Clinton administration's Whitewater scandal was increased in part by intensive media coverage of these issues.[51] The research in this area has not been as thorough, and the conclusions not as strong, as studies of the effect that the media have on what gets on the public's policy agenda. Furthermore, the research often suggests a two-way relationship: media coverage affects policy makers' agendas, but policy makers' agendas also affect what the media cover. Still, most of the research on the agenda-setting power of the media among policy makers, and particularly the most recent research, indicates that the media can exhibit a strong influence on the issues that policy makers choose to pay attention to.[52]

Three primary phenomena may limit the media's influence on attitudes and behaviors.

The early media effects research tended to assume that with enough exposure to a particular media message, individuals would eventually accept it. But this assumption was inconsistent with theories and findings from the fields of communications and psychology. Three phenomena limit the ability of media to influence attitudes and behaviors. The first is **selective exposure**, the tendency of people to expose themselves to information that is in accord with their beliefs.

continued on page 380 ▶

ThinkingCausally

Why are the effects of media on individuals' beliefs and opinions difficult to determine?

agenda-setting the media role in determining which issues the public considers important, by covering some issues and ignoring others.

priming a media effect in which the public assesses the performance of politicians and candidates in terms of the issues that the media have emphasized.

selective exposure the tendency of people to expose themselves to information that is in accord with their beliefs.

Do People React to Coverage of Events or to the Events Themselves?

10 Media and Politics

378

The Question

When it comes to measuring the agenda-setting power of the media, how do we know that people are reacting to media coverage of events rather than to events themselves? In times of economic recession, for example, many people will lose a job, know someone who has lost a job, or witness local companies going out of business. They have an understanding of the problems in the economy through direct, personal experience. At the same time, they are exposed to media coverage of the recession. So, when people tell researchers that they believe the performance of the economy is an important issue, are they reflecting their own experience, or are they responding to media coverage of the issue? In other words, the relationship between media coverage and public attention to certain issues might reflect reverse agenda-setting. Being profit-oriented businesses, media outlets need to appeal to a broad audience in order to sell advertising and subscriptions. A good way to ensure audience appeal is to cover issues the audience considers important. Therefore, the media may cover certain problems because the audience considers them important, rather than the audience's thinking certain problems are important because the media cover them. In addition to difficulties in identifying causality, scholars have also struggled with how to measure accurately who has been exposed to what sorts of media content.

▼ TUNING IN

Being exposed to messages from the media can affect how much importance people think an issue has. Fortunately, unlike this character in *A Clockwork Orange*, we are not all forced to be exposed to media messages.

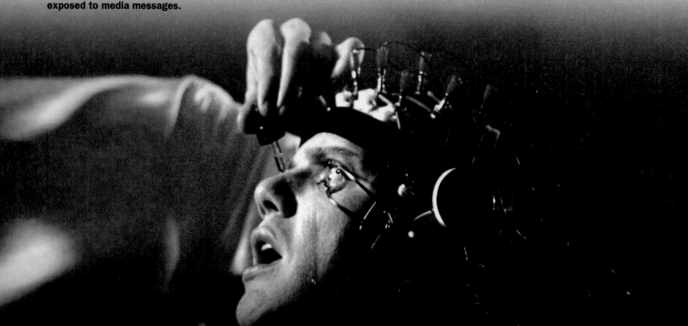

Why It Matters

The ultimate question in studying the various media in this country and the professional norms and legal frameworks that determine their content is whether the media influence political behavior. Even though most people and politicians assume that the media have extraordinary power to shape mass opinions and behavior, scholars have had a hard time finding evidence of significant effects. The failure to find media effects has been described by one scholar as "one of the most notable embarrassments of modern social science."[53]

Investigating the Answer

Experiments have been designed to disentangle the sort of "chicken or egg" causal puzzle that exists when examining the potential agenda-setting power of the media. The 1989 book *News That Matters* offered an experimental research approach that addressed concerns about both determining causality and accurately measuring exposure to particular media sources.[54] The researchers recruited hundreds of volunteers to participate in their experiment. They asked participants to complete a questionnaire covering a variety of topics relevant to politics and current events. Participants were then randomly divided into different groups.

Over the next four days, the different groups gathered and watched what they were told were videotaped recordings of the previous evening's network news. The researchers, however, had manipulated the news broadcasts to emphasize certain issues. For example, one group of participants saw broadcasts with a few added stories on American defense preparedness. Another group saw broadcasts with extra stories on pollution. Another saw additional stories on inflation. Because the groups were kept separate, they did not realize they were watching slightly different versions of the news. All assumed they were watching the same newscast.

To make the experience of watching the television news more realistic, the researchers sought to create a comfortable, home-like atmosphere for participants. They provided newspapers, magazines, and refreshments and asked questions in the survey that were designed to mask the true goal of their research.

After the groups had watched the manipulated broadcasts on four consecutive nights, the researchers again administered a questionnaire to participants. Answers to this second questionnaire revealed that individuals who had seen the broadcasts with added stories on defense preparedness considered that issue much more important than they had before the experiment began. The same held true for pollution, though not for inflation. (The authors argued that participants considered inflation such an important issue before the experiment that there was little room for them to show more concern after the experiment.) Thus, the agenda-setting hypothesis was largely supported; media emphasis on an issue could elevate the salience of that issue in the public mind.

The Bottom Line

The finding that media emphasis could elevate the salience of an issue was important. But just as important was the fact that this hypothesis was supported in an experimental setting. Because this controlled group could not in any way influence what the researchers' media people were reporting, it was clear that media coverage itself was driving the change in perceptions of issue salience. Therefore, it could not be argued that the media coverage reflected audience concerns. Given the difficulties in systematically measuring what the media are covering and what people are exposed to in the real world, experiments such as this have become a useful way for scholars to study media effects.

ThinkingCausally

Why do the media seem able to influence the attitudes and opinions of some individuals more than others?

selective perception the tendency of individuals to interpret information in ways consistent with their beliefs.

As we discussed at length above, the fragmented and increasingly partisan world of cable and Internet coverage of politics enables people to avoid information and arguments that might upset their belief system—and potentially change their opinions. This phenomenon has an important impact on the effect of Web-based communications and talk radio. Unlike an advertisement on television, individuals deliberately expose themselves to or actively seek out information from the Web or from a talk radio station. These sources may mobilize and energize base supporters (Republicans through talk radio, for example, and Democrats through liberal blogs), but because people probably already agree with the source, the persuasive effects are likely to be severely limited.

The second phenomenon is **selective perception**, the tendency of individuals to interpret information in ways consistent with their beliefs. Imagine, for example, a television news story depicting President George W. Bush comforting the victims of Hurricane Katrina in Louisiana. A Bush supporter likely would see this as evidence of the president's compassionate nature and rapport with everyday people. A Bush detractor, on the other hand, might see it as a politician seeking to score political points from a tragedy. Or consider the debates held during presidential election campaigns. Republicans and Democrats watch the very same debates, but Republicans inevitably conclude that the Republican performed better, and Democrats conclude that the Democrat performed better. In part, this is a consequence of selective perception.

▼ **SELECTIVE PERCEPTION**

As a result of selective perception, your previous attitudes toward President George W. Bush would likely influence what you think of this picture of the president inspecting Hurricane Katrina damage with two victims.

Finally, there is **selective retention**, the tendency of individuals to recall information that is consistent with existing beliefs and to discard information that runs counter to them. An admirer of President Ronald Reagan and his supply-side economics, for example, would recall the significant tax cuts enacted in Reagan's first and second terms but might well forget the substantial tax increases that were also enacted during Reagan's first term.

Note that there is a common element in these phenomena that limits the ability of the media to influence attitudes and behaviors. All represent efforts by individuals to avoid or reduce cognitive dissonance. Cognitive dissonance is a state in which some of one's attitudes, beliefs, or understandings are inconsistent with others. This dissonance leads to psychological discomfort, which people normally try to avoid or remedy.[55] The effect of selective exposure, selective perception, and selective retention is to render the information inside one's head more internally consistent, or consonant.

Think again about the example of selective exposure. If a conservative reader suddenly stopped listening to Rush Limbaugh and started reading the Daily Kos, she would be exposed to a number of arguments and ideas that were inconsistent with her existing worldview. This exposure might force her to question some of her beliefs. She might end up having doubts about matters on which she had held a settled opinion for years. On some issues, she might even be forced to change her mind. All of this could cause psychological discomfort. A sure way to avoid that discomfort, however, would be not to read the Daily Kos in the first place.

Selective exposure, selective perception, and selective retention all limit the impact that the mass media can have on individual attitudes. If people are inclined to see, hear, interpret, and retain only information that reinforces their existing beliefs, it becomes more difficult for the media to produce a large-scale attitude change.

Exposure, comprehension, and receptivity are preconditions for media effects.

Discovering the consequences of selective exposure, perception, and retention led political scientists to approach the study of media effects differently. Rather than simply assuming a direct link between the content of media messages and public opinion, they began studying the necessary preconditions for a message to change opinion. One of these is *exposure*—whether a person actually sees, hears, or reads a particular media message. Another is *comprehension*, understanding a message to which one has been exposed. A third is *receptivity*, which refers to an individual's openness to accepting a message communicated through the media.

Without exposure, comprehension, and receptivity, an individual cannot be influenced by a media message. If we look for media effects on public opinion among the public at large, we will probably be disappointed because many people, perhaps most, will not have been exposed to a particular media message, will not have comprehended it, or will not have been receptive to it. But if we look for effects among individuals who have been exposed to a message, who have comprehended it, and who are at least potentially receptive to it, then our search is likely to be more fruitful.

Moderately attentive and predisposed individuals are most likely to feel media influence.

In *The Nature and Origins of Mass Opinion*, political scientist John Zaller argues that the likelihood of exposure to and comprehension of a media message depends largely on **political attentiveness**, an individual's general attention to and

selective retention the tendency of individuals to recall information that is consistent with existing beliefs and to discard information that runs counter to them.

political attentiveness an individual's general attention to and knowledge of politics.

ThinkingCausally

What factors might influence an individual's ability to receive and process media messages?

political predisposition the interests, values, and experiences that help organize one's thinking about politics.

knowledge of politics.[56] An individual who is highly attentive to and knowledgeable about politics is likely to be exposed to, and understand, most politically oriented media messages. On the other hand, someone who pays little attention to politics and understands little of the political world will either miss most political messages in the media or fail to understand them if he or she should happen to come across them.

Receptivity also depends on one's **political predisposition**—the interests, values, and experiences that help organize one's thinking about politics. Someone who has very strong political predispositions is unlikely to be receptive to media messages that contradict those predispositions. For example, someone who is firmly convinced that U.S. troops should be used only to guard America's borders is unlikely to be receptive to media messages indicating the need for a deployment of troops to, say, the Middle East.

These insights have many interesting implications. Since data indicate that the most politically attentive individuals also tend to have the strongest political predispositions, individuals who are most likely to be exposed to and comprehend media messages (people who are most politically attentive) are least likely to be persuaded by them (because they have the strongest predispositions). The reverse is also true—the least politically attentive individuals tend to have the weakest political predispositions. Although the latter are most likely to be persuaded by media messages (because they have the weakest political predispositions), they are least likely to be exposed to and comprehend media messages (because they are least politically attentive). Figure 10-5 illustrates these relationships.

Who, then, are the most likely candidates for political persuasion by the media? People right in the middle—that is, individuals with a medium level of political attentiveness and political dispositions of medium strength. They will not be exposed to and comprehend every message that comes through the media, but they will encounter and understand many of them. And when they do, their political predispositions will be flexible enough to accept many of these messages. These realities suggest that part of the failure by political scientists to find strong media effects in the past was a failure to focus the search on this middle group.

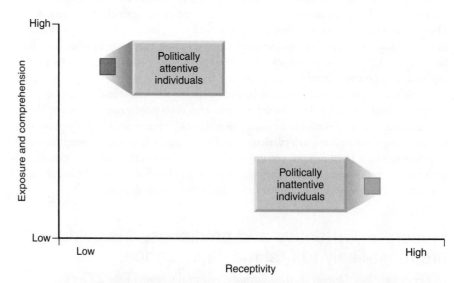

FIGURE 10-5. Those Most Likely to Be Influenced by the Media Are Less Likely to Be Exposed to and Understand Media Messages.

Zaller does not argue that this middle group is the only one that can be influenced by the media or that the media always influence this middle group. In some cases, when a message is particularly prominent (such as the coverage of Michael Jackson's death), even the least attentive person will be unable to miss it. The massive increase in President George W. Bush's job approval ratings after the September 11, 2001, terrorist attacks reflected the fact that everyone—from the most politically attentive to the least—had gotten the message about the attacks and the administration's strong response.

If a message is relatively "quiet," opinion change can still take place, but it will bypass all except the most politically attentive. Between 1964 and 1966, for example, press coverage of the Vietnam War became more negative. During that same period, some highly politically attentive individuals—but only highly politically attentive individuals—grew less supportive of the war. Why? Because only the highly attentive were exposed to and able to comprehend the change in the tone of media coverage. Individuals of middling and low attentiveness missed this shift, so their support for the war remained strong.

If we think in these terms, it becomes relatively easy to identify areas in which the media can have a large impact and those in which the impact is likely to be limited. For example, we know now that predispositions limit people's receptivity to media messages. If we want to look for media effects, then, we should look for cases in which predispositions are weak. Think, for example, about primary elections in which no incumbent is running—the 2008 Republican and Democratic presidential primaries, for example. In each primary race, all of the candidates were of the same party. Party identification, therefore, was useless as a tool for judging candidates. Furthermore, many of the candidates were unfamiliar to the public at large when the primary season began. Without partisanship and previous information about the candidates to draw on, voter predispositions toward candidates were weak. Accordingly, the potential for media influence was greatly enhanced. In fact, research has shown that the media do exert a strong influence on voter judgments during the presidential primary process.[57]

On the other hand, consider a case in which policy-maker and media discussions of an issue are largely balanced between a "pro" side and a "con" side. The general election between Republican and Democratic candidates for president usually fits this model. The campaigns and their supporters have roughly equal amounts of money to spend on their message, and the mainstream media present broadly balanced coverage of the campaigns. (See the discussion above on the absence of media bias in presidential election campaigns.) Under these circumstances, even if there were universal exposure to "the message," a balanced message would not challenge anyone's political predispositions because it would not convey a strong point of view. It would be unlikely, therefore, to result in large-scale opinion change.[58] Note, however, that in a country as closely politically divided as the United States, even small shifts in public opinion can have significant consequences. Thus, even if the "minimal effects" perspective still were considered accurate, "minimal" would not necessarily mean "inconsequential."

> "In a country as closely politically divided as the United States, even small shifts in public opinion can have significant consequences."

Media effects can be found if you look in the right places.

Scholars may have failed to find large media effects because they have been looking in the wrong places. First, we now know that, to find media effects, they should look for opinion change among people with moderate levels of political attentiveness and only moderately strong political predispositions. These people are likely to be exposed to most media messages, to have at least some comprehension of them, and to be somewhat receptive to them, even if the messages contradict their beliefs.

Second, opinion change occurs most often when the message is "loud," that is, when it is covered thoroughly, by a number of media outlets, for a long period of time. This tactic maximizes the chances of broad exposure to the message, which in turn maximizes the chances of broad-based opinion change. Recall the example of media coverage of the 9/11 terrorist attacks and the Bush administration's response.

Third, a media message that carries a largely one-sided point of view is more likely to lead to opinion change than balanced coverage. During the 1992 general election campaign between Bill Clinton and George H.W. Bush, for example, 90 percent of network news references to the economy were negative.[59] This kind of coverage can shift public opinion. On the other hand, coverage that is balanced— "some believe the economy remains weak, while others point to signs that it is in recovery"—would be unlikely to change opinions because it does not convey a particular point of view.

Fourth, opinion change occurs when media messages do not fit neatly with existing political predispositions. Recall the example of media coverage of presidential primary elections, in which partisanship and thorough knowledge of the candidates are generally not available to bolster predispositions. Another example would be media coverage of new or particularly complex issues, such as health care reform. The public can have difficulty determining how new or complex issues fit with their predispositions. With predispositions less of a factor, the chances for media influence on opinion are greatly enhanced.

Fifth, opinion change results from media messages to which people are most likely to be exposed. Recall that most Americans get their news from local television stations (refer again to Figure 10-4). Most studies of media influence, however, focus on messages delivered by network news and major newspapers, such as the *New York Times* and *Washington Post*. Why? Network news and newspaper content are monitored by various archiving and indexing services that are accessible online. Similar technology for archiving and tracking local news content is only beginning to be put in place. But Figure 10-4 suggests that local television news content holds the most promise for demonstrating the influence of media messages.

Sixth, opinion change takes two forms—gross and net. In an extreme example, imagine a society divided into two equal-sized groups—Group A and Group B. One hundred percent of Group A approves of the job the president is doing, while zero percent of Group B approves. This equal split puts the president's overall job approval at 50 percent. Imagine, though, that in a moment of weakness the president reveals to reporters that he finds members of Group A annoying and unattractive but finds members of Group B delightful and easy on the eyes. The media provide blanket coverage of the president's verbal indiscretion and the president's job approval falls to zero in Group A but rises to 100 percent in Group B. The president's overall approval rating remains at 50 percent, so there has been no net change, but there has been massive gross change, that is, change within Group A and Group B. By concentrating solely on net change, researchers can miss large but offsetting gross changes in opinion within subgroups of the population.

Finally, if a media message is particularly "quiet" or largely balanced between two sides, look for opinion change only among the most politically attentive. This is the only group likely to pick up on a quiet message in the first place, and the only group sophisticated enough to notice any subtle cues amid the largely balanced coverage that might induce a change in opinion.

CHAPTER SUMMARY

In this chapter, you have learned to:

10-1 Evaluate the unique role that the media play in American politics and society. The U.S. mass media differ from the media in other countries in several key ways. In the United States, the media are largely privately owned; there are different views about objectivity and taking sides; and the American media play a watchdog role. The American media also operate with relative freedom, and freedom from prior restraint is a particularly noteworthy characteristic.

10-2 Identify the legal constraints on American media. Despite their relative press freedom, the American media do operate under some constraints, including laws against defamation, the "equal time" rule, and the limited protection of shield laws. These limits are minor compared to those faced by American journalists in earlier centuries, when the media operated under much stricter government control. Beginning in the 1930s, this situation changed dramatically with a series of U.S. Supreme Court decisions expanding press freedoms.

10-3 Differentiate the types of media that exist today. Americans acquire information on politics and government from various types of media. Whereas newspapers once dominated, they were supplanted by broadcast television in the second half of the twentieth century. However, broadcast news has been in decline in recent years, with cable television, talk radio, and the World Wide Web gaining popularity as alternate news sources.

10-4 Analyze the nature of media coverage of politics and government. A few principles govern broadcast media coverage of American politics and government and distinguish broadcast media from other media sources. These include the tendency to focus on the president to the exclusion of Congress and the courts; the mediating role played by reporters in news coverage of elections; the negative tone of much television news coverage; and the tendency of television news to focus on the "horse race" and campaign strategies rather than candidates' policy positions and voting records. It is more difficult to make generalizations about the print media.

10-5 Determine whether the media are biased. Several kinds of evidence—anecdotal, survey data on journalists' beliefs, and the actual content of reporting—can be brought to bear on whether the media are biased. The best available evidence indicates a lack of bias in press reporting of presidential elections, but there is insufficient information to draw conclusions about other kinds of coverage.

10-6 Assess the effect of the media on political attitudes and behaviors. Early studies of media influence focused on voting behavior and produced evidence of only minimal effects. More recent studies of agenda-setting, framing, and priming have revealed more effects of media influence. However, selective exposure, selective perception, and selective retention limit media influence on attitudes and behavior. Research has also shown that individuals who are only moderately attentive to media coverage are likely to be the most influenced.

---

mypoliscilab **EXERCISES**

Apply what you learned in this chapter by starting with these resources on MyPoliSciLab.

Read on **mypoliscilab.com**

eText: Chapter 10

Study and **Review** on **mypoliscilab.com**

Pre-Test
Post-Test
Chapter Exam
Flashcards

Watch on **mypoliscilab.com**

Video: YouTube Politics
Video: The Pentagon's Media Message

Explore on **mypoliscilab.com**

Simulation: You Are the News Editor
Comparative: Comparing News Media
Timeline: Three Hundred Years of American Mass Media
Visual Literacy: Use of the Media by the American Public

KEY TERMS

SUGGESTED READINGS

J. N. Capella and K. H. Jamieson. 1997. *Spiral of Cynicism: The Press and the Public Good.* New York: Oxford University Press. Argues that a media focus on the horse race aspect of politics rather than substantive issues leads to citizens who are less trusting, less interested, and less inclined to participate.

Shanto Iyengar and Donald R. Kinder. 1989. *News That Matters: Television and American Opinion.* Chicago: University of Chicago Press. The ways in which television news programs set agendas, order priorities, shape opinions, and affect Americans' participation in political life.

Robert D. Putnam. 2000. *Bowling Alone: The Collapse and Revival of American Community.* New York: Simon & Schuster. Discusses changes in Americans' involvement with each other, their communities, politics, and government and suggests that TV, pressures of time and money, and urban sprawl may be the greatest contributing factors.

Larry Sabato, Mark Stencel, and Robert Lichter. 2001. *Peepshow: Media and Politics in an Age of Scandal.* Lanham, MD: Rowman and Littlefield. Argues that financial information, health that pertains to presidential duties, and public sexual encounters are fair game for press coverage. Family members, discrete extramarital sex, sexual orientation, and past drug and alcohol use are out of bounds.

John Zaller. 1992. *The Nature and Origins of Mass Opinion.* Cambridge University Press. How people acquire political information from the mass media and convert that information into political preferences.

SUGGESTED WEBSITES

ABC News Political Punch: http://blogs.abcnews.com/politicalpunch/

A political blog by Jake Tapper, ABC News senior White House correspondent, with sometimes controversial remarks on politics and the White House.

PoliWatch, Political Meanings: http://poliwatch.org/

A multipartisan political blog, with insight into political blogger assistance and training, publishing both experienced and newbie political bloggers. Also gives political news, research, polls, and more.

Mashable, The Social Media Guide: http://mashable.com/

Real-time updates on social media, including Facebook and Twitter, and reports on current issues in technology and the Internet, giving substantial coverage to the changing information age.

Public Broadcasting Systems: www.pbs.org

PBS serves 335 public noncommercial television stations and reaches nearly 73 million people each week through on-air and online content.

British Broadcasting Corporation: www.bbc.co.uk/info

The BBC, a public service broadcaster established by royal charter, is publicly owned and operated.

The Sun: www.thesun.co.uk/sol/homepage

The website of a British national newspaper.

Daily Kos: www.dailykos.com

A left-leaning daily political blog.

Hugh Hewitt: A Blog of Townhall: hughhewitt.townhall.com/blog

A right-leaning daily political blog.

Gallup: www.gallup.com

Gallup regularly conducts public opinion polls in the United States.

CHAPTER 11 Political Parties

A key causal relationship facing political parties is one between the relative strength of members of a party's coalition and the type of candidates and issues that are subsequently most likely to generate the enthusiasm and involvement of party supporters. Shifts in these coalitions lead to changes in candidate and party fortunes.

Consider the story of Joe Lieberman. Connecticut voters elected Lieberman to the U.S. Senate in 1988. Over the years, he compiled a record as a moderate Democrat and won re-election handily in 1994 and 2000. Tapped by Democratic nominee Al Gore to be his running mate in the 2000 presidential election, Lieberman broke a barrier by being the first Jew named to a major party ticket.

The Iraq War would prove to be Lieberman's undoing among Democratic supporters. Lieberman was a staunch supporter of the war prior to its onset in 2003, as were many other Democrats. Over time Democratic support waned, but Lieberman remained convinced that the war was a key battle in the fight against terrorism. His support for the war earned him public rebukes by Harry Reid and Nancy Pelosi, the leaders of the Senate and House Democrats, respectively. As the coalitional ground shifted beneath him and the party's anti-war activism grew, Lieberman did not move.

In 2006, Ned Lamont, a candidate heavily supported by MoveOn.org, a prominent political group pushing the Democratic Party to move in a more liberal direction, defeated Lieberman in the party primary. Running for reelection to the U.S. Senate as an independent, Lieberman prevailed in a three-way race in November. The man who was 537 votes away from being elected a Democratic vice president in 2000—the amount by which Gore and Lieberman lost Florida—was, six years later, no longer a Democrat. He campaigned for John McCain, the Republican presidential nominee, in 2008.

Although extreme, Lieberman's case is not unique.

Robert Bennett was first elected to the U.S. Senate, representing Utah, in 1992. He won reelection easily in 1998 and 2004 and was part of the Republican leadership team in the Senate. Bennett's ideological record over three terms was similar to that of Orrin Hatch, Utah's other Republican U.S. senator. But in 2010 this track record was not enough. Bennett was rejected by delegates at the state's party convention, where he lost to two political newcomers and failed to receive enough votes to proceed to the party primary.

Although receiving the endorsement of the National Rifle Association and some prominent conservative Republicans, Bennett had disappointed some of the party's support groups such as the Club for Growth, an organization that advocates for small government and low taxes. He had also upset supporters of the Tea Party movement that arose in 2009 and pushed Republican candidates to take more conservative positions, especially on the size of government. Sealing Bennett's fate were his vote in late 2008 for the Troubled Assets Relief Program, often referred to as "the Wall Street bailout"; his reintroduction in 2009, along with Democratic Senator Ron Wyden of Oregon, of an ultimately unsuccessful health insurance reform bill that required individuals to obtain coverage; and his history of actively pursuing federal earmarks or "pork" for spending projects in Utah.

Many Americans may appreciate Joe Lieberman's independent streak and the bipartisan gestures of Bob Bennett, but political activists that supported the Democrats and Republicans, respectively, did not. As events change, the issues and positions that energize or enrage party activists can change. The shifting balance of power within a party's coalition can have dramatic effects on electoral outcomes, as both Lieberman and Bennett learned. The public often expresses admiration for the politician who goes against the party tide or who casts unpopular votes, but to activists and fellow elected officials, these politicians are often derided as DINOs and RINOs—Democrats and Republicans In Name Only.

▼ THE FIGHT IS OVER

Delegates at the 2010 Republican convention in Utah rejected Senator Bob Bennett's bid for a fourth term in the U.S. Senate. Bennett was one of a number of Republican politicians nationally who faced serious challenges due to a resurgent conservatism among Republican voters.

CHAPTER LEARNING OBJECTIVES

After reading this chapter you will be able to:

11-1 Analyze the functions of political parties in American politics.

11-2 Determine why American electoral competition is dominated by two political parties rather than multiple parties.

11-3 Trace the evolution of American party organizations and their expanding role in campaigns.

11-4 Explain how parties achieve electoral success by building and maintaining coalitions of supporters.

What Political Parties Do

11-1 Analyze the functions of political parties in American politics.

Americans' views of parties have changed over time from fearful, to supportive, to skeptical. President George Washington, in his Farewell Address, warned Americans about the dangers of political parties. By the late nineteenth century, however, partisanship was a central aspect of Americans' identity, mentioned right alongside one's ethnicity, region, and religion. Today, Americans still have strong attachments to parties and do not fear them, but there is a pervasive skepticism that parties confuse issues more than clarify them—or alternately, that they are too polarized and stubborn and refuse to work together. What has provoked these strong reactions? What are political parties and what do they do?

Political parties are organized groups that seek to gain office and exercise political power through legislation, executive action, and control of government agencies, among other means. They aim to elect office holders who identify themselves by the group's common label and who consider themselves associated with that group. Candidates rally voters to their side who share the outlook or background of other supporters of the party.[1] Party activity occurs at all levels in American politics: from the individual voter who feels close to a party, to the candidate at the local, state, or national level who runs on the party label, to the public official who tries to rally fellow partisans around a policy proposal.

Defined narrowly, "the party" usually refers to its elected officials and the individuals working for official party organizations. More broadly, political parties are *networks* of people and groups who share common policy goals. The leadership of labor unions, trial lawyers, environmental groups, teachers, pro-choice groups, liberal think tanks, and the liberal blogosphere tend to align with the Democratic Party. The National Education Association (teachers' union), NARAL (pro-choice group), Center for American Progress (liberal think tank), and MoveOn.org (online liberal ideological group) are examples. Leaders of libertarian-leaning groups, business associations, gun rights' groups, veterans, pro-life groups, conservative think tanks, and conservative talk radio outlets tend to align with the Republican Party. The U.S. Chamber of Commerce (business group), the National Rifle Association (gun rights association), National Right to Life (pro-life group), and Heritage Foundation (conservative think tank) are examples. Dozens of other issue advocacy groups have close ties with one of the two major parties and actively seek to help the party's candidates win. These groups also expect that their voices will be heard as their party debates policy options. The party network thus involves the ongoing dialogue and mutual support between the party organizations, elected officials, party candidates, and political activists. In thinking of "the Republican Party" or "the Democratic Party," it is useful to keep in mind this entire party network of influence and conversation.[2]

political parties organized groups with public followings that seek to elect office holders who identify themselves by the group's common label, for the purpose of exercising political power.

Despite the negative attitudes the public often expresses about parties, political scientists generally offer a more positive assessment. Although not discounting parties' shortcomings, scholars see them as a vital part of democratic politics. Parties perform many roles in American politics, reflecting their construction as networks and their activity at all levels of politics. These roles serve the self-interest of party members, but they also produce benefits for the operation of American government and for the public.

Political parties fill gaps left by the Constitution.

The Constitution provided the basic structure for the selection of public officials. Elections, either direct or indirect, would determine the president, members of the House of Representatives, and U.S. senators. State constitutions, similarly, provided for a series of elections. But the Constitution stopped there. To say that elections are the selection mechanism is one thing—it was now up to candidates and voters to make it work. For the system established by the Constitution to gain credibility and legitimacy, some way had to be found to staff the offices of government and involve the public in politics.

Political parties filled this void. They were created by ambitious, hard-headed politicians to solve particular problems of candidate recruitment, to increase the likelihood of winning debates in the legislature, and to mobilize enough voter support to win elections.[3] They also serve as a vehicle for competing groups in the public—for example, a group advocating for more solar energy development and another advocating for more oil drilling—to influence the policy-making process. In serving the purposes of politicians and political activists, parties also assist political system legitimacy by contributing to a functioning system of electoral politics beyond what is specified in the Constitution.

Parties recruit candidates into the electoral process and nominate them for office.

Nationally and in most states, political parties take a very active role in identifying promising individuals and recruiting them to run for office. In the course of doing this, the party will assist both first-time and seasoned candidates with the various aspects of running a campaign, including raising money, dealing with the media, identifying potential supporters, developing positions on issues, and putting together a campaign organization to contact citizens and research opponents. In addition to the parties themselves, affiliated groups in the party's network contribute to candidate recruitment and training. For example, Emerge America is a group dedicated to recruiting and training women to run as Democratic candidates. The National Federation of Republican Women is its counterpart on the Republican side.

Parties also provide a ladder of opportunity up which candidates can climb, guiding them through a political career path. This helps sort out the potentially competing ambitions of many individual candidates by providing them with various offices to run for and a structure for moving up the party rungs to the next level of offices. Sometimes, for example, at the request of party leaders, a potential candidate will agree to step aside and run for office later or run for a different office.

Parties are engaged in finding candidates so that the party can increase its power. The party has the incentive to run as many candidates as it can in order to win control of as many offices as it can. But this self-interest also serves a social interest. Parties provide voters with choices, which are key to generating a sense of legitimacy for

American politics. Elections with choices make voters feel empowered. Candidates would emerge without parties, but parties, because of their competitive self-interest, increase the probability that candidates will be fielded systematically across an array of offices and levels of government, offering different policy solutions to entice voters. The Constitution could appear an empty promise if there were elections, but few candidates on the ballot.

After recruiting candidates, parties nominate them as the party's standard-bearers and put them on the ballot. Around the world, control of the nomination process is among the most significant powers of political parties: the power to filter who is elected to public office. In the United States, the nomination of candidates was first controlled by party leaders, then expanded to selection by delegates at party conventions, and now is determined in most cases by state-mandated primary elections.

Parties bridge constitutional gaps between institutions.

The Constitution deliberately spread power across institutions, across two houses of the legislature, across elected and unelected offices, and across the federal and state governments. It created a governing system that made the abuse of power difficult, but it also made law-making difficult. This diffusion of power is consistent with the limited government ethos of the American creed, as we discussed in Chapter 2.

Political parties bridge these institutional gaps by providing incentives for officials to cooperate in policy-making with each other, as shown in Figure 11-1. Officials who share a party label share a "brand name." When a president does well, members of his party in Congress enjoy some of the glow of that success. If he suffers from low approval ratings, the public's critical view can carry over to his fellow partisans in Congress. In 2010, with President Obama's approval low, health care reform unpopular, and the economy struggling, voters flipped over 65 House and Senate seats from Democratic to Republican control, and Republicans also gained big at the state level. Officials

▼ **PARTY SCHOOL**

Political party campaign schools teach candidates how to run for office and teach party workers and volunteers how to increase support for the party's candidates. James Carville, one of the best-known Democratic political consultants, spoke to participants at the Georgia Democratic Party's Grassroots Training program.

A. Institutional walls of separation in the Constitution

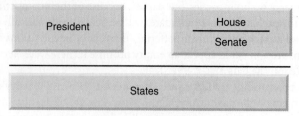

B. The party brand name provides incentives for coordination and cooperation across the constitutional walls

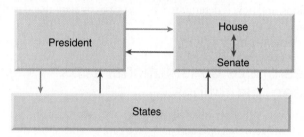

FIGURE 11-1. **Political Party Assistance to Policy-Making.** The Constitution created a set of institutions that would be involved in policy-making. It focused on the way these institutions could check each other's use of power. Left unstated was how the individuals in these institutions might work together. A political party provides a common "brand name" that encourages cooperation across institutional boundaries. Politicians know that when other members of their party are successful, the party brand name is enhanced and public approval and the probability of future election victories increase.

who share a party's brand name have a self-interest in seeing fellow partisans govern successfully.

This common bond does not undermine the Constitution's separation of powers, checks and balances, or federalism, but it does increase the ability to get things done. Because members of a party will usually share general goals and approaches, they start from a base of support when trying to enact policy. In that way, political parties contribute to governing by reducing some of the challenges to lawmaking in the American system. Members of a party do not always agree—but the shared party label increases the probability of cooperation. Without the connecting glue of partisanship, government might be even more hamstrung in acting.

This logic would seem to suggest that government gets more "big things" done when one party controls both Congress and the presidency—**unified government**—rather than when different parties control each of these branches—**divided government**. Does it? Certainly the passage and content of some of President Obama's major legislative victories—economic stimulus, health care reform, and financial industry reform—depended in part on his party's unified control of government. But the president also found himself stymied on issues like energy legislation and heard no enthusiasm from Congress when he suggested that immigration reform be on the table in 2010, an election year. Political scientists have extensively studied the causes and consequences of

unified government a situation where the presidency and both houses of Congress are controlled by the same party.

divided government a situation where the presidency is held by one party and at least one house of Congress is controlled by a different party.

unified and divided government and the contributing factors to legislative productivity. There is no guarantee that having the presidency and Congress controlled by the same party will result in a burst of significant legislation. Many other factors could lead to the government accomplishing more or less. A sense of crisis might inspire action; a shortage of revenue might discourage it. Public opinion may be calling for government action, or it might be calling for government to pull back. A president with high approval ratings might get more support from Congress, regardless of which party controls the House and Senate. A party with unified control of government might accomplish more early in its tenure rather than later. A president in his final years might find it difficult to get Congress to go along with him. And it matters whether a party is ideologically cohesive—a party can control the presidency and Congress, but if it suffers from internal dissension, legislative action will be difficult.

Studies by political scientists that take these and other factors into account generally conclude that unified government tends to increase the number of important laws enacted and reduces delay in various facets of legislative activity. The number is not large, maybe two or three additional significant enactments during a two-year congressional term. Over time, however, this can add up to a large number of enactments that may not have been possible under divided government.[4] Whether that is a good thing or not is a matter of one's personal political philosophy.

ThinkingCausally

Does unified or divided control of government have any impact on the number of significant laws that are enacted?

Political parties bring citizens into the electoral process.

Parties are self-interested bodies. They seek power to pursue their goals. To gain and assert power, parties need to win offices. To win offices, they need to win elections. And to win elections, they need more votes on Election Day than their opponents. Parties therefore have an incentive to get voters involved, and they do so in a number of ways.

Educate and inform voters   Historically, political parties have played a significant role in educating voters about candidates. In the nineteenth century, parties staged parades, festivals, and other events to attract a crowd to listen to candidates and party supporters deliver speeches. Given the limited entertainment options in the nineteenth century, these events were a big deal for a small town or city neighborhood. Voters would be entertained and energized by listening to detailed speeches explaining how the party was superior to its opponents.

In addition, political parties controlled much of the mass media of that era, newspapers in particular. Major party figures often urged the creation of newspapers as a means to communicate the party's message and assail the opposition. Publishers and editors had strong political and partisan views and saw the paper as a means to advance those views. The parties and the press were deeply intertwined, and the notion of "objective journalism" was still far in the future. So the positions of the party and its candidates were prominently available for citizens on a daily basis.

Parties today do not have the same kind of monopoly on information about their candidates. Nonetheless, they still attempt to educate voters through campaign

▼ **SENDING OUT THE MESSAGE**

Political parties use every communications technology at their disposal to get their message out to voters and create excitement about the party's candidates and office holders. Here, the Republican National Committee promotes its party's positions, such as its opposition to the Democrats' health care reform plan.

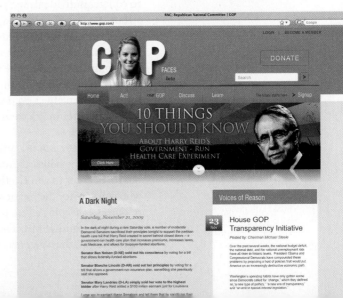

advertisements, leaflets and other literature, websites and blogs, e-mail and video and tweets, and frequent appearances by party officials and important party members on television and radio news and talk shows. They may coordinate candidate issues and messages across the country through advertising.

Deliver people to the polls   Parties work hard to convince supportive voters that something is at stake in the election and that the benefits of voting are so important that the voter best not stay at home. A party will point out to its supporters not only its positions and candidates, to show them the benefit of voting, but the positions and candidates of the other party, to show them the dire repercussion of failing to vote. More directly, with their get-out-the-vote (GOTV) efforts, party supporters—or sometimes hired telemarketing firms—make phone calls, send e-mail, and go door to door to remind people to vote and ask if they need assistance getting to the polling place. These activities may also inspire supporters of the opposing party to increase their efforts to get voters to the polls. Helping motivate people to get out and vote, whether through door-to-door, telephone, or electronic communications, is a major way for young people to be involved in party politics.

An individual voter might get a number of these reminders. Do any of these efforts matter? Studies show that individuals who are contacted by political parties, or by other groups, are more likely to say they voted than individuals who were not contacted. This correlation is not proof of causation, however: it is also the case that parties target their contacts to those individuals who they have reason to believe are more likely to vote.

Spending a significant amount of staff time and financial resources in the midst of a campaign to reach out to perpetual nonvoters or individuals highly uninterested in politics would rarely be a wise use of time and money. As communication costs drop significantly due to advances in technology, it may be that parties and candidates can increasingly reach out to a wider audience. Barack Obama's campaign made extensive use of newer technologies. Obama's campaign also used large rallies effectively to recruit new GOTV volunteers, and it placed more than 700 well-staffed local field offices around the country, mostly where the race was expected to be close. These offices located and trained volunteers who would contact voters, and they appear to have boosted Obama's vote total significantly in these areas.[5]

Sometimes parties take on a longer-term process of engaging new voters, conducting outreach regularly rather than only during campaigns. Generally, though, during the heat of a campaign it is sensible for parties, with their limited resources, to contact individuals with a prior history of voting or some other expression of strong interest. A better way to think of this relationship between contact and voting is that it is mutually reinforcing. Parties are likely to contact individuals with a higher than average likelihood of voting. The party contact can further increase this probability by stressing the importance of an election and the closeness of a contest. Research controlling for this possible reverse causation suggests that the contacts do indeed have an effect on driving up turnout.[6] Party contact is unlikely to turn a habitual nonvoter into a voter, but it can prompt an occasional voter to turn out.

Integrate new social groups   Political parties have an incentive to bring new groups into the political process, but they are selective about which groups to reach out to. In order to win elections, their main goal is to maximize the turnout of people who will vote for them, not to maximize overall turnout. They may even invest resources in keeping a group out of politics, as southern Democrats did with blacks through the mid-1960s. The logic of competition suggests that if one party is pushing a group away, the other major party would have an interest in integrating the group

ThinkingCausally

Does contact from a party or its candidates increase an individual's likelihood of voting?

into American politics, especially if it can do so without unduly alarming groups that already support the party. The Republican Party received strong support from black voters up through the 1950s, earning black votes because of its legacy as the party that ended slavery and began integrating blacks into the country's political life. Parties also saw other newly enfranchised groups, like women after 1920 and young voters after 1971, as opportunities for support.[7]

▲ JOIN THE PARTY

Parties seek to enlarge their vote totals by adding new groups of supporters. Following a naturalization ceremony in Miami, representatives from both major political parties and several advocacy groups urged new citizens to register to vote.

This process is also present with immigrant groups. In the waves of immigration across American history, the two major parties vied with each other to bring members of these groups into the electoral process and make them feel that the party represents them and cares about them.[8] Since the late twentieth century, the parties have reached out to different Hispanic groups. Cuban immigrants tend toward the Republicans, with one contributing factor being the party's hard line toward the communist regime in Cuba, an issue of great concern to these immigrants. Mexican immigrants have shown stronger support for the Democrats, due in part to a belief that the party's economic and immigration policies are preferable to those of the Republicans.

When it has suited their purpose, parties have also sought to make it hard for immigrant groups to enter politics. For example, in the 1890s, virtually every state enacted some form of personal voter registration. Often, these at first applied only to urban areas, where immigrant groups were concentrated. Although personal voter registration could make good policy sense—perhaps the risk of voter fraud is greater in areas of higher population—reformers also believed it would reduce immigrant influence in elections.[9] Today, some observers lodge the same charge at efforts to require photo identification prior to voting. Although reducing fraud is undoubtedly a good thing, these observers argue that one of the results of photo ID is to discourage voting by immigrants who are wary of U.S. legal authorities.

In recent elections, with the balance of power close in Congress and presidential elections hard fought, both major parties have worked to pull young adults into politics as volunteers and as voters. In the 1990s, the Republican Party was especially effective in reaching out to young adults through its network of support from rural-area church groups. More recently, the Democratic Party and its supporters have made extensive use of new technologies to reach out to young people—the Obama campaign in 2008 being especially effective. This trend was inaugurated primarily by people in their twenties who launched blogs, political meetup and fundraising sites, and social networking sites. Videos and podcasts on YouTube and other sites also enable party supporters to get young people involved in campaigning.

The public exerts leverage over public officials through use of the party label.

Parties benefit from the attachments and loyalty of the public. Candidates know they can count on 80 to 90 percent, or more, of their party loyalists to vote for them. They will need to spend some time energizing these loyalists and convincing them to vote, but the guaranteed support means they can devote more of their resources to appealing to undecided voters who do not have strong partisan leanings. Thus, party candidates benefit from having the party label.

Voters, in turn, can also use the party label to increase their leverage over public officials. The party label is a powerful tool for those voters with strong views who are highly attentive to politics. If voters believe that the parties are substantially different from each other in their policy priorities and preferences, they can consider this distinction when voting.[10] By voting for a Democrat, for example, they are roughly endorsing a particular approach to public policy. A Democratic public official seen as straying from this approach may face vigorous criticism from this attentive public. Thus, voters use the party label to hold officials accountable. Joe Lieberman and Bob Bennet, as described at the beginning of this chapter, learned this the hard way.

All voters, whether highly attentive or not, can use the party label to sweep one party out of office and put the other party in. This happened in 1994, when voters put Republicans in control of both the U.S. House and Senate for the first time in 40 years. In 2006, voters turned the tables and put the Democrats in control. Voters changed course again in 2010, giving Republicans big gains in the Senate and control of the House. The party label provides Americans with the simplest and most practical tool they have to make wide-ranging changes in the personnel of government and a possible new direction in public policy. The label frees voters from needing to know extensive information about each candidate, which is a hurdle relatively few voters could surmount. Although voting for a candidate because of his or her party label is often frowned upon in the media and popular culture—"I vote for the person, not the party" is a common refrain—political scientists have found the party label to be an effective, powerful, and usually accurate information shortcut.

The Two-Party System

11-2 Determine why American electoral competition is dominated by two political parties rather than multiple parties.

American electoral competition usually takes place between two major political parties. A major party has a large following, has endured over time, and is perceived to be electorally competitive by the public, potential candidates, and political observers. Minor parties, or "third parties," lack these features.

two-party system a system of electoral competition in which two parties are consistently the most likely to win office and gain power.

To say there is a **two-party system** in the United States does not mean that only two parties can compete but, rather, that it is a system of electoral competition in which two parties are consistently seen as the most likely to win office and gain power. If you were to predict who was going to win an election, and you predicted it would be either a Democrat or Republican, you would be right nearly every time.

Electoral systems outside the United States differ. In multiparty systems based on proportional representation, as discussed below, there might be several—not just two—parties that, in one election year or another, could potentially finish with the most votes. In addition, in those systems a party need not finish in first place to win seats in the legislature. Therefore, even smaller parties can be genuine contenders for power. To consider just a few examples, in their most recent legislative elections, Germany, Italy, Sweden, and Mexico each had six or more parties win seats in the national legislature. Each uses a form of proportional representation election.[11]

ThinkingComparatively

In proportional representation systems, smaller parties can win legislative seats.

Hundreds of political parties have competed over the years in the United States, but competition nationally has almost always been between two major parties. Across American history, there have been five major political parties: the Federalists (1789–1816); the Democratic-Republicans (1790–1824); the Democrats (1828 to the present); the National Republicans, later Whigs (1824–1854); and the Republicans

(1854 to the present). Third parties have included parties organized around ideology (Socialist Party, Progressive Party, Green Party, Libertarian Party), particular issues (Prohibition Party, Greenback Party), defection from a major party (States' Rights, also known as Dixiecrats), and parties built initially around a single presidential candidacy (American Independent Party for George Wallace in 1968; National Unity Party for John Anderson in 1980; United We Stand for Ross Perot in 1992, which led to the Reform Party in 1996). Wallace, Anderson, and Perot in 1992 were independents and the parties were built up around them after they had started running, rather than their candidacies emerging from the parties. At its very beginning, the Republican Party was a third party, but it quickly rose to ascendancy over the Whigs, which disbanded. Today the most significant third parties nationally are the Green Party and the Libertarian Party. These two parties contest a large number of offices, occasionally win elections, and have organizational structures from the local level to the national level that are somewhat similar to but not as extensive as the major parties.[12]

Third parties are rarely successful electorally but may be influential in other ways.

The electoral performance of American third parties can be summed up in one word: dismal. Third-party candidates rarely win elections and usually do not garner a significant share of the vote. Over the past 50 years, they rarely have received more than a few percent of the total national congressional vote. Their performance was strongest in the nineteenth century, with about 5 percent of House seats in the period from 1830 to 1870 held by third-party members. Over the past half-century, by contrast, there have only been nine times when a third-party candidate held a seat in the House, and eight of these were accounted for by Representative Bernard Sanders of Vermont, a member of the Socialist Party.[13]

Similarly, in presidential elections, third-party candidates rarely win states. No state has sided with a third-party candidate since 1968, when five southern states backed Alabama's Democratic governor, George Wallace, who was running as an independent candidate with the newly created American Independent Party.

Although third parties do not often win elections, they can still play significant roles in elections. Probably the most important of these roles is that third-party candidates, or independent candidates more generally, can introduce ideas and issues into the campaign that the major-party candidates might be neglecting or avoiding. Some analysts believe Democrat Al Gore struck a more populist tone in 2000 because of the solid showing of Green Party candidate Ralph Nader in polls.[14] Given this ability to introduce new ideas, one positive sign for third parties is that more voters today have the opportunity to hear from them in congressional elections (Figure 11-2), in large part because of ballot access lawsuits Perot filed in 1992.

Another possible but controversial role for third parties is to alter the election outcome

▼ A WASTED VOTE?

Many Democrats accused Green Party candidate Ralph Nader of helping elect President George W. Bush by diverting votes away from Al Gore, the Democratic nominee, in 2000. Would you vote for a third-party candidate if you thought he or she had no chance to win?

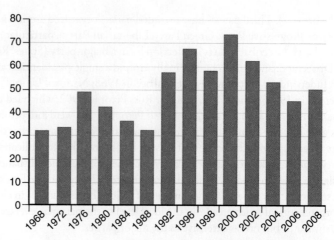

FIGURE 11-2. **Percent of U.S. House Districts with a Minor-Party or Independent Candidate Running.** Since 1992, voters in U.S. House elections have been more likely to see a third-party or independent candidate on the ballot than was true previously, with over half of all districts featuring a third-party or independent candidate. Prior to 1992, the proportion was more typically around 30 to 35 percent.

ThinkingCausally

Are third-party candidates to blame for the defeat of major party presidential candidates?

between the major parties. It was easy for Democrats in 1968 and Republicans in 1992 to blame George Wallace and Ross Perot for the defeat of Democrat Hubert Humphrey and Republican George H. W. Bush, respectively. Wallace and Perot received a large number of votes, and Humphrey and Bush lost; therefore, the argument goes, these third-party candidates cost Humphrey and Bush their elections by diverting votes from these two major party candidates. Many Democrats remain angry with Ralph Nader for his run in 2000, believing he cost Al Gore the presidency.

However, these are usually cases where correlation is mistaken for causality. First, these third-party candidates emerged and did well because of weaknesses in the major parties and their candidates. They may take advantage of those weaknesses, but they did not necessarily create them. Strong major party candidates discourage serious third-party challenges and deflate third-party performance. Humphrey in 1968, Bush in 1992, and Gore in 2000 failed to do so. The leap from correlation to causation also assumes that third-party candidates deliberately employ a spoiler strategy—seeking to cause the defeat of the major party they are ideologically closer to. This contention was made especially loudly by angry Democrats about the Nader candidacy in 2000 but is not well supported by political science research.[15] If Nader's goal was to contribute to Gore's defeat, he should have spent most of his time campaigning in states where the race between Bush and Gore was known to be close, in order to deny Gore victories in those states. Analysis of Nader's campaign travel and activity, however, found that he spent his time in states where he thought he could accumulate a large number of votes, not necessarily in states where the competition between Bush and Gore was expected to be tight. This pattern of campaign activity suggests that Nader's main goal was to reach 5 percent of the national vote to qualify the Green Party for public campaign financing, not to deny Gore the presidency.

Single-member districts with plurality elections favor two-party competition.

Certainly there is no constitutional prohibition on significant third parties. Indeed, the Constitution does not mention political parties at all. And Americans often say in surveys that they would welcome another major party—53 percent supported the idea in mid-2010, similar to the level seen for at least a decade.[16] Why would America's electoral competition tend to feature only two major parties as serious competitors? No single-factor explanation is sufficient. Rather, political scientists have identified a number of factors that push American party competition toward a two-party model.

In U.S. House elections, as with most American elections, **single-member districts** are the norm: voters elect one candidate to represent each congressional district. In addition, the candidate with the most votes (but not necessarily a majority) wins: these are **plurality elections**, sometimes referred to by scholars as first-past-the-post elections. Like in a race, the image suggests, what matters in an election is who crosses the finish line first, not how much she wins by or how long it took. Being first means you and only you win. Assume that politicians are ambitious and want to increase their chances of consistently winning office. What would be the best strategy: to remain in a small party that has the support of 5 percent of the population, or to join a larger party that can potentially obtain majority support? Joining a larger party is the likely answer, and two large, roughly evenly sized parties are the likely result.[17]

This line of argument holds up generally but not in every case. Canada and the United Kingdom, for example, have plurality elections but more than two major parties. Each has three major parties that are national in scope. In addition, each has parties strong in particular regions for reasons of nationality or language. Because of their strength in these regions, they earn seats in the national legislature. Within any particular district, competition might be primarily between two parties, but when summing the effects across the country, multiple parties win seats in the legislature. In the United Kingdom's 2010 elections to the House of Commons, the performance of the Liberal Party was so strong that it denied a majority to either the Conservative or the Labour Party. The Liberals joined a coalition government with the Conservatives and extracted promises of future electoral reforms, including a national referendum that would eliminate the system of plurality elections.

The idea that single-member districts and plurality elections push toward two-party politics assumes that parties have a way to nominate candidates to be on the November general election ballot. Nearly all states allow for party nominations, usually through a primary election or party convention. Louisiana and Washington, however, employ nonpartisan blanket primaries, in which all the candidates for an office, regardless of party, are in the same primary. Under this system, two candidates from the same party could win the primary and then face off in the next round of elections. California voters adopted Washington's version of this system in a 2010 referendum. Political scientists will need to wait for more election results from these states, and from other states that might adopt a form of nonpartisan blanket primary, before they can determine the long-term consequences for two-party competition and the fate of minor parties.

An alternative to the single-member plurality model is a system of **proportional representation** (PR), common in Europe and in many other democracies around the world. In this system, voters elect many representatives from the same district. The district, in fact, might be the entire country, as is the case in Israel. Depending on the

single-member districts electoral districts in which only one person is elected to represent the district in a representative body.

plurality elections elections in which the candidate with the most votes, not necessarily a majority, wins.

ThinkingComparatively
Despite the general tendency toward two-party competition, some plurality election systems have multiparty competition.

proportional representation an election system in which candidates are elected from multimember districts, with a party's share of seats from a district being roughly proportional to their share of the popular vote.

procedure used, voters may vote for a party but not specific candidates. Or, more commonly, they may be able to vote for specific candidates from a party's list. The number of representatives elected from a particular party will depend on that party's percentage of the vote on Election Day. If a party receives 35 percent of the vote in a district, it will send roughly 35 percent of the legislators from that district.[18] What this means is that the second- or third-place parties, or even more, may also be sending representatives to the legislature. Thus, in a PR system, an ambitious politician can remain in a smaller party and still have a chance to be elected to the legislature. Because there is a significant likelihood that no party will win a majority of the legislative seats, a majority coalition will need to be forged, further empowering smaller parties. Some countries, including Germany, used a mixed model, electing some seats by PR and some by the plurality system.

> **ThinkingCausally**
>
> Is two-party competition a result of rules like single-member-district plurality elections, or does two-party competition lead to those rules?

If single-member districts with plurality elections will generally be found in countries with predominantly two-party competition, a puzzle remains: is the two-party competition a consequence of these election rules or a cause of them? One study of the adoption of proportional representation systems found that countries with a prior history of diverse political competition between multiple groups adopted PR. In other words, the PR system was adopted as a result of what was effectively multiparty competition, rather than being the cause of that competition.[19] Iraq, for example, has numerous divisions among class, ethnic, religious, and regional lines. When devising Iraq's election rules in recent years, the writers of the new constitution created a system that gives a large number of parties a chance for representation in the legislature. Once in place, such a PR system would tend to encourage continued multiparty competition.

In the United States, on the other hand, political scientists have suggested that early political discourse was strongly oriented around fundamental debates about the proper role of government, and these debates tended to feature two competing views, one advocating a bigger role for the national government and the other a smaller role. A system like single-member districts with plurality elections works well in such an environment, reflecting rather than creating the nature of political competition between two predominant opposing viewpoints.[20] Overall, the research suggests that new electoral rules certainly can change outcomes—place a proportional representation system in the United States and it is feasible that third parties would win seats— but a society like Iraq with a history of multiple, deep political cleavages may be more likely to experience the political pressure to create these new rules.

The winner-take-all system in presidential elections favors two major parties.

Presidential elections pose a similar challenge to third parties. With the exception of Maine and Nebraska, all states allocate their electoral votes on a winner-take-all basis.[21] The popular vote winner of the presidential contest in these 48 states wins all the electoral votes from the state, no matter what the size of the popular vote victory. For a third-party candidate, this system makes it difficult to win electoral votes. Because a third party is not likely to be the leading vote winner in a state, it will win no electoral votes. With the winner of the presidency needing to win a majority of the electoral vote, the third-party path to the presidency is very challenging. And with the presidency and national government growing in stature and influence over the course of American political history, politicians throughout the country would want to be affiliated with a party that has a chance to win that powerful office. Voters also would want to have a say in choosing the president by voting for one of the major party candidates who has a plausible chance at victory.[22]

The structure of the presidential election process benefits third parties with strong regional appeals while hurting those with substantial national appeal. George Wallace in 1968 won 13 percent of the popular vote nationally, but he was the popular vote leader in five southern states and won their electoral votes over Republican Richard Nixon and Democrat Hubert Humphrey. In 1992, Ross Perot did even better nationally than Wallace, winning 19 percent of the popular vote, but he did not win a single electoral vote. He had broad national appeal but not a strong enough appeal in any single state or region to win electoral votes.

Legal and behavioral features of American elections reinforce two-party competition.

In addition to the basic structural features of American politics already discussed, statutes affecting elections, as well as the behavior of voters, politicians, and the media, reinforce the tendencies toward two-party politics.

Anti-fusion laws   Anti-fusion laws prohibit third parties from practicing **fusion** with a major party. Fusion, a common and successful strategy until banned in nearly all states around the turn of the twentieth century, allowed voters to vote for a candidate either under the third-party label or under the major party label. The strategy was to make voters comfortable voting for third-party candidates and to increase the influence the third party could exert on the candidates once they were in office.[23] Currently, only seven states allow fusion in its traditional form, most notably in New York where it is known as *cross-filing*. In 1997, the Supreme Court rejected a challenge to the constitutionality of anti-fusion laws.[24]

Ballot access   Prior to the 1880s, ballot access was not an issue. Parties printed their own ballots, which voters took to the polling place and dropped into the ballot box. Ballots could be a variety of shapes, sizes, and colors, and it was often easy to identify which party's ballot a voter was casting. Over a short period in the 1880s and 1890s, nearly every state adopted the **Australian ballot**, named for its country of origin. This is the ballot as we know it today—an official ballot printed by the government, provided at the polling place, listing all the candidates for every office, and cast secretly.

As soon as the ballot became an official, standardized government document, questions emerged. Would every candidate from every party, no matter how small, appear on the ballot? Or would the ballot list a limited set of candidates to prevent "ballot clutter"? Every state opted for the limited, clutter-free version and created rules to determine which candidates qualified for the ballot. In most states, parties could gain automatic ballot access if they did sufficiently well in prior elections— this rule largely benefited the major parties. Requirements to collect a large number of signatures to earn a spot on the ballot created a hurdle for minor parties. Over time, these restrictions have relaxed somewhat, usually as a direct result of lawsuits filed by third-party candidates.

401

▲ LOOKING FOR A LEGISLATIVE MAJORITY

German elections follow a two-part, mixed proportional representation procedure, in which voters select a specific party candidate who will represent a district and separately vote for a party, which also results in seats being awarded to a party. The overall distribution of seats is proportional to the party vote results. Here, Chancellor Angela Merkel, head of the Christian Democratic Union, confers with Guido Westerwelle, leader of the Free Democratic Party, over the terms for their parties to create a ruling coalition after the 2009 election.

fusion   a strategy in which third parties endorse a major party candidate but list that candidate separately on the ballot so that voters can vote for the candidate under the third-party label.

Australian ballot   an official government-produced ballot for elections that lists all offices and all the candidates and parties that have qualified to be on the ballot.

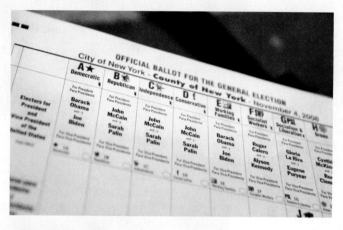

▲ **FUSION BALLOT**

New York State allows fusion, also known as cross-filing, in which a candidate can appear on a ballot separately as more than one party's nominee. Advocates of third parties hope fusion ballots will make voters comfortable with third-party candidates and that victorious candidates will realize they earned some of their votes as the nominee of a third party.

Campaign finance Running for office is expensive. Third-party candidates suffer from the fact that donors are usually not interested in contributing money to candidates they perceive as having no chance of winning. The public financing system for presidential candidates is also geared toward the major party candidates (see Chapter 9). Parties whose candidates received at least 25 percent of the vote in the prior presidential election get a full share of public financing for the general election in the fall. If a candidate received between 5 and 25 percent in the previous election, his or her party is entitled to a proportional share of public financing in the current election. Candidates falling below 5 percent, which is nearly always the case for third-party candidates, do not earn their party any share of public financing. Thus, third parties rarely qualify for public financing in presidential campaigns. The last one to do so was the Reform Party, due to Ross Perot's success in 1992 and 1996.

Voter, media, and candidate behavior The ways in which voters, the media, and candidates respond to the incentives created by these structural and legal aspects of American politics reinforce the tendency toward two-party politics. Voters unhappy with major party candidates often choose not to vote rather than vote for a third-party candidate who is likely to lose.[25] Other voters fear that voting for a third-party candidate amounts to throwing their vote away and helping their least favored of the two major party candidates—by denying a vote to one major party candidate, voters calculate, they are implicitly helping the other. Third parties face a very difficult time breaking through the psychology of nonvoting and the fear of the wasted vote.[26]

Media coverage is also problematic for third parties. Third-party officials often complain that if the media paid more attention to third parties, they would do better electorally. Media representatives respond that if third parties did better electorally, the news media would pay more attention to them. Each side is right. A media outlet that focuses a lot of attention on relatively obscure candidates may well find its readers, viewers, or listeners drifting to other media outlets. But more attention from the media would, overall, be at least marginally helpful for third-party candidates.

Ambitious, qualified candidates are much more likely to run for office as a Democrat or Republican than as a third-party candidate. Someone wanting to maximize her probability of winning, certainly someone who would like to make a career of elective office, is highly likely to affiliate with one of the major parties. Most voters, guided by their party identification with one of the major parties (see Chapter 9), are reluctant to vote for third-party candidates. Further, each major party has a network of supporters, consultants, experts, and fund-raisers to draw on. There are huge built-in advantages to running as a major party candidate.

Occasionally, third parties overcome these difficulties. Third-party candidates who have already become nationally visible as a former member of a major party or in some other way will often be talented, strong candidates, as Table 11-1 indicates. Theodore Roosevelt, George Wallace, and Ralph Nader all had significant name recognition. For some wealthy candidates, like Ross Perot in 1992 and 1996, campaign financing is not an obstacle.[27]

TABLE 11-1. Most Successful Third-Party Presidential Candidates, 1900–2008

Year	Candidate	Party	Percent of popular vote	Number of electoral votes
1912	Theodore Roosevelt	Progressive	27.4	88
1992	Ross Perot	Independent/ United We Stand	18.9	0
1924	Robert La Follette	Progressive	16.6	13
1968	George Wallace	American Independent	13.5	46
1996	Ross Perot	Reform	8.4	0
1980	John Anderson	Independent/ National Unity Party	6.6	0
1912	Eugene Debs	Socialist	6.0	0
1920	Eugene Debs	Socialist	3.4	0
1916	Allan Benson	Socialist	3.2	0
1904	Eugene Debs	Socialist	3.0	0
1908	Eugene Debs	Socialist	2.8	0
1948	Henry Wallace	Progressive	2.8	0
2000	Ralph Nader	Green	2.7	0
1948	Strom Thurmond	States' Rights	2.4	39
1932	Norman Thomas	Socialist	2.2	0

Source: Dave Leip's Atlas of U.S. Presidential Elections, www.uselectionatlas.org

Note: Includes all third-party presidential candidates who received at least 2 percent of the national vote.

Alternative voting rules might assist third-party electoral fortunes.

Supporters of an enhanced role for third parties argue that changes in voting rules could give these parties a better chance of winning elections. Whether this claim is accurate is difficult to determine because these alternative rules are not in wide use in the United States. The advocacy group FairVote put the number at 100 communities in 2008 using some form of alternative voting arrangement, but many of these are nonpartisan races such as school board elections.[28] Moreover, it may be that these reforms tend to be enacted in places already friendly to third parties—that is why they are enacted—rather than that they lead to support for third parties. Nonetheless, it seems plausible these rules would have some minor benefit for third parties.

ThinkingCausally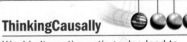

Would alternative voting rules lead to more third-party success?

Unlike full proportional representation, which would require the dismantling of single-member districts, preference voting and approval voting work within the American single-member district format.[29] Each aims to overcome the voter psychology that reinforces the two-party system and discourages casting a vote for a third-party candidate.

Preference voting In American elections, voters select their favored candidate among those on the ballot. An alternative arrangement would allow voters to rank their choices, indicating which candidate is their first pick, second, third, and so on. The idea is that voters could express support for a third-party candidate but need not indicate support for only that candidate.

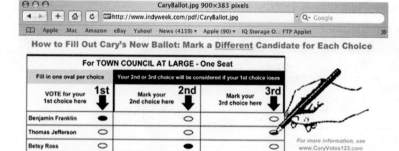

How to Fill Out Cary's New Ballot: Mark a **Different** Candidate for Each Choice

For TOWN COUNCIL AT LARGE - One Seat

Fill in one oval per choice | Your 2nd or 3rd choice will be considered if your 1st choice loses

	VOTE for your 1st choice here **1st**	Mark your 2nd choice here **2nd**	Mark your 3rd choice here **3rd**
Benjamin Franklin	●	○	○
Thomas Jefferson	○	○	○
Betsy Ross	○	●	○
Write-in: _____	○	○	○

For more information, see www.CaryVotes123.com or call Wake Co Board of Elections at 856-6240

Mark your 1st choice, then you may mark 2nd and 3rd choices as back-ups. Your back-up choices will never hurt your 1st choice. Back-up choices are only reviewed if an "instant runoff" occurs and your first-choice candidate gets eliminated and is not in the runoff.

▲ INSTANT RUNOFF VOTING BALLOT

Instant runoff voting has voters rank their preferences. If your top-ranked candidate finishes last in the first round of voting, your vote is reallocated to your second choice. This procedure continues until one candidate has received a majority of the votes. The city of Cary, North Carolina, used this sample ballot to help voters become acquainted with IRV. Should more cities and states be encouraged to adopt IRV?

Of the several varieties of preference voting arrangements, instant runoff voting is one that a handful of cities in the United States, including San Francisco and Minneapolis, have adopted. In this system, voters rank their choices. If no candidate receives a majority of the first-place votes, the candidate receiving the fewest first-place votes is eliminated, and the votes cast for him or her are redistributed to other candidates based on the preference ranking indicated by those voters. If a candidate now has a majority, he or she wins. If not, the last-place candidate is again removed and the votes redistributed.

Approval voting   Rather than ranking candidates, approval voting allows voters to indicate all candidates that they approve. The candidate receiving the most votes wins. As with preference voting, the logic is that voters might be interested in a third-party candidate but, because of their fear of wasting their vote, they would not want to commit their only vote to that candidate. Instead, with approval voting, they could vote for a third-party candidate and other candidates of their choosing—they would not have to worry about wasting their vote. Cumulative voting is a form of approval voting used primarily when voters are electing more than one official. For example, if a five-member school board is being elected, you as a voter could distribute votes as you please, ranging from giving all five of your votes to one candidate to casting one vote for each of five candidates, or any distribution of votes between those extremes. Currently, cumulative voting is used mainly in nonpartisan races such as school boards where multiple members are elected district-wide.

Whether promoting multiparty democracy in the United States through alternative voting rules is a good thing or not is a matter of dispute. To some political observers, multiparty democracy is more inclusive and produces higher voter turnout. To other observers, a two-party system produces more focused debates and a greater probability of decisive, majority victories rather than the plurality victories common to multiparty systems.

Party Organization

11-3 Trace the evolution of American party organizations and their expanding role in campaigns.

Scholars sometimes describe American political parties as a three-legged stool. The first leg is the party in the electorate: the party identification of voters, changes in their party attachments over time, and the influence of these attachments on political behavior (discussed in detail in Chapters 8 and 9). The second leg of the stool is party in government: the role of political parties in structuring the behavior, influence, and success of Congress, the president, the courts, and the bureaucracy (discussed in Chapters 13 through 16). The third leg of the stool is party organization, the focus of this section. Party organization is defined in different ways, but generally it refers to the formal structure that sets rules for party operations and provides services for various party units and candidates.

Party organization in the nineteenth century was informal.

Political parties in the early nineteenth century did not have large, official organizations. Prominent elected officials like governors or members of Congress usually held great sway over party activities. They would meet informally in small caucuses to select the party's candidates. In later years, parties sent large numbers of delegates to nominating conventions to select candidates, but elected officials still often handpicked the delegates to the convention.

During this era, the control was relatively tight over who could claim the party label as a candidate. Once candidates were in place, party workers were very involved in organizing parades, rallies, marches, and other events to motivate voters to get involved and support the ticket. These motivational efforts had the feel of "us against them" military campaigns and worked tremendously well. Turnout rates in the nineteenth century, especially its latter decades, were often in the range of 80 percent or more.[30]

Party machines provided organization in urban areas.

The era from 1870 to 1920 was the heyday of the local **party machine**. These organizations did not disappear entirely after that point, but they became less common and less powerful. One of the best-known survivors was that of Mayor Richard Daley of Chicago from 1955 to 1976. Daley combined his roles as mayor and as chair of the Cook County Democratic Party to wield tremendous influence on city affairs.

The word *machine* gives some hint as to their nature. Unlike the somewhat informal party organization common earlier in the nineteenth century at the state and national level, machines were disciplined organizations that selected candidates, got out the vote, and provided benefits to loyal constituencies. Usually the leader of the machine was an elected official, typically a mayor, but not always. Machines were hierarchical organizations with a reach all over a city, so that each precinct (usually a few city blocks) had a machine representative in charge, who reported to a ward boss. They were intensely local in focus, but they were willing to offer the backing of the machine and its supporters to a state or national politician who could return the favor in some way.

The machine spread benefits broadly. As a candidate or office holder, you knew that affiliation with the machine increased your likelihood of victory. Kicking back

party machine disciplined local party organizations that selected candidates; got out the vote; provided benefits to supporters including government workers, local constituents, and businesses; and served as social service agencies for their followers.

▼ **MONEY MAKES THE MACHINE GO 'ROUND**
Cartoonist Thomas Nast was a vigorous critic of party machines. Here he pans them as nothing more than corrupt organizations that bought the support of delegates at nominating conventions in order to get their favored candidates nominated.

THE "BRAINS"

THAT ACHIEVED THE TAMMANY VICTORY AT THE ROCHESTER DEMOCRATIC CONVENTION.

patronage awarding jobs in government on the basis of party support and loyalty rather than expertise or experience.

a portion of your salary to the machine would be an acceptable price to pay—it beat losing. As a worker, the promise of a city job awarded to you for your loyalty, known as **patronage**, made the machine a path to upward mobility. This was especially true for immigrants who might otherwise find it difficult to advance in the American economy. Businesspeople, lawyers, and bankers knew they would prosper through government contracts and favorable regulations if the machine was electorally successful. And individual voters were catered to by precinct captains who would provide them with groceries, financial and legal assistance, job contacts, help renting a facility for a wedding, or any other kind of help that would cement the voter's loyalty to the machine.

Party organizations were reformed at the beginning of the twentieth century.

Despite building deeply personal alliances with their supporters and serving important social service functions, machines had problems. Fiscal discipline was not one of their hallmarks. Nor were open and fair bids for contracts. The patronage system rewarded loyalty more than competence.

With the rise of professions and the middle class at the turn of the twentieth century, machines came under strong attack. Businesses that were not favored by the machines, rival politicians, and middle-class reformers joined forces in what became labeled the Progressive movement, to change civil service laws at the national, state, and local levels. These reforms protected government workers from removal when a new party came into power.

Progressive reforms a set of political and electoral reforms in the early twentieth century that had the combined effect of weakening political parties.

Parties at the state and local levels were the subject of a wide range of **Progressive reforms** during the first two decades of the twentieth century. Reforms included the introduction of nonpartisan elections; citywide rather than ward-based elections to city councils; the development of separate and often appointed rather than elected governing districts for services such as water, transportation, and schooling; and the hiring of city managers to run much of the day-to-day business of the city, taking that job away from elected mayors. At the state level, reforms included the widespread adoption of personal registration requirements for voting, requirements that primary elections determine party nominations, and the increased use of nonelected boards and commissions to make public policy. Reformers expected these changes to weaken political parties, or at least to weaken the control of their opponents over the parties and government. In this way, reformers and machine politicians were alike: each wanted to make it more difficult for their opponents to hold office and wield power.

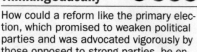

ThinkingCausally

How could a reform like the primary election, which promised to weaken political parties and was advocated vigorously by those opposed to strong parties, be enacted by state legislatures filled with party politicians?

As one political scientist suggests, it is misleading to describe machine politicians as determined to hoard power and reformers as determined to spread it widely. Instead, both represented coalitions of supporters who preferred that they hold power and their challengers do not. Each took advantage of opportunities to revise rules, laws, and political processes to create "political monopolies." And, by increasingly serving the narrow needs of its coalition while cities changed around them, each created the conditions for opposition to arise and lead to the monopoly's collapse.[31]

Because it was ardently pursued by reformers, the adoption of the primary election has usually been thought of by political scientists as an assault on a party's most defining power: control over nominations. Certainly, primaries do present challenges, as they create strife within parties and risk the nomination of weak candidates. There is also the curious fact of using a public process to select the candidates of a private organization, which political parties legally are—it is as

◄ CASTING A PRIMARY VOTE
Although political parties are legally considered private associations, state law often requires that party nominees be selected in primary elections. This is one of many ways in which state laws regulate political parties. States pay the costs of printing ballots and conducting the balloting on Election Day. They do not pay the costs associated with party caucuses and conventions, which are other ways party nominees are sometimes selected.

if nominations to the Board of Directors of the Sierra Club were a matter of a public vote rather than being left up to the Sierra Club. The correlation between the support of reformers and the adoption of the reform, however, is somewhat misleading. More recent research shows that major party officials welcomed the primaries in part because they had increasingly struggled to maintain control over their growing organizations and the conflicts about who "deserved" a nomination. Factional disputes within parties were becoming very common. It would be easier to sort out these disputes in primary elections.[32] Reformers advocated for primary elections, but party leaders also accepted primaries as a way to address serious organizational challenges.

The adoption of primaries as the dominant form of party nomination was part of a broader trend of state government regulation of political parties.[33] States established laws and rules concerning party committees, the selection process of party officials, how parties could raise and spend money, in what ways they could assist their candidates, how candidates would qualify for the party primary ballot, and who could vote in the primaries.

Party organizations have become more active in recent decades.

For decades after the introduction of Progressive movement reforms, party organizations were largely ineffective and inactive. The organizations were threadbare, rarely had a headquarters, and seemed to disappear between elections. Party functions such as recruiting, training, and assisting candidates fell by the wayside as candidates built their own campaign organizations, became less reliant on the resources of the formal party organizations, and deemphasized their link to their political parties. Voter mobilization by parties lagged in many areas. Organizations today have reversed these trends.

State party organizations   State parties challenged their legal status by arguing that they were not quasi-public utilities, but rather were private associations entitled to set their own rules. In a series of decisions beginning in the late 1980s, the Supreme Court agreed and granted state party organizations more autonomy from government regulations.[34] For example, the Court struck down the mandatory partisan blanket primary, in which voters could choose office by office in which party's primary to participate. As private associations, the Court argued, political parties had a right to decide who could be involved in selecting their nominees for office. The right of parties to spend unlimited sums on behalf of candidates was upheld, so long as candidates had no say in how the money was spent.[35]

To respond to the competitors for some of their key functions, state party organizations and legislative campaign committees increased their professionalism, hiring new staff and experts to recruit, train, and help finance candidates, and working more closely with the new web of pollsters, consultants, and media advisers.

National party organizations   The national party organizations include the Democratic and Republican national committees and the campaign committees for each party in the House and Senate, referred to as the Hill committees (Democratic Congressional Campaign Committee, National Republican Congressional Committee, Democratic Senatorial Campaign Committee, National Republican Senatorial Committee).

▼ **PARTY CHIEFS**

The national party committee establishes rules by which the party's business is conducted and provides support for recruiting, training, and financing candidates. The party chairs, such as Michael Steele and Tim Kaine, 2010 chairs of the RNC and DNC, respectively, are usually the most visible spokespersons for the national party organizations.

Starting in the mid-1970s, both parties began modernizing their operations and becoming more active in presidential campaigning, with the Republicans moving first. Both parties expanded their funding and staff. Voter contact, fund-raising, polling, advertising, candidate recruitment and training, opposition research, internal party communications, and fund transfer arrangements between the national and state parties all increased markedly. The key to this revival was that parties benefited from the complexity of campaigning in an era of high technology, constant media, large fund-raising demands, and intense demand from issue activists. Some candidates—especially new ones—simply cannot assemble on their own the necessary money and expertise needed to run a modern campaign, thus opening the door to national party organization involvement.[36]

In addition to contributing funds and providing services to their candidates, the national party organizations also acted independently. The national party committees spent anywhere from 3 to 15 times as much money in their independent spending than in their contributions to the party's candidates.[37] In total dollars, independent party expenditures were well over 100 times higher in 2010 than they had been in 2002.[38] In competitive congressional races, it was not unusual for the party organizations to spend more on a campaign than either of the candidates. The Hill committees expected safe incumbents to contribute some of their campaign funds to the party so the party could redeploy these funds to other contests. An expectation like this signals how far the national party organizations have come in increasing their discipline and focus.

Like political parties in the United States, parties in the Western European democracies traditionally relied on private funds from wealthy donors, trade unions, and party members to finance their campaigns. Over the past two decades, in contrast to the United States, government funding for party campaign activity has grown significantly in Europe at the national level. In the United States, only when candidates opt into the presidential public financing system do national tax dollars finance party campaign activity or, more precisely, the campaign activity of the party's nominee. Although especially a practice in the new democracies of Eastern Europe, western and southern European countries such as Germany, France, Italy, Spain, and Portugal also now provide large sums to parties. After 2010, the United Kingdom is expected to begin holding primary elections in legislative districts dominated by one party, with Parliament contributing funds for up to 200 of these races. Many of the newer democracies explicitly provide for political parties in their constitutions, and they support that guarantee through financial assistance.[39]

ThinkingComparatively

Unlike the United States, many countries explicitly recognize political parties in their constitutions and then support these parties with substantial funding provided by government.

For most Americans, the most visible activity of the national party organizations is running the **national party convention** held every four years to select the party's presidential and vice presidential nominees. The convention delegates pass the **party platform**, a statement of the party's principles, goals, and plans, and settle rules controversies within the party. Up through the mid-twentieth century, conventions were the place where rival factions within a party battled to select the party's presidential nominee. Multiple ballots were sometimes needed to determine the nominee; the Democrats famously took 104 ballots to select John Davis in 1924. Today, however, largely because of the reforms to the nominating process after 1968 (see Chapter 9), the nominee is usually known well in advance of the convention. The convention is a televised spectacle as well, and neither party wants a divisive internal battle broadcast across television screens like a bad reality TV show.

national party convention a meeting held over several days at which delegates select the party's presidential nominee, approve the party platform, and consider changes in party rules and policies.

party platform a document expressing the principles, beliefs, and policy positions of the party, as endorsed by delegates at the national party convention.

CaseStudy: Getting to Know Voters, One by One

One feature of the party machine praised by political scientists was its tight connections with voters. Machine precinct leaders knew each supporter in their area, checked in on them, helped them navigate through city government, and provided services such as attaining legal assistance, finding a doctor, and arranging for groceries during tough times. The machine was, in part, a social service or welfare agency. In exchange, the machine sought votes. It knew its voters.

Party organizations today also try to know their voters, but they do not have the deep personal connection with voters that the machine did. Nor do they provide social services. However, through microtargeting, they try to understand voters one by one to target messages to each. The hope is to persuade the undecided to support the party's candidate and to motivate the already decided to get out to vote.[40]

Microtargeting consists of building huge databases of information about voters. For each potential voter, party workers enter hundreds of bits of information, ranging from neighborhood characteristics available from the U.S. Census to consumer characteristics, such as purchasing habits, brand of car owned, television networks watched, magazine subscriptions, gun ownership, sports preferred, type of musical preference, and much more. Phone or direct contact from a party staffer or volunteer—known as party canvassing—might extract some additional information for the database. Canvassing is one of the main ways young people become involved in party activity. Today, volunteering for a political party is often as easy as visiting the party's website or its profile on a social networking site.

Examining voter databases, which are readily available from states, provides information on the voter's turnout history, party registration, and possibly which party primary she or he voted in. Voter visits to the party's website or, for example, its Facebook profile, provide additional information. The more information acquired about the voter, the better.[41] Public opinion data are then merged into the file, allowing data analysts to unearth connections between demographic, consumer, and other information and views on public issues.

These data are then analyzed to produce a specific message tailored to a voter's key interests. The database helps generate sophisticated and narrowly targeted advertising, mailings, phone contact, personal contact, and get-out-the-vote drives on behalf of a range of party candidates.[42] Analysts compute scores for each individual to estimate his or her likelihood of supporting the party's candidates, so the party can target its outreach efforts efficiently. Republicans found, for example, that viewers of Fox News or the Golf Channel, BMW drivers, health club visitors after work hours, and bourbon or Coors beer drinkers were more likely to support Republicans than Democrats. As one article title put it, "The GOP Knows You Don't Like Anchovies."[43] The party employed microtargeting to connect with millions of voters who leaned toward Republican candidates but had not voted regularly. Volunteers could be sent door to door to speak with these potential voters about how the party's agenda was consistent with their key concerns. Contact with the individual voter can help confirm whether the general relationship between demographics or consumer characteristics and policy preferences, known as "data mining," are true for this voter as well.

Republicans in 2002 were the first to use microtargeting in a systematic way, and it was a prominent part of the party's campaign effort in 2004. The Republican National Committee, in coordination with the Bush campaign and Republican state and local party organizations, purchased commercial databases that held hordes of information on individuals. The party also purchased or received from supporters the membership information from organizations expected to lean toward the party's positions, including groups like the National Rifle Association, churches, and clubs. All this information was entered into the national Republican database known as Voter Vault, which holds information on over 170 million voters.

◄ GETTING OUT THE VOTE
Political parties engage in extensive get-out-the-vote (GOTV) activities. Urging individuals to vote on Election Day is the culmination of a long and often precisely targeted effort to appeal to voters' key concerns. Through microtargeting, parties appeal to voters on issues of specific interest to them. The parties consult massive databases to discern what an individual's key issues might be.

The Democrats microtargeted extensively in 2006 as they regained majorities in the U.S. House and Senate. By 2008, the Democratic National Committee had built a national voter database known as DataMart that had grown tenfold since 2004 and that matched the Republicans' in size. Volunteers could log into the database over the Web and provide real-time updates to the information collected on potential voters. The database is also updated after primary elections, as candidates add new information they have collected over the course of the campaign. The Democrats' database benefited from the Obama campaign's heavy use of new media and technology to reach volunteers and supporters. The Obama campaign organization's outreach continued during his presidency in the form of Organizing for America, further boosting Democrats' data gathering.[44]

Creating and analyzing microtargeting databases are examples of jobs usually best performed by the national party organizations, because of their resource advantages. In 2008, this picture was reversed for the Democrats, as the huge financial resources of the Obama campaign allowed it to gather data on a scale that the DNC could not match, but these data were folded into the DNC database during September and October 2008. As a result of these efforts in previous elections, both parties in the 2010 midterm elections had billions of bits of voter information at their disposal.

ThinkingCritically

1. What might be some objections to parties tailoring their messages and appeals to individual voters? What are its virtues?

2. Are there circumstances under which you can imagine microtargeting not being an effective mobilization technique?

3. Is the advent of microtargeting a plus or a minus for third parties?

A new federalism of the parties is now in place.

Today, the national party organizations have more influence on the state organizations than was true previously. The Democratic and Republican national party organizations provide financing and technical assistance for their state parties. Each national party channels contributions to the state parties—when an individual or organization has maxed out on allowable contributions to the national party—with directions about how to employ these funds to benefit candidates for national office.

Both parties, but especially the Democrats, set mandatory rules at the national level. The Democrats have established rules for how delegates are apportioned among candidates in presidential primaries and caucuses, the demographic composition of state delegations to the national convention, and the procedures by which caucuses are run. The Republicans leave more of these matters to the state parties to determine. For 2012, however, the party is imposing rules on states that hold their nomination contest too early, rather than allowing the states to set their own rules. The goal is to encourage states to move their contests later into the spring.

As part of their increased activity in recent elections, national party organizations have created coordinated campaigns with state party organizations, in which the national party provides financial resources, expertise, and staff to help a state party's effort to win a congressional or other seat. Howard Dean, chair of the Democratic National Committee in 2006, adopted the "50-State Strategy" to signal to state party organizations that this kind of national assistance was possible across the country, not just in traditional Democratic strongholds. Rahm Emanuel, then the head of the Democratic Congressional Campaign Committee and more recently President Obama's chief of staff for two years, blasted the plan as squandering resources rather than focusing them on voter turnout in the most competitive races. Even after the Democrats' success in 2006, the 50-State Strategy remained controversial, but Barack Obama in 2008 followed Dean's lead by placing staff across the country, not just in loyal Democratic states and swing states.

The growing role of the national party organizations has been beneficial for state party organizations and candidates, particularly in providing resources and expertise. However, the new role has also created some strains. In 2010, national Democrats wanted Pennsylvania Congressman Joe Sestak to withdraw from his challenge to Senator Arlen Specter, the incumbent who had switched his party affiliation from Republican to Democrat in 2009 after spending decades as a Republican in Washington. Sestak had the support of many liberal activists in Pennsylvania even though state party officials supported Specter. He stayed in, defeated Specter in the Democratic primary, but lost in the November 2010 general election.

The Evolution of Party Competition and Party Coalitions

11-4 Explain how parties achieve electoral success by building and maintaining coalitions of supporters.

With two major parties in the United States, winning an election means getting more votes than the opponent, typically more than 50 percent. American parties, therefore, are large coalitions that bring together a wide range of groups with varied interests and policy perspectives under the same umbrella. Groups benefit by associating with a winning party because it increases the likelihood of action on the groups' key issues. The collection of groups under the party umbrella assists governing, because it forces some compromise among these groups—not every group's interest can be the top priority of the president and legislators. And bringing groups under the umbrella benefits parties, because it helps them win.

Bringing interests together does pose challenges, however. The larger the party, the more factions it is likely to have. For a while, these factions can reside in peaceful coexistence, but as groups in the coalition begin to believe that the party is marginalizing their issues and concerns, the coalition comes under strain. Coalition management presents complex challenges to party leaders.

The Republican Party during the presidency of George W. Bush, for example, had pulled together social conservatives, foreign policy conservatives, economic conservatives, and libertarians. Increasingly, these groups found it harder to support each other's causes or to let other groups' priorities be the party's main focus.[45]

President Obama has confronted the same problem keeping Democratic coalition members satisfied. Consider this list from a *Washington Post* columnist, who notes that, in addition to angering environmentalists with a decision to allow off-shore oil drilling (later revoked by the president after the 2010 oil spill in the Gulf of Mexico), the president also faced:

- "Unions unhappy that their top legislative priority, the Employee Free Choice Act, [was] stalled and that they had to swallow an excise tax on insurance plans as part of health-care reform.

- Gay rights advocates frustrated with the languid pace of progress on repealing 'don't ask, don't tell' and incensed . . . when the Obama Justice Department filed a brief defending the policy's constitutionality.

- Women's groups upset about the abortion restrictions in the new health-care law.

- Civil libertarians infuriated about the administration's legal positions in the war against terrorism, from indefinite detention to warrantless wiretapping to military commissions.

- African American groups concerned that the administration [had] not done enough for minorities, particularly in the area of job creation.

- Hispanic groups bemoaning the lack of action on immigration reform."[46]

The fact that American party coalitions need to be large has been the basis for a long-standing debate about American parties. Some analysts have called for candidates from a party to run as a team that offers a clear platform of proposals, works in a highly unified, disciplined fashion to enact them, and then runs on its record. Many political activists wish for the same. This is the **responsible party model**. One attraction of this model is that it improves accountability by forcing politicians to act in a cohesive way and then defend their record. Voters know where to point the finger of blame if things go wrong or whom to credit if they go right.

Some analysts, however, have said the broad nature of American party coalitions makes this kind of party behavior unlikely over an extended time because parties constantly need to adjust their positions to either become or maintain a majority. They need to respond to events and to the tactics of the other major party. And because some positions might be more popular in one part of the country than another, candidates of the same party will differ in their views from place to place. The practical reality, these critics say, is that successful parties will usually have to compromise and adjust their positions more than their most fervent supporters would like.[47]

▲ **TOUCHING BASE WITH ACTIVISTS**

Each party has particular groups whose support is important for candidates. The Conservative Political Action Conference provides a chance for Republican candidates to establish their conservative credentials with an audience of political activists. Here, former Massachusetts governor Mitt Romney, who ran for the Republican presidential nomination in 2008, addresses the group at its 2010 conference.

responsible party model   the idea that political parties should run as unified teams, present a clear policy platform, implement that platform when in office, and run on their record in the subsequent election.

Coalitions are dynamic, not static.

"The party coalition" is a general term that obscures the complicated nature of holding together a coalition. Coalitions come together in a wave of optimism—and perhaps in a wave of relief from removing the other party from power—because their members believe that their goals will be better achieved by joining forces. In general, they believe the party's approach to issues will advance their cause. They might even be willing to defer pressing their cause for a while as other coalition members take their turn.

A victorious party might wish for time to stand still while it revels in its unity—its coalition intact and the party a national majority. This is impossible. Party coalitions are always changing and facing strains. Like tectonic plates, the factions within a party shift and collide, sometimes creating minor rumbles, sometimes earthquakes. Cracks in the party foundation may appear immediately. At other times they may build up over decades. Unity tends to fracture. Waiting becomes less palatable, and the various parts of a coalition want their issues to be the party's primary concerns.

If a party knows that its success depends on serving the members of its coalition, what might prevent it from doing so? Media personalities, newspaper columnists, and bloggers often solve this puzzle by pinning the blame on unprincipled and spineless politicians. This explanation ignores the significant difficulty involved in holding together diverse coalitions of dozens of interest groups, hundreds of elected officials, and tens of millions of voters spread coast to coast. The explanation is appealing in its simplicity by focusing on character and personality, but it is misleading for that very reason. It ignores or wishes away the political realities faced by party leaders. Good analysis requires understanding these realities. There are several strategic factors explaining why a party might not serve all parts of its coalition equally.

First, a group might be so loyal to the party that it seems to have no serious options politically, which could reduce pressure on the party to advance the group's agenda. Leaders of black and labor organizations have had such complaints about

ThinkingCausally

Why would a political party seem to downplay the concerns of some members of its coalition, when it knows it needs the votes of these coalition members to win?

▼ BALANCING PARTY AND
INTEREST GROUP AGENDAS
Politicians want to appear
responsive to their support
groups, but they do not want to
create the impression they are
controlled by a group's agenda.
For national Democrats,
signaling support for the
NAACP's priorities at its annual
national convention is a long-
standing tradition. President
Barack Obama spoke to the
group in July 2009.

the Democratic Party.[48] Second, one group's interests might clash with the interests of other groups in the coalition—someone will have to be disappointed. Some of the desires of the Republican Party's conservative Christian followers, for example, would be objectionable to those Republicans who define themselves as libertarians and argue that government needs to stay out of individual decisions as much as possible. Third, as the mix of voters supporting a party changes over time, a group may become a smaller share of a party's voters and therefore be less central to the party's electoral strategies.

Lastly, a party that has lost recent elections will have conflicting internal interpretations about what lessons to learn from these defeats. The winning interpretation will favor some party groups and their issues more than others.[49] After the Republican Party's defeats in the 2006 and 2008 elections, the party's factions sparred over whether the party had pushed too far in a conservative direction or had strayed too far from conservative principles. By 2010, with the rise of the Tea Party movement—a conservative backlash to the policies of President Obama and congressional Democrats—the argument that the Republican Party had drifted too far from conservative thinking was dominant. Candidates supported by Tea Party followers captured Republican primaries through the spring and summer of 2010, sometimes with the support of prominent Republican elected officials and sometimes in defiance of them. The Tea Party movement and its supportive Republican politicians like former vice presidential nominee Sarah Palin and Senator Jim DeMint of South Carolina did not always field a winning candidate, but they did succeed in defeating some candidates preferred by powerful party leaders and pushing other candidates to take conservative stances. In Florida, the state's popular governor, Charlie Crist, left the U.S. Senate primary after Tea Party support swung behind Marco Rubio, the former speaker of the Florida House of Representatives, despite the support for Crist by Senator John Cornyn, head of the National Republican Senatorial Committee. Crist then lost in November 2010 as an independent.

All four of these factors contribute to parties changing their emphasis on particular issues, perhaps to the chagrin of some coalition members. At the extreme, a party might even reverse its position on an issue. Political scientists refer to flips in party positioning as **issue evolution**. Some examples of issue evolution are the support of

issue evolution a change in the partisan base of support for an issue over time, such that the positions of Democrats and Republicans switch.

civil rights by the Democratic Party beginning in the 1960s, a stance previously taken by Republicans; and the move by Republicans to a free trade position in the 1970s, after having been the party more supportive of protectionism since its founding in 1854. Issue evolution is a dramatic illustration of how party coalitions are always evolving. Sometimes party leaders calculate that maintaining and enlarging the party's base of support requires setting aside some groups' concerns or revising or even reversing a long-standing party position.[50]

American parties have evolved through six periods of party competition.

Over time, the key issues and relative strength of the two major parties have changed. Political scientists refer to the switch from one period of competition to another as **electoral realignment**—the shifting of support groups between the parties, the addition of new groups, and the rise of a new set of prominent issues. Political scientists dispute the process by which electoral realignment occurs and whether the most important change is sudden and dramatic, in the form of a "critical election," or slow building and gradual.[51] They more widely accept the view, however, that there are some roughly demarcated periods of competition.

electoral realignment a shift in the composition of party coalitions that produces a new, relatively durable pattern of party competition.

A common perspective among political scientists is that the United States has experienced six periods of party competition. The first was from 1801 to 1828. The Federalist Party of the 1790s, led by John Adams and Alexander Hamilton, advocated a larger, more active national government. Its support was strongest in the Northeast, among businesspeople and those of higher income. The Democratic-Republican Party, represented by Thomas Jefferson and James Madison, pushed to protect states' rights and limit national power. It prospered in the South and Mid-Atlantic states. The Democratic-Republicans were the dominant party and effectively the only major party for much of this period (see Table 11-2).

TABLE 11-2. Number of Years of Party Control of Congress and the Presidency, 1801–2012

	PRESIDENT		HOUSE		SENATE	
	DEMOCRATIC-REPUBLICANS	FEDERALISTS	DEMOCRATIC-REPUBLICANS	FEDERALISTS	DEMOCRATIC-REPUBLICANS	FEDERALISTS
1. 1801–1828	28	0	26	2	26	2
	DEMOCRATS	NATIONAL REPUBLICANS/ WHIGS	DEMOCRATS	NATIONAL REPUBLICANS/ WHIGS	DEMOCRATS	NATIONAL REPUBLICANS/ WHIGS
2. 1829–1860	24	8	24	8	28	4
	DEMOCRATS	REPUBLICANS	DEMOCRATS	REPUBLICANS	DEMOCRATS	REPUBLICANS
3. 1861–1896	8	28	6	30	14	22
a. 1861–1876	0	16	2	14	0	16
b. 1877–1896	8	12	4	16	14	6
4. 1897–1932	8	28	10	26	6	30
5. 1933–1968	28	8	32	4	32	4
6. 1969–2012	16	28	30	14	27	17
a. 1969–1992	4	20	24	0	18	6
b. 1993–2012	12	8	6	14	9	11

Source: Marjorie Randon Hershey, *Party Politics in America*, 13th ed. (New York: Pearson Longman, 2009), p. 119, and authors' calculations.

The Democratic-Republican Party split in two, inaugurating a new period of party competition from 1829 to 1860. The Democratic Party, represented by Andrew Jackson, continued the tradition of representing rural, low-income, and southern voters, but it also added support among the urban working class. It was the dominant party during this time. The National Republican Party, which would become the Whig Party, argued for an expansion of the national government's economic powers through such measures as funding railroad building and reestablishing the Bank of the United States after Jackson vetoed its renewal. It fared better among wealthier voters. John Quincy Adams was a major figure in this party.

The Whig Party collapsed when it was unable to heal internal divisions over the slavery issue. In 1854, the Republican Party, represented by Abraham Lincoln, emerged and quickly moved to major party status as the Whigs disappeared. The years 1861 through 1896 marked a third period of party competition. Slavery and then the Civil War and Reconstruction became the central issues. Party success was strongly regional, with Democrats prevailing in the South and Republicans in the Northeast and Midwest. The national government's role in economic development, and particularly its promotion of industrial capitalism through tariffs and other measures, also strongly divided the parties, with Republicans advocating a stronger government role and Democrats arguing for the primacy of states' rights and local economic development. Republicans dominated through 1876. After 1876, southern states were fully incorporated back into the Union and party strength was evenly divided.

In the 1890s, the Democratic Party adopted some of the populist economic views of the People's Party, most notably its views about the impact of the monetary system on farmers and agricultural workers. In 1896, the People's Party endorsed Democratic presidential candidate William Jennings Bryan on a fusion ticket. The 1896 presidential election was widely viewed at the time as a referendum on industrial capitalism. Would the United States continue down that path, with increasingly large corporations of national scope? The Republican Party and its candidate William McKinley, supporter of the view that industrial capitalism should be promoted and encouraged by the national government, prevailed, starting a new period of party competition in 1897 that lasted until 1932. Democrats remained the dominant, virtually the only, party in the South, and did well in many rural western states. They did well in some northern cities as well, especially among immigrant Catholic voters. Prior to 1932, their only presidential victories in this period were in 1912, when Woodrow Wilson benefited from the Progressive Party candidacy of former Republican president Theodore Roosevelt, and Wilson's reelection in 1916.

Franklin Roosevelt's landslide win in 1932, accompanied by large Democratic majorities in Congress, initiated a period of Democratic dominance from 1933 through 1968. The party won most presidential elections during this time and controlled Congress for all but four years. From 1969 through the present, political competition was closely fought and neither major party could claim the mantle of the undisputed majority party. Divided control of government was common, occurring in 30 of the 42 years between 1969 and 2010. Because these two periods are so important for understanding today's party politics, we discuss them in detail in the sections below.

The Democratic New Deal coalition dominated electoral politics for over 40 years.

The coalition brought together by Democratic presidential candidate Franklin Roosevelt in 1932 proved to be remarkably resilient. For over 40 years, this coalition produced victories in the House, Senate, and presidency. Galvanized by Roosevelt's promise to respond aggressively to the economic stress of the Great Depression,

Democratic supporters agreed that economic recovery through jobs, social welfare, and government spending—a collection of programs known as the New Deal—was the first and most important priority of government. The coalition included southern whites; agricultural workers; unionized labor; lower to lower-middle income individuals; big-city public officials and their ethnic group supporters such as the Irish and Poles; Catholics and Jews; and industries pleased by Roosevelt's free trade approach. These constituencies strongly supported the array of new government services, programs, and entitlements created by Roosevelt and the Democrats in response to the Depression.

Over time, the Democratic coalition shifted. With the civil rights achievements of Democratic presidents in the 1960s, blacks moved firmly into the Democratic column, support among white southerners fell, and Hispanic voters increased their support for Democrats. The prominence of new issues based on civil rights, women's rights, environmentalism, lifestyle, sexuality, the Vietnam War, and the use of American military power split the party. The 1968 Democratic National Convention descended into televised chaos as pro-war and anti-war factions shouted each other down and clashed over the party's internal democracy.

After 1968, upper-middle-class professionals, particularly in government, the nonprofit sector, law, the media, and academia, along with upper-income voters and college graduates, became a larger share of the Democratic Party coalition. Meanwhile, support began to wane among the original members of the New Deal coalition.[52] About 70 percent of Catholics favored Democratic candidates in the 1950s; by the 1980s, a little over 50 percent did. Support among white working-class voters—non-college-educated workers engaged in manual labor—also dropped.[53] And as union membership declined after the 1950s, especially in the private sector, the proportion of Democratic voters who were from union households dropped from nearly 35 percent to less than 15 percent.[54]

The coalition crafted by Ronald Reagan brought the Republicans to national parity.

Ronald Reagan in 1980 built a coalition that brought the Republicans to parity with Democrats nationally. In the wake of bad economic times and struggling U.S. foreign policy, Reagan encouraged new identities for disgruntled groups. He asked middle-class and working-class voters to think of themselves not as the beneficiaries of government programs, but as the taxpayers bearing the heavy cost of supporting these programs. Blue-collar workers were asked to focus not only on their economic concerns but on their patriotic concerns for the United States and their values that were "looked down on" by media and liberal elites. These "Reagan Democrats" joined conservative white southerners, conservative Christians, businesses frustrated by high taxes and regulation, and the Republicans' traditionally strong support groups of middle- to high-income individuals and small-town and rural residents.[55]

This coalition of voters produced presidential victories for Republicans Reagan (1980, 1984), George H. W. Bush (1988), and George W. Bush (2000, 2004). In 1994, Republicans gained control of the House and Senate for the first time in 40 years. Representative Newt Gingrich of Georgia played a leading strategic role in this electoral success. For over a decade, he had been pushing the party to take a more combative and conservative stance in Congress, encouraging conservative candidates to run, and providing them with financial assistance and training. The Republican congressional majority lasted until 2006 when the party lost its control of both the House and Senate due to economic concerns, the Iraq War, a series of scandals, and President Bush's low approval ratings.[56]

TABLE 11-3. Strongest Support Groups for Barack Obama in 2008

GROUP (SIZE IN ELECTORATE)	PERCENT VOTING FOR OBAMA	PERCENT VOTING FOR McCAIN	PRO-OBAMA GAP (% POINTS)
African-American (13%)	95	4	91
Democrat (39%)	89	10	79
Liberal (22%)	89	10	79
Oppose offshore oil drilling in new areas (28%)	86	12	74
Nonwhite (26%)	79	18	61
Jewish (2%)	78	21	57
Disapprove of Iraq War (63%)	76	22	54
Government should do more (51%)	76	23	53
No religious affiliation (12%)	75	23	52
Gay, lesbian, or bisexual (4%)	70	27	43
First-time voter (11%)	69	30	39
Latino (9%)	67	31	36
Age 18–29 (18%)	66	32	34
No gun in household (58%)	65	33	32
Single (34%)	65	33	32
Live in urban area (30%)	63	35	28
Not high school graduate (4%)	63	35	28
Asian (2%)	62	35	27
Very worried about impact of financial crisis (48%)	62	36	26
No investments in stock market (34%)	61	37	24
Income below $50,000 (38%)	60	38	22
Attend church occasionally or never (58%)	60	39	21
Moderate (44%)	60	39	21
Someone in household in union (21%)	59	39	20
Northeast (21%)	59	40	19
Postgraduate (17%)	58	40	18
West (23%)	57	40	17

Source: Voter News Survey exit polls, 17,836 respondents. Data available at www.cnn.com/election/2008.

The Democrats regained unified control of government in 2008.

Whereas the years from 1933 through 1968 consistently featured a Democratic majority, party competition since 1969 has been more complex. Divided government has been common. Rather than a party realignment, some analysts argued the first half of this period featured **dealignment**, with voters splitting tickets, feeling less attachment to the parties, increasingly identifying themselves as independents, and turning out less to vote. These behaviors peaked in the mid-1980s. After that, ticket splitting dropped: voters who identified as Democrats were increasingly likely to support the Democratic candidate for the House, Senate, or presidency, and similarly for Republicans. Generally, the Democrats were stronger in the Northeast and Pacific Coast, Republicans prevailed in the mountain and western states and the South, and the Midwest was a battleground between the two parties.[57]

dealignment a substantial reduction in the proportion of the voting population consistently voting for and identifying with one party.

Barack Obama's victory in 2008, coupled with Democratic gains in the House and Senate, had many Democrats hopeful that the chapter may have closed on the long period of balanced party competition from 1968 through 2008, signaling a realignment and the beginning of a seventh period of party competition. They pointed to the size of Obama's victory, the succession of two congressional elections with significant gains for Democrats, and 90 percent of the public in 2008 saying the country was headed in the wrong direction as possible signs pointing to an enduring sea change in American politics that would establish Democrats as a long-lasting majority party. Obama's 53–46 percent victory improved on John Kerry's 2004 performance in nearly every state and among most groups. In addition, Democrats suggested that the growing size of the black, Latino, and Asian American populations bodes well for continued Democratic victories, as these voters lean heavily Democratic, as does the party's strong support among voters age 18 to 29 in 2008 (Table 11-3). Add in voters' decreased tendency to split their tickets between the parties over the past 20 years, Democrats said, and the environment appeared even more conducive to continued strong Democratic performances.

Republicans were distressed by the extent of their defeat in 2008, not only for the presidency but in Congress as well. By 2010, however, Republicans were more optimistic, expecting to win significant numbers of seats from the Democrats, possibly enough to regain control of one or both houses of Congress. And that is precisely what happened. At the state level, Republican gains were sweeping, with the party gaining several governorships and flipping about 20 state legislative chambers to Republican control. Nationally, Republicans gained a majority in the House while improving their vote share in 393 of 435 districts. The party also added a number of seats in the Senate. Key support groups for the victory (see Table 11-4) were similar to those that reelected President George W. Bush in 2004. How do the parties

◄ DIVIDED GOVERNMENT

The 2010 midterm elections vaulted Republicans to a majority in the House of Representatives, with John Boehner becoming Speaker of the House. Since 1969, control of the presidency and Congress has more often been split between the two parties, rather than resting entirely in one party's hands as it did after the 2008 election. What might be the advantages and disadvantages of divided control of government?

TABLE 11-4. Strongest Support Groups for House Republican Candidates in 2010

GROUP (SIZE IN ELECTORATE)	PERCENT VOTING FOR REPUBLICAN	PERCENT VOTING FOR DEMOCRAT	PRO-REP GAP (% POINTS)
Republican (36%)	95	4	91
Support Tea Party movement (40%)	87	11	76
Repeal new health care law (48%)	87	11	76
Economic stimulus program hurt economy (33%)	86	12	74
Conservative (34%)	84	14	70
White evangelical/born-again (25%)	78	20	58
Government doing too much (56%)	77	20	57
Approve of Afghanistan war (40%)	74	25	49
Nation's economy in poor condition (37%)	71	26	45
Very worried about economy (50%)	70	28	42
No legal recognition for same-sex couples (54%)	69	28	41
Angry/dissatisfied with government (74%)	65	32	33
Family's financial situation worse (41%)	63	34	29
White men (37%)	63	35	28
White (78%)	60	37	23
South (31%)	60	38	22
Live in rural area or small town (20%)	60	38	22
Weekly church attendance or more (48%)	60	39	21
Protestant (54%)	60	39	21
Age 65 or older (23%)	59	38	21
Economic stimulus program made no difference (32%)	58	39	19
Independent (28%)	56	38	18
Income $100,000 or more (26%)	58	40	18
Fathers with children under 18 (16%)	58	40	18
White women (41%)	58	40	18
College degree, not postgraduate (28%)	56	41	15
Male (47%)	56	42	14
Income $75–100,000 (15%)	56	42	14
No union members in household (83%)	55	43	12

Source: Edison Research exit polls, 17,504 respondents. Data available at www.cnn.com/election/2010.

interpret these results? Republicans differ whether the Tea Party movement led to their success or prevented the party from winning even more seats. Democrats debate whether their policy philosophy is to blame or whether voters were simply expressing dissatisfaction with the pace of economic recovery. These debates will guide the parties' policy and electoral strategies in the run-up to the 2012 elections.[58]

Democrats and Republicans today have significant differences over public policy.

Despite the common criticism that they are just two peas in a pod, the two major parties do differ significantly on many policy issues. Indeed, if this were not so, it would be difficult to understand why the parties have different voting coalitions, different alliances of interest groups that support them, and different campaign contributors. Presumably, voters support candidates in part for their issue stances. Even if voters support party candidates for reasons of group affiliation—a sense that the party is friendly to "people like me"—that, too, is rooted in some sense that the party will behave in a way that voters will tend to approve.

There is strategic sense to the idea that parties will somewhat skew toward the center of public opinion, if that is where most of the voters are, rather than to the most extreme ends of the ideological spectrum. But parties also have an incentive to maintain the ideological distance between them. This distance keeps them attractive to supportive interest groups and voters, so that the party can count on, though not assume, their support in upcoming elections. This allows the party to focus its efforts on turnout and on persuading undecided voters. Like a business, a party wants to have "repeat customers" that it can count on—it will not achieve this goal by making its "product" a copycat of the other party.

Party differences vary at the national and state levels. Within a particular state, parties may adjust their position to be competitive. Republicans in the Northeast, for example, are generally more liberal than Republicans in the Southwest. Democrats in the South are generally more conservative than Democrats in the Pacific Northwest. Though the parties in a state may offer genuinely different positions, they may not mirror the range of ideological differences present at the national level. Democrats at the national level, for example, are more likely to support stronger gun control regulations, but in many states with widespread gun ownership, that would not be a viable position for Democrats to take.

> "Like a business, a party wants to have 'repeat customers' that it can count on—it will not achieve this by making its 'product' a copycat of the other party."

Nationally, Democrats tend to argue for a more expansive use of government in addressing social and economic problems. They are more inclined to define these problems as ones requiring a government solution. Republicans will lean toward a market-based, private sector solution to the problem and ask whether government policies are obstacles to individuals and businesses seeking to undertake desired behavior. When Democrats proposed a $787 billion economic stimulus plan in 2009, every Republican in the House and nearly all in the Senate rebelled at the size and scope of this government intervention. On social issues such as abortion, however, Democrats are less inclined to involve government in individual decision-making, whereas Republicans are more inclined to support government restrictions on abortion access. Democratic rhetoric will more often invoke equality and fairness, whereas Republican language will refer to individual opportunity and freedom. Democrats, for example, tend to consider tax arrangements that take a larger percentage of one's income as income rises to be a matter of fairness, while Republicans argue that increased tax rates amount to a penalty for individual hard work and success.

Although cultural and social issues like abortion or same-sex marriage receive significant attention in public discussion of parties and candidates, the contrasting agendas of the parties focus much more on economic, financial, and regulatory matters, including economic growth, prices, employment, taxes, regulating business, health care, retirement, and other issues such as education that can be defined as having economic significance.[59] In foreign policy, Republicans have generally supported a more aggressive use of military force to obtain desired goals; Democrats have expressed more reluctance in this area.[60]

In addition to different views on issues, party supporters also prioritize some issues differently. In early 2010, Republican and Democratic survey respondents agreed that terrorism, the economy, and more jobs were the top national priorities, with lesser but strong agreement that education, Medicare, Social Security, and cutting

continued on page 425 ▶

HOW DO WE KNOW?

Is America Polarized?

The Question

In the eyes of many Americans, politics in the United States has become nasty, bitter, and rife with conflict. In 2008, presidential candidates Barack Obama and John McCain both criticized the nature of political debate in the United States, with Obama deriding it as "do-anything, say-anything, divisive politics" and McCain labeling it as "mindless, paralyzing rancor."[61] "Two Americas," the "50/50 nation," "red and blue America," and "culture war" are labels said to define current American politics.[62] Is America polarized? How do we know?

Why It Matters

Both for citizens and for politicians looking to influence the policy process, it matters whether Americans are in two different worlds politically or have political differences that are modest in degree. If the country is polarized, then political success will depend on highly charged mobilization based on strong rhetoric. If the country is not, then success will depend more on mobilizing the support of those whose views are relatively moderate. Party differences might also influence one's appraisal of the health of American democracy. Some citizens might consider different viewpoints to be the lifeblood of a healthy democracy. Others might see high degrees of partisan conflict as an obstacle to solving problems and a blot on democracy.

Investigating the Answer

Television election result maps in 2000 and 2004 showing the country divided sharply into regions of Republican support (colored red) and Democratic support (colored blue) helped popularize the idea that Americans live in polarized worlds politically, with a vast gulf in their cultural values and political preferences.

Closer examination, however, showed that the maps were misleading. Some red states were barely red, and some blue states barely blue. Maps colored at the county level and shaded for their degree of support for Republican George Bush and Democrat John Kerry in

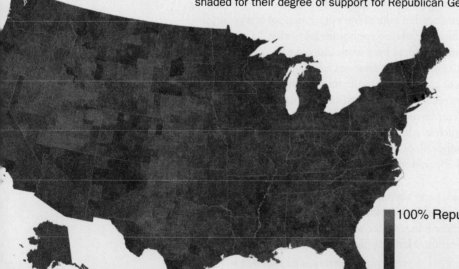

◄ **AMERICA THE PURPLE, 2004**

The red state/blue state dichotomy masks the varying level of party support throughout the country and within states. This map of county-level support for George W. Bush and John Kerry shows there are bright red (Bush) and bright blue (Kerry) counties, but most counties are lesser shades of red or blue or are purple.

100% Republican

100% Democrat

2004 showed that much of the country was a shade of purple rather than distinctly red or blue. Moreover, examination of maps of state legislative party control showed that the red-blue distinction did not carry over very well to that level, and the 2008 presidential election map showed nine states flipping color from red to blue.[63]

Despite the popularity of the red state/blue state language in media reports, it does not appear to get us very far in understanding whether America is polarized. Perhaps the place to look for polarization is not in the state-level pattern of party victories, but in public opinion. Does public opinion show more polarized views among the public?

One prominent study examines public opinion on a range of "hot button" issues like abortion and gay rights. The authors find that, when given the option, most Americans place themselves toward the middle of the scale rather than taking a position on the far left or far right. Even where opinion has become more polarized over time, the difference is not that great. For example, the National Election Study asks survey respondents to place themselves on a series of 7-point issue scales. The average difference between Democrats and Republicans has increased since the early 1970s, when it was half a point, but only to about 1 point. By that measure, public opinion among Democrats and Republicans is distinctive, but they are separated on average by only 1 point on the 7-point scale.[64]

Another study confirms that differences between Democrats and Republicans have grown—and uniquely so. The authors looked at public opinion on 35 issue areas since 1972. They found that by almost every measure—age, education, race, religious affiliation, region, and gender—there had been convergence rather than divergence of opinion between groups. The groups (old versus young, for example) did differ on their opinions, but the degree of difference had not grown. Partisanship was the exception. Only on this measure had opinion grown further apart.[65] This research suggests that public opinion may not be much more polarized now than previously, but that the political parties more precisely reflect the differences that do exist, making the dichotomy seem more pronounced. Political scientists refer to this as ideological sorting, meaning that the correlation between one's ideology and one's party identification is stronger today than previously: liberals are increasingly likely to identify with Democrats and conservatives with Republicans (see Figure 11-3).[66]

Partisans at the elite level have also moved further apart. Studies of legislative roll call voting show Democrats and Republicans in Congress are more ideologically distinct now

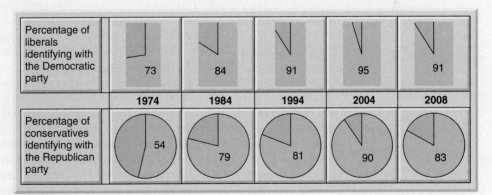

FIGURE 11-3. Partisan and Ideological Sorting, 1974–2008. Over time, liberals became more likely to identify with the Democratic Party and conservatives with the Republican Party. Liberal identification with the Democrats rose from 73 percent in 1974 to 95 percent in 2004, a 22 percentage point rise. Conservative identification with the Republicans rose from 54 to 90 percent over the same period, a 36 point increase. Ideological sorting dropped slightly in 2008.

than previously (see Chapter 15), with polarization of party voting patterns in the House and Senate at the highest levels since the end of Reconstruction.[67] Unlike the public, relatively few members of Congress fall in the ideological center, but—consistent with the trend in the public—liberals in Congress are now much more consistently in the Democratic Party and conservatives in the Republican Party—they are better sorted than previously. For example, in the U.S. Senate, all Republicans are now more conservative than all Democrats. This clear divide has not always been present. The opinion of party activists, as measured by a survey of delegates to the two parties' national conventions in 2008, is also strongly divergent, more so than among the public. Democratic delegates' support was 46 percentage points higher than was Republicans' for allowing illegal immigrants to stay in the United States and apply for citizenship, and 53 points higher for permitting abortion in all cases. Support among Republican delegates was 78 points higher than support among Democrats on military action in Iraq being the right thing to do. The partisan differences in the public were smaller, at 24, 21, and 57 points, respectively.[68]

So both elites and the public are better sorted ideologically into parties. That is the correlation. But what is the causality—what led to what? Did liberal and conservative voters begin the process by flocking more consistently to the Democratic and Republican parties, respectively, forcing the parties' candidates to respond by taking more extreme views? Or did candidates start the process by taking more extreme views, leading voters to respond by shifting and strengthening their party allegiance?

Political scientists have wrestled with these questions, exploring a number of explanations. Perhaps redistricting created safe partisan districts that encouraged legislators to behave in a more ideological fashion. Or perhaps congressional leaders began emphasizing partisan unity and ideology more after they adopted new leadership tools during congressional reforms in the 1970s and 1980s. Perhaps declining voter turnout signaled to parties that voters wanted stronger choices, and parties noticed that the public responded to fund-raising appeals when the ideological lines were drawn sharply. Or perhaps the story is really about the South and its emergence out of a one-party political competition in which nearly every voter, whether liberal or conservative, supported Democratic candidates. Scholars have tested many more possible explanations.[69]

Although the data are mixed, and each of the factors just mentioned likely played a role, overall it appears that elites led and the public followed. As political activists within the party networks—representatives of business groups, advocacy groups, nonprofits, unions—became better organized and more involved, candidates increasingly took the positions that would garner their support. With this relationship between activists and candidates occurring in both parties, the public was faced with candidates taking stronger ideological stances, and individual voters sorted themselves into the party closer to them ideologically. With a more ideologically unified base of support in the public, candidates then had further reason to distance themselves from the candidates in the other party and parties had further reason to recruit more conservative and liberal candidates, rather than moderates.[70] Voters responded by voting even more consistently for one party. Why? Imagine a voter who is slightly to the right of center. This voter might be open to voting for a mildly conservative Republican at some times and a mildly liberal Democrat at others. He might vote for the mildly liberal candidate over a more extreme conservative candidate. However, if the choices for this voter are now regularly between a strong liberal Democrat and a strong conservative Republican, he will likely vote Republican consistently.[71]

Thinking Critically

■ Is the trend toward greater ideological sorting among voters something to be applauded or feared?

■ If polarization is tied to the activities of party activists and supporters, is there any way to reverse it?

■ Would electoral reforms that increased the possibility for third-party success be likely to exacerbate or reduce polarization?

The Bottom Line

Public opinion overall is not dramatically more polarized now than previously. What has changed is that for both voters and politicians, opinion differences are now more sharply lined up by political party—fewer conservatives are aligned with the Democratic Party and fewer liberals identify with the Republican Party. Ideological sorting has led to a bigger philosophical gap between the typical Democratic and Republican politician and, to a lesser degree, a bigger gap between the typical Democrat and Republican in the public. Because of these trends, the cultural, economic, and other differences among Americans have become a more significant part of political debate. When, for example, voters with conservative (or liberal) cultural views were more spread across the two parties, it was less likely that cultural issues would be part of political debate. Today it is more likely. Polarized media rhetoric on high-profile economic and cultural issues attracts an audience. The election of Barack Obama did not reverse these trends. Public evaluations of Obama's job performance are just as polarized along party lines as were those for George W. Bush and Bill Clinton. Congress remains staunchly divided. Politics is a battle over big stakes and big outcomes. Issues matter. Because people do see the world differently, ideological sorting is likely to remain. Some observers say these developments in partisanship artificially create more conflict in government and leave moderate voters with unappealing choices. But others counter that ideological sorting has led to party competition that gives voters real choices, gives them a reason to vote, and encourages fellow partisans in government to work together.[72]

the budget deficit were also key concerns. Neither ranked tax cuts, international trade, global warming, or reducing the influence of lobbyists, as high on the priority list. Republicans named a stronger military as a top priority, while Democrats ranked this issue low. Democrats ranked poverty and national health insurance high on their list; Republicans did not. Independents agreed on the leading importance of the economy, jobs, and terrorism; on other issues they tended to fall in between Democrats and Republicans regarding the percentage who saw the issue as a top national priority.[73] When asked what issues posed an "extremely serious" threat to future U.S. well-being, terrorism, federal government debt, and the size and power of the federal government led the Republican list in mid-2010, whereas health care costs, terrorism, and the environment led the Democratic list. Federal debt led the independents' list.[74]

Voters identify some issues so much with one party that scholars say the party "owns" these issues. For example, the public has long identified Social Security and government assistance programs as Democratic strong suits—the Democrats have owned these issues. The public usually gives the Republicans a similar advantage on foreign policy and keeping taxes low. Prior to the 2010 midterm election, Republicans held more than a 10-point advantage on handling terrorism and the size and power of the federal government. Democrats had leads of about 30 points on the environment and discrimination against minority groups.[75] Not every issue is owned by a party—some bounce back and forth between the parties.

These "owned" issues will shape party competition. The party that owns an issue will emphasize the issue to maximize its advantage on it. Republicans in 2010 hammered away on the issues of the power of the federal government and the size of federal debt, issues that appealed to Republicans, independents, and some Democrats, and on which the Republicans held an advantage. Democrats sought to focus public attention on the benefits of health care and financial reform and the need for legislation to deal with climate change, and portraying Republicans as too cozy with big corporations, all issues owned by Democrats. Candidates may also try to deflect the other party's advantage on an issue, as when George W. Bush emphasized education reform in 2000 and Barack Obama pledged to cut taxes in 2008.[76]

In recent years, observers have suggested that party differences have become extreme. They depict this competition as a clash of values and culture between red America and blue America, or red states (Republican) and blue states (Democratic). Some observers, like television commentator Bill O'Reilly, refer to it as a culture war. To other observers, though, the nature of American public opinion and the breadth of party coalitions mean there is at best a culture skirmish rather than a culture war (see *How Do We Know? Is America Polarized?*).

CHAPTER SUMMARY

In this chapter you have learned to:

11-1 Analyze the functions of political parties in American politics. Political parties play a variety of roles. The Constitution provided for an electoral system but did not say how a sufficient number of candidates would emerge or how citizens would become engaged in the electoral process. Parties fill these roles. These functions of candidate recruitment and citizen mobilization, intended largely to advance the interests of the parties and their candidates, also enhance the legitimacy of American politics and government by bringing into practice the promise of electoral competition that was implicit in the Constitution. Political parties also contribute to American governance by giving public officials in different institutions and at different levels of government incentives to cooperate with each other to make public policy.

11-2 Determine why American electoral competition is dominated by two political parties rather than multiple parties. Two-party electoral competition has dominated American politics since the very beginning. The structure of American government, including single-member districts, plurality elections, and winner-take-all electoral votes in presidential elections, pushes electoral competition toward a two-party model. In addition, a number of laws as well as the behavior of voters, the media, and candidates, reinforce the tendency for two parties to be the serious competitors. Third parties are only rarely successful electorally, but they can make a mark in other ways, such as introducing issues to the campaign that the major party candidates have ignored.

11-3 Trace the evolution of American party organizations and their expanding role in campaigns. Party organization has gone through several phases. In early American history, party organizations were informal and largely implemented the wishes of important political leaders, especially regarding candidate nomination. Party machines emerged in the late nineteenth century. Machines thrived by developing a very personal form of politics but ran afoul of reformers who saw them as bastions of corruption. Progressive reformers passed a series of laws that weakened and regulated political parties in the early twentieth century. In recent decades, party organizations have become more active, especially by providing campaign services to party candidates.

11-4 Explain how parties achieve electoral success by building and maintaining coalitions of supporters. The broad and diverse nature of coalitions necessary to produce a majority and win elections creates a difficult job of political management for party leaders. They play the balancing act of maintaining the coalition and focusing on the key public policy concerns of coalition members, while also adapting to new circumstances and trying to keep the coalition growing. As they accommodate new issues and new groups, they risk unraveling the coalition by driving current supporters away. Neither party can produce victories today by simply relying on the coalitions of the past. American parties have evolved through six periods of party competition, with different issues and different major parties dominating.

---

mypoliscilab   EXERCISES

Apply what you learned in this chapter by starting with these resources on MyPoliSciLab.

Read on mypoliscilab.com

    eText: Chapter 11

Study and Review on mypoliscilab.com

    Pre-Test
    Post-Test
    Chapter Exam
    Flashcards

Watch on mypoliscilab.com

    Video: Republicans and Democrats Divide on Tax Cut
    Video: Senator Specter Switches Parties

Video: Tea Party Victories Concern for GOP
Video: Green Party Candidates Stay on Ballot
Video: New Ballots Bring New Complications in New York

Explore on mypoliscilab.com

Simulation: You Are a Campaign Manager: Help McCain Win Swing States and Swing Voters
Comparative: Comparing Political Parties
Timeline: Third Parties in American History
Timeline: The Evolution of Political Parties in the United States
Visual Literacy: State Control and National Platforms

KEY TERMS

Australian ballot, p. 401
dealignment, p. 418
divided government, p. 392
electoral realignment, p. 415
fusion, p. 401
issue evolution, p. 414

national party convention, p. 409
party machine, p. 405
party platform, p. 409
patronage, p. 406
plurality elections, p. 399
political parties, p. 389

Progressive reforms, p. 406
proportional representation, p. 399
responsible party model, p. 413
single-member districts, p. 399
two-party system, p. 396
unified government, p. 392

CHAPTER TEST

1. How do political parties bridge the gaps between institutions in American government?
2. In what ways do political parties bring citizens into the political process?
3. How does use of the party label increase voter leverage over the political system?
4. What is the general effect of single-member districts and plurality elections on the number of competitive parties?
5. How does the behavior of voters create challenges for third-party electoral success?
6. What innovations did Progressive reformers add to American politics and how did they affect political parties?
7. What are the major activities of party organizations today?
8. What are the major strategic dilemmas facing party leaders as they attempt to hold their coalition together?
9. In what ways do the policy orientations of Democrats and Republicans differ?
10. Why does the nature of coalition building sometimes frustrate those party supporters with strong ideological points of view?

427

SUGGESTED READINGS

Marty Cohen, David Karol, Hans Noel, and John Zaller. 2008. *The Party Decides: Presidential Nominations Before and After Reform*. Chicago: University of Chicago Press. Argues that political parties, conceived as a network of interest groups, activists, and elected officials and members of official party organizations, remain the dominant force in selecting presidential nominees.

Leon D. Epstein. 1986. *Political Parties in the American Mold*. Madison: University of Wisconsin Press. Thorough explanation of the functions and history of American political parties.

Paul Frymer. 1999. *Uneasy Alliances: Race and Party Competition in America*. Princeton, NJ: Princeton University Press. Argues that the American party system was built on racial considerations and inevitably marginalizes the interests of black Americans.

Andrew Gelman. 2008. *Red State, Blue State, Rich State, Poor State: Why Americans Vote the Way They Do*. Princeton, NJ: Princeton University Press. Examines party polarization, the role of culture and economics, and puzzles such as the Democrats' success in wealthy states while the Republicans do better among wealthy voters.

John Gerring. 1998. *Party Ideologies in America, 1828–1996*. New York: Cambridge University Press. Thorough account documenting the ideological distinctions between the major political parties, noting areas of continuity and change in the parties' philosophies.

Lawrence Goodwyn. 1978. *The Populist Moment: A Short History of the Agrarian Revolt in America*. New York: Oxford University Press. Wonderfully readable account of the rise of one of America's most important social movements and its eventual transformation into the People's Party, a third party with some short-lived success in the mid-1890s.

David Karol. 2009. *Party Position Change in American Politics: Coalition Management*. New York: Cambridge University Press. Challenges the idea that parties and politicians maintain persistent issue positions, and contends that parties frequently change issue stances as a means to maintain or expand their coalitions, redefining what liberal and conservative mean in the process.

Seth E. Masket. 2009. *No Middle Ground: How Informal Party Organizations Control Nominations and Polarize Legislatures*. Ann Arbor: University of Michigan Press. Analyzes the interaction of policy activists and politicians and argues that activists more than office holders push for stronger, ideologically cohesive parties.

David C. W. Parker. 2008. *The Power of Money in Congressional Campaigns, 1880–2006*. Norman: University of Oklahoma Press. Explores how the need for money and other resources to run campaigns has affected the relative power of parties, organized interests, and candidates and the nature of the interaction between these three groups.

Mark A. Smith. 2007. *The Right Talk: How Conservatives Transformed the Great Society into the Economic Society*. Princeton, NJ: Princeton University Press. How conservatives altered the discussion of key issues into economic terms and sparked the revival of the Republican Party.

James Sundquist. 1986. *Dynamics of the Party System: Alignment and Realignment of Political Parties in the United States*. Washington, DC: Brookings Institution Press.

Very readable account of the passage of the United States through various periods of party competition, including what might accelerate or stop these passages.

Jessica Trounstine. 2008. *Political Monopolies in American Cities: The Rise and Fall of Bosses and Reformers*. Chicago: University of Chicago Press. Uses case studies of Chicago and San Jose, and statistical analysis of a large number of cities, to argue that party machines and reform movements both seek to create uncompetitive political monopolies.

SUGGESTED WEBSITES

FairVote: www.fairvote.org

Advocacy group for proportional representation and alternative voting systems. Site provides explanation of various voting reforms.

Real Clear Politics: www.rcp.com

Analysis of politics and news featuring a good array of conservative and liberal writers.

Politics 1: www.politics1.com/parties.htm

Comprehensive list of links to political party websites, including capsule descriptions of third parties.

American Presidency Project: Political Party Platforms: www.presidency.ucsb.edu/platforms.php

Full text of platforms of all parties receiving electoral votes since 1840.

Campaign Finance Institute: www.cfinst.org

Extensive databases and helpful analysis of campaign finance, especially party revenues and spending.

ANES Guide to Public Opinion and Electoral Behavior: www.electionstudies.org/nesguide/nesguide.htm

Collection of tables presenting over 40 years of data on partisanship, evaluation of candidates, participation, and public opinion from the premier academic election survey.

Dave Leip's Atlas of U.S. Presidential Elections: www.uselectionatlas.org

Excellent collection of tables, data, graphs, and maps related to presidential election outcomes throughout American history. Also covers gubernatorial, U.S. Senate, and U.S. House elections.

Human Nature

First rule of human nature: people will always disagree. Name anything—a law, an event, even a plate of food—and people will have different opinions on the matter. This maxim, in essence, is the greatest challenge of a democratic government: how do you come to a consensus allowing the free-flow of ideas without letting the losing side feel cheated or worse, without people coming to blows—especially when factions are formed on opposing sides? And how do special interest groups—some with more money, power, or numbers—compete on a level playing field? Long before the power of electronic media was created, the founding fathers gave serious thought to the nature of political conflict and the fact that some groups have more resources and power than others. They specifically put in place rules that would make sure all voices—not just those of the powerful—were heard. Consider the following two examples.

In 1868, no women anywhere in the United States were allowed to vote. By 1920, however, women in every state had the same voting rights as men. How did this change take place—how did a completely disenfranchised group reach its goal? It came primarily through the efforts of an interest group—the women's suffrage movement. In 1869, after the Civil War, two organizations promoting women's suffrage were founded: the National Woman Suffrage Association (NWSA) and the American Woman Suffrage Association (AWSA). After two decades of pursuing their agendas separately, the groups merged in 1890 to form the National American Woman Suffrage Association (NAWSA) with Susan B. Anthony as its leader.

The suffrage movement grew as it accumulated legal victories at the state level. NAWSA was soon joined by other women's groups, including the General Federation of Women's Clubs and assorted professional women's organizations. This enhanced clout helped secure further victories, which won yet more converts to the cause, creating a positive momentum. Eventually, both the size of the movement and its repeated successes at the state level created irresistible momentum for a nationwide policy change. Congress proposed an amendment to the Constitution in 1919 that granted women the right to vote, and the amendment was ratified by the required 36 states in 1920.[1]

Admirers of American democracy look to this story with pride. In what other country, they ask, could a disenfranchised group force such dramatic changes in the law in such a short period of time? The success of the women's suffrage movement, they argue, shows the openness of the American political system to influence by groups of all political stripes—regardless of their resources

◄ **UNITED WE STAND**
Many women's groups came together to ensure passage of the Nineteenth Amendment to the U.S. Constitution. Their collective action and success in the states culminated in 1920 when they were formally granted the right to vote.

or their previous level of political involvement.

Now consider the immigration issue. The United States of America was established as a land that welcomed and benefited from immigration. But throughout its history laws were set up to control the flow of immigration. When cheap labor was needed at the turn of the twentieth century, the tap was opened, but then, mostly from Europe. By the 1920s and 1930s, the flow was cut off to a trickle.

In the latter half of the twentieth century, the flow of immigrants entering the country illegally began to expand exponentially, most coming across the southwest borders from Latin America. This change has created a highly emotional issue. On one side, the pro-immigration forces argue, correctly, that the country wants and benefits from the labor. And they point out that the vast majority of these immigrants are hard working and law abiding.

On the other side, critics say that these illegal immigrants strain already overburdened schools and hospitals, especially in border states like Arizona and California, and that the growing drug wars and human trafficking have increased problems with crime. Some critics question having immigration laws in the first place if no one is following them.

Neither side of this argument has been able to win the debate. The one thing that both sides agree on is that the immigration system in the first decade of the twenty-first century is not working, and no one seems able to fix it.

These two examples paint very different pictures of the political system in the United States. On the one hand, the story of the women's suffrage movement suggests that American politics is open to influence by any group with a reasonable agenda, even if it lacks the

▲ **IMMIGRATION STANDOFF**
Protestors in Arizona square off about the state's controversial immigration law.

power of the vote to hold as an implicit threat over the heads of policy makers. On the other hand, the immigration issue suggests that major policy issues are often difficult for our system to deal with. Furthermore, negative media coverage of lobbyists and the anti-lobbying rhetoric of many political leaders, including President Barack Obama, have spurred the popular perception that interest groups are too powerful and have a largely negative influence on public policy. In fact, President Obama, in an attempt to limit the control of lobbyists in Washington, has required employees to sign a pledge not to "participate in any particular matter on which I lobbied within the two years before the date of my appointment."[2]

Obama has openly criticized lobbyists, both in his campaign and as president. As the scope and power of interest groups and lobbyists have continued to grow over the years, so has Obama's rhetoric. Over the course of his campaign

and first year in office, Obama could be heard saying something similar to his remarks in his first State of the Union Address: "We face a deficit of trust—deep and corrosive doubts about how Washington works that have been growing for years. To close that credibility gap, we have to take action on both ends of Pennsylvania Avenue—to end the outsized influence of lobbyists; to do our work openly; to give our people the government they deserve."[3] This rhetoric has fueled much of the debate over how powerful and trustworthy lobbyists and interest groups are.

These competing narratives lead to a few important questions about the place of organized interests, or **interest groups**, in American politics. Are interest groups active and powerful, or passive and ineffective? Are they a positive or negative influence on American democracy? Do they encourage a healthy, broad-based consideration of a variety of interests, or do they promote the pursuit of narrow self-interest?

Guided by these questions, in this chapter we examine the role of interest groups in America.

CHAPTER LEARNING OBJECTIVES

After reading this chapter you will be able to:

12-1 Distinguish between pluralist theory's and James Madison's interpretation of the role of interest groups within American politics.

12-2 Describe how critics of pluralist theory view the role of interest groups today.

12-3 Explain how interest groups form and attract members.

12-4 Analyze the strategies and tactics interest groups use to impact elections and public policy.

12-5 Assess how much influence interest groups have over policy outcomes.

The Problem of Factions and the Pluralist Answer

12-1 Distinguish between pluralist theory's and James Madison's interpretation of the role of interest groups within American politics.

Almost every discussion of group politics in the United States begins with one of the most famous pieces of political rhetoric ever written by an American—*Federalist 10* by James Madison, one of the nation's founders. As we discussed in Chapter 3, this brief essay was part of a broader collection of writings known as *The Federalist Papers*. In *Federalist 10*, Madison noted the capacity of the proposed federal republic "to break and control the violence of faction." Madison's use of the word "faction" varied somewhat from modern usage. In more familiar language, Madison was referring to a group of individuals who share a belief that, if acted upon, would jeopardize the rights of individuals outside the group, or the interests of the community as a whole. Madison's concern was that factions would find ways to exercise their will through the mechanisms of government. If this happened, then individual rights might suffer, along with the long-term, collective interests of the new republic. Madison argued, therefore, that government—and by extension, Americans as individuals and the country as a whole—must be protected from the influence of factions.

Although Madison worried about the potential influence of factional interests on individual rights and the collective well-being of the country, he also believed that the American system was well designed to mute the influence of such interests.

Political scientists in the 1950s began to reconsider the place of group interests in politics. Like James Madison, scholars generally believed that the tendency toward factions in political life was inevitable. And they generally referred to factions as "groups," "interests," "organized interests," or "**interest groups**." These scholars were not preoccupied with keeping interest groups away from the corridors of power. Instead, they viewed the competition for influence in American politics as generally healthy, and a legitimate aspect of democratic governance.

This thinking on the place of group interests in America came to be known as **pluralism**, referring to the multiple groups and interests making demands on government (even if the demands were to be ignored). Pluralists assumed that groups and group struggle were the essence of politics. Pluralist thinkers believed that politics can be considered primarily as an organized effort to resolve conflicts among competing group interests.[4] Furthermore, they viewed political power and resources as being dispersed widely throughout society, with some groups more influential in certain issue areas, and a completely different set of groups influencing other issue areas. Because of this dispersion of power and resources, no one group or set of groups can achieve long-term supremacy across a significant number of issue areas.

interest groups organizations that seek to influence government decisions.

pluralism the theory that all groups are well represented and no single interest controls government decisions.

Pluralists also believed that the political system provides multiple access points for influence, consistent with the multiple interests it must accommodate. Groups are free to petition government at the local, state, and national levels, and through the offices of the executive, the legislature, and the judiciary. A group denied its policy preferences in one venue or at one level of government may take its argument to a different venue or to another jurisdiction—local, state, or federal. Because of this potential, almost every group can expect an opportunity to be heard and taken seriously somewhere in the political system.[5]

Finally, pluralists argued that, even if not organized into a formal group, individuals with a common interest can still have their needs addressed through politics. Policy makers recognize that such potential groups can become actual groups if their needs are not met, which may upset existing political arrangements. Thus, elected officials have an incentive to take into account the needs of unorganized interests, precisely to keep them from becoming organized.

Critics of Pluralism

12-2 Describe how critics of pluralist theory view the role of interest groups today.

Since at least the 1950s, pluralism has been a highly influential framework for thinking about American politics and government. Along with influence, however, comes scrutiny. Thus, as important as pluralism has been in structuring political scientists' thinking about American government, it has also attracted a significant number of criticisms: that the American political system is inherently resistant to change; that political resources are not distributed equally; that many important issues never make it onto the agenda; and that groups do not automatically form.

The American political system is resistant to change.

A fundamental critique of pluralism is that the American political system is resistant to change. The checks and balances designed by the Framers, coupled with the multiple decision points in the system, make it much more difficult to change the status quo than to defend the status quo. As we will see in detail in Chapter 13, on Congress, an individual or group wishing to defeat a new policy proposal has many opportunities to do so; for example, it can stop the proposal from:

being introduced as a bill in the first place.

being heard in committee.

being approved in committee.

being reported out of committee.

being heard on the House floor.

being heard on the Senate floor.

being approved by the House.

being approved by the Senate.

Even if the bill were to make it over all of these hurdles, an individual or group could still stop:

the reconciliation of any differences between the Senate and House versions of the bill.

the House from voting on the reconciled version.

- the Senate from voting on the reconciled version.
- the House from approving the reconciled version.
- the Senate from approving the reconciled version.
- the president from signing the reconciled version.

But even this list does not exhaust the possibilities for defeating a policy proposal. Programs and initiatives that make it through the legislative process can also be challenged in the court system, denied necessary funding in the appropriations process, or watered down or ignored by bureaucrats or state and local officials.

The bias against change in the American system should now be clear. Someone wishing to preserve the status quo need only succeed at one point to kill a policy initiative, but someone wishing to change the status quo must succeed at every point.

Because of this power to obstruct, critics of pluralism argue that the apparent openness of the American political system may not count for much. If a group succeeds in getting its policy preferences adopted, other groups with different preferences will have difficulty coming along later and altering the status quo. Thus, although the complex machinery of American government protects citizens against tyranny and factions, it also makes it hard for organized interests to bring about change.

Political resources are distributed unequally.

Pluralism is often viewed as a way of explaining how democracy works despite Americans' low levels of political knowledge and competence. The pluralists said that interest groups enable citizens who may not have high levels of political skill and interest to involve themselves in the issues that are most important to them. On issues that are less important to them, they can leave political participation to others.

Critics argue that some examples of nonparticipation are a result of insurmountable obstacles to participation, rather than a lack of interest. In the pre–civil rights era, for example, participation in politics by blacks was at strikingly low levels. We should not, however, interpret this as contentment with the status quo, or as a failure to see the relevance of politics to their own interests.[6] Indeed, for much of American history African Americans were deliberately excluded from the political system.

The political history of African Americans in America is an unusual case. But other, less extreme cases of political exclusion are indeed common. According to the most recent data, for example, more than 39 million Americans are in families with incomes below the poverty line.[7] Many of the impoverished are children, a group toward which the public is very sympathetic. Yet, while gun owners, nurses, attorneys, teachers, and the elderly are represented by vocal, highly successful interest groups in Washington, D.C., poor kids are not.

There are many reasons for this inequity. One is that effective political organization requires resources that the poor often do not have in abundance: money, time, knowledge, education, personal relationships, and political experience, among others. Critics of pluralism argue that, since critical political resources are not distributed

---

ThinkingCausally

What factors might keep other groups from participating?

▼ **BEHIND CLOSED DOORS**

Many complain that those rich in resources are better able to cope with the costs of lobbying and political participation than those without money and connections.

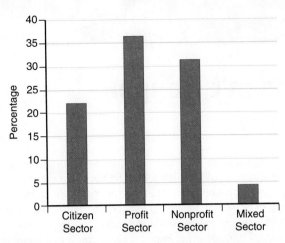

FIGURE 12-1. **Distribution of Groups by Sector.** Business interests working to increase profits are far better represented in Washington than organized groups advocating for civil rights, minorities, women, and other nonprofit interests.

equally across the population, the interest group system is biased in favor of upper- and middle-class groups, who have relatively easy access to the most important political resources and assets.

Even the pluralists acknowledged that political participation is costly in terms of resources, and that the upper and middle classes are better able to afford those costs. As political scientist E. E. Schattschneider famously said, "public activity of all kinds is a habit of the middle and upper classes."[8] Fellow political scientist Jack Walker determined that among all organized groups with a presence in Washington, D.C., 70 percent represented business interests trying to increase profits (Figure 12-1). Fewer than 5 percent represented civil rights groups, minority organizations, social welfare groups, poor people's organizations, and groups advocating on behalf of the handicapped, gays, and women.

▶ **IGNORING THE POOR**
Though poverty received political attention during the Great Depression and again under Lyndon Johnson's presidency, the poor and other marginalized groups are often left off the policy agenda.

Studying What Doesn't Happen

The Question

Sometimes in politics, things that do not happen are just as important as things that do. However, identifying and studying political fights that did not occur present no easy task. In fact, in the previous paragraph when we discussed this notion of studying nonevents in the context of a criticism of pluralism, we also presented the pluralists' response to this criticism. One of the pluralists' rejoinders was that nonevents—by definition, things that do not happen—are intrinsically difficult, if not impossible, to study. Is it possible to measure the impact of an issue's absence from the policy agenda? How do we know?

Why It Matters

We have already discussed certain "nonevents": nondecisions that result from the failure of groups to advance their interests when we might expect them to. Interest groups wield power by influencing what sorts of issues get talked about. Understanding power in the United States and the influence that interest groups might wield demands that we pay attention to the "dogs that are not barking."

Investigating the Answer

In The *Un-politics of Air Pollution*, Matthew Crenson examines why some cities take aggressive action against local pollution, while others neglect the issue. Crenson comes up with several useful ways to explore the failure of some cities to take the pollution issue

▶ **THE CAUSES OF INACTION**

Why didn't miners in Middlesboro, Kentucky, take action in the face of economic adversity? Answers to this question and others like it are often difficult to find, but creativity enables us to study political power, even when we don't see it directly exercised.

seriously. First, he uses the results of a 51-city survey of community leaders to identify the extent to which pollution was considered an important public issue in each city. With these results, he identifies cities that have put the pollution problem on their policy agenda and those that have largely ignored the issue. Crenson then seeks to develop explanations for these two different outcomes.

One possible explanation is that the cities that take pollution seriously have particularly bad pollution problems. In contrast, the cities that neglect the issue do so because pollution is not a serious problem there. Looking at pollution measures for each city, though, Crenson finds that this is no more than part of the explanation.

Next, for further explanation, he undertakes an intensive study of two cities that exhibited very different responses to their pollution problems: Gary and East Chicago, both in Indiana. The former city delayed action in tackling a serious pollution problem, while the latter acted quickly to address the issue. Why? Crenson's intensive study of the two cases led him to believe that the failure of industrial interests in Gary, Indiana, either to support or to oppose the city's anti-pollution plans left the pollution issue in limbo. Other stakeholders in town appeared to be paralyzed by the failure of industry to stake out a clear position.

Based on this finding, Crenson hypothesizes that the greater the relative influence of business interests in a community, the slower that community will be to respond to its air pollution problems. He then marshals survey data from local public figures to gain their assessment of local business influence. He matches that data against survey data indicating how seriously the community takes the issue of air pollution. Finally, Crenson finds that, indeed, in high pollution cities, the stronger the perceived influence of the business community, the less likely that city is to elevate the problem of air pollution to the public policy agenda.

In *Power and Powerlessness*, John Gaventa was occupied with the question of why miners in Middlesboro, Kentucky, did not take action in the face of miserable economic inequalities and poor working conditions. Part of Gaventa's explanation for this inaction was that the townsfolk internalized a system of beliefs and values propounded by powerful economic and political interests in their town. These beliefs and values were structured to keep the powerless miners quiet and submissive.

Gaventa has no difficulty demonstrating that the town's mining interests sought to cultivate a value system and ideology that would hold at bay any challenge to their power. What is more difficult to demonstrate, however, is that the townsfolk embraced that value system and ideology, and therefore did not seek to improve their situation. Gaventa applies two basic approaches in trying to demonstrate this latter point. First, like Crenson, he performs a comparative case study. He considers the behavior of miners in nearby communities that are not as dominated by economic interests as the town of Middlesboro. If his argument about Middlesboro is correct, then he should find greater tendency for protests, strikes, and even insurrections in these nearby communities. He finds precisely that.

However, Gaventa's finding need not indicate any ideological "brainwashing." Instead, it might simply indicate that miners in Middlesboro recognized the negligible likelihood of a successful strike, given the pervasive power of the mine owners. Acknowledging this, Gaventa analyzes the response of the Middlesboro townsfolk when the power of the mining interests weakens. We might expect the miners and their supporters to respond to this weakness with an increasing volume of demands. On the other hand, if the townsfolk had internalized the idea of subordination as their "natural" role, as Gaventa suspects, they might remain quiet when the power relationship changes. Gaventa finds the truth somewhere in the middle—there are limited demands for change when the power of the mine owners weakens, but not as numerous or vocal as we might expect if the miners fully tried to advance their own interests.

Thinking Critically

- In the two studies outlined above, explain how political power was manifested. How can you explain the direct correlation between wielding political power and action (or lack thereof)?
- Can you think of any examples of groups that hold little to no power to convince powerful interests to enact change?
- Explain how a "nonevent" can sometimes be more important than an actual event.

The Bottom Line

By definition, studying nonevents or nondecisions is difficult. That said, these two in-depth and creative studies show how it is possible to study political power even when we do not see it wielded directly. This is crucial because if we study only the winners and losers in battles that we can see, we miss two fundamental ways that power is wielded: through inaction and through the internalization of powerlessness by groups that fail to organize.

Pluralists ignore issues that policy makers ignore.

Another critique of pluralism begins with the observation that pluralists tend to study issue areas in which policy makers are debating solutions and groups are actively involved in the process. As the pluralists' critics have noted, however, some issues are not actually considered issues by political elites.[9]

Consider poverty as a political issue. In the Great Depression of the 1930s, and then again with Lyndon Johnson's declaration of a War on Poverty in 1964, the plight of the country's poor occupied center stage on the national agenda. But between these two periods—in the 1940s and 1950s—poverty virtually disappeared as a topic on the public policy agenda. Policy makers simply assumed (wrongly, as it turns out) that with the nation's return to prosperity in the 1940s, poverty had been largely vanquished. Thus, the attention of government decision makers turned to other issues.

This example illustrates the importance of what political scientists call **nondecisions**.[10] A nondecision can be defined as a decision not to put a particular issue on the **policy agenda**, which is the set of issues actively under consideration and discussion by policy makers. Whereas the pluralists focused on group participation in the decision-making process, their critics argue that one must take note of nondecisions as well. Quoting E. E. Schattschneider again, "Some issues are organized into politics while others are organized out."[11]

When government shunts some issues aside, the pluralist model breaks down. Group preferences on a particular issue cannot be taken into account if policy makers have chosen not to address that issue.

nondecisions decisions not to consider particular issues or incorporate them into the policy agenda.

policy agenda the set of issues under consideration by policy makers.

Groups do not automatically form.

In order for the pluralist model of democracy to work in optimal fashion, collections of individuals with interests that can be addressed by government need to come together to form groups. Since the political world is full of groups and associations actively pursuing their agendas at all levels of government, pluralists tend to take for granted the formation of diverse concerned groups. Pluralists explain the formation of groups through the **disturbance theory**, which holds that when social, political, and economic relationships are upset by some outside force, affected individuals often form a group in response.[12] In 2004, for example, as the American military position in Iraq steadily

disturbance theory the theory that when social, political, and economic relationships change, individuals form groups in response.

eroded, a group of veterans formed Iraq Veterans Against the War, which advocated a withdrawal of all U.S. troops from Iraq, reparations to Iraqis for the damage done to their country, and improved benefits for service members returning from Iraq.[13]

Groups do not always form, however, when there is a disturbance. In fact, when a potential group consists of a large number of individuals, the obstacles to group formation can be prohibitive. This argument was made most clearly in 1965 by economist Mancur Olson. Olson argued that "rational, self-interested individuals will not act to achieve their common or group interests."[14] Why? Because an individual's own efforts "will not have a noticeable effect on the situation of his organization, and he or she can enjoy any improvements brought about by others whether or not he has worked in support of his organization."[15]

Olson's argument is a statement of what is known, variously, as the public goods problem, the **free rider problem**, the collective action problem, the prisoner's dilemma, and the tragedy of the commons. College students as a whole may have an interest in increasing the pool of government scholarships available. But an individual student pursuing his or her own interests would just as soon not contribute time or money to help convince legislators to increase scholarships. Furthermore, if he or she did not work for better funding for higher education, the amount of funds available would hardly suffer. Moreover, and crucially, an individual who failed to contribute time or money to help convince the government to fund higher education would still be eligible for such funding and could still enjoy its benefits.

What does this example have to do with group formation? Imagine that you and your fellow students wish to have the school year shortened by two weeks. This requires a decision by school administrators. The best way of getting the decision you want is to form a group, organize rallies and e-mail campaigns, and lobby the relevant decision makers. From your perspective as an individual, however, it would be ideal if other students did all of the work and left you in peace. If the group consisted of, say, 500 active participants, your individual effort probably would not be missed anyway. Furthermore, if you failed to participate and the group succeeded without you, you would reap all of the benefits without having to give up any of your own time, money, or energy. What a great deal for you!

The obvious problem is that if everyone were to think this way, then everyone would leave it to others to do the work and the group would never form, get organized, bring attention to the issue, and lobby decision makers. The school year would remain two weeks longer than students would like it to be. And this would have happened even though members of the group had a collective interest in a shorter school year. Their individual interests in letting someone else do the work would have prevailed.

This is a simple statement of the free rider problem, but the free rider problem is a shot right at the heart of pluralism. If individuals with a common interest fail to organize to pursue that interest, they can hardly join in the competition for government attention that defines pluralism. If this happens often enough, the pluralist model collapses.

free rider problem a barrier to collective action because people can reap the benefits of group efforts without participating.

ThinkingCausally

What other factors inhibit participation and lead to the "collective action problem"?

Solving the Collective Action Problem: Group Formation and Maintenance

12-3 Explain how interest groups form and attract members.

We know, of course, that groups do form, get organized for political action, and participate in politics. These groups clearly have found a way to deal with the collective action problem, though the problem persists. In fact, the logic of group formation and maintenance is a central issue in the study of politics.

Groups overcome the collective action problem in a number of ways.

Political scientists have identified a variety of ways groups can overcome the collective action problem. These include (a) selective benefits provided to group members, typically material or monetary, but also social or ideological; (b) individual entrepreneurship, which can motivate individuals to get involved in a group's activities and stay involved; and (c) patronage from outsiders who support the group's mission.[16]

selective benefit benefit that can be accessed only by those who participate in or contribute to group activity.

material benefit a good or service offered to encourage participation in group activity.

Selective benefits   Groups often provide contributors with **selective benefits**, benefits not available to those who do not contribute. Remember, one of the key parts of the collective action problem is free riding: in certain circumstances, individuals can enjoy the benefits of group activity without having to bear any of the costs of that activity. Providing selective benefits is a way for groups to get around the free rider problem.

The most obvious kind of benefit that groups may provide is a **material benefit**. Benefits of this type can include publications, goods and services, discounts on products, and professional advice. For example, individuals who join the American Association of Retired Persons (AARP) become eligible for scores of benefits, simply by virtue of their membership. These include: discounts on hundreds of consumer products; members-only insurance plans; a subscription to AARP's monthly magazine; health and fitness tips; exclusive investment products, credit cards, and financial advice; tax preparation assistance; and dozens of others. The cost of all this? Anyone 50 years old or older can join AARP for as little as $8 per year.

Considering the low cost of membership, there are undoubtedly millions of AARP members who join the group for the benefits alone. In fact, a 1982 survey found that only 17 percent of members had joined primarily because of the group's work on behalf of the elderly. The rest were more interested in the material benefits.[17]

Associations of professionals—doctors, lawyers, teachers, nurses, accountants, social workers, and so on—provide similar material benefits, as well as professional certification and credentialing, which have a direct bearing on various professionals' ability to earn a living. Attorneys, for example, cannot practice law without first being admitted to their state bar, and they must meet continuing legal education requirements to remain bar members in good standing. State bar associations regulate these processes

▶ STAYING ACTIVE . . .
And solving the collective action problem. These seniors practice fitness tips available to members of AARP. This benefit, among others, can help the group to combat problems often associated with group formation and maintenance.

and charge members a fee for these services. The fees help subsidize the bar organizations' government-relations activities, which tend to be considerable. An attorney who does not wish to subsidize group political action can refuse to pay the fee, but the bar will deny him or her the ability to practice law. A state bar's control over this highly important selective benefit is one way it overcomes the collective action problem, enabling it to participate actively and effectively in the political process.

A group also can provide its members **social benefits**. Imagine, for example, that you are an avid environmentalist. Joining the Sierra Club, Greenpeace, or the Nature Conservancy would allow you to interact with people who are just as passionate about the environment as you are. If you were the owner of a small business, joining the National Federation of Independent Businesses could put you in touch with individuals who share many of the same challenges and successes.

Such group participation creates opportunities for you to socialize with people who have similar interests. Moreover, a sense of camaraderie can come from associating with others who are like you, and a sense of status from affiliating with people who share certain beliefs or values. If, for example, you are a member of the College Republicans or a contributor to EMILY's List (an organization that raises money for pro-choice women candidates), you are receiving the social benefit of solidarity while also working on behalf of group interests.

Olson considered material and social benefits to be powerful motivators of human behavior in a group setting. He even argued that for some groups, pursuit of group interests was a by-product of the group's selective benefits. Once the group solved the free rider problem through the use of selective benefits, it could pursue traditional political activities.

Some critics argue that Olson's focus on material and social benefits exaggerates the mercenary nature of actual and potential group members. Millions of people join groups because they believe in what the group stands for. Could Olson's theory account for these individuals, too?

Some interest group theorists believe so, arguing that the rewards such people seek are another kind of selective benefit, a **purposive benefit**. Purposive benefits are so called because they are connected to a group's stated purpose. Enjoying purposive benefits from group membership means getting satisfaction from contributing to a cause, or purpose, one believes in. For example, consider the following testimonial from a volunteer with Compassionate Action for Animals (CAA), an animal rights advocacy group:

> Through CAA I've come to realize that every little bit I do to end the suffering of animals makes a difference. But my efforts combined with others sets an example for a whole new generation, offering knowledgeable support in everything from raising positive awareness of farming to maintaining nutrition as a vegan. Through CAA I believe people give animals and our society a brighter, more socially responsible future. CAA has definitely given me hope for a better tomorrow.[18]

This person clearly derives satisfaction from helping promote animal rights. Of course, individuals need not volunteer or join a group in order to promote a cause that they believe in. Groups, however, make that process easier by creating, structuring, and supporting specific participation opportunities for members and volunteers. These allow members to enjoy unique purposive benefits not available to nonmembers.

Individual entrepreneurship   Selective benefits are an important mechanism for overcoming the collective action problem, but before a group can offer selective benefits, someone has to do significant organizational work to create the group. Some political scientists have argued that the collective action problem reasserts itself at this point. How do groups get started in the first place? Wouldn't everyone with a potential interest in organizing the group prefer to free ride, letting others bear the burden

social benefit   benefit that encourages individuals to join a group in order to enjoy the company of those who share similar opinions and interests.

purposive benefit   benefit that encourages group participation by connecting individuals to an organization's political purpose.

of group formation? And, again, if everyone thinks this way, how do groups come into being? One strain of the interest group literature provides a solution to this apparent problem: the **interest group entrepreneur**. This term refers to someone who launches and manages an interest group.[19]

interest group entrepreneur an individual who overcomes the costs of collective action by launching and managing an interest group.

Consider one of the most effective and well-known interest groups in America, the National Rifle Association (NRA). Though its primary interest today is in promoting and protecting the rights of gun owners, the NRA began with a very different agenda. Two Civil War veterans, William Conant Church and George Wood Wingate, had been alarmed by the poor shooting skills of Union troops. To address this perceived problem, Church and Wingate did much of the necessary "pushing"—seeking a charter from the New York legislature, along with $25,000 with which to purchase land and develop shooting ranges. Church urged New York's "citizen soldiers" to write their legislators and encourage approval of the charter and funding (a strategy the NRA follows to this day). The legislature ultimately obliged, and the NRA was born.[20]

The interest group entrepreneurs in this story were Church and Wingate. They invested the initial time and energy (and some cash) to get the NRA off the ground. Like business entrepreneurs, they gambled that their efforts would pay off, and that their initial investment would be returned, along with some "profit." Had they not done so, an NRA-style organization probably would have emerged at some point. But it would not have happened when it did, or in the form that it did, had Church and Wingate not assumed an entrepreneurial role.

patron an individual who supports an interest group by providing the resources needed to organize and flourish.

▼ AIM HIGH
Interest group entrepreneurs like the late actor Charlton Heston, former president of the NRA, help to launch or manage interest groups.

Patronage The decision by the New York state legislature to give the NRA $25,000 in start-up funds was critical. It may very well have made the difference between the NRA's sinking or swimming. If Church and Wingate had tried to raise the same amount of money—about $400,000 in today's dollars—from prospective NRA members in 1871, many would have balked at the price tag and some would have chosen to free ride: "Why should I contribute? Let others pick up the tab, and I'll just enjoy the benefits."

This is where **patrons** come into play. Patrons provide groups with the resources they need to get established. Patrons may work with an interest group entrepreneur to get a group started or may launch the group themselves but leave its management to others. Either way, they eliminate the need for groups to try to cobble together small contributions from potential members, all of whom are susceptible to free rider thinking.

Sometimes a patron is a single individual with a passion for an issue, and with resources to share. In 2004, for example, billionaire financier George Soros learned of a new organization called America Coming Together (ACT). The objective of this group was to increase voter turnout in an effort to defeat President George W. Bush's bid for reelection. Soros, who described the defeat of President Bush as "the central focus of my life," was intrigued. He knew that if ACT were to be successful, it would have to make a massive effort, reaching into key electoral battlegrounds across the United States. Accordingly, he pledged $10 million to help get the group up and running, effectively shifting ACT from idle to fifth gear with a stroke of his check-writing pen.[21]

Patrons need not be autonomous individuals. Corporations, units of government, foundations, and even other interest groups can act as patrons, founding new groups or helping start-ups get off the ground. Consider, for example, the National Association of Counties, which represents the interests of the nation's counties "on Capitol Hill and throughout the federal bureaucracy," and which was created with the patronage of county governments.[22]

Or consider the United States Chamber of Commerce, a membership group of businesses, associations, and state, local, and international chambers of commerce. The U.S. Chamber was created in 1912, in part as a result of the patronage of Secretary of Commerce and Labor Charles Nagel. Nagel had brought the idea of a national business organization to the attention of President William Howard Taft. At Nagel's encouragement, Taft publicly expressed his interest in the creation of a commercial group that could speak to Washington policy makers with a single voice. With the president on board, business had a strong incentive to act. But how to bring together diverse businesses from all over the country? Nagel provided the answer through an important act of patronage. He used the resources of his department to convene a national business conference to which approximately 1,000 associations were invited. Nagel and President Taft both spoke at the conference, once again promoting the idea of a consolidated national business group, and encouraging conferees to take advantage of the rare gathering. By the time the conference was adjourned, a new, nationwide business organization had been born: the United States Chamber of Commerce.[23] The Chamber of Commerce would grow into a very influential group and was a major player in the 2010 elections, criticized often and by name by President Obama and Democrats.

Even the casual observer of American politics knows that one way or another, tens of thousands of groups have succeeded in overcoming the collective action problem and have fended off threats to their survival (Figure 12-2). The challenges inherent in this are not the same for all groups, however. Some groups have ready access to desirable selective benefits, or to dynamic entrepreneurs, or to resource-rich patrons. Some have access to all three. Some have access to none. Some groups are very small and therefore do not have to struggle with the free rider problem. Some are so large that they must continually work to keep their members engaged. Some are organized around simple, high-profile, ideologically charged issues that naturally incite passions and attract attention. Others are focused on technical, abstract, nuanced issues that make the general public yawn.

443

▲ PUT YOUR MONEY WHERE YOUR MOUTH IS

With funding from patron George Soros, ACT made over 12 million phone calls to targeted voters and delivered 11 million pieces of literature at targeted doorsteps. ACT also maintained 86 offices, a staff of 4,000, and a goal of reinforcing an army of 45,000 paid canvassers. One patron made a huge difference in outreach, regardless of outcome.

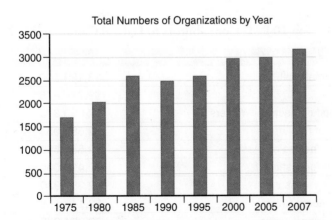

FIGURE 12-2. **Rise in the Number of Interest Groups over Last 40 Years.** In spite of the collective action problem, the number of interest groups in Washington has nearly doubled in the last 40 years.

In short, different groups face different challenges, and have strengths and weaknesses in different areas. Thus, groups must choose among various potential strategies and tactics to achieve their ends. We explore some of these choices in the next section.

What Groups Do, and Why They Do It

12-4 Analyze the strategies and tactics interest groups use to impact elections and public policy.

The ultimate goal of most politically oriented interest groups is to shape public policy in ways consistent with the group's interests, values, and beliefs. In general, groups use two primary strategies to do this. They attempt to influence either the selection of public officials (an electoral strategy) or the decisions of elected officials, bureaucrats, or members of the judiciary who have already been elected or appointed (a legislative strategy).

Of course, groups can pursue both strategies at once. Furthermore, as we will discuss later in the chapter, the two strategies often intertwine.

An electoral strategy consists of a variety of tactics.

In pursuing an electoral strategy, interest groups and their members may employ a number of tactics. The most familiar, and controversial, involve spending money in an effort to get certain candidates elected. Less controversial tactics include endorsements, voter mobilization efforts, voter education, and volunteering.

Political action committees   Many groups interested in election outcomes form **political action committees** (PACs), or encourage group members to donate to a PAC created by someone else. A PAC is an organization funded by 50 or more people, usually affiliated with a corporation, labor union, or some other special interest group. The PAC collects donations from individuals and then turns those donations into contributions to political parties and candidates for election (Table 12-1).

Groups form PACs, rather than contributing directly to a campaign or party, for several reasons. Federal law prohibits labor unions and corporations from contributing directly to political parties or candidates for federal office, but these groups may form a PAC and collect and distribute money from individuals sympathetic to their interests.

political action committee (PAC) a group that collects money from individuals and makes donations to political parties and candidates.

TABLE 12-1. Top 10 PAC Contributors to Federal Candidates in 2010

PAC	AMOUNT CONTRIBUTED
Honeywell International	$3,183,100
AT&T Inc	$2,776,875
Intl Brotherhood of Electrical Workers	$2,690,373
National Assn of Realtors	$2,685,054
National Beer Wholesalers Assn	$2,556,500
American Assn for Justice	$2,415,000
American Bankers Assn	$2,281,930
Operating Engineers Union	$2,149,258
Carpenters & Joiners Union	$2,004,875
American Crystal Sugar	$1,962,500

*From http://www.opensecrets.org/pacs/toppacs.php?cycle=2010&party=A
** Based on data released by the FEC on October 25, 2010.

PACs also allow individuals to multiply the effect of a campaign contribution. If you were to contribute $50 directly to a Senate campaign, you might feel that your contribution didn't amount to much. But if you were to donate that same $50 to a PAC supporting your favorite Senate candidate, and that PAC in turn donated $10,000 to the candidate by combining your contribution with many others, you might feel that you had gotten more bang for your buck.

Like individuals, PACs are limited in the amounts of money they can contribute to a political campaign (Table 12-2). PACs may give a maximum of $15,000 per year to a political party and a maximum of $5,000 per election to any federal election candidate. Because primaries and general elections are considered separate elections, however, a PAC may actually give a total of $10,000 to each federal candidate per election cycle. In the 2010 election, PACs contributed almost $375 million to candidates running for the House and Senate.[24] This represents about one-fourth of the funds that candidates for Congress raised during the 2009-2010 election cycle.

Competitive campaigns for Congress can be extraordinarily expensive. In 2010, for example, the most expensive House campaign cost more than $8.5 million (Michelle Bachmann, R-MN), and the most expensive Senate campaign cost more than $41 million (Linda McMahon, R-CT).[25] In a very costly race, then, the maximum PAC contribution will comprise a trifling amount of the total the campaign will spend.

Other spending options Groups can be involved in elections in ways other than PAC contributions in a variety of ways. For example, rather than contributing directly to a political campaign, a PAC can make unlimited **independent expenditures**, which are made with the explicit intent of advocating the election or defeat of a candidate. By law, such expenditures may not be coordinated with the candidate's campaign (hence the qualifier "independent"). Aside from that, however, they may serve exactly the same purpose as advertisements placed by candidates themselves.

Groups can also request that members write checks directly to a candidate's campaign. The group can then collect the individual checks and present them to the candidate all at once, a practice known as **bundling**. Considering that individuals can write candidate checks for up to $2,400 each, a bundle of checks from dozens of well-heeled donors can make quite an impression. In the 2008 presidential campaign, even

independent expenditures funds spent to elect or defeat candidates but not coordinated with any candidate's campaign.

bundling the practice of collecting individual checks and presenting them to a candidate at one time.

TABLE 12-2. **Summary of Campaign Donation Limits**

2010 CONTRIBUTION LIMITS	
Individuals can give:	
To candidate	$2,400
To national party committee	$30,400
To PAC/state or local party	$10,000 to state or local party
	$5,000 to each PAC
Aggregate total	$115,500 per two-year election cycle
	$45,600 to candidates
	$69,900 to all national party committees of which no more than $45,600 per cycle can go to PACs
Multicandidate PACs can give:	
To candidate	$5,000
To national party committee	$15,000
To PAC/state or local party	$5,000
Aggregate total	No limit

though Barack Obama raised large sums of money in small amounts over the Internet, the backbone of his fund-raising efforts was a group of supporters who gathered or "bundled" contributions to the Obama campaign.

Groups may also form and raise funds for **527 committees,** also called "527s," named for the relevant section of the Internal Revenue Code. A 527 is a tax-exempt, nonparty group that can raise and spend money on political activities and advertising with no effective limits.

527 committee an independent, nonparty group that raises and spends money on political activities.

In 2010, the Supreme Court decided in the Citizens United case to permit corporations and unions to have a much more direct role in campaigns. The Supreme Court rejected a major tenet of BCRA and now allowed groups who took corporate or union contributions to air ads within 30 days of primary and 60 days of a general election that depicted or mentioned a candidate for federal office. The Court went further though and also allowed corporations or unions to engage in direct advocacy (as defined by the magic word test in the Valeo decision) using money from their corporate or union treasuries. Although the decision was harshly criticized by President Obama, most observers thought it unlikely, that corporations would take advantage of the decision and air ads directly advocating the election or defeat of a particular candidate. The 2010 elections bore this out in some ways. For example, there were no television commercials that said "Defeat Jones, paid for by Gillette Shaving Cream." On the other hand, corporations such as News Corporation, among others, sent large checks to advocacy groups that aired ads praising or attacking candidates. Moreover, much of this was funded by groups who do not disclose their donors, making it hard to track the true extent of corporate activity. Unions in 2010 also took advantage of Citizens United, funding a lot of their electioneering with funds outside of their PACs.

In many ways, the effect of Citizens United was powerful in that it allowed groups to fund express advocacy with unregulated funds, and existing rules allowed many of these groups to avoid disclosing their donor lists. Still, it did not transform the overall look of campaigns. For years, organized interests had searched for loopholes to invest unregulated money into the electoral process, and Court decisions preceding Citizens United had already weakened the changes instituted by BCRA. No matter what the Court had decided, competitive races would still have cost lots of money, interest groups would have found ways to invest in their preferred candidate, and voters would have seen lots of political ads on television.

Other electoral tactics   Although campaign spending is probably the most high-profile and controversial tactic that interest groups use to pursue their electoral goals, it is just the beginning. Groups interested in electoral outcomes have a number of other tactics at their disposal. These include:

> *Endorsements*: Groups often publicize their support for a candidate, providing a valuable voting cue to group members, and to nonmembers who are sympathetic to the group's mission.
> *Voter mobilization*: As noted above, interest groups often dedicate themselves to increasing voter registration and turnout in competitive congressional races and in the important battleground states that decide presidential elections.
> *Voter education*: Sometimes groups seek to influence elections by disseminating educational materials to prospective voters. These materials may discuss a candidate's background, beliefs, or record; compare and contrast competing candidates; or rate a whole slate of candidates according to their votes or positions on various issues. Conservative Christian groups have been among the most active exponents of this approach, distributing voter guides in evangelical churches every election year.
> *Volunteer work*: Groups may provide volunteers to do some of the necessary day-to-day work on behalf of candidates they favor. This can include answering

phones, preparing campaign mailers, coordinating local meetings, reminding voters to do their civic duty on Election Day (for the preferred candidate, of course), and even driving voters to the polls.

Lobbying is the key ingredient in a legislative strategy.

As with the electoral strategy, groups that pursue a legislative strategy have a variety of tactics at their disposal. The most familiar of these is **lobbying**: communicating with government officials to persuade them toward a particular policy decision. Lobbying and lobbyists are sometimes stigmatized as sleazy, unseemly, and even undemocratic. For example, in his 2008 presidential campaign, Illinois Senator Barack Obama said:

> I am in this race to tell the corporate lobbyists that their days of setting the agenda in Washington are over. I have done more than any other candidate in this race to take on lobbyists—and won. They have not funded my campaign, they will not get a job in my White House, and they will not drown out the voices of the American people when I am president.[26]

President Obama, however, had to relax his stance somewhat. When pursued legally and ethically, lobbying is a legitimate tactic used to achieve a legitimate democratic end: influencing the deliberations, decisions, and actions of government officials. In fact, the right to lobby is guaranteed by the First Amendment, which prohibits Congress from interfering with the right of the people "to petition the government for a redress of grievances." Lobbying takes two general forms, inside lobbying and grass-roots lobbying. We shall examine each in some detail.

Inside lobbying and Congress   What most people think of as lobbying is technically called **inside lobbying**; it occurs when group representatives meet with public officials or their staff members. The lobbyist's job in these meetings is generally twofold: to present specific, evaluative information to the public official, and to request an action or a decision based on that information.

The lobbyist does not simply say, "We want you to know that our group is pro-environment, and we hope you will be, too." Instead, the lobbyist presents the group's position on a specific bill, amendment, nomination, budget item, or issue along with the reasons for that position: "The Sierra Club is opposed to this amendment because we think it will undercut some major provisions of the Clean Air Act that have nearly universal public support." To this statement, the lobbyist adds his or her request for action by the public official: "Because of that, we are asking that you vote against the amendment."

There are, of course, dozens of variations on this basic information/request-for-action two-step. Lobbyists recognize that public officials have a variety of goals. As discussed in more detail in Chapter 13, members of Congress value good public policy, reelection, and advancement within the institution (chairing a desirable committee, for example, or earning a spot in the party leadership). The information that lobbyists provide to legislators, then, is presented with these goals in mind. In the example above, the Sierra Club presented an evaluation of an amendment in terms of its soundness as public policy. Recognizing that members of Congress are interested in reelection, too, the lobbyist cited above might have added: "Furthermore, our research shows that the substance of this amendment is immensely unpopular within your district. If you vote for it, an opponent in the next election may beat you over the head with this issue all the way to November."

The type and amount of information that lobbyists provide will vary from situation to situation. Some policy makers want to see detailed studies supporting a

lobbying communicating with government officials to persuade them toward a particular policy decision.

inside lobbying meeting directly with public officials to influence political decisions.

group's position. Others are more interested in expressly political information on the issue: polling data, communications from voters, and activities of opposing groups. Some legislators want to know what recognized experts think. Some simply want a short list of talking points they can use to explain their vote. Others want to know what kind of media coverage the issue has received in national and home-town newspapers. Still others want to talk through hypothetical scenarios: "What if, instead of just voting against the amendment, we sent it back to committee for reconsideration with some specific suggestions for improving it?"

The lobbyist must be prepared to answer all such questions and provide supporting information when meeting with public officials or soon after. Lobbyists' ability to do so makes them immensely helpful to members of Congress. Faced with dozens of high-profile issues, each of which must pass through a long series of meetings, hearings, decisions, discussions, negotiations, and votes, representatives and senators cannot become experts in more than two or three issue areas. Having lobbyists available to provide information on other issues is like having a public policy encyclopedia at the ready.

Unlike an encyclopedia, however, a lobbyist has a point of view—a position that he or she is promoting—and often a broad philosophical orientation on issues of a certain type ("pro-labor," for example, or "pro-business"). This is actually helpful to public officials. They are far too busy to listen to lobbyists who present both sides and leave it up to the official to decide. Instead, they can hear the strongest arguments from the most passionate, well-informed advocates on both sides. These may help them evaluate an issue in ways that they otherwise could not because they lack the lobbyists' information, expertise, and familiarity with the most salient arguments.

The nature of the request for action by a lobbyist can also vary tremendously from situation to situation. Among other things, the lobbyist might ask a member of Congress to sponsor, amend, rewrite, or vote for or against a piece of legislation; talk to colleagues, hold hearings (or decline to hold hearings), or take a stand regarding an issue; support or oppose a nominee; or intervene with an agency.

Members of Congress may agree to do such work on behalf of an interest group because it is consistent with their goals, they are grateful for the lobbyist's or group's support in the past, or they are trying to build goodwill in anticipation of a request for support in the future. Whatever the case, by helping the lobbyist that comes to visit—and by extension, the group the lobbyist represents—members of Congress generally help themselves.

This kind of help is not a one-way street. A lobbyist who asks a member to sponsor a piece of legislation often provides a draft bill that the member can use as a starting point. The lobbyist might also volunteer to answer any questions on the legislation from the member's colleagues. If the member has agreed to meet with a regulatory agency, the lobbyist might offer to help set up the meeting and preview the major issues and arguments.

> "Whatever the case, by helping the lobbyist that comes to visit—and by extension, the group the lobbyist represents—members of Congress generally help themselves."

Furthermore, once a lobbyist has established a trusted relationship with a public official, that official may seek out the lobbyist for help. An official working on a pet issue may ask the lobbyist to supply information or suggest a subject-matter expert to provide congressional testimony, or talk to other groups involved with the issue in order to find out their position on a particular sticking point. Lobbyists are normally happy to oblige, knowing that a close, trusting, and mutually supportive relationship will benefit the groups they represent.

Inside lobbying and the executive branch   Although inside lobbying is most often thought of in relation to members of Congress and their staff, interest group lobbyists also devote resources to the executive branch. In some cases this focus means the president and White House personnel, but more often lobbying efforts focus on executive branch agencies. As we will see in Chapter 16, these agencies issue regulations, statutory interpretations, and quasi-legal decisions on issues as diverse as endangered species protection, the content of television and radio advertising, business accommodations for individuals with disabilities, and interstate speed limits. They also participate in the executive branch budget process, identifying programs for which they will seek to maintain funding at current levels, increase funding, or reduce or eliminate funding. Furthermore, executive agencies are responsible for administration of major federal programs and tax credits. Finally, they pursue policy agendas of their own, encouraging the president to promote and fund certain policy initiatives and to abandon others.

Obviously, interest groups and their members can have a significant stake in these executive agency decisions and activities. Some groups, therefore, devote major lobbying resources to the executive branch.

Inside lobbying and the judiciary   Inside lobbying of the judicial branch takes two primary forms. In one, an interest group may file *amicus curiae* briefs (discussed further in Chapter 15) on cases that involve an issue in which it has an interest. Such briefs present the group's analysis of legal or factual questions in the hope that judges, justices, or their clerks will take their arguments into account when deciding the case. One example involves the U.S. Supreme Court case of *Morse v. Fredrick*. Fredrick, a high school senior, had been suspended from school for hanging a banner school officials found offensive. Fredrick claimed that this was a violation of his First Amendment rights. When the case made its way to the Supreme Court, a number of groups, including the National Coalition Against Censorship, the Christian Legal Society, and Students for Sensible Drug Policy, filed briefs supporting Fredrick's position. They saw the case as an opportunity to establish important principles regarding freedom of speech in a public school setting. In the end, however, the Supreme Court ruled that Fredrick's First Amendment rights had not been violated by school administrators.

The other judiciary-related tactic available to interest groups is litigation. Although this is not lobbying per se, it can have important policy implications. During the 2004 Senate race, for example, Wisconsin Right to Life, Inc. (WRTL), an anti-abortion group, challenged the McCain-Feingold Act by using funds from its general treasury to broadcast television advertisements that mentioned Wisconsin senators Herb Kohl and Russ Feingold by name. Feingold was running in the September 14 primary, and after August 15 WRTL was in violation of McCain-Feingold, legislation prohibiting the use of general treasury funds to pay for advertisements that mentioned a federal candidate within 30 days of a primary election.

Believing these restrictions on political advertising to be unconstitutional, WRTL sued the Federal Elections Commission, the agency responsible for administering McCain-Feingold. The U.S. Supreme Court decided in favor of WRTL, effectively modifying a law enacted by Congress and signed by President Bush. Ultimately, this decision led to the previously discussed decision in Citizens United that further loosened campaign finance laws for corporations and unions. Thus, the suit resulted in fewer legal restrictions not just for the group involved in the litigation, but potentially for hundreds of similar groups around the country.

Grassroots lobbying   The other major tactic that groups use in support of a decision strategy is known as **grassroots lobbying** (also called outside lobbying). In this form of lobbying, rather than communicating directly with decision makers in government, interest groups and their lobbyists seek to influence opinion and stimulate action by the general public, specific groups, and the media. The goal is that public officials will be swayed by what they hear from influenced individuals, groups, and media outlets.

grassroots lobbying efforts to persuade citizens to contact their elected officials regarding a particular issue or piece of legislation.

Groups generally begin a grassroots lobbying effort with their own members. Group leaders have established communication channels with their members, and they know that most agree on the issues and many will also take action if asked. Thus, leaders bring new issues to members' attention, try to shape opinions on existing issues, and request phone calls, e-mails, and letters to policy makers in positions of influence.

Consider the example of LEAnet, a nationwide coalition of special education professionals and school administrators. LEAnet routinely notifies members of pending congressional actions that may affect group members' interests (primarily, the preservation of Medicaid funding for special needs students in public schools). These communications often include a call to action:

> Please send an e-mail to your Congressperson (if a Republican) or call her/his office as soon as possible. You can find the e-mail address and phone numbers of the Congressman you want to contact here or here. If you call, just ask for the staff person handling education or health and tell them you strongly support inclusion of the moratorium language and request their Congressperson's vote.

> If you e-mail, include on the subject line your address, which will tell the staff person in charge of reading e-mails that you are a constituent. Please respond to this call for help immediately. You can make a difference.

> An e-mail message as simple as "Please include moratorium language stopping CMS cuts to children's health programs in any appropriate legislation. Thank you" will make a difference.[27]

ThinkingComparatively

In what different ways might lobbyists influence the votes or opinions of legislators?

Some groups go further and encourage, or even arrange for, their members to meet policy makers in person. The American Public Health Association (APHA), for example, touts the value of such meetings on its website:

> One of the most effective ways to influence the policymaking process and make a lasting connection is to visit with your Senators and Representative, or their staff, in person.[28]

However, interest groups know that government officials respond to public opinion broadly, not just to opinions expressed by group members with an interest in a particular issue. They know, too, that policy makers react to what they see, hear, and read in the media. Because of these strengths, a grassroots lobbying campaign may be both extensive and multifaceted.

Consider, for example, a campaign launched in 2005 by Progress for America (PFA), a group that often advocated on behalf of President Bush and various Republican candidates and initiatives. Progress for America used grassroots tactics to build support for Samuel Alito, a Bush nominee to the U.S. Supreme Court. These included putting up a website and airing about $500,000 in television advertising. The group also hired consultants in 20 swing states to speak with editorial boards and sent over 10 million e-mail messages to Republican Party lists. The group also arranged for Judge Alito's former law clerks to visit Washington and lobby senators for their former boss. To generate favorable news stories, the group even sought out people from Judge Alito's past, including former teachers, coaches, and neighbors.[29]

This example illustrates many of the hallmarks of a textbook grassroots approach to lobbying. Progress for America attempted to influence the general climate of opinion through the use of paid advertising. It sought to educate and mobilize individuals that it thought might be willing to take action on behalf of Judge Alito. It tried to generate favorable stories and friendly interviews about

▼ BUILDING SUPPORT

Liberal group MoveOn.org used grass roots tactics to keep the pressure on Democrats to pass health care reform legislation.

Judge Alito in mass media outlets. It arranged for meetings between lawmakers and former clerks of Judge Alito, rather than meetings between lawmakers and paid professional lobbyists. In short, instead of using Washington-based, lobbyist-centered inside tactics, PFA tried to create a climate in which senators (who had to vote on Alito's nomination) would sense that there was significant support for Alito outside - Washington. Alito was ultimately confirmed. Although PFA's campaign was not the sole reason for Alito's Senate confirmation, it is a modern and textbook example of grassroots lobbying. The logic that drives grassroots lobbying was perhaps best summed up by former Illinois Senator Everett Dirksen. "When politicians feel the heat," Dirksen said, "they begin to see the light."[30]

CaseStudy: Health Care Lobbying

The cases of two different attempts at national health care reform—one in the Clinton White House and the other in the Obama administration—offer very different methods of dealing with this issue with very different results. In 1993, a new president made health care for all Americans his first signature piece of legislation. Although most Americans had health care coverage through their work, many Americans did not, and some unlucky people lost everything when catastrophic illness struck, wiping out their savings. The concept of national health insurance had been in debate since the New Deal, but in 1993 a particularly intense grassroots lobbying campaign emerged around President Clinton's proposal.

The campaign was focused on three committees: the Ways and Means Committee and the Energy and Commerce Committee in the House and the Finance Committee in the Senate. These committees were responsible for deciding whether any health care reform would pass, and if so, what shape it would take. Within these committees, lobbying efforts focused on those members (fewer than 20 in the House and 15 in the Senate) who were undecided, and also on a group of moderate Republican and Democratic senators, known as the "mainstream coalition," that was seeking a broadly acceptable compromise.

One crucial element in the grassroots lobbying effort against the Clinton proposal was a television commercial financed by the Health Insurance Association of America, a trade organization of health insurance providers. The commercial showed a typical married couple, Harry and Louise, sitting in their kitchen, seemingly loaded down with piles of papers. They worried aloud about some of the Clinton plan's features—not unlike millions of other Americans in their kitchens—trying to figure out if this bill would create a government monopoly over the health industry. Would health care involve a huge, intrusive, impersonal federal bureaucracy? Would government bureaucrats have the power to deny health care to some? The commercial ended by

exhorting people to get in touch with their congressional representative if they, too, were worried about the Clinton plan. "Harry and Louise" proved enormously effective. The producers claimed that the campaign "prompted 500,000 phone calls to a toll-free number, turned 50,000 of those callers into activists, and resulted in one-quarter million contacts with member of Congress."

The ad also led to a tremendous amount of media coverage in newspapers, on television, and on the radio. Thus, it received much wider exposure than it would have received from paid placements alone. As a result, policy makers and opinion shapers were forced to address the arguments in the Harry and Louise campaign.

Other radio and TV ads flooded targeted districts. An ad from Citizens for a Sound Economy, a free market/limited government advocacy group, told listeners, "If you don't want government gatekeepers telling you what doctor you can see, call Congressman [name] at [number] and tell him to vote no on the Clinton health care plan." These and similar efforts were directed not at Congress as a whole, but at the districts and states of members of Congress who were expected to be influential or persuadable in the health care debate. Groups also worked to identify constituents who were most likely to influence members of Congress.

Unlike a political activity such as voting, the letters or phone calls from different individuals are not equally influential. Letters most likely to influence congressional decision-making are those from local civic, business, or political leaders; from individuals or groups with a particular interest or expertise in an issue; or from individuals known to be highly involved and engaged in politics generally. Thus, interest groups seek to mobilize individuals with the most potential influence with their elected representatives—an approach sometimes referred to as a "grass tops" strategy.

Data indicate that such a strategy was at work during the Clinton health care debate. The National Federation of Independent Businesses, a key player in defeating the proposed legislation, created Guardian Advisory Council teams consisting of influential business people, college friends, neighbors, and former colleagues of targeted legislators, people who were thought to have extraordinary influence with those legislatures. The broader media efforts to defeat the Clinton plan were directed toward the "grass tops." Ben Goddard, who produced and placed the "Harry and Louise" ads, explained, "Our media buys were targeted on involved Americans, people who were registered to vote, wrote letters to the editor or public officials, attended meetings and made political contributions." These are the very people most likely to be taken seriously by policy makers.

The Clinton bill went down to a humiliating defeat for the new president, setting back his entire legislative agenda and hurting him in the polls. Sixteen years later, the outcome would be considerably different when another new president used health care as his first signature piece of legislation. Most Americans had not changed their view of national health care, but the political landscape had changed in that time. First, Barack Obama entered his office with a huge mandate (something Bill Clinton lacked), and more importantly, he had a super majority in the Senate with 60 Democrats along with a strong Democratic control of the House. Second, President Obama learned a lot from President Clinton's earlier defeat. And yet, even with those numbers in his favor, passing health care was no slam-dunk.

Perhaps the biggest story in the 2009 debate was what wasn't heard. Even with the numbers on their side, the Obama administration took no chances. Early on, they co-opted the earlier adversaries who defeated the Clinton bill. They quickly struck a deal with the large and powerful pharmaceutical industry, making sure their worries (financial compensation) were not a problem. They struck a deal with the American Medical Association (AMA), making it look as though all of the country's doctors were behind it. And, in perhaps the most brilliant and visible turn-around, Harry and Louise came back to the television screens, looking a bit older. The couple was still concerned about the bill, but—lo and behold—now they were more concerned for all of their fellow Americans out there who did not have health insurance.

In the House, a group of conservative Democrats known as "Blue Dog Democrats" was not onboard because they worried that federal dollars might pay for abortions, something they were against. After this group threatened to vote against the bill, President Obama held a special meeting with the leader of the group, Congressman Bart Stupak, and assured him that would not be the case. Stupak took the president at his word and brought in this small but important group.

Not taking any chances, there were also tremendous giveaways. The president promised individual congressmen and senators special deals—extra money for their states, pet

▲ HARRY AND LOUISE RETURN
The famous couple from the 1994 health care battle return—this time in a spot that encourages Congress to pass comprehensive health care reform.

projects, and even a ride in Air Force One seemed to be enough to sway one congressman.

The bill itself—well over 2,000 pages long—was so complicated that few members could read the entire piece of legislation. Polls showed a strong majority of Americans opposed the bill, so politicians understood that voting for it could have a huge impact on their futures. Indeed, Stupak, the anti-abortion congressman who faced abject anger in his district for supporting the president, was forced to end his political career.

When the final vote came, it was strictly across party lines. Not one Republican supported the measure and 34 Democrats opposed it. And there would be questions of its constitutionality. But in the end, the bill passed in the House by 7 votes, 219 to 212. President Obama had his first significant victory in his administration at a time when his approval numbers were falling. The United States would have national health care, but its actual cost would not be known for years to come. And Harry and Louise would go back to their kitchen, until the next significant controversy might use their talents.

Thinking Critically

1. Compare the tactics employed by both Clinton and Obama in their attempts to pass health care legislation. Why was Obama successful while Clinton failed? What lessons did Obama learn from Clinton's failed attempt?

2. Now compare the role that public interest groups played in both examples. How did interest groups help Obama and hurt Clinton? Do you think that their role was instrumental in getting a health care bill passed a second time around?

The electoral strategy and the legislative strategy intertwine.

Groups need not choose between an electoral strategy and a legislative strategy. Many pursue both strategies at once, and one often reinforces the other. A member of Congress who has been elected with the support of a particular group, for example, may be more open to entertaining that group's viewpoints on policy issues. He or she knows that maintaining a friendly relationship will likely ensure the group's support in the next campaign and so may feel obligated to meet with them. Thus, the group's electoral strategy can support its legislative strategy.

The reverse can be true as well. A group that wants a member of Congress to vote its way on a bill will often note the political appeal of that vote (or the political damage of opposition) in the next election. A group that engages in an outside lobbying strategy by encouraging communications to a legislator is, of course, registering its viewpoints on issues. At the same time, it is showing the kind of muscle it can flex—on behalf of the legislator or an opponent—in the next election.

In a similar vein, an interest group might seek to have legislation introduced on an issue both because it cares about the issue, but also because the legislation causes problems for political opponents. The proposed "partial birth abortion" ban, for example, first introduced by pro-life members of Congress in 1995, was designed in part to force pro-choice legislators to take a public position on a procedure that a large majority of the American public disapproved of. The same logic held with respect to the federal assault weapons ban passed in 1994. Most of the public approved of the ban, putting gun rights supporters in an awkward position if they opposed it.

Interest groups have a wide variety of tactics in their toolkits.

As the preceding discussion indicates, interest groups have a wide variety of tactics that they can choose from to try to influence the policy process. Their choice of tactics depends on the goals they are pursuing. All the various tactics try to convey some sort of information to policymakers—either on the substantive merits of their position or on the political consequences of a particular course of action. Table 12-3 summarizes the various tactics and how often they tend to be used.

Do Groups Matter?

12-5 Assess how much influence interest groups have over policy outcomes.

High-profile corruption cases have received significant media attention over the last few years. In these cases, some interest groups went well beyond the sorts of activities we have outlined here and attempted outright to bribe members of Congress. Randy Cunningham, a former representative from California, received a Rolls Royce and a yacht for steering Defense Department business toward a particular contract. Cunningham is currently biding his time in prison. Jack Abramoff, a well-known lobbyist in D.C. for many years, also earned prison time for his role in orchestrating bribes to members of Congress.

These sorts of blatant and illegal activities are rare, and as we have argued, interest groups and lobbyists have an important role in our political system as they engage in various legitimate strategies to influence the policy process. That said, and having examined what groups do and why they do it, we are left with a final question: do groups matter? That is, do group activities influence election results and public policy outcomes in the ways that groups intend? The answer to that question is surprisingly murky.

TABLE 12-3. Lobbying Techniques and Their Prevalence

LEGISLATIVE BRANCH	
Doing favors or providing gifts for legislators	–
Meeting personally with legislators or their aides	very often
Testifying at legislative hearings	very often
EXECUTIVE BRANCH	
Interacting with special agencies that advise the chief executive	–
Interacting with special liaison offices within the chief executive's office	–
Meeting personally with chief executive or aides	seldom
Meeting personally with executive agency personnel	very often
Serving on executive agency advisory boards or committees	occasionally
Submitting written comments on proposed rules or regulations	very often
Testifying at executive agency hearings	–
JUDICIAL BRANCH	
Attempting to influence judicial selections	–
Engaging in litigation	occasionally
Submitting *amicus curiae* ("friends of the court") briefs	occasionally
GRASSROOTS	
Arranging face-to-face meetings between group members/supporters and government officials	–
Dispatching a spokesperson to the media	–
Engaging in e-mail, letter, telegram, or telephone campaigns	very often
Engaging in demonstrations or protests	seldom
Running advertisements in the media	seldom
DIRECT DEMOCRACY	
Attempting to place an initiative or referendum on the ballot	–
Campaigning for or against an initiative or referendum	–
ELECTORAL	
Campaigning for or against candidates	seldom
Endorsing candidates	seldom
Engaging in election issue advocacy	seldom
Making in-kind contributions to candidates	seldom
Making monetary contributions to political parties	seldom
Making monetary contributions to candidates	occasionally
Mobilizing activists to work on a candidate's behalf	–
Issuing voter guides	seldom
OTHER	
Joining coalitions with other organizations or lobbyists	very often

Note: Dashes (–) indicate that there is little evidence with which to judge the frequency of such activities.

It is difficult to prove the impact of campaign contributions.

Few researchers doubt that if interest groups were to disappear from the American political landscape, different public officials would be elected and appointed, different issues would appear on the public agenda, different pieces of legislation would be approved, and budget items would be funded at different levels. For political scientists, however, the challenge comes in providing clear evidence that group activity caused a particular political outcome. Consider, for example, the case of interest-group spending on federal campaigns. The hundreds of millions of dollars that interest groups spend supporting and opposing candidates must surely have some impact, but political scientists cannot say as a general proposition that the more money a candidate spends, the more votes he or she gets.

Why this indecision? For one thing, candidates facing a highly competitive race tend to raise and spend more money, whereas candidates who are shoo-ins for reelection typically spend less. This paradox produces counterintuitive results: candidates who spend a lot of money often end up in very close races (they had to spend a lot of money because the race was close); and candidates who spend very little money often end up winning big (they could afford to spend so little because they faced little competition). Unfortunately, political scientists have not yet found their way out of this methodological thicket and therefore do not have a complete understanding of the impact of interest-group spending on election outcomes.

ThinkingComparatively
Why is it difficult for political scientists to determine the impact of candidate spending?

We find similar problems, but somewhat more satisfying answers, when we look at the impact of political action committee contributions on legislator behavior. Journalistic accounts of legislator voting sometimes note that legislators who receive large PAC contributions often vote as their donors wish. Members who receive large campaign contributions from tobacco PACs, for example, often cast votes in support of legislation advocated by the tobacco lobby. From this, we might infer that "big tobacco" is buying votes. Political scientists, however, have suggested an alternative explanation: tobacco PACs take note of legislators who support tobacco interests and distribute campaign dollars accordingly.

Which explanation is the right one? Most research finds that PAC contributions do not buy the votes of legislators. Again, there are logical reasons for this. First, a floor vote on a piece of legislation comes at the end of the legislative process. Important decisions, hearings, committee votes, negotiations, and coalition-building have to take place before a bill makes it this far. An interest group trying to buy influence after all of these steps have occurred would be like a football fan who pays full price for a Super Bowl ticket with only two minutes left in the game.

Second, members of Congress face other influences on their vote in addition to campaign contributions. These include their own policy preferences, the preferences of their constituents, the dictates of party leaders, and their voting records. These influences tend to be so strong that most political scientists consider it unlikely that an interest-group contribution could override them, turning a "yea" vote into a "nay," or vice versa.

Group influence may be strongest where it is hardest to observe.

If not floor votes, then what sorts of legislative outcomes might interest groups be buying? One insightful study of this question concluded that money buys time, that is, time the targeted legislator might spend working to incorporate an interest group's preferences into new legislation. Political scientists Richard Hall and Frank Wayman found that legislators who received campaign funds from an interest group were more likely to engage in the following activities on the group's behalf: "authoring or blocking a legislative vehicle; negotiating compromises behind the scenes, especially at the staff level; offering friendly amendments or actively opposing unfriendly ones; lobbying colleagues; planning strategy; and last and sometimes least, showing up to vote in favor of the interest group's position."[31] Hall and Wayman argued that such activities, rather than floor votes, were most likely to show evidence of group influence.

These activities can result not just in broad pieces of legislation that interest groups favor but in the provision of "private goods" for specific groups: government contracts, price increases, tax breaks, "earmarked" funds, exemptions from certain statutory provisions, and so on.[32] Private goods of this sort are typically distributed to groups behind the scenes, away from reporters, in private meetings and committee mark-up sessions, and without a formal vote. They are often buried in the fine print of massive appropriations bills and are therefore easily missed—even by political scientists.

In part, the challenge in finding effects is because political scientists tend to study highly contested issues in which the conflict is in plain view.[33] The politics surrounding these issues can be very dramatic. Accordingly, they seem interesting and important, and they generate readily available data, which makes them attractive subjects for study.

But groups probably have their greatest influence when the outcomes they seek are not contested by anyone; are negotiated or decided in low-profile settings; do not have a significant impact outside of the groups immediately affected; and cannot easily be observed or exposed by casual observers of politics. For obvious reasons, interest group influence is much harder to study in these situations.

Interest group influence is also most likely to be observable in marginal, unresolved cases. For example, if 10 of 11 committee members decided long ago how they would vote, interest groups would likely focus their lobbying efforts on the undecided one. A scholar looking for group influence on all 11 committee members would likely come up empty handed.

Similarly, in races for the House of Representatives, only a few dozen contests each year (out of 435) usually are competitive. These are the races where we would expect to find interest group influence, if it is to be found at all. Accordingly, a political scientist looking for the impact of groups across the full slate of congressional races would come up with little to show for his or her work.

In summary, political scientists clearly need to spend more time looking for group influence in less obvious settings, on lower-profile issues, in obscure but consequential legislative provisions, on decisions that do not require a vote, in discussions that typically take place behind closed doors, and in the marginal cases that tend to be decisive in determining an electoral or policy outcome. Reorienting interest group research in this way would undoubtedly demonstrate group influence in virtually every aspect of executive, legislative, judicial, and electoral activity.

That influence would show up not on all issues, but on select ones. It would be reflected not in every decision or in every setting, but in specific cases. In short, extensive interest group influence undoubtedly could be found, if political scientists were looking for it in the right ways and in the right places.

CHAPTER SUMMARY

In this chapter, you have learned to:

12-1 Distinguish between pluralist theory's and James Madison's interpretation of the role of interest groups within American politics. Founder James Madison was concerned about the negative influence of interest groups, what he termed factions, on individual rights and the collective good. However, he concluded that the American system was well designed to mute the influence of interest groups. The pluralists viewed politics as an organized effort to resolve conflicts among competing group interests, and they attempted to demonstrate empirically what Madison had argued theoretically. They concluded that political power and resources in the United States were dispersed widely, with some interest groups being influential and resource rich in some issue areas, and a completely different set being influential and resource rich in other issue areas.

12-2 Describe how critics of pluralist theory view the role of interest groups today. Critics of pluralism argue that the American system is resistant to change and retards certain issues from getting on the agenda. Furthermore, the free rider or collective action problem questions the assumption that groups automatically form and suggests some types of groups are more able to form than others.

12-3 Explain how interest groups form and attract members. Groups pursue a variety of strategies to get around the collective action problem. They provide selective benefits and material benefits, which members receive in return for joining. They also provide social benefits, in which members enjoy the camaraderie of being part of a group. And they provide purposive benefits, in which those who join get satisfaction from being involved in an important political struggle.

12-4   Analyze the strategies and tactics interest groups use to impact elections and public policy. Groups try to influence public policy in two ways. In an election strategy, groups try to influence which leaders achieve power and make public policy. In a legislative strategy, groups try to influence the behavior of elected officials, bureaucrats, and judges who are already in power.

12-5   Assess how much influence interest groups have over policy outcomes. Media coverage and public opinion suggest that interest groups are too powerful and often malevolent. They are neither. While particular lobbyists and legislators sometimes cross the line, groups in general play an important role in American politics, even though they are more likely to influence policy-making in small and subtle ways.

---

mypoliscilab EXERCISES

Apply what you learned in this chapter by starting with these resources on MyPoliSciLab.

Read on mypoliscilab.com

   eText: Chapter 12

Study and Review on mypoliscilab.com

   Pre-Test
   Post-Test
   Chapter Exam
   Flashcards

Watch on mypoliscilab.com

   Video: American Cancer Society Recommendation
   Video: California Teachers Stage Sit-Ins
   Video: Chicago Gun Laws
   Video: Murtha and the PMA Lobbyists

Explore on mypoliscilab.com

   Simulation: You Are a Lobbyist
   Comparative: Comparing Interest Groups
   Timeline: Interest Groups and Campaign Finance

KEY TERMS

527 committee, p. 446
bundling, p. 445
disturbance theory, p. 438
free rider problem, p. 439
grassroots lobbying, p. 449
independent expenditures,
   p. 445

inside lobbying, p. 447
interest group entrepreneur, p. 442
interest groups, p. 432
lobbying, p. 447
material benefit, p. 440
nondecisions, p. 438
patrons, p. 442

political action committee
   (PAC), p. 444
pluralism, p. 432
policy agenda, p. 438
purposive benefit, p. 441
selective benefit, p. 440
social benefit, p. 441

SUGGESTED READINGS

Frank Baumgartner and Beth Leech. 1998. *Basic Interests: The Importance of Groups in Politics and in Political Science.* Princeton, NJ: Princeton University Press. Reviews decades of political science research on interest groups, arguing for more large-scale empirical studies and that group behavior should be studied in tandem with Congress and other institutions that groups try to influence.

Jeffrey Berry and Clyde Wilcox. 2008. *Interest Group Society*, 5th ed. New York: Longman. A comprehensive summary of what scholars know about the role of interest groups in American politics, putting interest groups into context and discussing their strategies and tactics.

Michael Franz. 2008. *Choice and Changes*. Philadelphia, PA: Temple University Press. The impact of interest groups on electoral politics, with a particular focus on "soft money" contributions, issue ads, and "527s".

Mancur Olson. 1971. *The Logic of Collective Action*. Cambridge, MA: Harvard University Press. The hurdles that groups with collective goals face in forming and maintaining themselves, what sorts of groups are likely to form, and who in politics is advantaged by the collective action problem.

Jack L. Walker. 1991. *Mobilizing Interest Groups in America: Patrons, Professionals, and Social Movements*. Ann Arbor: University of Michigan Press. One of the most important empirical studies in interest group behavior, using a systematic survey of interest groups to outline the characteristics of the interest group world and identify what sorts of organizational factors influence the strategies that groups pursue.

SUGGESTED WEBSITES

Iraq Veterans Against the War: ivaw.org

Founded by Iraq War veterans in July 2004 at the annual convention of Veterans for Peace in Boston, IVAW has called for the immediate withdrawal of troops from Iraq, reparations for the human and structural damages in Iraq, and support for service members returning from Iraq.

AARP: www.aarp.org

The AARP website offers members tips on managing money, health care, family, and leisure and links to various resources related to these and other concerns of the retirement-age population.

Sierra Club: www.sierraclub.org

The Sierra Club is dedicated to protecting communities and the environment. It is America's oldest, largest, and most influential grassroots environmental organization.

EMILY's List: www.emilyslist.org

An acronym for "Early Money Is Like Yeast" (it makes the dough rise), EMILY's List has become the nation's biggest political action committee. Members work to elect pro-choice Democratic women to office by recruiting and funding viable women candidates, helping these women to build effective campaigns, and mobilizing women voters.

College Republican National Committee: www.crnc.org

The College Republican National Committee recruits and trains conservative student leaders to build a conservative movement to "fight against the radical left on campus."

College Democrats of America: www.collegedems.com

The College Democrats of America is the college outreach arm of the Democratic Party. They focus on electing Democrats to offices at all levels of government. This site offers links to local chapters and voter registration.

Compassionate Action for Animals: www.exploreveg.org

Compassionate Action for Animals works to inspire respect for animals and promote vegetarianism through outreach, education, and community building.

National Rifle Association: www.nra.org

The NRA represents millions of Americans who "believe in the Constitution" and "actively pursue some of the country's finest traditions—Hunting and Sports Shooting."

National Association of Counties: www.naco.org

A membership organization representing the nation's counties on Capitol Hill, NACO offers opportunities and services to affiliated businesses and corporations.

Swift Boat Veterans and POWs for Truth: www.swiftvets.com

Swift Vets and POWs for Truth has formally disbanded but the website is maintained, for historical purposes only, by New American Media Online Services (NAMOS).

Club for Growth: www.clubforgrowth.org

Club for Growth members believe that prosperity comes through economic freedom. The organization works to promote economic growth through legislative involvement, issue advocacy, research, training, and education. Club for Growth provides financial support to pro-growth candidates, particularly in Republican primaries.

Wisconsin Right to Life: www.wrtl.org

Wisconsin Right to Life works to prohibit abortion and assisted suicide.

LEAnet: www.theleanet.com

LEAnet is a coalition of Local Education Agencies dedicated to the protection and enhancement of school health programs.

American Veterinary Medical Association: www.avma.org

The AVMA is a nonprofit association representing more than 76,000 veterinarians.

Citizens for a Sound Economy: www.cse.org

FreedomWorks "recruits, educates, trains, and mobilizes hundreds of thousands of volunteer activists to fight for less government, lower taxes, and more freedom."

National Federation of Independent Businesses: www.nfib.com

The National Federation of Independent Businesses is a network of grassroots activists who send their views directly to state and federal lawmakers through member ballots.

Discover the Networks: A Guide to the Political Left: www.discoverthenetworks.org

This site with a conservative slant identifies individuals, organizations, and institutions of the political left, the paths through which the left exerts political influence, and its programmatic agendas, history, and platforms.

CHAPTER

13 Congress

Distributing Homeland Security Funds

In fiscal year 2010, the federal government spent $842 million on domestic counterterrorism.[1] On a per capita basis, though, these funds were not distributed equally across the country. Rather, one of the least populous states also received one of the largest per capita shares of federal anti-terrorism funds. Wyoming, not generally considered to be a terrorist target, secured funds amounting to $12.15 for each of its half-million residents from the Homeland Security Grant Program. New York, by contrast, received just $5.80 per resident, in spite of the fact that it was a site of the September 11, 2001, terrorist attacks.[2]

How did Wyoming manage to secure such a large chunk of federal funds to fight terrorism? The answer lies in the USA PATRIOT Act, more commonly known as the Patriot Act, which Congress passed in the

▼ OUTFITTING STATES TO FIGHT TERRORISM

In the aftermath of September 11, 2001, Congress distributed funds to every state in the country to combat terrorism. Nine years later, funds still are not allotted strictly according to assessed risk of a terrorist attack. Here, two New York City police officers stand watch in the aftermath of an attempted car bombing in Times Square. In your opinion, how should these funds be distributed around the nation?

aftermath of September 11, 2001. Among other things, the Patriot Act established a federal grant system to help state and local governments prepare for and respond to terrorist attacks. Eager to demonstrate their resolve to fight terrorism, members of Congress provided money for states to train first responders, purchase security equipment, and develop plans for emergency situations. However, the Patriot Act required the State Homeland Security Program (SHSP) to distribute almost 40 percent of its funds evenly among the 50 states, regardless of their population, size, or risk of being a terrorist target.[3]

When Congress passed the act in late October of 2001, no one objected to the funding distribution formula. In fact, members of Congress were eager to offer a swift, bold response to the September 11 attacks. The chair of the powerful Senate Judiciary Committee, Senator Patrick Leahy of Vermont, included in the state anti-terrorism program a distribution formula that would benefit the citizens of the small state he represented, and others just like it.

The Patriot Act met little resistance in Congress. It was introduced in the House of Representatives on October 23, 2001, and passed the very next day by a vote of 357 to 66. Although some senators opposed

other provisions of the bill, no one spoke out against the formula for distributing anti-terrorism funds to states. The Senate approved the bill with all but one vote in favor, and President George W. Bush signed it into law on October 26, 2001.

As the Department of Homeland Security devoted increasingly large sums of money to helping state and local governments prepare for a possible terrorist attack, the wastefulness of the Patriot Act's fund distribution formula became apparent. Common sense probably tells you that helping North Dakota buy a $200,000 remote-control bomb-disposal robot is not the most effective way of preparing the nation for a terrorist attack. Thomas H. Kean, chair of the September 11 Commission, agreed: "We've had some of this money spent to air condition garbage trucks. We've had some of the money spent for armor for dogs. This money is being distributed as if it's general revenue sharing."[4] Kean recommended that anti-terrorism funds be distributed not evenly among the states, but on the basis of threat and vulnerability.[5] Michael Chertoff, homeland security secretary at the time, further acknowledged that a uniform distribution of funds across states was not a good policy.[6]

Yet when Representative Christopher Cox of California tried to craft a new law in 2005 that would have distributed anti-terrorism funds on the basis of threat and risk, he could not get enough support from members of the Senate. Senators from smaller, less populous states lined up against the proposed measure, hoping to preserve the funding going to their states under the existing law. Senator Leahy argued that distribution based on the degree of terrorist threat would "shortchange rural states."[7] In July 2005, the Senate passed a milder version of the Cox bill, one that would have slightly reduced the guaranteed state minimum of annual SHSP funds. However, the

House and Senate were not able to agree on a compromise and the formula was not changed.

The failure of these efforts to address clear inefficiencies in the distribution of federal anti-terrorism funds seems to make little sense. When we think about the incentives that motivate individual members of Congress, however, their behavior is easier to understand. Opponents of the Cox proposal were representing the interests of the voters who put them into office. Whereas Cox represented an urban district outside of Los Angeles, Leahy spoke for a rural state. By arguing that Vermont *did* need to protect itself from terrorist attacks, he hoped

to secure federal funds for improving the state's police and fire protection services. Other members of Congress also wanted to secure funding to please voters who had the power to reelect them, even if it was not best for the country as a whole. As of 2010, SHSP anti-terrorism funds continued to be distributed by the same basic formula established by the Patriot Act.[8]

Neither irrationality nor happenstance is primarily responsible for the existing distribution of federal anti-terrorism funds. Rather, its origins lie in the strategic negotiations that occur every day on Capitol Hill. Congress is a collective decision-making body whose structure sometimes

inhibits effective problem solving. The individual members who serve in Congress work hardest on behalf of those who elected them. The laws they write represent compromises among hundreds of individuals fighting on behalf of districts and states. Sometimes, the final result is legislation that serves the interests of the country as a whole. Often, though, the pressure of pleasing the voters results in laws that do not address problems as effectively, or as efficiently, as many would like. To understand why these inefficiencies occur, and what might be done about it, we need to think about the structure of Congress and the incentives it creates for those who work within it.

CHAPTER LEARNING OBJECTIVES

After reading this chapter you will be able to:

13-1 Outline the basic structure of Congress.

13-2 Analyze the relationship of members of Congress to their constituencies, and distinguish between the trustee and delegate model of representation.

13-3 Assess the challenges that emerge when members of Congress set about working together.

13-4 Identify the resources and the committee and party structures that help Congress address its challenges.

13-5 Outline the lawmaking process in Congress.

13-6 Outline the appropriations process.

An Institution with Two Chambers and Shared Powers

13-1 Outline the basic structure of Congress.

Congress is a **bicameral** institution—that is, it consists of two chambers, a House of Representatives and a Senate. In the House, the 435 voting members (and the five nonvoting delegates) are elected every two years and represent state districts, which are remade every decade to reflect changes in the number of people living in different regions of the country. On average, each member of the House represents roughly 600,000 voters.[9] In the Senate, the 100 members are elected every six years and represent entire states.[10] Obviously, the size of states varies tremendously. As a consequence, senators from larger states like New York, Texas, and California represent tens of millions of voters, whereas senators from smaller states like North Dakota, Wyoming, and Montana represent far fewer.

For the most part, members of the House and Senate do similar things. As we discussed in Chapter 3, most powers enumerated in Article I of the Constitution, which concerns Congress, do not differentiate between the Senate and House. Both chambers have the responsibility of overseeing the bureaucracy, declaring war, regulating interstate commerce, raising and supporting armies, and most importantly, writing

bicameral an institution consisting of two chambers.

"all Laws which shall be necessary and proper for carrying into Execution the forego-ing power." Later in this chapter, we will consider the lawmaking process in detail.

There are some important differences, however, between the two chambers. In terms of duties, the Senate has the responsibility of ratifying foreign treaties. When brokering deals with foreign nations, presidents need only anticipate the reactions of senators, not representatives. Additionally, senators are charged with approving presidential appointments to the federal judiciary and executive branch. Therefore, before selecting federal judges, ambassadors, and members of their cabinet, presidents try to calculate their chances of securing the necessary approval of the Senate.

As part of the nation's system of checks and balances, Congress has the power to remove from office the president, vice president, and others immediately under their command. The removal process, however, is divided into two separate phases that are assigned to the House and Senate. In the first, members of the House decide whether to **impeach** the president—that is, determine that the charges against him or her are sufficiently credible and meet the standards laid out in the Constitution of "treason, bribery, or other high crimes and misdemeanors." Should the House impeach the president, the case goes before the Senate, where the chief justice of the Supreme Court then presides. For a conviction, two-thirds of the senators must vote against the president. In the nation's history, two presidents (Andrew Johnson in 1868 and Bill Clinton in 1998) have been impeached. The Senate, however, refused to convict either president. (See Chapter 14 for more on the impeachment process).

Members of the House and Senate also have different kinds of relationships with the people they represent. Because representatives are elected every two years and usually face a smaller (and typically more homogenous) group of voters than do senators, they tend to maintain closer relationships with the voters and work on behalf of a narrower band of interests. Senators, by contrast, hold office for six-year terms and represent larger (and typically more heterogeneous) populations. Senators, therefore, have more freedom to exercise their own judgment on policy matters, and are less beholden to a small group of people.

This difference is no accident. The Framers of the Constitution envisioned the House to be the "People's Chamber," where the interests of specific groups would be aired. The Senate was intended to be more deliberative than the House, allowing elected officials to reflect upon issues with national implications. Therefore, senators are more concerned with whether proposed legislation is consistent with long-standing principles of equality and individualism. Senators also reflect on the pros and cons of legislation for longer periods of time. "The use of the Senate," wrote James Madison in *Notes of Debates in the Federal Convention of 1787*, "is to consist in its proceedings with more coolness, with more system and with more wisdom, than the popular branch."[11] By "the popular branch," of course, Madison was referring to the House.

Congress is not the only bicameral legislature around. In fact, 49 of the country's 50 state governments have legislatures with two chambers. (The one exception is Nebraska.) Most large democracies around the globe also have bicameral legislatures, which go by many different names. India's parliament, for instance, consists of the Lok Sabha (House of the People) and the Rajya Sabha (Council of States). Japan's parliament, which is called the Diet, contains the House of Representatives and the House of Councillors. Switzerland's Federal Assembly contains the National Council and the Council of States.

To be sure, the U.S. Congress distinguishes itself from other bicameral legislatures in important ways. For instance, the upper chamber of Congress (the Senate) is

impeachment performed by the House of Representatives, the act of charging government officials with "treason, bribery, or other high crimes and misdemeanors." The Senate then decides whether to convict and remove the official from office.

ThinkingComparatively
Bicameral legislatures in other countries are also designed to promote competing notions of representation.

comprised of elected representatives, whereas the upper chambers of many European legislatures are appointed. Important similarities, nonetheless, persist. In most countries with bicameral legislatures, the lower chamber tends to have more individuals who represent smaller constituencies and who serve for shorter intervals, whereas the upper chamber tends to have fewer individuals who represent larger constituencies and who serve for longer intervals. The main reason for designing legislatures in this way is to promote competing notions of representation, the topic to which we now turn.

Principles and Dilemmas of Representation

13-2 Analyze the relationship of members of Congress to their constituencies, and distinguish between the trustee and delegate model of representation.

By design, the two chambers of Congress represent the people like no other branch of government. The federal judiciary is not elected—all judges are appointed. The executive branch sponsors just one election (for president and vice president) every four years—and because they can serve only two terms, presidents usually run for reelection at most once. Everyone else in the executive branch is either appointed or a civil servant. Congress, meanwhile, sponsors hundreds of elections. The public has more opportunities to evaluate members of Congress than any other group of politicians in the federal government. It should come as little surprise, then, that members of Congress are always focused on the next election.

Members of Congress share one objective: getting reelected.

Members of Congress are a diverse bunch, coming from all walks of life. But they have one thing in common. As David Mayhew, a political scientist who wrote one of the most influential books on Congress, writes, members are "single-minded seekers of reelection."[12] Every vote they cast, speech they write, argument they advance, favor they offer, and bill they sponsor is with an eye toward the next election—and the one after that, and the one after that.

Of course, members of Congress have other objectives as well. Some want to make a difference by reforming health care or pushing for prayer in public schools or cracking down on illegal immigration. Others want to direct government benefits to a particular population, such as college students, the poor, African Americans, or farmers. Others want to make names for themselves, and still others just enjoy sitting in a position of power. The mix of policy and personal objectives in Congress is as varied as the members.

To attain their individual goals, though, members must first win a seat and then hold onto it. In 2008 alone, in terms of spending, the top 10 interest groups contributed between $20 million and $91 million each to the reelection campaigns of representatives.[13] Hence, the motivation to be reelected precedes all other motivations. As Mayhew notes, reelection "has to be the proximate goal of everyone, the goal that must be achieved over and over if other ends are to be entertained."[14]

▼ **TERM LIMITS, BRINGING THE ELECTED CLOSER TO THE PUBLIC?**
Often, members of Congress are criticized for being out of touch with the interests of everyday citizens. In this regard, members of Congress are not unique. Here, a protester calls for the imposition of term limits in order to "end gridlock" in Montgomery County, Maryland.

To improve their reelection prospects, members serve their constituents.

Chapter 9 discusses the elections that determine who serves in Congress; and the Case Study in Chapter 2 examines the issue of redistricting, which can have important electoral consequences. In this chapter, we focus on what members of Congress actually do while they are in office in order to maximize their chances of winning the next election. More than anything else, successful members work hard on behalf of their **constituents**—that is, the individuals who reside within their political jurisdictions. To convince these people to vote for them, members generally support legislation that is popular in their home states or districts. Thus, members from the Midwest stand up for farm subsidies, members from Michigan advance the interests of autoworkers, and representatives in Florida attend to the elderly. For each, their political lives depend upon the voting habits of these populations.

Political scientists have shown that members' electoral fortunes critically depend on how well they represent their constituents. Members who represent liberal populations but who support conservative bills, and vice versa, are more likely to lose the next election than members who faithfully represent the interests of their constituents. The basic lesson: "out of step, out of office."[15]

Although political scientists have documented a clear link between the preferences of voters and the actions of Congress members, the exact nature of this link is less clear. It may be that individuals who share the policy objectives of most people in

constituents the people who reside within an elected official's political jurisdiction.

▼ STANDING WITH YOUR CONSTITUENTS
Members of Congress make a point of maintaining close relations, or at least the appearance thereof, with their constituents. Here, Florida Senator George LeMieux greets visitors while assessing the damage done to Pensacola Beach, Florida, by the British Petroleum Oil Spill in the summer of 2010.

their districts or states are more likely to run for office; for the same reason, when they run, they are more likely to win. On the other hand, members may adjust their views according to the opinions of those citizens who will shortly decide their political fate.

It stands to reason that **incumbents**—individuals who currently hold office—have more freedom to do as they please. It turns out that over 90 percent of Congress members are reelected, and they are usually reelected by large margins. In 2008, 94 percent of incumbents in the House and 83 percent of incumbents in the Senate were reelected. Incumbents who are confident of reelection might feel less bound by their constituents' views. We need to be careful, however, about the causal interpretations we draw from incumbent reelection rates. After all, does the fact that voters overwhelmingly approve of their representatives free them to do as they please, or are representatives reelected because they reflect the voters' views? If the latter is true, then members do not have that much freedom. When they disagree with large portions of their constituents, members may well face a tough challenge at the next election.

Beyond the positions they take on the issues of the day, members of Congress also serve their constituents through **casework**—direct assistance to individuals and groups within a district or state. The staffs that work for members of Congress will help constituents locate missing Social Security checks, direct constituents to federal agencies, and provide procedural support for dealing with these agencies, among other things. Obviously, members of Congress cannot address the individual needs of every constituent. In the House, after all, members serve hundreds of thousands of voters; most senators represent many more. Still, by performing casework for at least some of these constituents, members can hope to secure their votes (as well as those of their friends and families) at the next election.

To enhance their reelection prospects, members of Congress also direct federal benefits to their home districts and states. When new legislation is being considered that is intended to clean up the nation's streams, reduce poverty, or provide health insurance to children, members of Congress work hard to ensure that their own constituents reap the benefits of these initiatives. And as we saw at the chapter's outset, this also applies to legislation designed to combat terrorism. Rather than building a comprehensive program that devotes resources to cities in direct proportion to the threat of terrorism, members of Congress built one that ensured every district and state received a sizable chunk of the federal government's funds.

Serving constituents can mean different things.

The structural differences between the House and Senate reflect two broader conceptions of representation. According to the **delegate model of representation**, successful members of Congress share the same interests as the voters and promise to act upon them. If a majority of constituents supports affirmative action, then so will the Congress member; and if a majority subsequently opposes the same policy, that member will switch his or her position. Delegates must vote according to the expressed interests of their constituents even when their conscience or personal preferences dictate otherwise.

In contrast, according to the **trustee model of representation**, members of Congress are chosen for their judgment, experience, and skill. As Edmund Burke, an eighteenth-century Irish philosopher and member of England's Parliament, put it, voters ought to choose a legislator for "his unbiased opinion, his mature judgment, his enlightened conscience."[16] Rather than simply mirroring their constituents' opinions, trustees reflect deeply on the arguments for and against different policies before

incumbent the individual in an election who currently holds the contested office; as distinct from the challenger, who seeks to remove the incumbent from power.

ThinkingCausally

Do large election victories allow political actors to do as they choose once in office?

casework the direct assistance that members of Congress give to individuals and groups within a district or state.

465

delegate model of representation the type of representation by which representatives are elected to do the bidding of the people who elected them; representatives are "delegates" in that they share the same policy positions as the voters and promise to act upon them.

trustee model of representation the type of representation by which representatives are elected to do what they think is best for their constituents.

taking a position. To be sure, trustees still represent their constituents. They do so, however, by thinking about the longer-term implications that policies have both for their constituents and for the nation as a whole.

Roughly speaking, members of the House tend to act more like delegates, and members of the Senate behave more like trustees. They do so because of the electoral incentives they face. Because they face more homogenous constituents at more regular intervals, members of the House have stronger incentives to act on behalf of their public's current preferences. But senators, because they face more heterogeneous constituents over longer periods of time, can reflect on the deeper interests of a citizenry.

Not all constituents are represented equally well.

While all members have powerful incentives to represent their constituents, not all constituents are represented equally well. Instead, constituent groups who are likely to have a greater impact on a member's reelection bid tend to receive greater consideration on Capitol Hill.

Some constituents are less important because they cannot vote and therefore have fewer opportunities to influence the outcome of an election. Consider, for instance, the differences between the elderly and children. Older Americans tend to monitor the behavior of members of Congress quite closely and to vote in high numbers. Children, by contrast, pay little attention to politics. And even if they wanted to, children cannot vote until they officially become adults at age 18. Thus, it is not surprising that members of Congress tend to work harder on behalf of the elderly than they do on behalf of children. For every federal dollar spent to reduce poverty and poor health among children, four dollars are spent to accomplish the same objectives among the elderly.[17]

The citizens who organize, fund, and participate in interest groups—see Chapter 12—also figure prominently in members' reelection strategies.[18] Through financial contributions and endorsements, interest groups can influence both the number of people who come out on Election Day and the candidates they choose. In 1998, lobbyists spent $1.4 billion in their efforts to court members of Congress. A decade later, as shown in Figure 13-1, that number jumped to $3.5 billion. During this period, the number of congressional lobbyists also increased by roughly 30 percent.

▼ IN POLITICS, NOT EVERYONE IS REPRESENTED WELL

Members of Congress tend not to represent the interests of people who do not, or cannot, vote. Caught in the juvenile justice system, these youths cannot vote, and therefore have significantly fewer opportunities to put political pressure on members of Congress. In your view, should individuals who are incarcerated have the right to vote?

With the upsurge in interest group activity, members of Congress have stronger incentives to act on their behalf. Sometimes members do so by voting in ways that support these groups. More often, though, the influence of interest groups is more subtle, affecting which bills Congress considers, the amendments that are made to these bills, and the speed at which members deliberate.[20] Concerns about the undue influence of interest groups have spurred some reform-minded members to push for campaign finance legislation. For more on this topic, see Chapter 9.

Members of Congress also have strong incentives to listen to their core supporters and those who can be persuaded to vote on their behalf. By contrast, members have less incentive to work on behalf of those individuals

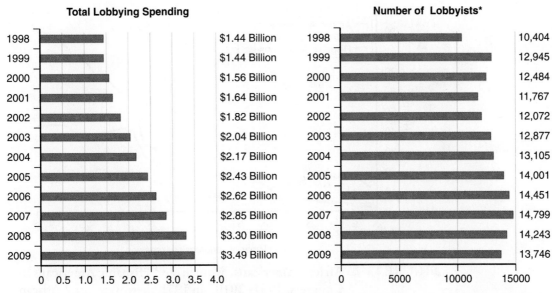

Total Lobbying Spending

1998	$1.44 Billion
1999	$1.44 Billion
2000	$1.56 Billion
2001	$1.64 Billion
2002	$1.82 Billion
2003	$2.04 Billion
2004	$2.17 Billion
2005	$2.43 Billion
2006	$2.62 Billion
2007	$2.85 Billion
2008	$3.30 Billion
2009	$3.49 Billion

Number of Lobbyists*

1998	10,404
1999	12,945
2000	12,484
2001	11,767
2002	12,072
2003	12,877
2004	13,105
2005	14,001
2006	14,451
2007	14,799
2008	14,243
2009	13,746

FIGURE 13-1. **Rise in the Number of Interest Groups.** In any given year, thousands of lobbyists, backed by billions of dollars, descend upon Capital Hill. And there are few signs of their abatement. Over the last decade, the number of lobbyists has increased by 30 percent, and the total amount of money spent on lobbying has nearly tripled.

*The number of unique, registered lobbyists who have actively lobbied.

Note: Figures on this page are calculations by the Center for Responsive Politics based on data from the Senate Office of Public Records.

who would not, under any circumstances, vote for them. Consequentially, a Republican would likely support different kinds of policy proposals than a Democrat who came from the same district two years earlier, despite the fact that they both technically represented the same people.[21] The Republican representative will tend to support policies that help the district's Republican citizens, and the Democratic representative will generally try to help the district's Democratic citizens. For example, when the Republican Party secured a majority of seats in Congress after the 1994 election, Republican members, many of whom had just won seats held by Democrats, worked to increase federal insurance and loan program funding, a type of government benefit that helps the farmers, entrepreneurs, and small businesses that form a core constituency of the Republican Party.[22]

Political scientists have also examined the ways in which people of different genders, races, ethnicities, and incomes are represented by members of Congress. Some argue that citizens are best represented by members who have much in common with them: women are best represented by women members, African Americans by African American members, and so forth.[23] And there is something to this claim. Female members, for example, are more likely than male members to sponsor laws concerning reproductive rights, women's health, and domestic violence.[24]

If the findings from these studies apply more generally, then recent Congresses should be doing a better job than past ones of representing the full spectrum of interests around the country. As Figure 13.2 (page 468) shows, members of Congress are reasonably diverse and are getting more so over time. The 111th Congress has a record 17 women in the Senate and 74 in the House of Representatives.

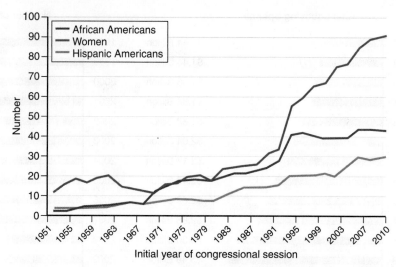

FIGURE 13-2. African Americans, Women, and Hispanic Americans in Congress, 1951–2010. In 1951, there were just 2 African Americans, 3 Hispanics, and 11 women serving in Congress. Two decades later, 11 African Americans, 6 Hispanics, and 11 women were serving. By 2010, there were 43 African Americans, 30 Hispanics, and 91 women in the House and Senate.

Note: Numbers including delegates, such as those from Washington, D.C., who do not have formal voting rights.

How Members Make Group Decisions

13-3 Assess the challenges that emerge when members of Congress set about working together.

Members of Congress do not work alone. To do so, in fact, would be foolhardy. Bills that rally the support of just a handful of other members are unlikely to impress most voters. To stand with confidence before their constituents, members of Congress must find ways to work together. For a variety of reasons, however, working together can be immensely challenging.

Members of Congress often disagree with one another.

Members of Congress hail from different regions of the country. They have wildly different views about the purposes of government. They represent different genders and ethnicities. They even follow different electoral calendars. To understand how Congress functions, it is vital to recognize the diversity of its membership.

Members' different views reflect in part the districts they serve. Members serving districts in northern California, Massachusetts, New York City, and Chicago are reliably much more liberal than are members serving districts in eastern Oklahoma, Utah, Orange County in southern California, and Dallas. The set of issues on which Barbara Boxer (a Democratic senator from California) and Jim DeMint (a Republican senator from South Carolina) agree is small indeed. But even senators representing the same state often disagree about public policy. In the 111th Congress, 14 states had senators from different parties. Members who represent the same state and come from the same party regularly disagree about all sorts of issues. For example, Lindsey Graham and Jim DeMint, both Republican senators from South Carolina, differ on issues ranging from immigration to the maintenance of the Guantanamo Bay detention facility.

Even members who share a common ideological orientation may disagree about what constitutes the most pressing issue of the day. For example, both Zach Wamp and Don Young are conservative Republicans. Wamp, though, represents the third district in Tennessee, whereas Young represents the entire state of Alaska.[25] For Wamp, the key issues are the restoration of the Chickamauga Dam, the ongoing support of the Tennessee Valley Authority (one of the nation's largest government corporations), the support of tobacco farmers, and the introduction of Moccasin Bend into the National Park System. For Young, the protection of the Tongass National Forest, the protection of citizens' rights to bear arms, the regulation of the fishing industry, and the right to drill for oil in the Arctic National Wildlife Refuge stand out as the most important issues. Disagreements between Wamp and Young have considerably less to do with their political outlooks or party affiliations. Rather, they concern the importance of local issues and the legislative priorities of Congress.

There are even differences in members' concerns about reelection—the core issue that supposedly unites them. As previously mentioned, some members come from less competitive states and districts, whereas others expect to face stiffer competition at the next election. In addition, members of Congress come up for reelection at different times. Every two years, all House members must face the electorate. Senators, however, serve six-year, staggered terms, with one-third up for election in each election year. Senators from the same state never come up for reelection in the same year. Because they all follow the same electoral calendar, House members therefore find it easier to coordinate their activities with one another. Senators, by contrast, must deal with the fact that every other year, one-third of the Senate's members are distracted by an election, while the other two-thirds can afford to focus on the obligations of governance.

◄ GULF OIL SPILL CONCERNS
U.S. Senator David Vitter (R-LA) surveys the oil damage to the coastline of Louisiana. In your view, what responsibilities do members of Congress have in disaster relief efforts?

Members of Congress confront basic challenges.

Although all members of Congress care greatly about their reelection prospects, the things that help one member get reelected are not the same things that help another. Members must find ways of sorting through their differences in order to satisfy their different constituents and thereby retain their seats. Unfortunately, members of Congress—like members of any collective decision-making body—confront a set of problems that makes it difficult to work together.

Collecting information   Imagine the challenges facing members of Congress each session. They must keep track of changes in everything from the domestic economy to crime to international trade to transportation networks to wars around the world. Having canvassed all of these and many more policy domains, members then must identify the biggest problems facing the country and the best solutions. To do this, they need information—and lots of it.

Take, for example, the minimum wage. This would appear to be a simple issue, requiring members only to figure out whether they think it ought to be increased or decreased. Minimum wage legislation, however, consists of much more than a single line identifying the smallest hourly wage that employers can pay their workers around the nation. It is filled with exemptions and qualifications.[26] To complete the legislation, members must address all kinds of questions: Should there be a different minimum for teenagers and for adults? What about for those who rely on tips for much of their earnings? What about for noncitizens? Should the government provide financial assistance to industries, such as hotels and restaurants, that rely on large numbers of low-wage workers? If so, then how much and for how long? Should new rates take effect immediately or be phased in? What kinds of penalties should apply to employers who fail to pay at least a minimum wage? Should the rate depend on the cost of living? If so, how should it be calculated and how often should it be updated?

Lawmakers must consider myriad issues when they do something seemingly as simple as changing the minimum wage. Imagine, then, the challenges of writing laws that address U.S. trade relations with China, immigration reform with Mexico, or urban redevelopment. Individually, members of Congress would appear ill equipped for the challenge. Though they may have some expertise in a handful of issues—typically ones that directly concern their constituents—members often know very little about most substantive issues they must confront. They must first collect the information they need to write the nation's laws.[27]

Having collected the relevant information, lawmakers find that the legislative process has just begun. To enact legislation, members must convince one another about the benefits of their preferred policies. They must bargain and negotiate with one another. To do this effectively, members need to learn about each other's preferences, which we now know can differ dramatically. Members need to anticipate what others will accept, what they will reject, and what they are willing to compromise over. Lacking this additional information, members of Congress would find it virtually impossible to legislate.

Acting collectively   It takes time and money to collect the information needed to write laws and evaluate how they will affect districts, states, and the nation at large. Because members of

▼ SETTING A MINIMUM WAGE

For many, minimum wage legislation strictly defines the hourly earnings they can expect to receive. The legislation itself, though, is extraordinarily complex, requiring members of Congress to develop and analyze lots of information about different industries.

Congress have a relatively short period of time to build a record of accomplishments, they must decide how to allot their scarce resources. Not surprisingly, some would prefer to let other members commit the resources and then take undeserved credit for the solutions.

Though the benefits of lawmaking generalize to all members of Congress, the costs do not. Specifically, the costs fall disproportionately on those who devote their own resources to researching an issue, devising possible solutions, and then building the coalitions needed to enact a policy. This, though, creates a basic **collective action problem**, which arises from the mismatch of individual and group incentives. As a group, members of Congress want to devise solutions for the nation's problems; individually, though, members would prefer that others pay the costs of formulating these solutions. And, because every member, individually, would prefer that other members pay these costs, there is a substantial risk of inaction.

A simple example serves to illustrate the point. Picture a common college student housing arrangement: four students, four bedrooms, a shared living area, and a very messy kitchen. Each of the students would prefer that the kitchen be cleaned. If all four students committed to cleaning the kitchen on any given evening, they could complete the job in relatively short order. The trouble is that each one of these students would be even better off if the other three did the work, leaving the fourth free to watch television. Because this basic incentive incompatibility applies to all of the housemates, the dishes just pile higher and higher. The collective benefit of a clean kitchen is never realized because the costs fall on the poor loser who finally gives up and begins scrubbing. Herein lies the tragedy of collective action problems. All four students would be better off if they all chipped in; however, because each one would be even better off reaping the rewards without doing the work, the dishes are never done.

So it is with lawmaking. Collectively, members of Congress would be better off if everyone contributed equally; individually, though, each member would be even better off if everyone else did the work, leaving her or him free to pursue a personal agenda. The problem is even more acute than the simple example of a dirty kitchen. Whereas the average dorm houses a handful of students, Congress houses hundreds of members, whose behavior is difficult to monitor. Some may claim to be working on comprehensive tax reform, for example, when they are actually focused on projects that will benefit one or two powerful interests in their districts. Without a clear and effective way of monitoring behavior, it is extremely difficult to overcome collective action problems.

Cycling   Members have very different ideas about what constitutes good public policy. Consequentially, they often have a difficult time making final decisions about public policy. A majority of members—that is, a group of at least 50 percent—would prefer some alternative to the existing policy. A second majority—that is, a different group that contains at least some members from the first majority—will then prefer a different alternative to the one first proposed. Yet a third majority will prefer still another alternative to the one proposed second. The result, which political scientists refer to as **cycling**, is that members cannot settle on a single change to existing policy.

In the world of lawmaking, the list of possible policy alternatives is seemingly limitless. And because it is almost always possible to identify another version of a policy that a majority might prefer, debate could go on and on without a decision ever being reached. Members therefore must figure out a way to conclude debates so laws can be written and enacted.

collective action problem a problem that arises when individuals' incentives lead them to avoid taking actions that are best for the group as a whole, and that they themselves would like to see accomplished.

cycling a phenomenon that occurs when multiple decision makers must decide among multiple options and cannot agree on a single course of action.

Imposing Structure on Congress

13-4 Identify the resources and the committee and party structures that help Congress address its challenges.

To effectively do their jobs, members of Congress must find ways of collecting information, making sure everyone does their part, and resolving differences. For when members are left to their own devices, too often they work at cross purposes and fail to satisfy their constituents. Members have devised structural solutions to make Congress in many ways ideally designed to deal with the problems of information, collective action, and cycling.

Committees establish a division of labor.

In both the House and Senate, members are assigned to different committees that oversee distinct policy areas. These committees draft versions of bills, hold hearings about policy issues, and investigate activities in the executive branch. The names of these committees suggest the policy issues that their members focus on: Agriculture; Armed Services; Environment and Public Works; Foreign Relations; Health, Education, Labor, and Pensions; and Veterans' Affairs, to name but a few in the Senate.

Types of committees In the 111th Congress, there were 16 standing committees in the Senate and 20 in the House. **Standing committees** have well-defined policy jurisdictions, which do not change markedly from Congress to Congress. Standing committees also are the real workhorses of Congress, developing, writing, and updating the most important legislation. Table 13-1 lists all the standing committees in the 111th Congress. **Select committees**, by contrast, are designed to address specific issues over shorter periods of time. Typically, they cease to exist once their members have completed their assigned task. So, for instance, in 2005 the House created the Select Bipartisan Committee to Investigate the Preparation for and Response to Hurricane Katrina. The committee was to conduct "a full and complete investigation" of the responses of local, state, and federal governments to Hurricane Katrina. One month after filing its report, the select committee was disbanded.

Whereas separate standing and select committees operate in the House and Senate, **joint committees** draw members from both chambers. Similar to select committees, joint committees focus on fairly narrow issue areas, but unlike select committees, joint committees are permanent. For example, the Joint Committee on the Library oversees the Library of Congress, and the Joint Committee on Taxation monitors tax policy. Joint committees tend to be weaker than either standing or select committees. Rather than develop bills that either the House or Senate subsequently considers, a process we consider in detail below, joint committees typically act as fact-finding entities. As such, the primary purpose of joint committees is to address Congress's need to collect information.

Committees consist of smaller, and more specialized, **subcommittees**. For example, the U.S. Senate Committee on Banking, Housing, and Urban Affairs contains five subcommittees: Securities, Insurance, and Investment; Financial Institutions; Housing, Transportation, and Community Development; Economic Policy; and Security and International Trade and Finance. Subcommittees allow for an even greater division of labor, which encourages the production of still more information. Because of their small size, it is easier to monitor members' behavior within subcommittees, improving the chances that all members do their share of the work.

Legislatures in other countries are organized much the same way. The organization of Britain's Parliament, in fact, looks quite like Congress. Parliament consists of two

standing committee a permanent committee with a well-defined, relatively fixed policy jurisdiction that develops, writes, and updates important legislation.

select committee a temporary committee created to serve a specific purpose.

joint committee a committee made up of members of both chambers of Congress to conduct a special investigation or study.

subcommittee a smaller organizational unit within a committee that specializes in a particular segment of the committee's responsibilities.

TABLE 13-1. Standing Committees of the 111th Congress. Committees divide the labor of lawmaking across members of the House and Senate.

HOUSE OF REPRESENTATIVES			SENATE		
COMMITTEE	SUBCOMMITTEES	MEMBERS	COMMITTEE	SUBCOMMITTEES	MEMBERS
Agriculture	6	46	Agriculture, Nutrition, and Forestry	5	20
Appropriations	13	66	Appropriations	12	28
Armed Services	7	66	Armed Services	6	24
Budget	0	39	Banking, Housing, and Urban Affairs	5	20
Education and Labor	5	49	Budget	0	22
Energy and Commerce	5	58	Commerce, Science, and Transportation	7	22
Financial Services	6	72	Energy and Natural Resources	4	22
Foreign Affairs	7	49	Environment and Public Works	7	18
Homeland Security	6	34	Finance	5	20
House Administration	2	9	Foreign Relations	7	20
Judiciary	6	40	Health, Education, Labor, and Pensions	3	20
Natural Resources	5	52	Homeland Security and Governmental Affairs	6	16
Oversight and Government Reform	5	41	Judiciary	7	18
Rules	2	13	Rules and Administration	0	18
Science and Technology	5	44	Small Business and Entrepreneurship	0	18
Small Business	5	36	Veterans' Affairs	0	14
Standards of Official Conduct	0	10			

chambers, the House of Commons (akin to the House of Representatives) and the House of Lords (akin to the Senate). Within each chamber are a variety of standing and select committees, whose purposes are defined by the types of policy that they write and oversee. Like Congress, Parliament has committees that focus on education, health, foreign affairs, and public works. Parliament also has committees devoted to issues that are particularly important to the United Kingdom, such as the Northern Ireland Affairs Select Committee and the European Union Select Committee.

ThinkingComparatively

Legislatures in other countries also have multiple committees that oversee specific public policies.

Committee membership On average, senators serve on four committees and representatives serve on two. Committee members develop expertise in a handful of policy areas that they can share with their colleagues, who develop expertise in other policy areas. With such a division of labor, Congress as an institution is able to collect more and better information.

▲ COLLECTING INFORMATION IN HEARINGS

In the summer of 2010, Joint Chiefs Chairman Admiral Mike Mullen, Defense Secretary Robert Gates, and Pentagon Comptroller Robert Hale testify before the Senate Appropriations Committee hearing on the Defense Department's fiscal 2011 budget.

Given what we know about members' concerns about reelection, it should not come as a surprise that members of Congress try to serve on committees that oversee policies that their constituents care the most about. Members who have large concentrations of veterans and active military personnel in their districts will often serve on the Veterans' Affairs or Armed Services committees; members from the Midwest who represent farming interests will tend to serve on the Agriculture committees.[28]

Other committees attract members not because of the policies that they oversee, but rather because of the power that they wield. The appropriations committees—Ways and Means in the House and Finance in the Senate—deal with tax and spending issues, which concern all sorts of government programs. Similarly, the Commerce Committee in the House provides members with lots of opportunities to influence a broad array of public policies. Joining these committees gives members prestige and influence that can serve them well at the next election.

A chair, who is always from the party with a majority of seats in his or her chamber, oversees each committee and subcommittee. Because they set the agenda, schedule hearings, and call meetings, chairs often exert special influence. For much of the twentieth century, chairs were selected on the basis of **seniority**—that is, the length of time that they had served in office. From the perspective of information gathering, this makes perfect sense. The persons who had served the longest on a committee tended to have the most expertise. Putting them in charge, therefore, would seem the ideal arrangement.

Historically, though, the process of selecting chairs has attracted some controversy. For most of the post–World War II period, the Democratic Party retained control of

seniority the length of time a legislator has served in office.

the House and Senate. In part, this occurred because the South was essentially a one-party region, electing Democrats year in and year out. Because they did not face substantial competition, southern Democrats tended to hold office for longer periods of time than northern Democrats. Committee chairs, therefore, were usually southern Democrats. These southern Democrats also were much more conservative than their northern brethren, and they often used their powers as chairs in order to kill bills that they did not like. For example, in 1962, House Rules Committee Chair Howard W. Smith (D-VA) led a coalition of Republicans and fellow southern Democrats in undermining legislation that would have created a Department of Urban Affairs. Southerners joined their GOP colleagues in expressing opposition to bigger government. The southerners also appeared to have worried about the possibility that President John F. Kennedy, a Democrat, would nominate an African American for the new Cabinet-level post. Kennedy attempted to create the department with an executive reorganization order, which automatically would have gone into effect if neither chamber had vetoed it within 60 days. The coalition of Republicans and southern Democrats in the House of Representatives, however, swiftly rejected the plan by a vote of 262 to 150.[29]

In response to this kind of obstructionist behavior, northern Democrats in the late 1960s and early 1970s forced through two reforms. First, the senior committee member of the majority party was no longer guaranteed to be chair; thus, it became possible for northern Democrats to assume control over some committees. Second, important powers were transferred from committees to subcommittees, making it easier to jump-start legislative activity that a committee chair might not support. During this period, the number of subcommittees in Congress rose from roughly 40 to over 300.

Parties impose order on their members.

As the discussion of committee organization makes clear, the two major parties in the United States, Democratic and Republican, provide still more order to Congress. The parties determine who will control the various committees and subcommittees, and thus determine which core issues Congress will consider, which it will disregard, and how the debate will proceed. Through parties, coalitions in favor of one policy or another are formed. And within parties, strategies are developed to promote the policies that best serve their members' reelection prospects. Parties, in short, help to overcome the collective action and cycling problems that otherwise would cripple Congress.

Party leadership   At the beginning of each term, congressional Democrats and Republicans gather to select their leadership. For Democrats, the gathering is called the **party caucus**; for Republicans, it is the **party conference**. In the House, the party with the most seats elects the **Speaker of the House**, which is the only position in the House that the Constitution specifically mentions. In the Senate, the majority party selects the **majority leader**. In both chambers, the party with fewer seats selects the **minority leader**.

The Speaker of the House and the majority leader of the Senate perform many of the same functions. They preside over their chambers when they are in session, communicate with the White House about the progress of different bills, and act as congressional spokespersons. Because they decide which committees will consider which legislative proposals, they also help set the legislative agenda. If they strongly oppose a particular proposal, they often find ways of delaying its consideration by Congress as a whole.

For the most part, the Speaker of the House plays a more important role in overseeing affairs in the House than the majority leader does in the Senate. The reason has to do with the differences in the size and culture of the two chambers. Because

party caucus   the gathering of all Democratic members of the House or Senate.

party conference   the gathering of all Republican members of the House or Senate.

Speaker of the House   the person who presides over the House and serves as the chamber's official spokesperson.

majority leader   the individual in each chamber who manages the floor; in the Senate, he or she is the most powerful member in the chamber; in the House, he or she is the chief lieutenant of the Speaker.

minority leader   the individual who speaks on behalf of the party that controls the smaller number of seats in each chamber.

▶ **THE PRESIDENT AND PARTY LEADERS**

President Barack Obama, flanked by House Speaker Nancy Pelosi (D-CA) and House Majority Leader Steny Hoyer (D-MD), arrive at Capitol Hill for a meeting with the Democratic caucus. Shortly after the Democrats lost control of House in the fall of 2010, Pelosi announced her decision to stand for minority leader in the next Congress, and Hoyer announced his decision to run for minority whip.

the House has 435 voting members whereas the Senate has just 100, it is much more important to have a stronger leader in the House overseeing the business of the day.

Party discipline   Second in command in the House is the House majority leader, whose responsibility it is to unify the party caucus and help deliver the party's message to the public. The majority and minority party leaders of both parties also have **whips** who deliver messages from the leaders to the rank-and-file members, keep track of their votes, and encourage them to stand together on key issues. The term comes from "whippers-in," whose job it is to control the dogs in a fox hunt.

whips designated members of Congress who deliver messages from the party leaders, keep track of members' votes, and encourage members to stand together on key issues.

The efforts of the House majority leader and whips to get party members to vote together are generally successful. Take a look at Figure 13-3. Over the last half-century, less than 30 percent of Republicans and Democrats have voted against their parties on so-called "party votes," votes on issues that are especially important to their leaders. And the percentage continues to drop. In 2004, less than 10 percent defected on party votes.

ThinkingCausally

Do parties force members of Congress to behave differently from the way they would prefer?

Political scientists debate how party discipline is achieved. Some emphasize the powers of the party leadership to direct their members to vote in certain ways.[30] Leaders have a variety of means by which to punish members for defecting, such as cutting off financial aid to reelection campaigns. And, by controlling the legislative agenda, party leaders can keep divisive issues from ever coming up for a vote. Moreover, these scholars argue, members benefit from party discipline, since it helps them achieve their goal of enacting laws that will satisfy constituents.

Other scholars suggest that party leaders have very little to do with the decline of party defections.[31] Instead, party members vote together because they agree with one another. These scholars argue that there is little evidence that members of Congress systematically vote against their constituents' interests in order to toe the party line. Nor should members vote this way. After all, to vote against one's constituents is to

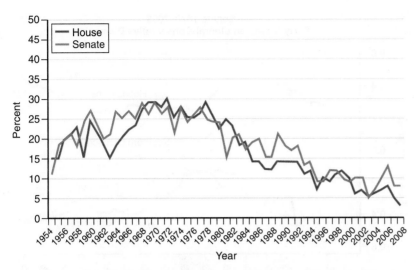

FIGURE 13-3. **Defections among Majority Party Members on "Party Votes," 1954–2008.** Since about 1970, both Democrats and Republicans in Congress vote with their party with increasing regularity.

Note: Southern Democrats not included in the analysis.

reduce one's chances of being reelected. By this account, the correlation between party positions and individual voting behavior is not causal but simply reflects the shared views of members of the same party.

In the United States, different parties can control the legislative and executive branches of government. In some other systems of government, however, they cannot. In the United Kingdom, for instance, executive and legislative powers are shared by one party. The party holding the majority of seats in the House of Commons (the lower chamber of Parliament) selects the nation's prime minister from within its own ranks, and the prime minister, in turn, often uses valuable positions in the Cabinet to reward loyal party members. Furthermore, the leaders of the Labour, Conservative, and Liberal Democratic parties wield substantial control over the distribution of campaign funds and the list of candidates who appear on the ballots. Although individual legislators occasionally defect on party votes, such defections are rare in the United Kingdom.

ThinkingComparatively

In parliamentary systems like that found in Britain, the same party controls both the executive and legislative branches. In presidential systems like that in the United States, however, different parties can control the two branches.

There has been a recent increase in party polarization.

One of the most striking trends in Congress during the past 30 years has been the increase in party polarization. As members have increased their tendency to vote together with their partisans, they in turn vote less frequently with members of the opposition party. As Figure 13.4 (page 478) shows, congressional Republicans in 2009 were significantly more conservative than they were in 1970. Northern congressional Democrats are slightly more liberal than their predecessors, and southern Democrats are much more liberal—largely because conservative southern Democrats, starting in the mid-1970s, switched parties and became Republicans.[32]

Why are Republican members of Congress more conservative, and Democratic members more liberal, than they were a generation ago? The question is especially

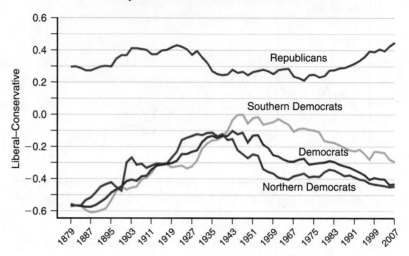

Senate 1879–2008
Party Means on Liberal-Conservative Dimension

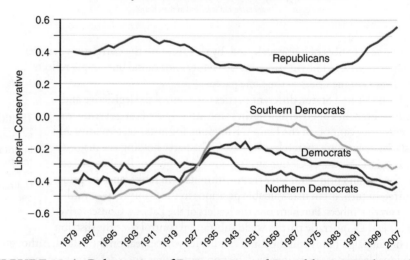

House 1879–2008
Party Means on Liberal-Conservative Dimension

FIGURE 13-4. **Polarization of Democratic and Republican Members of Congress, 1879–2008.** The two major parties are more polarized today than they have been in almost a century.

Note: The two major parties are more polarized today than they have been in almost a century. Here, we plot the average ideological score for Democratic and Republican members of Congress. Positive values indicate greater conservatism and negative values indicate greater liberalism.

ThinkingCausally

Why have Democrats and Republicans become more polarized over the past 30 years?

puzzling because there is very little evidence that citizens today are any more conservative or liberal than they were in 1970. According to one recent study, the root cause of this phenomenon is the rise in inequality around America.[33] Over the last century, partisan polarization has increased along with income inequality. It remains less clear, though, that inequality and polarization are causally related. Just because the two trends move together does not mean that inequality causes polarization. The authors of this study, in fact, recognize that the opposite might be true—polarization might generate inequality. They characterize the relationship between the two phenomena as one of "back and forth causality."

It is not clear whether party polarization strengthens or weakens democratic governance. On the one hand, polarized parties present voters with clear choices about different policy issues. And, with these clear choices, voters can more easily hold members of a party accountable for their performance in office. If they do not like the policies advanced by an incumbent, voters can shift their support to a challenger with reliably different policy positions. On the other hand, polarized parties can impede legislative processes. As William Galston laments, under conditions of rising polarization "Congress can become a haven for obstruction and gridlock rather than deliberation and compromise."[34] Moreover, as the two majorities drift to the extremes of the ideological spectrum, a rising share of the American public refuses to affiliate with either of them. Whereas 28 percent of the American public self-identified as independent in 1970, fully 36 percent did so in 2009.[35]

Although the rift between the Republican and Democratic parties in the United States has grown starker in recent years, polarization is not an overarching trend within democracies worldwide. In fact, a number of countries sustain three or more parties, offering different platforms in order to provide representation to diverse opinions about key political issues. The particular mix of parties in these democracies is constantly changing. Israel provides a recent and prominent example. In 2005, amid disagreements over his proposal to evacuate Jewish settlements in the Palestinian territories, then-prime minister Ariel Sharon withdrew from the conservative Likud Party and, with Shimon Peres of the liberal Labor Party, formed the backbone of a more centrist party called Kadima. Other democracies—such as France, Germany, and Canada—also sustain multiparty systems that offer voters wider options than does the United States.

ThinkingComparatively

In countries like Israel, France, Germany, and Canada, representatives from many different parties work within the legislature.

479

Staff and support agencies help collect and analyze information.

Members of Congress are assisted by roughly 11,000 staffers who perform all sorts of tasks, many of which concern the collection and analysis of information. On average, each senator has about 40 staffers working for him or her, and each House member has 17.[40] Some staffers work in a member's Washington, D.C., office, and others work back in the member's district or state. Those in D.C. tend to research public policies, write briefs, draft proposals, organize hearings, and interact with lobbyists. They also communicate with staffers for other members, helping to build coalitions in support of various policy initiatives. Staffers back home, meanwhile, interact with constituents about their concerns, their interests, and their ideas. These staffers then communicate this information back to the D.C. office.

Members also have access to several administrative agencies that provide vital information about public policy matters. The Congressional Research Service (CRS), established in 1914, handles hundreds of thousands of requests each year from members seeking information. Employees at CRS also take inventory of all the bills introduced in Congress and track their progress through the legislative process. The Government Accountability Office (GAO) also studies policy issues upon congressional request. Established in 1921, the GAO acts as an investigatory body for members who wish to know more about the spending habits of bureaucratic agencies. The Congressional Budget Office (CBO), established in 1974, provides members with information about the costs of policies that they are considering, the economic implications of different budget proposals, and the general state of the economy.

continued on page 482 ▶

HOW DO WE KNOW?

Has Congress Abdicated Its War-Making Authority?

The Question

The Constitution gives most war-making powers to Congress. Article I says that Congress shall have the power to declare war, raise and support armies, appropriate funds for war, and regulate the conduct of ongoing wars. By contrast, the war powers granted to the president are much shorter. Indeed, those Article II passages that refer explicitly to foreign policy merely identify the president as the commander in chief and authorize him to "receive ambassadors and other public ministers."

Today, though, the practice of war would not appear to follow the principles laid out in the Constitution. Most decisions about war are made by the president. And rarely does Congress formally restrict the president's ability to wage war abroad. Has Congress abdicated its war-making powers? How do we know?

Why It Matters

There is no greater government power than the ability to send citizens abroad to fight, kill, and perhaps die. For precisely this reason, the Founders worried a great deal about which branch of government would have the authority to wage war. If they vested too much authority

▼ CONGRESS'S WARS?

U.S. soldiers stand watch at the site of a bomb attack in Baghdad, Iraq, in January 2010. Article I of the Constitution grants members of Congress considerable authority over issues relating to war, including the funding of troops conducting ground-level operations. In overseeing the Iraq War, has Congress met its constitutional obligations?

in the president, the Founders worried that the system of checks and balances might one day collapse. As John Jay recognized in *Federalist 5*, "absolute monarchs will often make war when their nations are to get nothing by it, but for purposes and objects merely personal, such as a thirst for military glory, revenge for personal affronts, ambition, or private compacts to aggrandize or support their particular families or partisans." The Founders therefore looked to the legislative branch, which could be expected to better represent the will of the people in making decisions about war.

For much of U.S. history, this is exactly how decisions about whether to go to war were made. From the founding of the Republic to the mid-twentieth century, most major uses of force were approved by Congress. In the last half-century, though, the president has made most decisions involving war, and Congress has been pushed to the sidelines. If the Founders were right that war-making powers should not be entrusted to a president, then citizens ought to be greatly concerned about contemporary practice.

Investigating the Answer

One way to determine whether Congress has abdicated its war-making powers is to examine the declarations and actions of presidents and members of Congress. Who is setting the agenda, and who is following?

The answer appears clear: Congress has given up its war-making authority. After all, not since World War II has Congress formally declared war. It has authorized some wars (including the Vietnam, Persian Gulf, and Iraq wars) but not others (including the Korean War and conflicts in Panama, Kosovo, Bosnia, and Haiti).[36] Congress also has been reluctant to exercise its formal legislative and appropriations powers to influence wars that are under way. Though it has the constitutional authority to cut funding for a war, issue regular reports about a war's progress, and demand a withdrawal, Congress rarely takes advantage of these options—even when wars are unpopular.

In 1973, frustrated with the progress of the Vietnam War, members of Congress attempted to reassert their authority by passing the War Powers Resolution, which gave the president 60 to 90 days to secure formal authorization of a military deployment before troops would have to be withdrawn. Advocates believed the resolution would stop presidential incursions on congressional war powers and put members of Congress back in charge of decisions involving the use of military force. Instead, every president since the resolution was passed has refused to recognize its constitutionality. These presidents have launched one military initiative after another without securing congressional authorization. Only once, for Lebanon in 1983, was the War Powers clock even started; and then the president was granted an 18-month grace period. Rather than reestablishing Congress's constitutional role in matters involving war, says constitutional law expert Louis Fisher, the resolution "was a sellout, a surrender."[37]

More recently, political scientists have begun to examine subtle ways in which Congress nonetheless influences decisions about war. Though the president makes the case for war, members of Congress are not altogether silent. During the first three years of the Iraq War, for instance, members gave 5,000 speeches on the floors of the House and Senate. Such speeches, political scientists have shown, can have a profound impact on the ways in which the media cover a war, influencing the tone and content of news stories. By influencing the media, these speeches also can affect public opinion. And, over time, changes in public opinion can yield new governing majorities—as they did in 2006 when the Democrats regained control of the House and Senate, and in 2008 when the Democrats captured the White House.[38]

It also is difficult to interpret Congress's apparent reluctance to exercise its formal war-making powers. It could reveal weakness or strength. If presidents recognize that Congress is about to limit their war-making power, they may adjust their actions accordingly. In that case, congressional action may no longer be needed. Rather than demonstrating weakness, then, congressional silence sometimes might testify to the ongoing importance of the legislative branch in matters involving war.

Recent research also demonstrates that the partisan composition of Congress has important implications for the president's ability to wage war. Political scientists have observed the following patterns in military deployments following World War II: presidents whose party holds a large number of seats in the House and Senate tend to wage war more often than those whose party holds relatively few seats; presidents who enjoy lots of support within Congress tend to take military action more quickly.[39] The checks that Congress places on the president, then, are not constant. Rather, they vary according to the level of support that the president has.

Of course, partisan politics can be even more complicated when a war is passed off to a president of a different party. President Obama, a Democrat, inherited wars in Iraq and Afghanistan from former President Bush, a Republican. When these wars began, congressional Republicans almost uniformly supported them, while Democrats remained divided. Now Obama is the commander in chief, and in December 2009, he committed 30,000 additional troops to the war in Afghanistan. Speeches in Congress revealed the partisan strains that yesterday's decisions can place on today's politics. Both Republicans and Democrats appeared torn between the positions they had staked out under an earlier president and their allegiances to the current president. Republicans who called for more troops when Bush was president now went out of their way to criticize Obama's handling of the war, while Democrats who had previously contested the expansion of war made a point of complimenting Obama for the care and deliberation he exhibited in office.

Thinking Critically

- Has the emergent threat of terrorism made it more or less difficult for Congress to influence national decisions about the U.S. military?
- What kinds of members of Congress are likely to become most involved in debates about war?
- What kinds of evidence might demonstrate whether the work of these individuals influences the content of U.S. foreign policy?

The Bottom Line

The president's power to make decisions involving war has expanded dramatically during the past half-century, and congressional involvement in decisions involving war has declined. Congress, however, still represents an important check—arguably the most important check, at least domestically—on presidential war powers. The fact that military deployments tend to vary with the strength of the president's party in Congress says two important things about the domestic politics of war. First, Congress is a collection of diverse individuals with different assessments of the national interest and the value of war. Second, when evaluating how presidents conduct war or any other public policy, one must carefully monitor the ways in which they anticipate, and attempt to ward off, efforts by members of Congress to limit their authority.

Lawmaking

13-5 Outline the lawmaking process in Congress.

Members of Congress perform a variety of functions. As discussed in more detail in Chapter 16, they hold hearings and launch investigations to monitor goings-on in the executive branch. They help educate the public about the major issues of the day. They communicate with constituents and help resolve their problems. The single most important function that Congress serves, however, is to write the nation's laws.

The legislative process is long.

To become a law, a bill must travel a long road, which is outlined in Figure 13-5. To begin the process, a **sponsor** introduces a bill into either the House or Senate. Any member of Congress can serve as a bill's sponsor. A bill can originate in either chamber, and sometimes equivalent bills are introduced simultaneously to both.

sponsor a member of Congress who introduces a bill.

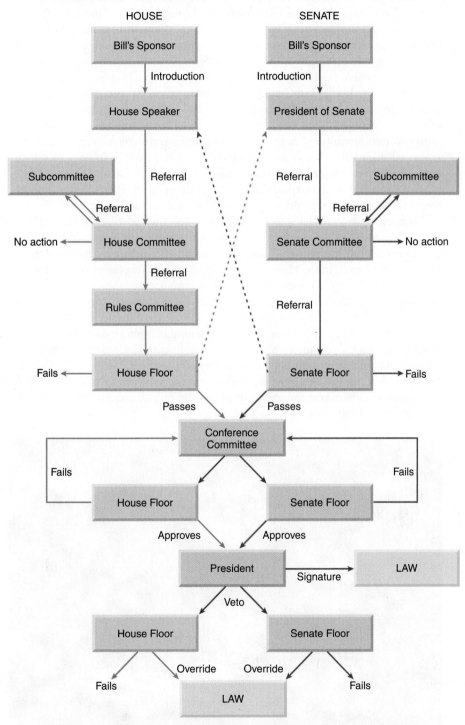

FIGURE 13-5. How a Bill Becomes a Law (or Not). The lawmaking process is long, and most introduced bills fail to become laws.

Subsequently, the bill must be referred to the appropriate committee for consideration. In the House, the Speaker decides which committee will take up the bill. In the Senate, the bill is assigned to a committee by the chamber's presiding officer, either the vice president or, more commonly, the president pro tempore. The president pro tempore is the most senior member of the majority party.

Bills typically are assigned to the committees that oversee the relevant policy domain. For example, bills on foreign conflicts are generally assigned to the Foreign Relations committee in the Senate and the Foreign Affairs committee in the House. Some bills are assigned to more than one committee—a practice called multiple referral.[41] In 2009, for example, the health care legislation that would mark the most significant legislative enactment of the 111th Congress was referred to three House committees: Ways and Means, Energy and Commerce, and Education and Labor. After assignment to one or more committees, a bill then is assigned to one or more subcommittees. The substance of a bill is typically first considered at the subcommittee level. Members of subcommittees carefully review the bill, holding hearings and conducting research on how it will likely affect their constituents and the nation as a whole. In a process called **markup,** members rewrite portions of the bill, delete others, and add still more. Once satisfied, the members then report the bill back to the full committee, whose members review the subcommittee's work and offer revisions of their own.

What happens next depends on which chamber is considering the bill. In the Senate, bills move straight from the committee of origin to the Senate floor, where the entire assembly of senators is given an opportunity to debate the merits of the proposed legislation. In the House, though, most bills coming out of committee are referred to the Rules Committee.[42] The Rules Committee decides how a bill will be debated on the floor by the entire membership of the House. It decides when the bill will go to the floor, how long members will debate the bill, and what kinds of amendments (if any) can be offered. When assigning an **open rule** to a bill, the Rules Committee allows for a wide range of amendments. Under a **closed rule**, the number and types of possible amendments are more restricted. Since bills assigned under an open rule can be altered significantly on the floor, supporters typically prefer a closed rule. Having completed its business, the Rules Committee then refers the bill to the House floor.

markup the process by which the members of a committee or subcommittee rewrite, delete, and add portions of a bill.

open rule the terms and conditions applied to a particular bill that allow members of Congress to make a wide range of amendments to it.

closed rule the terms and conditions applied to a particular bill that restrict the types of amendments that can be made to it.

▶ **MEETING THE PEOPLE**
Though congressional committees often solicit testimony from experts, they also meet with average citizens. In 2010, in the aftermath of a spate of accidents caused by sudden unintended acceleration in Toyota vehicles, a number of victims testified before the House Committee on Energy and Commerce.

On the floors of both the House and Senate, members typically give speeches about the bill, offer amendments (rules permitting, at least in the House), and eventually vote. To pass the House, a bill must receive the support of a majority of voting members. In the Senate, however, the threshold is somewhat higher. Technically, only a majority is needed to pass a bill. Any senator, though, may choose to **filibuster** a bill, which allows for indefinite debate. To end a filibuster—a process called invoking **cloture**—a supermajority of 60 votes is needed. If a majority of senators, but less than 60, support a filibustered bill, the bill will die.[43]

To become law, a bill must pass both chambers of Congress. But having gone through markups in subcommittees and committees and then having been subject to further amendments on the floor, Senate and House versions of the same bill often look quite different from one another at this stage. During the summer and fall of 2009, for example, Congress considered health care reforms that would increase coverage while curbing rising medical costs. The House version of the bill had language allowing government insurance, requiring employer responsibility, and creating subsidies for lower-income people, whereas the Senate's version did not. Such differences must be resolved before a bill becomes a law. Often, senators and representatives reconcile their differences informally. Party leaders play an important role in such negotiations, recommending elements of a bill to keep, to discard, and to amend. More formally, appointed members of each chamber serve on a **conference committee,** which has the job of producing a compromise version of the bill. Simple bills may have a relatively small conference committee, whereas complex and significant legislation may have hundreds of members serving on the conference committee. If conference committee members can come to an agreement—and sometimes they cannot—they send a revised version of the bill to the floors of the House and Senate, where it is subsequently voted on.

If the bill passes the House and Senate, it travels down Pennsylvania Avenue to the White House. The president can sign the bill, in which case it automatically becomes law. Alternatively, the president may **veto,** or reject, the legislation. Members can respond to a veto in three ways. First, they can refuse to reconsider the bill, in which case it dies. Second, they can make concessions to win over the president. In this case, both the House and Senate then vote on a new version of the bill, which is sent back to the president. Third, members can try to override the president's veto by securing the support of two-thirds of both houses. If they fail, the veto is sustained. Members of Congress may also select a combination of approaches. They might first write a revised version of a bill; if the president vetoes the bill again, they then might try to override him. If this fails, they may simply give up and move on to other issues.

Most bills are not enacted into law.

Traveling down this long legislative road, it is not surprising that bills often hit a pothole and veer onto an embankment. There are, after all, plenty of opportunities for a strategic politician, either working alone or with others, to derail a bill. Committees, minority factions in either the House or the Senate, and the president, too, can undermine the prospects of even those bills that enjoy the support of congressional majorities.

Let's begin with committees. Committee members who are assigned a bill they oppose could try to tailor the bill more to their liking or could refuse to do anything at all and "table" the bill indefinitely. This **gate-keeping authority** can give committees substantial power over the kinds of bills that come before the floor of either chamber. Despite the fact that a majority of either the House or the Senate, presumably, would like to see at least some of these bills enacted, in most congresses, upwards of 80 percent of all introduced bills never make it out of committee.[44]

filibuster a procedure by which senators delay or prevent action on a bill by making long speeches and engaging in unlimited debate.

cloture a mechanism by which 60 or more senators can end a filibuster and cut off debate.

conference committee a committee made up of members of both chambers that is responsible for ironing out the differences between House and Senate versions of a bill.

veto the president's rejection of a bill passed by both chambers of Congress, which prevents the bill from becoming law.

gate-keeping authority the power to decide whether a particular proposal or policy change will be considered.

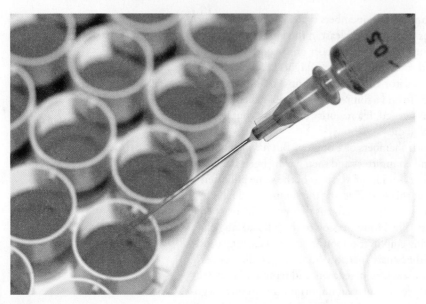

▲ STALEMATE

First in 2005 and again in 2007, Congress sent bills to President George W. Bush that would provide federal funding for medical research that uses human embryonic stem cells. Opposed to this research, Bush vetoed the Stem Cell Research Enhancement Acts of 2005 and 2007. In both instances, members of Congress sought to compromise with the president but could not reach common ground. To date, neither law has been enacted. In March 2009, President Barack Obama signed an executive order overturning Bush's ban on embryonic stem cell research. In August, 2010, however, a federal district judge issued an injunction blocking the use of federal funds for stem cell research.

Using a filibuster, just 41 opponents in the Senate can kill a bill—even if the other 59 senators and all 435 members of the House prefer to see it enacted. The filibuster is a powerful tool for minorities within Congress to check the powers of majorities, and minorities are making increasing use of it. During the first half of the twentieth century, only a handful of bills in each congressional session were subject to a filibuster. Beginning in the early 1970s, however, the average number increased to 22; during the 1990s, it increased to over 40.[45] During the 111th Congress, Republicans in the Senate threatened to filibuster numerous legislative initiatives. Indeed, the passage of health care reform in the winter of 2009, which is discussed at greater length in Chapter 14, hinged on the Democrats stitching together the necessary 60 votes to invoke cloture.

The president can often thwart the general interests of majorities in both chambers of Congress. If either chamber fails to override a presidential veto, a proposed bill fails to become law. During the nation's history, presidents have used this power with greater and greater frequency to influence the content of legislation. During the first half of the nineteenth century, presidents tended to use the veto power sparingly, and then only to ward off congressional efforts to usurp executive powers. By the middle of the twentieth century, however, presidents were not at all shy about vetoing bills they objected to on policy grounds. Not surprisingly, the vast majority of these vetoes were sustained. Almost every president has succeeded in having more than 75 percent of his vetoes upheld in Congress.[46]

Because lawmaking is so difficult, most bills are not enacted into law. As Figure 13-6 shows, between 1981 and 2004 roughly 10 percent of bills introduced to the House passed; even fewer were enacted into law. Though the figures fluctuate somewhat, enactment rates peaked at 11.4 percent (in 1987–1988), and bottomed out at 4.8 percent (in 1997–1998).

Not all bills that are enacted into law, however, follow the traditional path outlined in Figure 13-5. Indeed, a variety of parliamentary procedures enable members to occasionally circumvent the conventional approach. One such procedure is the "self-executing rule," colloquially called "deem and pass." First formulated in the House Rules Committee in the 1930s, deem and pass is a way of indirectly passing a bill through Congress without ever actually voting on it. If prior to the consideration of a bill the House votes in favor of a rule containing a self-executing provision, then passage of that rule ensures passage of the bill that it references. In other words, by adopting rules on how a bill would be debated on the floor, the House can treat the bill as if it had actually been voted on.

Since the 1930s, Republicans and Democrats alike have employed the self-executing rule. Although it was initially used as a way to make minor modifications to bills, deem and pass soon became a partisan tool to promote specific policies concerning immigration, smoking regulation, and the Internal Revenue Service.[47] Since the 95th Congress, over 200 self-executing rules have been used.[48] Most recently,

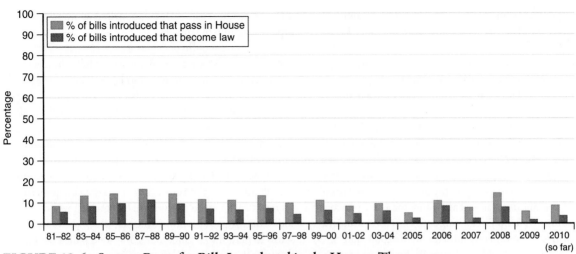

FIGURE 13-6. **Success Rates for Bills Introduced in the House.** The vast majority of bills introduced in Congress do not make it through the House; an even lower percentage of bills actually become law.

during the 2010 congressional debate over the health care bill, House Democrats toyed with the idea of using the self-executing rule in order to approve the Senate's version of the bill without ever voting on it. Ultimately, however, Speaker Pelosi opted against the measure, as Democrats realized that the scope of the bill was too broad for such maneuvers.[49]

Altogether different parliamentary procedures and political machinations were needed to enact health care reform in 2010. When Scott Brown, a Republican, won a special Senate election in Massachusetts in early 2010, prospects for enacting health care reform looked dim. By losing this one seat, Senate Democrats no longer had the votes they needed to overcome a threatened filibuster. To enact health care reform, therefore, Democrats would need to pursue some alternative to the traditional legislative process. They settled on the following: rather than hammering out differences in the House and Senate versions of the bill in conference committee and then revoting in each chamber, as is typically done, the House simply passed the Senate's version of the bill, which then went to the president for signature. To deal with a variety of objections to this law, meanwhile, Congress voted a separate set of "fixes" under a budget reconciliation, which requires only a majority of votes in both chambers and thereby avoids the threat of a Senate filibuster. Furthermore, to placate a handful of pro-life Democrats in the House, President Obama issued a separate executive order that reiterated language in the statute prohibiting the use of federal funds to pay for abortions.

CaseStudy: Immigration Reform

Today the Census Bureau reports more foreign-born residents—33 million—than ever before in its history. Some estimate that 12 million are in the country illegally, with that number growing by an average of 400,000 per year. Moreover, over 7 million of these illegal immigrants are employed, accounting for nearly 5 percent of the country's civilian labor force and constituting substantial portions of such industries as construction and agriculture.[50] More than once, Barack Obama has expressed his intention to address the various problems associated with illegal immigration and undocumented workers. As a candidate in 2008, Obama pledged to make immigration reform one of his top priorities during his first term as president. "Well, I don't know about you," he said, "but I think it's time for a president who won't walk away from comprehensive immigration reform when it becomes politically unpopular."[51] In a Cinco de Mayo speech in 2010, President Obama reiterated his commitment to enacting immigration reform: "I want to begin work this year, and I want Democrats and Republicans to work with me—because we've got to stay true to who we are, a nation of laws and a nation of immigrants."[52]

To date, however, Congress has not cooperated. In the spring and summer of 2010, with hundreds of thousands of gallons of oil pouring into the Gulf of Mexico as a result of a broken British Petroleum rig, Senate Majority Leader Harry Reid (D-NV) opted to prioritize the passage of a climate bill instead.[53] Perhaps this was well and good, for as the previous president learned in 2007, enacting comprehensive immigration reform is extraordinarily difficult. In his 2007 State of the Union Address, President George W. Bush proposed an overhaul of immigration rules, "without amnesty and without animosity," as one of four domestic policy priorities for the remainder of his second term. Though several previous immigration reform efforts had failed, Bush appeared hopeful that things this time would be different. In the 2006 midterm elections, control of the House and Senate switched to the Democrats, who looked more favorably upon the kinds of immigration reforms that Bush supported. During the spring, Bush sent Commerce Secretary Carlos Gutierrez and Homeland Security Secretary Michael

Chertoff to undertake closed-door deliberations with a bipartisan group of senators.

After three months of deliberation, Gutierrez, Chertoff, and members of Congress produced a draft bill. The proposed Comprehensive Immigration Reform Act of 2007 downplayed deportation and instead offered a path to citizenship for illegal immigrants. In an attempt to appease conservatives, the draft also outlined changes in the criteria for processing visa applications, created a business-backed guest worker program, and promised to bolster enforcement of immigration laws.

Senate Majority Leader Harry Reid agreed to introduce the bill directly to the Senate floor, bypassing the Judiciary Committee. Supporters mustered 66 votes in favor of the most controversial portion of the bill, which offered legal status to most illegal immigrants. But Reid pulled the bill from the floor on June 7, after three successive votes for cloture failed and only seven Republicans agreed to close debate. On June 26, the Senate voted 64–35 to reconsider the proposal, but two days later another cloture motion fell short, killing the bill.

Experts generally agree that the current immigration system is broken. Why, then, did the president's and Congress's reform efforts falter? A number of reasons emerge. For starters, the bill's opponents expressed their views more forcefully than did its proponents. As one researcher put it, the bill was "born an orphan in terms of

▶ **FAILING TO ACT**

To date, Congress has failed to pass comprehensive immigration reform of any kind. As a result, some states have taken it upon themselves to do so. Arizona's action on the matter in 2010 evoked widespread protests from supporters of immigration. In your view, how should Congress address the issue of immigration? And should the states have any say in the matter?

popular support."[54] A substantial portion of Americans did not feel strongly about the issue. Illegal immigrants could not vote, and their American employers, afraid of calling attention to their employment of undocumented workers, tended not to trumpet their support for amnesty. Opponents, by contrast, let their voices be heard, making well over 250,000 contacts with U.S. senators during the run-up to the June 28 vote.[55]

Disagreements between Democrats and Republicans about the immigration issue also made it difficult for Congress to enact needed reform. To make the U.S. economy less of a magnet for undocumented workers, both sides agreed to help employers fill jobs with government approved temporary laborers. However, many Republicans insisted that those workers eventually must leave, while many Democrats wanted to allow them to stay and become citizens. In an effort to strike a deal, the Senate draft outlined a path to citizenship for illegal immigrants as well as a number of hurdles, such as fines, waiting periods, and a merit-based application system. Nonetheless, most Republicans rejected anything that resembled amnesty, while Democrats balked, insisting that the U.S. visa system should do more to keep immigrant families together rather than to attract high-skilled workers.[56]

The immigration debates also revealed divisions within the two major parties. The desire of most Democrats to naturalize immigrants put them at odds with labor unions, while the inclination of most Republicans to send workers home pitted them against business owners. Labor unions maintained that foreign laborers drove down wages for American workers, while businesses argued that sending these laborers home would disrupt operations and increase production costs.[57]

A weakened presidency may also have contributed to the bill's failure. With low approval ratings, a controversial war in Iraq, and poor results in the 2006 midterm elections, President Bush could not overcome the objections of Republican members of Congress. As one moderate Republican dissenter, Representative Steve Pearce of New Mexico, put it: "I trust him, but I'm not going to vote for the bill as it currently stands. Out here, we have a saying, 'Trust your neighbor, but brand your cattle,' and the president will understand that."[58]

Immigration reform, then, ended in collapse rather than compromise. Members of both parties, as well as the executive and legislative branches, bemoaned the failure but were unable to prevent it. Without highlighting his own party's role in killing the bill, President Bush expressed disappointment in Congress's "failure to act."[59] But Senate Majority Leader Harry Reid may have summarized it best: "The big winner today was obstruction; the big winner today was inaction."[60]

ThinkingCritically

1. How does the fact that illegal immigrants cannot vote figure into the politics of immigration reform?

2. Why were some of President Bush's strongest critics members of his own party?

Laws, nonetheless, are enacted.

Just because lawmaking is difficult does not mean that it is impossible. In a typical year, Congress enacts several hundred laws. Though most of these laws concern rather mundane affairs, at least some have profound policy consequences. According to one study that categorized legislation into four different categories of significance, Congress each year enacts roughly 5 "landmark" laws, 6 "major" laws, 36 "ordinary" ones, and no less than 314 "minor" laws.

Political scientists have tried to determine the mix of political factors most likely to result in successful legislation. One of the most powerful predictors is the strength of the majority party's control in the House and Senate. When Democrats or Republicans control both chambers of Congress by wide margins, they find it much easier to overcome the various institutional challenges that derail so many bills. The single most productive Congress during the last half-century operated from 1965 to 1966. During this period, when Democrats maintained a whopping 295 seats in the House and 68 in the Senate, Congress enacted such landmark legislation as Medicare and Medicaid, the Immigration Act, the Elementary and Secondary Education Act (ESEA), the Housing and Urban Development Act, the Voting Rights Act, the Freedom of Information Act, and the National Traffic and Motor Vehicle Safety Act, to name but a few.

Though most laws live on indefinitely, laws with **sunset provisions** must be reauthorized after a specified number of years. The 2001 No Child Left Behind Act, the enactment of which is described in some detail in Chapter 14, was a reauthorization of

sunset provision a condition of a law that requires it to be reauthorized after a certain number of years.

the 1965 ESEA Act, which must be reconsidered by Congress every seven years. Given that existing laws maintain programs that are already up and running, that they have received political support in the past, and that they come up for formal consideration in a specified year, they are more likely to pass than other legislation. Moreover, Congress need not reauthorize these laws for full terms. Indeed, though the No Child Left Behind Act came up for reauthorization in 2008, Congress for two consecutive years put off amending, overturning, or formally authorizing the program for another seven.

The Appropriations Process

13-6 Outline the appropriations process.

The work of Congress is not complete after it enacts a law. Congress subsequently must commit funds so that the law can be set in motion. Every year, Congress uses money from the Treasury Department to fund federal agencies and programs.[61] According to Article I, section 9, of the Constitution, "no money shall be drawn from the treasury, but in consequence of appropriations made by law." But besides stipulating that "a regular statement and account of receipts and expenditures of all public monies shall be published from time to time," the Constitution has left most of the specifics to the legislature itself.

Spending is a two-step process.

authorization the granting of legal authority to operate federal programs and agencies.

appropriations the granting of funds to operate authorized federal programs and agencies.

Two steps must be taken for monies to make their way to different agencies and programs. First, these programs and agencies must receive **authorization** by the legislation that serves as the legal basis for their continued operation. The second step is **appropriations**, the actual granting of funds to federal agencies and programs. Authorization committees help determine the kinds of programs within their legislative jurisdiction that will be funded; appropriations committees determine the exact amounts of monies to be disbursed.

In principle, authorizations and appropriations are kept separate in order to reduce the chances that members of Congress will use federal monies to alter the actual operations of federal agencies and programs. In practice, though, the distinction between authorizations and appropriations often blurs—in part, because appropriations committee members make quite a habit of using limitations on the use of funds as a way to legislate indirectly. The phrase "none of the funds shall be used for . . ." has become an increasingly prominent feature in appropriations bills, effectively changing policy in spite of the prohibition against writing legislation in appropriations committees.[62]

Nonappropriations committees also use authorizing legislation to grant permanent budget authority to programs and agencies. As a result, a sizable fraction of each year's federal budget is dedicated to mandatory spending (often called entitlements) on these past obligations. The largest entitlements include such massive programs as Social Security, Medicare, and Medicaid, all of which are discussed at length in Chapter 17. The remainder of the budget—the portion not already promised elsewhere and therefore available for discretionary spending on new obligations—is the subject of deliberations within the appropriations committees.[63] Over time, a rising tide of entitlements has steadily shrunk the discretionary portion of the budget, reducing it to approximately 40 percent in fiscal year 2005.[64] Given that the federal budget is well over $2 trillion, however, this still leaves appropriations committees with a considerable amount of money to disburse.

Over time, a rising tide of entitlements has steadily shrunk the discretionary portion of the budget, reducing it to approximately 40 percent in fiscal year 2005.

Members also use **earmarks** to bypass executive agencies altogether and direct funds straight to their constituents. According to one watch-dog organization, Congress disclosed over 11,000 earmarks worth almost $15 billion in the 2008 fiscal year.[65] Texas alone received $2.2 billion in earmarks, including $294,000 for a Houston zoo program and $22 million for an army gymnasium near El Paso.[66] Facing substantial criticism for funding these "pork barrel" projects, the House in January 2007 passed new rules requiring public lists of every earmark, the recipient's name and address, and the individual who requested it.[67] Nevertheless, the practice is unlikely to disappear in the near future. Earmarks enable members of Congress to deliver benefits directly to their constituents, to take decisions out of the hands of executive officials, and to make bills more popular and passable.

What seems like pork to some citizens are essential services for others. Many legislators argue that earmarks support vital public works projects. Constituents benefit when their representatives obtain money to repair their roads and bridges, or to fund state colleges and universities, and community recreations centers. The positive aspects of regular earmarks, however, are occasionally outshined by reports of abuse. An infamous example from the 2008 presidential election is the Alaskan "Bridge to Nowhere" project that would have cost $398 million to connect the 50 residents living on Gravina Island to the mainland.

There have been many efforts to curb the use of earmarks. In 2006, Congress passed the Federal Funding Accountability and Transparency Act that, among other things, established a searchable database of earmarks.[68] More recently, President Obama proposed guidelines aimed to further increase transparency in the earmarking process, including a provision that requires members of Congress to publish their earmarks on their websites. Some lawmakers argue that Obama's guidelines, like past reform efforts, simply "fine-tune a fundamentally flawed process."[69]

Appropriations come in three forms.

There are three main types of appropriations. **Regular appropriations** are the main source of revenues that are disbursed to agencies and programs. Regular appropriations contain three standard features: an enacting clause that designates the fiscal year for which funds are given, a breakdown of budget authority by accounts, and general provisions that apply to all of the accounts. Small agencies might possess only one account, but larger ones usually are financed by several distinct accounts, designated with names such as "procurement" or "salaries and expenses." In general, agencies can "reprogram" funds (shift budget authority from one activity to another within a single account) by going through the proper notification and oversight channels. However, they cannot "transfer" funds (shift budget authority from one account to another) without statutory authorization.

A second type of appropriations is a **continuing resolution**, which disburses funding when regular appropriations have not been set by the close of the fiscal year on October 1. Continuing resolutions have become quite common. In fact, between 1977 and 2006, Congress and the president completed all of the regular appropriations on schedule only four times.[70] Traditionally, continuing resolutions were brief measures listing the agencies that had not yet received their regular funding and providing temporary assistance at the previous year's level or the president's budget request, whichever was lower. Today, however, continuing resolutions increasingly include omnibus measures that cover several of the regular appropriations bills at once.

Congress also provides **supplemental appropriations**, the third type, when regular appropriations do not cover certain activities or are deemed insufficient. In order to evade spending caps, Congress sometimes designates supplements as emergency funds. Franklin D. Roosevelt's New Deal used supplemental appropriations to

earmarks federal funds that support specific local projects.

regular appropriations the standard mode by which federal moneys are allotted to programs.

continuing resolution funds used to keep programs up and running when regular appropriations have not been approved by the end of the fiscal year.

supplemental appropriations the process by which Congress and the president can provide temporary funding for government activities and programs when funds fall short due to unforeseen circumstances.

create new government agencies and create new jobs. During World War II, the government used this type of appropriation to accelerate the production of fighter planes and other war weapons. In 2009, President Obama's economic stimulus package contained supplemental appropriations to stabilize the economy and preserve jobs. Much of the Iraq War has been funded not through regular defense appropriations but through a series of supplemental appropriations. Economists estimate that the upfront cost of the Iraq War was around $12 billion a month, as of March 2008, mostly consisting of emergency appropriations.[71] Many of the appropriations have gone toward operational costs, replacing military equipment, and caring for veterans.[72]

The appropriations process differs from the legislative process.

The process of appropriating federal funds looks quite a bit like the legislative process. Suggested appropriations are debated and marked up within committees, considered on the floors of the House and Senate, reconciled across chambers, and eventually sent to the president. In two important respects, however, the appropriations process differs from the lawmaking process.

First, appropriations are purposefully streamlined. Whereas a failure to legislate may disappoint key constituencies, a failure to appropriate funds can bring the federal government to a grinding halt. And, because appropriations are required every year, members of Congress have a vested interest in minimizing the procedural roadblocks—such as the Senate filibuster—that they are likely to encounter.

Second, the appropriations process is supposed to follow a strict timetable. The president initiates the process by submitting his annual budget proposal to Congress on or before the first Monday in February. The full House and Senate appropriations committees then have the option of conducting overview hearings to discuss the proposal with the Office of Management and Budget. From February to April, agencies meet with the relevant appropriations subcommittees to justify the difference between their newly requested amounts and the previous year's allotments. By April 15, Congress passes a resolution that determines the federal budget for the next five fiscal years and allocates that year's budget among all of its committees.

In May and June, the House chair, subcommittees, and lastly the full appropriations committee mark up the proposals, reporting regular bills to the entire House by July. The House debates, considers amendments, passes the bills, and sends them to the Senate, which passes the bills (perhaps with amendments) before the August congressional recess. In September, members of both chambers' appropriations committees hold conferences to resolve any remaining differences. Usually the House considers the conference report first, and the Senate decides whether to accept or reject the House's report. Once the two chambers have settled on the final appropriations bills, they are sent to the president, who has 10 days to sign or veto them in their entirety.

In practice, Congress and the president rarely abide by this strict schedule. In some years, the legislature does not pass the budget resolution by the April 15 deadline, delaying transmittal of explicit spending ceilings to the appropriations committees. In fact, in fiscal years 1999, 2003, and 2006, Congress did not complete the resolution at all. Rather than responding to the House's passed bills, the Senate sometimes creates its own proposals, which are inserted into the House bills as "amendments." Hampered by the August recess, the chambers might not resolve their differences by October 1. Last but not least, the president could kill the bill, either explicitly or, if Congress has adjourned, by taking no action within the 10-day timeframe. In December 1995, for example, Bill Clinton vetoed the reconciliation bill that would have enacted Republican-backed tax cuts and curtailed spending on social programs. When Congress failed to override the president's veto, portions of the federal government temporarily shut down.

CHAPTER SUMMARY

In this chapter you have learned to:

13-1 Outline the basic structure of Congress. As a bicameral institution, the U.S. Congress has two chambers: the House of Representatives and the Senate. Members in the House serve for two years, and Senators serve for six. Whereas members of the House represent congressional districts, Senators represent entire states. The Senate also has some duties (such as the ratification of treaties and approval of Supreme Court nominees) that members of the House do not have.

13-2 Analyze the relationship of members of Congress to their constituencies, and distinguish between the trustee and delegate model of representation. Congress represents the interests of some citizens more than others. Above all, members of Congress want to be reelected, and to be reelected, they must adequately represent the interests of their constituents. Depending on whether members follow a trustee or delegate model of representation, their relationship with their constituents will differ dramatically. Moreover, members do not represent all constituents equally. Depending on whether they vote, are organized, are Democrats or Republicans, or fit a certain demographic profile, some constituents receive more or less representation by the member of Congress who serves their district or state.

13-3 Assess the challenges that emerge when members of Congress set about working together. Members of Congress face important challenges when working together. They have different interests, priorities, and worldviews. To build a record of accomplishments that will serve them well at the next election, members of Congress must effectively navigate these differences. Additionally, they must overcome problems of information, collective action, and cycling that emerge when decisions require the participation of multiple members.

13-4 Identify the resources and the committee and party structures that help Congress address its challenges. The resources and structures that define Congress as an institution alleviate the challenges. Members of Congress have staffs that help collect information. They serve on committees and subcommittees that establish a division of labor. And most members belong to one of the two dominant parties, which provide further structure.

13-5 Outline the lawmaking process in Congress. The lawmaking process is long and difficult. To become a law, a bill must pass through multiple committees and subcommittees in both the House and Senate, the floors of both chambers, and a conference committee, before it lands on the president's desk for signature. Even then, though, the president may veto the bill, in which case it returns to Congress for reconsideration. Not surprisingly, most proposed bills fail to become law. Nonetheless, Congress does manage to enact laws on a regular basis—sometimes because its members agree about the solution to a particular problem, and sometimes because the business of the day (appropriations and reauthorizations) requires them to set about finishing the task.

13-6 Outline the appropriations process. The appropriations process differs from the lawmaking process. Because budgets must be approved every year, appropriations usually are easier to set than laws are to enact. Some of the roadblocks to lawmaking are eliminated, the budget has a permanent place on the congressional agenda, and the processes themselves are routinized. Still, delays are common. Increasingly, Congress has had to rely on continuing and supplemental appropriations to keep the government running.

PEARSON mypoliscilab **EXERCISES**

Apply what you learned in this chapter by starting with these resources on MyPoliSciLab.

Read on mypoliscilab.com
   eText: Chapter 13

Study and Review on mypoliscilab.com
   Pre-Test
   Post-Test
   Chapter Exam
   Flashcards

Watch on mypoliscilab.com
   Video: Kagan Hearing
   Video: Unknown Wins South Carolina Senate Primary

Explore on mypoliscilab.com
   Simulation: You Are a Member of Congress
   Simulation: How a Bill Becomes a Law
   Comparative: Comparing Legislatures
   Timeline: The Power of the Speaker of the House
   Visual Literacy: Congressional Redistricting
   Visual Literacy: Why Is It So Hard to Defeat an Incumbent?

KEY TERMS

CHAPTER TEST

1. How do structural differences between the Senate and House explain differences in behavior of those people who work in the two chambers of Congress?

2. What kinds of things can members of Congress do to increase their chances of being reelected?

3. When members of Congress challenge the president over matters involving war, are they behaving more consistently with the delegate model of representation or the trustee model? Why?

4. How do congressional committees help address the challenges of collecting information?

5. How do parties reduce collective action problems in Congress?

6. As long as a bill retains the support of a majority of members of Congress, will it necessarily be enacted into law?

7. How can the president influence the content of legislation?

8. Why do members of the same party typically vote the same way on legislative initiatives?

9. Through what mechanism does Congress direct funds to relief efforts for unforeseen emergencies?

10. In what ways is the appropriations process easier to navigate than the legislative process?

SUGGESTED READINGS

R. Douglas Arnold. 1992. *The Logic of Congressional Action*. New Haven: Yale University Press. Explores how legislation emerges from the individual incentives of members of Congress and the nature of different public policy problems.

Richard Fenno. 2002. *Homestyle: House Members in Their Districts*, new ed. New York: Longman. A classic examination of the relationship between members of Congress and their constituents.

David Mayhew. 2004. *Congress: The Electoral Connection*, 2nd ed. New Haven: Yale University Press. The classic statement on how members' concerns about reelection help explain their behavior in Congress.

Walter Oleszek. 2007. *Congressional Procedures and the Policy Process*, 7th ed. Washington, DC: CQ Press. Summarizes the rules and institutions that make up Congress.

Allen Schick. 2007. *The Federal Budget: Politics, Policy, Process*, 3rd ed. Washington, DC: Brookings Institution. Provides a comprehensive overview of the appropriations process.

Charles Stewart. 2001. *Analyzing Congress*. New York: Norton. Surveys the ways in which individual members act strategically to accomplish their objectives within Congress.

SUGGESTED WEBSITES

Library of Congress, Thomas: thomas.loc.gov

Includes a tremendous amount of information about the legislative process, including a searchable database of bills introduced to the House or Senate in recent congresses.

U.S. Senate: www.senate.gov
Official website of the U.S. Senate.

U.S. House: www.house.gov
Official website of the U.S. House.

C-SPAN: www.c-span.org

Includes a rich array of video footage of congressional debates, hearings, and investigations.

Congressional Research Service: opencrs.com

Access reports on a wide range of policy and political issues that are produced for members of Congress.

Surrounded by Challenges

"It has been a long time coming, but tonight, because of what we did on this date, in this election, at this defining moment, change has come to America."[1]

President-elect Barack Obama's words soared out to the crowd of 125,000 people gathered in Grant Park, Chicago, to celebrate the election of the new president of the United States. With the election of the nation's first African American president, expectations, particularly among young voters and intellectuals, ran high. Ban Ki-moon, UN secretary general, expressed his hopes after the vote: "I am confident that we can look forward to an era of renewed partnership and a new multilateralism. If ever before there were a time for the world to join together, it is now."[2]

As Obama concluded a campaign whose signature theme was "change," the nation remained mired in two wars and confronted a domestic economy in freefall. Much as he might have liked, he could not turn immediately to the domestic policy reforms that had figured so prominently in his campaign. He would admit one year later, "We have inherited the biggest set of challenges of any U.S. presidents since Franklin Delano Roosevelt."[3] In politics, the urgent often trumps the favored.

Presidents must manage an agenda in an uncooperative political world. They are responsible for setting and striving to meet the goals they campaigned on, while dealing with all the other issues that emerge when they are in office. By both today's public and tomorrow's historians, presidents are judged on how they balance their promises with their obligations.

In his inaugural address, President Obama outlined his plan for the nation. America, he promised, would rise from the ashes of the previous presidency and return to the world scene with a renewed image and reputation. By reducing troop commitments in Iraq, reaching out to the Muslim world, and increasing aid to the world's poorest, the United States would usher in a new era of peace. Domestically, Obama promised a drastic shift toward alternate forms of energy as well as a restructuring of the educational system with a renewed emphasis on science and technology.

Before he could do any of this, though, Obama had to stabilize a domestic economy in freefall. In February 2009, he pushed the Recovery and Reinvestment Act through

▼ A DELUGE OF CHALLENGES

Presidents are expected to identify and then offer solutions to every conceivable social problem. Here in June 2010, President Barack Obama spoke with Governor Charlie Crist of Florida about the environmental damage wrought by the British Petroleum oil spill.

Congress in an attempt to stimulate the depressed economy. The stimulus package was the largest in U.S. history, injecting $787 billion into the economy in the form of tax breaks, subsidies, and investments.

Obama's ability to immediately deliver on his earlier campaign promises was further limited by the paucity of formal powers granted to the president. The Constitution merely gives the power to veto legislation and appoint bureaucrats and judges, subject to the Senate's confirmation. For the most part, individuals outside the White House hold the responsibilities for writing, interpreting, and implementing

laws. Thus, to get things done, this current president, like all who preceded him, must curry their favor.

Realizing the promise of change is made all the more difficult by the intense and interminable scrutiny cast upon the president. Every appointment, speech, veto, executive order, and official visit attracts attention and debate. Like it or not, the president is the figure head of the federal government—and no matter how much praise he may garner for one decision, he always is at risk of shouldering blame the moment things go wrong.

In a speech delivered in Cairo, Egypt, in the fall of 2009, Obama

observed, "We have the power to make the world we seek, but only if we have the courage to make a new beginning, keeping in mind what has been written." Courage—yes, as a start.

But as we will learn in this chapter, it will also require a host of other qualities, both formal and informal, that are available to American presidents. And, as we shall soon see, successful leadership and the realization of change further depend upon the president's ability to rally support among the public and political actors that themselves have their own, independent bases of authority.

CHAPTER LEARNING OBJECTIVES

After reading this chapter you will be able to:

14-1 Trace the Constitutional origins and historical expansion of presidential power.

14-2 Distinguish between the formal and informal powers of contemporary presidents.

14-3 Analyze how presidents use public support, electoral victories, and congressional allies to push through their policies.

14-4 Assess the role of the Cabinet, the Executive Office of the President, and the White House staff in assisting the president.

Presidential Authority and Leadership

14-1 Trace the Constitutional origins and historical expansion of presidential power.

Americans project their hopes on the presidency. They expect their president to develop a legislative program and convince others to enact it. They expect the president to have, articulate, and defend policy ideas, all while unifying the country. They expect him (someday her), in the most general sense, to provide peace, prosperity, stability, and security. People want to feel that the country's leader has a plan, and they will credit him with good leadership if they believe that events are occurring in line with his plan. They want their leader to convey a firm sense of direction about his goals and priorities and the principles that will govern his decision-making. They want him to use the authority granted by the Constitution and historical precedent as he carries out his plan. (For qualities that the public considers "absolutely essential" in a president, see Figure 14.1.)

In the last half-century, an avalanche of expectations has fallen at the White House doorstep. When the *Challenger* space shuttle exploded in 1986, when terrorists attacked on September 11, 2001, when Hurricane Katrina devastated New Orleans and the Gulf Coast in 2005, and when hundreds of thousands of gallons of crude oil poured out of a busted British Petroleum rig in the Gulf of Mexico in 2010, the country turned to the president for reassuring words, for due expressions of outrage, for signs that the country was strong and would persevere. And in calmer

ThinkingComparatively

The president needs to combine the unifying role of head of state and the divisive role of head of government, but many other countries prefer to assign these roles to two different individuals.

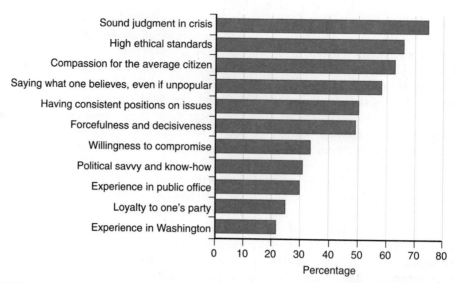

FIGURE 14-1. **"Absolutely Essential" Qualities in a President.** Presidential success in Congress is generally higher when the president's party has a majority in both houses of Congress. This chart shows the qualities the public thinks are "absolutely essential" in a president. The public is more concerned with a president's character and temperament than political or governmental experience.

times, citizens look to the president, more than anyone else, for guidance on the basic policy priorities that are needed to address the challenges of the day.

The Constitution created the office of the presidency.

How do presidents meet the extraordinary expectations laid before them? To begin to answer this question, we must first consult the document that created the presidency: the U.S. Constitution. When the delegates met in Philadelphia in 1787, they struggled mightily to create an executive office that would provide the needed "energy and dispatch" that was so sorely lacking in the Articles of Confederation, while also guarding against the very kinds of monarchical tendencies that had led to the American Revolution. (For more on this topic, see Chapter 3).

Creating the presidency   Wary of giving too much power to one individual, the Framers wrestled with whether one person should hold the office of president or whether an executive committee or council was more appropriate. Some delegates initially lined up behind the Virginia Plan, which called for a congressionally appointed executive council. The executive would not have any specific powers granted in the Constitution. Members of the council would serve for a single seven-year term. A special body would be created that included the executive council and the Supreme Court. This body, known as the council of revision, could veto (reject) bills passed by Congress, with Congress in turn able to override the veto.

Other delegates argued that accountability would be stronger and more focused if a single individual held the office. These delegates, however, differed among themselves about the relationship between the president and Congress. Some wanted the president to be selected by Congress and have no independent authority. To other

◄ **DEMOCRAT AL GORE CONCEDES DEFEAT TO GEORGE W. BUSH, 2000**

The Electoral College has often been criticized as undemocratic because it is possible for the person receiving the most popular votes nationally, like Gore, to fall short in electoral votes and lose the election.

delegates, the presidency needed to have its own set of constitutionally enumerated powers. There was general agreement among the delegates that the president would need to be able to check Congress, primarily through the veto power.

Selecting the president   After deciding that one person would hold the position, the Framers debated how to select that person. Direct election by the public had little support. Instead, indirect election dominated the discussion. With indirect election, the public does not directly elect the president but selects other individuals who, in turn, elect the president. Indirect election was intended to prevent the president from becoming an extension of public passions. One plan called for election of the president by Congress for a single term. He would gain office by appealing not to the public, but to members of Congress. With a one-term limit, his actions would not be geared toward reelection. Most delegates, however, believed this system would make the president too dependent on Congress.

The indirect election plan that prevailed was the **Electoral College**. In the Electoral College system, electors in each state vote for the president. Each state legislature could choose how to select its electors. In some states, the state legislatures chose the electors; in others the people voted for them. By 1856, every state allowed the people to vote for electors. Regardless of how they were chosen, the electors held the responsibility of selecting the president. This plan increased the president's independence from the legislature by not having Congress vote for the president and by allowing the president to run for reelection. If no individual received a majority of the electoral vote, only then would Congress have a say, with the House of Representatives choosing the president.

The Electoral College was initially thought of as a way for the country's leaders in each state to meet, deliberate, and vote for the president. Thus the selection of the president was insulated from direct public pressure. Rather, the people or the state legislature would be voting for "wise men" who would use their knowledge and wisdom to cast a vote for president. Today this distinction between the electors and the people is meaningless—electors almost always are required by state law to vote for the candidate who won the presidential popular vote in that state. Electors do not in any way today play the role of wise sages that was originally anticipated by the Framers.

Electoral College   the meeting, in each state and the District of Columbia, of electors who cast votes to elect the president.

Reaching compromise over the presidency   The American presidency as we know it today was a compromise that left no one at the Constitutional Convention entirely satisfied, but it contained elements that appealed to most delegates. The Constitution limited the presidency to individuals at least 35 years of age, born in the United States (or born abroad as the child of American citizens), and a resident of the United States for at least 14 years. The office was made more independent of the legislative branch than in earlier proposals. Indirectly elected by the people via the Electoral College, the president would serve a four-year term with the possibility of reelection.

Table 14-1 identifies the president's powers that are enumerated in Article II of the Constitution. Some constitutional powers, such as making treaties and appointing ambassadors and judges, are shared with the Senate. In these cases, the Senate must approve treaties negotiated by the president or confirm his nominees. Other powers, meanwhile, are reserved for the president alone. These include the power to commission officers in the military, to grant pardons to those convicted of crimes (or, preemptively, to those who might be charged with a crime), to receive foreign ambassadors, and to convene sessions of Congress.

TABLE 14-1.   Important Presidential Powers Enumerated in the Constitution.   With the exception of the veto power, which is located in Article I of the Constitution, all important sources of presidential authority are found in Article II.

EXCLUSIVE POWERS OF THE PRESIDENT

Pardon

The president can personally exonerate any individual from criminal charges or judicial pursuit. "He Shall have the Power to grant Reprieves and Pardons for Offenses against the United States."

Commander in Chief

The president is the ranking officer of the U.S. Armed Forces. He directs the military and is responsible for military strategy. "The President shall be the Commander in Chief of the Army and Navy of the United States, and of the Militia of the several States."

Implement Laws

The Constitution gives the president the power and responsibility to oversee the execution of laws passed by the Congress. He does so through his cabinet and its bureaucracy. "He [the President] shall take care that the laws be faithfully executed."

Executive Power (the Vesting Clause)

The president holds the "executive power," the exact meaning of which continues to be debated to this day. "The executive Power shall be vested in a President of the United States of America."

POWERS SHARED WITH CONGRESS

Veto

The president can send a bill he is unsatisfied with back to Congress for reconsideration. "Every Bill which shall have passed the House of Representatives and the Senate, shall, before it becomes a Law, be presented to the President of the United States; If he approve he shall sign it, but if not he shall return it, with his Objections to the House in which it shall have originated."

Treaties

Through the State Department, the president can negotiate treaties with other countries. However, they only take effect once they are ratified by a two-thirds vote of the Senate. "He shall have Power, by and with the Advice and Consent of the Senate to make Treaties."

Appointments

The president has the power to nominate and appoint U.S. officials, subject to Senate approval. "He shall nominate, and by and with the Advice and Consent of the Senate, appoint Ambassadors, other public Ministers and Consuls, Judges of the Supreme Court, and all other Officers of the United States."

The Constitution granted only limited specific powers to the president independent of Congress, but it included some open-ended and potentially power-enhancing clauses. One clause directed the president to "from time to time give to the Congress information of the State of the Union, and recommend to their Consideration such Measures as he shall judge necessary and expedient" (Article II, section 3). The first half of this statement was intended to ensure that the president did not remain aloof and distant from Congress. The second half provided an opening for presidential leadership of Congress. The **necessary and expedient clause**, which echoes the "necessary and proper" clause related to Congress, validates the president as a significant legislator—not merely an executive who is implementing and enforcing the law, but one who is instrumental in the creation and promotion of legislation.[4]

The Constitution also specified the president to "take care that the laws be faithfully executed." The vagueness of this **take care clause** allows strong independent action if the president believes laws are being ignored. For example, in 1981 President Ronald Reagan fired all the federal air traffic controllers who had, in violation of their contract, gone on strike.[5] The clause also invites the president to interpret exactly what would be necessary to "faithfully execute" a law passed by Congress, which means he might take much bolder, or much less bold, action than Congress would like.

Finally, the Constitution gives the president "executive power." Debates continue about the exact meaning of this clause. Advocates of the unitary theory of the executive, for instance, suggest that this clause gives the president complete control over the departments and agencies that operate in the executive branch, and moreover, that the formulation and implementation of most U.S. foreign policy falls within its domain.[6] Others, by contrast, argue that this clause merely recognizes the president's responsibility to execute those laws enacted by Congress.[7]

Presidents have stretched the language of the Constitution to expand their influence in American government.

In addition to the authority granted to the president in the Constitution, presidents have experimented to define the parameters of the office. A comparison of Article I in the Constitution (which concerns Congress) and Article II (which concerns the president) shows that the Framers had a much more detailed sense of the responsibilities and duties of Congress than they did of the president. Because Article II was written loosely, enterprising presidents have found ways to enlarge the powers and responsibilities of the office.

Put bluntly, presidents had to stretch a few constitutional clauses here and there to see what Congress, the courts, and the public would accept as legitimate exercises of presidential authority. Does being commander in chief, for instance, mean that the president can take the country into war? Does the power to appoint bureaucrats also imply the power to fire them? Can presidents refuse to implement laws that

necessary and expedient clause a clause in Article II, section 3, of the Constitution that authorizes the president to recommend legislation to Congress.

take care clause the constitutional clause that grants the president the authority and leeway to determine if laws are being "faithfully executed" and to take action if in his judgment they are not.

▼ **PRESIDENT BUSH SIGNS CONGRESSIONAL RESOLUTION REGARDING IRAQ, 2002**

The Constitution gives Congress the authority to declare war, but in practice Congress has not authorized war or military action without a prior request from the president. Here, Bush, surrounded by congressional leaders, including Senators John McCain and Joe Biden, signs a resolution that authorizes him to use force against Iraq if necessary.

they thought are unconstitutional? Does the power to "execute" laws include the power to interpret them? Presidents pushed and other institutions responded, and over time the office became more clearly defined. The process continues to this day. Through this pushing and prodding of the Constitution, the office eventually became what some early Americans feared: a powerful seat of executive authority. What some in Congress and the public might see as an expansion of presidential power, presidents are inclined to see as a practice of the office's inherent power—the chief executive inherently has certain authority due to the nature of the job that need not be spelled out explicitly in the Constitution.

The early presidency When George Washington took the oath of office as president in 1789, he began with the job as defined in the Constitution. Washington (1789–1797) was determined to protect the president's independence. For example, he was adamant that the Senate's job was to confirm his nominees to the courts, not dictate who those nominees would be. And he immediately established the president's key role as head of state—that is, the individual who represents the face of the federal government in diplomatic relations with other countries. Indeed, selected for the office primarily because of his enormous reputation throughout the country, Washington was in the eyes of most Americans the one figure to whom the early nurturance of this new political office could be entrusted. Although he was clearly also the head of government during many heated political and legislative battles, his establishment of the symbolic importance of the office as a representative of the nation was highly significant. This objective is clear in his founding of the two-term president tradition. Until 1951, the Constitution did not require a president to step down after a maximum of two terms, but all but one (Franklin Roosevelt) did. Washington began the tradition in part to establish the practice of shifting power, to reassure Americans that no concentrated monarchical powers were contained in the presidency.[8]

The stamp of other early presidents on the office also established the president's independence and made clear that the president would not simply be implementing congressional legislation. Thomas Jefferson (1801–1809) was actively involved in legislative matters. He arranged the Louisiana Purchase, which vastly expanded the geographical reach of the United States, with no congressional consultation. Andrew Jackson (1829–1837) employed aggressive use of vetoes on such politically explosive issues as the rechartering of the Bank of the United States. Before Jackson, presidential vetoes had been few and had centered on constitutional objections to legislation. Jackson, by contrast, rejected legislation that he found flawed as policy, and in doing so he established the use of the veto as a key tool of presidential power.

During the Civil War, Abraham Lincoln (1861–1865) took an expansive view of the authority of the presidency. To many of his critics, Lincoln's actions assaulted the nation's long-standing commitments to liberty and property rights. But in an emergency, Lincoln argued, Article II clauses concerning "executive power," "necessary and expedient," and "take care" had to be given very broad interpretation. Therefore, Lincoln initiated measures restricting civil liberties, including eavesdropping on telegraph lines and allowing prisoners to be held without charge.[9] To support the war effort, he launched the first national income tax not only in the absence of any constitutional language allowing such a policy but, in the eyes of many, directly contrary to constitutional language that seemed to prohibit this tax. It was not until 1913 that the Sixteenth Amendment would specifically allow the federal government to collect an income tax. Lincoln also created a national army that exceeded the size previously approved by Congress, helped found the state of West Virginia, declared a boycott of southern ports, and authorized the construction of warships, all without congressional approval. In most instances, though, Congress ultimately granted its subsequent approval of these actions.

Creation of the modern presidency   Theodore Roosevelt (1901–1909) was the first president to travel abroad during his term in office, cementing the president's role as the nation's chief diplomat. Roosevelt coupled this action with a foreign policy that sought to pull the United States more tightly into global politics and economics, including construction of the Panama Canal and a declaration that the Caribbean and Latin America were within the American sphere of influence. Roosevelt also was a pioneer of the tradition of the president's communicating directly to the public in easy-to-understand speeches about specific policy and legislative goals. In the nineteenth century, presidential speeches tended to be on broad topics that avoided controversy, rather than on specific legislation. Presidents presented themselves primarily as the head of state in their speaking tours around the country. Roosevelt, however, wanted to influence public opinion, which he believed would in turn influence members of Congress.

In the 1930s, crisis again dramatically reshaped the presidency—this time the economic crisis of the Great Depression. "This country wants action, and action now," new President Franklin Roosevelt declared in 1933, and he had no doubt that he was the one to provide it. At one time Americans would have recoiled from a president so determined to promise "action," but by the twentieth century, the idea sat more comfortably in people's minds—indeed, many saw the president's determination to act as a welcome change from previous presidents' cautious responses to the problems of the day.

Roosevelt (1933–1945) initiated a vast array of federal programs to deal with the collapse of the economy. He was blunt about his intentions. In his inaugural address in 1933, he declared that he was willing to work with Congress, but that if Congress failed to act, he would seek "broad executive power" to address the emergency. Roosevelt put the nation on notice that he intended the presidency to be the leading political institution in the United States and that he intended to experiment in bold ways to redefine the presidency. He would accomplish these goals not only through very active involvement in legislation, but through creating a set of supporting institutions in the Executive Office of the President. With a much larger staff at his disposal, the president could be even more active in policy-making, using government agencies to carry out his wishes, and communicating to the public, legislators, and interest groups.

Roosevelt also revolutionized the relationship between presidents and the people they represent. From the moment he assumed office, Roosevelt expressed a commitment to harnessing the powers of the federal government to promote the welfare of average citizens. And over the course of his presidency, Roosevelt made a habit of speaking directly to his constituents. Through his weekly radio addresses, commonly referred to as "fireside chats," the president's voice entered the living rooms of citizens across the nation, speaking to their everyday concerns and the government efforts to fix them.

Roosevelt's presidency, though, was not without its share of controversy. Several of the laws that he pushed through Congress were later declared unconstitutional by the Supreme Court. In response, Roosevelt proposed a plan that would give him a more favorable mix of justices on the Court. Rather than simply accept the Court's rulings, Roosevelt railed against Justices who, in his view, remained out of touch with Americans' concerns. In response, he proposed to increase the size of the Supreme Court, a plan that would allow him to appoint justices who would look more favorably upon his domestic policy agenda. Neither the public nor Congress supported this perceived power grab.[10] Despite the setback, the Court promptly shifted course and supported Roosevelt's policy agenda.

executive privilege the idea that executive branch officials need to be able to advise the president in confidence, and that the president has a right to prevent that advice from becoming public.

▼ **SUPREME COURT RULES AGAINST PRESIDENT NIXON, 1974**

The Supreme Court ruled unanimously that Richard Nixon's executive privilege did not allow him to withhold recordings of his conversations in the Oval Office. Two weeks later, Nixon became the only president to resign his position.

The postwar presidency   As the United States emerged from World War II as a world superpower, the president's power grew accordingly. During the Cold War between the United States and the Soviet Union, the president not only was the single most important person in American government but was commonly seen as the most powerful person in the world. This enormous stock of prestige helped the president domestically. Increasingly, his actions were portrayed as connected to and vital for national security. To protect America's national interests, presidents declared that they needed to act swiftly and forcefully around the world. Domestic policy became entwined with foreign policy—as the world's economic leader, actions of the U.S. government could have significant repercussions for allies and potential allies.

One area in which all presidents have expanded the boundaries of the office is the control of information, and the postwar presidency continued the trend. The administration of Dwight Eisenhower (1953–1961) was the first to use the now common phrase **executive privilege** to refer to the idea that executive branch officials need to be able to advise the president in confidence, and that the president has a right to prevent that advice from becoming public. The withheld information usually involves discussions in the White House. When invoking executive privilege, the president usually argues that, if members of Congress have access to private discussions, he and his staff are less likely to be fully forthcoming with one another. Moreover, if executive privilege is not permitted, Congress can request information merely out of a desire to discredit the president.

The most famous, or infamous, proponent of executive privilege was Richard Nixon (1969–1974). During the investigation of the scandal that became known as Watergate, Nixon claimed that he had the right to withhold from the public his notes, papers, and tapes of discussions in the White House.[11] In *U.S. v. Nixon* (1974), the Supreme Court rejected Nixon's claim of executive privilege. In this first judicial test of executive privilege, however, the Court did agree that presidents had such a privilege, but that it was not absolute and needed to be weighed against the public interest.

Early in his presidency, George W. Bush used the concept of executive privilege when Congress wanted information about the Energy Policy Task Force, headed by Vice President Dick Cheney. The refusal to disclose whom the task force had met with in 2001 and what recommendations it had received was the first instance in which an administration used the executive privilege concept to shield its conversations with corporate officials, as opposed to government officials. In December 2002, a U.S. district court sided with the administration, concluding that the doctrine of separation of powers was at stake.[12]

The Bush administration also expanded executive privilege by arguing that it applied broadly throughout the executive branch, not just to the president or vice president. President Bush used the take care and vesting clauses in Article II of the Constitution (Table 14-1) to argue for a view of the presidency known as the unitary executive. This doctrine, which the Bush administration propounded more strongly than other administrations, means that the president is in direct, hierarchical control of all executive power in American government. In this view, congressional control over the executive branch and delegation of authority to executive branch agencies that bypasses the president is limited. In 2007 and 2008, when Congress sought to investigate the firing of nine U.S. attorneys in the Justice Department, the administration would not comply with requests for information that it believed were covered by this broader view of executive privilege.

Despite these signs of increased strength, postwar presidents have faced significant obstacles to exercising power. The country has grown in population and complexity. The political environment contains powerful organized groups with diverse policy concerns. Numerous governmental programs are already in place, and attempts to remove them generate howls of protest. The federal budget is not limitless, nor is the public's willingness to tolerate increasing tax burdens. Presidents, therefore, often find themselves shackled by preexisting policy commitments that they inherit upon taking office. They cannot simply erase decades of history and start fresh. And as members of Congress forge their own power during long careers, presidents confront congressional challenges to their leadership. Unlike members of Congress in the nineteenth century, who were content with one or two terms in Washington, members in more recent eras have been inclined to make Congress a career.

Congress delegates authority to the president.

In addition to the Constitution, Congress yields additional authority to the president. Often, Congress defers to the president, either explicitly delegating policy-making tasks to him or deferring action until the president takes the initiative. Either way, the effect is to direct more public attention to the president as a leader. Through **delegation** of this sort, the president is given discretion to act in a particular area, typically within broad parameters of what is acceptable to Congress. If the president goes beyond these boundaries, Congress can find ways to indicate its displeasure, by either refusing to fund the implementation of the president's plan, setting stricter boundaries around future presidential action in this area, or being less cooperative in considering and passing a bill that is important to the president.

Congress has delegated especially vast powers in foreign affairs. For instance, Congress has delegated to the president the authority to negotiate foreign trade agreements, limiting itself to a single vote without the possibility of amending its language or engaging in a filibuster. The process has strict time limits, including how quickly committees must act and the number of hours the proposed trade agreement can be debated on the House or Senate floor. Known as fast-track authority, this is a significant concession of congressional power. Fast-track authority began in 1975, expired in 1994, was renewed in 2002, but expired once again in 2007.

What would cause legislators to give up their ability to amend trade agreements? Political scientists have offered several possible explanatory factors. Legislators may believe that negotiation with other countries works better when the United States presents a unified voice. Perhaps some of them fear that other members of Congress would be eager to protect industries in their districts, and the negotiations would unravel if the president then had to go back to other countries with a revised version of the treaty. Some legislators might consider trade to be a controversial subject and want the president to take the criticism. Because some of these reasons put the president at political risk, even a Congress controlled by the opposition party might grant presidents this authority. But if the congressional majority does not trust the president, it may refuse to delegate this authority. Democrat Bill Clinton wanted fast-track authority after its expiration in 1994, but the Republican-majority Congress refused to grant it to him. Similarly, Republican George W. Bush struggled unsuccessfully in 2007 to convince the Democratic-majority Congress to extend fast-track authority for another five years. Thus far, Obama has not sought fast-track authority, preferring instead to replace it with a process aimed at determining appropriate negotiating partners, as determined by their labor and environmental standards and the state of their civil society.

delegation the granting of authority by Congress to the president to be the first or main actor in a policy area, usually with implicit or explicit limits on actions that Congress would find acceptable.

ThinkingCausally

Considering that trade agreements potentially provide benefits to some constituents while imposing losses on others, why would reelection-minded legislators give up the power to amend these bills?

HOW DO WE KNOW?

Was President George W. Bush a Successful Leader?

The Question

In the tense hours after the terrorist attacks on September 11, 2001, Americans waited to hear from President George W. Bush. How would the country respond to the devastation in New York, at the Pentagon, and in Pennsylvania? On September 20, the president delivered a solemn, forthright speech to the nation. Soon after, with congressional support, he forged a coalition of allies to attack the Taliban regime in Afghanistan, believed to be a prime sponsor of terrorism and a haven for the perpetrators of the September 11 attacks. To most Americans at that time, Bush's actions after September 11 were the work of a strong, successful leader, someone who took charge of a situation and got things done. Public opinion surveys gave the president high marks for his leadership, and in 2004 the president made a case for his reelection that hinged in large part on his leadership skills. By the beginning of 2006, however, a string of negative news dragged down the president's reputation as a leader to the lowest point of his presidency, and the president limped through 2007 and 2008 with the lowest public approval of his presidency. Was George W. Bush a successful leader? How do we know?

▼ PRESIDENT BUSH ADDRESSES THE COUNTRY REGARDING SEPTEMBER 11

George W. Bush's speech on September 20, 2001, was widely considered a major triumph. His words expressed both the grim realization of what happened and his resolve to fight terrorism.

Why It Matters

Most Americans consider the election of the president to be among their most significant political acts. The more clearheaded and accurate we can be when casting these votes, the better. If we as citizens say we want strong and successful leadership, it helps to have standards by which to predict who will be the better leader or to determine whether a president has been a successful leader.

Investigating the Answer

Before researchers can determine whether a president is a strong leader, they first have to determine how to define and measure successful leadership. The public most often tends to think about presidential leadership in terms of impact: did the president's action alleviate a problem, have no impact, or make things worse? These assessments matter electorally. In November 2004, a majority of voters believed that President Bush had made the country safer than it had been prior to September 11, 2001, and rewarded him with their vote. By November 2006, however, voters swept Democrats to majorities in the House and Senate in part because of their doubt that the president's leadership had been wise and effective on that issue.

To political scientists, however, measuring success by impact is problematic for several reasons. First, whether the impact of a policy has been positive or negative can take a long time to determine and may change over time. Second, drawing the line between success and failure can seem arbitrary. What if the economic growth rate increases by 0.1 percent? By 1 percent? By 4 percent? Where does a researcher draw the line between success and failure, and why? Third, measuring presidential leadership by impact can be unreliable because the evaluation may be biased by political ideology. Consider Iraq. Iraq has deposed a dictator, held free elections, and written a constitution. It has also experienced brutal ongoing violence and a surge in terrorist activity that have damaged the image of the United States among our allies. Given the mixed results, your ideology might dictate whether you judge the president's actions as having an overall positive or negative impact. Lastly, the impact you see may not be the result of presidential action: the correlation of the president's action with a particular outcome does not prove causation.

Therefore, political scientists tend to define presidential leadership in terms of outcome rather than impact. They look at what the president has attempted to accomplish and they evaluate his success in those areas. Some researchers have compared the president's campaign promises with his actual performance. Others have studied the president's State of the Union Address as a measure of his highest priorities and tracked what he accomplished legislatively in those areas. Both of these methods are attractive because of the available data on campaign promises or State of the Union Addresses across several presidencies. Other researchers have chosen a broader measure, comparing the president's preferences on roll-call votes taken in Congress and calculating how often Congress agreed with the president's position. The focus in these outcome-oriented studies of leadership is not on whether the president's policies "worked," but on whether he was able to persuade Congress to enact them.

The most common political science measure of successful presidential leadership is the frequency with which Congress votes in accord with the president's preferences. The measure is not a perfect indicator of leadership success—the president might not have done much to produce the outcome in Congress, and the final outcome on a vote does not tell us whether the president had to abandon major aspects of his policy in the days or months leading up to the vote. One especially attractive feature of this measure, though, is that there are typically hundreds of congressional roll-call votes on which the president takes a position; thus, the frequency of presidential success can be calculated across time, across issue areas, and across different presidents, a method aiding political scientists in the kind of systematic analysis they prefer.

If we look at how often Congress voted the way the president wanted on roll-call votes, President Bush was a successful leader (see Figure 14-2). In 2005 and 2006, his success

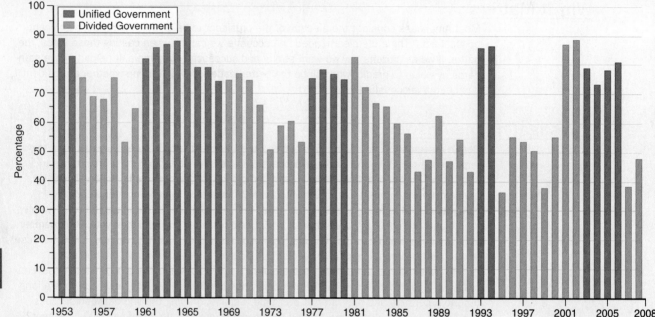

FIGURE 14-2. **Presidential Victories on Roll-Call Votes, House and Senate, 1953-2008.** Presidential success in Congress is generally higher when the president's party has a majority in both houses of Congress.

rate was higher than that of any other president in his fifth and sixth year since the Eisenhower administration (1953–1961).[13] His overall success rate from 2001 to 2005 rivaled that of Lyndon Johnson (1964–1968) and John Kennedy (1961–1963). But, unlike those two presidents, Bush achieved this result while facing a Senate narrowly controlled by the opposition party for 18 months of his first term; Bush's first-term success rate with the opposition party was substantially higher than that of any president since Richard Nixon, particularly within the Senate. In his second term in office, however, it declined substantially.[14]

Thinking Critically

■ How should we compare the success rates of two presidents, one of whom has an aggressive and far-reaching domestic policy agenda, and the other of whom has only a modest set of proposals that he would like Congress to enact?

■ When trying to assess Bush's success in Congress over time, how should we factor in the Democratic takeover of Congress in the 2006 elections?

■ How would you compare the legislative accomplishments of Bush's last year in office with Obama's first year? What accounts for the differences you observe?

The Bottom Line

When assessing presidential leadership, political scientists focus on tangible outcomes. This method avoids the ideological bias that influences the assessments made by political activists and zealous partisans. George W. Bush took a position on fewer congressional votes than did any other president since Dwight Eisenhower (1953–1961), but overall he was highly successful on those votes. By this measure, Bush can be considered a successful leader, despite his very low approval ratings. Focusing on other outcomes, such as his inability to get Congress to act on his Social Security reform initiative, supports different conclusions.

Importantly, Congress also delegated to the president significant powers in the federal budget process. Partly to help the president control executive branch agencies more effectively, and partly to help Congress think more systematically about the budget, Congress after 1921 required the president to submit an annual overall budget as a framework for congressional deliberation. In practice, this meant that the president set the parameters in which the federal budget and Congress worked. The overall budget, as passed by Congress in a series of separate spending bills, typically looked very much like the president's original plan. In 1974, Congress passed the Congressional Budget and Impoundment Control Act to return some of the leverage to Congress. From then on, Congress passed budget resolutions that established targets for revenue and spending across all policy areas. But the president's budget was still the first to reach Congress, so even the budget resolution was a response to the president's plan.

Successful leadership entails convincing people to do what the president wants them to do.

Broadening interpretations of the president's constitutional authority, coupled with the growth in Congress's delegation of power to the president, have increased public expectations about the president's ability to lead. These expectations can be a burden for the president: a president seen as falling short may find that a growing proportion of the public disapproves of his performance in office. But public expectations can be a blessing, too. Higher expectations may enhance the president's leadership potential by forcing the president to pressure Congress for cooperation. The president can appeal directly to the public, indicating he wants to meet their expectations but that Congress is obstructing him. Such appeals might generate public pressure on Congress to act and contribute to successful presidential leadership.

Leadership can be evaluated in terms of outcome (Did the president succeed in getting Congress to pass his plan to reduce crime?) or in terms of impact (Did the plan actually reduce the crime rate?).[15] Political scientists tend to focus more on the outcome side of leadership. Thought of this way, leadership involves convincing the public that action is needed and getting a favored piece of legislation passed in Congress. It can also involve stopping action in Congress or influencing the content of legislation. Thus, to political scientists, **leadership** means the ability of a president to influence and guide others to achieve some desired policy or action (see "How Do We Know? Was President George W. Bush a Successful Leader?").

leadership the ability to influence and guide others to achieve some desired policy or action.

Of course, it is easier to convince people to do what they already are inclined to do. In some situations, the president uses his skills to bring people together to do what, in effect, they already want to do but have not quite figured out how to do. Alternatively, presidents can attempt to lead while rebuking public and congressional opinion. Here the president tries to push the nation in a new direction and is often criticized for not being responsive to public opinion.

President Bush's effort in 2003 to engage the United States in military action against Iraq required this second type of leadership. He reassured the public that diplomatic efforts to resolve the crisis were under way, while raising the possibility that military action might be needed and that the United States might have to act alone. Public opinion polls showed that these efforts succeeded. For example, the percentage of Americans believing that the president had laid out a clear and convincing case for military action rose from 37 percent to 52 percent in a one-month period that included a major, highly publicized speech by President Bush to the United Nations.[16]

Powers of the President

14-2 Distinguish between the formal and informal powers of contemporary presidents.

Presidents invoke various powers in their efforts to set policy. Some of these—formal and expressed powers—are designated by law or the Constitution. Others—informal and inherent powers—derive from the unique advantages of the president as the sole public official in the United States elected by a national constituency. Presidential power is not limitless, however, and its use can be challenged by Congress and the courts.

Formal powers are defined in the Constitution and in law.

formal powers   specific grants of authority defined in the Constitution or in law.

As we have discussed, the president's **formal powers** are specific grants of authority defined in the Constitution or delegated by Congress. Others, though, were created through independent presidential initiative. The resulting mix of formal powers currently available to presidents establishes the first basis for leadership.

New legislation   The president shares with Congress the role of enacting new legislation. In his role as "chief legislator," a president is engaged in every part of the process. He and his staff can draft bills, although the president cannot himself introduce a bill in Congress; a member of Congress must do that on the president's behalf. During deliberations over the bill, the president and his staff typically contact members of Congress and encourage them to vote with the president. They will also appeal to the media, interest groups, and the public itself to apply pressure on Congress. If the bill passes, the president will need to sign it before it becomes law.[17]

> "The veto is powerful not only when it is used, but also when the president threatens its use."

veto   the president's power to reject legislation passed by Congress. Congress can override a veto with a two-thirds vote in both the House and Senate.

pocket veto   the president's veto of a bill without the opportunity for Congress to override the veto. It occurs if the president does not act on a bill within 10 days after passage by Congress and Congress adjourns during that time.

Presidential veto   One of the most important formal powers is the **veto**, which allows the president to reject bills enacted by Congress: the veto is the president's power to say no. When the president vetoes a bill, Congress can override the veto with a two-thirds vote of each chamber, but this step typically proves very difficult to do. In the case of a **pocket veto**, Congress does not even have that opportunity. The Constitution gives the president 10 days either to sign or to reject a bill. If he does neither, the bill becomes law. If, however, Congress has adjourned during that 10 days and the president does not act, the bill is rejected—the president kills the bill by keeping it in his pocket. Presidents can use their veto power to extract legislation more to their liking from Congress.[18]

The veto is powerful not only when it is used, but also when the president threatens its use. When the president threatens to veto a bill, Congress members, particularly those who are not in the president's party, must decide whether they want to revise the bill according to the president's preferences, or to refuse a compromise. If the bill is unchanged, the president will reject it. If they agree to revise the bill, the legislation will pass, but Congress members may be dissatisfied with the compromised version of the original bill. If they decide to allow the president to veto the bill, they are hoping that the public opinion backlash will force the president to reevaluate his stance or, if an election is near, that the president's position might hurt him or his fellow partisans running for office.

The president's threat of using the veto does not necessarily mean that he opposes a bill in that particular policy area, but rather that he does not like some provisions of the particular bill that was put on his desk for his signature. That was frequently true for President Clinton, who made effective use of vetoes and veto threats in his relationship with the Republican Congress beginning in 1995.

Presidents from John Kennedy through Bill Clinton vetoed legislation an average of nine times per year, but President George W. Bush made rare use of the veto power. He issued only 11 vetoes during his two terms in office. As of mid-2010, President Obama had not issued any formal vetoes, though he did issue one "pocket-veto," wherein he simply refused to sign a bill that Congress had passed at the end of the legislative calendar. In an effort to influence the legislative process, Obama also was not shy about making known his willingness to exercise his veto power. For instance, Obama threatened to veto bills requiring excessive military spending for fighter jets and military helicopters, forcing Senate Republicans to strip the initial bill of its multibillion-dollar line item.[19]

A veto is a big knife, but sometimes what the president really wants is a scalpel. Presidents have long sought a more delicate device for fine-tuning bills in the form of the **line-item veto,** which would allow them to veto portions of bills rather than entire bills. A 1996 law gave this power to presidents, but President Clinton enjoyed it for only a short time. In 1998, the U.S. Supreme Court ruled that the line-item veto unconstitutionally added to the president's powers by, in effect, allowing him to amend proposed legislation—a task limited to Congress in the Constitution. The president could only approve or reject proposed legislation in its entirety: if he wanted the power to approve legislation in part, the Court ruled, a constitutional amendment would be needed.

Commander in chief The president serves as the commander in chief of all the military services—the Army, Navy, Marines, Air Force, and Coast Guard. As commander in chief, the president has the authority to move American troops into combat. Being commander in chief requires the president to work in concert with Congress,

line-item veto the authority of a chief executive to reject part of a bill passed by the legislature.

▼ **PRESIDENT CLINTON VISITS TROOPS, 1996**
The president's commander-in-chief role over the world's largest military is a major part of his constitutional authority.

but in this role the president tends to lead while Congress follows. This presidential authority is not clearly spelled out in the Constitution. Rather, it is one of those areas that presidents claimed over time, often over the vigorous protest of partisan opponents and constitutional scholars.

As commander in chief, presidents have argued that they have inherent powers to respond to emergencies and protect the safety of Americans and the security of the United States. The nature of executive power is to act and use best judgment when emergency strikes, they argue. The Bush administration took controversial actions in response to terrorism, including indefinite detention of enemy combatants, denial of civilian court review of cases involving detainees, and surveillance of communications without prior judicial authorization. In defending these actions, President Bush and his spokespeople frequently argued that they fell squarely within the inherent powers of the president as commander in chief.

It does seem that the Framers intended for the president to be in charge of the armed forces and guide their conduct during war, but they intended Congress to declare war. Fearing that the president had become too dominant in this area and had turned a shared power into a presidential power, Congress passed the War Powers Act in 1973. This act requires the president to notify Congress and receive its approval within 60 days when he deploys American troops militarily. As a practical matter, however, Congress usually finds that by that time it is too late to change course, and the president's decision stands (see Chapter 13).

Executive agreements and executive orders   Two other formal powers available to presidents—the executive agreement and the executive order—enable them to enact public policy without the direct cooperation of Congress. These powers are not found in the Constitution but instead arise out of presidents' entrepreneurial efforts to expand their base of authority.

executive agreement   an international agreement in which the United States becomes a party once the president has signed it, without requiring approval from two-thirds of the Senate.

With an **executive agreement**, a president can negotiate an arrangement with a foreign government without formal approval by Congress. These agreements cannot require changes in U.S. law—in those instances, Congress must sign off on the change through a treaty. But many subjects of international diplomacy do not require such changes. Hence, as Figure 14-3 makes clear, presidents often substitute executive agreements for treaties. And they do so in lots of policy areas. In 2002, the Bush administration approved an executive agreement that committed the United States and Russia to specific nuclear arms reductions. In 2003, the United States and Vietnam reached an agreement to raise Vietnamese textile exports to the United States. And in 2009, President Obama and President Medvedev of Russia brokered an executive agreement to further reduce strategic offensive arms.

Executive agreements are not intended to be hidden from Congress and the public, although sometimes presidents have used them that way. A series of executive agreements between the United States and South Vietnam drew the United States more heavily into military involvement in Vietnam. Although the first of these agreements went into effect in the late 1950s under the administration of Dwight Eisenhower and continued through the 1960s under the administrations of John Kennedy and Lyndon Johnson, Congress was unaware of them until 1969. To forestall secret use of executive agreements in the future, Congress passed the Case Act in 1972 to require presidents to inform Congress of an executive agreement within 60 days of its inception (amended to 20 days in 1977).

executive order   a presidential directive or proclamation that has the force of law.

Executive orders (as well as proclamations, memoranda, and other directives) are presidential commands that have the force of law. Like executive agreements, they do not require Congress's approval; unlike executive agreements, they do not involve a foreign government. Executive orders apply to the executive branch and its employees, so the president, as head of the executive branch of government, is

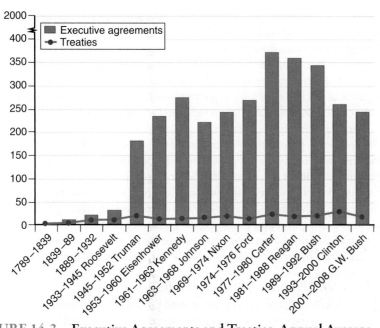

FIGURE 14-3. **Executive Agreements and Treaties, Annual Average, 1789–2008.** Presidents make much more extensive use of executive agreements than of treaties.

allowed to issue these, as would the chief executive of any organization. They can affect the private sector because private organizations interact with government, usually through contracts. For example, an executive order might state that companies wishing to provide goods or services to the government must have certain equal opportunity hiring policies in place. Although most orders are fairly routine matters of administrative procedure, the president can also use this tool to implement a wide range of policies, some of which aid constituencies important for the president's political success (see Table 14-2).[20]

In December 2002, for example, President Bush issued Executive Order 13279, designed to ensure that faith-based organizations—churches, synagogues, mosques, and

TABLE 14-2. **Examples of Policy Initiatives Implemented Using Executive Orders.**

EXECUTIVE ORDER	DATE	SUBJECT	ISSUED BY
9066	February 19, 1942	Internment of Japanese-American citizens	F. Roosevelt
9981	July 26, 1948	Segregation in the armed forces ended	Truman
10730	September 23, 1957	Enforcement of school desegregation using National Guard	Eisenhower
10925	March 6, 1961	Affirmative action to be used by government agencies and contractors to ensure nondiscriminatory hiring practices	Kennedy
11615	August 15, 1971	Wage and price controls	Nixon
13158	May 26, 2000	Development of national environmental system of marine protected areas	Clinton
13379	December 12, 2002	More participation by faith-based organizations in federal social programs	G. W. Bush
13507	April 8, 2009	Creation of a White House Office of Health Reform	Obama

other religious institutions—could compete for federal financing for programs that provide social services to the local community. Technically, the president required executive branch employees to treat these groups no differently from any other group applying for federal funding. By issuing the directive as an executive order, the president sidestepped potentially contentious congressional debate about the constitutionality of federal funding for religious organizations. Supporters saw the president's action as a vindication of the cultural support for religious rights and equality; opponents saw it as violating the American creed by forging too close a governmental link with religion.[21]

The president's power to use executive orders can be limited by Congress or by the U.S. Supreme Court. The Supreme Court can declare an executive order void if it finds that the president's action exceeded his statutory authority or is contrary to the Constitution. As with executive agreements, Congress can weaken executive orders by cutting off their funding. Congress can also define areas in which prior congressional approval is required, thus negating the possibility of an executive order. A future president also can overturn a prior executive order, as President Obama did with President Bush's order restricting federally funded stem cell research.

ThinkingComparatively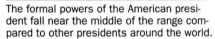

The formal powers of the American president fall near the middle of the range compared to other presidents around the world.

Formal powers compared to those of foreign presidents

Although dozens of countries around the world have systems of government headed by presidents, the exact form of the presidency and its power varies. Compared to other presidential systems, an American president's powers fall around the middle of the range. For example, like the American president, some presidents can issue a unilateral directive similar to an executive order and then veto legislative attempts to repeal it. Although the legislature can check presidential behavior, presidents in these countries are more powerful than those in countries where unilateral action is not possible. On the more powerful end of the range, in some countries presidents have the exclusive right to introduce policy in particular areas. Taiwan and South Korea, among others, constitutionally limit the legislature's ability to refine the president's budgetary allocations.

Presidential vetoes are particularly prone to international variation. In some systems, a president's veto power may be limited to particular forms of legislation. The Mexican president, for example, cannot veto the annual appropriations bill that sets government spending. And the strength of the veto also varies across countries. In Venezuela, an override requires only the same number of votes that originally passed the bill. In other countries, such as Colombia, an absolute majority is necessary. In the United States and Argentina, among others, a two-thirds vote of the legislature is required to override a presidential veto. Although this authority gives the U.S. president a relatively powerful veto, he does not have the line-item or partial veto available to some presidents of some other countries.

Informal powers include the power to persuade.

Presidents also have informal powers, which are not the result of an established rule, policy mechanism, or constitutional assignment of authority. Rather, informal powers derive from a president's personal experience, leadership style, reputation, or prestige. Most famously in the category of informal powers, presidents have the "power to persuade." Some political scientists go so far as to say that the president's power *is* the power to persuade. Presidents devote considerable resources (financial and otherwise) toward persuading elected officials and the public about the merits of their policy positions. Some presidents, like Lyndon Johnson and Franklin Roosevelt, had legendary bargaining skills. Others, like Jimmy Carter, struggled to compromise and understand the political pressures faced by members of Congress.

Presidents often need the cooperation of members of Congress, aides and advisers, officials in federal agencies, and fellow politicians on the state and local levels. On some issues, they will be more passionate and involved and less willing to see their plans thwarted. Despite decreasing public and congressional support for the Iraq War, for example, President Bush was determined to defend his strategy.[22] A president may trade success on more peripheral issues to defend his position on the key issue. To secure cooperation, a president tries to persuade other policy makers that his position is right. He may offer them some benefit if they will cooperate—perhaps federal funds for a favorite project, or fund-raising for a legislator facing reelection. He might threaten to withhold something from the legislator's district, or indicate that he will not throw his support behind one of the legislator's priorities. Presidents will also try to put pressure on a recalcitrant member of Congress by appealing directly to his or her constituents.[23]

Signing statements, which presidents can issue when they sign legislation, are one manner of persuading bureaucrats and judges. Most statements do little more than praise Congress for a job well done or emphasize the importance of the law itself. Increasingly, however, presidents have used these statements to reinterpret legislation in meaningful ways. For example, President Bush argued in signing statements that he retained the option to ignore certain provisions of laws if he concluded they unduly infringed on his constitutional role as commander in chief. The statements do not afford the president an opportunity—as some have charged—to actually rewrite the content of the law. They are attempts to persuade the bureaucrats who implement laws and the judges who may someday be called upon to interpret them.

Do signing statements cause bureaucrats to change their behavior? A congressional investigation in 2007 found some correlation between concerns raised in presidential signing statements and portions of legislation not implemented by federal agencies.[24] Although critics quickly asserted a direct causal relationship between statements and bureaucratic inaction, the facts at hand were more nuanced. It is not clear whether agencies ignored provisions of laws because of the signing statements or whether the statements were simply a convenient justification after the fact. It might also be that the president was more likely to issue a signing statement when an agency had already signaled its predisposition to ignore some aspect of a law. In that case, it would be the agency's planned behavior that caused the signing statement, rather than the other way around. Because the report did not examine laws passed without signing statements, there was no way to know whether bureaucratic inaction was more frequent when signing statements were issued than when they were not.

ThinkingCausally

Do presidential signing statements change bureaucratic behavior?

Congress and the courts can check presidential power.

Both Congress and the courts serve as a check on presidents who try to expand their authority too aggressively. When someone challenges a policy, ruling, or other action taken by the executive branch, the courts might declare it illegal or unconstitutional and therefore void. For example, in June 2004, the Supreme Court ruled in three cases that President Bush had exceeded his constitutional authority by indefinitely detaining noncitizens captured in Afghanistan as part of the U.S. campaign against terrorism. The detainees were held at the U.S. military base at Guantanamo Bay, Cuba, and were prohibited access to attorneys or the courts. The Supreme Court concluded that the detainees had the right to access the federal courts to challenge their incarceration.[25]

Congress can check the president's power through the normal legislative process by not acting on legislation he desires, refusing to approve judicial and other nominees, designing agencies to have some independence from presidential control, and withholding funding and thereby prohibiting the executive branch from taking certain actions of which Congress disapproves. The threat of these actions often leads presidents to adjust their plans and soothe congressional objections.

The most severe congressional check on presidential power is **impeachment**, a process through which the House of Representatives can vote to initiate a trial conducted by the Senate that can lead to the removal of the president from office.[26] Under the Constitution, impeachment is the appropriate remedy for presidents who have committed "high crimes and misdemeanors," treason, or bribery. The exact meaning of "high crimes and misdemeanors" is left for members of Congress to decide. For guidance, members can look to the discussions among the Framers of the Constitution, previous impeachment efforts, and previous incidences of presidents who seemed to exceed their authority.

The process of impeachment begins in the House of Representatives, based on "articles of impeachment" that describe the charges against the president. These articles are usually drafted by leaders in the opposition party, following a long period of strained relations with the president. The case against the president is first heard in the House Judiciary Committee. If that committee votes that there is a credible case against the president on all or some of the charges, it sends those articles to the full House to vote whether to proceed with impeachment. The impeachment trial is then held in the Senate, and senators vote whether the president is guilty and must be removed from office. Conviction in the Senate, not impeachment in the House, removes the president from office.

impeachment performed by the House of Representatives, the act of charging government officials with "treason, bribery, or other high crimes and misdemeanors." The Senate then decides whether to convict and remove the official from office.

▼ **PRESIDENT BILL CLINTON TESTIFIES BEFORE A FEDERAL GRAND JURY, 1998**

Minority Chief Investigative Counsel Abbe Lowell watches Bill Clinton's testimony to the House Judiciary Committee during the president's impeachment hearings.

Two presidents, Andrew Johnson in 1868 and Bill Clinton in 1998, have been impeached. In both cases, the Senate acquitted them. Johnson had antagonized congressional Republicans with his too lenient (in their view) approach toward the former Confederate states and with his attempts to derail Republican plans for reconstruction of the South. The impeachment case was based largely on his violation of the Tenure in Office Act, which required the president to receive the Senate's approval before dismissing any office holders, and which had been passed largely to keep reins on Johnson. The case against Clinton was based largely on the charge that he had lied to a federal grand jury about his sexual involvement with White House aide Monica Lewinsky, and that he had obstructed justice by stonewalling the case.

Two other presidents, John Tyler and Richard Nixon, were nearly impeached. Tyler was "censured" in 1843 by the Senate for alleged misuse of power, an option that many Democrats unsuccessfully suggested might be an alternative to impeachment in the case of Bill Clinton.[27] Nixon resigned in 1974 after the House Judiciary Committee voted to send articles of impeachment to the full House. The committee charged the president with obstructing justice in the Watergate investigation and with abuse of power by using agencies such as the Federal Bureau of Investigation and the Internal Revenue Service to intimidate opponents. Technically, then, Nixon was not impeached, but it was all but certain that he would have been both impeached and convicted had he not voluntarily resigned from office.

Public, Electoral, and Contextual Resources for Presidential Leadership

14-3 Analyze how presidents use public support, electoral victories, and congressional allies to push through their policies.

American presidents have varying degrees of success in leading the country, dealing with Congress, and achieving their goals. What explains these differing levels of success? Popular accounts often focus on a single factor—a president speaks well on television, or he is fortunate to have a growing economy, or he receives overwhelming support from "mindless partisans" in Congress. Political science research, in contrast, shows that multiple factors contribute to presidential leadership success. Pointing to just one factor can lead to misleading interpretations. A president might preside while the economy is growing but still have trouble passing his program. This coincidence, however, does not mean that economic growth leads to presidential weakness. Rather, it suggests that other factors that are less favorable may be overwhelming the generally positive impacts of economic growth.

Successful leadership often depends on the resources available to the president. These resources include the president's relationship with the public, electoral factors such as the strength of the president's victory and the size and support of his party in Congress, and historical and policy contexts such as presidential advantages in foreign policy. A president who has an abundant supply of these resources should be more successful with Congress than a president who does not.[28] But success is not automatic. A president with a favorable political environment must still manage that environment with skill.

ThinkingCausally

What factors explain the differing levels of success achieved by presidents in leading the country, dealing with Congress, and reaching their goals?

High levels of public approval are used to pressure Congress.

One of the president's most important resources is his relationship with the public. Since the late 1930s, the public's assessment of the president's job performance has been measured by his public **approval rating**. Public opinion firms conduct surveys and ask respondents whether they approve or disapprove of the job the president is doing. This initial question might be followed by questions relating to distinct policy areas such as the economy, foreign affairs, and the environment. The percentage of the respondents saying they approve of the president's job performance is the president's approval rating.

Approval and its consequences A key reason the president wants to maintain a positive relationship with the public is to exert pressure on members of Congress. The president hopes that high public approval will encourage members of Congress to cooperate with him because they fear the political consequences of challenging him. Conversely, legislators may not perceive much political risk in obstructing the plans of a president with low approval.

approval rating the percentage of the public that approves of the job the president is doing overall.

Among recent presidents, Bill Clinton best exemplifies both ends of the spectrum. Following the 1994 election, with his approval ratings low, Clinton struggled to maintain visibility as media attention focused more on Congress—where both chambers were controlled by the Republican Party for the first time in 40 years. The brash, outspoken new Speaker of the House, Newt Gingrich, was promising "revolutionary" changes in American government. Clinton famously, and meekly, replied that the president was still "relevant." Republicans pushed ahead with their legislative plan with little concern for Clinton's views. Less than a year later, however, Clinton rode a wave of public approval that resulted from his ability to portray himself as a reasonable moderate holding off the extremists in Congress. Finding that the public increasingly supported the president, congressional Republicans began to compromise with him more frequently.

Approval ratings tend to start high and drift down over time. During the early "honeymoon" period of a president's term, opposition to the president's plans has not yet solidified and the public is still likely to give him the benefit of the doubt. He will not likely be blamed, at least not immediately, for problems inherited from his predecessor. And, usually, he has not had time to make any major mistakes. As these mistakes happen, and as it gets harder to blame the predecessor, people find reasons to criticize the president's performance. When Obama first took office in January 2009, he enjoyed approval ratings of 68 percent, whereas just 15 percent of the American public actively disapproved of the president. A year later, both of these figures would change radically. In the early summer of 2010, as oil continued to pour into the Gulf of Mexico, persistently high unemployment rates and deficits fueled widespread anxiety, and large segments of the American public opposed the president's largest domestic policy initiatives from the previous year, the 2009 economic stimulus package and health care reform. Not surprisingly, the president's approval ratings registered at just 50 percent, and his disapproval numbers tripled during his short tenure in office.[29] (See top panel of Figure 14-4).

Party identification is a key factor in approval ratings. Democrats will be more likely to approve of President Obama's job performance, Republicans less likely, and independents somewhere in between. This pattern does not mean that Democrats will blindly approve of President Obama because of the party label, but rather that Democrats are more likely to agree philosophically with actions taken by a Democratic president than are Republicans. Never were these party divisions more pronounced than during George W. Bush's presidency, when Republicans tended to support the president, and Democrats overwhelmingly opposed him.[30]

Approval ratings and the economy   The economy is the most important determinant of a president's job approval rating. Improvements in the economy tend to improve people's assessments of the president. Though political scientists disagree about which economic indicator is paramount—unemployment, inflation, growth, or something else—virtually all concede that the economy's recent performance has a profound bearing on public assessments of the president.

These assessments, what is more, have important implications for people's vote choices on Election Day. When the national economy declines in the year before a presidential election, the incumbent president's vote share predictably declines. As the 2008 presidential election made clear, a flagging national economy also can have important implications for the electoral prospects of a presidential candidate from the same party as the incumbent. Already facing long odds, John McCain's chances of winning the presidency were all but dashed when the economy spiraled downward in early October 2008. (See Chapter 17 for a description of this event).

Approval ratings and rally events   Another factor in approval ratings are **rally events**, short-term international events or military actions that boost approval ratings.

rally event short-term international event or military action that boosts presidential approval ratings temporarily.

John F. Kennedy's rating surged 13 points in 1962 when the United States set up a blockade around Cuba after it was revealed that Soviet bases were being installed there. President George W. Bush's approval rating started out in the upper 50s and low 60s, substantially higher than his percentage of the vote in the 2000 election. It began drifting downward as perceived economic conditions deteriorated. Then, his approval rating rose enormously after the terrorist attacks on September 11, 2001 (see bottom panel of Figure 14-4). It also jumped sharply after the war with Iraq began in March 2003. Three days into the war, Bush's approval rating was 13 points higher than it had been before the war began. But by the summer of 2003, the president's approval rating was at about the level it was prior to September 11. After another short-lived rally event with the capture of Saddam Hussein, skepticism about the war in Iraq, the economy, and a series of missteps by the administration led to a steady decline in the president's approval rating.

Panel 1

Do you approve or disapprove of the job Barack Obama is doing as president?

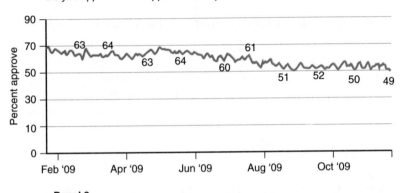

Panel 2

George W. Bush's Job Approval Ratings Trend

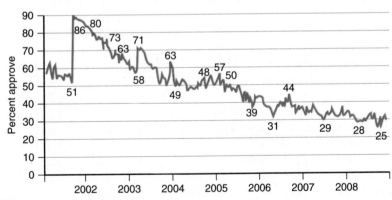

FIGURE 14-4. Percentage Approving of the President's Job Performance.

Panel 1, President Barack Obama's Job Performance, February 2009–December 2009. Over the course of Obama's first year in office, his job approval ratings steadily declined.

Panel 2, President George W. Bush's Job Performance, February 2001–November 2008.
President Bush's approval rating was defined by sharp increases during rally events and gradual erosion due to public dissatisfaction with his handling of the economy, the war, and other matters.

ThinkingCausally

Did scandal and impeachment lead paradoxically to higher approval ratings for President Clinton?

Scandal and approval ratings As expected, scandals usually depress presidential approval ratings. During the Watergate investigation of the early 1970s, Richard Nixon's job approval plummeted. However, scandals do not always cause ratings to drop. Bill Clinton's approval ratings went up during the investigation of the Monica Lewinsky matter and his subsequent impeachment. Did scandal actually cause higher approval? Not really. Many people, especially Democrats, saw the investigation as a partisan effort to weaken the president rather than a serious scandal, so the investigation and impeachment had little effect on their approval of Clinton. The usual tendency of scandals to depress approval was therefore weakened. Drawing a causal line from scandal to higher Clinton approval also overlooks an additional key factor that influences approval ratings. At the same time the impeachment drama was unfolding, the economy—a powerful predictor of presidential approval—was growing rapidly. The public rewarded Clinton primarily for the economy, not for being impeached.

Presidents seek popular support by "going public."

going public activities of presidents such as highly visible trips, press conferences, interviews, speeches, and public appearances in an attempt to raise public support for a policy agenda.

When **going public**, a president engages in a highly visible campaign of trips, press conferences, interviews, speeches, and appearances designed to galvanize support around his agenda. These campaigns are precisely plotted, scripted, choreographed, and timed to elicit a favorable response from the public and the media. Every symbol and prop on the platform from which the president speaks are carefully chosen.

Since World War II, presidents have gone public at an increasing rate. Dwight Eisenhower, in the 1950s, engaged in these activities about four times per month. The number 40 years later, during Bill Clinton's presidency, was nearly 30 times per month.

In these public appeals, the president has strong advantages over Congress. Simply put, he is more likely to attract media attention than are members of Congress. In part, the inherent significance of the presidency leads journalists to focus on this office. It is also due to the power of one—the president provides a single focal point that simplifies the task of presenting the news. Unlike 535 voting members of Congress, the president gives a journalist one story to tell.[31]

When President Bush advanced his case for tax cuts in April 2003, he made a one-day visit full of speeches and photo opportunities in Ohio, the home state of Republican Senator George Voinovich. The trip received heavy media coverage. The president hoped that generating public support for his tax plan in Ohio would put pressure on the senator to support the president's plan. Despite the president's pressure, the senator would not agree to the president's proposed tax cut—but he provided Bush the vote he needed for a tax cut of $350 billion, half of the original proposal. The plan passed the Senate 51–50, with Vice President Dick Cheney casting the deciding vote. Although going public did not completely succeed in this case, careful observers noted that it was remarkable that the president managed to persuade Congress—and a reluctant Senator Voinovich—to pass a tax cut during a time of war, with the budget deficit expanding sharply, just one year after the president's first major tax cut.[32]

Sizable election victories lead presidents to claim they have a mandate.

mandate the idea that the public provided clear policy guidance in the results of the prior election.

Presidents elected to office with sizable victories, and who ran on a clear policy platform, are often in an advantageous position when dealing with Congress. These presidents can claim that they have received a **mandate** from the American people; that is, the public spoke clearly in the election about the direction in which it wanted the country to move. Of course, the more consistent the election results are nationally, the stronger the president's case. It is a matter of perception: Can the president convince the country, or more immediately, Congress, that he has a mandate? Most will try.[33]

Barack Obama could make a compelling case for having received a popular mandate. Not only did he carry 28 states for a total of 365 electoral votes and 52.9 percent of the popular vote, he did so by winning states like North Carolina and New Mexico that traditionally have gone to Republicans. Furthermore, on Obama's coattails the Democratic Party in the 2008 elections strengthened its hold in both the House and Senate. When he assumed office, Obama's job-approval rating was 68 percent, second only to John F. Kennedy among newly elected presidents. Having campaigned expressly on the theme of change, Obama was poised to claim a mandate and tackle important elements of his policy agenda.[34] And so he would, as he quickly orchestrated the single largest stimulus package in the nation's history, a blend of infrastructure investments, tax cuts, and state funding that collectively carried a price tag of nearly $1 trillion. Later in the year, the president advanced a variety of education, stem cell research, and most dramatically, health care initiatives.

> "Can the president convince the country, or more immediately, Congress, that he has a mandate? Most will try."

Presidents rely on fellow partisans to promote their policies.

Normally, the president can count on the members of his party in Congress to help him enact his policy ideas. The more members of the president's party elected to Congress, the better his chances are for legislative victories. This is a valuable electoral resource. The president still needs to persuade his fellow partisans to go along with him, but that task will usually be simpler than convincing members of the other party.

Unified and divided control of government   Presidents, of course, do not choose the partisan balance in Congress, so they need to figure out how to work with the situation they face. Because his fellow partisans in Congress share many of his goals, presidents would prefer to have his party in control of both chambers of Congress. When Democrat Barack Obama became president, his party held a majority of seats in both the House and Senate, a situation known as **unified government**. The president thus was in a strong position to pass legislation to his liking. Success is not certain, however, because party members do not always fall in line. In most years since 1953, the president's fellow party members in the House voted against his position more than 20 percent of the time (Figure 14-5). Popular media accounts that criticize members of Congress for blindly supporting the president are therefore somewhat exaggerated. But why would fellow partisans defy their president? Multiple factors affect whether legislators support the president on a vote. Constituency pressure, district economic interests, public opinion, personal philosophy, and other factors may cause a member of the president's party to vote against the president. As discussed in Chapter 13, President George W. Bush had great difficulty unifying fellow Republicans around a single plan for immigration reform after his reelection in 2004. Similarly, significant accomplishments such as adding prescription drug benefits to Medicare were more popular among Democrats than Republicans. In both of these instances, many Republicans concluded that their electoral fortunes would be enhanced by challenging the president's position.

In **divided government**, the opposition party holds a majority of seats in one or both houses of Congress. If his party controls neither chamber, the president

ThinkingCausally

How do unified and divided government affect the likelihood of successful presidential leadership?

unified government   a situation where the presidency and both houses of Congress are controlled by the same party.

divided government   a situation where the presidency is held by one party and at least one house of Congress is controlled by a different party.

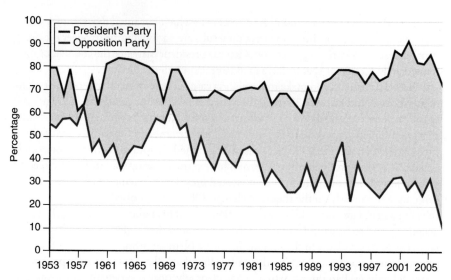

FIGURE 14-5. **Percentage of House Roll-Call Votes on Which Party Members Supported the President's Position, 1953–2007.** Presidents get the greatest support from their fellow partisans in Congress. The growing gap in support between the president's party and the opposition party, represented by the shaded area, means presidents have increasingly had to rely on support from their own party.

will typically face his most difficult challenges. Presidents may have some legislative success during this form of divided government, although less so than in unified government.[35] To succeed, the president needs to gain the support of a larger share of the opposition party by moving closer to their position, but without moving so far that he loses the support of his own partisans. The opposition party may want to deny the president victories, so it is likely to discourage its members from siding with the president. The president's success will be influenced by several factors, including how cohesive his party is, how cohesive the opposition party is, and the relative size of the two parties. The larger and more cohesive the opposition party is, the more difficult the president's legislative challenge will be.

Political scientists have found that party control of Congress complicates their analysis of presidential leadership. Politicians are strategic. In divided government, the president may have plans that he does not present to Congress because he believes they will have little chance at success. Or the president might offer a plan that he believes has as much or even more support in the opposition party than in his own. This was true for welfare reform during Bill Clinton's presidency and immigration reform during George W. Bush's. Similarly, during unified government, the president might offer bold legislative proposals that do not initially have strong support in the hope he can coax fellow party members to support him. Neither of these strategic actions changes the overall pattern that presidents have more legislative success in unified government. But the net effect of these actions would be some additional wins when the opposition party controls Congress and some additional losses when his party controls Congress.

Differences between presidential and parliamentary systems   These party dynamics make the president's relationship with Congress different from prime ministers' dealings with their legislatures in other countries. Whereas an American president is elected independently from Congress, and he can serve even if his own party is a minority in Congress, a prime minister will be in office only if his party is the majority. A president is elected in a national election, but in a parliamentary system, constituents elect only legislators.[36] The prime minister is then selected by his or her party peers within the parliament.[37] If the party loses control of the legislature in the next election, the prime minister will be replaced by someone from the new majority party. Should no single party secure a majority of the seats within Parliament, as occurred in the 2010 British elections, then a coalition government must be formed from at least two parties who constitute such a majority, and a Prime Minister is chosen from its ranks.

These differences make for significantly tighter ties between prime ministers and the legislators in their parties. Presidents Carter, Reagan, Clinton, and George W. Bush had all been state governors. Although somewhat familiar with national issues, they did not have strong ties with members of Congress. In contrast, prime ministers, as well as the heads of major government departments, emerge directly from the parliament. There is little need for "getting to know you" time. Not only do members of the party majority know the prime minister, but they have *chosen* him or her as the person they wish to lead the country. Typically, they are ready to work with that person from day one.

Because parliamentary elections are not bound to a fixed schedule, the prime minister must make a determined effort to keep these ties strong. The relative independence from Congress that American presidents prize is less attractive to prime ministers. Presidents rely heavily on their parties, but they also often need to forge ties across party lines to enact parts of their agenda. In many parliamentary systems, by contrast, crossing party lines to support another party's position is very rare and heavily punished by co-partisans. While co-partisans in Congress may try to separate their electoral fate from the president's, co-partisans in a parliament know that if the prime minister is seen as a failure, their party is almost certain to be relegated to minority status in the next election. They therefore have an even stronger incentive than the president's fellow partisans in Congress to support their chief executive.

ThinkingComparatively

Prime ministers have significantly tighter ties with their fellow partisans in the parliament than presidents do with their party members in Congress, which eases the policy-making process.

CaseStudy: Passing Health Care Reform

During the 2008 presidential election, Barack Obama promised sweeping changes to the American health care system, frequently discussing his mother's battle with insurance companies as she suffered ovarian cancer. Once in office, Obama set health care reform at the top of his domestic policy agenda. In his first year in office, he called for legislation that would impose new regulations on the insurance industry, control rising health care costs, and ensure quality and affordable health care for all Americans. To succeed, Obama would need to deploy virtually all the tools of leadership that were available to him.

Earlier U.S. presidents tried, and usually failed, to reform health care.[38] In the 1912 presidential elections, Theodore Roosevelt campaigned on a promise for national health insurance, but he lost the election to Woodrow Wilson. In 1945, President Harry Truman called on Congress to enact health care reform, including increasing the number of hospitals and doctors. His reform ideas, however, were never put into legislation. President John F. Kennedy also took on health care by trying to reform health benefits from Social Security coverage, but his proposal faced staunch opposition from the medical industry lobbyists and never passed Congress. In his first term, Bill Clinton famously tried and failed to overhaul the nation's health care system, which led to a Republican takeover of the House and Senate in 1994. Before President Obama, the last major successful reform effort was the creation of Medicare and Medicaid by President Lyndon B. Johnson in 1965.[39]

In March 2009, Obama formally announced his intention to seek health care reform. Although the failing economy demanded urgent attention, Obama pushed health care as a top domestic priority. As he put it, "I will not accept the status quo as a solution. Not this time. Not now."[40] Obama articulated some broad guidelines for reform—such as coverage for all Americans—but he left Congress with the responsibility of filling in the details. The president hoped that by actively currying Congress's involvement, he would rally the support of its members and thereby avoid the perceived mistakes of Bill Clinton's previous efforts at health care reform, which, critics charged, failed to include key members in its formulation.

With the House and Senate narrowly in Democratic control, Obama knew he would need every vote from within his party. To build public support for reform, Obama employed many of his grassroots organizing strategies from his 2008 presidential campaign, using a spin-off of his campaign organization to hold small rallies around the country. Obama spoke at length about the responsibility that members of Congress had to their constituents to bring about real change. "This is their moment, this is our moment, to live up to the trust that the American people have placed in us," Obama told reporters.[41] The president even called on Internet bloggers to pressure their representatives to support health care, telling them in a conference call: "It is important just to keep the pressure on members of Congress because what happens is there is a default position of inertia here in Washington," and the bloggers need to push "against that."[42]

However, Obama also faced significant grassroots opposition from conservatives. The Tea Party movement emerged in 2009 as a series of locally and nationally organized protests directed against what it saw as the administration's more intrusive policies. Centered around the themes of fiscal responsibility, limited government, and the free market, the Tea Party movement quickly gained national exposure by its vocal disapproval of not only the previous administration's bank bailouts but also President Obama's $787 billion stimulus package. In response to the White House's push for universal health care,

Tea Party members organized rallies throughout the country. Diana Reimer, a Tea Party leader, explained, "All I know is government was put here for certain reasons. They were not put here to run banks, insurance companies, and health care and automobile companies."[43] Using the same grassroots strategy employed by Obama during his campaign, Tea Party activists held numerous rallies outside the White House and members' offices in Washington, D.C. By pressuring local representatives and actively participating in political campaigns, the Tea Party hoped to defeat the bill.

When it came time for the House of Representatives to vote, Obama visited the chamber and made a rare personal appeal for lawmakers to support the bill. Just before the bill came up for a vote, Obama met with House Democrats to energize the party, reminding the representatives of the historic nature of the bill. He singled out those lawmakers who supported the bill knowing that their vote would not be popular with their constituents. Obama concluded his pep talk by expressing his confidence that they would be able to pass the bill, declaring that "each and every one of you will be able to look back and say, 'This was my finest moment in politics.'"[44] President Obama's lobbying paid off, as the bill narrowly passed with a vote of 220 to 215.

The president faced an even tougher battle in the Senate. In an effort to rally the caucus, Obama met with Democratic senators behind closed doors. Similar to the closed-door meeting with House Democrats before the vote in the House of Representatives, Obama stressed the urgency of the issue. The pep talk was even more necessary for the Senate than it was when the House voted because the Senate was even more divided over details over the bill. After heated debate in the late fall of 2009, the senators still had not settled on many contentious issues, such as how the new health care systems would cover abortions. The final vote fell along party lines with a 60–39 vote, bringing the

▶ **2010 PROTEST AGAINST HEALTH CARE BILL**

Though he ultimately prevailed, the president evoked widespread opposition when he tried to enact health care reform during 2009 and 2010. Here, Tea Party protestors rallied outside of Congress to the chant of "Kill The Bill."

health care bill even closer to reaching the goal of reform that Obama promised in his 2008 election campaign. The House and Senate versions of the bill now had to be reconciled.

In the weeks following the Senate's vote, Obama increased his campaign of personal appeals, this time enlisting the help of Democratic leaders Nancy Pelosi and Harry Reid. The three leaders met nonstop with the members of their caucus, sometimes issuing direct appeals to the constituents of swing voters within Congress. On March 23, 2010, the president finally signed health care reform into law. In Chapter 13, we discuss the parliamentary maneuvers within Congress that ultimately led to the enactment of health care reform in 2009. It is clear, though, that the passage would not have been possible absent the president's vigorous support.

Obama's work, however, was not finished. Having passed health care reform, the president sought to convince a skeptical American public of the value of the new law. To stave off a wave of attacks by conservative media outlets and

attorney generals seeking to undo as many provisions of the law as possible, the White House launched a multifaceted public relations campaign. The president created a new tax-exempt group to coordinate millions of dollars worth of publicity outreach both in the form of television advertisements and an interactive website comparing insurance plans. And Obama traveled the country, giving speeches and hosting nationally televised question-and-answer sessions on health care. These efforts continued well into the 2010 midterm congressional elections.

ThinkingCritically

1. Why did Obama's effort to enact comprehensive health care reform succeed when previous attempts had failed?

2. Did Obama's formal or informal powers play a more distinctive role in the effort to enact health care reform?

3. Will the enactment of health care reform strengthen or weaken the Tea Party movement? Why?

Presidents have advantages in foreign policy.

The context of policy-making differs between foreign and domestic policy. In foreign policy, which is discussed at greater length in Chapter 18, there are fewer interest groups, journalists, voters, and members of Congress who deeply care about these issues—a climate that gives the president a somewhat freer hand at advancing his agenda.[45] Because of this difference, the "two presidencies" theory argues that presidents exert significantly more influence over the writing and implementation of foreign policy than they do over domestic policy.

Does the different nature of the foreign policy-making environment lead to greater presidential success? Systematic evidence supports the two presidencies theory in some aspects of public policy-making but not in others. Presidential success on foreign policy votes in Congress has not been consistently better than in domestic policy votes. But more supportive of the theory, one analysis found that presidents are able to secure funding that better matches their budget priorities in foreign policy than they are in domestic policy. And when going public, presidents can sway public opinion more easily in foreign affairs than domestic affairs.

George W. Bush's tenure in office would appear to offer support for the two presidencies theory. In waging wars against governments in Afghanistan and Iraq and against terrorist networks worldwide, the president exerted his commander-in-chief authority, challenging the applicability of some U.S. laws and international treaties. But where these efforts had domestic implications, such as the trial and detention of terrorism suspects, Congress and the courts tended to resist the president's authority. And his stiffest legislative challenges were on domestic issues like Social Security reform.

▼ **HOPING TO STEER TOWARD ECONOMIC RECOVERY**

Not all presidents enter office with the right circumstances for enacting bold changes in policy, but a financial crisis and the public's desire for a change in direction may have given Barack Obama more opportunity than most. The public, though, proved quick to turn on the president, who saw his approval ratings drop by more than 20 points during his first 18 months in office.

ThinkingCausally

Does the nature of the foreign policy-making environment lead to greater presidential success in that policy area than in domestic policy?

Institutional Resources for Presidential Leadership

14-4 Assess the role of the Cabinet, the Executive Office of the President, and the White House staff in assisting the president.

To improve their chances at leading successfully, presidents rely on the established agencies and offices of the executive branch; they may also create an array of new supporting institutions. Think of these institutions as concentric circles, with the president in the center. The outer ring consists of the Cabinet departments (discussed in further detail in Chapter 16). Closer in to the president is the Executive Office of the President, established during the presidency of Franklin Roosevelt. Closest to the president is the White House Staff. These institutions provide different kinds of resources for presidential leadership efforts. All have grown in size over time, especially since World War II.[46]

The Cabinet departments implement federal programs.

Cabinet a group of the top-ranking officials of every major federal department, plus other officials included by the president, who meet periodically with the president to discuss major administration priorities and policies.

The outer ring of institutional resources, furthest away from the president, is the **Cabinet**, which includes departments that implement nearly all government programs and provide the vast majority of government services (see Figure 14-6). The Senate must approve the president's appointments to leadership positions in the 15 Cabinet departments. The heads of these departments are known as "secretaries" except for the Department of Justice, the head of which is the attorney general. These individuals are appointed, first, to run the major departments of the government and, second, to provide advice to the president and help him implement his agenda. Though the president often meets with the Cabinet as a group, he can also call on its members' individual expertise. Treasury, State, Defense, and Justice are generally considered the most important and powerful departments.

All department secretaries are permanent members of the Cabinet, but the president may also include other agencies that are not under the organizational control of any of the major departments. President Clinton, for example, included the Environmental Protection Agency. Presidents will add these agencies to the Cabinet primarily because they genuinely want to hear the input of these agencies at Cabinet meetings, they want to make a symbolic show of support for a particular issue, or both.

From the president's point of view, there is always a risk that a department secretary will become so closely attached to the interests and perspectives of his or her department—become "captured"—that, rather than communicating the president's viewpoint to the department, the secretary may push the department's views onto the president. When the president's ideas meet resistance from department personnel, will the secretary support the president or will he or she obstruct the president's agenda? One notable case during the George W. Bush presidency concerned Christine Todd Whitman, the administrator of the Environmental Protection Agency (who has Cabinet status). She resigned after a series of policy disagreements with the president and his closest advisers, including Vice President Dick Cheney, out of concern that the opinions of agency scientists were being overruled.

Because they are relatively high-profile figures, Cabinet officials also have the potential to put the president in the awkward situation of either defending or repudiating the Cabinet member. Statements by Defense Secretary Donald Rumsfeld, for example, created occasional controversy that forced a response from President Bush.

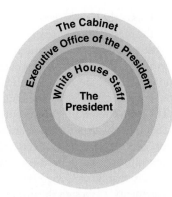

The Cabinet

Department Secretaries

State
Treasury
Defense
Justice
Health and Human Services
Labor
Commerce
Transportation
Energy
Housing and Urban Development
Veterans Affairs
Agriculture
Interior
Education
Homeland Security

Others Granted Cabinet Rank

Vice President
Administrator, Environmental
  Protection Agency
Director, Office of Management
  and Budget
U.S. Trade Representative
Director, Office of National Drug
  Control Policy

White House Staff

Chief of Staff
Press Secretary
Legislative Affairs
Political Affairs
Public Liaison
Communications Director
White House Counsel
Intergovernmental Affairs
Policy Planning and
  Development
Cabinet Liaison
Domestic and Economic Affairs
Science and Technology Policy
National Security Affairs
Strategic Initiatives

Executive Office of the President

Council of Economic Advisors
Office of Management and Budget
Office of National AIDS Policy
Office of National Drug Control Policy
United States Trade Representative
Council on Environmental Quality
National Security Council
Domestic Policy Council
National Economic Council
Office of Administration
Office of Science and
  Technology Policy
President's Foreign Intelligence
  Advisory Board
Office of Faith-Based and Community
  Initiatives
Homeland Security Council
Privacy and Civil Liberties Oversight
  Board
USA Freedom Corps
White House Fellows Office
White House Military Office
Office of the First Lady
White House Office of Health Reform

FIGURE 14-6. The Institutional Presidency, 2010. The president relies on the Cabinet departments to implement programs, the Executive Office of the President to provide policy advice, and the White House Staff to provide political advice.

In December 2004, Rumsfeld, hearing an American soldier's complaint that the military's vehicles in Iraq lacked adequate armor, replied that the Army was working as fast as it could to address the problem, but "you go to war with the Army you have. They're not the Army you might want or wish to have at a later time. . . . And if you think about it, you can have all the armor in the world on a tank and a tank can be blown up." Although in context Rumsfeld's comments expressed concern for the safety of troops, his seemingly aloof tone in the media's sound bites raised a firestorm of protest. White House officials found themselves defending the comments, and even the president was drawn into the fray in his press conference on December 20: "Listen, I know Secretary Rumsfeld's heart... Beneath that rough and gruff no-nonsense demeanor is a good human being who cares deeply about the military and deeply about the grief war causes."[47]

One sign of the strain between presidents and the Cabinet is the large turnover of Cabinet officials in presidents' second terms. Although sometimes a Cabinet official simply wants to move on to a new challenge, obtain a more lucrative job in the private sector, or have a less hectic lifestyle, often Cabinet turnover results from presidential displeasure with the official's performance. In the twentieth century, an average of about two Cabinet department heads served for both terms of a two-term presidency.[48] After being reelected in 2004, President George W. Bush replaced nine of 15 department

ThinkingComparatively 🌑⬤⬤⬤

Prime ministers usually know and have worked with their department heads because they served in the parliament together, but presidents usually need on-the-job training to get to know their department leaders.

secretaries. Of the six who continued, four had taken their positions at the start of the president's first term. One of these was Rumsfeld, who, long under fire from both Democratic and Republican legislators, resigned shortly after the Republicans' loss of the House and Senate in the 2006 elections. Only one department head, Elaine Chao at the Department of Labor, served for Bush's entire presidency.

The problems of directing department heads are more severe for the U.S. president than for prime ministers in European parliamentary systems. The U.S. president selects department heads from outside the legislature; the prime minister puts fellow legislators in charge of departments. The president cannot be sure that he or Congress will be able to work well with the heads of the Cabinet departments. Although the president appoints these officials, they are often people the president does not know well and has not worked with. The prime minister, on the other hand, chooses members of his or her party in the parliament to head the government departments. This would typically mean the prime minister has worked with these individuals and has confidence in them.

To avoid some of the challenges of working with Cabinet secretaries, some recent presidents have turned to policy "czars" for advice. These czars report directly to the president, do not require Senate confirmation, and assist in the coordination of policies across different departments. The use of the term "czar" dates back to the Franklin D. Roosevelt administration, but Richard M. Nixon was the first president to actually appoint one—a drug czar. Every president since has appointed multiple special advisers. During his tenure in office, President George W. Bush had 36 czars. And depending on the source, President Obama has had anywhere from 18 to 32 czars charged with policy responsibilities ranging from oversight of the car industry to executive compensation, Afghanistan, and climate change.[49]

According to White House Press Secretary Robert Gibbs, "Lots of these [positions] are designed to bring many different efforts together and coordinate them in a way that is more structured and more efficient than the governmental work chart might ordinarily allow."[50] Some members of Congress, however, do not see it that way. Republican Susan Collins of Maine complained, "Little information is available concerning their responsibilities and authorities. There is no careful Senate examination of their character and qualifications. And we are speaking here of some of the most senior positions within our government."[51] Collins has pursued an initiative to curb the amount of government spending on czars and to increase congressional oversight for the positions.

The Executive Office of the President provides policy advice to the president.

Executive Office of the President a group of agencies in the executive branch that primarily generate policy alternatives for the president's consideration.

The next closest concentric ring to the president is the **Executive Office of the President** (EOP), which consists of a number of policy-related groups that aid the president. Officials in the EOP generate policy alternatives and suggestions that are more faithful to the president's political agenda.[52] Their primary responsibility is to provide the president with trusted policy advice. Unlike Cabinet departments, EOP agencies generally do not administer programs (except in the sense of coordinating and directing the efforts of other federal agencies) and they do not have large staffs of career civil servants. Therefore, from the president's perspective, EOP officials do not have to wrestle with the pull of departmental loyalty that clouds the judgment of Cabinet secretaries. As Figure 14-6 indicates, the EOP provides advice and guidance across a number of policy areas, in some ways paralleling the areas covered by the Cabinet departments.

The single most important EOP agency is the Office of Management and Budget (OMB). OMB serves as a gateway through which departments must pass in making their budgetary requests, and it approves proposed regulations and testimony that a department wants to bring before Congress. In effect, OMB serves as a filter to make sure that departments are not seeking funds or regulations that are contrary to the president's program. Other especially important EOP agencies are the Central Intelligence Agency, the Council of Economic Advisers, and the National Security Council.

The vice president is officially part of the EOP. Most vice presidents, however, are selected not only to offer policy expertise but also to provide the president with electoral advantages. A president with no Washington experience, for example, might select a vice president who has held office in the nation's capital. Or a vice president might be chosen because he or she increases the president's chances of winning a key state or region. The vice presidency is an often maligned institution, mostly because it has only two defined duties: to break tie votes in the Senate and to succeed the president in case of the death, incapacity, or removal of the president from office. In some administrations, however, vice presidents do appear to play a greater role in policy-making. Bill Clinton delegated several significant policy tasks to Al Gore, and George W. Bush relied on the foreign policy advice of Vice President Dick Cheney, a former secretary of defense. The current Vice President, Joe Biden, offers extensive foreign policy recommendations to President Obama.

The offices of the White House Staff provide political advice to the president.

The institutional circle closest to the president is the **White House Staff** (WHS), sometimes referred to as the White House Office. The WHS provides the president with political advice, promotes the president's program with legislators and interest groups, and handles the president's public relations. With only about 420 employees in the Bush administration, the WHS was relatively small compared to the EOP, which had about 1,800 employees, and the Cabinet departments, which totaled 1.7 million civilian employees. The WHS consists of small units such as the offices of the press secretary, legislative affairs, public liaison, and intergovernmental affairs, to name a few. The primary concern of the WHS is the political well-being of the president. Whereas the EOP provides the president with policy advice and might be thought of as the president's policy filter, the White House Staff is the political filter. Figure 14-7 provides examples of the issues raised by the WHS when it considers policy proposals that emerge either from executive departments or Congress.

For President George W. Bush, Karl Rove was the key political confidante. A senior adviser since Bush's Texas days, Rove headed three WHS offices. In his words, "my job is to pay attention to the things that affect his political future."[53] He was credited with fostering close ties between the president and evangelical Christians. He also, however, came under fierce criticism in Bush's second term for the administration's political missteps concerning Hurricane Katrina, the war in Iraq, and allegations of government corruption.

White House Staff a group of offices in the executive branch that provides the president with political advice, promotes the president's program with legislators and interest groups, and handles the president's public relations.

▼ JOE BIDEN IN IRAQ
Vice President Biden has played a strong role advising President Obama on foreign policy. On July 4, 2010, he addressed troops in Baghdad, Iraq.

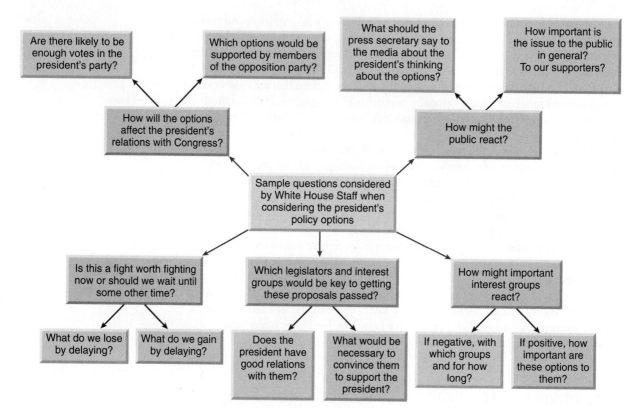

FIGURE 14-7. **Types of Questions Asked by the White House Staff.** The White House Staff provides the president an analysis of the political environment.

When he named Illinois Congressman Rahm Emanuel as his chief of staff, President Obama likewise tapped an accomplished political strategist for a leading WHS role. Emanuel was a senior adviser to President Clinton for seven years, led the Democratic Congressional Campaign Committee in 2006 when Democrats won a majority in the U.S. House, and as chair of the Democratic Congressional Caucus in 2007–2008 was instrumental in setting party strategy on policy positions and communications. Emanuel's time in the White House, however, would prove short lived. On October 1, 2010, just weeks after long-time Chicago mayor Richard Daley announced his own retirement from politics, Emanuel announced that he would leave the White House in order to run for Daley's former position.

CHAPTER SUMMARY

In this chapter you have learned to:

14-1 **Trace the Constitutional origins and historical expansion of presidency power.** The Constitution created the presidency, but the office subsequently underwent extraordinary changes. The American presidency was an attempt by the Framers to balance many competing ideas about executive power. As a compromise, it contains some inherent contradictions. It is the office that Americans demand the most from, but its constitutional list of specific duties is relatively meager. The very vagueness of the job description has accommodated a historical expansion of the meaning and

impact of the presidency from the time of the early republic to the present.

14-2 **Distinguish between the formal and informal powers of contemporary presidents.** Presidents have both formal and informal powers to reach their goals. Formal powers such as the veto, executive orders, and the role of commander in chief are specified in law or the Constitution, or are realized through independent executive initiative. The origins of informal powers are less easily identified. These powers include the president's skill at persuading others to do what he wants and the ability to tap into and strategically exploit the reservoir of support for basic values in American political culture. The manner in which presidents use their powers can be checked by the courts, which can declare presidential actions unconstitutional or inconsistent with law, and by Congress, which can use its legislative, budgeting, and, in extreme cases, impeachment powers to thwart presidents.

14-3 Analyze how presidents use public support, electoral victories, and Congressional allies to push through their policies. Presidents draw on a variety of public, electoral, and contextual resources to exercise leadership. The president's public approval receives substantial attention from politicians and political observers, and presidents devote significant amounts of time to appealing to the public to support their proposals. A president with a convincing election victory and his

party in the majority in the House and Senate is in a strong position for successful leadership. Other factors that affect a president's success are the support for existing policies as well as differences between foreign and domestic policy.

14-4 Assess the role of the Cabinet, the Executive Office of the President, and the White House staff in assisting the president. Presidents also rely on institutional resources to advance their policy agenda. The Cabinet departments implement nearly all federal programs and are therefore crucial to the president's agenda. The Executive Office of the President provides the president with policy advice. And the White House Staff specializes in providing the president political advice and services.

PEARSON
mypoliscilab

EXERCISES

Apply what you learned in this chapter by starting with these resources on MyPoliSciLab.

Read on **mypoliscilab.com**

   eText: Chapter 14

Study and **Review** on **mypoliscilab.com**

   Pre-Test
   Post-Test
   Chapter Exam
   Flashcards

Watch on **mypoliscilab.com**

   Video: Bush and the Congress
   Video: The Government Bails Out Automakers

Explore on **mypoliscilab.com**

   Simulation: Presidential Leadership: Which Hat Do You Wear?
   Simulation: You Are a President During a Nuclear Power Plant Meltdown
   Comparative: Comparing Chief Executives
   Timeline: The Executive Order Over Time
   Visual Literacy: Presidential Success in Polls and Congress

KEY TERMS

approval rating, p. 517
Cabinet, p. 526
delegation, p. 505
divided government, p. 521
Electoral College, p. 499
executive agreement, p. 512
Executive Office of the President,
   p. 528

executive order, p. 512
executive privilege, p. 504
formal powers, p. 510
going public, p. 520
impeachment, p. 516
leadership, p. 509
line-item veto, p. 511
mandate, p. 520

necessary and expedient clause,
   p. 501
pocket veto, p. 510
take care clause, p. 501
rally event, p. 518
unified government, p. 521
veto, p. 510
White House Staff, p. 529

CHAPTER TEST

1. Among the nation's Founders, what were the major points of disagreement about the design of the presidency?

2. What, in your view, was the most significant constitutional power granted to the president? Why?

3. How have presidents exploited the ambiguities of Article II in order to expand the powers of their office?

4. In what ways does the president play a formal role in the legislative process?

5. Do the president's formal and informal powers complement one another, or are they mutually exclusive?
6. Why would Congress delegate authority to the president?
7. Why do presidents tend to exert more influence over foreign policy than they do over domestic policy?
8. When is the American public most amenable to public appeals by the president?

9. Who provides presidents with the information they need in order to lead the country?
10. When formulating their policy agendas, why might presidents prefer to appoint policy "czars" rather than depend on Cabinet secretaries?

SUGGESTED READINGS

Edward Corwin. 1948. *The President, Office and Powers, 1787–1948: History and Analysis of Practice and Opinion.* New York: New York University Press. Classic treatment of the president's constitutional powers.

Marc Landy and Sidney Milkis. 2000. *Presidential Greatness.* Lawrence: University Press of Kansas. Careful assessment of the elements of presidential greatness and the individuals who achieved it.

Sidney Milkis and Michael Nelson. 2003. *The American Presidency: Origins and Development, 1776–2002.* Washington, DC: CQ Press. Thorough history of the evolution of the office of the presidency since the nation's founding.

Richard Neustadt. 1990. *Presidential Power and the Modern Presidents.* New York: Free Press. A highly influential analysis of the informal powers that presidents utilize to achieve their policy objectives in the modern era.

Richard Pious. 1995. *The Presidency.* New York: Longman. Overview of the office of the presidency, with special attention to historical developments.

Arthur M. Schlesinger Jr. 2004. *The Imperial Presidency,* reprint ed. New York: Mariner. A popular exploration of the growth of presidential power across American history.

Stephen Skowronek. 2007. *The Politics Presidents Make: Leadership from John Adams to Bill Clinton.* Cambridge, MA: Harvard University Press. A rich account of the various political environments facing presidents when they assume office and the limits and opportunities for leadership in those environments.

SUGGESTED WEBSITES

White House: www.whitehouse.gov
Provides overviews of the president's initiatives, text of presidential statements, and links to executive branch agencies and offices.

American President: An Online Reference Resource: www.millercenter.org/academic/americanpresident
Detailed biographical information on each president and key administration officials, with links to audio files of major presidential speeches and interviews with major figures from the presidencies of Jimmy Carter through Bill Clinton.

American Presidency Project: www.presidency.ucsb.edu
Outstanding collection of resources of nearly 80,000 documents related to the presidency, campaigns, and presidential activities in office.

National Archives: Presidential Libraries and Museums: www.archives.gov/presidential-libraries
Guide to the presidential library system, including links to online archival documents.

U.S. Presidency Links: http://cstl-cla.semo.edu/renka/presidencylinks.htm
Comprehensive and helpful A-to-Z guide to presidential information maintained by Russell Renka at Southeast Missouri State University.

The Courts Rule on Campaign Finance

On January 21, 2009, a deeply divided Supreme Court struck down limits on campaign funding by corporations, nonprofits, and labor unions. The groundbreaking 5–4 decision allows businesses and unions to spend millions on political campaigns. The case, *Citizens United v. Federal Election Commission*, centered on a dispute over whether the Federal Election Commission could regulate the communications of a documentary called *Hillary: The Movie*, which attacked the 2008 presidential candidate Hillary Clinton and was produced by a conservative non-profit organization. The Court ruled that regulating the documentary, and the funds used to create and disseminate it, constituted an infringement on free speech.[1]

Reaction to the ruling was split along ideological lines. Republicans praised the Court for upholding free speech. According to former Attorney General Theodore Olson, who represented Citizens United, the Court's decision will "invigorate political discourse . . . and, ultimately, strengthen the very foundations of our democracy."[2] Democrats, however, depicted the

decision as a setback for fair elections. Congressional Democrats, in particular, argued that the ruling gave corporations too much power over elections. "This will allow the biggest corporations in the United States to engage in the buying and selling of elections," declared Representative Chris Van Hollen from Maryland. President Barack Obama weighed in with criticisms of his own, condemning the Supreme Court in his first State of the Union Address: "With all due deference to separation of powers, last week, the Supreme Court reversed a century of law that I believe will open the floodgates for special interests, including foreign corporations, to spend without limit in our elections."[3]

The Court's rationale for ruling as it did focused on free speech and anti-regulation. Writing for the majority, Justice Kennedy explained that "when government seeks to use its full power, including the criminal law, to command where a person may get his or her information or what distrusted source he or she may not hear, it uses censorship to control thought." Referencing the First Amendment of the Constitution, the majority claimed that the regulation of corporate spending in elections inhibited political dialogue and debate.

Before President George W. Bush's two appointments, John Roberts and Samuel Alito, swung the Supreme Court in a conservative direction, the Court had ruled differently on similar cases on election spending. Former Justice John Paul Stevens cited this

factor in his scathing dissenting opinion: "The only relevant thing that has changed since *Austin* and *McConnell* [a past case on election spending] is the composition of this Court."

Many believe the Court's ruling will benefit the GOP, for the simple reason that big businesses traditionally support Republicans over Democrats.[4] Immediately after the Supreme Court's ruling, therefore, congressional Democrats promised legislation to curb the effects of corporate funding in elections. Only the Supreme Court can decide the constitutionality of the issue, but Democrats could craft bills to push for regulations on the spending. Some possible regulations include requiring shareholder approval of expenditures or the addition of limiting conditions to federal funds that go to corporations. According to many law experts, however, it will be difficult to craft new limits on corporations or union spending in elections in ways that comport with the Court's ruling.[5]

The tangible effects of the Court's ruling remain to be seen. The case itself, though, reveals two important facts about the Supreme Court. First, and most obviously, the Court adjudicates disputes that have extremely important political, and by extension policy, consequences. Second, factors that cause justices to rule one way or another often go beyond the legal and constitutional and into the ideological. Rather than being shielded from politics, as the Founders had hoped, the judiciary directly engages and often fuels some of the deepest ideological controversies.

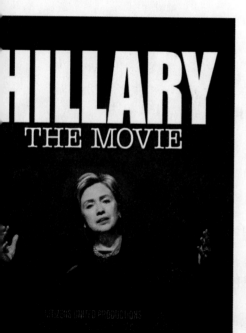

CITIZENS UNITED PRODUCTIONS

◄ HILLARY THE MOVIE

At the center of *Citizens United v. Federal Elections Commission*, a 2009 Supreme Court case involving the funding of political advertising, was a documentary that was critical of Hillary Clinton. In your view, was the Supreme Court correct in deciding that the Federal Elections Commission could not regulate documentaries such as this one?

CHAPTER LEARNING OBJECTIVES

After reading this chapter you will be able to:

15-1 Determine the role of the judiciary as established by the framers of the U.S. Constitution.

15-2 Outline the structure of the U.S. judiciary branch.

15-3 Distinguish between civil and criminal cases, and describe methods used to manage the judicial caseload.

15-4 Explain how judges decide cases that involve public policy.

15-5 Analyze the process of judicial appointment and selection.

The Constitutional Design of the Federal Judiciary

15-1 Determine the role of the judiciary as established by the Framers of the U.S. Consitution.

At the nation's founding, the Framers sought to build a federal judiciary that would serve the federal government in much the same way that state judiciaries had done in state governments for years. A federal judiciary was needed to perform the core functions of: (1) interpreting the laws that Congress and the president enacted; (2) issuing rulings over disputes where no guiding legislation previously existed; (3) ensuring that individuals who violated these laws and rulings were appropriately punished; and (4) compensating (where possible) the victims of these violations.

The first three articles of the Constitution lay out the powers, resources, and responsibilities of Congress (in Article I), then of the president (in Article II), and finally of the judiciary (in Article III). Last in order, Article III also is shortest in length. It establishes a "supreme Court" and "inferior Courts" operating underneath its jurisdiction; it recognizes a "judicial power" that applies to laws, treaties, and other formal acts of government; and it offers some brief guidelines about the prosecution of cases involving criminal behavior and treason. And that is all.

The Founders gave the judiciary a brief and rather vague mandate. A complete system of courts did not appear until 1789, when Congress enacted the Judiciary Act, which created a system of lower courts that would ease the workload of the one Supreme Court. It should not come as a surprise, then, that most of the Founders expected the judiciary would be the weakest of the three branches of government. According to Alexander Hamilton, the judiciary would be the "least dangerous branch." Whereas Congress had the power of the purse (that is, the power to levy taxes) and the president had the power of the sword (that is, control over the military), the judiciary had only its judgment. Thus, the ability of judges to exert political power ultimately depended on the persuasive appeal of the substantive rulings that they handed down. Recognizing its original design, the political scientist Robert Dahl concluded that the judiciary's "most important [base of power] is the unique legitimacy attributed to its interpretations of the Constitution."[6]

Consequentially, from the nation's beginning, judicial proceedings were structured to foster notions of respect and legitimacy. And so they are to this very day. Deliberations in courts are different from those in any other political institution. When judges enter courtrooms, parties to a case are required to stand. Judges are referred to as "your honor." When serving on the bench, judges wear robes. All of this symbolic imagery is meant to increase the chances that citizens and other political actors will accept court rulings as binding—for again, lacking the powers of either the purse or sword, the courts have little means by which to independently ensure that others heed their orders.

Perhaps most importantly, judges do everything possible to exude the qualities of a trustworthy and independent arbiter of justice. Judges go out of their way to distinguish themselves from elected political actors, whose job it is to represent the interests of a diverse and often fickle public. In the tumult of daily political life, courts protect individual rights, constitutional principles, and time-tested legal doctrine against the "tyranny of the majority." Judges do their utmost to rise above, rather than engage in, politics.

For the most part, such efforts of successive generations of judges seem to have borne fruit. Today, citizens hold the courts in higher regard than any other branch of government. According to national public opinion polls conducted in the summer 2010, 69 percent of Americans expressed favorable views of the Supreme Court. By comparison, roughly 45 percent of Americans approved of the job Barack Obama was doing as president, and only 21 percent had a favorable perception of Congress.[7] Even when public approval of the Supreme Court dips, it usually remains at least as high as that for the other branches. For instance, in September 2008, the Supreme Court's approval ratings fell to 50 percent. Yet even then, public support for the Supreme Court remained 19 percentage points higher than the president's job approval rating and 32 percentage points higher than support for Congress.[8]

With such strong public support, the courts stand at the center of some of the most pressing national controversies—about freedom of speech, reproduction, civil rights, the treatment of "enemy combatants," and the like. Failing to advance their preferred political reforms in the legislative and executive branches, interest groups often turn to the courts. Both state and federal law enforcement agencies prosecute criminal activities through the courts. And when individuals believe that their constitutional rights have been violated, they regularly seek redress in the judiciary.

This chapter examines how the federal court system is structured, and how federal judges make decisions about cases. When we analyze the latter issue, though, it will not do to simply take the supposed impartiality of the judiciary at face value. Just because judges claim to operate outside the realm of politics does not mean, as a matter of practice, that they do. In fact, politics plays an integral role in both the selection of judges and in judicial decision-making itself.

The Organization of the Federal Judiciary

15-2 Outline the structure of the U.S. judiciary branch.

The core elements of the federal judiciary consist of district courts, appellate courts, and the Supreme Court. These courts accept three kinds of cases: those in which the federal government is a party; those that involve a question about the U.S. Constitution, a federal law, or a federal treaty; and those involving a large civil suit between two parties from different states. In terms of sheer volume, district courts, appellate courts, and the Supreme Court collectively decide the vast majority of cases that come before the federal judiciary.

The federal judiciary is hierarchical.

Figure 15-1 on page 538 shows the three tiers of the federal judiciary. The bottom tier consists of 94 **district courts**. Every state contains at least one district court, and the most populous (California, Texas, and New York) contain as many as four. Individual judges oversee district court proceedings. In 2008, a total of 678 full-time federal judges worked in district courts. These judges are appointed by the president and

district courts   the first tier of the federal judiciary where most cases are decided.

can hold office for as long as they are alive. These life-term judges then have the power to appoint **magistrate judges**, who serve either four- or eight-year terms. By hearing and deciding minor cases, and by overseeing the early stages of major cases, magistrate judges help reduce the caseload of district court judges. In 2008, 557 magistrate judges worked in district courts around the nation.[9]

The second tier of the federal judiciary consists of **appellate courts**. Appellate courts, as discussed further below, primarily consider challenges to cases that have already been decided at the district level. Appellate courts are organized into 13 circuits. As shown in Figure 15-2, (on page 539) 12 circuits have regional jurisdictions; that is, the rulings of courts within these circuits are legally binding within a specified geographic area. Eleven of these circuits are referred to by number, and one is referred to as the "District of Columbia Circuit." There is also a federal circuit, which accepts cases based on subject matter rather than regional location. In 2008, a total of 178 appellate judges worked in the federal circuit courts. Typically, panels of three judges hear cases at the appellate level. To win a case, therefore, a party must secure the support of either two or three of the judges.

Standing atop the federal judiciary is the **Supreme Court**, which is the only court that is explicitly identified in Article III of the Constitution. Although there are many district and appellate courts, there is just one Supreme Court, which is located in Washington, D.C. In any given year, the Supreme Court considers only a small fraction of the cases that have proceeded through the district and appellate courts. Between 2004 and 2009, the Supreme Court never heard more than 92 cases per year, and it never offered a decision on more than 85.[10] Though the Supreme Court decides far fewer cases than the other courts, those that it does decide tend to have the biggest impact on society. Some of the most important have included *Brown v. Board of Education* (1954), which struck down state-mandated segregation in public schools; *Gideon v. Wainwright* (1963), which required the government to ensure that all individuals charged with criminal acts were granted adequate legal representation; *U.S. v. Nixon* (1974), which forced President Nixon to turn over White House audio recordings that would ultimately lead to his resignation from office; and *Bush v. Gore* (2000), which put George W. Bush in the White House.

magistrate judges   judges who support federal district judges by hearing and deciding minor cases at the district court level.

appellate courts   the second tier of the federal judiciary, primarily responsible for reviewing decisions rendered by the first tier of district courts.

▼ **CHALLENGING THE WAR ON TERROR**

The Supreme Court repeatedly shot down efforts by the Bush administration and Congress to establish an alternative court system to try individuals suspected of terrorism. On June 29, 2006, lawyers for Salim Ahmed Hamdan, an "enemy combatant" held in the U.S. military base at Guantanamo Bay, Cuba, left the Supreme Court after it issued its ruling on military tribunals. That day, the Court ruled that the president had overstepped his authority in ordering military war crimes trials for Guantanamo detainees. Two years later, the Court would once again strike down a similar law that had been enacted by Congress and signed by the president. What role, if any, do you think that the courts should play in defining national efforts to combat terrorism?

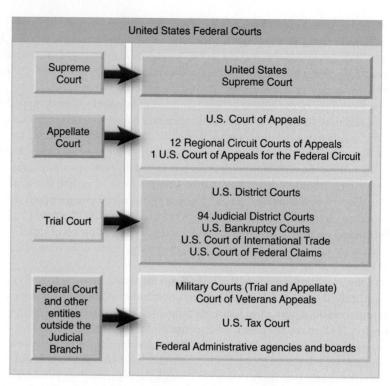

United States Federal Courts

| Supreme Court | → | United States Supreme Court |

| Appellate Court | → | U.S. Court of Appeals

12 Regional Circuit Courts of Appeals
1 U.S. Court of Appeals for the Federal Circuit |

| Trial Court | → | U.S. District Courts

94 Judicial District Courts
U.S. Bankruptcy Courts
U.S. Court of International Trade
U.S. Court of Federal Claims |

| Federal Court and other entities outside the Judicial Branch | → | Military Courts (Trial and Appellate)
Court of Veterans Appeals

U.S. Tax Court

Federal Administrative agencies and boards |

FIGURE 15-1. **The Federal Judiciary Is Hierarchical.** Most federal cases are decided in district courts. A portion of them are then appealed to appellate courts. A tiny fraction of these make it to the Supreme Court, which has final say over the outcome.

Supreme Court the highest court in the land, where all decisions are final.

In the United States, the three tiers of state-level courts mirror (in name and function) the three tiers of federal-level courts. Other countries, however, have structured their systems rather differently. In Israel, for example, religious courts—which deal with disputes about Jewish dietary laws, the necessary qualifications to become a rabbi, and other matters relating to religious law and custom—co-exist with secular magistrate, district, and supreme courts that focus on civil and criminal proceedings. Portugal's Supreme Court is at the top of a tiered system that handles civil and criminal cases, but a separate Constitutional Court is responsible for judging the constitutionality of legislative acts and international agreements. Finland has created special courts to handle certain types of civil cases, such as land, water, or labor disputes. Clearly, there is no single template for how a judicial system ought to be structured. Instead, countries tend to develop legal systems that reflect their political histories and cultural norms, and that best suit the particular kinds of local cases that require resolution.[11]

ThinkingComparatively 🌐 ⚫⚫⚫

Judicial systems in Israel and Europe look structurally quite different from those found in the United States.

District and appellate rulings can be appealed to the next level.

Almost all federal court cases start at the district level. District judges, though, do not have the final say about a case's outcome. The losing side always has the option of appealing to the appellate court, which can affirm the district court's decision, reverse

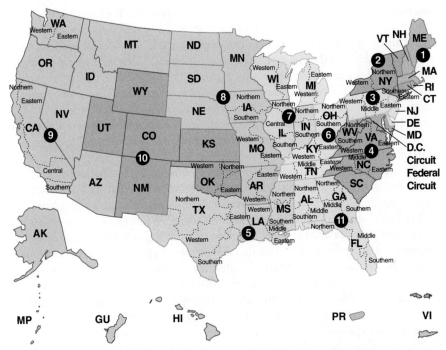

FIGURE 15-2. U.S. Federal Courts Are Divided into Circuits. Circuits serve different geographic regions, which vary dramatically in size. The first circuit includes only the northeastern portion of the country. The ninth, by contrast, includes the entire West, along with Alaska and Hawaii.

it, or refuse to take the case—in which case the district ruling stands. Whatever the outcome at the appellate level, the losing side has yet another opportunity to appeal— this time to the Supreme Court. The highest court to issue a ruling has the final say on the outcome of the case.

The vast majority of cases terminate at the district court, and therefore it is the district court's judgment that usually settles the matter. The high costs of litigation, combined with the fact that higher courts usually come to the same judgment as lower courts, generally convince the losing side to accept defeat. Trying cases, additionally, can take an extraordinary amount of time. It can take years for a case to wind its way through the federal judiciary.

The Supreme Court is especially choosy about which cases it will hear. Historically, the Supreme Court has accepted—or, to use the technical term, granted a **writ of certiorari** to—around 5 percent of petitions for appeals. Given the astronomical rise of cases filed with the Supreme Court in the last half-century, this number has dwindled down to about 1 percent. In 1945, just over 1,000 cases were appealed to the Supreme Court. By 2000, the number surpassed 9,000 cases, but it declined to 7,738 in 2008.[12]

The Supreme Court is the only judicial body that grants "cert," short for *writ of certiorari*. Doing so requires the support of four Supreme Court justices, the so-called "rule of four." Typically, the Court grants cert when either an important legal or constitutional issue is at stake, or when lower courts in different circuits come to different conclusions about a particular issue.[13] Such was the case in 2005 when the

writ of certiorari a formal acceptance by the Supreme Court to review a decision of a lower court.

Court chose to hear two cases dealing with the display of the Ten Commandments on government property. In *McCreary County v. ACLU of Kentucky*, the Sixth Circuit ruled that two Kentucky counties' displays of the Ten Commandments on the walls of their courthouses violated the establishment clause of the First Amendment. Around the same time, the Fifth Circuit in *Van Orden v. Perry* ruled that the display of the Ten Commandments on the grounds of the Texas State Capitol *was* constitutional. The Supreme Court intervened, clarifying that the intended purpose of such displays—whether purely religious or partially secular—must be taken into account in deciding matters of constitutionality with regard to the establishment clause.

Though most cases start at the district level, some go straight to the Supreme Court. Article III of the Constitution, for instance, stipulates that "all Cases affecting Ambassadors, other public Ministers and Consuls, and those in which a State shall be Party" shall be decided by the Supreme Court. When the Supreme Court has **original jurisdiction**, it is the first and last court to hear a federal case. The most common instance of original jurisdiction is when two states are in conflict with one another. North Carolina and South Carolina, for instance, have been fighting over the water from the Catawba River. The river originates in the mountains of North Carolina but then flows into South Carolina through Lake Wylie. South Carolina complained that North Carolina's use of more than its fair share of water was threatening the state's power and agriculture. In *South Carolina v. North Carolina* (2010), the Supreme Court ruled that a third-party private entity would be responsible for the fair distribution of the Catawba's water.

Other cases bypass the federal district courts for other reasons. Challenges to actions taken by federal administrative agencies, such as *Massachusetts v. EPA* (2007), often begin in the D.C. Court of Appeals. In other instances, as in *Bush v. Gore* (2000), which is this chapter's case study, the U.S. Supreme Court directly receives appeals to state supreme court rulings.

original jurisdiction the right of a court to be the first to hear a case rather than simply review the decision of a lower court.

▶ **WHOSE WATER IS IT?**
The Supreme Court often resolves disputes between states. As one example, North and South Carolina have been embroiled in a long-standing disagreement about rights to the water in the Catawba River. In your view, what right, if any, does South Carolina have to water from a river that originates in North Carolina?

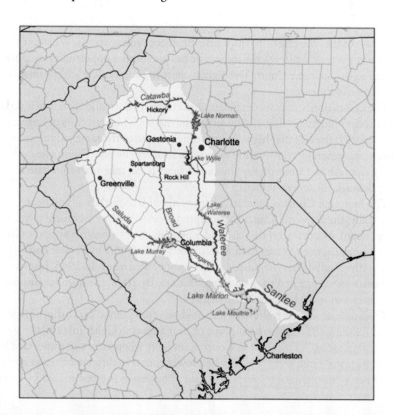

Supreme Court proceedings are highly scripted.

Whereas judges serve on district and appellate courts, justices serve on the Supreme Court. When a case makes it to the top of the federal judiciary, the nine justices who comprise the Supreme Court hear it. Once the Court has agreed to hear a case, both sides to a dispute submit **briefs**, which contain legal arguments about the dispute at hand. These briefs discuss relevant case law, outline the case's key facts, and present additional research that might bear on a particular policy issue. After they and their clerks have reviewed these briefs, the justices meet to hear **oral arguments** directly from the lawyers. During these sessions, the two lead lawyers are granted a half-hour each to make their arguments. Typically, though, the justices interrupt them, long before their time is up, to ask pointed questions.

Following oral arguments, the justices gather for **conference**, where they discuss their current thinking on the case and cast preliminary votes. This meeting provides each justice with some sense of where the other justices stand on the case. Conferences are completely confidential, however, and no formal record is kept of what is said or done during them.

The **chief justice**, who currently is John Roberts, presides over the conference. If he is part of the majority, he then selects which justice will write the majority opinion of the Court.[14] As its name implies, the **majority opinion** reflects the collective judgment of those justices—typically five or more—who are on the majority side of the vote.[15] The majority opinion represents the final determination of the Court. Whoever has the job of writing this opinion will do so with great care. It is not uncommon for justices to compose multiple drafts of an opinion. Usually, these drafts are written in ways that intentionally curry the support of every individual member of the majority.

In addition to the majority opinion, some members of the majority may decide to write **concurring opinions**, which outline additional considerations that they think are important and provide alternative rationales for the majority opinion. Members of the minority typically write **dissenting opinions**, which outline their reasoning on the case and often identify the flaws that they perceive in the majority or concurring opinions. Concurring and dissenting opinions are elements of the final record of the Court, but only the majority opinion is officially binding. Lawyers and judges in subsequent court cases, nonetheless, may cite elements of concurring and dissenting opinions to justify their positions. In fact, the most influential element of a court case can sometimes be a passing reference or footnote found in a concurring or dissenting opinion. Rather than the Court's majority opinion in *Youngstown Sheet and Tube Co. v. Sawyer* (1953), for instance, it was Justice Robert Jackson's concurring opinion that established an influential framework for subsequent courts to evaluate challenges to executive authority.

Having issued its decision, the Supreme Court typically sends a case back to a lower court for implementation. The justices tend to see their job as establishing broad principles that are meant to guide judicial decision-making at the district and appellate levels. As a consequence, the justices tend not to become especially involved in the details of the cases that come before them. Instead, having resolved the largest points of contention in a dispute, the justices rely on district and appellate judges to make sure that their ruling is appropriately implemented.

briefs documents that contain the legal arguments of a dispute.

oral argument a lawyer's spoken presentation to the court of the legal reasons that his or her side should prevail.

conference the confidential gathering of justices in which they discuss their thoughts about the case and cast preliminary votes.

Chief Justice the presiding member of the Supreme Court who serves as chair of the conference and, if in the majority, selects the justice who will write the majority opinion.

majority opinion the written document that reflects the collective judgment of the justices who are on the majority side of a ruling.

▼ **THE CURRENT SUPREME COURT**

Current members of the Supreme Court are, beginning in the top row at left, Sonia Sotomayor, Stephen Breyer, Samuel Alito, and Elena Kagan. In the bottom row are Clarence Thomas, Antonin Scalia, John Roberts (the chief justice), Anthony Kennedy, and Ruth Ginsburg.

concurring opinion   a document written by a justice on the majority side of a ruling which outlines additional considerations he or she thinks important.

dissenting opinion   a document written by a justice on the minority side of a ruling which outlines his or her own reasoning on the case and identifies perceived flaws in the majority opinion.

The Number and Types of Cases That Courts Process

15-3   Distinguish between civil and criminal cases, and describe methods used to manage the judicial caseload.

As should now be clear, the primary responsibility of judges is to resolve disputes. Judges play the role of referee both in society and, as we'll soon see, in politics as well. They identify when an individual, a group of individuals, or an organization has suffered because of actions that either are unlawful or violate established agreements; judges then determine the appropriate course of action. They take cases that determine whether one person stole money from another person, who was at fault in a car accident, and whether a business unlawfully fired an employee. In each instance, judges then decide the appropriate remedy—whether it be time spent in prison, financial compensation for automobile damages, or back pay for lost wages.

ThinkingComparatively

Lawyers play a much more proactive role in common law courts than they do in courts whose heritage traces back to Roman law.

In an adversarial system, judges decide criminal and civil cases.

U.S. courts have a rather peculiar way of resolving disputes. Rather than encouraging the two parties in the dispute to behave cooperatively, U.S. courts encourage the parties to behave adversarially. The legal counsel of each side independently decides what arguments and evidence to put forward. They do so, moreover, in an explicit effort to advance their own interests and undermine those of their adversary. This system sharply differs from the approach used in some European countries. In Germany and France, for example, judges lead the investigation, unearthing evidence and questioning witnesses. Lawyers, by contrast, play a relatively passive, supporting role.[16] The adversarial and inquisitorial systems derive from very different legal traditions. The U.S. adversarial system finds its historical roots in English common law, whereas the inquisitorial systems of Germany and France originate in Roman law.

plaintiff   the party who initiates a lawsuit by filing a complaint.

defendant   the party being sued or accused of a crime.

In U.S. court cases, the **plaintiff** brings the case before the court and, usually, makes accusations of wrongdoing. The **defendant** is the person or institution against whom the complaint is made. In a trial, both sides offer arguments and evidence to support their positions. A judge presides over the deliberations, deciding what kinds of evidence and arguments can be presented. At the end of a trial, a court ruling is made about which side made the stronger case and what should happen as a consequence.

The power to issue a court ruling is given to judges and juries. In the pages that follow, we will have much more to say about the ways in which judges go about making their decisions on matters of law. **Juries**, meanwhile, render decisions on matters of fact. Hence, juries typically decide whether the facts best support one party or another, and judges then determine the appropriate outcome of the case. Juries consist of private citizens who are selected to listen to the trial and as a group offer a final verdict. In the lead-up to a trial, lawyers for both the plaintiff and defendant select members of the jury by questioning candidates to ascertain which are most free from any bias or prejudice that may impair the jury's judgment. Lawyers tend to reject those who they think will rule unfavorably. Juries are meant to provide an impartial judgment about a defendant's actions by his or her peers. Whether the practice of jury trials reaches this objective, though, is the subject of considerable controversy.[17]

jury   a group of private citizens selected to listen to a trial and issue a final verdict.

criminal case   a case that involves a violation of the statutes that are intended to protect the public's health, order, safety, and morality.

Judges issue rulings on two kinds of cases: criminal and civil. **Criminal cases**, as the name implies, involve violations of the criminal code—that is, those statutes that are intended to protect the public's health, order, safety, and morality. In criminal cases, the plaintiff (also called the prosecutor) is always the government, and the defendant is the individual accused of committing a crime—whether it involves using illegal drugs or robbing a store or conducting fraudulent business practices. If the evidence suggests "beyond a reasonable doubt" that the defendant is guilty of committing a crime, then he or she faces punishments ranging from fines or probation to imprisonment, or even execution. The severity of the punishment, which is the purview of the judge, depends on the seriousness of the crime. If the jury decides that the evidence is not sufficiently strong, however, then the defendant may avoid punishment altogether.

Civil cases concern violations of the civil code, which summarizes the legal rights and obligations that individuals have toward one another. When an individual slips and falls in a grocery store, he might sue the owner for negligence; when a husband and wife get divorced, they might fight over the fair division of belongings; or when a stock holder loses money from an investment, she might sue the corporation for bad business practices. In civil cases, the plaintiff is not the government, but instead a private individual, group of individuals, or institution. To win a case, the plaintiff in a civil trial need only show that most—or more technically, a "preponderance"—of the evidence supports his or her position. If a jury finds in favor of the plaintiff, the defendant does not confront many of the punishments that accompany criminal violations. Rather, the defendant has to pay damages (typically monetary in nature) to the plaintiff. Occasionally, the defendant must also take certain corrective actions that reduce the chances that other individuals or groups will suffer similar harm.

In some instances, multiple individuals come together to bring a civil case to trial. In these **class action suits**, the plaintiff typically consists of a group that suffered a common injury. Examples might include residents of a small town whose water is polluted, members of a minority group who have been discriminated against, or parents of children who have been injured by a dangerous toy. If successful, the financial rewards of a class action suit are divided among the members of the group.

The 2000 movie *Erin Brockovich*, for which Julia Roberts won a Best Actress Oscar, is based on a large class action lawsuit that was settled in California in 1996. The case dates to the 1950s and 1960s, when the chemical chromium was used in a Pacific Gas and Electric (PG&E) pumping station and then leaked into the local groundwater. Over the next several decades, residents and visitors to the nearby town of Hinckley complained of serious illnesses that they believed were the result of drinking contaminated well water. Los Angeles lawyer Thomas Girardi, with the spirited assistance of his legal clerk, Erin Brockovich, represented 650 plaintiffs in their lawsuit against PG&E, who admitted the leakages but denied that the contamination was responsible for the complainants' problems. Following two years of negotiations, the utility company settled the dispute by agreeing to pay $333 million to a fund that would be distributed among the hundreds of plaintiffs.[18]

Courts do not resolve all disputes.

Not everyone can bring a civil case to trial. To do so, one must have **standing**—that is, one must personally have suffered a well-defined injury because of actions that violate the civil code. A pedestrian who watches two cars crash into one another from the safety of a nearby restaurant cannot sue the owners of the vehicles for reckless driving; and citizens who are outraged but personally unaffected by a business's hiring and firing decisions cannot sue for discrimination. To bring a case, the plaintiff must have experienced personal harm.

civil case   a case that concerns a violation of the legal rights or obligations of one individual toward another.

class action suit   a lawsuit in which the plaintiff is a group of individuals who have suffered a common injury.

standing   the requirement establishing that for a plaintiff to bring a case to court, he or she must have suffered a well-defined injury that is a result of violation of the civil code.

ripeness doctrine principle by which the courts will accept only cases where the actual harm has already taken place.

Even if an individual has standing, a judge may decide to dismiss a case on other grounds. A case, for instance, may not be "ripe" for consideration if an actual harm has not yet arisen. The **ripeness doctrine** is intended to "prevent the courts . . . from entangling themselves in abstract disagreements over administrative policies."[19] Before agreeing to accept a case, the ripeness doctrine says, judges must determine that a tangible harm has been inflicted upon an individual or group. So, for example, a citizen cannot sue a city for a poorly drafted law if that law has not been enforced, and a corporation cannot take another corporation to court for actions that it merely anticipates.

Many civil cases do not make it to trial because the two parties resolve their differences out of court. The plaintiff and defendant may decide that the costs of going to trial and the uncertainty of the outcome are too great, and they may negotiate a settlement. In these instances, the two parties are not required to disclose the terms of the settlement to either the court or the public.

plea bargain an agreement between the prosecutor and the defendant in a criminal case through which the parties agree to a specified crime and punishment.

Most criminal cases are also decided without going to trial because the prosecutor and the defendant's lawyer reach a deal outside the court. In such **plea bargains**, both parties agree to a specified crime and punishment. A judge must approve the terms of plea bargains, which are then put into the public record. The prosecutor benefits from plea bargains by locking in a conviction; the defendant benefits by typically receiving a lesser punishment; and the court system benefits by avoiding the considerable costs of holding a trial.

Today, the vast majority of criminal cases are resolved through plea bargains. In 1989, according to one report, 84 percent of federal criminal cases were settled via

▶ **THE REAL ERIN BROCKOVICH**

Erin Brockovich worked as a legal clerk in a class action suit against a company charged with contaminating the groundwater of several California communities. Brockovich won national acclaim when the actress Julia Roberts portrayed her in an Oscar-winning performance.

plea bargains. By 1995, the figure had risen to 90 percent, and by 2001, it had reached 94 percent. By the end of the twentieth century fewer than 6 percent of federal criminal cases went to trial.[20]

Federal courts process hundreds of thousands of cases each year.

Even though many cases do not make it to court, federal judges around the nation face massive caseloads. Each year from 1998 to 2004, for instance, about 65,000 criminal cases were filed in federal district courts.[21] In 2008, over 70,000 criminal cases were filed.[22] Meanwhile, litigants filed 267,000 civil cases per year in federal district courts.[23] In an average year, these cases came before just over 1,000 full-time and magistrate federal district judges. As a consequence, each judge processed an average of several hundred criminal and civil cases each year.

The total number of federal court cases was not always so large. In fact, caseloads have trended steadily upward in recent decades. From 1960 to 1995, federal district court filings more than tripled, and appeals to higher courts grew by more than 13 times over.[24] These trends have multiplied court costs and delayed the implementation of government policy. For example, the amount of money annually spent on legal services in the United States increased from $9 billion in 1960 to $54 billion in 1987.[25] Additionally, the budget of the Justice Department rose from $236 million in fiscal year 1962 to $27.7 billion in 2009.[26]

Federal appeals judges now must read 1,500 to 2,000 new opinions per year to remain up-to-date with legal developments.[27] Facing such a heavy workload, judges often have a difficult time keeping track of goings-on within their own courtrooms. Consider the experience of appellate judge Donald Lay: "A few months ago I was reading an opinion from our court; after reading several pages on a certain point, I wondered who wrote it. I was amazed to find that I had authored the opinion some 10 years before. The point is we read so much that we can no longer even recognize— let alone remember—our own opinions."[28]

The "litigation explosion" has led some observers to assert that "litigation has become the nation's secular religion."[29] Former Supreme Court Chief Justice Warren E. Burger warned in the late 1970s, "we may well be on our way to a society overrun by hordes of lawyers."[30] Similarly, President George W. Bush commented in 2003, "We're a litigious society. Everybody is suing, it seems like."[31] He also stated in 2004, "I'm deeply concerned about a legal system that is fraught with frivolous and junk lawsuits."[32] Thus far, however, President Obama has not followed Bush and called for tort reforms designed to reduce the number of cases coming before the judiciary.

Is the United States more litigious relative to other countries? The question has unleashed significant debate. Numerous studies conducted in the 1980s found that Americans were more likely than citizens of other democracies to bring disputes to court.[33] More recent scholarship, however, questions this view. One study concluded that the total volume of litigation in United States was actually comparable to that in Germany and Britain.[34] Like their counterparts in America, British government officials have expressed fears that Britain is developing a "compensation culture" in which "people with frivolous and unwarranted claims bring cases to court with a view of making easy money."[35] So although the United States is certainly more litigious now than it was 40 years ago, it remains unclear whether American legal culture is unusually litigious compared with other countries.

ThinkingComparatively

By some measures, the United States does not appear more litigious than other countries.

▲ **THE ANNALS OF LAW**

The sheer volume of existing case law requires lawyers and judges to conduct a tremendous amount of research in preparation for trial. What challenges does this expansion of case law present for lawyers and litigants?

common law   law made by judges when no legislation currently exists.

public law   those laws enacted by presidents and Congress that define the relationship between individuals (and organizations) and the state.

judicial review   the power of the judiciary to interpret and overturn actions taken by the legislative and executive branches of government.

The Judiciary Makes and Interprets the Law

15-4   Explain how judges decide cases that involve public policy.

In two ways, judges can influence public policy. The first is through actually making law. When no legislation exists, judges can develop rules that dictate how certain disputes are to be resolved. In these instances, judges create **common law** that becomes binding in future cases. For instance, most rulings in cases involving contracts, property, and personal injuries are based on common law.

Judges also resolve political disputes about **public law**, which deals with the statutes that presidents and Congress write and that bureaucrats implement. Sometimes judges help interpret the correct meaning of a statute; at other times they determine whether statutes are consistent with basic constitutional provisions, step in when state or local laws conflict with national laws, or intervene because bureaucrats failed to implement congressional statutes. Collectively, these cases provide judges with considerable influence over the policy-making process.

Through the power of **judicial review**, judges interpret and, when necessary, overturn actions taken by the legislative and executive branches of government. Unlike many of the court's other powers, however, this one cannot be found in Article III of the Constitution. It is a power, instead, that the judiciary claimed for itself in a landmark 1803 court case called *Marbury v. Madison*. The case is sufficiently important to warrant recounting in some detail. After losing the 1800 election, President John Adams appointed 42 individuals to the federal judiciary before his term expired. In the confusion of changing presidential administrations, however, the official commissions were never delivered to the new appointees. When the newly elected president, Thomas Jefferson, took office, he refused to do so. As a consequence, these individuals could not assume their new posts in the judiciary.

What recourse was available to these appointees whose commissions were never delivered? According to the Judiciary Act of 1789, the appointees could request that the federal courts issue an order forcing Jefferson and his secretary of state, James Madison, to finalize the appointments. One of the appointees, William Marbury, did so, which put the newly formed federal judiciary in a difficult spot. On the one hand, the Supreme Court was being asked to take on a popularly elected president who might well ignore a court order that he opposed. On the other hand, if it did not force the president to deliver the commissions, the Court might appear weak and ineffectual.

In a brilliant move, the Supreme Court managed to assert its own power without offending the new presidential administration. Rather than demand that the president appoint Marbury to his office, as the Judiciary Act seemed to require, the Supreme Court ruled that portions of the act itself were unconstitutional. In so doing, the judiciary claimed the power of deciding which laws were constitutional and which were not—transforming it from the weakest of the three branches of government to, perhaps, one on equal footing with the other branches. As Chief Justice John Marshall stated in the Supreme Court's opinion, "it is emphatically the province and duty of the judicial department to say what the law is." And when judges determine that a law enacted by Congress conflicts with the Constitution, they are obligated to rule that the law either be amended or be stricken from the books.

With the power of judicial review, the judiciary established a place for itself in the policy debates that would preoccupy the national government over time—debates about such issues as slavery, labor–management relations, racial and gender discrimination, and federalism. With the power of judicial review, the courts claimed the authority to have the final say about which laws violated the Constitution and which did not. But how would it use this power? How, exactly, would judges determine when a law was unconstitutional and when it was not? Political scientists have identified three models of judicial decision-making: legal, attitudinal, and strategic. As the discussion that follows makes plain, each model casts the courts in a very different light.

Judges develop and apply legal principles in the legal model.

The Constitution is a notoriously vague document. As a consequence, it is not always obvious whether a particular law does or does not violate it. According to the **legal model** of judicial decision-making, to which most constitutional law scholars adhere, judges rely on their judgment and expertise to decipher the correct interpretation of a law, the relevant portion of the Constitution, and whether there is any conflict between the two.

Different judges interpret the Constitution in different ways. Some pay careful attention to the intentions of those who wrote and ratified the document. For these judges, the Constitution can only be understood by reference to its historical record. Other judges think of the Constitution as a document that changes over time. For these judges, the Constitution has no fixed or final meaning. Rather, the correct meaning depends on the context in which it is applied. Still other judges prefer to concentrate on a literal reading of the Constitution's text. For them, neither the intentions of the Constitution's authors nor changing historical norms are relevant. Instead, they focus on the actual words of the Constitution and what implications they have for the dispute at hand.

Although judges may rely on different ways of interpreting the Constitution, they all try to apply basic principles of jurisprudence. The most important of these is **stare decisis**, which literally translates into "to stand by things already decided." According to this principle, judges deciding cases today must carefully

legal model a theory of judicial decision-making in which judges make decisions by deciphering the correct interpretation of the law and the relevant portion of the Constitution, and determining whether there is a conflict between the two.

stare decisis the principle that judges deciding a case must carefully weigh the decisions of their predecessors in similar cases and come to the same decision if the basic elements of the case before them are the same.

judicial restraint   the practice judges engage in when they limit the exercise of their own power by overturning past decisions only when they are clearly unconstitutional.

judicial activism   the tendency of judges to give themselves leeway in deciding whether to abide by past court decisions, which allows them to consider possible outcomes, public opinion, and their own preferences before issuing a ruling.

weigh the decisions made by their predecessors in similar cases. And if the basic elements of the case are the same, they come to the same decision about a law's constitutionality.

Of course, the principal of *stare decisis* is not a hard and fast rule. And different judges appear more or less willing to overturn established precedent. Advocates of **judicial restraint** insist that judges should almost never overturn past decisions; when they must, they should do so on the narrowest possible grounds. Advocates of **judicial activism**, by contrast, suggest that judges have considerably more leeway when deciding whether or not to abide by past court decisions. They suggest that the principle of *stare decisis* should not force judges to repeat mistakes from the past or apply the Constitution in ways that plainly are at odds with the dominant political culture at the time. Advocates of judicial restraint argue that the Supreme Court should stand by its ruling in *Roe v. Wade* (1973), which affirmed a woman's right to obtain an abortion, and which receives a longer discussion in Chapter 5. Advocates of judicial activism, by contrast, encourage the Court to abandon its previous position, which they view as legally flawed, and allow more restrictions on a woman's right to have an abortion. At times, though, the differences between advocates of judicial restraint and activism are not altogether clear. For instance, some people claim that *Roe v. Wade* itself was the product of judicial activism, and that legal restraint requires that the ruling be overturned to honor earlier precedent.

Evidence in support of the legal model would appear plentiful. Judges, after all, routinely cite legal principles and the relevant case law when making their arguments. Beyond *stare decisis*, judges apply many other principles to the cases that come before them. Some we have already discussed, such as standing and ripeness, which concern decisions about whether to hear a particular case. Others are developed to help guide judicial decision-making in particular areas of the law, such as employment, contracts, or copyright. It is extremely difficult, though, to show that such principles and precedents alone cause judges to rule as they do. Judges, after all, have a tremendous amount of discretion to choose which cases they want to cite, and how they want to cite them. Perhaps judges first figure out how they want to rule on a case, and then search existing case law for cases that best support their position. If true, then the observed relationship between past and present rulings misleads proponents of the legal model into thinking that the principle of *stare decisis* causes judges to rule as they do.

ThinkingCausally

Does past court precedence force current judges and justices to issue rulings with which they actually disagree?

Judges have their own policy preferences in the attitudinal model.

Many other political scientists argue that the legal principles that judges use to justify their rulings constitute nothing more than convenient fiction. Though judges try to project an image of neutrality and objectivity, they still use their powers to advance their policy preferences. According to the **attitudinal model** of judicial decision-making, courts "are not importantly different than legislatures and judges are no different than elected politicians."[36]

attitudinal model   the theory of judicial decision-making in which judges use their own policy preferences in deciding cases.

To justify their claims, political scientists have developed a variety of ways to measure judges' policy preferences. The most common of these is the party identification of the president who appointed the judge. Judges appointed by Republicans tend to be conservative, and judges appointed by Democrats tend to be liberal. Moreover, the great majority of judicial appointees identify with the same political party as the president who nominated them. Over the past 30 years, roughly 90 percent of district and appellate court appointees were members of

"Perhaps judges first figure out how they want to rule on a case, and then search existing case law for cases that best support their position."

the president's party. This pattern held for Republican and Democratic administrations alike. These judicial nominees, moreover, were not passive party members. Most of them actively supported their political parties in the past. In fact, more than 66 percent of appellate court appointees and 57 percent of district court appointees over this period had a record of party activism.[37]

Political scientists also have found an extremely strong relationship between judges' ideologies and the decisions they make—a fact that should not hold if judges are merely applying well-established legal principles to the cases that come before them. According to one study, judges rule on civil liberties cases in ways that are consistent with their ideological preferences roughly 80 percent of the time. Even after accounting for a wide range of other influences on judicial decision-making, judges' personal ideologies appear to be far and away the most important determinant of case outcomes.[38] As one political scientist notes, "even critics of the attitudinal model have conceded [the] exceptional explanatory ability" of judges' policy preferences.[39]

Conservative and liberal critics of the court system regularly accuse judges of projecting their own policy preferences onto the cases that come before them. "We still see judges ruling far too often on the basis of their personal opinions or their view of the good society," wrote Edwin Meese and Todd Gaziano of the conservative Heritage Foundation.[40] Adam Cohen, assistant editor for the liberal leaning *New York Times* editorial board, expressed dismay that many of the Supreme Court's decisions in 2006 were driven by ideology: "The most basic charge against activist judges has always been that they substitute their own views for those of the elected branches. The court's conservative majority did just that this term."[41]

The fact that judges' ideology is such a powerful predictor of case outcomes does not mean that ideology is the only, or even the most important, causal factor in the outcome of every case. Political scientists generally concede, for instance, that ideology plays little role in determining the outcome of criminal cases. Even among civil cases, ideology may not be the only relevant factor. For instance, if public opinion strongly leans in one direction or another, or if the nation is at war, or if the president indicates that he will ignore an objectionable court ruling, then judges may be persuaded to set aside their own policy preferences when formulating their decision.

Just the same, it is worth underscoring how radical the attitudinal model really is. In law schools, students spend years learning about the principles that are supposed to guide judicial decision-making; law journals are filled with articles about how the Constitution is appropriately interpreted; and when advancing arguments, both lawyers and judges constantly pay tribute to the relevant case law at hand. If the attitudinal model is correct, then all of these principles amount to little more than theater, merely dressing up what are, at their heart, political motivations and interests.

Judges pay attention to politics in the strategic model.

Most political scientists agree that judges issue rulings that are consistent with their policy preferences. Advocates of the **strategic model** of judicial decision-making, however, argue that judges also keep an eye to the long-term integrity of their rulings. Justices are strategic actors who recognize that their own ability to advance their policy preferences depends on the larger political environment in which they work.[42] Justices see that their word is not final on any policy matter. And they understand that other political institutions (most notably Congress) may subsequently amend or overturn their rulings. When a reversal is imminent, therefore, justices may craft opinions that do not perfectly reflect their policy preferences in order to avoid a clash with either adjoining branch of government.

strategic model the theory of judicial decision-making in which judges consider their own policy preferences as well as the possible actions of the other branches of government when making decisions.

continued on page 552 ▶

HOW DO WE KNOW?

Was *Bush v. Gore* a Political Decision?

The Question

A full month after the 2000 presidential election, the United States still had not declared a new president. The race between George W. Bush and Al Gore had been so close that determination of a winner rested entirely on which candidate was to receive Florida's 25 electoral votes. The day after the election, Florida announced that Bush had won by a mere 1,784 votes out of almost 6 million ballots cast. A statewide machine recount revealed that Bush's victory margin was even smaller.[43]

With the presidency hanging by a thread, Gore requested manual recounts of ballots in four Florida counties. Two of the four counties, however, did not complete the recounts by the deadline established under Florida state law. Moreover, each of the counties used different procedures to process ballots that the machines had failed to read. Despite the fact that the recounts turned up a few hundred additional votes for Gore, Florida Secretary of State Katherine Harris rejected the new figures from the two tardy counties. She declared Bush the winner on November 26, 2000.[44]

Gore next contested the election in the Florida state court system. The Florida Supreme Court ruled in his favor: the recount votes for Gore from the two tardy counties were to be added to his total, and all Florida counties were to conduct their own manual recounts. Bush immediately appealed this decision to the U.S. Supreme Court. Within days, a five-member majority of the Court ruled that the manual recounts were unconstitutional. The vote tallies announced by Harris on November 26 therefore became final.[45]

As a direct result of the Court's decision, George W. Bush became president of the United States. Unsurprisingly, Bush followers praised the Court, while Gore supporters were outraged. In *Bush v. Gore*, were the justices primarily motivated by political commitments? How do we know?

Why It Matters

Judges' decisions can have extremely important consequences: in *Bush v. Gore*, justices decided who would be president for the next four years. Because of their immense importance to society, we expect judges to be neutral and open-minded, free of all the influences of political bargaining and allegiance. But politics often seems to intrude. It is important, then, to understand how judges make decisions that give shape, meaning, and force to the nation's law and politics.

◀ **A PRESIDENTIAL ELECTION IN THE BALANCE**
Protesters gathered outside the Supreme Court as the Justices heard arguments for *Bush v. Gore*. This case, which many claim yielded a blatantly political decision, resolved the 2000 election disputes in Florida and put George W. Bush into the White House. Was it right, in your view, for the Supreme Court to intervene and settle the 2000 election dispute?

Investigating the Answer

The legal underpinnings of any Supreme Court decision can readily be found in the arguments made, the *amicus* briefs filed, and the opinions written in a case. A political scientist applying the legal model to a case would therefore want to determine whether the precedent the Court used was appropriate and whether the Court's interpretation of the law made sense. In deciding *Bush v. Gore*, the Supreme Court relied on the equal protection clause of the Fourteenth Amendment, discussed in greater detail in Chapter 5. Seven of the nine justices agreed that the use of different standards to recount votes violated Floridians' right to have their votes count equally. Two of these seven wanted to give the counties a chance to come up with a uniform method of recounting that would guarantee voters equal and fair treatment. The remaining five, however, opted to stop the recounting entirely. They cited the Florida Supreme Court's earlier decision that the state would abide by a federal law that required presidential election disputes to be settled by December 12, 2000. The U.S. Supreme Court decision was handed down that very day, leaving no time for additional recounts.

A political scientist applying the attitudinal model would argue that these legal explanations simply provided cover for the real reasons justices voted the way they did. Rather than analyzing the written opinions for a particular case, an attitudinalist typically uses data on many court decisions to show how often conservative judges make conservative choices, how often liberal judges make liberal choices, and how closely judges adhere to precedent. Jeffrey Segal and Harold Spaeth, for example, analyzed 40 years of Supreme Court justices' votes and found that justices who dissented in important cases rarely changed their stance when the same issue came up in later cases. If those justices had truly been abiding by *stare decisis*, Segal and Spaeth argued, they would have changed their stance in respect for precedent.[46] Segal and Spaeth later said of the *Bush v. Gore* decision, "Never in its history has a majority of the Court behaved in such a blatant politically partisan fashion."[47] The five most conservative justices, all appointed to the Court by Republican presidents, joined together in a decision that handed the presidency to the Republican candidate, while the Court's most liberal members dissented.[48]

The strategic model highlights the political context in which justices consider a case. The Supreme Court was under a great deal of pressure to hear and decide the case of *Bush v. Gore*. Many Americans worried that the impasse would raise doubts about the legitimacy of American government.[49] At the time, outgoing President Clinton felt the need to assure world leaders that there was "nothing to worry about."[50] In deciding the case, was the Court responding to a nationwide desire to have the matter resolved? The issue was so politically charged that the majority decided to hand down a *per curiam* decision, one that is not signed by any justice, suggesting that no justice wanted to be associated with its authorship, perhaps for fear the author would be a target for intense personal criticism.

Which view of the courts is correct? In a researcher's ideal world, a political scientist would be able to interview the justices and ask them directly. She or he might even conduct a survey of federal judges to ask about their true motivations in deciding cases. In the American political system, however, judges tend to stay out of the public eye. They conduct their deliberations in secret. When they finally reveal a decision, it is always grounded in legal reasoning. The legitimacy of the entire federal court system rests on the neutrality of the judges, and most judges would not admit to being influenced by politics.

Although conservative judges consistently vote conservatively and liberal judges vote liberally, this trend may not reveal political motivation. Perhaps conservative and liberal judges just use different methods of interpreting the Constitution. In other words, maybe judges divide not on political lines but on beliefs about interpreting the law. To test this proposition, one would ideally like to replay history and allow Gore to have a slight lead in Florida and Bush to call for a manual recount. If the attitudinal model is correct, this basic fact would cause the justices to rethink their positions. If the legal model is right, the underlying principles would stand and the votes would remain the same.

Thinking Critically

■ Had Bush, rather than Gore, stood to benefit from a recount of the Florida votes, do you think the Supreme Court would have ruled the same way?

■ Does carefully crafted legal reasoning in the Court opinions to *Bush v. Gore* rule out the possibility that the justices ultimately decided on the basis of political considerations?

■ In your view, are the political divisions in *Bush v. Gore* evident in the preponderance of cases that come before the Supreme Court? Or is *Bush v. Gore* exceptional?

The Bottom Line

Though judges go to great lengths to justify their opinions, it is extremely difficult to identify their true motivations. Taken at face value, the written record that judges leave behind suggests that legal and constitutional issues are paramount. But the inescapable fact is that judges' partisan identification is a powerful predictor of the votes they cast. This is abundantly clear in *Bush v. Gore*, where the selection of the next president was at stake. The conservative justices sided with the Republican candidate, and the liberal justices sided with the Democratic candidate. On this case in particular, then, judges' political views probably did influence the court's ruling.

Judges must also think about how their rulings will be implemented. Different administrative units in federal, state, and local governments may choose to interpret court orders either narrowly or broadly, depending on their own views about a policy dispute. When the court rulings appear entirely out of step with public opinion, administrative agencies and state governments may actively resist a court order. Hence, when the Supreme Court in 1955 required school districts to desegregate their schools "with all deliberate speed," responses varied widely across the country. Some districts promptly implemented the court edict, whereas others simply dragged their feet.

Not surprisingly, then, judges often monitor the political views of key political actors outside the judiciary. Consider, for instance, the impact of the **solicitor general**, who is appointed by the president and who represents the interests of the executive branch in the Supreme Court. The solicitor general's influence with the Supreme Court is so great that the position is sometimes referred to as "the tenth justice." The Court accepts only about 5 percent of all cases, but it accepts over 70 percent of the cases in which the solicitor general's office is the petitioning party.[51] And among those accepted cases, the office maintains an impressive record. According to one study, the executive branch won more than 60 percent of its cases in the nineteenth century and almost 70 percent from 1953 to 1983.[52] Another study of all Supreme Court cases to which the U.S. government was a party between 1933 and 2007 also put the solicitor general win-rate at nearly 70 percent.[53] The government's success is notable even when it is not a party to the case. According to some estimates, the side of a case that receives the endorsement of the solicitor general wins upward of 87 percent of the time.[54]

Courts also pay attention to the arguments made by relevant interest groups. Individuals and organizations that are not party to a court case may nonetheless express their opinions through **amicus curiae** ("friend of the court") briefs. The practice of *amicus curiae* allows arguments to be presented by groups that may not have standing, and hence may not be able to bring a case forward themselves. One study of court

solicitor general the individual who represents the federal government in the Supreme Court.

amicus curiae a brief written by someone who is not a party to a case but who submits information or an argument related to the dispute at hand.

◄ **THE SOLICITOR GENERAL**

When Elena Kagan left the Solicitor General's office to become the newest member of the Supreme Court, Neal Katyal took over as acting Solicitor General. As of November, 2010, President Obama has not selected a permanent replacement for Kagan.

challenges to executive orders found that courts were more likely to rule against the president when *amicus curiae* briefs were filed in opposition.[55]

Political scientists have generated a substantial body of evidence suggesting that judges are sensitive to public opinion. When the public overwhelmingly supports a particular policy, judges are less likely to overturn it; when the public opposes the policy, judges are more likely to do so. There probably is no starker example of the Supreme Court's setting aside legal and constitutional principles in order to cater to public opinion than the 1944 case *Korematsu v. United States.* As described in Chapter 6, during World War II, President Franklin Roosevelt unilaterally decided to place 120,000 Japanese Americans into internment camps. In the aftermath of the Japanese attack on Pearl Harbor, Roosevelt argued, Japanese Americans represented a latent security threat. The president's only cause of action, however, was their national origin. These individuals had done nothing at all to warrant their forced removal from their homes. The Supreme Court nonetheless ruled in favor of Roosevelt's policy. When the nation stood on a war footing, and the public stood squarely behind its president, the justices dared not intervene, even though the president's actions, most would agree, were unconstitutional.[56]

Studies of public opinion, in particular, require special sensitivity to issues of causation. It is not always clear, after all, whether the courts are following the public, or

◄ **CHALLENGING THE JAPANESE INTERNMENT IN WORLD WAR II**

Fred Korematsu, shown here in 1983, was the subject of one of the most important wartime cases ever decided by the Supreme Court. In a case that bore Korematsu's name, the Supreme Court upheld the internment of Japanese Americans during World War II.

ThinkingCausally

Does public opinion influence judicial decisions, or do judicial decisions shape public opinion?

the public is following the courts. A number of scholars have shown that public opinion changed in the direction of court rulings in the aftermath of important desegregation and abortion cases.[57] It is possible, though, that judges sensed or anticipated these shifts in public opinion, in which case the public may have influenced the court ruling.

Judicial Appointments

15-5 Analyze the process of judicial appointment and selection.

The Constitution gives the president the power to appoint judges and justices with "the advice and consent" of the Senate. Because judges hold office for life, these appointments enable presidents to have a lasting impact on the workings of government long after they have left office. And because of the stakes involved, presidents take great care when selecting individuals for federal judgeships.

Over the last half-century, each president has appointed scores of individuals to the federal judiciary. Recent presidents have had the opportunity to appoint even more. Every president since World War II has appointed more than 100 judges and justices (except Gerald Ford, who failed to do so only because he held office for just two years). Ronald Reagan and Bill Clinton, both of whom served two consecutive terms, appointed upwards of 400 individuals to the bench. During his two terms in office, George W. Bush appointed 328. In his first 16 months in office, Barack Obama appointed 35.[58] The power to appoint so many federal judges gives presidents some control over the policy preferences and priorities of those individuals who wield the extraordinary power of judicial review.

In terms of race and gender, judges look more and more like a cross section of America. Among Ronald Reagan's appointments, only 8 percent were women; 2 percent, African American; and 4 percent, Hispanic. Among George W. Bush's appointments, by contrast, fully 21 percent were women; 7 percent, African American; and 11 percent, Hispanic. In terms of other demographics, however, nominees to the federal judiciary continue to look very different from the rest of the population. Over 50 percent of both Bill Clinton's and George W. Bush's nominees, for instance, had a net worth over $1 million. The average age of a nominee has remained steady at about 50 years. And not surprisingly, almost all nominees worked in politics as either elected or appointed officials or as lawyers before being nominated to a judgeship.[59]

The process for making judicial appointments varies from country to country. In the United States, the president nominates judges and Congress votes to approve the appointment. In countries such as India and Israel, however, the heads of state have complete say over appointments to their highest courts. The president of Pakistan also appoints judges to the supreme court of Pakistan, but the Pakistani constitution stipulates that the president must at least first consult with the chief justice. The judges of Australia's highest court are officially appointed by the governor-general, who represents the British monarch, but it is more common for the prime minister to nominate judges in practice. Court systems of other countries also are constantly changing. For

▼ LOWER COURT CONTROVERSIES

Among the more controversial appointments made by President Obama to the appellate courts was Goodwin Liu, a constitutional law professor at U.C. Berkeley who has espoused traditionally liberal views on a variety of policy issues. Here he is seen greeting Senator Dianne Feinstein just before testifying before the Senate Judiciary Committee. As of November 2010, Congress still has not confirmed the appointment.

instance, the appointment process for the supreme court of the United Kingdom was reformed in 2005 to weaken the executive branch's influence over the process: the office of lord chancellor was stripped of some of its judicial powers and a selection commission was formed to make judicial appointments.

ThinkingComparatively
Different countries offer very different pathways to their highest courts of justice.

Confirmation hearings for district and federal courts are political.

Presidents try to appoint individuals who are competent at what they do, have legal expertise, and have a strong record of accomplishment. But politics also looms large in judicial appointments. Presidents regularly appoint judges who share their partisan affiliation. No less than 91 percent of Carter's appointments were Democrats, as were 88 percent of Bill Clinton's. Similarly, 92 percent of Ronald Reagan's appointments were Republicans, as were 89 percent of George H.W. Bush's and 83 percent of George W. Bush's during his first term in office.[60]

Despite this political favoritism, most lower-court nominees are confirmed. Take a look at Figure 15-3. In the 1980s and early 1990s, Congress confirmed the appointments of roughly four in five district and appellate nominees. With the Republican takeover of the 104th Congress (1995–96), however, and the advent of divided government, nominees for appellate courts were significantly less likely to be confirmed than nominees for district courts. Indeed, in every subsequent Congress, confirmation rates among appellate court nominees have been significantly lower than those among district court nominees.

Part of the reason most district nominees are confirmed is that senators play an important role in their selection. When choosing a judicial nominee for a district court,

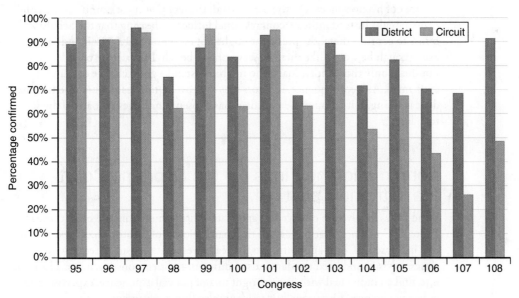

FIGURE 15-3 **Confirmation rates almost always appear higher among district court nominees than among appellate court nominees.** The actual number of district court nominees, meanwhile, ranges from 51 to 168 per Congress, with an average of 95. The number of circuit court nominees ranges from 13 to 60 per Congress, with an average of 30.

senatorial courtesy the custom by which the senior senator from the state in which there is a district court vacancy assists the president in selecting a replacement for that seat.

the president will often seek the approval of the senior senator who represents the state where the court is located. This norm, known as **senatorial courtesy**, tends to hasten the process of selecting and confirming district court judges around the nation.

Things get more complicated, however, at the appellate levels. For starters, senatorial courtesy applies only to district court appointments. Moreover, appellate court judges tend to be subject to greater scrutiny by both the president and the Senate. As a consequence, some individuals are easily confirmed at the district level but are denied assignment to an appellate judgeship.

The saga of Judge Charles Pickering is a case in point. In 1990, George H.W. Bush appointed Pickering to a federal district court in southern Mississippi. Twelve years later, George W. Bush nominated Pickering for a position on the Fifth Circuit court of appeals. At the time, the Democrats controlled the Senate, and they refused to confirm Pickering's nomination. Democrats levied a variety of charges against Pickering, including racial insensitivity and political views that were "out of step" with mainstream America. The next year, when the Republicans regained control of the Senate, Bush renominated Pickering for the position. This time Democrats filibustered the nomination, and the Republicans lacked the needed votes to cut off debate—a parliamentary procedure discussed in greater detail in Chapter 13. Not to be outdone, when the Senate was not in session in early 2004, Bush granted Pickering a recess appointment. This allowed him to hold the position until the end of the Congress's next session, December 8, 2004. When Congress got around to formally considering Pickering's case, concerns about his political positions were once again raised. Rather than drag the confirmation out any longer, Pickering withdrew his name from consideration and retired from the federal judiciary.

In this confirmation process, it is difficult to figure out just how much influence the president and the Senate wield. On the one hand, the fact that most presidential nominees are appointed would appear to be a clear testament to the president's influence. If the president were weak, the Senate might decide to block a greater number of his nominees. On the other hand, the fact that most nominees are confirmed might instead indicate congressional influence. Fearing that the Senate will refuse to confirm them, the president might not even nominate certain individuals—even though he would like them to serve on the bench. Instead, the president might nominate only those individuals who he thinks stand a good chance of being confirmed. As a consequence, senators may approve nominees not because the president is strong, but because the president has chosen candidates that are to the senators' liking.

Confirmation hearings for the Supreme Court are extremely political.

If the stakes involved in district and appellate court nominations are high, those in Supreme Court nominations are off the charts. Norms of senatorial courtesy play no role in Supreme Court appointments. Instead, presidents consult directly with their closest advisers and heed the demands of different political constituencies. The trick is to find an individual with just the right mix of judicial experience, expertise, and policy preferences. Occasionally, presidents also find it advantageous to select a candidate with a particular socioeconomic background. For example, George H.W. Bush in 1991 nominated Clarence Thomas to the Court. Thomas was a strong conservative who did not have a wealth of judicial experience.[61] Some political observers argued, however, that by selecting an African American, Bush managed to mute some liberals' criticisms of the nomination.

Once he comes up with a potential Supreme Court nominee, the president asks the Federal Bureau of Investigation to conduct a full background check on the individual. This check is intended to identify any evidence of unlawful behavior that a nominee might have engaged in. Recent presidents also have sent the names of prospective nominees to the American Bar Association (ABA), an interest group that represents the legal profession and that provides ratings of the qualifications of candidates. The ABA's Standing Committee on the Federal Judiciary typically rates nominees as either "well qualified," "qualified," or "not qualified." George W. Bush, however, opted not to ask the ABA to rate his candidates before they were publicly announced. Instead, he relied on the Federalist Society, a politically conservative organization of students and faculty at law schools around the nation. Barack Obama has reinstated the practice of working with the ABA.

▲ **CONFIRMING THOMAS**
Among Supreme Court confirmation hearings, Clarence Thomas's in 1991 was among the most politically charged in recent memory.

If a presidential nominee survives these background checks, he or she then must face the public. From the moment the president announces a name, a torrent of media scrutiny follows. Interest groups take out radio and television advertisements to highlight the candidate's strengths and foibles. Legal scholars write opinion pieces about the candidate's qualifications and judicial philosophies. Journalists investigate the candidate's personal and professional histories. When an individual is being considered for appointment to the Supreme Court, no element of his or her past is considered off-limits. During the 1991 Senate confirmation hearings for Supreme Court Justice Clarence Thomas, for instance, the media and politicians fixated on accusations that he had sexually harassed prior co-worker Anita Hill. The hearings became so personal and accusatory, in fact, that Thomas argued he was the victim of a "high-tech lynching" by the U.S. Senate.[62]

The real action of the judicial appointment process occurs during the confirmation hearings, which are open to the public. Members of the Senate Judiciary Committee have the opportunity to directly interrogate a nominee about decisions he or she made as a lawyer or lower court judge. They may ask about his or her views on issues ranging from abortion to the legal status of enemy combatants. Given that they may eventually issue rulings that fundamentally alter these public policies, it is perfectly appropriate that these nominees be interrogated on their views. Whether the nominees are completely forthcoming in their answers, however, is another matter.

In general, the Senate is less likely to confirm Supreme Court nominees than appellate or district court nominees. Since the nation's founding in 1789, presidents have formally submitted 158 nominations to the Court, including those for chief justice. Of these, the Senate confirmed 122, and 115 actually took office.[63] As Table 15-1 shows, dissenters can be found in all of the recent Supreme Court confirmation hearings. In some cases, such as Clarence Thomas's, full-blown controversies can erupt. Of late, however, nothing compares to the confirmation hearings of Robert Bork, whom Reagan nominated to the Supreme Court in 1987. No fewer than 86 different interest groups testified at his confirmation hearings.[64] Critics focused not on Bork's knowledge of the law—the ABA rated him "well qualified"—but on his political views on abortion, civil rights, and civil liberties. Less than an hour after Reagan announced Bork's nomination, Senator Edward Kennedy declared, "Robert Bork's America is a land in which women would be forced into back alley abortions, blacks would sit in segregated lunch counters, rogue police could break down citizens' doors in midnight raids."[65] For the next three and a half months, an avalanche of criticism fell upon the nominee. On October 23, 1987, the Senate rejected Bork's confirmation by a vote of 58–42.

TABLE 15-1. **Supreme Court Nominations Since World War II**

PRESIDENT	NOMINEE	SENATE VOTE DATE	VOTE COUNT	CONFIRMATION
Obama	Elena Kagan	August 5, 2010	63–37	Yes
	Sonia Sotomayor	August 6, 2009	68–31	Yes
G. W. Bush	Samuel Alito	January 31, 2006	58–42	Yes
	John Roberts	September 29, 2005	78–22	Yes
	Harriet Miers	None	None	**No**
Clinton	Stephen Breyer	July 29, 1994	87–9	Yes
	Ruth Bader Ginsburg	August 3, 1994	96–3	Yes
G.H.W. Bush	Clarence Thomas	October 15, 1991	52–48	Yes
	David Souter	October 2, 1990	90–9	Yes
Reagan	Anthony Kennedy	February 3, 1988	97–0	Yes
	Robert Bork	October 23, 1987	42–58	**No**
	Antonin Scalia	September 17, 1986	98–0	Yes
	Sandra Day O'Connor	September 21, 1981	99–0	Yes
Ford	John Paul Stevens	December 17, 1975	98–0	Yes
Nixon	William Rehnquist	December 10, 1971	68–26	Yes
	Lewis Franklin Powell Jr.	December 6, 1972	89–1	Yes
	Harry Blackmun	May 12, 1970	94–0	Yes
	G. Harrold Carswell	April 8, 1970	45–51	**No**
	Clement Haynesworth	November 21, 1969	45–55	**No**
	Warren E. Burger	June 9, 1969	74–3	Yes
L. Johnson	Homer Thornberry	None	None	**No**
	Thurgood Marshall	August 30, 1967	69–11	Yes
	Abe Fortas*	August 11, 1965	—	Yes
Kennedy	Arthur Goldberg	September 25, 1962	—	Yes
	Byron White	April 11, 1962	—	Yes
Eisenhower	Potter Stewart	May 5, 1959	70–17	Yes
	Charles E. Whittaker	March 19, 1957	—	Yes
	William J. Brennan Jr.	March 19, 1957	—	Yes
	John M. Harlan	March 16, 1955	71–11	Yes
	Earl Warren	March 1, 1954	—	Yes
Truman	Sherman Minton	October 4, 1949	48–16	Yes
	Tom C. Clark	August 18, 1949	73–8	Yes
	Fred M. Vinson	June 20, 1946	—	Yes
	Harold H. Burton	September 19, 1945	—	Yes

*Sitting justice also nominated in 1968 to be chief justice, but nomination was withdrawn. Where no vote count is listed, confirmation was by voice or otherwise unrecorded.

Source: David G. Savage, *Guide to the U.S. Supreme Court*, 4th ed., vol. 2 (Washington, DC: CQ Press, 2004), 1186–89.

CaseStudy: The Appointment of Sonia Sotomayor

Justice David Souter's decision to retire from the Supreme Court presented President Barack Obama with his first opportunity to appoint a justice to the Court. Souter was a member of the court's liberal wing. If the president wanted to maintain the Court's ideological balance, he would need to replace him with another liberal. On May 26, 2009, the president chose federal appellate Judge Sonia Sotomayor. Upon her confirmation, Sotomayor became the first Hispanic and third woman to serve on the Supreme Court.

Sotomayor, a child of Puerto Rican immigrants, grew up in a Bronx housing project. Her father, a factory worker with no education past third grade, died when she was nine years old. Thereafter, her mother worked two jobs to support the family. Sotomayor excelled in school, graduated from Princeton, and then attended Yale Law School. As a professional lawyer, she served for many years as a prosecutor and a corporate litigator. In 1991, President George H.W. Bush tapped her to serve on New York's U.S. District Court. President Bill Clinton nominated her for the 2nd Circuit in 1997, a position that she held until Obama nominated her for the Supreme Court. Obama recognized that her background was different from that of most Supreme Court justices when he announced her nomination: "What Sonia will bring to the Court, then, is not only the knowledge and experience acquired over a course of a brilliant legal career, but the wisdom accumulated from an inspiring life's journey."[66]

Because Democrats held a strong majority in the Senate, Republicans were not likely to successfully block the appointment of a liberal justice. But that did not keep them from trying. Typical of an appointment hearing, the nominee's past was scrutinized to determine whether she was qualified to serve on the nation's highest court. And Sotomayor's critics seized on two items from her past: a "wise Latina" comment and her ruling in a controversial court case over New Haven firefighters.

The controversial comment was from a lecture Sotomayor delivered at the University of California at Berkeley in 2001. Reflecting on her experience as a Latina judge, Sotomayor said, "I would hope that a wise Latina woman with the richness of her experiences would more often than not reach a better conclusion than a white male who hasn't lived that life."[67] The quote was repeated many times by the press, and some Republican members of Congress expressed concern that she believed that race and gender figured prominently in the capacity of justices to perform their duties in office.

The second controversy centered on her decision to uphold New Haven's actions to disregard the results of a firefighter's promotion exam out of concern that it was biased against lower-scoring minorities. The case eventually made its way to the Supreme Court, and Sotomayor's lower court decision was overturned. Critics argued that her written decision on the case was too short and did not fully explain her opinion, claims raising concerns over whether she would be an adequate and fair Supreme Court justice.[68]

Like most Supreme Court nominees, Sotomayor deflected accusations made about her ideological views. Her record as a district and appellate judge, she claimed, reflected her impartiality. She refused to answer a host of specific legal questions on the grounds that a similar case might soon come before the Supreme Court, and that therefore it would be inappropriate to stake out a position one way or another. With the successful navigation of these two challenges, and then the careful avoidance of controversial issues such as abortion, Sonia Sotomayor's appointment appeared secure. On August 6, 2009, by a 68–31 vote, the Senate confirmed the nation's first Hispanic Supreme Court justice.

In 2010, President Obama named his second nominee to the Supreme Court: Elena Kagan, the solicitor general. Kagan would become the fourth woman serving on the Supreme Court and its youngest justice. Though a former law school professor and aide to President Clinton, Kagan had never served on the bench. Moreover, throughout her legal career she left a thin paper trail. Because her views on the Constitution were not well known, the White House released over 150,000 pages of correspondence dating back to Kagan's time on President Clinton's staff. Despite the usual partisan wrangling in the media and the scoring of political points by the senators at her confirmation hearing, it seemed certain, even before the hearings began, that Kagan would soon follow Sonia Sotomayor to the Supreme Court. And so she did. In early August, the Senate confirmed her nomination by a vote of 63 to 37.

ThinkingCritically

1. Was Sotomayor's "wise Latina" comment relevant to her appointment to the Supreme Court? How much should a nominee's race, ethnicity, or gender matter?

2. Do you think Sotomayor would have had a more difficult time being confirmed if she were replacing a conservative member of the Supreme Court?

▲ A NEW SUPREME COURT JUSTICE

President Obama's first Supreme Court appointment, Sonia Sotomayor, smiles as she concludes her testimony before the Senate Judiciary Committee in July of 2009. One year later, the Senate would confirm his second nominee to the nation's highest Court, Elena Kagan.

CHAPTER SUMMARY

In this chapter you have learned to:

15-1 Determine the role of the judiciary as established by the framers of the U.S. Consitution. Many of the original framers of the Constitution anticipated that the federal judiciary would be the weakest of the three branches. Lacking the powers of both the sword and the purse, judges were left merely with the persuasive appeal of their judgment. From the nation's beginning, therefore, judges worked hard to promote the legitimacy of their institution. Over time, the public learned to hold the courts in high regard.

15-2 Outline the structure of the U.S. judiciary branch. The federal judiciary is organized hierarchically, with district courts at the bottom, appellate courts in the middle, and a Supreme Court on top. Most decisions are decided at the district court level. The losing party to a case, however, has the option of appealing the decision to appellate courts and the Supreme Court. Decisions made by higher courts are binding for lower courts.

15-3 Distinguish between civil and criminal cases, and describe methods used to manage the judicial caseload. In civil and criminal cases, the judiciary resolves disputes among individuals, organizations, and the government. Though many cases are settled before ever going to trial,

federal courts nonetheless process hundreds of thousands of cases each year.

15-4 Explain how judges decide cases that involve public policy. With the power of judicial review, judges exert considerable influence over the interpretation and implementation of laws. When deciding a case, judges rely on a variety of different considerations. They attempt to correctly interpret the Constitution and apply legal principles to the case at hand. They turn to their own political preferences and ideas about what constitutes good public policy. And they pay attention to politics more generally, trying to steer clear of certain decisions that are likely to evoke widespread opposition.

15-5 Analyze the process of judicial appointment and selection. Politics, in varying degrees, intrudes on the process of appointing judges to the federal judiciary. Presidents have strong incentives to select individuals who share their views and will advocate on behalf of these views long after the president has left office. As a consequence, the Senate confirmation process can be highly contentious. Nominees to the Supreme Court, in particular, face an extraordinary amount of public scrutiny. Occasionally, these nominees fail to be confirmed, either because the Senate votes against them or because the president withdraws the nominee.

PEARSON mypoliscilab   EXERCISES

Apply what you learned in this chapter by starting with these resources on MyPoliSciLab.

📖 Read on mypoliscilab.com

 eText: Chapter 15

✔ Study and Review on mypoliscilab.com

 Pre-Test
 Post-Test
 Chapter Exam
 Flashcards

👁 Watch on mypoliscilab.com

 Video: Prosecuting Corruption
 Video: Prosecuting Cyber Crime
 Video: Most Significant Abortion Ruling in 30 Years
 Video: Court Rules on Hazelton's Immigration Laws

✳ Explore on mypoliscilab.com

 Simulation: You Are a Clerk to Supreme Court Justice Judith Gray
 Simulation: You Are a Young Lawyer
 Simulation: You Are the President and Need to Appoint a Supreme Court Justice
 Comparative: Comparing Judiciaries
 Timeline: Chief Justices of the Supreme Court
 Visual Literacy: Case Overload

KEY TERMS

amicus curiae, p. 552
appellate courts, p. 537
attitudinal model, p. 548
briefs, p. 541
Chief Justice, p. 541

civil case, p. 543
class action suit, p. 543
common law, p. 546
concurring opinion, p. 542
conference, p. 541

criminal case, p. 542
defendant, p. 542
dissenting opinion, p. 542
district courts, p. 536
judicial activism, p. 548

CHAPTER TEST

1. What about Article III of the Constitution makes "legitimacy" so important to the judiciary?
2. What are the three levels of the federal judiciary? At what level are most court cases decided?
3. Must the Supreme Court accept all appeals?
4. What function do juries serve?
5. Do "plaintiffs" and "defendants" always consist of just one person or organization?
6. When interpreting the meaning of a congressional statute or constitutional provision, do judges rely on political considerations? How do you know?
7. Would the strategic model of judicial decision-making predict that the Supreme Court is more or less likely to overturn a policy issued by Barack Obama when Democrats hold a majority of seats within Congress?
8. What role, if any, do partisanship and ideology play in judicial appointments?
9. How do presidents go about selecting a nominee to a federal judgeship? How do these criteria differ, if at all, for Supreme Court nominees?
10. Are high rates of senatorial confirmation evidence that presidents are free to choose whomever they would like to serve on the federal judiciary?

SUGGESTED READINGS

Lawrence Baum. 2004. *The Supreme Court*, 8th ed. Washington, DC: CQ Press. A useful overview of the Supreme Court.

Cornell Clayton and Howard Gillman, eds. 1999. *Supreme Court Decision-Making: New Institutionalist Approaches*. Chicago: University of Chicago Press. A collection of essays on different aspects of the strategic model of judicial decision-making.

Lee Epstein and Jeffrey Segal. 2005. *Advice and Consent: The Politics of Judicial Appointments*. New York: Oxford University Press. A contemporary look at the politics of judicial appointments.

Herbert McCloskey. 2000. *The American Supreme Court*, 3rd ed. Chicago: University of Chicago Press. A careful analysis of the relationship between Supreme Court rulings and public opinion.

Shep Melnick. 1994. *Between the Lines: Interpreting Welfare Rights*. Washington, DC: Brookings Institution. Analysis of the ways in which judges interpret (and reinterpret) congressionally enacted laws.

H. W. Perry. 1994. *Deciding to Decide: Agenda Setting in the United States Supreme Court*, reprint ed. Cambridge, MA: Harvard University Press. A classic examination of the criteria used by the Supreme Court when deciding whether or not to grant cert.

Jeffrey Segal and Harold Spaeth. 2002. *The Supreme Court and the Attitudinal Model Revisited*. New York: Cambridge University Press. A thorough examination of the attitudinal model of judicial decision-making.

SUGGESTED WEBSITES

Official website of the Federal Judiciary: www.uscourts.gov

At this site, it is possible to track information about all courts and look up case rulings throughout the federal judiciary.

Federal Judicial Center: www.fjc.gov

This site houses research reports on a wide range of issues involving the federal judiciary and the law.

American Bar Association: www.abanet.org

This is the oldest and most prominent organization representing the interests of the legal profession.

Federalist Society: www.fed-soc.org

A conservative organization that professes to fight the "liberal orthodoxy" that pervades law schools and the legal profession.

CHAPTER 16

The Bureaucracy

Building a Bureaucracy to Combat Terrorism

Less than a month after the terrorist attacks of September 11, 2001, newly appointed presidential adviser Tom Ridge reminded fellow Homeland Security Council members about the dangers of political infighting. "The only turf we should be worried about protecting is the turf we stand on," he warned.[1] Ridge was rightly concerned, for observers increasingly suspected that certain departments of the federal government had jealously guarded information that might have prevented the attacks. Initiatives to prevent such turf battles included coordinating various agencies under a single homeland security umbrella, while also expanding the federal government's efforts to protect the country against terrorism. Ironically, however, early efforts not only failed to eliminate interagency squabbles but in fact fueled even more infighting: between the executive and legislative branches, and between Republicans and Democrats.

The seeds of the controversy were sown on September 21, when Senate Intelligence Committee Chair Bob Graham (D-FL) and several other Democrats introduced a proposal to create a National Office for Combating Terrorism. The new body would be charged with developing a comprehensive counterterrorism budget and coordinating different intelligence agencies. It was to be lodged within the Executive Office of the President. The office's director, however, would require Senate confirmation, and its activities would be subject to congressional oversight.

White House officials balked at this perceived intrusion by lawmakers. The Bush administration supported the creation of an organizational structure that would perform this task, but the president wanted to ensure that he, rather than Congress, would be in charge. Accordingly, on October 8, President Bush preempted congressional action by issuing an executive order that created an Office of Homeland Security (OHS) within the Executive Office of the President. Pennsylvania Governor Tom Ridge,

a longtime Bush ally, agreed to head the new body. The president's proposal differed from the Senate proposal in two important ways. Its director would be a special assistant to the president and thus would not be subject to Senate confirmation. And its activities would not require congressional oversight.

Many critics worried that the new agency, with only a small staff, few resources, and no clear authority over Cabinet-level partners, faced a challenge that would quickly overwhelm it. A few days later, Senators Arlen Specter (R-PA) and Joseph Lieberman (D-CT) issued a counterproposal. They introduced in the Senate a bipartisan bill that would establish a Cabinet-level position, subject to congressional confirmation and oversight. The White House opposed the Senate bill, and at the time, members of Congress lacked the votes needed to override a possible presidential veto.

The conflict between Capitol Hill and the White House intensified a few months later, when President Bush asked for an additional $38 million from Congress for his OHS. The legislators seemed prepared to fulfill the request but insisted that Ridge publicly and formally testify before Congress about the office's activities. The administration refused, insisting that Ridge's responsibility was to advise the president, and the president alone. Later, facing the threat of a subpoena, the administration relented and sent the homeland security adviser to provide informal testimony to the House Government Reform Committee.

After months of resisting congressional efforts to create a Cabinet-level position, on June 7 the administration blindsided legislators from both political parties by announcing a plan to create a Department of Homeland

▼ TRACKING SECURITY THREATS

In the spring of 2010, onlookers watch after parts of New York's Times Square were closed off. The sports utility vehicle that triggered the evacuation contained a large stash of explosive materials. How, in your opinion, might the federal bureaucracy better respond to the threat of domestic terrorism?

Security (DHS). The proposed DHS would have four divisions, responsible for border security, emergency preparedness, weapons of mass destruction, and intelligence. It would combine 22 federal agencies, programs, and research centers into a single organization. Importantly, though, it would not affect the Central Intelligence Agency and the Federal Bureau of Investigation. And because DHS would be a department rather than an office, it incorporated many elements from the bipartisan Specter-Lieberman bill that the president previously had opposed.

For the most part, Capitol Hill welcomed the White House proposal. Senator Charles Schumer (D-NY) went so far as to say that any executive initiative to enhance Ridge's authority would "pass the House and Senate like a hot knife through butter."[2] But because the new DHS would incorporate portions of eight current Cabinet-level departments, it fell under the authority of 88 congressional committees and subcommittees. Soon the proposal was mired in yet another political battle.

"Flexibility" proved to be the main sticking point in the deliberations that followed. The Bush administration wanted to be able to transfer money freely between homeland security accounts, to reorganize departmental operations without congressional approval, and to reduce the influence of labor unions on hiring practices. For the most part, Republicans in Congress supported these initiatives, while also admitting the need for traditional job protections for DHS staff. Democrats, however, were intent on further limiting the president's control over personnel matters. The job security of DHS employees stood out as one of the largest federal issues during the 2002 midterm elections.

As it turned out, Democrats lost control of the Senate after these elections, and they quickly saw fit to give the president most of what he wanted. On November 25, President Bush signed into law a bill that created the DHS, and he nominated Tom Ridge as its first secretary. The Senate confirmed the appointment, and Ridge took office in January 2003. Thus was born the first executive department since 1988, when President Reagan created the Department of Veterans Affairs to replace the Veterans Administration.[3] This department would take the lead in investigating all of the major terrorist threats that would follow, including most recently: a father and son team from Afghanistan who lived in Colorado and, in the fall of 2009, allegedly plotted an attack on a major U.S. transportation center; a Nigerian citizen who attempted to detonate plastic explosives hidden in his underwear while on board an airplane bound for Detroit on Christmas Day 2009; and a 30-year-old Bridgeport resident who failed to detonate a sports utility vehicle filled with explosives in New York City's Times Square in 2010.

The power struggles surrounding the birth of the DHS reveal the stumbling efforts of a federal government to more effectively address a pressing social need—in this case, the development of new, and the consolidation of existing, antiterrorism initiatives. Almost everyone agreed on the importance of creating a federal organization that would serve this goal. Nonetheless, deep concerns about how the organization would be structured and who would control it fueled drawn out and highly charged political battles between the president and Congress, Republicans and Democrats.

This is the stuff of bureaucratic politics. On the one hand, people recognize the extraordinary importance of experts who perform vital tasks, whether it means the protection of our environment, the education of our children, the enforcement of the nation's laws, the assurance of citizens' health and social welfare, or in this instance, the protection of our nation against terrorist attacks. On the other hand, serious disputes can rage over who is charged with overseeing the agencies that perform these activities and the amount of independence that is granted to them.

CHAPTER LEARNING OBJECTIVES

After reading this chapter you will be able to:

16-1 Identify the functions of the federal bureaucracy.

16-2 Outline the organization and the expansion of the bureaucracy.

16-3 Assess the role of the bureaucracy in public policymaking.

16-4 Evaluate the different approaches to overseeing and reforming the bureaucracy.

What Bureaucrats Do

16-1 Identify the functions of the federal bureaucracy.

bureaucracy a group of departments, agencies, and other institutions that for the most part are located in the executive branch of government and that develop and implement public policy.

What do bureaucrats do? The staggering number of functions that government bureaucracies perform might instead raise the question: What *don't* bureaucrats do? Bureaucrats, the individuals who work within a **bureaucracy**, run the nation's prisons and schools, collect garbage, maintain job training programs, write Social Security checks, monitor the pollution of our rivers, pave highways, patrol streets, regulate industries, put out fires, issue drivers' licenses, and so much more. When we experience government in our daily lives, we typically interact with employees of one or another local, state, or federal bureaucracy—teachers, police and parole officers, prison guards, firefighters, garbage collectors, auditors, inspectors, customer service representatives. Such interactions, however, reflect just a small portion of the things that bureaucrats actually do.

Bureaucrats interpret and implement laws.

When Congress enacts a law, when the president issues a unilateral directive, or when a court issues a decree of one sort or another, somebody must figure out what exactly these policies require in practice, and then they must ensure that the government actually takes the steps needed to realize them. Both of these tasks fall to bureaucrats. And both are remarkably difficult.

Laws, after all, are often quite vague. Take, for example, the Full Employment Act, which Congress enacted after World War II. Facing the transition from a wartime to peacetime economy, and anticipating the return of hundreds of thousands of discharged veterans, Congress sought to encourage the development of broad economic policy for the country. With the Full Employment Act, Congress mandated certain actions. It required the president to submit an annual economic report along with his proposed budget. It created the Council of Economic Advisors, an appointed board to advise and assist the president in formulating economic policy. And it established the Joint Economic Committee, composed of members of Congress and charged with reviewing the government's economic policy at least annually. The overriding purpose of the law, meanwhile, was to ensure that federal policies "promote maximum employment, production, and purchasing power."

What do all these legislative provisions mean? Consider the first clause: "promote maximum employment." What is maximum employment? Is 95 percent enough? Or does it require the employment of every single healthy adult who would like to work? Whatever the amount, is the specified goal of maximum employment fixed for all times? Or does the law allow for different objectives depending, for example, on whether the nation is at war or whether the economy is experiencing a downturn? And what does it mean to "promote" maximum employment? Are any means justified? Or should the government weigh the objective of maximizing employment against other objectives, such as reducing deficits or encouraging private enterprise?

It falls upon bureaucrats to formulate answers to these difficult questions, and they must do so in many other policy domains as well. Either when the language of a statute is vague, or when Congress expressly delegates the responsibility to them, bureaucrats must decipher the exact meaning of broad legislative pronouncements. They must determine the exact amount of various pollutants that an industry can release into the air, the precise number of questions that students must answer correctly on standardized tests in order to graduate from high school, the particular design of highway exit signs, and the regularity with which such signs must be replaced.

In the summer of 2010, bureaucrats were charged with making sense of the extraordinarily complex overhaul of the financial industries. Earlier in the year, Congress enacted legislation that increased regulations of various financial services in an attempt to guard against the economic meltdown associated with the housing crash of 2008. The law, however, is short on details. The legislation, for instance, requires banks to set aside funds in case of investment losses, but it leaves it up to bureaucrats to decide how much must be held in reserve. The legislation calls for caps on the amount of fees that banks can charge for ATM transactions, but it leaves it up to bureaucrats to set the exact level. As the *New York Times* reported, the law "is basically a 2,000-page missive to federal agencies, instructing regulators to address subjects ranging from derivatives trading to document retention. But it is notably short on specifics, giving regulators significant power to determine its impact."[4]

Having deciphered the meaning of laws, bureaucrats then are charged with putting them into practice—that is, with implementing them. The **implementation** of public policy constitutes the single biggest task assigned to bureaucrats. Laws, after all, constitute nothing more than words on paper until bureaucrats put them into practice. The implementation of public policy is where the "rubber hits the road."

Just as bureaucrats have considerable discretion to interpret laws, they also have considerable discretion when implementing them. Imagine, for example, a hypothetical agent working for the U.S. Drug Enforcement Administration (DEA) whose job is to enforce the nation's drug laws. This agent receives a tip that drugs are being sold out of an abandoned house on the outskirts of town. When he goes to investigate, he finds a teenage girl selling small amounts of cocaine. After arresting her, though, he learns that this teenager works for a well-known drug dealer in the region. To capture this dealer, the DEA agent will need the teenager's cooperation. To secure her cooperation, can the DEA promise not to prosecute her? Or must he enforce the law every time that he observes a violation?

implementation the process by which policy is executed.

▼ AFTER THE STORM

To uphold the law and ensure their own safety, police officers must make all sorts of decisions on the ground. Every day, they must discern when laws have been violated, who are the likely perpetrators, and what should be done about it. In the aftermath of Hurricane Katrina, basic law and order broke down in the streets of New Orleans. Here, police officers arrest a man who was found with stolen beer in his bags. How should police officers, sometimes called "street-level bureaucrats," go about assessing the threat posed by suspected criminals?

The laws that DEA agents are sworn to uphold provide little guidance on the matter. Instead, DEA agents—and bureaucrats everywhere—must draw on their expertise, their common sense, and whatever recommendations their superiors provide in order to determine the best way to enforce the laws of the land.

Bureaucrats make rules.

One of the principal ways in which bureaucrats flesh out the meaning of congressional statutes, presidential directives, and court orders is by issuing **rules**. Rules typically provide more specific directions about how policy is to be interpreted and implemented. Moreover, once rules are issued, they take on the weight of law. For this reason, political scientists refer to bureaucratic rules as "quasi-legislation."[5]

Rules have a dramatic effect on a vast array of policies—environmental, worker safety, food safety, to name only a few. They also influence the kinds of things we watch on television almost every day. Consider, for example, the efforts of the Federal Communications Commission (FCC) to regulate television and radio under the Communications Acts of 1934, the Communications Satellite Act of 1962, and the Telecommunications Act of 1996. Under these laws, the FCC is charged with "promoting safety of life and property and for strengthening the national defense." Part of this duty is the oversight of "obscene" and "indecent" programming. But what kind of programming qualifies as obscene or indecent? Does it matter whether the programming is aired when children are likely to be watching television? What, exactly, is to be done about violations? None of the three acts listed above provides clear answers to these questions. The FCC, therefore, has had to issue rules that clarify the original laws enacted by Congress.

Through such rules, the FCC has decided to forbid the airing of "obscene" programming at any time and the airing of "indecent programming" or "profane language" during certain hours. The FCC defines "obscene" material according to a three-pronged standard: (1) an average person, applying contemporary community standards, must find that the material, as a whole, appeals to prurient interests; (2) the material must depict or describe, in a patently offensive way, sexual conduct specifically defined by applicable law; and (3) the material, taken as a whole, must lack serious literary, artistic, political, or scientific value.[6] The FCC defines "indecent programming" as "language or material that, in context, depicts or describes, in terms patently offensive as measured by contemporary community standards for the broadcast medium, sexual or excretory organs or activities." It defines "profanity" as "language so grossly offensive to members of the public who actually hear it as to amount to a nuisance."[7] The FCC has further decided that neither indecent programming nor profanity can be aired between 6 a.m. and 10 p.m., when there is a reasonable risk that children may be in the audience.

After the FCC develops guidelines, however, its work is still not complete. It

rules administrative determinations about how laws will be interpreted and implemented.

▼ **STERN VERSUS THE FCC**
After receiving numerous fines from the FCC, popular shock-jock Howard Stern announced in 2004 that he would begin airing his show via satellite radio. So doing, he has avoided many of the rules and regulations that the FCC enforces. In your opinion, should the FCC also regulate the content of satellite radio?

must then ensure that media outlets abide by the rules. The FCC does so by monitoring the content of programming and then punishing infractions by issuing warnings, imposing fines, or revoking station licenses. As one example, comments made by Bono at the 2003 Golden Globe awards caught the attention of the FCC. During his televised acceptance speech, U2's lead singer used a well-known expletive to convey how excited he was to have won an award. Prior to the incident, the FCC had tolerated fleeting expletives in broadcasts. Prompted by complaints about Bono's language, however, the FCC declared that it would begin to fine networks that broadcast fleeting expletives. The FCC explained that the particular word used by Bono "invariably invokes a coarse sexual image and that its isolated and gratuitous utterance could be punished to safeguard the well-being of the nation's children from the most objectionable, most offensive language."[8] Fox Televisions Inc. challenged the new rule in court, claiming that it was arbitrary and contradicted the First Amendment of the Constitution.[9] But in 2009, in a 5–4 decision, the Supreme Court upheld the FCC's new rule.

The specific rules that the FCC developed are intended to guide bureaucrats who do the everyday work of implementing public policy. Obviously, though, these rules alone do not resolve the matter entirely. Considerable judgment is required to figure out whether a specific word or image on a television show meets the FCC's definitions of obscene, indecent, and profane, and if so, to decide what kind of punishment, if any, should apply. Such judgments involve *norms*, which are especially important when an agency's stated goals are vague. Norms come from an organization's culture and sense of mission. They are informal expressions of the customs, attitudes, and expectations put before people who work within a bureaucratic agency. Within the FCC, for example, norms help employees determine which specific words ought to be deemed indecent. They also play an important role in deciding how aggressively to prosecute violations.

In contrast to norms, rules emerge from a well-defined process. The 1946 Administrative Procedures Act lays out the specific steps that agencies must follow when they issue rules. To begin, rules are offered as proposals, allowing interested parties an opportunity to express their opinions. Agencies then must respond to each of the issues raised during the public comment period, which varies in length depending on the complexity of the rule. Further, the agency may be required to issue formal reports to Congress and the president to identify how, for instance, a rule will impact the economy. Final rules then are published in the *Federal Register*, a compendium of government rules, proposed rules, and notices. As agencies have issued increasing numbers of rules over the last 60 years, the *Federal Register* has grown longer and longer. To provide some indication of the volume of rules that the federal bureaucracy produces each year, Figure 16-1 shows the number of pages included in the *Federal Register* each year from 1945 to 2009. Note that whereas rules, notices of rules, and other executive branch policies required fewer than 8,000 pages in 1949, they now take up about 80,000 pages each year.[10]

Bureaucrats provide expert advice.

Bureaucrats in a particular area typically know a great deal more about the specifics of public policy than do members of Congress or the president. This know-how should come as no surprise, for bureaucrats usually are experts who have devoted their professional lives to a specific policy issue, while paying considerably less attention to most other issues. By contrast, members of Congress and presidents are policy generalists who have collected relatively small amounts of information on many different issues.

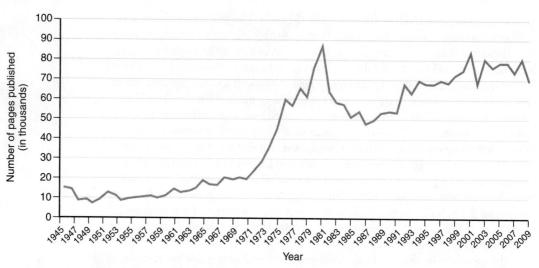

FIGURE 16-1. **The Size of the Federal Register.** During the past half-century, the federal bureaucracy has issued more and more rules.

When determining which public policies are most in need of change, and then figuring out how best to change them, members of Congress and presidents regularly consult bureaucrats. The main responsibility of the Government Accountability Office (GAO), for example, is to provide formal reports to members of Congress about specific policy issues. When a lawmaker wants to learn more about the test score achievement gap between blacks and whites or the threat of terrorism to our nation's seaports, she can request that the GAO investigate the issue. The GAO, then, consults with nongovernment experts, reads the relevant scholarship, and communicates with bureaucratic agencies that deal with the particular policy domain. Having completed its investigation, the GAO reports back to the lawmaker, who is then better equipped to address the issue at hand.

Often, though, members of Congress and presidents consult with bureaucrats through less formal means. Through either testimony in congressional hearings, advisory meetings, or simple conversations, bureaucrats provide lawmakers with vital information about how policies are affecting citizens, which policies seem to be working, which are not, and what should be done about it. Indeed, it is their expertise that makes bureaucrats so useful to lawmakers trying to figure out how best to solve the problems of the day.

Bureaucrats resolve disputes.

Just as bureaucrats serve core executive functions by implementing laws and core legislative functions by issuing rules and providing expertise, so too do they serve core judicial functions by resolving disputes. The National Labor Relations Board, for instance, regularly hears cases involving the unionization of workers and unfair labor practices. Similarly, the Social Security Administration has a well-established process by which citizens who are denied disability payments can appeal their cases. In these processes, both agencies act very much like a court, holding formal hearings, listening to testimony, evaluating evidence, and ultimately rendering a decision.

The FCC also resolves disputes. If a radio or television station wishes to challenge a punishment administered by the FCC for having violated its obscenity standards, it can appeal the matter directly to the agency's five commissioners. CBS Corporation did exactly this when the FCC fined the company $550,000 after the 2004 Super Bowl half-time performance, during which singer Janet Jackson's breast was briefly exposed to approximately 90 million television viewers. The FCC said that CBS had violated its rule governing the broadcast of indecent material. CBS appealed to the commission twice, arguing that the partial nudity was an accident, that Jackson was exposed for less than a second, and that the incident did not violate the FCC rule on indecency. On two separate occasions, the FCC rejected the appeals, saying that the incident was in fact indecent according to its rule and that CBS was at fault for not taking proper precautions to prevent it from happening. CBS, however, continued to insist that the indecency rule was vague.[11] After CBS exhausted its options for appealing directly to the FCC, in 2008 the federal courts stepped in and overturned the fine.[12]

Growth and Organization of the Bureaucracy

16-2 Outline the organization and the expansion of the bureaucracy.

Most of the federal bureaucracy is located within the executive branch of government. But the bureaucracy is not a unitary body operating in a single building down the street from Congress and the president. Rather, it is spread out all over the country and consists of many different units, some more independent than others. The type and number of those units, as well as the kinds of people who work within them, have evolved over time.

The bureaucracy has changed dramatically over the nation's history.

In most of Western Europe, national political systems were bureaucratized long before they were democratized. Particularly in France and Germany, bureaucracies served kings and emperors before they did presidents and prime ministers. With bureaucratic organizations already in place when these countries became democracies, elected officials merely had to redirect administrative activities to serve popular ends. Today, civil servants hold much more prominent positions in European governments, regularly serving in the British prime minister's office and cabinet office, the French president's Secretariat and prime minister's cabinet office, and the office of the German chancellor.[13]

The evolution of the U.S. bureaucracy looks quite different from that in Western Europe. In the United States, democratic political institutions were in place prior to the development of a fully fledged bureaucracy. In fact, America's Founders, disgusted by the British government's abuse of the colonies, intentionally restricted the size and powers of the bureaucracy. In the early years of the Republic, Congress assumed responsibility for most administrative decisions in the new nation. Although the legislature later recognized the need for a fully functional bureaucracy, members of Congress outnumbered civil servants in Washington until the 1820s.[14]

The modest beginnings of the U.S. bureaucracy should not come as a great surprise. The federal government in the nineteenth century, after all, was dramatically smaller than it is today. Its involvement in the daily lives of citizens was minimal by twenty-first-century standards. It produced and implemented far fewer policies than today. It provided little or no regulation of business practices. It also assumed very little responsibility for the welfare of average citizens.

ThinkingComparatively

Historically, bureaucrats have been more entrenched in most European governments than they have been in the U.S. government.

"In most of Western Europe, national political systems were bureaucratized long before they were democratized."

571

Growth and Organization of the Bureaucracy

spoils system a system of government in which a presidential administration awards jobs to party loyalists.

Nineteenth-century federal bureaucrats, therefore, had relatively little to do. Furthermore, they tended to be hired not for their expertise, but for their political allegiance to the party in power. The **spoils system**, as it came to be known, defined the common practice of handing out government jobs, contracts, and other favors not on the basis of merit, but on the basis of political friendships and alliances. When a new president was elected and a different political party assumed control of the executive branch, it would promptly fire most bureaucrats then in office and replace them with its own loyalists.

The spoils system served the political needs of people in power. Most obviously, it provided a basis on which to reward individuals for their political support. And with a growing number of citizens gaining the right to vote, it became more and more important to reward political activists who got people to the polls. Politicians also could raise money for their campaigns by promising jobs. By delivering jobs to key political allies, and thereby shoring up their own electoral fortunes, politicians often could secure the passage of a favorite law.

The spoils system had disadvantages as well. Because bureaucrats tended to be employed only as long as their party remained in office, turnover tended to be quite high. Rather than devoting their lives to a particular policy, bureaucrats often worked for just a few short years. This turnover, in combination with the fact that bureaucrats were selected on the basis of their party support rather than their skills, education, or experience, meant that agencies were less professional and often less capable of furnishing much-needed expertise about public policy.

civil service system a system of government in which decisions about hiring, promotion, and firing are based on individuals' work experience, skills, and expertise.

During the latter half of the nineteenth century, increasing pressure emerged to replace the spoils system with a **civil service system**, which awarded jobs primarily on the basis of merit. Decrying the abuses and waste of a bureaucracy filled with partisan hacks, a diverse group of professional elites pushed for reform. When President James Garfield was assassinated by a disgruntled (and mentally ill) office seeker in 1881, Congress finally saw fit to address their concerns. In 1883, Congress enacted the Pendleton Act, which established the Civil Service Commission (later the Office of Personnel Management). The Civil Service Commission oversaw the hiring and firing of federal bureaucrats on the basis of new procedures, examinations, and qualifications. Merit, rather than party allegiances, constituted the employment qualification that mattered most.

For the most part, though, the transition from the spoils system to a fully developed civil service was gradual. Since politicians still had incentives to reward their partisan backers with jobs, the spoils system was not eliminated overnight. Indeed, the spoils system's final death knell was not heard until 1939, when the vast majority of bureaucrats could truly be called civil servants, and when Congress enacted the Hatch Act, which forbade federal employees from engaging in blatantly partisan political activities like campaigning and fund-raising.

During the same time period that the management of federal bureaucracy personnel experienced dramatic reform, the size of the federal bureaucracy began to grow rapidly. Figure 16-2 tracks the growth in the number of executive branch employees from 1816 to 2008. As the government took on greater and greater responsibility, it needed more agencies and employees to administer public policy. In the late nineteenth and early twentieth centuries, the federal government created agencies to establish and enforce rules on industry, trade, commerce, and transportation so that it could keep pace with the expanding American economy.[15] In 1871, the entire executive branch had only about 50,000 employees. Fifty years later, it had more than 400,000 employees.

In the 1930s, Franklin D. Roosevelt created several new agencies through his "New Deal" program in an effort to lift the nation out of the Great Depression. The size of the bureaucracy skyrocketed when the United States became involved in

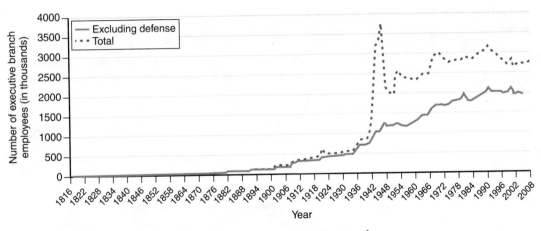

FIGURE 16-2. The Size of the Federal Bureaucracy. During the past century, the number of employees in the federal bureaucracy has increased dramatically. The dotted line includes all civilian executive branch employees. The solid line represents that total minus the number of civilian defense employees.

World War II. Since 1946, the total number of executive branch employees has remained fairly stable. However, the number of nondefense employees has continued to grow throughout the last 60 years.

The bureaucracy today consists of many different units.

Since the end of World War II, the size of the federal bureaucracy has leveled off. In 1946, roughly the same number of bureaucrats worked for the federal government as today—slightly over 2 million.[16] These bureaucrats work within very different kinds of governing structures: departments, independent agencies and regulatory commissions, and government corporations.

Departments   Most bureaucratic agencies are housed in a **department**, which is the largest organizational unit in the federal bureaucracy. Departments address broad areas of government responsibility, and the head of each department is appointed by the president to serve in his cabinet.

Today, there are 15 departments. The Department of Homeland Security, discussed at the beginning of this chapter, is the latest addition to the list. As Table 16-1 shows, at the nation's founding George Washington oversaw only three departments: Treasury, War (now Defense), and State. During the nineteenth century, three more departments were added: Interior, Justice, and Agriculture. But during the twentieth century, especially during the latter half, the number of departments really expanded. As citizens expected the federal government to do more and more on their behalf, departments were created to help write and implement policy. Health and Human Services, Housing

department   a major administrative unit that is composed of many agencies serving many policy functions, and that is headed by a secretary, who serves in the president's Cabinet.

▼ **A PRESIDENT'S CABINET**

In April 2010, President Obama meets with Labor Secretary Hilda Solis and other high-ranking bureaucrats to discuss issues involving mine safety.

TABLE 16-1. Founding Date and Purpose of Federal Departments

DEPARTMENT	YEAR FOUNDED	RESPONSIBILITIES
War Department, renamed Department of Defense in 1949	1789	Coordinates and oversees the U.S. Army, Navy, and Air Force as well as smaller agencies that are responsible for national security.
Department of the Treasury	1789	Manages the government's money; prints paper currency, mints coins, and collects taxes through the Internal Revenue Service.
Department of State	1789	Develops and executes the president's foreign policy agenda. The department head, the secretary of state, is the chief foreign policy adviser to the president.
Department of the Interior	1849	Conserves land owned by the federal government; manages cultural and natural resources like national parks, dams, wildlife refuges, and monuments.
Department of Justice	1870	The U.S. legal department that houses several law enforcement agencies, including the Federal Bureau of Investigation, Drug Enforcement Administration, and Federal Bureau of Prisons. Its lawyers represent the government in court. The chief lawyer of the federal government is the attorney general.
Department of Agriculture	1889	Develops policy to protect farmers, promote agricultural trade, and alleviate hunger in the U.S. and abroad. It also inspects food to ensure that it is safe to consume.
Department of Labor, reconstituted in 1913	1903	Oversees labor practices in the U.S.; makes sure that workplaces are safe, enforces a minimum wage, and provides unemployment insurance.
Department of Commerce, reconstituted in 1913	1903	Works to maintain the health of the U.S. economy; supports businesses, promotes the creation of jobs, gathers and provides economic data, and issues patents and trademarks.
Department of Health and Human Services	1953	Administers more than 300 federal programs to protect the health and safety of Americans; provides health insurance to the elderly and disabled, offers immunization services and treatment for substance abuse, and inspects drugs to ensure their safety.
Department of Housing and Urban Development	1965	Works to increase home ownership in the U.S. It also helps low-income individuals secure affordable housing.
Department of Transportation	1966	Ensures the safety, accessibility, and efficiency of air travel, the national highway network, railroads, and public transportation systems.
Department of Energy	1977	Oversees domestic energy production and conservation. It also manages the nation's nuclear weapons and reactors as well as the disposal of radioactive waste.
Department of Education	1980	Provides funding to education programs and enforces federal education laws such as No Child Left Behind.
Department of Veterans Affairs	1988	Provides a wide array of benefits to war veterans, including general compensation, health care, education, life insurance, and home loans.
Department of Homeland Security	2002	Responsible for protecting the U.S. from terrorist attacks and responding to natural disasters.

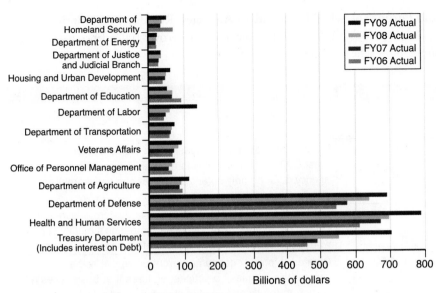

FIGURE 16-3. **Department Spending in 2009.** The sizes of the departments that make up the federal bureaucracy vary dramatically.

and Urban Development, Transportation, Energy, Education, Veterans Affairs, and finally Homeland Security were all created to confront concerns ranging from the mental and physical health of citizens to the looming threat of terrorism.

Now take a look at Figure 16-3, which shows the amount of money spent by each of the departments in fiscal year 2009. Among the groups, the department that spends the most annually is Health and Human Services, whose budget approached $800 billion in 2009. These costs covered such massive entitlement programs as Medicaid and Medicare, which are discussed at length in Chapter 17, as well as such prominent agencies as the Food and Drug Administration, the National Institutes of Health, and the Centers for Disease Control and Prevention. Together, the two departments that employ the largest numbers of people, Defense and Veterans Affairs, spent nearly $800 billion. Many of these funds covered the costs of ongoing wars in Afghanistan and Iraq. Education, Housing and Urban Development, and Energy, by contrast, are the three smallest agencies in terms of the number of people they employ. Combined, they spend roughly $150 billion each year and have fewer than 35,000 employees.

Independent agencies and regulatory commissions   Not all agencies operate within a department. Many **independent agencies and commissions** operate outside departments. These agencies and commissions are directed by administrators or boards who are appointed by the president, subject to Senate confirmation. The heads of these organizations, however, do not serve in the president's Cabinet. Unlike department heads, whom the president can select freely and who can be fired at any time, heads of independent agencies and regulatory commissions must meet well-defined qualifications, and they hold office for fixed periods. These restrictions on the hiring and firing of agency leaders tend to protect them from the efforts of presidents and members of Congress to meddle in their affairs—a topic we discuss further below.

Independent agencies, like those listed in Table 16-2, perform all sorts of functions. They manage national museums like the Smithsonian Institution.

independent agencies and commissions bureaucratic organizations that operate outside of Cabinet-level departments and are less subject to congressional or presidential influence.

TABLE 16-2. Founding Date and Purpose of Select Independent Agencies, Regulatory Commissions, and Government Corporations. The federal bureaucracy contains over 100 independent agencies and government corporations. The lists here contain some highlights.

	YEAR FOUNDED	RESPONSIBILITIES
Independent Agencies and Regulatory Commissions		
United States Postal Service (USPS), became an independent agency in 1971	1775	Delivers all first and third class mail. Was a department for almost 200 years before it was reorganized as an independent agency. It is the only organization that can deliver mail to private mailboxes.
Board of Governors of the Federal Reserve System	1913	Governing body of the Federal Reserve System, which is the central bank of the U.S. Manages the nation's money supply, working to control inflation and maintain economic growth.
Federal Trade Commission (FTC)	1914	Created to protect consumers from deceptive and anti-competitive business practices; ensures that businesses advertise truthfully and provide buyers with adequate information about their products and services.
Securities and Exchange Commission (SEC)	1934	Enforces laws against insider trading and accounting fraud; created to regulate the stock market after the stock market crash of 1929 that led to the Great Depression.
Federal Communications Commission (FCC)	1934	Regulates radio and television broadcasting as well as interstate wire, satellite, and cable telecommunications. Governed by five commissioners who are appointed by the president and confirmed by the Senate.
Social Security Administration, reinstated as an independent Agency in 1995	1935	Manages Social Security, the nation's social insurance program that delivers benefits to the elderly and disabled.
Central Intelligence Agency (CIA)	1947	Provides national security information on foreign governments, people, and corporations to senior officials in the federal government. Its secret operations are directed by the president and overseen by Congress.
National Aeronautics and Space Administration (NASA)	1958	Responsible for the nation's space program, including space exploration and scientific research.
Environmental Protection Agency (EPA)	1970	Protects Americans from the harmful health effects of air, water, and land pollution. Safeguards the natural environment by establishing and enforcing emissions standards for various types of pollutants.
Privacy and Civil Liberties Oversight Board	2007	Previously housed in the Executive Office of the President, this board was reconstituted in 2007 as an independent commission. It offers advice regarding civil liberties and privacy concerns in all matters involving anti-terrorism policies.
Government Corporations		
Tennessee Valley Authority (TVA)	1933	A federally owned power company that provides electricity to the Tennessee Valley, an area that includes most of Tennessee and parts of six other states in the region.
Federal Deposit Insurance Corporation (FDIC)	1933	Created during the Great Depression to promote confidence in the U.S. banking system; insures the money people deposit into checking and savings accounts in banks.

(Continued)

TABLE 16-2. Founding Date and Purpose of Select Independent Agencies, Regulatory Commissions, and Government Corporations (*Continued*)

	YEAR FOUNDED	RESPONSIBILITIES
Corporation for Public Broadcasting (PBS)	1967	Private, nonprofit corporation that distributes funding for public television and radio programming, including programming made available through the Public Broadcasting Service and National Public Radio (NPR). Funded almost entirely by the federal government.
Amtrak (National Railroad Passenger Corporation)	1971	Provides passenger train service between U.S. cities. Receives funding from both the federal government and ticket sales. Members of its board of directors are appointed by the president and confirmed by the Senate.
Overseas Private Investment Corporation (OPIC)	1971	Assists American businesses when they make investments abroad; helps companies manage the risk involved in overseas investments and promotes economic development in emerging markets. It gets most of its revenue from fees for its products.
Millennium Challenge Corporation (MCC)	2004	Provides funding to poverty-stricken countries in order to promote economic growth, infrastructure investment, and good government.

Through the Peace Corps, they send college graduates to volunteer in countries all over the globe. The National Aeronautics and Space Administration launches men and women into space, the Social Security Administration writes millions of checks each year, and the United States Postal Service delivers the mail. Recently, still more agencies have been created, which, as their names imply, serve an equally diverse array of responsibilities. Standouts include the Office of the Federal Coordinator for Alaska Natural Gas Transportation Projects, the U.S. Election Assistance Commission, and the Office of the National Counterintelligence Executive.

The first regulatory commission was the Interstate Commerce Commission, created in 1887 to regulate railroads. The nation subsequently experienced a rapid rise of commissions with the Administrative Procedures Act, which, as previously noted, established the governing framework for administrative agencies in the modern era. These commissions regulate all kinds of industries and organizations, ranging from toy manufacturers to stock markets to television stations. Among the especially important regulatory commissions are the Consumer Product Safety Commission, the Securities and Exchange Commission, the Federal Trade Commission, and as previously discussed, the Federal Communications Commission.

One of the newest independent agencies is the Financial Crisis Inquiry Commission, which was created in response to the national economic collapse of 2007 and 2008. The commission was a stipulation of the Fraud Enforcement and Recovery Act of 2009, signed into law by President Obama in May 2009. The FCIC was charged with examining "the causes of major financial institutions which failed, or were likely to have failed, had they not received exceptional government assistance."[17] The scope of the agency's inquiries went from fraud and abuse in the financial sector to the legal and regulatory structure of the U.S. housing market. Unlike some other commissions, the FCIC was granted subpoena power for witness testimony and the acquisition of documents. Any discoveries of unlawful activities by the commission in relation to the financial crisis were to be referred to the attorney general for further prosecution.

Government corporations Even more removed from presidential and congressional control are **government corporations**.[18] These organizations most closely

government corporation a corporation created and funded by the government to provide some public service that would be insufficiently provided by the private sector.

resemble private companies. Unlike private companies, however, government corporations receive steady streams of government funding and are subject to modest oversight. In most cases, Congress or the president has decided that the private marketplace does not provide sufficient monetary incentives to provide these services (especially to low-income individuals). As shown in Table 16-2, prominent examples of government corporations include the National Railroad Passenger Corporation (Amtrak), which takes citizens to work, and the Federal Deposit Insurance Corporation, which ensures the safety of bank deposits. The most recent government corporation to come into existence is the Millennium Challenge Corporation, which promotes economic development projects around the globe.

Challenges of Bureaucracy

16-3   Assess the role of the bureaucracy in public policymaking.

Bureaucrats provide vital services in an increasing number of policy areas. Indeed, hardly a day passes when we fail to interact with a bureaucrat of one type or another. But bureaucracy is not without its problems, which partially explains why so many politicians call for its reform. Sometimes bureaucrats attend to their own private interests or those of a narrow band of citizens rather than to the interests of the broader public. Sometimes, however, the organizations in which bureaucrats work are extraordinarily inefficient. As a result, the services that the government bureaucracy provides are often more expensive and less effective than we might like.

Bureaucrats have their own interests.

In principle, bureaucrats are supposed to implement the policies written by their political superiors. When needed, bureaucrats are also supposed to clarify the meaning of laws, either through rules or through norms. In practice, though, bureaucrats have their own interests, which may or may not align with those of the president or Congress. Because bureaucrats tend to have more expertise than the latter, they enjoy considerable discretion to pursue these ends, sometimes at a cost to the larger public.

To understand the problem of different interests, imagine that while you are driving home one day, your car suddenly breaks down. What do you do? If you are like most Americans, you do not have a clue how to fix the car yourself. So you have the car towed to the local mechanic to have it fixed. At this point, the interests of two people become involved. You need the mechanic for her expertise; the mechanic needs you for your money. The subsequent exchange, then, would appear perfectly straightforward. The mechanic fixes your car in exchange for a mutually agreed upon price.

But therein lies the rub. Precisely because you do not understand what is wrong with your car, you have little ability to determine how much it ought to cost to fix it. This would not ordinarily be a problem, at least not if the mechanic were honest and forthcoming. The trouble is that the mechanic's interests are different from yours. You want to pay the least amount of money for the most amount of work using the best possible parts. The mechanic, by contrast, wants to receive the most amount of money for the least amount of work using the least expensive parts. And because she knows more than you about what is wrong with your car and what is needed to fix it, the mechanic is often able to win out in this exchange.

The resulting inefficiencies are an example of what is commonly referred to as a **principal-agent problem**. In this example, you are the principal, and the mechanic is the agent. Both individuals are made better off by having the work done to the car at a fair price. But because the mechanic, as the agent, has private information that you,

principal-agent problem   the problem that occurs when one person (the principal) contracts with another person (the agent) to provide a service and yet cannot directly observe what the agent is actually doing; the agent, meanwhile, is motivated to take advantage of the principal.

as the principal, cannot know, the mechanic is made even better off, and you worse off—either because the mechanic charges you for services that your car does not really need, or because she does not do as good a job as promised on the work order.

This principal-agent problem fundamentally defines the relationship between Congress and the president (the principals), on the one hand, and the bureaucracy (the agent), on the other. Congress and the president, as policy generalists, need bureaucrats for their expertise. Bureaucrats, however, do not necessarily share the same interests as Congress and the president.[19] Bureaucrats may not want to work as hard as Congress and the president would like them to—generating what political scientists refer to as **slack**. Anyone who has stood for hours at the local post office can attest to its frustrations. Alternatively, bureaucrats may be perfectly willing to work hard, but they choose to do so in the service of objectives that Congress and the president oppose—generating what political scientists refer to as **drift**. Examples of drift include the district attorney who aggressively pursues white-collar criminals but prefers not to prosecute minor drug offenses, or the park ranger who uses funds to purchase new computers for his staff rather than to clean campgrounds, or the teacher who decides to stick with her tried and true lesson plans rather than teach a new state-mandated curriculum.

An essential element of what makes slack and drift possible is the principal's difficulty of monitoring the agent. Congress and the president cannot personally watch every decision of a district attorney, a park ranger, or a teacher. Moreover, outcomes are often hard to measure. Because all of the available measures of criminal activity, park cleanliness, and student learning are imperfect, it is difficult for Congress and the president to know for sure whether bureaucrats are working as effectively as they can in the service of their formal goals and responsibilities. Moreover, because there are so many contributors to each of these outcomes—what bureaucrats do, or do not do, is only part of the equation—bureaucrats can often explain away any observed failures to achieve stated objectives as being beyond their control. After all, as agents, they are the ones who are experts, whereas Congress and the president, as principals, are not.

The troubles, though, do not end there. In the example of the broken car, there is but one agent and one principal. In government, by contrast, at any given moment there are many principals and many agents. And the interests of each do not perfectly overlap. When Congress and the president disagree about a policy issue, as they typically do during periods of divided government, agents may be able to play off one principal against the other. And when multiple agents are responsible for a particular policy issue, each can attempt to blame the others when failures are observed.

Consider the extraordinary efforts of the federal government to monitor and improve student learning in public schools. Under the No Child Left Behind Act, discussed at length in Chapter 17, students are regularly evaluated on newly developed state tests; depending on student performance, schools may face consequences ranging from funding cuts to restructurings. Bureaucrats in local school districts, state education departments, and the federal government all work hard to implement the law. But given the stakes involved, and the controversies that surround standardized tests, these bureaucrats occasionally work at cross purposes: federal bureaucrats may blame state and local officials for refusing to fully incorporate the provisions of No Child Left Behind; local and state officials, meanwhile, blame the federal government for imposing undue burdens on schools without providing sufficient funding.

Compounding the principal-agent problem is the fact that in government the preferences of the principals change every two or four years. A coalition within Congress may set a bureaucratic agency's official mandate one year, but following an election the individuals who comprised this coalition may no longer be in power.

slack a situation in which bureaucrats do not work as hard as Congress or the president would like.

drift a situation in which bureaucrats create policy that does not match the policy preferences of Congress or the president.

"This principal-agent problem fundamentally defines the relationship between Congress and the president (the principals), on the one hand, and the bureaucracy (the agent), on the other."

Those individuals who replaced them, meanwhile, may have very different ideas about what bureaucrats ought to be doing. President Obama is under considerable pressure to substantially revise No Child Left Behind, raising the possibility that new state tests may be developed, the standards for evaluating student progress may shift, a new array of punishments for school failure may be introduced, and altogether new monitoring devices may be developed. For obvious reasons, such changes can place incredible burdens on those bureaucrats charged with interpreting and implementing a continually changing legislative mandate.

Bureaucrats sometimes serve the interests of unelected groups.

Bureaucrats occasionally stray from their mandate not in the pursuit of their own interests, but rather in the pursuit of someone else's. Sometimes it is a well-funded special interest group. At other times it is a highly mobilized segment of the population, or it might be the industry that a bureaucratic agency is supposed to be regulating. In any one of these instances, bureaucrats would appear to be taking their cues not from their political superiors, but instead from individuals and organizations that operate outside of government entirely.

agency capture the condition under which an agency primarily serves the interests of a nongovernmental group rather than those of elected officials.

Political scientists use the term **agency capture** to describe the situation when an agency primarily serves the interests of a nongovernmental group rather than those of elected officials. The possibility of agency capture is especially high under two conditions.[20] The first is when the benefits of agency actions are concentrated on a few individuals or organizations, while the costs are spread more or less evenly throughout society. Consider, for example, bureaucratic agencies that direct financial subsidies to farmers. These subsidies are not especially large. For the farmers who benefit from them, however, they mean a great deal. Thus, organizations like the American Farm Bureau Federation work hard to ensure that the federal government continues to dole out these benefits year in and year out, regardless of whether they serve a larger public purpose.

Agency capture also occurs when the costs of policy implementation fall on a small group of individuals or organizations, but the social benefits are more diffuse. Consider, for example, an agency that is charged with monitoring the air pollutants produced by an industry on the edge of a large city. If the agency vigorously enforces rules that limit pollution, the industry will incur the high costs of compliance. These costs include both the fines it may have to pay for violating clean air rules and the new machinery it may need to purchase in order to comply with the law. From the perspective of each city resident, though, the benefits of the agency's actions are relatively small. They certainly prefer that the industry produce less waste, but their daily lives are probably not deeply affected by the agency's efforts to reduce industrial pollutants. Consequently, the regulated industries have strong incentives to influence agency behavior, whereas the general public does not. The resulting mismatch between highly mobilized and organized interest groups and a less attentive public invites agency capture.

"Bureaucrats occasionally stray from their mandate not in the pursuit of their own interests, but rather in the pursuit of someone else's."

Some critics have argued that the Food and Drug Administration (FDA) has been captured by pharmaceutical companies, which help fund FDA activities, lobby members of Congress, and launch major public relations campaigns.[21] Pharmaceutical companies stand to make massive amounts of money when a drug is approved for public consumption. As a result, companies with existing drugs sometimes encourage raising the standards of evaluations, thereby reducing the opportunities for new treatments to enter the market. At other times companies pressure the FDA to approve drugs before the safety of those drugs has been conclusively established.

It is worth noting, though, that the FDA often is placed in an impossible position. If they do not approve drugs fast enough, they appear to be ignoring the needs of citizens in need of new treatments. But if they approve drugs hastily, they risk exposing the public to unsafe drugs. It often is difficult, therefore, to know whether the actions that the FDA takes are an attempt to balance these competing considerations, or whether the agency is ultimately guided by the very drug companies it is supposed to regulate.

Bureaucrats can be inefficient.

The most common complaint about bureaucrats is not that they serve their own interests or those of a narrow band of the U.S. public. Rather, it is that they do not do a good job of serving anyone's interest. For some, the very word *bureaucracy* has come to imply inefficiency, waste, and **red tape**.

Every few months, it seems, a story breaks in the news about a $1,000 hammer purchased by the federal government, a half-built bridge that never seems to be completed, a dozen agencies that are all supposed to be doing the same thing, piles of mail that sit for weeks in warehouses, or bureaucrats paid large amounts of money to do little but sit. A predictable set of charges follows: bureaucrats waste public funds, fail to complete their tasks, ignore pressing public needs, and live off the public's dole without any apparent justification.

Boston's "Big Dig" project stands out as one of the more recent and alarming examples of bureaucratic waste and mismanagement. Intended to reduce traffic in the downtown area and to clear space for parks, the public works project was officially launched in 1991, when Congress appropriated funds for the project over a presidential veto. Early plans for the project suggested an official price of $2.5 billion. In less than a decade, though, costs rose to $7.5 billion, and by 2006 costs reached an astronomical $14.6 billion. For all the money spent, the project has been awash (literally) in scandal.

continued on page 584 ▶

red tape the inefficiency and waste that result from excessive regulation and overly formal procedures.

▼ **GOVERNMENT WASTE**
Boston's Big Dig was hardly a paragon of government efficiency. In addition to high costs and delays, the public works project had numerous design setbacks. In 2006, a 12-ton portion of the tunnel collapsed and killed a driver.

HOW DO WE KNOW?

Did the Federal Bureaucracy Fail to Protect the City of New Orleans After Hurricane Katrina?

The Question

In August 2005, Hurricane Katrina tore through the Gulf Coast, devastating the city of New Orleans and other coastal areas in Louisiana, Mississippi, and Alabama. The collapse of several levees in New Orleans submerged much of the city under water. Survivors in the most ravaged sections of the city had no electricity, no way to communicate by telephone or radio, no roads or bridges on which to escape, and no functioning law enforcement to protect them from theft and violence. The disaster overwhelmed the response systems of the federal, state, and local bureaucracies. Thousands of residents who had not evacuated were left stranded on their rooftops for days without food or water, waiting to be rescued. More than 1,300 people died in the storm and its aftermath.

Americans were appalled by the slowness and inadequacy of the government's response to the disaster. In the months following, many questioned the effectiveness of multiple government agencies, especially the Federal Emergency Management Agency (FEMA), which had been moved into the Department of Homeland Security in 2003 after previously operating as an independent agency. Did the federal bureaucracy fail to protect the city of New Orleans after Hurricane Katrina? How do we know?

▼ STRANDED

Hurricane Katrina completely overwhelmed the capacities of local and state bureaucratic agencies. Following the hurricane, many residents of New Orleans were stuck on rooftops for days. Here, a woman is rescued from a school rooftop after she and dozens of others had been trapped by the rising waters.

Why It Matters

By objectively analyzing the effectiveness of the federal bureaucracy, we may contribute to policy discussions about what could be done better. These discussions shape decisions that affect us every time we take a prescription drug approved by the FDA, eat chicken inspected by the Department of Agriculture, or send a piece of mail through the U.S. Postal Service. Because we both consume those services and pay for them through taxes, we must think critically about whether our money is being spent well and whether the services provided by the bureaucracy meet our expectations.

Investigating the Answer

In the U.S. federalist system, power is shared among the federal government and 50 state governments. The state governments bear a great deal of responsibility for designing and implementing policy, and the executive branches of the state governments have their own bureaucracies with many of the same problems as the federal bureaucracy. Moreover, within the states, city and county governments have their own responsibilities. To evaluate the performance of the federal government, then, it is also important to account for the performance of state and local governments in the complex web of federalism. Cities, states, and the federal government share the responsibility of responding to natural disasters. Technically, it is the job of counties and cities to respond first. Only after local resources have been exhausted do the governor and the state bureaucracies provide further disaster assistance. The governor can call in the federal government to help if the state cannot handle the situation. Even when federal assistance is called for, however, federal agents must work with state and local agents to carry out relief. The shared nature of disaster relief makes it extremely difficult to sort out which level of government is most to blame for a poorly conducted relief effort.

Almost immediately after Hurricane Katrina struck New Orleans, local relief agencies realized that they could not possibly handle the crisis on their own. Nor was it clear that federal agencies were up for the task. In a statement to the American people, President Bush admitted, "It was not a normal hurricane, and the normal disaster relief system was not equal to it. . . . The system at every level of government, was not well coordinated and was overwhelmed in the first few days."[22]

The U.S. Army Corps of Engineers was singled out for criticism. It, after all, failed to detect a flaw in the designs of the 17th Street and London Avenue levees, a flaw that most likely caused the levees' collapse and the subsequent flooding of the city.

FEMA also came under heavy fire for its failure to respond to the crisis speedily and effectively. The catastrophe made clear that FEMA was entirely unprepared to handle the large-scale rescue operation. The competence and credentials of then-FEMA director Michael Brown were called sharply into question after the agency's inadequate response. The preponderance of evidence suggests that FEMA failed miserably in its responsibilities as a federal agency. In a hefty report issued several months after the disaster, Inspector General Richard Skinner ended up concluding, "Much of the criticism [of FEMA] is warranted."[23] The report cited a lack in manpower, a decline in preparation for natural disasters, and confusion over the roles and responsibilities of FEMA officials as reasons why the agency's response was so slow and inefficient.

It is not altogether clear, though, that the federal bureaucracy should bear the full brunt of criticism. The destruction of all communications infrastructure in New Orleans seriously impeded FEMA's ability to assess the full gravity of the situation and intervene appropriately. In addition, the magnitude of the hurricane was so great that arguably even an efficient and effective organization would have had difficulty dealing with the aftermath. By most accounts, some federal agencies performed quite well—in particular, the Coast Guard, the National Guard, and the military were instrumental in rescuing tens of thousands of people from their rooftops and their flooded homes.

Even the federal courts have entered the business of trying to assess blame. On November 18, 2009, a federal judge ruled on a case involving the Army Corps of Engineers and the people of New Orleans. The plaintiff's lawyers argued that the Army Corps had not exercised due care in maintaining the channel of levees that ran through the city. The judge apparently agreed. In the court's opinion, "the negligence of the corps, in this instance by failing to maintain the MR-GO properly, was not policy, but insouciance, myopia and shortsightedness." The judge granted six plaintiffs over $750,000 in reparations, opening the door for billions more to be given out. The case is currently on appeal.

Thinking Critically

Who, in your opinion, bears primary responsibility for responding to the devastation wrought by Hurricane Katrina?

When bureaucratic agencies have overlapping responsibilities, how can the American public best evaluate their individual performances?

Do the administrative failures associated with Hurricane Katrina have any resemblance to the problems associated with the oil spill in the Gulf of Mexico in the summer of 2010?

The Bottom Line

The devastation wrought by Hurricane Katrina would seem to speak for itself. Clearly the government failed to protect its citizens from the consequences of a natural disaster. Assigning blame, though, is complicated by the fact that multiple levels of government, and multiple agencies within any given level, are responsible for disaster relief. Furthermore, it is difficult to assess blame and prescribe structural reforms in the aftermath of atypical events. Given the inherent challenges of a bureaucratic system, the response of the government as a whole may not have been as bad as the horrifying images of the hurricane's aftermath would imply.

After the tunnels opened in January 2006, hundreds of water leaks sprung; multiple investigations uncovered the use of faulty materials; falling ceiling tiles killed a commuter; and charges of corruption and waste were leveled against both the companies who undertook the work and the government agencies charged with overseeing them.[24] In 2008, three of the private contractors involved in the Big Dig collectively paid almost half a billion dollars to the city of Boston and the state of Massachusetts for these various blunders and catastrophes.

Some critics blame these kinds of problems on a culture of inertia that exists within the government's bureaucracy. Culture, in this instance, emerges from worker incentives. Bureaucrats have strong job protections—a product of the civil service reforms previously discussed. And they are not driven by the profit motive. Quite the contrary. The culture of bureaucracy sometimes rewards individuals not for the impact that their labor has on the lives of citizens, but rather for their faithful adherence to a stated process for how things ought to be done. Indeed, it was not until Massachusetts's governor and attorney general stepped in that the head of the Massachusetts Turnpike Authority was fired, companies were sued for "shoddy work," and responsibility for the Big Dig project shifted to the state government.

Although the waste and mismanagement of the Big Dig were extreme, smaller versions of such failures are common. Moreover, they are entirely predictable. The bureaucracy, after all, is not designed merely for the sake of efficiency. It is also supposed to promote notions of fairness and equity. To ensure that individual bureaucrats follow these directives, politicians have insisted that bureaucrats follow painstaking procedures for even the simplest of tasks.

Take, for example, the job of purchasing a new computer. An individual working in the private industry need only find the company that will provide the best possible machine that suits his or her individual needs for the lowest price. In a government agency, by contrast, bureaucrats must solicit bids from government-approved vendors, choose from a select group of machines, and maintain careful documentation of all transactions. In this way, the public can rest assured that the companies that supply computers to the federal government do not discriminate against their workers, that bureaucrats are not spending lavish amounts of money, and that all monies are accounted for. The process is long and costly, but it exists to promote the important goals of fairness and equality.

Moreover, there are political explanations for certain bureaucratic failures or inefficiencies. Congress and the president often oversee agencies whose activities they would just as soon reduce, or even eliminate. So rather than appoint individuals who will vigorously pursue an agency's mission, they choose people who will take a more lax approach to regulatory enforcement. James Watt's tenure as secretary of the interior under President Ronald Reagan and Gale Norton's under President George W. Bush were both marked by such charges. Critics claimed that both Reagan and Bush were less interested in protecting federal lands and more interested in developing housing and increasing energy production. Accordingly, these presidents deliberately chose secretaries they knew would take a restricted (some supporters would argue, balanced) view of their duties to secure the well-being of the nation's parks and lands. Thus their choices for interior secretary were two former attorneys for the Mountain States Legal Foundation, an organization whose mission is to provide a "strong and effective voice for freedom of enterprise, the rights of private property ownership, and the multiple use of federal and state resources."[25]

Some political scientists argue that the very design of our system of governance undermines opportunities for effective bureaucracy. They claim that regular elections, multiple principals, and political compromise lend themselves to inefficiencies and mismanagement, even in domains that everyone agrees are essential to the nation's well-being. One political scientist, for instance, argues that the core agencies charged with intelligence-gathering—the Central Intelligence Agency, the Joint Chiefs of Staff, and the National Security Council—are "flawed by design."[26] The Joint Chiefs of Staff (JCS) emerged from "a brass-knuckle fight to the finish" pitting President Truman and the War Department (now the Department of Defense), who sought to bring the military services under one umbrella, against the Department of the Navy, which fiercely guarded its independence.[27] The resulting structure of the JCS pleased few and did little to quell interservice rivalry. Bureaucratic in-fighting during the Korean War was bitter enough that it "extended to conflicts over which service would operate a laundry in Alaska." More serious failures of the JCS included its approval of President Kennedy's disastrous Bay of Pigs invasion, as well as coordination problems during interventions in Iran, Grenada, and Beirut.[28]

Even the redundancy that pervades so much of the federal bureaucracy has a certain inherent political logic. Imagine the challenge faced by a president who assumes office after a long stretch of control by the opposition party. Should the newly elected president rely on individuals appointed under the former administrations to formulate his policy agenda? Or, after recognizing the awesome challenges of dismantling existing agencies, might he instead construct altogether new ones? Both options have advantages and disadvantages. Hence, when advancing a new policy initiative, presidents often spread out responsibilities across multiple agencies while also creating new ones. This tactic, in fact, is exactly what President George W. Bush followed when launching his "Faith-Based Initiative," a key plank in his 2000 campaign platform. In an effort to support social programs run by private and religion-based charities, Bush created new centers in existing Cabinet departments (Justice, Housing and Urban Development, Health and Human Services, Labor, and Education), as well as a White House Office of Faith-Based and Community Initiatives.[29]

Controlling and Reforming the Bureaucracy

16-4 Evaluate the different approaches to overseeing and reforming the bureaucracy.

Reformers have long sought solutions to the various problems of bureaucratic drift, slack, agency capture, and inefficiency. None works perfectly. But each manages to give the president, Congress, and the larger public somewhat more influence over the bureaucracy than would otherwise occur. These reforms generally fit into one of three categories: those that focus on the bureaucrats who work within agencies; those that focus on the structural relationship between agencies and their political superiors; and those that attempt to promote market forces of competition.

Presidents and Congress exercise control through appointments.

The secretaries of all Cabinet-level departments are appointed by the president, subject to Senate confirmation. The president is free to choose whomever he likes to fill these positions. The president also can select the individuals and boards that govern independent agencies, regulatory commissions, and government corporations, though these appointees often must satisfy various rules and restrictions. Moreover, all appointments can take a long time to complete. As late as July 2010, 19 months into Barack Obama's presidency, Congress had confirmed only 77 percent of his senior appointments.[30]

When making their selections, what criteria might Congress and the president consider? Both want to appoint individuals who are well qualified, who have expertise and experience in the given policy arena, and who are likely to inspire their workforce. All of these characteristics reflect the civil service reforms of the early twentieth century. The appointment process, however, remains deeply political. Precisely because bureaucrats have a tendency to drift away from their given mandate, Congress and the president have strong incentives to choose leaders on the basis of their expressed ideological views and policy commitments. In other words, Congress and the president try to solve the principal-agent problem by selecting agents who share their worldview, and who appear committed to seeing it realized by the department or agency that they will eventually run.

politicization a phenomenon that occurs when Congress and the president select bureaucracy leaders who share their political views.

Political scientists call this phenomenon the **politicization** of the bureaucracy.[31] Presidents and Congress select individuals they can trust to implement their wishes and ensure that their staff will follow suit. And they do so for good reason. What is the point, after all, of appointing someone who is highly skilled and experienced but has no interest in following your wishes? Competence is important, but in politics it is not enough. Presidents and Congress also need to know that those under their command will work hard on behalf of their interests, even when these individuals are not being watched.

Politicization, though, can come at a cost. By emphasizing loyalty, presidents may undermine an agency's ability to perform as well as its institutional memory. When political appointees replace policy experts, and when agency turnover increases, bureaucratic operations may founder. According to one recent study, agencies with larger proportions of political appointees were systematically less effective than agencies with fewer political appointees.[32]

Of course, presidents and members of Congress themselves may disagree about the kinds of policies that bureaucratic agencies ought to implement. In these instances, the appointment process can be highly controversial. Take, for example, President Clinton's decision to appoint California attorney Bill Lann Lee to head the Civil Rights Division of the Department of Justice. When Clinton first nominated Lee for the position in 1997, the Republican-controlled Senate Judiciary Committee balked. Contrary to the praise Lee received from civil rights groups and Democrats in Congress, Republicans argued that the former NAACP lawyer was far too liberal, particularly on the issue of affirmative action. Clinton tried to renominate Lee, but the Senate continued to deny Lee the position.[33]

When the Senate will not confirm a president's appointment, the president has two choices. He can withdraw the nomination and offer up an entirely new candidate. Or he can issue what is known as a **recess appointment**. Historically, presidents relied on recess appointments to ensure that the government continued to function when the Senate adjourned for longer periods of time. Increasingly, though, presidents have relied on recess appointments to circumvent political opposition within Congress, as Clinton did in the case of Lee.[34] Recess appointments can be used only under very specific conditions. Each year after the Senate term ends, the president may appoint individuals who immediately assume their positions of leadership in the federal bureaucracy. When Congress reconvenes, the Senate may choose whether to formally confirm these candidates. If a confirmation vote is not held, the candidate can remain in office at least until the end of Congress's session. Formally, presidents can repeatedly appoint the same individuals during Congress's recess. In practice, though, they tend not to do so.

Whether the result of presidents acting on their own or with Congress, the politicization of the bureaucracy has invited much criticism. Grumblings turned to heated condemnations when President George W. Bush selected Michael Brown to help run the Federal Emergency Management Agency. Brown, a former commissioner for the International Arabian Horse Association, had no prior experience running a major disaster relief organization. Many argued that Brown was selected because of his political allegiance to the president rather than on the basis of merit. When he failed to demonstrate clear leadership during the lead-up to and aftermath of Hurricane Katrina—a topic we discuss in the "How Do We Know?" section— many called for his resignation and attacked the Bush administration for having placed a purely political appointee in a position of such responsibility.

The politicization of the bureaucracy, however, concerns more than just the decision to hire individuals. It also relates to the decision to fire them. Again, the Bush administration is illustrative. When it came to light in 2006 that Attorney General Alberto Gonzales had dismissed eight U.S. attorneys for political reasons, a firestorm erupted in Washington, D.C., with Democrats leading the charge.[35] The attorneys had solid reputations and positive job evaluations. They purportedly clashed with the administration, however, on such issues as immigration and capital punishment. Many argued that these disagreements led to their dismissals. Because the attorney general was seen to be politicizing the Justice Department—a charge he vehemently denied—Democrats and even some Republicans called for his resignation.[36] According to one particularly harsh op-ed piece, "Gonzales, the nation's highest legal officer, has been point man for serial assaults against the rule of law, most recently in the crude attempt to politicize criminal prosecutions. Obstruction of a prosecution is a felony, even when committed by the attorney general."[37]

recess appointment the means by which the president fills a vacant position in the bureaucracy when Congress is not in session, thus avoiding the need for prior congressional approval.

Note, though, that the threat of firing individuals who do not share the president's mission helps address the basic problems of drift, slack, and agency capture. One could argue that if presidents (or their cabinet secretaries) discover that bureaucrats are not working hard or are implementing their own policies or those of an unelected subset of the population, the administration has cause to fire them. One might go so far as to argue that the attorney general has every right, and even the responsibility, to ensure that those individuals working within the Justice Department share the president's priorities about the prosecution of different crimes.

Of course, the high levels of turnover that result from all of these hirings and firings can create problems of their own. The election of each new president brings an entirely new set of appointments. Though the vast majority of workers within the bureaucracy enjoy strong job protection—the core result of the switch from the spoils system to the civil service system—many agency heads leave office at the end of a presidential term.[38] Such short tenures can diminish their ability to learn the culture of their agencies, secure the trust of their subordinates, and implement lasting policy changes.

In other countries, by contrast, a much more stable supply of policy experts runs the administrative apparatus. Take, for example, Canada. Whereas about 20 percent of American public servants leave their jobs in a typical year, only 4 percent of Canadian civil service employees do so.[39] One reason for this difference may be that the Canadian bureaucracy is comprised almost entirely of career civil servants (who serve for decades) rather than political appointees (who tend to serve shorter terms). In Canada, non-partisan career civil servants occupy all Canadian bureaucratic positions from the rank of deputy minister down the chain. Indeed, only the Cabinet-level ministers, of which there are about 30, can be appointed by the prime minister based on their partisan affiliation.[40] By contrast, in the United States, the president chooses roughly 3,000 political appointees to serve in the bureaucracy.[41] Although comprising less than 1 percent of the total civilian workforce, these partisan appointees dominate the highest echelons of agency management. Moreover, more than half of the 2.5 million American civil servants are "excepted" from the traditional merit-based guidelines, serving instead under agency-specific personnel systems.[42] Although these systems officially operate under the merit scheme, the flexibility they give to managers makes it easier to circumvent merit rules in hiring and promotion.[43] As a result, agency-based personnel systems "blur the line between appointees and careerists."[44] For all of these reasons, the U.S. civil service may not possess the same level of stability, independence, and expertise found in Canada and elsewhere.

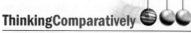

ThinkingComparatively

Bureaucratic turnover in Canada is significantly lower than in the United States.

Presidents and Congress use money, rules, and structure to control bureaucracies.

Between the hiring and firing of individuals who run the federal government's agencies, the president, Congress, and the courts have additional opportunities to influence bureaucratic behavior. Agencies do not run on their own. They require money to pay their employees; they must regularly report to their political superiors; they are situated within a larger bureaucratic structure; and their very survival often depends on continued political support. Each of these facts allows for even further control over the federal bureaucracy.

Budgets   Every year, the president must propose a budget, and Congress must enact it. (See Chapter 13 for a more thorough discussion of this process.) The budget process affords opportunities to reflect on the performance of each bureaucratic agency, and to punish or reward it accordingly. When agencies are doing well, Congress can reward them with higher budgets; when agencies are not performing effectively, Congress may decide to slash their budgets. With control of the purse strings, Congress can create strong incentives for agencies to abide by their interests.

Beyond adjusting the amount of money granted to different agencies, Congress can attach any number of stipulations on how these monies are to be spent. Rather than give each agency a lump-sum payment, which its employees then decide how to spend, Congress may write detailed instructions about which projects an agency should pursue and which it should abandon. In 2006, for instance, Congress required NASA to allocate $568.5 million of its budget for 198 special-interest items. A decade earlier, Congress had required that NASA devote just $74 million for six items.[45]

Oversight In a principal-agent relationship, you will recall, the agent's great advantages are information and expertise. So it is with the bureaucracy. Agencies are great reservoirs of expertise about a vast array of public policies. They know what should be done, what is being done, and what plans are in place for the future. As policy generalists, the principals (Congress and the president) to some extent must rely on that knowledge for their decisions and directives. To make sure that bureaucratic agencies use this information and expertise in ways that conform to the wishes of their political superiors, **oversight** is crucial. Through oversight, presidents and members of Congress monitor and supervise goings-on within the federal bureaucracy.

One of the best oversight mechanisms is **hearings**. Should an issue or a problem come to light, committees and subcommittees can call upon bureaucrats to testify in formal settings. Though members of Congress often use these opportunities to show off before the television cameras, they also direct pointed questions about agency actions, policies, and procedures. Members of Congress may also choose to bring in outside experts and former agency employees to verify or dispute the claims made by current bureaucrats. With the information they gather, members of Congress are in a better position to decide whether agency budgets need to be adjusted, whether their legislative mandates need to be revised, and sometimes whether criminal charges need to be brought forward.

In addition to hearings, members of Congress can choose to launch their own investigations into perceived abuses of power. A number of agencies have the specific responsibility of monitoring other agencies and reporting their findings back to Congress. The Government Accountability Office, the Congressional Research Service, and the Congressional Budget Office all provide independent sources of

oversight congressional and presidential efforts to monitor and supervise the actions of bureaucratic agencies.

hearing a formal process in which committees in Congress call upon bureaucrats and other experts to help them understand and oversee a particular agency.

589

◄ MONITORING THE BUREAUCRACY

Through hearings, members of Congress can monitor what is happening within the federal bureaucracy. In 2007, Representative Christopher Shays (R-CT) questioned witnesses at a congressional hearing on the treatment of wounded veterans at the Walter Reed Medical Center. What impact do you think these kinds of hearings have on actual public policy, if any?

information about public policy and agency behavior. Often, this information comes in the form of reports about specific issues that individual members request. With this information, members of Congress can further influence agency behavior and reduce problems that might arise from principal-agent relations.

Congress also has enacted a number of laws intended to make bureaucratic behavior more transparent. The 1976 Sunshine Law, for instance, requires that agency meetings be held in public, unless classified information is being discussed. Similarly, the 1967 Freedom of Information Act enables members of Congress (as well as all citizens) to inspect a wide variety of government documents. If agencies raise concerns about releasing these documents to the public, they must state their case before a federal judge. Both of these laws are designed to open to public scrutiny the federal government in general, and the bureaucracy in particular.

whistleblower a bureaucrat who witnesses and publicly exposes wrongdoing by either contacting his or her political superiors or tipping off the press.

Finally, members of Congress depend on **whistleblowers** to expose bureaucratic waste, mismanagement, and illegal behavior. The term refers to the bureaucrats who witness and publicly expose wrongdoing by either contacting their political superiors or tipping off the press. To encourage these individuals to come forward, Congress passed a number of laws (such as the 1989 Whistle-Blower Protection Act) making it illegal to demote, fire, or otherwise punish whistle-blowing bureaucrats.[46] In addition, Congress supports toll-free lines for bureaucrats working in different agencies to call and report problems that they witness. Congress has created an independent agency, the Office of Special Counsel, which is charged with investigating complaints about whistleblowers who have been punished by their immediate superiors.

These efforts to protect whistleblowers, however, are not foolproof. Bosses can find any number of ways of sanctioning whistleblowers without being detected. And the Supreme Court recently ruled that administrative agencies have a right to discipline at least some whistleblowers who exercise what might appear to be their First Amendment rights to free speech.

Centralization   Left to their own devices, bureaucrats may wander from their policy mandate. This behavior is especially true when their agencies are shielded from media scrutiny, and when Washington elites have few ways of directly monitoring their activity. These bureaucrats may well be advancing policies that improve the public's welfare. But what are political superiors to do when these bureaucrats resist their orders? One solution: round them up and bring them closer to home.

centralization the method of increasing the president's power by moving key administrative functions from the departments to the Executive Office of the President.

Political scientists have made much of presidents' use of **centralization**—that is, moving key functions from the departments to the Executive Office of the President (EOP), sometimes referred to as the "presidential branch." The core administrative structures in the EOP consist of the White House, the Office of Management and Budget, and the Council of Economic Advisors. It also contains the Office of National Drug Control Policy, the Office of Science and Technology Policy, the United States Trade Representative, the President's Foreign Intelligence Advisory Board, and many other units. In fact, throughout the EOP are people working on every imaginable policy. By relying on these individuals, the president can more easily monitor their behavior and ensure that they are advancing his core interests.[47]

When do presidents rely on individuals within the EOP for policy advice, and when do they turn to bureaucrats employed in the departments? The choice, some analysts argue, comes down to the perceived costs and benefits of loyalty and expertise. Individuals within the EOP are more likely to follow the president's lead, but they tend to know less about policy issues. By contrast, employees in the departments typically have extensive expertise about policy, but they cannot so easily be trusted to promote the president's interests. According to one study, presidents tend to worry more about the importance of expertise when an issue is either new or very complex; in these instances, the president turns to department bureaucrats when developing his policy agenda.[48] When large numbers of people from the opposition party hold seats in Congress, however, presidents worry more about loyalty; under these conditions, presidents are more likely to depend on EOP staffers.

This same study finds that the president's legislative initiatives are less likely to be enacted when the president centralizes authority. It is not clear why this is the case. Perhaps members of Congress are less likely to trust the president when he forsakes the expertise located in the departments in favor of the judgments of loyalists in the EOP. Alternatively, presidents may choose to centralize when they anticipate a difficult legislative road ahead. If so, then causality would appear to be reversed—expectations about legislative failure promote centralization, rather than centralization's leading to legislative breakdown.

Thinking Causally

Do presidential efforts to centralize authority in the Executive Office of the President improve the chances of enacting the president's policy agenda?

Beyond its impact on the likelihood of enacting presidential initiatives, centralization creates other problems. With increasing numbers of individuals and organizations working on any particular policy issue, lines of responsibility begin to blur. As the EOP grows, critics argue that there emerges "an unwieldy, tower hierarchy in which accountability is diffuse at best and the president is sometimes the last to know."[49] With the passage of time, one can well imagine presidents opting to centralize authority still further within the EOP—with loyalists working close by, and experts toiling away in the outer reaches of the presidential branch.

Agency eliminations   If all else fails, Congress and the president can eliminate an agency outright. Contrary to conventional wisdom, agencies are not immortal. In fact, agencies are eliminated with a fair amount of frequency.[50] According to one analysis, fully 60 percent of all agencies created between 1946 and 1997 had been eliminated by 2000. When President Nixon assumed office after eight years of Democratic control, for instance, he eliminated the Office of Economic Opportunity, which was then responsible for administering many of the social welfare programs created under President Johnson. In an effort to reduce the ability of the Environmental Protection Agency to regulate industries, President Reagan eliminated the Office of Enforcement.

Different kinds of agencies tend to survive for different amounts of time. Government corporations and independent agencies and commissions, which are intentionally given more autonomy, tend to live longer than do agencies located within the Executive Office of the President, which are subject to more presidential control. Congress and the president also have a more difficult time eliminating an agency when they are more constrained in their ability to hire and fire agency heads, either because these heads must be from a specific party or because they serve for fixed terms.

Thinking Causally

Why do some agencies live longer than others?

Politics also appears to contribute to the lifespan of different agencies. Agencies are more likely to be eliminated when the current president is of the opposite party of the president who was in power when the agency was created. It is unclear, though, what exactly to make of this finding. Perhaps presidents tend to kill programs that they oppose, and these programs tend to be created by predecessors from the opposition party. On the other hand, a switch from one party to another in the presidency may reflect broader changes in the public's spending priorities. If true, then the fact that agencies tend to die when a new party takes control of the White House has less to do with the independent policy agenda of the president and more to do with the efforts of elected officials to keep pace with public opinion.

CaseStudy: Tying the Hands of the Environmental Protection Agency

Sometimes, efforts by presidents and Congress to control the bureaucracy do not result in a more effective institution. Instead, such efforts undermine the work of an agency that is, by all accounts, faithfully attending to its mandate. The resulting problem has less to do with slack or drift, and more to do with political interference. The recent history of the Environmental Protection Agency (EPA) is a case in point.

Upon signing the first act of Congress of his administration, President Richard Nixon in 1969 declared that the 1970s would be the "environmental decade." The new law, the National Environmental Policy Act, was the first of several to dramatically expand the role of the federal government in protecting the environment. At the time, the president and Congress were eager to respond to a widely publicized environmental movement and a growing number of powerful environmental interest groups.[51]

In 1970, Congress established the EPA, whose most important responsibility was implementing the Clean Air Act. Under the act, EPA officials were charged with setting limits for the amount of pollution that could be emitted by steel mills, chemical plants, motor vehicles, and other sources. As Congress passed more and more environmental legislation, the EPA saw its budget grow from $500 million in 1973 to $1.3 billion in 1980. Bureaucrats within the agency worked hard to implement and enforce the new environmental policies. During the first 10 years of its existence, emissions of the five major air pollutants—particulates, nitrogen oxides, sulfur oxides, carbon monoxide, and hydrocarbons—decreased by 21 percent. By 1980, the EPA had 10,600 full-time employees who were committed to strict enforcement of the nation's clean air laws.[52]

When he won the presidential election in 1980, Ronald Reagan set out to change all that. During his campaign, Reagan had promised to address the nation's economic problems and drastically reduce the size of the federal government. He interpreted his victory against Jimmy Carter as a mandate to cut domestic program budgets and push business-friendly policies. One of his first targets was the EPA, an agency not well liked by business and industry leaders.[53]

Reagan started by filling EPA leadership positions with loyalists. Unlike President Carter, whose EPA appointees had mostly come from environmental organizations, Reagan appointed lobbyists, lawyers, and scientists who were closely tied to the very business interests the EPA was supposed to regulate.[54] In May 1981, he appointed Anne Gorsuch to run the EPA. Gorsuch did not try to conceal her plan to ease enforcement of the Clean Air Act.[55] She assured small oil refineries that they did not have to worry about her enforcing the EPA's lead-in-gasoline regulations.[56] She disbanded the agency's Office of Enforcement and then recreated it

▲ HAMSTRINGING THE REGULATORS

Sometimes, political principals seek to restrict the industrious work of bureaucratic agencies. During their time in office, Presidents Ronald Reagan and George W. Bush attempted to curtail the efforts of the Environmental Protection Agency to enforce federal clean air standards. What, in your view, should be done when political superiors try to undermine the effectiveness of agencies that have mandates with which they disagree?

with a smaller staff.[57] The decisions she made in the name of "administrative efficiency" outraged environmentalists, who accused her and Reagan of intentionally sabotaging the EPA.

Reagan did not stop with a few personnel replacements. He also pursued an aggressive legislative strategy through proposed budget cuts. During his first year in office, Republicans controlled the Senate, and few of the Democrats who held the majority in the House were willing to stand up against a president who had just won office with such a large victory margin.[58] As a consequence, the EPA operating budget was reduced by 24 percent in 1982. Funding for air pollution enforcement alone dropped by 42 percent between 1980 and 1983, and the number of EPA employees assigned to clean air responsibilities fell by 31 percent.[59]

Many analysts believed that the combination of drastic budget and staff cuts and Gorsuch's leadership would be the EPA's undoing. In the short run, Reagan's budget cuts produced the desired result—not a stronger, more effective organization, but a weaker, less effective one. The EPA conducted 41 percent fewer inspections and compliance tests of air pollution sources in 1982 than it had in 1981, and it took 69 percent fewer enforcement actions to rein in overpolluters. His initial personnel changes, however, did not appear to affect the enforcement activity of the EPA. When Gorsuch was first appointed, the agency's monitoring activities actually *increased*. EPA employees continued to do their jobs as they had before Reagan came into office. If anything, they increased the intensity of their enforcement activity, remaining committed to faithful implementation of the clean air policies of the 1970s.[60]

Reagan's attempts to curtail EPA enforcement ultimately failed. By the end of 1982, it had become clear that the public did not want federal clean air regulations to be relaxed: 48 percent of Americans thought the EPA's old air pollution policies were fine as they were, and 38 percent wanted the Clean Air Act to be made stricter.[61] In another blow to Reagan's agenda, the 1982 congressional elections brought more pro-environment Democrats to the House. They cited Gorsuch, who was then using her married name of Burford, for contempt of Congress for her mismanagement of the EPA hazardous waste program. Representative John Dingell, who had earlier supported Reagan's failed effort to revise the Clean Air Act, led a full investigation of the EPA, which resulted in Burford's resignation in March 1983.[62]

Immediately after, EPA employees renewed their previous levels of enforcement activity. Even before its budget was restored, the EPA's pollution monitoring and abatement activity recovered to levels *higher* than during the Carter administration of the late 1970s. By May, Reagan had replaced Burford with the original EPA administrator of the 1970s, William D. Ruckelshaus. Congress restored much of the EPA budget in 1983.[63]

Ultimately, Reagan was not able to reverse the tide of the "environmental decade." From its beginning, the EPA had been staffed with experts committed to the enforcement of federal environmental laws. In the early years of his administration, Reagan discovered that the culture of the EPA and its attentive environmentalist constituency could not be easily undone.

Reagan was not the last president to attempt to curb the EPA. President George W. Bush attempted to ease air pollution restrictions, relax enforcement of emissions standards, reduce requirements for industries' capital maintenance and upgrades, and roll back wilderness and wildlife regulations. His proposed policies led to clashes with EPA leaders—even with his own appointee, former EPA Administrator Christine Todd Whitman.[64] The Environmental Integrity Project, an organization founded by former EPA Regulatory Enforcement Director Eric Schaeffer, reported in 2007 that enforcement of environmental standards declined substantially during Bush's time in office in comparison to enforcement during the years of Clinton's presidency.[65]

The election of Barack Obama revitalized the federal government's efforts to protect the environment. Soon after he took office, Obama proposed a $10.5 billion budget for the EPA—the largest in the agency's history—signaling that environmental protection and enforcement would be a priority for the new president. During the president's first year in office, the EPA reversed numerous pro-industry rules from the prior Bush administration.[66] In 2009, the president attended an international conference on climate change, at which he recognized the human causes of climate change. In the aftermath of one of the nation's greatest environmental disasters—the oil spill in the Gulf of Mexico in 2010—Obama imposed a six-month moratorium on deep-well, offshore drilling, pressured British Petroleum to set aside $20 billion to begin compensating U.S. citizens whose livelihoods were affected by the spill, and renamed the Minerals Management Service (the federal agency charged with overseeing offshore drilling) the Bureau of Ocean Energy Management, Regulation, and Enforcement, an act that many viewed as a precursor to an even more vigorous regulatory regime of the oil industry.

ThinkingCritically

1. From the perspective of President Reagan, were the EPA's activities examples of slack, drift, or something else entirely?

2. Is it necessarily a bad thing when bureaucrats do things that Congress and the president oppose?

3. How should lifetime bureaucrats respond to the ideological and policy changes that accompany transitions in presidential administrations, such as the one from Bush to Obama?

Reformers seek to introduce market forces.

All of the methods that presidents and Congress use to control the bureaucracy represent efforts to reform the existing system of bureaucratic governance. Increasingly, though, reformers are suggesting that the problems of bureaucracy, especially those that involve inefficiencies, are best solved by looking beyond the individuals and agencies that work within the federal government. These reformers suggest that increased effectiveness and efficiency can only come about through deregulation or privatization.

Deregulation   Some people argue that the best way to deal with the bureaucracy is to temper its impulse to regulate more and more areas of business activity. Claiming that government regulations cripple the entrepreneurial spirit of private industries,

deregulation the process of decreasing the number of agency rules that apply to a particular industry or group of industries so as to introduce market forces to their operations.

reformers argue that rather than restructuring these agencies or introducing better oversight mechanisms, political leaders ought to scale back their activities altogether.

Through **deregulation**, the government reduces the workload of bureaucrats. It cordons off certain areas of business activity, insisting that bureaucrats not interfere with market forces of supply and demand. During the 1970s and 1980s, substantial efforts were made to deregulate the airline, trucking, telecommunications, and financial services industries. Through these efforts, the government encouraged new companies to form, providing more choices and cheaper services to consumers. For example, the deregulation of the telecommunications industry made possible the emergence of companies like Sprint and MCI (and later, Verizon, T-Mobile, and others).

Occasionally, though, deregulation can backfire. When the government deregulated the financial services industry in the early 1980s, savings and loan companies suddenly had many of the powers of traditional banks—such as the ability to issue credit cards, borrow money from the Federal Reserve, and make commercial loans—without the regulations of traditional banks. With their new powers, savings and loan companies began to invest large amounts of money in highly risky ventures. Not surprisingly, many of these ventures failed, and savings and loan companies were left without the money needed to pay back their investors. In total, these defaults cost the federal government (and the taxpayers) over $100 billion. Congress responded in 1989 by enacting the Financial Institutions Reform Recovery and Enforcement Act, which reintroduced many of the regulations that had been eliminated earlier in the decade.

privatization the transfer of government functions from the federal government to private companies.

Privatization   Whereas deregulation concerns the relaxation of bureaucratic oversight of different industries, **privatization** concerns the transfer of government functions from the federal government to private companies. Rather than government bureaucrats providing certain services, private companies do so. In communities around the country, private contractors have replaced government agencies to run prisons, provide security services, and manage hospitals. As we discuss in Chapter 17, some people call for the privatization of public schools as well.

Note that privatization is not an all-or-nothing arrangement. Many bureaucratic agencies turn to private companies to perform selected tasks. The military, for instance, pays billions of dollars each year to private contractors that build parts, conduct research, and provide strategic advice. Even when it decides to hand over complete responsibility for a certain public service to private companies, the government may continue to fund their work. When writing contracts with these companies, moreover, the government may introduce any number of requirements about how they conduct their business. The key question, then, is not whether a government service has been privatized, but how much it has been privatized.

CHAPTER SUMMARY

In this chapter you have learned to:

16-1 Identify the functions of the federal bureaucracy.
Bureaucrats serve a wide variety of vital functions for the American public. They implement the policies that Congress and the president write; they write rules that clarify these policies; they provide expert advice to their political superiors; and they help resolve disputes. Thus the bureaucracy serves quasi-legislative, executive, and judicial functions.

16-2 Outline the organization and the expansion of the bureaucracy.
During much of the nineteenth century, the bureaucracy was quite small and tended to employ individuals better known for their political ties than for their experience or expertise. At the turn of the twentieth century, however, the nation witnessed the transformation of the spoils system into a merit-based system. During this period, the federal bureaucracy also expanded dramatically. Today, the bureaucracy consists of Cabinet departments, independent agencies, regulatory commissions, and government corporations.

16-3 **Assess the role of the bureaucracy in public policy-making.** Though the bureaucracy serves important functions, it also presents serious challenges. Because bureaucrats know more about the policy issues that they oversee, they can act in ways that do not always represent the interests of Congress, the president, the courts, or the American public. Sometimes bureaucrats act on behalf of their own policy interests, sometimes they serve the interests of other unelected officials, sometimes they do not work especially hard, and often they are less efficient than the public would like.

16-4 **Evaluate the different approaches to overseeing and reforming the bureaucracy.** Congress and the president have devised a number of ways to address the problems of bureaucracy. Through appointments, they put like-minded individuals in charge of federal agencies. Through budgets, oversight hearings, and centralization efforts, Congress and the president reshape the incentives of bureaucrats and monitor their actions. When all else fails, Congress and the president can eliminate agencies, substantially reduce their regulatory powers, or turn to the private marketplace for help in providing public services.

PEARSON
mypoliscilab

EXERCISES

Apply what you learned in this chapter on MyPoliSciLab.

Read on **mypoliscilab.com**

   eText: Chapter 16

✓ **Study** and **Review** on **mypoliscilab.com**

   Pre-Test
   Post-Test
   Chapter Exam
   Flashcards

Watch on **mypoliscilab.com**

   Video: The CDC and the Swine Flu
   Video: Internal Problems at the FDA
   Video: Making Environmental Policy

Explore on **mypoliscilab.com**

   Simulation: You Are a Deputy Director of the Census Bureau
   Simulation: You Are the Head of FEMA
   Simulation: You Are the President of MEDICORP
   Simulation: You Are a Federal Administrator
   Comparative: Comparing Bureaucracies
   Timeline: The Evolution of the Federal Bureaucracy
   Visual Literacy: The Changing Face of the Federal Bureaucracy

---

KEY TERMS

agency capture, p. 580
bureaucracy, p. 566
centralization, p. 590
civil service system, p. 572
department, p. 573
deregulation, p. 594
drift, p. 579
government corporation, p. 577

hearing, p. 589
implementation, p. 567
independent agencies and
   commissions, p. 575
oversight, p. 589
politicization, p. 586
principal-agent problem, p. 578

privatization, p. 594
recess appointment, p. 587
red tape, p. 581
rules, p. 568
slack, p. 579
spoils system, p. 572
whistleblower, p. 590

CHAPTER TEST

1. Is it possible to implement laws without first interpreting them? And if not, how can agencies figure out the meaning of different statutes?

2. In what ways are bureaucratic agencies' responsibilities similar to those of members of Congress?

3. In what ways are bureaucratic agencies' responsibilities similar to those of judges?

4. What were the essential features of the spoils system?
5. What are the most important merits of a civil service system?
6. Why is bureaucracy often equated with inefficiency?
7. In what ways does the relationship between Congress and the federal bureaucracy resemble a principal-agent problem?

8. In what ways do appointments enable members of Congress and the president to gain control over administrative units?
9. How can members of Congress find out what bureaucratic agencies are doing?
10. Why might presidents want to rely on officials within the Executive Office of the President rather than departmental bureaucrats for policy advice?

SUGGESTED READINGS

Peri Arnold. 1998. *Making the Managerial Presidency: Comprehensive Reorganization Planning, 1905–1996*, 2nd ed. Lawrence: University Press of Kansas. A comprehensive summary of presidents' efforts to reorganize the federal bureaucracy during the twentieth century.

Herbert Kaufman. 2006. *The Forest Ranger: A Study in Administrative Behavior*, special reprint ed. Washington, DC: Resources for the Future. A classic study of how top-level managers within the bureaucracy maintain control over lower-level bureaucrats whose day-to-day activities are not easily monitored.

David Lewis. 2008. *The Politics of Presidential Appointments: Political Control and Bureaucratic Performance*. Princeton, NJ: Princeton University Press. Provides a detailed empirical account of the politicization of the bureaucracy.

Michael Lipsky. 1983. *Street Level Bureaucracy*. New York: Russell Sage. A bottom-up approach to studying the bureaucracy, with special attention to lower-level bureaucrats.

James Q. Wilson. 1991. *Bureaucracy: What Government Agencies Do and Why They Do It*. New York: Basic Books. A contemporary classic that examines how politics contributes to bureaucratic organization and behavior.

SUGGESTED WEBSITES

Federal Emergency Management Agency: www.fema.gov

The primary federal agency that assumes responsibility for overseeing disaster relief.

Environmental Protection Agency: www.epa.gov

This organization oversees the implementation of environmental and energy legislation.

Government Accountability Office: www.gao.gov

This agency monitors goings-on through the federal bureaucracy.

Executive Office of the Presidency: www.whitehouse.gov/government

This bureaucracy houses, among other units, the Council of Economic Advisors, the Domestic Policy Council, and the National Security Council.

OMB Watch: www.ombwatch.org

A nonpartisan watchdog organization that pays particular attention to regulatory and budgetary processes in the federal bureaucracy.

USA.gov: http://www.usa.gov/Agencies/Federal/Executive.shtml

A listing of all the major departments, agencies, and commissions in the federal bureaucracy.

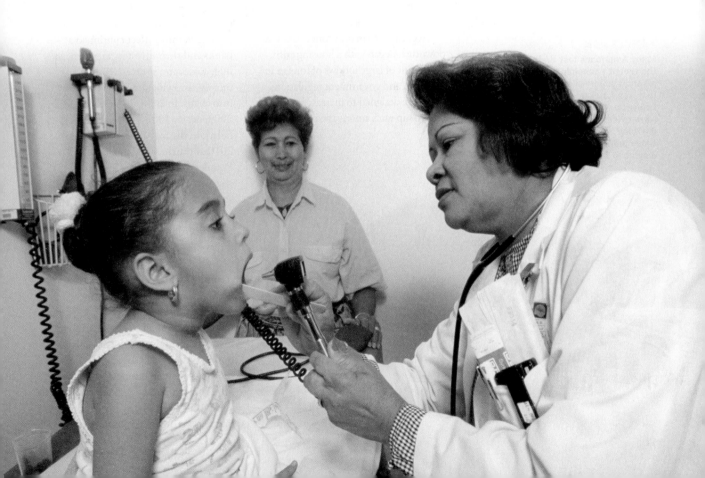

An Economy in Collapse

Over the course of 2008, the U.S. economy stumbled, gasped, and then utterly collapsed. In March, Bear Stearns, one of the nation's most important investment banks, announced that its "liquidity position in the last 24 hours had significantly deteriorated" and it needed to turn to the federal government and rival JP Morgan Chase for emergency bailout funds. In September, the government assumed control of two of the nation's largest mortgage finance companies, Fannie Mae and Freddie Mac. Lehman Brothers filed for bankruptcy shortly thereafter, marking the largest bankruptcy filing in U.S. history. Washington Mutual then went under, the biggest bank failure in history. In October, the stock market fell 22 percent in just eight days.[1]

The effects of the financial meltdown rippled across the country. Housing foreclosures skyrocketed, and millions of Americans lost their

jobs. Those banks that did not shut down nonetheless cut way back on their credit, making it extraordinarily difficult for students to secure education loans and entrepreneurs to acquire business loans. In October 2008, the unemployment rate was 6.2 percent. A year later, unemployment shot up to 9.8 percent, the highest in 26 years.

Across the nation, local governments struggled to cope with the economic meltdown and were forced to cut basic services. Philadelphia, for example, slashed its sanitation costs by limiting residential street cleaning and eliminating leaf, bulk, and tire collections. In October 2009, New York Governor David Paterson announced a cost-saving plan that would reduce aid to schools by $686 million for the 2009–2010 academic year. In early 2010, it was Los Angeles's turn to cut back on services. In January, the city was forced to drastically reduce its public transportation sector, eliminating 10 Metrolink train lines and curtailing bus traffic.[2]

According to many economists, the downturn began with a housing crisis. As a result of large inflows of foreign investment and government regulations that were designed to increase home ownership rates among the poor, the

housing market in the early 2000s experienced rapid and widespread growth. Banks went out of their way to extend loans to an ever increasing proportion of the American public, some of whom were ill equipped to make the mortgage payments. The lenders then sold these mortgage loans to investors such as Fannie Mae and Freddie Mac for huge profits. Still more investment firms sold complex insurance packages, sometimes called derivatives, on these loans—tying vast swaths of the domestic and international economy to the U.S. housing market.

The housing growth proved to be unsustainable. Beginning in 2006, housing prices nationwide began to fall as people defaulted on loans that they could no longer afford. Then the "housing bubble" popped. Housing prices in one year dropped by 11.8 percent in Tampa and 12.4 percent in Miami. Los Angeles, one of the nation's largest metropolitan areas, suffered an 8.8 percent drop over the same time span.[3]

The domino effect continued as banks and their investors experienced huge losses and stopped lending money, throwing the entire economy into chaos. In 2008, 25 banks failed; in 2009, nearly 100 additional banks failed; in the first seven months of 2010, more than 100 more did so.[4] Retailers such as Linens 'n Things were forced into bankruptcy as lenders stopped giving out more credit.[5]

As is typical during times of crisis, Americans' appetite for government intervention grew ravenous. And many government officials were happy to feed it. Some called for the indictment of top hedge fund managers and for new regulations to oversee the incredibly complex financial arrangements that supported the housing boom. Others wanted new stimulus funding for small business and bailout funds for major banks. But some Americans protested against any major governmental intervention.

▼ RECESSION

Many Americans lost their homes in the recent economic recession. Here, a sheriff supervises as a landlord removes furniture from a home in Lafayette, Colorado, after the tenants were evicted. In your opinion, what, if anything, should be done on behalf of those individuals who have been displaced from their homes?

In a major national address in the fall of 2008, President George W. Bush proposed a $700 billion bailout to prevent an economic collapse. Although typically a champion of free enterprise, the Bush administration now emphasized that in these extraordinary circumstances, government intervention was essential. In October 2008, Congress approved the bailout, which purchased unwanted assets that were clogging the financial system. The bailout, the president argued, would reduce the financial burden on banks and encourage them to resume lending.

Government efforts to curtail the economic meltdown did not end there. Soon after he became president in 2009, Barack Obama proposed the American Recovery and Reinvestment Plan, which aimed to create jobs and encourage long-term growth. Approved by Congress, the plan included a $787 billion stimulus to the economy and tax cuts for working families. In addition, Obama sought to jumpstart the economy by repairing schools, creating a clean energy program, and improving the quality of health care.

Obama also underscored the need to rebuild the nation's financial regulatory framework. He declared in a televised speech in January 2009, "No longer can we allow Wall Street wrongdoers to slip through regulatory cracks."[6] As the public call to fix the economic corruption continued to gather support, Obama reminded bank CEOs in April 2009, "My administration is the only thing between you and the pitchforks."[7] These changes, however, were slow in coming. Unemployment continued to rise and important segments of the economy continued to contract throughout 2009.[8] It was not until the summer of 2010 that Congress enacted regulatory reform for the nation's financial institutions.

The hubbub over the financial meltdown reveals a basic fact about domestic policy-making: the wheels of policy-making whirl fastest during periods of crisis. Spurred by pressing social needs, politicians entertain all sorts of economic and social reforms. In this instance, the financial crisis introduced new political pressure for economic reforms. As we saw in Obama's economic recovery plan, reforms in education, energy, and health care can follow at the heels of a crisis. And as we shall soon see, these kinds of social programs almost always live longer than the crises that created them.

This chapter examines domestic policies supported by the federal government. Although domestic policy covers issues ranging from environmental protection to patent law, here we focus on economic policy and social programs—programs purposefully designed to enhance the well-being of U.S. citizens.

CHAPTER LEARNING OBJECTIVES

After reading this chapter you will be able to:

17-1 Identify the conditions under which policy innovations are created.

17-2 Assess efforts by the federal government to manage the domestic economy.

17-3 Trace the development of the largest federal social program, which assists the elderly.

17-4 Analyze changes in welfare policy within the United States.

17-5 Trace the federal government's expanding involvement in education.

17-6 Evaluate the government's efforts to provide health care to the poor and aged.

Possibilities for Enacting Economic and Social Policies

17-1 Identify the conditions under which policy innovations are created.

What prompts the federal government to create new public policies? Detailed histories of individual policy interventions often highlight the idiosyncrasies that lead to public policy-making. In retrospect, major policy innovations often appear to arise from chance meetings between key politicos or a particularly well-timed protest in Washington, D.C. For such seemingly random occurrences to bear fruit, however, at least three factors must converge: a problem warranting a governmental response must be identified; a solution to the problem must be articulated; and some kind of focusing event must prod politicians into action. In this section, we reflect on each of these ingredients of domestic policy-making.[9]

Identifying a problem is the first step in developing a policy.

There are lots of facts about the world that we may wish were not true. Apple iPads are more expensive than we would like. Our friends do not always act like friends. Our grandparents have a difficult time paying for their medication. When the economy hits a rough spot, some relatives lose their jobs. It is difficult to imagine the federal government passing a law that requires Apple to lower its prices or that requires friends to be more responsive to one another's needs. But what of the other problems? Which of them warrant government action? Much depends on public opinion, which varies over time and across the country. Historically, though, those problems that appear to violate basic elements of the American creed or that threaten the nation's security have stood the best chance of attracting the attention of politicians in Washington, D.C.

The American creed   Problems are especially likely to attract the attention of the federal government when they violate elements of the American creed. Concerns about equity stand out in this regard. Many social programs funded by the government aim to reduce long-standing inequalities—whether they involve access to sports programs among men and women, the relative incomes of the rich and poor, or the test scores of white and black schoolchildren. Of course, certain inequalities are inevitable. Some are even desirable. But the federal government is especially likely to enact social programs designed to reduce gross and persistent inequalities that systematically limit the life chances of certain citizens. Although the federal government may accept some inequality of outcomes, it often intervenes in the lives of citizens in order to promote a base level of equality of opportunities.

In the last half-century, concerns about equality were never more prominent than during Lyndon Johnson's presidency in the 1960s. Johnson sought to create a **Great Society** "where the demands of morality, and the needs of the spirit, can be realized in the life of the Nation."[10] He called upon the nation to tackle the problems of poverty, racial discrimination, environmental degradation, and urban decay. Only

Great Society   a set of large-scale social initiatives proposed by President Lyndon Johnson in the 1960s to reduce poverty, racial discrimination, environmental degradation, and urban decay.

▶ **FOOD STAMPS**

In 1970, when this photo was taken, the federal government launched the federal Food Stamp program. This customer used the stamps to purchase a supply of groceries.

by doing so, Johnson argued, could the ideals of the Founders, enshrined in the Declaration of Independence and U.S. Constitution, be realized. With strong Democratic support within Congress, Johnson managed to enact more large-scale social programs than any other president since Franklin Roosevelt. Many of these programs are described in this chapter.

National security   Above all else, the federal government's fundamental objective is to protect its citizens from foreign harm. Military threats, terrorist activity, the proliferation of nuclear weapons, and the like rise to the top of governmental concerns. Domestic problems that potentially link into U.S. security interests, either directly or indirectly, gain an important advantage in the contest to attract the attention of federal politicians.

To understand these priorities, recall the discussion of energy in the 2008 presidential election. Both Democratic candidate Barack Obama and Republican candidate John McCain claimed it was risky for the nation to depend on imported oil from the Middle East, and they proposed various means to increase the use of renewable and alternative forms of energy. "By relying on foreign oil," declared McCain during a campaign stop, "we enrich bad actors in the world, some of whom finance terrorists."[11] By linking energy independence to national security concerns, there was growing pressure on the federal government to solve energy issues.

Environmental interests, of course, are not unique in making demands. Immigration activists regularly argue that stemming the flow of undocumented workers across U.S. borders is an important element of national security. Presidents Lyndon Johnson and Ronald Reagan did not merely support anti-poverty and anti-drug programs—they waged self-declared "wars" against these looming threats.[12] National security interests spurred the federal government's initial foray into public education as well. At every step, advocates for policy change justified the importance of deploying significant resources to combat a perceived security problem.

Identifying a government solution is the next step in developing policy.

For social legislation to emerge, problems must have solutions. Lacking solutions, politicians can offer little more than their sympathies for those who suffer from society's ailments and injustices.

Policy entrepreneurs play an important role in identifying solutions and linking them to observed problems.[13] These individuals work in think tanks, universities, lobbying organizations, unions, and interest groups. Backed by data, conviction, and persuasive skills, they design solutions for the many problems facing the federal government. Often, like-minded entrepreneurs form networks that operate at the local, state, and federal levels of government. These entrepreneurs coordinate with one another, with the intention of convincing politicians to adopt one policy reform or another.

Take, for example, the activities of the American Federation of Teachers (AFT) and the National Education Association (NEA), the two largest teachers unions in the nation. Both advocate policies to support teachers, such as higher pay and fewer restrictions on how they perform in the classroom. Lobbyists for both unions work at all levels of government to convince politicians about the merits of their preferred policies, emphasizing the ways they will solve problems in education.

In most areas of life, there is a logical ordering of problems and solutions. We devise solutions for problems, not the other way around. When the problems disappear, the solutions usually are discarded. In politics, though, things do not always work this

policy entrepreneurs professionals working in think tanks, universities, lobby groups, unions, and interest groups who propose solutions to policy problems and persuade politicians to adopt them.

way. If one day the nation no longer suffered from a shortage of public school teachers, the NEA and AFT, like all policy entrepreneurs, would look for other problems to attach their solutions to. In this sense, solutions in politics can arise independently of problems and often outlive the problems they were intended to solve.

Focusing events spark government action.

At any given moment, many domestic problems demand government action. Many solutions also float about the corridors of Congress. Bringing problems and solutions together often requires some kind of focusing event. As we have already seen, the failure of the nation's largest banking institutions and the collapse of housing markets in 2008 put the topic of financial regulatory reform front and center. These events infused the issue with a new urgency, to which politicians felt compelled to respond.

Focusing events can take many forms. Human tragedies, foreign crises, and even the weather can serve the role. As we discussed in Chapter 16, the devastation wrought by Hurricane Katrina exposed deep problems of poverty, crime, and corruption in New Orleans. Policy entrepreneurs descended upon the region, insisting that they could assist the government's efforts to solve these problems. The images of families stuck on rooftops days after the levees broke infused the ensuing deliberations with a genuine sense of urgency. We also considered whether the responses of local, state, and federal governments effectively solved the problems surrounding Hurricane Katrina. That the hurricane itself was a focusing event, though, is undeniable.

Among twentieth-century focusing events, nothing had more impact than the **Great Depression**, which was a period of unprecedented economic hardship for the nation. The stock market collapse in 1929 led to the utter devastation of the domestic economy. When Franklin Roosevelt became president four years later, the banks in 32 states had been closed by state government edict, and bank operations in the remaining 16 states remained severely curtailed. No fewer than 15 million Americans—roughly 25 percent of the total workforce at the time—were unemployed. The gravity of the nation's problems spurred the federal government into action never before experienced. As many of the social policies described in this chapter attest, federal government agencies assumed altogether new responsibilities for the management of the economy and the welfare of the nation's citizens.

Great Depression a period of severe economic recession in the United States precipitated by the stock market crash in October 1929.

Economic Policy

17-2 Assess efforts by the federal government to manage the domestic economy.

One of the government's greatest responsibilities involves regulating the domestic economy. After all, the domestic economy fundamentally determines the well-being of a citizenry. The ability of manufacturers to sell their goods at a profit, the ability of consumers to purchase them, and the willingness of intermediaries to facilitate the exchange critically depend on a healthy domestic economy.

Economists monitor different aspects of the domestic economy.

When gauging the health of the economy, economists tend to monitor three main indicators. First, they focus on unemployment trends, which reveal the percentage of people who would like to work but do not have a job. The unemployment rate typically has been 4–6 percent. In the early 1990s, though, it reached as high as 8 percent, and in

both the early 1980s and late 2009, it reached double digits. In the first quarter of 2010, the U.S. unemployment rate hovered just below 10 percent, on par with France's unemployment rate, a couple of points higher than Canada's, Germany's, and the United Kingdom's, but dramatically lower than either Ireland's or Spain's, both of which lingered in the teens.[14]

Second, economists also monitor inflationary trends, which concern how the costs of basic goods and services change over time. When inflation is high, the costs increase at a rapid rate; when inflation is low, costs increase at a more moderate pace. The government tends to measure inflation through the Consumer Price Index (CPI), which tracks the costs of food, clothing, medical services, and other essential items from year to year. For all goods and services, the annual CPI in December 2007 was 4.1 percent, which is somewhat higher than the annual average of 2.8 percent recorded between 1913 and 2007.[15]

Third, analysts monitor the overall growth of the economy. A prime indicator is the **gross domestic product (GDP)**, a statistic that measures all goods and services produced by individuals and businesses within the United States.[16] Between 2003 and 2005, GDP hovered around $13 trillion, which surpasses that of any other country. Indeed, the U.S. GDP constitutes almost 20 percent of all spending worldwide. Economists, though, tend to focus on annual changes in GDP, which in recent history have ranged between 2 and 4 percent. The first few quarters of 2009, however, actually recorded negative growth, confirming analysts' expectations of a deepening recession. By mid-2010, however, growth rates returned to the positive side of the ledger.

Economists have different ideas about how to improve the economy.

How might the government respond to fluctuations in the economy, as reflected in changes in unemployment, inflation, or GDP? Economists, like all social scientists, regularly disagree about the best course of action. The first option is to do nothing—or at least very little. This is the governing philosophy of **laissez-faire economics**. According to this theory, the private marketplace experiences natural periods of expansion and decline, and the best thing for the government to do, by and large, is to stay out of the way. When the government tries to regulate the otherwise free exchange of goods and services between private parties, this theory suggests, fundamental distortions and inefficiencies are introduced. In the long run, the public benefits most by minimal government involvement in the economy.

Most economists, however, admit that a vibrant economy requires at least some government intervention. The government, for instance, might alter the supply of money in the marketplace, which is the central objective of **monetary policy**. The national bank system, called the Federal Reserve, retains the power to set interest rates, which affect the flow of money in the domestic economy. By

▲ **ECONOMIC TURMOIL**
In October 2008, the U.S. economy, as well as the economies of most other industrialized nations, experienced a sharp downturn. The crisis was defined by housing foreclosures, a credit crunch, plunging stock prices, and the collapse of major companies in the financial industry. Here, Federal Reserve Chair Benjamin Bernanke testifies before Congress about the economic crisis.

gross domestic product (GDP) a statistic that measures all goods and services produced by a nation's economy.

laissez-faire economics a theory that discourages the government from becoming involved in the economy.

monetary policy policy designed to improve the economy by controlling the supply of available money.

increasing interest rates, the Federal Reserve can restrain economic growth and inflationary pressures. By decreasing interest rates, the Federal Reserve can stimulate economic activity, though at the risk of increasing inflation rates. The president has the power to appoint the chair of the Federal Reserve, who currently is Ben Bernanke. For the most part, though, the Federal Reserve is kept independent from political pressures.

Finally, the government can directly intervene into the economy through taxing and spending, the central elements of **fiscal policy**. The government can attempt to stimulate economic activity either by spending in the marketplace (as Obama did early in 2009) or by decreasing taxes (as Bush did over the course of his presidency). Conversely, in more prosperous times, when inflationary trends may need to be curbed, the government may opt to cut spending or increase taxes.

When the government spends less than it recovers through taxes, it incurs a surplus. More commonly, though, the government spends more than it recovers through taxes. In so doing, it contributes to the annual **deficit**, which represents the total amount of money that the federal government had to borrow from U.S. citizens and foreign governments in order to meet its spending obligations. President George W. Bush assumed office in 2001 after four consecutive years of surpluses. Tax cuts, a declining economy, foreign wars, and economic stimulus packages, however, have reinstated deficits on the order of several hundred billion dollars each year.

Over time, of course, these deficits mount. The **public debt** refers to the total amount of money that the federal government owes. As of 2008, the public debt surpassed a whopping $10 trillion—no less than 70 percent of the nation's GDP. This amounts to approximately $30,000 per person living in the United States, or $60,000 per member of the working population. Just to finance the interest on the debt, the federal government must pay hundreds of billions of dollars each year.[17] With recent efforts to stimulate the economy, the debt has only increased in magnitude. Projections for 2010 put public debt at fully 94 percent of GDP, a pace that Federal Reserve Chair Ben Bernanke has called "unsustainable."[18]

With the U.S. economy increasingly dependent on foreign sources of revenues, particularly from China, some scholars have raised concerns about the impact of rising national debt on U.S. foreign policy. China currently holds $755 billion in U.S. Treasury securities, making it the second largest foreign investor in the United States, just behind Japan. If we add Hong Kong's holdings, however, China becomes the single largest foreign financer of U.S. debt. As long as the United States remains beholden to Chinese debtors, some worry, the U.S. government lacks the necessary leverage to press for a variety of human rights reforms on issues ranging from control of the press, the status of Tibet, and the treatment of prisoners within China, or to confront China on its efforts to artificially depress the value of its currency, which contributes to its widening trade gap with the United States.[19] Others, however, insist that such fears are ungrounded. Just as the United States needs China, so does China need the United States. And should it divest from the United States, China would suffer substantial economic losses.[20]

The total amount of U.S. debt is higher now than it has ever been. As a percentage of GDP, it is quickly approaching the historical highs witnessed in the 1940s. By international standards, however, the current U.S. debt appears more moderate. Though some countries such as South Korea and Luxemburg have much lower debt levels, others such as Switzerland, Japan, Greece, Belgium, France, and Italy hold debt levels that, as a percentage of their GDP, surpass that of the United States.

fiscal policy policy designed to improve the economy through spending and taxation.

deficit the amount of money a government spends in a year, above and beyond what it brings in through taxation and other means.

public debt the total amount of money that the federal government owes.

ThinkingComparatively
Though the U.S. national debt is larger today than it has been in half a century, as a percentage of GDP it remains lower than in a number of other Western industrialized nations.

Economists have long debated the relative benefits of fiscal and monetary policy.[21] As a matter of course, though, the federal government does not have to choose between the two. It regularly implements both. In early 2008, economists worried about the onset of a **recession**, which exists when the GDP declines for two successive quarters. To encourage economic growth, the Federal Reserve decreased interest rates by 0.75 point. Shortly thereafter, Congress enacted an economic stimulus package that disbursed funds to individuals and families around the country in the hopes of jumpstarting the economy. The tax rebates, the president promised, would give the economy a much-needed "shot in the arm."[22] In 2009, a newly elected President Obama enacted a massive stimulus package, the American Recovery and Reinvestment Plan, which was discussed at this chapter's outset. Concurrently, the Federal Reserve kept interest rates at historic lows.

Different people are affected by the economy in different ways. In the pages that follow, we examine a variety of social programs that are designed to address the specific challenges facing different populations within the United States.

recession an economic downturn, which technically exists when the gross domestic product drops in size for two successive quarters.

Social Security

17-3 Trace the development of the largest federal social program, which assists the elderly.

Think what it must have been like for the elderly during the Great Depression. After working for decades and putting money aside for their eventual retirement, they watched as their savings vanished overnight. The collapse of the banking system drained the money they expected to live on during their golden years. Unlike younger people, the elderly could not readily start over again and recover what they had lost, and many spent their last years in poverty.

The **Social Security Act**, enacted in 1935, attempted to correct this state of affairs. The act established the framework for the Social Security Administration (SSA), charged with providing a reliable income stream for the elderly.[23] Social Security is perhaps best thought of as an anti-poverty program for the elderly. Today, most individuals qualify for Social Security benefits either when they turn 67 or when they become disabled and cannot work.[24] The benefits come in the form of a monthly check, the size of which varies according to the amount of money that the individual paid into the Social Security fund during years of employment.

Funding for Social Security is different from that for other social programs that we will review later in the chapter. During the course of their working lives, employees pay a portion of their income into a fund, which the SSA maintains. These payments, however, are not like deposits in a bank. A worker's contributions do not sit in the fund until he or she wishes to withdraw them. Rather, most of the contributions made today are promptly paid out to today's beneficiaries. This "pay as you go" system means that funds flow into and out of the Social Security fund at a continual rate.

Social Security benefits are **entitlements**—benefits that all qualifying individuals have a legal right to obtain. Social Security beneficiaries include people as young as 62 who have paid into the system (or, if they are deceased, their survivors). Thus, to receive Social Security benefits, one does not need to demonstrate financial need. Indeed, the size of the payments is unrelated to the amount of private savings an individual has. With this design, Social Security checks are an essential form of income for some people, and a welcome supplementary income for others.

Social Security Act a 1935 law that established Social Security, an entitlement program providing retirees with a monthly income in order to reduce poverty among the elderly.

entitlements benefits that all qualifying individuals have a legal right to obtain.

Social Security benefits have steadily expanded.

Since its enactment in 1935, Social Security has grown from a modestly sized government program to a massive one. Originally, the Social Security Act excluded many different types of workers, including farm workers, government employees, the self-employed, and individuals working for small businesses. Indeed, roughly one-half of the civilian labor force was excluded from the Social Security system. In 1950, farmers became qualified for Social Security. Since then, virtually all industry restrictions have been lifted. In 2006, almost 50 million individuals received Social Security benefits in the United States.[25]

The size of the benefits has also increased. In part, this reflects the natural maturation of the program. During the program's early years, retired workers had paid into the system for relatively short periods of time. Upon retirement, therefore, these individuals qualified for relatively small payments. As their total contributions increased, however, workers stood to receive larger benefits when they retired. And workers who have contributed into the system over their entire working lives can expect to receive, on average, around $1,000 each month.[26]

The government itself also contributed to increases in Social Security benefits. The most important action occurred in 1975, when Congress revised the act to account for changes in the cost of living. Automatic increases in the size of benefits—COLAs, short for "cost of living adjustments"—were mandated. However, the COLAs eventually exceeded inflation, so that average benefits in 2010 were roughly 41 percent larger than they were in 1975, even after accounting for inflation.[27]

▼ **THE BIRTH OF SOCIAL SECURITY**
Several members of the House and Senate look on as President Franklin Roosevelt signs the Social Security Act in August 1935.

Obviously, total Social Security outlays have increased dramatically over the past 70 years. In 1935, Social Security expenditures hovered at around $1 million. They broke the $1 billion mark in 1950, and the $100 billion mark in 1980. In 2009, the Social Security system paid out over $564 billion in benefits.[28]

The future of Social Security is uncertain.

Changing demographics in the United States have introduced new challenges to the Social Security system. Recall that the program critically depends on the ability of today's workers to fund the payments to today's elderly. The balance of workers to beneficiaries, however, has changed markedly over time. When the Social Security Act went into effect, roughly nine workers supported each elderly beneficiary. Today, just over three workers support each beneficiary. By some projections, this number will drop to only two workers per beneficiary by 2030.[29]

Because workers dramatically outnumbered the elderly for so long, Social Security managed to build up substantial reserves, known as Old-Age, Survivors, and Disability Insurance (OASDI) trust funds. As Figure 17-1 shows, though, these reserves will begin to fall in the not-too-distant future. By some economists' projections, Social Security expenditures will exceed both receipts and available reserves by as soon as 2037. The effects of a large Baby Boom generation entering retirement, COLAs that mandate higher payments each year, and longer life expectancies are straining the Social Security system. Some leaders, such as former Vice President Dick Cheney, warned the program is heading for a "financial train wreck."[30] Or, as President Bush put it, "If you're 20 years old, in your mid-twenties, and you're beginning to work, I want you to think about a Social Security system that will be flat bust, bankrupt, unless the United States Congress has got the willingness to act now."[31] Thus far, however, President Obama has not cast much public attention on the looming Social Security problem.

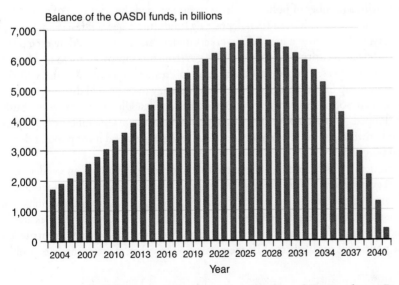

Balance of the OASDI funds, in billions

FIGURE 17-1. Social Security Reserves Are Predicted To Decline. Based on the current policy and the best available information about the size of the contributing workforce and the number of retired individuals, Social Security reserves will continue to increase until approximately 2028, at which time they will begin to rapidly decline.

What can the government do about these dwindling reserves? For starters, it can reduce the size of Social Security benefits doled out each year. To do this, it could raise the age at which individuals qualify for benefits—thereby reducing the number of beneficiaries. Alternatively, the government could decrease the benefits that it gives to each individual. Neither option, though, is especially attractive. Having paid into the Social Security system throughout their working lives, the elderly rightly expect to receive their due. And should they feel slighted, they will likely punish the offending politicians at the next election. So charged is the issue of Social Security reform, in fact, that it is referred to as the "third rail" of American politics—should you touch it, you can expect to be toast!

Although cutting Social Security benefits is difficult, it is not impossible. In 1983, after several years of stagflation—periods of high unemployment and high inflation—the federal government decided to reduce Social Security outlays. Such periods take an especially heavy toll on Social Security because high inflation triggers larger COLAs than normal and high unemployment means that fewer workers are paying into the Social Security system. To ensure the program's solvency, the government for the first time began to tax Social Security benefits, increased the eligible age for full benefits from 65 to 67, and added federal civil employees to the workers who could contribute to Social Security. However, these amendments may not solve the longer-term challenges facing the program.

Another way to protect Social Security would be to increase taxes. Historically, this has been the approach most commonly adopted. When the Social Security Act was enacted in 1935, the Social Security tax was set at 1 percent of the first $3,000 earned. Over the next 65 years, both the tax rate and the maximum taxable earning were increased 20 times. In 2008, the rate for individuals who are not self-employed was 6.2 percent of the first $102,000 earned.[32] Of course, there are political costs associated with increasing taxes, and these explain why both political parties at the national level tout their records at cutting taxes, not raising them.

Finally, a number of politicians have recommended the adoption of private investment accounts. Rather than depositing funds into a general reserve account, which typically receives a low yield, workers under this scheme could invest a portion of their Social Security contributions into government-approved stocks and bonds. This reform represented the core innovation in President George W. Bush's 2005 effort to shore up Social Security. Under Bush's plan, workers could direct up to 5 percent of their Social Security taxes into private accounts. Ultimately, however, Bush's plan flopped. Worried about the risks of private investments, members of Congress proved unwilling to fundamentally restructure the largest and most popular domestic social program.

Earlier in this chapter, we suggested that a focusing event is often needed to propel government action. We now see that this event often needs to underscore a problem that the American public faces in the here and now. From the vantage point of most politicians, several decades—the time when Social Security reserves are expected to run out—is a virtual eternity. Consequently, and perhaps unfortunately, these politicians are likely to shift their attention to other, more immediate problems.

Welfare

17-4 Analyze changes in welfare policy within the United States.

The federal government supports a wide range of programs designed to assist the poor. Collectively, these public assistance programs are often referred to as "welfare." Some of these programs involve direct cash transfers to the poor, others provide the equivalent of food vouchers, and others supply modest income subsidies. In one way or another, though, all attempt to alleviate the hardships experienced by the poor.

Who are the poor?

All of the programs described in this section are **means tested**—that is, they target those who demonstrate a lack of financial resources. To qualify for benefits, individuals must prove either that they are unemployed or that their income falls below a certain level. Means-tested programs are quite different from Social Security, which distributes benefits to all who have paid into the fund, no matter how well off they might be.

To ascertain eligibility for welfare programs, the federal government has developed a standard measure for identifying the poor: the poverty level. The poverty level varies according to a family's size: the larger the family, the higher the threshold. The precise level is calculated according to the cost of a family's basic needs. Specifically, it equals three times the cost of a minimally nutritious diet for a family of a given size. In 2009, the federal government calculated that a family of four would need to pay a minimum of $7,904 for food.[33] For such a family, therefore, the pre-tax poverty threshold was set at $22,128.[34] This way of calculating poverty does not do a good job of accounting for unreported incomes, which often include earnings from tips or domestic work.[35]

Figure 17-2 shows the percentage of the U.S. population in poverty since 1960. The number peaks early and then steadily declines. Indeed, poverty rates continued to drop until the early 1970s, when they leveled off at roughly 12 percent. As the U.S. population has increased in size, however, the number of people living in poverty has steadily increased since the early 1970s.

means-tested program any program that targets the poor and for which eligibility is based on financial need.

Welfare

609

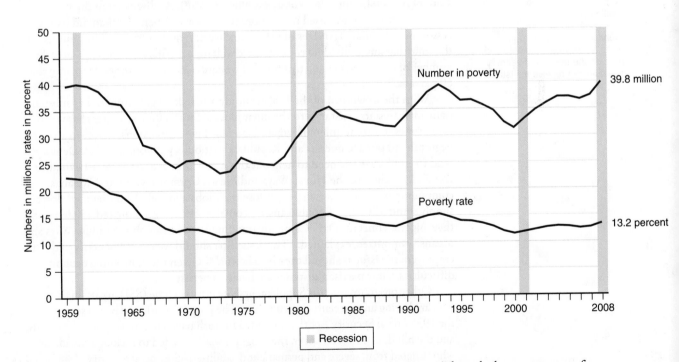

FIGURE 17-2. Number and Percentage of U.S. Population in Poverty. Though the percentage of Americans in poverty declined during the 1960s, it has remained steady every since. Because of population increases, meanwhile, the number of individuals in poverty since 1970 has increased by over 10 million.

Note: The data points are placed at the midpoints of the respective years.

The poor do not represent a random sample of U.S. adults. Young people, non-white adults, and single parents are disproportionately represented among the poor. No less than 18 percent of those under the age of 18 live in poverty, as compared to 10 percent of adults over the age of 65. Roughly one in four African Americans and Hispanics are poor, as compared to one in 10 whites. Five percent of married couples live in poverty, as compared to 13 percent of male single parents and 29 percent of female single parents.[36]

The federal government supports a variety of welfare programs.

Aid to Families with Dependent Children (AFDC) a federal program in effect from 1935 to 1996 that provided assistance to households with needy children.

The federal government has devised a variety of ways to help the poor. Historically, the most significant effort was **Aid to Families with Dependent Children (AFDC)**. Enacted in 1935 as part of the Social Security Act, this program provided assistance to needy children whose mother or father was missing from the home, physically handicapped, deceased, or unemployed. In 1950, the program was expanded to direct benefits to the parents of children in need as well. Not surprisingly, this reform led to a marked rise in expenditures. By 1962, AFDC distributed upward of half a billion dollars in benefits nationwide. Expenditures rose steadily through the 1970s. The Reagan administration cut AFDC benefits slightly, but by the mid-1990s the program was distributing over $16 billion to citizens living in poverty around the nation.[37]

Throughout its history, AFDC attracted considerable controversy. Critics charged that it discouraged parents from working and staying together.[38] In 1996, therefore, the federal government replaced AFDC with a new program entitled **Temporary Assistance for Needy Families (TANF)**. As discussed in the Case Study, this program imposed many more restrictions on benefits than did its predecessor. In particular, TANF established new work requirements and firm limits on the time that any individual could receive welfare benefits. As a consequence, the number of citizens receiving this form of welfare benefit has dropped by more than 60 percent.[39]

Temporary Assistance for Needy Families (TANF) a program replacing AFDC in 1996 that established new work requirements for welfare recipients and limits on the number of years an individual can receive assistance.

With the downturn of the U.S. economy, the federal government has substantially increased its assistance to the unemployed. Since 2008, Congress has voted seven times to extend unemployment benefits. These extensions, however, are beginning to put Democrats and Republicans at odds with one another. Democrats tend to emphasize the need to help out those most in need. As Sander Levin, the Democratic chair of the House Ways and Means Committee, put it, "We are a community of people. When people lose their jobs and can't find them, we don't simply stand idly by."[40] Republicans, by contrast, cite the growing federal deficit as their biggest concern. Dave Camp, the ranking Republican on the House Ways and Means Committee, explained, "This issue isn't should we extend benefits to the unemployed, the issue is should they be paid for."[41] Given the continuing economic difficulties, these partisan disputes are likely to persist.

Other programs, such as Supplemental Security Income (SSI), focus on those who are having an especially difficult time. The program's origins lay in a section of the 1935 Social Security Act that provided for cash payments to the poor, the elderly, and the blind. In 1950, however, the program was expanded to include individuals who suffered from severe and permanent disabilities. The Social Security Administration runs the program, but aid comes from general tax revenues rather than from Social Security contributions. To qualify for SSI support, individuals must demonstrate not only that they are poor, but also that they have few possessions. To qualify in 2010, a single individual or child usually could not own in excess of $2,000 worth of goods, and married couples could not own more than $3,000.[42] SSI is really directed toward reaching the destitute. In 2010, SSI disbursed a total of $47 billion in aid.[43]

Other federal programs assist the poor in obtaining specific necessities. The federal government supports a variety of food programs for the needy, including a nutritional program for women, infants, and children (WIC) and a school breakfast and lunch program. The largest, though, is the Supplemental Nutrition Assistance Program (SNAP), formerly the Food Stamp Program. After operating briefly in the late 1930s and early 1940s, the program became a permanent component of the welfare landscape in 1964. Administered by the Department of Agriculture, it provides the poor with coupons that can be redeemed at local grocery stores to purchase approved food items. The income restrictions for SNAP are not quite as strict as those for AFDC, TANF, or SSI. Consequently, the program benefits more U.S. residents. Over the last 40 years, the program has grown dramatically. In 1969, 3 million individuals received food stamps whose costs totaled $250 million. By 2010, 33 million people received them at a total cost of $53 billion.[44]

Other programs are designed expressly to support the working poor. The Earned Income Tax Credit (EITC), created in 1974, subsidizes the wages of low-income individuals. Specifically, it reduces the amount of income taxes they must pay; for some individuals, the EITC results in a government refund. Throughout its history, the EITC has received bipartisan support, largely because it encourages work, unlike other welfare programs (notably AFDC). EITC eligibility requirements have both an income ceiling and a floor. Although the ceiling is as much as twice the poverty threshold for a household, the floor requires that families have a nonzero income. Consequentially, individuals who are unemployed for the entirety of a year cannot receive EITC benefits. When filing their taxes in 2010, over 25 million individuals claimed EITC benefits that totaled $54 billion.[45]

▲ **MAKING ENDS MEET**

Welfare programs, which underwent significant revision in 1996, are directed toward the poor. Under the new system, mothers such as this one must secure paid employment in order to maintain welfare benefits.

U.S. welfare programs are small by international standards.

By European standards, the U.S. welfare system is quite young. Whereas most U.S. welfare programs were created in the 1930s and 1960s, many European programs trace back to the nineteenth century. Germany pioneered early welfare efforts, enacting laws in the 1880s to aid poor people who could not work because of industrial accidents, illness, or old age. Other countries soon followed. These programs mainly resulted from the dramatic socioeconomic changes going on in Europe at the time. The emergence of factories, the rise of the working classes, and massive migration from rural areas into cities brought new social problems to the fore and exacerbated the hard conditions facing workers. Welfare assistance served as a way of quelling discontent among the working classes, who many feared might rise up against their governments. By the eve of World War I in 1914, Austria, Belgium, Britain, Denmark, Finland, France, Germany, Italy, the Netherlands, Norway, Sweden, and Switzerland all had some form of welfare in place. These programs expanded greatly in the years between the world wars, and then again after World War II.[46]

The American welfare system is also smaller than that in other countries. The amount of money the U.S. government devotes to social programs lags far behind

ThinkingComparatively

European welfare systems are typically older and more expansive than those found in the United States.

the sums spent in Western Europe, Australia, and Canada. In 2000, the United States ranked last out of 10 Western democracies in public welfare expenditures, spending little more than half of the average expenditure of the other Western democracies.[47] In 2010, the United States contributed 15 percent of its national income to government welfare programs.[48] According to two Harvard University economists, as a percentage of its national income, France spends almost double what the United States spends on social programs, and Nordic countries spend even more.[49]

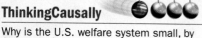

ThinkingCausally

Why is the U.S. welfare system small, by international standards?

Scholars continue to debate the causes of the differences between U.S. and European welfare systems. Some have argued that American political culture, which prizes individualism and personal responsibility, is less amenable to social welfare programs than European cultures, which stress collective values. Others contend that the American system of checks and balances makes it harder to enact major social legislation. Both of these explanations, however, have obvious limitations. Programs like Social Security, which provides government support for all older Americans, remain wildly popular despite the individualistic culture of the United States. And sweeping anti-poverty measures such as Lyndon Johnson's Great Society initiative managed to overcome both cultural and institutional hurdles.[50]

Education

17-5 Trace the federal government's expanding involvement in education.

The U.S. Constitution does not discuss the education of children. The obligation to educate, therefore, fell upon state and local governments. Since the nation's founding, public schools in this country have been locally controlled. As public education took hold in the 19th century, school boards contended with a loosely knit assembly of schools whose principals and teachers retained considerable freedom to do as they pleased. As the education historian David Tyack notes, public education constituted "more a miscellaneous collection of village schools than a coherent system."[51] Metaphorically, public schools around the nation looked less like peach trees in an orchard and more like brightly colored and misshapen stones in a mosaic.

During the nineteenth century, the federal government granted public lands to states for educational use, but it had little say over what happened within the newly constructed schoolhouses. The Office of Education, established in 1870, collected descriptive statistics on public schools but otherwise rarely interfered. More than half a century later, though, all of this localism would change, and the federal government burst onto the education scene.

The needed focusing event occurred on October 4, 1957, when the Soviet Union stunned the world with its successful launch of *Sputnik I*, the first satellite to circle the globe. The feat left many Americans deeply concerned about their ability to compete with the communist regime. Within a few months, President Dwight Eisenhower responded by outlining education reforms designed to improve U.S. schools. "As never before," he warned, "the security and continued well-being of the United States depend on extension of scientific knowledge."[52] Concerns about national security spurred the federal government's entry into the business of education.

On September 2, 1958, Eisenhower signed into law the National Defense Education Act. The act, the president declared, would "do much to strengthen our American system of education so that it can meet the broad and increasing demands imposed upon it by considerations of basic national security."[53] Most of the aid went to science, math, and foreign language training, though smaller amounts went to school construction and low-interest loans. Though the act did not change the curriculum or method of instruction of any public school, it opened the door for increased federal involvement in public education.

The federal government seeks to equalize education funding.

In principle, states and municipalities were supposed to provide a basic education to all children. For much of U.S. history, however, they did not. Boys had greater opportunities to join sports teams than girls. The amount of money spent on schools varied dramatically across school districts and states. And the educational options granted to white citizens were usually superior to those of African Americans, Hispanics, and other ethnic minorities. Testifying before a Senate subcommittee in 1963, Commissioner of Education Frances Koppel cited a troubling statistic: whereas nearly 75 percent of the young white population had completed high school, only 40 percent of nonwhites had done so. Such inequalities in education, moreover, perpetuated inequalities in the workplace. For example, although African Americans then comprised 11 percent of the total population, they made up only 3.5 percent of all professional workers.[54]

During the 1960s and 1970s, the federal government sought to redress such inequalities. Most importantly, in 1965 it enacted the **Elementary and Secondary Education Act (ESEA)**, which provided direct aid to local school districts with large concentrations of poor residents. The original law and its subsequent amendments funneled additional assistance to Native Americans and to students whose primary language was not English.

In the 1970s, the federal government turned its attention to the educational needs of the physically handicapped. In 1975, Congress enacted what is now called the Individuals with Disability Education Act (IDEA). The act proclaimed

Elementary and Secondary Education Act (ESEA) a federal law passed in 1965 designed to reduce educational inequities by directly aiding school districts with large numbers of poor citizens.

▼ **THE VANGUARD OF INTEGRATION**

Pictured are eight of the nine African American students who helped integrate Central High School in Little Rock, Arkansas, in 1957.

that all citizens are entitled to a "free appropriate public education." It then mandated public schools to make the accommodations needed to ensure that students with disabilities received this. As a consequence, public schools needed to change their buildings, alter their curricula, and introduce classes that would suit the needs of disabled students. However, the federal government covers just a fraction of these costs. As a consequence, the IDEA is often referred to as an **unfunded mandate**.

unfunded mandate a law requiring certain actions without appropriating the necessary funds to carry them out.

Educational inequities persist. For example, high school dropout rates for the 2003–2004 academic year hovered around 3 percent for whites but ranged between 5 and 8 percent for blacks.[55] In 2003, Hispanics constituted 18 percent of elementary school students but less than 11 percent of college students.[56] Among college graduates who obtained bachelor's degrees in computer science or engineering during the 2004–2005 school year, men outnumbered women by about 4 to 1.[57]

Other historical inequalities, meanwhile, have actually flipped. Women today outnumber men at colleges and universities across the country. In 2006, women represented no less than 58 percent of the nation's college students.[58] Women also, on average, perform better and have higher graduation rates than their male counterparts. If current trends persist, by 2020 women will earn 156 Bachelor of Arts degrees to men's 100.[59] Educators say that the top male students are just as competent as the top female students, but that struggling males crowd the other end of the spectrum.[60]

The federal government attempts to impose standards.

ThinkingComparatively

By international standards, U.S. students do not perform especially well on standardized tests.

In the early 1980s, concerns about the ability of U.S. citizens to compete with others around the globe again intensified. In *A Nation at Risk*, a report that was sufficiently influential to be considered a focusing event, a panel of education experts complained about the "rising tide of mediocrity" infecting U.S. schools. International comparisons of student achievement, which had been completed a decade earlier, revealed that "on 19 academic tests American students were never first or second and, in comparison with other industrialized nations, were last seven times."[61] At the turn of the millennium, lackluster performance remained an issue. In a test administered in 2006 to 15-year-olds in 31 countries, the United States ranked 21 in science, and 25 in mathematics. As Table 17-1 shows, when averaging across the two subjects, the United States ranked 24. Increasingly, it seemed, states and local districts could not be counted on to provide the level of excellence required to keep pace with students abroad.

ThinkingCausally

What accounts for cross-national differences in student performance?

The precise reasons why U.S. students fail to keep pace with their peers abroad remain something of a mystery. Some plausible reasons can be readily eliminated. For instance, a lack of public school funding is probably not the cause, as per-pupil expenditures in the United States are higher than in the vast majority of other industrialized nations, including those like Japan and South Korea that regularly rank near the top of international tests.[62]

And within the United States, some of the highest performing students come from states like Utah, which spend relatively little on their public schools. What, then, explains the gap? Some people emphasize the lack of discipline in U.S. public schools. Others fault poor teacher recruitment and training. For many, though, the primary culprit is the lack of strict standards to which students are held accountable.

TABLE 17-1. U.S. Students Lag Behind Their International Counterparts on Standardized Tests

RANK	COUNTRY	AVERAGE MATH AND SCIENCE SCORES ON THE PROGRAM FOR INTERNATIONAL STUDENT ASSESSMENT FOR 15-YEARS-OLDS IN OECD COUNTRIES
1	Finland	552.85
2	Korea, Republic of	541.88
3	Canada	529.50
4	New Zealand	524.47
5	Netherlands	520.75
6	Australia	519.89
7	Japan	517.48
8	Switzerland	513.49
9	Belgium	510.54
10	Ireland	509.04
11	Germany	504.79
12	Sweden	504.33
13	Austria	502.17
14	Czech Republic	501.81
15	United Kingdom	501.77
16	Denmark	501.13
17	Poland	500.29
18	Iceland	493.59
19	France	492.82
20	Hungary	492.41
21	Norway	486.89
22	Luxembourg	485.23
23	Slovak Republic	482.30
24	**United States**	**481.63**
25	Spain	476.40
26	Portugal	470.92
27	Italy	468.54
29	Greece	464.10
30	Turkey	431.64
31	Mexico	408.60

Source: *Digest of Education Statistics*, 2009, Table 402, http://nces.ed.gov/programs/digest/d09/tables/dt09_402.asp.

The demand for standards and accountability came to a head in 2001, when Congress enacted the **No Child Left Behind Act (NCLB)**.[63] For the first time, the federal government assumed the responsibility of monitoring individual schools and doling out punishments and rewards on the basis of their performance. Specifically, NCLB requires states to establish a testing regime that evaluates student learning trends from year to year. Furthermore, states must identify the percentage of students who perform at a certain level each year. Schools that fail to meet designated benchmarks are deemed "in need of improvement." If a public school fails to attain testing standards for two years, its attendees may transfer to higher-performing schools within their district. After three years, students qualify for supplemental tutoring services. Schools that fail for longer periods of time face harsher sanctions still.

No Child Left Behind Act (NCLB) a 2001 federal law that rewards public schools for meeting certain educational benchmarks and punishes schools that fail to do so.

No Child Left Behind has not yet produced dramatic improvements in the educational performance of U.S. students. According to some research, math scores of U.S. fourth graders have increased, while reading scores have remained stagnant.[64] Nonetheless, NCLB has had a dramatic effect on the U.S. education system. Two consequences are especially noteworthy. First, the federal government has become an important agenda setter in public education. Rather than merely providing support services and ensuring a roughly even playing field, the federal government now plays an important role in determining the curricula of schools around the nation. Second, NCLB has raised the stakes of standardized testing dramatically. Never before has so much ridden on children's performance on state-mandated standardized tests.

CaseStudy: Obama's "Race to the Top" Initiative

States retain the constitutional responsibility to provide public education. Hence, the federal government typically relies on financial inducements to influence public education. Historically, the federal government has offered funds that are slated for specific programs and projects that it supports. In 2009, however, President Obama tried a slightly different tack. Rather than providing all states with funds for specific initiatives, the president announced a competition that would reward just a handful of reform-minded states.

Obama announced his "Race to the Top" initiative in July 2009. The competition unlocked $4.35 billion in grants to be distributed to the states that demonstrated the greatest improvements to their educational systems. More specifically, the initiative was designed to "encourage and reward States that are implementing significant reforms in four education areas: enhancing standards and assessments, improving the collection and use of data, increasing teacher effectiveness and achieving equity in teacher distribution, and turning around struggling schools."[65] It was left up to states, meanwhile, to figure out how they would pursue these four broad objectives.

Initially, 41 states submitted applications. In early March 2010, a list of 16 finalists was announced. Several weeks later, Secretary of Education Arne Duncan declared Delaware and Tennessee the competition's first two winners. According to Duncan, "Both states have statewide buy-in for comprehensive plans to reform their schools. They have written new laws to support their policies. And they have demonstrated the courage, capacity, and commitment to turn their ideas into practices that can improve outcomes for students."[66] Accounting for their differences in sizes, Delaware received roughly $100 million in new federal funds, and Tennessee received $500 million.

Both states stood out for their commitment to a variety of education reforms—primarily accountability and merit

▲ THE FEDERAL GOVERNMENT GETS INTO THE EDUCATION BUSINESS

Student journalist Gopa Praturi, age 10, interviews U.S. Secretary of Education Arne Duncan on the first day of classes at Wakefield High School in Arlington, Virginia, September 8, 2009. In your view, how much influence should the federal department of education have over public schools?

pay—that the Obama administration hoped to encourage. Tennessee had passed a new law that linked teacher evaluations with objective student assessment and student growth on standardized tests. Similarly, Delaware outlined plans to implement regular testing to more accurately gauge students' learning trajectories. And like Tennessee, Delaware promised to reward teachers based on performance rather than seniority and credentials.

Though the Obama administration hailed the first round of the competition as a glowing success, others appeared more critical. Colorado's Democratic governor led the charge, complaining about the opaque judging process and the criteria for success. According to the competition's rules, widespread support by teacher unions as well as increased state control over failing schools improves a state's chances of success. But these criteria, critics charged, discriminated against larger and Republican-controlled states. Large states found it more difficult to garner the support of a majority of its districts. And Republican-controlled states often found it more difficult to secure the support of teachers unions.[67, 68]

Union support, however, came at a price. As Earl Winam, president of the Tennessee Education Association, noted, "It was just facing up to the political reality that you just can't beat the hope of $500 million. We did buy into it, but it was more because of the political reality."[69] In exchange for their full support, the union in Tennessee secured a plurality of seats on the legislative advisory committee and thereby strengthened their influence over state education policy.

In the summer of 2010, the Obama administration evaluated a second round of applications. And in August, they announced 10 winners, including Florida and Louisiana. Colorado, however, was once again among the losers. Indeed, the only western state to win the competition was Hawaii, raising speculation among some about geographic bias. Given the political fallout associated with advancing the kinds of reforms supported by the Obama administration,[70] it remains to be seen whether the federal government will support additional rounds of the competition.

ThinkingCritically

1. The Obama administration could have directed the funds used in the Race to the Top initiative to any states willing to implement its preferred education reforms. What are the advantages, then, of holding a competition for these funds? What are the disadvantages?

2. For those people interested in either advancing or retarding merit pay for teachers and school accountability, what are the relative costs and benefits of focusing their lobbying efforts on the federal government?

Reformers challenge the "public school monopoly."

During the last two decades, reformers have issued a series of challenges against public schools. According to these reformers, public schools fail to perform well because they are not subject to competition. For the most part, government-run schools can count on a steady supply of students, even when these schools perform poorly. As a result, public schools lack the competitive incentive to improve that drives most industries in the private marketplace. These reformers have proposed two policy innovations to increase the schooling options available to parents, especially those in urban settings. The first concerns **charter schools**, which are public schools that are exempted from many rules and regulations faced by traditional public schools. For instance, when hiring teachers and choosing their curriculum, charter schools tend to have greater freedom than do traditional public schools. Charter schools are directly responsible to a chartering board, which oversees their operations. Though their character varies, most charter schools focus on a particular population of students (such as those with special needs) or offer a distinctive curriculum (such as one that emphasizes science).

In 1991, the first charter school opened in Minnesota. Since then, over 40 states have enacted charter school legislation. The highest concentration of such schools is in Washington, D.C., where almost 20 percent of children attend a charter school. The devastation wrought by Hurricane Katrina in southern states along the Gulf of Mexico created new opportunities to replace many of the affected region's traditional public schools with charter schools.

charter schools public schools, administered by chartering boards, that are exempt from many rules and regulations applicable to traditional public schools.

continued on page 620 ▶

HOW DO WE KNOW?

Are Private Schools Better than Public Schools?

The Question

Almost everyone believes that the federal government should support the education of children. A vibrant economy and a functioning democracy, after all, depend on an educated citizenry. Less clear is whether the government should be in the business of actually running the schools. Currently, roughly 90 percent of children attend public schools, most of which serve children within well-defined neighborhood boundaries. The remaining 10 percent of children, however, attend private schools. Most of these are Catholic schools, but others adhere to different religious denominations, and some are secular. Do students attending these schools perform better on standardized tests than their public school peers? How do we know?

Why It Matters

Local, state, and federal governments contribute a total of $9,762 per year, on average, to educate a public school student.[71] Most private schools charge parents approximately $3,000 a year to send a child to school. Private schools also are not subject to the kinds of rules and regulations that govern public schools. Private schools, for instance, do not participate in any of the NCLB testing regimes. If private school students perform as well as or better than comparable public school students, then one way to increase student performance may involve increasing the educational options available to parents, especially those who cannot currently afford the cost of a private education. Moreover, there may be substantial savings associated with doing so.

◄ PUBLIC VERSUS PRIVATE SCHOOLS
Tax credits and vouchers have the potential to help students attend private schools such as this one, in Poughkeepsie, New York.

Investigating the Answer

The most straightforward way of assessing the relative quality of public and private schools would seem to involve simply comparing the test scores of a random sample of students in each sector. If private school students score higher, we might conclude that private schools do a superior job of educating students. Unfortunately, things are not nearly so simple.

There is good reason to expect that private school students differ systematically from public school students. Private schools, after all, charge tuition, whereas public schools are nominally free. Moreover, private schools enjoy considerable discretion to select which students to admit. Traditional public schools, by contrast, typically accept all students within a defined geographic region. Given these facts, it is extraordinarily difficult to know whether observed differences between public and private school students arise from differences in the quality of education or from differences in student backgrounds that influence whether they attend private or public school in the first place.

How might scholars go about distinguishing between these two possibilities? One option involves carefully controlling for a wide range of background characteristics when comparing public and private school test scores. Pursuing this approach, analysts have built large datasets and employed complex statistical techniques that allow them to account for differences in students' family backgrounds. These studies attempt to hold constant a wide range of observable qualities, such as race and ethnicity, parental involvement, and family education and employment levels.

The trouble with these studies, however, is that we can never be entirely sure that the analysts have correctly accounted for all relevant characteristics. In surveys, for instance, people regularly misreport their income. Studies that rely on survey income data, then, may not effectively control for this dimension. Moreover, such research could omit other important background characteristics, such as a parent's commitment to education. In either case, these studies may generate biased estimates of the quality of public and private schools.

The most effective way to solve these selection problems, then, is to randomly assign students to public and private schools. By conducting a randomized field trial, researchers could ensure that the two populations are exactly alike in all respects, both observable and unobservable, before the experiment. Subsequently, differences that arise between the two populations could be attributed to the education experience and not to the children's backgrounds.

Randomized field trials are commonplace in medical studies, in which subjects are randomly assigned to receive a pill or placebo. In the last decade, this approach has come to education. Private philanthropists launched school voucher programs in New York City, Dayton, Ohio, and Washington, D.C., during the 1990s. Rather than give out the vouchers on a first-come-first-serve basis, however, the administrators conducted lotteries. Among qualified applicants, some students were randomly offered a voucher and some were not. The only thing that distinguished the "treatment" and "control" groups was the opportunity to attend a private school. By tracking the performance of these two groups over time, researchers stood the best chance of overcoming the self-selection problems described above.

What did these three programs teach us about the quality of public and private schools? Interestingly, the answer very much depends on the ethnicity of the students. Across the three cities, white students who attended private schools did not score any higher than white students who attended public schools. The performances of Hispanic students in the two sectors also appeared indistinguishable from one another. However, private schools did seem to benefit African American students. After three years, African American students in private schools scored significantly higher on standardized tests than African Americans in public schools.[72]

Though randomized field trials are the gold standard of social research, we still need to be careful when interpreting their results. It is not always clear that the observed findings from one study apply to a larger population. Randomized field trials of voucher programs in other cities might yield very different results. Second, social scientists encounter a variety of challenges when conducting randomized field trials. Over time they may lose track of certain students and thereby compromise the original randomization.[73] Finally, the private school advantage remains unclear. What is it about private schools that disproportionately benefits African American students? The mere documentation of the private-school effect does not explain what caused the effect.

Thinking Critically

- What are the best indicators of student learning? How might we go about assessing whether different kinds of schools perform better or worse along these indicators?
- When assessing school quality, should policy analysts account for how much money is spent on students?
- If private schools, on average, perform better than public schools, does this mean that all private schools are better than all public schools? If not, what are the policy implications of studies that demonstrate average differences in school performances?

The Bottom Line

In this instance, there appears to be a fair amount of consensus.[74] In both randomized field trials and observational studies, the test-score advantages of attending a private school appear to be concentrated among African Americans. Policy makers interested in improving the educational lives of African American children, then, might consider expanding the array of public and private schooling options available to them.

Since 2005, roughly half of the schools reopening in New Orleans are charter schools.[75] As Figure 17-3 shows, over 5,000 charter schools now serve upward of 1.5 million students around the country.[76]

vouchers tuition subsidies that reduce the costs of sending children to private schools.

The second innovation is school **vouchers**, which are tuition subsidies that reduce the costs of sending a child to a private school. The first voucher experiment in the United States began in 1990 in Milwaukee, which offered tuition subsidies of (initially) up to $2,500 to low-income families. For the first eight years, the program could legally serve no more than 1.5 percent of the city's public school population (approximately 1,700 students) and only secular schools were allowed to participate. In 1996, the state of Wisconsin permitted up to 15 percent of the public school population to participate in the program, expanded the menu of private schooling options to include religious institutions, and increased the monetary value of the vouchers.

Other publicly funded voucher programs now operate in Ohio, Florida, and Washington, D.C. Vermont and Maine have voucher-like programs that assist children in rural districts to attend either a secular private school or a public school in another district. In the 2005–2006 school year, thousands of nonspecial education students made use of the voucher program. That same year, tens of thousands more received scholarships, roughly equivalent to vouchers, through tax credit programs.[77] And thousands more pupils have enrolled in privately funded voucher programs. Such

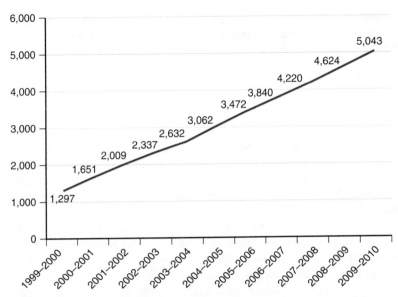

FIGURE 17-3. **Thousands of Charter Schools Operate Around the Nation.** Since the early 1990s, the number of charter schools has steadily risen.

efforts include a national program operated by the Children's Scholarship Fund, as well as local initiatives in several cities.

Although controversial within the United States, vouchers have attracted widespread support in other nations. In 1980, Chile enacted the equivalent of a national voucher program. Private schools in Chile are fully subsidized, while public schools face significantly fewer regulations than their U.S. counterparts. As a result, almost 40 percent of students in Chile attend private schools, as compared to just 10 percent in the United States. Whether Chilean students have benefited from these new educational opportunities, however, remains a subject of continued academic debate. Some scholars have found that the private school students outperform their public school peers, whereas others argue that the differences are negligible.[78]

ThinkingComparatively

Students in Chile are four times as likely to attend a private school as students in the United States.

Though they are all prominent education reforms, NCLB, vouchers, and charters have important differences. NCLB increases the government's involvement in schools. Because of NCLB, schools must regularly test children, report their results, and then be graded accordingly. Moreover, a central premise of NCLB is that principals and teachers in failing schools will change their behavior because of the law's direct intervention in their schools. Vouchers and charters, on the other hand, are intended to reduce the role of the government in the administration of schools. In both instances, participating students attend schools with considerably less oversight than traditional public schools.

Health Care

17-6 Evaluate the government's efforts to provide health care to the poor and aged.

In addition to attending to the elderly, the poor, and the young, the federal government also assists the infirm. Many U.S. citizens receive private health insurance for themselves and their families through their workplace. Millions, though, rely on the two largest government insurance programs: Medicare, which assists the elderly, and Medicaid, which assists the poor.

Medicare and Medicaid provide coverage to the elderly, poor, and disabled.

Though Lyndon Johnson's Great Society legislation tackled poverty, education, and discrimination, its most sweeping achievements were reserved for the infirm. Through two programs enacted in 1965, Johnson put the government firmly into the health care business. **Medicare** provided government health insurance to the elderly, and **Medicaid** did so to the poor and disabled.[79]

When originally enacted, Medicare covered physicians' fees and the costs of compulsory hospitalization for citizens over the age of 65. Over time, though, the program has expanded dramatically. Today it allows the elderly to secure a wide range of services, including inpatient hospital care, certain kinds of home health care, hospice assistance, and outpatient hospital care. In 2003, the government added prescription drug benefits to Medicare. These benefits constitute the single largest expansion of Medicare in decades.

By any calculation, Medicare is a massive government program. In 2007, Medicare assisted 42 million citizens at a total cost of $430 billion—almost as much as all Social Security outlays, and far more than any other federal education or welfare program.[80] Medicare is financed through a variety of means. As with Social Security, workers must pay a Medicare-specific tax. Additionally, for those receiving such medical services as x-rays, laboratory and diagnostic tests, and influenza and pneumonia vaccinations, the federal government deducts a portion of their Social Security payments and then covers the remaining costs with general revenues.

In many ways, though, Medicaid is even bigger than Medicare. In 2006, Medicaid provided health insurance to 54 million low-income and disabled citizens. It also assumed responsibility for providing a larger proportion of health care services. For instance, Medicaid now covers one-third of the nation's childbirths, nearly 40 percent of long-term care expenses, and more services for AIDS patients than any other provider in the country.[81]

Medicaid expenditures, however, are quite a bit lower than those of Medicare. In 2009, Medicaid cost federal and state governments a total of $218 billion, roughly $200 billion less than Medicare.[82] Two primary reasons explain why Medicaid today is less expensive than Medicare, even though it provides more services to more people. First, Medicaid does not offer as generous a prescription drug benefit program. Indeed, before Medicare's 2003 drug benefit enhancement, the costs of the two programs tracked one another quite closely. Second, the costs of caring for the elderly have steadily increased over time. Today, the elderly are living eight years longer, on average, than they did when Medicare began. The elderly, moreover, typically require more expensive medical procedures than does the rest of the citizenry. And Medicare is picking up most of these extra costs.

Certain populations—such as the disabled and poor seniors—qualify for both Medicare and Medicaid. And because the two programs cover different kinds of medical services, these individuals draw benefits from both. In important respects, though, the two programs operate very differently from one another. Whereas Medicare is an entitlement program for the elderly, Medicaid is a means-tested program for the needy. And whereas Medicare is run exclusively by the federal government, Medicaid

Medicare a federally funded entitlement program that offers health insurance to the elderly.

Medicaid a means-tested program, funded by federal and state governments, that extends health insurance to the poor and disabled.

also receives funding from the states. Consequently, whereas Medicare looks exactly the same across the country, Medicaid programs differ markedly from state to state.[83]

U.S. health care and health are poor by international standards.

Despite massive government programs like Medicare and Medicaid, as well as the patchwork of private insurance plans, many Americans lack health insurance. In every year between 1995 and 2005, more than 15 percent of U.S. citizens lacked any health insurance. Every other major industrialized nation in the world, by comparison, has some form of universal health care. The United Kingdom was the first nation to offer universal medical coverage. In 1948, it established the National Health Service, which uses general tax revenue to support hospitals that serve all citizens. Thus far, over 30 other European countries have followed suit with universal programs of their own, as have tens of other countries, including Israel, Uruguay, India, and Japan.

ThinkingComparatively
Thirty-six other nations have "better" health care systems than does the United States.

Coverage rates in the United States are all the more troubling given the extraordinary costs of its health care. In 2003, the United States spent close to 16 percent of its gross national product (GNP) on health costs. As a percentage of their economies, this proportion is higher than any other advanced industrialized nation. Indeed, U.S. costs are 50 to 80 percent higher than those in Germany, Canada, the United Kingdom, and France, all of which provide universal health care to their citizens.

Though they pay a great deal for health care, U.S. citizens remain comparatively unhealthy. Consider, for example, the number of years that people in different nations can expect to live. In 2004, the life expectancy of U.S. citizens trailed that of 24 other major industrialized nations. Ranking just above citizens of Poland, Mexico, and the Czech Republic, U.S. men live an average of 75 years, and U.S. women, 80. Both figures trailed those of every nation in Western Europe.[84] American citizens also have much less healthy lifestyles than their international counterparts. In 2005, for instance, U.S. obesity rates eclipsed those of every other industrialized nation in the world. Fully 32 percent of U.S. citizens were deemed obese, as compared to just 3 percent of the Japanese, 8 percent of the Swiss, 10 percent of the French, and 23 percent of the English.[85]

Given international differences in coverage rates and lifestyles, it is difficult to assess the overall quality of different health care systems. Those who have tried to do so, however, have not given the United States high marks. Table 17-2 ranks the quality of health care systems in the top 50 countries, according to the World Health Organization (WHO). The United States ranks 37 in the world for the overall performance of its health care system. This places the American system behind those of all Western European countries as well as Canada, Australia, and Japan. A number of South and Central American countries, including Colombia, Chile, and Costa Rica, also outperform the United States by this measure.

By international standards, the United States health care system appears mediocre. Nevertheless, overall system performance is just one of many ways to evaluate national health care quality. The WHO report, for instance, bases its rankings on a composite measure that includes factors such as the health of a nation's citizens, the responsiveness of a health care system to patients' nonhealth concerns, and the extent to which health care systems accommodate patients' financial limitations. Although the United States performs poorly on financing, ranking 54, it comes in at 24 in health attainment and at 1 in system responsiveness.[86]

TABLE 17-2. Overall Health System Performance, World Health Organization Estimates (1997)

RANK	COUNTRY	RANK	COUNTRY
1	France	26	Saudi Arabia
2	Italy	27	United Arab Emirates
3	San Marino	28	Israel
4	Andorra	29	Morocco
5	Malta	30	Canada
6	Singapore	31	Finland
7	Spain	32	Australia
8	Oman	33	Chile
9	Austria	34	Denmark
10	Japan	35	Dominica
11	Norway	36	Costa Rica
12	Portugal	**37**	**United States**
13	Monaco	38	Slovenia
14	Greece	39	Cuba
15	Iceland	40	Brunei Darussalam
16	Luxembourg	41	New Zealand
17	Netherlands	42	Bahrain
18	United Kingdom	43	Croatia
19	Ireland	44	Qatar
20	Switzerland	45	Kuwait
21	Belgium	46	Barbados
22	Colombia	47	Thailand
23	Sweden	48	Czech Republic
24	Cyprus	49	Malaysia
25	Germany	50	Poland

Source: World Health Organization, "The World Health Report 2000: Health Systems: Improving Performance," http://www.who.int.

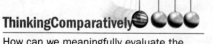

ThinkingComparatively

How can we meaningfully evaluate the quality of different health care systems?

Moreover, ranking a nation's health care system based partly on the wellness of its population, as the WHO does, can be tricky. On the one hand, a healthy citizenry could indicate that the system is working effectively. Residents may be living longer and healthier lives because of good preventive medicine or access to excellent doctors and facilities. On the other hand, it could reflect considerations that have little to do with the health care system, such as culture, the environment, or economic development. For instance, people may live longer in a nation where the traditional diet consists of low-fat foods like fish, fruits, and vegetables. Conversely, populations of developing countries may be exposed to higher levels of pollution, which can trigger a variety of ailments.

Comprehensive health care reform was eventually achieved in 2010.

Almost everyone agrees that something needs to be done about the state of U.S. health care. It is too costly. Too many people are uninsured. For many, the quality of care is unacceptable. What people cannot agree about is the right way to go about improving this state of affairs. Some suggest that allowing U.S. citizens to purchase prescription drugs from foreign countries might drastically reduce costs. Others push for closer regulation of the pharmaceutical industry. The most ambitious, however, advocate government-provided health insurance that covers every U.S. citizen.

Advocates of universal health care are generally liberals. They couch their arguments in terms of traditional American values about fairness and equity, asking, "Isn't health the most basic right?" Indeed, doesn't the exercise of all other rights depend on citizens being healthy? And if so, how can we deny health insurance to millions of U.S. citizens?[87] Advocates also note that the United States is the only major industrialized nation in the world not to offer health care to all of its citizens.

There are powerful opponents, however, to universal health care. Most conservatives are deeply suspicious of what they call "socialized medicine."[88] Libertarian organizations, such as the Cato Institute, oppose reforms that would increase federal regulations of hospitals. And the American Medical Association is wary of any plan that would reduce the role of private insurance. Moreover, critics insist, government-provided health insurance threatens to reduce the number of hospital and doctor options available to the public. In this sense, universal health care violates other basic tenets of the American creed, notably individualism and freedom of choice. These individuals do not dispute the importance of decreasing the number of uninsured individuals around the country. But they insist that private insurers, rather than the federal government, should assume primary responsibility for achieving this important goal.

These forces set the stage of an epic showdown on health care reform during the fall of 2009 and spring of 2010. The national debate evoked long-standing disputes about the effect of government-provided health insurance on private insurance markets. According to proponents of a vigorous government intervention, a single-payer system, which would pay for all medical fees from a single government source, is best. Others advocated for a two-tier system in which the government provides for basic health services, and people can purchase other health care coverage in the private marketplace. Still others argued for nonprofit, health care co-ops, which constitute something of a compromise between a genuine government insurance option and purely private providers.

Ultimately, Democrats in Congress and President Obama managed to overcome nearly unanimous Republican opposition and enact sweeping health care reform. In Chapters 13 and 14, we detail some of the extraordinary political maneuverings required to enact the Patient Protection and Affordable Care Act (PPACA). Here we merely summarize some of its main provisions. The act extends health care coverage to 32 million uninsured Americans and expands Medicaid to cover families of four that earn less than roughly $29,327 per year.[89] Uninsured and self-employed citizens, as well as small businesses, will be able to buy into state-based insurance plans. By 2014, the act mandates that every American have health insurance, else they pay a yearly fine of $695. Similarly, employers with more than 50 workers will have to provide insurance or pay a yearly fine of $2,000 per worker. The legislation also regulates the practices of insurance companies. Under the PPACA, starting in 2014 insurance companies can no longer deny patients coverage because of preexisting conditions. Moreover, insurance companies are obligated to allow children to stay under their parent's plan until the age of 26.

Just after the president signed the bill into law on March 23, 2010, Senate Majority Leader Harry Reid proclaimed, "We have worked and waited for this moment for over a century. This, of course, was a health bill. But it was also a jobs bill. It was also an

► **HEALTH CARE REFORM**
Flanked by members of Congress and his cabinet, president Barack Obama signs the health care bill in the East Room of the White House on March 23, 2010.

economic recovery bill. It was a deficit reduction bill. It was truly a bill of rights. And now it is the law of the land."[90] Others, though, were not nearly so effusive. Republican opposition remains strong and is increasingly vocal. Raising concerns about its costs and the expansion of government involvement in health care, some opponents began calling for the legislation's repeal just hours after its enactment. The legislation's fate, though, surely depends on its ability to deliver on its promises to reform the U.S. health care system—an eventuality we have yet to witness.

CHAPTER SUMMARY

In this chapter you have learned to:

17-1 Identify the conditions under which policy innovations are created. For social policies to be enacted, problems must be identified, solutions must be suggested, and a focusing event must propel action. Problems are most likely to attract government attention when they raise concerns about national security or equity. Politically viable solutions typically require the backing of organized interest groups. And focusing events can take a wide range of forms, ranging from environmental disasters to high-profile government reports.

17-2 Assess efforts by the federal government to manage the domestic economy. The government regularly monitors the health of the economy, paying particular attention to unemployment rates, inflation trends, and the gross domestic product. Depending on how well the economy is performing, the government may alter fiscal or monetary policy. Some economists recommend that the government intervene in the economy as little as possible, so as to allow markets to adjust to new economic realities.

17-3 Trace the development of the largest federal social program, which assists the elderly. As the backbone of the modern welfare state, Social Security provides a steady income stream to the nation's elderly. During their working lives, individuals pay into the system with the expectation that they can

draw from it when they retire. Over the past 70 years, the number of people paying into the system has increased markedly, but so has the amount of the benefits paid out. This, in combination with recent demographic changes, has raised deep concerns about the program's long-term sustainability.

17-4 Analyze changes in welfare policy within the United States. The U.S. welfare system consists of a patchwork of programs, each of which directs benefits to a different segment of the U.S. population. These programs provide varying levels and types of support, including direct cash transfers and subsidies for life necessities. Whereas most social programs expand over time, welfare has experienced some cutbacks. In 1996, President Clinton fulfilled his campaign promise to "end welfare as we know it" by replacing AFDC with the more restrictive TANF.

17-5 Trace the federal government's expanding involvement in education. Historically, state and local governments assumed primary responsibility for the education of their residents. Although these governments continue to cover the vast majority of education expenses, over the last half-century the federal government has increased its aid to public schools and its regulatory demands on them. Contemporary efforts to reform public schools focus on raising standards and increasing accountability (which further augment the federal government's involvement in public education), and expanding choice and competition (which reduces government regulations over where children attend school).

17-6 Evaluate the government's efforts to provide health care to the poor and aged. More money is spent on health care than any other social program. Total expenditures of the two largest programs, Medicare and Medicaid, reached upward of $800 billion in 2007. Run exclusively by the federal government, Medicare provides medical insurance to the elderly. A joint venture of federal and state governments, Medicaid assists the poor and disabled. Unlike all other major industrialized nations, however, the United States does not provide universal health care. Consequently, approximately 15 percent of the U.S. population lacks any medical coverage.

PEARSON mypoliscilab **EXERCISES**

Apply what you learned in this chapter on MyPoliSciLab.

📖—**Read** on **mypoliscilab.com**

eText: Chapter 17

✓—**Study** and **Review** on **mypoliscilab.com**

Pre-Test
Post-Test
Chapter Exam
Flashcards

👁—**Watch** on **mypoliscilab.com**

Video: Fed Approves Mortgage Crackdown
Video: Economic Policy Debate at the G20
Video: Recession Hits Indiana
Video: The Stimulus Breakdown
Video: America's Aging Population
Video: Raising the Minimum Wage
Video: Health Care Plan

✳—**Explore** on **mypoliscilab.com**

Simulation: You Are an Environmental Activist
Simulation: Making Economic Policy
Simulation: You Are the President and Need to Get a Tax Cut Passed
Comparative: Comparing Economic Policy
Comparative: Comparing Health Systems
Comparative: Comparing Social Welfare Systems
Timeline: Growth of the Budget and Federal Spending
Timeline: The Evolution of Social Welfare Policy
Visual Literacy: Where the Money Goes
Visual Literacy: Evaluating Federal Spending and Economic Policy

---

KEY TERMS

Aid to Families with Dependent
  Children (AFDC), p. 610
charter schools, p. 617
deficit, p. 604
Elementary and Secondary Education
  Act (ESEA), p. 613
entitlements, p. 605
fiscal policy, p. 604
Great Depression, p. 602

Great Society, p. 600
gross domestic product (GDP), p. 603
laissez-faire economics, p. 603
means-tested program, p. 609
Medicaid, p. 622
Medicare, p. 622
monetary policy, p. 603
No Child Left Behind Act
  (NCLB), p. 615

policy entrepreneurs, p. 601
public debt, p. 604
recession, p. 605
Social Security Act, p. 605
Temporary Assistance for Needy
  Families (TANF), p. 610
unfunded mandate, p. 614
vouchers, p. 620

CHAPTER TEST

1. What factors improve the chances that the government will formulate a public policy response to a perceived problem?
2. What role for government intervention into the economy do advocates of fiscal and monetary policy envision?

3. What is the difference between the national deficit and national debt?
4. Why are at least some political analysts worried about the future of Social Security?
5. Historically, what have been the largest federal anti-poverty programs?

6. How has the federal government interjected itself into public education, which historically has been a matter of local and state control?
7. How do charter schools differ from traditional public schools?
8. Who are the primary beneficiaries of the federal government's health care policies Medicare and Medicaid?
9. How does the U.S. health system stack up against those found in other industrialized countries?
10. What were the most significant elements of the health care reforms enacted into law in March 2010?

SUGGESTED READINGS

Nancy Altman. 2005. *The Battle for Social Security: From FDR's Vision to Bush's Gamble*. Hoboken, NJ: Wiley. Reviews the history of Social Security while offering a spirited critique of recent efforts to privatize the program.

John Chubb and Terry Moe. 1990. *Politics, Markets, and America's Schools*. Washington, DC: Brookings Institution. A probing and controversial account of how politics undermines the nation's public schools and of how markets might improve the educational lives of children.

Martin Gilens. 2001. *Why Americans Hate Welfare: Race, Media, and the Politics of Antipoverty Policy*. Chicago: University of Chicago Press. Examines the foundations of public attitudes toward welfare policy and welfare recipients.

Jeffrey Grogger and Lynn Karoly. 2005. *Welfare Reform: Effects of a Decade of Change*. Cambridge, MA: Harvard

University Press. A careful assessment of how the poor have fared under the 1996 welfare reforms.

Jacob Hacker. 2002. *The Divided Welfare State: The Battle over Public and Private Social Benefits in the United States*. New York: Cambridge University Press. Surveys the historical roots of welfare programs, searching to explain why the U.S. welfare state is smaller than its European counterparts.

John Kingdon. 1995. *Agendas, Alternatives, and Public Policies*, 2nd ed. New York: HarperCollins. The preconditions needed for major policy change.

Jonathan Oberlander. 2003. *The Political Life of Medicare*. Chicago: University of Chicago Press. The politics of Medicare and the possibilities for comprehensive health care reform.

SUGGESTED WEBSITES

Social Security Administration: www.ssa.gov

This organization governs the single largest entitlement program run by the federal government.

World Health Organization: www.who.int

This organization oversees global trends in different health indicators.

U.S. Department of Education: www.ed.gov

This department monitors, among other laws, the recently enacted No Child Left Behind Act.

Board of Governors of the Federal Reserve System: www.federalreserve.gov

This agency oversees U.S. monetary policy.

Economics and Statistics Administration: www.economicindicators.gov

A vast array of statistics on the state of the U.S. economy is available at this site.

Robert Wood Johnson Foundation: www.rwjf.org

A private foundation that focuses on issues involving health and health care.

18

Foreign Policy

Afghanistan

When candidate Barack Obama first hit the presidential campaign trail in 2007, the United States was engaged in two wars halfway around the world. In response to the September 11 terrorist attacks, the United States joined a NATO coalition to invade Afghanistan on October 7, 2001. The military forces sought to capture and prosecute those responsible for the attacks while dismantling both the al-Qaeda terrorist organization that had orchestrated the attacks and the Taliban regime that had harbored the group.

On March 20, 2003, President George W. Bush initiated another military campaign, this one in Iraq. Though the initial rationale for the war centered on the country's weapons of mass destruction (WMD) program, investigations soon concluded that Iraq had ended all of its WMD programs in the early 1990s. In this second war, the United States quickly toppled the regime led by Saddam Hussein but soon found itself governing a violent and unstable nation.

Both of these wars exacted increasing financial resources and loss of life. In Afghanistan, the United States maintained close to 26,500 troops on the ground, which constituted roughly 50 percent of the International Security Assistance Force.[1] Another 140,000 U.S. troops continued to patrol Iraq.[2] Bush's last budget proposal for FY2008 brought the total costs for both conflicts to over $800 billion since September 11, 2001.[3] By the end of Bush's presidency, only 25 percent of the American public approved of the Iraq War, and fully 58 percent thought that the war in Afghanistan was going badly.[4]

Picking up on the popular dissatisfaction, Barack Obama campaigned on the theme of change, promising to redirect Bush's foreign policy commitments. "We have to understand that the situation is precarious and urgent in Afghanistan. And I believe this has to be our central focus, the central front on our battle against terrorism," declared Obama on the campaign trail.[5]

The Afghanistan war continued to present profound security challenges.

Both al-Qaeda and the Taliban established operations in Pakistan. Allied forces progressively lost control of the country's provinces, especially in the south.[6] Given the weak and floundering economy, a black-market opium trade had become the driving source of Afghanistan's income, empowering regional drug lords.[7] The sudden increase in illegal wealth led to widespread corruption in President Hamid Karzai's government, to the point where the rule of law did not extend far beyond Kabul, the nation's capital.

Once elected, President Barack Obama declared that he would send 30,000 additional troops to Afghanistan. The plan, crafted with Secretary of Defense Robert Gates, Secretary of State Hillary Clinton, and Chair of the Joint Chiefs Mike Mullen, provided additional forces and posited an explicit goal of transitioning the security responsibility to the Afghan army after 18 months. The president hoped that the timetable would pressure the Afghan government to root out corruption within its ranks while also reducing the number of U.S. troops in the region in time for America's 2012 elections.[8]

A number of congressional Democrats, however, expressed doubts about the president's plan. Senator Carl Levin (D-MI), chair of the Armed Services Committee, stated after returning from a trip to Afghanistan, "I just think we should hold off on a commitment to send more combat troops until these additional steps to strengthen the Afghan security forces are put in motion."[9] Other high-ranking Democrats, including Vice President Biden, echoed calls for accelerating the training of Afghan forces. Still others objected to the war's rising financial costs.[10]

Many Republicans, meanwhile, criticized the president for establishing

▼ UPPING THE ANTE IN AFGHANISTAN.

During his presidency, Barack Obama has significantly increased the number of troops operating in Afghanistan. Upon arrival to Southern Afghanistan in May of 2010, U.S. Marines seen here leave a V-22 Osprey transport helicopter. In your view, was Obama's decision justified?

a "rigid" and "irresponsible" exit date.[11] Several weeks after Barack Obama's announcement, two Senate Republican delegations toured Afghanistan. Upon their return, the senators strongly supported the idea of a troop increase. Senator John McCain, however, firmly rejected the establishment of a fixed timetable, which, in his view, was "artificial, and should only be based by conditions on the ground."[12]

The president, however, remained the single most important political actor in U.S. foreign policy-making. With the strong support of General David Petraeus, who later would have overall command of U.S. forces in the area, the troop increase proceeded as planned. The larger

military plan, crafted in collaboration with the Afghan government, focused heavily on counterinsurgency operations in the south, the training of Afghan security forces, and the integration of Taliban fighters into civil society.[13]

It is difficult to assess how the president's plan is going. On the one hand, U.S. casualties remain high (well over 1,000 as of May 2010), and the Taliban have intensified their efforts to destabilize the government.[14] On the other hand, some signs point toward progress. In February 2010, for instance, 6,000 U.S. marines accompanied Afghan forces in a large and mostly successful invasion of the Mara section of southern Afghanistan, an area overwhelmingly controlled

by the Taliban.[15] Other evidence of progress in the region included the increased attendance at and vibrancy of outdoor markets, and rising attendance of women at the country's 22 universities.[16]

We have yet to see whether U.S. efforts to stabilize Afghanistan and purge the region of al-Qaeda and Taliban influences will ultimately succeed. But the changes in the nation's military and diplomatic operations in Afghanistan reveal important aspects of how U.S. foreign policy is made. In this chapter, we examine the key players in U.S. foreign policy-making, offering examples of some of these policies and the domestic political struggles that they engender.

631

CHAPTER LEARNING OBJECTIVES

After reading this chapter you will be able to:

18-1 Recount the history of U.S. foreign policy.

18-2 Identify the powers of the president to direct foreign policy and the executive agencies that support the president.

18-3 Identify the power of Congress to shape foreign policy.

18-4 Analyze the role of interest groups in foreign policy-making.

18-5 Assess the foreign policy challenges that face the U.S. today.

A Brief History of U.S. Foreign Policy

18-1 Recount the history of U.S. foreign policy.

Since its founding, the United States has formulated **foreign policies** that define its political and economic relationships with other nations. At the heart of foreign policy debates lie concerns about the nation's **grand strategy**, the larger, organizing principles that define national interests, outline possible threats to those interests, and recommend military and diplomatic policies to protect those interests.

Until the twentieth century, the United States followed a grand strategy of **isolationism**, a policy of minimizing the nation's involvement in world affairs. The alternative policy, **internationalism**, is based on the belief that intervention in the affairs of other nations is sometimes necessary to protect one's own interests. The nation's Founders, however, feared that alliances with European countries could entangle the nation in overseas wars—or even worse, draw European wars to the North American continent. As a result, early American leaders sought to distance the country from European politics and conflicts. In his farewell address, President George Washington

foreign policy the mix of military, diplomatic, and economic policies that define U.S. relations with other nations around the world.

grand strategy a plan that determines American national security interests, outlines possible threats to those interests, and recommends military and diplomatic policies to attain them.

isolationism the grand strategy of minimizing a nation's involvement in world affairs.

internationalism the grand strategy of actively engaging in world affairs.

set the tone for this policy, famously urging the country to avoid the mischiefs of foreign intrigue.[17]

Although subsequent presidents stayed out of European affairs, they actively intervened in the Western Hemisphere throughout the nineteenth century. "Manifest Destiny," the belief that the United States should expand across North America, took hold of the nation. In pursuit of this goal, the United States purchased large portions of land from Spain, France, and Britain. The largest such acquisition, the 1803 Louisiana Purchase, more than doubled the size of U.S. territory. The United States tried to seize Canada from Britain in the War of 1812, although this attempt failed. In December 1823, American leaders issued the Monroe Doctrine, a policy statement that warned European countries not to meddle in the Western Hemisphere. The United States fought a war with Mexico from 1846 to 1848, which resulted in the gain of California and other territory in the southwest. By 1900, the United States had become the most powerful country west of the Atlantic Ocean.[18]

In the early twentieth century, U.S. involvement in world politics was sporadic.

At the dawn of the twentieth century, internal and external pressures were forcing American leaders to reconsider their grand strategy of isolationism. Industrialization and the expansion of the financial sector led to increased trade and investment abroad.[19] Economic ties to Europe then grew exponentially with the onset of World War I in 1914. The United States lent money and supplies to Britain and France as they fought Germany in one of the bloodiest wars in modern times. As a result, exports as a share of American national income doubled from 6 percent in 1914 to 12 percent in 1916. In 1916, fully 83 percent of those exports were bound for Britain, France, Italy, and the Russian Empire.[20]

Ultimately, concerns about trade with European allies convinced the United States to enter World War I. The German decision to launch unrestricted submarine warfare in January 1917 jeopardized American shipments to Britain and France. In April, the United States declared war on Germany.[21] The vast resources the United States brought to the war effort sealed the victory over Germany, Austria-Hungary, and the Ottoman Empire in 1918.

World War I officially concluded with the Treaty of Versailles in 1919. Believing that the United States and its allies should use the historic occasion to reshape the world political order, President Woodrow Wilson urged acceptance of his "Fourteen Points" proposal for peace. Wilson called for a new international system based on the principles of democracy, self-determination, and the rule of law. He also championed the establishment of the League of Nations, a collective security institution designed to uphold European peace.

This brief turn toward internationalism in American foreign policy, however, did not last. Although Wilson's ideas received support in Europe, they foundered back home. The American public and many members of Congress were unwilling to give up their vision of a United States that remained apart from European power struggles. In the biggest defeat of his presidency, Wilson failed to secure Senate approval of accession to the League of Nations, and a spirit of isolationism once again infused U.S. foreign policy.[22]

The next 25 years saw great political and economic instability in Europe. The Great Depression, discussed in Chapter 17, devastated European economies. Hyperinflation, massive unemployment, and mandatory reparations established under the Treaty of Versailles brought ruin to the Weimar Republic, the weak democratic government established in Germany after the war. Ultimately, the Weimar government could not survive the turmoil unleashed by the Depression, and the ultra-nationalist Nazi party under Adolf Hitler came to power in 1933. Around the same time, Italy descended into fascism under Benito Mussolini, and Spain became engulfed in civil war. The United States remained largely distant from these developments as it dealt with its own economic difficulties.

As the 1930s wore on, increasingly aggressive Japan, Germany, and Italy brought Europe and Asia to the brink of war. Japan's invasion of China, Italy's invasion of Ethiopia and Albania, and German expansion into Austria and Czechoslovakia raised serious concerns in the United States. Yet optimists hoped that the strong coalition of Russia, France, and Great Britain could contain Germany, Italy, and Japan.

This hope, however, did not materialize. World War II officially began on September 1, 1939, when Germany invaded Poland, provoking a declaration of war from Britain and France. In 1940, Hitler's forces quickly overran France, "divert[ing] the flow of history into darker channels."[23] British forces then departed from the continent at Dunkirk, leaving Western Europe to Hitler's devices. To humiliate the French, who had lost to the Nazis despite superior manpower and materiel, Hitler forced the country's leaders to formally capitulate in the same railcar in which the Germans had surrendered in 1918.[24] The following year, Nazi armies invaded deep into the Soviet Union.

The U.S. president, Franklin Roosevelt, was highly sympathetic to the plight of the British, French, and Soviets.[25] He recognized that a Europe dominated by Hitler posed a great threat to American national security. If Hitler conquered all of Europe, he could readily secure the resources needed to challenge U.S. supremacy in North America. Still, the American public had little appetite for war. Roosevelt was able to assist the allies through his lend-lease program, which provided war materiel to the British, and eventually to the Soviets and Chinese. But even this aid faced resistance in Congress.

Any such hesitancy changed with Japan's surprise attack on Pearl Harbor in the early morning hours of December 7, 1941—a day that President Roosevelt said would "live in infamy." During the battle, Japanese planes damaged or destroyed 347 of the roughly 400 American aircraft stationed on Oahu, Hawaii. In all, 2,400 American service members were killed and 1,200 were injured. Most of the destruction had occurred within a scant 30 minutes.[26]

The attack on Pearl Harbor catapulted the United States into World War II. The United States spent the next four years fighting Germany, Italy, and Japan. Yet, the impact of Pearl Harbor reached far beyond American entry into the war. It ushered in a new era of American leadership in world affairs.

The United States enters the world stage for the long term.

In 1945, the United States and its allies emerged victorious after years of war in Europe and Asia. The war transformed American foreign policy. Politically, isolationism was no longer generally viewed as a viable option. Even though the United States and the Soviet Union had collaborated to defeat Hitler, goodwill between the countries quickly evaporated after the war. The looming presence of the Soviet army in Europe raised fears that an American departure from the continent would lead to Soviet domination. Economically, the United States was the only country to survive the war with its major industries intact. World War II had reduced Europe to shambles. Through the **Marshall Plan**, the United States supported vast reconstruction efforts in Western Europe, helping its war-torn allies to rebuild their economies, with an eye toward bolstering their security against the Soviet communist threat.

Marshall Plan a program that provided aid to rebuild Western European economies after World War II.

North Atlantic Treaty Organization (NATO) established in 1949, a military alliance of the United States and a number of European nations that pledge to join forces against an attack by any external threat.

containment the strategy of guarding against Soviet power by adopting policies that limited the geographic expansion of Soviet power.

Cold War the period, from the late 1940s to the late 1980s, in which the United States and the Soviet Union engaged in diplomatic and economic hostility but not full-fledged war.

Over time, there emerged a new type of conflict that divided Europe along ideological lines. In the east, the Soviet Union established communist satellite governments in Bulgaria, Romania, Yugoslavia, Hungary, Poland, East Germany, and Czechoslovakia.[27] This alliance was formalized by the Warsaw Pact. In Western Europe, the United States constructed a web of democratic allies, including Great Britain, France, the Netherlands, Italy, and West Germany. In 1949, the United States and its allies created the **North Atlantic Treaty Organization (NATO)** to solidify their common defense. Signatories to the NATO treaty pledged to come to each other's aid if attacked by the Soviet Union. Through NATO, the United States maintained a strong combat presence in Europe for over 40 years.

In the late 1940s, the United States adopted a grand strategy of **containment**, a particular type of internationalism meant to counter the threat the Soviet Union posed to Europe and America. Hitler's near takeover of Europe convinced America's leaders that the United States could not afford the rise of a hostile power that spanned the Eurasian continent. Such a country would possess vast economic resources and could threaten the American homeland. Advocated by State Department diplomat George F. Kennan, containment sought to guard against Soviet expansion by adopting policies that checked Soviet power. Kennan thought that the Soviets could not be negotiated with, but that the Soviet economic system bore within itself "the seeds of its own decay, and . . . the sprouting of these seeds is well advanced." The United States needed only to bide its time until the Soviet system of government inevitably faltered. So although the United States would not directly confront the Soviets or their allies, American foreign policy would meet Soviet challenges at every turn.[28]

Tensions ran high between America and the Soviet Union for the better part of 40 years, from the end of World War II until the revolutionary year of 1989. This period has been dubbed the **Cold War**—a state of diplomatic and economic hostility between the superpowers but not open, "hot" warfare. Both sides consistently accused the other of unprovoked aggression as they competed for allies and influence throughout the world. This competition, however, never erupted into direct military confrontation.[29] After nearly 50 years of political upheaval, Europe returned to an era of stability not seen since the early nineteenth century.[30]

While Europe remained in a state of fragile peace, the rest of the world was not so fortunate. Indeed, the first major conflict between the East and West arose in Korea in 1950, when the Soviet-backed government of North Korea invaded South Korea, an American ally. The Korean War, which lasted from 1950 to 1953, confirmed the fears of many Americans that the Soviet Union was determined to spread its power and ideology across the globe. From the standpoint of American foreign policy, the Korean War was the final nail in the coffin of isolationism. Containment was widely viewed as a necessary policy that would require an extensive investment of American blood and treasure.

The United States vastly expanded its involvement in international affairs over the next several decades. The government sponsored coups in Iran (1953), Guatemala (1954), and the Dominican Republic (1956). It aided governments fighting communist insurgencies in the Philippines (1954), Chile (1964), and El Salvador (1980s). And it funded anti-communist insurgencies in Chile (1973), Ghana (1961), Cuba (1960s), and Nicaragua (1980s). American policy makers viewed nearly every problem through the lens of the Cold War. International politics became a zero-sum game between Soviet interests and American ones.

The largest and most extensive conflict in the developing world would unfold in Vietnam, a former French colony. Throughout the late 1950s and early 1960s, the United States sent military aid to South Vietnam in an effort to curb the influence of Soviet-backed North Vietnam and an insurgency group called the National Front for

the Liberation of South Vietnam. South Vietnam's leaders became completely dependent on American military support for their power. This reliance turned much of the population of South Vietnam against its own government. In 1964, after a purported attack by the North on American military personnel, known as the Gulf of Tonkin incident, President Lyndon Johnson asked Congress for the authority needed to conduct "all necessary action to protect our Armed Forces."[31] Congress granted Johnson's request and the Vietnam War began in earnest. At its height, the war would involve over half a million American troops. The war would last until 1973 and result in nearly 60,000 American casualties and another 3 million South and North Vietnamese dead.[32]

The Vietnam War was a watershed event for American foreign policy. It is, after all, the first major foreign war that the United States is perceived to have lost. Many Americans questioned the strategic interests in sending young men and women to fight and die in a distant land. And with television crews for the first time showing the carnage wrought by the war, protests mounted against the emergence of an "imperial presidency" in foreign affairs.[33] Congress, the media, and the public sought ways to restrict the president's foreign policy powers, lest America find itself mired in another unpopular, seemingly unwinnable war.[34]

In the aftermath of Vietnam, both the Soviet Union and the United States started to rethink whether fighting wars in far-off lands was worth the steep costs in money and lives. Many in the United States began to question whether the Soviets presented such a large threat. Meanwhile, the financial costs of the Cold War were taking their toll on the Soviet economy. In response to these changes in both states, a move toward more peaceful relations took place. This period of easing of tensions, known as **détente**, fostered Soviet-American cooperation on issues ranging from agricultural trade to space exploration.

▲ **STORMING THE BEACH HEAD**

While under enemy fire in November 1965, American soldiers of the 7th Marines waded ashore at Cape Batangan, Vietnam. Though the United States had sent thousands of "military advisors" to Vietnam in the early 1960s, the Vietnam War began in earnest in the middle of the decade. How did the nation's experience in Vietnam inform the nation's conduct of subsequent wars in Iraq and Afghanistan?

détente a period of reduced Cold War tensions in the 1970s.

While the 1970s were marked by declining tensions between the Soviet Union and the United States, the era of cooperation would not last forever. The 1979 Soviet invasion of Afghanistan soured relations between the two superpowers. American leaders, especially President Ronald Reagan, viewed the Soviets as aggressively pursuing expansion at the expense of the United States and its allies. Referring to the Soviet Union as the "evil empire," Reagan's administration launched a military buildup that nearly doubled Pentagon spending from 1980 to 1985.[35] This resurgence of Cold War hostilities, however, did not last long.

The Cold War ends, but new conflicts surface.

Nearly as quickly as détente faded, the Cold War came to a close. In 1985, reform-minded Mikhail Gorbachev took over as Soviet premier. Over the next four years, Gorbachev passed numerous political and economic reforms intended to shore up the flagging Soviet economy. He withdrew Soviet troops from Afghanistan, agreed to arms control with the United States, and permitted democratic reform in the member states of the Warsaw Pact. By the end of 1989, the Berlin Wall, which had long divided communist East Berlin from capitalist West Berlin, had fallen. And by the end of 1991, East and West Germany had reunited and the Soviet Union had dissolved.

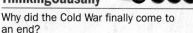

ThinkingCausally

Why did the Cold War finally come to an end?

Scholars continue to argue about why the Cold War ended in the way that it did. Some, echoing Kennan, claim that the demise of the Soviet Union was inevitable. A system of centralized government and tight economic controls simply was not sustainable. Others argue that the inability of the Soviet Union to keep pace with American ingenuity proved decisive. According to this line of argumentation, left to its own devices the Soviet Union might have persisted indefinitely. Competition from the West, however, provided the needed pressure to topple the communist regime. Whatever the precise cause, the peaceful revolutions of 1989–1991 were the most important international events since Pearl Harbor. For four decades, American foreign policy had focused almost exclusively on the Soviet threat. Now the United States was suddenly the world's lone superpower.

The dramatic end of the Cold War spurred a vigorous debate among scholars and policy makers over what America's new grand strategy should be. Four main options arose from this debate. Some proposed a return to isolationism, arguing that geography and the U.S. nuclear arsenal made America secure enough to disengage from Europe. Others advocated a strategy of *selective engagement*, whereby the United States would monitor Europe and the Middle East and intervene only if a clear threat emerged. A third option was *cooperative security*, which envisioned the United States as the leader of a "new world order" that would check aggression anywhere in the world. Finally, some recommended a strategy of American *primacy*, designed to maintain America's overwhelming military and economic power advantage.[36]

In practice, the American grand strategy during the 1990s consisted of a mix of all these policies. The 1991 Persian Gulf War, for instance, combined elements of selective engagement and cooperative security. In 1990, Iraq, then led by President Saddam Hussein, invaded and occupied oil-rich Kuwait. The invasion surprised the international community and drew criticism from nearly every country in the world. By conquering Kuwait, Hussein controlled 20 percent of the world's oil reserves. If he conquered Saudi Arabia next, that number would jump to 40 percent—allowing Hussein to manipulate world oil prices and threaten American interests.[37] The invasion also constituted an act of naked aggression, setting a troubling precedent for the post–Cold War world.

"It was not until September 11, 2001, that U.S. foreign policy makers would fundamentally redefine the grand strategy. The simultaneous attacks that day on the Pentagon and New York's World Trade Center changed the course of American foreign policy."

In response to the invasion, the United States led a United Nations–sponsored military force to liberate Kuwait and drive back Hussein's Iraqi forces. For many, this successful military campaign signaled the beginning of a new collective security system led by the United States and the United Nations. Japan, Russia, and European Union members all participated in some fashion. Many analysts hoped that a newly empowered United Nations could put a stop to territorial aggression, civil wars, and humanitarian disasters. This had been the organization's founding purpose, and in the Persian Gulf War it succeeded.

Unfortunately, cooperative security proved to be short lived. For decades, tensions between the Soviet Union and the United States had kept regional conflicts in check. Local populations dared not provoke either superpower in their desire for independence or domination over other populations. With the Cold War's demise, however, these tensions quickly flared, and the United States found itself involved in regional wars in Somalia, Bosnia, Serbia, Croatia, and Kosovo.

It was not until September 11, 2001, that U.S. foreign policy makers would fundamentally redefine the grand strategy. The simultaneous attacks that day on the Pentagon and New York's World Trade Center changed the course of American foreign policy—focusing attention on terrorist groups and nonstate actors as never before. Turning away from the previous strategy of collective security, President George W. Bush announced a series of principles that collectively would become known as the **Bush Doctrine**. When formulating foreign policy, the president said, the United States would treat nations that harbored terrorists the same as it treated the terrorists themselves. The United States would no longer wait for terrorist activities to occur; it would instead launch preemptive strikes (military and otherwise) against emergent threats. And finally, the United States would not allow the United Nations or any other international organization to dictate when the United States could flex its military muscle. If need be, the United States would wage unilateral wars to protect its interests at home and abroad.

In the immediate aftermath of the attacks, the United States began a war to evict al-Qaeda, the terrorist organization responsible for the September 11 attacks, from its safe haven in Afghanistan. Osama bin Laden and his followers had

Bush Doctrine a grand strategy pursued after September 11, 2001, that emphasized an aggressive posture toward nations that provide safe haven for terrorists, preemptive action, and a willingness to unilaterally launch military actions.

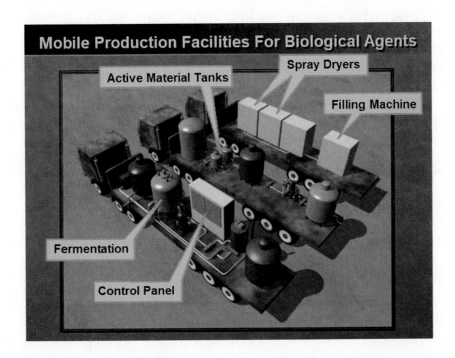

Mobile Production Facilities For Biological Agents

Spray Dryers
Active Material Tanks
Filling Machine
Fermentation
Control Panel

◄ **MAKING THE CASE FOR WEAPONS OF MASS DESTRUCTION**

In February 2003, Secretary of State Colin Powell came before the United Nations Security Council to make the case for war against Iraq. Just over a year later, Powell acknowledged that the "most dramatic" part of his presentation, that which focused on mobile chemical weapons laboratories, was based on flawed intelligence. Shown here is a slide from Powell's presentation. Knowing now that Iraq did not possess WMDs, should the United States nonetheless have invaded the country in 2003?

benefited from ties to the Taliban government, which sympathized with their cause. The Taliban allowed the terrorist group to recruit and train members, as well as plan attacks, from their bases in the country. America's allies and the U.S. public strongly supported the war in Afghanistan, which they saw as a necessary response to September 11.

America's next choice of target, however, stirred controversy. In the spring of 2003, President Bush launched a war against the Saddam Hussein regime in Iraq. The Bush administration based its case for war on intelligence suggesting that Hussein had weapons of mass destruction (WMDs) and ties to al-Qaeda operatives. Bush warned that a preventive war against Iraq was necessary, claiming, "we cannot wait for the final proof—the smoking gun—that could come in the form of a mushroom cloud."[38] Critics argued that the administration was manipulating intelligence, that Hussein had no relationship with al-Qaeda, and that he could be contained through diplomacy.[39]

The initial invasion of Iraq went quite well for the Americans. However, the process of rebuilding the country and achieving political stability there proved far more difficult. Over the first four years of occupation, American forces suffered nearly 4,000 casualties—this after losing only 138 during the initial invasion.[40] Moreover, extensive investigations found no evidence of WMDs in Iraq, suggesting that the rationale for the invasion was misguided. The lack of WMDs and the struggle to stabilize Iraq led to dissatisfaction with the Bush administration over the war. In January 2008, polls showed that only 30 percent of the American public approved of Bush's handling of Iraq.[41]

Even as the United States continues its efforts to stabilize Iraq, new threats and challenges have emerged. These include domestic instability in Pakistan, a nuclear nation and a major American ally in the "war on terror"; concerns over the rising power of a nondemocratic China; the ongoing hostilities in Afghanistan; Russia's backsliding toward totalitarianism; and continued violence between Israelis and Palestinians. At the end of this chapter, we further examine a handful of the many daunting challenges that now face the United States.

The Role of the Foreign Policy Bureaucracy

18-2 Identify the powers of the president to direct foreign policy and the executive agencies that support the president.

No other individual dominates U.S. foreign policy-making as much as the president. As discussed in Chapter 14, presidents exercise extraordinary power in foreign affairs. As commander in chief, the president regularly decides when troops will be deployed, for how long, and what their mission will be. As chief diplomat, the president often holds summits with foreign heads of state about the major issues of the day. As chief administrator, the president appoints many of the individuals who are charged with developing and implementing foreign policy. Serving the president in these various roles is a massive foreign policy bureaucracy.

The National Security Council advises the president.

Thousands of individuals within the executive branch oversee foreign affairs, as discussed in the chapters on the presidency and the bureaucracy. In many ways, the executive agency closest to the president on issues of foreign policy is the

National Security Council (NSC). Formed in 1947, the NSC coordinates the activities of the armed forces and other executive agencies (e.g., the Departments of State and Defense and the CIA) to increase national security cooperation. The NSC assists the president in gathering advice from agencies and departments.

By law, the NSC must include the vice president, the national security advisor, the secretaries of state and defense, and the chair of the Joint Chiefs of Staff. In practice, most presidents have chosen to include more individuals than these. In addition to the formal council, the NSC also includes staff assistants, whose roles have grown in size and importance over the years. Over time, the formal decision-making council of the NSC has declined in importance.

The State Department oversees U.S. diplomacy.

At its core, foreign policy is about **diplomacy**—the ongoing negotiation of economic and political relationships between different countries. Historically, the State Department has held primary responsibility for U.S. diplomacy. The **State Department** is the agency home of diplomats, embassies, and most foreign aid programs run by the U.S. government. The primary job of the State Department is to represent U.S. interests overseas and in various international organizations. In so doing, it communicates with foreign governments and publics, and it provides analysis on events abroad and their implications for American foreign policy. The State Department also negotiates treaties and agreements, makes policy recommendations, and takes steps to implement them. Finally, the department coordinates with the Agency for International Development (USAID) to oversee American foreign aid.

As Figure 18-1 highlights, the State Department operates hundreds of foreign embassies and consulates all over the globe. Roughly 30,000 employees, of which 3,500 are foreign service officers (FSOs), work in these outposts. These FSOs work alongside personnel from other federal departments and agencies, including Defense, Commerce, Agriculture, Homeland Security, USAID, and the Peace Corps.[42]

The State Department is very hierarchical. The secretary of state leads the department and is the most visible and notable figure of American diplomacy. Beneath the secretary is the deputy secretary and then several undersecretaries in charge of planning and coordination. State Department bureaus are organized in two ways: by issue and by region. Some bureaus focus on particular regions, whereas others are tasked with particular issues cutting across regions (such as AIDS policy or counterterrorism). Bureaus charged with regions then coordinate desk officers and personnel who focus on particular countries.

The Defense Department focuses on the military.

The primary responsibility of the **Defense Department** is to defend the nation from external attack. Increasingly, though, the United States also has relied on the Defense Department to pursue a wide variety of other objectives. In just the last two decades, the military has conducted counterterrorism efforts in the Middle East, provided assistance to war-torn areas in Africa, trained other militaries for anti-drug operations in South America, and as we saw at this chapter's outset, struggled to maintain stability in Afghanistan. This expansive set of missions has increased the importance of the American military and raised conflicts between the military and its civilian leaders over the appropriate uses of American military personnel.

continued on page 644 ▶

National Security Council (NSC) an advisory body, formed in 1947 by the National Security Act, that assists the president in gathering information from military services and other security-related executive agencies.

diplomacy the peaceful negotiation of economic and political relationships between different countries.

State Department the agency home of diplomats, embassies, treaty negotiators, and most foreign aid programs run by the U.S. government.

Defense Department the agency created by the National Security Act in 1947 that replaced the Departments of War and the Navy.

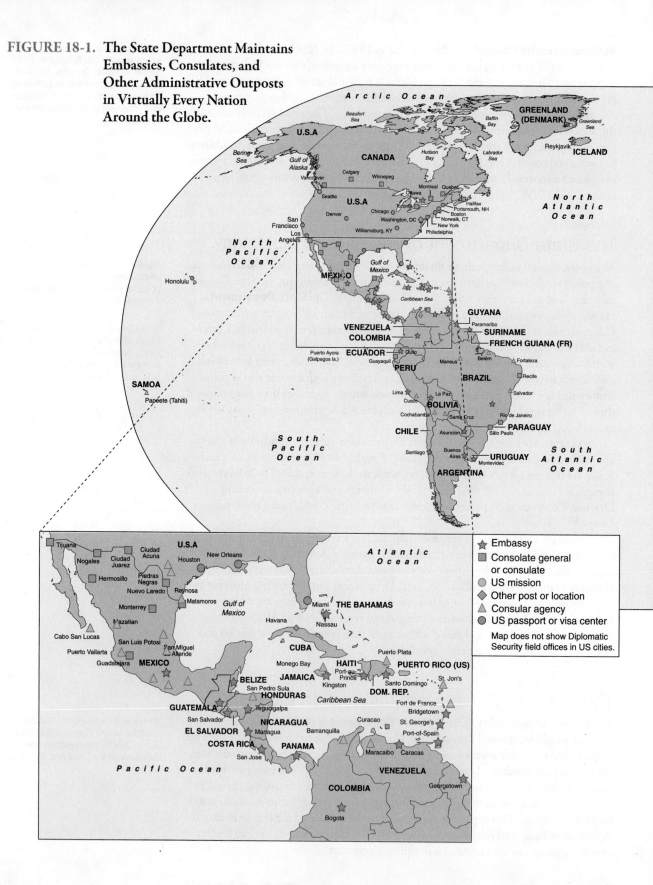

FIGURE 18-1. The State Department Maintains Embassies, Consulates, and Other Administrative Outposts in Virtually Every Nation Around the Globe.

Embassy

Consulate general or consulate

US mission

Other post or location

Consular agency

US passport or visa center

Map does not show Diplomatic Security field offices in US cities.

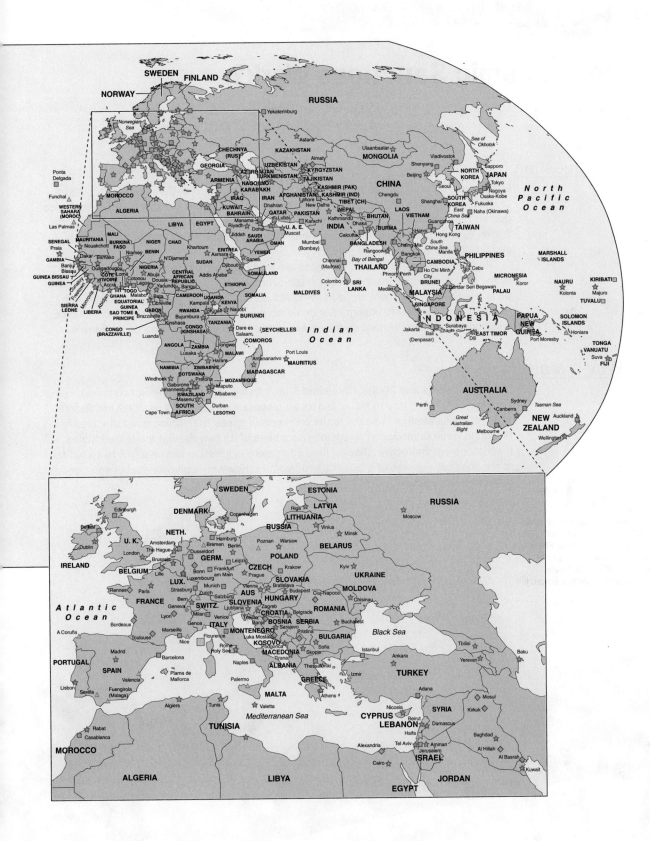

Do Economic Sanctions Work?

The Question

Effective diplomacy includes the right blend of carrots and sticks. Carrots typically consist of things like foreign aid, preferential trade agreements, and promises of military assistance that are meant to reward other governments for doing things that the United States supports. Sticks, by contrast, consist of various forms of punishment that are meant to discourage certain kinds of behaviors and policies.

In foreign affairs, economic sanctions are some of the most frequent sticks employed by the U.S. government against either single countries or groups of countries. Through sanctions, the State Department can pursue objectives ranging from signaling its displeasure toward other countries to undermining domestic support for another government. Although sanctions have a long history, do they achieve their intended goals? How do we know?

Why It Matters

During the 1990s and 2000s, the United States levied sanctions against countries ranging from Iran to Cuba to Iraq to India. And as we discuss in detail below, in 2002 the George W. Bush administration imposed tariffs on imported goods from China and India, leading the World Trade Organization to organize sanctions of its own against the United States. If sanctions are ineffective, though, then other more aggressive tactics might be called for, at the possible expense of U.S. lives and treasure. However, a primary goal of sanctions is to avoid military action.

▶ **NOT TO BE PUSHED AROUND**

While addressing the United Nations General Assembly in 1979, Cuban Premier Fidel Castro points his finger in defiance of a U.S. trade embargo against his country.

Investigating the Answer

How might we determine whether sanctions are effective tools of foreign policy? Scholars began to assess the effectiveness of sanctions by building a large data set that cataloged incidents of sanctions, their goals, and their effects. This initial work, by Gary Hufbauer, Jeffrey Schott, and Kimberly Elliot, found 116 episodes of economic sanctions placed by all states in the world from World War I to 1990.[43] These scholars concluded that sanctions could be effective as long as the goals were modest. Sanctions that were designed to change aspects of a foreign government's trade policies, for instance, stood some chance of success. But sanctions put in place to achieve more difficult goals, such as unseating powerful and entrenched regimes, have not performed as well. Moreover, Hufbauer and his colleagues argued that more recent sanctions have been less successful overall—likely owing to increasing globalization and the ease with which states can find new trade partners to replace those cut off by sanctions.

Numerous scholars, however, have questioned these conclusions. Daniel Drezner has argued that the key to success is the threat of future conflict between the sanctioner and the sanctioned.[44] If sanctions are part of a larger pattern of conflict between states (that is, they are placed after a war or years of disagreement), they are unlikely to work.

Later, Dean Lacy and Emerson Niou challenged the earlier scholars, claiming the sanctions data were incomplete.[45] They argued that potential targets of sanctions, hoping to prevent damage to their economy, may give in to international pressure prior to sanctions' taking effect. If this response is common, then we are likely to see sanctions levied only in the most difficult cases, when the target state does not back down on the threat of sanctions. Because unneeded sanctions are never levied, they are not cataloged in the sanctions data set; therefore, scholars did not account for those instances when the threat of sanctions is sufficient to cause change.

Even if a complete data set of sanctions were assembled, though, it would remain difficult to systematically evaluate their success. How, after all, should analysts go about determining whether sanctions achieved their stated goals? On the one hand, assessment seems straightforward—states adopt sanctions to force other states to change their behavior in reasonably clear ways, and scholars observe whether target states change their behavior or not. On the other hand, however, such assessment is more complicated.

Sanctions, it bears emphasizing, are often multilateral—that is, they are levied by multiple states, frequently with different goals. This fact makes it all the more difficult to assess whether sanctions have succeeded. For example, were the sanctions placed on Iraq after its 1990 invasion of Kuwait successful? They did not bring about a withdrawal from Kuwait—that took a war in 1991 led by the United States and a large coalition of other states. After the war, many states continued the sanctions in order to pressure Saddam Hussein not to attack Kurds and Shiites, to undermine his ability to rebuild his army, and ultimately to unseat him. Not only did states have different justifications for the sanctions, but they also had different assessments of whether the sanctions were working, leading some to lift sanctions against Iraq long before others were willing to do so. Much of the existing scholarship on sanctions has not dealt with this complication. Rather, most scholars continue to use the Hufbauer data, which treats each sanction episode as one unified sender and target, even if multiple states are senders or targets.

Thinking Critically

- When trying to assess whether sanctions work, how should we compare historical cases when sanctions were merely threatened with cases where they were actually imposed?
- Other than sanctions, what foreign policy options are available to the United States when another country behaves in ways that are objectionable? How might we go about evaluating the effectiveness of sanctions vis-à-vis these other options?

The Bottom Line

The debate over the effectiveness of economic sanctions is complex, but it is important. Given the frequent use of sanctions by foreign policy makers, it is crucial to be able to evaluate their effectiveness. The general conclusion is that, under certain circumstances, sanctions can be effective: namely, when the goals are modest, when the sanctions are against an ally, and when the costs to the sanctioned state are very high. Research continues in this area, and future studies will no doubt further refine our knowledge of the conditions under which economic sanctions are likely to be successful.[46]

As shown in Figure 18-2, expenditures by the Department of Defense far eclipse expenditures by the Department of State. Although defense spending has varied with historical events—such as the escalation of the Vietnam War in the mid-1960s and the Reagan buildup of the 1980s—it trends clearly upward. State Department spending has also grown over time, but at a much slower rate.

At the end of the Cold War, military spending fell significantly, creating a small "peace dividend" brought by declining superpower tensions. This trend, however, quickly reversed with the terrorist attacks of 2001. Military expenditures now outstrip even those observed during the Cold War, surpassing $400 billion annually, not even counting the costs of wars in Afghanistan and Iraq. In 2006, the United States accounted for 46 percent of the world's total military expenditures. America now spends more on its military than the next 14 nations combined.[47]

Despite its size, the Defense Department is relatively young. It was created in 1947 to replace the Department of War, a weak institution that did not include the U.S. Navy and usually lay dormant until a ma-

ThinkingComparatively

By international standards, the U.S. military is astoundingly large.

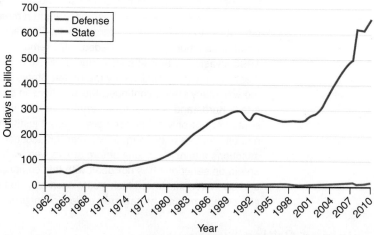

FIGURE 18-2. The Defense Department Has Always Been Bigger than the State Department. Shown here are the annual Defense and State Department outlays between 1962 and 2010. The Defense Department has always had a larger budget than the State Department, but the discrepancy between the two increased substantially beginning in the Reagan administration.

jor conflict arose. In the Cold War era, when the United States sought to meet any threat presented by the Soviet Union, a more permanent military establishment was needed. Thus began the growth of the Department of Defense into the largest executive branch agency—an agency that employed over 35 percent of all federal government workers in 2007.[48]

One of the most influential secretaries of defense in modern times was Donald Rumsfeld, who served under George W. Bush. Rumsfeld argued that recent changes in military technology made large armies less important to military victory. He thus pressured the military to give up its conception of war as battles of attrition and instead focus on becoming a smaller, more mobile, but highly lethal fighting force. Military leaders resisted this goal, as well as Rumsfeld's tendency to micromanage. Rumsfeld resigned in November 2006, the day after Democrats gained control of Congress in that year's midterm election.

Numerous executive agencies provide intelligence services.

To formulate U.S. foreign policy, the government needs reliable information about goings-on around the globe—about the activities and objectives of other states, the creation of new alliances between states and the dissolution of old ones, possible threats to U.S. economic and political interests, and many other things. This "intelligence" crucially facilitates the State Department's diplomatic efforts and the Defense Department's war planning.

Since World War II, the **Central Intelligence Agency (CIA)** has had primary responsibility for collecting and analyzing foreign intelligence. The CIA is a fairly large organization, although the exact size of its budget and staff is classified. The popular conception of the CIA depicts the agency's employees as shadowy figures staging

Central Intelligence Agency (CIA) the cornerstone of U.S. efforts to gather and analyze data in order to confront America's real and potential enemies.

▼ A CIVILIAN LEADER OF THE U.S. MILITARY
On May 7, 2009, U.S. Secretary of Defense Robert Gates spoke to U.S. troops in the Kandahar province of Afghanistan.

cloak-and-dagger operations to overthrow foreign governments. This reputation is not altogether undeserved. In the immediate aftermath of World War II, for instance, the CIA engaged in activities as diverse as influencing election outcomes, sponsoring coups, and assassinating foreign leaders. The CIA's success in these endeavors led to its increased use as an operational foreign policy tool, sometimes replacing traditional military forces.

For the most part, though, CIA employees undertake far more mundane operations: monitoring overseas news for signs of crises, reading and analyzing reports from field offices abroad, briefing executive branch members or Congress of looming threats to American interests, or simply distilling the massive amounts of information it gathers. Historically, the CIA has enjoyed tremendous power and latitude to conduct such operations, yet it is subject to considerable scrutiny and occupies a challenging role. When a surprise event occurs, Congress often holds the CIA accountable for neglecting to anticipate it. If the CIA fails, all Americans see the outcome—a revolution, bombing, or other incident that harms American interests. Yet when the agency succeeds in thwarting secret threats, it receives no public accolades. The CIA must walk a fine line between "crying wolf" and keeping the White House prepared for potential problems.

It is not surprising, then, that the agency received substantial blame for failing to foresee the September 11 terrorist attacks. Some criticisms, though, were perhaps unwarranted. After all, the CIA had been taking steps since the late 1990s to capture al-Qaeda ringleader Osama bin Laden, who justified terrorist methods on the basis of perceived Western imperial designs and Islamic doctrine. During the summer of 2001, American intelligence had intercepted 34 al-Qaeda messages referencing an upcoming event. This "chatter" indicated something was brewing, but it did not provide the date or location of the attack.[49]

The CIA, however, is not the only agency charged with collecting and analyzing national security intelligence. In fact, a veritable alphabet soup of agencies has such responsibilities. The National Security Agency (NSA) is one of the more prominent ones. Formed in 1952, the NSA monitors communications coming into and out of the United States. The NSA also specializes in cryptography—the making and breaking of secret codes.[50] For decades, denial of the agency's existence by the U.S. government led many to quip that NSA stood for "No Such Agency."

The Departments of State and Defense also include their own intelligence arms. The Defense Department operates the Defense Intelligence Agency (DIA). Founded in 1961, the DIA is supposed to supply intelligence and analysis to the secretary of defense and the Joint Chiefs. Similarly, each military service branch conducts its own intelligence activities. The U.S. Army, Navy, Air Force, and Marines regularly contribute to the development of foreign policy strategies. In the State Department, the Bureau of Intelligence and Research (INR) does not gather intelligence directly, but it creates intelligence reports for the secretary of state based on the knowledge of its area experts. Even the Federal Bureau of Investigation (FBI), which is supposed to focus on domestic security issues, is involved in intelligence. The FBI tracks international terrorism suspects who travel to the United States and keeps tabs on any terrorist group that may attempt to find resources in America.

With so many different agencies pursuing overlapping mandates, the foreign policy bureaucracy is neither as efficient nor as effective as many critics would like. In the aftermath of September 11, therefore, the Office of National Intelligence (ONI) was created to oversee the many intelligence agencies in the federal government. In theory, the ONI coordinates the analysis of intelligence from *all* sectors of the intelligence community, including the CIA, FBI, INR, and all Defense Department agencies.

In practice, this goal is difficult, since each agency attempts to protect its turf (and thereby its budget). Although the Office of National Intelligence has worked hard to coordinate the activities of all these executive branch agencies, it continues to encounter significant resistance.

The **Department of Homeland Security (DHS)** was also created in the aftermath of September 11. Like the ONI, the DHS coordinates the work of agencies involved in preventing and responding to attacks on the United States. The director of homeland security is a Cabinet-level official who, in theory, has the power to coordinate intelligence, analysis, and response to strikes against the United States. Creation of the DHS merged 22 agencies with over 177,000 employees. It combined agencies as varied as the Secret Service, U.S. Customs, the Immigration and Naturalization Service (INS), the Federal Emergency Management Agency (FEMA), and the Coast Guard. It has yet to be seen whether the ONI and the DHS, in combination, can effectively coordinate the efforts of their respective agencies charged with collecting the information needed to protect the country.

Department of Homeland Security (DHS) the agency created in the aftermath of September 11 to coordinate the work of agencies involved in preventing and responding to attacks on the United States.

The Role of Congress

18-3 Identify the power of Congress to shape foreign policy.

Presidents stand front and center in debates about foreign policy. Congress, nonetheless, often appears as a worthy adversary. True, legislators may be less involved in foreign policy than in domestic policy, but it would be incorrect to claim, even during the Cold War, that Congress sat silently by, ceding all authority to the president. As we survey the various foreign policy powers of Congress, we will highlight historical examples in which Congress attempted to check presidential influence over foreign policy.

Congress enacts foreign policy statutes.

Congress legislates on a variety of foreign policy topics: weapons programs, foreign aid, environmental standards, and numerous other issues. Sometimes Congress wields influence by crafting legislation. The energy bill that became law in December 2007, for instance, sought to reduce America's dependence on foreign oil by mandating conservation measures, greater fuel efficiency in vehicles, and funding for alternative energy sources. At other times, Congress uses appropriations bills to provide more or less funding than the president has requested for specific projects, ranging from military operations in the Middle East to humanitarian ventures in Southeast Asia.

Members of Congress tend to pay special attention to foreign trade, for it has immediate implications for the nation's economic growth, unemployment, and the cost of goods to the average citizen. The key issue in trade policy concerns **tariffs**, which are taxes on goods exchanged between nations. High tariffs tend to discourage trade, whereas lower tariffs tend to promote it.

tariff a tax on goods exchanged between nations.

The most significant trade agreement in recent history is the **North American Free Trade Agreement (NAFTA)**. NAFTA's roots lie in the 1988 Canada-U.S. Free Trade Agreement, which aimed to steadily decrease tariffs and other barriers to trade and investment between the two countries. In the early 1990s, Mexican President Carlos Salinas expressed strong interest in extending the agreement to his own country. Salinas, U.S. President George H. W. Bush, and Canadian Prime Minister Brian Mulroney worked to build domestic support for the trilateral measure, and the three executives signed NAFTA in December 1992. Bush's failed reelection bid could have

North American Free Trade Agreement (NAFTA) an agreement, signed in 1992, to reduce tariff and nontariff barriers to trade and investment among Canada, Mexico, and the United States.

derailed congressional ratification, but instead the incoming president, Bill Clinton, took up the cause in 1993. In November 1993, NAFTA passed in both the House and the Senate.[51]

ThinkingCausally

How does international trade affect the domestic U.S. economy?

How has NAFTA affected the U.S. economy? Some areas of the country benefit from freer trade because their industries produce goods that are export oriented—that is, most of the goods made are sold overseas. Given that free trade agreements also mean that the other countries in the agreement will cut their own tariffs, this step decreases the price of American goods overseas and leads to more sales. These can increase revenue, create jobs, and cut the costs of goods to consumers. Other industries, though, may suffer from free trade. The increased competition inspired by NAFTA means that domestic factories that are less efficient may close, jobs may be lost, and economic growth may falter. Further, different countries and districts have different specializations, which NAFTA also stands to disrupt. Thus, free trade can be seen as good or as bad, depending on the particular district in question and the country with which the United States is signing the agreement.

Congress also influences the foreign policy-making process through procedural legislation—legislation that changes how institutions in the executive branch are structured or operate on a day-to-day basis. For example, after a number of high-profile military operations were carried out in a haphazard manner, Congress passed the Goldwater-Nichols Act, which mandated that the chair of the Joint Chiefs of Staff be the primary military adviser to the president and be in charge of long-term military planning and budget coordination. It also required that the staff of the Joint Chiefs serve only the chair, rather than the commanders of the individual service branches. With this act, members of

▼ **THE COSTS OF FREE TRADE**

With the reduction of tariff barriers and the rise of globalization, numerous U.S. manufacturing plants have relocated abroad. Here, auto workers rally to keep a domestic Chrysler assembly plant open. How should policymakers weigh the relative costs and benefits of free trade?

Congress hoped to give the chair more institutional powers, thereby reducing interbranch competition for budget and operations and leading to better military advice and performance.

Finally, Congress occasionally enacts symbolic resolutions that have implications for foreign policy. On March 4, 2010, for instance, the House Foreign Affairs Committee passed a resolution labeling as a "genocide" the mass killings of Armenians in Turkey in 1915. Despite last-minute pressure by the Obama administration, the nonbinding resolution passed the committee by a vote of 23–22. Turkey reacted negatively to the vote, endangering the normalization of relations between the two countries.[52]

Congress retains the power to declare war.

Congress's constitutional authority to declare war places it in the middle of debates over proposed uses of force by the American military. Perhaps no area of congressional–presidential politics has received more attention than the question of who has the ultimate authority to initiate and oversee the conduct of war.[53] One reason for the pitched debate is that the Constitution is vague by design: whereas Congress is given the power to declare war, the president is the commander in chief of the military. Consequently, leadership of the military and its mission is divided. By constitutional design, Congress and the president must share the power to initiate and sustain armed conflict against an adversary.

Undoubtedly, the president maintains important advantages over Congress in the realm of military policy. For example, Congress can call hearings to gather information about a potential or actual military conflict; however, a president has the NSC, including all the major military and civilian figures, at his or her beck and call at a moment's notice. As a result, the president is able to respond to foreign crises more quickly—and with more information—than is Congress.

Congress, however, occasionally challenges the president's war powers. In response to what many critics argued was a failed deployment in Vietnam, Congress passed the War Powers Act in 1973. The law, passed over President Nixon's veto, placed several legal constraints on the executive's ability to initiate international conflict. First, the president must consult with Congress *before* committing armed forces into hostile situations. Second, the president must report to Congress within 48 hours after troops are introduced into an area where hostilities exist or are imminent. Third, and most important, the troops must be withdrawn within 60 days unless Congress authorizes them to stay longer.[54]

On paper, the War Powers Act would appear to be a significant constraint on executive authority. In practice, though, the act has constrained presidents less than its designers had hoped. Never has the act been used to end a military venture. Indeed, the 60-day clock has been started only once, after the 1983 invasion of Lebanon. But in that case, Congress immediately approved an 18-month extension. The infrequency of its use has led some scholars to condemn the War Powers Act as "a sellout, a surrender."[55] Other scholars, however, argue that the act has caused at least some presidents to limit military actions to shorter, smaller campaigns—an issue that is examined further in the "How Do We Know?" section of Chapter 13.[56]

ThinkingCausally

Has the War Powers Act aided Congress's efforts to constrain the president's use of the U.S. military on the international stage?

Congress confirms nominees for foreign policy positions.

As explained in Chapter 13, the Senate has the power to confirm individuals nominated to various Cabinet-level and ambassadorial posts. Although the vast majority is

▲ **TESTIFYING ON CAPITOL HILL**

U.S. Ambassador to the United Nations John Bolton testified during a Senate Foreign Relations Committee hearing on October 18, 2005. At the time, the committee was considering plans for restructuring the United Nations.

confirmed, the hearings often reveal pointed disagreements over aspects of foreign policy. Controversy is especially likely when a nominee seems underqualified or espouses views that substantially diverge from the policy positions held by members of the Senate Committee on Foreign Relations, which must first approve the nomination.

Occasionally, a high-profile nominee is rejected or held up to such scrutiny that a president opts to withdraw the nomination. In August 2005, President George W. Bush took advantage of a congressional recess to appoint John Bolton as ambassador to the United Nations until the sitting Congress concluded its business in January 2007. Bolton had faced five months of strong opposition from Senate Democrats, who expressed concern over his confrontational temperament and allegations that he had manipulated intelligence while working at the State Department. The Bush administration cited the large number of recess appointments made by other presidents and portrayed the Bolton decision as a necessary move to avoid further "partisan delaying tactics."[57] Nevertheless, recess appointments for such high-level positions have been rare. Foreign states and international organizations, after all, want to have assurances that the U.S. officials with whom they negotiate have the full backing of the U.S. government.

Congress provides advice and consent on international treaties.

treaty an international agreement in which the United States becomes a party once the president has signed and two-thirds of the Senate has ratified it.

The Senate also has the power to ratify **treaties** signed by the president. There have been several high-profile instances of the Senate rejecting treaties signed by a president, thus dealing a blow to the ongoing conduct of foreign policy. In the most famous instance, as mentioned earlier, the Senate rejection of American involvement in the League of Nations after World War I returned the United States to a course of isolationism for another two decades. In 1999, the Comprehensive Test Ban Treaty (CTBT) was rejected by the U.S. Senate after Republicans objected to several provisions.

executive agreement an international agreement in which the United States becomes a party once the president has signed it, without requiring approval from two-thirds of the Senate.

Rejection is rare, however. In fact, the Senate itself reports that it rejected only 21 of the approximately 1,500 treaties it has considered since 1789.[58] Still, if they are worried about Congress's reaction, presidents can bypass the treaty ratification process by signing an **executive agreement**, which automatically is binding on state signatories. Of the 18,000 international agreements entered into by the United States between 1789 and 2000, only 2,000 have been in the form of a treaty requiring consent of the Senate.[59] As discussed in Chapter 14, the ratio of executive agreements to treaties has steadily increased during the past half-century. Presidents have made executive agreements involving security alliances, trade, finance, and a variety of other areas.

Executive agreements, however, do not allow presidents to do exactly as they please. Congress may pass a law that rescinds an executive agreement, or it may refuse to appropriate the funds needed to implement it. In addition, executive agreements tend to survive for shorter periods of time, as future presidents are free to overturn them unilaterally.

Congress oversees foreign policy bureaucracies.

Congress also influences foreign policy through oversight. At any point, either chamber can convene hearings on topics related to the conduct of foreign policy. Although legislation may or may not result from these fact-finding exercises, the hearings themselves sometimes generate tremendous publicity about issues. This power of investigation can be highly influential in setting the stage for new laws or in simply bringing the public's attention to a particular issue.

In September 2007, for example, General David Petraeus and Ambassador Ryan Crocker provided much-anticipated testimony concerning the ongoing war in Iraq. Democrats and Republicans alike used the hearings to trumpet their positions.[60] Through the hearings, the American public also learned of some nagging uncertainties. Asked whether ethnic reconciliation in Iraq appeared likely, Ambassador Crocker pointed to encouraging signs but admitted, "How long that is going to take and . . . whether it will succeed, I can't predict." When Senator John Warner (R-VA) inquired whether Petraeus's proposed troop surge would make the U.S. safer, the general replied, "Sir, I don't know, actually."[61]

In April 2008 General Petraeus and Ambassador Crocker returned to the Hill to brief Congress on the developing situation in Iraq. In the midst of a contested presidential election, Petraeus pleaded his case for maintaining substantial troops on the ground, claiming that "withdrawing too many forces too quickly could jeopardize the progress of the past year."[62] Senators on both sides of the aisle used the testimony as an opportunity to elaborate their own foreign policy positions. Senator McCain, who would become the Republican nominee for president, called the withdrawal "reckless and irresponsible," while Democratic presidential candidate Senator Clinton warned about

▼ ON THE STREETS OF BAGHDAD

During his presidency, Barack Obama has dramatically reduced the number of U.S. combat soldiers in Iraq. Seen here in March 2009, a U.S. soldier visits with Iraqi children as he patrols a neighborhood in Baghdad.

perpetuating a "same failed policy." George Voinovich (R-OH) claimed that "the American people have had it up to here" with the war and demanded a more precise timeline for withdrawal.[63] Petraeus counseled continued patience, insisting that progress remained possible but that it would require continued military and diplomatic investments.

The Role of Interest Groups

18-4 Analyze the role of interest groups in foreign policy-making.

The federal government does not create foreign policy in a vacuum. Indeed, numerous interest groups weigh in with advice of their own. And given their organization and funding, foreign policy interest groups often exert a tremendous amount of influence. They include three major types: ethnic lobbies, business groups, and think tanks.

Ethnic lobbies advocate foreign policies that concern a specific country.

ethnic lobby an interest group that advocates policies focusing on specific foreign states.

Some of the most prominent foreign policy interest groups are **ethnic lobbies**. These groups advocate policies that focus on specific foreign states. In some instances, ethnic lobbies encourage U.S. assistance to a foreign state. In other instances, they pressure the federal government to take a hard line against the foreign state's governing regime.

One of the more controversial interest groups in American foreign affairs is the American-Israeli Public Affairs Committee (AIPAC). Founded in 1953, AIPAC promotes close ties between Israel and the United States. Detractors have long criticized it for pressuring American decision makers to support and aid Israel even when its policies disrupt American relations with other Middle Eastern countries. However, the close relationship between the United States and Israel would likely have developed and prospered without AIPAC. After all, the United States began sending large quantities of weapons to Israel in the mid-1960s, well before AIPAC was a major player in U.S. politics. Even then, U.S. decision makers saw Israel as one of the few stable, pro-Western allies in a hostile region. The Soviet Union had garnered staunch allies such as Syria and Egypt, and other pro-Western states such as Lebanon and Jordan faced consistent internal threats.[64]

Cuban Americans make up another powerful ethnic lobby. Following Fidel Castro's 1959 communist revolution, many Cubans fled to the United States, particularly to Florida. Initially, the exiles hoped to return to their homeland once democracy had been restored. As Castro solidified one-party communist rule, however, the focus turned to isolating Cuba in the international arena. By 1962, the United States had enacted an economic embargo against its neighbor to the south, and in 1996 the embargo was bolstered by the Helms-Burton Act, which placed even more stringent restrictions on U.S. relations with Cuba.

To be sure, the Cuban American ethnic lobby exhibits a number of characteristics that could contribute to foreign policy influence: it is well organized, geographically concentrated, well funded, and motivated by involuntary exile.[65] However, in light of the anti-communism atmosphere of the Cold War, one could question whether the lobby was decisive in U.S. efforts to isolate Cuba. Just because American foreign policy choices support the interests of a pressure group does not mean the pressure group was instrumental in the outcome. Consider the classic political science

ThinkingCausally

Do ethnic lobbies dictate foreign policy between the United States and other countries?

definition of power paraphrased from the political scientist Robert Dahl: power is the ability to convince others to do things they would otherwise not do.[66] To show that an interest group has power or influence, one must show that a policy would have been different without the group's pressure. This is difficult to determine, for it requires us to intuit how the world would differ in the absence of a particular interest group.

Business groups increasingly attempt to influence foreign policy.

Perhaps the most powerful set of foreign policy pressures arises from multinational business and defense firms. Traditionally, some of the more powerful lobbying groups in America have been those involved in the production and sale of military goods. In his farewell address, President Eisenhower warned against "the acquisition of unwanted influence, whether sought or unsought, by the military-industrial complex."[67] The "military-industrial complex" has become a pejorative catchphrase used by those who oppose the influence of big business, especially in the realm of national security policy.

The phrase suggests a handful of business and military elites conspiring to drive up (possibly unnecessary) defense spending. The fact is, though, that numerous segments of American society—including Congress, academia, business, and the military establishment—have aligned interests concerning defense spending. Various interests clearly benefit from defense spending: the military can be ready to defend the national interest, businesses can make money and spur economic growth, individuals can find and keep jobs, and each of these benefits helps members of Congress get reelected. One analysis of defense spending during the Cold War concluded that 1 in 10 jobs in the United States relied, either directly or indirectly, on federal defense spending.[68] At a time when defense budgets are nearing $500 billion, the dependence of many businesses on defense spending is clearly enormous.

> "One analysis of defense spending during the Cold War concluded that 1 in 10 jobs in the United States relied, either directly or indirectly, on federal defense spending."

Other businesses lobby the government on a host of foreign policy issues, but perhaps no issue is more common than trade. As previously discussed, because so many individuals benefit *and* suffer from trade, thousands of industry-based groups have formed to lobby Congress and the president for more or less protection. Each time free trade discussions begin with a new country, lobbying groups support or oppose the proposals, based on whether their industries will be helped or harmed.[69]

Think tanks offer foreign policy advice.

Think tanks support and publicize the work of scholars, many of whom have significant foreign policy expertise. Drawing on their government experience or academic research, these scholars contribute to newsletters, magazines, journals, and opinion pieces advocating particular policies. Under certain circumstances, their opinions resonate widely.

One of America's most prominent think tanks is the New York-based Council on Foreign Relations (CFR), which publishes the influential journal *Foreign Affairs*. Founded in 1921, the CFR grew out of an informal band of foreign policy experts who advised President Woodrow Wilson toward the end of World War I. In planning for a postwar world, this group helped to formulate Wilson's Fourteen Points initiative, planting the seed for the United Nations and other innovations in international relations. Following World War II, the CFR again demonstrated its influence. In an anonymous *Foreign Affairs* article, George Kennan—a council member and State Department official—made the case that the United States should limit the Soviet Union's expansionist tendencies.[70] Containment, as discussed above, became the key American grand strategy during the Cold War.

The Council on Foreign Relations is not alone in offering foreign policy insights. In July 2007, two members of the Brookings Institution, a left-of-center think tank based in Washington, D.C., published a striking op-ed in the *New York Times*. Following an eight-day visit to Iraq, Michael O'Hanlan and Kenneth Pollack praised the "surge" in U.S. troop levels and chided opponents for ignoring encouraging changes. "We are finally getting somewhere in Iraq, at least in military terms," they declared.[71] The opinion piece drew attention to improvements that numerous observers had overlooked. Because it was written by critics of George W. Bush's prior handling of the Iraq War, the opinion piece had a dramatic influence on Washington debates about the war.

CaseStudy: Interest Groups Call for Funds to Combat AIDS in Africa

In early 2003, President George W. Bush announced a major effort to fight AIDS overseas. The president's Emergency Plan for AIDS Relief focused on 15 countries: Botswana, Cote d'Ivoire, Ethiopia, Kenya, Mozambique, Namibia, Nigeria, Rwanda, South Africa, Tanzania, Uganda, Zambia, Haiti, Guyana, and Vietnam. The initiative, which called for $15 billion over five years to fund prevention, treatment, and orphan care, surpassed the aid of any previous administration.[72] In 2008, Congress enthusiastically exceeded Bush's request by another $4 billion.[73]

Congress is not always so eager to provide such generous allotments of foreign aid. Only a few years earlier, the Clinton administration fought with Congress to secure just $225 million in global AIDS spending.[74] What explains such a remarkable turn of events? Interest groups, it seems, put pressure on the president and congressional leaders to do something about the spread of AIDS in developing countries. The most prominent of these interest groups, however, were not ethnic lobbies, business groups, or think tanks. Rather, they consisted of Christian organizations and an especially entrepreneurial rock star.

In February 2002, Franklin Graham—the son of evangelist Billy Graham and founder of the charity Samaritan's Purse—sponsored the first "international Christian conference on HIV/AIDS." Graham announced that it was his Christian duty to "bring healing, to bring love, to bring compassion" to the sick and dying.[75]

Bono, the lead singer of the Irish rock band U2, subsequently advocated for combating AIDS, framing the issue as a moral imperative for Christians. In a meeting with conservative Senator Jesse Helms (R-SC), Bono pointed out that 2,103 verses of Scripture pertain to the poor, but Jesus mentions judgment only once.[76] Helms was moved by such

arguments. In March, the influential senator published an op-ed piece in the *Washington Post* renouncing his lifelong skepticism of foreign aid and arguing for increased federal government spending on programs to combat AIDS abroad. This development was "like Nixon going to China," according to Patrick Cronin, a former assistant administrator at the Agency for International Development.[77]

Other conservative politicians also played instrumental roles. Senator Jeff Sessions (R-AL) held two congressional hearings about the role of unsafe health care in spreading the disease.[78] Senator Bill Frist (R-TN), a physician, co-sponsored a bill offering millions of dollars to prevent mother-to-child transmissions. In addition, key members of the Bush administration embraced the issue. Chief of Staff Josh Bolten and National Security Advisor Condoleezza Rice supported expanding foreign aid to fight AIDS.[79] Treasury Secretary Paul O'Neill ended his fact-finding trip to Africa by concluding that "there could no longer be any excuse for failure to address the basic needs of the world's poorest people."[80] President Bush himself compared AIDS to genocide, implying that fighting it was a moral imperative.[81] Expressing solidarity with his religious constituents, he declared that "everybody has worth, everybody matters, everybody was created by the Almighty."[82]

The president also had strategic reasons for backing the policy. In 2002, Bush highlighted the danger of allowing Africa to become a haven for terrorists.[83] Bush further hoped that AIDS relief would improve America's tarnished international reputation. Among members of the Organization for Economic Cooperation and Development, the United States had ranked last or near last in terms of foreign development aid as a percentage of gross national income (GNI) for many years. Whereas countries such as Denmark, the Netherlands, Sweden, Norway, and Luxembourg donated around 1

▲ WALK ON, AFRICA
Bono is greeted at a school in South Africa. In May 2006, the Irish rock star toured six African nations in an attempt to draw attention to the issues of HIV and AIDS. In your view, how successful are celebrities in drawing attention to global issues?

percent of their GNI, the United States contributed only about *one-tenth of* 1 percent.[84]

The administration and its congressional allies brought more than rhetoric to the table. Republican leaders introduced an ambitious five-year, $15 billion plan that moved beyond mother-to-child transmission and the traditional focus on prevention. The resulting legislation—the U.S. Leadership Against HIV/AIDS, Tuberculosis, and Malaria Act of 2003— allocated 55 percent of the funds to treatment, 20 percent to prevention, 15 percent to care for the dying, and 10 percent to orphans.[85] It aimed to treat 2 million people, provide care for 10 million, and prevent 7 million new infections.[86]

The increase in foreign assistance to combat AIDS shows how the preferences of an interest group can align with broader strategic goals held by the executive or legislative branch. Would AIDS have become a major priority without pressure from religious organizations? Possibly, but this pressure certainly helped.

ThinkingCritically

1. What other opportunities are there for religious organizations to join forces with other interest groups in order to further influence U.S. commitments of foreign aid?

2. What are some other ways in which religious organizations affect U.S. foreign policy?

Contemporary Foreign Policy Challenges

18-5 Assess the foreign policy challenges that face the U.S. today.

The United States continues to face extraordinary foreign policy challenges. It oversees a remarkably complex and dangerous international environment. And because the United States is the world's only superpower, foreign nations regularly look to it to formulate solutions. This section highlights recent efforts of presidents, the foreign policy bureaucracy, Congress, interest groups, and other domestic political actors to confront three of the many critical foreign policy challenges faced by the United States today: how to reduce the threats of a North Korean nuclear program; how to balance the costs and benefits of free trade; and how to handle individuals who are suspected of terrorist activities.

Diplomatic efforts to halt North Korea's nuclear program have not proceeded smoothly.

On August 6, 1945, during World War II, a U.S. military plane dropped an atomic bomb code-named "Little Boy" that leveled the Japanese city of Hiroshima, killing tens of thousands almost immediately. Three days later, another U.S. plane dropped the atomic bomb code-named "Fat Man" on the Japanese city of Nagasaki. The United States thereby became the first—and to date the only—country to use a nuclear weapon against another country. The demonstration of such weapons' devastating strength, coupled with the crystalizing Cold War, fueled an international race for nuclear weapons. In 1949, the Soviet Union tested bombs of its own. By 1964, the United Kingdom, France, and China had acquired nuclear capabilities. Developments in rocket science made the specter of nuclear-armed states, able to project their power to far corners of the globe, much more real. And U.S. foreign policy needed to contend not only with the ramifications of America's own nuclear capability but also with that of its allies and rivals.

Some observers saw this dilemma as a benefit for U.S. foreign policy. Perhaps the overwhelming might of nuclear weapons actually made them integral for *deterring* open hostilities between the East and West. By pursuing certain tactics—such as dividing up arsenals and placing warheads in underground facilities—nuclear powers could maintain second-strike capabilities. Thus, states would think hard about offensive moves, for while the instigator might wreak havoc on its enemy, it would bring similarly devastating retaliation upon itself. This notion of "mutually assured destruction" may be one of the key reasons why the Cold War remained cold.

Diplomatic efforts to stem the proliferation of nuclear weapons were codified in the Nuclear Non-Proliferation Treaty, which opened for signature in 1968. The United States, the United Kingdom, and the Soviet Union signed almost immediately. The treaty stipulates that nonnuclear countries will not seek nuclear capabilities, pre-existing nuclear states will not facilitate proliferation to more states, countries can acquire nuclear technology for peaceful uses such as energy, and all will work toward a somewhat vague disarmament goal. Currently, 189 different countries are signatories.[87]

ThinkingComparatively

Over time, different countries have come to different conclusions about the benefits of a nuclear program.

Still, considerable uncertainties persisted. Miscalculations, laxity, or accidents in *any* of the five nuclear-capable states promised dire consequences. Moreover, nonnuclear countries reacted strongly. Although some called for total disarmament, others were eager to obtain nuclear power for themselves. During the 1970s, 1980s, and 1990s, countries such as South Africa, Libya, and Iraq launched, and then subsequently abandoned, efforts to acquire nuclear weapons. More recently, other countries, such as Iran and North Korea, have been accused of concealing weapons development behind civilian energy programs.

Since the end of the Cold War, concerns about nuclear proliferation have only intensified. The breakup of the Soviet Union scattered a massive stockpile among the newly independent countries. Even though much of the arsenal has been returned to Russia, part remains missing. And ensuring the stability of nuclear states such as Pakistan and ascertaining the motivations of "rogue states" are key priorities in U.S. foreign policy.

North Korea represents a key challenge for U.S. efforts to hinder the proliferation of nuclear weapons. Since the Korean War, relations between the United States and North Korea have fluctuated between strained and nonexistent. In 1990, satellite photos revealed a facility that appeared capable of producing weapons-grade plutonium from fuel rods. Deeply concerned, the United States, South Korea, and a number of other countries pushed for United Nations sanctions. The Clinton administration also engaged North Korean president Kim Il-Sung diplomatically, reaching a pact called the "Agreed Framework" in late 1994.[88]

Neither side, however, fulfilled all of its obligations. In the aftermath of the terrorist attacks of September 11, 2001, new intelligence indicated that North Korea was still pursuing a nuclear weapons program. In his 2002 State of the Union Address, President Bush denounced the developments and designated North Korea (as well as Iraq and Iran, which also were suspected of developing nuclear weapons) as a lynchpin of the "Axis of Evil."[89] A year later, North Korea announced its withdrawal from the Nuclear Non-Proliferation Treaty, declaring that it absolutely needed nuclear weapons to protect itself from U.S. "hostility."[90]

657

▲ **TENSIONS RISE AGAIN**
On July 2, 2009, North Korea test launched two short-range missiles, further heightening tensions in the region. Here, two South Koreans watch a televised broadcast of the event.

In 2007, North Korea detonated a nuclear bomb in an underground test. The following year, in return for fuel oil, North Korea agreed to dismantle its facilities and disclose its nuclear programs, and President Bush held out the prospect of open trade and political engagement if North Korea upheld its obligations under the agreement. Further signs of progress surfaced in June 2008, as the cooling tower at the country's main nuclear weapons plant was destroyed—a visible indication that Kim Jong-Il was willing to back off from his nuclear program. President Bush called the event "a moment of opportunity for North Korea," and presumably the United States as well.

Tensions between North Korea and the United States resurfaced in April 2009, however, when North Korea test-launched a long-range ballistic missile. As an early challenge for President Obama, all eyes were on Washington to see how the new administration would respond. Obama criticized Kim's violations of international law and declared that "now is the time for a strong international response."[91] It proved difficult to turn words into actions, however, as the United States failed to rally the United Nations to punish North Korea for its actions.

Secretary of State Hillary Clinton subsequently offered to reconvene talks, but North Korea rejected the invitation, further isolating itself from the United States. In May 2009, news broke that North Korea successfully tested its second nuclear weapon. This time, the international response was much stronger as many nations condemned the test. Obama used the event to strengthen ties with South Korea and other international allies. The United Nations Security Council tightened sanctions on North Korea, and Japan enacted additional economic sanctions on exports to the country.[92] If past is prologue, the rest of Obama's presidency is likely to witness a continued rocky relationship between North Korea and the United States.

Domestic lobbying groups push for protective tariffs.

The United States has been a vocal advocate of "free trade," which involves lowering or eliminating tariffs and other mechanisms that impede the movement of goods and services. Certainly, freer trade increases consumer choices, but there is a precise economic rationale as well. In his 1776 book *The Wealth of Nations*, the economist Adam Smith argued that countries should export according to their relative advantage. Thus, if Britain was the lowest-cost producer of wool while Portugal was the lowest-cost producer of port wine, then the former should export wool in exchange for the latter's wine, and both parties would be better for it.

As Smith makes clear, free trade has a powerful economic justification. But political realities complicate matters. Widespread exchange, after all, involves reliance on other countries. Some sectors, most obviously weapons producers, raise important security concerns that can prompt governments to entertain less-efficient domestic production in order to avoid such dependence.[93] Furthermore, even when gains from trade outweigh losses, those gains and losses may not be equally distributed across different populations. Widespread unemployment in a particular part of the country, for instance, can affect everything from crime rates to electoral fortunes. And when politically connected groups sustain significant losses, they make sure that politicians take notice.

As a result, even countries that advocate free trade may pursue selective **protectionism**—that is, the imposition of specific tariffs to protect the interests of domestic industries. The case of U.S. steel tariffs illustrates this point well. In the late 1990s, a number of countries in Asia and elsewhere suffered financial crises that diminished the value of their currencies. The devaluation made exports from those countries relatively cheap and encouraged companies to sell their products quickly before their home currencies fell even further. Many tried to sell to the world's largest economy, the United States, which relies on steel to manufacture all sorts of products. This abundance caused a drop in steel prices, benefiting steel consumers but hurting U.S. steel producers.

Economists estimated that low steel prices resulted in higher gains than losses for the economy as a whole. Lots of consumers enjoyed small gains, but a reasonably small but well-organized group of producers suffered substantial losses. Labor (represented by unions) and capital (represented by producers' associations) in the steel sector teamed up to petition the Clinton administration for help. They accused South Korea, Russia, and others of "dumping," an outlawed practice in which countries sell exports for less than their production cost or home-market price.[94] Politicians from steel-producing states also joined the chorus, frequently advancing concerns about national security.

President Clinton, however, remained unconvinced that the steel producers had a strong legal case, and he declined to take action. Given traditional alliances between blue-collar labor and the Democratic Party, many lobbyists felt betrayed by Clinton and his vice president, Al Gore. In the closely contested 2000 presidential election, some citizens used their vote to punish the Democrats. Indeed, the Republican candidate, George W. Bush, defeated Gore in steel-producing states such as Indiana, Ohio, and West Virginia.

In the spring of 2001, just months after Bush took office, steel lobbyists launched another political offensive.[95] This time, the lobbyists met with greater success. The Bush administration anticipated political payoffs from siding with steel producers—including inroads with traditionally Democratic voters and 2002 midterm election support in key states such as Pennsylvania and Ohio. He initiated a move that gave the International Trade Commission, an independent American panel, six months to investigate the allegations and provide recommendations to the White House.[96]

In December, American steel production was still hemorrhaging. Prices had dropped by about one-third during 2001, and numerous companies—including the giant Bethlehem Steel—were declaring bankruptcy.[97] The International Trade Commission, having determined that imports had injured the U.S. industry, recommended

protectionism the practice of imposing selective tariffs on trade in an effort to protect specific domestic industries from international competition.

that the president impose import quotas, as well as tariffs ranging from 15 to 40 percent.[98]

The administration struggled to determine its course of action, given a wide range of reactions from advisors and congressional leaders. In March 2002, the president finally decided on three-year tariffs as high as 30 percent (depending on the type of steel) against countries such as Japan, China, South Korea, Russia, Ukraine, and Brazil. He asserted that the action was within the World Trade Organization (WTO) allowance for temporary "safeguard provisions" and exempted many developing nations, in addition to NAFTA trading partners Canada and Mexico.[99]

▲ **THE GOVERNMENT BACKS STEEL**

Early in his first term, President Bush sought to protect the domestic steel industry by increasing tariffs on foreign production. Subsequent retaliatory actions by the World Trade Organization, however, led to the retraction of the U.S. tariffs. In your view, when should the federal government take steps to protect domestic industries from foreign competition?

This action, however, did not permanently resolve matters. In fact, an all-out trade war loomed. Almost immediately, China—the world's largest steel producer—filed a complaint with the World Trade Organization. Then the European Union, Japan, and China threatened to impose tariffs on other U.S. goods without waiting for the WTO's ruling, accurately pointing out that U.S. steel imports had in fact declined rather than risen over the past three years. Russia hinted that the tariffs would reduce its willingness to cooperate in the war on terror.[100]

In November 2002, the WTO rejected the U.S. government's protectionist policies, authorizing other countries to impose countervailing tariffs as punishment. The following month, the Bush administration relented. Facing a full-blown trade war, Bush repealed the tariffs 15 months before their scheduled expiration.[101]

This episode reveals important lessons about the politics of trade. Despite the economic rationality of free trade, political realities may lead to selective protectionism. The steel case highlights a number of reasons for this: national security concerns, powerful interest groups, and the difficulties of transferring workers from one industry to another. As Gary Hufbauer of the Institute for International Economics points out, a free trade president who seeks quotas and tariffs may be uncharacteristic, "but it's a way of trying to keep moving on the bigger goal while dealing with the truly squeaky wheels—and steel is truly a squeaky wheel."[102]

ThinkingComparatively

Other countries occasionally protest against U.S. protectionist policies.

The president, Congress, and the courts argue about the legal status of "enemy combatants."

The September 11 terrorist attacks spurred the Bush administration into a new kind of war, an ongoing "global war on terrorism." President Bush has called this struggle "a different kind of conflict with a different kind of enemy," a war "without battlefields or beachheads."[103] As a multifaceted initiative, the war on terrorism has included diplomatic efforts to freeze terrorist assets overseas, tougher law enforcement at home and abroad, and heightened homeland security.

Many aspects of the war on terrorism have garnered broad support. A few, however, have provoked significant political controversy. One of the most heated debates concerns the legal rights of U.S. citizens who are accused of plotting terrorist attacks or fighting for al-Qaeda, the organization responsible for the 9/11 attacks. The Bush administration contends that these individuals should be recognized as "enemy combatants" who can be detained indefinitely under the auspices of military law. Critics, however, claim that the "enemy combatant" designation deprives suspects of their civil right to due process, and that they should be tried in civilian courts under the U.S. criminal justice system.

This debate has provoked legal battles that have made it all the way to the Supreme Court, with members of the president's administration, the foreign policy bureaucracy, Congress, and numerous interest groups all weighing in. One of the first important cases was *Hamdi v. Rumsfeld*. At issue was the fate of Yaser Esam Hamdi, an American citizen who was captured in Afghanistan in November 2001. Government officials claimed he was carrying an assault weapon when he surrendered to the Northern Alliance, an ally of the United States. But his father, Esam Fouad Hamdi, insisted that his son had traveled to Afghanistan only for religious study and humanitarian work.

Originally sent to the U.S. Navy base in Guantanamo Bay, Cuba, Hamdi was transferred to a military brig in Norfolk, Virginia, upon confirmation of his U.S. citizenship. There he was held for years without any charges filed against him. Hamdi's case entered the U.S. court system when his father filed a petition for a writ of habeas corpus on his behalf, requesting a chance for Hamdi to contest his designation as an enemy combatant in court. In 2004, the case came before the Supreme Court.[104]

The administration's case rested on a few key claims. First, government lawyers insisted that the president's constitutional war powers gave Bush the right to designate citizens as enemy combatants and detain them. Second, the 2001 congressional Authorization on the Use of Military Force (AUMF) explicitly delegated authority to the president to exercise "all necessary and appropriate force" against "persons" and organizations involved in terrorist actions against the United States. The government counsel claimed the AUMF authority included the detention of citizens. Finally, the administration and its supporters insisted that national security concerns dictated the selective use of military detentions.

Hamdi's public defender vehemently objected to the claim that an American citizen could be denied both access to an attorney and a habeas review simply by being declared an enemy combatant. He further argued that if the AUMF permitted the president to hold suspects without trial indefinitely, "we could have people locked up all over the country tomorrow without any due process, without any opportunity to be heard. There is no indication that Congress intended any such thing."[105] Several civil liberties groups and lawyers' organizations also backed Hamdi.[106]

In its decision in *Hamdi v. Rumsfeld*, the Court ruled against the administration.[107] The justices found that suspects retained the right to contest the charges against them before a "neutral decision maker." The Court, however, set aside deeper questions about the limits of presidential power in wartime. It argued that AUMF did in fact permit the president to detain enemy combatants, but said nothing about whether that authority held in absence of an explicit congressional authorization. Hamdi himself, however, never got his day in court. Following the Supreme Court ruling, the administration released Hamdi to Saudi Arabia in exchange for renouncing his U.S. citizenship.[108]

The Court's decision in *Hamdi v. Rumsfeld*, while significant, was far from the last word in the conflict between national security and civil liberties. The following year, Congress got involved through passage of the Detainee Treatment Act of 2005. The law sought to reaffirm the president's wartime power by limiting the judiciary's ability to intervene in matters involving military tribunals, and by preventing it from hearing habeas petitions filed by Guantanamo detainees.

The Detainee Treatment Act faltered under legal challenge just one year later, in yet another landmark Supreme Court ruling. The central protagonist in *Hamdan v. Rumsfeld* was a Yemeni citizen, Salim Ahmed Hamdan, who had been captured in Afghanistan and was suspected of being Osama bin Laden's bodyguard and driver. Hamdan was among the first Guantanamo prisoners to be tried in a military commission. But before the commission issued a ruling, Hamdan appealed to the U.S. civilian court system by filing a writ of habeas corpus that claimed the special military courts were illegal. Eventually, his case made its way up to the Supreme Court.

The Supreme Court found that the 2005 Detainee Treatment Act could not strip the Court of jurisdiction over cases, including Hamdan's, that were already pending in the federal courts system at the time the law was passed. Moreover, the Court found that the 2001 AUMF declaration by Congress did not give the president authority to try detainees under military tribunals.[109]

The Court's ruling appeared to present the president with two options: try the detainees using the regular process of military court-martial or get express permission from Congress to use different means. In its wake, the administration and its supporters opted to collaborate with Congress.[110] A few months later, Congress enacted the Military Commissions Act, which specifically granted presidential authority to try detainees under special military commissions.

But again the Supreme Court halted the administration in its tracks. In an extraordinary case involving Lakhdar Boumediene, a detainee from Bosnia-Herzegovina, the Court went farther than it ever had before in challenging the system of military commissions. The Court in June 2008 decided that the Military Commissions Act amounted to unlawful suspension of habeas corpus. This decision paved the way for Guantanamo prisoners to challenge their detainment in civilian courts.[111] *Boumediene v. Bush* dealt a heavy blow to the administration's anti-terrorism policies.[112] Immediately after the court's ruling, the defense lawyers for several other detainees filed legal challenges in U.S. civilian courts.

The appropriate tradeoff between national security and civil liberties continues to attract widespread attention in the war on terror. And considering the long period the United States expects to be engaged in this global struggle, the question of legal status of detainees will loom large for some time to come. Without a doubt, we can expect members of all three branches of government, as well as a wide variety of organized interest groups, to continue to participate in the ongoing debate.

CHAPTER SUMMARY

In this chapter you have learned to:

18-1 Recount the history of U.S. foreign policy.
Throughout the nineteenth century, U.S. foreign policy was guided by a grand strategy of isolationism. After fighting two world wars in the first half of the twentieth century, the country was gripped by a new spirit of internationalism. During the Cold War, the United States sought to contain the spread of communism, but it never fought directly against the Soviet Union. Since the Cold War ended in 1989, the United States has been the world's only superpower, with economic and military interests that span the globe.

18-2 Describe the powers of the president to direct foreign policy, and identify the executive agencies that support the president.
As commander in chief, chief diplomat, and chief administrator, the president has extraordinary powers and responsibilities in foreign policy. Moreover, a vast network of agencies and departments assists the president in formulating and implementing his foreign policy agenda.

18-3 Understand congressional efforts to shape foreign policy.
Congress has a variety of means at its disposal to influence U.S. foreign policy-making. By enacting statutes, retaining the power to declare war, confirming bureaucratic nominees,

ratifying treaties, and exercising its oversight responsibilities, Congress can influence U.S. foreign policy in important ways.

18-4 Understand the role of interest groups in foreign policy-making.
Interest groups also contribute to foreign policy. Business groups, ethnic lobbies, and think tanks, in particular, can provide important insights. They also can shape national conversations about particularly pressing foreign policy issues; in so doing, they occasionally put pressure on Congress to challenge presidential powers in foreign policy.

18-5 Probe the foreign policy challenges that face the United States today.
Presidents, officials in the State and Defense Departments, Congress, a wide variety of interest groups, and the courts all participate in ongoing foreign policy debates. Issues range from the spread of nuclear weapons to the protection of U.S. industries against foreign competition to the legal status of enemy combatants in the ongoing war against terrorism.

---

mypoliscilab EXERCISES

Apply what you learned in this chapter by starting with these resources on MyPoliSciLab.

Read on mypoliscilab.com

  eText: Chapter 18

Study and Review on mypoliscilab.com

  Pre-Test
  Post-Test
  Chapter Exam
  Flashcards

Watch on mypoliscilab.com

  Video: Three Vivid Years-But Progress?
  Video: Sanctions on Iran
  Video: NYC's Subway Surveillance System

Explore on mypoliscilab.com

  Simulation: You Are President John F. Kennedy
  Simulation: You Are the Newly Appointed Ambassador to the Country of Dalmatia
  Simulation: You Are the President of the United States
  Comparative: Comparing Foreign and Security Policy
  Timeline: The Evolution of Foreign Policy
  Visual Literacy: Evaluating Defense Spending

KEY TERMS

Bush Doctrine, p. 637
Central Intelligence Agency (CIA), p. 645
Cold War, p. 634
containment, p. 634
Defense Department, p. 639
Department of Homeland Security (DHS), p. 647
détente, p. 635

diplomacy, p. 639
ethnic lobby, p. 652
executive agreement, p. 650
foreign policy, p. 631
grand strategy, p. 631
internationalism, p. 631
isolationism, p. 631
Marshall Plan, p. 633
National Security Council (NSC), p. 639

North American Free Trade Agreement (NAFTA), p. 647
North Atlantic Treaty Organization (NATO), p. 634
protectionism, p. 658
State Department, p. 639
tariff, p. 647
treaty, p. 650

CHAPTER TEST

1. How did the grand strategy of isolationism influence U.S. foreign policy in the nineteenth and early twentieth centuries?

2. After World War II, how did internationalism change the conduct of U.S. foreign policy?

3. How do the responsibilities of the State Department and Defense Department differ from one another?

4. Short of military action, what kinds of things can the United States do in response to objectionable behavior by other nations?

5. In the aftermath of the September 11 terrorist attacks, what kinds of changes were made to the U.S. foreign policy bureaucracy?

6. What is the difference between a treaty and an executive agreement?
7. How can Congress influence the conduct of U.S. military policy?
8. What are ethnic lobbies?

9. What are the central subjects of dispute between the United States and North Korea?
10. In what ways does U.S. trade policy pit the interests of consumers and U.S. industries against one another?

SUGGESTED READINGS

Graham Allison and Philip Zelikow. 1999. *Essence of Decision*, 2nd ed. New York: AB Longman. An updated edition of the classic study of the Cuban missile crisis. Three models (rational actor, organizational processes, bureaucratic politics) are developed to explain foreign policy decision-making and the behavior that results from the process.

James F. Hoge and Gideon Rose, eds. 2003. *America and the World: Debating the New Shape of International Politics*. Washington, DC: Foreign Affairs. A compendium of arguments about the role of American primacy, the clash of civilizations, and the future of democracy.

Stephen Hook and John Spanier. 2007. *American Foreign Policy Since World War II*, 17th ed. Washington, DC: CQ Press. A classic book tracing the major phases of American foreign policy since World War II through September 11, with special attention to the political process and context in which decisions were made.

William Howell and Jon Pevehouse. 2007. *While Dangers Gather: Congressional Checks on Presidential War Powers*.

Princeton, NJ: Princeton University Press. Examines the proposition that the president has become all-powerful in formation of policies concerning use of military force, and shows that Congress has a definite, if circumscribed, influence over decisions involving troop deployments abroad.

David A. Welch. 2005. *Painful Choices: A Theory of Foreign Policy Change*. Princeton, NJ: Princeton University Press. Outlines organizational and psychological theories about when foreign policy decision-makers attempt to make major changes in policy, and uses historical case studies to examine each theory.

Amy Zegart. 1999. *Flawed by Design: The Evolution of the CIA, JCS, and NSC*. Stanford, CA: Stanford University Press. Reviews the creation and evolution of several executive branch agencies, and argues that pressures from Congress, the White House, and voting public have undermined effective operation of certain security institutions, while bureaucratic politics limit the sharing of expertise and coordination of actions across agencies.

SUGGESTED WEBSITES

Department of Defense: www.defenselink.mil

Assumes primary responsibility for the U.S. military.

State Department: www.state.gov

Assumes primary responsibility for U.S. diplomatic relations with foreign countries.

Council on Foreign Relations: www.cfr.org

Provides substantial research and commentary on foreign policy issues.

Brookings Institution: www.brookings.edu/ foreign-policy.aspx

The foreign affairs wing of the Brookings Institution, another prominent policy think tank.

United Nations: www.un.org

The most prominent international organization to facilitate diplomatic relations between nations.

Senate Foreign Relations Committee: www.foreign. senate.gov

Primarily responsible for overseeing the foreign policy apparatus within the executive branch.

Nestor and his guidance counselor at South High School in Denver were frustrated and angry. It didn't seem fair. Nestor had worked diligently to pursue a college-bound track of courses and earn a 3.5 grade point average. Teachers all agreed he was a bright, responsible, and highly motivated student who was bound to do well at a good university. But Nestor faced hurdles having nothing to do with academics or with choices that he had made. His concern was how the state defined who was a resident of Colorado.

When Nestor was only five years old, his parents moved to Colorado from Guatemala to seek refuge from political turmoil and to take advantage of employment opportunities in the state. They did not go through the required immigration procedures, however, and thus were illegal immigrants. Nestor's dad had a job arranging and removing tables and chairs people rented for parties, and his mother worked at a candy store. They could not afford to

pay for a college education. Nestor worked summers and did odd jobs during the school year, but his savings were only a little over $12,000. The lack of resources was especially important: even though Nestor had been in Colorado since he was five years old and was graduating from a public high school in Colorado, because his parents were illegal immigrants he did not qualify for resident tuition at the state's public universities. Although the national government makes the determination of which immigrants are in the country legally and which are not, state governments set policies about who has resident status for public universities and state financial aid programs.

In contrast to Colorado, in 2010 ten states allowed any student graduating from a state high school to pay resident tuition rates, regardless of their immigration status or that of their parents. Colorado, Georgia, and Arizona, however, explicitly ban in-state tuition for undocumented students. In April 2008, the General Assembly (the lower legislative house) of Virginia debated six different proposals, ranging from considering children of illegal immigrants as eligible for financial aid to prohibiting state universities from even admitting these students. Bob McDonnell, Virginia's attorney general, issued a legal opinion that fueled some of the debate. He noted some ambiguities in the state's current law and then told public university officials that they should presume that children of undocumented immigrants are legally not residents of Virginia, but allowed the universities to make exceptions on a case-by-case basis. The opinion was controversial

◄ DEMONSTRATORS ON IMMIGRATION POLICIES

States, as well as the national government, determine the rights and status of immigrants. What recent policies has your state adopted that address the immigration issue?

because it was a response to the plea of a student who was born in Virginia. Anyone born in Virginia is a citizen of that state and of the United States, regardless of whether the parents entered the country legally. According to the attorney general, it was the status of the boy's parents that mattered.

Both educational opportunities and immigration are emotional issues. During times of economic hardship, those who are unemployed or underemployed sometimes resent the presence of immigrant workers, especially those who are not in the country legally. Some employers rely heavily on workers from other countries who will work for relatively low wages, and employers are more concerned about having these workers than about whether they entered the country legally or have a visa that is still valid. A complicating concern regarding tuition for public universities is that children, who obviously do not control the decisions of their parents, are affected. It seems more appropriate to penalize those who are guilty of negligence or malfeasance than those who played no role in the decision. The counterargument is that states can provide a disincentive for parents to be in the country illegally by denying resident status to their children. Commonly, states that do grant children of illegal immigrants resident status for tuition require these students to become U.S. citizens, if they are not already. Students who do not become citizens within five years of qualifying for resident status must pay the state the difference between resident and nonresident tuition. This approach aims at increasing the coun-

try's pool of highly educated people and thereby helping the economy.

The states also differ in defining residence for circumstances other than immigration. States like California are generally very generous in granting residency status. A person qualifies by showing financial independence and demonstrating intent to make California home by getting a driver's license, registering to vote, listing the state as residence on official records, or some similar act. At the other extreme are states like Wisconsin, which has a policy that defines anyone who enters the state to attend college as a nonresident regardless of financial independence or where he or she votes or gets a driver's license.

State differences regarding higher education and immigrant status do not follow any particular patterns. Southern border states like California, Arizona, New Mexico, and Texas have the largest number of immigrants from Mexico and Central America. Of these, Arizona has passed the most controversial and restrictive laws on providing services to those who are not citizens. Other states with stringent policies are scattered around the country and include some that are highly urbanized and others that are very rural, some controlled by Republicans and some by Democrats.

Not only do state policies regarding tuition, scholarships, and residency vary, but the ways states establish these policies also do so. All states have legislatures that pass bills and present them to a governor for approval or veto. In addition, Arizona, California, and 22 other states enact laws through the direct initiative, in which voters can get a

proposal on a statewide ballot without any involvement of their legislature or governor. In eight states, legislatures place proposals on the ballot and create laws without governors participating. These forms of direct democracy sometimes give interest groups undue influence over higher education policies in a state that otherwise would probably not give serious consideration to their ideas. The point is not that state governments are likely to act one way and citizens another, but that states offer advocates a number of arenas for pursuing their ideas. Understanding state policies requires knowledge of the actors and the avenues for achieving change.

This chapter describes how state and local governments function. Most of the public policies that directly affect us are made and implemented by state and local governments. Street maintenance, park services, garbage collection, police and fire protection, education from kindergarten through college, marriage and divorce, highway safety, and the many other critical, daily governmental services and regulations we experience are primarily the products of state and local governments. Policies in arenas like the environment, energy, and commerce are typically made by the national government but are then implemented by state and local agencies. When the national government does not resolve issues like health care and climate change, state and even city governments have stepped in. In short, to understand the roles government plays in our lives requires an appreciation of the nature of governance in the 50 states and more than 89,000 local governments.

CHAPTER LEARNING OBJECTIVES

After reading this chapter you will be able to:

19-1 Explain how state constitutions and local government charters provide the structure and operations of state and local governments.

19-2 Compare and contrast the various forms of executive and legislative branches in state and municipal government.

19-3 Outline the structure of state courts and their relationship with national courts.

19-4 Classify the methods of direct democracy used by some states.

The Making of State and Local Governments

19-1 Explain how state constitutions and local government charters provide the structure and operations of state and local governments.

Northwest Ordinance of 1787 law passed by Congress under the Articles of Confederation that established the process by which the territories of Ohio, Indiana, Illinois, Michigan, and Wisconsin would be governed and admitted as states.

As the national Congress that existed under the Articles of Confederation adjourned to allow the writing of the Constitution, it passed the **Northwest Ordinance of 1787**, which was critical in shaping the United States and the state governments. In Article 5 of the Ordinance, Congress provided for the admission of additional states to the Union with the full status of the first 13. This provision meant that all states would have the same rights and privileges:

> **Article 5:** . . . . And, whenever any of the said States shall have sixty thousand free inhabitants therein, such State shall be admitted, by its delegates, into the Congress of the United States, on an equal footing with the original States in all respects whatever, and shall be at liberty to form a permanent constitution and State government: Provided, the constitution and government so to be formed, shall be republican, and in conformity to the principles contained in these articles; and, so far as it can be consistent with the general interest of the confederacy, such admission shall be allowed at an earlier period, and when there may be a less number of free inhabitants in the State than sixty thousand.

The other major provision of Article 5 was the requirement that new states have constitutions acceptable to Congress. Thus, territories petitioning for statehood had an incentive to adopt constitutions similar to those of the states already in the Union. The five states that were carved out of the Northwest Territory—Ohio, Indiana, Illinois, Michigan, and Wisconsin—submitted constitutions almost identical to those of New York and Massachusetts, the states from which most of the initial settlers in the territory had originated. The strategy of each of the territories was to propose constitutions that members of Congress would recognize. Ohio was the first to join the Union (in 1803) and Wisconsin the last of the Northwest Territories (1848). States that emerged out of the Louisiana Purchase also modeled their governments and constitutions on those of existing states.

State constitutions primarily limit the power of government.

The first state constitutions were drafted before the passage of the U.S. Constitution, which lays out the relationship between states and the national government. When the authors of the constitutions of the original 13 states did their work, their primary concern was to make certain that state governments did not have the power and discretion of their colonial predecessors. The Founders had the tyranny of the British crown in mind as they formed the state governments that would succeed the colonial governors. The American Revolution was about providing power to the governed and limiting that of the government. As new states formed, they drafted constitutions that maintained this perspective, and as new policy issues emerged over time, states amended their constitutions to address them.

Evolution of the state constitutions From the beginning, state constitutions included clauses that limit officials from placing restrictions on an individual's speech and assembly, participating in unreasonable searches and seizures, and using cruel and inhuman punishment. New Hampshire's constitution even makes clear that citizens have a right to revolt. The major limiting clauses of the U.S. Constitution are the first 10 amendments, the Bill of Rights, which were added as a condition for ratification by the first 13 states. The states considered individual liberties and limits on government power important enough to include in the national as well as the state constitutions.

The first state constitutions designed weak government institutions to prevent the kind of government tyranny that characterized colonial rule.[1] Legislatures were part time and governors served only two-year terms. Governors of the new states had nothing close to the authority and discretion of colonial governors. State constitutions stipulated that these offices be primarily ceremonial and made legislatures the primary center of decision-making authority. Initially only South Carolina, New York, and Massachusetts allowed their governors to veto legislation.

The tradition of weak state governments continued with the adoption of constitutions in the aftermath of the Civil War, as the country expanded westward.[2] Former Confederate states had to write new constitutions that did not include the right of individuals to own slaves. Individual southern states adopted and repealed as many as four different constitutions between 1865 and 1880. With white southern economic and social elites still smarting from federal government intrusions of the Reconstruction era, the end results were state constitutions severely limiting the power and role of government, allowing elites to govern informally.

When western states joined the Union, the **Progressive movement** attempted to prevent the emergence of political machines by again limiting the authority of state governments. Progressives added new techniques: empowering voters with the **initiative**, which allows voters to enact new laws by putting a proposal on the ballot if enough people sign a petition, and the **recall**, which allows for the removal of elected officials through popular vote rather than impeachment. Although these mechanisms of direct democracy are most common in western states, nine states in other regions eventually adopted them.

It has only been with constitutional changes adopted in the 1960s and 1970s that state institutions have increased in power.[3] As discussed below, a 1962 U.S. Supreme Court ruling mandated legislative redistricting in the states, prompting reforms that give state governments a larger role in policy-making. All governors now have veto authority and, except for New Hampshire and Vermont, now serve four-year terms. More legislatures are full-time, and state courts have become more streamlined and professional. But the historic distrust of powerful government continues and state constitutions still include many restrictions.

In contrast to many countries in Asia and Europe, the political culture in the United States is generally cynical and cautious about government, a feature born from its revolutionary origins. The initial distrust toward government emerged in response to what was regarded as arbitrary and excessive control by colonial governments. The revolt against the monarchy further cemented the feelings of distrust toward government embodied in state constitutions. This central feature of state constitutions continues because reforms have tended to focus on specific issues rather than wholesale rewritings.

Other attributes of state constitutions State constitutions do more than protect the rights of individual citizens and establish the institutions of state governments. Constitutions are meant to deal with basic functions of government. However, almost all

Progressive movement advocated measures to destroy political machines and instead have direct participation by voters in the nomination of candidates and the establishment of public policy.

initiative a process in which a proposal for legislation is placed on the ballot and voters can either enact or reject the proposal without further action by the governor or legislature.

recall a process in which voters can petition for a vote to remove officials between elections.

669

▼ TEDDY ROOSEVELT FIGHTING CORRUPTION AND MACHINE POLITICS
This cartoon depicts one of the leaders of the Progressive movement, President Theodore Roosevelt, in the fight against political machines and big corporations. What institutions and policies did the movement create in state and local government?

NO MOLLY-CODDLING HERE

ThinkingComparatively ●●●●

The political culture in the United States is more cynical toward government than in most other countries. This has led to state constitutions with explicit limits on governments.

state constitutions include a potpourri of policies and details that are more appropriate as laws and regulations, not constitutional provisions. California has a clause that dictates the length of a wrestling match. More importantly, California led the way in embedding into state constitutions limits and formulas that restrict government taxing and spending patterns. In some states, farmers and ranchers have protected their special interests in constitutions. In others, the oil and mining industries have embedded their concerns.[4]

In part because of the inclusion of policy and administrative detail, state constitutions are lengthier than the U.S. Constitution. The average length of state constitutions is over 27,000 words, whereas the U.S. Constitution is 8,700 words. Unlike the U.S. Constitution, most state constitutions are relatively easy to amend. The major reason for this is that states do not need the approval of other states in order to change their own constitutions. In addition, most states have relatively simple procedures for amending their constitutions. All states allow for the calling of a constitutional convention and all require that proposals for change be ratified by voters in a statewide referendum. In 40 of the states, the legislature can vote to submit a proposal to the voters in just one session. Ten states require the proposed amendment to pass two legislatures. Twenty states require only a majority vote in the legislature for approval, whereas the others require a supermajority, usually two-thirds.

Charters authorize local governments to make and enforce laws.

Alexis de Tocqueville, a popular nineteenth-century French philosopher and historian who visited the new nation, is widely cited as capturing the spirit and principles of early American democracy. He conveyed, however, a romantic but misleading picture of the place of local governments in the United States. He wrote that individuals established social contracts to formulate the basic terms and conditions of government and that "the township was organized before the county, the county before the state, the state before the union."[5]

In fact, local governments are not the building blocks of states; rather, they are the creatures of the states. Judge John F. Dillon articulated this doctrine in 1868. The case challenged whether Iowa violated a constitutional principle when it established local commissions that both applied regulations to railroads and then ruled on appeals from the railroads objecting to the enforcement of the regulations. Dillon stated that, according to the U.S. Constitution and the state constitution of Iowa, because local governments did not enjoy sovereignty or inherent powers, they did not have to conform to a basic set of characteristics, such as separation of powers. **Dillon's rule** summarizes the legal status of local governments in all 50 states. He said, "The true view is this: Municipal corporations owe their origins to and derive their power and rights wholly from the (state) legislature. It breathes into them the breath without which they cannot exist. As it creates, so it may destroy. If it may destroy, it may abridge and control."[6]

Dillon's rule principle articulated in a court ruling that local governments do not have any inherent sovereignty but instead must be authorized by a state government.

State governments recognize the existence of local governments by granting them **charters**, which are similar to constitutions. Charters may be found in a state statute that relates to cities, counties, school districts, and the like, or they may be written by a community and submitted for approval by the state legislature. Charters describe the institutions of government, the processes used to make legally binding decisions, the scope of issues and services that will be provided, and the ways in which the expenses of government will be funded.

charter a document that, like a constitution, specifies the basic policies, procedures, and institutions of a local government.

TABLE 19-1. Types and Numbers of Local Governments

TYPES OF LOCAL GOVERNMENTS	NUMBER
County	3,033
Townships and towns	16,519
Municipalities	19,492
Special districts (School districts)	37,381 (13,051)

Source: U.S. Bureau of the Census, "Local Governments and Public School Systems by Type and State: 2007," April 27, 2010, http://www.census.gov.

Some local governments are created top-down. A legislature will divide the state into counties, for example, and write a charter that guides how they will operate. States use **counties** as basic administrative units for welfare and environmental programs, courts and law enforcement, registering land, births, and deaths, and for holding elections (see Table 19-1). All states except Connecticut and Rhode Island have counties, although in Louisiana they are called parishes and in Alaska they are called boroughs. County boundaries are typically arbitrary and have no relation necessarily to where people live. Texas and Kansas drew county boundaries so that everyone in the state could ride by horse and reach their county seat within one day. In other states, there are some cities in which the boundaries of as many as three different counties converge. These shared boundaries require counties to cooperate in order to provide effective governance. For example, since counties are typically responsible for 911 emergency services, cooperation is essential.

Local governments can also be created by a bottom-up process. When businesses and families cluster in a particular area or when a city grows in land and population, residents must petition the state legislature to be recognized as a legal entity with powers to pass and enforce laws, collect taxes and fees, and provide services. Such a petition must include either a standard charter available from the state or a charter written for that proposed government. Municipal governments, which include towns, villages, and cities, emerge from this process. States typically distinguish between these governments based on the size of the population, but they provide more authority in charters to cities than in charters for towns and villages. The Northwest Ordinance of 1787 attempted to export the model of the New England **town** by creating a grid of **townships** over the territories. Townships are geographic entities 6 miles by 6 miles. When people settled in a township, they usually, but not always, formed a town government and petitioned for a charter. The former Northwest Territory still has some townships or parts of townships, but as urbanization has increased, cities and villages have acquired authority over most of the former townships.

Most local governments are **special districts**—that is, they focus on a particular function or service. The most common special district is a school district. Other examples are water districts, sewerage districts, park districts, and lake districts.[7] Not only are these governments restricted in what they control or provide, but they are also limited in how they may get revenue. Often special districts rely on a fee, like a charge for using water, or on grants from other governments. School districts typically levy a tax on property and otherwise rely on state and national funds. Municipal and county governments also rely heavily on property taxes.

Other local governments, like counties, towns, and cities, have a wide scope of responsibilities. Almost all states offer **home rule** charters to these jurisdictions.[8] These charters allow local governments to make and enforce public policy on any issue not under the mandate of a special district or explicitly prohibited under state law. Traditional

county a district created by state government for establishing a local government responsible for implementing a variety of state laws and for providing general governmental services.

town a local government with general responsibilities for order and services in a medium-sized community.

township a 6-mile by 6-mile area created by the Northwest Ordinance of 1787 to be used for local governance in the territories of Ohio, Indiana, Michigan, Illinois, and Wisconsin.

special district a local government created for a narrowly defined purpose and with a restricted source of revenue.

home rule a local government with authority to pass laws and provide services as long as those laws or services are not provided by a special district or otherwise prohibited under state law.

► **CHARTER SCHOOL**
Some states authorize public schools to operate with special rules, known as a charter.

charter schools public schools, administered by chartering boards, that are exempt from many rules and regulations applicable to traditional public schools.

charters itemized what kinds of policies municipalities were authorized to develop and enforce. Home rule uses the approach that anything goes unless it is prohibited.

School districts are special districts created to divide an entire state into smaller educational units, and boundaries can be arbitrary. There are cities and towns in which neighbors send their children to different schools simply because a street in the neighborhood is the boundary between two different school districts. Whereas counties have a general set of responsibilities, school districts are established by state legislatures to deal only with public education.

In 1991, Minnesota's state government passed a law allowing the creation of **charter schools**, which are also discussed in Chapter 17. By 2008, 39 other states, plus the District of Columbia and Puerto Rico, followed this lead. School districts are governed in accordance with charters. These districts—or in a few cases, a state agency—may, in turn, charter individual public or private schools to operate independently but within the school district. Usually these charters are for a three- to five-year period. Parents, teachers, or even entrepreneurs, when allowed by state law, may propose a charter that provides for a special approach to education or exempts a school from certain standard regulations. Some charter schools rely exclusively on computer-based instruction, emphasize the arts in all courses, or focus primarily on science. Most, but not all, states require that teachers meet state certification requirements, and states like Minnesota insist that charter schools have the same diversity among their students as exists in other public schools. Educators and parents favor a particular approach to learning, because they want to escape what they regard as defective public schools, or both. If the school district or state approves a proposal, the school receives public funding but it has authority to operate in accordance with its own unique charter.

Executives and Legislatures

19-2 Compare and contrast the various forms of executive and legislative branches in state and municipal government.

State and local governments make laws and implement them through enforcing regulations and providing services. To accomplish this, state governments generally follow the model of the national government by having separate branches for making laws on the one hand and implementing them on the other. This separation includes checks, such as the authority of the executive to veto legislation and the administrative oversight responsibilities of the legislature. In local governments, however, executive and legislative responsibilities are not always separate, and the structures of these institutions take a variety of forms.

Governors are the chief elected executive in state governments.

The primary role of a **governor** is to set the agenda for state governments. Even when the office was weak and largely ceremonial, governors were the most visible elected officials in state governments. Even the most flamboyant or outrageous legislator could not command the attention of a governor. From the time they campaign until the time they leave office, governors speak to and for statewide audiences. If a governor declares there is an urgent energy problem or a crisis in public schools, the focus inevitably will turn to those issues. Other gubernatorial powers, such as budgeting authority, appointments to administrative agencies, and modifying court actions, allow governors to go beyond agenda setting.

governor the chief elected executive official in state governments.

Budget authority Budgets provide governors with an opportunity to set agendas and move toward solutions. Until the 1920s, state legislative committees, not governors, initiated the budget process and then the legislature as a whole presented a budget bill to the governor for approval or veto. As discussed below, when the U.S. Supreme Court issued a mandate in 1962 that state legislatures had to use districts representative of the population, state governments became more relevant and important policy makers. The increase in the responsibilities of state governments required more effective executive branches to set the policy agenda and to implement the laws

ThinkingCausally

Although a common perception is that governors appoint friends and campaign contributors to senior posts, any such inclination is balanced by the need to run government competently.

◄ **GUBERNATORIAL TRANSITION**

New Jersey Governor Chris Christie speaks after being sworn into office on January, 19, 2010. Governor Christie defeated a Democratic incumbent in a state that is heavily Democratic.

passed by legislatures and thus led to efforts to strengthen the powers of governors. Governors gained the authority to initiate the budget process and make decisions about how to generate revenues and allocate funds.[9] Legislators can amend what the governor submits, but debates begin with the governor's ideas. Moreover, state budgets in the twenty-first century commonly consist of hundreds of pages of detail. Inevitably most of that detail will escape scrutiny and change, and thus governors tend to get most of what they want.

The authority to veto considerably enhances the role of the governor in the budget process. Like presidents, governors have **package or general veto** authority, allowing them to reject an entire bill. Governors of 43 states also have the authority to exercise a **line-item veto** over bills that affect taxing and spending, an authority the U.S. president does not have. This allows governors to balance budgets by revising financially relevant legislation without rejecting it wholesale. Numbers as well as words may be eliminated in a line-item veto. Although general and line-item vetoes can be overridden by the legislature, an override usually takes a two-thirds majority in both houses and thus happens rarely.[10]

package or general veto the authority of a chief executive to void an entire bill that has been passed by the legislature.

line-item veto the authority of a chief executive to reject part of a bill passed by the legislature.

674

ThinkingCausally

Is the power to hire and fire agency heads a way of allowing governors to reward their friends or to run state governments more effectively?

Appointment powers   Many department and agency heads are appointed by governors and serve at their pleasure. Although a common perception is that governors appoint friends and campaign contributors to senior posts, any such inclination is balanced by the need to run government competently. Although governors sometimes will use appointment powers for political patronage, the more important purpose is to allow a governor to follow through on his or her campaign promises and provide leadership in state government.[11] The reasoning is that if we elect governors at least in part because we favor their policy agendas, then we need to give them an opportunity to exercise control over the agencies of government. Nevertheless, most state employees have job security through civil servant protections that allow them to have careers that can span many different governors. Conceivably they could render elections meaningless by ignoring the governor's direction. As part of the post-1962 reforms to make state governments work more effectively and enhance gubernatorial leadership, many governors were given authority to assemble their own policy and management teams by determining who headed major state agencies.

Although the appointment powers of governors provide direction and control over administrative agencies, limits to this power reflect the legacy of historic efforts to check the authority of governors. Unlike the national government, most states fill a number of agency head positions through statewide elections rather than gubernatorial appointment. Agency heads may be from a party other than the governor's and may even be planning to run against the governor. The most common and significant elected agency head is the attorney general. Forty-three states elect their attorneys general. Other elected positions include secretary of state; treasurer; education, labor, and agriculture commissioners; and even commissioner of charities.[12] Reforms to enhance gubernatorial powers have left largely untouched the provisions to elect heads of some state agencies.

Role in the judicial system   Governors are also major actors in the judicial system but with limited powers. Only the governors of California, Maine, and New Jersey appoint judges in a way similar to the U.S. president, but some judges also make appointments based on panel recommendations. Judges in still other states are elected for fixed terms, but governors generally appoint someone to complete a term when a judge leaves the bench. Because an incumbent judge running for reelection has considerable advantages over an opponent, the power to appoint an interim judge can be valuable.

The most substantial power of governors in the judicial system applies after someone is convicted of a crime. A governor has the authority to **pardon** someone, thereby voiding a conviction in court and eliminating all punishment. Governors also have the option of leaving the conviction in place and reducing the sentence. They may **parole** prisoners who have served part of their term, releasing them from behind bars but keeping them under supervision, or **commute** all or part of a sentence, releasing someone from both prison and supervision. Some governors may also commute a death penalty and replace it with life in prison. Governors may not, however, increase the severity of a sentence.

The power to pardon has sometimes been abused by governors. In Texas some governors have used pardons as part of political wheeling and dealing and as a way of augmenting their state salaries. Governor James E. Ferguson granted 2,253 pardons between 1915 and 1917 as part of gubernatorial bargains.[13] When his wife, Miriam "Ma" Ferguson, took office two years later, she granted almost 3,800. In response, Texas voters amended the state constitution and placed authority for granting pardons in the hands of a board, thus making the Lone Star governor weaker in this arena than any other governor in the country.

The U.S. Constitution provides governors with the discretion to **extradite** individuals, that is, to deliver an individual to another state where he or she is wanted for a particular crime. Extradition is not routinely granted and frequently highlights differences in how states treat criminal justice issues, especially the death penalty. In December 2007, Governor Matt Blunt of Missouri asked Governor Rod Blagojevich of Illinois to extradite Timothy Krajcir, who was in prison in Illinois for rape and murder. Governor Blagojevich, however, had serious misgivings about the death penalty and was concerned that extraditing Krajcir might lead to his execution in Missouri. The issue

pardon   the authority of a governor to cancel someone's conviction of a crime and eliminate all sanctions and punishments.

parole   the authority of a governor to release a prisoner before his or her full sentence has been completed. A parole is for a specific period and includes restrictions and supervision.

commute   the action of a governor to cancel all or part of a sentence while keeping a conviction on the record.

extradite   the action of a governor to send someone against his or her will to another state to face criminal charges.

FIGURE 19-1. **Political Party of State Governors, July 2010.** Although Democrats held more gubernatorial offices than Republicans in 2010, the balance between the parties continued to be relatively even.

was resolved when Krajcir, who was 63 in 2007, pled guilty to the Missouri murders and yet another in Illinois and was sentenced to serve consecutively two 40-year terms.

Between 1945 and 1990, Democrats usually had about 10 percent more governors than did Republicans. Since 1990, however, governors have been relatively evenly split between Republicans and Democrats. After the 2008–2009 elections, as shown in Figure 19-1, 26 governors were Democrats and 24 were Republicans.

State legislatures pass laws and monitor the activities of state agencies.

As explained above, in order to make state governments more effective, the power and authority of governors has increased since the 1960s. In turn, state legislatures have seen their powers decrease. The nation began with state legislatures that were very strong and governors that were primarily ceremonial. Legislatures formulated budgets, appointed judges and agency heads, and even elected U.S. senators. These legislators were initially true citizen policy makers, farmers and lawyers who traveled to the state capitol for several weeks each year to do their work.

Representation   In the first half of the twentieth century, the need for agricultural labor declined, and population shifted from rural to urban areas, but the boundaries of districts from which legislators were elected did not change to reflect this shift. As a result, state legislatures were increasingly unrepresentative of the population. In the same state legislature, one legislator could represent 50,000 people while another had 500,000 constituents. Not surprisingly, overrepresentation of rural areas led to a neglect of the issues and concerns of urban areas.

In the 1960s, a number of Supreme Court rulings began to address the imbalance of representation. In 1962, the Court ruled in *Baker v. Carr* that all legislative districts in a state had to have roughly the same number of constituents. This ruling prompted significant efforts to make state legislatures more representative and state governments more competent. In 1964, the Court made clear that this decision applied to elections generally. *Reynolds v. Sims* (1964) prohibited states from following the national model in which one legislative house is based on population and another on geography. Areas within a state do not have the same sovereignty that states within the federal system have, and so, the Court ruled, each chamber in a state legislature must be based on the one-person, one-vote principle. In *Westbury v. Sanders* (1964), the Court ruled that districts for the U.S. House of Representatives and local governments must also be based on population.

The one-person, one-vote principle articulated in *Baker v. Carr* led to policy agendas more relevant to states' needs and opportunities. Political scientists have examined the changes that occurred in policy agendas, state budgets, and legislative actions with the redrawing of districts to implement the Court's ruling.[14] They found an increased willingness to address the concerns of growing urban areas, as the voices of urban constituents became more accurately reflected by the new district system. The growth of urban areas requires major investments in water and sewerage systems, streets, schools, and parks. These require not only some state funding, but changes in state laws authorizing municipalities to generate their own revenues. Issues of police and fire protection, public health, and traffic congestion also are special to urban areas. States inevitably have to allow cities to expand their jurisdiction over larger areas and to encourage regional forms of government. Legislatures ignored these issues until *Baker v. Carr* provided more urban representation.

ThinkingCausally

How did *Baker v. Carr* influence the representation of urban versus rural interests in state legislatures?

The legislators   Ironically, as legislatures became more representative and state governments became more relevant to the needs and wishes of the people, it was necessary to create more powerful gubernatorial offices and cede some legislative authority to the executive branch. Nonetheless, modern legislatures have more responsibilities and more issues to resolve. In response, with few exceptions, state legislatures have increased their activity and hired more staff. In 1960, only 18 states met annually. By 2010, all but seven met every year. In most states, sessions are longer, there is more committee work on proposed legislation, task forces examine issues in greater depth throughout the year, and legislators and their committees have more staff to help with constituent services and legislative research than prior to 1960.[15] The legislatures generally are attracting people who are more professional and eager to play a meaningful role in public problem solving.[16]

Nevertheless, in contrast to the U.S. Congress, state legislatures are still primarily part-time citizen bodies. Some states, like Alabama and Montana, do not pay their legislators any salary but instead pay travel expenses and a set fee for every day the legislator meets either in committee or in a floor session. States with salaries for legislators pay from $8,000 in Texas to $120,000 a year in California.[17] Even in states where legislators have floor sessions and committee meetings throughout the year, compensation is usually set as a percentage of the salaries of senior administrators, and legislators receive reimbursement or special allowances for every time they leave home and travel to the state capitol. States explicitly recognize that their legislators typically have jobs in addition to their positions as representatives or senators, and they have issued guidelines to avoid conflicts of interest.[18]

Terms of office   In the 1980s and 1990s, 21 states adopted **term limits** for their legislators, limiting the number of years someone might serve as a state legislator. The

term limits   restrictions that exist in some states about how long an individual may serve in an elected office.

677

▼ **POLITICS NEVER SLEEPS**
State legislators negotiated over amendments during a break in debate on a bill. How might legislative term limits influence elections and policy-making in the 15 states that have them?

TABLE 19-2. Term Limits for State Legislators

STATE	YEAR ENACTED	HOUSE LIMIT	SENATE LIMIT
Arkansas	1992	6	8
Arizona	1992	8	8
California	1990	6	8
Colorado	1990	8	8
Florida	1992	8	8
Louisiana	1995	12	12
Maine	1996	8	8
Michigan	1992	6	8
Missouri	1992	8	8
Montana	1992	8	8
Nebraska	2000	n/a	8
Nevada	1996	12	12
Ohio	1992	8	8
Oklahoma	1990	12	12
South Dakota	1992	8	8

Source: National Council of State Legislatures, http://www.ncsl.org.

argument fueling the drive for term limits was that individuals who made a career of elective politics amassed powers and advantages that made it difficult for someone to challenge them successfully in the polls. Representation, it was argued, would be enhanced by a regular rotation of people in and out of elective office. Some critics argued that limiting terms would weaken legislatures by decreasing institutional memory and policy expertise, and lobbyists and career administrators would gain influence.[19] The counterargument prevailed in six states, where state supreme court rulings and changes in political sentiment led to the abandonment of term limits. Table 19-2 lists the states that still have term limits with the years that apply to each house.

All states except Nebraska have two legislative chambers. The upper chamber is usually called the senate, and all have larger districts and thus fewer members than the lower chamber, which is usually called the house or assembly. Most states simply cluster three or four adjoining house or assembly districts to constitute a senate district, but some states draw entirely different boundaries for the two bodies. The most common ratio of members between senate and house chambers is 1:3, although New Hampshire has one senator for every 16 representatives.

Terms of office sometimes vary between the houses. Thirty-four states have four-year terms for senators and two-year terms for representatives. The other 16 states have the same length of terms for all state legislators: 11 have two-year terms for everyone and the other five, including Nebraska, have four-year terms.

Partisan control   Nebraska's legislature is also unique in that elections to its senate are **nonpartisan**—candidates do not run as nominees of any party. Some states and regions of the country have historically been dominated by one political party. Democrats, for example, controlled southern states from after the Civil War until the 1990s, while Republicans were predominant in New England states. As each party has become less ideologically diverse, party control in different regions of the country has shifted, with the South becoming more Republican and New England

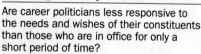

ThinkingCausally

Are career politicians less responsive to the needs and wishes of their constituents than those who are in office for only a short period of time?

nonpartisan an election in which candidates run without formal identification or association with a political party.

becoming more Democratic. Minnesota and Wisconsin once had very strong third parties—the Farmer Labor Party in the former and the Progressive Party in the latter—that eventually merged with the Democratic Party.

The Democratic Party generally controlled substantially more state legislatures from 1952 to 1992, but Republican gains in the 1990s, especially in the South, have led to a much more competitive picture. White southerners had supported the Democratic Party since the presidency of Franklin D. Roosevelt, but they started abandoning the party when it supported the civil rights movement in the 1960s. Beginning with the Republican candidacy of Richard Nixon in 1968, many white southern Democrats felt comfortable with the GOP and helped that party become more competitive in what had been a solidly Democratic region. In 2004, Republicans had a majority in both houses in 21 of the 49 bicameral state legislatures, Democrats in 17, and party control was split in 11. However, in 2006, Democrats gained control of both houses in 23 states, in contrast to Republican control in 15 and split control in 11 states. As Figure 19-2 shows, after the 2008–2009 elections, Democrats controlled both houses in 27 states, Republicans in 14, and the parties split control in 8. Nebraska is nonpartisan.

As with the U.S. Congress, party control of a state legislative chamber is critical to determining who will chair committees and control the agenda. Defining which issues have priority and how concerns are framed depends on who is in charge. Most states reflect the increasingly partisan nature of conflict and deliberation over policies that have characterized the national government. Being in the minority party may mean being unable to achieve passage or even consideration of a proposal. Leaders of the majority party are likely to ignore and exclude legislators from the minority. Winners, of course, have always had the advantages in policy-making, the essence of representative democracy. At times the partisan divide in state legislatures has become so wide and bitter, however, that the potential for stalemates and unresolved problems is rising.[20]

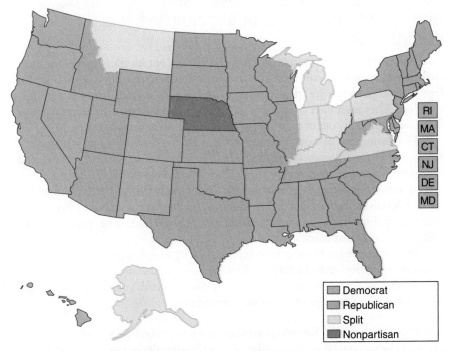

FIGURE 19-2. Party Control of State Legislatures, July 2010. Democrats fared well in the 2008 elections and secured control over almost twice as many state legislative chambers as Republicans.

Policy Experimentation in the States.

States are often viewed as laboratories of democracy. One state might attempt to address a problem faced by many states or even the entire country. If the state's experiment successfully addresses the problem, other states might soon follow. The policy idea may even percolate up and make its way into a new national policy. This was the pattern for many social welfare reforms in the 1990s. However, a state's experiment may fail or cause additional problems, such as budget deficits. In these cases, other states can still learn from the experience, and only the experimenting state's population is affected.

But what leads one state to innovate, or adopt a policy early, while other states stand by? Indeed, why do some states adopt a particular policy while other states never act? Social scientists view the states as laboratories of democracy not simply because the states experiment. Instead, because the states are very similar in many ways, such as institutional design, but are different in many others, such as political culture, partisan control, professionalization of the state legislation, and so on, the variation in state policy allows social scientists to test theories about the policy-making process. For example, does California have stricter environmental protection laws than other states because it has a highly professionalized legislature, because its residents are more liberal, because it allows for the initiative process, or some combination of factors?

Using a variety of statistical methods, social scientists can test specific hypotheses about what state characteristics are important for determining outcomes of the policy-making process. These allow them to better understand the roles of everything from electoral institutions to importance of rules within the state legislature.

Local government executives and legislatures enact and implement public policies for communities.

Local governments follow a variety of patterns and, except for the largest cities and counties, are even more part time than their state counterparts. Local government legislators in particular are friends and neighbors of their constituents and have full-time jobs. They meet once a week or once a month, depending on community issues. They serve primarily out of civic duty or interest in a particular set of issues.

The institutions of local governments do not always follow the principles of separation of powers or checks and balances that we associate with the national and state governments. A single body, like a school board or village board, can have legislative, executive, and even judicial powers. For example, school boards commonly adopt rules on student conduct and adjudicate any conflicts or appeals when a student is disciplined for not following those rules. School boards hire and fire administrators and, in many cases, teachers.

The composition of local governments can vary greatly but generally will include an elected executive, such as a mayor, village president, or county executive; an elected council, such as a city council, school board, or county board; and an appointed manager, such as a city manager or school superintendent.

Elected executives   Executives may be elected by voters in a community or be chosen by other council members. Almost three-fourths of the cities have a directly elected mayor. The common pattern among towns and villages is to have a mayor or president elected from among council members. Mayors of cities are usually full-time positions, whereas elected executives in smaller municipalities are part time.

Most local government executives are elected in nonpartisan contests. Although party identification is not on the ballot in nonpartisan elections, candidates in fact may be linked to a political party. In some cases, political parties make clear who their preferred candidate is in a nonpartisan election. Campaign managers and political consultants who work for candidates of a particular political party may run campaigns in nonpartisan as well as partisan elections. Individuals and organizations providing financial support to candidates may have a history of funding those using a given party label.

Like governors, local government executives have an opportunity to set the agenda since they are the most visible figures in their jurisdictions, but they do not have many of the powers of a governor. They do not, for example, have authority to amend or nullify court actions and most do not have veto powers. Some city charters explicitly provide for a **weak mayor** system by establishing two-year terms, no veto authority, and no authority to appoint the heads of administrative agencies. Mayors in such systems have little more than a ceremonial role. Other charters, primarily in large municipalities, have a **strong mayor**, with four-year terms, veto authority, and the opportunity to hire and fire top administrators. Strong elected executives may also have the power to appoint members of the legislative council to committees, thereby influencing what kinds of proposals are likely to be successful. Committee assignments are extremely important to council or board members.

Elected councils   Communities can elect representatives to a city council, school board, or other local legislative body by using geographically defined districts. Local council elections are also nonpartisan in many states.[21] **District-based elections** have the advantage of reflecting the needs and concerns of the different neighborhoods in a community. People who live in apartments in densely populated areas are likely to have different concerns from those in single-family residences. Neighborhoods commonly differ from one another in ethnicity, income, and age of residents. Boundaries can be drawn to reflect these differences, or they can fragment a particular ethnic group so that it becomes a minority in several districts and a majority in none. The Progressive movement sought to avoid district-based councils as a way of breaking up political machines based on wards with white ethnic bloc voting. The more contemporary concern is the impact of district boundaries on African American, Hispanic, Asian American, and other non-European ethnic groups. As with the earlier white ethnic groups, legislators can ensure the election of an African American or Hispanic, for example, by designing districts that have substantial majorities of those groups, or they can fragment these groups into several districts so that they are minorities in each one. Ethnic and racial representation is valued for its symbolic nature and because research suggests it makes public policies more responsive to the needs of minorities. Studies by political scientists demonstrate that the policy agendas and budget issues addressed in cities with minority mayors and minority district representation in city councils include more attention to minority neighborhood concerns than in similar communities that have few minority elected officials.[22]

The alternative to district-based elections is **at-large elections**. Here candidates run to represent the city or other jurisdiction as a whole, rather than as a specific part of the city. In some communities there are designated—usually numbered—positions so that candidates are running against one or more opponents for specific at-large positions. In other communities the election is more of a free for all in which the top vote getters fill whatever positions are available. Research consistently shows that ethnic and racial minority candidates are disadvantaged in at-large elections.

weak mayor   a governance system in which the elected chief executive has little formal authority to veto legislation or appoint administrators.

strong mayor   a governance system in which the elected chief executive has significant authority to veto legislation and appoint administrators.

district-based election   election in which candidates run for an office that represents only the voters of a specific district within the jurisdiction.

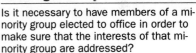

ThinkingCausally

Is it necessary to have members of a minority group elected to office in order to make sure that the interests of that minority group are addressed?

at-large election   election in which candidates for office must compete throughout the jurisdiction as a whole.

commission form of local government in which voters elect individuals to act as legislators and to head administrative agencies.

Only 3 percent of communities have a **commission** form of government, with at-large elections for positions that have both legislative and administrative responsibilities.[23] Voters elect commissioners to head departments of transportation, finance, economic development, and social services, for example. These commissioners form the equivalent of a city council and each commissioner is the head of a city agency. The commission form of government first emerged in Galveston as a response to a hurricane in 1900 that devastated southern Texas and killed almost 10,000 people. The model received positive reviews, and by 1917 almost 500 cities around the country adopted this form of government. Gradually a number of communities, including Galveston, abandoned the commission because agency heads ideally should be selected based on their expertise and managerial background, whereas elections are fundamentally about which candidate is most popular. In 2008, 176 cities had a commission. Portland, Oregon, is the largest city that still has the commission form of government.

Appointed managers.   In part because the elected executives and legislators in most local governments serve part time, many cities, counties, school boards, and the like hire full-time, professional managers. Progressive reformers advocated using appointed managers as part of their efforts to destroy political machines, which functioned to provide jobs and services in return for electoral support. Progressives believed that having professionals in charge of providing services and hiring employees would reduce the patronage on which machines depended. Typically, city or village managers and school superintendents initially gain employment in a relatively small community and then move to larger jurisdictions. Some large and troubled school districts have contracted with national firms that specialize in the management of educational institutions and programs.

Managers head agencies within local governments as well as serve as executives for a city or county government as a whole. Most of these managers are appointed, but as in state governments, some are elected. Chiefs of city police departments, for example, are usually appointed professionals, but county sheriffs are elected. The Case Study reminds us of how critical it is to have well-run law enforcement agencies.

CaseStudy: Shootings on Campus

On Valentine's Day, 2008, at Northern Illinois University, a graduate returned to campus dressed in black, stepped from behind a curtain on a stage in a lecture hall, and opened fire. About 150 students were in the class, taking notes. Steven Kazmierczak, armed with a shotgun hidden in a violin case and three handguns concealed under a coat, shot 23 people, killing five. He then turned one of his handguns on himself and committed suicide.[24]

Less than a year earlier, on April 16, 2007, Seung-Hui Cho had killed 32 people on the campus of Virginia Polytechnic Institute and State University (Virginia Tech), before killing himself. In the decade prior to the Northern Illinois tragedy, there were 38 school shootings in 24 states.[25] The incident at Virginia Tech was the deadliest—and it also was the deadliest shooting rampage by a single person in U.S. history.

The responsibility for maintaining safety on campuses and for responding to emergencies like school shootings falls on local government and state officials. University administrators, especially at public colleges and universities, are included among these officials. Police at Virginia Tech and Northern Illinois were the first responders. Area police and medical personnel went into action as soon as 911 was called. Governors in both states declared official emergencies, thereby making counseling and recovery services available to the injured victims and to others affected by the incidents. State governments also reimbursed the towns of Blacksburg and DeKalb for some of the expenses they incurred in responding to the shootings.

Northern Illinois, like universities and colleges across the country, had reexamined and refined its emergency response plans in light of lessons learned at Virginia Tech.

Kazmierczak entered the lecture hall at 3:06 p.m. Police responded within three minutes after the shooting began. At 3:20 the campus was notified, via e-mail, text messages, the university website, and other warning systems, about a gunman on campus, and everyone was told to seek safety. At 3:40 the campus was locked down—no one other than emergency and law enforcement personnel was allowed on campus, and classes and all other events were cancelled.

In contrast, the response at Virginia Tech had been criticized by a state-appointed task force for missing opportunities that might have saved some lives.[26] Cho's first two victims were shot in a dormitory about 7:15 a.m. Cho then went back to his dorm room, changed out of his blood-stained clothes, deleted his e-mail, and filled his backpack with guns, ammunition, and other supplies. Then he went to a post office and mailed a package of writings and video recordings to NBC News. About two hours after the initial shootings, Cho went to Norris Hall and chained the three main entrance doors shut. He placed a note on the barricaded entrance saying that a bomb would explode if the doors were opened. A faculty member found the note and notified the school's administration, but no one called 911. Cho went from one classroom in Norris Hall to another, shooting students and faculty. In a 12-minute period, he fired at least 174 rounds, killing 29 and wounding 17; Cho then fatally shot himself in the head. It took police almost five minutes to enter the barricaded building once they arrived on the scene.

The task force that reviewed the shootings at Virginia Tech faulted not only the response, but also the failures of state and university officials to heed signs that Seung-Hui Cho was troubled. In middle school, he had been diagnosed with a severe anxiety disorder. He continued therapy until his junior year in high school. While in college, he was declared mentally ill by a judge and ordered to receive therapy. In part, the court action was a response to accusations in 2005 that he was stalking two female students. Because state authorities thought federal laws protecting the privacy of the mentally ill kept them from notifying gun dealers, Cho was able to purchase the guns and ammunition he used in the shootings. Similarly, university officials were not informed about his past. The shooter at Northern Illinois University also suffered from mental illness, although he did not have a history similar to Cho's and there were no warning signs of the danger he posed.

▼ **VIRGINIA TECH SHOOTINGS**
After the 2007 shootings on the campus of Virginia Tech, state and local governments worked with university officials to make students safer. Do you think allowing students, faculty, and staff to bring firearms on campus would make a campus more safe or less safe?

Prompted by the Virginia Tech shootings, state and local governments, including universities, assessed their abilities to respond to shootings and other emergencies and considered preventive measures that might make such incidents less likely. Some state legislators and the National Rifle Association argued for allowing students and faculty to carry concealed weapons on campuses, contending that an armed student could have shot Cho or Kazmierczak and prevented further carnage. Local and state governments examined, as they typically do after any emergency or natural disaster, their protocols and procedures for response. University task forces around the country considered changes to admission policies to screen out or monitor applicants with histories of violence. Universities also reviewed mental health services available to students. A major concern for universities, too, was to reassure students and their families that campuses were safe places for living and learning.

ThinkingCritically

1. What additional steps, if any, can be taken to reduce the likelihood of shootings at schools and college campuses?

2. What should local police forces, hospitals, and trauma counselors do to be prepared for the shootings that might occur? Can you identify if any additional steps have been taken in your area?

3. Should state and local governments allow individuals to carry concealed weapons on college campuses?

Forms of municipal government   Municipal government may take various forms. As Table 19-3 shows, almost 56 percent of municipalities use the combination of a mayor and an elected council. This is the most traditional form of city, town, and village government. Of the mayors, 72 percent are directly elected and the others are council members who have been elected by their peers. Mayors and councils are common in the smallest and largest municipalities.

Most mid-sized cities, with populations between 25,000 and 250,000, have the council–manager form of government, in which there is either no mayor or only a weak ceremonial mayor. Elected councils hire professional managers to run their governments in this form. With very few exceptions, school districts follow the council–manager model—that is, elected school boards hire a superintendent to manage the schools.

In New England and the Midwest, most of the smallest municipalities have **town meetings** to consider budgets and laws. All voters are invited to attend a meeting, which might be annual or monthly, and conduct the public business of the community. Whoever attends determines the fate of the town. Frequently, very few actually take advantage of this opportunity for direct democracy.

A very small number of communities have **representative town meetings**. In these communities, located primarily in New Hampshire, Massachusetts, Connecticut, and Vermont, voters choose representatives by precinct or district to participate in the town meeting. This form of government differs from the open town meeting in that not all residents are allowed to vote. It differs from an elected council because no one serves a term of office. The representatives simply go to the

town meeting   form of local government in which all eligible voters are invited to attend a meeting to pass budgets and ordinances.

representative town meeting   form of local government in which voters select someone from their precinct or district to participate in a meeting that considers and approves budgets and ordinances. Representatives do not hold an office or serve a term after the meeting adjourns.

TABLE 19-3. **Major Forms of Municipal Government, 2008**

FORM OF GOVERNMENT	NUMBER	PERCENTAGE
Mayor–council	3,686	55.8
Council–manager	2,290	34.7
Commission	176	2.7
Town meeting	370	5.6
Representative town meeting	81	1.2

Note: Only those municipalities with populations of at least 2,500 are included.

Source: International City/County Management Association, *The Municipal Year Book 2008* (Washington, DC: ICMA, 2008), 39–45.

meeting, deliberate, and return home as citizens without a title or set of ongoing responsibilities.

Informal power   The most powerful and influential people in a community are not necessarily those who hold offices in government. Especially in small or medium-sized communities, a single family or employer can commonly be the major decision maker, whether or not the family or the company holds a formal position.[27] Social and economic elites in these communities typically need to support changes if they are to succeed. For example, they must be comfortable with plans to develop residential and commercial areas in the community. They must also approve police policies like whether to focus attention on certain racial groups or outsiders and whether to give priority to white-collar crimes, drug use, or sexual misconduct between consenting adults. A newly elected mayor or village president would be naïve to think that he or she could govern as if the informal sources of power did not exist. When the informal and formal powers are in alignment on policies, those policies are likely to be adopted and implemented. If someone in a formal position of authority wants to oppose a family or company with informal power, he or she had better be prepared for a battle.

Ad hoc, issue-specific organizations are also important and relatively frequent sources of power at local levels of government. Individuals may, for example, come together to oppose a particular road project or to promote a program in the public schools. Their activity can be intense and highly visible as they advocate their cause. Once the decision has been made and the issues resolved—win or lose—this ad hoc organization will generally disband and no longer exert influence on local officials.

Informal power is also important when certain personalities play a role that exceeds their formal positions. This happened, for example, in San Diego in the 1970s when Pete Wilson was mayor. San Diego has a council–manager form of government, with a weak, ceremonial mayor. The city manager had been an advocate for rapid growth, but Mayor Wilson was opposed to this. He provided effective leadership in the community and on the city council and was able to stop the manager.[28] Pete Wilson used his political skills, not the powers of his office. In fact, he gained attention outside the San Diego area and went on to become a U.S. senator and then governor of California.

State Courts

19-3   Outline the structure of state courts and their relationship with federal courts.

Almost everyone will be in a courtroom at some point. It may be as a judge, a juror, a litigant, an attorney, or a witness. A dispute—or an administrative function, such as the processing of a will, a name change, or an adoption—may bring us to court. Most likely, these events will take place in a state or local court, not a national court. The notable exception is that for people who live in Washington, D.C., where all courts are national.

The primary function of courts is to settle disputes and enforce laws. Most disputes involve state laws, which cover criminal behavior; family matters such as divorce or child custody; business issues such as contracts, liability, and land use; and, of course, traffic, parking, and speeding citations.

State and national courts are separate but sometimes overlap.

inclusion   the principle that state courts will apply federal laws when those laws directly conflict with state laws.

dual jurisdiction   when two different courts (state, tribal, national) have the authority to try someone for crimes committed in the same incident.

National and state laws may sometimes be interrelated, with national courts involved in what would otherwise be a state issue. In contradictions between national and state laws, national law usually prevails. Through a rule known as **inclusion**, state courts are obliged to enforce the prevailing national law. National courts resolve any disputes about the application of national law. Occasionally national and state laws apply to the same crime, as is the case in most states regarding drug use and drug trafficking. These situations are called **dual jurisdiction**, in which the individual could be brought before both a state and a national court. On these occasions, national and state prosecutors generally agree to bring the accused to one of the two courts for trial and sentencing. Such agreements may well be based on whether the state or the national government has the harsher penalties.

Since the 1970s, the U.S. Supreme Court has generally taken the position that state courts should regard its rulings concerning individual rights, such as freedom of speech and protection from unreasonable search and seizure, as minimums that might be enhanced by state governments. If, for example, a state law required officers making an arrest to remind the accused not only that they have a right to remain silent and have representation by an attorney, but that they also could call a friend or employer to post bail (something not guaranteed by federal law), then the extra requirement must be honored. If, on the other hand, a state did not require arresting officers to say anything about a right to remain silent, then the federal protection—known here as Miranda rights—must be applied by state courts.

▼ COURT TRIAL

A judge and jury watch an attorney question a witness. Juries evaluate the credibility of testimony. What is the primary function of state courts?

Court structures in states provide routes for appeals.

States reorganized their courts in the 1970s to follow a model that simplified the handling of cases and appeals and allowed state supreme courts to refuse to take certain cases so that they had manageable workloads. Prior to these reforms, cases commonly took years, even decades, to resolve.[29] In some cases, parties to litigation about wills or land died before the courts resolved the disputes. Figure 19-3 presents the structure that describes most state courts since the simplification of the 1970s.

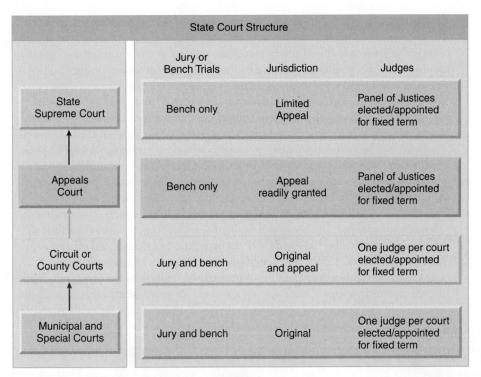

State Court Structure			
	Jury or Bench Trials	Jurisdiction	Judges
State Supreme Court	Bench only	Limited Appeal	Panel of Justices elected/appointed for fixed term
Appeals Court	Bench only	Appeal readily granted	Panel of Justices elected/appointed for fixed term
Circuit or County Courts	Jury and bench	Original and appeal	One judge per court elected/appointed for fixed term
Municipal and Special Courts	Jury and bench	Original	One judge per court elected/appointed for fixed term

FIGURE 19-3. State Court Structure. State courts are organized to provide at least one appeal and to make the workload of supreme courts manageable.

Urban areas typically have courts that handle traffic and parking citations, small claims (disputes seeking damages less than a certain sum—commonly $5,000), family issues, and probate (wills). Small towns and rural areas usually do not have their own courts, but if they do the judges are generally part time. Cases in these communities are heard in a county court. Municipal courts and courts that specialize in something like probate or small claims do not have juries. A single judge hears the cases. When a judge hears a case without a jury, it is referred to as a **bench trial**.

Most cases in state courts begin in county or circuit courts. State courts may also hear appeals from municipal or specialized courts. The trials in county or circuit courts are what most people envision when they think of what happens in a courtroom. In most states, either party to a dispute has the right to ask for a jury. Lawyers make arguments, call witnesses, and present evidence to the jury, with the judge presiding and ruling on whether the lawyers are following procedure. The main role of the jury (or judge if the parties do not want a jury) is to evaluate the credibility of witnesses and evidence and then determine guilt or innocence, and liability, if any.

In the common state model, appeals courts are panels of several judges. Appeals courts typically must take all cases presented to them. There are no juries at this level. Appellate courts hear arguments of lawyers about whether correct procedures were followed and whether laws and precedents were correctly applied.

State supreme courts are also appellate courts, but following the reforms of the 1970s they can select which cases they will hear. This freedom allows them to consider a manageable number of cases and to focus on cases where appeals courts rulings on similar issues disagree with one another or where major constitutional and legal issues are raised. If the state supreme court decides not to hear a case, then the appeals court ruling stands.

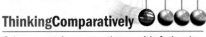
ThinkingComparatively
Other countries, even those with federal governments, usually have a single, national court system.

bench trial a court trial in which a judge hears and rules on a case without a jury.

justice the term used to refer to a state supreme court judge.

merit plan a method of selecting judges in which a governor must appoint someone from a list provided by an independent panel. Judges are then kept in office if they get a majority of yes votes in general elections; also called Missouri plan.

Selection of judges and justices   Most state judges and **justices** (the term for members of state supreme courts) are elected to their positions for a specific term. Of course, this pattern is different from that in the national government, where judges are appointed by the president, confirmed by the Senate, and serve indefinitely. The first states had their legislatures place judges and justices on the bench for fixed terms of six to 10 years, still the case in South Carolina and Virginia (Table 19-4). Governors in Maine and New Jersey appoint judges, subject to legislative confirmation, for seven-year terms. When a term expires, the governors may reappoint for another seven-year term. California's governor appoints appellate judges and supreme court justices for 12-year terms. When a term expires, the judge or justice must be elected for another 12 years.

Nineteen states elect their judges and justices on nonpartisan ballots. As with nonpartisan races for local government positions, party identification and support may be linked to candidates even though party labels do not appear on the ballot. In 12 states, judicial elections are in fact explicitly partisan and nominees may have to win a party primary just like candidates running for other, nonjudicial offices (see "How Do We Know? Do Campaign Supporters Influence Decisions by Judges?").

Concerned about the possibility of partisanship in judicial elections compromising the role and prestige of the court, 24 states use the **merit plan**, sometimes called

TABLE 19-4. Judicial Selection Patterns

PARTISAN ELECTION	NONPARTISAN ELECTION	ELECTION BY LEGISLATURE	APPOINTMENT BY GOVERNOR	MISSOURI OR MERIT PLAN
Alabama	Arkansas	South Carolina	California	Alaska
Illinois	California	Virginia	Maine	Arizona
Indiana	Florida		New Jersey	Colorado
Kansas	Georgia			Connecticut
Louisiana	Idaho			Delaware
Missouri	Indiana			Florida
New York	Kentucky			Hawaii
Ohio	Michigan			Indiana
Pennsylvania	Minnesota			Iowa
Tennessee	Mississippi			Kansas
Texas	Montana			Maryland
West Virginia	Nevada			Massachusetts
	North Carolina			Missouri
	North Dakota			Nebraska
	Oregon			New Hampshire
	South Dakota			New Mexico
	Utah			New York
	Washington			Oklahoma
	Wisconsin			Rhode Island
				South Dakota
				Tennessee
				Utah
				Vermont
				Wyoming

Note: Some states use different selection systems for different courts.

Source: Adapted from *The Book of the States, 2008* (Lexington, KY: Council of State Governments, 2008), 251–4.

the Missouri plan, to select judges. In this system, the governor appoints a committee of judges, attorneys, and citizens to nominate individuals they consider highly qualified for a judicial position. The governor then selects someone from the list of nominees. That person may have to be approved by one chamber of the legislature and serves for one year and then voters are presented with the question: "Shall Judge (name of the judge who had been serving) be retained in office?" If the majority says yes, the judge serves a full term. If the majority says no, then the governor must select someone else from the original list of nominees, who then serves a year before being subject to voter approval (called a retention election).

Another response to concerns about the possibility of elections compromising the impartiality of courts is to avoid conflicts of interest, on a case-by-case basis. Frequently, one party in a case has a business or personal link to the judge that rules on it. Judicial codes of conduct in all states stipulate that in such a situation, the judge should make sure both sides know about the ties and can object to the judge's continuing to handle the case. Moreover, judges are themselves encouraged to **recuse** themselves from the case—that is, voluntarily abstain or excuse themselves and let other judges or justices decide.

Recusal was a key issue in West Virginia in 2008 when Chief Justice Elliott E. Maynard received financial support for his reelection campaign and was photographed vacationing with Don L. Blankenship, chief executive of a coal company that was a litigant in cases before the state's supreme court. Justice Maynard voted with the majority in a 3–2 decision favoring Blankenship's company and only recused himself after publicity about the conflict of interest prompted the court to reconsider the case. Voters regarded the recusal as too late and too reluctant, and Justice Maynard was defeated in the Democratic primary in his bid for a new term.

States prohibit judicial candidates from indicating how they would rule in a pending or likely lawsuit. All states have such prohibitions. The U.S. Supreme Court in *Republican Party of Minnesota v. White* (2002) ruled that states cannot prohibit candidates from discussing legal issues or telling voters how they would handle certain types of cases, but the Court agreed it was inappropriate to make promises about specific cases.

recuse the act of abstaining or not participating in a decision. This applies primarily to judges who avoid a conflict of interest by not participating in cases where they have a personal or financial interest.

Direct Democracy

19-4 Classify the methods of direct democracy used by some state governments.

Some state and local governments provide their citizens with opportunities for participating directly in public policy-making, rather than relying solely on elected representatives. The town meeting in small communities in New England and the Midwest, discussed earlier, is one form of direct democracy. However, there are several other forms as well, which we will examine here.

Initiatives allow voters to enact laws. In 19 states, most of them in the West, citizens can use the **direct initiative** to enact state laws (Table 19-5). Western states wrote their constitutions and were admitted to the United States at the height of the Progressive movement, which sought to empower voters rather than bosses of political machines. The direct initiative is also available at the local government level in 28 states. Under this procedure, if enough citizens sign a petition supporting a particular policy proposal, the policy question will be placed on a ballot and will become law if approved by a majority of those voting. The governor and legislature are not involved in direct initiatives.

The number of signatures required to get a measure on a ballot varies by state but is typically 8 to 10 percent of the number of people who voted in the most recent gubernatorial election. Wyoming requires 15 percent. North Dakota places the minimum at 2 percent of the voting-age population.

direct initiative a process in which voters can place a proposal on a ballot and enact it into law without involving the legislature or governor.

continued on page 692 ▶

Do Campaign Supporters Influence Decisions by Judges?

The Question

When judges are elected rather than appointed, they need financial and other forms of support in their campaigns. If interest groups, corporations, or wealthy individuals support a judicial candidate, they might expect that they will be treated favorably by the judge once he or she is elected. This expectation can threaten public confidence in the fairness of judicial decisions. Do campaign contributors influence decisions by judges? How do we know?

Why It Matters

Ideally, judges are regarded as neutral, third-party arbiters of disputes. Unlike legislators or governors, judges are not considered to have constituents that they serve, because they serve society as a whole and the state constitution. Judges are to interpret and apply the law to specific cases, not to reward supporters. The functioning of the court depends heavily on a general sense that everyone is treated fairly and impartially. As in an athletic contest, it is important that referees or umpires are not blamed for being biased and ruling for one side because of that bias.

The potential for bias remains even when judges disclose conflicts of interest in cases involving campaign supporters. In fact, we might interpret these attempts as an acknowledgement of the power behind the notion that campaign supporters influence judges. Political scientists have addressed this issue in a number of studies, using different research designs.

▼ JUDICIAL ELECTIONS
In many states judges must face voters at least once in order to obtain or retain a state judicial seat.

Investigating the Answer

One scholar focused on states with a partisan election process for judicial selection. He then identified which state courts were dominated by Republicans, which by Democrats, and which were fairly even. Then he looked at whether decisions made by these courts favored criminal defendants, corporations, government agencies, and poor people.[30] He hypothesized that courts dominated by Republicans would tend to favor corporations and rule against criminal defendants, government agencies, and poor people; courts dominated by Democrats would have the opposite tendencies; and evenly split courts would be mixed. He found no significant correlations between the partisan character of a court and its judicial decisions.

Another scholar used a similar but more detailed approach in a study of the Texas Supreme Court. Texas uses partisan elections to select members of its supreme court. He correlated campaign contributors with the decisions of specific judges. Although there were some notable exceptions, he found a clear and systematic pattern in which the judges ruled in favor of groups who had made significant contributions to their campaigns.[31] This study was about just one state, but it had the advantage of looking closely at the votes of individual justices and at their respective supporters.

Yet another scholar completed a comprehensive study of the influence of elections and campaign contributions on the behavior of state supreme court justices. Her study included states using different selection processes and, like the Texas study, analyzed the relationship between the decisions of individual justices and the groups providing campaign support. She, too, found a pattern suggesting that campaign contributions matter.[32] Justices rarely recused themselves from cases in which groups that had made substantial contributions had an interest. Moreover, they generally ruled in favor of those groups. The pattern in partisan elections was stronger than that for nonpartisan elections, but the relationship between contributions and rulings was evident in both systems.

This study also compared what happens in states in which justices are elected and those in which they are appointed. This analysis is important because the appointments are made by elected governors and legislators who usually draw support from particular sets of interest groups. The finding was that appointed justices tended to rule in favor of the groups who supported the governors and legislators responsible for their appointment. This was even somewhat the case with states that use the merit (or Missouri) plan. The degree to which appointed justices favored the groups who supported those who appointed them, however, was considerably less than occurred for elected justices, where the relationship to campaign contributors was more direct.[33]

The studies cited above examined state supreme courts. Many critical decisions are, of course, made at the appellate and trial court levels. It is reasonable to infer that the patterns discovered in looking at supreme courts also apply to other courts, but we do not know that for certain, given the complexity of studying such a relationship.

Another difference between the decisions of state supreme court justices and those of appellate and trial judges is that the reasoning provided in the written opinions of supreme court justices uses general principles. In large part, this is because state supreme courts set precedents that are supposed to be followed by other courts in their respective states. The issue of judicial reasoning also raises another caveat in the studies done by political scientists—and by those engaged in judicial campaigns. Disputes typically raise several important legal issues, and it is sometimes misleading to characterize a justice as being for business interests or biased toward defendants in criminal cases. A vote that results in a victory for an insurance company may be based on how a state statute is written, rather than on a bias in favor of companies who made campaign contributions. What appears to be a ruling freeing a convicted criminal or reducing a sentence may be based on procedures that were not followed, not sympathy for someone who has had a rough life.

Finally, and importantly, determining whether or not campaign contributions influence judicial decisions almost inevitably involves making reasonable interpretations of why a correlation does or does not exist. We simply do not have e-mails or taped conversations between justices and their campaign contributors that reveal negotiations or motivations for particular decisions. If there was a pattern of justices ruling in favor of their supporters, we can conclude that there may be influence. However, it may also be that interest groups make contributions to candidates who would likely rule in their favor even if no contribution were made. The contribution, in other words, is designed to get a sympathetic candidate elected rather than to influence behavior on the bench.

Thinking Critically

◼ What do you think? Do judicial elections make judges biased toward the interests of their campaign supporters?
◼ If judicial elections can bias judges, will using an appointment process or merit plan eliminate the problem?
◼ If judges are biased, because of campaigns or any other reason, does it mean that they cannot represent the general interests of society at the same time?

The Bottom Line

The most comprehensive, systematic research does show a positive relationship between campaign contributions to judicial candidates and the decisions those candidates make if they get on the bench. This finding is especially important because the relationship is stronger than that between the rulings of justices who are appointed to state supreme courts and the campaign supporters of those who appoint them. Also, this finding is important because studies indicate that those who are elected are more likely to set new precedents than those who are appointed. Even though we lack direct evidence of motivation or negotiation, and there may be reasons for the correlation between support and judicial decisions, as discussed above, it is reasonable to be concerned that elected justices seem to act like other elected officials, for whom we expect and accept constituent relations.

The direct initiative was one of the reforms that came out of the Progressive era. The idea was that, to combat political machines and interest groups that might control governors or legislators, direct democracy would enable people to take action by themselves. However, interest groups still have an impact. For example, business groups, labor unions, and single-issue advocacy organizations pay individuals as much as $5 for every signature they get on a petition to put a proposal on a ballot. As pointed out in Chapter 9, political advertising is central to campaigns, and its importance applies to campaigns for and against ballot initiatives as well as candidates. Ideally, the advertisements inform the electorate, but unequal access to funds may mean that one side cannot get its message out to voters as effectively as the other.[34] In some states, like California, it is common for each side to spend about $35 million on ballot initiatives. Despite the drawbacks, the direct initiative has been used to legalize medical use of marijuana, physician-assisted suicide, property tax limits, life sentences for repeat offenders, bans on same-sex marriage, and a ban on confining pregnant pigs.

One concern about the direct initiative is that there is no opportunity for the deliberation and revision process that occurs in a legislature. Voters have to accept or reject the proposal as presented on the ballot. When issues like the status of

TABLE 19-5. Authority for Instruments of Direct Democracy

STATE	DIRECT INITIATIVE	INDIRECT INITIATIVE	POPULAR REFERENDUM	RECALL
Alabama			X	
Alaska	X		X	X
Arizona	X		X	X
Arkansas	X		X	
California	X		X	X
Colorado	X			X
Florida	X			
Georgia				X
Idaho			X	X
Illinois	X			
Kansas				X
Kentucky			X	
Louisiana				X
Maine		X	X	
Maryland			X	
Massachusetts		X	X	
Michigan	X	X	X	X
Minnesota				X
Missouri	X		X	
Montana	X		X	X
Nebraska	X		X	
Nevada	X	X	X	X
New Mexico			X	
North Dakota	X		X	X
Ohio	X	X	X	
Oklahoma	X		X	
Oregon	X		X	X
Rhode Island				X
South Dakota	X		X	
Utah	X	X	X	
Washington	X	X	X	X
Wisconsin				X
Wyoming		X	X	

Source: Based on *The Book of the States, 2008* (Lexington, KY: Council of State Governments, 2008), 308–27.

children of illegal immigrants, described in the chapter opening, are dealt with in an initiative, there are no opportunities for dealing with subtleties or complexities through debate and amendment. The **indirect initiative**, available in eight states—including five that also have the direct initiative—addresses this concern. This process starts with action by the legislature, which introduces, debates, amends, and passes a proposal just like any other bill. Instead of sending the bill to the governor for approval, however, the legislature puts the measure on the ballot for approval by voters.

indirect initiative a process in which the legislature places a proposal on a ballot and allows voters to enact it into law, without involving the governor or further action by the legislature.

▶ **PETITION FOR DIRECT INITIATIVE**

In order to get a proposed initiative on the ballot, supporters must get the signatures of eligible voters on a petition. What are some of the drawbacks of direct democracy, including initiatives?

Referenda are another form of direct democracy that allow voters to veto state legislation and authorize borrowing money.

popular referendum a process by which voters can veto a bill recently passed in the legislature by placing the issue on a ballot and expressing disapproval. Also called direct referendum.

The **popular referendum**, sometimes called the direct referendum, is an opportunity for voters to veto actions by the legislature and governor. Voters in 24 states may circulate a petition objecting to a bill passed in a recent legislative session; if enough people sign the petition, the question of whether to uphold or veto the bill will appear on the ballot. For example, in South Dakota in 2007, the legislature and governor agreed on a bill that was designed to bring the question before the U.S. Supreme Court of whether states could ban abortions. The governor and a majority of legislators believed that two new appointments to the Court by President George W. Bush probably meant that *Roe v. Wade* (1973) would be overturned. Voters in South Dakota objected, however, to what they thought were excessive restrictions on the privacy rights of women. They used the popular referendum to veto the law in a 2008 statewide vote and keep it from becoming the basis of a test case in court.

bond referendum a process of seeking voter approval before a government borrows money by issuing bonds to investors.

When governments have to borrow money to complete a large project like a new school or a bridge, they often have to get voter approval in a **bond referendum**. This step is especially true for local governments. The debates about whether to approve the issuance of bonds include not only whether the project is needed but how much taxpayers will be billed to pay back the loans and interest.

advisory referendum a process in which voters cast nonbinding ballots on an issue or proposal.

Sometimes legislators place an **advisory referendum** on the ballot. As the term implies, the results of an advisory referendum are not binding. Legislators may genuinely want to test voter sentiment before deciding whether to initiate a change in a law. Another reason for having an advisory referendum is political. An issue may be placed on the ballot to mobilize some voters to go to the polls in the hopes that they will support certain candidates as well as vote on the referendum. Such a strategy was used in advisory referenda on ending the U.S. involvement in Iraq in 2006 in over 2,500 local and state elections. Obviously, however, cities and states have no control over U.S. military and foreign policy. The referenda were designed to mobilize antiwar sentiment and advantage certain candidates.

One concern about initiatives and referenda is that the rights of minority groups may be threatened by the "tyranny of the majority." The issue is complex, but research does suggest that minorities are likely to lose when their rights are decided at the ballot box versus legislative institutions.[35]

Recall allows voters in some states to remove elected officials from their positions before their terms expire.

Finally, most states allow their citizens to recall elected local government officials and 18 states allow state officials such as judges, legislators, and governors to be recalled. A recall is a procedure in which an elected official is voted out of office before his or her term expires. In 11 of the 17 states that allow it, the recall does not require any particular grounds, such as a crime or scandal. In Alaska, Georgia, Kansas, Minnesota, Montana, Rhode Island, and Washington, specific grounds are required and a judge determines whether the alleged misconduct or malfeasance is serious enough to warrant a recall. The judge makes the determination after a hearing in which both sides are able to make arguments and offer evidence. In all situations, however, the issue of guilt or innocence and the decision whether to retain or remove the official are up to voters. Legislatures can also remove officials from office, but they must use an impeachment process, which requires formal charges of wrongdoing and follows procedures similar to a court trial. State legislators have been recalled for raising taxes and supporting subsidies for professional baseball teams. Judges have been recalled for

▼ **RECALL**
Shortly after his reelection in 2002, California Governor Gray Davis had to campaign to keep his job in a recall election. He lost and Arnold Schwarzenegger became governor. Some states allow for recall elections only under certain conditions. Should states limit the situations under which a recall election can be held?

blaming victims of rape for the assault they suffered, rather than those who committed the crime. Only two governors have been recalled: North Dakota's Lynn Frazier in 1921 and California's Gray Davis in 2003.

In most states, a person must serve for one year in the office before he or she can be recalled, and there are separate ballots to recall someone and to choose a replacement. The more common process is first to decide whether to recall someone. If a majority favors recall, voters then go to the polls three to four weeks later for a primary election to determine which names will be on the final ballot. After another three to four weeks, voters choose between winners of the primary.

The irony of all forms of direct democracy is that enhanced access to government does not translate into higher rates of participation. Even in visible, colorful recall elections like the one in California in 2003, less than half of eligible voters tend to go to the polls. And although school board members, city council members, mayors, and state legislators are approached with suggestions, complaints, and concerns when they shop for groceries, go for a walk, or attend church, those who make the effort to express themselves in these ways and to attend meetings and hearings are a small percentage of those who could participate in grassroots governance.

ThinkingCausally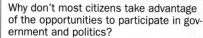

Why don't most citizens take advantage of the opportunities to participate in government and politics?

CHAPTER SUMMARY

In this chapter you have learned to:

19-1 Explain how state constitutions and local government charters provide the structure and operations of state and local governments. State constitutions and local government charters provide frameworks in much the same way that the U.S. Constitution guides the national government. The constitutions specify individual rights that state governments must respect and describe the basic institutions and processes for selecting officials and enacting public policies. In large part because territories that petitioned to join the Union as states had to have a constitution acceptable to Congress, states have borrowed from one another and their constitutions are generally similar. Like the national government, states have separate legislative, judicial, and executive branches. Local governments do not inherently have a right to exist nor do they hold automatic powers. State governments use charters to authorize specific local governments and outline the extent of their power and authority, including whether they can levy taxes or enforce laws.

19-2 Compare and contrast the various forms of executive and legislative branches in state and municipal government. State and local legislative branches and executive branches typically have similar structures and functions, but significant variations have developed over the last 40 years. Governors, in particular, have emerged as very powerful actors in some states, with greatly expanded powers such as budgetary and veto powers, while mayors in many cities have ceded power to legislatures or city managers. In many states the executive branch also includes separately elected officials, such as an attorney general, and these elected offices weaken the governor's institutional position. All state legislatures (except in Nebraska) are bicameral and have similar functions. Because of the application of the one-person, one-vote principle for drawing district boundaries, state legislatures have become more representative of a state's population, often have more staff and compensation, and more have become full-time, remaining in session for much of the year. Local governments may have executive, judicial, and legislative branches located in the same building and even the same body. Other than the largest cities, most local governments are run by individuals who serve part time as elected leaders. Any specific local government is likely to have one or more of the following: elected executive, elected council, and appointed manager.

19-3 Outline the structure of state courts and their relationship with national courts. Most legal disputes are settled in state courts. National courts and national laws have some impact on what happens in state courts, but only where national and state laws converge. Almost all states use a hierarchical system with trial courts at the bottom, district or county courts, intermediate appellate courts, and a supreme court of last resort at the top. Intermediate and supreme courts deal almost exclusively with questions of law and procedure. Although some states appoint judges as in the national system, many states elect their judges for specific terms of office. Still other judges are appointed and then face one-time retention elections. Campaigns have the potential for compromising the fair and impartial role that judges are supposed to play in deciding cases.

19-4 Classify the methods of direct democracy used by some state governments. Some states allow voters to place on the ballot proposals to enact laws or to veto recently passed legislation. When local governments borrow money, they generally have to seek voter approval following legislative action in a form of direct democracy usually called a referendum. Some state and local governments also allow citizens to place policy questions directly on the ballot to be decided by voters; this is usually referred to as a citizen initiative process, and the requirements for placing questions on the ballot vary significantly across the states. Another form of direct democracy is the opportunity voters have to remove an elected official from office before his or her term expires. A recall differs from an impeachment, which is done by legislatures rather than voters. In most cases, there does not have to be any specified grounds for a recall, and in the seven states that do require that there be grounds, it is still up to voters to decide whether to retain or recall the official.

Although direct democracy is not the norm for governance in any jurisdiction, ballot initiatives and recalls can and are used to pursue far-reaching policy and political objectives. Indeed, observers have noted the risks to the rights of minority groups in making policy through direct democracy, while some proponents have demonstrated that the existence of direct democracy in a state constrains the policy-making choices of legislators, whether the direct democracy process is actually used or not.

PEARSON mypoliscilab EXERCISES

Apply what you learned in this chapter by starting with these resources on MyPoliSciLab.

Read on mypoliscilab.com

eText: Chapter 19

Study and Review on mypoliscilab.com

Pre-Test
Post-Test
Chapter Exam
Flashcards

Watch on mypoliscilab.com

Video: Battling City Corruption
Video: Wisconsin Governor Seeks to Remove 'Sexting' DA

Explore on mypoliscilab.com

Simulation: You Are Attempting to Revise the California Constitution
Simulation: You Are Attempting to Revise the Texas Constitution
Simulation: You Are the Director of Economic Development for Los Angeles
Simulation: You Are the Mayor and Need to Get a Town Budget Passed
Simulation: You Are a Governor
Simulation: You Are a State Legislator
Comparative: Comparing State and Local Governments
Comparative: Comparing Executive Branches
Comparative: Comparing Judicial Systems
Timeline: Initiatives and Referendums
Visual Literacy: Explaining Differences in State Laws

KEY TERMS

advisory referendum, p. 694
at-large election, p. 681
bench trial, p. 687
bond referendum, p. 694
charter, p. 670
charter school, p. 672
commission, p. 682
commute, p. 675
county, p. 671
Dillon's rule, p. 670
direct initiative, p. 689
district-based election, p. 681
dual jurisdiction, p. 686

extradite, p. 675
governor, p. 673
home rule, p. 671
inclusion, p. 686
indirect initiative, p. 693
initiative, p. 669
justice, p. 688
line-item veto, p. 674
merit plan, p. 688
nonpartisan, p. 678
Northwest Ordinance of 1787, p. 668
package or general veto, p. 674
pardon, p. 675

parole, p. 675
popular referendum, p. 694
Progressive movement, p. 669
recall, p. 669
recuse, p. 689
representative town meeting, p. 684
special district, p. 671
strong mayor, p. 681
term limits, p. 677
town, p. 671
town meeting, p. 684
township, p. 671
weak mayor, p. 681

CHAPTER TEST

1. Discuss the central elements of state constitutions, why some states have very long constitutions, and the relevance of the timing of a state's founding to the contents of its constitution.

2. What is Dillon's rule?

3. How and why has representation in state legislatures changed since the 1960s?

4. What are the powers of a governor and how do they differ across the states?

5. How has partisan control of governor's offices and state legislatures changed over the past 25 years? What implications do these changes have for policy-making? What has been the trend in your state?

6. Local governments use different types of elections for local legislatures. What are these, and what are the implications of using different systems?

7. State and local government institutions allow for many points of access to policy-making for citizens. Does having more points of access encourage greater participation, or does it overwhelm citizens? What changes might encourage more or less participation?

8. Using local resources or the Internet, investigate the structure of local governments in your area. How do they compare to one another? Are there differences that are associated with the size of the population served?

9. What is your opinion of the different methods for selecting judges? Do you favor one method over another? Explain why or why not.

10. What forms of direct democracy are used in states and localities? What are some of the drawbacks of direct democracy institutions such as the initiative and referenda?

SUGGESTED READINGS

Thomas E. Cronin. 1999. *Direct Democracy: The Politics of Initiative, Referendum, and Recall.* Cambridge, MA: Harvard University Press. The origins and development of the major instruments of direct democracy.

Todd Donovan, Christopher Mooney, and Daniel A. Smith. 2010. *State and Local Politics: Institutions and Reform,* 2nd ed. Belmont, CA: Wadsworth. A textbook covering the institutions, processes, and major public policies of state and local governments.

V. O. Key Jr. 1949. *Southern Politics in State and Nation.* New York: Vintage. A classic study of regional politics that pioneered in the use of qualitative research.

John G. Matsusaka. 2004. *For the Many or the Few: The Initiative, Public Policy, and American Democracy.* Chicago: University of Chicago Press. The role of interest groups and corporations in the initiative process.

Alan Rosenthal. 2004. *Heavy Lifting: The Job of the American Legislature.* Washington, DC: CQ Press. A critique of the challenges faced by state legislatures and recent trends toward partisanship.

Ralph G. Wright. 2005. *Inside the Statehouse: Lessons from the Speaker.* Washington, DC: CQ Press. Reflections of the former Speaker of the Vermont General Assembly, both on dynamics within the legislature and relations with governors.

Peverill Squire and Keith E. Hamm. 2005. *101 Chambers: Congress, State Legislatures, and the Future of Legislative Studies.* Columbus: Ohio State University Press. A comprehensive look at legislatures in the states relative to the U.S. Congress.

SUGGESTED WEBSITES

www.stateline.org

A daily source of news analysis and links to stories related to states.

Congressional Quarterly Press: www.governing.com

A service providing links to news stories about state governments and politics.

Council of State Governments: www.csg.org

A nonpartisan organization serving all three branches of state governments and the public with information and issue analyses.

National Conference of State Legislatures: www.ncsl.org

A nonpartisan organization serving state legislatures and the public with information, issue analyses and election results.

National Governors Association: www.nga.org

A nonpartisan organization serving governors and the public with information and issue analyses.

1 Annotated Declaration of Independence*

In Congress, July 4, 1776
The Unanimous Declaration of the Thirteen United States of America

The Declaration of Independence marked the break of the 13 American colonies away from Great Britain. After decades of disputes, the colonists announced to the world the beginning of a new country. The chief goals of the Declaration were to announce and provide the reasons for separating the colonies from the British Empire and to cement support in the colonies for independence. Ensuring this support was not an easy task. Historians' estimates place the proportion of colonists returning to Britain following the start of the Revolutionary War as somewhere between one-quarter and one-third. The writers of the Declaration sought to build a sense of national identity among the colonists as Americans. The document has four sections: a preamble, a statement of principles that should guide a political system, a list of grievances against the British government, and a statement that the states are now independent.

The preamble is the introduction to the Declaration. The writers explain that they wish to detail why the colonies are separating from Britain.

When in the Course of human events it becomes necessary for one people to dissolve the political bands which have connected them with another, and to assume among the powers of the earth, the separate and equal station to which the Laws of Nature and of Nature's God entitle them, a decent respect to the opinions of mankind requires that they should declare the causes which impel them to the separation.

The Declaration in its second section provides a statement of the principles that should guide a political system. In this section, the Declaration quickly makes the claim that some rights are natural, they are inherent in people and cannot be given away (they are "unalienable"); that there is a social contract between the governed and the rulers (governments derive their power from the peoples' consent); that the people are sovereign, have a right to revolution, and have the right to self determination—to create a new system that reflects their principles when the contract is broken. The authors then explain that the colonists were patient and suffered many abuses before taking the step of independence.

We hold these truths to be self-evident, that all men are created equal, that they are endowed by their Creator with certain unalienable Rights, that among these are Life, Liberty and the pursuit of Happiness.—That to secure these rights, Governments are instituted among Men, deriving their just powers from the consent of the governed,—That whenever any Form of Government becomes destructive of these ends, it is the Right of the People to alter or to abolish it, and to institute new Government, laying its foundation on such principles and organizing its powers in such form, as to them shall seem most likely to effect their Safety and Happiness. Prudence, indeed, will dictate that Governments long established should not be changed for light and transient causes; and accordingly all experience hath shewn that mankind are more disposed to suffer, while evils are sufferable, than to right themselves by abolishing the forms to which they are accustomed. But when a long train of abuses and usurpations, pursuing invariably the same Object evinces a design to reduce them under absolute Despotism, it is their right, it is their duty, to throw off such Government, and to provide new Guards for their future security.

Such has been the patient sufferance of these Colonies; and such is now the necessity which constrains them to alter their former Systems of Government. The history of the present King of Great Britain is a history of repeated injuries and usurpations, all having in direct object the establishment of an absolute Tyranny over these States. To prove this, let Facts be submitted to a candid world.

The Declaration now provides a lengthy list of grievances against the British king and Parliament. The charges it lodges are serious. The king has trivialized any notion that the consent of the governed should be taken into account. He has interfered with all branches of government in the colonies, and even shut some down. He has elevated military power over the people's power. Despite the colonists' attempts to manage their affairs, he has frequently revised or overthrown their decisions. The theme that legitimate government must be based on the consent of the governed runs strongly throughout the 27 charges. The first 12 charges are directed toward the king.

He has refused his Assent to Laws, the most wholesome and necessary for the public good.

He has forbidden his Governors to pass Laws of immediate and pressing importance, unless suspended in their operation till his Assent should be obtained; and when so suspended, he has utterly neglected to attend to them.

He has refused to pass other Laws for the accommodation of large districts of people, unless those people would relinquish the right of Representation in the Legislature, a right inestimable to them and formidable to tyrants only.

*This text retains the spelling, capitalization, and punctuation of the original.

He has called together legislative bodies at places unusual, uncomfortable, and distant from the depository of their Public Records, for the sole purpose of fatiguing them into compliance with his measures.

He has dissolved Representative Houses repeatedly, for opposing with manly firmness his invasions on the rights of the people.

He has refused for a long time, after such dissolutions, to cause others to be elected; whereby the Legislative Powers, incapable of Annihilation, have returned to the People at large for their exercise; the State remaining in the mean time exposed to all the dangers of invasion from without, and convulsions within.

He has endeavored to prevent the population of these States; for that purpose obstructing the Laws for Naturalization of Foreigners; refusing to pass others to encourage their migration hither, and raising the conditions of new Appropriations of Lands.

He has obstructed the Administration of Justice, by refusing his Assent to Laws for establishing Judiciary powers.

He has made Judges dependent on his Will alone, for the tenure of their offices, and the amount and payment of their salaries.

He has erected a multitude of New Offices, and sent hither swarms of Officers to harass our people, and eat out their substance.

He has kept among us, in times of peace, Standing Armies without the Consent of our legislatures.

He has affected to render the Military independent of and superior to the Civil power.

The next set of charges are leveled against the king and Parliament ("he has combined with others"). The first paragraph establishes the colonists' view that Parliament's actions are not binding on the colonies. "Their acts of pretended legislation" refers to laws passed by Parliament, to which the king gave his approval. The colonists had no representation in Parliament and, since government depends on the consent of the governed, any actions of Parliament are but "pretend" legislation. The long list of complaints includes, among many others, the famous charge that the king and Parliament imposed taxes on the colonists without their consent. "No taxation without representation" soon became a symbolic reference for generations of Americans to understand the principles that led to Revolution.

He has combined with others to subject us to a jurisdiction foreign to our constitution, and unacknowledged by our laws; giving his Assent to their Acts of pretended Legislation:

For quartering large bodies of armed troops among us:

For protecting them, by a mock Trial, from punishment for any Murders which they should commit on the Inhabitants of these States:

For cutting off our Trade with all parts of the world:

For imposing Taxes on us without our Consent:

For depriving us in many cases, of the benefits of Trial by Jury:

For transporting us beyond Seas to be tried for pretended offences:

For abolishing the free System of English Laws in a neighboring Province, establishing therein an Arbitrary government, and enlarging its Boundaries so as to render it at once an example and

fit instrument for introducing the same absolute rule into these Colonies:

For taking away our Charters, abolishing our most valuable Laws, and altering fundamentally the Forms of our Governments:

For suspending our own Legislatures, and declaring themselves invested with power to legislate for us in all cases whatsoever.

The next five charges address the king's conduct of war and violence against the colonists.

He has abdicated Government here, by declaring us out of his Protection and waging War against us.

He has plundered our seas, ravaged our Coasts, burnt our towns, and destroyed the lives of our people.

He is at this time transporting large Armies of foreign Mercenaries to compleat the works of death, desolation and tyranny, already begun with circumstances of Cruelty & perfidy scarcely paralleled in the most barbarous ages, and totally unworthy the Head of a civilized nation.

He has constrained our fellow Citizens taken Captive on the high Seas to bear Arms against their Country, to become the executioners of their friends and Brethren, or to fall themselves by their Hands.

He has excited domestic insurrections amongst us, and has endeavored to bring on the inhabitants of our frontiers, the merciless Indian Savages, whose known rule of warfare, is an undistinguished destruction of all ages, sexes and conditions.

The writers end the section on grievances by noting that the colonists have tried to make the arrangement with Britain work, but they have been rejected. They have petitioned the king and conveyed to their fellow Britons the unique nature of the colonies. The authors note that neither the British ruler nor the British people have been responsive to these pleas.

In every stage of these Oppressions We have Petitioned for Redress in the most humble terms: Our repeated Petitions have been answered only by repeated injury. A Prince, whose character is thus marked by every act which may define a Tyrant, is unfit to be the ruler of a free people.

Nor have We been wanting in attention to our British brethren. We have warned them from time to time of attempts by their legislature to extend an unwarrantable jurisdiction over us. We have reminded them of the circumstances of our emigration and settlement here. We have appealed to their native justice and magnanimity, and we have conjured them by the ties of our common kindred to disavow these usurpations, which would inevitably interrupt our connections and correspondence. They too have been deaf to the voice of justice and consanguinity. We must, therefore, acquiesce in the necessity, which denounces our Separation, and hold them, as we hold the rest of mankind, Enemies in War, in Peace Friends.

The Declaration concludes in its fourth section by establishing American independence. On behalf of the American people and as representatives of the United States, the writers declare the colonies are now free and independent states, with all political connection between them and Great Britain dissolved. They pledge to each other to join in the battle to achieve independence.

We, therefore, the Representatives of the United States of America, in General Congress, Assembled, appealing to the Supreme Judge of the world for the rectitude of our intentions, do, in the Name, and by Authority of the good People of these Colonies, solemnly publish and declare, That these United Colonies are, and of Right ought to be Free and Independent States; that they are Absolved from all Allegiance to the British Crown, and that all political connection between them and the State of Great Britain, is and ought to be totally dissolved; and that as Free and Independent States, they have full Power to levy War, conclude Peace, contract Alliances, establish Commerce, and to do all other Acts and Things which Independent States may of right do. And for the support of this Declaration, with a firm reliance on the protection of divine Providence, we mutually pledge to each other our Lives, our Fortunes and our sacred Honor.

JOHN HANCOCK,
President of the Congress

NEW HAMPSHIRE
Josiah Bartlett,
Wm. Whipple,
Matthew Thornton.

MASSACHUSETTS BAY
Saml. Adams,
John Adams,
Robt. Treat Paine,
Elbridge Gerry.

RHODE ISLAND
Step. Hopkins,
William Ellery.

CONNECTICUT
Roger Sherman,
Samuel Huntington,
Wm. Williams,
Oliver Wolcott.

NEW YORK
Wm. Floyd,
Phil. Livingston,
Frans. Lewis,
Lewis Morris.

NEW JERSEY
Richd. Stockton,
Jno. Witherspoon,
Fras. Hopkinson,
John Hart,
Abra. Clark.

PENNSYLVANIA
Robt. Morris,
Benjamin Rush,
Benjamin Franklin,
John Morton,
Geo. Clymer,
Jas. Smith,

Geo. Taylor,
James Wilson,
Geo. Ross.

DELAWARE
Caesar Rodney,
Geo. Read,
Tho. M'kean.

MARYLAND
Samuel Chase,
Wm. Paca,
Thos. Stone,
Charles Caroll of
Carrollton.

VIRGINIA
George Wythe,
Richard Henry Lee,
Th. Jefferson,

Benjamin Harrison,
Thos. Nelson, Jr.,
Francis Lightfoot Lee,
Carter Braxton.

NORTH CAROLINA
Wm. Hooper,
Joseph Hewes,
John Penn.

SOUTH CAROLINA
Edward Rutledge,
Thos. Heyward, Jr.,
Thomas Lynch, Jr.,
Arthur Middleton.

GEORGIA
Button Gwinnett,
Lyman Hall,
Geo. Walton.

2 Annotated *Federalist No. 10**

The Utility of the Union as a Safeguard Against Domestic Faction and Insurrection (continued)
Daily Advertiser
Thursday, November 22, 1787
[James Madison]
TO THE PEOPLE OF THE STATE OF NEW YORK

Federalist No. 10 is often regarded as offering the Framers' clearest theoretical defense of the Constitution. James Madison's writing contains some of the most important and often quoted sections of the Federalist Papers. Relying upon a view that suggests the natural imperfections of people, Madison, in Federalist No. 10, addresses how the core concepts of a republican form of government and federalism partially remedy those imperfections.

Among the numerous advantages promised by a well constructed Union, none deserves to be more accurately developed than its tendency to break and control the violence of faction. The friend of popular governments never finds himself so much alarmed for their character and fate, as when he contemplates their propensity to this dangerous vice. He will not fail, therefore, to set a due value on any plan which, without violating the principles to which he is attached, provides a proper cure for it. The instability, injustice, and confusion introduced into the public councils, have, in truth, been the mortal diseases under which popular governments have everywhere perished; as they continue to be the favorite and fruitful topics from which the adversaries to liberty derive their most specious declamations. The valuable improvements made by the American constitutions on the popular models, both ancient and modern, cannot certainly be too much admired; but it would be an unwarrantable partiality, to contend that they have as effectually obviated the danger on this side, as was wished and expected. Complaints are everywhere heard from our most considerate and virtuous citizens, equally the friends of public and private faith, and of public and personal liberty, that our governments are too unstable, that the public good is disregarded in the conflicts of rival parties, and that measures are too often decided, not according to the rules of justice and the rights of the minor party, but by the superior force of an interested and overbearing majority. However anxiously we may wish that these complaints had no foundation, the evidence, of known facts will not permit us to deny that they are in some

degree true. It will be found, indeed, on a candid review of our situation, that some of the distresses under which we labor have been erroneously charged on the operation of our governments; but it will be found, at the same time, that other causes will not alone account for many of our heaviest misfortunes; and, particularly, for that prevailing and increasing distrust of public engagements, and alarm for private rights, which are echoed from one end of the continent to the other. These must be chiefly, if not wholly, effects of the unsteadiness and injustice with which a factious spirit has tainted our public administrations.

The proposed United States Constitution, then awaiting ratification, would, according to Madison, address three central problems that had plagued most governments, including the then existing state constitutions. Those problems were (1) instability in governments, by which he chiefly means governments failing to function effectively and being replaced by a new set of governing institutions, (2) rulers who legislate against the common good, and (3) majority interests that trample the rights of the minority. Madison casts blame almost entirely at the feet of factions. Madison, in the next sentence below, provides his definition of faction.

By a faction, I understand a number of citizens, whether amounting to a majority or a minority of the whole, who are united and actuated by some common impulse of passion, or of interest, adversed to the rights of other citizens, or to the permanent and aggregate interests of the community.

A faction can be either a minority or a majority of the population. The key is that a faction is motivated by a passion or self-interest that negatively affects the rights of other citizens or the public interest in general.

There are two methods of curing the mischiefs of faction: the one, by removing its causes; the other, by controlling its effects.

If factions are dangerous, what is to be done about them? The dangers of factions can be addressed either by removing the causes of factions, or by making sure the effects of factions are not destructive. Madison first considers how the causes of factions could be eliminated.

There are again two methods of removing the causes of faction: the one, by destroying the liberty which is essential to its existence; the other, by giving to every citizen the same opinions, the same passions, and the same interests. It could never be more truly said than of the first remedy, that it was worse than the disease. Liberty is to faction what air is to fire, an aliment without which it instantly expires. But it could not be less folly to abolish liberty, which is essential to political life, because it nourishes faction, than it would be to wish the annihilation of air, which is essential to animal life, because it imparts to fire its destructive agency.

---

*Annotations by Martin Sweet, Florida Atlantic University, and the authors.

Just as one might wish to eliminate air because it has the potentially dangerous effect of feeding fire, one might wish to eliminate factions by abolishing personal liberty. But, according to Madison, the destructive powers of faction are far less severe than what would happen should the government abolish personal liberty. "Liberty is to faction what air is to fire" may be one of the best lines in all of *the Federalist Papers*. To abolish liberty in order to remove factions is, he says, a cure worse than the disease. Madison next considers the second way of removing the causes of factions—giving all people the same opinions and interests.

The second expedient is as impracticable as the first would be unwise. As long as the reason of man continues fallible, and he is at liberty to exercise it, different opinions will be formed. As long as the connection subsists between his reason and his self-love, his opinions and his passions will have a reciprocal influence on each other; and the former will be objects to which the latter will attach themselves. The diversity in the faculties of men, from which the rights of property originate, is not less an insuperable obstacle to a uniformity of interests. The protection of these faculties is the first object of government. From the protection of different and unequal faculties of acquiring property, the possession of different degrees and kinds of property immediately results; and from the influence of these on the sentiments and views of the respective proprietors, ensues a division of the society into different interests and parties.

Here Madison states that factions are, in fact, natural. They are part and parcel of what makes us human. People cannot be given the same opinions and interests. We are all born with different talents and abilities, and those differences will manifest themselves in different ways—including how much money one makes, how much property one might accumulate, or what one's opinions might be. According to Madison, the government must, chief among all of its myriad responsibilities, protect property rights. In doing so, government protects the individual differences that inevitably lead to different abilities to acquiring that property. Madison continues exploring how factions are a natural outcome of our humanness.

The latent causes of faction are thus sown in the nature of man; and we see them everywhere brought into different degrees of activity, according to the different circumstances of civil society. A zeal for different opinions concerning religion, concerning government, and many other points, as well of speculation as of practice; an attachment to different leaders ambitiously contending for pre-eminence and power; or to persons of other descriptions whose fortunes have been interesting to the human passions, have, in turn, divided mankind into parties, inflamed them with mutual animosity, and rendered them much more disposed to vex and oppress each other than to co-operate for their common good. So strong is this propensity of mankind to fall into mutual animosities, that where no substantial occasion presents itself, the most frivolous and fanciful distinctions have been sufficient to kindle their unfriendly passions and excite their most violent conflicts. But the most common and durable source of factions has been the various and unequal distribution of property. Those who hold and those who are without property have ever formed distinct interests in society. Those

who are creditors, and those who are debtors, fall under a like discrimination. A landed interest, a manufacturing interest, a mercantile interest, a moneyed interest, with many lesser interests, grow up of necessity in civilized nations, and divide them into different classes, actuated by different sentiments and views. The regulation of these various and interfering interests forms the principal task of modern legislation, and involves the spirit of party and faction in the necessary and ordinary operations of the government.

People are bound to fall into disputes, Madison explains in the preceding paragraph. He again notes that the unequal distribution of property has been especially likely to lead to factions—"those who hold and those who are without property have ever formed distinct interests in society." Managing the disputes between these factions is one of government's chief activities.

No man is allowed to be a judge in his own cause, because his interest would certainly bias his judgment, and, not improbably, corrupt his integrity. With equal, nay with greater reason, a body of men are unfit to be both judges and parties at the same time; yet what are many of the most important acts of legislation, but so many judicial determinations, not indeed concerning the rights of single persons, but concerning the rights of large bodies of citizens? And what are the different classes of legislators but advocates and parties to the causes which they determine? Is a law proposed concerning private debts? It is a question to which the creditors are parties on one side and the debtors on the other. Justice ought to hold the balance between them. Yet the parties are, and must be, themselves the judges; and the most numerous party, or, in other words, the most powerful faction must be expected to prevail. Shall domestic manufactures be encouraged, and in what degree, by restrictions on foreign manufactures? are questions which would be differently decided by the landed and the manufacturing classes, and probably by neither with a sole regard to justice and the public good. The apportionment of taxes on the various descriptions of property is an act which seems to require the most exact impartiality; yet there is, perhaps, no legislative act in which greater opportunity and temptation are given to a predominant party to trample on the rules of justice. Every shilling with which they overburden the inferior number, is a shilling saved to their own pockets.

It is in vain to say that enlightened statesmen will be able to adjust these clashing interests, and render them all subservient to the public good. Enlightened statesmen will not always be at the helm. Nor, in many cases, can such an adjustment be made at all without taking into view indirect and remote considerations, which will rarely prevail over the immediate interest which one party may find in disregarding the rights of another or the good of the whole.

Key in the three preceding paragraphs is the premise that the natural differences among men will result in wide variety of factions—sometimes divided by occupation, other times by wealth, religion, or a belief in the role of government—and that those same factions will find their way into the government. Therefore it is natural that our representatives themselves will be influenced and divided by their own interest—the same interests that are readily apparent among the people. Even the most well-intentioned rulers cannot be relied upon to stamp out their own natural inclinations, and we cannot always be sure a well-intentioned ruler is in charge.

The inference to which we are brought is, that the causes of faction cannot be removed, and that relief is only to be sought in the means of controlling its effects.

> Recall that Madison had written above that there are two ways to deal with factions: eliminating their causes or reducing their bad effects. He concludes in this paragraph that there is no desirable way to eliminate the causes of factions. Our attention should instead, he says, be focused on making sure they do not have dangerous effects.

If a faction consists of less than a majority, relief is supplied by the republican principle, which enables the majority to defeat its sinister views by regular vote. It may clog the administration, it may convulse the society; but it will be unable to execute and mask its violence under the forms of the Constitution. When a majority is included in a faction, the form of popular government, on the other hand, enables it to sacrifice to its ruling passion or interest both the public good and the rights of other citizens. To secure the public good and private rights against the danger of such a faction, and at the same time to preserve the spirit and the form of popular government, is then the great object to which our inquiries are directed. Let me add that it is the great desideratum by which this form of government can be rescued from the opprobrium under which it has so long labored, and be recommended to the esteem and adoption of mankind.

> Madison suggests that minority factions can be thwarted in governments based on popular rule, because they can be outvoted. He is more concerned with what happens when a majority faction forms under such a government. His goal, he writes, is to find a way that popular rule can exist without producing majority factions that will harm the minority or the public good.

By what means is this object attainable? Evidently by one of two only. Either the existence of the same passion or interest in a majority at the same time must be prevented, or the majority, having such coexistent passion or interest, must be rendered, by their number and local situation, unable to concert and carry into effect schemes of oppression. If the impulse and the opportunity be suffered to coincide, we well know that neither moral nor religious motives can be relied on as an adequate control. They are not found to be such on the injustice and violence of individuals, and lose their efficacy in proportion to the number combined together, that is, in proportion as their efficacy becomes needful.

> A way needs to be found to make majority factions less likely to come together and execute their "schemes of oppression." Hoping that moral or religious values will stop a majority faction is inadequate.

From this view of the subject it may be concluded that a pure democracy, by which I mean a society consisting of a small number of citizens, who assemble and administer the government in person, can admit of no cure for the mischiefs of faction. A common passion or interest will, in almost every case, be felt by a majority of the whole; a communication and concert result from the form of government itself; and there is nothing to check the in-

ducements to sacrifice the weaker party or an obnoxious individual. Hence it is that such democracies have ever been spectacles of turbulence and contention; have ever been found incompatible with personal security or the rights of property; and have in general been as short in their lives as they have been violent in their deaths. Theoretic politicians, who have patronized this species of government, have erroneously supposed that by reducing mankind to a perfect equality in their political rights, they would, at the same time, be perfectly equalized and assimilated in their possessions, their opinions, and their passions.

> A pure democracy, or a system in which all of the people share ruling power by voting on all laws, provides no safeguard to check the power of majority factions. This form of government makes it easy for majority factions to form and easy for them to win.

A republic, by which I mean a government in which the scheme of representation takes place, opens a different prospect, and promises the cure for which we are seeking. Let us examine the points in which it varies from pure democracy, and we shall comprehend both the nature of the cure and the efficacy which it must derive from the Union.

> A republic, on the other hand, or what we might today label a representative democracy, offers a greater hope of deterring the negative effects of majority factions. Madison in the following paragraphs explains how republics differ from democracies and why these differences are helpful in deterring majority factions.

The two great points of difference between a democracy and a republic are: first, the delegation of the government, in the latter, to a small number of citizens elected by the rest; secondly, the greater number of citizens, and greater sphere of country, over which the latter may be extended.

> The differences are: (1) instead of voting directly on public matters as in a pure democracy, citizens in a republic elect representatives to vote for them on public matters, and (2) the population and geographical size of a republic can be larger than in a pure democracy.

The effect of the first difference is, on the one hand, to refine and enlarge the public views, by passing them through the medium of a chosen body of citizens, whose wisdom may best discern the true interest of their country, and whose patriotism and love of justice will be least likely to sacrifice it to temporary or partial considerations. Under such a regulation, it may well happen that the public voice, pronounced by the representatives of the people, will be more consonant to the public good than if pronounced by the people themselves, convened for the purpose. On the other hand, the effect may be inverted. Men of factious tempers, of local prejudices, or of sinister designs, may, by intrigue, by corruption, or by other means, first obtain the suffrages, and then betray the interests, of the people. The question resulting is, whether small or extensive republics are more favorable to the election of proper guardians of the public weal; and it is clearly decided in favor of the latter by two obvious considerations:

In the first place, it is to be remarked that, however small the republic may be, the representatives must be raised to a certain number, in order to guard against the cabals of a few; and that, however large it may be, they must be limited to a certain number, in order to guard against the confusion of a multitude. Hence, the number of representatives in the two cases not being in proportion to that of the two constituents, and being proportionally greater in the small republic, it follows that, if the proportion of fit characters be not less in the large than in the small republic, the former will present a greater option, and consequently a greater probability of a fit choice.

In the next place, as each representative will be chosen by a greater number of citizens in the large than in the small republic, it will be more difficult for unworthy candidates to practice with success the vicious arts by which elections are too often carried; and the suffrages of the people being more free, will be more likely to centre in men who possess the most attractive merit and the most diffusive and established characters.

> In the preceding three paragraphs, Madison discusses the first difference between a republic and a democracy: the presence of representatives. He argues that in a republic, representatives offer a filter to weed out dangerous and unwise ideas. The result may be more consistent with the public good than, ironically, if the people made the laws themselves in a pure democracy. He then asks whether small or large republics make the election of representatives who will make wise and just decisions more likely. He argues that there is a happy medium between too few representatives—which might be susceptible to corruption or other vices—and too many representatives—which might lead to confusion or chaos. Madison suggests that a larger republic in terms of population and size is more desirable than a smaller republic. First, there will be a greater number of wise candidates in a large republic than in a small one. The likelihood that unfit individuals will be elected is thus lower in a large republic. Second, because there are more voters and proportionally fewer representatives in a large republic—in other words, each district is larger than in a small republic and each representative will have to represent a larger number of people—such a republic is better suited to withstand the deception and sometimes ugliness that can mar elections. It is easier for candidates to be deceptive when appealing to small groups of people in a small area.

It must be confessed that in this, as in most other cases, there is a mean, on both sides of which inconveniences will be found to lie. By enlarging too much the number of electors, you render the representatives too little acquainted with all their local circumstances and lesser interests; as by reducing it too much, you render him unduly attached to these, and too little fit to comprehend and pursue great and national objects. The federal Constitution forms a happy combination in this respect; the great and aggregate interests being referred to the national, the local and particular to the State legislatures.

> Madison again notes it is important that the ratio of voters to representatives be neither too large nor too small. The proposed Constitution provides an admirable compromise: national government will address broad issues of general importance, while state governments will focus on the more narrow concerns of their respective states.

The other point of difference is, the greater number of citizens and extent of territory which may be brought within the compass of republican than of democratic government; and it is this circumstance principally which renders factious combinations less to be dreaded in the former than in the latter. The smaller the society, the fewer probably will be the distinct parties and interests composing it; the fewer the distinct parties and interests, the more frequently will a majority be found of the same party; and the smaller the number of individuals composing a majority, and the smaller the compass within which they are placed, the more easily will they concert and execute their plans of oppression. Extend the sphere, and you take in a greater variety of parties and interests; you make it less probable that a majority of the whole will have a common motive to invade the rights of other citizens; or if such a common motive exists, it will be more difficult for all who feel it to discover their own strength, and to act in unison with each other. Besides other impediments, it may be remarked that, where there is a consciousness of unjust or dishonorable purposes, communication is always checked by distrust in proportion to the number whose concurrence is necessary.

> Madison now discusses the second difference between a republic and a democracy: a republic can govern a larger geographical area. Why is this a good thing? The larger the area, Madison argues, the less likely majority factions will exist. As a country expands, so does the diversity of its citizens—"extend the sphere, and you take in a wider variety of parties and interests." This expanding diversity means a diffusion of interests and an expansion of the number of factions and a lower likelihood of a common interest uniting a majority of the population. Moreover, even if a majority faction were to emerge, the vast land mass of a large republic would make it harder for citizens to realize that they shared this interest and to come together to impose their will on the minority. He then applies this logic to the proposed national government and the states in the following two paragraphs.

Hence, it clearly appears, that the same advantage which a republic has over a democracy, in controlling the effects of faction, is enjoyed by a large over a small republic,—is enjoyed by the Union over the States composing it. Does the advantage consist in the substitution of representatives whose enlightened views and virtuous sentiments render them superior to local prejudices and schemes of injustice? It will not be denied that the representation of the Union will be most likely to possess these requisite endowments. Does it consist in the greater security afforded by a greater variety of parties, against the event of any one party being able to outnumber and oppress the rest? In an equal degree does the increased variety of parties comprised within the Union, increase this security. Does it, in fine, consist in the greater obstacles opposed to the concert and accomplishment of the secret wishes of an unjust and interested majority? Here, again, the extent of the Union gives it the most palpable advantage.

The influence of factious leaders may kindle a flame within their particular States, but will be unable to spread a general conflagration through the other States. A religious sect may degenerate into a political faction in a part of the Confederacy; but the variety of sects dispersed over the entire face of it must secure the national councils against any danger from that source. A rage for paper money, for an abolition of debts, for an equal division of property, or for any other improper or wicked project, will be less apt to pervade the whole body of the Union than a particular member of it; in the same proportion as such a malady is more likely to taint a particular county or district, than an entire State.

Madison summarizes that republics are better at controlling the effects of factions than are pure democracies, that larger republics are preferable to smaller republics, and that a federal system—with government at both the state and the national level—is superior to the alternative of a single central government (which would be insensitive to local needs) and to a diffused system of state governments (which would be insensitive to broad, national needs). For those who were concerned about the concentration of power in this new national government, Madison provides an argument that suggests this new large government will actually better protect individual rights and the common good than would governments like the states that are smaller and close to the people. An "improper or wicked project"—Madison references some examples that would be familiar to his audience, including the issuance of worthless paper money and the dismissal of debts—is more likely to take hold and inflame in people's passions in one state than it is in an entire country, just as it is more likely in a single district or county within a state. The bigger the area, the more difficult for factious leaders to succeed. Under the proposed Constitution, the ability of factions to succeed would be dim.

In the extent and proper structure of the Union, therefore, we behold a republican remedy for the diseases most incident to republican government. And according to the degree of pleasure and pride we feel in being republicans, ought to be our zeal in cherishing the spirit and supporting the character of Federalists.

PUBLIUS

3 Annotated *Federalist No. 51**

The Structure of the Government Must Furnish the Proper Checks and Balances Between the Different Departments

Independent Journal
Wednesday, February 6, 1788
[James Madison]

TO THE PEOPLE OF THE STATE OF NEW YORK

Federalist No. 51 revolves around the key concept of power. One of the primary reservations about the proposed United States Constitution, particularly from the Anti-Federalists, was the fear of the power of a centralized government. James Madison in *Federalist No. 51* continues an argument that had begun in earlier essays, especially Nos. 47 and 48. One of the complaints against the Constitution was that it was providing not a true separation of powers but a blended system in which each major branch of government interfered with the other. Critics saw this as a threat to liberty, but Madison in this essay emphasizes the benefits of this arrangement for protecting the peoples' rights. He argues that the separation of powers among the three branches of the national government, the checks and balances built into the structure of each branch and their relationship to the other branches of government, federalism (two distinct levels of government, each with some sovereign authority), and pluralism (the proliferation of and competition among interest groups) will each and together refute the criticism that the government proposed in the Constitution threatens liberty by centralizing power.

To what expedient, then, shall we finally resort, for maintaining in practice the necessary partition of power among the several departments, as laid down in the Constitution? The only answer that can be given is, that as all these exterior provisions are found to be inadequate, the defect must be supplied, by so contriving the interior structure of the government as that its several constituent parts may, by their mutual relations, be the means of keeping each other in their proper places. Without presuming to undertake a full development of this important idea, I will hazard a few general observations, which may perhaps place it in a clearer light, and enable us to form a more correct judgment of the principles and structure of the government planned by the convention.

How can the distinction between the executive, legislative, and judicial branches be preserved? Madison says that neither merely writing down the distinctions on paper nor holding elections—"the exterior provisions"—will be sufficient. In addition, the government must be designed so that each branch is "keeping each other in their proper places"—that is, through checks and balances.

In order to lay a due foundation for that separate and distinct exercise of the different powers of government, which to a certain extent is admitted on all hands to be essential to the preservation of liberty, it is evident that each department should have a will of its own; and consequently should be so constituted that the members of each should have as little agency as possible in the appointment of the members of the others. Were this principle rigorously adhered to, it would require that all the appointments for the supreme executive, legislative, and judiciary magistracies should be drawn from the same fountain of authority, the people, through channels having no communication whatever with one another. Perhaps such a plan of constructing the several departments would be less difficult in practice than it may in contemplation appear. Some difficulties, however, and some additional expense would attend the execution of it. Some deviations, therefore, from the principle must be admitted. In the constitution of the judiciary department in particular, it might be inexpedient to insist rigorously on the principle: first, because peculiar qualifications being essential in the members, the primary consideration ought to be to select that mode of choice which best secures these qualifications; secondly, because the permanent tenure by which the appointments are held in that department, must soon destroy all sense of dependence on the authority conferring them.

It is equally evident, that the members of each department should be as little dependent as possible on those of the others, for the emoluments annexed to their offices. Were the executive magistrate, or the judges, not independent of the legislature in this particular, their independence in every other would be merely nominal.

One of the primary reasons that Madison and the Federalists favored the new Constitution was the need for strong national government power. The Framers, however, realized that such power would be ripe for abuse, and they made a concerted effort to create structures within the Constitution that would limit the opportunity for such abuse. One of those structural limitations on the abuse of power would later come to be known as the "separation of powers" doctrine. Under separation of powers, each branch of government has its own unique powers and is limited in its ability to absorb the functions of the other branches of government. How can each branch resist the encroachment of the other branches of government? Madison explores the defense against encroachment in the following paragraph. Checks and balances provide the methods of this interinstitutional defense and a strong security that no single branch will gradually take on all the major functions—executive, legislative, judicial—of government.

---

*Annotations by Martin Sweet, Florida Atlantic University, and the authors.

But the great security against a gradual concentration of the several powers in the same department, consists in giving to those who administer each department the necessary constitutional means and personal motives to resist encroachments of the others. The provision for defense must in this, as in all other cases, be made commensurate to the danger of attack. Ambition must be made to counteract ambition. The interest of the man must be connected with the constitutional rights of the place. It may be a reflection on human nature, that such devices should be necessary to control the abuses of government. But what is government itself, but the greatest of all reflections on human nature? If men were angels, no government would be necessary. If angels were to govern men, neither external nor internal controls on government would be necessary. In framing a government which is to be administered by men over men, the great difficulty lies in this: you must first enable the government to control the governed; and in the next place oblige it to control itself. A dependence on the people is, no doubt, the primary control on the government; but experience has taught mankind the necessity of auxiliary precautions.

> This paragraph has two key quotes. First, "Ambition must be made to counteract ambition." One of the aims of the Constitution was to craft a healthy competition among the branches of government—such that the very natural human impulses contained within individuals in one branch of government would limit those very natural human impulses contained within individuals in another branch of government. Government is only an aggregation of fallible individuals and thus needs limitations. This precept led Madison to remark in the second key quote, "If men were angels, no government would be necessary." Because people are not angels, a government of mortal humans needs to be controlled. Elections and the sovereignty of the people provide the greatest control, but others are necessary as well.

This policy of supplying, by opposite and rival interests, the defect of better motives, might be traced through the whole system of human affairs, private as well as public. We see it particularly displayed in all the subordinate distributions of power, where the constant aim is to divide and arrange the several offices in such a manner as that each may be a check on the other — that the private interest of every individual may be a sentinel over the public rights. These inventions of prudence cannot be less requisite in the distribution of the supreme powers of the State.

But it is not possible to give to each department an equal power of self-defense. In republican government, the legislative authority necessarily predominates. The remedy for this inconveniency is to divide the legislature into different branches; and to render them, by different modes of election and different principles of action, as little connected with each other as the nature of their common functions and their common dependence on the society will admit. It may even be necessary to guard against dangerous encroachments by still further precautions. As the weight of the legislative authority requires that it should be thus divided, the weakness of the executive may require, on the other hand, that it should be fortified. An absolute negative on the legislature appears, at first view, to be the natural defense with which the executive magistrate should be armed. But

perhaps it would be neither altogether safe nor alone sufficient. On ordinary occasions it might not be exerted with the requisite firmness, and on extraordinary occasions it might be perfidiously abused. May not this defect of an absolute negative be supplied by some qualified connection between this weaker department and the weaker branch of the stronger department, by which the latter may be led to support the constitutional rights of the former, without being too much detached from the rights of its own department?

If the principles on which these observations are founded be just, as I persuade myself they are, and they be applied as a criterion to the several State constitutions, and to the federal Constitution it will be found that if the latter does not perfectly correspond with them, the former are infinitely less able to bear such a test.

> Today we often think of the three branches of government as "co-equal" branches. Yet Madison writes that in a republic—a representative democracy—the legislative branch must be dominant. But to make sure the legislative branch does not exert too great a power, special constraints would be imposed on it. It will consist of two different legislative bodies (the House of Representatives and the Senate), each elected by different means and with some difference in function. To prevent the executive branch from being too weak compared to the legislative branch, the president should be given a veto power (an "absolute negative"). The executive branch and the Senate ("the weaker branch of the stronger department") should also have an arrangement that protects the power of the executive while also allowing the Senate to honor its legislative function. Madison does not mention these examples, but this relationship appears in the treaty approval process and executive branch appointments, both of which require Senate but not House approval. To the critics of the Constitution, Madison notes in the previous paragraph that although the systems of checks and balances proposed in the new system to protect the separation of powers may not be perfect, it is superior to that found in the state constitutions.

There are, moreover, two considerations particularly applicable to the federal system of America, which place that system in a very interesting point of view.

First. In a single republic, all the power surrendered by the people is submitted to the administration of a single government; and the usurpations are guarded against by a division of the government into distinct and separate departments. In the compound republic of America, the power surrendered by the people is first divided between two distinct governments, and then the portion allotted to each subdivided among distinct and separate departments. Hence a double security arises to the rights of the people. The different governments will control each other, at the same time that each will be controlled by itself.

> The separation of powers in the American system is twofold. First, powers are to be separated horizontally—among the executive, legislative, and judicial branches. Second, powers are to be separated vertically—between the federal government and the state governments. The American federal system, the "compound republic" with two distinct sovereigns at the national and state levels, serves to further diffuse government power. And just as the competition among the national branches of government serves to

counteract the power of any one branch, so will the competition between the federal and state governments serve to counteract the concentration of power in one location. Madison refers to this as a "double security" that will protect the rights of the people.

Second. It is of great importance in a republic not only to guard the society against the oppression of its rulers, but to guard one part of the society against the injustice of the other part. Different interests necessarily exist in different classes of citizens. If a majority be united by a common interest, the rights of the minority will be insecure. There are but two methods of providing against this evil: the one by creating a will in the community independent of the majority — that is, of the society itself; the other, by comprehending in the society so many separate descriptions of citizens as will render an unjust combination of a majority of the whole very improbable, if not impracticable. The first method prevails in all governments possessing an hereditary or self-appointed authority. This, at best, is but a precarious security; because a power independent of the society may as well espouse the unjust views of the major, as the rightful interests of the minor party, and may possibly be turned against both parties.

Madison begins his long concluding paragraph by noting that the people need to be protected from each other just as much as they need to be protected from their rulers. How can this be accomplished? One way is for an independent "will" in the society that represents the society's interests but is independent of it. Systems based on hereditary rule are one example but, Madison writes, such a solution is unsatisfactory. Such a ruler might still promote the unjust views of the majority rather than do what is best for all, or such a ruler might turn against both the majority and minority, not in the interests of society but in the ruler's own self-interest. Madison continues, in the remainder of the paragraph, by asserting the advantages of the second method to protect the people from each other—making it difficult for a majority faction to form. Madison summarizes some of his conclusions from *Federalist No. 10*.

The second method will be exemplified in the federal republic of the United States. Whilst all authority in it will be derived from and dependent on the society, the society itself will be broken into so many parts, interests, and classes of citizens, that the rights of individuals, or of the minority, will be in little danger from interested combinations of the majority. In a free government the security for civil rights must be the same as that for religious rights. It consists in the one case in the multiplicity of interests, and in the other in the multiplicity of sects. The degree of security in both cases will depend on the number of interests and sects; and this may be presumed to depend on the extent of country and number of people comprehended under the same government. This view of the subject must particularly recommend a proper federal system to all the sincere and considerate friends of republican government, since it shows that in exact proportion as the territory of the Union may be formed into more circumscribed Confederacies, or States oppressive combinations of a majority will be facilitated: the best security, under the republican forms, for the rights of every class of citizens, will be diminished: and consequently the stability and independence of some

member of the government, the only other security, must be proportionately increased. Justice is the end of government. It is the end of civil society. It ever has been and ever will be pursued until it be obtained, or until liberty be lost in the pursuit. In a society under the forms of which the stronger faction can readily unite and oppress the weaker, anarchy may as truly be said to reign as in a state of nature, where the weaker individual is not secured against the violence of the stronger; and as, in the latter state, even the stronger individuals are prompted, by the uncertainty of their condition, to submit to a government which may protect the weak as well as themselves; so, in the former state, will the more powerful factions or parties be gradually induced, by a like motive, to wish for a government which will protect all parties, the weaker as well as the more powerful. It can be little doubted that if the State of Rhode Island was separated from the Confederacy and left to itself, the insecurity of rights under the popular form of government within such narrow limits would be displayed by such reiterated oppressions of factious majorities that some power altogether independent of the people would soon be called for by the voice of the very factions whose misrule had proved the necessity of it. In the extended republic of the United States, and among the great variety of interests, parties, and sects which it embraces, a coalition of a majority of the whole society could seldom take place on any other principles than those of justice and the general good; whilst there being thus less danger to a minor from the will of a major party, there must be less pretext, also, to provide for the security of the former, by introducing into the government a will not dependent on the latter, or, in other words, a will independent of the society itself. It is no less certain than it is important, notwithstanding the contrary opinions which have been entertained, that the larger the society, provided it lie within a practical sphere, the more duly capable it will be of self-government. And happily for the republican cause, the practicable sphere may be carried to a very great extent, by a judicious modification and mixture of the federal principle.

Madison defends what we label today as "pluralism" or the division of society into such a large number of varied interest groups that the concept of "majority" is rendered suspect. If most individuals are part of these smaller interest groups, these divided interests are difficult to combine into any single organized majority. Without a single organized majority, power cannot concentrate in a centralized location and factions among the people are less likely to threaten fellow citizens. Madison intends for his earlier argument in this essay concerning separation of powers and checks and balances to combine with these points about pluralism, leading the reader to conclude that the proposed Constitution is desirable. A federal system ensures that power does not concentrate within the national or state governments. Separation of powers ensures that power does not concentrate within any single branch of government. Without centralization of power, with this double security, the opportunity is maximized for the government to achieve justice, and, according to Madison, "Justice is the end [goal] of government. It is the end [goal] of civil society."

PUBLIUS

4 Presidents of the United States

YEAR ELECTED	PRESIDENTIAL CANDIDATES	POLITICAL PARTY	ELECTORAL VOTE	PERCENTAGE OF POPULAR VOTE
1789	1. **George Washington**	—	69	—
	John Adams		34	
	Others		35	
1792	**George Washington**	—	132	—
	John Adams		77	
	Others		55	
1796	2. **John Adams**	Federalist	71	—
	Thomas Jefferson	Democratic-Republican	68	
	Thomas Pinckney	Federalist	59	
	Aaron Burr	Democratic-Republican	30	
	Others		48	
1800	3. **Thomas Jefferson**	Democratic-Republican	73	—
	Aaron Burr	Democratic-Republican	73	
	John Adams	Federalist	65	
	C. C. Pinckney	Federalist	64	
	John Jay	Federalist	1	
1804	**Thomas Jefferson**	Democratic-Republican	162	—
	C. C. Pinckney	Federalist	14	
1808	4. **James Madison**	Democratic-Republican	122	—
	C. C. Pinckney	Federalist	47	
	George Clinton	Independent-Republican	6	
1812	**James Madison**	Democratic-Republican	128	—
	De Witt Clinton	Federalist	89	
1816	5. **James Monroe**	Democratic-Republican	183	—
	Rufus King	Federalist	34	
1820	**James Monroe**	Democratic-Republican	231	—
	John Q. Adams	Independent-Republican	1	
1824	6. **John Q. Adams**	Democratic-Republican	84	30.5
	Andrew Jackson	Democratic-Republican	99	
	Henry Clay	Democratic-Republican	37	
	W. H. Crawford	Democratic-Republican	41	
1828	7. **Andrew Jackson**	Democratic	178	56.0
	John Q. Adams	National Republican	83	
1832	**Andrew Jackson**	Democratic	219	55.0
	Henry Clay	National Republican	49	
	William Wirt	Anti-Masonic	7	
	John Floyd	Independent Democrat	11	

YEAR ELECTED		PRESIDENTIAL CANDIDATES	POLITICAL PARTY	ELECTORAL VOTE	PERCENTAGE OF POPULAR VOTE
1836	8.	**Martin Van Buren**	Democratic	170	50.9
		William H. Harrison	Whig	73	
		Hugh L. White	Whig	26	
		Daniel Webster	Whig	14	
1840	9.	**William H. Harrison***	Whig	234	53.0
		Martin Van Buren	Democratic	60	
	10.	(**John Tyler**, 1841)			
1844	11.	**James K. Polk**	Democratic	170	49.6
		Henry Clay	Whig	105	
1848	12.	**Zachary Taylor***	Whig	163	47.4
		Lewis Cass	Democratic	127	
	13.	(**Millard Fillmore**, 1850)			
1852	14.	**Franklin Pierce**	Democratic	254	50.8
		Winfield Scott	Whig	42	
1856	15.	**James Buchanan**	Democratic	174	45.3
		John C. Frémont	Republican	114	
		Millard Fillmore	American	8	
1860	16.	**Abraham Lincoln**	Republican	180	39.8
		J. C. Breckinridge	Democratic	72	
		Stephen A. Douglas	Democratic	12	
		John Bell	Constitutional Union	39	
1864		**Abraham Lincoln***	Republican	212	55.0
		George B. McClellan	Democratic	21	
	17.	(**Andrew Johnson**, 1865)			
1868	18.	**Ulysses S. Grant**	Republican	214	52.7
		Horatio Seymour	Democratic	80	
1872		**Ulysses S. Grant**	Republican	286	55.6
		Horace Greeley	Democratic	**	
1876	19.	**Rutherford B. Hayes**	Republican	185	47.9
		Samuel J. Tilden	Democratic	184	
1880	20.	**James A. Garfield***	Republican	214	48.3
		Winfield S. Hancock	Democratic	155	
	21.	(**Chester A. Arthur**, 1881)			
1884	22.	**Grover Cleveland**	Democratic	219	48.5
		James G. Blaine	Republican	182	
1888	23.	**Benjamin Harrison**	Republican	233	47.8
		Grover Cleveland	Democratic	168	
1892	24.	**Grover Cleveland**	Democratic	277	46.0
		Benjamin Harrison	Republican	145	
		James B. Weaver	People's	22	
1896	25.	**William McKinley**	Republican	271	51.0
		William J. Bryan	Democratic	176	
1900		**William McKinley***	Republican	292	51.7
		William J. Bryan	Democratic	155	
	26.	(**Theodore Roosevelt**, 1901)			

YEAR ELECTED		PRESIDENTIAL CANDIDATES	POLITICAL PARTY	ELECTORAL VOTE	PERCENTAGE OF POPULAR VOTE
1904		**Theodore Roosevelt**	Republican	336	56.4
		Alton B. Parker	Democratic	140	
1908	27.	**William H. Taft**	Republican	321	51.6
		William J. Bryan	Democratic	162	
1912	28.	**Woodrow Wilson**	Democratic	435	41.8
		Theodore Roosevelt	Progressive	88	
		William H. Taft	Republican	8	
1916		**Woodrow Wilson**	Democratic	277	49.2
		Charles E. Hughes	Republican	254	
1920	29.	**Warren G. Harding***	Republican	404	60.3
		James M. Cox	Democratic	127	
	30.	**(Calvin Coolidge**, 1923)			
1924		**Calvin Coolidge**	Republican	382	54.1
		John W. Davis	Democratic	136	
		Robert M. La Follette	Progressive	13	
1928	31.	**Herbert C. Hoover**	Republican	444	58.2
		Alfred E. Smith	Democratic	87	
1932	32.	**Franklin D. Roosevelt**	Democratic	472	57.4
		Herbert C. Hoover	Republican	59	
1936		**Franklin D. Roosevelt**	Democratic	523	60.8
		Alfred M. Landon	Republican	8	
1940		**Franklin D. Roosevelt**	Democratic	449	54.7
		Wendell L. Willkie	Republican	82	
1944	33.	**Franklin D. Roosevelt***	Democratic	432	53.4
		Thomas E. Dewey	Republican	99	
		(Harry S Truman, 1945)			
1948		**Harry S Truman**	Democratic	303	49.5
		Thomas E. Dewey	Republican	189	
		J. Strom Thurmond	States' Rights	39	
1952	34.	**Dwight D. Eisenhower**	Republican	442	55.1
		Adlai E. Stevenson	Democratic	89	
1956		**Dwight D. Eisenhower**	Republican	457	57.4
		Adlai E. Stevenson	Democratic	73	
1960	35.	**John F. Kennedy***	Democratic	303	49.7
		Richard M. Nixon	Republican	219	
	36.	**(Lyndon B. Johnson**, 1963)			
1964		**Lyndon B. Johnson**	Democratic	486	61.0
		Barry M. Goldwater	Republican	52	
1968	37.	**Richard M. Nixon**	Republican	301	43.4
		Hubert H. Humphrey	Democratic	191	
		George C. Wallace	American Independent	46	
1972		**Richard M. Nixon**†	Republican	520	60.7
		George S. McGovern	Democratic	17	
	38.	**(Gerald R. Ford**, 1974)†			
1976	39.	**James Earl Carter**	Democratic	297	50.1
		Gerald R. Ford	Republican	240	

YEAR ELECTED		PRESIDENTIAL CANDIDATES	POLITICAL PARTY	ELECTORAL VOTE	PERCENTAGE OF POPULAR VOTE
1980	40.	**Ronald Reagan**	Republican	489	50.7
		James Earl Carter	Democratic	49	
		John B. Anderson	Independent	—	
1984		**Ronald Reagan**	Republican	525	58.8
		Walter Mondale	Democratic	13	
1988	41.	**George H.W. Bush**	Republican	426	53.4
		Michael Dukakis	Democratic	112	
1992	42.	**William Clinton**	Democratic	370	43.0
		George H.W. Bush	Republican	168	
		H. Ross Perot	Independent	—	
1996		**William Clinton**	Democratic	379	49.2
		Robert Dole	Republican	159	
		H. Ross Perot	Reform	—	
2000	43.	**George W. Bush**	Republican	271	47.8
		Albert Gore	Democratic	266	
		Ralph Nader	Green		
		Patrick J. Buchanan	Reform		
2004		**George W. Bush**	Republican	286	50.7
		John Kerry	Democratic	251	
		Ralph Nader	Independent	—	
2008	44.	**Barack Obama**	Democratic	365	53.4
		John McCain	Republican	173	

Note: Winning candidates and succeeding vice presidents are shown in boldface

*Died in office, succeeding vice president follows in parentheses.

**Horace Greeley died between the popular vote and the meeting of the presidential electors.

†Resigned, succeeding vice president follows in parentheses.

5 Party Control of the Presidency, Senate, and House of Representatives

| CONGRESS | YEARS | PRESIDENT | SENATE* | | | HOUSE* | | |
			D	R	OTHER	D	R	OTHER
57th	1901–03	McKinley	29	56	3	153	198	5
		T. Roosevelt						
58th	1903–05	T. Roosevelt	32	58	—	178	207	—
59th	1905–07	T. Roosevelt	32	58	—	136	250	—
60th	1907–09	T. Roosevelt	29	61	—	164	222	—
61st	1909–11	Taft	32	59	—	172	219	—
62nd	1911–13	Taft	42	49	—	228†	162	1
63rd	1913–15	Wilson	51	44	1	290	127	18
64th	1915–17	Wilson	56	39	1	230	193	8
65th	1917–19	Wilson	53	42	1	200	216	9
66th	1919–21	Wilson	48	48†	1	191	237†	7
67th	1921–23	Harding	37	59	—	132	300	1
68th	1923–25	Coolidge	43	51	2	207	225	3
69th	1925–27	Coolidge	40	54	1	183	247	5
70th	1927–29	Coolidge	47	48	1	195	237	3
71st	1929–31	Hoover	39	56	1	163	267	1
72nd	1931–33	Hoover	47	48	1	216††	218	1
73rd	1933–35	F. Roosevelt	59	36	1	313	117	5
74th	1935–37	F. Roosevelt	69	25	2	322	103	10
75th	1937–39	F. Roosevelt	75	17	4	333	89	13
76th	1939–41	F. Roosevelt	69	23	4	262	169	4
77th	1941–43	F. Roosevelt	66	28	2	267	162	6
78th	1943–45	F. Roosevelt	57	38	1	222	209	4
79th	1945–47	Truman	57	38	1	243	190	2
80th	1947–49	Truman	45	51†	—	188	246†	1
81st	1949–51	Truman	54	42	—	263	171	1
82nd	1951–53	Truman	48	47	1	234	199	2
83rd	1953–55	Eisenhower	47	48	1	213	221	1
84th	1955–57	Eisenhower	48†	47	1	232†	203	—
85th	1957–59	Eisenhower	49†	47	—	234†	201	—
86th†††	1959–61	Eisenhower	64†	34	—	283†	154	—
87th†††	1961–63	Kennedy	64	36	—	263	174	—
88th	1963–65	Kennedy	67	33	—	258	176	—
		Johnson						
89th	1965–67	Johnson	68	32	—	295	140	—
90th	1967–69	Johnson	64	36	—	248	187	—

CONGRESS	YEARS	PRESIDENT	SENATE* D	SENATE* R	OTHER	HOUSE* D	HOUSE* R	OTHER
91st	1969–71	Nixon	58†	42	—	243†	192	—
92nd	1971–73	Nixon	55†>	45	—	255†	180	—
93rd	1973–75	Nixon / Ford	57†	43	—	243†	192	—
94th	1975–77	Ford	61†	38	—	291†	144	—
95th	1977–79	Carter	62	38	—	292	143	—
96th	1979–81	Carter	59	41	—	277	158	—
97th	1981–83	Reagan	47	53	—	243†	192	—
98th	1983–85	Reagan	46	54	—	269†	166	—
99th	1985–87	Reagan	47	53	—	253†	182	—
100th	1987–89	Reagan	55†	45	—	258†	177	—
101st	1989–91	G. H.W. Bush	55†	45	—	260†	175	—
102nd	1991–93	G. H.W. Bush	56†	44	—	267†>	167	1
103rd	1993–95	Clinton	57	43	—	258	176	1
104th	1995–97	Clinton	46	54†	—	202	232†	1
105th	1997–99	Clinton	45	55†	—	206	228†	1
106th	1999–01	Clinton	45	55†	—	211	223†	1
107th	2001–03	G. W. Bush	50#	50	—	212	221	2
108th	2003–05	G. W. Bush	48	51	1	205	229	1
109th	2005–07	G. W. Bush	44	55	1	202	232	1
110th	2007–09	G. W. Bush	50†	49	1	233†	202	—
111th	2009–11	Obama	57	41	2	257	178	—
112th**	2011–13	Obama	51	46	3	192	243	—

*Excludes vacancies at beginning of each session. Party balance immediately following election.

**Projection as of November 6, 2010.

†Chamber controlled by party other than that of the president.

††Republicans won a majority of seats in the 1930 election, but because of deaths and subsequent special elections, Democrats held a majority by the time the 72nd Congress was seated.

†††The 437 members of the House in the 86th and 87th Congresses are attributable to the at-large representative given to both Alaska (January 3, 1959) and Hawaii (August 21, 1959) prior to redistricting in 1962.

#Republicans controlled the Senate until mid-2001. Party control switched to the Democrats when Republican Senator James Jeffords became an independent and began caucusing with the Democrats, making the party balance 50 Democrats, 49 Republicans, and 1 independent.

D = Democrat

R = Republican

6 Supreme Court Justices

NAME	NOMINATED BY	SERVICE
John M. Harlan	Hayes	1877–1911
Horace Gray	Arthur	1882–1902
Melville W. Fuller*	Cleveland	1888–1910
David J. Brewer	Harrison	1890–1910
Henry B. Brown	Harrison	1890–1906
George Shiras Jr.	Harrison	1892–1903
Edward D. White	Cleveland	1894–1910
Rufus W. Peckham	Cleveland	1895–1909
Joseph McKenna	McKinley	1898–1925
Oliver W. Holmes	T. Roosevelt	1902–1932
William R. Day	T. Roosevelt	1903–1922
William H. Moody	T. Roosevelt	1906–1910
Horace H. Lurton	Taft	1910–1914
Edward D. White	Taft	1910–1921
Charles E. Hughes	Taft	1910–1916
Willis Van Devanter	Taft	1911–1937
Joseph R. Lamar	Taft	1911–1916
Mahlon Pitney	Taft	1912–1922
James C. McReynolds	Wilson	1914–1941
Louis D. Brandeis	Wilson	1916–1939
John H. Clarke	Wilson	1916–1922
William H. Taft	Harding	1921–1930
George Sutherland	Harding	1922–1938
Pierce Butler	Harding	1922–1939
Edward T. Sanford	Harding	1923–1930
Harlan F. Stone	Coolidge	1925–1941
Charles E. Hughes	Hoover	1930–1941
Owen J. Roberts	Hoover	1930–1945
Benjamin N. Cardozo	Hoover	1932–1938
Hugo L. Black	F. Roosevelt	1937–1971
Stanley F. Reed	F. Roosevelt	1938–1957
Felix Frankfurter	F. Roosevelt	1939–1962
William O. Douglas	F. Roosevelt	1939–1975
Frank Murphy	F. Roosevelt	1940–1949
Harlan F. Stone	F. Roosevelt	1941–1946
James F. Byrnes	F. Roosevelt	1941–1942

NAME	NOMINATED BY	SERVICE
Robert H. Jackson	F. Roosevelt	1941–1954
Wiley B. Rutledge	F. Roosevelt	1943–1949
Harold H. Burton	Truman	1945–1958
Fred M. Vinson	Truman	1946–1953
Tom C. Clark	Truman	1949–1967
Sherman Minton	Truman	1949–1956
Earl Warren	Eisenhower	1953–1969
John M. Harlan	Eisenhower	1955–1971
William J. Brennan Jr.	Eisenhower	1956–1990
Charles E. Whittaker	Eisenhower	1957–1962
Potter Stewart	Eisenhower	1958–1981
Byron R. White	Kennedy	1962–1993
Arthur J. Goldberg	Kennedy	1962–1965
Abe Fortas	Johnson	1965–1969
Thurgood Marshall	Johnson	1967–1991
Warren E. Burger	Nixon	1969–1986
Harry A. Blackmun	Nixon	1970–1994
Lewis F. Powell Jr.	Nixon	1971–1987
William H. Rehnquist	Nixon	1971–1986
John Paul Stevens	Ford	1975–2010
Sandra Day O'Connor	Reagan	1981–2006
William H. Rehnquist	Reagan	1986–2005
Antonin Scalia	Reagan	1986–
Anthony M. Kennedy	Reagan	1988–
David H. Souter	G. H.W. Bush	1990–2009
Clarence Thomas	G. H.W. Bush	1991–
Ruth Bader Ginsburg	Clinton	1993–
Stephen G. Breyer	Clinton	1994–
John G. Roberts Jr.	G. W. Bush	2005–
Samuel A. Alito Jr.	G. W. Bush	2006–
Sonia Sotomayor	Obama	2009–
Elena Kagan	Obama	2010–

*Boldface type indicates service as chief justice.

Glossary

A

advisory referendum: a process in which voters cast nonbinding ballots on an issue or proposal.

affirmative action: efforts to reach and attract applicants for jobs, college admissions, and business contracts from traditionally underrepresented groups, ranging from extensive publicity and outreach to quota plans.

agency capture: the condition under which an agency primarily serves the interests of a nongovernmental group rather than those of elected officials.

agenda-setting: the media role in determining which issues the public considers important, by covering some issues and ignoring others.

Aid to Families with Dependent Children (AFDC): a federal program in effect from 1935 to 1996 that provided assistance to households with needy children.

American creed: the dominant political culture in the United States, marked by a set of beliefs in individualism, democracy, liberty, property, and religion, tied together by the value of equality.

amicus curiae: a brief written by someone who is not a party to a case but who submits information or an argument related to the dispute at hand.

Anti-Federalists: individuals opposed to the proposed Constitution, fearing it concentrated too much power in the national government.

appellate courts: the second tier of the federal judiciary, primarily responsible for reviewing decisions rendered by the first tier of district courts.

appropriations: the granting of funds to operate authorized federal programs and agencies.

approval rating: the percentage of the public that approves of the job the president is doing overall.

Articles of Confederation: the first constitution of the United States, which based most power in the states.

at-large election: election in which candidates for office must compete throughout the jurisdiction as a whole.

attitudinal model: the theory of judicial decision-making in which judges use their own policy preferences in deciding cases.

Australian ballot: an official government-produced ballot for elections that lists all offices and all the candidates and parties that have qualified to be on the ballot.

authoritarian (or totalitarian) system: a political system in which one person or group has absolute control over the apparatus of government, and in which popular input in government is minimal or nonexistent.

authorization: the granting of legal authority to operate federal programs and agencies.

autocracy: a form of government in which a single person rules with effectively unlimited power.

B

bad tendency standard: a free speech standard which took as its starting point a presumption that government restrictions on speech were reasonable and constitutional, thus leaving the burden of proof to those who objected to the restriction.

balancing test: used by the Supreme Court in free exercise of religion cases, this two-part test first determined whether a government action or law was a burden on religious practice and, if it was, whether a compelling government interest was at stake that would make the burden constitutionally acceptable.

battleground states: competitive states in which no candidate has an overwhelming advantage, and therefore Electoral College votes are in play.

bench trial: a court trial in which a judge hears and rules on a case without a jury.

bias: favorable treatment to certain politicians, policy positions, groups, and political outcomes.

bicameral: an institution consisting of two chambers.

Bill of Rights: the first 10 amendments to the U.S. Constitution, intended to protect individual liberties from federal government intrusion.

block grant: funds provided by the federal government to a state or local government in general support of a broad government function such as education or transportation.

blue states: largely uncontested states in which the Democratic candidate for president is very likely to win.

bond referendum: a process of seeking voter approval before a government borrows money by issuing bonds to investors.

briefs: documents that contain the legal arguments of a dispute.

Brown v. Board of Education: Supreme Court ruling in 1954 that in public education, mandatory separation of children by race results in inherently unequal education. The decision overturned the separate but equal doctrine.

bundling: the practice of collecting individual checks and presenting them to a candidate at one time.

bureaucracy: a group of departments, agencies, and other institutions that for the most part are located in the executive branch of government and that develop and implement public policy.

Bush Doctrine: a grand strategy pursued after September 11, 2001, that emphasized an aggressive posture toward nations that provide safe haven for terrorists, preemptive action, and a willingness to unilaterally launch military actions.

C

Cabinet: a group of the top-ranking officials of every major federal department, plus other officials included by the president, who meet periodically with the president to discuss major administration priorities and policies.

casework: the direct assistance that members of Congress give to individuals and groups within a district or state.

categorical grant: funds provided by the federal government to a state or local government for a specific, defined purpose.

caucus: a small meeting at which registered political party members select delegates to attend the national party convention and nominate a presidential candidate.

causal question: a question regarding the factors responsible for a particular outcome.

causation: a relationship between variables such that change in the value of one is directly responsible for change in the value of the other.

Central Intelligence Agency (CIA): the cornerstone of U.S. efforts to gather and analyze data in order to confront America's real and potential enemies.

centralization: the method of increasing the president's power by moving key administrative functions from the departments to the Executive Office of the President.

charter: a document that, like a constitution, specifies the basic policies, procedures, and institutions of a local government.

charter schools: public schools, administered by chartering boards, that are exempt from many rules and regulations applicable to traditional public schools.

checks and balances: the principle that each branch of the federal government has the means to thwart or influence actions by other branches of government.

Chief Justice: the presiding member of the Supreme Court who serves as chair of the conference and, if in the majority, selects the justice who will write the majority opinion.

civic skills: the skills of writing, speaking, analyzing, and organizing that reduce the cost of political participation.

civil case: a case that concerns a violation of the legal rights or obligations of one individual toward another.

civil disobedience: strategy of breaking law nonviolently in order to protest a law one considers unjust and draw attention to one's cause.

civil liberties: individual rights and freedoms that government is obliged to protect, normally by not interfering in the exercise of these rights and freedoms.

civil rights: guarantees of equal opportunities, privileges, and treatment under the law that allow individuals to participate fully and equally in American society.

civil service system: a system of government in which decisions about hiring, promotion, and firing are based on individuals' work experience, skills, and expertise.

class action suit: a lawsuit in which the plaintiff is a group of individuals who have suffered a common injury.

clear and present danger standard: used in free speech cases, this standard permitted government restrictions on speech if public officials believed that allowing the speech created a risk that some prohibited action would result from the speech.

closed primary: an election in which only registered members of a political party can participate in the party's primary election.

closed rule: the terms and conditions applied to a particular bill that restrict the types of amendments that can be made to it.

cloture: a mechanism by which 60 or more senators can end a filibuster and cut off debate.

Cold War: the period, from the late 1940s to the late 1980s, in which the United States and the Soviet Union engaged in diplomatic and economic hostility but not full-fledged war.

collective action problem: a problem that arises when individuals' incentives lead them to avoid taking actions that are best for the group as a whole, and that they themselves would like to see accomplished.

collective benefit: a benefit everyone enjoys, regardless of whether or not they contributed to its attainment.

commerce clause: a provision in the U.S. Constitution that gives Congress the power to regulate commerce with other countries, among the states, and with Indian tribes.

commission: form of local government in which voters elect individuals to act as legislators and to head administrative agencies.

527 committee: an independent, nonparty group that raises and spends money on political activities.

common law: law made by judges when no legislation currently exists.

communitarianism: the view that the needs of the community are of higher priority in government than the needs of the individual, even if the result is a restriction of individual liberties.

commute: the action of a governor to cancel all or part of a sentence while keeping a conviction on the record.

compact theory: a theory of the founding of the American government that argues states were sovereign units that joined together in the new national government but did not give up their status as sovereign, independent governments.

concurring opinion: a document written by a justice on the majority side of a ruling which outlines additional considerations he or she thinks important.

confederation: a loose grouping of independent political units, such as states or countries, whose main purpose is to govern the relationship between those units.

conference committee: a committee made up of members of both chambers that is responsible for ironing out the differences between House and Senate versions of a bill.

conference: the confidential gathering of justices in which they discuss their thoughts about the case and cast preliminary votes.

constituents: the people who reside within an elected official's political jurisdiction.

constitutional democracy: a form of democracy in which there is a foundational document (such as the U.S. Constitution) that describes the structure, powers, and limits of government.

containment: the strategy of guarding against Soviet power by adopting policies that limited the geographic expansion of Soviet power.

continuing resolution: funds used to keep programs up and running when regular appropriations have not been approved by the end of the fiscal year.

cooperative federalism: a form of federalism in which the national and state governments share many functions and areas of authority.

coordinated expenditures: legally limited purchases or payments made by a political party on behalf of, and in coordination with, a specific campaign.

correlation: a relationship between factors such that change in one is accompanied by change in the other.

county: a district created by state government for establishing a local government responsible for implementing a variety of state laws and for providing general governmental services.

criminal case: a case that involves a violation of the statutes that are intended to protect the public's health, order, safety, and morality.

cycling: a phenomenon that occurs when multiple decision makers must decide among multiple options and cannot agree on a single course of action.

D

dealignment: a substantial reduction in the proportion of the voting population consistently voting for and identifying with one party.

Declaration of Independence: the document announcing the intention of the colonies to separate from Great Britain based on shared grievances about the treatment of the colonists by the British government.

de facto segregation: racial segregation that results not because of explicit law, policy, or procedures, but from patterns of behavior that have the effect of segregating the races.

defendant: the party being sued or accused of a crime.

Defense Department: the agency created by the National Security Act in 1947 that replaced the Departments of War and the Navy.

deficit: the amount of money a government spends in a year, above and beyond what it brings in through taxation and other means.

de jure segregation: racial segregation that occurs because it is written into law, policy, or government procedures.

delegate model of representation: the type of representation by which representatives are elected to do the bidding of the people who elected them; representatives are "delegates" in that they share the same policy positions as the voters and promise to act upon them.

delegates: individuals who represent a state's voters in the selection of a political party's presidential candidate.

delegation: the granting of authority by Congress to the president to be the first or main actor in a policy area, usually with implicit or explicit limits on actions that Congress would find acceptable.

democracy: a form of government in which the people rule. This can take place directly, through participation by the people in actual lawmaking, or indirectly, through free elections in which the people choose representatives to make laws on their behalf.

department: a major administrative unit that is composed of many agencies serving many policy functions, and that is headed by a secretary, who serves in the president's Cabinet.

Department of Homeland Security (DHS): the agency created in the aftermath of September 11 to coordinate the work of agencies involved in preventing and responding to attacks on the United States.

deregulation: the process of decreasing the number of agency rules that apply to a particular industry or group of industries so as to introduce market forces to their operations.

détente: a period of reduced Cold War tensions in the 1970s.

devolution: a process in which the authority over a government program's rules and implementation is largely transferred from a higher-level government to a lower-level government.

Dillon's rule: principle articulated in a court ruling that local governments do not have any inherent sovereignty but instead must be authorized by a state government.

diplomacy: the peaceful negotiation of economic and political relationships between different countries.

direct democracy: a form of democracy in which the people themselves make the laws and set the policies adopted by the government.

direct initiative: a process in which voters can place a proposal on a ballot and enact it into law without involving the legislature or governor.

direct mail: political advertising in which messages are sent directly to potential voters in the form of mail or e-mail, rather than using a third-party medium.

direction: in public opinion, the tendency for or against some phenomenon.

discrimination: the view that not all groups in society are deserving of equal rights and opportunities.

dissenting opinion: a document written by a justice on the minority side of a ruling which outlines his or her own reasoning on the case and identifies perceived flaws in the majority opinion.

district courts: the first tier of the federal judiciary where most cases are decided.

district-based election: election in which candidates run for an office that represents only the voters of a specific district within the jurisdiction.

disturbance theory: the theory that when social, political, and economic relationships change, individuals form groups in response.

divided government: a situation where the presidency is held by one party and at least one house of Congress is controlled by a different party.

Dred Scott v. Sandford: Supreme Court decision in 1857 declaring that neither slaves nor the descendants of slaves could be U.S. citizens.

drift: a situation in which bureaucrats create policy that does not match the policy preferences of Congress or the president.

dual citizenship: the idea that an individual is a citizen of both his or her state and the United States. Rights and responsibilities can vary from state to state and can be different on the state and national levels.

dual federalism: a form of federalism in which the national and state governments have distinct areas of authority and power, and individuals have rights as both citizens of states and citizens of the United States.

dual jurisdiction: when two different courts (state, tribal, national) have the authority to try someone for crimes committed in the same incident.

dual sovereignty: the idea that both the national and state governments have sovereignty, but over different policy areas and functions.

due process: procedural safeguards that government officials are obligated to follow prior to restricting rights of life, liberty, and property.

E

earmarks: federal funds that support specific local projects.

Electoral College: the meeting, in each state and the District of Columbia, of electors who cast votes to elect the president.

electoral realignment: a shift in the composition of party coalitions that produces a new, relatively durable pattern of party competition.

Elementary and Secondary Education Act (ESEA): a federal law passed in 1965 designed to reduce educational inequities by directly aiding school districts with large numbers of poor citizens.

entitlements: benefits that all qualifying individuals have a legal right to obtain.

enumerated powers: the specifically listed duties that the U.S. Constitution assigns to Congress.

equal privileges and immunities clause: a clause in the Constitution stating that states are to treat equally their citizens and the citizens of other states.

equal protection clause: clause in the Fourteenth Amendment stating that states are not to deny any person equal treatment under the law.

equality: the value that all Americans should be treated the same under the law, be able to influence government, and have equal opportunity to succeed in life.

establishment clause: a clause in the First Amendment that prevents government from establishing an official religion, treating one religion preferably to another, proselytizing, or promoting religion over nonreligion.

ethnic lobby: an interest group that advocates policies focusing on specific foreign states.

exclusionary rule: principle established by the Supreme Court, according to which evidence gathered illegally cannot be introduced into trial, and convictions cannot be based on this evidence.

executive agreement: an international agreement in which the United States becomes a party once the president has signed it, without requiring approval from two-thirds of the Senate.

Executive Office of the President: a group of agencies in the executive branch that primarily generate policy alternatives for the president's consideration.

executive order: a presidential directive or proclamation that has the force of law.

executive privilege: the idea that executive branch officials need to be able to advise the president in confidence, and that the president has a right to prevent that advice from becoming public.

extradite: the action of a governor to send someone against his or her will to another state to face criminal charges.

F

federalism: a form of government that distributes power across a national government and subnational governments and ensures the existence of the subnational governments.

Federalists: individuals who supported the proposed Constitution and favored its ratification.

field operations: the "ground war" intended to produce high turnout among party loyalists, particularly in battleground states.

filibuster: a procedure by which senators delay or prevent action on a bill by making long speeches and engaging in unlimited debate.

fiscal federalism: a technique of persuasion in which the federal government offers resources to states that agree to take certain actions.

fiscal policy: policy designed to improve the economy through spending and taxation.

focus group: in-depth interview with a small number of people representing important voter constituencies.

foreign policy: the mix of military, diplomatic, and economic policies that define U.S. relations with other nations around the world.

formal powers: specific grants of authority defined in the Constitution or in law.

free exercise clause: a clause in the First Amendment that prohibits government from interfering with individuals' practice of their religion.

free rider problem: a barrier to collective action because people can reap the benefits of group efforts without participating.

full faith and credit clause: a clause in the Constitution stating that states are to honor the official acts of other states.

fusion: a strategy in which third parties endorse a major party candidate but list that candidate separately on the ballot so that voters can vote for the candidate under the third-party label.

G

gate-keeping authority: the power to decide whether a particular proposal or policy change will be considered.

generational effect: the situation in which younger citizens are influenced by events in such a fashion that their attitudes and beliefs are forever rendered distinct from those of older generations.

get-out-the-vote (GOTV): term used by campaign professionals to describe the various activities candidates, political parties, activists, and interest groups use to make sure their likely supporters go to the polls on Election Day.

going public: activities of presidents such as highly visible trips, press conferences, interviews, speeches, and public appearances in an attempt to raise public support for a policy agenda.

government: the institutions that have the authority and capacity to create and enforce public policies (rules) for a specific territory and people.

government corporation: a corporation created and funded by the government to provide some public service that would be insufficiently provided by the private sector.

governor: the chief elected executive official in state governments.

grand strategy: a plan that determines American national security interests, outlines possible threats to those interests, and recommends military and diplomatic policies to attain them.

grassroots lobbying: efforts to persuade citizens to contact their elected officials regarding a particular issue or piece of legislation.

gravity of the danger standard: a free speech standard in which the Supreme Court allowed restrictions on speech if the danger espoused by the speech was sufficiently evil, even if that evil was unlikely to occur.

Great Compromise: the agreement between small states and large states that representation in the Senate would be equal for each state, as small states preferred, and representation in the House would be based on population, as large states preferred.

Great Depression: a period of severe economic recession in the United States precipitated by the stock market crash in October 1929.

Great Society: a set of large-scale social initiatives proposed by President Lyndon Johnson in the 1960s to reduce poverty, racial discrimination, environ mental degradation, and urban decay.

gross domestic product (GDP): a statistic that measures all goods and services produced by a nation's economy.

H

hard money: funds to be used for the express purpose of running an election campaign, or advocating for or against the election of a specific candidate.

hearing: a formal process in which committees in Congress call upon bureaucrats and other experts to help them understand and oversee a particular agency.

home rule: a local government with authority to pass laws and provide services as long as those laws or services are not provided by a special district or otherwise prohibited under state law.

horse race: a focus in election coverage on who and what are up or down in the latest poll numbers.

I

ideology: a consistent set of ideas about a given set of issues.

impeachment: performed by the House of Representatives, the act of charging government officials with "treason, bribery, or other high crimes and misdemeanors." The Senate then decides whether to convict and remove the official from office.

implementation: the process by which policy is executed.

implied powers: functions and actions that Congress could perform in order to implement and exercise its enumerated powers.

inclusion: the principle that state courts will apply federal laws when those laws directly conflict with state laws.

incorporation process: the application, through the Fourteenth Amendment, of the civil liberties protections in the Bill of Rights to state governments.

incumbent: the individual in an election who currently holds the contested office; as distinct from the challenger, who seeks to remove the incumbent from power.

independent agencies and commissions: bureaucratic organizations that operate outside of Cabinet-level departments and are less subject to congressional or presidential influence.

independent expenditures: funds spent to elect or defeat candidates but not coordinated with any candidate's campaign.

indirect election: an election in which voters select other individuals who directly vote for candidates for a particular office; U.S. Senate and presidential elections were of this type in the Constitution, but Senate elections are now direct elections.

indirect initiative: a process in which the legislature places a proposal on a ballot and allows voters to enact it into law, without involving the governor or further action by the legislature.

individualism: a belief that all individuals should be able to succeed to the maximum extent possible given their talents and abilities, regardless of race, religion, or other group characteristics.

initiative: a process in which a proposal for legislation is placed on the ballot and voters can either enact or reject the proposal without further action by the governor or legislature.

inside lobbying: meeting directly with public officials to influence political decisions.

intensity: the strength of the direction of public opinion.

interest group entrepreneur: an individual who overcomes the costs of collective action by launching and managing an interest group.

interest groups: organizations that seek to influence government decisions.

internationalism: the grand strategy of actively engaging in world affairs.

invisible primary: the race to raise the most money and achieve frontrunner status before the primary season begins.

isolationism: the grand strategy of minimizing a nation's involvement in world affairs.

issue evolution: a change in the partisan base of support for an issue over time, such that the positions of Democrats and Republicans switch.

issue voting: voting style in which the voter judges candidates based on the voter's and the candidates' opinions on specific issues and preferences for certain policies.

J

Jim Crow: system of laws that separated the races in schools, public accommodations, and other aspects of daily life.

joint committee: a committees made up of members of both chambers of Congress to conduct a special investigation or study.

judicial activism: the tendency of judges to give themselves leeway in deciding whether to abide by past court decisions, which allows them to consider possible outcomes, public opinion, and their own preferences before issuing a ruling.

judicial restraint: the practice judges engage in when they limit the exercise of their own power by overturning past decisions only when they are clearly unconstitutional.

judicial review: the power of the judiciary to interpret and overturn actions taken by the legislative and executive branches of government.

jury: a group of private citizens selected to listen to a trial and issue a final verdict.

justice: the term used to refer to a state supreme court judge.

L

laissez-faire economics: a theory that discourages the government from becoming involved in the economy.

leadership: the ability to influence and guide others to achieve some desired policy or action.

legal model: a theory of judicial decision-making in which judges make decisions by deciphering the correct interpretation of the law and the relevant portion of the Constitution, and determining whether there is a conflict between the two.

Lemon test: a three-part establishment clause test used by the Supreme Court that states that, to be constitutional, a government action must have a plausible nonreligious purpose; its primary or principal effect must be to neither advance nor inhibit religion; and it must not foster excessive government entanglement with religion.

libertarianism: a view that emphasizes the importance of individual choice and responsibility, the private sector, and the free market, in which government's primary obligations are to defend the country militarily, protect individuals from crime, and ensure that people fulfill contracts entered into freely.

liberty: the belief that government should leave people free to do as they please and exercise their natural rights to the maximum extent possible.

life cycle effect: attitudes or physical characteristics that change as one ages, no matter the time period or generation. The graying of one's hair is a life cycle effect.

limited government: the idea that the scope of government activities should be narrow and that government should act only when the need is great and other sectors of society are unable to meet the need.

line-item veto: the authority of a chief executive to reject part of a bill passed by the legislature.

lobbying: communicating with government officials to persuade them toward a particular policy decision.

M

magistrate judges: judges who support federal district judges by hearing and deciding minor cases at the district court level.

majority leader: the individual in each chamber who manages the floor; in the Senate, he or she is the most powerful member in the chamber; in the House, he or she is the chief lieutenant of the Speaker.

majority opinion: the written document that reflects the collective judgment of the justices who are on the majority side of a ruling.

majority-minority districts: legislative districts in which district boundaries are drawn in a manner to ensure that a majority of the district residents are members of minority groups, intended to increase the probability of minorities being elected.

mandate: an order from the federal government that requires state governments to take a certain action.

mandate (electoral): the idea that the public provided clear policy guidance in the results of the prior election.

margin of error: the range surrounding a sample's response within which researchers are confident the larger population's true response would fall.

markup: the process by which the members of a committee or subcommittee rewrite, delete, and add portions of a bill.

Marshall Plan: a program that provided aid to rebuild Western European economies after World War II.

mass media or media: various modes of communication intended to reach a mass audience—including television, radio, newspapers, newsmagazines, and the Internet.

matching funds: public monies given to qualifying candidates to match a certain percentage of the funds they have raised from private donors.

material benefit: a good or service offered to encourage participation in group activity.

means-tested program: any program that targets the poor and for which eligibility is based on financial need.

Medicaid: a means-tested program, funded by federal and state governments, that extends health insurance to the poor and disabled.

Medicare: a federally funded entitlement program that offers health insurance to the elderly.

merit plan: a method of selecting judges in which a governor must appoint someone from a list provided by an independent panel. Judges are then kept in office if they get a majority of yes votes in general elections; also called Missouri plan.

minimal effect: the theory that change in voting intent as a result of mass media exposure was relatively rare.

minority leader: the individual who speaks on behalf of the party that controls the smaller number of seats in each chamber.

miracle of aggregation: the phenomenon that occurs when a group consists of individuals who are largely ignorant of a particular issue, but their collective opinion tends to makes sense.

Miranda warning: ruling that requires police, when arresting suspects, to inform them of their rights, including the right to remain silent and have an attorney present during questioning.

modified open primary: an election in which registered voters who are not affiliated with either party can vote in either party's primary.

momentum: the boost in media coverage, name recognition, fund-raising, and perceptions of electability that accompanies unexpected and repeated primary success.

monetary policy: policy designed to improve the economy by control-ling the supply of available money.

multiculturalism: the view that group identity influences political beliefs and that, because groups are naturally diverse in their beliefs, the idea of a shared or dominant political culture merely reflects the imposition of a dominant group's beliefs on subordinate groups.

N

nation: A shared sense of understanding and belonging among a people, that they are different and separate from other peoples with particular characteristics and that they have a right to self-government over a defined territory.

national party convention: a meeting held over several days at which delegates select the party's presidential nominee, approve the party platform, and consider changes in party rules and policies.

National Security Council (NSC): an advisory body, formed in 1947 by the National Security Act, that assists the president in gathering information from military services and other security-related executive agencies.

nationalist theory: a theory of the founding of the American government that sees the Constitution more as the joining together of the people than the joining together of the states.

natural rights: rights inherent in the essence of people as human beings; government does not provide these rights but can restrict the exercise of them.

necessary and expedient clause: a clause in Article II, section 3, of the Constitution that authorizes the president to recommend legislation to Congress.

necessary and proper clause: a provision in the U.S. Constitution that gives Congress the authority to make the laws needed to carry out the specific duties assigned to Congress by the Constitution.

neutrality test: the Supreme Court's most recent approach to deciding free exercise of religion cases, this test declares that a government law or action with a neutral intent and application is constitutional, even if it burdens religion and there is no compelling government interest at stake.

New Jersey Plan: one of the rival plans at the Constitutional Convertion, it called for, among other things, equal representation of the states in a single-house legislature.

No Child Left Behind Act (NCLB): a 2001 federal law that rewards public schools for meeting certain educational benchmarks and punishes schools that fail to do so.

nondecisions: decisions not to consider particular issues or incorporate them into the policy agenda.

nonpartisan: an election in which candidates run without formal identification or association with a political party.

nonresponse bias: a nonrandom error that occurs when people who choose to participate in a survey have different attitudes from those of people who decline to participate.

North American Free Trade Agreement (NAFTA): an agreement, signed in 1992, to reduce tariff and nontariff barriers to trade and investment among Canada, Mexico, and the United States.

North Atlantic Treaty Organization (NATO): established in 1949, a military alliance of the United States and a number of European nations that pledge to join forces against an attack by any external threat.

Northwest Ordinance of 1787: law passed by Congress under the Articles of Confederation that established the process by which the territories of Ohio, Indiana, Illinois, Michigan, and Wisconsin would be governed and admitted as states.

nullification: the theory that states have the right to nullify national laws to which they object and believe violate the U.S. Constitution.

O

open primary: an election in which a voter can participate in either party's primary (but not both), regardless of party registration.

open rule: the terms and conditions applied to a particular bill that allow members of Congress to make a wide range of amendments to it.

opinion leaders: individuals with high levels of interest and expertise in politics who seek to communicate their political beliefs to others.

oral argument: a lawyer's spoken presentation to the court of the legal reasons that his or her side should prevail.

original jurisdiction: the right of a court to be the first to hear a case rather than simply review the decision of a lower court.

oversight: congressional and presidential efforts to monitor and supervise the actions of bureaucratic agencies.

P

package or general veto: the authority of a chief executive to void an entire bill that has been passed by the legislature.

pardon: the authority of a governor to cancel someone's conviction of a crime and eliminate all sanctions and punishments.

parliamentary system: a political system in which the head of the executive branch is selected by members of the legislature rather than by popular vote.

parole: the authority of a governor to release a prisoner before his or her full sentence has been completed. A parole is for a specific period and includes restrictions and supervision.

party caucus: the gathering of all Democratic members of the House or Senate.

party conference: the gathering of all Republican members of the House or Senate.

party machine: disciplined local party organizations that selected candidates; got out the vote; provided benefits to supporters including government workers, local constituents, and businesses; and served as social service agencies for their followers.

party platform: a document expressing the principles, beliefs, and policy positions of the party, as endorsed by delegates at the national party convention.

patron: an individual who supports an interest group by providing the resources needed to organize and flourish.

patronage: awarding jobs in government on the basis of party support and loyalty rather than expertise or experience.

period effect: an event that influences the attitudes and beliefs of people of all ages.

persistence: the principle that political lessons, values, and attitudes learned early in life tend to structure political learning later on in life.

plaintiff: the party who initiates a lawsuit by filing a complaint.

plea bargain: an agreement between the prosecutor and the defendant in a criminal case through which the parties agree to a specified crime and punishment.

Plessy v. Ferguson: Supreme Court decision in 1896 upholding the constitutionality of laws and government policies that required segregated facilities for blacks and whites.

pluralism: the theory that all groups are well represented and no single interest controls government decisions.

plurality elections: elections in which the candidate with the most votes, not necessarily a majority, wins.

plurality rule: rule by which a candidate wins office by getting more votes than his or her opponent, even if that candidate does not receive an absolute majority of the votes.

pocket veto: the president's veto of a bill without the opportunity for Congress to override the veto. It occurs if the president does not act on a bill within 10 days after passage by Congress and Congress adjourns during that time.

police power: the protection of public safety, health, welfare, and morality by a government.

policy agenda: the set of issues under consideration by policy makers.

policy entrepreneurs: professionals working in think tanks, universities, lobby groups, unions, and interest groups who propose solutions to policy problems and persuade politicians to adopt them.

political action committee (PAC): a group that collects money from individuals and makes donations to political parties and candidates.

political attentiveness: an individual's general attention to and knowledge of politics.

political culture: the values and beliefs of citizens toward the political system and toward themselves as actors in it.

political efficacy: an individual's belief that he or she can influence what happens in the political world.

political parties: organized groups with public followings that seek to elect office holders who identify themselves by the group's common label, for the purpose of exercising political power.

political predisposition: the interests, values, and experiences that help organize one's thinking about politics.

political socialization: the learning process in which individuals absorb information and selectively add it to their knowledge and understanding of politics and government.

politicization: a phenomenon that occurs when Congress and the president select bureaucracy leaders who share their political views.

politics: individual and collective efforts to influence the workings of government.

poll tax: fee assessed on each person who wishes to vote; prohibited by the Twenty-fourth Amendment in 1964.

popular referendum: a process by which voters can veto a bill recently passed in the legislature by placing the issue on a ballot and expressing disapproval. Also called direct referendum.

preemption legislation: legislation that declares, or mandates, certain actions off-limits for state governments.

preferred position: the idea, endorsed by the Supreme Court, that the First Amendment predominates over the other amendments and that First Amendment protections predominates over the other protections of rights, meaning that speech restriction should be done narrowly and reluctantly and speech generally should prevail when in conflict with other rights.

presidential system: a political system in which the head of the executive branch is selected by some form of popular vote and serves a fixed term of office. The United States has a presidential system.

primacy: the principle that what is learned first is learned best and lodged most firmly in one's mind.

primary: election in which voters choose the candidate that will represent their political party in the general election.

priming: a media effect in which the public assesses the performance of politicians and candidates in terms of the issues that the media have emphasized.

principal-agent problem: the problem that occurs when one person (the principal) contracts with another person (the agent) to provide a service and yet cannot directly observe what the agent isactually doing; the agent, meanwhile, is motivated to take advantage of the principal.

prior restraint: government intervention to prevent the publication of material it finds objectionable.

privatization: the transfer of government functions from the federal government to private companies.

Progressive movement: advocated measures to destroy political machines and instead have direct participation by voters in the nomination of candidates and the establishment of public policy.

progressive reforms: a set of political and electoral reforms in the early twentieth century that had the combined effect of weakening political parties.

property rights: the belief that people should be able to acquire, own, and use goods and assets free from government constraints, as long as their acquisition and use does not interfere with the rights of other individuals.

proportional representation: an election system in which candidates are elected from multimember districts, with a party's share of seats from a district being roughly proportional to their share of the popular vote.

prospective voting: voting style in which voters judge a candidate based on their assessment of what the candidate will do in office if elected.

protectionism: the practice of imposing selective tariffs on trade in an effort to protect specific domestic industries from international competition.

public debt: the total amount of money that the federal government owes.

public goods: goods (and services) that are enjoyed by all citizens and unlikely to be provided by any organization other than government.

public law: those laws enacted by presidents and Congress that define the relationship between individuals (and organizations) and the state.

public money: taxpayer funds used to help finance presidential campaigns.

public opinion: the collective political beliefs and attitudes of the public, or groups within the public, on matters of relevance to government.

purposive benefit: benefit that encourages group participation by connecting individuals to an organization's political purpose.

R

rally event: short-term international event or military action that boosts presidential approval ratings temporarily.

random sample: a population sample in which it is equally likely that each member of the population will be included in the sample.

recall: a process in which voters can petition for a vote to remove officials between elections.

recess appointment: the means by which the president fills a vacant position in the bureaucracy when Congress is not in session, thus avoiding the need for prior congressional approval.

recession: an economic downturn, which technically exists when the gross domestic product drops in size for two successive quarters.

recuse: the act of abstaining or not participating in a decision. This applies primarily to judges who avoid a conflict of interest by not participating in cases where they have a personal or financial interest.

red states: largely uncontested states in which the Republican candidate for president is very likely to win.

red tape: the inefficiency and waste that result from excessive regulation and overly formal procedures.

Regents of the University of California v. Bakke: Supreme Court decision in 1978 that a rigid quota plan for admissions violates the Constitution's equal protection guarantee, but race could be considered a "plus factor" in college admissions to increase student body diversity.

religious freedom: a belief that individuals should be free to choose and practice their religious faith and that government should not establish any particular religion as the official or preferred religion.

representative democracy: a form of democracy in which the people, through free elections, select representatives to make laws on their behalf and set policies adopted by the government; also known as a republic.

representative town meeting: form of local government in which voters select someone from their precinct or district to participate in a meeting that considers and approves budgets and ordinances. Representatives do not hold an office or serve a term after the meeting adjourns.

republic: a system in which people elect representatives to make policy and write laws; also known as a representative democracy.

reserved powers: Tenth Amendment guarantee to state governments of any powers other than those granted to the national government or those specifically prohibited for the states.

responsible party model: the idea that political parties should run as unified teams, present a clear policy platform, implement that platform when in office, and run on their record in the subsequent election.

retrospective voting: voting style in which voters judge candidates based on the performance of the candidates or their parties rather than issue stands and assessments of what each candidate would do if elected.

ripeness doctrine: principle by which the courts will accept only cases where the actual harm has already taken place.

rules: administrative determinations about how laws will be interpreted and implemented.

S

salience: an issue's importance to a person or to the public in general.

sampling error: the difference between the reported characteristics of the sample and the characteristics of the larger population that result from imperfect sampling.

sampling: taking a small fraction of something that is meant to represent a larger whole: e.g., a group of people that represents a larger population.

select committee: a temporary committee created to serve a specific purpose.

selective benefit: benefit that can be accessed only by those who participate in or contribute to group activity.

selective exposure: the tendency of people to expose themselves to information that is in accord with their beliefs.

selective incorporation: the process by which protections in the Bill of Rights were gradually applied to the states, as the Supreme Court issued decisions on specific aspects of the Bill of Rights.

selective perception: the tendency of individuals to interpret information in ways consistent with their beliefs.

selective retention: the tendency of individuals to recall information that is consistent with existing beliefs and to discard information that runs counter to them.

senatorial courtesy: the custom by which the senior senator from the state in which there is a district court vacancy assists the president in selecting a replacement for that seat.

seniority: the length of time a legislator has served in office.

separate but equal doctrine: Supreme Court doctrine that laws or policies requiring segregated facilities for the races are constitutionally acceptable as long as the facilities are of equal quality.

separation of powers: the principle that the executive, legislative, and judicial functions of government should be primarily performed by different institutions in government.

Shays's Rebellion: a protest by farmers in western Massachusetts in 1786–1787 to stop foreclosures on property by state courts; it convinced many political leaders that the Articles of Confederation were insufficient to govern the United States.

single-member districts: electoral districts in which only one person is elected to represent the district in a representative body.

slack: a situation in which bureaucrats do not work as hard as Congress or the president would like.

social benefit: benefit that encourages individuals to join a group in order to enjoy the company of those who share similar opinions and interests.

social contract: an agreement among members of a society to form and recognize the authority of a centralized government that is empowered to make and enforce laws governing the members of that society.

Social Security Act: a 1935 law that established Social Security, an entitlement program providing retirees with a monthly income in order to reduce poverty among the elderly.

socioeconomic status (SES): a combination of an individual's occupation, income, and education levels.

soft money: funds to be used for political purposes other than running a campaign, for example, get-out-the-vote efforts.

solicitor general: the individual who represents the federal government in the Supreme Court.

sovereign immunity: the principle that state governments cannot be sued by private parties in federal court unless they consent to the suits or Congress has constitutionally provided an exemption that allows suits to be filed.

sovereign power: the individual or institution in a political system whose decisions are binding and unable to be overturned by other individuals or institutions.

sovereignty: having the ultimate authority to make decisions within one's borders, without interference by other governments.

Speaker of the House: the person who presides over the House and serves as the chamber's official spokesperson.

special district: a local government created for a narrowly defined purpose and with a restricted source of revenue.

spoils system: a system of government in which a presidential administration awards jobs to party loyalists.

sponsor: a member of Congress who introduces a bill.

spurious relationship: a relationship between variables that reflects correlation but not causation.

stability: the likelihood that public opinion will change, the speed with which the change would occur, and the likelihood that the new opinion would endure.

standing: the requirement establishing that for a plaintiff to bring a case to court, he or she must have suffered a well-defined injury that is a result of violation of the civil code.

standing committee: a permanent committee with a well-defined, relatively fixed policy jurisdiction that develops, writes, and updates important legislation.

stare decisis: the principle that judges deciding a case must carefully weigh the decisions of their predecessors in similar cases and come to the same decision if the basic elements of the case before them are the same.

state action: Supreme Court interpretation of the equal protection clause that holds the clause prohibited unfair discriminatory actions by government, not by private individuals.

State Department: the agency home of diplomats, embassies, treaty negotiators, and most foreign aid programs run by the U.S. government.

strategic model: the theory of judicial decision-making in which judges consider their own policy preferences as well as the possible actions of the other branches of government when making decisions.

strong mayor: a governance system in which the elected chief executive has significant authority to veto legislation and appoint administrators.

subcommittee: a smaller organizational unit within a committee that specializes in a particular segment of the committee's responsibilities.

substantive due process: an interpretation of the due process clause in the Fourteenth Amendment that says the clause's guarantee of "life, liberty, and property" provides a means to discover new rights not mentioned elsewhere in the Constitution, and that these rights would exist at both the national and state levels of government.

suffrage: the right to vote.

sunset provision: a condition of a law that requires it to be reauthorized after a certain number of years.

supplemental appropriations: the process by which Congress and the president can provide temporary funding for government activities and programs when funds fall short due to unforeseen circumstances.

supremacy clause: a clause in the Constitution that declares that national laws and treaties have supremacy over state laws and treaties.

supreme court: the highest court in the land, where all decisions are final.

T

take care clause: the constitutional clause that grants the president the authority and leeway to determine if laws are being "faithfully executed" and to take action if in his judgment they are not.

tariff: a tax on goods exchanged between nations.

Temporary Assistance for Needy Families (TANF): a program replacing AFDC in 1996 that established new work requirements for welfare recipients and limits on the number of years an individual can receive assistance.

term limits: restrictions that exist in some states about how long an individual may serve in an elected office.

Three-fifths Compromise: an agreement between slave states and free states that a state's slave population would be counted at 60 percent for purposes of determining a state's representation in the house of representatives.

town meeting: form of local government in which all eligible voters are invited to attend a meeting to pass budgets and ordinances.

town: a local government with general responsibilities for order and services in a medium-sized community.

township: a 6-mile by 6-mile are acreated by the Northwest Ordinance of 1787 to be used for local governance in the territories of Ohio, Indiana, Michigan, Illinois, and Wisconsin.

treaty: an international agreement in which the United States becomes a party once the president has signed and two-thirds of the Senate has ratified it.

trustee model of representation: the type of representation by which representatives are elected to do what they think is best for their constituents.

two-party system: a system of electoral competition in which two parties are consistently the most likely to win office and gain power.

U

unfunded mandate: a law requiring certain actions without appropriating the necessary funds to carry them out.

unified government: a situation where the presidency and both houses of Congress are controlled by the same party.

unitary system: a form of government in which government at the highest level has the power to create, combine, or disband lower-level governments and determine what powers will be allowed at the lower levels.

V

valence issues: issues on which virtually everyone agrees.

veto: the president's power to reject legislation passed by Congress. Congress can override a veto with a two-thirds vote in both the House and Senate.

veto: the president's rejection of a bill passed by both chambers of Congress, which prevents the bill from becoming law.

Virginia Plan: one of the rival plans at the Constitutional Convention, it argued for a two-house legislature, with representation based on a state's population; the lower house would be elected directly by the people, and that house would then select the members of the upper house.

Voting Rights Act of 1965: legislation that abolished literacy tests as a requirement to register to vote.

vouchers: tuition subsidies that reduce the costs of sending children to private schools.

W

watchdog: the media's role in keeping a close eye on politicians and presenting stories and information that politicians might not willingly reveal to the media on their own.

weak mayor: a governance system in which the elected chief executive has little formal authority to veto legislation or appoint administrators.

whips: designated members of Congress who deliver messages from the party leaders, keep track of members' votes, and encourage members to stand together on key issues.

whistleblower: a bureaucrat who witnesses and publicly exposes wrongdoing by either contacting his or her political superiors or tipping off the press.

White House Staff: a group of offices in the executive branch that provides the president with political advice, promotes the president's program with legislators and interest groups, and handles the president's public relations.

white primary: primary elections in southern states in which only white voters were allowed to participate.

winner-take-all: election in which the candidate who gets the most votes wins, while any other candidate loses and receives nothing.

writ of certiorari: a formal acceptance by the Supreme Court to review a decision of a lower court.

Notes

CHAPTER ONE

1. Thomas Hobbes, *Leviathan*, ed. Richard Tuck (New York: Cambridge University Press, 1996).
2. See Hobbes, *Leviathan*; John Locke, *Second Treatise on Government*, ed. C. B. Macpherson (Indianapolis: Hackett, 1980); and Jean-Jacques Rousseau, *Basic Political Writings*, ed. Donald A. Cress (Indianapolis: Hackett, 1987).
3. Judge Learned Hand, "We Seek Liberty," address in Central Park, New York, May 21, 1944.

CHAPTER TWO

1. Steven Erlanger, "France Debates Its Identity, but Some Question Why," *New York Times*, November 29, 2009, p. A16.
2. The creed is grounded in the "classical liberal" political theory of the seventeenth and eighteenth centuries. See Louis Hartz, *The Liberal Tradition in America: An Interpretation of American Political Thought Since the Revolution* (New York: Harcourt Brace, 1955); David F. Ericson and Louisa Bertch Green, eds., *The Liberal Tradition in American Politics: Reassessing the Legacy of American Liberalism* (New York: Routledge, 1999). Seymour Martin Lipset. *American Exceptionalism: A Double-Edged Sword* (New York: W. W. Norton, 1997).
3. Peter A. Morrison, "A Demographic Perspective on Our Nation's Future," RAND Report, 2001, http://www.rand.org/publications/DB/DB320/. See also Laura B. Shrestha, "The Changing Demographic Profile of the United States," Congressional Research Service, May 5, 2006 (http://www.fas.org/sgp/crs/misc/RL32701.pdf); and Jeffrey S. Passel and D'Vera Cohn, "U.S. Population Projections: 2005–2050," Pew Research Center, February 11, 2008 (http://pewhispanic.org/files/reports/85.pdf).
4. Daniel J. Hopkins, "Politicized Places: Explaining Where and When Immigrants Provoke Local Opposition," *American Political Science Review* 104, 1 (2010): 40–60; Jens Hainmueller and Michael J. Hiscox, "Attitudes toward Highly Skilled and Low-skilled Immigration: Evidence from a Survey Experiment," *American Political Science Review* 104, 1 (2010): 61–84.
5. Werner Sombart's argument was published in German in 1905. It appears in English as *Why Is There No Socialism in the United States?* trans. Patricia M. Hocking (Armonk, NY: M. E. Sharpe, 1976).
6. See Theda Skocpol, "The Origins of Social Policy in the United States: A Polity-Centered Analysis," in Lawrence C. Dodd and Calvin Jillson, eds., *The Dynamics of American Politics: Approaches and Interpretations* (Boulder, CO: Westview Press, 1994); Adam Przeworski, "The Material Bases of Consent," in Adam Przeworski, *Capitalism and Social Democracy* (New York: Cambridge University Press, 1985).
7. Edward S. Herman and Noam Chomsky, *Manufacturing Consent: The Political Economy of the Mass Media* (Pantheon, 2002); Robert Justin Goldstein, *Political Repression in Modern America: From 1870 to 1976* (Champaign: University of Illinois Press, 2001); Victoria Hattam, *Labor Visions and State Power: The Origins of Business Unionism in the United States* (Princeton, NJ: Princeton University Press, 1992).
8. See Michael Lind, "The American Creed: Does It Matter? Should It Change?" *Foreign Affairs*, March/April 1996; and Forrest Church, "The American Creed," *The Nation*, September 16, 2002.
9. Pew Research Center for the People and the Press, 2009 Values Survey, http://people-press.org/reports/questionnaires/517.pdf); Pew Forum on Religion and Public Life, Religion and Public Life Survey, 2002, http://people-press.org/reports/display.php3?PageID=388.
10. Richard M. Merelman, *Partial Visions: Culture and Politics in Britain, Canada, and the United States* (Madison: University of Wisconsin Press, 1991).
11. Survey data from International Social Science Programme, 2006. Question wording: "On the whole, do you think it should or should not be the government's responsibility to reduce income differences between the rich and the poor."
12. Data collected in 2007 survey for Benjamin I. Page and Lawrence R. Jacobs, *Class War? What Americans Really Think about Economic Inequality* (Chicago: University of Chicago Press, 2009), question QWAG3. http://www.press.uchicago.edu/books/page/Class_War_Marginal_Frequencies.pdf.

13. Lars Osberg and Timothy Smeeding, "An International Comparison of Preferences for Leveling," October 3, 2003, http://www-cpr.maxwell.syr.edu/seminar/fall03 /osberg.pdf; Lars Osberg and Timothy Smeeding, "'Fair' Inequality? An International Comparison of Attitudes to Pay Differentials," November 2, 2004, http://www.cpr .maxwell.syr.edu/faculty/smeeding/selectedpapers/ Economicaversion27October2004.pdf.

14. See James Morone, In *The Democratic Wish: Popular Participation and the Limits of American Government*, revised edition (New Haven, CT: Yale University Press, 1998).

15. John Locke, *Two Treatises of Government*, originally published in 1689.

16. See Jeffrey A. Winters and Benjamin I. Page, "Oligarchy in the United States?" *Perspectives on Politics* 7, 4 (2009): 731–52, and Martin Gilens, "Preference Gaps and Inequality in Representation," *PS* 42, 2 (2009): 335–42.

17. Pew Values Survey, 2009, Pew Research Center. http://people-press.org/reports/questionnaires/ 517.pdf

18. Surveys in late 2009 frequently showed support in the range of two-thirds to three-quarters of Americans supporting restrictions on pay if a company had received federal bailout funds. In cases where funds had been paid back, or the question did not mention bailouts, the public was evenly split on whether any pay limitations were appropriate. A CBS News Poll in August 2009 found a 46%–46% split. A Time/Abt SRBI Poll in October 2009 found a 49%–45% split.

19. A classic articulation of this view is by Milton Friedman, *Capitalism and Freedom* (Chicago: University of Chicago Press, 1962).

20. Anne Norton, *Republic of Signs: Liberal Theory and American Popular Culture* (Chicago: University of Chicago Press, 1993).

21. James T. Kloppenberg, "The Virtues of Liberalism: Christianity, Republicanism, and Ethics in Early American Political Discourse," *Journal of American History* 74 (1987): 9–33.

22. "President Discusses Stem Cell Research," Office of the Press Secretary, August 9, 2001, http://www.whitehouse .gov/news/releases/2001/08/20010809-2.html.

23. Pew Center for the People and the Press, 2009 Values Survey, http://people press.org/reports/questionnaires/ 517.pdf.

24. Pew Research Center for the People and the Press and Pew Forum on Religion and Public Life, Religion and Public Life Survey, August 2008, http://people-press. org/reports/questionnaires/445.pdf.

25. Critics argue that individualist beliefs obscure perceptions of structural problems in the economy and society.

See Jack Turner, "American Individualism and Structural Injustice: Tocqueville, Gender, and Race," *Polity* 40, 2 (2008): 197–215.

26. Paul C. Light, *The True Size of Government* (Washington, DC: Brookings Institution Press, 1999).

27. See Benjamin I. Page and Lawrence R. Jacobs, *Class War? What Americans Really Think About Economic Inequality* (Chicago: University of Chicago Press, 2009).

28. Pew Center for the People and the Press surveys in 2009 for spending preferences; Pew 2009 Values Survey for evaluations of government effectiveness, http://people-press.org/reports/questionnaires/517.pdf.

29. See Steven Rathgeb Smith and Michael Lipsky, *Nonprofits for Hire: The Welfare State in the Age of Contracting* (Cambridge, MA: Harvard University Press, 1995); Irwin Garfinkel, Lee Rainwater, and Timothy Smeeding, *Wealth and Welfare States: Is America a Laggard or Leader?* (New York: Oxford University Press, 2010).

30. The ANES (American National Election Studies) Guide to Public Opinion and Electoral Behavior provides a handful of measures of political trust over time: http://www.electionstudies.org/nesguide/gd-in-dex.htm#5.

31. CNN/Opinion Research Corporation Poll, February 2010; Quinnipiac University Poll, March 2010.

32. Joseph S. Nye Jr., Philip D. Zelikow, and David C. King, eds., *Why People Don't Trust Government* (Cambridge, MA: Harvard University Press, 1997); and Pew Research Center for the People and the Press, "How Americans View Government: Deconstructing Distrust," March 10, 1998, http://people-press.org /reports/print.php3?ReportID=95; Russell J. Dalton, "The Social Transformation of Trust in Government," unpublished manuscript, 5, http://www. worldvaluessurvey.org.

33. Marc J. Hetherington, "The Political Relevance of Political Trust," *American Political Science Review* 92, 4 (December 1998): 791–808.

34. Richard J. Ellis, *American Political Cultures* (New York: Oxford University Press, 1993).

35. Daniel J. Elazar, *American Federalism: A View from the States*, 3rd ed. (New York: HarperCollins, 1984). A map is available at http://www.valpo.edu/geomet/pics /geo200/politics/elazar.gif.

36. Daniel T. Rodgers, *Contested Truths: Keywords in American Politics Since Independence* (Cambridge, MA: Harvard University Press, 1998).

37. There have been multi-legislator districts in some states at some times, but they have been a very small share of the total.

38. *Wesberry v. Sanders* and *Reynolds v. Sims*.

39. Matthew Hayes, Matthew V. Hibbing, and Tracy Sulkin, "Redistricting, Responsiveness, and Issue Attention," *Legislative Studies Quarterly* 35, 1 (2010): 91–116.

40. *Vieth v. Jubilerer*.

41. Four cases were consolidated as *League of United Latin American Citizens v. Perry*.

42. Communitarianism is a modern version of a political philosophy known as classical republicanism. Although there are some distinctions between communitarianism and classical republicanism, they are similar enough for us to use the single label in this discussion.

43. Cited in Gordon S. Wood, *The Creation of the American Republic, 1776–1787* (New York: W.W. Norton, 1969), 61.

44. Wood, *The Creation of the American Republic, 1776–1787*; Bernard Bailyn, *The Ideological Origins of the American Revolution* (Cambridge, MA: Harvard University Press, 1992).

45. In the words of a colonist in 1776, "No man is a true republican that will not give up his single voice to that of the public." Cited in Wood, *The Creation of the American Republic, 1776–1787*, 61.

46. One of the best-known popularizers of communitarian ideas is Amitai Etzioni. See, for example, his *The Spirit of Community: The Reinvention of American Society* (New York: Touchstone, 1993).

47. Karl Polanyi, *The Great Transformation: The Political and Economic Origins of Our Times*, 2nd ed. (Boston: Beacon Press, 2001); Andrew Stark, "The Consensus School, Its Critics, and Welfare Policy: A Study of American Political Discourse," *Journal of Politics* 71, 2 (2009): 627–43.

48. Pew Values Survey 2009 (http://people-press.org/reports/questionnaires/517.pdf).

49. Francesca Colombo and Nicole Tapay, "Private Health Insurance in OECD Countries: The Benefits and Costs for Individuals and Health Systems," OECD Health Working Paper no. 15, 2004, 11–12.

50. See polls at http://www.pollingreport.com/health3.htm, and David W. Brady and Daniel P. Kessler, "Who Supports Health Reform?" *PS* 43, 1 (2010): 1–6.

51. CBS News/New York Times Poll, April 22–26, 2009; CNN/Opinion Research Corporation Poll, March 12–15, 2009.

52. See John T. Scott and Brian H. Bornstein, "What's Fair in Foul Weather and Fair? Distributive Justice across Different Allocation Contexts and Goods," *Journal of Politics* 71, 3 (2009): 831–46.

53. See Sven Steinmo and Jon Watts, "It's the Institutions, Stupid! Why Comprehensive National Health Insurance Fails in America," *Journal of Health Politics, Policy and Law* 20, 2 (1995): 329–72.

54. See Colin Gordon, *Dead on Arrival: The Politics of Health Care in Twentieth-Century America* (Princeton, NJ: Princeton University Press, 2003); Jacob S. Hacker, "The Historical Logic of National Health Insurance: Structure and Sequence in the Development of British, Canadian, and U.S. Medical Policy," *Studies in American Political Development* 12, 1 (1998): 57–130.

55. See Chapter 8 for a discussion of the interest group politics surrounding President Bill Clinton's health care plan.

56. Bunford and Fuchs, "Who Favors National Health Insurance? Who Opposes It? And Why?" talk delivered at the Center for Health Policy and Center for Primary Care and Outcomes Research, Stanford University, March 8, 2006. http://chppcor.stanford.edu/events/4436.

57. Remarks by the President to the House Democratic Congress, March 20, 2010. www.whitehouse.gov/the-press-office/remarks-president-house-democratic-congress. See also Jacob S. Hacker, "The Road to Somewhere: Why Health Reform Happened," *Perspectives on Politics* 8, 3 (2010): 861–76.

58. Rogers M. Smith, "Beyond Tocqueville, Myrdal, and Hartz: The Multiple Traditions in America," *American Political Science Review* 87, 3 (1993): 549–66. Survey data in this paragraph are from the General Social Survey.

59. See the 2009 survey data in "A Place to Call Home: What Immigrants Say Now About Life in America," Public Agenda, http://www.publicagenda.org/pages/immigrants and Maria Hsia Chang, "Multiculturalism, Immigration and Aztlan," paper presented at the Second Alliance for Stabilizing America's Population Action Conference, Breckenridge, Colorado, August 6, 1999, http://www.diversityalliance.org/docs/Chang-aztlan.html.

60. Doriane Lambelet Coleman, "Individualizing Justice Through Multiculturalism: The Liberals' Dilemma," *Columbia Law Review* 96, 5 (1996): 1093–1167.

61. Susan Moller Okin, "Is Multiculturalism Bad for Women?" in Joshua Cohen and Matthew Howard, eds., *Is Multiculturalism Bad for Women?* (Princeton, NJ: Princeton University Press, 1999). See also Cynthia Lee, "Cultural Convergence: Interest Convergence Theory Meets the Cultural Defense?" *Arizona Law Review* 49, 4 (2007).

CHAPTER THREE

1. In a 2006 legislative compromise, President Bush agreed to submit the program to the FISA Court for a one-time review on its constitutionality, but he did not agree to obtain warrants for each individual target of surveillance. A 2008 revision of FISA reaffirmed this procedure. See Eric Lichtblau, "Bush Would Let Secret Court Sift Wiretap

Process," *New York Times*, July 14, 2006; Charles Babington and Peter Baker, "Bush Compromises On Spying Program," *Washington Post*, July 14, 2006.

2. Michael Isikoff, "Obama Secrecy Watch II: A State Secrets Affidavit Straight from the Bush Era," *Newsweek* blog, November 2, 2009. http://blog.newsweek.com/

3. Declan McCullagh, "Feds Push for Tracking Cell Phones," *CNet News*, February 11, 2010. http://news.cnet.com/

4. Bernard Bailyn, *The Ideological Origins of the American Revolution* (Cambridge, MA: Harvard University Press, 1967), 160.

5. Bailyn, *Ideological Origins*, x.

6. See Gordon S. Wood, *The Creation of the American Republic, 1776–1787* (New York: W. W. Norton, 1969), 7–8.

7. Edmund S. Morgan, *Inventing the People: The Rise of Popular Sovereignty in England and America* (New York: W. W. Norton, 1989).

8. Bailyn, *Ideological Origins*, 173.

9. All colonies except Georgia sent representatives to the Congress.

10. Social scientists label this the "state," but that terminology is complicated by the fact that in the United States the word "state" is most often used in reference to state governments.

11. See Merrill Jensen, *The Articles of Confederation* (Madison: University of Wisconsin Press, 1970).

12. On the despair of the 1780s, see Wood, *Creation of the American Republic*, chap. 10.

13. He is also famously, or infamously, known for losing his life in a duel with Aaron Burr.

14. Michael Kammen, *The Origins of the American Constitution: A Documentary History* (New York: Penguin Books, 1986); Catherine Bowen, *Miracle at Philadelphia: The Story of the Constitutional Convention, May–September 1787* (Boston: Little, Brown, 1966); Jack Rakove, *Original Meanings: Politics and Ideas in the Making of the Constitution* (New York: Alfred A. Knopf, 1996).

15. Some historians believe that the Framers were influenced by the governing practices of the Six Nations, known more commonly as the Iroquois Confederacy, which included the Cayuga, Mohawk, Oneida, Onondaga, Seneca, and Tuscarora tribes. Certainly many of the features of U.S. government were present in the Confederacy: checks and balances, federalism, participation, and civil liberties protections. The preamble to the Constitution echoes the language in a 1520 Iroquois treaty: "We the people, to form a union, to establish peace, equity, and order." The Iroquois occupied territory now in New York State. Members of the Iroquois visited the Continental Congress in June 1776. See Bruce E. Johansen, *Forgotten Founders: Benjamin Franklin, the Iroquois and the Rationale for the American Revolution* (Ipswich, MA: Gambit, 1982).

16. Randolph presented a resolution at the outset of the Convention that served, in effect, as a draft for a new system of government.

17. The New Jersey Plan was geared more toward revising the Articles rather than discarding them, but delegates had already gravitated toward the idea that a new system was needed.

18. The three-fifths calculation would also apply for federal taxation purposes.

19. See Mark A. Graber, *Dred Scott and the Problem of Constitutional Evil* (New York: Cambridge University Press, 2008), and Justin Buckley Dyer, "After the Revolution: *Somerset* and the Antislavery Tradition in Anglo-American Constitutional Development," *Journal of Politics* 71, 4 (2009): 1422–1434.

20. See Bryan D. Jones, Heather Larsen-Price, and John Wilkerson, "Representation and American Governing Institutions," *Journal of Politics* 71, 1 (2009): 277–90.

21. In everyday language, when people think "democracy" they are thinking along the lines of republican government. "Direct democracy" is often used to describe democracy in which the people themselves make law.

22. Nolan McCarty, "Presidential Vetoes in the Early Republic: Changing Constitutional Norms or Electoral Reform?" *Journal of Politics* 71, 2 (2009): 369–84.

23. Mark A. Graber, "Establishing Judicial Review? *Schooner Peggy* and the Early Marshall Court," *Political Research Quarterly* 51, 1 (1998): 221–39. For judicial review and its relationship to democracy, see J. Mitchell Pickerill, *Constitutional Deliberation in Congress: The Impact of Judicial Review in a Separated System* (Durham, NC: Duke University Press, 2004); Annabelle Lever, "Democracy and Judicial Review: Are They Really Incompatible?" *Perspectives on Politics* 7, 4 (2009): 805–22.

24. In *Federalist 51*, Madison notes that the legislature predominates, but its power can be moderated by creating two houses with different modes of election.

25. *Federalist 51*.

26. *Federalist 51*.

27. The Supreme Court verified national supremacy on this issue in its decision in *Lorillard Tobacco Company v. Reilly* (2001).

28. See David J. Siemers, *Ratifying the Republic: Antifederalists and Federalists in Constitutional Time* (Stanford, CA: Stanford University Press, 2002).

29. William Riker, *Federalism: Origin, Operation, Significance* (Boston: Little, Brown, 1964).

30. Iain McLean, "William H. Riker and the Invention of Heresthetic(s)," *British Journal of Political Science* 32 (2002): 535–58.

31. These names are misnomers. Federalism connotes a sharing of power across the national and state governments, and the Anti-Federalists ardently advocated this position.

32. Herbert Storing, *What the Anti-Federalists Were For: The Political Thought of the Opponents of the Constitution* (Chicago: University of Chicago Press, 1981).

33. See Robert W. T. Martin, "James Madison and Popular Government: The Neglected Case of the 'Memorial,'" *Polity* 42, 2 (2010): 185-209; Tiffany Jones Miller, "James Madison's Republic of 'Mean Extent' Theory: Avoiding the Scylla and Charybdis of Republican Government," *Polity* 39, 4 (2007): 545–69.

34. Charles A. Beard, *An Economic Interpretation of the Constitution of the United States* (New York: Macmillan, 1913); Jerry Fresia, *Toward an American Revolution: Exposing the Constitution and Other Illusions* (Boston: South End Press, 1988).

35. Karen Orren and Stephen Skowronek, *The Search for American Political Development* (New York: Cambridge University Press, 2004), 53–54.

36. John P. Roche, "The Founding Fathers: A Reform Caucus in Action," *American Political Science Review* 55, 4 (1961): 799–816; Calvin C. Jillson and Cecil L. Eubanks, "The Political Structure of Constitution Making: The Federal Convention of 1787," *American Journal of Political Science* 28, 3 (1984): 435–58.

37. Robert E. Brown, *Charles Beard and the Constitution: A Critical Analysis of "An Economic Interpretation of the Constitution"* (Princeton, NJ: Princeton University Press, 1956).

38. Colleen A. Sheehan, "Madison v. Hamilton: The Battle Over Republicanism and the Role of Public Opinion," *American Political Science Review* 98, 3 (2004): 405–20.

39. David Brian Robertson, "Madison's Opponents and Constitutional Design," *American Political Science Review* 99, 2 (2005): 405–20.

40. Keith L. Dougherty and Jac C. Heckelman, "A Pivotal Voter from a Pivotal State: Roger Sherman at the Constitutional Convention," *American Political Science Review* 100, 2 (2006): 297–302.

41. Nathalie Behnke and Arthur Benz, "The Politics of Constitutional Change between Reform and Evolution," *Publius* 39, 2 (2009): 213–40.

42. John R. Vile, "The Long Legacy of Proposals to Rewrite the U.S. Constitution," *PS: Political Science and Politics*, June 1993, 208–11.

43. Christopher P. Manfredi, "Institutional Design and the Politics of Constitutional Modification: Understanding Amendment Failure in the United States and Canada," *Law & Society Review* 31, 1 (1997): 111–36.

44. The discussion in this case study draws extensively on Alexander Keyssar, *The Right to Vote: The Contested History of Democracy in the United States* (New York: Basic Books, 2000).

45. Caldeira, "Constitutional Change in America: Dynamics of Ratification under Article V."

46. See Gregory A. Caldeira, "Constitutional Change in America: Dynamics of Ratification under Article V," *Publius* 15, 4 (1985): 29–49.

47. The average length of state constitutions is about three times that of the federal document, and the average number of amendments is over four times that of the U.S. Constitution.

48. See Bruce Ackerman, *We The People, Volume One: Foundations* and *We the People, Volume Two: Transformations* (Cambridge: Harvard University Press, 1993 and 2000, respectively).

CHAPTER FOUR

1. The lead attorneys who sought to overthrow the ban were Theodore Olson and David Boies—the combatants who took opposite sides in the court clash between George Bush and Al Gore to decide the 2000 presidential election.

2. They charge that same-sex marriage is not consistent with the traditional conceptual understanding of marriage.

3. Helen Dewar and Alan Cooperman, "Senate Scuttles Amendment Banning Same-Sex Marriage," *Washington Post*, July 14, 2004.

4. According to an October 2009 survey, nearly 60 percent of Americans under age 30 favor same-sex marriage, compared to about 35 percent for those age 30 to 64, and 22 percent among Americans 65 or over. See Pew Research Center for the People and the Press, "Majority Continues to Support Civil Unions," October 2009, http://people-press.org/report/553/same-sex-marriage.

5. See National Conference of State Legislatures, http://www.ncsl.org/Issues Research/HumanServices/SameSexMarriage/tabid/16430/Default.aspx#DOMA); and the Pew Forum on Religion and Public Life, http://pewforum.org/Gay-Marriage-and-Homosexuality/Gay-Marriage-Around-the-World.aspx).

6. Nullification made its first appearance in 1798 when Virginia and Kentucky nullified the Alien and Sedition Acts.

7. The president indicated his support for a new public insurance plan that would compete with private insurance companies. Some of the presidents' more liberal

supporters wanted the president to push for a single-payer system, in which all payment for health care would be routed through government.

8. See Virginia Gray, David Lowery, James Monogan, and Erik K. Godwin, "Incrementing Toward Nowhere: Universal Health Care Coverage in the States," *Publius* 40 (2010): 82–113, for a review of state efforts to achieve universal coverage.

9. Other states had constitutions prior to the U.S. Constitution but have had subsequent constitutions written and adopted.

10. Stefan Voigt, "Explaining Constitutional Garrulity," *International Review of Law and Economics* 29 (2009): 290–303.

11. The District has been given some state-like features, such as votes in the Electoral College, but it does not have formal voting representation in the House and Senate.

12. *United States v. E. C. Knight Co. et al.* (1895).

13. The Court's language is clearly that of dual federalism: "The relief of the citizens of each state from the burden of monopoly and the evils resulting from the restraint of trade among such citizens was left with the states to deal with, and this court has recognized their possession of that power . . . . On the other hand, the power of Congress to regulate commerce among the several states is also exclusive."

14. Specifically, the law forbade the interstate transport of a product from a factory that, within the previous 30 days, had employed children under the age of 14 or permitted children ages 14 through 16 to work more than eight hours in a day, more than six days a week, after 7 P.M., or before 6 A.M.

15. *Hammer v. Dagenhart* (1918).

16. Any employee working for a business involved in interstate commerce is covered, as is any employee working for a business with sales volume exceeding $500,000.

17. See Suzanne Mettler, *Dividing Citizens: Gender and Federalism in New Deal Public Policy* (Ithaca, NY: Cornell University Press, 1998).

18. See also the Marshall Court decisions in *Martin v. Hunter's Lessee* (1816) and *Cohens v. Virginia* (1821).

19. *United States v. Darby* (1941). See also Donald F. Kettl, "Real-Life Federalism," *Governing Magazine*, August 2001.

20. *United States v. Mazurie* (1975).

21. See U.S. Department of Energy, Office of Environmental Management, "American Indian Executive Orders (1994 to Present)," http://web.em.doe.gov/public/tribal/orders.html; U.S. Department of Justice, Office of Tribal Justice, "Department of Justice Policy on Indian Sovereignty and Government-to-Government

Relations with Indian Tribes," http://www.usdoj.gov/otj/sovtrb.htm.

22. See http://www.bia.gov for information and statistics on Indian tribes.

23. Kim Isaac Eisler, *Revenge of the Pequots: How a Small Native American Tribe Created the World's Most Profitable Casino* (New York: Simon and Schuster, 2001).

24. Generally speaking, state criminal law is considered binding on the reservations, but gambling law is considered to be regulatory rather than criminal. The exception to this rule is the Organized Crime Control Act of 1970, which provides federal criminal prosecution against certain gambling activity.

25. *Washington v. Confederated Tribes of Colville Indian Reservation* (1980).

26. Recall that the Supreme Court concluded in *McCulloch v. Maryland* that the power to tax was the power to destroy.

27. Douglas Roger Nash, "Indian Gaming," FindLaw, 1999, http://library.findlaw.com/1999/Jan/1/241489.html.

28. See Steven Andrew Light and Kathryn R. L. Rand, *Indian Gaming and Tribal Sovereignty: The Casino Compromise* (Lawrence: University Press of Kansas, 2007).

29. Fox Butterfield, "Indian Casino Revenues Grow to Sizable Segment of Industry," *New York Times*, June 16, 2005, A18; *The Economic Impact of Indian Gaming in 2008*, National Indian Gaming Association, 2009, http://www.indiangaming.org/info/pr/press-releases-2009/NIGA_08_Econ_Impact_Report.pdf).

30. Patrick Marshall, "Gambling in America," *CQ Researcher*, 13, 9 (2003): 201–24.

31. Onell R. Soto, "Court Backs Rincon Tribe in Gambling Revenue Dispute," *San Diego Union-Tribune*, April 20, 2010.

32. Paul Rogers, "Increase in National Gas Mileage Standards Announced; California Drove Obama Policy," *Silicon Valley Mercury News*, April 1, 2010.

33. Robert L. Fischman, "Cooperative Federalism and Natural Resources Law," *NYU Environmental Law Journal* 14 (2005): 179–231.

34. The National Conference of State Legislatures tracks immigration law, http://www.ncsl.org. See also Lina Newton and Brian E. Adams, "State Immigration Policies: Innovation, Cooperation or Conflict?" *Publius* 39 (2009): 408–31.

35. Douglas Elmendorf, "A Review of CBO's Activities in 2009 Under the Unfunded Mandates Reform Act," April 1, 2010, Director's Blog Archive, Congressional Budget Office, http://cboblog.cbo.gov/?m=201004.

36. Angela Antonelli, "Promises Unfulfilled: Unfunded Mandates Reform Act of 1995," *Regulation* 19, 2 (1996); David S. Broder, "Those Unfunded Mandates," *Washington Post*, March 17, 2005, A25.

37. U.S. Government Accountability Office, *Unfunded Mandates: Views Vary About Reform Act's Strengths, Weaknesses, and Options for Improvement*, GAO-05-454, March 31, 2005, http://www.gao.gov/products /GAO-05-454. See also U.S. Government Accountability Office, *Unfunded Mandates: Analysis of Reform Act Coverage*, GAO-04-637, May 2004, http://www.gao .gov/new.items/d04637.pdf.

38. James Dao, "Rebellion of the States: Red, Blue, and Angry All Over," *New York Times*, January 16, 2005. See also http://www.ncsl.org/standcomm/scbudg /manmon.htm.

39. United States House of Representatives, Committee on Government Reform, Minority Staff Special Investigations Division, "Congressional Preemption Of State Laws And Regulations," June 2006. See also the Preemption Monitor published regularly by the National Conference of State Legislatures, http://www .ncsl.org.

40. U.S. Government Accountability Office, *Formula Grants: Funding for the Largest Federal Assistance Programs Is Based on Census-Related Data and Other Factors*, December 2009, GAO-10-263, http://www. gao.gov/new.items/d10263.pdf.

41. U.S. Census Bureau, *Statistical Abstract of the United States 2010*, table 419, http://www.census.gov/ compendia/statab/cats/state_local_govt_finances_ employment/federal_aid_to_state_and_local_ governments.html.

42. Budget of the United States Government: Historical Tables Fiscal Year 2011, Table 12-2, http://www .gpoaccess.gov/usbudget/fy11/hist.html

43. Daniel B. Wood, "California's Education Reforms Hand More Power to Parents," *Christian Science Monitor*, January 7, 2010.

44. Within each region, states vary in whether they receive more than they pay, or pay more than they receive.

45. Under revenue sharing, the federal government provided funds to the states based on a formula that considered population, per capita income, and the property tax base. States were dropped from the program in 1981, and revenue sharing was completely eliminated in 1987.

46. Wisconsin officials, for instance, have expressed concerns that the state was becoming a magnet for out-of-state parents seeking educational and medical services for their autistic children.

47. See Sanford F. Schram and Samuel H. Beer, eds., *Welfare Reform? A Race to the Bottom?* (Princeton, NJ: Woodrow Wilson Center Press, 1999); Joe Soss, Sanford F. Schram, Thomas P. Vartanian, and Erin O'Brien, "Welfare Policy Choices in the States: Does the Hard Line Follow the Color Line? *Focus* 23, 1 (2004): 9–15.

48. Michael A. Bailey and Mark Carl Rom, "A Wider Race? Interstate Competition Across Health and Welfare Programs," *Journal of Politics* 66, 2 (2004): 326–47, find that in basic welfare programs, there is a race to the bottom on benefits and access; on Medicaid, on overall costs; and on supplemental security income (for individuals with medical or other disabilities), on all three.

49. Race-to-the-bottom research and findings are discussed in William D. Berry, Richard C. Fording, and Russell L. Hanson, "Reassessing the 'Race to the Bottom' in State Welfare Policy," *Journal of Politics* 65, 2 (2003): 327–49; Michael A. Bailey, "Depressing Federalism: Re-Assessing Theory and Evidence on the 'Race to the Bottom,'" manuscript, April 2002. John Kennan and James R. Walker, "Wages, Welfare Benefits, and Migration," *Journal of Econometrics* 156, 1 (2010): 229–38.

50. Stephen C. Fehr, "The United Regions of America," Pew Center on the States, Stateline.org, April 22, 2010, http://www.stateline.org/live/details/story?contentId= 478959. See also Rebecca M. Blank, *It Takes a Nation: A New Agenda for Fighting Poverty* (Princeton, NJ: Princeton University Press, 1997).

51. Paul Peterson, *The Price of Federalism* (Washington, DC: Brookings Institution Press, 1998); Kevin M. Esterling, "Does the Federal Government Learn from the States? Medicaid and the Limits of Expertise in the Intergovernmental Lobby," *Publius* 39 (2009): 1–21.

52. Adeed I. Dawisha and Karen Dawisha, "How to Build a Democratic Iraq," *Foreign Affairs* 82, 3 (2003); Bryan Carroll and David A. Anderson, "Afghanistan Governed by a Federal System with Autonomous Regions: A Path to Success?" *Small Wars Journal*, December 2009, 1–29.

53. Richard Simeon, "Constitutional Design and Change in Federal Systems: Issues and Questions," *Publius* 39, 2 (2009): 241-61.

54. Nancy Bermeo, "Position Paper for the Working Group on Federalism, Conflict Prevention and Settlement," n.d; Nicholas Charron, "Government Quality and Vertical Power-Sharing in Fractionalized States," *Publius* 39 (2009): 585–605.

55. Dean E. McHenry Jr., "Federalism in Africa: Is It a Solution to, or a Cause of, Ethnic Problems?" Paper presented at the annual meeting of the African Studies Association, Columbus, Ohio, November 1997.

56. The *Federal Register* lists pending regulations and also the period for public comment on them.

57. The case concerned Alfonso Lopez Jr., a grade 12 student at Edison High School in San Antonio who brought a concealed handgun and ammunition to school and was charged with violating the Gun-Free School Zone Act.

58. Section 5 of the Fourteenth Amendment provides the authority to override this immunity.

59. *Alden v. Maine* (1999); *Gregory v. Ashcroft* (1991); *Kimel v. Florida Board of Regents* (2000); *Board of Trustees of the University of Alabama v. Garrett* (2001); and *Seminole Tribe v. Florida* (1996).

60. Keith E. Whittington, "Taking What They Give Us: Explaining the Court's Federalism Offensive," *Duke Law Journal* 51, 1 (2001): 477–520.

61. Christine Vestal, "States Try New Approaches, Feds Cool," http://www.stateline.org/live/ViewPage.action?siteNodeId=136&languageId=1&contentId=44968.

62. See http://www.ncsl.org/realid/.

63. Priscilla M. Regan and Christopher J. Deering, "State Opposition to REAL ID," *Publius* 39, 3 (2009): 476–505.

64. Paul Posner, "The Politics of Coercive Federalism in the Bush Era," *Publius* 37, 3 (2007): 390–412.

65. Universal Right to Vote by Mail Act, H.R. 1604.

66. http://www2.ed.gov/programs/racetothetop/index.html.

67. See, for example, Barry Rabe, "Environmental Policy and the Bush Era: The Collision Between the Administrative Presidency and State Experimentation," *Publius* 37, 3 (2007): 413–31; Posner, "The Politics of Coercive Federalism in the Bush Era."

68. In *Nevada Department of Human Resources v. Hibbs* (2003).

69. Marci Hamilton, "The Supreme Court's Federalism Cases This Term: A String of Decisions Upholding Federal Power Show the Portrayal of the Court as Extreme Is a Caricature," FindLaw, June 3, 2004, http://writ.news.findlaw.com/hamilton/20040603.html.

70. *American Insurance Association v. Garamendi* (2004).

71. See http://medicalmarijuana.procon.org/view.resource.php?resourceID=000881.

CHAPTER FIVE

1. See Ronald Dworkin, "The 'Devastating' Decision," *New York Review of Books*, January 25, 2010, and "The Decision That Threatens Democracy," *New York Review of Books*, May 13, 2010; and Bradley Smith, "Newsflash: First Amendment Upheld," *Wall Street Journal*, January 22, 2010, and "*Citizens United* We Stand," *American Spectator*, May 2010. The quotations are taken from Dworkin and Smith's January 2010 articles. DISCLOSE stood for "Democracy Is Strengthened by Casting Light on Spending in Elections."

2. See, for example, Stephen Ansolabehere, John M. de Figueiredo, and James M. Snyder Jr., "Why Is There So Little Money in U.S. Politics?" *Journal of Economic Perspectives* 17, 1 (2003): 105–30; Jeffrey Milyo, David Primo, and Timothy Groseclose, "Corporate PAC Campaign Contributions in Perspective," *Business and Politics* 2, 1 (2000): 75–88. For a study arguing that there is a statistically significant impact of contributions, see Thomas Stratmann, "Some Talk: Money in Politics, A (Partial) Review of the Literature," *Public Choice* 124 (2005): 135–56.

3. John J. Coleman, "*Citizens United* and Political Outcomes," manuscript, February 2, 2010, http://users.polisci.wisc.edu/coleman; Timothy Werner, "The Sound, the Fury, and the Non-event: Business Power and Market Reactions to the *Citizens United* Decision," *American Politics Review,* forthcoming, Carol D. Leonnig, "Political Ads Are Tough Sell For Image-Conscious Corporations," *Washington Post*, June 1, 2010.

4. We discuss freedom of the press in Chapter 10.

5. Where rights come from is a matter of philosophical dispute.

6. Freedom House's 2010 report can be found at www.freedomhouse.org/template .cfm?page=505. For civil liberties, Freedom House assesses a country's freedom of expression and belief, association and organization rights, rule of law and human rights, and personal autonomy and economic rights.

7. See also the twin studies by Robert Barro, "Determinants of Democracy," *Journal of Political Economy* 107, 6 (1999); and *Determinants of Economic Growth: A Cross-Country Empirical Study* (Cambridge, MA: MIT Press, 1997).

8. See Akhil Reed Amar, *The Bill of Rights: Creation and Reconstruction* (New Haven, CT: Yale University Press, 2000) for an overview.

9. Seventeen amendments had been adopted in the House of Representatives; 12 of these were accepted by the Senate. Ten were ratified by the states in December 1791.

10. Two cases kicked off the incorporation process: *Chicago, Burlington, and Quincy Railroad Company v. Chicago* (1897) and *Gitlow v. New York* (1925).

11. The language of the due process clause in the Fourteenth Amendment is based on a nearly identically worded clause in the Fifth Amendment.

12. *Chicago, Burlington, and Quincy Railroad v. Chicago* (1897); *Gitlow v. New York* (1925).

13. See Shawn Francis Peters, *Judging Jehovah's Witnesses: Religious Persecution and the Dawn of the Rights Revolution* (Lawrence: University Press of Kansas, 2000); Ken I. Kirsch, *Constructing Civil Liberties: Discontinuities in the Development of American Constitutional Law* (New York: Cambridge University Press, 2004).

14. *McDonald v. Chicago* (2010).

15. See Lawrence Baum, "Membership Change and Collective Voting Change in the United States Supreme Court," *Journal of Politics* 54, 1 (1992): 3–24.

16. Federal courts only rarely agree to prior restraint.

17. Arati Korwar, *War of Words: Speech Codes at Public Colleges and Universities* (Nashville, TN: Freedom Forum First Amendment Center, 1994).

18. *R.A.V. v. City of St. Paul* (1992).

19. A government can regulate the nature of these activities by requiring permits, but it must be content neutral toward what it allows.

20. *Virginia v. Black* (2003).

21. See Jon B. Gould, *Speak No Evil: The Triumph of Hate Speech Regulation* (Chicago: University of Chicago Press, 2005); Martin P. Golding, *Free Speech on Campus* (Lanham, MD: Rowman and Littlefield, 2000).

22. Geoffrey R. Stone, "The Origins of the 'Bad Tendency' Test: Free Speech in Wartime," *Supreme Court Review* (2002): 411–53.

23. Herbert McClosky and Alida Brill, *Dimensions of Political Tolerance: What Americans Believe About Civil Liberties* (New York: Russell Sage, 1983), 203; Herbert McClosky and John Zaller, *The American Ethos: Public Attitudes Toward Capitalism and Democracy* (Cambridge, MA: Harvard University Press, 1984), 25, 37, 38, 74, 75; Pew Center for the People and the Press surveys.

24. See Geoffrey R. Stone, *Perilous Times: Free Speech in Wartime from the Sedition Act of 1798 to the War on Terrorism* (New York: W. W. Norton, 2004).

25. Darren W. Davis and Brian D. Silver, "Civil Liberties vs. Security: Public Opinion in the Context of the Terrorist Attacks on America," *American Journal of Political Science* 48, 1 (2004): 28–46. See also Cindy D. Kam and Donald R. Kinder, "Terror and Ethnocentrism: Foundations of American Support for the War on Terrorism," *Journal of Politics* 69, 2 (2007): 320–38.

26. FOX News/Opinion Dynamics Poll, May 18–19, 2010, 900 registered voters nationwide; FOX News/Opinion Dynamics Poll, May 4–5, 2010, 900 registered voters nationwide; Ipsos/McClatchy Poll, January 7–11, 2010, 1,336 adults nationwide; USA Today/Gallup Poll, January 8–10, 2010, 1,023 adults nationwide; CBS News Poll, January 6–10, 2010, 1,216 adults nationwide.

27. For example, see Thomas E. Nelson, Rosalee A. Clawson, and Zoe M. Oxley, "Media Framing of a Civil Liberties Conflict and Its Effect on Tolerance," *American Political Science Review* 91, 3 (1997): 567–83; W. Kip Viscusi and Richard J. Zeckhauser, "Sacrificing Civil Liberties to Reduce Terrorism Risks," *Journal of Risk and Uncertainty* 26, 2–3 (2003): 99–120.

28. CBS News Poll, April 13–16, 2005; Pew Research Center survey, May 21, 2009, http://people-press.org/reports/questionnaires/517.pdf, question Q33F1, 1,492 adults nationwide.

29. See Paul Sniderman, Joseph Fletcher, et al., *The Clash of Rights: Liberty, Equality, and Legitimacy in Pluralist Democracy* (New Haven: Yale University Press, 1996); and Robert W. Jackman, "Political Elites, Mass Publics, and Support for Democratic Principles," *Journal of Politics* 54, 3 (1992): 753–73.

30. George E. Marcus, John L. Sullivan, and Elizabeth Theiss-Morse, *With Malice Toward Some: How People Make Civil Liberties Judgments* (New York: Cambridge University Press, 1995).

31. Researchers can infer support for these measures from public opinion surveys or, for times prior to polling, letters in newspapers, election results, and policy statements by organized groups with large memberships.

32. David Corn, "The 'Suicide Pact' Mystery," *Slate*, January 4, 2002, http://www.slate.com/id/2060342.

33. In *Terminiello v. Chicago* (1949), the Court declared that speech should be punished only when it creates a clear and present danger of a "serious substantive evil that rises far above public inconvenience, annoyance, or unrest."

34. *American Communications Association v. Douds* (1950); *Dennis v. United States* (1951). See Ken I. Kersch, "'Guilt by Association' and the Post War Civil Libertarians," *Social Philosophy and Policy* 25, 2 (2008).

35. See *Konigsberg v. State Bar of California* (1961).

36. *Murdock v. Pennsylvania* (1943).

37. *Chaplinsky v. New Hampshire* (1942).

38. *Beauharnais v. Illinois* (1952).

39. *New York Times Co. v. Sullivan* (1964); *Gertz v. Robert Welch, Inc.* (1974); *Milkovich v. Lorain Journal Co.* (1990).

40. *Valentine v. Chrestensen* (1942); *Greater New Orleans Broadcasting Association v. United States* (1999); *Lorillard Tobacco v. Reilly* (2001).

41. *Tinker v. Des Moines* (1969).

42. *U.S. v. Stevens* (2010). The decision struck down a federal law that prohibited the distribution or possession of videos that depicted animal cruelty.

43. *Roth v. United States* (1957).

44. In 2002, the Supreme Court overturned the Child Pornography Prevention Act of 1996, concluding that the act attempted to restrict materials that were not necessarily obscene as defined in previous court decisions.

45. *Jacobellis v. Ohio* (1964).

46. *Reno v. American Civil Liberties Union* (1997).

47. *Ashcroft v. American Civil Liberties Union* (2004).

48. *United States et al. v. American Library Association, Inc., et al.* (2003).

49. David M. O'Brien, *Constitutional Law and Politics: Civil Rights and Civil Liberties*, 5th ed. (New York: W.W. Norton, 2003), 506.

50. As noted above, Article VI of the Constitution prohibits religious tests or oaths for public office.

51. Frank Lambert, *The Founding Fathers and the Place of Religion in America* (Princeton, NJ: Princeton University Press, 2003).

52. Article 11 of the 1797 Treaty with Tripoli States that "the government of the United States of America is not in any sense founded on the Christian Religion." Although there is substantial dispute about precisely how and when this article was inserted into the treaty, this text was approved unanimously by the Senate and signed into law by President John Adams.

53. *Aguilar v. Felton* (1985).

54. If improper behavior by a teacher was discovered, the school could react or a case could be brought to court.

55. *Engale v. Vitale* (1962); *Abington School District v. Schempp* (1963); *Lee v. Weisman* (1992); *Wallace v. Jaffrie* (1985); *Santa Fe Independent School District v. Doe* (2000).

56. *County of Allegheny v. ACLU Greater Pittsburgh Chapter* (1989). The Texas case is *Van Orden v. Perry* (2005); the Kentucky case is *McCreary County v. A.C.L.U. of Kentucky* (2005).

57. O'Brien, *Constitutional Law and Politics*, 782–85.

58. BBC News, "The Islamic Veil Across Europe," April 22, 2010, news.bbc.co.uk/.

59. In *Wisconsin v. Yoder* (1971), the Supreme Court determined that Amish religious exercise was burdened by Wisconsin's requirement that students remain in school until age 16, and that the states, interest was not compelling enough to justify the burden.

60. *Rosenberger v. University of Virginia* (1995).

61. *United States v. American Friends Service Committee*, 1974; *United States v. Lee*, 1982. Congress has on occasion allowed exemptions from the law based on religious beliefs.

62. The Court's decision noted that the laws did not make clear why the Santeria practice should be treated differently from a number of similar practices.

63. *Christian Legal Society v. Martinez* (2010). See Jonathan Turley, "Inequality, in the Name of Equality," *Washington Post*, April 18, 2010, for a discussion of the issues in the case. See also Stanley Fish, "Being Neutral is Oh So Hard to Do," *New York Times*, July 29, 2010, http://opinionator.blogs.nytimes.com.

64. *City of Boerne v. Flores* (1997).

65. *Gonzales v. O Centro Espírita Beneficente União do Vegetal* (2006).

66. The law also granted churches great leeway in building projects, which had been the subject matter in the case that overturned RFRA. This aspect of the law will likely appear before the Court soon.

67. *California v. Greenwood* (1988).

68. *Michigan Department of State Police v. Sitz* (1990).

69. *Illinois v. Caballes* (2005); *Kyllo v. United States* (2001).

70. *Mapp v. Ohio* (1961).

71. http://www.nytimes.com/2008/07/19/us/19exclude.html?_r=1.

72. *Davis v. United States* (1994). See also *Arizona v. Fulminante* (1991) and *Dickerson v. United States* (2000).

73. *Coker v. Georgia* (1977); *Kennedy v. Louisiana* (2008).

74. *Atkins v. Virginia* (2002) concerns the mentally retarded. *Roper v. Simmons* (2005) overturned the Court's *Stanford v. Kentucky* (1989) decision on capital punishment for minors.

75. *Graham v. Florida* (2010).

76. *Rompilla v. Beard* (2005).

77. When Timothy McVeigh, one of the bombers of an Oklahoma City federal building in 1995, was executed in 2001, it was the first execution by the federal government in nearly 40 years.

78. Death Penalty Statistics, Amnesty International, http://www.amnesty.org/en/death-penalty/abolitionist-and-retentionist-countries.

79. See http://thomas.loc.gov/cgibin/bdquery/z?d107:HR03162:@@@L&summ2=m& for a brief description of the sections of the act.

80. Harris Poll, 1,015 adults nationwide, June 7–12, 2005, and September 19–24, 2001.

81. For a timeline of events, see http://www.bespacific.com/mt/archives/cat_patriot_act.html.

82. Sherly Gay Stolberg, "Senate Passes Legislation to Renew Patriot Act," *New York Times*, March 3, 2006, A14.

83. *Holder v. Humanitarian Law Project* (2010).

84. See Philippa Strum, *Privacy: The Debate in the United States Since 1945* (New York: Harcourt Brace, 1998); Ken I. Kersch, "The Right to Privacy," in James W. Ely Jr. and David Bodenhamer, eds., *The Bill of Rights in Modern America*, 2nd edition (Bloomington: Indiana University Press, 2008).

85. The anti-obscenity law was known as the Comstock Act.

86. *Eisenstadt v. Baird* (1972).

87. The Court's opinion famously stated that "specific guarantees in the Bill of Rights have penumbras, formed by emanations from those guarantees that help give them life and substance." Penumbras are partial

shadings or shadows that are cast on outlying regions or peripheries.

88. The Court did not rule whether a fetus is a person, but stated that throughout the early nineteenth century, "prevailing legal abortion practices were far freer than they are today, persuad[ing] us that the word 'person,' as used in the Fourteenth Amendment, does not include the unborn."

89. In *Webster v. Reproductive Health Services* (1989), the Court declared constitutional a Missouri law outlawing abortions in public hospitals and prohibiting public employees from being involved in abortion services.

90. *Gonzales v. Carhart* (2007).

91. Lance Whitney, "Consumer Groups: Online Tracking at "Alarming Levels,'" CNet, May 4, 2010, http://news .cnet.com; Julia Angwin and Tom McGinty, "Sites Feed Personal Details to New Tracking Industry," Wall Street Journal, July 30, 2010, http://online.wsj.com.

92. *City of Ontario v. Quon* (2010).

93. *Washington v. Glucksberg* (1997); *Vacco v. Quill* (1997); *Gonzales v. Oregon* (2006).

94. The relevant cases are, respectively, *NAACP v. Alabama* (1958); *Boy Scouts of America v. Dale* (2000); *West Virginia v. Barnette* (1943); *Pierce v. Society of Sisters* (1925); *Miranda v. Arizona* (1966); and *Skinner v. Oklahoma* (1942). The Court's opinion in *Washington v. Glucksberg* (1997) provides a good discussion of substantive due process.

95. *Palko v. Connecticut* (1937) and *Moore v. East Cleveland* (1977), respectively.

96. Note the Court's comment in *Roe*: "This right of privacy, whether it be founded in the Fourteenth Amendment's concept of personal liberty and restrictions upon state action, as we feel it is, or, as [others have] determined, in the Ninth Amendment's reservation of rights to the people."

97. *Collins v. Harker Heights* (1992); *Sacramento County v. Lewis* (1998); *Kansas v. Hendricks, 1997.*

98. For example, the Court concluded in *Troxel v. Granville* (2000) that a law in the state of Washington that allowed "any person" "at any time" to petition for visitation rights with children violated the parents' "fundamental right to rear children," a right previously established by substantive due process.

CHAPTER SIX

1. *Korematsu v. United States* (1944).
2. This discussion is based on Steven Kelman et al., "Against All Odds: The Campaign in Congress for Japanese-American Redress," Case Program, Kennedy School of Government, C16-90-1006.0.

3. See Janice Fine and Daniel J. Tichenor, "A Movement Wrestling: American Labor's Enduring Struggle with Immigration, 1866–2007," *Studies in American Political Development* 23, no. 2 (2009): 218–48.

4. Abraham Hoffman, *Unwanted Mexican Americans in the Great Depression: Repatriation Pressures 1929-1939* (Tucson: University of Arizona Press, 1974); Camille Guerin-Gonzales, *Mexican Workers and American Dreams: Immigration, Repatriation, and California Farm Labor, 1900-1939* (New Brunswick, NJ: Rutgers University Press, 1994); Francisco E. Balderama and Raymond Rodriguez, *Decade of Betrayal: Mexican Repatriation in the 1930s*, rev. ed. (Albuquerque: University of New Mexico Press, 2006); Wendy Koch, "U.S. Urged to Apologize for 1930s Deportations," *USA Today*, April 5, 2006.

5. The question of public apologies or reparations for past actions is one facing governments outside the United States as well.

6. Article I, section 2; I, 9; and IV, 2, respectively.

7. This position was consistent with the stance of the northern states that considered slaves to become free when they traveled in free states.

8. The act was a response to so-called Black Codes passed by southern states in 1865 and 1866.

9. Fearing that the act might be declared unconstitutional, supporters moved quickly to include its major provisions in the Fourteenth Amendment.

10. Eric Foner, *A Short History of Reconstruction, 1863–1877* (New York: Harper and Row, 1990).

11. The Thirteenth Amendment was particular to slavery, not private racial discrimination in general, the Court ruled, so it could not be pointed to as justification for the act.

12. To free blacks prior to the Thirteenth Amendment, the Court argued, "[m]ere discriminations on account of race or color were not regarded as badges of slavery."

13. Plessy was one-eighth black, so one issue in the case was whether he should be considered white or black. The Supreme Court concluded that what constitutes "black" or "white" should be determined by the laws of each state, so on those grounds Louisiana could consider Plessy to be black.

14. See Jeffery A. Jenkins, Justin Peck, and Vesla M. Weaver, "Between Reconstructions: Congressional Action on Civil Rights, 1891–1940," *Studies in American Political Development* 24, 1 (2010): 57–89.

15. Executive Order 8802. Executive Order 9346 expanded the FEPC's budget and enforcement power. See Kevin J. McMahon, *Reconsidering Roosevelt on Race: How the Presidency Paved the Road to Brown* (Chicago: University of Chicago Press, 2004).

16. *State of Missouri ex rel. Gaines v. Canada* (1938).

17. The Texas decision is *Sweatt v. Painter*.

18. The Oklahoma decision is *McLaurin v. Oklahoma State Regents for Higher Education*.

19. Seventeen states required segregation; another four allowed it as a local option.

20. The timetable applied to the District of Columbia also. On the same day as *Brown I*, the Court ruled that segregated schools in the District, a federal entity, violated the Fifth Amendment's guarantee of due process in *Bolling v. Sharpe* (1954).

21. Gary Orfield and Chungmei Lee, "Racial Transformation and the Changing Nature of Segregation," The Civil Rights Project at Harvard University, January 2006, http://www.civilrightsproject.ucla.edu/research/deseg/Racial_Transformation.pdf.

22. *Green v. County School Board of New Kent County* (1968).

23. *Milliken v. Bradley* (1974).

24. The two cases were consolidated as *Parents Involved in Community Schools v. Seattle School District No. 1* (2007).

25. Erica Frankenberg and Chungmei Lee, "Race in American Public Schools: Rapidly Resegregating School Districts," The Civil Rights Project at Harvard University, August 2002. See also the document submitted to the Supreme Court in the Seattle and Louisville case by a group of social scientists: "Brief of 553 Social Scientists as Amici Curiae in Support of Respondents," October 2006.

26. The use of Congress's commerce clause and spending powers in the Civil Rights Act of 1964 was upheld by the Supreme Court in *Heart of Atlanta Motel v. United States* (1964) and *Katzenbach v. McClung* (1964).

27. The Voting Rights Act of 1965 was upheld by the Supreme Court in *South Carolina v. Katzenbach* (1965).

28. *Harper v. Virginia Board of Elections* (1966).

29. Executive Orders 10925 (Kennedy), 11246 and 11375 (Johnson), 12106 (Carter), 13087 and 13152 (Clinton).

30. Executive Orders 10925 (Kennedy), 11246 and 11375 (Johnson), and 11478 (Nixon).

31. John David Skrentny, *The Ironies of Affirmative Action: Politics, Culture, and Justice in America* (Chicago: University of Chicago Press, 1996).

32. Vincent L. Hutchings and Nicholas A. Valentino, "The Centrality of Race in American Politics," *Annual Review of Political Science* 7 (2004): 383–408.

33. Hutchings and Valentino, "The Centrality of Race in American Politics," 389.

34. Two pivotal figures in the debate have been Paul Sniderman and Donald Kinder. See Paul M. Sniderman and Edward G. Carmines, *Reaching Beyond Race* (Cambridge: Harvard University Press, 1997); Snider-

man and Thomas Piazza, *The Scar of Race* (Cambridge, MA: Harvard University Press, 1993); and Donald R. Kinder and Lynn M. Sanders, *Divided by Color: Racial Politics and Democratic Ideals* (Chicago: University of Chicago Press, 1996).

35. A number of alternative terms have been employed, including new racism, symbolic racism, and covert racism.

36. See Stanley Feldman and Leonie Huddy, "Racial Resentment and White Opposition to Race-Conscious Programs: Principles or Prejudice?" *American Journal of Political Science* 49, 1 (2005): 168–83; Christopher Tarman and David O. Sears, "The Conceptualization and Measurement of Symbolic Racism," *Journal of Politics* 67, 3 (2005).

37. Paul M. Kellstedt, "Media Framing and the Dynamics of Racial Policy Preferences," *American Journal of Political Science* 44, 2 (2000): 258; Kenneth Prewitt, "When Social Inequality Maps to Demographic Diversity, What Then for Liberal Democracies?" *Social Research* 77, 1 (2010): 1–20.

38. A related area of study is whether diversity and interracial trust are connected. See Thomas J. Rudolph and Elizabeth Popp, "Race, Environment, and Interracial Trust," *Journal of Politics* 72, 1 (2010): 74–89.

39. Paul M. Kellstedt, *The Mass Media and the Dynamics of American Racial Attitudes* (New York: Cambridge University Press, 2003); Rene P. Rocha and Rodolfo Espino, "Racial Threat, Residential Segregation, and the Policy Attitudes of Anglos," *Political Research Quarterly* 62, 2 (2009): 415–26.

40. Jason Barabas and Jennifer Jerit, "Are Survey Experiments Externally Valid?" *American Political Science Review* 104, 2 (2010): 226–42.

41. Robert C. Lieberman, *Shaping Race Policy: The United States in Comparative Perspective* (Princeton, NJ: Princeton University Press, 2005); Erik Bleich, *Race Politics in Britain and France: Ideas and Policymaking Since the 1960s* (New York: Cambridge University Press, 2003); Martin A. Schain, "Managing Difference: Immigrant Integration Policy in France, Britain, and the United States," *Social Research* 77, 1 (2010): 205–36.

42. See Richard M. Valelly, *The Two Reconstructions: The Struggle for Black Enfranchisement* (Chicago: University of Chicago Press, 2004).

43. King was arrested at the protest, and it was at this time that he penned his famous essay, "Letter from Birmingham Jail, 1963." He included it in his book *Why We Can't Wait* (New York: Harper Collins, 1964).

44. See Dennis Chong, *Collective Action and the Civil Rights Movement* (Chicago: University of Chicago Press, 1991), and Taeku Lee, *Mobilizing Public Opinion: Black Insurgency and Racial Attitudes in the Civil Rights*

Era (Chicago: University of Chicago Press, 2002) as examples of these two research styles.

45. Mark I. Lichbach, "Where Have All the Foils Gone? Competing Theories of Contentious Politics and the Civil Rights Movement," in Anne N. Costain and Andrew S. McFarland, eds., *Social Movements and American Political Institutions* (Lanham, MD: Rowman and Littlefield, 1998).

46. *Smith v. Allright* (1944).

47. Alan Ware, *The Democratic Party Heads North, 1877–1962* (New York: Cambridge University Press, 2006).

48. Edward G. Carmines and James A. Stimson, *Issue Evolution: Race and the Transformation of American Politics* (Princeton, NJ: Princeton University Press, 1990).

49. Lieberman, *Shaping Race Policy: The United States in Comparative Perspective.*

50. Bruce J. Dierenfield, *The Civil Rights Movement* (Harlow, England: Pearson, 2004), 104.

51. The argument is most forcefully made in Paul Frymer, *Uneasy Alliances: Race and Party Competition in America* (Princeton, NJ: Princeton University Press, 1999).

52. *Shaw v. Reno* (1993); *Miller v. Johnson* (1995); *Hunt v. Cromartie* (2001).

53. Hutchings and Valentino, "The Centrality of Race in American Politics."

54. David Epstein and Sharyn O'Halloran, Columbia University, "The Voting Rights Act: Here Today, Gone Tomorrow?" manuscript, 2005.

55. See John D. Griffin and Brian Newman, *Minority Report: Evaluating Political Equality in America* (Chicago: University of Chicago Press, 2008).

56. *Bartlett v. Strickland* (2009).

57. *United States v. Carolene Products* (1938), footnote 4.

58. *Reed v. Reed* (1971); *Craig v. Boren* (1976).

59. See *Nordinger v. Hahn* (1992).

60. *Yick Wo v. Hopkins* (1886).

61. Gary M. Segura and Helena Alves Rodrigues, "Comparative Ethnic Politics in the United States: Beyond Black and White," *Annual Review of Political Science* 9 (2006): 375–95; Rodney E. Hero and Robert R. Preuhs, "Beyond (the Scope of) Conflict: National Black and Latino Advocacy Group Relations in the Congressional and Legal Arenas," *Perspectives on Politics* 7, 3 (2009): 501–18.

62. *Elks v. Wilkins* (1884).

63. In 1961, the Supreme Court ruled in *Hoyt v. Florida* that Florida could exclude women from jury service.

64. *Meritor Savings Bank FBD v. Vinson* (1986).

65. Gohar Grigorian, "Women and the Law in Comparative Perspective," UCLA International Institute, July 4, 2004, http://www.international.ucla.edu/article.asp?parentid=13036.

66. Mark R. Daniels and Robert E. Darcy, "As Time Goes By: The Arrested Diffusion of the Equal Rights Amendment," *Publius* 15, 4, (1985): 51–60.

67. *Gregory v. Ashcroft* (1991).

68. A Supreme Court decision in 2000 (*Kimel v. Florida Board of Regents*) narrowed the law by stating that it did not apply to state government employees.

69. Samuel R. Bagenstos, "Comparative Disability Employment Law from an American Perspective," *Comparative Labor Law and Policy Journal* 24 (2003): 650.

70. This discussion relies heavily on Bagenstos, "Comparative Disability Employment Law from an American Perspective."

71. *Oncale v. Sundowner Offshore Services* (1998).

72. *Boy Scouts of America v. Dale* (2000).

73. Richard Socarides, "Obama Is Missing in Action on Gay Rights," *Wall Street Journal*, June 25, 2010; David Badash, "Obama's Gay Rights Come with an Expiration Date," June 24, 2010, http://gayrights.change.org.

74. See Section 8 of Department of Defense Instruction 1332.14, March 29, 2010, http://www.dtic.mil/whs/directives/corres/pdf/133214p.pdf.

75. Charles McLean and P. W. Singer, "Don't Ask. Tell," *Newsweek*, June 4, 2010.

76. *Wong Wing v. U.S.* (1896); *Yick Wo v. Hopkins* (1886).

77. Some of the key cases are cited by Eugene Volokh, "Free Speech and Non-Citizens," August 8, 2005, http://volokh.com/posts/1123520953.shtml.

78. *Plyler v. Doe* (1982).

79. *Ward's Cove Packing Co. v. Atonio* (1989).

80. *St. Mary's Honor Center v. Hicks* (1993).

CHAPTER SEVEN

1. Excerpted, with edits, from James Surowiecki, *The Wisdom of Crowds* (New York: Random House, 2004).

2. Quoted in "Campaign 2008: Public Opinion and Foreign Policy," Council on Foreign Relations transcript from *News Hour with Jim Lehrer*, September 26, 2008.

3. Bruce Drake, "Analysis: Health Care Polls Don't Tell Whole Story," Kaiser Health News, December 23, 2009, http://www.kaiserhealthnews.org./Stories/2009/December/23/analysis-health-care-polls.aspx

4. Robert S. Erikson and Kent L. Tedin, *American Public Opinion* (New York: Pearson Education, 2005), 6.

5. Pew Research Center for People and the Press, "Unabated Economic Gloom, Divides on Afghanistan and Health Care," December 16, 2009, http://people-press.org./reports/pdf/572.pdf

6. "U.S. Online MR Gains Drop," *Inside Research* 20, no. 1 (2009): 11–134, http://blogs.abcnews.com/thenumbers/2010/04/study-group-issues-a-warning-on-optin-online-surveys.html.

7. L. Rainie, "Internet, Broadband, and Cell Phone Statistics," Pew Internet and American Life Project, Pew Research Center, 2010.

8. AAPOR Report on Online Panels, 2010, http://aapor.org/AM/Template.cfm?Section=AAPOR_Committee_and_Task_Force_Reports&Template=/CM/ContentDisplay.cfm&ContentID=2223.

9. AAPOR Report on Online Panels.

10. David Easton and Jack Dennis, *Children in the Political System* (Chicago: University of Chicago Press, 1969), 236.

11. Easton and Dennis, *Children in the Political System*, 115.

12. Edward Greenberg, "Black Children in the Political System," *Public Opinion Quarterly* 34 (1970): 335–48; Chris F. Garcia, *Political Socialization of Chicano Children* (New York: Praeger, 1973); Dean Jaros, Herbert Hirsch, and Frederick Fleron, "The Malevolent Leader: Political Socialization in an American Sub-Culture," *American Political Science Review* 62 (June 1968): 564–75; and Erikson and Tedin, *American Public Opinion*, 121, but see also 122.

13. Erikson and Tedin, *American Public Opinion*, 146; and Fred Greenstein, *Children and Politics* (New Haven, CT: Yale University Press, 1965), 58–59.

14. Greenstein, *Children and Politics*, 58–59; and Easton and Dennis, *Children in the Political System*, 138.

15. Easton and Dennis, *Children in the Political System*, 254–70.

16. Easton and Dennis, *Children in the Political System*, 256.

17. M. Kent Jennings and Richard G. Niemi, *The Political Character of Adolescence* (Princeton, NJ: Princeton University Press, 1974), 274; and Greenstein, *Children and Politics*, 55.

18. Robert W. Connell, *The Child's Construction of Politics* (Melbourne: Melbourne University Press, 1971), 46–49, 59, 62.

19. Robert D. Hess and Judith V. Torney, *The Development of Political Attitudes in Children* (Chicago: Aldine, 1967), 215.

20. Connell, *The Child's Construction of Politics*, 58.

21. Greenstein, *Children and Politics*, 68, 73.

22. Connell, *The Child's Construction of Politics*, 50.

23. Jennings and Niemi, *The Political Character of Adolescence*, 266.

24. Jennings and Niemi, *The Political Character of Adolescence*, 271.

25. Jennings and Niemi, *The Political Character of Adolescence*, 275–76.

26. Roberta S. Sigel, *Learning About Politics* (New York: Random House, 1970), 103.

27. Kenneth P. Langton, *Political Socialization* (New York: Oxford University Press, 1969), 53.

28. M. Kent Jennings and Richard Niemi, *Generations and Politics* (Princeton, NJ: Princeton University Press, 1981), 90.

29. Hess and Torney, *Development*, 134–37; Frank J. Sorauf and Paul Allen Beck, *Party Politics in America* (New York: Harper Collins Publishers, 1988), 180–82.

30. Sigel, *Learning*, 412.

31. Hess and Torney, *The Development of Political Attitudes in Children*, 137–43; Erikson and Tedin, *American Public Opinion*, 127–28.

32. For an overview of the role of school and education in the socialization process, see Hess and Torney, *The Development of Political Attitudes in Children*, 120–32.

33. M. Kent Jennings, "Residuals of a Movement: The Aging of the American Protest Generation," *American Political Science Review* 81 (June 1987): 365–81.

34. "Americans More Upbeat About U.S. Defense Readiness," Gallup, March 26, 2009, http://www.gallup.com./poll/117100/americans-upbeat-defense-readiness.aspx#2

35. William G. Mayer, *The Changing American Mind* (Ann Arbor: University of Michigan Press, 1992), 252–54.

36. Erikson and Tedin, *American Public Opinion*, 142.

37. Erikson and Tedin, *American Public Opinion*, 140.

38. "Political Knowledge Update Survey," Pew Research Center, January 14–17, 2010.

39. Michael X. Delli Carpini and Scott Keeter, *What Americans Know About Politics and Why It Matters* (New Haven, CT: Yale University Press, 1996), 101–2.

40. "What Americans Know: 1987–2007," Pew Research Center, April 15, 2007.

41. Delli Carpini and Keeter, *What Americans Know About Politics and Why It Matters*, 101–2.

42. "What Americans Know: 1987–2007," Pew Research Center, April 15, 2007.

43. "Awareness of Iraq War Fatalities Plummets," Pew Research Center, March 12, 2008.

44. Henry E. Brady, James S. Fishkin, and Robert C. Luskin, "Informed Public Opinion About Foreign Policy: The Uses of Deliberative Polling," The Brookings Institute, 2003, http://www.brookings.edu./articles/2003/summer_elections_brady.aspx

45. Phillip Converse, "The Nature of Belief Systems in Mass Publics," in David E. Apter, *Ideology and Discontent* (New York: Free Press, 1964), 206–61.

46. Donald R. Kinder, "Diversity and Complexity in American Public Opinion," in Ada W. Finiter, ed., *Political Science: The State of the Discipline* (Washington, DC: American Political Science Association, 1983), 397.

47. John Zaller and Stanley Feldman, "A Simple Theory of the Survey Response: Answering Questions Versus Revealing Preferences," *American Journal of Political Science* 36, no. 3 (1992): 379.

48. George F. Bishop, Robert W. Oldendick, and Alfred J. Tuchfarber, "Pseudo-Opinions on Public Affairs," *Public Opinion Quarterly* 51 (Summer 1980): 198–209.

49. The question asked by Gallup was, "Next, thinking about the issue of global warming, sometimes called the 'greenhouse effect,' how well do you feel you understand this issue—would you say very well, fairly well, not very well, or not at all?"

50. See also Jim Yang and Gerald Stone, "The Powerful Role of Interpersonal Communication in Agenda Setting," *Mass Communications and Society* 6, no. 1 (2003): 57–74; and Hans- Bernd Brosius and Gabriel Weimann, "Who Sets the Agenda?" *Communication Research* 23, no. 5 (1996): 561–80.

51. Benjamin I. Page and Robert Y. Shapiro, *The Rational Public* (Chicago: University of Chicago Press, 1992), 341–48.

52. One of the most important and influential discussions of the role of party identification in shaping Americans' thinking about politics appears in Angus Campbell, Philip E. Converse, et al., *The American Voter* (New York: Wiley, 1960). See especially chap. 6.

53. Campbell, Converse, et al., *The American Voter*, 201. Reference is to 1980 reprint.

54. For a discussion of this phenomenon as applied to presidential economic performance, see Campbell, Converse, et al., *The American Voter*, chap. 14.

55. James A. Stimson, *Tides of Consent: How Public Opinion Shapes American Politics* (Cambridge: Cambridge University Press, 2004), 163.

CHAPTER EIGHT

1. Alabama Department of Archives and History, "Application for Registration," 1965, http://www.alabamamoments.state.al.us/sec59pstrans.html (accessed March 17, 2005). While a graduate student at University of Michigan, one of us, Goldstein, first came across these questions when his advisor, Steven Rosenstone, gave them as a pop quiz in an introduction to American Politics course.

2. Steven F. Lawson, *Black Ballots: Voting Rights in the South, 1944–1969* (New York: Columbia University Press, 1976).

3. United States Election Project, "2008 Current Population Survey Voting and Registration Supplement," November 20, 2009, http://elections.gmu.edu /CPS_2008.html.

4. Sidney Verba, Kay Shlozman, and Henry Brady, *Voice and Equality* (Boston: Harvard University Press, 2006), 127.

5. Anthony Downs, *An Economic Theory of Democracy* (New York: Harper, 1957), 267–68.

6. It was political scientist Mancur Olson who introduced the idea of selective benefits, which he called "selective incentives," in a classic work: *The Logic of Collective Action*. We have much more to say about this book in Chapter 12 on interest groups.

7. Riker and Ordeshook elaborated on this article in a 1973 book entitled *Introduction to Positive Political Theory*. Their logic does not apply as well to other forms of political behavior—writing a letter to a member of Congress, for example, or gathering signatures on a petition. The concept of "civic duty" does not apply as well to such activities. To cover these other kinds of participation, therefore, political scientists have tended to talk about their "psychic benefits." "Psychic benefits" is just another way of saying that people derive satisfaction from participating in politics, regardless of whether or not their participation has any effect on relevant political outcomes.

8. Verba et al., *Voice and Equality,* 115, 550.

9. United States Election Project, "2008 Current Population Survey Voting and Registration Supplement," November 20, 2009, http://elections.gmu.edu /CPS_2008.html.

10. Michael McDonald and Samuel Popkin, "The Myth of the Vanishing Voter," *American Political Science Review* 95 (2001).

11. Shirley Zilberstein, "Ballot, Machine Problems to Blame for Uncounted Votes in 2000 Election," CNN, July 17 2001, http://archives.cnn.com/2001/ ALLPOLITICS/07/16/voting.problems/index.html.

12. Verba et al., *Voice and Equality,* 349.

13. Some states allowed women and those aged 18 to 20 to vote prior to these amendments.

14. Roger Clegg, "Felon Disenfranchisement Is Constitutional, and Justified," National Constitution Center, http://www.constitutioncenter.org/education/ForEducators/Viewpoints/FelonDisenfranchisementIsConstitutional,AndJustified.shtml.

15. NBC/Wall Street Journal poll, "Tea Party Tops Democrats and Republicans," December 16, 2009.

16. United States Election Project, "2008 Current Population Survey Voting and Registration Supplement," November 20, 2009. http://elections.gmu.edu/CPS_ 2008.html.

17. Mark A. Smith, "The Contingent Effects of Ballot Initiatives and Candidate Races on Turnout," *American Journal of Political Science* 45 (2001): 700–6; Caroline Tolbert, John Grummel, and Daniel Smith, "The

Effects of Ballot Initiatives on Voter Turnout in the American States," *American Politics Review* 29 (2001): 625–48; and Caroline Tolbert, Ramona McNeal, and Daniel A. Smith, "Enhancing Civic Engagement: The Effect of Direct Democracy on Political Participation and Knowledge," *State Politics and Policy Quarterly* 3 (2003): 23–41.

18. Robert A. Jackson, "The Mobilization of State Electorates in the 1988 and 1990 Elections," *Journal of Politics* 59 (1999): 520–37; Richard W. Boyd, "The Effects of Primaries and Statewide Races on Voter Turnout," *Journal of Politics* 51 (1989): 730–39.

19. Priscilla L. Southwell, "Voter Turnout in the 1986 Congressional Elections: The Media as a Demobilizer?" *American Politics Quarterly* 19 (1991): 96–108; and Dean Lacy and Barry C. Burden, "The Vote-Stealing and Turnout Effects of Ross Perot in the 1992 U.S. Presidential Election," *American Journal of Political Science* 43 (1999): 233–55.

20. Gary W. Cox and Michael C. Munger, "Closeness, Expenditures, and Turnout in the 1982 U.S. House Elections," *American Political Science Review* 83 (1989): 217–31; Mark N. Franklin and Wolfgang P. Hirczy de Mino, "Separated Powers, Divided Government, and Turnout in U.S. Presidential Elections," *American Journal of Political Science* 42 (January 1998): 316–26; and Gregory A. Caldeira and Samuel C. Patterson, "Getting Out the Vote: Participation in Gubernatorial Elections," *American Political Science Review* 77 (1982): 675–89.

21. American National Election Studies, "The NES Guide to Public Opinion and Electoral Behavior," American National Election Studies, http://www.electionstudies.org/nesguide/gd-index.htm#6.

22. Steven J. Rosenstone and John M. Hansen, *Mobilization, Participation, and Democracy in America* (New York: Macmillan, 1993), 29.

23. "The Great Schlep," http://www.thegreatschlep.com.

24. "Yes We Can," Wikipedia, http://en.wikipedia.org/wiki/Yes_We_Can.

25. "Phone Booking for the Modern Political Campaign," What Are You Looking At? http://whatareyoulookingatpolitics.blogspot.com/2009/07/phone-banking-for-modern-political.html.

26. Rosenstone and Hansen, *Mobilization, Participation, and Democracy in America*, 44.

27. "Voter Turnout: An International Comparison," *Public Opinion Quarterly* (1984).

28. Robert Stein and Greg Vonnahme, "Early, Absentee, and Mail in Voting," in *The Oxford Handbook of American Elections and Political Behavior* (Oxford: Oxford University Press, 2010), 185.

29. National Center for Education Statistics, Digest of Education Statistics, http://nces.ed.gov/pubs2002/digest2001/tables/dt008.asp.

30. Rosenstone and Hansen, *Mobilization, Participation, and Democracy in America*, 215.

31. Rosenstone and Hansen, *Mobilization, Participation, and Democracy in America*.

32. M. Margaret Conway, *Political Participation in the United States* (Washington, DC: CQ Press, 1991), 171.

33. Rosenstone and Hansen, *Mobilization, Participation, and Democracy in America*, 163.

34. Paul R. Abramson, John H. Aldrich, and David W. Rohde, *Change and Continuity in the 2004 Elections* (Washington, DC: CQ Press, 2006), 85.

35. For a review of the existing literature and a report on some new research findings, see Alan S. Gerber and Donald P. Green, "The Effects of Canvassing, Direct Mail, and Telephone Contact on Voter Turnout: A Field Experiment," *American Political Science Review* 94 (2000): 653–63.

36. Rui Texeira, *The Disappearing American Voter* (Washington, DC: Brookings Institution, 1992), 7, 36.

37. Rosenstone and Hansen, *Mobilization, Participation, and Democracy in America*, 156.

38. As quoted in Kenneth M. Goldstein, *Interest Groups, Lobbying, and Participation in America* (New York: Cambridge University Press, 1999).

CHAPTER NINE

1. D. W. Miller, "Election Results Leave Political Scientists Red-Faced over Their Forecasting Models," *Chronicle of Higher Education*, November 8, 2000.

2. Robert G. Kaiser, "Gore to Win Election?" *Washington Post*, May 26, 2000, A1.

3. This isn't so in two states: Louisiana and Washington both use a "top two" system in which the two final candidates (if no candidate receives over 50 percent in the first round) could both be Democrats or both be Republicans.

4. "New Hampshire Primary," Wikipedia, http://en.wikipedia.org/wiki/New_Hampshire_primary#Democrats.

5. Ron Gunzburger, "Presidency 2000: Arizona Primary Results," Politics 1, http://www.politics1.com/vote-az.htm.

6. Lawrence D. Longley and Neal R. Peirce, *The Electoral College Primer 2000* (New Haven: Yale University Press, 1999), 18–19.

7. Gary L. Gregg II, *Securing Democracy: Why We Have an Electoral College* (Wilmington, DE: ISI Books, 2001), 6.

8. Gregg, *Securing Democracy*, 7, 8.

9. Gregg, *Securing Democracy*, 27–29. Originally the second-place finisher became the vice president. This was changed by constitutional amendment in 1804 so that electors cast votes separately for president and vice president. By awarding the vice presidency to the second-place finisher, the previous system set up the possibility for severe disharmony in the executive branch.

10. "U.S. Electoral College," Wikipedia, http://en.wikipedia.org/wiki/U.S._Electoral_College#Maine-Nebraska_method.

11. "US President, National, Exit Poll," CNN, http://www.cnn.com/ELECTION/2004/pages/results/states/US/P/00/epolls.0.html.

12. William H. Flanigan and Nancy H. Zingale, *Political Behavior of the American Electorate* (Washington, DC: CQ Press, 2002), 93.

13. Michael Gant and Norman Luttbeg, "The Cognitive Utility of Partisanship," *Western Political Quarterly* 40 (1987): 499–517.

14. Flanigan and Zingale, *Political Behavior of the American Electorate*, 78.

15. Michael R. Alvarez, *Information and Elections* (Ann Arbor: University of Michigan Press, 1998), 8.

16. V.O. Key, *The Responsible Electorate, Rationality in Presidential Voting, 1936–1960* (Cambridge, MA: Belknap Press, 1966); Gregory B. Markus and Philip Converse, "A Dynamic Simultaneous Equation Model of Electoral Choice," *American Political Science Review* 73 (1979).

17. Edward G. Carmines and James A. Stimson, *Issue Evolution: Race and the Transformation of American Politics* (Princeton, NJ: Princeton University Press, 1989).

18. Donald E. Stokes, "Some Dynamic Elements of Contests for the Presidency," *American Political Science Review* 60 (1966): 19–28.

19. Larry M. Bartels, "Impact of Candidate Traits in American Presidential Elections," in *Leaders' Personalities and the Outcomes of Democratic Elections*, Anthony King, ed. (New York: Oxford University Press, 2002), 46.

20. Angus Campbell et al., *The American Voter* (Chicago: University of Chicago Press, 1980), 44–45.

21. Markus and Converse, "A Dynamic Simultaneous Equation Model of Electoral Choice."

22. Campbell et al., *The American Voter*; Stanley Kelley Jr. and Thad W. Mirer, "The Simple Act of Voting," *American Political Science Review* 68 (1974): 572–91; Markus and Converse, "A Dynamic Simultaneous Equation Model of Electoral Choice"; Warren E. Miller and J. Merrill Shanks, *The New American Voter* (Cambridge, MA: Harvard University Press, 1996), chap. 17.

23. Kelley and Mirer, "The Simple Act of Voting"; Markus and Converse, "A Dynamic Simultaneous Equation Model of Electoral Choice."

24. Markus and Converse, "A Dynamic Simultaneous Equation Model of Electoral Choice."

25. Larry M. Bartels, *Presidential Primaries and the Dynamics of Public Choice* (Princeton, NJ: Princeton University Press, 1998).

26. American Political Science Association, "6 of 9 Presidential Election Forecasts Predict Obama Will Win 2008 Popular Vote," October 16, 2008, http://www.apsanet.org/content_58969.cfm.

27. James E. Campbell, "Forecasting the Presidential Vote in the States," *American Journal of Political Science* 36 (1992): 386–407.

28. Randall J. Jones Jr., *Who Will Be in the White House: Predicting Presidential Elections* (New York: Longman, 2002), 31.

29. Jones, *Who Will Be in the White House.*

30. Morris P. Fiorina, "Parties and Partisanship: A 40-Year Retrospective," *Political Behavior* 24 (June 2002): 93–115.

31. Fiorina, "Parties and Partisanship."

32. Dan Balz, "Bad Signs for Bush in History, Numbers Approval Rating Is Lowest of His Term," *Washington Post*, May 13, 2004.

33. Jimmy Carter, "Remarks Accepting the Presidential Nomination at the 1980 Democratic National Convention," August 14, 1980, Public Papers of the Presidents of the United States: Jimmy Carter: 1977–1981, 9 vols. (Washington, DC: Government Printing Office, 1977–1982), http://www.4president.org/speeches/carter1980convention.htm.

34. Stan Greenberg and Jim Gerstein, "Focus Group Report: Findings from Recent Discussions with Voters," April 9, 2004, Democracy Corps, http://archive.democracycorps.com/focus/Democracy_Corps_April_2004_Focus_Group_Report.pdf.

35. "Stats at a Glance," OpenSecrets, http://www.opensecrets.org/overview/index.php.

36. "http://www.cfinst.org/pdf/federal/PostElec2010_Table4_.pdf .

CHAPTER TEN

1. Bill Carter, "CNN Fails to Stop Fall in Ratings," *New York Times*, March 29, 2010.

2. D. C. Hallin and R. Giles, "Presses and Democracies," in *The Press*, ed. G. Overholser and K. Hall Jamieson (New York: Oxford University Press, 2005), 7.

3. S. Djankov et al., *Who Owns the Media?* 2001, http://siteresources.worldbank.org.

4. Hallin and Giles, "Presses and Democracies."

5. Carter, "CNN Fails to Stop Fall in Ratings."

6. T. Patterson, "Political Roles of the Journalist," in *The Politics of News: The News of Politics*, ed. D. A. Graber, D. McQuail, and P. Norris (Washington, DC: CQ Press, 2007); R. E. Horn, *Visual Language: Global Communication for the 21st Century* (Bainbridge, WA: MacroVU, 1999).

7. Hallin and Giles, "Presses and Democracies," 8–9.

8. Hallin and Giles, "Presses and Democracies," 10.

9. Patterson, "Political Roles of the Journalist," 22, table 1.1.

10. Patterson, "Political Roles of the Journalist," 23.

11. F. Esser and B. Pfetsch, eds., "Comparing Political Communication: Theories, Cases, and Challenges," *Communication, Society, and Politics* (New York: Cambridge University Press, 2005); Graber et al., *The Politics of News.*

12. *New York Times Co. v. United States*, 403 U.S. 713 (1971).

13. http://www.law.ou.edu/hist/sedact.html.

14. Margaret A. Blanchard, "Freedom of the Press," in *American Journalism: History, Principles, Practices,* ed. W. David Sloan and Lisa Mullikin Parcell (Jefferson, NC: McFarland, 2002), 127.

15. Richard W.T. Martin, *The Free and Open Press* (New York: New York University Press, 2001), 132.

16. W. D. Sloan and L. M. Parcell, eds., *American Journalism: History, Principles, Practices* (New York: McFarland, 2002); Martin, *The Free and Open Press.*

17. Samuel D. Warren and Louis D. Brandeis. "The Right to Privacy," *Harvard Law Review* 4, no. 5 (1890): 195.

18. W. Overbeck, *Major Principles of Media Law* (Belmont, CA: Wadsworth, 2007).

19. Patterson, "Political Roles of the Journalist," 22, table 1.1.

20. Blanchard, "Freedom of the Press."

21. "Press Freedom Day by Day," http://www.rsf.org.

22. H. W. Stanley and R. G. Niemi, eds., *Vital Statistics on American Politics 1999–2000* (Washington, DC: CQ Press, 1999).

23. The State of the News Media in 2004: An Annual Report on American Journalism, http://www.stateofthe-newsmedia.org.

24. M. Schudson and S. E. Tifft, "American Journalism in Historical Perspective," in Overholser and Jamieson's *The Press*, 32.

25. Scotti Williston, "Global News and the Vanishing American Correspondent," TBS Archives, Spring 2001, http://www.tbsjournal.com.

26. Paul Farhi, "Limbaugh's Audience Size? It's Largely Up in the Air," *Washington Post*, March 7, 2009, http://www.washingtonpost.com.

27. Schudson and Tifft, "American Journalism in Historical Perspective," 33.

28. Pew Research Center for the People and the Press, "Press Accuracy Rating Hits Two Decade Low," September 13, 2009, http://people-press.org.

29. Lichter and McGinnis, "Government in and out of the News," 48–49.

30. Schudson and Tifft, "American Journalism in Historical Perspective," 33.

31. Schudson and Tifft, "American Journalism in Historical Perspective."

32. T. Patterson, *Out of Order: An Incisive and Boldly Original Critique of the News Media's Domination of America's Political Process* (New York: Vintage, 1994).

33. J. N. Cappella and K. H. Jamieson, *Spiral of Cynicism: The Press and the Public Good* (New York: Oxford University Press, 1997).

34. J. T. Hamilton, "The Market and the Media," in *The Press*, 358.

35. Pew Research Center for the People and the Press, "Media Metric: Obama's 100 Days of Press," April 29th, 2009, http://pewresearch.org.

36. Albert Hunt, "Tension in Hillaryland Grows as Plan Goes Awry," http://www.bloomberg.com.

37. S. J. Farnsworth and S. R. Lichter, *The Nightly News Nightmare: Network Television's Coverage of U.S. Presidential Elections, 1988–2000* (New York: Rowman and Littlefield, 2002).

38. S. R. Lichter, *Good Intentions Make Bad News: Why Americans Hate Campaign Journalism* (New York: Rowman and Littlefield, 1996).

39. T. Patterson and P. Seib, "Informing the Public," in *The Press*, 194.

40. Patterson and Seib, "Informing the Public," 195; Patterson, *Out of Order.*

43. S. Tiner, "Why Editors Are Dumber than Mules," 1999, http://www.asne.org.

44. R. Parry, "Media Mythology: Is the Press Liberal?" 1997, http://www.consortiumnews.com.

45. D. D'Alessio and M. Allen, "Media Bias in Presidential Elections: A Meta-Analysis," *Journal of Communication* 50, no. 4 (2000): 148.

46. D'Alessio and Allen, "Media Bias in Presidential Elections," 145.

47. J. Bryant and D. Zillman, eds., "Media Effects: Advances in Theory and Research," Lea's Communication Series (Mahwah, NJ: Lawrence Erlbaum, 2002).

48. Bryant and Zillman, eds., "Media Effects."

49. Angus Campbell, Philip E. Converse, Warren E. Miller, and Donald Stokes, *The American Voter* (New York: Wiley, 1960).

50. John Zaller, "The Myth of Massive Media Impact Revived: New Support for a Discredited Idea," in *Political Persuasion and Attitude Change*, ed. Diana C. Mutz, Paul M. Sniderman, and Richard A. Brody (Ann Arbor: University of Michigan Press, 1996), 17.

51. C. Trumbo, "Longitudinal Modeling of Public Issues: An Application of the Agenda-Setting Process to the Issue of Global Warming," Journalism and Communications Monographs, 1995, 152; Larry Bartels, "Politicians and the Press: Who Leads, Who Follows?" Annual Meeting of the American Political Science Association, San Francisco, 1996.

52. Time of Presidential Election Vote Decision 1948–2004, 2005, http://www.electionstudies.org.

53. Larry Bartels, "Messages Received: The Political Impact of Media Exposure," *American Political Science Review* 87, no. 2 (1993): 267.

54. S. Iyengar and D. R. Kinder, *News That Matters: Television and American Opinion*, American Politics and Political Economy Series (Chicago: University of Chicago Press, 1989).

55. L. Festinger, *Theory of Cognitive Dissonance* (Stanford, CA: Stanford University Press, 1957).

56. John Zaller, *The Nature and Origins of Mass Opinion* (New York: Cambridge University Press, 1992). Zaller's work forms the basis for much of the discussion in this section.

57. Bartels, "Politicians and the Press"; T. Patterson, *Mass Media Election* (New York: Praeger, 1980); S. J. Farnsworth and S. R. Lichter, "No Small Town Poll: Network Coverage of the 1992 New Hampshire Primary," *Harvard International Journal of Press/Politics* 4 (1999): 51–61.

58. Bartels, "Politicians and the Press"; Zaller, *The Nature and Origins of Mass Opinion*, 23, 37, 48.

59. Patterson, *Out of Order*.

CHAPTER ELEVEN

1. The definition here is based on William N. Chambers, "Party Development and the American Mainstream," in William N. Chambers and Walter Dean Burnham, eds., *The American Party Systems: Stages of Political Development*, 2nd ed. (New York: Oxford University Press, 1975), 5; and Leon D. Epstein, *Political Parties in the American Mold* (Madison: University of Wisconsin Press, 1986), 18–19.

2. See Gregory Koger, Seth Masket, and Hans Noel, "Partisan Webs: Information Exchange and Party Networks," *British Journal of Political Science* 39 (2009): 633–53; Paul S. Herrnson, "The Roles of Party Organizations, Party-Connected Committees, and Party Allies in Elections," *Journal of Politics* 71, 4 (2009): 1207–24.

3. John H. Aldrich, *Why Parties? The Origin and Transformation of Political Parties in America* (Chicago: University of Chicago Press, 1995). See also Seth E. Maskett, "It Takes an Outsider: Extralegislative Organization

and Partisanship in the California Assembly, 1849–2006," *American Journal of Political Science* 51, 3 (2007): 482–97.

4. John J. Coleman, "Unified Government, Divided Government, and Party Responsiveness," *American Political Science Review* 93, 4 (1999): 821–35; Sarah A. Binder, "The Dynamics of Legislative Gridlock, 1947–96," *American Political Science Review* 93, 3 (1999): 519–33; William G. Howell, E. Scott Adler, Charles Cameron, and Charles Riemann, "Divided Government and the Legislative Productivity of Congress, 1945–1994," *Legislative Studies Quarterly* 25, 2 (2000): 285–312. See David R. Mayhew, *Divided We Govern: Party Control, Lawmaking, and Investigations, 1946–2002,* 2nd ed. (New Haven, CT: Yale University Press, 2005), for a contrary view.

5. Seth E. Masket, "Did Obama's Ground Game Matter? The Influence of Local Field Offices During the 2008 Presidential Election," *Public Opinion Quarterly* 73, 5 (2009): 1023–39.

6. Kenneth M. Goldstein and Travis Ridout, "The Politics of Participation: Mobilization and Turnout over Time," *Political Behavior* 24, 1 (2002): 3–29; R. Michael Alvarez, Asa Hopkins, and Betsy Sinclair, "Mobilizing Pasadena Democrats: Measuring the Effects of Partisan Campaign Contacts," *Journal of Politics* 72, 1 (2010): 31–44.

7. Anna Harvey, *Votes Without Leverage: Women in American Electoral Politics, 1920–1970* (New York: Cambridge University Press, 1998).

8. See, for example, Richard Jensen, *The Winning of the Midwest, 1888–1896* (Chicago: University of Chicago Press, 1971); Paul J. Kleppner, *The Cross of Culture: A Social Analysis of Midwestern Politics, 1850–1900* (New York: Free Press, 1970).

9. Michael E. McGerr, *The Decline of Popular Politics: The American North, 1865–1928* (New York: Oxford University Press, 1986).

10. Alan S. Gerber and Gregory A. Huber, "Partisanship, Political Control, and Economic Assessments," *American Journal of Political Science* 54, 1 (2010): 153–73.

11. On voting systems, see the list at www.idea.int/esd/world.cfm and the analysis by Gary W. Cox, *Making Votes Count: Strategic Coordination in the World's Electoral Systems* (New York: Cambridge University Press, 1997).

12. For overviews, see Alan Ware, *Political Parties and Party Systems* (New York: Oxford University Press, 1996); and Steven J. Rosenstone, Roy L. Behr, and Edward H. Lazarus, *Third Parties in America: Citizen Response to Major Party Failure*, 2nd ed. (Princeton, NJ: Princeton University Press, 1996).

13. Harold W. Stanley and Richard G. Niemi, *Vital Statistics on American Politics, 2007–08* (Washington, DC: CQ Press, 2008), 43.

14. Candidates of third parties that are relatively large, such as the People's Party of the 1890s or the Progressive Party of the early twentieth century, may eventually absorb back into the major parties and can work to change the major parties' positions from within.

15. Barry C. Burden: "Minor Parties and Strategic Voting in Recent U.S. Presidential Elections," *Electoral Studies* 24, 4 (2005): 603–18; and "Ralph Nader's Campaign Strategy in the 2000 U.S. Presidential Election," *American Politics Research* 33, 5 (2005): 672–99.

16. Pew Research Center for the People and the Press, people-press.org/reports/questionnaires/630.pdf, question 22.

17. William H. Riker, "The Two-Party System and Duverger's Law: An Essay on the History of Political Science," *American Political Science Review* 76 (1982): 753–66; and William Roberts Clark and Matt Golder, "Rehabilitating Duverger's Theory: Testing the Mechanical and Strategic Modifying Effects of Electoral Laws," *Comparative Political Studies* 39, 6 (2006): 679–708.

18. Most systems employ a threshold and deny seats to very small parties.

19. Josep M. Colomer, "It's Parties That Choose Electoral Systems (Or, Duverger's Laws Upside Down)," *Political Studies* 53, 1 (2005): 1–21; Kenneth Benoit, "Electoral Laws as Political Consequences: Explaining the Origins and Change of Electoral Institutions," *Annual Review of Political Science* 10 (2007): 363–90.

20. Aldrich, *Why Parties?* See also Anthony Downs, *An Economic Theory of Democracy* (New York: Harper, 1957).

21. Maine and Nebraska award two electoral votes to the presidential candidate who wins the state, and one electoral vote for winning a congressional district.

22. Pradeep Chhibber and Ken Kollman, "Party Aggregation and the Number of Parties in India and the United States," *American Political Science Review* 92, 2 (1998): 329–42.

23. Lisa Disch, *The Tyranny of the Two-Party System* (New York: Columbia University Press, 2002).

24. *Timmons v. Twin Cities Area New Party* (1997). The seven states are Connecticut, Delaware, Idaho, Mississippi, New York, South Carolina, and Vermont.

25. See Rosenstone et al., *Third Parties in America: Citizen Response to Major Party Failure*, 254–6.

26. John Zaller and Mark Hunt, "The Rise and Fall of Candidate Perot: Unmediated Versus Mediated Politics—Part I," *Political Communication* 11, 4 (1994): 357–90; Paul R. Abramson, John H. Aldrich, Philip Paolino, and David W. Rohde, "Challenges to the American Two-Party System: Evidence from the 1968, 1980, 1992, and 1996 Presidential Elections," *Political Research Quarterly* 53, 3 (2000): 495–522.

27. Rosenstone, Behr, and Lazarus, *Third Parties in America*.

28. See www.fairvote.org for discussion of a number of alternative voting systems.

29. Designed for use in multimember districts such as school board elections, especially to increase minority representation, cumulative voting could potentially be modified for single-member district use.

30. Ronald P. Formisano, "The 'Party Period' Revisited," *Journal of American History* 86, 1 (1999): 93–120.

31. Jessica Trounstine, *Political Monopolies in American Cities: The Rise and Fall of Bosses and Reformers* (Chicago: University of Chicago Press, 2008).

32. Alan Ware, *The American Direct Primary: Party Institutionalization and Transformation in the North* (New York: Cambridge University Press, 2002); and "Anti-partism and Party Control of Political Reform in the United States: The Case of the Australian Ballot," *British Journal of Political Science* 30, 1 (2000): 1–29.

33. Epstein, *Political Parties in the American Mold*; Amy Bridges, *Morning Glories: Municipal Reform in the Southwest* (Princeton, NJ: Princeton University Press, 1997); and Byron E. Shafer, *Quiet Revolution: The Struggle for the Democratic Party and the Shaping of Post-Reform Politics* (New York: Russell Sage Foundation, 1983).

34. See Cornelius P. Cotter, James L. Gibson, John F. Bibby, and Robert J. Huckshorn, *Party Organizations in American Politics* (New York: Praeger, 1984); and Paul S. Herrnson, "The Revitalization of National Party Organizations," in L. Sandy Maisel, ed., *The Parties Respond* (Boulder, CO: Westview Press, 1994).

35. *California Democratic Party v. Jones* (2000); *Tashjian v. Connecticut* (1986).

36. Paul S. Herrnson, *Party Campaigning in the 1980s* (Cambridge, MA: Harvard University Press, 1988); John J. Coleman, "Party Organizational Strength and Public Support for Parties," *American Journal of Political Science* 40, 3 (1996): 805–24.

37. Marjorie Randon Hershey, *Party Politics in America*, 13th ed. (New York: Longman, 2009), 76.

38. Campaign Finance Institute, www.cfinst.org/data/pdf/VitalStats_t12.pdf.

39. See Ben Clift and Justin Fisher, "Comparative Party Finance Reform: The Cases of France and Britain," *Party Politics* 10, 6 (2004): 677–99; Susan E. Scarrow, "Explaining Political Finance Reforms: Competition and Context," *Party Politics* 10, 6 (2004): 653–75.

40. Matthew J. Burbank, Ronald J. Hrebenar, and Robert C. Benedict, *Parties, Interest Groups, and Political Campaigns* (Boulder, CO: Westview Press, 1999), 149.

41. The discussion in this case study relies extensively on Hershey, *Party Politics in America*, 205–06; and Matthew J. Burbank et al., *Parties, Interest Groups, and Political Campaigns*, 148–

42. David Paul Kuhn, "DNC Blunts GOP Microtargeting Lead," May 23, 2008, www.politico.com.

43. Hershey, *Party Politics in America*, 205; Peter Wallsten and Tom Hamburger, "The GOP Knows You Don't Like Anchovies," *Los Angeles Times*, June 25, 2006.

44. David Talbot, "The Democrats' New Weapon," *Technology Review*, December 18, 2008; Jim Rutenberg and Christopher Drew, "National Push by Obama on Ads and Turnout," *New York Times*, June 22, 2008.

45. See Pew Research Center's political typology groups, www.people-press.org, for a thorough overview of intra-party frictions in the public.

46. Ruth Marcus, "President Obama Is Making Nobody Happy," *Washington Post*, April 3, 2010.

47. Nicol C. Rae, "Be Careful What You Wish For: The Rise of Responsible Parties in American National Politics," *Annual Review of Political Science* 10 (2007): 169–91.

48. Paul Frymer, *Uneasy Alliances: Race and Party Competition in America* (Princeton, NJ: Princeton University Press, 1999).

49. Philip A. Klinkner, *The Losing Parties: Out-Party National Committees, 1956–1993* (New Haven: Yale University Press, 1994); Zeynep Somer-Topcu, "Timely Decisions: The Effects of Past National Elections on Party Policy Change," *Journal of Politics* 71, 1 (2009): 238–48.

50. Edward G. Carmines and Michael W. Wagner, "Political Issues and Party Alignments: Assessing the Issue Evolution Perspective," *Annual Review of Political Science* 9 (2006): 67–81; David Karol, *Partisan Position Change in American Politics: Coalition Maintenance* (New York: Cambridge University Press, 2009).

51. For an overview and critique, see David R. Mayhew, *Electoral Realignments: A Critique of an American Genre* (New Haven, CT: Yale University Press, 2002).

52. See James L. Sundquist, *Politics and Policy: The Eisenhower, Kennedy, and Johnson Years* (Washington, DC: Brookings Institution Press, 1968) and Donald Green, Bradley Palmquist, and Eric Schickler, *Partisan Hearts and Minds: Political Parties and the Social Identities of Voters* (New Haven, CT: Yale University Press, 2002).

53. William G. Mayer, *The Divided Democrats: Ideological Unity, Party Reform, and Presidential Elections* (Boulder, CO: Westview Press, 1996), chap. 5; Paul R. Abramson, John H. Aldrich, and David W. Rohde, *Change and Continuity in the 2004 Elections* (Washington, DC: CQ Press, 2006), chap. 5.

54. Larry M. Bartels, "Where the Ducks Are: Voting Power in a Party System," in John G. Geer, ed., *Politicians and Party Politics* (Baltimore: Johns Hopkins University Press, 1998); Alan I. Abramowitz and Kyle L. Saunders, "Ideological Realignment in the U.S. Electorate," *Journal of Politics* 60, 3 (1998): 634–52; Abramson, Aldrich, and Rohde, *Change and Continuity in the 2004 Elections*.

55. Walter Dean Burnham, "The 1980 Election: Realignment, Reaction, or What?" in Thomas Ferguson and Joel Rogers, eds., *The Hidden Election: Politics and Economics in the 1980 Presidential Campaign* (New York: Pantheon, 1981). See also Brett M. Clifton, "Romancing the GOP: Assessing the Strategies Used by the Christian Coalition to Influence the Republican Party," *Party Politics* 10, 5 (2004): 475–98.

56. Democrats controlled the Senate from mid-2001 until the end of 2002 after James Jeffords, a Republican senator from Vermont, declared himself an independent and aligned with the Democrats.

57. Larry M. Bartels, "Partisanship and Voting Behavior, 1952–1996," *American Journal of Political Science* 44, 1 (2000): 35–50; Joseph Barfumi and Robert Y. Shapiro, "A New Partisan Voter," *Journal of Politics* 71, 1 (2009): 1–24; David A. Hopkins, "The 2008 Election and the Political Geography of the New Democratic Majority," *Polity* 41, 3 (2009): 368–87.

58. Robert S. Erikson, Michael B. MacKuen, and James A. Stimson argue that public opinion tends to push against the ideological grain of current policy. See *The Macro Polity* (New York: Cambridge University Press, 2002).

59. www.voteview.com/polarized_america. htm#Politicalpolarization.

60. CBS News/New York Times Poll, August 31, 2008, www.cbsnews.com/htdocs/pdf/RNCDelegates_issues. pdf. See also Hershey, *Party Politics in America*, 187.

61. Edward G. Carmines and Geoffrey Layman, "Issue Evolution in Postwar American Politics: Old Certainties and Fresh Tensions," in Byron E. Shafer, ed., *Present Discontents: American Politics in the Very Late Twentieth Century* (Chatham, NJ: Chatham House, 1997).

62. See John Gerring, *Party Ideologies in America, 1828–1996* (New York: Cambridge University Press, 1998).

63. Analysis based on percentage of the population rating these issues as a "top priority" in the Pew Research Center's January 2010 survey; cited in "Public's Priorities for 2010: Economy, Jobs, Terrorism," January 25, 2010, people-press.org/report/584/policy-priorities-2010.

64. Lydia Saad, "Federal Debt, Terrorism Considered Top Threats to U.S.," Gallup Poll, June 4, 2010,

www.gallup.com/poll/139385/Federal-Debt-Terrorism-Considered-Top-Threats.aspx.

65. Saad, "Federal Debt, Terrorism Considered Top Threats to U.S."

66. John R. Petrocik, William L. Benoit, and Glenn J. Hansen, "Issue Ownership and Presidential Campaigning, 1952–2000," *Political Science Quarterly* 118, 4 (2003–04): 599–626.

67. David Wright, Andy Fies, and Sunlen Miller, "Obama: 'Old Politics Just Won't Do'—Democratic Contender Frames Race Against Clinton as 'Past Versus the Future,'" January 30, 2008, www.abcnews.go.com; Associated Press, "McCain Outlines Vision of Iraq Victory, Reduced Partisanship," May 15, 2008, http://elections.foxnews.com.

68. The "two Americas" label was used by Democratic presidential candidate John Edwards in 2004 and 2008 and "culture war" by 1992 Republican presidential candidate Patrick Buchanan.

69. Pietro S. Nivola and David W. Brady: *Red and Blue Nation? Characteristics and Causes of America's Polarized Politics* (Washington, DC: Brookings Institution Press, 2006) and *Red and Blue Nation? Consequences and Correction of America's Polarized Politics* (Washington, DC: Brookings Institution Press, 2008).

70. Morris P. Fiorina, Samuel J. Abrams, and Jeremy C. Pope, *Culture War? The Myth of a Polarized America*, 2nd ed. (New York: Longman, 2005).

71. Paul DiMaggio, John Evans, and Bethany Bryson, "Have Americans' Social Attitudes Become More Polarized?" *American Journal of Sociology* 102, 3 (1996): 690–755.

72. Matthew Levendusky, *The Partisan Sort: How Liberals Became Democrats and Conservatives Became Republicans* (Chicago: University of Chicago Press, 2009).

73. Geoffrey C. Layman, Thomas M. Carsey, and Juliana Menasce Horowitz, "Party Polarization in American Politics: Characteristics, Causes, and Consequences," *Annual Review of Political Science* 9 (2006): 83–110.

74. For a small sample of this large body of studies, see Marc J. Hetherington, "Resurgent Mass Partisanship: The Role of Elite Polarization," *American Political Science Review* 95, 3 (2001): 619–31; Sean M. Theriault, *Party Polarization in Congress* (New York: Cambridge University Press, 2008); and Nolan McCarty, Keith T. Poole, and Howard Rosenthal, "Does Gerrymandering Cause Polarization?" *American Journal of Political Science* 53, 3 (2009): 666–80.

75. Morris P. Fiorina, "Parties and Partisanship: A 40-Year Retrospective," *Political Behavior* 24, 2 (2002): 93–115.

76. David R. Jones, "Partisan Polarization and Congressional Accountability in House Elections," *American Journal of Political Science* 54, 2 (2010): 323–37.

CHAPTER TWELVE

1. Adapted from M. Margaret Conway, *Political Participation in the United States*, 3rd ed. (Washington, DC: CQ Press, 2000), 108–11; and Nancy E. McGlen and Karen O'Connor, *Women, Politics, and American Society* (Englewood Cliffs, NJ: Prentice Hall, 1995), chap. 1.

2. Brody Mullins and Jane Zhang, "Nomination Tests Antilobbyist Policy," *Wall Street Journal*, May 4, 2009, http://online.wsj.com/article/SB124139960819782109.html.

3. Bob Cusack, "After Obama Rips Lobbyists, K Street Insiders Get Private Policy Briefings," *The Hill*, January 28, 2010, http://thehill.com./homenews/administration/78509-after-obama-rips-k-street-administration-invites-lobbyists-to-private-briefings.

4. Earl Latham, *The Group Basis of Politics: A Study in Basing-Point Legislation* (New York: Octagon, 1965), 221.

5. David B. Truman, *The Governmental Process: Political Interests and Public Opinion* (New York: Knopf 1951), 507.

6. Truman, *The Governmental Process*, 289.

7. U.S. Census Bureau News, "Household Income Rises, Poverty Rate Declines, Number of Uninsured Up," August 28, 2007, http://www.census.gov/Press-Release/www/releases/archives/income_wealth/010583.html (accessed August 11, 2008).

8. Nelson W. Polsby, "How to Study Community Power: The Pluralist Alternative," in Roderick Bell, David V. Edwards, and R. Harrison Wagner, eds., *Political Power: A Reader in Theory and Research* (New York: Free Press, 1969), 33. Excerpted from *Journal of Politics* 22 (1960): 474–84; and Nelson W. Polsby, *Community Power and Political Theory* (New Haven: Yale University Press, 1980), 116.

9. Peter Bachrach and Morton S. Baratz, "Two Faces of Power," *American Political Science Review* 56, no. 4 (1962): 947–52.

10. Peter Bachrach and Morton S. Baratz, "Decisions and Nondecisions: An Analytical Framework," *American Political Science Review* 57, no. 3 (1963): 632–42.

11. Polsby, *Community Power and Political Theory*, 71.

12. Truman, *The Governmental Process*.

13. Iraq Veterans Against the War, http://ivaw.org/about (accessed August 11, 2008).

14. Mancur Olson, *The Logic of Collective Action: Public Goods and the Theory of Groups* (Cambridge, MA: Harvard University Press, 1965), 2.

15. Olson, *The Logic of Collective Action*, 16.

16. Olson, *The Logic of Collective Action*, 51. Olson coined "selective incentives."

17. Paul C. Light, *Artful Work: The Politics of Social Security Reform* (New York: Random House, 1985), 76.

18. Compassionate Action for Animals, "Volunteer Testimonials," http://www.exploreveg.org/help/volunteer-testimonials (accessed August 11, 2008).

19. Robert H. Salisbury, "An Exchange Theory of Interest Groups," *Midwest Journal of Political Science* 13, no. 1 (1969): 1–32.

20. Violence Policy Center, "National Rifle Association Information," http://www.vpc.org/nrainfo/chapter1.html (accessed August 11, 2008).

21. Hoover Institute Public Policy Inquiry, "Campaign Finance: Current Structure," March 8, 2004, http://www.campaignfinancesite.org/structure/opinions16.html (accessed August 11, 2008); Jerry Seper, "Soros-Supported Voter-Registration Drive Probed," *Washington Times*, October 18, 2004, http://www.mdfva.org/2004News/Washtimes041018_041024.html#M041020%20%20%20Soros-supported%20voter-registration%20drive (accessed August 11, 2008).

22. National Association of Counties, "About NACO," http://www.naco.org/Content/NavigationMenu/About_NACo/Membership/Membership.htm; http://congressional.energy.gov/state_local.htm (accessed August 11, 2008).

23. Richard Hume Werking, "Bureaucrats, Businessmen, and Foreign Trade: The Origins of the United States Chamber of Commerce," *Business History Review* 52, no. 3, *Corporate Liberalism* (Autumn 1978): 321–41.

24. Opensecrets.org, Center for Responsible Politics, "Stats at a Glance," http://www.opensecrets.org/overview/index.php.

25. Opensecrets.org, Center for Responsible Politics, "Most Expensive Races," http://www.opensecrets.org/overview/topraces.php.

26. BarackObama.com, "Ethics," November 10, 2007, http://www.barackobama.com/issues/ethics/ (accessed August 11, 2008).

27. LEAnet alert, December 11, 2007, www.theleanet.com.

28. American Veterinary Medical Association, "News," March 1, 2004, http://www.avma.org/onlnews/javma/mar04/040301j.asp (accessed August 11, 2008).

29. Glen Justice and Aron Pilhofer, "Unwavering Bush Ally Acts Quickly on Court Choices," *New York Times*, November 14, 2005, http://www.nytimes.com/2005/11/14/politics/politicsspecial1/14progress.html?pagewanted=print (accessed August 11, 2008).

30. Jeffrey Birnbaum, "Returning to the Game He Started," Washington Post, November 28, 2004, http://www.washingtonpost.com/wp-dyn/articles/A18417-2004Nov28.html (accessed August 11, 2008).

31. Richard L. Hall and Frank W. Wayman, "Buying Time: Moneyed Interests and the Mobilization of Bias in Congressional Committees," American Political Science Review 84, no. 3 (1990): 802.

32. R. Kenneth Godwin and Barry J. Seldon, "What Corporations Really Want from Government," http://72.14.253.104/search?q=cache:nartLRj_rsYJ:www.politicalscience.uncc.edu/godwink/RecentPublications/What%2520Corporations%2520Really%2520Want%2520from%2520Government.pdf+%22what+corporations+really+want+from+government%22&hl=en&ct=clnk&cd=1&gl=us (accessed August 11, 2008).

33. Godwin and Seldon, "What Corporations Really Want from Government."

CHAPTER THIRTEEN

1. Shawn Reese, Congressional Research Service Report for Congress, *Fiscal Year 2005 Homeland Security Grant Program: State Allocations and Issues for Congressional Oversight* (Washington, DC: Congressional Research Service, 2004). See also "FY 2010 Homeland Security Grant Program," Federal Emergency Management Agency, http://www.fema.gov.

2. These figures are based on spending figures found in "Homeland Security and Grant Program, Guidance and Application Kit," Department of Homeland Security, 27; and population figures found in "Annual Estimates of the Resident Population for the United States, Regions, and Puerto Rico," U.S. Census Bureau, January 26, 2009. See also Kathleen Hunter, "Per Capita, New Anti-terror Funds Still Favor Wyoming," Pew Research Center, December 16, 2004, http://www.stateline.org.

3. The remaining 60 percent of the funds are distributed by formula according to population.

4. "U.S. Not 'Well-prepared' for Terrorism," December 5, 2005, http://www.cnn.com.

5. Judy Holland, "Anti-terror Funding open to 'Pork Barrel' Politics," *Milwaukee Journal Sentinel*, August 22, 2004, 18A.

6. Kathleen Hunter, "Budget Would Revise Anti-terrorism Funding," Pew Research Center, February 8, 2005, http://www.stateline.org.

7. Veronique de Rugy, "Homeland-Security Scuffle," *National Review*, October 15, 2004, http://www.nationalreview.com/comment/rugy200410150840.asp.

8. The Homeland Security Grant Program, however, has gradually reduced the total amount of money distributed through SHSP and has increased the amount of anti-terrorism funding awarded through another of its programs, the Urban Areas Security Initiative, which is

relatively free to distribute federal anti-terrorism funding to the cities that need it most. U.S. Department of Homeland Security, Office of Grants and Training, *Overview: FY 2007 Homeland Security Grant Program*, January 5, 2007.

9. Nonvoting members come from the District of Columbia, American Samoa, Guam, Puerto Rico, and the Virgin Islands.

10. At the nation's founding, state legislatures appointed senators to office. In 1913, however, the states ratified the Seventeenth Amendment, which required the direct election of senators. Representatives in the House have always been popularly elected.

11. Max Farrand, ed., *The Records of the Federal Convention of 1787* (New Haven: Yale University Press, 1966), 151.

12. David Mayhew, *The Electoral Connection* (New Haven: Yale University Press, 1974).

13. "Lobbying: Top Spenders," Open Secrets: Center for Responsive Politics, http://www.opensecrets.org /lobby/top.php?showYear=2008&indexType=s.

14. Mayhew, *The Electoral Connection*, 16.

15. Brandice Canes-Wrone, David Brady, and John Cogan, "Out of Step, Out of Office: Electoral Accountability and House Members' Voting," *American Political Science Review* 96, no. 1 (2002): 127–40.

16. Edmund Burke, "Speech to the Electors of England" in *The Works of the Right Honorable Edmund Burke*, vol. 2. (New York: Oxford University Press, 1774 [1907]).

17. Based on figures from fiscal year 2000. Congressional Budget Office, "Federal Spending on the Elderly and Children," July 2000, http://cbo.gov/ftpdocs/23xx /doc2300/fsec.pdf.

18. Gary Jacobson, *The Politics of Congressional Elections*, 6th ed. (New York: Longman, 2003).

19. Brody Mullins, "Growing Role for Lobbyists: Raising Funds for Lawmakers," *Wall Street Journal*, January 27, 2006, 1.

20. Kenneth Goldstein, *Interest Groups, Lobbying, and Participating in America* (New York: Cambridge University Press, 1999); John Mark Hansen, *Gaining Access: Congress and the Farm Lobby, 1919–1981* (Chicago: University of Chicago Press, 1991).

21. Keith T. Poole and Thomas Romer, "Ideology, 'Shirking,' and Representation," *Public Choice* 77 (1993): 185–96.

22. Kenneth N. Bickers and Robert M. Stein, "The Congressional Pork Barrel in a Republican Era," *Journal of Politics* 62, no. 4 (November 2000): 1070–86.

23. For more on descriptive or numerical representation, see Jane Mansbridge, "Should Blacks Represent Blacks and Women Represent Women? A Contingent 'Yes,'" *Journal of Politics* 61, no. 3 (August 1999): 628–57.

24. Michele Swers, *The Difference Women Make* (Chicago: University of Chicago Press, 2002).

25. Because of its small population, Alaska has just one House representative.

26. Daniel Gitterman, *Boosting Paychecks: The Politics of Supporting America's Working Poor* (Washington, DC: Brookings Institution, 2009).

27. For one study of the role of information in Congress, see Keith Krehbiel, *Information and Legislative Organization* (Ann Arbor: University of Michigan Press, 1992).

28. Kenneth Shepsle, *The Giant Jigsaw Puzzle: Democratic Committee Assignments in the Modern House* (Chicago: University of Chicago Press, 1978).

29. Robert C. Albright, "Two-Stage Battle, If Necessary, Planned for Urban Affairs Unit," *Washington Post, Times Herald*, January 24, 1962, A2; Russell Baker, "Kennedy Accused on Urban Moves: G.O.P Sees Racism in Plan to Create Cabinet Post," *New York Times*, January 26, 1962, 14; Richard L. Lyons, "House Kills Urban Plan by 262-150." *Washington Post, Times Herald*, February 22, 1962, A1; Chalmers M. Roberts, "Anguish in Urban Affairs: Kennedy Nudges GOP into Own Booby Trap," *Washington Post, Times Herald*, January 26, 1962, A2; and House of Representatives Committee on Rules, "Committee on Rules: A History," http://www.rules.house.gov/archives/rules_history .htm.

30. Gary Cox and Mathew McCubbins, *Setting the Agenda: Responsible Party Government in the U.S. House of Representatives* (New York: Cambridge University Press, 2005).

31. See, for example, Keith Krehbiel, "Where's the Party?" *British Journal of Political Science* 23 (1993): 235–66.

32. Since the Civil War, southern politicians retained strong loyalties to the Democratic Party. Ideologically, however, they had more in common with northern Republicans. Beginning in the 1970s, over a century after the Civil War's end, southern Democrats began to abandon their former partisan commitments in order to join the ranks of the Republican Party.

33. Nolan McCarty, Keith Poole, and Howard Rosenthal, *Polarized America: The Dance of Ideology and Unequal Riches* (Cambridge, MA: MIT Press, 2005).

34. William A. Galston, "The GOP's Grassroots Obstructionists," *Washington Post*, May 16, 2010.

35. Figures are available at http://people-press.org/party-identification-trend/.

36. For a profile of congressional staffers in 2007, see "The Hill People 2007: A Special Report," *National Journal*, June 23, 2007.

37. By declaring war, Congress asserts that a state of war currently exists. By authorizing war, Congress typically

grants the president the authority to decide whether to respond militarily to a perceived foreign crisis.

38. Louis Fisher, *Congressional Abdication on War and Spending* (College Station: Texas A&M University Press, 2000), 65.

39. William Howell and Douglas Kriner, "Political Elites and Public Support for War," University of Chicago typescript, 2007.

40. William Howell and Jon Pevehouse, *While Dangers Gather: Congressional Checks on Presidential War Power* (Princeton, NJ: Princeton University Press, 2007). See also William Howell and Jon Pevehouse, "When Congress Stops Wars," *Foreign Affairs* 86, no. 5 (2007): 95–108.

41. Barbara Sinclair, *Unorthodox Lawmaking: New Legislative Processes in the U.S. Congress* (Washington, D.C.: CQ Press, 1997).

42. It is possible to bypass the Rules Committee. With a two-thirds vote, members can send a bill directly to the floor, where only 40 minutes of debate are allowed and all amendments are forbidden. To enact the bill under this fast-track procedure, though, supporters must garner the support of two-thirds of the House. Typically, only those bills that are either trivial in importance or that enjoy widespread support are thus considered.

43. The Senate also offers its members several other ways of prolonging the legislative process. For instance, senators can place anonymous holds on bills, which prevent them from moving forward. Additionally, senators have more opportunities to introduce amendments to bills than do representatives in the House, where the party leadership exercises more control over deliberations.

44. It is worth noting, though, that floors have some powers to check such tendencies—for example, the discharge petition allows a majority of floor members to force a committee to release a bill for a floor vote.

45. Norman Ornstein, Thomas Mann, and Michael Malbin, *Vital Statistics on Congress, 1995–1996* (Washington, DC: CQ Press, 1996), 169. For more on the filibuster, see Gregory Wawro and Eric Schickler, *Filibuster: Obstruction and Lawmaking in the U.S. Senate* (Princeton, NJ: Princeton University Press, 2006).

46. The two exceptions: Franklin Pierce, who ranks near the bottom of most ratings of presidential greatness; and Andrew Johnson, who ranks no higher and whom the House went on to impeach. See Lyn Ragsdale, *Vital Statistics on the Presidency* (Washington, DC: CQ Press, 1998), 27–28.

47. "Self-Executing Rules Reported by the House Committee on Rules," Walter J. Oleszek, December 21, 2006, http://usgovinfo.about.com/library/PDF/self _executing.pdf.

48. Don Wolfensberger, "Bimonthly Column on Procedural Politics," June 19, 2006, http://www .wilsoncenter.org/index.cfm?topic_id=1412&fuseaction =topics.publications&doc_id=190504&group_id =180829.

49. Adam Nagourney, "Political Maneuvering and Public Opinion," *New York Times*, March 19, 2010.

50. Rachel L. Swarns, "Split over Immigration Reflects Nation's Struggle," *New York Times*, March 29, 2006, A17; Robert Pear, "Bush Ties Drop in Illegal Immigration to His Policies," *New York Times*, April 10, 2007, A18; and Robert Pear, "Many Employers See Flaws as Immigration Bill Evolves," *New York Times*, May 27, 2007, 1.23.

51. T. W. Farnam, "Obama Pitches Immigration Policy," *Wall Street Journal*, September 10, 2010.

52. "Remarks by the President at Cinco de Mayo Reception," President Barack Obama, May 5, 2010.

53. Eric Zimmerman, "Obama Uses Cinco De Mayo to Call for Immigration Reform," *The Hill*, May 5, 2010.

54. Julia Preston, "Grass Roots Roared, and an Immigration Plan Fell," *New York Times*, June 10, 2007, A.1.

55. Jeff Zeleny, "Immigration Bill Prompts Some Menacing Responses," *New York Times*, June 28, 2007, A18.

56. David Rogers and Sarah Lueck, "Immigration Bill Might Be Dead After Failing Pivotal Senate Test; Barring White House Push, Political Climate May Halt Overhaul Effort for Now," *Wall Street Journal*, June 8, 2007, A3; David Rogers, "Politics and Economics: White House Courts Kyl to Back Immigration Bill," *Wall Street Journal*, April 30, 2007, A4.

57. June Kronholz and Sarah Lueck, "State of the Union: Immigration Proposals Reverse Party Loyalties," *Wall Street Journal*, January 24, 2007, A2.

58. Carl Hulse, "An Immigration Compromise Divides Republican Senators," *New York Times*, June 7, 2007, A31.

59. Jonathan Weisman, "Immigration Bill Dies in Senate; Bipartisan Compromise Fails to Satisfy the Right or the Left," *Washington Post*, June 29, 2007, A1.

60. Peter Baker, "Bush May Be out Of Chances for a Lasting Domestic Victory," *Washington Post*, June 29, 2007, A1.

61. Sandy Streeter, CRS Report 97-684, *The Congressional Appropriations Process: An Introduction* (Washington, DC: Congressional Research Service, 2006), 4.

62. Allen Schick and Felix LoStracco, *The Federal Budget: Politics, Policy, and Progress* (Washington, DC: Brookings Institution, 2000), 235, 236, 238.

63. See http://appropriations.senate.gov/budgetprocess.cfm.

64. Streeter, *The Congressional Appropriations Process*, 17.

65. See Taxpayer's for Common Sense, http://www .taxpayer.net.

66. Bennet Roth and Patrick Brendel, "Texas Reaps $2.2 Billion in Earmarks," *Houston Chronicle*, March 23,

2008, http://www.chron.com/disp/story.mpl
/headline/metro/5641050.html.

67. See http://appropriations.house.gov.

68. This database is available at http://earmarks.omb.gov.

69. Quote can be found online at http://www.washington-post.com/wp-dyn/content/article/2009/03/11/AR2009031101499.html.

70. Streeter, *The Congressional Appropriations Process*, 14.

71. Linda Bilmes and Joseph E. Stiglitz. "The Iraq War Will Cost Us $3 Trillion, and Much More," *Washington Post*, March 9, 2008.

72. Joseph Stiglitz and Linda Bilmes, *The Three Trillion Dollar War: The True Cost of the Iraq Conflict* (New York: Norton, 2008).

CHAPTER FOURTEEN

1. "Obama: Victory Speech," *New York Times*, November 5, 2008.

2. "In Quotes: US Election Reaction," BBC, November 5, 2008. Available online at: http://news.bbc.co.uk/2/hi/americas/us_elections_2008/7710020.stm.

3. Interview with Oprah Winfrey, CNN, December 13, 2009.

4. See Richard Pious, *The Presidency* (New York: Longman, 1995).

5. For an analysis of the president's place in the American political system, see Charles O. Jones, *The Presidency in a Separated System* (Washington, DC: Brookings Institution, 1994).

6. See, for example, John Yoo. 2010. *Crisis and Command: A History of Executive Power from George Washington to George W. Bush* (New York: Kaplan; Steven Calabresi and Christopher Yoo, 2008), *The Unitary Executive: Presidential Power from Washington to Bush* (New Haven: Yale University Press).

7. See, for example, James Pfiffner. 2009. *Power Play: The Bush Presidency and the Constitution*. (Washington, DC: Brookings Institution).

8. The Twenty-second Amendment, a reaction to Franklin Roosevelt's four-term presidency, limited the president to two terms in office.

9. Technically, Lincoln suspended the writ of habeas corpus. A defendant can request a writ of habeas corpus, which is a court order that requires a government official to explain to a judge why an individual is incarcerated.

10. Roosevelt proposed that for every justice over the age of 70, the president could nominate one additional justice until the Supreme Court reached a maximum size of 15. The plan would have allowed Roosevelt to offset older, more conservative justices with those more likely to accommodate his proposals. For more on this "court

packing" plan, see Jeff Shesol, *Supreme Power: Franklin Roosevelt vs. the Supreme Court* (New York: Norton, 2010).

11. The scandal was so named because of the break-in at the Democratic National Committee's headquarters at the Watergate Hotel in Washington, D.C., on June 17, 1972. The president's aides were responsible for arranging the break-in, and the president engineered a cover-up designed to keep the truth from coming out. The discovery of that break-in prompted investigations that revealed a wide range of White House abuses of power, ultimately leading to Nixon's resignation in August 1974.

12. *Walker v. Cheney* (2002).

13. On different leadership styles, see Fred I. Greenstein, *The Presidential Difference: Leadership Style from FDR to George W. Bush* (Princeton, NJ: Princeton University Press, 2004).

14. For a skeptical view of the president's ability to change public opinion, see George Edwards, *On Deaf Ears: The Limits of the Bully Pulpit* (New Haven: Yale University Press, 2003).

15. Isaiah J. Poole, "Two Steps Up, One Step Down," *CQ Weekly*, January 9, 2006, 80.

16. Harold W. Stanley and Richard G. Niemi, *Vital Statistics on American Politics 2009–2010* (Washington, DC: CQ Press, 2009), 246–7.

17. Whether the bill was originally one of interest to the president or not, to become law both the Congress and the president must approve of the legislation.

18. Charles M. Cameron, *Veto Bargaining: Presidents and the Politics of Negative Power* (New York: Cambridge University Press, 2000).

19. "Senate Blocks Financing for F-22s," *New York Times*, July 21, 2009, http://thecaucus.blogs.nytimes.com/2009/07/21/senate-blocks-financing-for-f-22s/?scp=7&sq=F-22&st=Search.

20. William G. Howell, *Power Without Persuasion: The Politics of Direct Presidential Action* (Princeton, NJ: Princeton University Press, 2003).

21. For a summary of Bush's early faith-based initiatives, see Anne Farris, Richard Nathan, and David Wright. 2004. "The Expanding Administrative Presidency: George W. Bush and the Faith-Based Initiative," report issued by the Rockefeller Institute of Government, Albany, N.Y.

22. Craig Crawford, "Stubborner than a Donkey," *CQ Weekly*, May 28, 2007, 1638.

23. See Richard Neustadt, *Presidential Power and the Modern Presidents: The Politics of Leadership from Roosevelt to Reagan* (New York: Free Press, 1991).

24. U.S. Government Accountability Office, "Presidential-Signing Statements Accompanying the Fiscal Year 2006 Appropriations Acts," June 18, 2007,

http://www.gao.gov/decisions/appro/308603.pdf. The investigation looked at appropriations bills only. Of the 12 bills, the president questioned a total of 160 provisions in 11 of the bills. The investigation tracked 19 of these and found noncompliance on 6 of those 19.

25. *Rasul v. Bush* (2004); *al Odah v. United States* (2004); *Hamdi v. Rumsfeld* (2004).

26. Congress can also impeach other executive branch officials or members of the judiciary.

27. Tyler was the first vice president to assume the office of president, and his tenure was uncertain: the Constitution did not make it clear whether he should be an acting president until another was chosen or whether he was in fact president. A former Democrat, he was elected to the vice presidency as a member of the Whig party, but he soon antagonized the Whigs, leading to the resignation of his entire Cabinet and heated battles with Congress. After a series of controversial vetoes, an attempt was made to impeach him for misusing his power and not taking care to pass legislation fundamental to the government's operation. The failure of this attempt led to his censure by the Senate.

28. George Edwards, *At the Margins: Presidential Leadership of Congress* (New Haven: Yale University Press, 1990).

29. The exact figures are available at http://www.gallup .com/poll/113980/Gallup-Daily-Obama-Job-Approval .aspx.

30. Gary Jacobson, *A Divider, Not a Uniter: George W. Bush and the American People* (New York: Longman, 2006).

31. Samuel Kernell, *Going Public: New Strategies of Presidential Leadership*, 3rd ed. (Washington, DC: CQ Press, 1997).

32. The bill achieved the $350 billion figure by assuming that some tax cuts would be phased out after a few years, but it was widely expected that Congress, fearful of appearing to increase taxes, would vote to extend the cuts when the time came, resulting in a cost closer to $1 trillion. This made the achievement even more remarkable given rising concerns over deficits.

33. Patricia Heidotting Conley, *Presidential Mandates: How Elections Shape the National Agenda* (Chicago: University of Chicago Press, 2001).

34. Chris Cillizza, "The White House Cheat Sheet: The Obama Mandate," *Washington Post*, January 27, 2009. Available online at: http://voices.washingtonpost.com /thefix/cheat-sheet/white-house-cheat-sheet-pollin.html.

35. See John J. Coleman, "Unified Government, Divided Government, and Party Responsiveness," *American Political Science Review* 93, no. 4 (1999): 821–35, for an overview of literature on lawmaking during unified and divided government.

36. As was demonstrated in 2000, the presidential election is not technically a national election in which the candidate receiving the most popular votes nationally wins. Instead, it is 51 separate elections—each state and the District of Columbia—selecting electors to the Electoral College, and the candidate amassing a majority of electoral votes might not be the one who received a majority of the popular vote. The election is national in the sense that voters from around the country will be voting for president.

37. Although still distinctive from the presidential system, recent elections in Great Britain have had the appearance of presidential races, with the faces and words of the leading contenders for prime minister plastered around the country, even though the population at large is unable to vote for these candidates.

38. For a useful historical timeline on U.S. health care reform, see the health timeline at: http://www.nytimes .com/interactive/2009/07/19/us/politics/20090717 _HEALTH_TIMELINE.html.

39. For a complete discussion of these programs, see Chapter 17.

40. "Remarks by the President to a Joint Session of Congress on Health Care," White House, Office of the Press Secretary, September 9, 2009. Available online at: http://www.whitehouse.gov/the_press_office/remarks- by-the-president-to-a-joint-session-of-congress-on- health-care/.

41. "House Passes Health Care Reform Bill," CNN, November 8, 2009. Available online at: http://www .cnn.com/2009/POLITICS/11/07/health.care/index .html.

42. "Obama Calls On Bloggers to Keep Health Care Pressure on Congress," Huffington Post, July 20, 2009. Available online at: http://www.huffingtonpost.com /2009/07/20/obama-calls-on-bloggers-t_n_241570 .html.

43. "With No Jobs, Plenty of Time for Tea Party," Kate Zernike, *New York Times*, March 27, 2010.

44. David M. Herszenhorn and Sheryl G. Stolberg, "Obama Rallies House Democrats," *New York Times*, November 7, 2009. Available online at: http:// prescriptions.blogs.nytimes.com/2009/11/07 /obamas-in-the-house/?scp=5&sq=obama%20health %20care%20personal%20appeal%20house%20of %20representatives&st=cse.

45. Representative Tammy Baldwin of Wisconsin expresses this sentiment in these remarks: "I think one of the challenges I've had as I've moved from working on domestic issues to now having a vote and a say on international issues is, I would say, a frustration with the limits to your information sources. If I look at almost any

domestic issues imaginable, I can easily obtain information from a variety of perspectives and weigh the pros and cons of most policy decisions. It's much more difficult on a wide range of international issues, be they trade issues, global environmental issues, issues of war and peace. The information that's easiest to obtain is usually through the filter of the State Department, the military, or an agency of the United States government. It has been a real challenge for me to try to get information from a broader array of resources." *Badger Herald*, July 8, 1999, University of Wisconsin.

46. John P. Burke, *The Institutional Presidency: Organizing and Managing the White House from FDR to Clinton* (Baltimore: Johns Hopkins University Press, 2000).

47. Department of Defense, "News Transcript: Secretary Rumsfeld Town Hall Meeting in Kuwait," December 8, 2004, http://www.dod.mil/transcripts/2004 /tr20041208-secdef1761.html; Richard Tomkins, "Analysis: Bush Cheerleads Iraq, Rumsfeld," *Washington Times*, December 20, 2004, http://www.washtimes. com/upi-breaking/20041220-040901-4646r.htm; CNN, "Troops Put Thorny Questions to Rumsfeld," December 9, 2004, http://www.cnn.com/2004 /WORLD/meast/12/08/rumsfeld.troops/.

48. Charles O. Jones, "Clinton's Cabinet: Stability in Disorder," *PRG Report* 24, no. 1 (2001): 13–16.

49. One such list is available at http://www.glennbeck .com/content/articles/article/198/29391/.

50. Michael A. Fletcher and Brady Dennis, "Obama's Many Policy 'Czars' Draw Ire from Conservatives," *Washington Post*, September 16, 2009.

51. Fletcher and Dennis, "Obama's Many Policy 'Czars' Draw Ire from Conservatives," 19. See also Mimi Hall, "Number, Role of Obama's Policy 'Czars' Spark Debate," *USA Today*, September 30, 2009.

52. Like the secretaries of Cabinet departments, the president's appointments of the heads of the various EOP offices must be confirmed by the Senate.

53. James Carney and John F. Dickerson, "The Busiest Man in the White House," *Time*, April 22, 2001, Time Online Edition, http://www.time.com/time/nation /article/0,8599,107219,00.html.

CHAPTER FIFTEEN

1. *Citizens United v. Federal Election Commission*, 558 U.S. —(2010).

2. Jess Bravin, "Court Kills Limits on Corporate Politicking," *Wall Street Journal*, January 22, 2010. Web. <http://online.wsj.com/article/SB10001 4240527487036992045750169429300090152 .html>.

3. Barack Obama, "Remarks of President Barack Obama—As Prepared for Delivery," Address to Joint Session of Congress, February 24, 2009.

4. David D. Kirkpatrick, "Courts Roll Back Limits on Election Spending," *New York Times*, January 8, 2010. Web. <http://www.nytimes.com./2010/01/09/us /politics/09donate.html>.

5. Keith Perine and Alex Knott, "Court Loosens Campaign Spending Law," *CQ Weekly* (2010): 238–239. *CQ Weekly*. Web. 7 Feb. 2010. <http: //library.cqpress.com/cqweekly/weeklyreport111- 000003283407>.

6. Robert A. Dahl, "Decision-Making in a Democracy: The Supreme Court as a National Policy-Maker," *Journal of Public Law* 6, no. 2 (1957): 279–95. Quote on p. 293.

7. These are the last available data on public approval ratings for the judiciary. Approval ratings for Congress and the president remained reasonably constant through June 2010. See http://www.realclearpolitics.com /polls/.

8. When it comes to the judicial branch as a whole, Americans hold similarly positive views. Over the past 25 years, a majority of Americans have reported a "great deal" or "fair amount" of confidence in the courts. From 1973 to 2005, levels of public trust ranged from a low of 63 percent in 1976 to a high of 80 percent in 1999. Confidence in the judiciary was consistently higher than trust in either the executive branch or the legislative branch during the same period. See Joseph Carroll, "Slim Majority of Americans Approve of the Supreme Court: Approval Rating Still Lower Following Partial-Birth Abortion Ban Earlier This Year," *Gallup News Service*, September 26, 2007, http://www.gallup.com /poll/28798/Slim-Majority-Americans-Approve- Supreme-Court.aspx.

9. See Judicial Facts and Figures, http://www.uscourts. gov/uscourts/Statistics/JudicialFactsAndFigures/2008 /Table101.pdf.

10. "Workload of the Courts," *Third Branch* 39, no. 1 (January 2007), http://www.uscourts.gov/ttb/2007-01 /workload/index.html. Figure for 2009 available at http://otd.oyez.org/cases/2009.

11. U.S. Library of Congress, Federal Research Division, "Country Studies," http://lcweb2.loc.gov/frd/cs/.

12. Most recent data available at http://www. supremecourt.gov/publicinfo/year-end/2009year- endreport.pdf.

13. Strictly speaking, appellate court rulings in one circuit are not binding for appellate courts in other circuits. As a result, different circuits can produce different appellate rulings on similar cases.

14. If the chief justice is part of the minority, then the justice in the majority who has the most seniority makes the assignment.

15. If a justice recuses himself or herself from a case, a majority can be achieved with less than five supporters.

16. Timothy L. Hall, ed., *The U.S. Legal System* (Pasadena, CA: Salem, 2004).

17. For a sampling of the arguments made for and against jury trials, see Jeffrey Abramson, *We, the Jury: The Jury System and the Ideal of Democracy* (Cambridge, MA: Harvard University Press, 2000); William Dwyer, *In the Hands of the People: The Trial Jury's Origins, Triumphs, Troubles, and Future in American Democracy* (New York: St. Martin's Griffin, 2004); Stephen Adler, *The Jury: Trial and Error in the American Courtroom* (New York: Times Books, 1994).

18. Frank Clifford, "Utility to Pay $333 Million to Settle Suit," *Los Angeles Times*, July 3, 1996, 3.

19. *Abbott Laboratories v. Gardner*, 387 U.S. 136 (1967), at 148.

20. George Fisher, *Plea Bargaining's Triumph: A History of Plea Bargaining in America.* (Stanford, CA: Stanford University Press, 2003), 222.

21. See Judicial Facts and Figures, http://www.uscourts .gov/judicialfactsfigures/2006.html. During the same period, fully 7.7 million criminal cases were filed in state trial courts.

22. See Judicial Facts and Figures, http://www.uscourts.gov /uscourts/Statistics/JudicialFactsAndFigures/2008 /Table501.pdf.

23. See Judicial Facts and Figures, http://www.uscourts.gov /uscourts/Statistics/JudicialFactsAndFigures/2008 /Table401.pdf. For data between 1998 and 2004, see table 6.1 at http://www.uscourts.gov/judicialfactsfigures /2006.html. During the same period, nearly 11 million civil cases were filed per year in state trial courts. State trial court data include limited and general jurisdiction courts. Sources: *Judicial Business of the United States Courts*, vols. 2001–2005 (Washington, DC: Administration of the United States Courts); *Examining the Work of State Courts: A National Perspective from the Court Statistics Project*, vols. 1999–2006 (Washington, DC: Administration of the United States Courts), http://www. ncsconline.org/D_Research/csp/CSP_Main_Page.html.

24. Richard A. Posner, *The Federal Courts: Challenge and Reform* (Cambridge, MA: Harvard University Press, 1996), 59–61.

25. Figures are in constant 1983 dollars. Source: Robert A. Kagan, "American Lawyers, Legal Cultures, and Adversarial Legalism," in Lawrence M. Friedman and Harry N. Scheiber, *Legal Culture and the Legal Profession* (Boulder: Westview, 1996), 13–14.

26. These figures are in current dollars. Office of Management and Budget, "Historical Tables, Budget of the United States Government, FY 2011," 77, 83, available online at http://www.gpoaccess.gov/usbudget/fy11 /pdf/hist.pdf.

27. David M. O'Brien, "The Dynamics of the Judicial Process," in David M. O'Brien, ed., *Judges on Judging: Views from the Bench* (Chatham, NJ: Chatham House, 1997), 34.

28. Quoted in O'Brien, "The Dynamics of the Judicial Process," 34.

29. Quoted in Jethro K. Lieberman, *The Litigious Society* (New York: Basic Books, 1981), xi.

30. Quoted in Lieberman, *The Litigious Society*, 8.

31. "President Calls for Medical Liability Reform," White House Press Release, January 16, 2003, http://www .whitehouse.gov/news/releases/2003/01/20030116-1. html.

32. "President Outlines Path for Lasting Prosperity in Wednesday Speech," White House Press Release, April 21, 2004, http://www.whitehouse.gov/news/releases/ 2004/04/20040421-5.html.

33. Kagan, "American Lawyers, Legal Cultures, and Adversarial Legalism," 8–10.

34. The only notable difference was the rate of tort filings, which was much lower in Britain. The British filed 1,200 tort claims—which concern personal injuries to one's property, body, or rights—for every million of the British population, while Americans filed 3,750 suits per million and Germany, 3,278. See Basil S. Markensinis, *Foreign Law and Comparative Methodology: A Subject and a Thesis* (Oxford: Hart, 1997), 452. Herbert M. Kritzer similarly shows that the British are no less likely to litigate than Americans, except in cases of personal injury torts. Herbert M. Kritzer, "Courts, Justice, and Politics in England," in Herbert Jacob et al., eds., *Courts, Law, and Politics in Comparative Perspective* (New Haven: Yale University Press, 1996), 125–35.

35. Catherine Elliot and Frances Quinn, *English Legal System*, 7th ed. (Harlow, UK: Pearson Education, 2006), 474. See also Martin Partington, *Introduction to the English Legal System*, 3rd ed. (Oxford: Oxford University Press, 2006), 206–07.

36. John Ferejohn and Barry Weingast, "A Positive Theory of Statutory Interpretation," *International Review of Law and Economics* 12 (1992): 265.

37. Averages calculated from data found in Sheldon Goldman, Elliot Slotnick, Gerard Gryski, and Sara Schiavoni, "W. Bush's Judiciary: The First Term Record," *Judicature* 88, no. 6 (May–June 2005): 269, 274.

38. Jeffrey Segal, Lee Epstein, Charles Cameron, and Harold Spaeth, "Ideological Values and the Votes of

U.S. Supreme Court Justices Revisited," *Journal of Politics* 57, no. 3 (1995): 812–23.

39. Jeffrey Segal, "Separation-of-Powers Games in the Positive Theory of Congress and Courts," *American Political Science Review* 91 (1997): 33.

40. Edwin Meese III and Todd Gaziano, "Restoring the Proper Role of the Courts," *Issues 2006: The Candidate's Briefing Book* (Washington, DC: Heritage Foundation, 2006), http://www.heritage.org/research/features /issues/index.cfm.

41. Adam Cohen, "Last Term's Winner at the Supreme Court: Judicial Activism," *New York Times*, July 9, 2007.

42. See Lee Epstein and Jack Knight, *The Choices Justices Make* (Washington, DC: CQ Press, 1998); Forrest Maltzman, James Spriggs, and Paul Wahlbeck, "Strategy and Judicial Choice: New Institutionalist Approaches to Supreme Court Decision Making," in Cornell W. Clayton and Howard Gillman, eds., *Supreme Court Decision-Making: New Institutional Approaches* (Chicago: University of Chicago Press, 1999).

43. Abner Greene, *Understanding the 2000 Election* (New York: New York University Press, 2001).

44. Greene, *Understanding the 2000 Election.*

45. Greene, *Understanding the 2000 Election.*

46. Jeffrey A. Segal and Harold J. Spaeth, "The Influence of Stare Decisis on the Votes of United States Supreme Court Justices," *American Journal of Political Science* 40, no. 4 (1996): 971–1003.

47. Jeffrey A. Segal and Harold J. Spaeth, *The Supreme Court and the Attitudinal Model Revisited* (New York: Cambridge University Press, 2002), 171.

48. Segal and Spaeth, *The Supreme Court and the Attitudinal Model Revisited*, 172–74.

49. See, for example, Richard Z. Chesnoff, "Europe Worries as U.S. Re-Counts," *Daily News*, November 12, 2000; "The Nation's Mood: Get It Resolved, but Get It Right; Americans Express Faith in the Electoral System, but Many Say, 'We Need to Move On,'" *Grand Rapids Press*, November 12, 2000.

50. Terrence Hunt, "Election Impasse 'Nothing to Worry About,' Clinton Tells Putin," *Star-Ledger*, November 15, 2000, 11.

51. For more on the solicitor general, see Rebecca Mae Salokar, *The Solicitor General: The Politics of Law* (Philadelphia: Temple University Press, 1992).

52. Lincoln Caplan, *The Tenth Justice: The Solicitor General and the Rule of Law* (New York: Knopf, 1987), 295.

53. William Howell and Faisal Ahmed, 2010. "Voting for the President: The Supreme Court during War," University of Chicago Typescript.

54. David G. Savage, *Guide to the U.S. Supreme Court*, 4th ed., vol. 2 (Washington, DC: CQ Press, 2004), 809.

55. See Chapter 6 of William Howell, *Power Without Persuasion: The Politics of Direct Presidential Action* (Princeton, NJ: Princeton University Press, 2003).

56. Decades later, the U.S. government would officially apologize for the internment of Japanese Americans and pay upward of $1 billion in reparations to their families. In 1998, President Bill Clinton selected Fred Korematsu as a recipient of the Presidential Medal of Freedom.

57. Timothy Johnson and Andrew Martin, "The Public's Conditional Response to Supreme Court Decisions," *American Political Science Review* 92 (1998): 299–309; Jennifer Hochschild, *The New American Dilemma: Liberal Democracy and School Desegregation* (New Haven: Yale University Press, 1984).

58. Data available at Judges and Judgeships, http://www.uscourts.gov/JudgesAndJudgeships/Viewer.aspx?doc= /uscourts/JudgesJudgeships/docs/apptsbypres.pdf.

59. Goldman et al., "W. Bush's Judiciary," 269.

60. Goldman et al., "W. Bush's Judiciary." See also Harold Stanley and Richard Niemi, *Vital Statistics on American Politics 2009–2010* (Washington, DC: CQ Press, 2009), 270. As of this writing, information on Barack Obama's appointments are not yet available.

61. The ABA refused to give Thomas a "well-qualified" rating.

62. "Hearing of the Senate Judiciary Committee on the Nomination of Clarence Thomas to the Supreme Court," Electronic Text Center, University of Virginia Library, October 11, 1991, http://etext.lib.virginia. edu.

63. Seven justices who were confirmed nonetheless declined to serve, the most recent being Roscoe Conkling in 1882. Data available online at http://www.senate.gov/pagelay-out/reference/nominations/Nominations.htm.

64. Karen O'Connor, Alixandra Yanus, and Linda Mancillas Patterson, "Where Have All the Interest Groups Gone? An Analysis of Interest Group Participation in Presidential Nominations to the Supreme Court of the United States," in Allan Cigler and Burdett Loomis, eds., *Interest Group Politics*, 7th ed. (Washington, DC: CQ Press, 2007).

65. Manuel Miranda, "The Original Borking: Lessons from a Supreme Court Nominee's Defeat," *Wall Street Journal*, August 24, 2005, http://www.opinionjournal. com/nextjustice/?id=110007149.

66. Transcript of Obama-Sotomayor announcement, May 26, 2009. Available online at: http://www.cnn.com /2009/POLITICS/05/26/obama.sotomayor.transcript /index.html.

67. Sonia Sotomayor, "A Latina Judge's Voice," University of California, Berkeley, School of Law, 26 Oct. 2001.

Available online at: <http://berkeley.edu/news/media/releases/2009/05/26_sotomayor.shtml>.

68. Seth Stern and Keith Perine, "Sotomayor a Steady Hand at Hearings," *CQ Weekly* (2009): 1712–1713. *CQ Weekly*. Web. 7 Feb. 2010. Available online at: http://library.cqpress.com/cqweekly/weeklyreport111-000003170512.

CHAPTER SIXTEEN

1. Elizabeth Becker and Elaine Sciolino, "A Nation Challenged: Homeland Security; A New Federal Office Opens Amid Concern That Its Head Won't Have Enough Power," *New York Times*, October 9, 2001, B11.

2. Bill Miller, "Ridge Lacks Power to Do His Job, Says Panetta at Hearing; Cabinet Rank, Budget Clout Urged," *Washington Post*, April 18, 2002, A19.

3. Having created the department, the work of Congress and the president was not complete. New crises would bring new reforms. In the aftermath of Katrina, Congress and the president enacted the Post-Katrina Emergency Reform Act. Signed into law by President Bush on October 4, 2006, the act created new leadership positions, revamped FEMA, and reallocated functions to different parts of the department. For more on these changes, see: http://www.dhs.gov/xabout/structure/gc_1169243598416.shtm.

4. Binyamin Appelbaum, "On Finance Reform Bill, Lobbying Shifts to Regulations," *New York Times*, June 26, 2010.

5. Cornelius Kerwin, *Rulemaking: How Government Agencies Write Law and Make Policy* (Washington, DC: CQ Press, 2003).

6. The FCC adopted its three-prong definition of obscenity from a 1973 U.S. Supreme Court case, *Miller v. California*.

7. FCC rules can be found at http://ecfr.gpoaccess.gov/cgi/t/text/text-idx?c=ecfr&tpl=/ecfrbrowse/Title47/47tab_02.tpl.

8. Jess Bravin, "Court Backs Fines for On-Air Expletives," *Wall Street Journal*, April 29, 2009.

9. Joan Biskupic, "High Court Hears FCC Obscenity Case," *USA Today*, November 4, 2008.

10. Some of the increase in the length of the *Federal Register* can be explained by the introduction of stricter requirements for publication of final rules. In 1973, the Administrative Committee of the Federal Register decided that every rule must include a summary of its subject matter in its preamble. As of 1977, the preamble of a rule must also include a summary of public comments about the rule as well as the agency's answers to questions raised by the public.

11. Federal Communications Commission, Order on Reconsideration, May 31, 2006.

12. "FCC Reaffirms Its Indecency Fine for CBS," *Wall Street Journal*, June 1, 2006; "FCC Rebuffs Second CBS Appeal for Super 'Wardrobe Malfunction,'" *Houston Chronicle*, June 1, 2006.

13. James Fesler, "The Higher Public Service in Western Europe," in Ralph Clark Chandler, ed., *A Centennial History of the American Administrative State* (New York: Free Press, 1987).

14. Michael Nelson, "A Short, Ironic History of American National Bureaucracy," *Journal of Politics* 44, no. 3 (1982): 747–78. See also William Nelson, *The Roots of American Bureaucracy, 1830–1900* (Cambridge, MA: Harvard University Press, 1982).

15. Stephen Skowronek, *Building a New American State: The Expansion of National Administrative Capabilities, 1877–1920* (New York: Cambridge University Press, 1982).

16. The number of bureaucrats working for state and local government, however, has increased dramatically. At the local level, there were approximately 3 million bureaucrats in 1946. By 2003, that number climbed to upward of 14 million. During the same period, state bureaucrats grew from less than 1 million to over 5 million. Source: U.S. Bureau of the Census, *Historical Statistics of the United States: Colonial Times to 1970* (Washington, DC: Government Printing Office, 1975); *Statistical Abstract of the United States, 2006* (Washington, DC: GPO, 2006).

17. "About the Commission," Financial Crisis Inquiry Commission, http://www.fcic.gov/about/

18. All in all, the 2006–2007 edition of the *U.S. Government Manual* lists 110 independent agencies and government corporations. However, the actual number may be larger than 110. It is particularly difficult to determine the number of government corporations in operation; actual counts vary significantly. National Archives and Records Administration, Office of the Federal Register, *U.S. Government Manual 2006–2007* (Washington, DC: Government Printing Office, 2006), 361–554. Available online at, http://www.gpoaccess.gov/gmanual/browse-gm-06.html. See also General Accountability Office, *Government Corporations: Profiles of Existing Government Corporations*, GAO/GGD-96-14 (Washington, DC: General Accounting Office, 1995). Available online at: http://www.gao.gov/archive/1996/gg96014.pdf.

19. For a classic treatment of this topic, see Max Weber, "Bureaucracy," in H. H. Gerth and C. Wright Mills, eds., *From Max Weber: Essays in Sociology* (New York: Oxford University Press, 1946).

20. This idea was developed most fully by the Nobel Prize-winning economist George Stigler. See, for example, *Citizen and the State: Essays on Regulation* (Chicago: University of Chicago Press, 1975).

21. John Carey, "A Shot at Making Drugs Safer: Congress Could Revamp the Cozy Ties Between Drugmakers and the FDA. Will It?" *Business Week*, May 21, 2007, 71.

22. Address to the Nation, President Bush, New Orleans, Louisiana, September 15, 2005.

23. Mike Ahlers, "Criticism of FEMA's Katrina Response Deserved," CNN, April 14, 2006.

24. Michael Powell, "Boston's Big Dig Awash in Troubles: Leaks, Cost Overruns Plague Project," *Washington Post*, November 19, 2004, A3; Elizabeth Taurasi, "Boston's Big Dig: One of Engineering's Biggest Mistakes?" *Design News*, July 28, 2006, http://www.designnews.com/index.asp?layout=article&articleid=CA6357443.

25. See http://www.mountainstateslegal.org/mission.cfm.

26. Amy Zegart, *Flawed by Design: The Evolution of the CIA, JCS, and NSC* (Stanford, CA: Stanford University Press, 1999).

27. Zegart, *Flawed by Design*, 57.

28. Zegart, *Flawed by Design*, 159–60.

29. See Dana Milbank, "Bush Unveils 'Faith-Based' Initiative; Effort Will Team Agencies, Nonprofits on Social Issues," *Washington Post*, January 30, 2001, A1. Bush's work has carried over into the Obama administration. On February 5, 2009, Obama signed an executive order creating the White House Office of Faith-based and Neighborhood Partnerships. Headed by Joshua DuBois, a former associate pastor and adviser to the president, the new office is charged with enlisting the help of community groups in the economic recovery, addressing issues of family planning, and fostering interfaith dialogue with leaders and scholars around the world.

30. Appointment trends during Obama's presidency are available at http://projects.washingtonpost.com/2009/federal-appointments/.

31. Thomas Weko, *The Politicizing Presidency: The White House Personnel Office, 1948–1994* (Lawrence: University Press of Kansas, 1995); Terry Moe, "The Politicized Presidency," in John Chubb and Paul Peterson, eds., *New Directions in American Politics* (Washington, DC: Brookings Institution, 1985); David Lewis, *The Politics of Presidential Appointments: Political Control and Bureaucratic Performance* (Princeton, NJ: Princeton University Press, 2008).

32. Lewis, *The Politics of Presidential Appointments*.

33. Mark Johnson, "Rights Lawyer Faces New Senate Showdown," *Tampa Tribune*, March 14, 1999, 6; John C. Henry, "President Resubmits Nomination; Choice for Civil Rights Post Rejected by GOP," *Houston Chronicle*, March 6, 1999, 10.

34. Randall Mikkelsen, "Clinton Shuns the GOP in Naming Lee as Civil Rights Enforcer," *Star-Ledger*, August 4, 2000, 15; Christopher Marquis, "Clinton Sidesteps Senate to Fill Civil Rights Enforcement Job," *New York Times*, August 4, 2000, A14.

35. Dan Eggen, "Justice Department Fires 8th U.S. Attorney: Dispute over Death Penalty Cited," *Washington Post*, February 24, 2007, A2; Richard Schmitt, "Gonzales Gets Rare Rebuke from Bush," *Los Angeles Times*, March 15, 2007, A14.

36. Richard Serrano, "Gonzales to Admit Mistakes in Firings," *Los Angeles Times*, April 16, 2007, A1.

37. Robert Kuttner, "Gonzales Should Be Impeached," *Boston Globe*, March 24, 2007, A11.

38. See Lewis, *The Politics of Presidential Appointments*.

39. U.S. Office of Personnel Management, *Federal Civilian Workforce Statistics: The Fact Book, 2005 Edition*, http://www.opm.gov/FedData/factbook/index.asp; Government of Canada Privy Council Office, *Fifteenth Annual Report to the Prime Minister on the Public Service of Canada*, March 31, 2008, http://www.pco-bcp.gc.ca/index.asp?lang=eng&Page=information&Sub=publications&Doc=ar-ra/15-2008/table_e.htm.

40. See Donald J. Savoie, *Breaking the Bargain: Public Servants, Ministers, and Parliament* (Toronto: University of Toronto Press, 2003), 28, 136.

41. Lewis, *The Politics of Presidential Appointments*, 98.

42. Lewis, *The Politics of Presidential Appointments*, 20–21.

43. Lewis, *The Politics of Presidential Appointments*, 25.

44. Lewis, *The Politics of Presidential Appointments*, 218.

45. "NASA's Greedy Overseers," *New York Times*, April 30, 2006.

46. In 2007, the House passed the Whistleblower Protection Enhancement Act of 2007. It would have amended the original Whistleblower Protection Act by providing protections for national security, government contractor, and science-based agency whistleblowers and by enhancing the existing whistleblower protections for all federal employees. The bill, however, never passed the Senate. For more on the legislative history of this bill, see L. Paige Whitaker, "The Whistleblower Protection Act: An Overview," *Congressional Research Service*, March 12, 2007.

47. John Hart, *The Presidential Branch: Executive Office of the President from Washington to Clinton*, 2nd ed. (Chatham, NJ: Chatham House, 1995); Matthew Dickinson, *Bitter Harvest: FDR, Presidential Power, and the Growth of the Presidential Branch* (New York: Cambridge University Press, 1997).

48. Andrew Rudalevige, *Managing the President's Program: Presidential Leadership and Legislative Policy Formation* (Princeton, NJ: Princeton University Press, 2002).

49. Paul Light, *Thickening Government: Federal Hierarchy and the Diffusion of Accountability* (Washington, DC: Brookings Institution, 1995), 1.

50. David Lewis, *Presidents and the Politics of Agency Design: Political Insulation in the United States Government Bureaucracy, 1946–1997* (Stanford, CA: Stanford University Press, 2003); David Lewis, "The Adverse Consequences of the Politics of Agency Design for Presidential Management in the United States: The Relative Durability of Insulated Agencies," *British Journal of Political Science* 34 (2004): 377–404.

51. Norman J. Vig and Michael E. Kraft, "Environmental Policy from the Seventies to the Eighties," in Norman J. Vig and Michael E. Kraft, eds., *Environmental Policy in the 1980s: Reagan's New Agenda* (Washington, DC: CQ Press, 1984), 3–26.

52. Vig and Kraft, "Environmental Policy from the Seventies to the Eighties."

53. Michael E. Kraft, "A New Environmental Policy Agenda: The 1980 Presidential Campaign and Its Aftermath," in Vig and Kraft, *Environmental Policy in the 1980s*, 29–50.

54. Norman J. Vig, "The President or the Environment: Revolution or Retreat?" in Vig and Kraft, *Environmental Policy in the 1980s*, 77–95.

55. J. Clarence Davies, "Environmental Institutions and the Reagan Administration," in Vig and Kraft, *Environmental Policy in the 1980s*, 143–60.

56. Richard J. Tobin, "Revising the Clean Air Act: Legislative Failure and Administrative Success," in Vig and Kraft, *Environmental Policy in the 1980s*, 227–49.

57. Davies, "Environmental Institutions and the Reagan Administration."

58. Kraft, "A New Environmental Policy Agenda"; Henry C. Kenski and Margaret Corgan Kenski, "Congress Against the President: The Struggle over the Environment," in Vig and Kraft, *Environmental Policy in the 1980s*, 97–120.

59. B. Dan Wood, "Principals, Bureaucrats, and Responsiveness in Clean Air Enforcements," *American Political Science Review* 82, no. 1 (1988): 213–34; Kenski and Kenski, "Congress Against the President."

60. Wood, "Principals, Bureaucrats, and Responsiveness in Clean Air Enforcements."

61. Tobin, "Revising the Clean Air Act: Legislative Failure and Administrative Success."

62. Davies, "Environmental Institutions and the Reagan Administration."

63. Wood, "Principals, Bureaucrats, and Responsiveness in Clean Air Enforcements."

64. See Joel A. Mintz, "'Treading Water': A Preliminary Assessment of EPA Enforcement During the Bush II Administration," *Environmental Law Institute*, 2004, http://www.eli.org.

65. Eric Schaeffer, "Paying Less to Pollute: Environmental Enforcement Under the Bush Administration," Environmental Integrity Project, May 23, 2007, http://www.environmentalintegrity.org/pub443.cfm.

66. See, for example, Edward Felker, "EPA Rapidly Reversing Bush Policies," *Washington Times*, May 1, 2009; Charles Duhigg, "E.P.A. Vows Better Effort on Water," *New York Times*, October 15, 2009.

CHAPTER SEVENTEEN

1. Statement by Secretary Henry M. Paulson, Jr. on Treasury and Federal Housing Finance Agency Action to Protect Financial Markets and Taxpayers. Department of the Treasury, September 7, 2008. Available online at: http://www.treas.gov/press/releases/hp1129.htm. *Lehman folds with record $613 billion debt.* MarketWatch, September 15, 2008. Available online at: <http://www.marketwatch.com/story/lehman-folds-with-record-613-billion-debt?siteid=rss>. "WaMu Is Seized, Sold Off to J.P. Morgan, In Largest Failure in U.S. Banking History." *Wall Street Journal*, September 26, 2008. p. A1. "Misery math: Great Recession by the numbers." *MSNBC*. Associated Press, October 11, 2009. Available online at: <http://www.msnbc.msn.com/id/33266915>.

2. City of Philadelphia. City of Philadelphia's *Response to the Financial Crisis.*. November 6, 2008. Available online at: http://www.transformgov.org/assets/0/72/1412/723e5502-c3ac-4ee4-b3ce-0acc5a2fc8e4.pdf. New York State Governor's Office. *Governor Paterson Proposes Two-Year, $5.0 Billion Deficit Reduction Plan to Address Current-Year Budget Gap, Improve New York's Long-Term Fiscal Stability.* October 15, 2009. Available online at: http://www.state.ny.us/governor/press/press_1015091.html. Rich Connell, "Metrolink Cuts 10 Trains but Fares Stay Put," *Los Angeles Times*, January 9, 2010.

3. Vikas Bajaj, "Home Prices Fall for 10th Straight Month." *New York Times*, December 26, 2007. Available online at: http://www.nytimes.com/2007/12/26/business/27home-web.html.

4. The list of 2010 bank failures is available online at http://www.fdic.gov/bank/individual/failed/banklist.html.

5. Jonathan D. Glater, "Credit Crisis Cuts Bankruptcy Lifeline." *The New York Times*, October 19, 2008. Available online at: http://www.nytimes.com/2008/11/19/business/worldbusiness/19iht-bankruptcy.4.17967473.html sec.

6. Obama's Speech on the Economy, as recorded by Federal News Service. January 8, 2009. Transcript available online at: http://www.nytimes.com/2009/01/08/us/politics/08text-obama.html?pagewanted=1.

7. Faye Fiore, "Obama begins leading America in a new direction." *Los Angeles Times.* April 19, 2009. Available online at: http://www.latimes.com/news/nationworld/nation/la-na-obama-presidency19-2009apr19,0,6718107.story.

8. David Cho, "Summers Comes Out Swinging on Economic Policy." *The Washington Post.* October 13, 2009. Available online at: http://www.washingtonpost.com/wp-dyn/content/article/2009/10/12/AR2009101203019.html?hpid=topnews.

9. For further reading on this topic, see John Kingdon, *Agendas, Alternatives, and Public Policies*, 2nd ed. (New York: Harper Collins, 1995).

10. The full text of Johnson's University of Michigan speech on the Great Society is available in *Public Papers of the Presidents of the United States: Lyndon B. Johnson, 1963–64*, vol. 1, entry 357, 704–7 (Washington, DC: Government Printing Office, 1965).

11. *McCain's Speech on Energy Security and National Security.* Council on Foreign Relations, June 23, 2008. Available online at: http://www.cfr.org/publication/16626/.

12. In a 1988 ceremony honoring slain drug-enforcement officers, President Reagan drew vivid parallels between the War on Drugs and the American Revolution: "America's liberty was purchased with the blood of heroes [and] our release from the bondage of illegal drug use is being won at the same dear price. The battle is ultimately over what America is and what America will be. At our founding, we were promised the pursuit of happiness, not the myth of endless ecstasy from a vial of white poison." Public Papers of the President, "Remarks at a White House Ceremony Honoring Law Enforcement Officers Slain in the War on Drugs, April 19, 1988," http://www.presidency.ucsb.edu/ws/index.php?pid=35698&st=war+on+drugs&st1=.

13. In our own lives, we typically devise solutions after having recognized the existence of a specific problem. In politics, though, policy entrepreneurs often advocate on behalf of specific policies that they deem solutions to a wide variety of problems.

14. These figures come from the U.S. Department of Labor, http://www.bls.gov/fls/intl_unemployment_rates_monthly.pdf.

15. Figures available at http://www.bls.gov/cpi/cpid0712.pdf.

16. More specifically, GDP is the sum of all domestic consumption spending, investment spending, government spending, and the differences between export and import spending.

17. For the latest figures, see http://www.treasurydirect.gov/govt/reports/pd/feddebt/feddebt_ann2009.pdf.

18. The latest government figures are available at http://www.whitehouse.gov/omb/budget/Historicals/. For Bernanke quote, see Sewell Chan, "Bernanke Warns of 'Unsustainable' Debt," *New York Times*, June 9, 2010.

19. For a longer discussion of these latter issues, see http://www.cfr.org/publication/20758/confronting_the_chinaus_economic_imbalance.html.

20. For more on this debate, see http://ricks.foreignpolicy.com/posts/2010/03/02/debt_s_life_debt_s_what_all_the_people_say_big_squeeze_coming_from_china.

21. In the 1940s and 1950s, there persisted a lively debate among two of the century's greatest economists, Milton Friedman and John Maynard Keynes, about the relative benefits of fiscal and monetary policy.

22. Associated Press, "Bush Calls for $145 Billion Stimulus Package," January 18, 2008, http://www.msnbc.msn.com/id/22725498/.

23. The Social Security Act also provided grants-in-aid and health and welfare services to states. The most important elements of the act, though, concern the establishment of a retirement account, which we focus on here.

24. Individuals born after 1938 qualify for full benefits at the age of 67.

25. Figures available at http://www.ssa.gov/OACT/STATS/OASDIbenies.html.

26. Figures available at http://www.ssa.gov/cgi-bin/awards.cgi.

27. Figures available at http://ssa.gov/cgi-bin/awards.cgi.

28. Figures available at http://ssa.gov/OACT/STATS/table4a1.html.

29. Social Security Administration, *The 2007 Annual Report of the Board of Trustees of the Federal Old-Age and Survivors Insurance and Federal Disability Insurance Trust Funds*, http://www.ssa.gov/OACT/TR/TR07/.

30. White House Press Release, "Vice President and Chairman Thomas' Remarks at a Town Hall Meeting on Social Security," March 21, 2005, http://www.whitehouse.gov/news/releases/2005/03/20050321-14.html.

31. Michael A. Fletcher, "Bush Promotes Plan for Social Security," *Washington Post*, January 12, 2005, A4.

32. Tax rates available at http://www.ssa.gov/OACT/ProgData/taxRates.html. Maximum taxable earning available at http://www.ssa.gov/OACT/COLA/cbb.html#Series.

33. Figures available at http://www.census.gov/compendia/statab/2010/tables/10s0716.pdf.

34. Figures available at http://www.census.gov/hhes/www /poverty/data/threshld/thresh09.html.

35. These problems have led some scholars to conclude that poverty rates should be calculated on the basis of consumption patterns rather than reported income. See, for example, Bruce Meyer and James Sullivan, "Measuring the Well-Being of the Poor Using Income and Consumption," *Journal of Human Resources* 38 (2004): 1180–1220.

36. Figures available at http://www.census.gov/hhes/www /poverty/poverty06/table3.pdf.

37. Figures available at http://aspe.hhs.gov/hsp/AFDC /baseline/4spending.pdf.

38. For an especially influential critique, see Charles Murray, *Losing Ground: American Social Policy, 1950–1980* (New York: Basic Books, 1984).

39. Figures available at http://www.acf.hhs.gov/program s/ofa/caseload/2007/tanf_family.htm.

40. Stephen Ohlemacher, "House Rejects Extension of Un-employment Benefits," Associated Press, June 29, 2010.

41. Stephen Dinan, "Extension of Unemployment Benefits Rejected," *Washington Times*, June 29, 2010.

42. Figures available at http://socialsecurity.gov/ssi/text-eligibility-ussi.htm.

43. Figures available at http://www.whitehouse.gov/omb /budget/fy2011/assets/socsec.pdf.

44. Figures available at http://www.fns.usda.gov/fns/key _data/april-2010.pdf.

45. Figures available at http://www.cbpp.org/cms/index .cfm?fa=view&id=2992.

46. For the origins of European welfare programs, see Peter Flora and Jens Alber, "Modernization, Democratization, and the Development of Welfare States in Western Europe," in Peter Flora and Arnold J. Heidenheimer, eds., *Development of Welfare State in Europe and America* (New Brunswick: Transaction Books, 1981); and Philip Manow, "Germany: Co-operative Federalism and the Overgrazing of the Fiscal Commons," in Herbert Obinger, Stephan Leibfried, and Francis G. Castles, eds., *Federalism and the Welfare State: New World and European Experiences* (Cambridge: Cambridge University Press, 2005).

47. See Figure 1 of Irwin Garfinkel, Lee Rainwater, and Timothy M. Smeeding, "Equal Opportunities for Chil-dren: Social Welfare Expenditures in the English-speak-ing Countries and Western Europe," *Focus* 23, no. 3 (2005); and Jacob S. Hacker, *The Divided Welfare State: The Battle over Public and Private Social Benefits in the United States* (Cambridge: Cambridge University Press, 2002), 13–15.

48. Figure available at: http://www.usgovernmentspending .com/us_welfare_spending_40.html.

49. Alberto Alesina and Edward Glaeser, "Why Are Welfare States in the U.S. and Europe So Different?" *Horizons stratégiques* 2, no. 2 (2006): 51–61, http: //www.cairn.info/article.php?ID_ARTICLE= HORI_002_0051.

50. Jacob Hacker, *The Divided Welfare State*.

51. David Tyack, *The One Best System: A History of American Urban Education* (Cambridge, MA: Harvard University Press, 1974).

52. Bess Furman, "President to Give Education Plans: Will Forward His Message to Congress Tomorrow on Spurring Science Study," *New York Times*, January 26, 1958, 60.

53. Public Papers of the President, American Presidency Project, "President Eisenhower's Statement upon Sign-ing the National Defense Education Act," September 2, 1958, http://www.presidency.ucsb.edu/ws/.

54. Marjorie Hunter, "More School Aid for Negro Urged," *New York Times*, June 26, 1963, 21.

55. National Center for Education Statistics, "Numbers and Rates of Public School Dropouts: School Year 2004–05," December 2007, http://nces.gov.edu/pubs2008 / hsdropouts/tables/table_7.asp.

56. National Center for Education Statistics, "Race/Ethnic-ity of Students," October 2003, http://nces.ed.gov/programs /youthindicators/Indicators.asp?PubPageNumber=10& ShowTablePage=TablesHTML/10.asp.

57. National Center for Education Statistics, "Bachelor's, Master's, and Doctor's Degrees Conferred by Degree-granting Institutions, by Sex of Student and Field of Study: 2004–05," July 2006, http://nces.ed.gov /programs/digest/d06/tables/dt06_258.asp.

58. Tamar Lewin, "At Colleges Women Are Leaving Men in the Dust," *New York Times*, July 9, 2006.

59. "Leaving Men Behind: Women Go to College in Ever-Greater Numbers," *Education Portal*, November 13, 2007, http://education-portal.com/articles/Leaving _Men_Behind:_Women_Go_to_College_in_Ever-Greater_Numbers.html.

60. Data on enrollment and degrees come from the U.S. Department of Education and are available at http://nces.ed.gov/fastfacts/display.asp?id=98 and http://nces.ed.gov/fastfacts/display.asp?id=72.

61. U.S. Department of Education, *A Nation at Risk*, http: //www.ed.gov/pubs/NatAtRisk/risk.html.

62. National Center for Education Statistics, http: //nces.ed.gov/programs/digest/d07/tables/dt07 _404.asp.

63. Frederick Hess and Michael Petrilli, *No Child Left Behind: A Primer* (New York: Peter Lang, 2006).

64. OECD Program for International Student Assessment, *PISA 2006 Science Competencies for Tomorrow's World,*

December 2007, http://www.pisa.oecd.org/document
/2/0,3343,en_32252351_32236191_39718850_
1_1_1_1,00.html.

65. "Race to the Top Program," U.S. Department of Education, January 13, 2010, http://www2.ed.gov/programs
/racetothetop/faq.pdf.

66. "Delaware and Tennessee Win First Race to the Top
Grants," Arne Duncan, March 29, 2010, U.S.
Department of Education.

67. Sam Dillon, "U.S. Names Education Grant Winners,"
New York Times, March 29, 2010.

68. Nick Anderson, "Input of Teachers Unions Key to Successful Entries in Race to the Top," *Washington Post*,
April 3, 2010.

69. Leslie Postal, "Tennessee's Teachers Union on Race to
the Top," *Orlando Sentinel*, April 5, 2010.

70. For a discussion of some of the disputes surrounding
new applications for federal education funding, see
Gerry Shih, "Educators Are Opposed to Obama's
School Plan," *New York Times*, June 5, 2010.

71. National Center for Education Statistics, *The Condition
of Education Annual Reports 2000–2007*, http://nces
.ed.gov/programs/coe/2007/section4/table.asp?
tableID=733.

72. William G. Howell and Paul E. Peterson, *The
Education Gap: Vouchers and Urban Schools*, rev. ed.
(Washington, DC: Brookings Institution, 2006).

73. For a discussion of these problems in the voucher studies referenced above, see Appendices A and E to Howell
and Peterson, *The Education Gap*.

74. See, for example, Jeffrey Grogger and Derek Neal, "Further
Evidence on the Effects of Catholic Secondary Schooling,"
in *Brookings-Wharton Papers on Urban Affairs: 2000*
(Washington, DC: Brooking Institution, 2000).

75. Joseph Berger, "A Post-Katrina Charter School in New
Orleans Gets a Second Chance," *New York Times*,
October 17, 2007.

76. For more figures, see www.edreform.com.

77. For a survey of tax credit programs, see William Howell
and Mindy Spencer, "Choice Without Vouchers:
Expanding Education Options Through Tax Benefits,"
Pioneer Institute White Paper, October 2007, http:
//www.pioneerinstitute.org/pdf/wp41.pdf.

78. See Patrick McEwan and Martin Carnoy, "The
Effectiveness and Efficiency of Private Schools in Chile's
Voucher System," *Education Evaluation and Policy
Analysis* 22, no. 3 (2000): 213–39; Gregory Elacqua,
Dante Contreras, and Felipe Salazar, "The Effectiveness
of Private School Franchises in Chile's National Voucher
Program," Princeton University Typescript, 2007.

79. In addition to the elderly, Medicare also provides some
assistance to the disabled.

80. Figures available at http://www.cms.hhs.gov
/DataCompendium/17_2007_Data_Compendium.asp.

81. Alan Weil, "There's Something About Medicaid,"
Health Affairs 22, no. 1 (2003), http://content.
healthaffairs.org/cgi/reprint/22/1/13.pdf.

82. Figures available at http://www.hhs.gov/budget
/09budget/2009BudgetInBrief.pdf.

83. Centers for Medicare and Medicaid Services, U.S.
Department of Health and Human Services, *Medicaid
At-a-Glance, 2005*, http://www.cms.hhs.gov
/MedicaidDataSourcesGenInfo/Downloads/
maag2005.pdf.

84. Figures available at http://caliban.sourceoecd.org
/vl=2555969/cl=18/nw=1/rpsv/health2007/g2-1-02
.htm.

85. Figures available at http://masetto.sourceoecd.org
/vl=4048346/cl=15/nw=1/rpsv/health2007/g3-3-01
.htm/.

86. World Health Organization, "The World Health
Report 2000: Health Systems: Improving Performance,"
176–84, 189, http://www.who.int/whr/2000/en
/whr00_en.pdf.

87. See, for example, Center for Economic and Social
Rights, "The Right to Health in the United States of
America: What Does It Mean?" October 29, 2004,
http://cesr.org/ushealthright?PHPSESSID=91 . . .
a78f9969da61bd9.

88. See, for example, John Goodman, "Five Myths of
Socialized Medicine," Cato Institute, *Cato's Letter*,
Winter 2005, http://www.cato.org/pubs/catosletter
/catosletterv3n1.pdf.

89. Longer description of the legislation's main provisions
can be found at http://energycommerce.house.gov
/Press_111/20090714/hr3200_summary.pdff and
http://www.cbsnews.com/8301-503544_162-
20000846-503544.html. The legislation itself is available at http://democrats.senate.gov/reform
/patient-protection-affordable-care-act-as-passed.pdf.

90. Shailagh Murray, "Congress Approves Fixes to Health
Care Bill," *Washington Post*, March 26, 2010.

CHAPTER EIGHTEEN

1. "International Security Assistance Force and Afghan
National Army Strength and Laydown," North Atlantic
Treaty Organization, April 3, 2009, available online at:
http://www.understandingwar.org/themenode/
international-security-assistance-force-isaf.

2. Josh White, "New Troops in Iraq Will Keep Number at
140,000," *Washington Post*, May 20, 2008.

3. Josh White and Ann Scott Tyson, "Increase in War
Funding Sought," *Washington Post*, September 27, 2007.

4. "Bush's Final Approval Rating," CBS/New York Times Poll, January 16, 2009, available online at: http://www.cbsnews.com/htdocs/pdf/Bush_poll_011609.pdf?tag=contentMain;contentBody.

5. "Obama Calls Situation in Afghanistan Urgent," CNN, July 21, 2008, available online at: http://www.cnn.com/2008/POLITICS/07/20/obama.afghanistan/.

6. Greg Bruno, "NATO in Afghanistan," Council on Foreign Relations, February 19, 2009, available online at: http://www.cfr.org/publication/18560/nato_in_afghanistan.html.

7. For a more detailed discussion on Afghanistan's economy, see, "The Opium Economy in Afghanistan: An International Problem," United Nations Office on Drugs and Crime, 2003, available online at: http://www.reliefweb.int/library/documents/2003/unodc-afg-31jan.pdf.

8. Peter Spiegel, "Obama Bets Big on Troop Surge," *Wall Street Journal*, December 2, 2009.

9. Eric Schmitt and David Sanger, "Obama Faces Doubts from Democrats on Afghanistan," *New York Times*, September 10, 2009.

10. Jim McGovern, Russ Feingold, and Walter Jones, "Letter to Obama," December 9, 2009, available online at: http://www.boston.com/news/politics/politicalintelligence/2009/12/mcgovern_leads.html.

11. Ken Dilanian, "Afghanistan Plan Leaves Democrats Doubtful, Republicans Critical," *USA Today*, December 2, 2009.

12. Roy Gutman, "Senate Democrats Leave Kabul Still Wary of US Troop Surge," *McClatchy*, January 14, 2010, available online at: http://www.mcclatchydc.com/2010/01/13/82306/senate-democrats-leave-kabul-still.html.

13. Rod Nordland and Alissa Rubin, "Karzai Closing in on Taliban Reconciliation Plan," *New York Times*, January 17, 2010.

14. A breakdown of all Afghan War casualties can be found online at: http://www.icasualties.org. See also Dexter Filkins, "Kabul Attack Shows Resilience of Afghan Militants," *New York Times*, January 18, 2010.

15. Mark Mazzetti, "Secret Joint Raid Captures Taliban's Top Commander," *New York Times*, February 15, 2010.

16. Anna Nemstova, "Women and Higher Education Make Steady Progress in Afghanistan," *Chronicle of Higher Education*, March 28, 2010.

17. Washington's Farewell Address, 1796; available online at: http://www.yale.edu/lawweb/avalon/washing.htm.

18. John J. Mearsheimer, *The Tragedy of Great Power Politics* (New York: Norton, 1999), 236–49.

19. Jeff Frieden, "Sectoral Conflict and Foreign Economic Policy: 1914–1940," *International Organization* 41, no. 2 (1988): 63.

20. Benjamin O. Fordham, "Revisionism Reconsidered: Exports and American Intervention in World War I," *International Organization* 61 (Spring 2007): 286.

21. Fordham, "Revisionism Reconsidered."

22. For more on World War I, see Donald Kagan, *On the Origins of War and the Preservation of Peace* (New York: Anchor, 1996).

23. Williamson Murray and Allan R. Millet, *A War to Be Won: Fighting the Second World War* (Cambridge, MA: Harvard/Belknap Press, 2000), 75.

24. Murray and Millet, *A War to Be Won*, 82.

25. For World War II, the Allied nations were Great Britain, France, the Soviet Union, and eventually the United States. The Axis nations were Germany, Italy, and Japan.

26. Murray and Millet, *A War to Be Won*, 177–8.

27. Murray and Millet, *A War to Be Won*, 82.

28. George F. Kennan, "The Sources of Soviet Conduct," in *American Diplomacy*, expanded ed. (Chicago: University of Chicago Press, 1984), 115–20, 125.

29. The Cold War has also been called the "Long Peace." Coined by Yale historian John Lewis Gaddis, the Long Peace referred to the prolonged lack of war in Europe. John Lewis Gaddis, "The Long Peace: Elements of Stability in the Postwar International System," *International Security* 10, no. 4 (1986): 99–142.

30. For an overview of Cold War history, see John Lewis Gaddis, *The Cold War: A New History* (New York: Penguin, 2005).

31. President Johnson's message to Congress, August 5, 1964, available online at: http://www.mtholyoke.edu/acad/intrel/tonkinsp.htm.

32. Casualty data available online at: http://www.archives.gov/research/vietnam-war/casualty-statistics.html.

33. Arthur Schlesinger Jr., *The Imperial Presidency* (New York: Mariner, 2004).

34. For more on the war in Vietnam, see George C. Herring, *America's Longest War: The United States and Vietnam, 1950–1975*, 3rd ed. (New York: McGraw-Hill, 1996); and Leslie H. Gelb and Richard K. Betts, *The Irony of Vietnam: The System Worked* (Washington, DC: Brookings Institution, 1979).

35. Gaddis, *The Cold War*, 225.

36. For the post–Cold War grand strategy debate, see Michael E. Brown et al. eds., *America's Strategic Choices*, rev. ed. (Cambridge, MA: MIT Press, 2000).

37. Robert Pape, *Bombing to Win: Air Power and Coercion in War* (Ithaca, NY: Cornell University Press, 1996), 214.

38. "President Bush Outlines Iraqi Threat," White House Press Release, October 7, 2002, available online at: http://www.whitehouse.gov/news/releases/2002/10/20021007-8.html.

Notes

39. John J. Mearsheimer and Stephen M. Walt, "An Unnecessary War," *Foreign Policy* 134 (January/February 2003): 51–59.

40. Data on U.S. casualties in Iraq available online at: http://www.globalsecurity.org/military/ops/iraq_casualties.htm.

41. Michael Abramowitz, "Economy, War to Dominate State of the Union; Bush's Challenge May Be Getting People to Listen," *Washington Post*, January 28, 2008, A1.

42. Consulates can be thought of as "subembassies," usually located in large noncapital cities abroad to help American citizens or support the main embassy. Many employees of foreign embassies and consulates are foreign nationals providing support for American personnel.

43. Gary Hufbauer, Jeffrey Schott, and Kimberly Elliot, *Economic Sanctions Reconsidered: History and Current Policy*, Peterson Institute, 1990.

44. Daniel Drezner, *The Sanctions Paradox: Economic Statecraft and International Relations* (New York: Cambridge University Press, 1999).

45. Dean Lacy and Emerson M. S. Niou, "Theory of Economic Sanctions and Issue Linkage: The Roles of Preferences, Information, and Threats," *Journal of Politics* 66, no. 1 (2004): 25–42.

46. For additional reading, see: David Baldwin, *Economic Statecraft* (Princeton, NJ: Princeton University Press, 1985); Robert Pape, "Why Economic Sanctions Do Not Work," *International Security* 22, no. 2 (1997): 90–136; A. Cooper Drury, "Sanctions as Coercive Diplomacy: The U. S. President's Decision to Initiate Economic Sanctions," *Political Research Quarterly* 54, no. 3 (2001): 485–508.

47. Stockholm International Peace Research Institute (SIPRI), "The Fifteen Major Spenders in 2006," available online at: http://www.sipri.org/contents/milap/milex/mex_trends.html.

48. This number excludes U.S. Postal Service employees, as well as those working for the CIA, NSA, Defense Intelligence Agency, and National Imagery and Mapping Agency. These latter four agencies do not make their employment figures public for national security reasons. See U.S. Department of Labor, Bureau of Labor Statistics, *Career Guide to Industries: Federal Government, Excluding the Postal Service*, available online at: http://www.bls.gov/oco/cg/cgs041.htm.

49. Bob Woodward, *Bush at War* (New York: Simon and Schuster, 2002), 3–4.

50. The National Reconnaissance Office (NRO) is also in charge of data monitoring, but its tools are spy aircraft and reconnaissance satellites. Also unacknowledged for many years, the NRO operates under the cover of the U.S. Air Force.

51. I. M. Destler, *American Trade Politics*, 3rd ed. (Washington, DC: Institute for International Economics, 1995).

52. Brian Knowlton, "House Panel Says Armenian Deaths Were Genocide," *New York Times*, March 4, 2010, available online at: http://www.nytimes.com/2010/03/05/world/europe/05armenia.html?_r=1&scp=2&sq=armenian%20genocide&st=cse.

53. See, for example, Louis Fisher, *Presidential War Power*, 2nd ed. (Lawrence: University Press of Kansas, 2004).

54. This 60-day clock can be extended for another 30 days if the president certifies that the time is necessary for the troops' safety.

55. Louis Fisher, *Congressional Abdication on War and Spending* (College Station: Texas A&M University Press, 2000), 65.

56. David Auerswald and Peter Cowhey, "Ballotbox Diplomacy: The War Powers Resolution and the Use of Force," *International Studies Quarterly* 41, no. 3 (1997): 505–28.

57. Jim VandeHei and Colum Lynch, "Bush Names Bolton U.N. Ambassador in Recess Appointment," *Washington Post*, August 2, 2005, A1.

58. Figures available online at: http://www.senate.gov/artandhistory/history/common/briefing/Treaties.htm.

59. Jerel Rosati and James Scott, *The Politics of United States Foreign Policy*, 4th ed. (Belmont, CA: Wadsworth, 2007), 333.

60. Previous two quotes can be found in Carl Hulse, "Political Fault Line Emphasized by Timing of Hearings," *New York Times*, September 11, 2007, A18.

61. Two quotes can be found in Warren P. Strobel, "Two Days of Iraq Testimony, but No Answer to 'How This Ends,'" Knight Ridder Tribune News Service, September 11, 2007, 1.

62. Peter Baker and Jonathan Weisman, "A Plea from Petraeus," *Washington Post*, April 9, 2008.

63. Guy Raz, "Petraeus, Crocker Continue Testimony on Iraq," NPR, April 9, 2008.

64. For a more critical assessment, see John Mearsheimer and Stephen Walt, *The Israeli Lobby and U.S. Foreign Policy* (New York: Farrar, Straus and Giroux, 2008).

65. James M Lindsay, "Getting Uncle Sam's Ear: Will Ethnic Lobbies Cramp America's Foreign Policy Style?" Brookings Institution, 2002, available online at: http://www.brookings.edu/articles/2002/winter_diplomacy_lindsay.aspx.

66. Robert Dahl, *Who Governs? Power and Democracy in an American City* (New Haven: Yale University Press, 1961).

67. As quoted in Alan Curtis, ed., *Patriotism, Democracy, and Common Sense* (New York: Rowman and Littlefield, 2005), xii.

68. Rone Tempest, "Servants or Masters? Revisiting the Military-Industrial Complex," *LA Times*, July 10, 1983, H1.

69. Elizabeth Becker and Larry Rohter, "U.S. and Chile Reach Free Trade Accord," *New York Times*, December 12, 2002, C1.

70. Council on Foreign Relations, "History," available online at: http://www.cfr.org/about/history/cfr/index.html.

71. Michael E. O'Hanlon and Kenneth M. Pollack, "A War We Just Might Win," *New York Times*, July 30, 2007, A17.

72. Donald G. McNeil, "Audit Finds Bush's AIDS Effort Limited by Restrictions," *New York Times*, March 31, 2007, A12.

73. Sheryl Gay Stolberg, "In Global Battle on AIDS, Bush Creates Legacy," *New York Times*, January 5, 2008, A1.

74. Sheryl Gay Stolberg, "Getting Religion on AIDS," *New York Times*, February 2, 2003, 4.1.

75. Stolberg, "Getting Religion on AIDS."

76. Marc Sandalow, "Jesse Helms, Global AIDS Activist," *San Francisco Chronicle*, April 1, 2002, B7.

77. Elizabeth Becker, "With Record Rise in Foreign Aid Comes Change in How It Is Monitored," *New York Times*, December 7, 2003, A10.

78. Holly Burkhalter, "The Politics of AIDS: Engaging Conservative Activists," *Foreign Affairs* 83, no. 1 (2004): 10.

79. Stolberg, "In Global Battle on AIDS, Bush Creates Legacy."

80. Richard Stevenson, "Middle Path Emerges in Debate on Africa Aid," *New York Times*, June 9, 2002, C4.

81. Joseph Kahn, "A Star Close to the Heart of Aid Policy," *New York Times*, March 15, 2002, A8.

82. Stolberg, "Getting Religion on AIDS."

83. Becker, "With Record Rise in Foreign Aid Comes Change in How It Is Monitored."

84. Stevenson, "Middle Path Emerges in Debate on Africa Aid."

85. McNeil, "Audit Finds Bush's AIDS Effort Limited by Restrictions."

86. Stolberg, "In Global Battle on AIDS, Bush Creates Legacy."

87. United Nations, "NPT Treaty Status," available online at: http://disarmament.un.org/TreatyStatus.nsf/NPT%20(in%20alphabetical%20order)?OpenView&Start=1.

88. Carnegie Endowment for International Peace, "Nonproliferation: Agreed Framework," available online at: http://www.carnegieendowment.org/static/npp/agreed_framework.cfm.

89. American Presidency Project, "George W. Bush: Address Before a Joint Session of the Congress on the State of the Union, January 29, 2002," available online at: http://www.presidency.ucsb.edu.

90. CNN, "Timeline: North Korea's Nuclear Weapons Development," January 6, 2004, available online at: http://www.cnn.com/2003/WORLD/asiapcf/east/08/20/nkorea.timeline.nuclear/.

91. "Korea's Obama Test." *Wall Street Journal*. May 26, 2009, p. A18, available online at: http://online.wsj.com/article/SB124329265169452457.html.

92. "Path of peace available to North Korea, Obama says." *CNN*, June 16, 2009, available online at: http://www.cnn.com/2009/POLITICS/06/16/south.korea.meeting/index.html.

93. Stephen Brooks, *Producing Security: Multinational Corporations, Globalization, and the Changing Calculus of Conflict* (Princeton, NJ: Princeton University Press, 2005).

94. The lobbyists themselves disagreed about which remedy they desired under U.S. trade law. Some called for anti-dumping measures, which required minimal evidence of injury but could be applied only against specific products and countries. Others wanted to pursue a "Section 201" complaint, which would offer more comprehensive protection to the sector, but only if a much higher burden of proof was met.

95. Richard W. Stevenson, "Big Steel: An Invalid That Can Roar in Washington," *New York Times*, December 11, 2001, C1.

96. Paul Blustein, "Bush to Seek Protection for U.S. Steel Firms; President Yields to Industry Pressure," *Washington Post*, June 6, 2001, E1.

97. Edmund Andrews, "To Little Avail, U.S. Presses for Steel Output Cut Abroad," *New York Times*, December 18, 2001, C2.

98. Steven Perlstein and Mike Allen, "Bush Faces Tough Choices on Steel Imports; Under Lobbying Pressure, President Must Decide by Wednesday Whether to Act to Aid U.S. Industry," *Washington Post*, February 28, 2002, A4.

99. Mike Allen and Steven Perlstein, "Bush Settles on Tariff for Steel Imports," *Washington Post*, March 5, 2002, A1.

100. Paul Blustein, "U.S. Indignant over EU Threat; Retaliatory Tariffs Would Be 'Hypocritical,' Official Says," *Washington Post*, April 18, 2002, E2.

101. Jonathan Weisman, "Bush Rescinds Tariffs on Steel; Trade War Averted; Industry Angry," *Washington Post*, December 5, 2003, A1.

102. Blustein, "Bush to Seek Protection for U.S. Steel Firms."

103. Transcript of George W. Bush's address to the nation on September 15, 2001. See "After the Attacks, the President's Message: A Different Battle Awaits," *New York Times*, September 16, 2001.

104. Katharine Q. Seelye, "Threats and Responses: The Detainee; Court to Hear Arguments in Groundbreaking Case of U.S. Citizen Seized with Taliban," *New York Times*, October 28, 2002, A13.

105. Linda Greenhouse, "Court Hears Case on U.S. Detainees," *New York Times*, April 29, 2004, A1.

106. American Bar Association brief to Supreme Court, quoted in Linda Greenhouse, "The Imperial Presidency and the Constraints of the Law," *New York Times*, April 18, 2004, A7.

107. The full transcript of the Court's ruling in *Hamdi v. Rumsfeld* is available at http://www.law.cornell.edu/supct/html/03-6696.ZS.html.

108. Noah Feldman, "Who Can Check the President?" *New York Times Magazine*, January 8, 2006, 52.

109. The full transcript of the court's ruling in *Hamdan v. Rumsfeld* is available online at: http://www.supreme-courtus.gov/opinions/05pdf/05-184.pdf.

110. Quoted in Linda Greenhouse, "Justices, 5-3, Broadly Reject Bush Plan to Try Detainees," *New York Times*, June 30, 2006, A1.

111. The full transcript of the court's ruling in *Boumediene v. Bush* is available online at: available online at: http://www.supremecourtus.gov/opinions/07pdf/06-1195.pdf.

112. Quoted in William Glaberson, "Lawyers for Detainees Plan to Use Justices' Ruling to Mount New Attacks," *New York Times*, June 14, 2008, A14.

CHAPTER NINETEEN

1. G. Alan Tarr, *Understanding State Constitutions* (Princeton, NJ: Princeton University Press, 1999).

2. Albert L. Sturm, "The Development of State Constitutions," *Publius* 12 (Winter 1982): 60–67.

3. Albert L. Sturm, *Thirty Years of State Constitutions-Making 1938–1968* (New York: National Municipal League, 1970).

4. David C. Nice, "Interest Groups and State Constitutions—Another Look," *State and Local Government Review* 20 (Winter 1988): 21–29.

5. Alexis de Tocqueville, *Democracy in America*, ed. Phillips Bradley (New York: Knopf, 1945), 40.

6. *City of Clinton v. Cedar Rapids and Missouri River Railroad Co.* (Iowa, 1868).

7. Kathryn A. Foster, *The Political Economy of Special Purpose Government* (Washington, DC: Georgetown University Press, 1997); and Nancy Burns, *The Formation of American Local Governments: Private Values in Public Institutions* (New York: Oxford University Press, 1994).

8. Dale Krane, Platon N. Rigos, and Melvin B. Hill Jr., *Home Rule in America: A Fifty State Handbook* (Washington, DC: CQ Press, 2001).

9. Dall Forsyth, *Memos to the Governor: An Introduction to State Budgeting* (Washington, DC: Georgetown University Press, 1997).

10. Alan Rosenthal, *Governors and Legislators: Contending Powers* (Washington, DC: CQ Press, 1990).

11. Norma M. Riccucci and Judith R. Saidel, "The Demographics of Gubernatorial Appointees: Toward an Explanation of Variation," *Policy Studies Journal* 29 (January 2001): 11–22; and Thad L. Beyle, "Enhancing Executive Leadership in the States," *State and Local Government Review* 27 (Winter 1995): 18–35.

12. Council of State Governments, *The Book of the States, 2008* (Lexington, KY: Council of State Governments, 2008), 201–6, http://www.csg.org.

13. Leon W. Blevins, *Texas Government in National Perspective* (Englewood Cliffs, NJ: Prentice-Hall, 1987), 169.

14. Ann O'Bowman and Richard C. Kearney, "Dimensions of State Government Capability," *Western Political Quarterly* 41 (June 1988): 341–62; Timothy G. O'Rourke, *The Impact of Reapportionment* (New Brunswick, NJ: Transaction, 1980); and David M. Hedge, *Governance and the Changing American States* (Boulder, CO: Westview, 1998).

15. Council of State Governments, *The Book of the States, 2008*, 145–76. http://www.csg.org.

16. Glenn Abney and Thomas P. Lauth, *The Politics of State and City Administration* (Albany: State University of New York Press, 1986), 65–89.

17. Council of State Governments, *The Book of the States, 2008*, 142–5. http://www.csg.org.

18. National Conference of State Legislatures, "Dual Employment," http://www.ncsl.org/programs/pubs/summaries/08LBFeb_Dual-sum.htm.

19. For a discussion of the effects of term limits, see Karl T. Kurtz, Bruce Cain, and Richard G. Niemi, eds., *Institutional Change in American Politics: The Case of Term Limits* (Ann Arbor: University of Michigan Press, 2007); and Rick Farmer, John David Rausch Jr., and John C. Green, eds., *The Test of Time: Coping with Legislative Term Limits* (Lanham, MD: Lexington, 2008).

20. Alan Rosenthal, *Heavy Lifting: The Job of the American Legislature* (Washington, DC: CQ Press, 2004).

21. Kimberly L. Nelson, *Elected Municipal Councils: Special Data Issue* (Washington, DC: International City/County Management Association, 2002); and Brian F. Schaffner, Gerald Wright, and Matthew Streb, "Teams Without Uniforms: The Nonpartisan Ballot in State and Local Elections," *Political Research Quarterly* 54 (March 2001): 7–30.

22. Susan Welch, "The Impact of At-Large Elections on the Representation of Blacks and Hispanics," *Journal of Politics*, 52 (November 1990): 1050–7; and Susan A. MacManus and Charles S. Bullock III, "Women and Racial/Ethnic Minorities in Mayoral and Council Positions," in *Municipal Year Book, 1993* (Washington, DC: International City/County Management Association, 1993), 57–69.

23. See http://www.census.gov/govs/cog/GovOrgTab03ss .html.

24. Stories, video, timeline, and photographs are archived by *Northwest Herald*, http://www.nwherald.com, under "Tragedy on Campus."

25. Complete coverage of the shootings and their aftermath is available from the *Chronicle of Higher Education*, http://www.chronicle.org, under "Virginia Tech shootings."

26. The state-appointed Virginia Tech Review Panel's report and background material are available at http://www.vtreviewpanel.org.

27. Floyd Hunter, *Community Power Succession* (Chapel Hill: University of North Carolina Press, 1980); and Robert Dahl, *Who Governs?* (New Haven: Yale University Press, 1961).

28. Glen Sparrow, "The Emerging Chief Executive: The San Diego Experience," *National Civic Review* 74 (December 1985): 538–47.

29. American Bar Association, *Standards Relating to Court Organization* (New York: American Bar Association, 1974).

30. Stuart Nagel, "Unequal Party Representation in State Supreme Courts," *Journal of the American Judicature Society* (September 1961): 62–65.

31. Madhawi McCall, "The Politics of Judicial Elections: The Influence of Campaign Contributions on the Voting Patterns of Texas Supreme Court Judges," *Politics and Policy* 31 (June 2003): 314–33.

32. Medina Gann Hall, "Justices as Representatives: Elections and Judicial Politics in the American States," *American Politics Quarterly* 23 (October 1995): 427–46.

33. Melinda Gann Hall, "Electoral Politics and Strategic Voting in State Supreme Courts," *Journal of Politics* 54 (Fall 1992): 508–18; and Melinda Gann Hall, "Toward an Integrated Model of Judicial Voting Behavior," *American Politics Quarterly* 20 (March 1992): 147–68.

34. Elisabeth R. Gerber, Arthur Lupia, Matthew D. McCubbis, and D. Roderick Kiewiet, *Stealing the Initiative: How State Government Responds to Direct Democracy* (Upper Saddle River, NJ: Prentice-Hall, 2001).

35. Donald P. Haider-Markel, Alana Querze, and Kara Lindaman, "Lose, Win, or Draw? A Reexamination of Direct Democracy and Minority Rights," *Political Research Quarterly* 60, no. 2 (2007): 304–14.

Text and Art Credits

Chapter 2

Table 2-1. General Social Survey 2000. Reprinted with permission. Table 2-3. Questions and wording adapted from the National Election Study, 2002; data presented in Larry Bartels, "Homer Gets a Tax Cut: Inequality and Public Policy in the American Mind," paper presented at the annual meeting of the American Political Science Association, Philadelphia, August 2003. Figure 2-1. Survey data: Pew Center for the People and the Press, http://people-press.org/reports/display.php3?ReportID=167. Income data (Gross national income per capita, 2003): World Bank, http://siteresources.worldbank.org/DATASTATISTICS/Resources/GNIPC.pdf. Figure 2-2. The American National Election Studies (www.electionstudies.org). THE 1948-2004 ANES CUMULATIVE FILE [dataset]. Stanford University and the University of Michigan [producers and distributors], 2008.

Any opinions, findings, and conclusions or recommendations expressed in these materials are those of the author(s) and do not necessarily reflect the views of the funding organizations. Figure 2-3. Data from Pew Center on the People and the Press, various surveys 1987–2009. Figure 2-4. Data from Pew Center on the People and the Press. Figure 2-5. Map from http://www.jenner.com. Reprinted with permission from Jenner & Block LLP. Figure 2-6. Organisation for Economic Co-operation and Development, *OECD Health Data 2009*. Updated April, 2010.

Chapter 4

Table 4-1. Paul L. Posner, The Politics of Unfunded Mandates: Whither Federalism? Washington, DC: Georgetown University Press, 1998. Figure 4-2. US Department of Labor, http://www.dol.gov/esa/minwage/america.htm. Figure 4-3. Budget of the United States Government: Historical Tables Fiscal Year 2011,

Table 12-2, http://www.gpoaccess.gov/usbudget/fy11/hist.html. Figure 4-4. Consolidated Federal Funds Report, 2008, Table 13, http://www.census.gov/govs/cffr/; Internal Revenue Service, IRS Data Book, Table 5, http://www.irs.gov/taxstats/article/0,id=206488,00.html; Statistical Abstract of the United States 2010, Population, Table 12, http://www.census.gov/compendia/statab/cats/population.html.

Chapter 5

Table 5-4. Herbert McClosky and Alida Brill, *Dimensions of Political Tolerance: What Americans Believe About Civil Liberties* (New York: Russell Sage, 1983), p. 203; Herbert McClosky and John Zaller, *The American Ethos: Public Attitudes Toward Capitalism and Democracy* (Cambridge: Harvard University Press, 1984), p. 25, 37, 38, 74, 75; Pew Center for the People and the Press surveys. Figure 5-1. From Freedom House, www.freedomhouse. Reprinted by permission.

Chapter 6

Figure 6.1. Gary Orfield and Chungmei Lee, "Why Segregation Matters: Poverty and Educational Inequality," The Civil Rights Project at Harvard University, January 2005, Table 7. Figure 6.2. Doug McAdam, POLITICAL PROCESS AND THE DEVELOPMENT OF BLACK INSURGENCY 1930–1970 (Chicago: University of Chicago Press, 1982), p. 121. Copyright © 1982 by the University of Chicago. Reprinted by permission.

Chapter 7

Table 7-1. Pew Research Center for the People and the Press, "Unabated Economic Gloom, Divides on Afghanistan and Health Care." December 16, 2009.

http://people-press.org. Table 7-2. "Political Knowledge Update Survey," Pew Research Center, January 14–16, 2010, and "What Americans Know: 1987–2007," Pew Research Center, April 15,2007. Table 7-3. Michael X. Delli Carpini and Scott Keeter, *What Americans Know About Politics and Why It Matters* (New Haven, CT: Yale University Press, 1996), p. 91. Copyright © 1996 by Yale University. Reprinted with permission. Table 7-4. Michael X. Delli Carpini and Scott Keeter, *What Americans Know About Politics and Why It Matters* (New Haven, CT: Yale University Press, 1996), p. 91. Copyright © 1996 by Yale University. Reprinted with permission.

Chapter 8

Table 8-1. Authors' analysis of 2008 National Election Study, http://electionstudies.org). Table 8-2. Authors' analysis of 2008 National Election Study, http://electionstudies.org). Table 8-3. Reprinted by permission of the publisher from VOICE AND EQUALITY: CIVIC VOLUNTARISM IN AMERICAN POLITICS by Sidney Verba, Kay Lehman Schlozman, and Henry E. Brady, p. 135, Cambridge, Mass.: Harvard University Press, Copyright © 1995 by the President and Fellows of Harvard College. Table 8-4. Erikson, Robert S. and Tedin, Kent L. *American Public Opinion* p. 201–203. Reprinted with permission from Pearson Higher Education. Table 8-5. Authors' analysis of 2008 National Election Study, http://electionstudies.org). Figure 8-1. Verba, Sidney, Kay Scholzman, and Henry Brady. 2006. *Voice and Equality*, Boston: Harvard University Press, p. 70. Figure 8-2. Verba, Sidney, Kay Scholzman, and Henry Brady. 2006. *Voice and Equality*, Boston: Harvard University Press, p. 135. Figure 8-3. Social Science Research Council, http://election04.ssrc.org/research/csae_2004_final_report.pdf. Reprinted with permission. Figure 8-4. Center for the Study of the American Electorate,

http://www.american.edu/ia/cdem/csae/pdfs/csae061109.pdf. Figure 8-5. The American National Election Studies (www.electionstudies.org). THE 1948–2004 ANES CUMULATIVE FILE [dataset]. Stanford University and the University of Michigan [producers and distributors], 2005. Any opinions, findings, and conclusions or recommendations expressed in these materials are those of the author(s) and do not necessarily reflect the views of the funding organizations. Figure 8-6. Verba, Sidney, Kay Scholzman, and Henry Brady. 2006. *Voice and Equality*, Boston: Harvard University Press, p. 233.

Chapter 9

Table 9-1. Stephen J. Wayne, *The Road to the White House,* 1996 (New York: St. Martin's Press, 1996), table 6.2. Data from 1996 from Harold W. Stanley and Richard G. Niemi, Vital Statistics on American Politics, 2003–04 (Washington, DC: Congressional Quarterly Press, 2003), table 1.23, p. 66. Data from 2004 from the US Federal Election Commission. Figure 9-1. The American National Election Studies (www.electionstudies.org). THE 1948–2004 ANES CUMULATIVE FILE [dataset]. Stanford University and the University of Michigan [producers and distributors], 2005.

Text and Art Credits

Any opinions, findings, and conclusions or recommendations expressed in these materials are those of the author(s) and do not necessarily reflect the views of the funding organizations. Figure 9-2. American National Election Study, Cumulative File. Figure 9-3. American National Election Study, Cumulative File.

Chapter 10

Table 10-2. Public figures from August 2008 Pew Media Believability Study (N=1800) And http://www.stateofthemedia.org.

Chapter 11

Table 11.1. David Leip's Atlas of US Presidential Elections, www.uselectionatlas.org. Reprinted with permission. Table 11.2. Marjorie Randon Hershey, *Party Politics in America*, 13/e (New York: Pearson Longman, 2009), p. 119. Reprinted with permission. Table 11.3. Voter News Survey exit polls, 13, 660 respondents. Data available at http://www.cnn.com/ELECTION/2004/pages/results/states/US/P/00/epolls.0.html. Table 11.4. Voter News Survey exit polls, 17,836 respondents. Data available at www.cnn.com/election/2008. Figure 11.1. Christian Collett and Martin P. Wattenberg, "Strategically Unambitious: Minor Party and Independent Candidates in the 1996 Congressional Electionas," in John C. Green and Daniel M. Shea, eds., *The State of the Parties: The Changing Role of Contemporary American Parties* (Lanham, MD: Rowman and Littlefield, 1999). Reprinted with permission.

Chapter 12

Figure 12.1. Walker, Jack L., *Mobilizing Interest Groups in America: Patrons, Professionals, and Social Movements*, p. 59, Fig. 4.1. Copyright © by the University of Michigan 1991. Ann Arbor: University of Michigan Press, 1991. Reprinted with permission.

Chapter 13

Figure 13-1. From http://www.opensecrets.org. Reprinted by permission of Center for Responsive Politics. Figure 13-2. Mildred L. Amer, Congressional Research Service Report for Congress, *Membership of the 109th Congress: A Profile*, May 31, 2006. Mildred L. Amer. CRS Report for Congress: Black Members of the United States Congress, 1870–2007. Washington, DC: Congressional Research Service; Carmen E. Enciso, 1995. Hispanic Americans in Congress, 1822–1995. Washington, DC: Library of Congress. Updated information, through 2007, is available at: http://www.loc.gov/rr/hispanic/congress/chron.html. Accessed October 18, 2007. Figure 13.4. Nolan McCarty, Keith T. Poole, and Howard Rosenthal., POLARIZED AMERICA: THE DANCE OF IDEOLOGY AND UNEQUAL RICHES, figure: "Polarization of Democratic and Republican Members of Congress 1879–2007", © 2006 Massachusetts Institute of Technology, by permission of The MIT Press.

Chapter 14

Figure 14-1. Princeton Research Associates survey, 1995, data presented in Jeffrey Cohen and David Nice, *The Presidency* (Boston: McGraw Hill, 1995), p. 215 Copyright © McGraw-Hill Companies, Inc. Reprinted with permission. Figure 14-2. Harold W. Stanley and Richard G. Niemi, VITAL STATISTICS ON AMERICAN POLITICS 2005–2006 (Washington, DC: CQ Press, 2006), pp. 258–59. Copyright © 2006 CQ Press, a division of SAGE Publications. Reprinted with permission. Figure 14-3. Harold W. Stanley and Richard G. Niemi, VITAL STATISTICS ON AMERICAN POLITICS 2005–2006 (Washington, DC: CQ Press, 2006), p 339. Copyright © 2006 CQ Press, a division of SAGE Publications. Reprinted with permission. Figure 14-4.

(PENDING) Gallup Poll. Reprinted with permission. Figure 14-5. Harold W. Stanley and Richard G. Niemi, VITAL STATISTICS ON AMERICAN POLITICS 2005–2006 (Washington, DC: CQ Press, 2006), pp. 260–61. Copyright © 2006 CQ Press, a division of SAGE Publications. Reprinted with permission.

Chapter 15

Table 15-1. Savage, David G. *Guide to the US Supreme Court*, 4th ed., Vol. II Washington, DC: CQ Press, 2004, pp. 1186–1189. Copyright © 2004 CQ Press, a division of SAGE Publications. Reprinted with permission. Figure 15-1. Administrative Office of the U.S. Courts, http://uscourts.gov outreach/structure.jpg. Figure 15-2. Administrative Office of the U.S. Courts, http://www.uscourts.gov/courtlinks. Figure 15-3. Wendy L. Marinek, "The Lower Federal Court Confirmation Database, 1977–2004," Center on Democratic Performance, August 22, 2005. Reprinted with permission.

Chapter 16

Figure 16-1. Office of the Federal Register, National Archives and Records Administration, The *Federal Register*, Vols. 1–71," Washington, DC. Available online at: http://www.heinonline.org (accessed June 18, 2007). Figure 16-2. US Bureau of Census, *Historical Statistics of the United States: Colonial Times to 1970* (Washington, DC: Government Printing Office, 1975), 1102–1103, series 312–314. US Bureau of the Census, *Statistical Abstract of the United States: 2008*, (Washington, DC: Government Printing Office, 2006). Figure 16-3. US Bureau of the Census, (Washington, DC: Government Printing Office).

Chapter 17

Table 17-1. Digest of Education Statistics, 2009, Table 402, http://nces.ed.gov/programs/digest/d09/tables/dt09_402.asp. Table 17-2. "The World Health Report 2000: Health Systems: Improving Performamce." *World Health Organization*. http://www.who.int/whr/2000/en/whr00_en.pdf. Figure 17-1. Sidor, Gary. "Social Security: Brief Facts and Statistics" *CRS Report for Congress*. January 26, 2006. http://price.house.gov/issues/uploadedfiles/socialsecurity2.pdf. Figure 17-2. US Census Bureau, Current Population Survey, 1960–2008 Annual Social and Economic Supplements. Figure 17.3. Reprinted with permission of The Center for Education Reform, www.edreform.com.

Chapter 18

Figure 18-1. US Department of State, available online at: http://www.state.gov/cms_images/fy2006par_DoS_LocationsMap.gif. Accessed March 6, 2008. Figure 18-2. *Historical Tables: Budget of the United States Government: Fiscal Year 2008*, pp. 73–78. Available online from: http://www.gpoaccess.gov/usbudget/fy08/browse.html. Accessed February 8, 2008.

Chapter 19

Table 19-1. U.S. Bureau of the Census, "Local Governments and Public School Systems by Type and State: 2007," April 27, 2010,http://www.census.gov. Table 19-2. © National Conference of State Legislatures. Reprinted with permission. Table 19-3. International City/County Management Association, The Municipal Year Book 2008 (Washington, DC: ICMA, 2008). Table 19-4. Adapted from *The Book of the States 2008* (Lexington, KY: Council of State Governments, 2008), pp. 251–254. Reprinted with permission. Table 19-5. Based on *The Book of the States, 2008* (Lexington, KY: Council of State Governments, 2008) 308–327. Reprinted with permission. Figure 19-1. © National Conference of State Legislatures. Reprinted with permission.

Photo Credits

Chapter 1

1 (Clockwise from top right): Brooks Kraft/Corbis, Chris Hondros/Getty, Scott Gries/Getty, Sean Gallup/Getty, Joe Raedle/Newsmakers/Getty, Paula Bronstein/Getty, Chris Jackson/Getty, Chip Somodevilla/Getty, Chris Helgren/Reuters/Corbis, Robert Michael/Corbis, Chip Somodevilla/Getty, Win McNamee/Getty, Gabriel Bouys/AFP/Getty, Christopher Simon/AFP/Getty, Corbis/Getty/NBC/Landov, Win McNamee/Getty; 2: CBS News/Landov; 6: David McNew/Getty Images; 7: iStockphoto; 8: AFP/Getty Images; 9 circle inset: David Madison/Getty Images; 9: Robert Michael/Corbis; 10 left: Dario Lopez-Mills/AP Photo; 10 right: Norm Dettlaff/Las Cruces Sun-News/AP Photo; 12 both: Time & Life Pictures/Getty Images; 13: Corbis; 14: Claude Paris/AP Photo; 15: Larry Downing/Reuters/Landov; 17: Mike Simmons/Getty Images; 19: Image Source/Corbis

Chapter 2

23: Newscom; 24: E. Jason Wambgans/MCT/Landov; 28: Rob Evans/AP Photo; 29: Tannen Maury/Corbis; 31: Justin Sullivan/Getty Images; 32: U.S. Army; 34: Larry Downing/Reuters/Corbis; 35: Mike Segar/Reuters/Corbis; 36: Pensacola News Journal/SipaUSA; 38: Corbis RF/Alamy; 40: Bettmann/Corbis; 46: Mark Wilson/Getty Images; 52: Paul Sakuma/AP Photo; 54: Pablo Martinez Monsivais/AP Photo; 58: The Granger Collection; 60: AP Photo; 61: Karl Merton Ferron/MCT/Landov; 62: AFP/Getty Images

Chapter 3

67: George Widman Photography; 68: Alex Segre/Alamy; 70: The Granger Collection; 73: Elaine Thompson/AP Photo; 74: The Granger Collection; 76: The Granger Collection; 81: The Granger Collection; 82: Sven Creutzmann/Mambo Photo/Getty Images; 85: Yale University Art Gallery/Art Resource, NY; 86: Scott J. Ferrell/Congressional Quarterly/Getty Images; 88: Matthew Staver/Bloomberg via Getty Images; 91 both: National Portrait Gallery, Smithsonian Institution/Art Resource, NY; 93: Chris Keane/Reuters/Landov; 94: The Granger Collection; 100: Larry Burrows/Time Magazine/Time & Life Pictures/Getty Images

Chapter 4

121: John David Mercer/Corbis; 122: Robert Galbraith/Reuters/Corbis; 124: Charles Dharapak/AP Photo; 128: © Bob Daemmrich/Photoedit; 131: drtphotoslive/Newscom; 132: Spencer Platt/Getty Images; 134: Beathan/Corbis RF; 137: Joel Stettenheim/Corbis; 138: Jeff Gentner/Reuters/Corbis; 140: Image Source/Getty RF; 143: Robert Galbraith/Reuters/Corbis; 146: Tony Freeman/Phototake, Inc.; 153: Fotosearch; 150: Rich Pedroncelli/AP Photo; 155: Matt York/AP Photo; 158: Teri Stratford/Six-Cats Research Inc.; 159: Erich Schlegel/Corbis

Chapter 5

165: George Steinmetz/Corbis; 166: afplivethree/Newscom; 170: Mosefros/The New York Times/Redux; 172: AP Photo; 175: Bettmann/Corbis; 178: Elaine Thompson/AP Photo; 181: Michael Curlett/Tribune Star/AP Photo; 182: Brendan McDermid/Reuters/Corbis; 186:

Bettmann/Corbis; 188: Clay Good/Zuma Press; 191: Liberty Legal Institute, Henry and Wanda Sandoz/AP Photo; 194: George Steinmetz/Corbis; 197: Chang W. Lee/The New York Times/Redux; 200: California Department of Corrections/Reuters; 201: Kurt Rogers/San Francisco Chronicle; 204: Mark Kegans/The New York Times/Redux; 207: Harry Cabluck/AP Photo; 208: David Radlubowski/The New York Times/Redux

Chapter 6

213: Bruce Davidson/Magnum Photos; 214: The Granger Collection; 215: Library of Congress; 217: The Granger Collection; 219: The Granger Collection; 220: Library of Congress; 223: Bettmann/Corbis; 228: Stefanie Deutsch/Getty Images; 232: Abbas/Magnum Photos; 234: Newscom; 237: AP Photo; 240: Librado Romero/Redux; 241: Jeff Greenberg/The Image Works; 243: Image 100/Corbis RF; 246: Roman Milert/Alamy; 247: Zumawirewestphotos/Newscom

Chapter 7

253: Shawn Baldwin/The New York Times/Redux; 254: Library of Congress; 256: Jason Reed/Reuters/Landov; 258: Brooks Kraft/Corbis; 262: Nancy G. Spirit Wolf Photography/Alamy; 263: David Young Wolff/Photoedit; 264: Norbert von der Groeben/The Image Works; 265: Roger Maloch/Magnum Photos; 266: Time & Life Pictures/Getty Images; 271: Getty Images; 272 left: Jason Hornick/The Potomac News/Washington Examiner/AP Photo; 272 right: Joey Richardson/Oakland Tribune/Landov; 273: © Bob Gorrell, Creators Syndicate, Inc.; 275: Brooks Kraft/Corbis

Chapter 8

279: Newscom; 280: Bettmann/Corbis; 282: Jim West/Alamy; 284: Ross D. Franklin/AP Photo; 289 top: Kevork Djansezian/Getty Images; 289 bottom: Chip Somodevilla/Getty Images; 286: Grant Faint/Getty Images RF; 291 top: Susan Van Etten/Photoedit; 291 bottom: Bill Bachman/Photo Researchers, Inc.; 293: Ullstein Bild/The Granger Collection; 294: Courtesy of CNBC; 296: Roger L. Wollenberg/UPI/Landov; 300: Jewish Council for Education and Research, www.jcer.info; 303: Paul White/AP Photo; 310: AP Photo; 312: Newscom

Chapter 9

315: Robyn Beck/AFP/Getty Images; 316: Steve Sack/Star Tribune/Creators Syndicate; 318: Reuters/Landov; 320: Popperfoto/Getty Images; 321: John Gress/Reuters; 322: Steve Sack/Star Tribune/Creators Syndicate; 327: Ronald Reagan Presidential Library; 331: Museum of History and Technology; 338: AP Photo; 341: Jay LaPrete/AP Photo; 348: Justin Sullivan/AP Photo

Chapter 10

353: Kevin Lamarque/Reuters/Landov; 354 left: Frank Micelotta/Getty Images for Fox; 354 right: Win McNamee/Getty Images; 356: Charlie Neibergall/AP Photo; 357: The Granger Collection; 359: Dog Mills/The New York Times/Redux; 362: Alex Wong/Getty Images; 364: Teri Stratford/Six-Cats

Research, Inc.; 367 top: Edward M. Pio/UPI/Landov; 367 bottom: Photo courtesy of Rush Limbaugh/AP Photo; 368: Steve Helber/AP Photo; 370: Getty Images; 371: Jewel Samad/Getty Images; 376: Hulton Archive/Getty Images; 378: Warner Bros./Courtesy Neal Peters Collections; 380: Jim Watson/Getty Images

Chapter 11

387: Alexis C. Glenn/UPI/Landov; 388: Monica Almeida/The New York Times/Redux; 391: Erik S. Lesser/AP Photo; 393: Republican National Committee; 395: J. Pat Carter/AP Photo; 397: Steven E. Frischling/Corbis; 401: Andreas Rentz/Getty Images; 402: Lucas Jackson/Reuters/Landov; 405: Bettmann/Corbis; 407: Carlos Barria/Reuters/Landov; 408 left: Brendan Smialowski/Getty Images; 408 right: Yuri Gripas/Reuters/Corbis; 410: Mike Mergen/Bloomberg via Getty Images; 413: Cliff Owen/AP Photo; 414: Kevin Lamarque/Corbis; 419: Larry Downing/MAI/Landov

Chapter 12

429: Ron Edwards/AP Photo; 430: Bettmann/Corbis; 431: Earl S. Cryer/UPI/Landov; 434: Stephen Crowley/The New York Times/Redux; 435: AP Photo; 436: Newscom; 440: Chuck Savage/Corbis; 442: Scott Houston/Corbis/Sygma; 443: AP Photo; 450: Andy Kropa/Redux

Chapter 13

459: Jim Young/Reuters/Landov; 460: Craig Ruttle/AP Photo; 463: Leslie E. Kossoff/AP Photo; 464: Michael Spooneybarger/AP Photo; 466: Michael Ainsworth/Dallas Morning News/Corbis; 469: Times-Picayne/Landov; 470: Rachel Epstein/Photoedit; 474: Pablo Martinez Monsivais/AP Photo; 476: Manuel Balce Ceneta/AP Photo; 480: Saad Shalash/Reuters/Corbis; 484: Benjamin J. Myers/Corbis; 486: Science Photo Library/Alamy; 488: Jim Ruymen/Landov

Chapter 14

495: Christopher Farina/Corbis; 496: Stephen Crowley/The New York Times/Redux; 499: Mark Wilson/Getty Images; 501: Kevin Lamarque/Reuters; 504: Bettmann/Corbis; 506: Win McNamee/Reuters; 511: Diana Walker/Time & Life Pictures/Getty Images; 516: Luke Frazza/AFP/Getty Images; 525: Newscom; 524: Aristide Economopoulos/The Star Ledger/Corbis; 529: Ali Al-Saadi/AFP/Getty Images

Chapter 15

533: Jacquelyn Martin/AP Photo; 534: Citizens United; 537: Jamie Rose/The New York Times/Redux; 541: Chip Somodevilla/Getty Images; 544: Stephen Strickler/Corbis; 546: JG Photography/Alamy; 553 top: Alex Wong/Getty Images; 553 bottom: Bettmann/Corbis; 550: Tom Williams/Getty Images; 554: Charles Dharapak/AP Photo; 557: Reuters/Corbis; 559: J. Scott Applewhite/AP Photo

Chapter 16

563: Construction Photography/Corbis; 564: Cary Horowitz/Reuters/Corbis; 567: Irwin Thompson/Dallas Morning News/Corbis; 568: spnphotos/Newscom; 573: Pete Souza/The White House; 581: Darren McCollester/Getty Images; 582: Mario Tama/Getty Images; 589: Doug Mills/The New York Times/Redux; 592: Alamy RF

Chapter 17

597: Jacques M. Chenet/Corbis; 598: John Moore/Getty Images; 600: Bettmann/Corbis; 603: Chip Somodevilla/Getty Images; 606: AP Photo; 611: Mark Richards/Photoedit; 613: Fred Kaufman/AP Photo; 616: Jonathan Ernst/Reuters/Corbis; 618: Kathy McLaughlin/The Image Works; 626: J. Scott Applewhite/AP Photo

Chapter 18

629: Joshua Roberts/Bloomberg via Getty Images; 630: Asmaa Waguih/Reuters/Landov; 635: Paul Schutzer/Time & Life Pictures/Getty Images; 637: Reuters/Landov; 642: Bettmann/Corbis; 645: Jim Young/Getty Images; 648: Jim West/Alamy; 650: Mark Wilson/Getty Images; 651: Ahmad Al-Rubaye/AFP/Getty Images; 655: Mike Hutching/Reuters/Corbis; 657: Gao Haorona/Xinhua/AP Photo; 659: M.E. Warren/Photo Researchers

Chapter 19

665: Rudi Von Briel/Photoedit; 666: Brian Snyder/Reuters/Landov; 669: The Granger Collection; 672: Joe Raedle/Getty Images; 673: Tim Larsen/Office of the Governor of New Jersey; 677: Bob Daemmrich/The Image Works; 683: Chip Somodevilla/Getty Images; 685: Dan Habib/Concord Monitor/Corbis SABA; 686: John Neubauer/Photoedit; 690: Dave Caldwell/The Minot Daily News/AP Photo; 694: Ron Campbell/Johnson City Press/AP Photo; 695: Kenneth James/Corbis

Index

Page numbers followed by *f* or *t* indicate material in figures or tables, respectively.

commander-in-chief of, 112, 480–482, 500*t*, 511–512, 511*f*
homosexuals in, 247–248, 412
integration of, 222
as Republican issue, 421
spending on, 575, 575*f*, 644, 644*f*, 653
as public good, 13–14, 14*f*
public opinion on, 266, 267*f*
women in, 242
Military Commissions Act, 661
Military courts, 538*f*
Military-industrial complex, 653
Millennium Challenge Corporation (MCC), 577*t*, 578
Miller, Bill, 761n2
Miller, D. W., 746n1
Miller, Judith, 362–363, 362*f*
Miller, Sunlen, 752n67
Miller, Tiffany Jones, 735n33
Miller, Warren, 325, 747n22, 748n49
Millet, Allan R., 767nn23–24, 767nn26–27
Milliken v. Bradley (1974), 225*t*
Mills, C. Wright, 761n19
Milwaukee, school vouchers in, 620
Milyo, Jeffrey, 738n2
Minerals Management Service, 593
Miners, political inaction by, 436*f*, 437–438
Mine Safety Health Administration (MSHA), 138*f*
Minimal effects, of media, 376–377
Minimum wage, 135, 136*f*, 470, 470*f*
Minneapolis, preference voting in, 404
Minnesota
charter schools in, 617, 672
cross-burning in, 180
2010 midterm elections in, 445
preference voting in, 404
prior restraint in, 179
recall election in, 695
third parties in, 679
Mino, Wolfgang P. Hirczy de, 746n20
Minority leader, 109, 475
Minority population, 28
Minority rights, 16–17. *See also specific minorities*
Minor laws, 489
Minors
abortion access for, 179, 205
death penalty prohibited for, 199–200
protection of student speech, 187, 188*f*, 449
tobacco sales to, 146*f*
Minton, Sherman, 558*t*
Mintz, Joel A., 763n64

Minutemen, in border patrol, 10*f*
Miracle of aggregation, 274
Miranda, Manuel, 760n65
Miranda v. Arizona (1966), 198
Miranda warning, 198–199, 686
Mirer, Thad W., 747nn22–23
Mississippi
school integration in, 227
violence against civil rights activists in, 236–237
voting by blacks in, 281
Missouri
extradition to, 675–676
mandatory retirement in, 245
separate but equal in, 222
Missouri Compromise of 1820, 217–218
Missouri plan, for judicial selection, 688–689, 688*t*
Mobilization efforts, 296–300, 305–306, 310, 340, 341*f*, 345
by interest groups, 444, 446
personal connectedness and, 298–299, 299*f*, 305
by political parties, 394, 410–411, 410*f*
in 2008 presidential campaign, 296–299, 310, 394
social media and, 297–298
Tea Party movement and, 294–295
viral videos and, 299, 300*f*
Mobocracy, 75–76
Modified open primary, 319
Moe, Terry, 762n31
Momentum, primary, 334–335
Mondale, Walter, 322
Le Monde, 356, 356*f*
Monetary policy, 603–605
Monogan, James, 736n8
Monroe Doctrine, 632
Montana
legislators in, 677
midterm elections in, 2006, 310
recall election in, 695
Montejo v. Louisiana (2009), 198
Montgomery, Alabama, bus boycott, 233
Moralistic culture, 49
Morgan, Edmund S., 734n7
Morone, James, 732n14
Morrison, Peter A., 731n3 (chap. 2)
Morse v. Frederick (2007), 188*f*, 449
Mortgage crisis (2008–), 31*f*, 294, 598–599, 598*f*, 602, 603*f*
Motor Voter Act of 1993, 158, 294, 304, 314
Mountain States Legal Foundation, 585
MoveOn.org, 278, 314, 388, 389, 450*f*
MSHA. *See* Mine Safety Health Administration

MSM. *See* Mainstream media
MSNBC, 354–355, 356–357, 366, 367*f*, 372
Mullen, Mike, 474*f*, 630
Mullins, Brody, 752n2, 754n19
Mulroney, Brian, 647
Multiculturalism, 59–62
vs. American creed, 59–62, 61*f*
defining characteristics of, 59–60
definition of, 60
Multiparty systems
vs. polarization, 479
and political participation, 302, 303*f*
and proportional representation, 396, 399–400
vs. two-party system, 396, 399–400, 404
Multiple referral, of bills, 484
Munger, Michael C., 746n20
Municipal courts, 687, 687*f*
Municipal governments, 671, 671*t*.
See also Local government
appointed managers of, 680, 682
commissions of, 682
elected councils of, 680, 681–682
elected executives of, 680–681
forms of, 684–685, 684*t*
Murdoch, Rupert, 354, 356
Murray, Charles, 765n38
Murray, Shailagh, 766n90
Murray, Williamson, 767nn23–24, 767nn26–27
Mussolini, Benito, 376, 633
Mutual assured destruction, 656
Mutz, Diana C., 748n50
MySpace, 297–298

N

NAACP. *See* National Association for the Advancement of Colored People
Nader, Ralph, 316, 397–398, 397*f*, 402, 403*t*
NAFTA. *See* North American Free Trade Agreement
Nagel, Charles, 443
Nagel, Stuart, 771n30
Nagourney, Adam, 755n49
Napolitano, Janet, 158, 573*f*
NARAL, 389, 429*f*
NASA. *See* National Aeronautics and Space Administration
Nash, Douglas Roger, 736n27
Nast, Thomas, 405*f*
Nathan, Richard, 756n21
Nation, definition of, 74
National Aeronautics and Space Administration (NASA), 576*t*, 577, 589

National American Woman Suffrage Association (NAWSA), 311, 430
National Archives: Presidential Libraries and Museums, 532
National Association for the Advancement of Colored People (NAACP), 252, 414*f*
and black separatists, 237
founding of, 221
Legal Defense and Educational Fund, 222
legal strategy of, 222
National Association of Counties, 144, 443, 458, 753n22
National Broadcasting Company. *See* MSNBC; NBC
National Center for Education Statistics, 746n29, 765nn55–57, 765n62, 766n71
National Coalition Against Censorship, 449
National Conference of State Legislatures (NCSL), 144, 163, 698, 735n5, 736n34, 770n18
National Council of La Raza, 252
National defense
Constitution and, 90
as public good, 13–14, 14*f*
spending on, 575, 575*f*, 644, 644*f*, 653
as public good, 13–14, 14*f*
public opinion on, 266, 267*f*
National Defense Education Act of 1958, 612–613
National Education Association (NEA)
and Democratic Party, 389
as policy entrepreneur, 601–602
on voting age, 100
National Election Studies, 43, 305
National Environmental Policy Act of 1969, 592
National Federation of Independent Businesses, 441, 451–452, 458
National Federation of Republican Women, 390
National Front for the Liberation of South Vietnam, 634–635
National Governors Association, 124*f*, 698
National health insurance. *See* Health care/health insurance
National Health Service (United Kingdom), 623
National Highway and Traffic Safety Administration (NHTSA), 88*f*
National identity, 46*f*
National Indian Gaming Association, 736n29
National Institute on Money in State Politics, 352
National Institutes of Health, 575
Nationalists, black, 237